Contract Law

Practice, Interpretation, and Enforcement

First Edition

Willy E. Rice

cognella® academic publishing

Bassim Hamadeh, CEO and Publisher
Michael Simpson, Vice President of Acquisitions
Jamie Giganti, Managing Editor
Jess Busch, Graphic Design Supervisor
Marissa Applegate, Acquisitions Editor
Jessica Knott, Project Editor
Luiz Ferreira, Licensing Associate

First published in the United States of America in 2014 by Cognella, Inc.

9781621312413

cognella academic publishing

www.cognella.com 800-200-3908

CONTENTS

Part 1

The Formation and Enforcement of Contracts Under the Common Law

PART I

INTRODUCTION

Like walking, human beings make promises quite regularly and effortlessly. In fact, we make a variety of *stand-alone promises*: unilateral, bilateral, express (oral and written), implied-in-fact, and implied-in-law. Similarly, humans form an assortment of *contracts*: unilateral, bilateral, express (oral and written), implied-in-fact, and implied-in-law. Put simply, this casebook has two broad purposes. First, it outlines the legal principles that parties must use to construct "valid" and "legally enforceable" stand-alone promises and contracts.

Although this casebook discusses legally enforceable stand-alone promises and contracts, the title of the casebook is merely CONTRACTS. In fact, one would be hard pressed to find a first-year casebook entitled, THE LAW OF CONTRACTS AND PROMISES. Yet, there are major differences between a "*legally enforceable, valid stand-alone promise*" and a "*legally enforceable, valid contract*." To be sure, those distinctions are covered in the text. However, at this point, it is sufficient to understand a few general propositions regarding a promise: A promise is a party's *one-sided decision* to act or to abstain from acting for the benefit of another party. To be legally enforceable, a promise must be "valid." Consequently, a promise is not *valid*, if it evolves out of duress, violates public policy, or involves fraudulent, unconscionable, or illegal acts.

Even more importantly, to prove a valid promise in a court of law, a plaintiff need only to establish *a single element*: Proof that the defendant unilaterally represented—orally or in writing—to act or to abstain from acting for the plaintiff's benefit. However, as discussed more fully in this part, to prove a valid contract, a litigant must satisfy a substantially higher burden of proof.

Additionally, this casebook outlines and discusses both common-law and statutory rules that courts of law and equity use to determine whether or not promises and contracts are enforceable. In particular, PART I outlines common-law rules, which govern the construction, interpretation, and enforcement of valid promises and contracts. Also, PART I presents a discussion of common-law affirmative defenses and denials that defendants may employ in courts of law and equity.

On the other hand, PART II covers statutory rules that govern the "sale of goods" under Article 2 of the Uniform Commercial Code (UCC).[a] Put simply, sellers and buyers of goods may form agreements. And, if one party breaches an agreement, the complaining party may seek numerous remedies under the UCC, rather than litigating under the common law. Briefly stated, the UCC "relaxes" many of the "iron clad" procedural and substantive barriers that a plaintiff must overcome under the common law. Nevertheless, under Article 2, a complainant must still prove specific elements of her theory of recovery if she intends to prevail. Similarly, under Article 2, a defendant still has the burden to prove that a plaintiff's Article 2 claims and theories of recovery have no basis in law. However, the UCC embraces or codifies many common-law affirmative defenses.[b] Therefore, as discussed more fully in PART II, Article 2 does not substantially increase a defendant's burden of proof.

---

a The American Law Institute (ALI) and the National Conference of Commissioners on Uniform State Laws (NCCUSL) drafted the Uniform Commercial Code (UCC), including Article 2. Put simply, the purpose of the UCC is to "simplify, clarify and modernize the law governing commercial transactions" and "to make uniform the law among the various jurisdictions." UCC § 1-102(2). Barring Louisiana, all states have codified Article 2 of the UCC. And, although some variance exists among the states, the differences are minor and do not contravene the UCC drafters' stated purpose. *See Pennzoil Co. v. Fed. Energy Regulatory Comm'n*, 789 F.2d 1128, 1142 (5th Cir. 1986). In 2003, the ALI and NCCUSL promulgated a revised version of the UCC. Uniform Commercial Code: *Official Text and Comments*, app. XX, 1964–65, 1978 (West 2008). Some states, however, have retained the prior version of Article 2.

b *See Branch Banking & Trust Co. v. Witmeyer*, No. 3:10CV55-HEH-DWD, 2011 WL 3297682, at *6 (E.D. Va. 2011):

> Although BB&T's motion for summary judgment does not directly challenge each of Witmeyer's affirmative defenses, the central challenge to all common law claims essentially precludes each of the enumerated defenses. Specifically, BB&T argues that the UCC displaces the common law defense of equitable estoppel. Here, the Court is compelled to determine an issue of first impression under Virginia state law, as no Virginia Court has explicitly addressed the precise issue in question, and there is no other controlling authority that is applicable. BB&T urges, in essence, that all common law claims are displaced if the UCC has established any rules for a particular type of transaction. However, the UCC, as applied in Virginia, incorporates no such rule. To the contrary, Va. Code § 8.1A–103(b) specifically provides:

Of course, the introduction would be incomplete if it failed to squarely address three questions that students present early on in a first-year contracts course: 1) What is the distinction between unilateral and bilateral contracts?; 2) What are the major differences between proof of a *prima facie case* and, say, the ancient, common-law *action of debt* or *action in assumpsit*?; and 3) What distinguishes a "contort" action from an *action sounding in contract* or *an action sounding in tort*? Some less-than-bright-line answers appear in the following sections.

SECTION ONE: UNILATERAL VERSUS BILATERAL CONTRACTS

The False Distinction Between Bilateral and Unilateral Contracts

64 Yale L.J. 512 (1955)
Samuel J. Stoljar

The distinction between bilateral and unilateral contracts has long been considered fundamental. It has been regarded as an axiomatic truth revealing the basic order of the contractual system. First enunciated by Professor Langdell, it has gained almost universal recognition, and achieved its final glory when laid as a theoretical cornerstone in the RESTATEMENT OF CONTRACTS. But the time has come to look once more at this distinction. For, as we shall see, it incorporates an important error, error the effect of which has been to precipitate complicated, though unnecessary, problems as well as to obstruct a consistent and comprehensive theory of bargain. This article is an attempt to unravel and remove some of our "dogmatic" muddles.

> Unless displaced by the particular provisions of this subtitle, the principles of law and equity, including the law merchant and the law relative to capacity to contract, principal and agent, estoppel, fraud, misrepresentation, duress, coercion, mistake, bankruptcy, or other validating or invalidating cause shall supplement its provisions.

The Supreme Court of Virginia interprets the provision to displace common law remedies only where it creates an alternative statutory remedy. Where no UCC provision otherwise applies or explicitly forecloses such a defense, the common law defense "survives." Where there is more than one transaction involved, common law claims arising out of those transactions governed by specific provisions of the UCC are displaced, but common law claims arising out of other transactions, not subject to UCC control, are not. Moreover, it is significant that Va. Code § 8.1A-103(b) explicitly references common law estoppel as one of the "principles of law and equity" that is not invalidated.

Analysis is best begun with an examination of two well-known definitions. A contract is called bilateral if "there are mutual promises between two parties to the contract; each party being both a promisor and a promisee." On the other hand, a contract is unilateral "in which no promisor receives a promise as consideration for his promise." In the former case, there is a promise for promise; in the latter, a promise for an act.

However, these definitions explain nothing of real value, for they merely describe a dichotomy of *existing contracts*. If *ex hypothesi* a contract does exist, what difference does it make, in terms of legal consequences, whether two promises were consideration for each other, or no promise was consideration for the promisor's promise? *Of course, the definitions do, indirectly, tell us something: in the bilateral contract, there being two enforceable promises, either promisor may commit a breach of contract, while in the unilateral contract only one party may fail in his performance, the other having already performed his side of the bargain.* But this is, to say the least, scant information. And, at any rate, it is not the kind of knowledge which deserves a grandiose distinction.

Furthermore, and this is the main objection, the bilateral–unilateral distinction generates an erroneous conception of the nature of contractual formation. The distinction assumes that a contract can be "formed" in two ways only: either by the sequence of a promise and a counter-promise or by the sequence of a promise and an act. But promises, counter-promises, and acts are purely physical events which in themselves are neutral. It is therefore necessary to explain why these events are singled out and given a special legal significance. It is necessary, in other words, to elucidate the interests which these events represent and inquire whether and to what extent, they are legally protected.

While this objection is theoretically fundamental, it must be at once admitted that it has no practical relevance for what is perhaps the vast majority of cases. In the usual situation it makes no difference whether we say that a contract is formed by a promise for a promise, a promise for an act, or, more broadly, by offer and acceptance; or whether we say, on the other hand, that a bargain is set afoot by the presence of certain interests to which the law accords protection.

SECTION TWO: FORMS OF ACTIONS IN EARLY ENGLISH COURTS AND THE "MODERN" PRIMA FACIE CASE

Discussing the differences between the *writs of trespass* and *trespass on the case*, the Nevada Supreme Court wrote the following in *Aftercare of Clark County v. Justice of Las Vegas Tp. ex rel. County of Clark*, 120 Nev. 1, 82 P.3d 931, 936–937 (Nev. 2004) (emphasis added):

> Under the common law, "tort actions were brought under the *writs of trespass* and *trespass on the case*." "*Trespass* remedied direct, forcible tortious injuries, while the later developed *trespass on the case* remedied indirect or consequential harms." Tort actions involving a claim for money damages were generally triable to a jury at common law. However, if the amount of the claim was insignificant, a jury trial was not required.

Moreover, under a *writ of trespass*, plaintiffs could recover a remedy only for the following torts or "invasions": battery, trespass to land, trespass to chattel, and assault. Remedies for negligence were not permitted. Furthermore, the *writ of trespass* provided relief between strangers if a defendant's unauthorized use of physical force caused plaintiff's injuries directly and immediately.

Conversely, a *writ of trespass on the case* or *action on the case* allowed litigants—who had a contractual or status-based relationship—to litigate their differences in a court of law. *See* S.F.C. Milsom, HISTORICAL FOUNDATIONS OF THE COMMON LAW 393 (2d ed. 1981). Quite simply, the *action on the case* evolved from a need to protect persons who were allegedly victims of other torts: conversion, false imprisonment, slander, libel, deceit, defamation, or intentional infliction of emotional distress. Much later, negligence and strict-liability actions evolved under the *writ of trespass on the case*.

Now consider what a Connecticut court penned in *Rocque v. Sound Mfg., Inc.,* 2002 WL 1371038,*3 (Conn. Super. Ct. 2002) (emphasis added):

> A common law *action in debt* lies where there [is] due a sum certain or capable of reduction to certainty. ... A principal characteristic of an *action in debt*, therefore, is that the sum to be recovered is certain and liquidated: Debt is an action founded on contract, express or implied, in which the certainty of the sum, or duty appears, and in which the plaintiff is to recover the sum in numero, and not in damages.

Briefly put, an *action of debt* was proper if the complaining party could prove one of the following: 1) defendant breached an express promise to pay a specific price for goods which had been delivered, or 2) defendant breached an express promise to pay a specific price for services which has been performed. Additionally, in pre-sixteenth-century England, an *action of debt* was viable only if a plaintiff could prove that a defendant promised to pay a specific sum of money under a seal.

To be sure, from a plaintiff's point of view, the early common-law *action of debt* had its procedural limitations. Quite simply, a trial could be resolved through compurgation. Stated differently, a defendant could successfully defend himself by 1) swearing in open court that he did not owe the debt and 2) asking ten friends—"compurgators"—to take an oath and swear that the defendant was telling the truth. Certainly, securing the requisite number of "oath swearers" or compurgators determined whether or not this affirmative defense was effective. *See* JAMES BRADLEY THAYER, A PRELIMINARY TREATISE ON EVIDENCE AT THE COMMON LAW 24–28 (1898).

Given those procedural and substantive barriers in English common-law courts, many plaintiffs took their complaints to English courts of equity. A trial by judge occurred in the latter tribunals. Consequently, in courts of equity, a plaintiff could commence an *action of debt* and receive damages—even if the plaintiff failed to establish that the defendant expressly promised to pay a specific amount of money for delivered goods or for services performed.

Additionally, if a party breached a contract, a complaining party could file an *action of covenant* under the common law. However, there was a proviso: The covenant had to be under a seal. Simple contracts—without seals—were not enforceable. Therefore, to correct the latter problem, English courts embraced, yet, another form of action—the *action of assumpsit*. In *Alternatives Unlimited, Inc. v. New Baltimore City Bd. of School Com'rs,* 843 A.2d 252, 284 (Md. Ct. Spec. App. 2004) (emphasis added), the Maryland court described the *assumpsit's* evolution and purpose this way:

> [T]he early common law recognized no cause of action for the breach of a simple contract. To fill a void that desperately needed filling, there gradually developed the form of action known as *Assumpsit*. It is Latin for "he assumed" or "he undertook." The fuller form is *Indebitatus Assumpsit*: "He assumed the debt; he undertook to pay the debt." ... Early on, *Assumpsit* came to cover the case of an actual, though simple, contract, written or oral. From the coverage of an *express contract*, it then expanded to cover *a contract that was not express* but that could be inferred from the circumstantial behavior of the contracting parties. It ultimately was stretched to cover certain instances of unjust enrichment, where the *law was willing to create a contract, as a legal fiction*, where none in fact existed, even inferentially.

Overwhelmingly, modern American courts have abandoned English courts' early forms of pleadings. Today, if a plaintiff wants a court of law to award damages or other remedies for a breach-of-promise or a breach-of-contract claim, the plaintiff must file a complaint. And, in the complaint or pleading, the aggrieved party must establish a "*prima facie* case."[c]

---

c *See Goldstein v. Sachs*, 114 A. 593, 596 (Md. 1921) ("Where plaintiff has established *a promise and a breach* [resulting in a] loss, a *prima facie* case

NOTES AND QUESTIONS

1. **Advantages of Litigating in Courts of Equity**. Are there major differences between courts of law and courts of equity? And if so, what are the advantages and disadvantages of a person's litigating their disputes in courts of law and equity?

2. **Equity and Remedies.** Courts of equity have a long history of fashioning equitable remedies that address the uniqueness of each conflict. More specifically, equitable remedies "are distinguished for their flexibility, their unlimited variety, their adaptability to circumstances, and the natural rules which govern their use. There is in fact no limit to their variety and application; the court of equity has the power of devising its remedy and shaping it so as to fit the changing circumstances of every case and the complex relations of all the parties." *Sears, Roebuck & Co. v. Camp*, 124 N. J. Eq. 403, 411–12, 1 A.2d 425 (N.J. 1938), quoting JOHN N. POMEROY, EQUITY JURISPRUDENCE § 109 (4th ed. 1918).

3. **The Vanishing Bright Line Between Courts of Law and Equity.** In most jurisdictions, the distinction between courts of law and equity has been abandoned. However, in England, Delaware, and Mississippi the tradition persists. In addition, "Tennessee has preserved the distinction between courts of law and courts of equity and courts of equity generally enjoy broad power to dismiss actions with or without prejudice." *Calaway ex rel. Calaway v. Schucker* 395 Fed. Appx. 251 (6th Cir. 2010), citing *Long v. Kirby-Smith*, 292 S.W.2d 216, 220–21 (Tenn. Ct. App. 1956). But note: "Federal courts are courts in law and in equity, and a court of equity has traditionally had the power to fashion any remedy deemed necessary and appropriate to do justice in a particular case." *Carter-Jones Lumber Co. v. Dixie Distrib. Co.*, 166 F.3d 840, 846 (6th Cir. 1999).

---

is made ..., thus throwing on defendant the burden of vindicating himself."); *Burns v. Am. Nat'l Ins. Co.*, 280 S.W. 762, 765 (Tex. Comm'n App. 1926) ("[B] efore there can be a 'claim for damages,' ... there must be made *a prima facie case* by the *pleading and proof that the contract* upon which the suit is based [has] been *breached* by the party against whom the claim is made.").

SECTION THREE: CONTRACT- AND NEGLIGENCE-BASED THEORIES OF RECOVERY VERSUS "CONTORTS"

Southwestern Bell Telephone Co. v. DeLanney
809 S.W.2d 493
(Tex. 1991)

Phillips, Chief Justice. Eugene DeLanney advertised his real estate business in the Galveston Yellow Pages for several years. For the 1980–1981 directory, he again contracted with Bell for a Yellow Pages advertisement. At this time DeLanney had two business phones, a rotary line and a single line. Prior to publication of the 1980–1981 directory, DeLanney's wife asked Bell to cancel the single line and add a third number to their existing rotary line. The Yellow Pages advertisement was billed to DeLanney's single line. When that line was canceled, DeLanney's Yellow Pages advertisement was automatically deleted from the directory due to Bell's internal procedures.

When the advertisement was not published as promised, DeLanney sued Bell, alleging negligence and violation of the Texas Deceptive Practices—Consumer Protection Act (DTPA), Tex. Bus. & Com. Code §§ 17.41–17.63. Bell answered and urged by special exception that DeLanney's petition failed to state a cause of action for negligence. No ruling was made on this special exception, and DeLanney proceeded to trial on both claims.

After DeLanney rested his case in chief, Bell moved for a directed verdict on both theories of liability. The trial court granted Bell's motion as to the DTPA claim, but denied it as to negligence. The remaining issues were submitted to a jury.

The jury found that Bell was negligent in omitting DeLanney's advertisement from the Yellow Pages and that such negligence was a proximate cause of damages to DeLanney. The jury assessed these damages at $109,000 for lost profits in the past and $40,000 for lost profits in the future. After ordering a partial remittitur which reduced future lost profits to $21,480, the trial court rendered judgment for DeLanney. Bell appealed.

Breach of Contract or Negligence

The court of appeals, with one justice concurring and one justice dissenting, affirmed. A majority of the court held that Bell's cancellation of DeLanney's Yellow Pages advertisement was correctly submitted as a negligence claim. The dissenting justice argued that because DeLanney sought damages for breach of a duty created under the contract, rather than a duty imposed by law, the claim sounded only in contract. We agree with the dissent.

The majority below relied on *Montgomery Ward & Co. v. Scharrenbeck,* 204 S.W.2d 508, 510 (Tex. 1947), where we quoted from 38 Am. Jur. *Negligence* § 20 (1941) as follows:

> Accompanying every contract is a common-law duty to perform with care, skill, reasonable expedience and faithfulness the thing agreed to be done, and a negligent failure to observe any of these conditions is a tort, as well as a breach of the contract.

In *Scharrenbeck*, the defendant agreed to repair a water heater in plaintiff's home. A short time after repair, the heater ignited the roof, destroying the house and its contents. Although the contract obligated the defendant to put the water heater back in good working order, the law also implied a duty to the defendant to act with reasonable skill and diligence in making the repairs so as not to injure a person or property by his performance. In failing to repair the water heater properly, the defendant breached its contract. In burning down plaintiff's home, the defendant breached a common-law duty as well, thereby providing a basis for plaintiff's recovery in tort.

The principle recognized in *Scharrenbeck* has also been recognized by commentators in this area. As one prominent authority has explained: "Tort obligations are in general obligations that are imposed by law—apart from and independent of promises made and therefore apart from the manifested intention of the parties—to avoid injury to others." W. Keeton, D. Dobbs, R. Keeton & D. Owen, Prosser and Keeton On the Law of Torts § 92 at 655 (5th Ed. 1984). If the defendant's conduct—such as negligently burning down a house—would give rise to liability independent of the fact that a contract exists between the parties, the plaintiff's claim may also sound in tort. Conversely, if the defendant's conduct—such as failing to publish an advertisement—would give rise to liability only because it breaches the parties' agreement, the plaintiff's claim ordinarily sounds only in contract.

In determining whether the plaintiff may recover on a tort theory, it is also instructive to examine the nature of the plaintiff's loss. When the only loss or damage is to the subject matter of the contract, the plaintiff's action is ordinarily on the contract. We applied this analysis in *Jim Walter Homes, Inc. v. Reed,* 711 S.W.2d 617, 618 (Tex.1986), where we wrote:

> The acts of a party may breach duties in tort or contract alone or simultaneously in both. The nature of the injury most often determines which duty or duties are breached. When the injury is only the economic loss to the subject of a contract itself the action sounds in contract alone.

Bell's duty to publish DeLanney's advertisement arose solely from the contract. DeLanney's damages, lost profits, were only for the economic loss caused by Bell's failure to perform. Although DeLanney pleaded his action as one in negligence, he clearly sought to recover the benefit of his bargain with Bell. We hold that Bell's failure to publish the advertisement was not a tort. Under our analysis in *Reed*, DeLanney's claim was solely in contract.

DeLanney, however, did not request jury questions on breach of contract. Because the jury was asked only questions as to liability resulting from Bell's negligence, DeLanney waived any claim for breach of contract. *Ramos v. Frito-Lay, Inc.*, 784 S.W.2d 667, 668 (Tex. 1990) (the plaintiff has the "burden to obtain affirmative answers to jury questions as to the necessary elements of his cause of action") (citing Tex. R. Civ. P. 279).

DeLanney did obtain an affirmative answer to the question whether there was a disparity in bargaining power between the parties in negotiating the Yellow Pages agreement. The court of appeals correctly determined that disparity in bargaining power is irrelevant in a negligence suit. Perhaps the issue was submitted because DeLanney pled that Bell's conduct was unconscionable under the DTPA. Because of his failure to comply with the notice requirements of the DTPA, however, DeLanney's entire cause of action under the DTPA, including any claim of unconscionability, was dismissed by a directed verdict. For this reason, and because DeLanney submitted no contract issues, the jury finding concerning disparity of bargaining power is of no effect.

For the foregoing reasons, the judgment of the court of appeals is reversed, and judgment is rendered that DeLanney take nothing.

* * *

Gonzalez, Justice, concurring.

I agree with the court that Bell's failure to publish the advertisement was not a tort and that it sounded solely in contract. I also agree that DeLanney failed to discharge his burden to obtain affirmative findings to jury questions on the contract. However, I do not fault the court of appeals for its confusion. We have muddled the law of "contorts" and an all-encompassing bright line demarcation of what constitutes a tort distinct from breach of contract has proven to be elusive. ... DeLanney and the court of appeals rely heavily on the statement in *Montgomery Ward & Co. v. Scharrenbeck*, 204 S.W.2d 508, 510 (Tex. 1947), that:

> Accompanying every contract is a common-law duty to perform with care, skill, reasonable expedience and faithfulness the thing agreed to be done, and a negligent failure to observe any of these conditions is a tort, as well as a breach of the contract.

Despite this broad language, not every breach of contract accompanied by negligence creates a cause of action in tort. In *International*

Printing Pressman & Assistants' Union v. Smith, 198 S.W.2d 729, 735 (1946), we acknowledged that no single concise rule will define the rights of parties in every situation. We nonetheless wrote:

> [G]enerally speaking, "actions in contract and in tort are to be distinguished in that an action in contract is for the breach of a duty arising out of a contract either express or implied, while an action in tort is for a breach of duty imposed by law. ..." "[I]f the action is not maintainable without pleading and proving the contract, where the gist of the action is the breach of the contract, either by malfeasance or nonfeasance, it is, in substance an action on the contract, whatever may be the form of the pleading." *Id.*

I believe that this formulation comes closer than *Scharrenbeck* to stating a general rule to distinguish contract from tort and that the broad language in *Scharrenbeck* must be read in light of the particular circumstances of that case. The opinion in *Scharrenbeck* is correct in its observation that a contract may be the occasion that brings the parties together, but it is the relationship or situation of the parties that gives rise to a duty in law, the breach of which is a tort. *See Greater Houston Transp. Co. v. Phillips,* 801 S.W.2d 523 (Tex. 1990). Had Montgomery Ward repaired the water heater gratuitously, it would have owed Scharrenbeck a duty not to create a dangerous condition. Thus the duty to not create a dangerous condition existed independent of any contractual relationship.

In summary, when a party must prove the contents of its contract and must rely on the duties created therein, the action is "in substance an action *on the contract*, even though it is denominated an action for negligent performance of the contract." *Bernard Johnson, Inc. v. Continental Constructors, Inc.,* 630 S.W.2d 365, 368 (Tex. App.—Austin 1982, writ ref'd n.r.e.) (emphasis in original).

* * *

Mauzy, Justice, dissenting.

I respectfully dissent. The contractual relationship creates duties not only under contract law, but under tort law as well. A contract may create the state of things which furnishes the occasion for the tort. *Montgomery Ward & Co. v. Scharrenbeck,* 204 S.W.2d 508, 510 (Tex. 1947).

Every contract is accompanied by a duty to perform that contract with care, skill, reasonable expedience and faithfulness. The negligent failure to observe any of the conditions imposed by this duty constitutes a tort. *Id.* In determining whether the action is one in contract or tort or both, the court must look to the substance of the cause of the action, and not necessarily the manner in which it was pleaded. *Jim*

Walter Homes, Inc. v. Reed, 711 S.W.2d 617, 617–18 (Tex. 1986) (citing *International Printing Pressman and Ass't Union v. Smith,* 198 S.W.2d 729 (Tex. 1946). When the injury involves failure to perform a contract and the only loss is that economic loss that is the substance of the contract itself, the action sounds only in contract and not in tort. *Jim Walter Homes,* 711 S.W.2d at 618.

This case involves more than the mere failure to perform or negligent performance of the Yellow Pages contract. The action of Bell that gave rise to DeLanney's tort cause of action was the negligent performance of its contract to provide telephone service to DeLanney, not the negligent performance of its contract to provide the Yellow Pages advertisement.

* * *

To confine DeLanney to recovery in contract, when his damages clearly extend beyond the contract itself, is to step back into the days of the common-law forms of action. Originally, forms of action were rigidly prescribed, and a plaintiff had no cause of action unless he could fit his claim "into the form of some existing and recognized writ." PROSSER AND KEETON ON THE LAW OF TORTS § 6 at 28 (5th ed. 1984).

Texas, though, has never adopted the old forms of action; thus, "it makes no difference in what shape a plaintiff presents his cause of action, the courts will look to the substance of it, and not be controlled by the mere form in which it is set forth." *Rector v. Orange Rice Mill Co.,* 102 S.W. 402, 403 (Tex. 1907). The option to proceed in contract or tort is available not to diminish the plaintiff's rights, but rather to afford the plaintiff a suitable remedy.

"In jurisdictions where the old forms of action have been totally abolished, there should be nothing left of the whole doctrine excepting a few historical echoes." Corbin, *Waiver of Tort and Suit in Assumpsit,* 19 Yale L.J. 221, 246 (1910). The echo heard from the majority today is out of tune with modern jurisprudence, and wrongly deprives DeLanney of an adequate remedy at law.

This case was correctly tried in the trial court. The jury's verdict formed the basis of the trial court's judgment, which the court of appeals rightly affirmed. I would affirm the judgment of the court of appeals.

CHAPTER ONE

Cause of Action for Breach of Promise: Plaintiff's Burden to Establish Prima Facie Proof of an Enforceable Promise

Once more, a *stand-alone* promise appears in two forms: 1) one's promising to perform an act for another party's benefit; and 2) one's promising to abstain from acting for the benefit of another person. Of course, not all promises are enforceable in a court of law or in a court of equity. To increase one's likelihood of securing a monetary award or equitable relief for a defendant's breach of a promise, a plaintiff must establish *a prima facie case* in *a court of law*. Specifically, a plaintiff must prove the following elements: 1) defendant made a valid unilateral promise or both parties made valid bilateral promises; 2) plaintiff gave good consideration for the promise; 3) defendant breached the promise; and 4) defendant's breach was the cause in fact and proximate cause of plaintiff's injury and damages. *See Mead v. Johnson Group, Inc.*, 615 S.W.2d 685, 687 (Tex. 1981); *Coombs v. Fazzio,* 386 S.W.2d 650, 652–654 (Tex. Civ. App.—San Antonio, 1965); *Stewart v. Basey,* 245 S.W.2d 484, 486 (Tex. 1952); and *Glasscock v. Shell*, 57 Tex. 215 (Tex. 1882), 1882 WL 9491, *8 (Tex.).

In a court of equity, a plaintiff may file an action to secure one or a combination of the following remedies: cancellation, disaffirmance, declaratory relief, injunctive relief, restitution, reformation, indemnification, reinstatement, specific performance, and *quantum meruit*—to name a few. On the other hand, the plaintiff does not have to prove a *prima facie* case. The party simply asks the equity court to examine the relevant facts in the complaint, apply the law, and reward relief. Still, the plaintiff must establish that a *stand-alone promise* or *a contractual promise* was valid. If the movant does not satisfy this minimum requirement, both courts of law and equity will rule in favor of the opposing party.

A. Valid Promises, Mental Incapacity, and Voidable Promises

Bucchi v. Gleason
74 A.2d 212
(Conn. 1950)

O'Sullivan, Judge. The complaint is in two counts. By the first, [Adolph Bucchi sued Roger F. Gleason, administrator of the estate of Alice M. Judd] to recover the reasonable value of services claimed to have been performed for ... Alice M. Judd, under an alleged agreement to compensate him by her will. The second count seeks equitable relief which, in effect, would require the defendant Mrs. Theo L. Pyle to return to the defendant administrator the personalty and realty received from Mrs. Judd during her life, on the ground that these transfers have rendered the decedent's estate insufficient to provide for the payment to which the plaintiff is entitled under the first count. Shortly after the return day, the court, upon motion, ordered that Stanley Goddard, a brother of Mrs. Pyle, be joined as codefendant.

The answers of all three defendants were in the nature of general denials. Goddard filed with his answer a counterclaim setting forth that the gifts received by [his] sister were induced by undue influence practiced upon the decedent, and, as relief, he sought their return to the decedent's estate. The case was tried to the court. Judgment was entered on the complaint in favor of all defendants, and, except as to the realty involved, in favor of Goddard on the counterclaim. The plaintiff and Mrs. Pyle have taken separate appeals to this court.

The finding, which is attached in each appeal but which is not subject to material correction, discloses these facts: [Adolph Bucchi] went to work for Rollin D. Judd in 1922. There he remained until Judd died in 1929. A few days before his impending death, Judd obtained a promise from the plaintiff that he would remain in Mrs. Judd's employ as long as she lived. The plaintiff did as he had promised, working for Mrs. Judd as a gardener, chauffeur and handyman. While in her employ, he occasionally took on other part-time jobs for various people. This was done with her knowledge and consent, but this additional work was always subordinate to her right to have first call upon his time.

Originally, Mrs. Judd paid him $28 weekly. Later, she increased this wage to $30. On several occasions she presented him with a yearly bonus of $100. During his employment she gave him $1100 to buy two accordions for his children. This latter sum with others received by him from time to time made a total of about $1450 which Mrs. Judd paid him in excess of his regular wage. On many occasions, she told the plaintiff that she was not paying him enough but that she would see he was well paid at her death. He believed she would do so. He rendered at all times loyal and faithful service to her.

In 1931, Mrs. Judd told the plaintiff that she had left him $1000 in her will. Two years later, she executed another will in which she bequeathed to him $3000 and her automobile. She informed the plaintiff of these bequests. In 1941, she made a third will wherein she devised to the plaintiff the home in which she lived and bequeathed to him $5000 and her automobile. Previous to executing the will, Mrs. Judd had told him of these contemplated testamentary gifts and had asked him if he was satisfied with them. He replied that he was. Each of the three wills she had executed up to this time provided for only a small legacy to her niece, Mrs. Pyle.

On August 15, 1944, Mrs. Pyle, who had been living in Florida, came to New Britain at her aunt's request. This request was prompted by the fact that Mrs. Judd's housekeeper was obliged to leave. Upon her arrival, Mrs. Pyle took over the management of Mrs. Judd's household. At the end of six weeks, Mrs. Pyle discharged the plaintiff. He was never thereafter permitted to enter the house or speak to Mrs. Judd alone.

For many years, Mrs. Judd's financial affairs had been cared for by a local bank, and, from 1940 on, under a general power of attorney. She owned her own home, which was worth $13,000, government bonds of the value of $15,000, cash and bank deposits in excess of $10,000, an automobile and personal effects of substantial value. She was also the beneficiary of an annuity under which she was entitled to receive $325 monthly as long as she lived.

Three weeks after her arrival in New Britain, Mrs. Pyle received from Mrs. Judd a deed of the house. This conveyance was made in consideration of Mrs. Pyle's written agreement to care for Mrs. Judd and act as her companion for the rest of her life. On September 27, 1944, Mrs. Judd revoked the power of attorney held by the bank, and Mrs. Pyle told the bank's representative that she would henceforth handle her aunt's finances. On October 9, 1944, Mrs. Judd gave her niece a power of attorney, and from that date on Mrs. Pyle took complete charge of all of her aunt's financial affairs. Between the last mentioned date and the following February, the bank accounts and government bonds were changed so as to make them payable to Mrs. Judd and Mrs. Pyle, or the survivor. On February 13, 1945, Mrs. Judd destroyed her will and at the same time executed a memorandum by which she attempted to give all of her personal property to Mrs. Pyle.

From August, 1944, until her death in December, 1946, Mrs. Judd was at times mentally confused, forgetful, suffering from infirmities of age and readily susceptible to suggestion. She died intestate, leaving as her only asset five shares of stock valued at $500. Her death was attributed to generalized causes, with arteriosclerosis and paralysis agitans specified. The named defendant is the administrator of her estate.

Upon these facts, the court concluded that there was no basis for a finding that Mrs. Judd agreed to compensate the plaintiff by her will, and that she had paid him compensation, while he was in her employ, which was not less than his services were reasonably worth. It further concluded that the personalty which Mrs. Pyle received from her aunt was acquired through undue influence. It entered judgment on the complaint against the plaintiff. On the counterclaim, the judgment incorporated an order that Mrs. Pyle turn over to the administrator on Mrs. Judd's estate all of the personalty received as gifts and, further, that she render an account.

We first dispose of the assignment of errors raised in Mrs. Pyle's appeal. As indicated above, the facts found have ample support in the evidence, and those which Mrs. Pyle seeks to incorporate in the finding, even if added, would not affect the result.

Another assignment challenges the court's conclusion that Mrs. Ryle obtained the gifts in question by exerting undue influence upon her aunt. "Any influence brought to bear upon a person … consenting to a disposal of property, which, having regard to the age and capacity of the party, the nature of the transaction, and all the circumstances of the case, appears to have been such as to preclude the exercise of free and deliberate judgment, is considered by courts of equity to be undue influence, and is a ground for setting aside the act procured by its employment." Pollock, Contracts (8th Eng. Ed.) p. 640; *Preston v. Preston*, 102 Conn. 96, 109, 128 A. 292.

The ultimate question before the court was whether Mrs. Judd's mind was so dominated by Mrs. Pyle as to prevent the exercise of an independent judgment. The burden of proof rested on Goddard. *Sullivan v. Clear,* 101 Conn. 603, 612, 127 A. 14. Such burden is not ordinarily met by direct and positive evidence. When it is sustained, it is usually owing to proof by logical and reasonable inferences from all the facts and circumstances of the case.

The conclusion of the court that Mrs. Pyle unduly influenced her aunt was reasonable and logical. The speed with which she acted and the totality of her operations are impressive. Within a matter of weeks she received from Mrs. Judd all but $500 of the latter's assets. She kept her aunt in practical isolation from friends and former confidants. At this time Mrs. Judd was frequently confused and forgetful. The infirmities, both mental and physical, of which her advanced age was the cause rendered her an apt subject for a scheming woman, who, unfortunately, was in a most advantageous position to exercise undue influence.

The court had the further advantage of reading several letters written by Mrs. Pyle to her brother Goddard. In them she related some of her activities in language of a most damaging nature. For example, in one she said, "I've tried to fix things so as to get everything for the best for you & I." Again she wrote, "If I could only find the certificates for that bank stock we'd be O.K. without going to probate court." In another letter she said that she was going to keep Mrs. Judd's "checking acct drawn out & put it in [Mrs. Pyle's] name in a savings acct." The evidence as to the issue of undue influence was such as thoroughly to justify the court in the conclusion it reached.

* * *

We now turn to the appeal of [Adolph Bucchi]. The court reached the conclusion that there was no agreement on Mrs. Judd's part to compensate the plaintiff by her will. It further concluded that the compensation paid to him by Mrs. Judd, while he was in her employ, was not less than the reasonable value of the services performed. Whatever merit there may be in the assignment of error attacking the first conclusion is dissipated by our view of the second.

If we assume that the plaintiff and Mrs. Judd entered into the claimed agreement, her failure to comply with her promise would entitle him to recover no more than the reasonable value of the services he performed. *Spurr's Appeal*, 116 Conn. 108, 111, 163 A. 608. On conflicting evidence as to the extent of the work he had done, the court concluded that he had been paid what his services were reasonably worth. Every week he received the amount of salary agreed upon. In several of the years he was given a bonus of $100. In all, Mrs. Judd paid him $1450 above his specified salary. That she may have intended to be more generous by her will and he may have expected her to do so is immaterial. He could recover, for her breach, only the reasonable value of his services. For these Mrs. Judd had already paid him. *Yantz v. Dyer*, 120 Conn. 600, 605, 181 A. 717. There is no error.

Notes and Questions

1. **Impending Death and One's Mental Capacity.** Mrs. Judd executed three wills before her death, bequeathing various sums of cash and property to Bucchi. Did she have the mental capacity to

make those wills? Did the Supreme Court of Connecticut discuss her mental ability or inability to fashion those legal documents?

2. **Promisor's Impending Death and Reliance on a Promise.** The Connecticut Supreme Court reported: "Rollin D. Judd in 1922. There he remained until Judd died in 1929. A *few days* before [Rollin D. Judd's] impending death, Judd obtained a promise from [Bucchi] that he would remain in Mrs. Judd's employ as long as she lived." Did Rollin Judd have the mental capacity to make a promise or understand Bucchi's promise immediately before dying?

3. **An Affirmative Defense to a Dying Person's Promise.** Assume that Rollin Judd promised in writing—a few days before his death—that Bucchi would be compensated for helping Mrs. Judd after Rollin's death. Would the Supreme Court of Connecticut enforce that written promise? Would mental incapacity be a good defense to bar the enforcement of a "dying man's promise"?

4. **Promisee's Insanity and Promisor's Continuing Obligation.** Consider what the Supreme Court of Georgia penned in *Hudson v. Hudson*, 13 S.E. 583 (Ga. 1891):

> An old and infirm father proposed to one of his sons that if the latter would remove from his own home to that of the former, and attend to and take care of him during his life-time, he would will to the son his home place. The son accepted this offer, and, according to the evidence, complied faithfully with his part of the contract. Sometime after his removal to his father's place, the old man became insane, and remained in that condition until his death, so that it was impossible for him to make the promised will. Nevertheless the son continued his ministrations until the father's death.
>
> * * *
>
> [W]hen the arrangement between the father and son was originally entered into both parties contemplated that the son would be entitled to and should receive compensation for his services, and it was not a case in which it was expected that the services would be performed on account of mere filial duty and affection.
>
> * * *
>
> It was certainly not incumbent on the son, after the father became insane, and consequently incapable of making the promised will, to abandon his part of the contract; but he had the right, and it was his duty, to continue taking care

of his father as he had agreed to do. The latter having become unable to comply with his part of the contract, the son had a right to regard it as one that never could be literally performed; and the existing circumstances were such as to justify him in continuing to render the necessary services to his father, with the right to be paid for the same.

B. The Infancy Doctrine and Voidable Promises

Kiefer v. Fred Howe Motors, Inc.
158 N.W.2d 288
(Wis. 1968)

Wilkie, Justice. Three issues are presented on this appeal. They are:

1. Should an emancipated minor over the age of eighteen be legally responsible for his contracts?

2. Was the contract effectively disaffirmed?

3. Is the plaintiff liable in tort for misrepresentation?

Legal Responsibility of Emancipated Minor

The law governing agreements made during infancy reaches back over many centuries. The general rule is that "the contract of a minor, other than for necessaries, is either void or voidable at his option." 2 Williston, Contracts, 2 § 223 (3d ed.). The only other exceptions to the rule permitting disaffirmance are statutory or involve contracts which deal with duties imposed by law such as a contract of marriage or an agreement to support an illegitimate child. The general rule is not affected by the minor's status as emancipated or unemancipated.

Appellant does not advance any argument that would put this case within one of the exceptions to the general rule, but rather urges that this court, as a matter of public policy, adopt a rule that an emancipated minor over eighteen years of age be made legally responsible for his contracts.

The underpinnings of the general rule allowing the minor to disaffirm his contracts were undoubtedly the protection of the minor. It was thought that the minor was immature in both mind and experience and that, therefore, he should be protected from his own bad judgments as well as from adults who would take advantage of him. The doctrine of the voidability of minors' contracts often seems commendable and just. If the beans that the young naive Jack purchased from the crafty old man in the fairy tale "Jack and the Bean Stalk" had been worthless rather than magical, it would have been only fair to allow Jack to disaffirm the bargain and reclaim his cow. However, in today's modern and sophisticated society the "infancy doctrine" seems to lose some of its gloss.

Paradoxically, we declare the infant mature enough to shoulder arms in the military, but not mature enough to vote; mature enough to marry and be responsible for his torts and crimes, but not mature enough to assume the burden of his own contractual indiscretions. In Wisconsin, the infant is deemed mature enough to use a dangerous instrumentality—a motor vehicle—at sixteen, but not mature enough to purchase it without protection until he is twenty-one.

No one really questions that a line as to age must be drawn somewhere below which a legally defined minor must be able to disaffirm his contracts for nonnecessities. The law over the centuries has considered this age to be twenty-one. Legislatures in other states have lowered the age. We suggest that the appellant might better seek the change it proposes in the legislative halls rather than this court. A recent law review article ... explores the problem of contractual disabilities of minors and points to three different legislative solutions leading to greater freedom to contract. The first approach is one gleaned from the statutes of California and New York, which would allow parties to submit a proposed contract to a court which would remove the infant's right of disaffirmance upon a finding that the particular contract is fair. This suggested approach appears to be extremely impractical in light of the expense and delay that would necessarily accompany the procedure. A second approach would be to establish a rebuttable presumption of incapacity to replace the strict rule. This alternative would be an open invitation to litigation. The third suggestion is a statutory procedure that would allow a minor to petition a court for the removal of disabilities. Under this procedure a minor would only have to go to court once, rather than once for each contract as in the first suggestion.

Undoubtedly, the infancy doctrine is an obstacle when a major purchase is involved. However, we believe that the reasons for allowing that obstacle to remain viable at this point outweigh those for casting it aside. Minors require some protection from the pitfalls of the market place. Reasonable minds will always differ on the extent of the protection that should be afforded. For this court to adopt a rule that the appellant suggests and remove the contractual disabilities from a minor simply because he becomes emancipated, which in most cases would be the result of marriage, would be to suggest that the married minor is somehow vested with more wisdom and maturity than his single counterpart. However, logic would not seem to dictate this result especially when today a youthful marriage is oftentimes indicative of a lack of wisdom and maturity.

Disaffirmance

The appellant questions whether there has been an effective disaffirmance of the contract in this case. Williston, while discussing how a minor may disaffirm a contract, states:

> Any act which clearly shows an intent to disaffirm a contract or sale is sufficient for the purpose. Thus a notice by the infant of his purpose to disaffirm … a tender or even an offer to return the consideration or its proceeds to the vendor … is sufficient.

The testimony of Steven Kiefer and the letter from his attorney to the dealer clearly establish that there was an effective disaffirmance of the contract.

Misrepresentation

Appellant's last argument is that the respondent should be held liable in tort for damages because he misrepresented his age. Appellant would use these damages as a setoff against the contract price sought to be reclaimed by respondent.

The 19th-century view was that a minor's lying about his age was inconsequential because a fraudulent representation of capacity was not the equivalent of actual capacity. This rule has been altered by time. There appear to be two possible methods that now can be employed to bind the defrauding minor: He may be estopped from denying his alleged majority, in which case the contract will be enforced or contract damages will be allowed; or he may be allowed to disaffirm his contract but be liable in tort for damages. Wisconsin follows the latter approach.

In *Wisconsin Loan & Finance Corp. v. Goodnough*, 228 N.W. 484 (Wis. 1930), the defendant minor was a co-partner in a business who had defaulted on a note given to the plaintiff in exchange for a loan. The defendant had secured the loan by fraudulently representing to the plaintiff that he was twenty-one years old. In adopting the tort theory and declining to adopt the estoppel theory, Mr. Chief Justice Rosenberry said:

> It is a matter of some importance, however, to determine whether an infant who secures benefits by misrepresenting his age to the person from whom he secured them is estopped to set up his infancy in order to defeat the contract or whether he becomes liable in an action for deceit for damages. In this case, if there is an estoppel which operates to prevent the defendant from repudiating the contract and he is liable upon it, the damages will be the full amount of the note plus interest and a reasonable attorney's fee. If he is held liable, on the other hand, in deceit, he will be liable only for the damages which the plaintiff sustained in this case, the amount of

> money the plaintiff parted with, which was $352 less the $25 repaid. There seems to be sound reason in the position of the English courts that to hold the contract enforceable by way of estoppel is to go contrary to the clearly declared policy of the law. But as was pointed out by the New Hampshire court, that objection lies no more for wrongs done by a minor by way of deceit than by way of slander or other torts. The contract is not enforced. He is held liable for deceit as he is for other torts such as slander, trover, and trespass. ... [T]he sounder rule is [to hold] an infant under such circumstances liable in tort for damages.

Having established that there is a remedy against the defrauding minor, the question becomes whether the requisites for a tort action in misrepresentation are present in this case.

The trial produced conflicting testimony regarding whether Steven Kiefer had been asked his age or had replied that he was "twenty-one." Steven and his wife, Jacqueline, said "No," and Frank McHalsky, appellant's salesman, said "Yes." Confronted with this conflict, the question of credibility was for the trial court to decide, which it did by holding that Steven did not orally represent that he was "twenty-one." This finding is not contrary to the great weight and clear preponderance of the evidence and must be affirmed.

Even accepting the trial court's conclusion that Steven Kiefer had not orally represented his age to be over twenty-one, the appellant argues that there was still a misrepresentation. The "motor vehicle purchase contract" signed by Steven Kiefer contained the following language just above the purchaser's signature: "I represent that I am 21 years of age or over and recognize that the dealer sells the above vehicle upon this representation." Whether the inclusion of this sentence constitutes a misrepresentation depends on whether elements of the tort have been satisfied. They were not.

In *First Nat. Bank in Oshkosh v. Scieszinski*, 131 N.W.2d 308 (Wis. 1964) it is said: "A party alleging fraud has the burden of proving it by clear and convincing evidence. The elements of fraud are well established: 'To be actionable the false representation must consist, first of a statement of fact which is untrue; second, that it was made with intent to defraud and for the purpose of inducing the other party to act upon it; third, that he did in fact rely on it and was induced thereby to act, to his injury or damage.'" No evidence was adduced to show that the plaintiff had an intent to defraud the dealer. To the contrary, it is at least arguable that the majority of minors are, as the plaintiff here might well have been, unaware of the legal consequences of their acts.

Without the element of scienter being satisfied, the plaintiff is not susceptible to an action in misrepresentation. Furthermore, the reliance mentioned in *Scieszinski* must be, as Prosser points out, "justifiable reliance." We fail to see how the dealer could be justified in the mere reliance on the fact that the plaintiff signed a contract containing a sentence that said he was twenty-one or over. The trial court observed that the plaintiff was sufficiently immature looking to arouse suspicion.

The appellant never took any affirmative steps to determine whether the plaintiff was in fact over twenty-one. It never asked to see a draft card, identification card, or the most logical indicium of age under the circumstances, a driver's license. Therefore, because there was no intent to deceive, and no justifiable reliance, the appellant's action for misrepresentation must fail. Judgment affirmed.

Hallows, Chief Justice (dissenting)

The majority opinion on the issue of whether an emancipated minor legally should be responsible for his contracts "doth protest too much." After giving very cogent reasons why the common-law rule should be abandoned, the opinion refrains from reshaping the rule to meet reality. Minors are emancipated by a valid marriage and also by entering military service. If they are mature enough to become parents and assume the responsibility of raising other minors and if they are mature enough to be drafted or volunteer to bear arms and sacrifice their life for their country, then they are mature enough to make binding contracts in the market place. The magical age limit of 21 years as an indication of contractual maturity no longer has a basis in fact or in public policy.

My second ground of the dissent is that an automobile to this respondent was a necessity and therefore the contract could not be disaffirmed. Here, we have a minor, aged 20 years and 7 months, the father of a child, and working. While the record shows there is some public transportation to his present place of work, it also shows he borrowed his mother's car to go to and from work. Automobiles for parents under 21 years of age to go to and from work in our current society may well be a necessity and I think in this case the record shows it is. An automobile as a means of transportation to earn a living should not be considered a nonnecessity because the owner is 5 months too young. I would reverse.

NOTES AND QUESTIONS

1. **Voidable Promises and the Infancy Doctrine.** The common-law doctrine of necessaries is a multifaceted doctrine—imposing duties on spouses and on parents and their minor children. First, it imposes a duty on minors. Generally, minors' contractual

obligations are voidable. *McBriety v. Spear*, 60 A.2d 528 (Md. 1948). However, the doctrine of necessaries requires a minor to pay the value of necessaries which were furnished to him or her. The minor's contract is not voidable. *Monumental Bldg. Ass'n v. Herman,* 33 Md. 128 (1870).

2. **Definition of Necessaries.** What are necessaries? What is the test to determine whether or not a certain good or service is necessary or essential for life, safety, and well-being? In *Keifer*, the emancipated minor was a "family man." Therefore, was the car a necessity? Did the court's majority in *Keifer* address this point? One court fashioned the following test:

   The scope of "necessaries" ... is not restricted to what may be considered the bare essentials required to hold body and soul together. Things required for and suitable in light of the rank and position of the spouses to maintain their lifestyle are also included. The kind and amount of such necessaries is to be determined on a case-by-case basis by considering the means, ability, social position and circumstances of both spouses. *See In re Olexa,* 317 B.R. 290, 294 (Bankr.W.D.Pa. 2004) (citing *Gimbel Brothers, Inc. v. Pinto,* 188 Pa. Super. 72, 145 A.2d 865, 869 (1958)).

3. **The Infancy Doctrine and Parental Obligations.** The doctrine of necessaries also imposes a duty on parents to pay third parties for furnishing services to minors. *Sansone v. Sansone*, 67 Pa. D. & C.4th 129, 134 (Pa. Com. Pl. 2004). Moreover, the Pennsylvania Supreme Court has a long history of applying the doctrine of necessaries and forcing parents to pay third parties when the *latter form contracts* with minors and deliver necessary goods and services which the parents could not give to the minors. *Johnson v. Lines*, 6 Watts & Serg. 80, 1843 Pa. Lexis 116 (Pa. Sup. Ct. 1843).

4. **Common-Law Doctrine of Necessaries and Parental Obligations After a Child's Death.** But does a parent's obligation to pay for a child's necessaries continue after a child's death? Appellate courts in Alabama, Illinois, Indiana, Ohio, and Tennessee have declared that a parent's duty to support a minor child includes the obligation to pay reasonable medical and funeral expenses for any child who dies before reaching the age of majority. *See Jones v. Jones*, 2003 WL 21488825 (Ala. Civ. App.), *Graul v. Adrian*, 32 Ill. 2d 345 (1965), *Kaplon v. Harris*, 567 N.E.2d 1130 (Ind. 1991), *In re Terrell*, 48 Ohio App. 2d 352 (1976), and *Rose Funeral Home v. Julian*, 176 Tenn. 534 (1940).

5. **The Codification of the Doctrine of Necessaries:** The Tex. Fam. Code Ann. § 2.501 reads: "(a) Each spouse has the duty to support the other spouse, and (b) A spouse who fails to discharge the duty of support is liable to any person who provides necessaries to the spouse to whom support is owed." In other states, the common-law doctrine of necessaries allows a third party to collect damages from, say, a husband, if the third party delivers food, shelter, and medical services to a wife without the husband's consent or knowledge. *See, e.g. St. Francis Regional Med. Center, Inc. v. Bowles*, 251 Kan. 334, 335 (1992).

C. Illegality, the Doctrine of Unclean Hands, and Voidable Promises

During the Elizabethan era in England, the rule regarding the unenforceability of illegal stand-alone and contractual promises was settled. For example, in *Fish v. Sadler*, 74 Eng. Rep. 165, 166 (1589), the court declared rather inelegantly: "when the unlawful act [begins], the illegal agreement afterwards ... is unlawful also." A shorter version of the same principle appears in *Rex v. Allen*, 86 Eng. Rep. 738, 738 (1670): "The corrupt agreement makes the contract void." Furthermore, early on, the Parliament of England codified the principle in various statutes, thereby making it applicable to the formation of illegal promises and contracts between English subjects within and beyond Great Britain. To underscore the gravity of Parliament's enactment, Chief Justice Lord Holt declared in *Bartlett v. Vinor*, 90 Eng. Rep. 750, 750 (1692): "Every contract made for or about *any matter or thing* which is prohibited and made unlawful by any statute, is a void contract, *though the statute itself doth not mention that it shall be so.*"

In America, Colonial and later courts of law and equity approved the English illegality rule. For instance, in 1804, the Pennsylvania Supreme Court decided *Mitchell v. Smith,* 2 Am. Dec. 417 (Pa. 1804). Citing Chief Justice Holt's declaration in *Bartlett*, the Supreme Court held: "[A] contract or agreement is unlawful if it ... encourage[s] unlawful acts or omissions." That same year, the New York Court of Appeals reaffirmed the same principle in *Belding v. Pitkin,* 1804 Cai. R. 147, 149 (N.Y. Sup. Ct. 1804): "A contract, in order to be binding, must be lawful. Whenever the consideration ... is unlawful, the whole contract is void."

Following the rulings in *Mitchell* and *Belding*, other state supreme courts adopted the principle that illegal stand-alone and contractual promises are void from their inception. *See Wheeler v. Russell*, 1821 WL 1489, *12 (Mass.) (embracing the New York Court of Appeals' ruling in *Belding*); *Carrington v. Caller*, 1829 WL 372, *11 (Ala. 1829) (citing the Massachusetts Supreme Court's decision in *Wheeler v. Russell,* 17

Mass. 258, 263–63 (1821) and concluding: "Every contract against public policy, or adverse to the enactments of the legislature, is illegal and void."); *Cheney v. Duke*, 1838 WL 1975, *5 (Md. 1838) (citing *Wetherell v. Jones*, 110 Eng. Rep. 82, 84 (1832) and concluding: "A contract to be void must be expressly prohibited or declared to be void, or be 'contrary to justice, morality, or sound policy'"); and, *Wooten v. Miller*, 1846 WL 1700, *4 (Miss. 1846) ("The principle is established beyond controversy that a contract in violation of law, or against public policy, cannot be enforced in the courts of the country.").

The doctrine of unclean hands or *in pari delicto*—"equal fault or criminality"—is closely related to the general proposition that illegal stand-alone and contractual promises are void. Generally, the doctrine of unclean hands prevents persons from commencing a legal action in courts of law and equity if their dispute evolved from illegal promises or contracts.

Even before the reign of Queen Elizabeth in the mid- to late 1500s, the doctrine of unclean hands was a major pillar in English law. To illustrate, in 1589, the Court of King's Bench Court decided *Fish v. Sadler*, 74 Eng. Rep. 165, 166 (1589) and held: All agreements to defraud or harm a third party are "abhorred in law"; as a result, courts will not hear any action arising out of such illegality. Furthermore, during the Elizabethan era, the rule against asking courts to enforce or to award relief under a *covin* was settled. Simply put, a *covin* is a secret agreement between two or more persons to injure or defraud another individual. *See Anonymous*, 84 Eng. Rep. 1171 (1678) ("Fraud and *covin* make legal acts illegal and void").

England's celebrated Chief Justices Lord Mansfield and Lord Kenyon wrote many majority opinions in the 1700s. And in several cases those learned jurists consistently ruled: Courts will not hear controversies or award remedies if an action and alleged injuries evolve from illegal or immoral promises, contracts, transactions, or conduct. *See Faikney v. Reynous*, 96 Eng. Rep. 366, 367 (1767) (Chief Justice Lord Mansfield's ruling: "Where a thing is prohibited by Act of Parliament, it is void as between the parties, and no court of justice will allow a man to recover for what is made unlawful to be done."); *Steers v. Lashley*, 101 Eng. Rep. 435, 436 (1794) (Chief Justice Lord Kenyon's ruling: "[If one knows that a contract is illegal,] he cannot be permitted to recover on the bill in a court of law."); and, *Booth v. Hodgson*, 101 Eng. Rep. 619, 621 (1795) (Chief Justice Lord Kenyon's holding, "[I]t is the great duty of every court of justice to administer justice as well as [it] can between the litigating parties.... [But it] is a maxim in [English] law that a plaintiff must [show] that he stands on ... fair ground when he calls on a court of justice to administer relief to him").

In 1899, the Supreme Court decided *McMullen v. Hoffman*, 174 U.S. 639, 654 (1899). Writing for the majority, Associate Justice Rufus Peckham stressed: "The authorities from the earliest time to the present unanimously hold that no court will lend its assistance in any way towards carrying out the terms of an illegal contract [;] ... courts will not enforce it, nor will they enforce any alleged rights directly springing from such contract."

Yet, during the height of the Transatlantic Slave Trade between the 1600s and 1800s, English and American courts of law and equity allowed insurers, slave traders, and owners of slave ships to enter court and settle heated disputes surrounding illegal promises and contracts. *See generally*, Willy E. Rice, *"Commercial Terrorism" From the Transatlantic Slave Trade to the World Trade Center Disaster: Are Insurance Companies & Judges "Aiders and Abettors" of Terror?—A Critical Analysis of American and British Courts' Declaratory and Equitable Actions, 1654–2002*, 6 SCHOLAR: ST. MARY'S LAW REVIEW ON MINORITY ISSUES 1 (2003).

Why? Are there exceptions to the illegality and unclean-hands doctrines? Consider the following cases. Do they provide bright-line rules?

Plumlee v. Paddock
832 S.W.2d 757
(Tex. App.—Fort Worth 1992)

Farris, Justice. [Michael Paddock, Jim Loveless, and Charles Roach were lawyers and members of a partnership (Paddock). Joe Plumlee sued Paddock for breaching a referral contract. Plumlee owned an ambulance company. And he alleged that Paddock refused to pay an up-front fee and a percentage of Paddock's fees for personal-injury case referrals. Paddock answered and filed a joint motion for summary judgment denying the existence of the contract and asserted even if there were such a contract that such contract was incapable of enforcement because it would be an illegal barratry contract. The trial court ordered a take-nothing judgment in favor of Paddock.

The Court of Civil Appeals set forth the law very early on this subject, and it has remained the same: Ordinarily, a contract between an attorney and one not an attorney, providing that the latter shall procure the employment of the former by a third person for the prosecution of suits to be commenced in consideration of a fee to be procured or collected therein, is void as against public policy, independent of statutes prohibiting same. *See Montgomery v. Utilities Ins. Co.*, 117 S.W.2d 486, 491 (Tex. Civ. App.—Beaumont 1938), *rev'd on other grounds*, 138 S.W.2d 1062 (Tex. 1940) (declaring that Texas courts will not enforce contract made for illegal practice of law).

In addition, the sharing of fees with a layman by a lawyer is prohibited by statute, as well as by disciplinary rule. *See* TEX. PENAL CODE ANN. § 38.12 (Vernon Supp. 1992); SUPREME COURT OF TEXAS, STATE BAR RULES art. X, § 9 (TEXAS DISCIPLINARY RULES OF PROFESSIONAL CONDUCT), Rule 5.04 (1989) [hereinafter TEX. DISCIPLINARY RULES OF PROF. CONDUCT] (located in the pocket part for Volume 3 of the TEXAS GOVERNMENT CODE in title 2, subtitle G app., following § 83.006 of the Government Code).

Moreover, courts generally will not enforce illegal contracts. *See Lewis v. Davis*, 199 S.W.2d 146, 148–49 (Tex. 1947). The policy is not to protect or punish either party to the contract, but is for the benefit of the public. "In Texas there is a presumption that contracting parties are knowledgeable of the law and contract accordingly." *Cherokee Water Co. v. Forderhause*, 727 S.W.2d 605, 615 (Tex. App.—Texarkana 1987), rev'd on other grounds, 741 S.W.2d 377 (1987). Accordingly, the courts will generally leave the parties as they find them. *After Hours, Inc. v. Sherrard*, 456 S.W.2d 227, 229 (Tex. Civ. App.—Austin 1970). Courts are no more likely to aid one attempting to enforce such a contract than they are disposed in favor of the party who uses the illegality to avoid liability. *Loggins v. Stewart*, 218 S.W.2d 1011, 1015 (Tex. Civ. App.—El Paso 1949, writ ref'd).

On appeal, Plumlee attempts to avoid the well-settled law by arguing summary judgment was improper because he was not *in pari delicto* with [Paddock]; denial of recovery affords [Paddock] unjust enrichment; and denial of recovery is against public policy. However, none of these arguments is valid.

It is true there are cases which hold when the parties to an illegal contract are not *in pari delicto*, the party least culpable may recover. *See American Nat'l Ins. Co. v. Tabor*, 230 S.W. 397, 400 (Tex. 1921). However, such cases depend upon the knowledge of peculiar facts by the defendant, not known by the party seeking to enforce the contract, in other words, a mistake of fact. *See Graham v. Dean*, 188 S.W.2d 372, 373 (Tex. 1945). This case does not involve any mistake of fact. Both parties were aware of the facts surrounding the entering of their contract. It is simply irrelevant that Plumlee maintains ignorance that this type of contract was illegal. *See Cherokee Water Co.*, 727 S.W.2d at 615 ("Ignorance of the law is no excuse").

In addition, courts have required parties—who wish to recover on an illegal contract—to prove their case without reliance on their own illegal act. *See Kokernot v. Gilstrap*, 187 S.W.2d 368, 370 (Tex. 1945). Plumlee cannot prove the existence of a contract, nor his right to recover, without proving his own illegal conduct in entering a barratry contract. *See* TEX. PENAL CODE ANN. § 38.12 (Vernon Supp. 1992).

As to Plumlee's unjust enrichment argument, courts generally will not lend their equity powers to enforcing contracts which violate sound public policy. *Stone v. Boone*, 160 S.W.2d 578, 581 (Tex. Civ. App.—Fort Worth 1942, writ ref'd w.o.m.). Moreover, equity requires "clean hands" of the party who is seeking enforcement of the contract. The Penal Code makes barratry an offense for the attorney as well as the other party who enters the contract with the attorney. Thus, Plumlee hardly comes to court with "clean hands."

Lastly, Plumlee uses a public policy argument which he argues is a complement to his unjust enrichment argument. Plumlee contends that State Bar Disciplinary Rules prevent lawyers from entering into fee agreements with non-lawyers, and by not allowing him to recover, this court would be condoning what the Supreme Court has forbidden. *See* TEX. DISCIPLINARY RULES OF PROF. CONDUCT, RULE 5.04 (1989).

The Supreme Court, in its comment following Rule 5.04, states the reasons for this rule: "The provisions of Rule 5.04(a) express traditional limitations on sharing legal fees with nonlawyers. The principal reasons for these limitations are to prevent solicitation by lay persons of clients for lawyers and to avoid encouraging or assisting nonlawyers in the practice of law." With that in mind, we fail to see how Plumlee believes this court can afford him any relief.

Plumlee's point of error is overruled and the judgment of the trial court is affirmed.

Packard v. OCA, Inc.
624 F.3d 726
(5th Cir. 2010)

Edith Brown Clement, Circuit Judge. OCA, Inc. and Orthodontic Centers of Texas, Inc. (OCA) appealed the district court's grant of summary judgment in favor of Robert Packard, D.M.D., M.S. and Packard Orthodontics, P.A., doing business as Apple Orthodontix (Packard). This appeal arises out of an illegal business relationship between a corporation from Delaware and a dentist from Texas.

The facts underlying this relationship are complicated, but largely undisputed. Dr. Packard, his former partner, and their professional corporation entered into a long-term service agreement with Apple Orthodontix, Inc. (Apple). Apple provided "practice management services" to orthodontic practices in seventeen states before filing for bankruptcy in 2000. With the bankruptcy court's blessing, Apple sold some of its assets, including the Packard-Apple contract, to OCA.

Shortly thereafter, Packard and OCA entered into several agreements. OCA paid to Packard almost five million dollars in exchange for, among other things and relevant here, the entry into a long-term management services agreement that superseded the Packard-Apple contract. This new agreement, the Business Services Agreement (BSA), included a twenty-five-year term for which OCA would provide Packard with business and administrative support and services. The BSA also called for OCA to develop up to seven new offices with Packard, with OCA agreeing to advance Packard the money needed to develop the new offices.

Five years into the BSA, Packard terminated the BSA and sued for a declaratory judgment that the Packard-OCA agreements were illegal, and therefore void. OCA counterclaimed for breach of contract, conversion, unjust enrichment, promissory estoppel, money had and received, account stated, declaratory judgments that the contracts were legal, breach of warranty and indemnity, and attorney's fees. OCA introduced evidence that it had paid Packard approximately $4,992,674.00 in up-front affiliation payments and advances, and argued that—taking into account the sums Packard paid OCA during the five years of the BSA—Packard retained a net benefit of approximately $2,279,275.00. Packard moved for summary judgment as to the illegality of contract.

The district court then stayed the proceedings pending the outcome of a related appeal to this court that required us to pass on the legality of OCA's standard contracts. In December 2008, this court declared OCA's standard contracts illegal under Texas law, concluding that the agreements allowed OCA to engage in the unlicensed practice of dentistry. *In re OCA, Inc.*, 552 F.3d 413, 424 (5th Cir. 2008) (holding "the subject matter of the [BSA] runs afoul of [Texas Occupations Code] section 251.003(a)(4)'s prohibition of unlicensed persons from owning, operating, or maintaining a premises at which those persons also employ or engage another person to practice dentistry"). The district court then lifted its stay of the proceedings in this case.

OCA conceded the illegality of the agreements, leaving its equitable counterclaims as the only remaining issues for resolution. Packard moved for summary judgment as to the counterclaims, and the district court referred the matter to a magistrate judge for preparation of a report and recommendation (R&R). The magistrate judge reasoned that, under Texas law, the general rule is that a court will not assist parties to an illegal contract. Recognizing several narrow exceptions to the general rule, the magistrate judge concluded that no evidence supported the application of any exceptions, and recommended that summary judgment be granted in favor of Packard on OCA's counterclaims. The district court adopted the amended report and recommendation over OCA's objections. OCA timely appealed as to its counterclaims for unjust enrichment and money had and received. OCA does not appeal the district court's grant of summary judgment on the illegality of the contract or the remaining counterclaims.

* * *

B. Illegal Contracts Under Texas Law

The general rule under Texas law is that "no accounting or recovery of profits can be had by one party to an illegal transaction against another." *Lewis v. Davis*, 145 Tex. 468, 199 S.W.2d 146, 150 (1947) (quotations omitted); *see also Beer v. Landman*, 88 Tex. 450, 31 S.W. 805, 806 (1895) ("[N]either a court of law nor a court of equity will aid either [party to an illegal transaction] to recover or reinvest himself with any title or interest which he, in consideration of such unlawful contract, has vested in the other, but will leave them in the same condition as to vested interests as they, by their own acts, have placed themselves").

This rule springs from a judicial "unwillingness to afford the matter an initial examination [which] flows from the failure of the illegal contract to confer upon the parties rights to be examined and determined by a court ... and from a refusal to aid a plaintiff who stands *in pari delicto* with the defendant." *Burks v. State*, 795 S.W.2d 913, 914 (Tex. App.—Amarillo 1990, pet. ref'd).

Texas law recognizes limited exceptions to the general prohibition. First, "[a] test, sometimes used in determining whether a demand connected with an illegal transaction can be enforced, is whether the plaintiff requires any aid from the illegal transaction to establish his case." *Lewis*, 199 S.W.2d at 151. Second, an illegal contract will not preclude recovery if the parties are not *in pari delicto*. *Graham v. Dean*, 188 S.W.2d 372, 373 (Tex. 1945) ("The rule that a court will not entertain a suit growing out of an illegal transaction is not always applicable where the parties are not *in pari delicto*").

Finally, "even where the parties are *in pari delicto* relief will sometimes be granted if public policy demands it." *Lewis*, 199 S.W.2d at 151. In reaching that decision, the question "often involved" is "[whether] the policy against assisting a wrongdoer outweighs the policy against permitting unjust enrichment of one party at the expense of the other. The solution of the question depends upon the peculiar facts and the equities of the case, and the answer usually given is that which it is thought will better serve public policy."

It is undisputed that the Packard-OCA contract is illegal, and therefore triggers the general prohibition against recovery. We turn then to whether OCA should be afforded relief according to one of the aforementioned exceptions.

1. Whether OCA Can Establish a Right to Recover Independent of the Illegal Transaction

Texas law distinguishes between a party who must rely on an illegal contract to establish his right to recover and a party that merely needs to incidentally refer to an illegal contract to explain the transaction, allowing the latter to recover. *See, Beer*, 31 S.W. at 807 ("The plaintiff cannot recover when it is necessary for him to prove, as a part of his cause of action, his own illegal contract, or other illegal transaction; but if he can show a complete cause of action without being obliged to prove his own illegal act, although such illegal act may incidentally appear, and may be important even as explanatory of other facts in the case, he may recover").

We hold that OCA cannot invoke this exception because the calculation of any recovery would require proof as to each party's satisfaction of the illegal agreement over a period of several years—thus requiring far more than the incidental reference permitted under Texas law.

* * *

We agree with the district court that, under these facts, any recovery by OCA would be intertwined with the illegal contract and hold that the first exception to the general prohibition against recovery by parties to an illegal contract is inapplicable in this case.

2. Whether the Parties Are In Pari Delicto

"Texas courts recognize that where parties to an illegal contract are not *in pari delicto*, the party least culpable may recover." *Villanueva v. Gonzalez*, 123 S.W.3d 461, 467 (Tex. App.—San Antonio 2003). The district court concluded that "there is no summary judgment evidence here to show that OCA was any less culpable than Packard." We agree.

In *Bateman Eichler, Hill Richards, Inc. v. Berner*, the Supreme Court addressed the contours of the *in pari delicto* doctrine. 472 U.S. 299, 310 (1985). The Court explained that the *in pari delicto doctrine* applies to bar a private action for damages in the securities context "only where 1) as a direct result of his own actions, the plaintiff bears at least substantially equal responsibility for the violations he seeks to redress, and 2) preclusion of suit would not significantly interfere with the effective enforcement of the securities laws and protection of the investing public." Bateman Eichler, 472 U.S. at 310–11.

Courts have traditionally applied the *in pari delicto* doctrine to allow plaintiffs who engaged in illegal acts to recover when: One party may act under circumstances of oppression, imposition, hardship, undue influence, or great inequality of condition or age; so that his guilt may be far less in degree than that of his associate in the offence.

Texas courts have applied the exception "where one party is unaware of the true facts and believes the contract is lawful, the general rule that an illegal contract is unenforceable does not apply." *Int'l Bank of Comm. v. Int'l Energy Dev. Corp.*, 981 S.W.2d 38, 52 (Tex. App.—Corpus Christi 1998).

The relevant issue is whether there is any genuine issue of material fact as to whether OCA and Packard do not bear "substantially equal responsibility" for the illegal contract, such that they are not *in pari delicto*. Specifically, the critical issue is the relative culpability of the parties as to the illegal contract. OCA sets forth two arguments in support of its claim that it is not *in pari delicto* with Packard: 1) that OCA subjectively believed that the contract was legal; and 2) that Packard, as a licensed dentist, had a heightened obligation under the Texas Administrative Code to prevent the unlicensed practice of dentistry.

As to OCA's first argument, the district court properly noted that "there has been no showing, and none is alleged, that Packard had knowledge of peculiar facts not known to OCA. Both parties were aware of the facts surrounding the entering of the contract." While "[r]elief from the effect of an illegal contract has been given in some cases to a party induced to enter the contract by means of fraud or undue influence," *Sherrard v. After Hours, Inc.*, 464 S.W.2d 87, 90 (Tex. 1971), even assuming, arguendo, that Packard knew of the illegality of the contract prior to entry and OCA did not, OCA does not allege that Packard concealed that knowledge from it or induced it into entering into the contract. Indeed, it appears from the record that both parties were sophisticated entities that entered into an illegal agreement that inured to each of their benefit. Moreover, "[s]ince every man is presumed to know the law, [OCA] had no right to assume that the contract [with Packard] was legal." *Nystel v. Gully*, 257 S.W. 286 (Tex. Civ. App. 1923).

As to Packard's alleged violation of the Texas Administrative Code section requiring dentists to prevent the unauthorized practice of dentistry, OCA argues that "the Packard Contract would have never been consummated if Packard had simply followed the proscriptions [the code] mandated." We find this argument unpersuasive.

* * *

As a matter of law, OCA and Packard bear "substantially equal responsibility" for the illegal contract and are therefore *in pari delicto*. We hold that the second exception to the general prohibition against recovery by parties to an illegal contract is inapplicable in this case.

3. Whether Public Policy Demands Relief for OCA

"[E]ven where the parties are *in pari delicto* relief will sometimes be granted if public policy demands it." *Lewis*, 199 S.W.2d at 151. Determining whether "the policy against assisting a wrongdoer outweighs the policy against permitting unjust enrichment ... depends upon the peculiar facts and the equities of the case, and the answer usually given is that which it is thought will better serve public policy." "[I]t is not the purpose of this rule of law to benefit or punish either of the parties. ..." *Norman,* 363 S.W.2d at 178.

* * *

The focus of the public policy exception to the rule general prohibiting recovery by parties to illegal contracts is properly on the public's interest, not the parties'. We therefore look to whether the "higher right of the public" will be best served by allowing OCA to recover and ask whether such relief would "discourage such transactions by others." Id.

* * *

The "higher public right" at the center of this case is the public's interest in the prevention of the unlicensed practice of dentistry. Indeed, the very reason this contract was deemed illegal is because its terms allowed OCA to engage in the illegal practice of dentistry. OCA fails to explain how the public interest of preventing the unlicensed practice of dentistry is best served by allowing it, a corporation that engaged in the unlicensed practice of dentistry, to recover monies it paid in order to do so.

* * *

Finally, the public policy exception to the general prohibition requires us to determine whether the policy against assisting a wrongdoer outweighs the policy against permitting unjust enrichment. We note that the "wrong" here is the unlicensed practice of dentistry. Under the "peculiar facts and equities of the case," we find a situation in which one of two parties, *in pari delicto* and substantially equally guilty of the wrong, has allegedly been unjustly enriched at the expense of the other.

We hold that allowing that party, OCA, to recover from Packard would not serve the "higher public right" by discouraging future illegal arrangements like the one before us. Therefore, we cannot say that "public policy demands [OCA's recovery]." We agree with the district court that this exception is inapplicable.

We are cognizant that this holding may permit Packard to be unjustly enriched at OCA's expense, but hold that the policy against permitting unjust enrichment does not outweigh the policy against courts assisting a wrongdoer based upon the peculiar facts and equities of this case. The judgment of the district court is affirmed.

NOTES AND QUESTIONS

1. **Criminality and Minors' Gaining Access to Courts of Law and Equity.** Assume that a state's penal or criminal code prohibits wagering, gaming, betting, or gambling. Now, assume that a seventeen-year-old high school student promises to pay an illegal $500 bet if Duke University's Blue Devils did not win the NCAA Championship. In the course of events, the Blue Devils do not prevail and the promisor refuses to pay the bet. May the promisee

obtain relief in a court of law or equity? May the promisor successfully defend herself against the promisee's action by raising the doctrine of unclean hand and illegality? Consider what the Massachusetts Supreme Court wrote in *Babcock v. Thompson,* 20 Mass. 446, 449 (Mass. 1826): "All gaming is unlawful; and money lost at gaming, whether by fair or by foul play, cannot be recovered back by the loser."

2. **Disaffirmance and Exceptions to the In Pari Delicto Doctrine**. In *Lewy v. Crawford*, 23 S.W. 1041 (Tex. Civ. App. 1893) a group of men illegally wagered on the outcome of a gubernatorial election. The gamblers placed their wagers with Lewy, a stakeholder. The bet violated a Texas penal statute. After the election, Crawford asked Lewy to return his wager to him. Lewy refused. However, at the time of the lawsuit, Lewy had not paid the money to anyone. The court in *Lewy* reaffirmed the general rule against permitting parties to an illegal contract to invoke the aid of the courts. But, the court found that the stakeholder (Lewy) still retained the illegal bet. In the end, the court allowed Crawford to disaffirm his illegal act and ordered Lewy to return the money to Crawford.

   The court stressed: "A gaming contract being illegal and void, courts have invariably refused to interfere between the parties to the wager, who, being *in pari delicto*, cannot invoke the aid of the courts in carrying out their contracts. The question, however, presented to this court is not whether it will enforce or affirm a gambling contract, but whether it will permit one of the parties to disaffirm it. We have investigated a large number of American cases, and in nearly all of them the rule is laid down that, as long as the money is in the hands of a stakeholder, either party has a right to demand his part of the money, and, if refused, can maintain an action at law, whether demand is made on the stakeholder before or after the happening of the contingency upon which the wager is suspended. This is the English rule, and is fortified by age, and hallowed by precedent."

D. Violation of Public Policy and Voidable Promises

In *Packard v. OCA*, Judge Clement wrote: "'[E]ven where the parties are *in pari delicto* relief will sometimes be granted if public policy demands it.' Determining whether 'the policy against assisting a wrongdoer outweighs the policy against permitting unjust enrichment … depends upon the peculiar facts and the equities of the case. … The focus of the public policy exception ... is properly on the public's interest, not the parties.' We therefore look to whether the 'higher right of the public' will be best served[.]"

But, a careful reading of Judge Clements' opinion reveals two public policies: 1) a policy against courts' assisting parties who fashion illegal promises and contracts; and 2) a policy against allowing one of several wrongdoers from crafting an illegal promise and becoming unjustly enriched. Of course, this leads one to ask: Which public policy is superior? Which public interest should receive the greatest amount of protection from a court? What is the test? Judge Clement tells us: An answer "depends upon the *peculiar facts* and the *equities* of the case." Consider the dispute in the next case. Are there competing public policies?

Y.W., a Minor, by and Through Vearl D. Smith v. National Super Markets, Inc.
876 S.W.2d 785
(Mo. App. Ct. 1994)

Pudlowski, Judge. On September 25, 1991, Y.W., an eleven-year-old child, was observed by National Super Markets, Inc.'s security personnel shoplifting candy. While the minor was still detained by National's employee, her mother entered into a stipulated release whereby National agreed not to prosecute the minor in consideration for the minor's agreement not to bring civil charges against National. Subsequently, the minor, by and through her duly-appointed next friend, filed a civil suit against National alleging an assault and battery upon her.

The trial court granted National's motion to dismiss on the ground that the minor's right to bring suit against National had been contracted away. Although both the parent's and the minor's names appear on the signature line of the release, it is unclear from the contract, and contested by the parties, whether the minor actually signed the agreement or the mother signed both names in a representative capacity. For the reasons hereinafter stated, such a determination is unnecessary.

In reviewing the lower court's dismissal of Y.W.'s petition, we must determine if there are any grounds for relief in either the facts pleaded or the inferences reasonably drawn therefrom. In this assessment we treat the facts averred as true and construe all averments liberally and favorably [for the minor]. [Y.W.] first alleges that because she lacked the capacity to execute a binding release the agreement is voidable. We agree.

An infant's contractual capacity is limited. Their agreements are either void, or more often, voidable. Assuming that the signature appearing on the release is appellant's, she has the ability to void the contract and pursue her claim. Point one sustained.

The second claim of error is that [Y.W.'s] mother had no authority to execute a release on behalf of her minor child and such action is in violation of § 507.184 RSMo Cum.Supp. 1993. Put another way, does a parent, without court appointment as a guardian or next friend, have authority to contract away the minor child's claim for damages?

Neither party has submitted authority concerning this precise issue and this court's research has not disclosed any authority which would clearly indicate the answer to this question. However, in deciding this issue, we must keep in mind that in any proceeding involving minors, they are to be considered "wards of the court and their rights are to be jealously guarded as provided by statute." *Morgan v. Morgan*, 289 S.W.2d 151, 153 (Mo. App. Spr.D. 1956). The requirements for the settlement of a minor's claim are dictated by § 507.184 RSMo 1986.

* * *

Based upon our research the terms "next friend," "guardian" and "conservator" in this statute must refer to duly-appointed persons and that a natural guardian would not be able to enter into a binding settlement of a minor's claim. *See Cox v. Wrinkle*, 267 S.W.2d 648, 652–53 (Mo. 1954). The requirement that even a parent be judicially-appointed the minor's representative gives the court the opportunity to determine whether the parent is qualified to enter into a settlement agreement on the child's behalf. The court may consider first, whether the parent has the necessary knowledge and ability to act under the circumstances and, second, whether a conflict of interest exists between the parent and the child.

* * *

National notes that § 507.184 RSMo 1986 has never been, and argues that it should never be, applied to pre-action settlements. We disagree. The statute is concerned with "contracts on behalf of the minor for a settlement of the minor's claim, action or judgment." [emphasis added]. The word "claim" is defined as "Right to payment, whether or not such right is reduced to judgment, liquidated, unliquidated, fixed, contingent, legal, equitable, mature, unmature, secure or unsecure." BLACK'S LAW DICTIONARY 247 (6th ed. 1990).

It therefore may include either a pending or a pre-filed cause of action. Furthermore, the statutory scheme is replete with evidence of the legislative intent to maximize the protection afforded minor's legal actions. If §§ 507.184, 507.110 and 507.190 exist to protect a minor's rights during a suit, the legislature must certainly have intended to safeguard a minor's legal right to bring a suit. ... We, therefore, hold that a parent cannot bargain away a minor's right to bring a civil action against an alleged tortfeasor without being duly appointed. Point two sustained.

* * *

[Y.W.] third claim is that the release is contrary to public policy in Missouri and therefore it is unenforceable. [Y.W.] argues that such an agreement is void due to illegality since "[a] contract made with the purpose and upon the consideration that a criminal prosecution shall be suppressed, stifled or stayed will not be enforced." *Ensminger v. Burton*, 805 S.W.2d 207, 217 (Mo. App. W.D. 1991), citing *McCoy v. Green*, 83 Mo. 626, 632 (1884).

In response, National cites *Town of Newton v. Rumery*, 480 U.S. 386, 392 in which the United States Supreme Court held that release-dismissal agreements are not per se illegal and argues that because the state has limited resources, it is sometimes in the public's interest for a merchant to refrain from pressing criminal charges against a minor.

National claims that in arriving at such a decision the merchant can take into consideration factors such as: whether the merchandise was recovered; the value of the goods taken; whether the perpetrator is a first-time offender; whether the perpetrator appears repentant; and, in a case in which the perpetrator is a minor, whether a parent is available to take custody of the child and exhibits concern and an interest in dealing with the problem on his/her own.

National argues that a shopkeeper may feel that the circumstances do not warrant pressing criminal charges but fear that the alleged perpetrator would use the merchant's decision to forego prosecution as evidence in a later civil action against the merchant. This concern, however, has been alleviated by our legislature. Merchants detaining suspected shoplifters are protected from frivolous civil actions by § 537.125.2 RSMo 1986 which reads:

> Any merchant, his agent or employee, who has reasonable grounds or probable cause to believe that a person has committed or is committing a wrongful taking of merchandise or money from a mercantile establishment, may detain such person in a reasonable manner and for a reasonable length of time for the purpose of investigating whether there has been a wrongful taking of such merchandise or money. Any such reasonable detention shall not constitute an unlawful arrest or detention, nor shall it render the merchant, his agent or employee, criminally or civilly liable to the person so detained.

Furthermore, under § 570.087.6 RSMo Cum.Supp. 1992: "[n]o owner or agent or employee of the owner may attempt to gain an advantage in a civil action by threatening to initiate a criminal prosecution pertaining to the same incident." Under § 575.020.1(1)–(2) RSMo 1986, the merchant, the minor child and her mother would be guilty of the crime of concealing an offense since the merchant conferred, and the minor or the mother accepted, "pecuniary benefit or other consideration in consideration of his concealing any offense, refraining from initiating or aiding in the prosecution of an offense or withholding any evidence thereof."

Moreover, National's reliance on *Town of Newton v. Rumery* is misplaced. ... We therefore follow *Ensminger* for its holding that a private citizen or entity may not contract away his/her right to press criminal charges against the perpetrator of a crime. National argues that the release should still be upheld because it could also be interpreted to be a lawful agreement by National not to institute a civil action against the minor, which National had the right to do under § 570.087.2–.3 RSMo 1986.

We note that a contract which has several items of consideration, one sufficient and one insufficient, may be upheld on the strength of the valid consideration. However, "one who gives illegal consideration for a promise is not given a remedy to enforce [the contract] ..." even if he or she offers a second and lawful consideration. National's inability to enforce the release is not due to lack of consideration, but rather it is due to public policy reasons. Furthermore, since the minor or her parent violated the law by entering into such a contract, they are also unable to enforce National's promise. Judgment reversed and remanded.

NOTES AND QUESTIONS

1. **Illegal Contracts and the Public Policy Against Prosecuting Minors Who Commit Crimes**. National argued that the court should have enforced the "illegal" release-dismissal agreement, because "it is sometimes in the public's interest for a merchant to refrain from pressing criminal charges against a minor." How can an illegal contract between a merchant and a minor serve the "public's interest"? Which public?

2. **Public Policy, Lack of Consideration, and Illegal Releases.** The Missouri Court of Appeals wrote: "National's inability to enforce the [illegal] release is not due to lack of consideration, but rather it is due to public policy reasons." Did the court clearly identify and outline those "public policy reasons"?

3. **Immorality and the Doctrine of In Pari Delicto.** Assume that two unmarried people promised to live together forever and share resources. Is the promise valid? If one person breaches the promise after ten years, may the other person commence a successful

action in equity to secure remedies? Would the doctrine of *in pari delicto* bar the action?

4. **Public Policy vs. Immorality**. What is the distinction between "public policy" and the "immorality doctrine"? Consider *Marvin v. Marvin*, 557 P. 2d 106 (Cal. 1978). Lee Marvin was a celebrated actor. Between 1964 and 1970, Lee and Michelle Marvin "held themselves out as husband and wife." Michelle verbally promised expressly to do wifely chores and duties. And allegedly, both Marvin and Michelle promised expressly to share and combine all accumulated property. Lee Marvin, however, breached the verbal promise. Michelle sued, accusing Lee of breaching an interspousal, express verbal promise. Lee Marvin's affirmative defense was not novel: He asserted that he and Michelle were *paramours living in sin*. Therefore, the express verbal promise was not enforceable because it *violated the public policy* of California. The trial Court agreed, granted Lee Marvin's motion for judgment on the pleadings, and dismissed Michelle's action. The California Supreme Court reversed the lower court's ruling, holding that *express verbal promises as well as implied contracts* between two unmarried partners—who live together—are valid. On the other hand, the California Supreme Court declared: Verbal promises between unmarried partners—which are based on "tasteless" or "chintzy" consideration—are not enforceable. On remand, the trial court found: Marvin did not promise Michelle expressly or impliedly to share his property. In fact, the trial court held: Over the years, Michelle had already received "adequate compensation" for her services. Therefore, the court ordered Marvin to pay to damages for "rehabilitation purposes." Ultimately, an appellate court reversed that ruling.

5. Nearly three years after *Marvin*, the Illinois Supreme Court decided *Hewitt v. Hewitt*, 394 N.E.2d 1204 (Ill. 1979). For fifteen years, Victoria and Robert Hewitt held themselves out as a married couple. They were not legally married. Yet, they had three children. Victoria decided to leave Robert and filed a breach-of-promise lawsuit. She asserted that Robert promised to "share his life, his future, his earnings and his property" with her. She also asserted that equity required Robert to transfer a one-half share of all the property they accumulated during their "family relationship." The trial court found that Illinois law and public policy required Victoria's claims to be based on a valid marriage. The appellate court reversed. Noting that the Criminal Code of 1961 made fornication an offense only if the behavior was open and notorious, the appellate court concluded that public policy did not bar her relief. In fact, the appellate court adopted the California

Supreme Court's reasoning in *Marvin v. Marvin*. In the end, the Supreme Court of Illinois reversed the appellate court, refusing to embrace the analysis in *Marvin*. Instead, Illinois' highest court concluded that Victoria's claims were unenforceable. They contravened the public policy, which disfavors courts' granting mutually enforceable property rights to knowingly unmarried cohabitants.

E. Duress, Economic Necessity, and Voidable Promises

Wright v. Sydow
173 S.W.3d 534
(Tex. App.—Houston [14th Dist.] 2004)

Wanda Mckee Fowler, Justice. [Under the False Claim Act (FCA), individual citizens—relators—may bring a *qui tam* action[a] in the name of the government, seeking damages for fraudulent acts against the government. *See* 31 U.S.C. §§ 3729–3733 (1994). In exchange for these efforts, a relator receives a portion of the recovery—up to thirty percent—plus reasonable expenses, costs, and attorney's fees. *Id.* § 3730(d). Don Kennard and Harrold Wright (Wright) filed an action under the FCA against a large number of oil and gas companies. (*FCA lawsuit*). Wright alleged that the companies underpaid royalties after producing oil, gas, and natural gas on federally owned onshore, Indian, and outer-continental-shelf lands. Wright hired attorney Michael Sydow and the law firm of *Verner, Liipfert, Bernhard McPherson & Hand, Chartered* (Sydow) to file the FCA lawsuit.]

* * *

The relationship soured rather quickly. Among other complaints, Wright [accused Sydow of misrepresenting their legal experience and failing to disclose the lawyers' conflict of interests. Less than a year after hiring Sydow, Wright discharged the attorneys]. ... Sydow filed motions to withdraw as counsel for Wright and Kennard and motions to intervene in the three pending lawsuits. ... United States District Judge John Hannah, Jr., the presiding judge over the three lawsuits ... granted Sydow's request to withdraw as counsel.

* * *

Several months later, ... the parties executed a Settlement Agreement releasing and discharging one another "from any and all

---

a A *qui tam* action is one authorized by statute in which a private citizen sues an individual or business to recover a penalty, part of which the government or a public institution will receive. *See* BRYAN A. GARNER, A DICTIONARY OF MODERN LEGAL USAGE 728 (2d ed. 1995).

claims, demands and causes of actions, including, but not limited to, those in contract, warranty or tort, of negligence or gross negligence, of *quantum meruit*, under common law or statute, based upon any acts and/or omissions" of the parties.

More than a year after executing the Settlement Agreement, Wright sued Sydow, asserting legal malpractice, fraud, negligent misrepresentation, negligence, breach of contract, breach of fiduciary duty, conversion, negligent supervision, fraudulent inducement, and Texas Deceptive Trade Practices Act (DTPA) violations.

* * *

Sydow filed a motion for summary judgment arguing that … Wright's and Kennard's claims had been settled and released by the Settlement Agreement. … The trial court granted summary judgment in favor of Sydow, holding in part that 1) all claims asserted by Wright and Kennard had been released by the Settlement Agreement; and 2) no genuine issue of fact existed regarding the alleged fraud and/or duress. … This appeal ensued.

* * *

IV. WRIGHT'S AND KENNARD'S SUBSTANTIVE CLAIMS RELATED TO THE SETTLEMENT AGREEMENT

We now turn to Wright's and Kennard's substantive issues related to the Settlement Agreement. First, they claim the trial court erred in dismissing their claims because the Settlement Agreement was procured by duress and fraud, and therefore was not enforceable. They then claim the court should not have dismissed some of their fraud claims because the claims arose after the effective date of the Settlement Agreement. Finally, relying on Texas Disciplinary Rule 1.08, they argue the court should not have dismissed Kennard's claims because Sydow violated the rule when they entered into the Settlement Agreement with Kennard, who claims he had no counsel at the time. We address each issue in turn.

A. The Settlement Agreement Is Enforceable; It Was Not Procured Through Duress or Fraud

Sydow and Verner, Liipfert moved for summary judgment arguing, in part, that Wright and Kennard settled and released their claims by executing the Settlement Agreement.

A release that is valid on its face is a complete bar to any action based on matters covered in the release. *McMahan v. Greenwood*, 108 S.W.3d 467, 478 (Tex. App.—Houston [14th Dist.] 2003, pet. denied). Only when it is set aside does the release become ineffective. In a summary judgment context, once a release is properly pleaded, the burden shifts to the other party to offer proof that the release should be set aside. Therefore, once Sydow pleaded and proved the Settlement Agreement, Wright and Kennard had the burden to present evidence raising a fact issue as to duress and fraud. Wright and Kennard presented evidence they believed showed the Settlement Agreement was unenforceable because it had been procured through duress or fraud. In its final judgment, the trial court found that "[a]ll claims of Wright and Kennard asserted in this lawsuit were released by those parties' execution of the Settlement Agreement."

We review the evidence below, and, as we explain, we agree with the trial court that the facts of this case reveal no duress or fraud.

a. Duress

Wright and Kennard argue that they executed the Settlement Agreement under economic duress. They claim Sydow created the duress by intervening in the FCA suits and claiming—in "bad faith"—an interest in Wright's and Kennard's potential recoveries in the FCA litigation. According to Wright and Kennard, the interventions jeopardized Wright's and Kennard's ability to continue with the pending suits because they were unable to find lawyers willing to prosecute the inherently expensive and risky FCA litigation while Sydow asserted an interest in the proceeds.

Wright and Kennard contend that Sydow asserted the claims to coerce a settlement and gain proceeds they knew were not theirs. According to Wright and Kennard, Sydow knew their intervention was wrongful, so they cannot assert they had a "legal right" to intervene. And, Wright and Kennard claim, Sydow confirmed their bad intent by filing the intervention and motion to withdraw and fraudulently representing they had sent notice of the intervention to all attorneys of record when they had not.

b. The Law Governing Economic Duress.

Generally, when one coerces another to execute a contact by taking undue or unjust advantage of the person's economic necessity or distress, the contract may be invalid or unenforceable. *Brown v. Cain Chem., Inc.*, 837 S.W.2d 239, 244 (Tex. App.—Houston [1st Dist.] 1992, writ denied). This legal theory is called economic duress. It requires both the acts/conduct of the opposing party and the necessities of the alleged victim or his fear of what a third person might do. The victim's plight alone will not suffice; it must be coupled with the bad acts of the transgressor.

What constitutes duress is a question of law for the court. *Windham v. Alexander, Weston & Poehner, P.C.*, 887 S.W.2d 182, 185 (Tex. App.—Texarkana 1994, writ denied). However, whether duress exists in a particular situation is generally a fact question dependent upon all the circumstances surrounding the situation, including the mental effect on the party claiming duress.

Economic duress consists of (1) a threat to do something a party has no legal right to do, (2) an illegal exaction or some fraud or deception, and (3) an imminent restraint that destroys the victim's free agency and leaves him without a present means of protection. *Dale v. Simon*, 267 S.W. 467, 470 (Tex. Comm'n App. 1924). Wright and Kennard had the burden to raise a fact issue as to each of these elements.

Finally, one additional rule is relevant and important. When a party making a demand has to resort to the courts to enforce the demand, no duress occurs—even if the demand is wrongful or unlawful—because the courts provide the victim with adequate protection. *Cont'l Cas. Co. v. Huizar*, 740 S.W.2d 429, 430 (Tex. 1987) (Under Texas law, "[a] threat to institute a civil suit or even the actual institution of suit does not, as a matter of law, constitute duress."); *Ward v. Scarborough*, 236 S.W. 434, 437 (Tex. Comm'n App. 1922) ("The courts have drawn a distinction between the cases where, although the claim asserted ... is wrongful or unlawful, the party asserting the claim ... is compelled to resort to the courts to enforce [it], and the cases where the party making [the] demand possesses ... the power to enforce the demand ... without resort to the courts. In the former case it is held ... with uniformity ... that there is no duress").

* * *

In sum, we find Wright and Kennard failed to establish that the Settlement Agreement was signed under duress.

Lewis v. Lewis
387 So. 2d 1206
(La. Ct. App. 1980)

Lottinger, Judge. The plaintiff-husband brought this suit for divorce and the defendant-wife reconvened, claiming that a post-separation community property settlement was invalid because she had been threatened into signing it by her husband. The validity of the settlement is the sole issue on appeal. From a judgment nullifying the community property settlement, the plaintiff-husband has appealed.

The Lewises were legally separated on November 7, 1977, in a judgment rendered in favor of Mrs. Lewis on the grounds of cruel treatment. On December 23, 1977, the Lewises entered into a community property settlement, authentic in form, to settle and liquidate the *community of acquets and gains*.[b] An authentic "Act of Correction" dated January 24, 1978, was later signed, and both documents were recorded in the St. Tammany Parish clerk of court's office on January 25, 1978.

In the community property settlement, Mrs. Lewis received a 1974 automobile, all her personal belongings, a television set, certain household appliances, and $10,000.00 payable in $400.00 monthly installments, with the balance due at the time of the final divorce. Mr. Lewis assumed all the community debts and agreed to hold Mrs. Lewis harmless from all the debts. Mr. Lewis also received certain immovable property owned by the community, some of which was apparently used to stable horses owned by Mr. Lewis and other persons who rented stalls from him. In the act of correction, Mrs. Lewis received one registered quarter horse in return for her signing over to Mr. Lewis three businesses operated by him—Lewis Feed and Tack, Lewis Stables, and Lewis Trailer Sales.

On April 12, 1979, Mr. Lewis brought this suit for divorce based upon living one year separate and apart following judgment of separation without reconciliation. The wife answered on April 26, 1979, and reconvened, claiming the community property settlement had been signed by her under duress and fear for her life. She also claimed the settlement was invalid because of *lesion beyond moiety*[c] and because she was not represented by an attorney, but these claims were dismissed during trial. Mr. Lewis generally denied the allegations of threats and duress.

Mrs. Lewis testified that most of the threats against her regarding the community property settlement were made before she moved to Shreveport from her Slidell home. She said her husband also threatened her once over the telephone. She said Mr. Lewis's threat was that if she did not sign the community property settlement and peacefully accept what she received in the settlement, she "would be taken care of."

---

b *See* BLACK'S LAW DICTIONARY (9th ed. 2009) (Under the civil law, an acquet is property acquired by purchase, gift, or any means other than inheritance. The term is most commonly used to denote a marital acquisition that is presumed to be community property.)

c BLACK'S LAW DICTIONARY (9th ed. 2009) (Under the civil law, laesio enormis or lesion beyond moiety is the sale of a thing for which the buyer paid less than half of its real value. In Louisiana and elsewhere, lesion beyond moiety allows "a seller [to] rescind a contract if he [has] received less than half its real value. [I]n spite of its imperfections, lesion not only was adopted in all modern civilian systems but became the means of testing the validity of contracts generally by their fairness.")

Such a test is no more difficult to apply in law than in equity, where it has long been established in our system. As the Romans applied it, it was a clumsy and inadequate way of reaching this result. In modern courts, in civil-law countries, it invests judges with a discretion not very likely to be abused, but sufficient to act as a deterrent to the grosser forms of economic exploitation." MAX RADIN, HANDBOOK OF ROMAN LAW 233–34 (1927).

Both documents relating to the community property settlement were prepared by Mrs. Lewis's attorney and mailed to her in Shreveport, where she signed them out of the presence of her husband, who retained the family residence in Slidell.

She explained that she felt forced to sign the documents because her husband told her he would quit sending her money until she signed. Jobless and with a young child to raise, Mrs. Lewis said she had no other choice but to sign the agreements. She admitted, however, that her husband had sent her a number of checks timely before the community property settlement was prepared and signed; that her husband never visited her in Shreveport, nor bothered her there; and that her husband never interfered in her request to see her son, who was living with the husband.

Mrs. Lewis also testified she was "scared to death" of her husband. She said the separation judgment was based on cruel treatment because her husband beat her, cursed her in front of others and slapped her around. Mrs. Lewis did not know whether her husband would carry out the threats, but she apparently concluded that he would not because he had made the threats in front of so many other people:

"At the time (of the threats) I thought he would (carry out the threats), but when I thought about it, that he said it in front of so many people, I didn't think he would."

Nevertheless, she added: "Right now, I'm afraid of him."

Two close friends of both of the Lewises testified that Mr. Lewis had a short, easily aroused temper. One witness, said he heard Mr. Lewis threaten Mrs. Lewis, but only out of her presence. He added, too, that he never heard any threats made concerning the community property settlement. Another witness said she heard Mr. Lewis threaten Mrs. Lewis regarding the community property settlement, but she did not know what community property settlement was being referred to. She admitted on cross examination that the "threats" were made during a husband/wife argument, and that Mr. Lewis did not actually threaten to kill his wife.

Mr. Lewis testified that if he ever said his wife would be taken care of, he only meant he would take care of her financially. He said that though he and Mrs. Lewis had numerous arguments, he never intended to inflict bodily harm upon her. He said he never denied her any money and never bothered her in Shreveport. He was never arrested for threatening his wife or for any other offenses against her.

James R. Strain, Jr., the attorney who drafted the community property settlement, said that he always considered himself to be Mrs. Lewis's attorney, and that he refused to answer Mr. Lewis's questions without Mrs. Lewis's consent. Strain said Mrs. Lewis never told him she was forced to sign the community property settlement. On the contrary, the document was discussed at length between the parties before it was signed. "In my conferences with Mr. Lewis and Mrs. Lewis, she never indicated in her actions, mannerisms, or questions that she was in any way duressed or forced." Not until three to six months after the documents were executed did Mrs. Lewis complain to Mr. Strain about the amount of money she had received in the settlement.

In oral reasons for judgment, the trial court accepted the testimony of Mrs. Lewis and her two witnesses concerning the alleged threats, and concluded that Mrs. Lewis had been coerced into signing the documents. He ruled that the documents should be rescinded since Mrs. Lewis's consent was not freely and voluntarily given.

The law governing the rescission of contracts because of consent induced by violence or threats is found in Articles 1850 and 1851 of the Louisiana Civil Code of 1870.

Article 1850 provides: "Consent to a contract is void, if it be produced by violence or threats, and the contract is invalid."

Article 1851 states: "It is not every degree of violence or every kind of threat that will invalidate a contract; they must be such as would naturally operate on a person of ordinary firmness, and inspire a just fear of great injury to person, reputation or fortune. The age, sex, state of health, temper and disposition of the party, and other circumstances calculated to give greater or less effect to the violence or threats, must be taken into consideration."

Exactly what standard courts are to apply to determine whether violence or threats have vitiated consent to a contract is difficult to determine, given the apparent contradictory standards in Article 1851. The first sentence of Article 1851 lays down an objective standard: Only that degree of violence or those types of threats which would lead a person of "ordinary firmness" into fearing great harm to person, reputation or property will be found to undermine his free and voluntary consent. The second sentence, however, requires courts to give weight to the subjective characteristics of the individual who claims his or her consent was coerced by violence or threats. Among these characteristics are age, sex, state of health, temper and the situation of the party.

In the few Louisiana cases which have interpreted this article as it applies to contracts between husband and wife, the courts seem to have placed greater weight on the subjective characteristics listed in Article 1851.

* * *

Despite the apparently inconsistent standards in Article 1851, our goal is to attempt to reconcile the standards without emasculating either one. The redactors of the code probably realized that applying an objective standard to all situations could result in an injustice to those individuals who sincerely fear they will suffer great harm if they do not consent to an obligation, but whose fear would not be shared by a person of ordinary firmness. This may be the reason the redactors added the subjective qualities to the objective standard of Article 1851.

On the other hand, the redactors probably felt that a defense based on threats or violence should not be taken lightly because of the relative ease with which a person can claim he or she has been forced into agreeing to a contract. This may have been the reason for giving Article 1851 its predominantly objective flavor. As a compromise, the redactors adopted both standards, and a proper interpretation of this Article must necessarily focus on objective and subjective characteristics. This can be done by first determining the subjective characteristics of the individual who claims he or she was forced by violence or threats into agreeing to a contract and then deciding whether other reasonable persons with the same subjective characteristics would have felt forced into signing the contract under the same type of threat or violence.

In the case at bar, the wife—whose age was not in the record—was separated from her husband on the grounds of cruel treatment. A meager amount of evidence indicated some physical cruelty was involved. At the time she signed the agreement, the wife was living in Shreveport many miles away from her husband. She admitted she was in fairly dire need of money. The wife and two witnesses testified that the husband threatened to "take care of" the wife if she failed to sign the community property settlement. But the same two witnesses admitted either that the threats were not made in connection with the community property settlement or that the threats were made during a normal husband–wife argument in the presence of other persons.

And even the wife could not testify to any degree of certainty that she felt her husband would carry out his threats. At one point in her testimony, Mrs. Lewis claims that it was not necessarily the fear of violence but the lack of money which caused her to sign the documents. As noted previously, there is no evidence in the record to show that Mrs. Lewis was unfairly treated in the settlement agreements.

We find that, under this set of circumstances, a reasonable person with the subjective characteristics of Mrs. Lewis would not have felt forced by violence of threats into signing the community property settlement upon which this suit is based. We realize that the trial judge in matters of this nature must, of necessity, be given great discretion. He alone observes the witnesses and notices their demeanor.

The trial judge in this case chose to believe the testimony of the wife and the two witnesses in finding that Mrs. Lewis had been coerced by threats of violence to sign the community property settlement. The facts as presented above, particularly the fact that Mrs. Lewis received

$10,000.00 in the settlement and the fact that she signed the settlement in Shreveport, lead us inexorably to the conclusion that the trial judge was clearly wrong in his determination.

Mrs. Lewis has presented no evidence that the settlement was lesionary. In fact she abandoned such a claim at trial. Her basic complaint, it seems, is that she signed the settlement because she was in need of money. The court in *Wilson v. Aetna Casualty and Surety Company*, 228 So.2d 229 (La. App. 3rd Cir. 1969)—under circumstances of duress which seem much more severe than those in this case—found that strong economic duress, by itself, was insufficient to vitiate the consent given to an otherwise valid contract. We feel the same rule must be applied in the case of the community property settlement between the husband and the wife.

Therefore, for the above and foregoing reasons, the decision of the trial court is reversed and the defendant-wife's claim is dismissed. The appellee will pay the costs of this appeal.

NOTES AND QUESTIONS

1. **Proving Duress—The "Subjective" Versus the "Objective" Test.** As discussed in *Lewis v. Lewis*, courts apply both a subjective and an objective standard to determine whether a stand-alone or contractual promise evolved from duress. Therefore, what is a person's burden of proof if she raises duress or undue influence as an affirmative defense and the court applies the "subjective test"? Consider what the court wrote in *Cintron v. New Jersey*, No. 10-195(NLH/JS), 2011 WL 4549147, at *4 (D.N.J. 2011):

> Plaintiff's burden of proof to show that she signed the settlement agreement under duress is a heavy one. A court may set aside a settlement agreement only if a party can show, by clear and convincing evidence, that the agreement was achieved through "coercion, deception, fraud, undue pressure, or unseemly conduct."
>
> Undue pressure constituting duress does not require an actual threat, nor does it require that the defendant engage in unlawful conduct. For a court to find duress, however, the plaintiff must suffer "a degree of constraint or danger, either actually inflicted or threatened and impending, sufficient in severity or in apprehension to overcome the mind or will of a person of ordinary firmness." Where a party claims to have suffered duress in the form of moral compulsion or psychological pressure, the pressure must be "so oppressive under

given circumstances as to constrain one to do what his free will would refuse."

From a subjective standpoint, the pressure must be of a type sufficient to effect the actual control of a party's will. Additionally, a court must find that the pressure in question was of sufficient intensity that "a person of reasonable firmness in plaintiff's situation would have been unable to resist." Smith, 343 N.J. at 499

2. **Undue Influence.** What is a person's burden of proof if he raises duress or undue influence as an affirmative defense and a court applies the "objective test"? Consider what the federal district court wrote in *Comeau v. Mt. Carmel Medical Center, Inc.*, 869 F. Supp. 858, 865 (D. Kan. 1994):

The elements of economic duress, as articulated by the Tenth Circuit as a general rule, are: 1) a wrongful act or improper threat; 2) the absence of a reasonable alternative to entering the agreement; and 3) the lack of free will. The only variant which an economic duress claim adds which is not explicit in the Kansas duress test is "the absence of a reasonable alternative to entering the agreement". However, this is essentially an objective form of the free-will prong of the well-accepted test and is consistent with the rule set out in Restatement (Second) of Contracts § 175.

The determination of reasonable alternatives, then, is an objective inquiry into the range of possible alternatives, whether or not the plaintiff actually considered such alternatives, and it is the party asserting duress who must show why there was an absence of such alternatives in order to avoid a contract because of economic duress. *See Libel v. Libel*, 5 Kan.App.2d 367, 368 (1980) (generally one who asserts duress to avoid an agreement has the burden of proof to establish that claim and such evidence must be of a substantial nature).

F. Fraud, Unconscionable Acts, Deception, False Pretense, and Voidable Promises

Schindler v. United Services Auto. Ass'n (USAA) Inc.
254 P.3d 583
(Mont. 2011)

Justice Michael E. Wheat delivered the opinion of the court.

A jury in the Second Judicial District Court, Silver Bow County, returned a verdict for United Services Automobile Association (USAA), concluding USAA did not breach its homeowner's insurance policy with Gregory and Grace Schindler (Schindlers) ... Schindlers appeal from the District Court's orders denying their motion for summary judgment. ... We affirm.

Background

After securing a loan from Provident Financial (Provident), Gregory Schindler (Greg) bought a house located at 307 West Granite Street, Butte, Montana (House), in November 2006. Provident required Greg to insure the House, and, if he did not, Provident could force-place insurance at his expense. The initial insurance policy Greg secured was cancelled in October 2007, and Provident subsequently force-placed insurance. Greg was unable to afford the force-placed policy and sought other insurance.

On November 13, 2007, Greg—a retired Marine captain—telephoned USAA, a members-only association that provides insurance to current and former members of the United States military and their dependents. Greg's call was randomly routed to USAA customer service representative Leeann Williams (Williams). Williams asked Greg a series of questions and, based upon his answers, provided Greg with a quote for a homeowner's policy. The call was not recorded. Greg subsequently paid the required premium and received a written policy in the mail.

The House was destroyed by fire on July 29, 2008, after a tenant left a smoldering cigarette on a couch. Greg notified USAA, and general adjuster Rick Aufrecht (Aufrecht) was assigned to adjust Schindlers' loss. During his investigation, Aufrecht determined that the policy limit of $502,000 was not sufficient to cover the cost of rebuilding the House. Aufrecht also discovered that the description of the House's structure in the policy differed significantly from the description given to USAA by Greg and upon which USAA had based its policy valuation.

For example, the policy described the House as having a single kitchen and four bathrooms, when, in fact, the House had six kitchens and six bathrooms. Although these discrepancies were apparent to Aufrecht, he proceeded with his investigation and submitted Schindlers' claim for payment approval. While the investigation was pending, USAA advanced $104,000 to Provident to discharge Schindlers' mortgage and paid Greg $15,000 to help with his losses.

In December 2008, after concluding its claim investigation, including examining Greg under oath, USAA denied coverage on the basis that Greg had committed fraud during his application conversation with Williams. Specifically, USAA determined that Greg had misrepresented that the House was his primary residence and was a single family dwelling with one kitchen and four bathrooms, when, in fact, it was not his primary residence and had been divided into eight apartment units, which were inhabited by approximately ten tenants at the time of the fire.

Greg testified under oath that he had told Williams the House had been divided into apartments; it contained six kitchens and six bathrooms; tenants were living at the House; and, that Greg intended to remodel the House to restore it to a single family residence. USAA asserted that had Greg divulged this information in his application conversation with Williams, as he claimed, he would not have met underwriting criteria, and the policy would not have been issued.

Schindlers filed suit against USAA in December 2008, asserting USAA breached the insurance contract and the implied obligation of good faith and fair dealing. Schindlers subsequently amended their complaint to include equitable estoppel. USAA defended on the basis that Greg committed fraud in the application process and sought reimbursement of the money it had advanced to Schindlers.

Before trial, Schindlers moved for summary judgment on their equitable estoppel claim, arguing that because USAA violated § 33–1–501, MCA, by not filing its application form with the Montana Insurance Commissioner (Commissioner), USAA should be estopped from defending with the application information. The District Court denied Schindlers' motion. USAA subsequently disclosed a physical copy of the computer entries made during the application conversation, which contained the prompts and/or questions that Williams had asked Greg and his answers (screen shots). Schindlers moved in limine to exclude any evidence of the screen shots. The District Court excluded the physical copy of the screen shots from evidence, but permitted Williams to testify about Greg's answers during the application conversation. Schindlers filed another motion in limine to preclude USAA from introducing any evidence of fraud on the basis that USAA could not produce an application in support of its fraud defense. The District Court denied the motion.

The case was tried before a jury in June 2010. Greg testified that he bought the House with the intention of residing there with his family after he remodeled the apartments. Greg admitted that he told Williams the House was his primary residence, although he had not slept there since approximately June 2007; he had been residing in a rental home since September 2007; and, six weeks after he spoke with Williams, he placed the House on the market, advertising it as having been converted to apartments. Greg testified he told Williams the House contained six kitchens and six bathrooms. Greg's explanation for the discrepancies between the description of the House as contained in the USAA policy/as recollected by Williams and the actual structure of the House was that Williams had somehow changed his answers.

Williams testified that she remembered Greg because his profile contained a warning note indicating that he was in the business [of] "flipping" homes, and a previous homeowner's insurance application of his had been declined in April 2006. Due to the warning note and Greg's request for a home insurance quote, Williams asked Greg additional questions, including whether he was going to be living in the House. Greg told her he intended to live there for three to five years. Williams relayed this information to underwriting and received permission to proceed with a quote.

Williams, based on prompts generated by USAA's electronic application system, continued to ask Greg a series of questions and entered each of his answers into USAA's computerized system. Williams testified that Greg told her the House was a single family dwelling (as opposed to an apartment); that it was his year-round primary residence; and that he did not have boarders. Greg told her the House had one kitchen and four bathrooms. Williams testified that had Greg told her the House had six bathrooms and six kitchens, it "would have put a red flag up to [her]" because six kitchens was not typical for a single family home. More questions would have been asked, and, had Williams discovered the House had been broken up into apartments, the application would have been declined because it was not a single family dwelling.

Based on Greg's answers, USAA's computerized system calculated the cost of rebuilding the House at approximately $502,000. Greg accepted that liability amount and was quoted an annual premium of $1,836.40. Williams testified that she never changed the information Greg had given her.

The jury unanimously found that USAA did not breach the insurance contract or the obligation of good faith and fair dealing and that Greg had committed fraud in the application process and awarded USAA the monies it had advanced to Schindlers. Schindlers appealed following the entry of judgment and ordered transcripts from oral arguments on their motion for summary judgment and motion in limine and the District Court's oral ruling on their motion in limine to preclude evidence of fraud.

USAA moved the District Court to require Schindlers to order and pay for additional transcripts on appeal, including opening and closing statements, all evidentiary rulings and motions made during trial, jury polling, and testimony of all the witnesses. The District Court granted USAA's motion, and, as a result, Schindlers paid $2,382.75 for the additional transcripts.

* * *

DISCUSSION

Issue One: Did the District Court err in denying Schindlers' motion for summary judgment?

Schindlers filed a motion for summary judgment on their equitable estoppel claim, arguing USAA should be estopped from claiming Greg misrepresented material facts during the oral application process because USAA, in violation of § 33–1–501, MCA, used an application form that had not been approved by the Commissioner. The District Court declined to invoke the doctrine of equitable estoppel as a matter of law or fact, concluding (1) that USAA's oral application process did not have to be approved by the Commissioner and, further, (2) that summary judgment was not appropriate because issues of material fact existed.

We conclude the District Court appropriately denied Schindlers' motion for summary judgment on their equitable estoppel claim on the basis that issues of material fact existed, which precluded summary judgment. Accordingly, we need not address the District Court's determinations regarding Schindlers' § 33–1–501, MCA, arguments.

Equitable estoppel, although generally not favored, is a doctrine based upon principles of equity and good faith and serves to prevent a party from suffering gross injustice at the hands of another party who created the situation or condition. *Avanta Fed. Credit Union v. Shupak*, 223 P.3d 863 (Mont. 2009). A court sitting in equity is empowered to fashion just results. *Kauffman-Harmon v. Kauffman*, 36 P.3d 408 (Mont. 2001). This Court has consistently recognized that "one who seeks equity must do equity." A party may not expect equitable relief unless he or she comes into court with clean hands.

Here, issues of material fact existed regarding whether Greg possessed "clean hands" when applying for the policy, as evinced in the documents USAA attached to its brief in opposition to summary judgment: 1) Greg's statement taken under oath and 2) Schindlers' insurance policy. While Greg stated under oath that he described the House as a six kitchen and six bathroom single family dwelling that had been converted to apartments, the insurance policy indicates Greg represented otherwise. Furthermore, Greg, for whatever reason, failed to notify USAA of the alleged errors in the policy. Because genuine issues of material fact existed regarding whether Greg applied for the policy in good faith, Schindlers were not entitled to estop USAA from defending itself.

* * *

Issue Three: Did the District Court abuse its discretion in denying Schindlers' motion in limine to preclude USAA from introducing evidence of Greg's fraud?

Schindlers moved in limine that USAA be prevented from defending itself pursuant to § 33–15–403, MCA, which precludes an insured's recovery if he or she committed fraud in the application process, because 1) the District Court had concluded the screen shots did not constitute an application within § 33–1–501, MCA, and 2) USAA could not produce an application due to the District Court's exclusion of the screen shots. The District Court denied the motion.

On appeal, Schindlers argue that the District Court erred in interpreting § 33–1–501, MCA, and, therefore, this Court should overturn the District Court's ruling. We decline to do so.

Entirely depriving USAA of its § 33–15–403, MCA, fraud defense is not the appropriate remedy because Greg's statements relating to the description and character of the House provided the basis for the type of policy USAA issued. The District Court acted within its discretion in permitting USAA to defend itself via § 33–15–403, MCA, by allowing Williams to testify about Greg's alleged fraudulent statements. The District Court did not abuse its discretion in denying Schindlers' motion in limine. * * * For the foregoing reasons, we affirm.

NOTES AND QUESTIONS

1. **Fraudulent Inducement.** In *Wright v. Sydow*, 173 S.W.3d 534 (Tex. App.—Houston [14 Dist.] 2004), Justice Fowler discussed the law regarding fraud and the enforceability of stand-alone and contractual promises. She wrote: "Under Texas law, a person has a duty to abstain from fraudulently inducing another to enter into a contract. *See Haase v. Glazner*, 62 S.W.3d 795, 798 (Tex. 2001). When one individual fraudulently induces another to enter into a contract, no contract results because the one who was fraudulently induced gave no real consent to the agreement. *See Schlumberger Tech. Corp. v. Swanson*, 959 S.W.2d 171, 178 (Tex. 1997). A settlement agreement or release is a contract and, like other contracts, may be avoided if it was procured through fraud."

2. **Definition of Fraud.** But, what is fraud? What is the test for determining whether a person's words are fraudulent? In *Wright v. Sydow*, 173 S.W.3d 534 (Tex. App.—Houston [14 Dist.] 2004), Justice Fowler wrote: "Fraud requires a material false representation that the speaker knew was false or that was made recklessly without any knowledge of the truth and as a positive assertion.

Johnson & Higgins of Tex., Inc. v. Kenneco Energy, Inc., 962 S.W.2d 507, 524 (Tex. 1998). The speaker must intend that the other party act upon the statement. *Id.* The party must act in reliance upon the representation and suffer injury. *Id.* In addition, implicitly, the rule requires that the victim not know that the statement is false. *McMahan v. Greenwood*, 108 S.W.3d 467, 479–81 (Tex. App.—Houston [14th Dist.] 2003, pet. denied) (finding that knowledge of the alleged fraud defeated a claim that a settlement agreement was procured through fraud)."

3. **Procedural Versus Substantive Unconscionable Conduct.** Legally, there are two categories of unconscionable behaviors—procedural and substantive. Consider the following discussion, which appears in 8 WILLISTON ON CONTRACTS § 18:10 (4th ed.):

> The concept of unconscionability was meant to counteract two generic forms of abuses. ... [T]he first ... relates to procedural deficiencies in the contract formation process, such as deception or a refusal to bargain over contract terms. ... [T]he second ... relates to the substantive contract terms themselves and whether those terms are unreasonably favorable to the more powerful party. ... [T]his formulation requires a showing that the contract was both procedurally and substantively unconscionable when made. ... [A] finding of a procedural abuse, inherent in the formation process, must be coupled as well with a substantive abuse, such as an unfair or unreasonably harsh contractual term which benefits the drafting party at the other party's expense.... The distinction between procedural and substantive abuses, however, may become quite blurred. ... [O]verwhelming bargaining strength or use of fine print or incomprehensible legalese may reflect procedural unfairness [because] it takes advantage of or surprises the victim of the clause[.] [On the other hand], the terms contained in the resulting contract—whether in fine print or legal "gobbledygook"—would hardly be of concern unless they were substantively harmful to the nondrafting party as well.

CHAPTER TWO

Cause of Action for Breach of Contract

This chapter discusses common-law rules that govern the construction, interpretation, and enforcement of "valid" contracts. Many legally binding written contracts contain a "scope of undertaking" clause. Typically, an undertaking clause will encompass *one or several unilateral or bilateral promises*. On the other hand, the scope-of-undertaking language and the entire scope of the parties' performance under the contract often do not mirror each other precisely. *See, e.g., In re Bond & Mortgage Guarantee Co.*, 196 N.E. 313, 314 (N.Y. 1935) ("[I] t is no longer true that the scope of an undertaking is necessarily to be fixed in absolute accordance with the literal meaning of the language used.").

There is more. Under the common law, a party may unilaterally construct a contract, which binds him and one or more parties. Such agreements are widespread and are called "adhesion contracts" or "non-negotiated contracts." For example, under Kansas law, an adhesion contract is a standardized contract, which sellers of goods and services offer to consumers on an essentially take-it-or-leave-it basis. Consumers do not have an opportunity to bargain and they cannot secure products or services without acquiescing to the terms and conditions appearing in boilerplate or form contracts. *See Ed Bozarth Chevrolet, Inc. v. Black*, 96 P.3d 272, 279 (Kan. Ct. App. 2003).

Apartment leases, automobile insurance contracts, and federal student loan contracts are excellent examples of adhesion contracts.

On the other hand, face-to-face negotiated contracts are exceedingly more prominent among small businesses and in some large business sectors. For instance, one would be hard pressed to find adhesion contracts, which outline parties' respective rights, obligations, and intentions, within the large financial-services industry.

And to repeat, unlike *stand-alone promises*, contracts generally comprise one or more promises, plus a multiplicity of supplementary provisions: acceleration, appraisal, arbitration, "AS IS," attorney-fee, cancellation, choice of law, condition precedent, condition subsequent, disclaimer, disclaimer of reliance, exceptions, exclusion, indemnification, limited warranty, liquidated damages, merger and integration, non-waiver, option, release, savings, severability, statute of limitations, time of performance, waiver, and warranty clauses.

But even more importantly, under the common law, a plaintiff must prove multiple elements if she expects to prevail in a court of law. Specifically, she must prove the following: 1) a "valid" contractual agreement between the parties; 2) "sufficient" consideration was exchanged for the contractual promise; 3) defendant breached the contractual promise or another provision in the contract; 4) the breach was the cause in fact of plaintiff's injury and damages; 5) defendant's breach was the proximate cause of plaintiff's injury and damages; and 6) monetary damages.

Of the six major elements, establishing that the parties formed a "valid" contract is arguably the toughest burden to overcome. And the reason is not terribly complicated. To prove that a contract is "valid," a party must present *prima facie* or probative evidence of seven additional sub-elements: 1) each party's intent to be mutually obligated and be bound under the terms of a contract; 2) one party's offer; 3) the other party's acceptance of the offer; 4) the parties' meeting of the minds regarding the "undertaking"; 5) each party's consent to the terms of the contract; 6) the execution of the contract; and 7) the "delivery" of the contract. *See Copeland v. Alsobrook,* 3 S.W.3d 598, 604 (Tex. App. Ct.—San Antonio, 1999). Discussions of the latter sub-elements appear in this chapter. And the remaining major elements—plus corresponding common-law, affirmative defenses—will be discussed in PART I, CHAPTERS 3–7.

SECTION ONE. DEFINING THE LEGAL CONTOURS OF VARIOUS CONTRACTS

In *Legros v. Tarr,* 540 N.E.2d 257, 263–64 (Ohio 1989), the Ohio Supreme Court reaffirmed legal principles that it had embraced more than a half-century earlier. In relevant part, the court wrote:

> [I]t is well-established that there are three classes of simple contracts: express, implied in fact, and implied in law. "In express contracts the assent to its terms is actually expressed in offer and acceptance. In contract implied in fact *the meeting of the minds,* manifested in express *contracts by offer and acceptance*, is shown by the surrounding circumstances which made it inferable that the contract exists as a matter of tacit understanding.
>
> In contracts implied in law there is no meeting of the minds, but civil liability arises out of the obligation cast by law upon a person in receipt of benefits which he is not justly entitled to retain and for which he may be made to respond to another in an action in the *nature of assumpsit*. Contracts implied in law are not true contracts; the relationship springing therefrom is not in a strict sense contractual but *quasi-contractual or constructively contractual*. In truth contracts implied in law are often called quasi contracts or constructive contracts." *See Columbus, Hocking Valley & Toledo Ry. Co. v. Gaffney*, 61 N.E., 152, 153–55 (Ohio 1901), and *Hummel v. Hummel*, 14 N.E.2d 923, 925–926 (Ohio 1938).

Now, consider the definitive statement of law that the Iowa Supreme Court penned in *Hunter v. Union State Bank*, 505 N.W.2d 172, 177 (Iowa 1993) just four years later:

> Contracts are either express or implied. A contract is express if the parties reach it by words. In contrast, a contract is implied if the parties *manifest it by their conduct*. There are two types of implied contracts: implied in fact and implied in law. ... As to these, all of the traditional rules of contract law—*offer and acceptance, consideration*, and breach—apply.

In contrast, implied in law contracts—also known as constructive or quasi-contracts—rest on *a legal fiction* arising from considerations of justice and the equitable principle of unjust enrichment. Such contracts do not arise from bargaining. And so, they are not real contracts. For that reason, the general rules of contracts do not apply to them. In short, a quasi-contract is "simply a rule of law that requires restitution to the plaintiff of something that came into the defendant's hands but belongs to the plaintiff." Dan B. Dobbs, HANDBOOK ON THE LAW OF REMEDIES § 4.2, at 235 (1973)

The overwhelming majority of state supreme courts have adopted Ohio's and Iowa's definitions and statements of law, barring a few words and phrases. Yet, litigants continue to file lawsuits, asking courts to declare whether certain agreements are express, implied-in-fact, or implied-in-law contracts. To illustrate the courts' challenges, consider the controversy and rulings in the next case.

Bailey v. West
249 A.2d 414
(R.I. 1969)

Aolino, Justice. This is a civil action wherein the plaintiff alleges that the defendant is indebted to him for the reasonable value of his services rendered in connection with the feeding, care and maintenance of a certain race horse named "Bascom's Folly" from May 3, 1962 through July 3, 1966. The case was tried before a justice of the superior court sitting without a jury, and resulted in a decision for the plaintiff for his cost of boarding the horse for the five months immediately subsequent to May 3, 1962, and for certain expenses incurred by him in trimming its hoofs. The cause is now before us on the plaintiff's appeal and defendant's cross appeal from the judgment entered pursuant to such decision.

The facts material to a resolution of the precise issues raised herein are as follows. In late April 1962, defendant, accompanied by his horse trainer, went to Belmont Park in New York to buy race horses. On April 27, 1962, defendant purchased "Bascom's Folly" from a Dr. Strauss and arranged to have the horse shipped to Suffolk Downs in East Boston, Massachusetts. Upon its arrival defendant's trainer discovered that the horse was lame, and so notified defendant, who ordered him to reship the horse by van to the seller at Belmont Park. The seller refused to accept delivery at Belmont on May 3, 1962, and thereupon, the van driver, one Kelly, called defendant's trainer and asked for further instructions. Although the trial testimony is in conflict as to what the trainer told him, it is not disputed that on the same day Kelly brought "Bascom's Folly" to plaintiff's farm where the horse remained until July 3, 1966, when it was sold by plaintiff to a third party.

While "Bascom's Folly" was residing at his horse farm, plaintiff sent bills for its feed and board to defendant at regular intervals. According to testimony elicited from defendant at the trial, the first such bill was received by him some two or three months after "Bascom's Folly" was placed on plaintiff's farm. He also stated that he immediately returned the bill to plaintiff with the notation that he was not the owner of the horse nor was it sent to plaintiff's farm at his request. The plaintiff testified that he sent bills monthly to defendant and that the first notice he received from him disclaiming ownership was "... maybe after a month or two or so" subsequent to the time when the horse was left in plaintiff's care.

In his decision the trial judge found that defendant's trainer had informed Kelly during their telephone conversation of May 3, 1962, that "... he would have to do whatever he wanted to do with the horse, that he wouldn't be on any farm at the defendant's expense. ..." He also found, however, that when "Bascom's Folly" was brought to his farm, plaintiff was not aware of the telephone conversation between Kelly and defendant's trainer, and hence, even though he knew there was a controversy surrounding the ownership of the horse, he was entitled to assume that "... there is an implication here that, 'I am to take care of this horse.'"

Continuing his decision, the trial justice stated that in view of the result reached by this court in a recent opinion [*Strauss v. West*, 216 A.2d 366 (R.I. 1966)] wherein we held that the instant defendant was liable to the original seller, Dr. Strauss, for the purchase price of this horse, there was a contract "implied in fact" between the plaintiff and defendant to board "Bascom's Folly" and that this contract continued until plaintiff received notification from defendant that he would not be responsible for the horse's board. The trial justice further stated that "... I think there was notice given at least at the end of the four months, and I think we must add another month on there for a reasonable disposition of his property."

In view of the conclusion we reach with respect to defendant's first two contentions, we shall confine ourselves solely to a discussion and resolution of the issues necessarily implicit therein, and shall not examine other subsidiary arguments advanced by plaintiff and defendant.

I

The defendant alleges in his brief and oral argument that the trial judge erred in finding a contract "implied in fact" between the parties. We agree.

The following quotation—from 17 C. J. S. CONTRACTS § 4 at pp. 557–560—illustrates the elements necessary to the establishment of a contract "implied in fact":

> "A 'contract implied in fact,' ... or an implied contract in the proper sense, arises where the intention of the parties is not expressed, but an agreement in fact, creating an obligation, is implied or presumed from their acts, or, as it has been otherwise stated, where there are circumstances which, according to the ordinary course of dealing and the common understanding of men, show a mutual intent to contract.
>
> "It has been said that a contract implied in fact must contain all the elements of an express contract. So, such a contract is dependent on mutual agreement or consent, and on the intention of the parties: and a meeting of the minds is required. A contract implied in fact is to every intent and purpose an agreement between the parties, and it cannot be found to exist unless a contract status is shown. Such a contract does not arise out of an implied legal duty or obligation, but out of facts from which consent may be inferred; there must be a manifestation of assent arising wholly or in part

> from acts other than words, and a contract cannot be implied in fact where the facts are inconsistent with its existence."

Therefore, essential elements of contracts "implied in fact" are mutual agreement, and intent to promise, but the agreement and the promise have not been made in words and are implied from the facts. *St. Paul Fire & M. Ins. Co. v. Indemnity Ins. Co. of No. America*, 158 A.2d 825 (N.J. 1960); *St. John's First Lutheran Church v. Storsteen*, 84 N.W.2d 725 (S.D. 1957).

In the instant case, plaintiff sued on the theory of a contract "implied in law." There was no evidence introduced by him to support the establishment of a contract "implied in fact," and he cannot now argue solely on the basis of the trial justice's decision for such a result.

The source of the obligation in a contract "implied in fact"—as in express contracts—is in the intention of the parties. We hold that there was no mutual agreement and "intent to promise" between the plaintiff and defendant so as to establish a contract "implied in fact" for defendant to pay plaintiff for the maintenance of this horse. From the time Kelly delivered the horse to him plaintiff knew there was a dispute as to its ownership, and his subsequent actions indicated he did not know with whom, if anyone, he had a contract. After he had accepted the horse, he made inquiries as to its ownership and, initially, and for some time thereafter, sent his bills to both defendant and Dr. Strauss, the original seller.

There is also uncontroverted testimony in the record that prior to the assertion of the claim which is the subject of this suit neither defendant nor his trainer had ever had any business transactions with plaintiff, and had never used his farm to board horses. Additionally, there is uncontradicted evidence that this horse, when found to be lame, was shipped by defendant's trainer not to plaintiff's farm, but back to the seller at Belmont Park. What is most important, the trial justice expressly stated that he believed the testimony of defendant's trainer that he had instructed Kelly that defendant would not be responsible for boarding the horse on any farm.

From our examination of the record we are constrained to conclude that the trial justice overlooked and misconceived material evidence which establishes beyond question that there never existed between the parties an element essential to the formulation of any true contract, namely, an "intent to contract." *Compare Morrissey v. Piette*, 241 A.2d 302, 303 (R.I. 1968)

II

The defendant's second contention is that, even assuming the trial justice was in essence predicating defendant's liability upon a quasi-contractual theory, his decision is still unsupported by competent evidence and is clearly erroneous.

The following discussion of quasi-contracts appears in 12 AM. JUR., CONTRACTS, § 6 (1938) at pp. 503 to 504:

> "A quasi contract has no reference to the intentions or expressions of the parties. The obligation is imposed despite, and frequently in frustration of, their intention. For a quasi contract neither promise nor privity, real or imagined, is necessary. In quasi contracts the obligation arises, not from consent of the parties, as in the case of contracts, express or implied in fact, but from the law of natural immutable justice and equity. The act, or acts, from which the law implies the contract must, however, be voluntary. Where a case shows that it is the duty of the defendant to pay, the law imputes to him a promise to fulfil that obligation. The duty, which thus forms the foundation of a quasi-contractual obligation, is frequently based on the doctrine of unjust enrichment." ...
>
> The law will not imply a promise against the express declaration of the party to be charged, made at the time of the supposed undertaking, unless such party is under legal obligation paramount to his will to perform some duty, and he is not under such legal obligation unless there is a demand in equity and good conscience that he should perform the duty."

Therefore, the essential elements of a quasi-contract are a benefit conferred upon defendant by plaintiff, appreciation by defendant of such benefit, and acceptance and retention by defendant of such benefit under such circumstances that it would be inequitable to retain the benefit without payment of the value thereof. *Home Savings Bank v. General Finance Corp.*, 103 N.W.2d 117 (Wis. 1960).

The key question raised by this appeal with respect to the establishment of a quasi-contract is whether or not plaintiff was acting as a "volunteer" at the time he accepted the horse for boarding at his farm. There is a long line of authority which has clearly enunciated the general rule that "... if a performance is rendered by one person without any request by another, it is very unlikely that this person will be under a legal duty to pay compensation." 1 A Corbin, CONTRACTS § 234.

The RESTATEMENT OF RESTITUTION, §2 (1937) provides: "A person who officiously confers a benefit upon another is not entitled to restitution therefor." COMMENT A in the above-mentioned section states in part as follows:

> "Policy ordinarily requires that a person who has conferred a benefit ... by way of giving another services ... should not be permitted to require the other to pay therefor, unless the

> one conferring the benefit had a valid reason for so doing. A person is not required to deal with another unless he so desires and, ordinarily, a person should not be required to become an obligor unless he so desires."

Applying those principles to the facts in the case at bar it is clear that plaintiff cannot recover.

The plaintiff's testimony on cross-examination is the only evidence in the record relating to what transpired between Kelly and him at the time the horse was accepted for boarding. The defendant's attorney asked plaintiff if he had any conversation with Kelly at that time, and plaintiff answered in substance that he had noticed that the horse was very lame and that Kelly had told him: "That's why they wouldn't accept him at Belmont Track." The plaintiff also testified that he had inquired of Kelly as to the ownership of "Bascom's Folly," and had been told that "Dr. Strauss made a deal and that's all I know."

It further appears from the record that plaintiff acknowledged receipt of the horse by signing a uniform livestock bill of lading, which clearly indicated on its face that the horse in question had been consigned by defendant's trainer not to plaintiff, but to Dr. Strauss's trainer at Belmont Park. Knowing at the time he accepted the horse for boarding that a controversy surrounded its ownership, plaintiff could not reasonably expect remuneration from defendant, nor can it be said that defendant acquiesced in the conferment of a benefit upon him. The undisputed testimony was that defendant, upon receipt of plaintiff's first bill, immediately notified him that he was not the owner of "Bascom's Folly" and would not be responsible for its keep.

It is our judgment that the plaintiff was a mere volunteer who boarded and maintained "Bascom's Folly" at his own risk and with full knowledge that he might not be reimbursed for expenses he incurred incident thereto.

The plaintiff's appeal is denied and dismissed, the defendant's cross appeal is sustained, and the cause is remanded to the superior court for entry of judgment for the defendant.

NOTES AND QUESTIONS

1. **Distinguishing the Litigants.** Who is the plaintiff in *Bailey v. West*? Who is the appellant? Generally, at the trial-court level, the plaintiff's name will appear first. And, at the appellate level, the appellant's name appears first. However, fairly often, a trial court's ruling will dissatisfy both the plaintiff and defendant. Therefore, both litigants will appeal the judge's ruling. For example, in

Bailey, we find: "The case was tried before a justice of the superior court sitting without a jury. ... The cause is now before us *on the plaintiff's appeal and defendant's cross appeal from the judgment* entered pursuant to such decision." Customarily, the title of the appellate decision will have the names of both litigants who appealed. And generally, the name of the litigant who appealed first will appear first in the title.

2. **Distinguishing Agents from Principals.** In *Bailey*, the Rhode Island Supreme Court embraced the following findings:

> [West]—accompanied by his horse trainer—went to Belmont Park ... [West] ***purchased*** "Bascom's Folly" from a Dr. Strauss and arranged to have the horse shipped to Suffolk Downs. ... Upon its arrival [West's] trainer discovered that the horse was lame. ... [The trainer] notified [West] who ordered [the trainer] to reship the horse by van to the seller [Strauss] at Belmont Park. [Strauss] refused to accept delivery at Belmont. ... [T] hereupon, the van driver, one Kelly, called [West's] trainer and ***asked for further instructions***. Although the trial testimony is in conflict as to what the trainer told [Kelly], it is not disputed that on the same day Kelly brought "Bascom's Folly" to [Bailey's] farm where the horse remained until July 3, 1966, when it was sold by plaintiff to a third party.

Was West a principal and were the trainer and Kelly agents for West? Did the Rhode Island Supreme Court discuss the law of agency?

3. **Agents' Common-Law Authority.** May agents negotiate and form temporary and permanent contracts—express and implied-in-fact—on behalf of principals? May agents bind principals under contractual agreements?

4. **Agency and Privity of Contract.** An agent may make a contract for an undisclosed principal in his own name, and the principal may sue or be sued on the contract. *Latch v. Gratty, Inc.*, 107 S.W.3d 543, 546 (Tex. 2003) (citing *First Nat'l Bank of Wichita Falls v. Fite*, 115 S.W.2d 1105, 1109–10 (Tex. 1938). *See also*, RESTATEMENT (SECOND) OF AGENCY § 320 (1958) ("Unless otherwise agreed, a person making or purporting to make a contract with another—as agent for a disclosed principal—does not become a party to the contract."); and, 17A CORPUS JURIS SECUNDUM CONTRACTS § 364 (West 2007) ("An individual who signs a corporate contract and indicates the name of the corporation and the nature of his or her representative capacity on the contract is generally not subject to personal liability on the contract.").

5. **Insurance Agents' Right to Bind Under the Common Law.** Consider the conflict and court's ruling in *Lucadou v. Time Ins. Co.* 758 S.W.2d 886, 887 (Tex. App.—Houston [14 Dist.], 1988)

> [Lucadou] charged that Time, through Melchor (agent), made misrepresentations. ... [She thought that] she and her son were covered by a Time health insurance policy (contract), and only became aware that she lacked coverage ... after she hospitalized her son. ... [He] suffered from a terminal brain disorder. ... Time denied coverage for her son. [She] applied and paid an initial premium for health insurance ... but ... Melchor failed to forward the application and accompanying premium to Time, although he did give her a conditional receipt. ... [T]he conditional receipt ... provided that insurance coverage could "become effective prior to policy (contract) delivery" on satisfaction of three conditions:
>
> 1. The proposed insured(s) must be, on the effective date ... a risk acceptable to the company under its rules, standards and practices for the exact policy (contract) and premium applied for, without any modification.
> 2. The amount of the payment taken with the application must be equal to the amount of the full first premium according to the mode of premium payment selected.
> 3. The policy (contract) is issued exactly as applied for within 60 days from the date of the application.
>
> If each and every one of the above conditions shall have been fulfilled, then insurance as provided by the terms and conditions of the policy (contract) applied for will become effective, prior to policy (contract) delivery. ... "Effective date" as used herein: Means the later of (a) the date the application is signed, (b) the date of completion of all medical examinations, if required, and (c) the Requested Contract Date shown on the application, but for Health Insurance, not more than 10 days prior to the receipt of the application by the Company.
>
> Relying on the conditional receipt, Time's literature, and Melchor's representations, [Lucadou] claimed that Time—through Melchor (Agent)—committed misrepresentation, *breach of contract*, and fraud.

4. **Insurance Agents' Right to Bind Under Statutes.** VERNON'S TEXAS INSURANCE CODE § 4001.052

> (a) A person who solicits an application for life, accident, or health insurance or property or casualty insurance is *considered the agent of the insurer* issuing a policy on the application

and not the agent of the insured in any controversy between the insurer and the insured, the insured's beneficiary, or the insured's dependents.

(b) The agent may not alter or waive a term or condition of the application or policy (contract).

SECTION TWO: PLAINTIFF'S BURDEN TO ESTABLISH PRIMA FACIE PROOF OF A "VALID" AGREEMENT

To repeat, a plaintiff must prove several elements to establish that he and another party formed a "valid" contract. On the other hand, if one searches large legal databases, one would find an interesting development: The *rules* that govern the formation of a valid contract are rarely litigated in courts of law. One explanation for the paucity of litigation is terribly simple: The greater majority of rules regarding offer, acceptance, intent, mutuality, etc., are settled. Consequently, they generate little debate among litigants.

Second, when considering the entirety and volume of lawsuits involving breached contracts, a researcher finds remarkably few disputes in courts of appeals over another issue: whether lower courts *apply* intent-to-contract, offer, acceptance, mutuality, and meeting-of-minds rules correctly or incorrectly. And quite simply, this result has materialized because the increasing use of boilerplate or standard-form contracts has reduced significantly plaintiffs' obligation to prove that she and another party formed a valid contract.

Beginning with the insurance industry, boilerplate, standardized, or standard-form contracts have been in use for more than two centuries.[a] Today, standardized contracts are pervasive, governing commercial transactions in many industries. *See, e.g., College of Notre Dame of Maryland, Inc. v. Morabito Consultants, Inc.*, 752 A.2d 265, 273–74 (Md. Ct. App. 2000) ("The standard form contracts drafted by the American Institute of Architects (AIA) are widely used."); *U.S. Fidelity & Guaranty Co. v. Treadwell Corp.* 58 F. Supp. 2d 77, 84 (S.D.N.Y. 1999) (reporting that the insurance industry began using standard-form comprehensive general liability contracts in the 1960s). In fact, one commentator estimated that standard-form contracts comprise ninety-nine percent of all written contracts.[b]

a *See* Michael I. Meyerson, *The Reunification of Contract Law: The Objective Theory of Consumer Form Contracts*, 47 U. Miami L. Rev. 1263, 1263–64 (1993).

b *See* W. David Slawson, *Standard Form Contracts and Democratic Control of Lawmaking Power*, 84 Harv. L. Rev. 529, 529 (1971) "Standard form contracts

Therefore, in light of the meteoric rise of standardized contracts and decline of negotiated agreements, courts do not have to spend precious resources determining whether or not a plaintiff has established a valid contract. However, novel issues have arisen and continue to arise, involving the construction of boilerplate contracts as well as the formation of negotiated contracts. Discussions of those issues appear below.

A. Proof of the Parties' Intent to Be Bound

1) Competing and Conflicting Legal Doctrines to Uncover Intent

The King v. The Inhabitants of Shinfield
104 Eng. Rep. 709, 14 East 541
(K.B. 1811)

Martha—the wife of Richard Lanesbury, a private in the Royal Berks Militia—was removed by an order of justices from the parish of Saint Giles in Reading to Shinfield, in the county of Berks. [The] order was confirmed by the sessions, on appeal, subject to the opinion of this Court on the following case.

The pauper's husband in June 1806—before his marriage [and] then a minor—hired himself for a year to James Palmer of Shinfield, brick maker. ... [The husband worked] upwards of a year in Palmer's service. On the 29th of September 1806 the pauper's husband—being still a minor—and Palmer signed the following agreement on unstamped paper, and not under seals, under which the pauper's husband served the whole three years.

A Memorandum and Agreement Between
James Palmer and Richard Lanesbury

> This agreement made the 29th of September 1806 between James Palmer, brick maker of Shinfield in the county of Berks, and Richard Lanesbury of Sonning, &c. I, Richard Lanesbury, do hereby covenant and agree to serve James Palmer for three years, to learn to make bricks, and the art of burning, on condition of the said James Palmer's finding me the said Richard Lanesbury sufficient victuals, drink, lodging and clothes, and to be decently clothed in the habit of a working

probably account for more than ninety-nine percent of all the contracts now made. Most persons have difficulty remembering the last time they contracted other than by standard form; except for casual oral agreements, they probably never have. But if they are active, they contract by standard form several times a day. Parking lot and theater tickets, package receipts, department store charge slips, and gas station credit card purchase slips are all standard form contracts."

> man at the expiration of the three years, on condition of my helping to attend the kiln on nights. Whereas I have hereunto set my hand this 29th of September 1806.
>
> *Signed*: Richard Lanesbury, and attested by two witnesses.

[I]n the margin of the paper, near the attestation, was written, "I James Palmer consenting to the above agreement."

The appellants produced Richard Lanesbury's mother, who swore that Palmer came to her, and asked her if she had any objection to her son being apprenticed to him and she said "No."

Abbott and Cooper, in support of the orders. Admitting first, ... if the original parol agreement by Lanesbury to serve Palmer as a servant for a year were meant to be abandoned, and another contract for service—as an apprentice substituted in the place of it by the written agreement entered into between them in three months after the commencement of the service, no settlement was gained by Lanesbury in Shinfield. [T]hey denied that such was the intention of the parties, or the operation of the written contract.

For where one is retained to serve another generally—and not as an apprentice *eo nomine* [c]—though ... the contract [states that he will] be taught a trade, it only operates as a contract of hiring and service, and not of apprenticeship. This ... is now the established rule. The conversation between Lanesbury's mother and Palmer cannot vary the written contract.

In *Rex v. Highnam*, 99 Eng. Rep. 859, 4 Douglas 238 (K.B. 1785), it was expressly stated that the parties meant to constitute an apprenticeship, which prevented the gaining of a settlement as a hired servant. In this view of the case, it is immaterial whether the written contract [was] valid or not. [I]f valid, a settlement was gained as a hired servant under it. [I]f invalid, as not being stamped, then the pauper continued to serve in Shinfield for more than a year under the original contract as a yearly servant, and gained his settlement there. But supposing the written contract would in its terms constitute an apprenticeship, then, not being stamped, it could not be received in evidence, to do away the former good agreement by parol.

Burrough, Wakefield, and Burnal, contra. Though the instrument of the 29th of September 1806 [was] invalid as an apprenticeship, yet if in fact Lanesbury intended to serve, and did serve, his master from that time in the supposed character of an apprentice, that put an end to the relation of master and servant. ... [S]o there was no service for a year under the first contract. The question therefore turns upon the

---

c BLACK'S LAW DICTIONARY (9th ed. 2009) *eo nomine* is Latin and it means "in the name of" or "by or in that name."

true construction of the written contract, whether the parties intended by the terms of it to create a hiring or an apprenticeship.

The distinctive character of the latter—in addition to the service of the master which is common to both—is for the master to teach the person retained some trade or business; and that was stipulated for by the contract in question. [N]o technical words can be necessary to create such a contract. ... So it was in *Rex v. Laindon*, 104 Eng. Rep. 1444, 8 Term Rep. 379 (K.B. 1799) and *Rex v. Rainham*, 102 Eng. Rep. 205, 1 East 531 (K. B. 1801).

Le Blanc, J. In *R. v. Laindon* a premium was given to the master, which was relied on as shewing the intention of the contracting parties to create an apprenticeship. The reserving a premium is no necessary part of such a contract; and the circumstance that no wages are to be paid equally indicates the same intention in this case. [F]or if a mere hiring and service were meant, as under the first general contract, though no particular sum was mentioned at the time, the mere relation of master and servant would have entitled the servant to wages upon a quantum meruit, which would not result from a mere contract of apprenticeship.

Bayley, J. The boy was to have clothes provided for him as well as board and lodging, and he was to be so employed as to enable him to learn the trade. [T]here was therefore an equivalent for wages.

Lord Ellenborough, C.J. There are no terms in this contract by which the master binds himself to teach the boy his trade. The boy is to have the opportunity of learning it by serving the master in his trade for three years. [B]ut it does not therefore follow that an action would lie against the master for not teaching him. In the Laindon case, the master did not undertake to teach the party serving; and yet the Court thought that an apprentice was intended, though defectively made.

* * *

Grose, J. Here there was originally a good contract of hiring and service; and that was not done away with by the subsequent instrument, whereby the parties merely prolonged the duration of the contract, and fixed the compensation to be made by the master for the service.

Le Blanc, J. To give a settlement by hiring and service, there must be a contract of hiring for a year; and this case is distinguishable from all the former cases, in which the question has been whether the contract was to serve as an apprentice, or as a hired servant. ... [I] if the Court considered that the contract was to serve as an apprentice, it could not enure to give a settlement as in case of a hired servant. [I]n none of those cases was there any valid contract of hiring and service existing before independent of the instrument in question.

But here the husband of the pauper had first entered into a good contract by parol as a hired servant for a year; and pending that contract, he and his master entered into a written agreement, by which it is contended that the parties meant to contract for an apprenticeship. [A] nd though invalid for the purpose of creating an apprenticeship, [this] changed the nature of the service under the former hiring into a service as an apprentice, and therefore prevented the gaining of a settlement as a hired servant.

But I do not accede to that argument, because if there were at one time a subsisting valid contract of hiring and service for a year, and, pending that, the parties enter into an invalid agreement, I do not see how that can do away the former valid contract. But even upon the construction of the written instrument itself, I do not think that it is to be taken as a contract of apprenticeship.

In all the former cases, where the instrument in question has been so construed, it has been stated that the parties intended to contract in the relation of master and apprentice, only they had contracted informally in order to avoid the stamp duties. But here the contract is for Lanesbury to serve Palmer for three years to learn the art of a brick maker, on condition of Palmer's finding him in board, lodging, and clothes. [T]here is no contract by the master to teach him, but only for the boy to have the opportunity of learning the business.

It is said that no wages are reserved. [B]ut that is no more than what often happens with boys at service: [T]hey get less at first, because they must first learn their business before they can be of use to their masters in it. Then, though it is stated here that the boy was to serve his master to learn his business, that would not prevent [the agreement] from operating as a contract of hiring and service. I do not think therefore that this was … an agreement for an apprenticeship, so as to supersede the former contract of hiring and service. But even if it were intended as an apprenticeship, yet the instrument, being invalid, would not supersede the former valid contract.

Bayley, J. I consider the instrument as a contract of service, and not as an apprenticeship. There was an original good contract for a year between the parties as master and servant generally, and after three months' service under it. [T]hey entered into a new agreement, by which the boy was to serve his master for three years, not generally, but to learn to make bricks and the art of burning, upon condition of being found in board, lodging, and clothes.

The meaning of the parties therefore was that the general service before contracted for should be restrained to such service as would enable the boy to learn his master's business. If an apprenticeship had been intended, there would have been words introduced into the agreement binding the master to teach the boy; and there being no such words of obligation on the master, and the written contract not having the ordinary words of binding to serve as an apprentice, and the intent of the parties, as collected from the terms of it, being at least equivocal.

[W]e are warranted by the cases in saying that the object of it was merely to confine the general service before contracted for to such parts of the master's employ as would enable the boy to learn his business. If this therefore were to give an extraordinary benefit to the servant, the master might well stipulate for receiving such service without the payment of wages.

Orders confirmed.

NOTES AND QUESTIONS

1. **Proving Intent in Courts of Equity.** Consider the Iowa Supreme Court's declaration in *LaFontaine v. Developers & Builders, Inc.*, 156 N.W.2d 651, 657 (Iowa 1968): "Equity courts will not hesitate to indulge in inferences which will avoid unfair or inequitable results. On this matter we have stated[:] ... 'an agreement will not be construed so as to give one party an unfair, oppressive or inequitable advantage over the other, ... unless the terms of the contract clearly require it, an interpretation will not be given which places one party at the mercy of the other, ... [and] courts will endeavor to give the contract that interpretation most equitable to the parties. ...'") Quoting *Freese v. Town of Alburnett*, 125 N.W.2d 790, 792–93 (Iowa 1964).

2. **Proof of an Intent to Contract: Question of Law or Question of Fact?** In *LaFontaine v. Developers & Builders, Inc.*, 156 N.W.2d 651, 654–55 (Iowa 1968), the Iowa Supreme Court ruled: "[To prove the real intent of the parties to an agreement], the parties are entitled to the benefit of [an] interpretation of their evidence, and of all reasonable inferences most favorable to their case. ... [I] f reasonable minds may differ as to the conclusions to be drawn from that evidence, a question of fact exists. 'The existence of a contract, meeting of the minds, intention to assume an obligation—[T]he understanding is to be determined not alone from words used, but in the situation, acts, and conduct of the parties, and from their situation and the attending circumstances, and by the inferences which mankind would ordinarily and reasonably draw therefrom.'"

3. **Intent and "Reasonably Certain Proof".** In *Jensen v. Taco John's Int'l, Inc.,* 110 F.3d 525, 527 (8th Cir. 1997), the Eighth Circuit declared: "An alleged contract 'which is so vague, indefinite,

and uncertain as to place the meaning and intent of the parties in the realm of speculation is void and unenforceable.'" Therefore, to be enforceable, an oral contract "requires reasonably certain proof of parties' intent on fundamental terms." Quoting *King v. Dalton Motors, Inc.*, 109 N.W.2d 51, 52 (Minn. 1961).

4. **Proving Intent Using Clear and Precise Evidence.** Consider the federal district court's ruling in *Reynolds v. University of Pennsylvania*, 684 F. Supp. 2d 621, 629 (E.D. Pa. 2010): "In order to prove the existence of an agreement, Reynolds must show that: '1) both parties manifested an intention to be bound by the terms of the agreement; 2) the terms of the agreement are sufficiently definite to be specifically enforced; and 3) there is mutuality of consideration.' The existence of an oral contract must be established by clear and precise evidence." Citing *Channel Home Ctrs. v. Grossman,* 795 F.2d 291, 298–99 (3d Cir. 1986). *See also Greene v. Oliver Realty, Inc.*, 363 Pa. Super. 534, 543 (1987) ("The party claiming that an agreement is for a definite period has the burden of proving that fact. ... This requirement is satisfied by clear proof that the parties contracted for a specific duration.").

5. **Proving Intent by Examining the Parties' Words and Circumstances.** In *Tallmadge Bros., Inc. v. Iroquois Gas Transmission System, L.P.,* 746 A.2d 1277, 1288 (Conn. 2000), the Connecticut Supreme Court concluded: "A contract must be construed to effectuate the intent of the parties, which is determined from the language used interpreted in the light of the situation of the parties and the circumstances connected with the transaction. ... [T]he intent of the parties is to be ascertained by a fair and reasonable construction of the written words and ... the language used must be accorded its common, natural, and ordinary meaning and usage where it can be sensibly applied to the subject matter of the contract. ... Where the language of the contract is clear and unambiguous, the contract is to be given effect according to its terms. A court will not torture words to import ambiguity where the ordinary meaning leaves no room for ambiguity. ... Similarly, any ambiguity in a contract must emanate from the language used in the contract rather than from one party's subjective perception of the terms." Citing *Lawson v. Whitey's Frame Shop*, 241 Conn. 678, 686 (1997).

6. **Proof of Intent and the "Objective Manifestation Theory".** Again, courts must determine "the mutual intentions of the contracting parties." *See Grant County Constructors v. E. V. Lane Corp.*, 77 Wash. 2d 110, 459 P.2d 947 (Wash. 1969). The Supreme Court of Washington has a long history of employing the objective

manifestation theory of contracts to achieve that end. Under the theory, a court "impute[s] to a person an intention corresponding to the reasonable meaning of his words and acts. ... In ascertaining the parties' intentions, [a] trial court must confine itself to the evidence before it. If no relevant evidence is presented, the party having the burden of proving the mutual intentions has not met that burden, and the relief sought must be denied. The court cannot speculate as to the parties' mutual intentions for this speculation may result in a contract which does not reflect the parties' true intentions at the time they entered into the contract." *See Dwelley v. Chesterfield,* 560 P.2d 353, 355 (Wash. 1977).

7. **Proving Insurers' and Insureds' Intent Using "Extraneous Evidence."** In *O'Reilly v. Physicians Mut. Ins. Co.,* 992 P.2d 644, 647 (Colo. Ct. App. 1999), the appellate court stated: "Extraneous evidence is admissible to prove the intent of the parties only when the terms of the instrument are ambiguous." *See also U.S. Fid. & Guar. Co. v. Hollerich & Walgenbach Co.,* 22 Ill. App. 3d 156, 161 (Ill. Ct. App. 1974) ("As a general rule a company manual is not a part of an insurance policy. It may, however, become so, provided it is embodied in the policy or an endorsement by clear and unmistakable terms, or by a reference thereto as governing the rights of the parties.").

8. **Using Extrinsic Parol (Oral) Evidence to Uncover the Parties' Intention.** Consider the court's holding in *Richmond Farms, Inc. v. Foremost Dairies, Inc.,* 224 N.Y.S.2d 266, 268 (N.Y. Special Term 1962) ("[C]ourts are not permitted to explore the actuality of the intent of the parties where the words employed in a contract have a precise, definite, and well understood meaning when used in connection with the subject matter of the contract. ... [However] where the language employed is imprecise, or is susceptible of more than one reasonable interpretation, parol proof may be received to ascertain intent.")

2) Proving an Intent to Contract Using Memoranda of Understanding and Other Preliminary Agreements

Before parties complete final negotiated contracts, they may fashion preliminary or temporary agreements. Some familiar examples are "memoranda of understanding (MOU)," "earnest money agreements," "deposit receipts," "temporary insurance binders," "conditional binding receipts," "letters of intent," "commitment letters," and "agreements in principle." *See Teachers Ins. and Annuity Ass'n of America v. Tribune Co.*, 670 F. Supp. 491, 497 (S.D.N.Y. 1987) (discussing letters of intent and commitment letters). A less familiar preliminary agreement is entitled "heads of agreement." *See Global Seafood Inc. v. Bantry Bay Mussels Ltd.*, 659 F.3d 221, 223 (2nd Cir. 2011).

Simply put, preliminary agreements allow parties to outline their intentions, weigh their options, circumvent ambiguities, escape liabilities, and consider the consequences of an undertaking before binding themselves to a permanent enforceable contract. In fact, letters of intent, insurance binders, and similar temporary instruments are often called "agreements with open terms" or "agreements to negotiate." *See generally* E. Allan Farnsworth, *Precontractual Liability and Preliminary Agreements: Fair Dealing and Failed Negotiations*, 87 Colum. L. Rev. 217, 250–51 (1987) (discussing various preliminary agreements).

But even more importantly, a preliminary agreement may or may not be a legally binding and enforceable contract. *See Global Seafood Inc.*, at 223 (2nd Cir. 2011) ("Bantry Bay and Global Seafood signed a document entitled 'Heads of Agreement,' which contains provisions relating to the marketing and sale of Bantry Bay mussels in North America. Global Seafood contends that the agreement is a binding contract establishing it as Bantry Bay's exclusive North American marketing agent. ... Bantry Bay disputes that the Heads of Agreement was a binding agreement, insisting that under Irish law so-called 'Heads of Agreements' are treated as non-binding letters of intent.").

In *Shinfield*, the parties signed a memorandum of understanding. Lanesbury asserted that the memorandum stated the parties' respective intent and was a binding apprenticeship contract. Defendant Palmer and the King's Bench disagreed. When are courts more likely to "enforce" an MOU or another preliminary agreement? Consider the next case.

Brown v. Cara
420 F.3d 148
(2nd Cir. 2005)

Straub, Circuit Judge.

BACKGROUND

Plaintiff-Appellant Jeffrey M. Brown (Brown), a citizen and resident of Pennsylvania, is CEO of Plaintiff-Appellant Jeffrey M. Brown Associates, Inc. (collectively "JMB"), a development and construction contractor with its principal place of business in Pennsylvania. Defendant-Appellee Charles Cara (Cara), a citizen and resident of New York, is owner and President of Defendant-Appellee Tracto Equipment, Corp. (Tracto), a New York corporation with its principal place of business in New York. During all times relevant to this appeal Tracto owned a parcel of land located at 100 Jay Street, Brooklyn, New York ("Jay Street Property" or the "Property").

In March 2000 the Jay Street Property was in use as a parking lot and was subject to zoning limitations that made it unsuitable for substantial commercial or residential development. At some time prior to March 2000, JMB and Cara together contemplated developing the Jay Street Property for commercial and residential use. The discussions that followed culminated in a two-page Memorandum of Understanding (MOU)—signed by Brown for "Jeffrey M. Brown Associates, Inc., and his companies, entities, etc.," and by Cara for "Charles Cara and his companies, entities, etc.," on March 27, 2000—by which the parties agreed to "work together to develop, build, market and manage a new real estate venture planned for an existing site at 100 Jay Street in Brooklyn, NY."

The MOU—referring to prior meetings between the parties—sets forth a general working framework for the Project, including basic design parameters and provisions for the division and distribution of future proceeds. According to the stated terms, Cara is to "provide[ ] the property at no cost to the partnership (or whatever combined entity is formed in the future to develop the project)." Brown is to "provide[ ] his company and individual experience, lender relationships, architect/engineering relationships, legal relationships and governmental relationships to lead the development effort ... [including] the rezoning process, conceptual design of the project, conceptual budgeting, arranging for possible financing avenues and helping to establish an effective marketing plan."

The MOU sets forth Cara's responsibility for compensating a named consultant and Brown's responsibility to compensate another named consultant. It provides that "Brown will build the project with union labor, if needed," and establishes that "Cara will act in the capacity of an Owner's representative on the project." "Brown agrees to front the costs of development up to an amount not exceeding $175,000," and the parties agree to pursue jointly the provision of necessary financing. Finally, the MOU declares that "time is of the essence," and states the parties' intent to "enter into a formal contract shortly."

In a letter dated April 5, 2000, and addressed to Brown, Cara states his desire to negotiate final terms of the partnership, design, and project financing. None of the proposed terms were settled, however, allegedly because the parties agreed that the costs associated with the negotiations would be wasted if the Property was not suitably rezoned.

Consistent with the terms outlined in the MOU, JMB commissioned the design of a multi-use, two-tower, building, which came to be known as the "Light Bridges at Jay Street." JMB subsequently sought, through a process of applications, publicity, community meetings, lobbying, and presentations to community boards, rezoning of the Property to allow construction of the Light Bridges Project. Cara was aware of these efforts and attended some of the meetings. In November and December 2001, the Project received the needed approvals.

Ready to move forward, the parties attempted to negotiate the necessary corporate, financing, construction, and operating agreements. Negotiations proceeded through 2002 and into 2003. During the spring of 2003, Cara requested from JMB a proposed construction management agreement. JMB complied, but Cara was not pleased with the terms described in that document. JMB claims that the wrong document was sent to Cara and that JMB so informed Cara at the time. However, Cara's displeasure and offense were so deep that he refused to continue with negotiations and ceased all communication and collaboration with JMB.

In June 2003 JMB brought this diversity action seeking declaratory judgment, a permanent injunction, specific performance of the MOU, and, in the alternative, damages in *quantum meruit*. Defendants moved for summary judgment. ... Plaintiffs cross-moved for summary judgment. ... [The magistrate judge concluded] that summary judgment should be granted in favor of defendants as to plaintiffs' first and second causes of action seeking enforcement of the MOU. [The magistrate judge] ... also recommended dismissing all claims against Tracto. The Report further recommended that the parties proceed to discovery on the remaining claims.

The parties filed timely objections to the Report and Recommendation. ... [T]he district court judge, issued brief orders, adopting in substance the recommendations of the magistrate judge. The district court dismissed all causes of action against Tracto and all causes of action against Cara, save plaintiffs' claim for relief in *quantum meruit* against Cara. JMB subsequently filed a motion for entry of final judgment pursuant to Rule 54(b), Fed. R. Civ. P. The unopposed motion was granted; and JMB filed a timely notice of appeal. We assert jurisdiction under 28 U.S.C. § 1291, affirm, in part, reverse, in part, vacate, in part, and remand.

DISCUSSION

Neither party disputes that New York law applies in this diversity case. ... Because this case involves enforcement of an alleged contract, the intentions of the parties are at issue. While this is frequently a source of persistent disputes of fact, "[w]here a question of intention is determinable by written agreements, the question is one of law, appropriately decided on a motion for summary judgment." *Arcadian Phosphates, Inc. v. Arcadian Corp.*, 884 F.2d 69, 73 (2d Cir. 1989).

* * *

I. Enforceability of the MOU

The first question presented on appeal is whether the MOU is an enforceable preliminary agreement. *See Adjustrite Sys., Inc. v. GAB Bus. Servs., Inc.*, 145 F.3d 543, 548 (2d Cir. 1998); Arcadian, 884 F.2d at 72–73; *Teachers Ins. & Annuity Ass'n. v. Tribune Co.*, 670 F. Supp. 491, 498 (S.D.N.Y. 1987). The district court found that it is not. We agree that the MOU does not bind the parties to complete the Jay Street Project but disagree insofar as the district court found that the MOU does not bind the parties to negotiate in good faith open terms that must be settled in order for the development to proceed within the framework described by the MOU.

"Ordinarily, where the parties contemplate further negotiations and the execution of a formal instrument, a preliminary agreement does not create a binding contract." *Adjustrite*, 145 F.3d at 548. There is no dispute that this is the situation here. At the signing of the MOU, JMB and Cara knew that further negotiations would be required. The MOU itself contemplates a "formal contract" to be entered into in the future. Further, only days after the MOU was signed, Cara solicited JMB to enter negotiations toward the execution of significant and necessary agreements, demonstrating the parties' contemporary understanding that, though they had signed the MOU, further negotiations and formal agreements were necessary.

"In some circumstances, however, preliminary agreements can create binding obligations." *Adjustrite*, 145 F.3d at 548. The extent of the obligations created depend on the preliminary agreement in question, though, in general, "binding preliminary agreements fall into one of two categories." *Id.* These two types are most authoritatively described in *Tribune*, where Judge Leval—collecting the relevant New York law—describes "Type I" preliminary agreements as "complete," reflecting a meeting of the minds on "all the issues perceived to require negotiation." 670 F. Supp. at 498. Because it is complete, a Type I preliminary agreement "binds both sides to their ultimate contractual objective." *Adjustrite*, 145 F.3d at 548.

"Type II" preliminary agreements, by contrast, are "binding only to a certain degree," reflecting agreement "on certain major terms, but [leaving] other terms open for further negotiation." *Id.* Type II agreements "do ... not commit the parties to their ultimate contractual objective but rather to the obligation to negotiate the open issues in good faith in an attempt to reach the ... objective within the agreed framework." *Id.*

A. The MOU Is Not a Binding Type I Preliminary Agreement

The district court ... found that the MOU is not a "Type I" preliminary agreement. We agree. The hallmark of a Type I agreement is that the parties have agreed to all necessary elements of the contract and are, therefore, bound to the ultimate objective despite the fact that a more formal or elaborate writing has yet to be produced. *Adjustrite*, 145 F.3d at 548. However, "'[t]here is a strong presumption against finding binding obligation in agreements which include open terms, call for future approvals and expressly anticipate future preparation and execution of contract documents.'" *Arcadian*, 884 F.2d at 73. *See also Carmon v. Soleh Boneh Ltd.*, 614 N.Y.S.2d 555, 556 (1994) ("[W]here an agreement contains open terms, calls for future approval, and expressly anticipates future preparation and execution of contract documents, there is a strong presumption against finding a binding and enforceable obligation."). The category of Type I preliminary agreements is, then, limited to agreements that are "preliminary" in name only. *Adjustrite*, 145 F.3d at 548.

There are four factors relevant to determining whether a preliminary agreement is enforceable as to the "ultimate contractual objective":

1. whether there is an expressed reservation of the right not to be bound in the absence of a writing;

2. whether there has been partial performance of the contract;

3. whether all of the terms of the alleged contract have been agreed upon; and

4. whether the agreement at issue is the type of contract that is usually committed to writing.

See Adjustrite, 145 F.3d at 549.

The first factor—which is frequently the most important—requires the court to determine whether the language of the contract discloses an intention by the parties to be bound to the ultimate objective. *Adjustrite*, 145 F.3d at 549. This factor is frequently determined by explicit language of commitment or reservation. However, the "fact that [a] preliminary agreement contains no express reservation of the right not to be bound is not dispositive of whether it is binding [because] a reservation of right not to be bound presumes that there is some expression of commitment or agreement in the writing." WILLISTON ON CONTRACTS, § 4:8. Where there is no language that may be read to bind the parties to the ultimate goal, an explicit reservation would serve no purpose.

There is no explicit reservation in the MOU. Rather, the language is decidedly non-committal, suggesting, at most, a promise to "work together." As plaintiffs admit, all of the critical design, business, construction, and financing details were utterly contingent upon the rezoning. In comprehension of this uncertainty, the language of the MOU is scrupulously reserved. For example, rather than committing the parties "to develop, build, market, and manage the Light Bridges of Jay Street," the MOU only purports to "outline the terms under which [the parties] will work together to develop, build, market, and manage a new real estate venture." The MOU goes on to foretell entrance "into a formal contract," and concludes by stating that the parties "agree to work together." Because the language is so non-committal, the absence of an expressed reservation is of little significance, particularly in view of the MOU's statement that a formal contract is forthcoming.

* * *

There can be no serious dispute that the second factor weighs heavily in favor of plaintiffs. JMB expended significant time and energy to design the Project and to clear a number of political and regulatory hurdles. Cara was contemporaneously aware of this performance and, on some occasions at least, was present for presentations conducted by JMB before various boards and citizen groups. These efforts bore fruit and constitute significant partial performance by JMB, which was accepted by Cara and has resulted in significant benefits accruing to the Property.

The third factor, by contrast, falls in favor of defendants. No credible case can be made that the MOU documents a "complete agreement ... on all the issues perceived to require negotiation." *Tribune*, 670 F. Supp. at 498. To the contrary, the MOU reaches almost none of the terms of the Light Bridges Project that require negotiation. For example, the MOU is silent on critical terms of design, financing, construction, compensation, corporate form, and ownership. The several-years-long process of negotiation that followed the rezoning is ample evidence that much is missing from the MOU.

JMB argues that, given the circumstances, this level of detail was impossible to achieve when the MOU was signed. Assuming this to be true does not make the MOU a more binding contract, however. Moreover, we are not convinced that, had they so desired, the parties could not have negotiated a fully binding contract regardless of the unknown. Contracting parties faced with similar uncertainty routinely negotiate objective methodologies by which open terms are later to be determined. *See, e.g., Carmon*, 614 N.Y.S.2d at 556 ("It is well settled that an agreement to agree, in which material terms are left for future negotiations, is unenforceable unless a methodology for determining the material terms can be found within the four corners of the agreement or the agreement refers to an objective extrinsic event, condition, or standard by which the material terms may be determined."). JMB may claim that such an exercise would have been pointless until the rezoning process was completed. Of course, that says no more than that JMB, rather than expending the resources necessary to achieve a fully-binding agreement, decided to assume the risk that the parties would not, in the end, be able to "work together."

The fourth factor also weighs in favor of defendants. New York courts have recognized that the "complexity and duration of [an] alleged agreement" is particularly significant in determining whether it must be reduced to formal writing in order to be fully enforceable. *See Warwick Assocs. v. FAI Ins. Ltd.*, 713 N.Y.S.2d 178 (2000). As contemplated by the parties, the Light Bridges is a project of enormous complexity that would likely span decades were it pursued to completion. All parties admit that the two-page MOU is not sufficient to the task of developing and managing the final Project.

* * *

For these reasons, we agree with the district court and hold that the MOU is not a binding Type I preliminary agreement. We affirm the judgment of the district court to the extent that it is consistent with this holding.

B. *The MOU Is a Binding Type II Preliminary Agreement.*

We agree with the lower courts that the MOU is not a binding Type I preliminary agreement. We hold, however, that the intention of the parties to create a "Type II" preliminary agreement is patent in the language of the MOU, presenting us with a pure issue of law. *See Arcadian Phosphates, Inc. v. Arcadian Corp.*, 884 F.2d 69, 73 (2d Cir. 1989). We reverse the judgment of the District Court to the extent that it finds to the contrary.

In *Tribune*, Judge Leval identified two core—but often competing—policy concerns relevant to preliminary agreements. The first is to "avoid trapping parties in surprise contractual obligations that they never intended." The second is the "[enforcement and preservation of] agreements that were intended as binding, despite a need for further documentation or further negotiation." *Adjustrite*, 145 F.3d at 548. The path between this Scylla and Charybdis is, of course, to enforce a preliminary agreement only to the extent that the parties intend it to be binding.

In this regard, "giving legal recognition to [Type II agreements] serves a valuable function in the marketplace ... [permitting parties] to make plans in reliance upon their preliminary agreements and present market conditions ... [without expending] enormous sums negotiating every detail of final contract documentation before knowing whether they have an agreement, and if so, on what terms." *Tribune*, 670 F.

Supp. at 499. In our view, this is exactly what these parties did when they signed the MOU.

This flexibility comes with limitations, of course. While a Type I preliminary agreement is fully binding as to the final contractual goal, a Type II agreement "does not commit the parties to their ultimate contractual objective but rather to the obligation to negotiate the open issues in good faith in an attempt to reach the ... objective within the agreed framework." *Adjustrite*, 145 F.3d at 548. "This obligation does not guarantee that the final contract will be concluded if both parties comport with their obligation, as good faith differences in the negotiation of the open issues may prevent a reaching of final contract." *Tribune*, 670 F. Supp. at 498. Whether the differences that have terminated the parties' working relationship in this case reflect good faith is a question for the district court on remand.

The considerations relevant to whether a preliminary agreement is a binding Type II agreement are:

1. whether the intent to be bound is revealed by the language of the agreement;

2. the context of the negotiations;

3. the existence of open terms;

4. partial performance; and

5. the necessity of putting the agreement in final form, as indicated by the customary form of such transactions.

See Arcadian, 884 F.2d at 72

While some of these factors are the same as those applied to determine whether a document is a Type I preliminary agreement, they "have a somewhat different significance where ... the nature of the contract alleged is that it commits the parties in good faith to negotiate the open terms." *Tribune*, 670 F. Supp. at 499. More to the point, if the question posed is whether the parties have agreed to proceed within an open framework toward a contractual goal, leaving necessary terms for later negotiation, rather than whether the parties have agreed to achieve the ultimate contractual goal, then the language of the agreement, its contents and omissions, and the context in which it was negotiated and signed, may lead to different conclusions.

The essence of a Type II preliminary agreement is that it creates an "obligation to negotiate the open issues in good faith in an attempt to reach the [ultimate contractual objective] within the agreed framework." *Tribune*, 670 F. Supp. at 498. Measuring the MOU by the relevant factors in light of this limited contractual goal, it is clear that it is a binding preliminary agreement to work toward the goal of developing the Jay Street Property within defined framework, preserving for later negotiation in good faith business, design, financing, construction, and management terms necessary to achieve the ultimate goal of developing and exploiting the Jay Street Property.

As to the first factor, while the MOU does not disclose an intention by the parties to be bound to the ultimate goal of the contract, it clearly states the parties' agreement to "work together to develop, build, market, and manage [the Jay Street Property]" and to "work together in accordance with the terms and conditions outlined [in the MOU]." We cannot imagine more clear evidence of an intention to be bound to the MOU as a general framework in which the parties will proceed in good faith toward the goal of developing the Property while preserving for later negotiation the specific details of necessary business, design, construction, financing, and management terms.

The second factor also supports a finding that the MOU is a binding Type II agreement. As the parties agree, at the time the MOU was signed, the Jay Street Project was subject to numerous contingencies that had the potential to dramatically affect planning, execution, and management. It was in this context that the parties elected to negotiate a general framework within which they could proceed while preserving flexibility in the face of future uncertainty. While it was possible in the abstract to negotiate a more definitive contract, using determinative methodologies to be applied to open issues, the context of the negotiations did not require derivation of such algorithms if the parties opted instead for a more open arrangement. The MOU is evidence of such an arrangement, and, as a Type II agreement, is consistent with the context of the negotiations.

Turning to the third factor, where the existence of open terms creates a presumption against finding a binding contract as to the ultimate goal, these same omissions may actually support finding a binding Type II agreement. *See Adjustrite*, 145 F.3d at 548, and *Tribune*, 670 F. Supp. at 499. The MOU leaves open terms—critical to every aspect of the Jay Street Project, from design, to business structure, to ownership and management. However, these omissions do not warrant against finding the MOU enforceable as a Type II agreement. In view of indeterminate regulatory and market conditions, JMB and Cara simply elected to pursue rezoning first, leaving finalization of project design and execution for later negotiation within the framework described in the MOU.

Consistent with views expressed in our discussion of the MOU as a Type I agreement, we find that the fourth prong, partial performance, cuts strongly in favor of finding the MOU to be a Type II agreement.

JMB provided extensive and valuable performance within the framework described by the MOU. Plaintiffs are entitled to demand defendants' good faith in negotiating remaining open terms.

Finally, while the requirement for a more formal future contract may be terminal to a Type I claim, Type II agreements—by definition—comprehend the necessity of future negotiations and contracts. Here, there can be little debate that creation of the holding corporation, construction, financing, and management of the Property, all required more formal and extensive contracts, both practically and as matters of customary form. The MOU clearly contemplated these future agreements, and, after rezoning, the parties expended considerable effort to negotiate some of these agreements.

* * *

CONCLUSION

For the foregoing reasons, the judgment of the district court is affirmed in part, reversed in part, vacated in part, and remanded for further proceedings consistent with this order.

B. Proof of an Offer

RESTATEMENT (SECOND) OF CONTRACTS § 24 reads: "An offer is the manifestation of willingness to enter into a bargain, so made as to justify another person in understanding that his assent to that bargain is invited and will conclude it." On the other hand, "[a] manifestation of willingness to enter into a bargain is not an offer if the person to whom it is addressed knows or has reason to know that the person making it does not intend to conclude a bargain until he has made a further manifestation of assent." RESTATEMENT (SECOND) OF CONTRACTS § 26.

Generally, state supreme courts have embraced those restatements of laws. Consequently, among state and federal courts, there is little debate about or conflict over the definition of an offer. However, several offer-related issues have spawned and continue to generate disagreements among state and federal courts. Discussions of those issues and disagreements appear in the following subsections.

1) Distinguishing Serious Offers from Joking, Needling, Jesting, or Daring Remarks

Lucy v. Zehmer
84 S.E.2d 516
(Va. 1954)

Buchanan, J. This suit was instituted by W. O. Lucy and J. C. Lucy, complainants, against A. H. Zehmer and Ida S. Zehmer, his wife, defendants, to have specific performance of a contract by which it was alleged the Zehmers had sold to W. O. Lucy a tract of land owned by A. H. Zehmer in Dinwiddie county containing 471.6 acres, more or less, known as the Ferguson farm, for $50,000. J. C. Lucy, the other complainant, is a brother of W. O. Lucy, to whom W. O. Lucy transferred a half interest in his alleged purchase.

The instrument sought to be enforced was written by A. H. Zehmer on December 20, 1952, in these words: "We hereby agree to sell to W. O. Lucy the Ferguson Farm complete for $50,000.00, title satisfactory to buyer," and signed by the defendants, A. H. Zehmer and Ida S. Zehmer.

The answer of A. H. Zehmer admitted that at the time mentioned W. O. Lucy offered him $50,000 cash for the farm, but that he, Zehmer, considered that the offer was made in jest; that so thinking, and both he and Lucy having had several drinks, he wrote out "the memorandum" quoted above and induced his wife to sign it; that he did not deliver the memorandum to Lucy, but that Lucy picked it up, read it, put it in his pocket, attempted to offer Zehmer $5 to bind the bargain, which Zehmer refused to accept, and realizing for the first time that Lucy was serious, Zehmer assured him that he had no intention of selling the farm and that the whole matter was a joke. Lucy left the premises insisting that he had purchased the farm.

Depositions were taken and the decree appealed from was entered holding that the complainants had failed to establish their right to specific performance, and dismissing their bill. The assignment of error is to this action of the court.

* * *

Mr. and Mrs. Zehmer were called by the complainants as adverse witnesses. Zehmer testified in substance as follows: He bought this farm more than ten years ago for $11,000. He had had twenty-five offers, more or less, to buy it, including several from Lucy, who had never offered any specific sum of money. He had given them all the same answer, that he was not interested in selling it.

On this Saturday night before Christmas it looked like everybody and his brother came by there to have a drink. He took a good many drinks during the afternoon and had a pint of his own. When he entered the restaurant around eight-thirty Lucy was there and he could see that he was "pretty high." He said to Lucy, "Boy, you got some good liquor, drinking, ain't you?" Lucy then offered him a drink. "I was already high as a Georgia pine, and didn't have any more ... sense than to pour another great big slug out and gulp it down, and he took one too."

After they had talked a while Lucy asked whether he still had the Ferguson farm. He replied that he had not sold it and Lucy said, "I bet you wouldn't take $50,000.00 for it." Zehmer asked him if he would give $50,000 and Lucy said yes. Zehmer replied, "You haven't got $50,000 in cash." Lucy said he did and Zehmer replied that he did not believe it. They argued "pro and con for a long time," mainly about "whether he had $50,000 in cash that he could put up right then and buy that farm."

Finally, said Zehmer, Lucy told him if he didn't believe he had $50,000, "you sign that piece of paper here and say you will take $50,000.00 for the farm." He, Zehmer, "just grabbed the back off of a guest check there" and wrote on the back of it. At that point in his testimony Zehmer asked to see what he had written to "see if I recognize my own handwriting." He examined the paper and exclaimed, "Great balls of fire, I got 'Firgerson' for Ferguson. I have got satisfactory spelled wrong. I don't recognize that writing if I would see it, wouldn't know it was mine."

After Zehmer had, as he described it, "scribbled this thing off," Lucy said, "Get your wife to sign it." Zehmer walked over to where she was and she at first refused to sign but did so after he told her that he "was just needling him [Lucy], and didn't mean a thing in the world, that I was not selling the farm." Zehmer then "took it back over there ... and I was still looking at the dern thing. I had the drink right there by my hand, and I reached over to get a drink, and he said, 'Let me see it.' He reached and picked it up, and when I looked back again he had it in his pocket and he dropped a five dollar bill over there, and he said, 'Here is five dollars payment on it.' ... I said, 'Hell no, that is beer and liquor talking. I am not going to sell you the farm. I have told you that too many times before.'"

Mrs. Zehmer testified that when Lucy came into the restaurant he looked as if he had had a drink. ... She heard Lucy ask Zehmer if he had sold the Ferguson farm, and Zehmer replied that he had not and did not want to sell it. ... Zehmer came back to where she was standing and said, "You want to put your name to this?" She said "No," but he said in an undertone, "It is nothing but a joke," and she signed it.

* * *

The defendants insist that the evidence was ample to support their contention that the writing sought to be enforced was prepared as a bluff or dare to force Lucy to admit that he did not have $50,000; that the whole matter was a joke; that the writing was not delivered to Lucy and no binding contract was ever made between the parties.

It is an unusual, if not bizarre, defense. When made to the writing admittedly prepared by one of the defendants and signed by both, clear evidence is required to sustain it.

In his testimony Zehmer claimed that he "was high as a Georgia pine," and that the transaction "was just a bunch of two doggoned drunks bluffing to see who could talk the biggest and say the most." That claim is inconsistent with his attempt to testify in great detail as to what was said and what was done. It is contradicted by other evidence as to the condition of both parties, and rendered of no weight by the testimony of his wife that when Lucy left the restaurant she suggested that Zehmer drive him home. The record is convincing that Zehmer was not intoxicated to the extent of being unable to comprehend the nature and consequences of the instrument he executed, and hence that instrument is not to be invalidated on that ground. 17 C.J.S., CONTRACTS, § 133 b., p. 483; *Taliaferro v. Emery*, 124 Va. 674, 98 S.E. 627 (1919). It was in fact conceded by defendants' counsel in oral argument that under the evidence Zehmer was not too drunk to make a valid contract.

The evidence is convincing also that Zehmer wrote two agreements, the first one beginning "I hereby agree to sell." Zehmer first said he could not remember about that, then that "I don't think I wrote but one out." Mrs. Zehmer said that what he wrote was "I hereby agree," but that the "I" was changed to "We" after that night. The agreement that was written and signed is in the record and indicates no such change. Neither are the mistakes in spelling that Zehmer sought to point out readily apparent.

The appearance of the contract, the fact that it was under discussion for forty minutes or more before it was signed; Lucy's objection to the first draft because it was written in the singular, and he wanted Mrs. Zehmer to sign it also; the rewriting to meet that objection and the signing by Mrs. Zehmer; the discussion of what was to be included in the sale, the provision for the examination of the title, the completeness of the instrument that was executed, the taking possession of it by Lucy with no request or suggestion by either of the defendants that he give it back, are facts which furnish persuasive evidence that the execution of the contract was a serious business transaction rather than a casual, jesting matter as defendants now contend.

On Sunday, the day after the instrument was signed on Saturday night, there was a social gathering in a home in the town of McKenney at which there were general comments that the sale had been made. Mrs. Zehmer testified that on that occasion as she passed by a group of people, including Lucy, who were talking about the transaction, \$50,000 was mentioned, whereupon she stepped up and said, "Well, with the high-price whiskey you were drinking last night you should have paid more. That was cheap."

Lucy testified that at that time Zehmer told him that he did not want to 'stick' him or hold him to the agreement because he, Lucy, was too tight and didn't know what he was doing, to which Lucy replied that he was not too tight; that he had been stuck before and was going through with it. Zehmer's version was that he said to Lucy: "'I am not trying to claim it wasn't a deal on account of the fact the price was too low. If I had wanted to sell $50,000.00 would be a good price, in fact I think you would get stuck at $50,000.00.'" A disinterested witness testified that what Zehmer said to Lucy was that "he was going to let him up off the deal, because he thought he was too tight, didn't know what he was doing. Lucy said something to the effect that 'I have been stuck before and I will go through with it.'"

If it be assumed, contrary to what we think the evidence shows, that Zehmer was jesting about selling his farm to Lucy and that the transaction was intended by him to be a joke, nevertheless the evidence shows that Lucy did not so understand it but considered it to be a serious business transaction and the contract to be binding on the Zehmers as well as on himself. The very next day he arranged with his brother to put up half the money and take a half interest in the land. The day after that he employed an attorney to examine the title. The next night, Tuesday, he was back at Zehmer's place and there Zehmer told him for the first time, Lucy said, that he wasn't going to sell and he told Zehmer, "You know you sold that place fair and square." After receiving the report from his attorney that the title was good he wrote to Zehmer that he was ready to close the deal.

Not only did Lucy actually believe, but the evidence shows he was warranted in believing, that the contract represented a serious business transaction and a good faith sale and purchase of the farm.

In the field of contracts, as generally elsewhere, "We must look to the outward expression of a person as manifesting his intention rather than to his secret and unexpressed intention. 'The law imputes to a person an intention corresponding to the reasonable meaning of his words and acts.'" *First Nat. Bank v. Roanoke Oil Co.*, 169 Va. 99, 114, 192 S.E. 764, 770 (1937).

At no time prior to the execution of the contract had Zehmer indicated to Lucy by word or act that he was not in earnest about selling the farm. They had argued about it and discussed its terms, as Zehmer admitted, for a long time. Lucy testified that if there was any jesting it was about paying $50,000 that night. The contract and the evidence show that he was not expected to pay the money that night. Zehmer said that after the writing was signed he laid it down on the counter in front of Lucy. Lucy said Zehmer handed it to him. In any event there had been what appeared to be a good faith offer and a good faith acceptance, followed by the execution and apparent delivery of a written contract. Both said that Lucy put the writing in his pocket and then offered Zehmer $5 to seal the bargain. Not until then, even under the defendants' evidence, was anything said or done to indicate that the matter was a joke. Both of the Zehmers testified that when Zehmer asked his wife to sign he whispered that it was a joke so Lucy wouldn't hear and that it was not intended that he should hear.

The mental assent of the parties is not requisite for the formation of a contract. If the words or other acts of one of the parties have but one reasonable meaning, his undisclosed intention is immaterial except when an unreasonable meaning which he attaches to his manifestations is known to the other party. RESTATEMENT OF THE LAW OF CONTRACTS, Vol. I, § 71, p. 74. "The law, therefore, judges of an agreement between two persons exclusively from those expressions of their intentions which are communicated between them." CLARK ON CONTRACTS, 4 ed., § 3.

An agreement or mutual assent is of course essential to a valid contract but the law imputes to a person an intention corresponding to the reasonable meaning of his words and acts. If his words and acts, judged by a reasonable standard, manifest an intention to agree, it is immaterial what may be the real but unexpressed state of his mind. 17 C.J.S., CONTRACTS, § 32, p. 361; 12 AM. JUR., CONTRACTS, § 19, p. 515.

So a person cannot set up that he was merely jesting when his conduct and words would warrant a reasonable person in believing that he intended a real agreement, 17 C.J.S., CONTRACTS, § 47, p. 390; CLARK ON CONTRACTS, 4 ed., § 27, at p. 54.

Whether the writing signed by the defendants and now sought to be enforced by the complainants was the result of a serious offer by Lucy and a serious acceptance by the defendants, or was a serious offer by Lucy and an acceptance in secret jest by the defendants, in either event it constituted a binding contract of sale between the parties.

Defendants contend further, however, that even though a contract was made, equity should decline to enforce it under the circumstances. These circumstances have been set forth in detail above. They disclose some drinking by the two parties but not to an extent that they were unable to understand fully what they were doing. There was no fraud, no misrepresentation, no sharp practice and no dealing between unequal parties. The farm had been bought for $11,000 and was assessed for taxation at $6,300. The purchase price was $50,000. Zehmer admitted that it was a good price. There is in fact present in this case none of the grounds usually urged against specific performance.

Specific performance, it is true, is not a matter of absolute or arbitrary right, but is addressed to the reasonable and sound discretion of the court. *First Nat. Bank v. Roanoke Oil Co., supra*, 169 Va. at p. 116,

192 S.E. at p. 771. But it is likewise true that the discretion which may be exercised is not an arbitrary or capricious one, but one which is controlled by the established doctrines and settled principles of equity; and, generally, where a contract is in its nature and circumstances unobjectionable, it is as much a matter of course for courts of equity to decree a specific performance of it as it is for a court of law to give damages for a breach of it. *Bond v. Crawford*, 193 Va. 437, 444, 69 S.E.2d 470, 475 (1952).

The complainants are entitled to have specific performance of the contracts sued on. The decree appealed from is therefore reversed and the cause is remanded for the entry of a proper decree requiring the defendants to perform the contract in accordance with the prayer of the bill. Reversed and remanded.

2) Distinguishing Serious Offers from Non-Binding Opinions, Advertisements, and Promotions

Leonard v. Pepsico
88 F. Supp. 2d 116
(S.D.N.Y. 1997)

Kimba M. Wood, District Judge. Plaintiff brought this action seeking, among other things, specific performance of an alleged offer of a Harrier Jet, featured in a television advertisement for defendant's "Pepsi Stuff" promotion. Defendant has moved for summary judgment pursuant to Federal Rule of Civil Procedure 56. For the reasons stated below, defendant's motion is granted.

I. Background

This case arises out of a promotional campaign conducted by defendant, the producer and distributor of the soft drinks Pepsi and Diet Pepsi. The promotion, entitled "Pepsi Stuff," encouraged consumers to collect "Pepsi Points" from specially marked packages of Pepsi or Diet Pepsi and redeem these points for merchandise featuring the Pepsi logo. Before introducing the promotion nationally, defendant conducted a test of the promotion in the Pacific Northwest from October 1995 to March 1996. A Pepsi Stuff catalog was distributed to consumers in the test market, including Washington State. Plaintiff is a resident of Seattle, Washington. While living in Seattle, plaintiff saw the Pepsi Stuff commercial that he contends constituted an offer of a Harrier Jet.

* * *

A. The Alleged Offer

Because whether the television commercial constituted an offer is the central question in this case, the Court will describe the commercial in detail. The commercial opens upon an idyllic, suburban morning, where the chirping of birds in sun-dappled trees welcomes a paperboy on his morning route. As the newspaper hits the stoop of a conventional two-story house, the tattoo of a military drum introduces the subtitle, "MONDAY 7:58 AM." The stirring strains of a martial air mark the appearance of a well-coiffed teenager preparing to leave for school, dressed in a shirt emblazoned with the Pepsi logo, a red-white-and-blue ball. While the teenager confidently preens, the military drumroll again sounds as the subtitle "T–SHIRT 75 PEPSI POINTS" scrolls across the screen.

Bursting from his room, the teenager strides down the hallway wearing a leather jacket. The drumroll sounds again, as the subtitle "LEATHER JACKET 1450 PEPSI POINTS" appears. The teenager opens the door of his house and, unfazed by the glare of the early morning sunshine, puts on a pair of sunglasses. The drumroll then accompanies the subtitle "SHADES 175 PEPSI POINTS." A voiceover then intones, "Introducing the new Pepsi Stuff catalog," as the camera focuses on the cover of the catalog.

* * *

Finally, the Harrier Jet swings into view and lands by the side of the school building, next to a bicycle rack. Several students run for cover, and the velocity of the wind strips one hapless faculty member down to his underwear. While the faculty member is being deprived of his dignity, the voiceover announces: "Now the more Pepsi you drink, the more great stuff you're gonna get." ... A few seconds later, the following appears in more stylized script: "Drink Pepsi—Get Stuff." With that message, the music and the commercial end with a triumphant flourish.

Inspired by this commercial, plaintiff set out to obtain a Harrier Jet. Plaintiff explains that he is "typical of the 'Pepsi Generation.' ... [H]e is young, has an adventurous spirit, and the notion of obtaining a Harrier Jet appealed to him enormously." Plaintiff consulted the Pepsi Stuff Catalog. ... The Catalog specifies the number of Pepsi Points required to obtain promotional merchandise. The Catalog includes an Order Form which lists, on one side, fifty-three items of Pepsi Stuff merchandise redeemable for Pepsi Points. Conspicuously absent from the Order Form is any entry or description of a Harrier Jet.

Although plaintiff initially set out to collect 7,000,000 Pepsi Points by consuming Pepsi products, it soon became clear to him that he "would not be able to buy (let alone drink) enough Pepsi to collect the necessary Pepsi Points fast enough." Reevaluating his strategy, plaintiff "focused for the first time on the packaging materials in the Pepsi Stuff promotion," and realized that buying Pepsi Points would be a more promising option. Through acquaintances, plaintiff ultimately raised about $700,000.

B. Plaintiff's Efforts to Redeem the Alleged Offer

On or about March 27, 1996, plaintiff submitted an Order Form, fifteen original Pepsi Points, and a check for $700,008.50. Plaintiff appears to have been represented by counsel at the time he mailed his check; the check is drawn on an account of plaintiff's first set of attorneys. At the bottom of the Order Form, plaintiff wrote in "1 Harrier Jet" in the "Item" column and "7,000,000" in the "Total Points" column. In a letter accompanying his submission, plaintiff stated that the check was to purchase additional Pepsi Points "expressly for obtaining a new Harrier jet as advertised in your Pepsi Stuff commercial."

On or about May 7, 1996, defendant's fulfillment house rejected plaintiff's submission and returned the check, explaining that:

> The item that you have requested is not part of the Pepsi Stuff collection. It is not included in the catalogue or on the order form, and only catalogue merchandise can be redeemed under this program.
>
> The Harrier jet in the Pepsi commercial is fanciful and is simply included to create a humorous and entertaining ad. We apologize for any misunderstanding or confusion that you may have experienced and are enclosing some free product coupons for your use.

Plaintiff's previous counsel responded on or about May 14, 1996, as follows:

> Your letter of May 7, 1996 is totally unacceptable. We have reviewed the video tape of the Pepsi Stuff commercial … and it clearly offers the new Harrier jet for 7,000,000 Pepsi Points. Our client followed your rules explicitly. …
>
> This is a formal demand that you honor your commitment and make immediate arrangements to transfer the new Harrier jet to our client. If we do not receive transfer instructions within ten (10) business days of the date of this letter you will leave us no choice but to file an appropriate action against Pepsi. …

This letter was apparently sent onward to the advertising company responsible for the actual commercial, BBDO New York ("BBDO"). In a letter dated May 30, 1996, BBDO Vice President Raymond E. McGovern, Jr., explained to plaintiff that:

> I find it hard to believe that you are of the opinion that the Pepsi Stuff commercial (Commercial) really offers a new Harrier Jet. The use of the Jet was clearly a joke that was meant to make the Commercial more humorous and entertaining. In my opinion, no reasonable person would agree with your analysis of the Commercial.

Litigation of this case initially involved two lawsuits, the first a declaratory judgment action brought by PepsiCo in this district (the "declaratory judgment action"), and the second an action brought by Leonard in Florida state court (the "Florida action"). PepsiCo brought suit in this Court on July 18, 1996, seeking a declaratory judgment stating that it had no obligation to furnish plaintiff with a Harrier Jet. ...

In response to PepsiCo's suit in New York, Leonard brought suit in Florida state court on August 6, 1996, although this case had nothing to do with Florida. That suit was removed to the Southern District of Florida in September 1996. ... The Florida suit was transferred to this Court on December 2, 1996. ... PepsiCo moved for summary judgment pursuant to Federal Rule of Civil Procedure 56. The present motion thus follows three years of jurisdictional and procedural wrangling.

II. Discussion

A. The Legal Framework

On a motion for summary judgment, a court "cannot try issues of fact; it can only determine whether there are issues to be tried." Donahue v. Windsor Locks Bd. of Fire Comm'rs, 834 F.2d 54, 58 (2d Cir. 1987) (citations and internal quotation marks omitted). To prevail on a motion for summary judgment, the moving party therefore must show that there are no such genuine issues of material fact to be tried, and that he or she is entitled to judgment as a matter of law. *See* Fed. R. Civ. P. 56(c); *Celotex Corp. v. Catrett*, 477 U.S. 317, 322 (1986). The party seeking summary judgment "bears the initial responsibility of informing the district court of the basis for its motion," which includes identifying the materials in the record that "it believes demonstrate the absence of a genuine issue of material fact." *Celotex Corp.,* 477 U.S. at 323

Once a motion for summary judgment is made and supported, the non-moving party must set forth specific facts that show that there is a genuine issue to be tried. *See Anderson v. Liberty Lobby, Inc.*, 477 U.S. 242, 251–522 (1986). Although a court considering a motion for summary judgment must view all evidence in the light most favorable to the non-moving party, and must draw all reasonable inferences in that party's favor, the nonmoving party "must do more than simply show that there is some metaphysical doubt as to the material facts." *Matsushita Elec. Indus. Co. v. Zenith Radio Corp.*, 475 U.S. 574, 586 (1986). If, based on the submissions to the court, no rational fact-finder could find in the non-movant's favor, there is no genuine issue of material fact, and summary judgment is appropriate. *See Anderson,* 477 U.S. at 250, 106 S.Ct. 2505.

* * *

B. Defendant's Advertisement Was Not an Offer

1. Advertisements as Offers

The general rule is that an advertisement does not constitute an offer. THE RESTATEMENT (SECOND) OF CONTRACTS explains that:

> Advertisements of goods by display, sign, handbill, newspaper, radio or television are not ordinarily intended or understood as offers to sell. The same is true of catalogues, price lists and circulars, even though the terms of suggested bargains may be stated in some detail. It is of course possible to make an offer by an advertisement directed to the general public (see § 29), but there must ordinarily be some language of commitment or some invitation to take action without further communication. RESTATEMENT (SECOND) OF CONTRACTS § 26 cmt. b (1979).

Similarly, a leading treatise notes that:

> It is quite possible to make a definite and operative offer to buy or sell goods by advertisement, in a newspaper, by a handbill, a catalog or circular or on a placard in a store window. It is not customary to do this, however; and the presumption is the other way. ... Such advertisements are understood to be mere requests to consider and examine and negotiate; and no one can reasonably regard them as otherwise unless the circumstances are exceptional and the words used are very plain and clear.
>
> 1 Arthur Linton Corbin & Joseph M. Perillo, CORBIN ON CONTRACTS § 2.4, at 116–17 (rev. ed. 1993). *See also*, 1 E. ALLAN FARNSWORTH, FARNSWORTH ON CONTRACTS § 3.10, at 239 (2d ed. 1998)

An advertisement is not transformed into an enforceable offer merely by a potential offeree's expression of willingness to accept the offer through, among other means, completion of an order form. In *Mesaros v. United States*, 845 F.2d 1576 (Fed. Cir. 1988), for example, the plaintiffs sued the United States Mint for failure to deliver a number of Statue of Liberty commemorative coins that they had ordered. When demand for the coins proved unexpectedly robust, a number of individuals who had sent in their orders in a timely fashion were left empty-handed.

The court began by noting the "well-established" rule that advertisements and order forms are "mere notices and solicitations for offers which create no power of acceptance in the recipient." *Id.* at 1580. *See also Foremost Pro Color, Inc. v. Eastman Kodak Co.*, 703 F.2d 534, 538–39 (9th Cir. 1983) ("The weight of authority is that purchase orders such as those at issue here are not enforceable contracts until they are accepted by the seller."); RESTATEMENT (SECOND) OF CONTRACTS §

26 ("A manifestation of willingness to enter a bargain is not an offer if the person to whom it is addressed knows or has reason to know that the person making it does not intend to conclude a bargain until he has made a further manifestation of assent.").

The spurned coin collectors could not maintain a breach of contract action because no contract would be formed until the advertiser accepted the order form and processed payment. *See also Alligood v. Procter & Gamble*, 72 Ohio App.3d 309, 594 N.E.2d 668 (1991) (finding that no offer was made in promotional campaign for baby diapers, in which consumers were to redeem teddy bear proof-of-purchase symbols for catalog merchandise); *Chang v. First Colonial Savings Bank*, 242 Va. 388, 410 S.E.2d 928 (1991) (newspaper advertisement for bank settled the terms of the offer once bank accepted plaintiffs' deposit, notwithstanding bank's subsequent effort to amend the terms of the offer).

Under these principles, plaintiff's letter of March 27, 1996, with the Order Form and the appropriate number of Pepsi Points, constituted the offer. There would be no enforceable contract until defendant accepted the Order Form and cashed the check.

The exception to the rule that advertisements do not create any power of acceptance in potential offerees is where the advertisement is "clear, definite, and explicit, and leaves nothing open for negotiation," in that circumstance, "it constitutes an offer, acceptance of which will complete the contract." *Lefkowitz v. Great Minneapolis Surplus Store*, 86 N.W.2d 689, 691 (1957).

* * *

The present case is distinguishable from *Lefkowitz*. First, the commercial cannot be regarded in itself as sufficiently definite, because it specifically reserved the details of the offer to a separate writing, the Catalog. The commercial itself made no mention of the steps a potential offeree would be required to take to accept the alleged offer of a Harrier Jet. The advertisement in *Lefkowitz*, in contrast, "identified the person who could accept." Corbin, supra, § 2.4, at 119. *See generally United States v. Braunstein*, 75 F. Supp. 137, 139 (S.D.N.Y. 1947) ("Greater precision of expression may be required, and less help from the court given, when the parties are merely at the threshold of a contract."); Farnsworth, *supra*, at 242 ("The fact that a proposal is very detailed suggests that it is an offer, while omission of many terms suggests that it is not.")

Second, even if the Catalog had included a Harrier Jet among the items that could be obtained by redemption of Pepsi Points, the advertisement of a Harrier Jet by both television commercial and catalog would still not constitute an offer. As the *Mesaros* court explained, the absence of any words of limitation such as "first come, first served," renders the alleged offer sufficiently indefinite that no contract could be formed. *See Mesaros*, 845 F.2d at 1581. "A customer would not usually have reason to believe that the shopkeeper intended exposure to the risk of a multitude of acceptances resulting in a number of contracts exceeding the shopkeeper's inventory." Farnsworth, *supra*, at 242. There was no such danger in *Lefkowitz*, owing to the limitation "first come, first served."

The Court finds, in sum, that the Harrier Jet commercial was merely an advertisement.

* * *

III. CONCLUSION

In sum, there are three reasons why plaintiff's demand cannot prevail as a matter of law. First, the commercial was merely an advertisement, not a unilateral offer. Second, the tongue-in-cheek attitude of the commercial would not cause a reasonable person to conclude that a soft drink company would be giving away fighter planes as part of a promotion. Third, there is no writing between the parties sufficient to satisfy the Statute of Frauds.

For the reasons stated above, the Court grants defendant's motion for summary judgment. The Clerk of Court is instructed to close these cases. Any pending motions are moot.

NOTES AND QUESTIONS

1. **Proving an Offer Using an Objective, Reasonable Person Standard.** In *Pepsico*, the district court judge did not find an offer, because "no objective person could reasonably have concluded that the commercial actually offered consumers a Harrier Jet." So, what is the "Objective Reasonable Person Standard"? The judge stated:

   > In evaluating [a] commercial, a [court] must not consider defendant's subjective intent in making the commercial, or plaintiff's subjective view of what the commercial offered, but what an objective, reasonable person would have understood the commercial to convey. *See Kay–R Elec. Corp. v. Stone & Webster Constr. Co.*, 23 F.3d 55, 57 (2d Cir. 1994) ("[W]e are not concerned with what was going through the heads of the parties at the time [of the alleged contract]. Rather, we are talking about the objective principles of contract law." ... "A basic rule of contracts holds that whether an offer has been made depends on the objective reasonableness of the alleged

offeree's belief that the advertisement or solicitation was intended as an offer.") (Citations omitted)

2. **Rewards as Offers.** In *Pepsico*, the plaintiff cited, relied, and fashioned his argument on a species of law involving unilateral offers. Specifically, these cases center on public offers and a promisor's duty to pay a reward when a nonspecific listener performs a specified act. Because these cases generally involve public declarations regarding the efficacy or trustworthiness of specific products, one court has aptly characterized these authorities as "prove me wrong" cases. *See Rosenthal v. Al Packer Ford,* 36 Md. App. 349, 374 A.2d 377, 380 (Md. Ct. Spec. App. 1977). Consider, for example, *Carlill v. Carbolic Smoke Ball Co.*, 1 Q.B. 256 (Court of Appeal 1892). In that case, Mrs. Carlill saw and relied upon the following advertisement, which stated:

> 100£ reward will be paid by the Carbolic Smoke Ball Company to any person who contracts the increasing epidemic influenza, colds, or any diseases caused by taking cold, after having used the ball three times daily for two weeks according to the printed directions supplied with each ball. 1000£ is deposited with the Alliance Bank, Regent Street, shewing our sincerity in the matter.

During the last epidemic of influenza many thousand carbolic smoke balls were sold as preventives against this disease, and in no ascertained case was the disease contracted by those using the carbolic smoke ball. "On the faith of this advertisement," Mrs. Carlill purchased the smoke ball and used it as directed, but contracted influenza nevertheless. The lower court held that she was entitled to recover the promised reward. Generally, offers-of-rewards rules require the offeror to pay the reward because the offer induces a party to perform a specific action for noncommercial reasons.

3. **Standards for Distinguishing Serious Offers from Jokes.** In *Lucy v. Zehmer*, the court concluded that the offer was serious and not a joke. Conversely, in *Pepsico*, the court concluded that the "Harrier Jet commercial" did not present a serious offer. Essentially, the latter was a joke: "If it is clear that an offer was not serious, then no offer has been made." So, "[w]hat kind of act creates a power of acceptance and is therefore an offer?" Consider the district court's statement in *Pepsico*:

> It must be an expression of will or intention. It must be an act that leads the offeree reasonably to conclude that a power to create a contract is conferred. This applies to the content of the power as well as to the fact of its existence. It is on this ground that we must exclude invitations to deal or acts

of mere preliminary negotiation, and acts evidently done in jest or without intent to create legal relations. CORBIN ON CONTRACTS, § 1.11 at 30

An obvious joke, of course, would not give rise to a contract. *See, e.g., Graves v. Northern N.Y. Pub.* Co., 260 A.D. 900, 22 N.Y.S.2d 537 (1940) (dismissing claim to offer of $1000, which appeared in the "joke column" of the newspaper, to any person who could provide a commonly available phone number). On the other hand, if there is no indication that the offer is "evidently in jest," and that an objective, reasonable person would find that the offer was serious, then there may be a valid offer. *See Barnes*, 549 P.2d at 1155 ("[I]f the jest is not apparent and a reasonable hearer would believe that an offer was being made, then the speaker risks the formation of a contract which was not intended.").

3) Litigation Involving Allegedly Discriminatory Offers

Lefkowitz v. Great Minneapolis Surplus Store
86 N.W.2d 689
(Minn. 1957)

Murphy, Justice. This is an appeal from an order of the Municipal Court of Minneapolis denying the motion of the defendant for amended findings of fact, or, in the alternative, for a new trial. The order for judgment awarded the plaintiff the sum of $138.50 as damages for breach of contract.

This case grows out of the alleged refusal of the defendant to sell to the plaintiff a certain fur piece which it had offered for sale in a newspaper advertisement. It appears from the record that on April 6, 1956, the defendant published the following advertisement in a Minneapolis newspaper:

Saturday 9 A.M. Sharp

3 Brand New Fur Coats Worth to $100.00

First Come First Served

$1 Each

On April 13, the defendant again published an advertisement in the same newspaper as follows:

Saturday 9 A.M.

2 Brand New Pastel Mink 3-Skin Scarfs Selling for $89.50

Out they go Saturday. Each ... $1.00

1 Black Lapin Stole Beautiful, worth $139.50 ... $1.00

First Come First Served

The record supports the findings of the court that on each of the Saturdays following the publication of the above-described ads the plaintiff was the first to present himself at the appropriate counter in the defendant's store and on each occasion demanded the coat and the stole so advertised and indicated his readiness to pay the sale price of $1. On both occasions, the defendant refused to sell the merchandise to the plaintiff, stating on the first occasion that by a "house rule" the offer was intended for women only and sales would not be made to men, and on the second visit that plaintiff knew defendant's house rules.

The trial court properly disallowed plaintiff's claim for the value of the fur coats since the value of these articles was speculative and uncertain. The only evidence of value was the advertisement itself to the effect that the coats were "WORTH TO $100.00," how much less being speculative especially in view of the price for which they were offered for sale. With reference to the offer of the defendant on April 13, 1956, to sell the "1 BLACK LAPIN STOLE ... WORTH $139.50," the trial court held that the value of this article was established and granted judgment in favor of the plaintiff for that amount less the $1 quoted purchase price.

The defendant contends that a newspaper advertisement offering items of merchandise for sale at a named price is a "unilateral offer" which may be withdrawn without notice. He relies upon authorities which hold that, where an advertiser publishes in a newspaper that he has a certain quantity or quality of goods which he wants to dispose of at certain prices and on certain terms, such advertisements are not offers which become contracts as soon as any person to whose notice they may come signifies his acceptance by notifying the other that he will take a certain quantity of them.

Such advertisements have been construed as an invitation for an offer of sale on the terms stated, which offer, when received, may be accepted or rejected and which therefore does not become a contract of sale until accepted by the seller; and until a contract has been so made, the seller may modify or revoke such prices or terms. *Montgomery Ward & Co. v. Johnson*, 209 Mass. 89, 95 N.E. 290; *Nickel v. Theresa Farmers Co-op. Ass'n*, 247 Wis. 412, 20 N.W.2d 117; *Lovett v. Frederick Loeser & Co. Inc.*, 124 Misc. 81, 207 N.Y.S. 753; *Schenectady Stove Co. v. Holbrook,* 101 N.Y. 45, 4 N.E. 4; *Georgian Co. v. Bloom*, 27 Ga. App. 468, 108 S.E. 813; *Craft v. Elder & Johnson Co.*, 38 N.E.2d 416, 34 Ohio L.A. 603; Annotation, 157 A.L.R. 746.

The defendant relies principally on *Craft v. Elder & Johnston Co. supra*. In that case, the court discussed the legal effect of an advertisement offering for sale, as a one-day special, an electric sewing machine at a named price. The view was expressed that the advertisement was "not an offer made to any specific person but was made to the public generally. Thereby it would be properly designated as a unilateral offer and not being supported by any consideration could be withdrawn at will and without notice." 38 N.E.2d 417, 34 Ohio L.A. 605.

It is true that such an offer may be withdrawn before acceptance. Since all offers are by their nature unilateral because they are necessarily made by one party or on one side in the negotiation of a contract, the distinction made in that decision between a unilateral offer and a unilateral contract is not clear. On the facts before us we are concerned with whether the advertisement constituted an offer, and, if so, whether the plaintiff's conduct constituted an acceptance.

There are numerous authorities which hold that a particular advertisement in a newspaper or circular letter relating to a sale of articles may be construed by the court as constituting an offer, acceptance of which would complete a contract. *J. E. Pinkham Lumber Co. v. C. W. Griffin & Co.*, 212 Ala. 341, 102 So. 689; *Seymour v. Armstrong & Kassebaum*, 62 Kan. 720, 64 P. 612; *Payne v. Lautz Bros. & Co., City Ct.*, 166 N.Y.S. 844, affirmed, 168 N.Y.S. 369, affirmed, 185 App. Div. 904, 171 N.Y.S. 1094; *Arnold v. Phillips*, 1 Ohio Dec. Reprint 195, 3 West. Law J. 448; *Oliver v. Henley,* Tex. Civ. App., 21 S.W.2d 576; Annotation, 157 A.L.R. 744, 746.

The test of whether a binding obligation may originate in advertisements addressed to the general public is "whether the facts show that some performance was promised in positive terms in return for something requested." 1 Williston, CONTRACTS (Rev. ed.) § 27.

The authorities above cited emphasize that, where the offer is clear, definite, and explicit, and leaves nothing open for negotiation, it constitutes an offer, acceptance of which will complete the contract. The most recent case on the subject is *Johnson v. Capital City Ford Co.*, La. App., 85 So.2d 75, in which the court pointed out that a newspaper advertisement relating to the purchase and sale of automobiles may constitute an offer, acceptance of which will consummate a contract and create an obligation in the offeror to perform according to the terms of the published offer.

Whether in any individual instance a newspaper advertisement is an offer rather than an invitation to make an offer depends on the legal intention of the parties and the surrounding circumstances. Annotation, 157 A.L.R. 744, 751; 77 C.J.S., Sales, § 25b; 17 C.J.S., CONTRACTS, § 389. We are of the view on the facts before us that the offer by the defendant of the sale of the Lapin fur was clear, definite, and explicit, and left nothing open for negotiation. The plaintiff having successfully managed to be the first one to appear at the seller's place of business to be served, as requested by the advertisement, and having offered the stated purchase price of the article, he was entitled to performance on the part of the defendant.

We think the trial court was correct in holding that there was in the conduct of the parties a sufficient mutuality of obligation to constitute a contract of sale.

The defendant contends that the offer was modified by a "house rule" to the effect that only women were qualified to receive the bargains advertised. The advertisement contained no such restriction. This objection may be disposed of briefly by stating that, while an advertiser has the right at any time before acceptance to modify his offer, he does not have the right, after acceptance, to impose new or arbitrary conditions not contained in the published offer. *Payne v. Lautz Bros. & Co., City Ct.*, 166 N.Y.S. 844, 848; *Mooney v. Daily News Co.*, 116 Minn. 212, 133 N.W. 573, 37 L.R.A.,N.S., 183. Affirmed.

NOTES AND QUESTIONS

1. **Discriminatory Offers Based on Gender.** In *Lefkowitz*, the defendant refused to sell certain merchandise to the male plaintiff, stating that—under a "house rule"—the specific offer was intended for women only. And, on a second visit, the merchant refused to sell the items to plaintiff, because the plaintiff "knew defendant's house rules." Put simply, the defendant practiced gender discrimination. Is that legal? The Minnesota Supreme Court used common-law contract principles—rather than federal constitutional and statutory laws—to resolve the conflict. Do discriminatory offers violate federal law?

2. **Discriminatory Offers and Federal Antidiscrimination Statutes**. The Civil Rights Act of 1866, § 1981 reads as follows:

   (a) All persons within the jurisdiction of the United States shall have the same right in every State and Territory to make and enforce contracts, to sue, be parties, give evidence, and to the full and equal benefit of all laws and proceedings for the security of persons and property as is enjoyed by white citizens, and shall be subject to like punishment, pains, penalties, taxes, licenses, and exactions of every kind, and to no other.

   (b) For purposes of this section, the term "make and enforce contracts" includes the making, performance, modification, and termination of contracts, and the enjoyment of all

> benefits, privileges, terms, and conditions of the contractual relationship.

However, in *Patterson v. McLean Credit Union*, 491 U.S. 164, 164 (1989), the Supreme Court wrote the following about the scope of § 1981:

> The most obvious feature of the provision is the restriction of its scope to forbidding discrimination in the "making and enforcement" of contracts alone. ... Where an alleged act of discrimination does not involve the impairment of one of these specific rights, § 1981 provides no relief. ... Section 1981 cannot be construed as a general proscription of *racial discrimination* in all aspects of contract relations, for it expressly prohibits discrimination only in the making and enforcement of contracts.

3. **Discriminatory Offers in Advertisements Based on Ethnicity.** Put simply, federal laws do not prohibit all discriminatory offers in advertisements which are based on ethnicity. To illustrate, consider the facts and holding in *Ragin v. The New York Times Co.*, 726 F. Supp. 953 (S.D.N.Y. 1989):

> Black prospective home purchasers and equal opportunity in housing organization brought action against newspaper publisher, alleging newspaper's real estate advertisements violated the Fair Housing Act, and asserting other civil rights claims. On publisher's motion to dismiss, the District Court held that: 1) Fair Housing Act—Title VIII of Civil Rights Act of 1968—claim was stated for newspaper's alleged practice of printing and publishing real estate advertisements with virtually all human white models in city with significant population of blacks and other minorities, and 2) alleged discrimination in real estate advertising was not actionable under either §§ 1981 or 1982
>
> * * *
>
> The Times maintains that discrimination in the advertising of real estate is not actionable under either §§ 1981 or 1982. The weight of authority supports defendant's position. Accordingly, these claims will be dismissed.
>
> In *Jones v. Alfred H. Mayer Co.*, 392 U.S. 409 (1968), which held that § 1982 reaches private conduct, the Court defined the statute's scope. In particular, the Court indicated that § 1982 does not reach discrimination in advertising. The Court wrote:
>
> Whatever else it may be, 42 U.S.C. § 1982 is not a comprehensive open housing law. In sharp contrast to the Fair Housing

Title (Title VIII) of the Civil Rights Act of 1968, Pub. L. 90–284, 82 Stat. 81, the statute in this case deals only with racial discrimination and does not address itself to discrimination on grounds of religion or national origin. It does not deal specifically with discrimination in the provision of services or facilities in connection with the sale or rental of a dwelling. It does not prohibit advertising or other representations that indicate discriminatory preferences. 392 U.S. at 413

* * *

Despite plaintiffs' contentions, the Supreme Court's recent decision in *Patterson v. McLean Credit Union*, 491 U.S. 164 (1989) does not support their claim under §§ 1981 and 1982. Plaintiffs contend that *Patterson* reinterpreted the scope of § 1981 to apply only to the formation stage of a contract.

Relying on a passage of the opinion that states "[§ 1981] prohibits, when based on race, the refusal to enter into a contract with someone, as well as the offer to make a contract only on discriminatory terms," plaintiffs argue that advertisements pertain to the formation stage of the contract and are thus covered by § 1981. Plaintiffs' argument is without merit. ... Clearly, the holding in *Patterson* does not help the plaintiffs. Nor does the rationale of *Patterson* favor plaintiffs.

PROOF OF AN OFFER AND ACCOMPANYING AFFIRMATIVE DEFENSES IN A NUTSHELL

Proof of the Sub-Element: Offer

The Offer Must Be Sufficiently Specific, Definite, or Certain

Once more, a plaintiff who commences a breach-of-contract action must establish that the parties formed a valid contract. At the outset, the plaintiff must prove that one of the parties made an offer to perform or an offer to sell, purchase, and/or deliver goods or services. In particular, the plaintiff or movant must produce evidence of the following: 1) the offeree is a specific person; 2) the offeror used specific language to communicate terms and conditions; 3) the time to perform was definite; and 4) the time to deliver the goods or services was fixed. In some jurisdictions, these requirements are called the "specificity" rules. *See, e.g., MacGill v. Blue Cross of Maryland, Inc.*, 551 A.2d 501, 503 (Md. Ct. Spec. App. 1989) ("In short, notwithstanding the generality of their expression, the policies were—in the final analysis—employee specific. Moreover, implicit in the personnel policies was a promise, made to each employee, of a definite and specific benefit should the company's proposed contractual undertaking be accepted.").

Other courts have stated that "an offer must be sufficiently definite." *See, e.g., In re Stone & Webster, Inc.*, 279 B.R. 748,787 (Bankr. D. Del. 2002) ("To constitute an 'offer,' a proposal must be sufficiently defined ... to manifest a willingness to enter into a bargain, such that the offeree would understand that its assent to that bargain is invited and will conclude the bargain"); *Searles v. Trustees of St. Joseph's College*, 695 A.2d 1206, 1211 (Me. 1997) ("[I]t is necessary that the offer ... contain[s] all the terms of the contract to be made"); and *Alexander v. Codemasters Group Limited,* 104 Cal. App. 4th 129, 141 (Cal. Ct. App. 2002) ("To form a contract, an 'offer must be sufficiently definite ... that the performance promised is reasonably certain.'").

In *General Auto Parts Co., Inc. v. Genuine Parts Co.,* 979 P.2d 1207, 1215 (Idaho 1999), the Idaho Supreme court stated the "specificity" rules slightly more generally:

> The general rule is a contract is enforceable, if it is "complete, definite and certain in all [of] its material terms, or contain[s] provisions which are capable in themselves of being reduced to certainty." *Giacobbi Square v. PEK Corp.*, 670 P.2d 51, 53 (Idaho 1983). "[C]ourts will not hold the contracting parties to a standard of absolute certainty relative to every detail of a contract. Rather only reasonable certainty is necessary before a contract will be given legal effect." *Barnes v. Huck*, 540 P.2d 1352, 1357 (Idaho 1975). The parties' obligations must be identified so that the adequacy of performance can be ascertained. *See Dale's Serv. Co. v. Jones*, 534 P.2d 1102, 1105 (Idaho 1975).

The Offer Must Embody the Parties' "Mutual Understanding and Assent" or "Meeting of Minds"

Courts also require plaintiffs to prove "mutuality." To be sure, this term generates confusion because it is also associated with another element—"consideration." Still, in *Domingo v. Mitchell*, 257 S.W.3d 34, 39–40 (Tex. App.—Amarillo 2008), the Texas appellate court provides an intelligible discussion of the connection between an *offer* and *mutuality*:

> The threshold question is whether Mitchell and Domingo entered into a contract. For a contract to exist there must be an offer, acceptance, and consideration. ... To determine whether there was an offer and acceptance, and therefore a "meeting of the minds," courts use an objective standard, considering what the parties did and said, not their subjective states of mind.

* * *

> To prove that an offer was made, a party must show 1) the offeror intended to make an offer, 2) the terms of the offer were clear and definite, and 3) the offeror communicated the essential terms of the offer to the offeree.
>
> * * *
>
> A "meeting of the minds" is not an independent element of a valid contract. It is merely *a mutuality* subpart of the offer and acceptance elements. A "meeting of the minds" is *a mutual understanding and assent* to the expression of the parties' agreement. If evidence of the parties' *mutual* agreement consists of their conduct and course of dealing with one another, their *mutual* agreement may be inferred from the circumstances, in which case the contract is "implied" as opposed to "express." An implied contract involves an inference from circumstantial evidence and is a question of fact.

The Offer May Not Leave Any Issues or Terms for Further Negotiation

In addition, there must be probative evidence of the parties having "nothing left to negotiate." *See Evans v. Bank of New York Mellon*, 2011 WL 4007386, *4 (E.D. Wash. Sept. 8, 2011) ("A valid contract requires mutual assent, offer ... [and] acceptance. ... A condition on an offer does not change the offer into an invitation to deal or a preliminary negotiation, if the contract is otherwise complete and there is nothing left to negotiate."), and *Lefkowitz v. Great Minneapolis Surplus Store*, 86 N.W.2d 689, 691 (Minn. 1957) ("Whether in any individual instance a newspaper advertisement is an offer rather than an invitation to make an offer depends on the legal intention of the parties and the surrounding circumstances. We are of the view on the facts before us that the offer by the defendant of the sale of the Lapin fur was clear, definite, and explicit, and left nothing open for negotiation. ... [T]here was in the conduct of the parties a sufficient mutuality of obligation to constitute a contract of sale").

The Offer May Not Contain Any Conditions Precedent

Finally, the plaintiff also must establish that the parties have not attached any conditions precedent to the offer. *See Nodolf v. Nelson*, 103 Wis. 2d 656, 658–59 (Wis. Ct. App. 1981) (finding that the language—"[The above] offer is subject to obtaining financing"—in the offer to purchase created a condition precedent to the buyer's performance and, therefore, concluding that the contract was unenforceable), and *Woodland Realty, Inc. v. Winzenried*, 262 N.W.2d 106, 108–09 (Wis. 1978) (concluding that the "subject to financing" clause was a condition precedent, because an offer ripens into a valid and enforceable contract only when the financing terms are actually met).

Proof of an Offer and Accompanying Affirmative Defenses

Revocation, Retractation, Retraction, Rejection, Rescission, and Withdrawal of an Offer Before Acceptance

There are several affirmative defenses to the assertion: "An offer was made." First, if a party revokes, retracts, withdraws, or rescinds an offer before it is accepted, the offer dies or terminates. Consider the following common-law rules:

- ***Revocation and Retractation***: *Berthiaume v. Doe*, 133 P. 515, 516 (Cal. Dist. Ct. App. 1913) ("[T]he owner of the lost property was under no legal obligation to make an offer of reward. ... [But] having done so, he became liable upon such offer upon its acceptance by the finder. The offer of reward, however, could be *revoked* before it was acted upon. The facts of this case ... show no *retractation* of the offer.").
- ***Retraction***: *Cooper v. Lansing Wheel Co.*, 54 N.W. 39, 39 (Mich. 1892) (reaffirming the principle that a "continuing offer ... may be *retracted* at any time. But if, at any time before it is retracted, it is accepted, such offer and acceptance constitute a valid contract.").
- ***Rejection***: *Figueroa v. Davis*, 318 S.W.3d 53, 69 (Tex. App.—Hous. [1st Dist.] 2010) ("Under contract principles, once an offer is *rejected*, it is terminated, and the rejecting party cannot thereafter accept it.").
- ***Revocation, Rescission, and Withdrawal***: *C.A. Bryant Co. v. Hamlen I.S.D.,* 14 S.W.2d 53, 56 (Tex. 1929) ("Ordinarily, until an offer is accepted, it can be *withdrawn*"); and, *Collins v. Morgan Grain Co.*, 16 F.2d 253, 254 (9th Cir. 1926) ("[A]ll the authorities agree that the offer may be *rescinded* or *revoked* at any time before the corporation is formed and the offer accepted. ... [I]t takes two parties to make a contract, and ... if one is not bound, the other is not. ... [A] mere unaccepted offer cannot in the nature of things constitute a binding contract.").

Of course, there is a general counterargument. One may argue that the other party did not *expressly* reject, revoke, retract, or withdraw the offer. And there is some support for that view. For example, in *Pepsi-Cola Bottling Co. v. NLRB*, 659 F.2d 87, 89–90 (8th Cir. 1981), the Eighth Circuit stated:

> [A] contract offer is not automatically terminated by the other party's rejection or counterproposal, but may be accepted within a reasonable time unless it was *expressly withdrawn* prior to acceptance, was *expressly* made contingent upon some condition subsequent, or was subject to intervening circumstances which made it unfair to hold the offeror to his bargain. Under this policy, an offer, once made, will remain on

> the table *unless explicitly withdrawn by the offeror* or unless circumstances arise which would lead the parties to reasonably believe that the offer had been withdrawn.

On the other hand, several courts have not embraced the Eighth Circuit's rule wholeheartedly. To illustrate, in *Lasco v. Town of Winfield*, 2007 WL 2349685, *2 (N.D. Ind. Aug. 14, 2007), the federal district court concluded: "An offer can be revoked prior to its acceptance if the offeror either *expressly revokes the offer or implicitly revokes* the offer by clearly manifesting an unwillingness to enter into the proposed bargain" *Id.* at *2 (citing RESTATEMENT (SECOND) OF CONTRACTS § 42, cmt. d).

Additionally, in *First Development Corp. of Kentucky v. Martin Marietta Corp.*, 959 F.2d 617, 621 (6th Cir. 1992), the Sixth Circuit wrote: "Under Kentucky law, an offer must be accepted 'before any intimation is received that offer is withdrawn'; *express notice or use of the word 'revoke' is not necessary to revoke an offer*. An offer is revoked when the offeree learns of acts by the offeror that are inconsistent with the continuance of the offer or that imply that the offer has been revoked", Id. at 621 (citing *Shaw v. Ingram-Day Lumber Co.*, 53 S.W. 431, 434 (Ky. 1913) and, RESTATEMENT (SECOND) OF CONTRACTS §§ 42 & 43 (1979)).

Finally, in addition to asserting that an offer was terminated or withdrawn, a defendant may raise the following affirmative defenses:

- ***Alleged Offer Was Only a Joke***: *Barnes v. Treece*, 549 P.2d 1152, 1155 (Wash. App. [Div. 1] 1976) ("When expressions are intended as a joke and are understood or would be understood by a reasonable person as being so intended, they cannot be construed as an offer and accepted to form a contract. However, if the jest is not apparent and a reasonable hearer would believe that an offer was being made, then the speaker risks the formation of a contract which was not intended. It is the objective manifestations of the offeror that count and not secret, unexpressed intentions.").
- ***Alleged Offer Was Only an Invitation to Negotiate***: *In re Merrill Lynch Auction Rate Securities Litigation*, 758 F. Supp. 2d 264, 285 (S.D.N.Y. 2010) ("'[If] a proposal [is] to qualify as an offer, it must reflect the intent of the author to give to the other party the right of concluding the contract by assent.' ... [A] proposal is 'only an invitation to negotiate or an expression of willingness to receive offers from others.'").
- ***Mere Price Quotations and Estimates Are Not Offers***: *Rhenalu v. Alcoa, Inc.*, 224 F. Supp. 2d 773, 802 (D. Del. 2002) ("Generally, mere price quotations without other contractual terms—time and place of delivery, terms of payment, etc.—do not constitute offers. ... An estimate is not ... an offer or a quotation.").

- ***Alleged Offer Was Only a Naked Offer Without Sufficient Consideration***: *Hotel Longview v. Pittman*, 276 S.W.2d 915, 921 (Tex. Civ. App.—Texarkana 1955) ("No consideration is recited in ... the lease. We find it to be just a naked offer which appellant had a right to withdraw at any time before its acceptance"); and, *Bosshardt & Wilson Co. v. Crescent Oil Co.*, 32 A. 1120, 1121 (Pa. 1895) ("There being no consideration for the offer in this case, the defendant had a clear right to withdraw it at any time before there was an acceptance of it.").
- ***Offer Was Revoked Before Full Performance***: *Hutchinson v. Dobson-Bainbridge Realty Co., Inc.*, 217 S.W.2d 6, 9 (Tenn. Ct. App. 1946) ("[Some authorities hold that ... the offeror may revoke his offer at any moment before full performance, whatever the hardship that may result to the offeree.").
- ***Offeror Had No Capacity to Make Offer***: *Sphere Drake Ins. Ltd. v. All American Life Ins. Co.*, 2004 WL 442640,*2 (N.D. Ill. 2004) ("In Sphere Drake's view, All American had made a judicial admission that Stirling Cooke did not have the capacity to make a valid offer ... and, thus, there were no binding contracts.").

C. Proof of an Acceptance

In *Embree, Inc. v. Southwestern Bell Media, Inc.*, 772 S.W.2d 209, 210 (Tex. App.—Dallas 1989, writ denied), the appellate court stated succinctly: "[N]o contract can result from an offer until it is accepted by the other party." In *Silber v. New York Life Ins.* Co., 938 N.Y.S.2d 46, 50 (N.Y. App. Div. 2012), the court reaffirmed that general principle and added a few more:

> It is a fundamental principle of contract law that a valid acceptance must comply with the terms of the offer. Where the offer specifies the mode of acceptance, an acceptance in any other manner is wholly nugatory and ineffectual. Furthermore, a purported acceptance—that is "qualified with conditions"—is a rejection of the offer. Whenever a purported acceptance is even slightly at variance with the terms of an offer, the qualified response operates as a rejection and termination of the initially offered terms.

THE RESTATEMENT (SECOND) OF CONTRACTS § 29 reads:

1. The manifested intention of the offeror determines the person or persons in whom is created a power of acceptance.

2. An offer may create a power of acceptance in a specified person or in one or more of a specified group or class of persons, acting

separately or together, or in anyone or everyone who makes a specified promise or renders a specified performance.

In addition, RESTATEMENT (SECOND) OF CONTRACTS § 30(1) states: "An offer may invite or require acceptance to be made by an affirmative answer in words, or by performing or refraining from performing a specified act." And section 50(1) reads: "Acceptance of an offer is a manifestation of assent to the terms thereof made by the offeree in a manner invited or required by the offer."

Certainly, these principles are not terribly difficult to understand. Still, from time to time, they generate conflicts among litigants. And, in the end, courts of law and equity must review probative facts, interpret these principles, and apply them to resolve breach-of-contract disputes. The controversies in the next two cases illustrate the types of conflicts that arise when one party asserts that another party "did not accept an offer."

1) "Acceptance Must Comply with the Terms of the Offer"

Aon Risk Services, Inc. v. Meadors
267 S.W.3d 603
(Ark. Ct. App. 2007)

Larry D. Vaught, Judge. A Pulaski County jury awarded appellee John Meadors $2,509,127.60 on several breach of contract claims against his employer, appellant Aon Risk Services, Inc., of Arkansas (ARS Arkansas). In post-trial proceedings, the circuit judge reduced the award to $1,281,930.90. … ARS Arkansas appeals, arguing that the jury's verdict was not supported by substantial evidence. … On cross-appeal, Meadors asks us to reinstate the jury's original damage award … and reverse several summary judgments that were entered prior to trial.

Background Facts

Meadors is a veteran of the insurance-brokerage industry. On May 1, 1997, he executed a five-year employment contract with ARS Arkansas, a Little Rock insurance brokerage firm whose parent company is Aon Corporation. ARS Arkansas's managing director, Mark Brockington, described Meadors's job as that of a producer, meaning that he was responsible for attracting business and making sales. The contract provided that Meadors would be compensated by a base salary plus an annual bonus calculated on a percentage of new, first-year commissions earned and collected by ARS Arkansas.

For twenty-five to thirty years prior to 1997, Meadors cultivated a business relationship with Dillard's department stores in hopes of brokering insurance benefits for Dillard's employees. His patience was rewarded in the fall of 1999, while he was employed at ARS Arkansas.

In August and September of that year, he put Dillard's in touch with Combined Insurance Companies, another subsidiary of Aon Corporation. Combined offered a package called Workplace Solutions in which Dillard's employees could purchase life, disability, and other types of insurance policies through workplace enrollment. Dillard's and Combined ultimately executed a five-year agreement on March 24, 2000, giving Combined access to Dillard's employees for that length of time.

Before the agreement was signed, however, Meadors obtained a copy of what is referred to as the "Interdependency Memorandum." This document, dated February 9, 2000, was sent by Aon to all Aon Risk Services Managing Directors, including Mark Brockington at ARS Arkansas. Its intent was to promote "interdependency" among Aon entities, that is, to encourage ARS brokerage offices to place insurance business with Aon-affiliated companies. The Memo recited the following:

> [A] financial rewards system has now been put in place with almost all Aon companies. ARS Management has agreed with the various Aon companies listed on the following page that it will receive from these companies bonus pool monies representing the listed percentage of interdependence revenues generated on new fees and commissions.

The following page was headlined "Interdependency Compensation Agreements for 2000," and it listed, among others, Combined Insurance Companies. Combined agreed to pay "30% of annualized premium on all life products over 15 year term plus 15% [during the] 1st year for all other products to pool." The Memo then explained how the bonus pool would operate:

> Such funds will be paid out in entirety to ARS staffers in the form of annual bonus pool payments under the following conditions:
>
> 1. The Aon Company will credit these monies to the ARS office(s) practice group(s) as appropriate to their involvement in the procurement of revenue.
>
> 2. The credit is made as the income is booked and, if not booked on the accrual method, for 12 full months of income booking.
>
> 3. No formulaic bonus will be accrued to any individual ARS employee.
>
> 4. Each office/practice group will accumulate its "bonus pool" through year end at which time each Managing Director will allocate 100% of the fund balance in the pool to those employees who have been the most responsible

> for the professional production and/or marketing, servicing and/or maintenance of the client accounts generating the bonus pool funds and who have done so in a manner consistent with Aon's stated policies of professional excellence, cooperative behavior, and ethical conduct.
>
> 5. Shared introduction with an office/practice or between and office/practice generates a single payment only, which may be split as agreed by the MDs [Managing Directors].
>
> 6. Each Managing Director's recommendation as to the allocation of the bonus funds in the pool is subject to sign off by the President or CEO of ARS Americas for audit purposes, but the Managing Director's recommendation will not be altered without assumed "extreme prejudice." In any case, the entire pool in each office or practice will be paid.
>
> On a quarterly basis we will share the bonus pool figures with ARS professional staff so that employees are aware of the magnitude of the rewards accruing to them from serving client needs via interdependence efforts.

Additionally, the Memo declared that "local/practice group management is now authorized to make the proper call 'on the ground' as to just how to allocate bonus monies." Managing Directors were asked to "carefully discuss this enhanced compensation structure with all professional staff" and to "share this message as soon as possible."

According to Meadors, when he saw the Memo sometime in February 2000, he was enthused about the program and "absolutely" believed that it would entitle him to compensation over and above his basic employment contract compensation. However, after the Dillard's/Combined agreement was signed in March 2000, Combined placed no monies in the bonus pool based on Dillard's premiums.

Mark Brockington explained that, in order for Combined to acquire the Dillard's account, it had to buy out another broker or insurance company for $1.6 million. Thus, Combined told him, it could not pay normal commissions. Following negotiations that lasted well beyond the signing of the Dillard's agreement, Combined and ARS Arkansas agreed to a $240,000 commission, of which Meadors received fifteen percent, or $36,000, as called for in his basic employment contract.

In 2005, Meadors sued ARS Arkansas, Combined, and several other Aon companies, alleging that the Interdependency Memorandum was a unilateral contract, which was breached when he did not receive bonus-pool monies generated by the Dillard's agreement. Combined and the other Aon entities were dismissed by summary judgment, as were Meadors's claims for unjust enrichment, fraud, and breach of contract as a third-party beneficiary.

However, the case against ARS Arkansas went to trial. There, Meadors testified that, had the appropriate monies been placed in the bonus pool, he would have received $2,406,522.60 on the Dillard's transaction. The jury awarded him that amount, plus additional damages based on other claims. In post-trial proceedings, the trial judge reduced the Dillard's award by almost fifty percent. This appeal followed.

We begin our discussion of the issues with ARS Arkansas's direct appeal from the jury's verdict pertaining to the Dillard's transaction and Meadors's cross-appeal from the trial judge's reduction of the damages on that same transaction.

I. Formation of Contract

ARS Arkansas argues that the Interdependency Memorandum did not form a contract because: 1) it was not sufficiently definite to constitute an offer; 2) if it was an offer, Meadors did not accept it; [and], 3) if a contract was created, it was not an agreement between ARS Arkansas and Meadors. ARS presents these arguments in the context of the trial court's denial of its motion for a directed verdict.

* * *

Meadors's theory at trial was that the Interdependency Memorandum formed a unilateral contract. There are several instances where unilateral contracts commonly appear, such as where a reward is offered, e.g., *Ark. Bankers' Ass'n v. Ligon*, 295 S.W. 4 (Ark. 1927), where a contest is announced, e.g., *Mears v. Nationwide Mut. Ins. Co.*, 91 F.3d 1118 (8th Cir. 1996), or where changes are made and disseminated in an employee manual. *See Crain Indus., Inc. v. Cass*, 810 S.W.2d 910 (Ark. 1991). In those situations, the offeree does not accept the offer by express agreement but by his performance.

For example, in the case of a reward, the offeree accepts by performing the particular task, such as the capture of a fugitive, for which the reward is offered. Even though he has not directly communicated his acceptance, a contract is formed as the result of his performance. See 17 C.J.S. CONTRACTS § 9 (1999) (recognizing that a unilateral contract is composed of an offer that invites acceptance in the form of actual performance); 17A AM. JUR. 2D CONTRACTS § 5 (2d ed. 1991) (stating that, if performance occurs, then the offer has been accepted, and a contract is formed). The performance also constitutes consideration for the contract. 17A AM. JUR. 2D CONTRACTS § 5.

A. Definiteness of Offer

ARS Arkansas argues first that the Interdependency Memorandum was not sufficiently definite to constitute an offer for a unilateral contract. An offer is the manifestation of willingness to enter into a bargain, so made as to justify another person in understanding that his assent to the bargain is invited and will conclude it. *ERC Mtg. v. Luper*, 795 S.W.2d 362 (Ark. App. 1990). An offer cannot be accepted so as to form a contract unless the terms are reasonably certain. RESTATEMENT (SECOND) OF CONTRACTS § 33 (1981). *See also Pine River State Bank v. Mettille*, 333 N.W.2d 622 (Minn. 1983). To bind the employer, an offer must be definite in form and must be communicated to the offeree. *See Hardie v. Cotter & Co.*, 849 F.2d 1097 (8th Cir. 1988). Whether a proposal is meant to be an offer for a unilateral contract is determined by the outward manifestations of the parties, and not by their subjective intentions. The principal issue is whether the employer's statements are intended [to be] an offer and accepted as such or are merely statements of policy and practice.

ARS Arkansas contends first that, because the trial court determined that the Interdependency Memo was ambiguous in some respects, it was too indefinite to constitute an offer. We disagree that an ambiguous offer is necessarily indefinite. A writing that is indefinite is incomprehensibly vague or incapable of being understood. *Barnes v. Barnes*, 627 S.W.2d 552 (Ark. 1982); and such indefiniteness is an impediment to the formation of a contract. *See Mgmt. Comp. Servs., Inc. v. Hawkins, Ash, Baptie, & Co.*, 206 Wis.2d 158 (1996).

But, ambiguity does not prevent the formation of a contract; rather, it calls for interpretation of a contract. An ambiguous writing may be understood and enforced by applying the rules of contract construction. *See generally Smith v. Farm Bureau Mut. Ins. Co.*, 194 S.W.3d 212 (Ark. App. 2004), and *Shibley v. White*, 104 S.W.2d 461 (Ark 1937) (recognizing that, while a contract was ambiguous, it was not uncertain). We therefore see no error in the trial court's refusal to grant a directed verdict on this basis.

ARS Arkansas also argues that the Interdependency Memo lacked definiteness, because it merely expressed general concepts of teamwork and provided for judgment calls in the allocation of bonus-pool money. ARS cites several cases in which statements by employers were deemed too indefinite to constitute an offer. ... We believe that the Memo contains terms far more definite than these vague statements. The Memo expressly states that "a financial rewards system has now been put in place." It also sets out specific percentages of amounts to be contributed to the bonus pool by each participating Aon entity, and it contains the precise means by which those pool funds will be distributed to ARS staffers. It is therefore more than a mere statement of policy or a vague promise regarding future events.

* * *

B. Acceptance of Offer

ARS Arkansas claims that, even if the Memo constituted an offer, Meadors did not accept it. ARS first cites *MDH Builders, Inc. v. Nabholz Construction Corp.*, 17 S.W.3d 97 (Ark. App. 2000), which states that, to create a binding contract, an acceptance must unconditionally agree to all the material provisions of the offer. ARS contends that Meadors did not unconditionally agree to the provisions of the offer because he testified as follows:

> QUESTION: When you received this document [the Memo], did you ever unconditionally agree to its terms?
>
> MEADORS: That was not a conscious thought that I had when I—the first time I looked at that.
>
> QUESTION: And so whether it's when you received it in February or whether you received it in April, that's never a decision you made to unconditionally agree to the terms of [the Memo]?
>
> MEADORS: Not in that, no, I didn't think about that.

ARS's reliance on *MDH* is misplaced. The language in *MDH* does not lend itself to a unilateral contract, which is accepted by performance rather than by express agreement. Additionally, the point we were making in *MDH* was that an acceptance cannot vary the terms of the offer. There is no claim that Meadors attempted to vary the terms of the Memo. In any event, we believe that ARS reads too much into Meadors's statement that when he first saw the Memo, he simply did not think about whether he unconditionally agreed to its terms.

We turn now to ARS's contention that Meadors could not have accepted the offer in the Interdependency Memorandum because, by the time he learned of the Memo, he had already performed his brokerage task of referring Dillard's to Combined as a client.

A unilateral contract is not formed where a party's performance is not made "on the faith of" the offer or "in consequence of" the offer. However, unless the offeror manifests a contrary intention, an offeree who learns of an offer after he has rendered part of the performance requested by the offer may accept by completing the requested performance. *See* RESTATEMENT (SECOND) OF CONTRACTS § 51 (1981). Meadors contends that, even though he began brokering the deal between Dillard's and Combined before the Memo was in existence, he did not complete performance until after he received the Memo. Thus, he claims, he accepted the Memo's offer. We agree that substantial evidence supported the jury's verdict on this point.

There was evidence at trial that Meadors was aware of the Memo before the Dillard's/Combined deal was finalized in March 2000. ARS managing director Mark Brockington testified that he assumed that he received the Memo on or about February 9, 2000, and he agreed that it directed him to share its message with his eligible professional staff, which would have included Meadors. Meadors testified that he obtained a copy of the Interdependency Memorandum from Combined Insurance Companies in February 2000, although he did not receive a copy directly from ARS Arkansas until April or May 2000.

There was also evidence from which the jury could have concluded that Meadors continued or completed his performance on the Dillard's account after learning of the Interdependency Memo. Combined Insurance Companies executive Heather Gardere said that Meadors played a role in the Dillard's transaction other than the initial referral. She also said that he was involved in the coordination of the overall strategy, the sales process, and was ultimately responsible for the overall relationship. Neil Mayfield, who worked for the enrollment division of Combined, said that Meadors called him after the contract had been signed, asking how the enrollments were going. Moreover, the Interdependency Memorandum provided that bonus-pool monies would go to employees who were responsible not only for production of accounts but for servicing and maintaining accounts.

Though the evidence on this point is spare, it was the jurors' prerogative to believe or disbelieve it and to accord it whatever weight and value they deemed appropriate. Our task on appeal is not to substitute our view of the evidence for the jury's but to determine whether the jury's verdict was supported by substantial evidence. *See Rathbun v. Ward*, 866 S.W. 2d 403 (Ark. 1993). With that standard to guide us, we cannot say that ARS Arkansas was entitled to a directed verdict on this point.

C. Parties to the Contract

Finally, ARS Arkansas argues that neither it nor Meadors is named in the Memo and, therefore, the Memo does not constitute a contract between them. However, the Memo imposed certain duties on ARS Arkansas, as it did on all ARS offices, such as accumulating bonus-pool monies and distributing them to deserving employees. And, as already discussed, the Memo was accepted as a unilateral contract by Meadors, thereby making him a party to it. There was, therefore, substantial evidence from which the jury could conclude that Meadors and ARS Arkansas had rights and obligations under the Memo.

* * *

IX. CONCLUSION

We affirm the jury's verdict for breach of a unilateral contract against ARS Arkansas and reinstate Meadors's damages of $2,406,522.60 pertaining to the Dillard's transaction. Affirmed in part; reversed and remanded in part.

NOTES AND QUESTIONS

1. ***Mandatory Requirement to Accept an Offer Within a Certain Time Period.*** Consider the facts and ruling in *Bowles v. Fickas*, 167 S.W.2d 741, 743 (Tex. 1943). The seller offered to sell land. But there was a condition. The buyer had to sign a written contract and deposit $1,000 in earnest money at a particular bank. The buyer received the offer and signed the contract at the end of April. However, the buyer did not deliver the $1,000. On May 15th, the seller "declared the deal off." Still, on May 17th, the buyer deposited $1,000 with the bank. The Texas Supreme Court declared that the parties never entered into a contract. According to the court, the seller "had the absolute right to withdraw the offer at any time before [the buyer] accepted same in the manner prescribed. Since, no such acceptance had occurred, [the seller] still retained the right ... to withdraw the offer as she did and thus prevent any contract from arising between her and [buyer]."

2. ***Lapse of Time Terminates Power to Accept an Offer.*** In *Texas Pipe Line Co. v. Miller*, 84 S.W.2d 550, 551 (Tex. Civ. App.—Eastland 1935, no writ), the Texas appellate court declared: "The acceptance must come within the terms of the offer. In other words, if the offer contains a specific time limitation within which it must be accepted, the plaintiff must allege and prove that the acceptance [came] within such time." *See also* RESTATEMENT (SECOND) OF CONTRACTS § 36(1)(a)(2) (1981). It reads: "An offeree's power of acceptance may be terminated by ... lapse of time. ... In addition, an offeree's power of acceptance is terminated by the non-occurrence of any condition of acceptance under the terms of the offer."

3. ***No Withdrawal of Offers or Cancellation of Contracts After Acceptance.*** Consider the Connecticut court's ruling in *Hoye v. DeWolfe Companies*, 1999 WL 608671, *3 (Conn. Super. Ct. Aug. 3, 1999): "[An] attempt to cancel the contract was made subsequent to the plaintiff's acceptance of the offer. A contract cannot be rescinded by attempts to withdraw an offer subsequent to acceptance by the other party."

2) Methods of Acceptance

Overman v. Brown
372 N.W.2d 102
(Neb. 1985)

Per Curiam. Rhonda K. Overman-Plaintiff filed [a] suit in the municipal court of Omaha alleging [that] defendants B.G. Brown and Patsy J. Brown breached a real estate purchase contract. Following the overruling of defendants' demurrer to the amended petition, defendants elected not to plead further and default judgment was entered against them. On appeal to the district court the judgment was affirmed, and defendants have appealed to this court.

"A general demurrer tests the substantive legal rights of the parties upon admitted facts, including proper and reasonable inferences of law and fact which may be drawn from facts which are well pleaded." *Blanchard v. White*, 351 N.W.2d 707, 709 (Neb. 1984). However, in ruling on a demurrer the courts are obliged to accept plaintiff's well-pleaded facts, as distinguished from conclusions, as true. *Allen v. County of Lancaster*, 352 N.W.2d 883 (Neb. 1984).

The pertinent portion of plaintiff's amended petition reads as follows:

> [O]n or about October 12, 1983, Plaintiff and Defendant Patsy J. Brown entered into an agreement wherein said Defendant was to purchase certain premises from the Plaintiff commonly known as 4915 North 118th Street, Omaha, Douglas County, Nebraska. A Uniform Purchase Agreement was executed by the parties as evidence of the agreement, a copy of which is attached hereto and incorporated herein as Exhibit "A". Thereafter, on November 4 [sic], 1983—by agreement of the parties, a second Uniform Purchase Agreement was entered into by the Plaintiff and Defendants Patsy J. Brown and B.G. Brown, which replaced the first purchase agreement.
>
> A copy of the second Uniform Purchase Agreement is attached hereto and incorporated herein as Exhibit "B". The second Uniform Purchase Agreement was accepted on November 4, 1983, by the Plaintiff on a separate authorization, a copy of which is also attached hereto and incorporated herein as Exhibit "C".

The pleading goes on to allege a breach by the defendants and damages suffered by the plaintiff.

The bare facts alleged in the amended petition state the existence of a valid purchase agreement, i.e., the execution of a purchase agreement, including the acceptance by the plaintiff. It is only when reference is made to the actual documents involved—as exhibits to the pleading—that a suggestion of an anomaly appears.

Both of the offers to purchase were made on a "Uniform Purchase Agreement"—a printed form, which contained the terms of the offer and the signature of Patsy J. Brown on the October agreement and those of both Patsy and B.G. Brown on the November agreement. Following the signatures of the defendants, still on the first page of the form, is a receipt of the offer and down payment signed by the real estate agent.

Contained within that receipt is the language: "[T]he above proposition is taken subject to the written approval and acceptance by the owner. ..." Immediately following that signature, and at the very bottom of page 1, are the words: "ACCEPTANCE ON REVERSE SIDE."

The agreement—dated October 12th—was signed by the plaintiff, following the heading "ACCEPTANCE" located at the top of the second page, in which plaintiff simply accepted the "foregoing proposition."

The November 3rd agreement was not accepted in this same manner. Rather, there does appear in the record a letter—dated November 4th—[which was] written on the letterhead of Wurdeman of Omaha. ... [It was] signed by the plaintiff [and stated]: "This is authorization of WURDEMAN OF OMAHA to exchange [the] Original contract dated October 12, 1983 between PATSY J. BROWN-Purchaser and RHONDA K. OVERMAN-Seller for newly signed contract on 4915 North 118th Street, Omaha, Nebraska. Copy of which is attached."

Defendants argue that an offeror is the "master of his offer" and that failure to accept such offer in the prescribed manner is ineffective to create a binding agreement. However, we do not construe the offer to have required an acceptance in any mandatorily assigned manner other than that it is to be in writing.

"If an offer prescribes the place, time or manner of acceptance, its terms in this respect must be complied with in order to create a contract. If an offer merely suggests a permitted place, time or manner of acceptance, another method of acceptance is not precluded." RESTATEMENT (SECOND) OF CONTRACTS § 60 at 147 (1981).

In other words, an offeror is entitled to prescribe an exclusive method of acceptance of an offer, but when the offer as fairly interpreted merely suggests without explicitly directing a particular method of acceptance, the offer can be accepted in any reasonable manner. *David J. Tierney v. T. Wellington Carpets*, 392 N.E.2d 1066 (Mass. App. 1979); *Vaulx v. Cumis Ins. Society, Inc.*, 407 A.2d 262 (D.C. 1979).

We do not view the directory language "ACCEPTANCE ON REVERSE SIDE" to be a mandatory requirement for the acceptance of the offer.

Defendants argue that regardless of the allegations in the petition, the purported acceptance by the plaintiff of the November 3rd offer—by means of a separate letter—was ambiguous and ineffective. We do not agree.

Although it was perhaps ill advised and a clumsy and complicated method of performing a simple task, it could be construed to express an unequivocal intent on the part of the plaintiff to be bound by the terms of the November 3rd agreement, sufficiently so that it would withstand the challenge of a demurrer.

"Acceptance may be made in several different ways, and ordinarily need not be express or formal, but may be shown by words, conduct, or acquiescence indicating agreement." 17 C.J.S. CONTRACTS § 41 at 666 (1963). The act constituting the alleged acceptance of an offer must be judged by whether that communication by the offeree would lead a reasonable person to conclude that the offer has been accepted. *In re Mapes Enterprises, Inc.,* 15 B.R. 192 (D. Nev. 1981). …

The judgment of the district court is correct and is affirmed.

NOTES AND QUESTIONS

1. **Acceptance by Acquiescence.** The law is clear: An express or formal acceptance is not required. Instead, acceptance may be made in different ways—"by words, conduct, or acquiescence." In *Schreiber v. Olan Mills*, 627 A.2d 806 (Pa. Super. Ct. 1993), the court rejected the plaintiff's assertion that defendant's alleged acquiescence culminated in an enforceable contract. Olan Mills operates a nationwide chain of family portrait studios, relying heavily upon "telemarketing." A representative of Olan Mills phoned Allen Schreiber and he wrote a letter. In pertinent part, it read:

   Mrs. Linda Borelli

   Olan Mills

   547 Clairton Blvd.

   Pittsburgh, Pa. 15236

   Dear telemarketer:

   Today, you called us attempting to sell a product or a service. We have no interest in the product or service that you are selling. Please don't call us again. Please remove us from your telemarketing list and notify the provider of the list to also remove our name and number since we do not appreciate

> receiving telemarketing phone calls. We rely on the availability of our phone lines which have been installed for our convenience and not for the convenience of telemarketers. We pay for these phone lines and instruments. You do not. Please don't tie up our phone lines.
>
> Should we receive any more phone calls from you or from anyone connected with your firm of a telemarketing nature, we will consider that you have entered into a contract with us for our listening services and that you have made those calls to us and expect us to listen to your message on a "for hire" basis. If we receive any additional telemarketing phone calls from you, you will be invoiced in accordance with our rates which are $100.00 per hour or fraction thereof with a $100.00 minimum charge. Payment will be due on a net seven (7) day basis.

There were two subsequent calls. Schreiber sued to collect $479, alleging that Olin Mills breached a contract. The lower court concluded that the parties did not form a contract. There was "no true and actual meeting of the minds" and no "ordinary course of dealing and common understanding of men showing a mutual intention to contract." The appellate court agreed, citing settled principles of offer and acceptance. The elemental aspects necessary to give rise to an enforceable contract are "offer," "acceptance," "consideration," and "mutual meeting of the minds." "Further, when seeking to enforce an agreement, one may look to the 'conduct' of the parties to ascertain the acceptance of the agreement. … [A] contract is not binding unless there is an offer and an acceptance. … [I]t is equally well-established that 'an offer may be accepted by conduct; and what the parties do pursuant to the offer' is germane to show whether the offer is accepted. … [I]t is evident from the tenor of the plaintiff's communique to the defendant that it was in the nature of a 'cease and desist' request rather than an 'offer' to 'listen … "for hire"' to the solicitations of the defendant. … Consequently, as a matter of law the parties did not enter into a contract. … There was no 'unconditional' manifestation on the part of Olan Mills or its representative that a *contract was acknowledged by behavior* of the defendant."

2. **Silence or Dominion as Acceptance.** In *B.J. Kadrmas, Inc. v. Oxbow Energy, LLC,* 727 N.W.2d 270, 274 (N.D. 2007), the North Dakota Supreme Court discussed silence and inaction as evidence of acceptance: "It is a general rule of law that silence and inaction, or mere silence or failure to reject an offer when it is made, do not constitute an acceptance of the offer. However, under some circumstances, silence and inaction operate as an acceptance … where … an inference of assent is warranted, or … where, under the circumstances, such an inference is required or is necessary."

See also 17A AM. JUR .2D CONTRACTS § 103 (1991), citing *Lechler v. Montana Life Ins. Co.*, 186 N.W. 271 (N.D. 1921). "[W]here the relations between parties have [caused the offerer to expect a reply justifiably], or where the offeree has ... some duty to communicate either a rejection or acceptance, his failure to communicate his rejection or to perform this duty may result in a legal assent to the terms of the offer." *Lechler*, 186 N.W. at 274.

3. **Voluntary Acceptance.** "A voluntary acceptance of the benefit of a transaction is equivalent to a consent to all the obligations arising from it so far as the facts are known or ought to be known to the person accepting." NORTH DAKOTA CENTURY CODE § 9-03-25.

4. **Common-Law Mailbox or Postal-Acceptance Rule: General Principles.** The Maryland Court of Special Appeals gives a cogent discussion of the "mailbox rule" in *U.S. Life Ins. Co. in City of New York v. Wilson*, 18 A.3d 110, 124–25 (Md. Ct. Spec. App. 2011): "At common law, what is often called the 'mailbox rule,' the 'dispatch rule,' or sometimes the 'postal acceptance rule' is the widely-adopted convention for pinpointing the time that an offer is accepted and a contract is formed." Illinois, like Maryland, recognizes the rule that ... "the mailed acceptance of an offer is effective when mailed, not when received or acknowledged." *See Martin v. Gov't Employees Ins. Co.*, 206 Ill. App. 3d 1031, 1042 (Ill. App. Ct. 1990). *See also Reserve Ins. Co. v. Duckett,* 238 A.2d 536, 540 (Md. 1968) (explaining that the "postal acceptance rule" was adopted initially in *Adams v. Lindsell*, 1 Barn & Ald. 681, 106 Eng. Rep. 250 (King's Bench 1818)).

5. **Acceptance, Private Carriers, and the "Dispatch Rule".** "The private delivery service ... would have to be independent of the offeree, reliable both in terms of its delivery obligations and record keeping. ... [And, the carrier must be] of a type that would customarily be used to communicate messages of this sort. Such agencies as the United Parcel Service, Federal Express, or even private messenger services in urban areas would qualify. ... [And] as soon as the communication leaves the offeree's possession and is placed with an authorized recipient of the instrumentality, an effective dispatch will be deemed to have occurred." *U.S. Life Ins. Co. in City of New York v. Wilson*, 18 A.3d 110, 124–25 (Md. App. 2011). *See also* CORBIN ON CONTRACTS § 3.24, at 440 (Joseph M. Peillo ed., Revised ed. 1993) (stating that the dispatch rule establishes when the contract is formed so as to uniformly and definitely designate which of the parties is to carry the risk of "loss and inconvenience").

6. **RESTATEMENT (SECOND) OF CONTRACTS § 30(2) (1981).** "Unless otherwise indicated by the language or the circumstances, an offer invites acceptance ... by any medium reasonable in the circumstances."

7. **RESTATEMENT (SECOND) OF CONTRACTS § 63(a) (1981).** "Unless the offer provides otherwise, an acceptance made in a manner and by a medium invited by an offer is operative and completes the manifestation of mutual assent as soon as put out of the offeree's possession, without regard to whether it ever reaches the offeror[.]"

---

3) Mirror Image Rule, Counteroffers, Modifications, Rejections, New Conditions, and New Provisions

The majority of state supreme courts adopted the common-law "mirror image rule": "[A]n acceptance must be coextensive with the offer and may not introduce additional terms or conditions." *See, e.g., Podany v. Erickson*, 39, 49 N.W.2d 193, 194 (Minn. 1951). Or stated slightly differently, to form a valid contract, one's acceptance of an offer must be absolute and unconditional. In addition, the acceptance must mirror the terms of the offer. *Montgomery v. English*, 902 So.2d 836, 837 (Fla. 5th Dist. Ct. App. 2005).

Still, the mirror image rule has generated several important questions: 1) whether or not one's altering or varying the terms of an offer always constitutes a rejection of the offer; and 2) whether or not the slightest alteration of an offer is a counteroffer. *See Rose v. Guerdon Indus., Inc.*, 374 N.W.2d 282, 284 (Minn. Ct. App. 1985) (acceptance that seeks to vary, add to, or qualify the terms of an offer constitutes a rejection of the offer and a counteroffer.) Are there exceptions to the mirror image rule? The following case provides some answers.

Gresser v. Hotzler
604 N.W.2d 379
(Minn. Ct. App. 2000)

Lansing, Judge. Michael Gresser sued Calvin and Cheryl Hotzler for specific performance of a purchase agreement for commercial real estate and, alternatively, for breach of contract. On the Hotzlers' motion for partial summary judgment on Gresser's specific-performance claim, the district court held that the purchase agreement was invalid and entered final judgment against Gresser pursuant to MINN. R. CIV. P. § 54.02, dismissing both the specific-performance and breach-of-contract claims. Gresser appeals from the judgment.

FACTS

The property in dispute includes five acres of land and a building that formerly housed the Stagecoach Theatre in Shakopee. In early 1998, Michael Gresser—a real estate investor—began negotiating with landowners Calvin and Cheryl Hotzler to purchase the property. In July, Gresser submitted to the Hotzlers an unsigned, proposed purchase agreement. ... [Among] other items, [it] required the Hotzlers to deliver a recertified survey on August 10, 1998, and provided for closing on September 1, 1998. The Hotzlers changed several terms, initialed the changes, signed the purchase agreement, and returned it to Gresser's attorney on August 4, 1998.

On August 10, 1998, Gresser initialed the Hotzlers' changes and signed the purchase agreement. Gresser, however, made two additional changes. He changed the survey delivery date to September 10, 1998, and the closing date to October 15, 1998. Gresser initialed both date changes. Gresser made these changes on the advice of his attorney, who had talked to the Hotzlers' realtor. The attorney and the realtor agreed that—because of the time that had elapsed—the original survey and closing dates had become impractical. The attorney knew that the realtor had not consulted the Hotzlers about the changes, and both Gresser and his attorney knew that the realtor did not have the power to bind the Hotzlers.

Gresser's attorney returned the signed purchase agreement to the realtor on August 12, 1998, along with $2,000 earnest money. Gresser and his attorney expected that the Hotzlers would initial the date changes and return the purchase agreement to them. The realtor delivered the purchase agreement to Calvin Hotzler on August 12, 1998, but testified that he did not indicate whether Gresser had signed the counteroffer. Calvin Hotzler assumed the parties had a deal, but he did not read the purchase agreement. Instead, he placed it on the kitchen counter to await the return of Cheryl Hotzler, who was out of town. Later that day, Calvin Hotzler showed Gresser the property and introduced him to tenants as the buyer.

On the afternoon of August 12, 1998, the realtor received another offer for the property, which he forwarded to the Hotzlers. Calvin Hotzler placed this document on the kitchen counter as well. On August 13, the Hotzlers reviewed both documents, decided to accept the new offer, and signed that purchase agreement.

ISSUES

I. Given the undisputed facts in the record, did the district court err by concluding that the purchase agreement between the Hotzlers and Gresser was not legally binding?

II. Did the district court err by refusing to apply equitable estoppel?

* * *

ANALYSIS

I

Whether a contract is formed is judged by the objective conduct of the parties and not their subjective intent. *Cederstrand v. Lutheran Bhd.,* 117 N.W.2d 213, 221 (1962). Minnesota has followed the "mirror image rule" in analyzing acceptance of offers. Under that rule, "an acceptance must be coextensive with the offer and may not introduce additional terms or conditions." *Podany v. Erickson*, 49 N.W.2d 193, 194 (1951). When the offer is positively accepted, however, a requested or suggested modification does not prevent contract formation, regardless of whether the modification is accepted. *Alpha Venture / Vantage Properties v. Creative Carton Corp.*, 370 N.W.2d 649, 652 (Minn. App. 1985). *See also* RESTATEMENT (SECOND) OF CONTRACTS § 61 (1981).

* * *

Gresser primarily argues that his changes to the purchase agreement are within the modification exception to the mirror-image rule because he unconditionally accepted the Hotzlers' counteroffer and merely suggested the date changes. According to Gresser, he accepted unconditionally because he would have been willing to comply with the original dates, the realtor encouraged Gresser to make the changes, and Calvin Hotzler introduced Gresser as the owner of the property on August 12th.

Viewed objectively, these facts do not demonstrate that Gresser positively accepted the purchase agreement. First, Gresser's uncommunicated subjective intent is not relevant, and, second, these facts do not suggest that the Hotzlers knew or should have known that Gresser offered the change in dates only as a suggestion. To the contrary, the undisputed facts regarding absence of any express communication, the method of initialing the changes, and the prior course of dealings between the parties indicate that the changes were part of the series of counteroffers.

Minnesota has applied the modification exception sparingly and only to those cases in which objective manifestations of acceptance existed separately from the suggestions for modifications. *See Podany*,

49 N.W.2d at 195 (offeree's written acceptance clearly stated it had elected to exercise option to purchase property); *Alpha Venture*, 370 N.W.2d at 651–52 (offeree's acceptance letter attached to signed letter termination of lease agreement). Gresser proposed his changes on the face of the purchase agreement and provided no objective indication that his acceptance was not conditioned on them.

Gresser alternatively argues that his changes to the purchase agreement did not preclude contract formation because the changes were immaterial. The mirror-image rule historically has been strictly construed to forbid even minor variations between offer and acceptance. Many modern courts have relaxed the rule, holding that only an acceptance that differs materially from the terms of the original offer prevents contract formation. *See, e.g., Raydon Exploration, Inc. v. Ladd*, 902 F.2d 1496, 1500 (10th Cir. 1990) (Oklahoma law); *Hoyt R. Matise Co. v. Zurn*, 754 F.2d 560, 566 (5th Cir. 1985) (Texas law); *Northwest Television Club v. Gross Seattle, Inc.*, 640 P.2d 710 (Wash. 1982).

The corollary to this modern rule is that an immaterial variation in the acceptance does not impede contract formation. For instance, several courts have held that, under this exception, variations implied in the offer do not interfere with the completed contract. *Northwest Television Club*, 634 P.2d at 841–42; *Karas v. Brogan*, 378 N.E.2d 470, 471 (Ohio 1978); *Northwest Properties Agency, Inc. v. McGhee*, 462 P.2d 249, 253 (Wash. App. 1969).

The Minnesota Supreme Court used the language of the immateriality exception in *Markmann v. H.A. Bruntjen Co.*, 81 N.W.2d 858, 862 (Minn. 1957). In *Markmann*, the court held that "an acceptance which differs substantially and materially from the terms of the original offer does not give rise to a completed contract." The *Markmann* court did not, however, find an immaterial variation or make clear that it was diverging from its former strict construction of the mirror-image rule.

The Hotzlers argue that Minnesota caselaw has retained the strict mirror-image rule for real estate contracts, while tempering the rule in its application to other types of contracts. Although we note that the supreme court and this court have more often applied the strict-construction standard in cases involving real estate, caselaw provides no explicit distinction. *Compare Rose v. Guerdon Indus., Inc.,* 374 N.W.2d 282, 284 (Minn. App. 1985) (applying strict construction to acceptance of offer to sell real estate), *with Markmann*, 81 N.W.2d at 862 (using material-difference standard to analyze contract for sale of product distribution rights). It is, however, unnecessary to define the scope of an immateriality exception unless the changes to the purchase agreement are immaterial.

"Authority on what constitutes a material variation is meager." *Northwest Television Club*, 634 P.2d at 841. BLACK'S LAW DICTIONARY defines "material alteration" as "a change in a legal instrument sufficient to alter the instrument's legal meaning or effect." BLACK'S LAW DICTIONARY, 78 (7th ed. 1999). Similarly, the Florida Court of Appeals found the addition of "and/or assignees" did not constitute a material variation because it did not "change the legal effect of the contract." *Kitsos v. Stanford*, 291 So.2d 632, 634 (Fla. Dist. Ct. App. 1974). We agree that the focus should be on the legal operation of the contract. Thus, only minor changes that do not substantially alter the performance obligations of the parties may be immaterial.

Under this principle, the date changes Gresser made are material. The changes directly affect Gresser's performance obligations under the contract, postponing his duty to perform by almost six weeks. The law of contracts is not advanced by allowing a contracting party to manipulate the finality of an obligation by rejecting an insubstantial change, but few terms are more important to sellers of real estate than the date on which they will receive the purchase money. The purchase agreement's inclusion of a time-is-of-the-essence clause further evidences the materiality of the performance date. As a matter of law, the exception to the mirror-image rule for immaterial variations does not apply to the changes Gresser made to the purchase agreement.

In retrospect, Gresser may have been very willing to expressly note that the changed dates were proposals rather than conditions or to retain the earlier closing date rather than risk the loss of the property. But contract formation proceeds on an objective basis and courts should not reconstruct—much less call back—the written word. The high volume of real estate transactions in Minnesota reinforces the importance of identifying and preserving a bright line in the formation of purchase agreements.

II

The district court rejected Gresser's argument that the Hotzlers should be equitably estopped from denying the validity of the purchase agreement. We note at the outset that "it is questionable whether a contract can be created in the first instance by estoppel." *St. Paul Fire & Marine Ins. Co. v. Bierwerth*, 175 N.W.2d 136, 142 (Minn. 1969). But the equitable estoppel argument itself is flawed in its reliance on agency and ratification.

Equitable estoppel arises when "one by his acts or representations, or by his silence when he ought to speak, intentionally or through culpable negligence, induces another to believe certain facts to exist, and such other rightfully acts on the belief so induced in such a matter that if the former is permitted to deny the existence of the facts it will prejudice the latter." *Transamerica Ins. Group v. Paul*, 267 N.W.2d 180, 183 (Minn. 1978). The first element necessary to establish estoppel is a misrepresentation. Gresser does not allege the Hotzlers made misrepresentations directly, but contends that the realtor's statements that the changes would not affect the deal are attributable to the Hotzlers under agency theories.

The general rule is that real estate agents have no implied authority to contract on behalf of their principals. *La Plant v. Loveland*, 170 N.W. 920, 921 (Minn. 1919). And apparent authority must be founded on the principal's actions "since no agent by his own act can create evidence of authority." *West Concord Conservation Club, Inc. v. Chilson*, 306 N.W.2d 893, 897 (Minn. 1981). *See also Hagedorn v. Aid Ass'n for Lutherans*, 211 N.W.2d 154, 158 (Minn. 1973). Gresser has not identified any conduct or statements by the Hotzlers that would support a variance from the general rule on implied authority or a finding of apparent authority.

We also reject Gresser's argument that any deficiencies in the proof of implied or apparent authority were cured by ratification when Hotzler introduced Gresser as the buyer of the property after receiving the purchase agreement with the changed dates. "Ratification occurs when one having full knowledge of all material facts confirms, approves or sanctions a previous act done on behalf of the principal without authority." *Centennial Ins. Co. v. Zylberberg*, 422 N.W.2d 18, 21 (Minn. App. 1988). Conversely, ratification cannot occur when the principal does not have full knowledge of all material facts, unless constructive knowledge is imputed by the principal's acceptance of a transaction's benefits. *Anderson v. First Nat'l Bank of Pine City*, 228 N.W.2d 257, 259 (Minn. 1975) (lack of knowledge defeats ratification claim); *Cooney v. Milwaukee Mut. Ins. Co.*, 397 N.W.2d 352, 355 (Minn. App. 1986) (insurance company ratified unauthorized acts of agent by accepting premiums).

The record does not support Gresser's claim that Hotzler had actual notice of the changes to the contract when he showed Gresser the property and introduced him as the buyer. *See Jackson v. Badger*, 26 N.W. 908, 909 (Minn. 1886) (no ratification when principal continued with sale but had no knowledge that agent had made deal on different terms than he authorized). Nor does the record support Gresser's claim that Hotzler accepted the benefits of the transaction. The mere delivery of a check as earnest money is insufficient to constitute a benefit.

* * *

Gresser's equitable estoppel claim also fails on the essential element of reasonable reliance. *See Transamerica*, 267 N.W.2d at 183 (listing reasonable reliance as element of equitable estoppel). Both Gresser and his attorney admit that they knew real estate agents are not authorized to contract on behalf of their principals. And Gresser's attorney also knew that the realtor had not contacted the Hotzlers before making the assurances. On these facts, any reliance on the realtor's assurances was unreasonable as a matter of law. *See West Concord Conservation Club*, 306 N.W.2d at 897 (to invoke estoppel doctrine, "truth must have been unknown" to party when he acted).

DECISION

Because the date changes to the purchase agreement precluded contract formation as a matter of law, and because Gresser failed to assert facts sufficient to support an equitable estoppel claim, the district court properly granted summary judgment to the Hotzlers. Affirmed.

NOTES AND QUESTIONS

1. **The Mirror Image Rule.** Consider the Supreme Court of the Territory of Guam's review in *Blas v. Cruz*, 2009 WL 4282909 (Guam 2009): "It is hornbook law that, to ensure mutual consent of the parties to an offer, an offer must be mirrored by its acceptance to create a binding contract. Because the offeror is entitled to receive what it has bargained for, if a purported acceptance includes additional terms to which the offeror did not assent, the consequence is not merely that the addition is not binding and that no contract is formed, but that the offer is rejected, and that the offeree's power of acceptance thereafter is terminated."

2. **Counteroffers—New Conditions or New Provisions.** *See Benya v. Stevens & Thompson Paper Co., Inc.*, 468 A.2d 929, 931 (Vt. 1983) ("The law relative to contract formation has long been well settled. ... An acceptance that modifies or includes new terms is not an acceptance of the original offer; it is a counteroffer by the offeree that must be accepted or rejected by the original offeror."), and *C.H. Leavell & Co. v. Grafe & Assocs., Inc.*, 414 P.2d 873, 878 (Idaho 1966) ("An acceptance of an offer, in order to create a binding contract, must unqualifiedly and unequivocally agree to all the material terms of the offer and must not include any new conditions or provisions.").

3. **The Rejection of Common-Law "Mirror Image Rule."** In *Medical City Dallas, Ltd. v. Carlisle Corp.*, 251 S.W.3d 55, 60 & n. 3 (Tex. 2008), the Texas Supreme Court noted that the Uniform Commercial Code governs contracts involving the sale of movable goods. *See also Glenn Thurman, Inc. v. Moore Const., Inc.*, 942 S.W.2d 768, 771 (Tex. App.—Tyler 1997, no pet.) ("When parties enter into a contract for the sale of goods, [the U.C.C.] controls the

conduct of the parties. Where the U.C.C. applies, it displaces all common law rules of law regarding breach of contract and substitutes instead those rules of law and procedure set forth in the U.C.C."). Consequently, TEX. BUS. & COM. CODE § 2.207 rejects the common law "mirror image" rule and allows a contract to be formed even though the parties' exchanged documents contain varying terms. However, the formation is subject to the following qualifications: 1) the offer may not expressly limit an acceptance of the terms in the offer; 2) the varying terms may not materially alter the contract; or 3) neither party objects to the varying terms.

4. **The Last Shot Doctrine**. In *Step-Saver Data Sys., Inc. v. Wyse Tech.*, 939 F.2d 91, 99 (3rd Cir. 1991), the Court of Appeals for the Third Circuit explained the doctrine:

> Under the common law of sales, and to some extent still for contracts outside the UCC, an acceptance that varied any term of the offer operated as a rejection of the offer, and simultaneously made a counteroffer. This common law formality was known as the mirror image rule, because the terms of the acceptance had to mirror the terms of the offer to be effective. If the offeror proceeded with the contract despite the differing terms of the supposed acceptance, he would, by his performance, constructively accept the terms of the "counteroffer," and be bound by its terms. As a result of these rules, the terms of the party who sent the last form, typically the seller, would become the terms of the parties' contract. This result was known as the "last shot rule." ... The UCC, in § 2-207, reject[s] this approach.

5. **The Knockout Rule.** Consider the Kentucky court's explanation of the knockout doctrine in *General Steel Corp. v. Collins*, 196 S.W.3d 18, 21 (Ky. Ct. App. 2006):

> [Under the] common law the disparity between the fine-print terms in the parties' forms would have prevented the consummation of a contract when these forms are exchanged. ... [However, a] court may conclude that the parties have formed a contract even where the acceptance of the offer contains terms additional to or different from those stated in the offer. As long as the parties demonstrate their mutual assent to the essential terms of an agreement, a written contract is deemed to exist. ... A majority of jurisdictions holds that the conflicting terms between an offer ... and [an] acceptance are properly subject to the "knockout" rule. Where the terms of

the offer and acceptance are clearly at odds, they cancel out one another, and neither becomes a part of the contract.

PROOF OF AN ACCEPTANCE AND ACCOMPANYING AFFIRMATIVE DEFENSES IN A NUTSHELL

Again, "mutual assent," offer and acceptance rules govern whether a valid contract has been formed. Consequently, parties who want to fashion a valid contract must agree about the same things or terms. Additionally, an offer must be accepted. And the offeree's acceptance will not bind the offeror, unless the acceptance conforms to certain rules. To be sure, there are exceptions to these general rules as well as exceptions to the exceptions. Generally, the exceptions are called "affirmative defenses." This nutshell outlines some general rules—regarding the proper way to accept an offer—and some corresponding defenses.

Proof of the Sub-Element: Acceptance

An Acceptance Must Comply Strictly to the Terms of Offer

Under the common law, the "mirror image" rule applies to the formation of contracts. Put simply, the terms of an acceptance must precisely imitate or "mirror" the terms of an offer. If the offeree's terms are different from or add to those in the offer, it is a counteroffer and not an acceptance. *Gardner Zemke Company v. Dunham Bush, Inc.*, 850 P.2d 319, 322 (N.M. 1993).

An Acceptance May Not Be Conditional

Generally, a conditional acceptance of an offer is considered to be a rejection and counteroffer. *See United Concrete Pipe Corp. v. Spin–Line Co.*, 430 S.W.2d 360, 363–64 (Tex. 1968). *See also Homayouni v. Banque Paribas*, 241 A.D.2d 375, 376, 660 N.Y.S.2d 413 (1997) ["[W]henever a purported acceptance is even slightly at variance with the terms of an offer, the qualified response operates as a rejection and termination of … the initially offered terms").

An Offeror Has Exclusive Power to Determine the Method of Acceptance

If an offer prescribes the place, time, or manner of acceptance, the offeree's acceptance must comply with the terms. Or an acceptance is "wholly nugatory and ineffectual" if it varies from the stated method of acceptance, which appears in the offer. *Rochester Home Equity v. Guenette*, 6 A.D.3d 1119, 1120, 775 N.Y.S.2d 680 (2004).

Proof of Acceptance and Accompanying Affirmative Defenses

There are several general affirmative defenses to the assertion: "An acceptance of the offer was communicated effectively and legally to the offeror." Consider the following common-law defenses:

- ***The Method of Acceptance Was Only a Suggestion.*** *See Allied Steel & Conveyors, Inc. v. Ford Motor Co.*, 277 F.2d 907, 911 (6th Cir. 1960) ("[If an] offeror prescribes an exclusive manner of acceptance, an attempt on the part of the offeree to accept the offer in a different manner does not bind the offeror in the absence of a meeting of the minds on the altered type of acceptance. On the other hand, if an offeror merely suggests a permitted method of acceptance, other methods of acceptance are not precluded.")
- ***A Formal Acceptance of an Offer Is Not Mandatory***: An acceptance of an offer may occur in different ways. Therefore, an express or a formal acceptance is not required. Words, conduct, or acquiescence may be used to show an acceptance of an offer. *See Pleines v. Franklin Const. Co., Inc.*, 621 A.2d 759, 762 (Conn. App. 1993) ("The law ... does not require an express acceptance. Acceptance may be shown by acts or conduct indicating assent to an offer or, under appropriate circumstances, acceptance may be implied by the offeree's silence and inaction.")
- ***Conditional Acceptances Are Valid.*** *See* 2 RICHARD A. LORD, WILLISTON ON CONTRACTS § 6.15 at 122–24 (4th ed. 1991) ("Occasionally an offeree, out of ignorance or an abundance of caution, will insert a condition in his acceptance which merely expresses what would otherwise be implied in fact or in law from the offer. Because such a condition involves no qualification of the offeree's assent to the terms of the offer, it is not in truth a conditional acceptance, and it does not preclude the formation of a contract.")
- ***Acceptance Was Only an Immaterial Deviation from the Stated Mode of Acceptance.*** Many courts have relaxed the mandatory, method of acceptance rule and allowed a party to show that her acceptance did not deviate materially from the terms appearing the offer. *See, e.g., Nungesser v. Bryant*, 153 P.3d 1277, 1288(Kan. 2007) ("[I]mmaterial or minor differences or variances between an offer and acceptance will not prevent the formation of a contract").

CHAPTER THREE

PROOF OF CONSIDERATION

Nearly one hundred years ago, a Texas appellate court crafted the opinion in *J. M. Radford Grocery Company v. Jamison*, 221 S.W. 998, 1000 (Tex. Civ. App.—El Paso 1920). The opinion contains this passage:

> A declaration in an action on a contract must aver every material part of it. ... The material facts of a contract cannot be presumed; they must be alleged, in order to show a breach or nonperformance. A declaration in an action on a contract which does not state the time at which the defendant should have performed is bad on demurrer. Where no time for performance is specified in a contract, it should be averred that it was to be performed on request, or within a reasonable time, and that such request was made or that a reasonable time has elapsed. ... In our system of pleading no presumption of consideration exists, and *one seeking to enforce a contract*, or to recover damages for its breach, is required to both plead and prove a valid consideration for the undertaking.

Certainly, those principles outlined in the *Jamison* opinion still apply today, if one expects to secure breach-of-promise or breach-of-contract damages. But, there is a pressing initial question: What is consideration? And second, how does a plaintiff "prove a valid consideration for an undertaking"? Or, what is the plaintiff's burden of proof in a court of law? The discussion in this chapter answers these and several related questions.

To start the discussion, consider the definition of consideration in RESTATEMENT (SECOND) OF CONTRACTS §§ 71(1)–(3) (1981):

1. To constitute consideration, a performance or a return promise must be bargained for.

2. A performance or return promise is bargained for if it is sought by the promisor in exchange for his promise and is given by the promisee in exchange for that promise.

3. The performance may consist of

   (a) an act other than a promise, or

   (b) a forbearance, or

   (c) the creation, modification, or destruction of a legal relation.

Now consider RESTATEMENT (SECOND) OF CONTRACTS § 90(1) (1981):

§90 (1)—Promise Reasonably Inducing Action or Forbearance

> A promise which the promisor should reasonably expect to induce action or forbearance on the part of the promisee or a third person and which does induce such action or forbearance is binding if injustice can be avoided only by enforcement of the promise. The remedy granted for breach may be limited as justice requires.

RESTATEMENT § 71 outlines the so-called bargained-for-exchange doctrine and § 90 lays the foundation for the promissory estoppel doctrine.

SECTION ONE: PROOF OF CONSIDERATION AND THE BARGAINED-FOR-EXCHANGE DOCTRINE

A. Distinguishing Consideration from a Gift or a "Mere Gratuity"

Briefly put, if two parties exchange promises to act or not act for the benefit of each other, the exchanges may serve as consideration. In addition, consideration can evolve when a promisor and a promisee deliver and exchange goods or services among themselves. But, an exchange of goods or services might be evidence of a gift rather than consideration. Therefore, what is the test for distinguishing a "mere gratuity" from a bargained-for consideration?

1. Consideration Clauses as Evidence of Bargained-for Consideration Rather Than a Mere Gratuity

Thomas v. Thomas
114 Eng. Rep. 330
2 Q.B. 851 (1842)

Assumpsit. At the trial, before [Judge Coltman at the Glamorganshire Lent Assizes], it appeared that John Thomas—the deceased husband of the plaintiff [Eleanor Thomas] at the time of his death in 1837—was possessed of a row of seven dwelling houses in Merthyr Tidvil. ... [B]y his will, he appointed his brother Samuel Thomas—since deceased—and the defendant executors thereof, to take possession of all his houses ..., subject to certain payments in the will ... for the benefit of the plaintiff. In the evening before the day of his death, he expressed orally a wish to make some further provision for his wife; and on the following morning he declared orally, in the presence of two witnesses, that it was his will that his wife should have either the house in which he lived and all that it contained, or an additional sum of 100*l*. instead thereof.

This declaration [was] shortly afterwards brought to the knowledge of Samuel Thomas and the defendant—the executors and residuary legatees[.] They consented to carry the intentions of the testator so expressed into effect; and, after the lapse of a few days, they and the plaintiff executed the agreement ... which—after stating the parties, and briefly reciting the will—proceeded as follows:

> "And, whereas the said testator, shortly before his death, declared, in the presence of several witnesses, that he was desirous his said wife should have and enjoy during her life, or so long as she should continue his widow, all and singular the dwelling house," &c., "or 100*l*. out of his personal estate," in addition to the respective legacies and bequests given her in and by his said will; "but such declaration and desire was not reduced to writing in the lifetime of the said John Thomas and read over to him; but the said Samuel Thomas and Benjamin Thomas are fully convinced and satisfied that such was the desire of the said testator, and are willing and desirous that such intention should be carried into full effect[.]
>
> '[N]ow these presents witness, and it is hereby agreed and declared by and between the parties, that, in consideration of such desire and of the premises," the executors would convey the dwelling house, &c. to the plaintiff and her assigns during her life, or for so long a time as she should continue a widow and unmarried: "provided nevertheless, and it is hereby further agreed and declared, that the said Eleanor Thomas, or her assigns, shall and will, at all times during which she shall have possession of the said dwelling house, &c., pay to the

> said Samuel Thomas and Benjamin Thomas, their executors, &c., the sum of 1*l*. yearly towards the ground rent payable in respect of the said dwelling house and other premises thereto adjoining, and shall and will keep the said dwelling house and premises in good and tenantable repair:" with other provisions not affecting the questions in this case.

The plaintiff was left in possession of the dwelling house and premises for some time: but the defendant, after the death of his co-executor, refused to execute a conveyance tendered to him for execution pursuant to the agreement; and, shortly before the trial, [the defendant] brought an ejectment, under which he turned the plaintiff out of possession. [The defendant] argued that one part of the consideration was omitted in the declaration. ... [Consequently,] there was a fatal variance.

The learned Judge overruled the objection, reserving leave to move to enter a nonsuit. Ultimately a verdict was found for the plaintiff [Eleanor] on all the issues; and, in Easter term ..., a rule *nisi* was obtained pursuant to the leave reserved.

Chilton and W. M. James now shewed cause. ... The objection taken at the trial was[:] [T]he consideration for the agreement—instead of being that which is alleged in the declaration—was, as stated in the agreement itself, a respect for the testator's intentions. ... [In that] case, this would be a mere voluntary agreement. ... [T]he defendant now appears to contend that respect for the testator's intentions is a part of the legal consideration, and ought to have been set out. But it could not be so characterized. All that a plaintiff is required to do is to set out the legal effect of the contract, and to shew performance on the plaintiff's part. ... [H]ere she was in possession for three or four years, paying rent, under an undertaking to pay rent and keep the premises in repair. ... [T]hat is a good consideration. ... Parties are often influenced by motives which form no part of the legal consideration, such as the character of a tenant, or the merits or distresses of the party intended to be benefited; and the circumstance that such motives happen to be stated in the agreement cannot affect the legal rights of the parties, nor make it necessary to state those motives in the declaration.

* * *

E. V. Williams, contra. The consideration alleged in the declaration is solely the promise to pay rent and repair: therefore it lay[s] on the plaintiff to prove that to have been the true and sole consideration. ... But the evidence shews that the testator's declaration—as brought before and recognized by the executors—was part, if not the whole, of the consideration. It is conceded that where there is a good legal consideration conjoined with a moral one, it is not necessary to state both. [B]ut here, regard for the testator's intentions was not—under the circumstances—a mere moral consideration. ... If the testator's expressed wish was part or the whole of the consideration, the declaration should have so alleged it, and a nonsuit ought to be entered. But, in fact, if it [is] not the consideration, there is no legal consideration at all: this is a mere gift. …

* * *

Patteson J. The rent—if issuing out of the house—might follow the gift. … [B]ut the obligation to repair does not. The expressions in the agreement—with reference to the ground rent, and the evidence of one of the witnesses—shew that the property was held under a superior landlord. … [T]he assignee's obligation to pay rent and repair would therefore be implied from the very nature and state of things which existed between the parties.

* * *

Coleridge J. The concessions made in the course of the argument have … disposed of the case. It is conceded that mere motive need not be stated; and we are not obliged to look for the legal consideration in any particular part of the instrument, merely because the consideration is usually stated in some particular part. … [W]e may look to any part. In this instrument, in the part where it is usual to state the consideration, nothing certainly is expressed but a wish to fulfil the intentions of the testator. … [B]ut in another part, we find an express agreement to pay an annual sum for a particular purpose and also a distinct agreement to repair. If these had occurred in the first part of the instrument, it could hardly have been argued that the declaration was not well drawn, and supported by the evidence. As to the suggestion of this being a voluntary conveyance, my impression is that this payment of 1*l*. annually is more than a good consideration. It is a valuable consideration. It is clearly a thing newly created, and not part of the old ground rent.

Rule discharged [and affirmed for plaintiff].

NOTES AND QUESTIONS

1. **Consideration Clauses in Contracts.** In *Thomas*, the defendants argued that Eleanor could not produce evidence of any consideration because Eleanor and the defendants' agreement did not contain a "consideration clause." Customarily, to protect themselves from a no-consideration defense, parties insert consideration clauses in contracts. An excellent example of the practice appears in *In re Greene* 45 F.2d 428 (S.D.N.Y. 1930). However, as the court in *Thomas* stressed: "[Courts] are not obliged to look for the legal consideration in any particular part of [an] instrument,

merely because the consideration is usually stated in some particular part." Quite simply, courts may look in any part of an agreement to find evidence of consideration.

2. **Proving Bargained-for Consideration Between a Deceased Grantor and Grantee.** In *Thomas*, the deceased husband was the grantor and Eleanor was the grantee under the husband's will. Also, the grantor "declared orally" or promised that his wife would receive the house and all of the contents. How did Eleanor prove bargained-for consideration to enforce the grantor's promise? What did she exchange?

2. Forbearance: Loss of Time and Options as Bargained-for Consideration

Kirksey v. Kirksey
8 Ala. 131
(Ala. 1845)

Assumpsit by the defendant, against the plaintiff in error. The question is presented in this court, upon a case agreed, which shows the following facts:

The plaintiff was the wife of defendant's brother, but had for some time been a widow, and had several children. In 1840, the plaintiff resided on public land, under a contract of lease, she had held over, and was comfortably settled, and would have attempted to secure the land she lived on. The defendant resided in Talladega county, some sixty, or seventy miles off. On the 10th October, 1840, he wrote to her the following letter:

> Dear sister Antillico—Much to my mortification, I heard, that brother Henry was dead, and one of his children. I know that your situation is one of grief, and difficulty. You had a bad chance before, but a great deal worse now. I should like to come and see you, but cannot with convenience at present. ... I do not know whether you have a preference on the place you live on, or not. If you had, I would advise you to obtain your preference, and sell the land and quit the country, as I understand it is very unhealthy, and I know society is very bad. If you will come down and see me, I will let you have a place to raise your family, and I have more open land than I can tend; and on the account of your situation, and that of your family, I feel like I want you and the children to do well.

Within a month or two after the receipt of this letter, the plaintiff abandoned her possession, without disposing of it, and removed with her family, to the residence of the defendant, who put her in comfortable houses, and gave her land to cultivate for two years, at the end of which time he notified her to remove, and put her in a house, not comfortable, in the woods, which he afterwards required her to leave.

A verdict being found for the plaintiff, for two hundred dollars, the above facts were agreed, and if they will sustain the action, the judgment is to be affirmed, otherwise it is to be reversed.

Ormond, J. (dissenting):

The inclination of my mind, is, that the loss and inconvenience, which the plaintiff sustained in breaking up, and moving to the defendant's, a distance of sixty miles, is a sufficient consideration to support the promise, to furnish her with a house, and land to cultivate, until she could raise her family. My brothers, however think, that the promise on the part of the defendant, was a mere gratuity, and that an action will not lie for its breach. The judgment of the court below must therefore be reversed, pursuant to the agreement of the parties.

NOTES AND QUESTIONS

1. **The Mystery of Kirksey v. Kirksey**. Professor William R. Casto and attorney Val D. Ricks wrote the following in *"Dear Sister Antillico": The Story of Kirksey v. Kirksey*, 94 Geo. L.J. 321, 324 (2006):

   > *Kirksey* truly is a famous case. ... Although the case seems straightforward and even simple, many ambiguities and puzzles lie beneath its still surface. Countless professors in countless classes have queried: Why did Isaac Kirksey invite his sister-in-law "Antillico" (an aberrant spelling of Angelico) down to Talladega? Was he bargaining for something when he did? How many children did Angelico bring? Did Isaac mean for the children to work on his plantation (did he bargain for their labor)? Did Isaac and Angelico have an affair (was the consideration meretricious)? Why did Isaac move to evict his sister-in-law? Was she unbearable as a neighbor? Why did she sue? What result was she seeking? What evidence was presented at trial? Did she have evidence of consideration other than her trip to Talladega? Was her lawyer incompetent? Did the law of the time support Angelico's legal position, or is Ormond's conclusion based on something other than legal authority? Did the appellate court usurp the jury's factfinding role? Why did the dissenting judge write the majority opinion? Whatever happened to Angelico and her small children?

2. **Bargained-for Consideration as Forfeiting an Option to Purchase Land or a Property Interest in Land.** Consider the following discussion in *"Dear Sister Antillico": The Story of Kirksey v. Kirksey*, 94 Geo. L.J. at 342–43:

> [I]n September 1841 Congress passed a standing preemption law—Preemption Act of Sept. 4, 1841, ch. 16, 5 Stat. 453 (repealed 1891). Under this law, any head of a family, widow, or single man over the age of twenty-one years who settled on surveyed public lands, improving and building or using a house on them, was given a preemption right to 160 acres including the dwelling. ...
>
> The statute only granted one preemption right per person. ... Isaac Kirksey was legally astute and well-acquainted with these laws and informal practices. ... In October 1840, Angelico was living on public land under a "contract of lease," not with the United States, but "with another." This last phrase in fact denotes that she was leasing from the holder of a preference. But Angelico had "held over," meaning that her term as a tenant had ended. If she was possessing adversely to her lessor, she may well have been the legal equivalent of a squatter against the United States. The *Kirksey* Court stated that had Isaac not offered her a place, *Angelico "would have attempted to secure [the title to] the land she lived on."* What was obvious to the Court—too obvious to mention, but not at all obvious to readers now—was that *Angelico as a squatter may have already earned a preference in the property*, perhaps under the Act of June 1, 1840, in which case the land might have been hers for the minimum price of $1.25 per acre. Alternately, her continued possession may have given her a preference under a later act had she remained.

3. **Loss of Time and an Extension of Time as Consideration.** *See Farmers & Merchants State Bank v. Higgins*, 89 P.2d 916, 918 (Kan. 1939) ("By extending the time of payment for a period of two years the bank may have lost other opportunities to collect or to acquire other securities. We think the extension of time, under the circumstances, was sufficient to make the bank a purchaser for a valuable consideration. Our statute G.S.1935, 52-302, provides: 'Value is any consideration sufficient to support a simple contract.'").

4. **Inconvenience as Bargained-for Consideration.** *See Smith v. Mountjoy*, 694 S.E.2d 598, 602 (Va. 2010) ("We have long defined '[a] gift ... as a contract without a consideration.' Consideration may arise from '[a]ny act done at the defendant's request, and for

his convenience, or at the inconvenience of the plaintiff.'"), and *Oscar v. Simeonidis*, 800 A.2d 271, 276 (N.J. Super. Ct. 2002) (reaffirming that one's inconvenience for another party is adequate consideration for a contract.).

3. Forbearance: Waiving, Suspending, and Forfeiting Legal Rights and Other Interests as Bargained-for Consideration

Hamer v. Sidway
27 N.E. 256
(N.Y. 1891)

Appeal from an order of the general term of the supreme court in the fourth judicial department, reversing a judgment entered on the decision of the court at special term in the county clerk's office of Chemung county on the 1st day of October, 1889. The plaintiff presented a claim to the executor of William E. Story, Sr., for $5,000 and interest from the 6th day of February, 1875. She acquired it through several mesne assignments from William E. Story, 2d.

The claim being rejected by the executor, this action was brought. It appears that William E. Story, Sr., was the uncle of William E. Story, 2d; that at the celebration of the golden wedding [anniversary] of Samuel Story and wife, father and mother of William E. Story, Sr., on the 20th day of March, 1869, in the presence of the family and invited guests, he promised his nephew that if he would refrain from drinking, using tobacco, swearing, and playing cards or billiards for money until he became 21 years of age, he would pay him the sum of $5,000. The nephew assented thereto, and fully performed the conditions inducing the promise.

When the nephew arrived at the age of 21 years, and on the 31st day of January, 1875, he wrote to his uncle, informing him that he had performed his part of the agreement, and had thereby become entitled to the sum of $5,000. The uncle received the letter, and a few days later, on the 6th day of February, he wrote and mailed to his nephew the following letter:

> Buffalo, Feb. 6, 1875
>
> W. E. Story, Jr.
>
> Dear Nephew:
>
> Your letter of the 31st ult. came to hand all right, saying that you had lived up to the promise made to me several years ago. I have no doubt but you have, for which you shall have five thousand dollars, as I promised you. I had the money in the bank the day you was twenty-one years old that I intend for

> you, and you shall have the money certain. Now, Willie, I do not intend to interfere with this money in any was till I think you are capable of taking care of it, and the sooner that time comes the better it will please me. I would hate very much to have you start out in some adventure that you thought all right and lose this money in one year.
>
> The first five thousand dollars that I got together cost me a heap of hard work. You would hardly believe me when I tell you that to obtain this I shoved a jack-plane many a day, butchered three or four years, then came to this city, and, after three months' perseverance, I obtained a situation in a grocery store. I opened this store early, closed late, slept in the fourth story of the building in a room 30 by 40 feet, and not a human being in the building but myself. All this I done to live as cheap as I could to save something.
>
> I don't want you to take up with this kind of fare. … All the money I have saved I know just how I got it. It did not come to me in any mysterious way. … Willie, you are twenty-one, and you have many a thing to learn yet. This money you have earned much easier than I did, besides acquiring good habits at the same time, and you are quite welcome to the money. Hope you will make good use of it. … Hope you can make out what I have written. Today is the seventeenth day that I have not been out of my room, and have had the doctor as many days. Am a little better today. Think I will get out next week. You need not mention to father, as he always worries about small matters.
>
> Truly yours,
>
> W. E. Story
>
> P. S. You can consider this money on interest.

The nephew received the letter, and thereafter consented that the money should remain with his uncle in accordance with the terms and conditions of the letter. The uncle died on the 29th day of January 1887, without having paid over to his nephew any portion of the said $5,000 and interest.

Parker, J. … The defendant contends that the contract was without consideration to support it, and therefore invalid. He asserts that the promisee, by refraining from the use of liquor and tobacco, was not harmed, but benefited; that that which he did was best for him to do, independently of his uncle's promise,—and insists that it follows that, unless the promisor was benefited, the contract was without consideration—a contention which, if well founded, would seem to leave open for controversy in many cases whether that which the promisee did or omitted to do was in fact of such benefit to him as to leave no consideration to support the enforcement of the promisor's agreement. Such a rule could not be tolerated, and is without foundation in the law.

The Exchequer Chamber in 1875 defined "consideration" as follows:

> A valuable consideration, in the sense of the law, may consist either in some right, interest, profit, or benefit accruing to the one party, or some forbearance, detriment, loss, or responsibility given, suffered, or undertaken by the other.

Courts, "will not ask whether the thing which forms the consideration does in fact benefit the promisee or a third party, or is of any substantial value to anyone. It is enough that something is promised, done, forborne, or suffered by the party to whom the promise is made as consideration for the promise made to him." ANSON. CONT. 63. "In general waiver of any legal right at the request of another party is a sufficient consideration for a promise." PARS. CONT. 444. "Any damage, or suspension, or forbearance of a right will be sufficient to sustain a promise." 2 KENT. COMM. (12th Ed.) 465.

Pollock in his work on CONTRACTS (page 166), after citing the definition given by the Exchequer Chamber, already quoted, says:

> The second branch of this judicial description is really the most important one. 'Consideration' means not so much that one party is profiting as that the other abandons some legal right in the present, or limits his legal freedom of action in the future, as an inducement for the promise of the first.

Now, applying this rule to the facts before us, the promisee used tobacco, occasionally drank liquor, and he had a legal right to do so. That right he abandoned for a period of years upon the strength of the promise of the testator that for such forbearance he would give him $5,000.

We need not speculate on the effort which may have been required to give up the use of those stimulants. It is sufficient that he restricted his lawful freedom of action within certain prescribed limits upon the faith of his uncle's agreement, and now, having fully performed the conditions imposed, it is of no moment whether such performance actually proved a benefit to the promisor, and the court will not inquire into it; but, were it a proper subject of inquiry, we see nothing in this record that would permit a determination that the uncle was not benefited in a legal sense. Few cases have been found which may be said to be precisely in point, but such as have been, support the position we have taken. ...

Order appealed from reversed, and judgment of the special term affirmed.

NOTES AND QUESTIONS

1. **The Test for Uncovering Bargained-for-Exchange Consideration**. The appellate courts in *Thomas* and *Hamer* ruled in favor of plaintiffs, concluding that each proved a bargained-for exchange. In *Kirksey*, the Alabama Supreme Court declared that Antillico Kirksey did not prove consideration. Did each court identify a specific legal standard, which determined whether bargained-for-exchange consideration was present or absent?

2. **Proving the Underage Child's Legal Rights in Hamer**. The *Hamer* court reaffirmed settled law: "A valuable consideration, in the sense of the law, may consist [of] some right ... accruing to the one party." The court concluded that 15-year-old Willie had legal rights—to drink alcohol, use tobacco, swear, and play cards or billiards for money. Willie forfeited those allegedly legal rights until he became 21 years of age. Where did 15-year-old Willie get the *legal rights* to engage in the stated activities?

3. **Common-Law Legal Rights: Tangible and Intangible Property Interests.** Legal rights are not moral or natural rights. In addition, only legal rights are enforceable in a court of law or in a court of equity. Tangible and intangible property interests are legal rights. Under the common law, some examples of tangible property interests are one's "ownership" or "possession" of the surface of land, air, and space over one's land, minerals below one's land, and minerals on the surface of land. Some intangible property interests are:

   a) one's legal title to land or to other tangible property—contingent, defeasible, or indefeasible title;

   b) one's equitable title to land or to other tangible property;

   c) one's qualified right to use land or other tangible property;

   d) one's possessory right to use land or other tangible property; and

   e) one's expectancy interest in land or in other tangible property—a lien on a car or a house, or an option to purchase a stock or to buy a house.

4. **Legal Rights or Constitutional Rights Under the U.S. Constitution.** Under the "Equal Protection of the Laws" Doctrine, the following legal rights are created:

   a) AMENDMENTS—1 thru 9 (Protection from Federal Government)

b) 13th AMENDMENT—(Protection from Private Discrimination)

1) Civil Rights Act of 1866—[42 U.S.C § 1982]

2) Civil Rights Act of 1870—[42 U.S.C § 1981]

3) Civil Rights Act of 1871—[42 U.S.C §§ 1983 & 1985]

4) Civil Rights Act of 1875—[18 U.S.C § 243]

c) 14th AMENDMENT—(Protection from "State Action")

1) Legal Right: "Equal Protection of the Laws" Clause

2) "Right to Be Free" from Impermissible Discrimination (Classification) Based on Race, Ancestry, or National Origin

d) 14th AMENDMENT—"Due Process of Law" Clause

1) Procedural Due Process of Law—

(i) Right to Sue or File a Lawsuit

(ii) Right to Trial by Jury

(iii) Right to a Speedy Trial

2) Substantive Due Process of Law—

(i) The Right to Marry

(ii) The Right to Travel

(iii) The Right to Procreate

(iv) Other Fundamental Rights

5. **Whose Burden to Prove Bargained-for-Exchange Consideration**. In *Hamer*, the plaintiff is a female. "The plaintiff presented a claim to the executor of William E. Story, Sr., for $5,000 and interest. ... She acquired it through several mesne assignments from William E. Story, 2d." Who was she? And who had the burden to prove a bargained-for exchange between the uncle and nephew? In *Hamer v. Sidway,* 11 N.Y.S. 182, 186–87 (New York Gen. Term 1890), New York's intermediate court provides some insight:

Action by Louisa W. Hamer against Franklin Sidway, as executor of William E. Story, deceased. Judgment for plaintiff, and defendant appeals. It seems to us that the evidence ... discloses an unexecuted promise by the testator to give William $5,000 when he became of age, if he proved himself worthy of it, and that, upon his attaining his majority, the testator again promised to make the same gift, with the addition of the interest, when he should consider his nephew capable of taking care of it.

Moreover, the evidence in this case is far from satisfactory. It tends to show quite clearly that the testator, during his lifetime, had fulfilled his promise to his nephew. Soon after the letter of the testator was written, we find William engaged in business with his father. He had borrowed $2,500 of the testator, for which he gave his promissory note. Subsequently, he and his father failed in business, and were declared bankrupts. …

After this the testator transferred to William and his father $11,000 worth of goods, for which he received two 1,000-dollar notes, and a general release, under seal, executed by both, which was broad enough to cover this claim. The plaintiff seeks to avoid the effect of this evidence by proving that the plaintiff's claim had been previously assigned by William to his wife, and that the testator knew of such assignment when the release was given.

The credibility of that testimony is materially shaken by the fact that when this action was brought no such assignment was alleged, but the plaintiff alleged in her complaint that she acquired title to this claim directly from William by an assignment made February 3, 1887. The plaintiff's attorney, who drew that complaint, also swears that such an assignment was before him when he drew it. It may be that the assignment was made by William to his wife, as alleged and proved, but it is certainly very remarkable that that fact should have been forgotten by them until the defendant pleaded a release as a defense to this action.

It would seem that either William, his wife, or the plaintiff must have remembered the fact, if it existed, either when the claim against the testator's estate was made, verified, and presented, or when the original complaint in this action was prepared. Without stating the evidence in further detail, it certainly is not satisfactory to us. … We are, however, of the opinion that there was no legal contract between the parties sufficient to uphold the recovery in this case, and that the judgment should be reversed. Judgment reversed, and a new trial granted, with costs to abide the event.

PROBLEM

Jasper purchased an automobile insurance contract from Allstate. Under the policy, Allstate promised to pay "up to $20,000 to cover each third-party claim, even if the claim is groundless, false, or fraudulent."

In the course of events, Jasper's Ford F-150 Truck collided with Barry's BMW. Jasper's truck was not damaged. Barry and his passenger were slightly injured. Later, Barry reported without presenting verifiable evidence: 1) "It will take $25,000 to pay the 'combined medical bills' and 2) it will cost $27,566 to repair my BMW." Allstate refused to pay anything, asserting that 1) Barry caused the accident and 2) Barry's calculations were fraudulent. Texas law prevents a third party from filing a "direct action" against a liability insurer. On the other hand, an assignment agreement between an insured and a third party would allow a third party to sue an insurer directly. Therefore, Jasper and Barry agreed to "combine forces" and file a lawsuit against Allstate. The pleading outlined several theories of recovery, including a breach-of-contract action. They asked for $60,000 in damages. But, a month after filing the suit, "Jasper disappeared in thin air." Still, the suit continued without Jasper. Early in the proceedings, Allstate filed a motion for summary judgment, asking the court to dismiss the breach-of-contract action. According to Allstate, there was no evidence of a contractual relationship between Barry and Allstate. And, assuming a valid contract was formed, Allstate maintained that Barry could not produce any probative evidence of consideration in a jury trial. Should the trial judge grant or deny Allstate's motion for summary judgment? Explain.

SECTION TWO: PROOF OF CONSIDERATION AND THE DOCTRINE OF PROMISSORY ESTOPPEL

The majority of state supreme courts have adopted RESTATEMENT (SECOND) OF CONTRACTS § 90(1). To repeat, this section lays the foundation for the doctrine of promissory estoppel, which actually contains two theories of consideration: 1) consideration based on a promisee's "change of position" or "change in position" following a promisor's promise to deliver a benefit, and 2) consideration based on a promisee's detrimental reliance on a promisor's promise to confer a benefit. But it is extremely important to reiterate a point that the Court of Appeals for the Ninth Circuit stressed in *Barnes v. Yahoo!, Inc.*, 570 F.3d 1096, 1106 (9th Cir. 2009): "Promissory estoppel is not a cause of action in itself; rather it is a subset of a theory of recovery based on a breach of contract and serves as a substitute for consideration." Yet, most courts require plaintiffs to prove several sub-elements to establish a "*change of position*" as well as "*detrimental reliance*." Below, both theories are discussed.

A. A "Change of Position" as Consideration

Ricketts v. Scothorn
77 N.W. 365
(Neb. 1898)

Sullivan, J. In the district court of Lancaster county, the plaintiff—Katie Scothorn—recovered judgment against the defendant—Andrew D. Ricketts—as executor of the last will and testament of John C. Ricketts, deceased. The action was based upon a promissory note, of which the following is a copy: "May the first, 1891. I promise to pay to Katie Scothorn on demand, $2,000, to be at 6 per cent. per annum. J. C. Ricketts."

In the petition the plaintiff alleges that the consideration for the execution of the note was that she should surrender her employment as bookkeeper for Mayer Bros., and cease to work for a living. She also alleges that the note was given to induce her to abandon her occupation, and that, relying on it, and on the annual interest, as a means of support, she gave up the employment in which she was then engaged. These allegations of the petition are denied by the administrator.

The material facts are undisputed. They are as follows: John C. Ricketts, the maker of the note, was the grandfather of the plaintiff. Early in May—presumably on the day the note bears date—he called on her at the store where she was working. What transpired between them is thus described by Mr. Florence, one of the plaintiff's witnesses:

> A. Well, the old gentleman came in there one morning about nine o'clock, probably a little before or a little after, but early in the morning, and he unbuttoned his vest, and took out a piece of paper in the shape of a note; that is the way it looked to me; and he says to Miss Scothorn, 'I have fixed out something that you have not got to work anymore.' He says, none of my grandchildren work, and you don't have to.
>
> Q. Where was she?
>
> A. She took the piece of paper and kissed him, and kissed the old gentleman, and commenced to cry.

It seems Miss Scothorn immediately notified her employer of her intention to quit work, and that she did soon after abandon her occupation. The mother of the plaintiff was a witness, and testified that she had a conversation with her father—Mr. Ricketts—shortly after the note was executed, in which he informed her that he had given the note to the plaintiff to enable her to quit work; that none of his grandchildren worked, and he did not think she ought to.

For something more than a year the plaintiff was without an occupation. [B]ut in September, 1892, with the consent of her grandfather, and by his assistance, she secured a position as bookkeeper with Messrs.

Funke & Ogden. On June 8, 1894, Mr. Ricketts died. He had paid one year's interest on the note, and a short time before his death expressed regret that he had not been able to pay the balance. In the summer or fall of 1892 he stated to his daughter, Mrs. Scothorn, that if he could sell his farm in Ohio he would pay the note out of the proceeds. He at no time repudiated the obligation.

We quite agree with counsel for the defendant that upon this evidence there was nothing to submit to the jury, and that a verdict should have been directed peremptorily for one of the parties. The testimony of Flodene and Mrs. Scothorn—taken together—conclusively establishes the fact that the note was not given in consideration of the plaintiff pursuing, or agreeing to pursue, any particular line of conduct. There was no promise on the part of the plaintiff to do, or refrain from doing, anything. Her right to the money promised in the note was not made to depend upon an abandonment of her employment with Mayer Bros., and future abstention from like service.

Mr. Ricketts made no condition, requirement, or request. He exacted no *quid pro quo*. He gave the note as a gratuity, and looked for nothing in return. So far as the evidence discloses, it was his purpose to place the plaintiff in a position of independence, where she could work or remain idle, as she might choose. The abandonment of Miss Scothorn of her position as bookkeeper was altogether voluntary. It was not an act done in fulfillment of any contract obligation assumed when she accepted the note. The instrument in suit, being given without any valuable consideration, was nothing more than a promise to make a gift in the future of the sum of money therein named.

Ordinarily, such promises are not enforceable, even when put in the form of a promissory note. *Kirkpatrick v. Taylor*, 43 Ill. 207; *Phelps v. Phelps*, 28 Barb. 121; *Johnston v. Griest*, 85 Ind. 503; *Fink v. Cox*, 18 Johns. 145. But it has often been held that an action on a note given to a church, college, or other like institution, upon the faith of which money has been expended or obligations incurred, could not be successfully defended on the ground of a want of consideration. *Barnes v. Perine*, 12 N. Y. 18; *Philomath College v. Hartless*, 6 Or. 158; *Thompson v. Board*, 40 Ill. 379; *Irwin v. Lombard University*, 56 Ohio St. 9, 46 N. E. 63. In this class of cases the note in suit is nearly always spoken of as a gift or donation, but the decision is generally put on the ground that the expenditure of money or assumption of liability by the donee on the faith of the promise constitutes a valuable and sufficient consideration.

It seems to us that the true reason is the preclusion of the defendant—under the doctrine of estoppel—to deny the consideration. Such seems to be the view of the matter taken by the Supreme Court of Iowa in the case of *Simpson Centenary College v. Tuttle*, 71 Iowa, 596, 33 N. W. 74, where Rothrock, J., speaking for the court, said:

> Where a note, however, is based on a promise to give for the support of the objects referred to, it may still be open to this defense [want of consideration], unless it shall appear that the donee has, prior to any revocation, entered into engagements, or made expenditures based on such promise, so that he must suffer loss or injury if the note is not paid. This is based on the equitable principle that, after allowing the donee to incur obligations on the faith that the note would be paid, the donor would be estopped from pleading want of consideration.

And in the case of *Reimensnyder v. Gans*, 110 Pa. St. 17, 2 Atl. 425, which was an action on a note given as a donation to a charitable object, the court said: "The fact is that, as we may see from the case of *Ryerss v. Trustees*, 33 Pa. St. 114, a contract of the kind here involved is enforceable rather by way of estoppel than on the ground of consideration in the original undertaking." It has been held that a note given in expectation of the payee performing certain services, but without any contract binding him to serve, will not support an action. *Hulse v. Hulse,* 84 E. C. L. 709. But when the payee changes his position to his disadvantage in reliance on the promise, a right of action does arise. *McClure v. Wilson*, 43 Ill. 356; *Trustees v. Garvey*, 53 Ill. 401.

Under the circumstances of this case, is there an equitable estoppel which ought to preclude the defendant from alleging that the note in controversy is lacking in one of the essential elements of a valid contract? We think there is. An estoppel *in pais* is defined to be "a right arising from acts, admissions, or conduct which [has] induced a change of position in accordance with the real or apparent intention of the party against whom they are alleged." Mr. Pomeroy has formulated the following definition:

> Equitable estoppel is the effect of the voluntary conduct of a party whereby he is absolutely precluded, both at law and in equity, from asserting rights which might, perhaps, have otherwise existed, either of property, of contract, or of remedy, as against another person who in good faith relied upon such conduct, and has been led thereby to change his position for the worse, and who on his part acquires some corresponding right, either of property, of contract, or of remedy." 2 POM. EQ. JUR. 804.

According to the undisputed proof, as shown by the record before us, the plaintiff was a working girl, holding a position in which she earned a salary of $10 per week. Her grandfather—desiring to put her in a position of independence—gave her the note, accompanying it with the remark that his other grandchildren did not work, and that she would not be obliged to work any longer. In effect, he suggested that she might abandon her employment, and rely in the future upon the bounty which he promised.

He doubtless desired that she should give up her occupation. [B]ut, whether he did or not, it is entirely certain that he contemplated such action on her part as a reasonable and probable consequence of his gift. Having intentionally influenced the plaintiff to alter her position for the worse on the faith of the note being paid when due, it would be grossly inequitable to permit the maker, or his executor, to resist payment on the ground that the promise was given without consideration.

The petition charges the elements of an equitable estoppel, and the evidence conclusively establishes them. If errors intervened at the trial, they could not have been prejudicial. A verdict for the defendant would be unwarranted. The judgment is right, and is affirmed.

Feinberg v. Pfeiffer Company
322 S.W.2d 163
(Mo. Ct. App. 1959)

Doerner, Commissioner. This is a suit brought in the Circuit Court of the City of St. Louis by plaintiff—a former employee of the defendant corporation—on an alleged contract whereby defendant agreed to pay plaintiff the sum of $200 per month for life upon her retirement. A jury being waived, the case was tried by the court alone. Judgment below was for plaintiff for $5,100, the amount of the pension claimed to be due as of the date of the trial, together with interest thereon, and defendant duly appealed.

The parties are in substantial agreement on the essential facts. Plaintiff (Anna Sacks Feinberg) began working for the defendant—a manufacturer of pharmaceuticals—in 1910, when she was but 17 years of age. By 1947 she had attained the position of bookkeeper, office manager, and assistant treasurer of the defendant, and owned 70 shares of its stock out of a total of 6,503 shares issued and outstanding. Twenty shares had been given to her by the defendant or its then president. [S]he had purchased 20, and the remaining 30 she had acquired by a stock split or stock dividend. Over the years she received substantial dividends on the stock she owned, as did all of the other stockholders. Also, in addition to her salary, plaintiff from 1937 to 1949, inclusive, received each year a bonus varying in amount from $300 in the beginning to $2,000 in the later years.

On December 27, 1947, the annual meeting of the defendant's Board of Directors was held at the Company's offices in St. Louis, presided over by Max Lippman—its then president and largest individual stockholder. The other directors present were George L. Marcus, Sidney Harris, Sol Flammer, and Walter Weinstock—who with Max Lippman—owned 5,007 of the 6,503 shares then issued and outstanding. At that meeting the Board of Directors adopted the following resolution, which, because it is the crux of the case, we quote in full:

> The Chairman thereupon pointed out that the Assistant Treasurer, Mrs. Anna Sacks Feinberg, has given the corporation many years of long and faithful service. Not only has she served the corporation devotedly, but with exceptional ability and skill. The President pointed out that although all of the officers and directors sincerely hoped and desired that Mrs. Feinberg would continue in her present position for as long as she felt able, nevertheless, in view of the length of service which she has contributed provision should be made to afford her retirement privileges and benefits which should become a firm obligation of the corporation to be available to her whenever she should see fit to retire from active duty, however many years in the future such retirement may become effective.
>
> It was, accordingly, proposed that Mrs. Feinberg's salary which is presently $350.00 per month, be increased to $400.00 per month, and that Mrs. Feinberg would be given the privilege of retiring from active duty at any time she may elect to see fit so to do upon a retirement pay of $200.00 per month for life, with the distinct understanding that the retirement plan is merely being adopted at the present time in order to afford Mrs. Feinberg security for the future and in the hope that her active services will continue with the corporation for many years to come.

After due discussion and consideration, and upon motion duly made and seconded, it was—

> Resolved, that the salary of Anna Sacks Feinberg be increased from $350.00 to $400.00 per month and that she be afforded the privilege of retiring from active duty in the corporation at any time she may elect to see fit so to do upon retirement pay of $200.00 per month, for the remainder of her life.

At the request of Mr. Lippman, his sons-in-law—Messrs. Harris and Flammer—called upon the plaintiff at her apartment on the same day to advise her of the passage of the resolution. Plaintiff testified on cross-examination that she had no prior information that such a pension plan was contemplated, that it came as a surprise to her, and that she would have continued in her employment whether or not such a resolution had been adopted. It is clear from the evidence that there was no contract, oral or written, as to plaintiff's length of employment, and that she was free to quit, and the defendant to discharge her, at any time.

Plaintiff did continue to work for the defendant through June 30, 1949, on which date she retired. In accordance with the foregoing resolution, the defendant began paying her the sum of $200 on the first of each month. Mr. Lippman died on November 18, 1949, and was succeeded as president of the company by his widow. Because of an illness, she retired from that office and was succeeded in October, 1953, by her son-in-law, Sidney M. Harris. Mr. Harris testified that—while Mrs. Lippman had been president—she signed the monthly pension check paid plaintiff, but fussed about doing so, and considered the payments as gifts.

After his election, he stated: [A] new accounting firm employed by the defendant questioned the validity of the payments to plaintiff on several occasions; and in the spring of 1956, upon its recommendation, he consulted the Company's then attorney, Mr. Ralph Kalish. Harris testified that both Ernst and Ernst—the accounting firm—and Kalish told him there was no need of giving plaintiff the money. He also stated that he had concurred in the view that the payments to plaintiff were mere gratuities rather than amounts due under a contractual obligation, and that following his discussion with the Company's attorney plaintiff was sent a check for $100 on April 1, 1956. Plaintiff declined to accept the reduced amount, and this action followed.

* * *

We come, then, to the basic issue in the case. While otherwise defined in defendant's third and fourth assignments of error, it is thus succinctly stated in the argument in its brief: "[W]hether plaintiff has proved that she has a right to recover from defendant based upon a legally binding contractual obligation to pay her $200 per month for life."

It is defendant's contention, in essence, that the resolution adopted by its Board of Directors was a mere promise to make a gift, and that no contract resulted either thereby, or when plaintiff retired, because there was no consideration given or paid by the plaintiff. It urges that a promise to make a gift is not binding unless supported by a legal consideration; that the only apparent consideration for the adoption of the foregoing resolution was the "many years of long and faithful service" expressed therein; and that past services are not a valid consideration for a promise. Defendant argues further that there is nothing in the resolution which made its effectiveness conditional upon plaintiff's continued employment, that she was not under contract to work for any length of time but was free to quit whenever she wished, and that she had no contractual right to her position and could have been discharged at any time.

Plaintiff concedes that a promise based upon past services would be without consideration, but contends that there were two other elements which supplied the required element: First, the continuation by plaintiff in the employ of the defendant for the period from December 27, 1947, the date when the resolution was adopted, until the date of her retirement on June 30, 1949. And, second, her change of position—i.e., her retirement and the abandonment by her of her opportunity to continue in gainful employment, made in reliance on defendant's promise to pay her $200 per month for life.

We must agree with the defendant that the evidence does not support the first of these contentions. There is no language in the resolution predicating plaintiff's right to a pension upon her continued employment. She was not required to work for the defendant for any period of time as a condition to gaining such retirement benefits. She was told that she could quit the day upon which the resolution was adopted, as she herself testified, and it is clear from her own testimony that she made no promise or agreement to continue in the employ of the defendant in return for its promise to pay her a pension. Hence there was lacking that mutuality of obligation which is essential to the validity of a contract.

But as to the second of these contentions, we must agree with plaintiff. By the terms of the resolution, defendant promised to pay plaintiff the sum of $200 a month upon her retirement. Consideration for a promise has been defined in the RESTATEMENT OF THE LAW OF CONTRACTS § 75, as:

1) Consideration for a promise is

(a) an act other than a promise, or

(b) a forbearance, or

(c) the creation, modification or destruction of a legal relation,

or

(d) a return promise, bargained for and given in exchange for the promise.

As the parties agree, the consideration sufficient to support a contract may be either a benefit to the promisor, or a loss or detriment to the promisee. *Industrial Bank & Trust Co. v. Hesselberg*, Mo., 195 S.W.2d 470 (Mo. 1946).

Section 90 of the RESTATEMENT OF THE LAW OF CONTRACTS states:

> A promise which the promisor should reasonably expect to induce action or forbearance of a definite and substantial character on the part of the promisee and which does induce such action or forbearance is binding if injustice can be avoided only by enforcement of the promise.

This doctrine has been described as … "promissory estoppel," as distinguished from that of equitable estoppel or estoppel in pais, the reason for the differentiation being stated as follows:

> It is generally true that one who has led another to act in reasonable reliance on his representations of fact cannot afterwards in litigation between the two deny the truth of the

> representations, and some courts have sought to apply this principle to the formation of contracts, where, relying on a gratuitous promise, the promisee has suffered detriment. It is to be noticed, however, that such a case does not come within the ordinary definition of estoppel. If there is any representation of an existing fact, it is only that the promisor at the time of making the promise intends to fulfill it. As to such intention, there is usually no misrepresentation and if there is, it is not that which has injured the promisee. In other words, he relies on a promise and not on a misstatement of fact; and the term "promissory" estoppel or something equivalent should be used to make the distinction. 1 WILLISTON ON CONTRACTS, REV. ED., § 139

In speaking of this doctrine, Judge Learned Hand said in *Porter v. Commissioner of Internal Revenue*, 60 F.2d 673, 675 (2nd Cir. 1932) that "'promissory estoppel' is now a recognized species of consideration." As pointed out by our supreme court in *In re Jamison's Estate*, 202 S.W.2d 879, 887 (Mo. 1947), it is stated in the MISSOURI ANNOTATIONS TO THE RESTATEMENT § 90 that: "There is a variance between the doctrine underlying this section and the theoretical justifications that have been advanced for the Missouri decisions." That variance, as the authors of the Annotations point out, is that:

> This § 90, when applied with § 85, means that the promise described is a contract without any consideration. In Missouri the same practical result is reached without—in theory—abandoning the doctrine of consideration. In Missouri three theories have been advanced as ground for the decisions: 1) Theory of act for promise. The induced "action or forbearance" is the consideration for the promise; 2) Theory of promissory estoppel. The induced "action or forbearance" works an estoppel against the promisor; and, 3) Theory of bilateral contract. When the induced "action or forbearance" is begun, a promise to complete is implied, and we have an enforceable bilateral contract, the implied promise to complete being the consideration for the original promise.

Was there such an act on the part of plaintiff, in reliance upon the promise contained in the resolution, as will estop the defendant, and therefore create an enforceable contract under the doctrine of promissory estoppel? We think there was.

One of the illustrations cited under § 90 of the RESTATEMENT is:

> A promises B to pay him an annuity during B's life. B thereupon resigns a profitable employment—as A expected that he might. B receives the annuity for some years, in the

> meantime becoming disqualified from again obtaining good employment. A's promise is binding.

This illustration is objected to by defendant as not being applicable to the case at hand. The reason advanced by it is that in the illustration, B became "disqualified" from obtaining other employment before A discontinued the payments, whereas in this case the plaintiff did not discover that she had cancer and thereby became unemployable until after the defendant had discontinued the payments of $200 per month.

We think the distinction is immaterial. The only reason for the reference in the illustration to the disqualification of A is in connection with that part of Section 90 regarding the prevention of injustice. The injustice would occur regardless of when the disability occurred. Would defendant contend that the contract would be enforceable if the plaintiff's illness had been discovered on March 31, 1956, the day before it discontinued the payment of the $200 a month, but not if it occurred on April 2nd, the day after?

Furthermore, there are more ways to become disqualified for work, or unemployable, than as the result of illness. At the time she retired, plaintiff was 57 years of age. At the time the payments were discontinued she was over 63 years of age. It is a matter of common knowledge that it is virtually impossible for a woman of that age to find satisfactory employment, much less a position comparable to that which plaintiff enjoyed at the time of her retirement.

The fact of the matter is that plaintiff's subsequent illness was not the "action or forbearance" which was induced by the promise contained in the resolution. As the trial court correctly decided, such action on plaintiff's part was her retirement from a lucrative position in reliance upon defendant's promise to pay her an annuity or pension. In a very similar case, *Ricketts v. Scothorn*, 77 N.W. 365, 367 (Neb. 1898), the Supreme Court of Nebraska said:

> According to the undisputed proof, as shown by the record before us, the plaintiff was a working girl, holding a position in which she earned a salary of $10 per week. Her grandfather, desiring to put her in a position of independence, gave her the note accompanying it with the remark that his other grandchildren did not work, and that she would not be obliged to work any longer. In effect, he suggested that she might abandon her employment, and rely in the future upon the bounty which he promised. He doubtless desired that she should give up her occupation, but, whether he did or not, it is entirely certain that he contemplated such action on her part as a reasonable and probable consequence of his gift. Having intentionally influenced the plaintiff to alter her position for the worse on the faith of the note being paid when due,

> it would be grossly inequitable to permit the maker, or his executor, to resist payment on the ground that the promise was given without consideration.

The Commissioner therefore recommends, for the reasons stated, that the judgment be affirmed. *Per curiam.* The foregoing opinion by Doerner, C., is adopted as the opinion of the court. The judgment is, accordingly, affirmed.

NOTES AND QUESTIONS

1. **Competing Rules: Elements of the Promissory Estoppel Doctrine.**

   California Law—*See Lawther v. OneWest Bank*, FSB, 2012 WL 298110, *17(N.D. Cal.) ("Under California law, ... [w] here consideration is lacking, a contract may nonetheless be enforceable under the doctrine of promissory estoppel. ... A claim for promissory estoppel requires that the following elements be established: "1) a promise clear and unambiguous in its terms; 2) reliance by the party to whom the promise is made; 3) his reliance must be both reasonable and foreseeable; and 4) the party asserting the estoppel must be injured by his reliance." *Laks v. Coast Fed. Sav. & Loan Ass'n.,* 60 Cal. App. 3d 885, 890 (1976).

   Illinois Law—*See Wagner Excello Foods, Inc. v. Fearn Int'l, Inc.,* 601 N.E.2d 956, 963 (Ill. Ct. App. 1994) (In Illinois, "to establish ... promissory estoppel, the plaintiff must prove 1) an unambiguous promise by the defendant to the plaintiff, 2) the plaintiff's reliance on such promise, 3) that the plaintiff's reliance was expected and foreseeable by the defendant, 4) that the plaintiff's ***reliance was detrimental***, and 5) that the plaintiff's reliance was reasonable and justified.").

   Oregon Law—*See Natkin & Co. v. H.D. Fowler Co.*, 876 P.2d 319, 321 (Or. Ct. App. 1994) ("Promissory estoppel is not an independent cause of action. It is a substitute for consideration, and provides a basis for enforcing a promise as a contract despite a lack of consideration[.]"), and *Neiss v. Ehlers*, 223, 899 P.2d 700, 703–704 (Or. Ct. App. 1995) (To prove promissory estoppel under Oregon law, a plaintiff must prove the following: 1) defendant made a promise, 2) the defendant reasonably understood that the promise would cause plaintiff to rely on the promise, and 3) reliance caused a substantial change in plaintiff's position.).

Texas Law—*See Aubrey v. Workman*, 384 S.W.2d 389, 393 (Tex. Civ. App.—Fort Worth 1964) ("[Promissory estoppel is] a substitute for consideration. The elements of this brand of estoppel are set forth as follows in § 90 of the RESTATEMENT OF THE LAW (CONTRACTS). ... A true application of the doctrine of promissory estoppel consists of three elements which must be alleged and proved to support it, and they are: 1) a promise, 2) foreseeability of reliance thereon by the promisor, and 3) ***substantial reliance by the promisee to his detriment***. ... In 20 TEX. LAW REVIEW 479, it is stated that Texas courts have reiterated the general rule that the consideration given must be the consideration requested by the promisor and thus have applied the estoppel theory only to donative promises and refused to do so where there is a request for a ***bargained-for exchange*** even though the three elements of promissory estoppel are present.").

2. **Proof of Consideration and Competing "Change of Position" Rules.**

Tennessee Law—*See Alden v. Presley,* 637 S.W.2d 862, 864 (Tenn. 1982) ("A promisor who induces ***substantial change of position*** by the promisee in reliance on the promise is estopped to deny its enforceability as lacking consideration.").

Texas Law—*See Davis v. Campbell*, 524 S.W.2d 790, 793 (Tex. Civ. App.—Dallas 1975) ("[A] vendor may be entitled to enforce [an] oral contract if he shows performance of the contract by delivery of possession to the purchaser and a ***detrimental change of position***, for which the vendor has no adequate remedy.).

Washington Law—*See Young v. Frank*, 2012 WL 1798451, *5 (Wash. App. [Div. 3]) ("Promissory estoppel can render a promise enforceable without the usual requirement of [bargained-for] consideration. ... There must be a promise [and the] ... promisee must *actually change his position based on that promise*.").

B. "Detrimental Reliance" as Consideration

Hayes v. Plantations Steel Company
438 A.2d 1091
(R.I. 1982)

Shea, Justice. The defendant employer—Plantations Steel Company (Plantations)—appeals from a Superior Court judgment for the plaintiff employee, Edward J. Hayes (Hayes). The trial justice—sitting without a jury—found that Plantations was obligated to Hayes on the basis of an implied-in-fact contract to pay him a yearly pension of $5,000. The award covered three years in which payment had not been made. The trial justice ruled, also, that Hayes had made a sufficient showing of detrimental reliance upon Plantations's promise to pay, to give rise to its obligation based on the theory of promissory estoppel. The trial justice, however, found in part for Plantations in ruling that the payments to Hayes were not governed by the Employee Retirement Income Security Act, 29 U.S.C.A. §§ 1001–1461 (West 1975), and consequently he was not entitled to attorney's fees under s 1132(g) of that act. Both parties have appealed.

* * *

Plantations is a closely held Rhode Island corporation—engaged in the manufacture of steel reinforcing rods for use in concrete construction. The company was founded by Hugo R. Mainelli, Sr., and Alexander A. DiMartino. A dispute between their two families in 1976 and 1977 left the DiMartinos in full control of the corporation. Hayes was an employee of the corporation from 1947 until his retirement in 1972 at age of sixty-five. He began with Plantations as an "estimator and draftsman" and ended his career as general manager, a position of considerable responsibility. Starting in January 1973 and continuing until January 1976, Hayes received the annual sum of $5,000 from Plantations. Hayes instituted this action in December 1977, after the then company management refused to make any further payments.

Hayes testified that in January 1972, he announced his intention to retire the following July—after twenty-five years of continuous service. He decided to retire because he had worked continuously for fifty-one years. He stated, however, that he would not have retired had he not expected to receive a pension. After he stopped working for Plantations, he sought no other employment.

Approximately one week before his actual retirement Hayes spoke with Hugo R. Mainelli, Jr., who was then an officer and a stockholder of Plantations. This conversation was the first and only one concerning payments of a pension to Hayes during retirement. Mainelli said that the company "would take care" of him. There was no mention of a sum of money or a percentage of salary that Hayes would receive. There was no formal authorization for payments by Plantations's shareholders and/or board of directors. Indeed, there was never any formal provision for a pension plan for any employee other than for unionized employees, who benefit from an arrangement through their union. The plaintiff was not a union member.

Mr. Mainelli, Jr. testified that his father—Hugo R. Mainelli, Sr.—had authorized the first payment "as a token of appreciation for the many years of (Hayes's) service." Furthermore, "it was implied that that check would continue on an annual basis." Mainelli also testified that it was his "personal intention" that the payments would continue for "as long as I was around."

Mainelli testified that after Hayes's retirement, he would visit the premises each year to say hello and renew old acquaintances. During the course of his visits, Hayes would thank Mainelli for the previous check and ask how long it would continue so that he could plan an orderly retirement.

The payments were discontinued after 1976. At that time a succession of several poor business years plus the stockholders' dispute, resulting in the takeover by the DiMartino family, contributed to the decision to stop the payments.

The trial justice ruled that Plantations owed Hayes his annual sum of $5,000 for the years 1977 through 1979. The ruling implied that barring bankruptcy or the cessation of business for any other reason, Hayes had a right to expect continued annual payments.

The trial justice found that Hugo Mainelli, Jr.'s statement that Hayes would be taken care of after his retirement was a promise. Although no sum of money was mentioned in 1972, the four annual payments of $5,000 established that otherwise unspecified term of the contract. The trial justice also found that Hayes supplied consideration for the promise by voluntarily retiring, because he was under no obligation to do so.

From the words and conduct of the parties and from the surrounding circumstances, the trial justice concluded that there existed an implied contract obligating the company to pay a pension to Hayes for life. The trial justice made a further finding that even if Hayes had not truly bargained for a pension by voluntarily retiring, he had nevertheless incurred the detriment of foregoing other employment in reliance upon the company's promise. He specifically held that Hayes's retirement was in response to the promise and held also that Hayes refrained from seeking other employment in further reliance thereon.

The findings of fact of a trial justice sitting without a jury are entitled to great weight when reviewed by this court. His findings will not be disturbed unless it can be shown that they are clearly wrong or that the trial justice misconceived or overlooked material evidence. *Lisi v. Marra*, 424 A.2d 1052 (R.I. 1981); *Raheb v. Lemenski*, 350 A.2d 397 (R.I. 1976). After careful review of the record, however, we conclude that the trial justice's findings and conclusions must be reversed.

Assuming for the purpose of this discussion that Plantations in legal effect made a promise to Hayes, we must ask whether Hayes did supply the required consideration that would make the promise binding?

And, if Hayes did not supply consideration, was his alleged reliance sufficiently induced by the promise to estop defendant from denying its obligation to him? We answer both questions in the negative.

We turn first to the problem of consideration. The facts at bar do not present the case of an express contract. As the trial justice stated, the existence of a contract in this case must be determined from all the circumstances of the parties' conduct and words. Although words were expressed initially in the remark that Hayes "would be taken care of," any contract in this case would be more in the nature of an implied contract. Certainly the statement of Hugo Mainelli, Jr., standing alone is not an expression of a direct and definite promise to pay Hayes a pension. Though we are analyzing an implied contract, nevertheless we must address the question of consideration.

Contracts implied in fact require the element of consideration to support them as is required in express contracts. The only difference between the two is the manner in which the parties manifest their assent. *Bailey v. West*, 249 A.2d 414 (R.I. 1969). In this jurisdiction, consideration consists either in some right, interest, or benefit accruing to one party or some forbearance, detriment, or responsibility given, suffered, or undertaken by the other. Valid consideration furthermore must be bargained for. It must induce the return act or promise. To be valid, therefore, the purported consideration must not have been delivered before a promise is executed, that is, given without reference to the promise. Consideration is therefore a test of the enforceability of executory promises, and has no legal effect when rendered in the past and apart from an alleged exchange in the present. *Zanturjian v. Boornazian*, 55 A. 199 (R.I 1903).

In the case before us, Plantations's promise to pay Hayes a pension is quite clearly not supported by any consideration supplied by Hayes. Hayes had announced his intent to retire well in advance of any promise, and therefore the intention to retire was arrived at without regard to any promise by Plantations. Although Hayes may have had in mind the receipt of a pension when he first informed Plantations, his expectation was not based on any statement made to him or on any conduct of the company officer relative to him in January 1972. In deciding to retire, Hayes acted on his own initiative. Hayes's long years of dedicated service also is legally insufficient because his service too was rendered without being induced by Plantations's promise.

Clearly then this is not a case in which Plantations's promise was meant to induce Hayes to refrain from retiring when he could have chosen to do so in return for further service. Nor was the promise made to encourage long service from the start of his employment. Instead, the testimony establishes that Plantations's promise was intended "as a token of appreciation for (Hayes's) many years of service." As such it was in the nature of a gratuity paid to Hayes for as long as the company chose. In *Spickelmier Industries, Inc. v. Passander*, 359 N.E.2d 563 (Ind. App. 1977), an employer's promise to an employee to pay him a year-end bonus was unenforceable because it was made after the employee had performed his contractual responsibilities for that year.

* * *

Hayes also argues that the work he performed during the week between the promise and the date of his retirement constituted sufficient consideration to support the promise. He relies on *Ulmann v. Sunset-McKee Co.*, 221 F.2d 128 (9th Cir. 1955), in which the court ruled that work performed during the one-week period of the employee's notice of impending retirement constituted consideration for the employer's offer of a pension that the employee had solicited some months previously. But there the court stated that its prime reason for upholding the agreement was that sufficient consideration existed in the employee's consent not to compete with his employer. These circumstances do not appear in our case. Hayes left his employment because he no longer desired to work. He was not contemplating other job offers or considering going into competition with Plantations. Although Plantations did not want Hayes to leave, it did not try to deter him, nor did it seek to prevent Hayes from engaging in other activity.

Hayes argues in the alternative that even if Plantations's promise was not the product of an exchange, its duty is grounded properly in the theory of promissory estoppel. This court adopted the theory of promissory estoppel in *East Providence Credit Union v. Geremia*, 103 R.I. 597, 601, 239 A.2d 725, 727 (1968) (quoting 1 RESTATEMENT CONTRACTS § 90 at 110 (1932)) stating:

> A promise which the promisor should reasonably expect to induce action or forbearance of a definite and substantial character on the part of the promisee and which does induce such action or forbearance is binding if injustice can be avoided only by enforcement of its promise.

In *East Providence Credit Union,* this court said that the doctrine of promissory estoppel is invoked "as a substitute for a consideration, rendering a gratuitous promise enforceable as a contract." To restate the matter differently, "the acts of reliance by the promisee to his detriment (provide) a substitute for consideration."

Hayes urges that in the absence of a bargained-for promise the facts require application of the doctrine of promissory estoppel. He stresses that he retired voluntarily while expecting to receive a pension. He would not have otherwise retired. Nor did he seek other employment.

We disagree with this contention largely for the reasons already stated. One of the essential elements of the doctrine of promissory estoppel is that the promise must induce the promisee's action or forbearance. The particular act in this regard is plaintiff's decision whether or not to retire. As we stated earlier, the record indicates that he made the decision on his own initiative. In other words, the conversation between Hayes and Mainelli which occurred a week before Hayes left his employment cannot be said to have induced his decision to leave. He had reached that decision long before. An example taken from the RESTATEMENT provides a meaningful contrast:

> A promises B to pay him an annuity during B's life. B thereupon resigns profitable employment, as A expected that he might. B receives the annuity for some years, in the meantime becoming disqualified from again obtaining good employment. A's promise is binding. 1 RESTATEMENT CONTRACTS § 90 at 111 (1932).

In *Feinberg v. Pfeiffer Co.*, 322 S.W.2d 163 (Mo. App. 1959), the plaintiff-employee had worked for her employer for nearly forty years. The defendant corporation's board of directors resolved, in view of her long years of service, to obligate itself to pay "retirement privileges" to her. The resolution did not require the plaintiff to retire. Instead, the decision whether and when to retire remained entirely her own. The board then informed her of its resolution. The plaintiff worked for eighteen months more before retiring. She sued the corporation when it reduced her monthly checks seven years later.

The court held that a pension contract existed between the parties. Although continued employment was not a consideration to her receipt of retirement benefits, the court found sufficient reliance on the part of the plaintiff to support her claim. The court based its decision upon the above restatement example, that is, the defendant informed the plaintiff of its plan, and the plaintiff in reliance thereon, retired. Feinberg presents factors that also appear in the case at bar. There, the plaintiff had worked many years and desired to retire; she would not have left had she not been able to rely on a pension; and once retired, she sought no other employment.

However, the important distinction between *Feinberg* and the case before us is that in *Feinberg* the employer's decision definitely shaped the thinking of the plaintiff. In this case the promise did not. It is not reasonable to infer from the facts that Hugo R. Mainelli, Jr., expected retirement to result from his conversation with Hayes. Hayes had given notice of his intention seven months previously. Here there was thus no inducement to retire which would satisfy the demands of § 90 of the RESTATEMENT.

Nor can it be said that Hayes's refraining from other employment was "action or forbearance of a definite and substantial character." The underlying assumption of Hayes's initial decision to retire was that upon leaving the defendant's employ, he would no longer work. It is impossible to say that he changed his position any more so because of what Mainelli had told him in light of his own initial decision. These circumstances do not lead to a conclusion that injustice can be avoided only by enforcement of Plantations's promise.

Hayes received $20,000 over the course of four years. He inquired each year about whether he could expect a check for the following year. Obviously, there was no absolute certainty on his part that the pension would continue. Furthermore, in the face of his uncertainty, the mere fact that payment for several years did occur is insufficient by itself to meet the requirements of reliance under the doctrine of promissory estoppel.

For the foregoing reasons, the defendant's appeal is sustained and the judgment of the Superior Court is reversed. The papers of the case are remanded to the Superior Court.

NOTES AND QUESTIONS

1. **Competing Doctrines of Detrimental Reliance and Their Elements.**

   Louisiana Law. *See State Farm Mut. Auto. Ins. Co. v. Coard*, 2012 WL 1037944, *2 (La. App. [4th Cir.]) ("'A party may be obligated by a promise when he knew or should have known that the promise would induce the other party to rely on it to his detriment and the other party was reasonable in so relying.' ... Thus, in order to invoke the doctrine of detrimental reliance, the claimant must prove three elements: 1) a representation by word or conduct; 2) justifiable/reasonable reliance; and 3) a change in position to one's detriment because of the reliance. ... The doctrine of detrimental reliance is designed to prevent injustice by barring a party from taking a position contrary to his prior acts, admissions, representations, or silence.").

   Pennsylvania Law. *See Lehigh Valley Hospital v. County of Montgomery*, 768 A.2d 1197, (Pa. Cmwlth. Ct. 2001) ("[A] detrimental reliance or promissory estoppel [claim] arises 'when a party relies to his detriment on the intentional or negligent representations of another party, so that in order to prevent the relying party from being harmed, the inducing party is estopped from showing that the facts are not as the relying party understood them to be.' ... The elements of promissory estoppel or detrimental reliance are: 1) misleading words, conduct or silence by the party against whom estoppel is asserted; 2) unambiguous proof of reasonable reliance on the misrepresentation by the party seeking to assert the estoppel; and 3) no duty on the party seeking to assert estoppel.").

New York Law. *See BWA Corp. v. Alltrans Exp. U.S.A., Inc.*, 493 N.Y.S.2d 1, 3 (N.Y.App. Div. 1985) ("In order for estoppel to exist, three elements are necessary: '1) Conduct which amounts to a false representation or concealment of material facts, or, at least, which is calculated to convey the impression that the facts are otherwise than, and inconsistent with, those which the party subsequently seeks to assert; 2) intention, or at least expectation, that such conduct will be acted upon by the other party; 3) and, in some situations, knowledge, actual or constructive, of the real facts. The party asserting estoppel must show with respect to himself: '1) lack of knowledge of the true facts; 2) reliance upon the conduct of the party estopped; and 3) a prejudicial change in his position.'").

2. **Competing Standards for Proving "Detrimental Reliance".** The rules for establishing promissory estoppel are clear enough. But what is "detrimental reliance"? After all, "[d]etrimental reliance is an element of both equitable and promissory estoppel." 4 AM. JUR. 2D PROOF OF FACTS § 641, 1 (1975). Put simply, there is no universal standard. To underscore this point, consider the variance among the following standards:

District of Columbia. *See Law Mathematics & Tech., Inc. v. United States*, 779 F.2d 675, 678–79 (Fed. Cir. 1985) ("To prove detrimental reliance, [a party] must demonstrate that its action or forbearance amounted to a substantial change of position. … [A] speculative claim of damage does not amount to a 'substantial change of position' so as to prove detrimental reliance within the meaning of the doctrine of promissory estoppel.").

Minnesota Law. *See Spice Corp. v. Foresight Marketing Partners, Inc.*, 2011 WL 6740333, *17 (D. Minn.) ("[A plaintiff] must show that it reasonably relied on [defendant's] promise to [plaintiff's] detriment. … [The plaintiff] 'must demonstrate some detriment—damage—caused by [its] reliance.' To prove detrimental reliance, [the plaintiff] must show 'an actual change in … position. … Mere speculation is insufficient to show reliance.' In actions based on promissory estoppel, '[r]elief may be limited to damages measured by the promisee's reliance.'"), quoting *Krutchen v. Zayo Bandwidth Northeast, LLC*, 591 F. Supp. 2d 1002, 1017 (D. Minn. 2008), *Gauff v. Wimbley*, 2011 WL 1363981 (D. Minn. Apr. 11, 2011), and *Dallum v. Farmers Union Cent. Exchange, Inc.*, 462 N.W.2d 608, 613 (Minn. Ct. App. 1990).

Texas Law. *See Hinds v. Orix Capital Markets, L.L.C.*, 2003 WL 22132791, *5 (N.D. Tex. 2003) ("The elements of promissory estoppel are: 1) a promise, 2) foreseeability of reliance on the promise by the promisor; and 3) detrimental reliance by the promisee. In order to prove detrimental reliance in the context of promissory estoppel, reliance on the promise must be reasonable and justified.), citing *American Tobacco Co. v. Grinnell*, 951 S.W.2d 420, 436 (Tex. 1997).

3. **The Employment-at-Will Doctrine**. Generally, if a contract does not exist between an employer and an employee, the doctrine of employment-at-will allows an employer or an employee to terminate the employment at any time for any lawful reason. *See, e.g., Phipps v. IASD Health Servs. Corp.*, 558 N.W.2d 198, 202 (Iowa 1997). Or, if an oral employment agreement has no fixed duration, it is an at-will agreement; therefore, an employee is free to seek work elsewhere and the employer may discharge the employee without cause. *See Henkel v. Educational Research Council of America*, 344 N.E.2d 118, 120 (Ohio 1976).

4. **Exceptions to the Employment-at-Will Doctrine**. Three exceptions to the employment-at-will doctrine have evolved: the public-policy, implied-contract, and covenant-of-good-faith exceptions. First, the public-policy exception permits an at-will employee to commence a wrongful-discharge suit if an employer terminates the employee because 1) the employee refused to participate in illegal activity or 2) the employee reported his employer's or anyone else's illegal activity. *See Buchanan v. Ameristar Casino Vicksburg, Inc.*, 852 So. 2d 25, 26–27 (Miss. 2003). Second, the implied-contract exception allows an employee to cite an employer's personnel manual and argue that the language in the manual modified the employment-at-will relationship and became part of an employment contract. *See Leikvold v. Valley View Community Hosp.*, 688 P.2d 170, 174 (Ariz. 1984). And finally, the covenant-of-good-faith exception prevents an employer from terminating an at-will employee summarily—with or without cause. Instead, an employer's decision to terminate its at-will employee must be made in good faith, because "parties to contracts and commercial transactions must act in good faith toward one another." *See Fortune v. National Cash Register Co.*, 373 Mass. 96, 101–102 (1977).

5. **Employment-at-Will Doctrine in Missouri and Rhode Island.** When the courts decided *Feinberg* and *Hayes*, in 1959 and 1982, respectively, the employment-at-will doctrine was alive and well in Missouri and in Rhode Island. *See Quinn v. Buchanan*, 298 S.W.2d 413, 418 (Mo. 1957) ("[I]n the absence of a contract for

employment for a definite term or a contrary statutory provision, an employer may discharge an employee at any time, without cause or reason, or for any reason and, in such case, no action can be maintained for wrongful discharge."); and, *Booth v. National India Rubber Co.*, 36 A. 714, 715 (R.I. 1897) (reaffirming the rule that one's employment continues on the terms of an original contract if one enters into the service of another for a definite period, continues to work after the expiration of that period, without any new contract and stressing that employment is at-will hiring when the hiring is for an indefinite period and may be terminated at any time by either party.). Yet, the *Feinberg* and *Hayes* courts spent valuable judicial resources and a lot of paper and ink explaining why the doctrine of promissory estoppel applied or did not apply. Would the conflicts have been resolved more quickly and efficiently if the two courts had applied the employment-at-will rather than the promissory estoppel doctrine?

6. **Promissory Estoppel as Independent Cause of Action in Texas**. Consider the appellate court's controversial conclusion in *Ford v. City State Bank of Palacios*, 44 S.W.3d 121, 140 (Tex. App.—Corpus Christi, 2001):

> PROMISSORY ESTOPPEL AS AN INDEPENDENT CAUSE OF ACTION
>
> Promissory estoppel is primarily a defensive theory; it is a plea in confession and avoidance. However, promissory estoppel is also a cause of action available to a promisee who has acted to his detriment in reasonable reliance on an otherwise unenforceable promise. *Wheeler v. White*, 398 S.W.2d 93, 96–97 (Tex. 1965); *David McDavid Nissan, Inc. v. Subaru of Am., Inc.,* 10 S.W.3d 56, 73 (Tex. App.—Dallas 1999, pet. granted); *Henderson v. Texas Commerce Bank—Midland, N.A.*, 837 S.W.2d 778, 781–82 (Tex. App.—El Paso 1992, writ denied). Generally, promissory estoppel is a viable alternative to a breach of contract. *Allied Vista, Inc. v. Holt*, 987 S.W.2d 138, 141 (Tex. App.—Houston [14th Dist.] 1999, pet. denied).

However, in *Wheeler*, the Texas Supreme Court does not state categorically that "promissory is [estoppel] also a cause of action." Instead, the supreme court wrote:

> The binding thread which runs through the cases applying promissory estoppel is the existence of promises designedly made to influence the conduct of the promisee, tacitly encouraging the conduct, which conduct, although not necessarily constituting any actual performance of the contract itself, is something that must be done by the promisee before he could begin to perform, and was a fact known to the promisor. *As to*

> *the argument that no new cause of action may be created by such a promise regardless of its established applicability as a defense,* it has been answered that where one party has by his words or conduct made to the other a promise or assurance which was intended to affect the legal relations between them and to be acted on accordingly, then, once the other party has taken him at his word and acted on it, the party who gave the promise cannot afterward be allowed to revert to the previous relationship as if no such promise had been made. This does not create a contract where none existed before, but only prevents a party from insisting upon his strict legal rights when it would be unjust to allow him to enforce them. *See* 1 WILLISTON, CONTRACTS, §§ 139–40 (Rev. ed. 1936)

CLASHING DOCTRINES: PROMISSORY ESTOPPEL VERSUS EMPLOYMENT-AT-WILL

Employers Beware! The Emerging Use of Promissory Estoppel as an Exception to Employment-at-Will
49 Baylor L. Rev. 197 (1997)
Cortlan H. Maddux

Cortlan H. Maddux, Comment, EMPLOYERS BEWARE! The Emerging Use of Promissory Estoppel as an Exception to Employment-at-Will, 49 Baylor L. Rev. 198 (1997).

A majority of employees in Texas are at-will employees. In theory, their employers may discharge them at any time, for any reason, without fear of recourse. But because of the harsh impact that may result, employees often attempt to alter the at-will relationship and seek relief for wrongful discharge. Increasingly, employees are using promissory estoppel as a theory of recovery in wrongful discharge claims. ... The traditional goal of the promissory estoppel doctrine is accomplished when a party invokes its reliance on a promise to prevent the opposing party from asserting the absence of a traditional contract requirement. ... Some courts, however, have expanded the promissory estoppel doctrine beyond its traditional use as a defensive shield. ... Broadening the use of promissory estoppel has become common in the area of employment relations. ...

Employment at Will

The employment-at-will doctrine became prevalent in the late nineteenth century as a result of an abundance of labor created by the Industrial Revolution. The first articulation of the doctrine is generally considered to be Horace G. Wood's 1877 employment law treatise, in which he stated:

> With us the rule is inflexible, that a general or indefinite hiring is prima facie a hiring at will, and if the servant seeks to make it out a yearly hiring, the burden is on him to establish it by proof. A hiring at so much a day, week, month or year, no time being specified, is an indefinite hiring, and no presumption attaches that it was for a day even, but only at the rate fixed for whatever time the party may serve. ... (U)nless their understanding was mutual that the service was to extend for a certain fixed and definite period, it is an indefinite hiring and is determinable at the will of either party. ...

The employment-at-will doctrine in Texas provides that an employment relationship is "terminable at any time by either party, with or without cause, absent an express agreement to the contrary." Texas first recognized the at-will doctrine in 1888, and since then Texas courts have vigorously adhered to the doctrine and sought to preserve it. The reverence among courts toward employment at will is evident in that only one judicially-created exception exists to the doctrine, despite its long existence.

In contrast, the Texas Legislature has enacted several statutory exceptions to the doctrine. A close examination of these statutory exceptions, however, reveals that they are narrowly tailored to prohibit dismissal based on either (1) inclusion in a specific group such as race, religion, sex, or national origin, or (2) engagement in a specific activity such as jury duty, union involvement, or political activity. By codifying only these narrow exceptions, the Texas Legislature has, for the most part, maintained the viability of employment at will in Texas. A successful claim of promissory estoppel, however, limits an employer's right to discharge an at-will employee, and acts as an additional exception to employment at will. ...

Promissory Estoppel and Modification of Employment at Will

The use of promissory estoppel has become increasingly prevalent in two employment contexts: (1) prehiring promises to employ and (2) posthiring promises not to discharge. Cases involving prehiring promises to employ almost always stem from an employee leaving his current job in reliance on a promise of future employment. Such promises often cause the employee to relocate and abandon other opportunities in preparation for the new position. Given the significant reliance on the promise to employ, these situations give rise to an ideal use of promissory estoppel. Because employment has not begun, however, the at-will presumption has not yet attached to the relationship. For this reason, although cases involving prehiring promises to employ are instructive as to the emerging uses of promissory estoppel, they do not erode employment at will.

A posthiring promise not to discharge occurs after the at-will presumption has attached to the employment relationship. This seems to create an inherent inconsistency: how can an employee claim reasonable reliance on a promise not to discharge when the law says that an employer can discharge at any time and for any reason? This inconsistency presents policy concerns between protecting an employee's reliance and preserving the employer's right to terminate at will.

Historically, in the absence of one of the express exceptions to at-will employment discussed above, a Texas employee attempting to enforce a promise not to discharge was left with only the option of trying to prove the formation of a contract and a breach of that contract. If the employee could not prove a contract, the at-will presumption prevailed and the employee could be discharged without the employer incurring liability. Using promissory estoppel defensively, the employee's reliance can only maintain the enforceability of a promise against the statute of frauds or in a failure of consideration.

Promissory estoppel keeps the employer from denying the existence of a contract. The emergence of promissory estoppel as a cause of action, however, has given employees an additional vehicle by which they can limit employers' right to discharge at will. A promissory estoppel cause of action allows employees to sue their employers for wrongful discharge without even alleging a contract, completely circumventing employment at will. …

Texas's Confusion Regarding Promissory Estoppel in the Employment Context

The Texas Supreme Court has articulated the requirements of promissory estoppel as (1) a promise, (2) the promisor's foreseeability of the promisee's reliance thereon, and (3) substantial reliance by the promisee to his detriment. However, confusion exists in Texas as to whether promissory estoppel should be used as an independent cause of action or as a defensive theory in response to an employer's assertion of either a failure of traditional contract requirements or the statute of frauds defense. Conflicting language among Texas courts causes this confusion. …

Promissory Estoppel as a Cause of Action

Other authorities in Texas, however, challenge the view that promissory estoppel is only a defensive action. The TEXAS PATTERN JURY CHARGES presents the question on promissory estoppel as: "Did (employee) substantially rely to his detriment on (employer's) promise, if any, and was this reliance foreseeable by (the employer)?" This language follows the elements of promissory estoppel as articulated by the Texas Supreme Court. The comment that follows in the TEXAS PATTERN JURY CHARGES, however, states that "(t)he doctrine of promissory estoppel may be invoked as a cause of action. It is appropriate if a promisee has acted to his detriment in reasonable reliance on an otherwise unenforceable promise." In addition, some Texas courts have suggested that promissory estoppel is a cause of action. ...

Conclusion

Courts should remember that promissory estoppel began not as a separate cause of action, but as a defensive tool to allow enforcement of a promise when an element of the traditional contract principles was missing or when a promise lacked the writing requirement imposed by the statute of frauds. This approach makes promissory estoppel a doctrine within traditional contract law, not parallel to it. Given that the express language of the Texas Supreme Court supports this position, Texas courts should act with caution when employing the doctrine to extend greater protection to Texas employees. ... If the Texas Supreme Court has the opportunity to address this issue, it should balance the competing policy interests discussed in this Comment. Requiring employees to show traditional contract requirements when attempting to hold an employer liable for an alleged promise is not unreasonable.

SECTION THREE: ADEQUACY OF CONSIDERATION

Assume these facts: A plaintiff files a breach-of-promise or a breach-of-contract cause of action against an employer. The plaintiff proves that the contract or promise is valid. And the plaintiff employs the bargained-for-exchange or promissory-estoppel doctrine to prove consideration. Now, assume that the employer files a timely motion for summary judgment. Among other assertions, the employer argues that plaintiff's cause of action should be dismissed because the plaintiff did not prove "sufficient consideration." Or the employer raises this affirmative defense: Plaintiff gave "insufficient consideration" for the exchange or the bargain. How much consideration must parties exchange before a court will enforce a valid promise or contract? What is adequate consideration? This section discusses this and related questions.

A. "Adequacy of Consideration" Versus "Legal Sufficiency of Consideration"

Browning v. Johnson
422 P.2d 314
(Wash. 1967)

Langenbach, Judge. This is the tale of two osteopaths who attempted a business transaction. The heart of the case is a certain promise which Dr. Browning made to Dr. Johnson. The sole issue is whether Dr. Browning is to be bound by his promise.

Browning and Johnson entered into a contract of sale whereby Browning was to sell his practice and equipment to Johnson. Both parties and their attorneys believed the contract made to be completely valid and enforceable. Before the contract's effective date, Browning changed his mind about selling and sought to be released from the obligations he had undertaken. Johnson, at first, demurred. Later, however, upon Browning's promise to pay Johnson $40,000 if Johnson would give up the contract of sale, the parties entered into a contract (the contract here in issue) canceling the contract of sale.

Some months later Browning tired of his bargain and brought this action for declaratory judgment and restitution. In the course of this action the trial court concluded that the canceled sale contract had lacked mutuality and had been too indefinite in its terms for enforcement. Nevertheless, it concluded that the contract canceling the sale contract was supported by "adequate consideration." Browning has appealed from that decision. He brought 24 errors which pertain mainly to the trial court's failure to adopt his proposed findings. He insists that his promise to pay Johnson was unsupported by consideration and that the promise was a child of mutual mistake.

We should first say a word about terminology. Courts are loath to inquire into the "adequacy" of consideration, that is, into the comparative value of the promises and acts exchanged. As we said in *Rogich v. Dressel*, 278 P.2d 367, 374 (Wash. 1954): "(W)e must apply the rule followed in this state that parties who are competent to contract will not be relieved from a bad bargain they make unless the consideration is so inadequate as to be constructively fraudulent."

But "adequacy" of consideration, into which courts seldom inquire, is to be distinguished from the legal "sufficiency" of any particular consideration. The latter phrase is concerned not with comparative value but with that which will support a promise. "[A]nything which fulfils the requirements of consideration will support a promise whatever may be the comparative value of the consideration, and of the thing promised." 1 WILLISTON, CONTRACTS § 115, cited in *Puget Mill Co. v. Kerry*, 49 P.2d 57, 64 (Wash. 1935). "[T]he relative values of a promise and the consideration for it, do not affect the sufficiency of consideration." RESTATEMENT, CONTRACTS § 81 (1932). This distinction is sometimes lost sight of.

In the instant case, Browning bargained for Johnson's act of giving up the contract of sale. The issue is whether the law regards Johnson's act of giving up that contract as legally "sufficient" consideration to support Browning's promise to pay him for such an act. The trial court concluded that giving up the contract of sale was 'adequate' consideration for Browning's promise.

Whether there exists something which will support a promise and which therefore may be called legally sufficient consideration is obviously prior to the question of whether that consideration is adequate when compared to the value of the promise given in exchange for it. Therefore, whether the trial court meant (1) that giving up the contract of sale was a bargained-for act legally sufficient to support Browning's promise, or (2) that giving up the contract of sale was sufficient consideration—consideration not so inadequate as to be constructively fraudulent—is not important. We hold that Browning's promise was supported by sufficient consideration and there is nothing in this case which induces us, under the *Rogich* formulation, to consider the relative values of the things exchanged.

This is a unilateral contract. *See Cook v. Johnson*, 221 P.2d 525 (Wash. 1950). A unilateral contract is one in which a promise is given in exchange for an act or forbearance. Here, Browning gave Johnson a promise to pay $40,000 in exchange for Johnson's act of giving up the contract of sale. Sufficiency of consideration in unilateral contracts is discussed by Professor Williston in his treatise, CONTRACTS § 102 (3d ed. 1957). There he indicates that the requirement of sufficient consideration to support a promise is met by a detriment incurred by the promisee (Johnson) or a benefit received by the promisor (Browning) at the request of the promisor.

"That a detriment suffered by the promisee at the promisor's request and as the price for the promise is sufficient, though the promisor is not benefited, is well settled." Williston, *supra*. This has been the law in Washington for over 50 years. *Harris v. Johnson*, 75 Wash. 291, 294 (1913). The question then becomes the nature of a detriment. Detriment is defined by Williston as the giving up of "something which immediately prior thereto the promisee was privileged to retain, or doing or refraining from doing something which he was then privileged not to do, or not to refrain from doing." Williston, *supra*, § 102A. We have already had occasion to quote this definition with approval. *Luther v. Nat'l Bank of Commerce*, 2 Wash. 2d 470, 483 (1940).

We have employed the definition for many years. *See, e.g., Harris v. Johnson, supra*, where we said: "Indeed there is a consideration if the promisee, in return for the promise, does anything legal which he is not bound to do, or refrains from doing anything which he has a right to do, whether there is any actual loss or detriment to him or actual benefit to the promisor or not." citing 9 Cyc. 311 *et seq*.

The problem presented by this case is not a new one. Over a century ago, in England, Brooks obtained a certain document from Haigh believing that it was a guarantee, and promised to pay a certain sum of money in consideration of Haigh's giving it up. The guarantee proved to be unenforceable. Haigh sued Brooks for the money promised. The court said:

> [T]he plaintiffs were induced by the defendant's promise to part with something which they might have kept, and the defendant obtained what he desired by means of that promise. Both being free and able to judge for themselves, how can the defendant be justified in breaking this promise, by discovering afterwards that the thing in consideration of which he gave it did not possess that value which he supposed to belong to it? It cannot be ascertained [whether] that value was what he most regarded. He may have had other objects and motives; and of their weight he was the only judge. *Haigh v. Brooks*, 10 A. & E. 309, 320 (1839).

Similarly here, of Browning's objects and motives, he was the only judge.

Over a quarter of a century ago, in Washington, Fleishbein's sister—Bertha—purchased some land which was subject to a first mortgage. Fleishbein later purchased the mortgage. Bertha wanted to obtain a loan by executing a first mortgage on the property and so she asked her brother to release his mortgage on the property and promised to give him a second mortgage as soon as she had obtained her loan. Fleishbein, in consideration of that promise, released the mortgage. At the time, the mortgage and mortgage note were barred by the statute of limitations. The trial court held that the release of the unenforceable mortgage was "sufficient consideration." This court affirmed. *Fleishbein v. Thorne*, 193 Wash. 65, 74 P.2d 880 (1937).

In 1935 the case of *Puget Mill Co. v. Kerry*, *supra*, came before this court. The following discussion—appearing in 49 P.2d at 63–64—while not entirely necessary ... is persuasive here. So much so that we feel justified in quoting at some length[:]

> It clearly appears that appellants, represented as they were by able counsel, procured respondent's consent to their purchase of the lease. * * * Appellants state that at the time of their purchase of the lease all parties believed that respondent still had the right to object to an assignment thereof, and that its consent was necessary to a valid assignment. ...

> [Appellants argue] that the giving of an unnecessary consent by respondent cannot be held sufficient consideration for appellants' promise. In the first place, this assumes that the consent which respondent accorded was unnecessary. ... In determining the question, the position of the parties in 1923 must be considered, not the situation as it exists now. Appellants then, of course, believed that they were making a good bargain, and anything which tended to make their position more secure would appear to them to be to their advantage.
>
> Then, it is well settled that a consideration sufficient to support a promise need not always—in the last analysis—have an actual value. In this instance, it may be assumed that whether or not respondent had the right to refuse its consent to an assignment of the lease could only ultimately be determined by the courts. The giving of its consent by respondent would constitute a valuable consideration for a promise, even though a possibility existed that at the end of protracted litigation, it might be held that respondent had lost its right to accept or reject a new tenant. Of course, a consideration cannot be sham or frivolous or manifestly false; but in the case at bar, we are satisfied that a real controversy might have been waged before the courts as to the rights of respondent as they existed in 1923.

The matter is discussed in 1 WILLISTON ON CONTRACTS, §§ 102, 102-a and 115.

The Supreme Court of the United States case of *Sykes v. Chadwick*, 18 Wall. 141, 149 (1873) is [on] point. In the case cited, the Court used the following language:

> At all events, the defendant when he was endeavoring to negotiate the sale of his property deemed it of sufficient importance to give the note in question in consideration of the plaintiff joining in the deed, and releasing any contingent right she might have. This very act of hers may have been necessary, and we have a right to infer that it was deemed important, to the closing up of the transaction and securing the sale of the property. If any release is deemed requisite to confirm the title of lands with which one has been connected, though by a proper construction of the law he has no interest in them whatever, still such release will be a good consideration for a promise or for the payment of money.

That the parties cited none of the above cases in their briefs makes these cases no less appropriate. It is clear that at the time of contracting, the parties, equally informed, of equal bargaining power and equally assisted by able counsel, freely bargained for, and freely settled upon an exchange which each felt would be beneficial to him. Their mutual assent proved this mutual expectation of benefit for the law must presume that no man bargains against his own interest.

Subsequent events revealed that the contract, fully acceptable to both parties when made, was less beneficial to the promisor than he and his attorney had, at the time of contracting, thought. But this alone cannot be reason enough for allowing the promisor to avoid it. There was no misrepresentation, no fraud, and no duress. The promisor Browning wanted Johnson to give up the sale contract and to secure the performance of that act, he solemnly promised to pay Johnson $40,000. Johnson, induced by Browning's urgent pleas and solemn promise, gave up the sale contract. The legal detriment suffered by Johnson through Browning's inducement will support Browning's promise to pay.

* * *

The judgment is affirmed.

NOTES AND QUESTIONS

1. **Additional Examples: Distinguishing Adequate Consideration from Legally Sufficient Consideration.**

   - *Wartenburg Trust v. Elrod*, 2005 WL 3462785, *4 (Wash. App. Div. 1) ("Courts rarely inquire into the adequacy of consideration. But the adequacy of consideration is different from the legal sufficiency of consideration. *The legal sufficiency of consideration is a question of law.* ... [For example, a benefit] to the guarantor on the one hand, or some detriment to the guarantee on the other ... is sufficient consideration for a contract of guaranty. But a promise to carry out an already existing duty does not constitute consideration.") (Emphasis added)
   - *Tumarkin v. Goldstein*, 109 A.2d 435, 437 (N.J. Super. App. Div. 1954) ("[A]ssuming that there [was] an agreement, ... there was no consideration to support it. The rule is established. ... [T]here must be a valid consideration for an agreement—a detriment incurred by the promisee or a benefit received by the promisor. ... [L]egal sufficiency does not depend upon the comparative value of the consideration and of what is promised in return. ... The controlling factor is the element of bargain or exchange. ... [U]nder the circumstances here, there is a complete absence of that element. ... In effect, consideration is the price bargained and paid for the promise—something

given in exchange for the promise. The rule—to the necessity for the element of bargain and exchange—is settled in New Jersey.").

2. **Peppercorn Theory of Consideration.** How much consideration is adequate? Consider the court's explanation in *Sfreddo v. Sfreddo*, 720 S.E.2d 145, 152–154 (Va. Ct. App. 2012):

"[A] gift has been defined as a contract without a consideration." *Ott v. L & J Holdings, LLC*, 654 S.E.2d 902, 905 (Va. 2008). Indeed, "by definition, a deed of gift requires no consideration." *Hill v. Brooks*, 482 S.E.2d 816, 823 (Va. 1997). Consideration represents "the price bargained for and paid for a promise." *Smith v. Mountjoy*, 53, 694 S.E.2d 598, 602 (Va. 2010). It may come in "a benefit to the party promising or a detriment to the party to whom the promise is made." *GSHH-Richmond, Inc. v. Imperial Assocs.*, 480 S.E.2d 482, 484 (Va. 1997). ... Virginia has long followed the "peppercorn" theory of consideration, under which even a peppercorn suffices as consideration. *See Richmond Eng'g & Mfg. Corp. v. Loth*, 115 S.E. 774, 787 (Va. 1923). A peppercorn has been equated with a cent. *Whitney v. Stearns*, 16 Me. 394, 397 (1839). The dictionary states that "[i]n English law, the reservation of a merely nominal rent, on a lease, was sometimes expressed by a stipulation for the payment of a peppercorn." Black's Dictionary, at 1135. In *Barker v. Keete*, 89 Eng. Rep. 179 (1678), the court held that "[t]he reservation of a peppercorn rent on a lease for years is a sufficient consideration to transfer the possession." The principle also dates from early American jurisprudence. *See Perkins v. Parker*, 1 Mass. (1 Tyng) 117, 126 (1804).

Under this theory, "[i]t matters not to what extent the promisor is benefited or how little the promisee may give for the promise." *Sager v. Basham*, 401 S.E.2d 676, 677 (Va. 1991). "A very slight advantage to the one party or a trifling inconvenience to the other is generally held sufficient to support the promise." *Brewer v. First Nat'l Bank of Danville*, 120 S.E.2d 273, 279 (Va. 1961). "The owner of the historic estate of 'Blackacre' can give it away, and he can sell it for a peppercorn. Courts, though they have long arms, cannot relieve one of the consequences of a contract merely because it was unwise." *Planters Nat'l Bank of Fredericksburg, Va. v. E. G. Heflin Co.*, 184 S.E. 216, 219 (Va. 1936).

3. **Peppercorn Consideration as Evidence of Unauthentic Bargaining**. Some have suggested that contracts which are based

solely on exchange of peppercorns may be evidence of an unauthentic bargaining between parties. *See* 1 ARTHUR LINTON CORBIN, CORBIN ON CONTRACTS § 127, at 546 (1963):

> The gross inadequacy of the consideration, as measured by the opinions of other men; may tend to support the conclusion that the parties did not actually agree upon an exchange, that the "peppercorn" was not in fact bargained for by the promisor. If it was not bargained for, it was not a consideration, according to the definition that makes agreed bargain the test. Persons sometimes say that they have bargained, when their other conduct shows that they have not. ... Courts must first determine the fact of bargain and agreed exchange before they can properly apply the rules of consideration as a bargained exchange. The rule that market equivalence of consideration is not required, and that the value of the consideration is to be left solely to the free bargaining process of the parties, leads in extreme cases to seeming absurdities. When the consideration is only a "peppercorn" or a "tomtit" or a worthless piece of paper, the requirement of a consideration appeared to Holmes to be as much of a mere formality as is a seal.

B. Nominal Consideration

In re Greene
45 F.2d 428
(2d Cir. 1930)

Woolsey, District Judge. The petition for review is granted, and the order of the referee is reversed.

I. The claimant—a woman—filed proof of claim in the sum of $375,700, based on an alleged contract, against this bankrupt's estate. The trustee in bankruptcy objected to the claim. A hearing was held before the referee in bankruptcy and testimony taken.

The referee held the claim valid and dismissed the objections. The correctness of this ruling is raised by the trustee's petition to review and the referee's certificate.

II. For several years prior to April 28, 1926, the bankrupt—a married man—had apparently lived in adultery with the claimant. He gave her substantial sums of money. He also paid $70,000 for a house on Long Island acquired by her, which she still owns.

Throughout their relations the bankrupt was a married man, and the claimant knew it. The claimant was well over thirty years of age when the connection began. She testified that the bankrupt has promised to marry her as soon as his wife should get a divorce from him; this the bankrupt denied. The relations of intimacy between them were discontinued in April, 1926, and they then executed a written instrument under seal which is alleged to be a binding contract and which is the foundation of the claim under consideration.

In this instrument, which was made in New York, the bankrupt undertook 1) to pay to the claimant $1,000 a month during their joint lives; 2) to assign to her a $100,000 life insurance policy on his life and to keep up the premiums on it for life, the bankrupt to pay $100,000 to the claimant in case the policy should lapse for nonpayment of premiums; and 3) to pay the rent for four years on an apartment which she had leased.

It was declared in the instrument that the bankrupt had no interest in the Long Island house or in its contents, and that he should no longer be liable for mortgage interest taxes, and other charges on this property. The claimant on her part released the bankrupt from all claims which she had against him. The preamble to the instrument recites as consideration the payment of $1 by the claimant to the bankrupt, "and other good and valuable consideration."

The bankrupt kept up the several payments called for by the instrument until August, 1928, but failed to make payments thereafter,

III. In the proof of claim it is alleged that a total of $375,700 was due because of breach of the agreement, made up as follows: $250,000 for failure to pay $1,000 a month; $99,200 for failure to maintain the insurance policy; and $26,500 for failure to pay the rent. The claim was sustained by the referee for the full amount.

It seems clear that the $250,000 allowed as damages for failure to pay $1,000 a month was excessive. The bankrupt's undertaking was to pay $1,000 a month only so long as both he and the claimant should live; it was not an annuity for the claimant's life alone, as she seems to have assumed. There is nothing in the record to indicate the bankrupt's age, and consequently there is a failure of proof as to this element of damage. In view of my conclusion that the entire claim is void, however, the matter of damages is of no present importance.

IV. A contract for future illicit cohabitation is unlawful. There is consideration present in such a case, but the law strikes the agreement down as immoral. WILLISTON ON CONTRACTS § 1745.

Here the illicit intercourse had been abandoned prior to the making of the agreement, so that the above rule is not infringed. This case is one where the motive which led the bankrupt to make the agreement on which the claim is based was the past illicit cohabitation between him and the claimant.

The law is that a promise to pay a woman on account of cohabitation which has ceased is void, not for illegality, but for want of consideration. The consideration in such a case is past. The mere fact that past cohabitation is the motive for the promise will not of itself invalidate it, but the promise in such a case, to be valid, must be supported by some consideration other than past intercourse. WILLISTON ON CONTRACTS, §§. 148, 1745.

The problem in the present case, therefore, is one of consideration, not of illegality, and it is clear that the past illicit intercourse is not consideration.

The cases dealing with situations where there is illegitimate offspring or where there has been seduction are of doubtful authority, for the doctrine that past moral obligation is consideration is now generally exploded. But these cases and others speaking of expiation of past wrong, cited by the referee, are not in point.

Here there was not any offspring as a result of the bankrupt's union with the claimant; there was not any seduction shown in the sense in which that word is used in law. Cf. New York Penal Law, art. 195, § 2175. There was not any past wrong for which the bankrupt owed the claimant expiation—*volenti non fit injuria.* Cases involving deeds, mortgages, and the like are not analogous, because no consideration is necessary in an executed transaction.

V. The question, therefore, is whether there was any consideration for the bankrupt's promises, apart from the past cohabitation. It seems plain that no such consideration can be found, but I will review the following points emphasized by the claimant as showing consideration:

1. The $1 consideration recited in the paper is nominal. It cannot seriously be urged that $1, recited but not even shown to have been paid, will support an executory promise to pay hundreds of thousands of dollars.

2. "Other good and valuable consideration" are generalities that sound plausible, but the words cannot serve as consideration where the facts show that nothing good or valuable was actually given at the time the contract was made.

3. It is said that the release of claims furnishes the necessary consideration. So it would if the claimant had had any claims to release. But the evidence shows no vestige of any lawful claim. Release from imaginary claims is not valuable consideration for a promise. In this connection, apparently, the claimant testified that the bankrupt had promised to marry her as soon as he was divorced. Assuming that he did—though he denies it—the illegality of any such promise, made while the bankrupt was still married, is so

obvious that no claim could possibly arise from it, and the release of such claim could not possibly be lawful consideration.

4. The claimant also urges that by the agreement the bankrupt obtained immunity from liability for taxes and other charges on the Long Island house. The fact is that he was never chargeable for these expenses. He doubtless had been in the habit of paying them, just as he had paid many other expenses for the claimant; but such payments were either gratuitous or were the contemporaneous price of the continuance of his illicit intercourse with the claimant.

   It is absurd to suppose that, when a donor gives a valuable house to a donee, the fact that the donor need pay no taxes or upkeep thereafter on the property converts the gift into a contract upon consideration. The present case is even stronger, for the bankrupt had never owned the house and had never been liable for the taxes. He furnished the purchase price, but the conveyance was from the seller direct to the claimant.

5. Finally, it is said that the parties intended to make a valid agreement. It is a non sequitur to say that therefore the agreement is valid. A man may promise to make a gift to another, and may put the promise in the most solemn and formal document possible; but, barring exceptional cases, such, perhaps, as charitable subscriptions, the promise will not be enforced.

   The parties may shout consideration to the housetops, yet, unless consideration is actually present, there is not a legally enforcible contract. What the bankrupt obviously intended in this case was an agreement to make financial contribution to the claimant because of his past cohabitation with her, and, as already pointed out, such an agreement lacks consideration.

VI. The presence of the seal would have been decisive in the claimant's favor a hundred years ago. Then an instrument under seal required no consideration, or, to keep to the language of the cases, the seal was conclusive evidence of consideration. In New York, however, a seal is now only presumptive evidence of consideration on an executory instrument. This presumption was amply rebutted in this case, for the proof clearly shows, I think, that there was not in fact any consideration for the bankrupt's promise contained in the executory instrument signed by him and the claimant.

NOTES AND QUESTIONS

1. **Legally Sufficient Consideration Under New York's Law.** In *Greene*, the federal district judge concluded that the "$1 consideration recited in the paper" was only "nominal"; therefore, it could not support "an executory promise to pay hundreds of thousands of dollars." Which body of law did the federal judge use to reach that conclusion? Is nominal consideration legally sufficient to enforce a valid contract under New York's law? *See Jackson ex dem. Hudson v. Alexander*, 3 Johns. 484, (N.Y. Sup. Ct. 1808) ("The rule requiring a consideration ... has become merely nominal. ... [T]he smallest sum possible is sufficient: nay, it has been solemnly adjudged, that a pepper-corn was sufficient to raise a use.").

2. **Affirmative Defense: "Consideration Was Stated, But Not Paid".** In *Greene*, the federal district judge also concluded that the "$1 consideration [was] recited but not paid. Generally, do courts force plaintiffs to prove that consideration has been paid before enforcing a valid contract? Answers appear in the following cases:

   - *Jackson ex dem. Hudson v. Alexander*, 3 Johns. 484 (N.Y. Sup. 1808) ("The rule requiring a consideration ... has become merely nominal, and a matter of form; for if a sum of money be mentioned, it is never an inquiry whether it was actually paid, and the smallest sum possible is sufficient: nay, it has been solemnly adjudged, that a pepper-corn was sufficient ...").
   - *Hofland v. Gustafson*, 282 P.2d 1039, 1041 (Cal. Super. 1955) ("The fact that the consideration was not paid until a few days after the release was executed did not constitute such a material failure of consideration. ... 'Although failure of consideration may be a ground for rescinding the contract, ... the contract is not void. ... [A]n unsubstantial failure of consideration does not give the other party the right to rescind the contract but is only the basis for damages. ... Where time is not of the essence of the contract, payment within a reasonable time is sufficient.").
   - *1464–Eight, Ltd. v. Joppich*, 154 S.W.3d 101, 109–10 (Tex. 2004) (declaring that a failure to pay recited nominal consideration does not preclude enforcement of an option contract).

3. **Majority and Minority Rules.** In *Smith v. Wheeler*, 210 S.E.2d 702, 703–04 (Ga. 1974), the Supreme Court of Georgia presented a synopsis of majority and minority rules:

   > The option agreement—signed by both parties—states that it is "In consideration of the sum of one ($1.00) dollar to me in hand paid, receipt whereof is hereby acknowledged. ..."

> It is undisputed that the one dollar consideration cited in the agreement was not paid at the time of execution. ... The majority of cases from other jurisdictions hold that the offeror may prove that the consideration had not been paid and that no other consideration had taken its place. However, the minority rule—and what we consider to be the best view—is that even if it is shown that the dollar was not paid it does not void the contract. We have held many times that the recital of the one dollar consideration gives rise to an implied promise to pay which can be enforced by the other party.

4. **Affirmative Defense: "Love and Affection Are Not Consideration".** May "love and affection" in very personal relationships quality as legally sufficient consideration? Consider the Ohio Supreme Court's explanation in *Snyder v. Warde*, 86 N.E.2d 489, 494–96 (Ohio 1949):

> We know of no rule by which it is necessary for an employer and employee to dislike or hate each other and not to be kindly and generous toward each other in order for the services of the employee to be monetarily compensable by the employer. In the present case, ... the services to be rendered by plaintiff after the agreement—[the making of a will]—[would] be the same as those which she was performing ... [original] contract of $40 per month and a home with board for herself and her family. ... [We have] we stated that there may be times when a contract may be enforced when the consideration for the contract "[has] been paid in personal services, not intended to be, and not susceptible of being, measured by a pecuniary standard. ... In order for services to be such as are not compensable in money they must be of a kind which are rendered as a result of a sacrifice by the one performing them, generally being rendered because of love and affection."

C. Illusory Promises as Consideration

Again, to enforce a valid promise or contractual agreement, there must be evidence of consideration or mutuality of obligation between parties. As we have discovered, consideration may be forbearance—some detriment for another party's benefit. Or consideration may be an exchange of various rights, interests, and currencies. Put simply, when illusory promises are the only the exchanges that have occurred between parties, a valid contract may not be enforced.

What is an illusory promise? Courts have given a variety of definitions. *See In re 24R, Inc.,* 324 S.W.3d 564, 567 (Tex. 2010) ("A promise is illusory if it does not bind the promisor [and] the promisor retains the option to discontinue performance."); *Metro. Park Dist. of Tacoma v. Griffith*, 723 P.2d 1093, 1099 (Wash. 1986) (reiterating that a promise is illusory if its performance is optional or discretionary); *Bryant v. City of Atlantic City*, 309 N.J. Super 596, 620 (N.J. Super. Ct. App. Div. 1998) (declaring that an illusory promise gives a promisor an unfettered option to perform, regardless of what happens or regardless of the promisor's course of conduct); and *Petition of Department of Public Service*, 596 A.2d 1303, 1309 (Vt. 1991) ("A promise is illusory only if the promisor's future action is not limited in any way"), citing 1 A. CORBIN, CORBIN ON CONTRACTS § 149, at 657 (1963).

Again, under RESTATEMENT (SECOND) OF CONTRACTS § 71(2), a promisee's "return promise" that is "bargained for" and exchanged for a promisor's promise is consideration. However, fairly often, an initial as well a "return promise" is subjected to numerous contingencies. Consequently, the "return promise" is an "illusory promise" and there is no bargained-for-exchange consideration. On the other hand, a promise is not illusory if, say, a promisor's "power to terminate is conditioned upon some factor outside the promisor's unfettered discretion, such as the promisee's non-performance, or the happening of some event such as a strike, war, decline in business, etc." *Bryant v. City of Atlantic City*, 309 N.J. Super. at 620. Which rule did the court apply in the following renowned case?

Wood v. Lucy, Lady Duff-Gordon
118 N.E. 214
(N.Y. 1917)

Cardozo, J. The defendant styles herself "a creator of fashions." Her favor helps a sale. Manufacturers of dresses, millinery, and like articles are glad to pay for a certificate of her approval. The things which she designs, fabrics, parasols, and what not, have a new value in the public mind when issued in her name. She employed the plaintiff to help her to turn this vogue into money. He was to have the exclusive right, subject always to her approval, to place her indorsements on the designs of others. He was also to have the exclusive right to place her own designs on sale, or to license others to market them.

In return she was to have one-half of "all profits and revenues" derived from any contracts he might make. The exclusive right was to last at least one year from April 1, 1915—and thereafter from year to year unless terminated by notice of 90 days. The plaintiff says that he kept the contract on his part, and that the defendant broke it. She placed her indorsement on fabrics, dresses, and millinery without his knowledge, and withheld the profits. He sues her for the damages, and the case comes here on demurrer.

The agreement of employment is signed by both parties. It has a wealth of recitals. The defendant insists, however, that it lacks the elements of a contract. She says that the plaintiff does not bind himself to anything. It is true that he does not promise in so many words that he will use reasonable efforts to place the defendant's indorsements and market her designs. We think, however, that such a promise is fairly to be implied. The law has outgrown its primitive stage of formalism when the precise word was the sovereign talisman, and every slip was fatal. It takes a broader view today. A promise may be lacking, and yet the whole writing may be "instinct with an obligation," imperfectly expressed. *See* Scott, J., in *McCall Co. v. Wright*, 133 App. Div. 62, 117 N. Y. Supp. 775; *Moran v. Standard Oil Co.*, 211 N. Y. 187, 198, 105 N. E. 217). If that is so, there is a contract.

The implication of a promise here finds support in many circumstances. The defendant gave an exclusive privilege. She was to have no right for at least a year to place her own indorsements or market her own designs except through the agency of the plaintiff. The acceptance of the exclusive agency was an assumption of its duties. *Phoenix Hermetic Co. v. Filtrine Mfg. Co.*, 164 App. Div. 424, 150 N. Y. Supp. 193; *W. G. Taylor Co. v. Bannerman*, 120 Wis. 189, 97 N. W. 918; *Mueller v. Mineral Spring Co.*, 88 Mich. 390, 50 N. W. 319. We are not to suppose that one party was to be placed at the mercy of the other. *Hearn v. Stevens & Bro.*, 111 App. Div. 101, 106, 97 N. Y. Supp. 566; *Russell v. Allerton*, 108 N. Y. 288, 15 N. E. 391.

Many other terms of the agreement point the same way. We are told at the outset by way of recital that: "The said Otis F. Wood possesses a business organization adapted to the placing of such indorsements as the said Lucy, Lady Duff-Gordon, has approved."

The implication is that the plaintiff's business organization will be used for the purpose for which it is adapted. But the terms of the defendant's compensation are even more significant. Her sole compensation for the grant of an exclusive agency is to be one-half of all the profits resulting from the plaintiff's efforts. Unless he gave his efforts, she could never get anything. Without an implied promise, the transaction cannot have such business "efficacy, as both parties must have intended that at all events it should have." *See* Bowen, L. J., in the *Moorcock*, 14 P. D. 64, 68.

But the contract does not stop there. The plaintiff goes on to promise that he will account monthly for all moneys received by him, and that he will take out all such patents and copyrights and trade-marks as may in his judgment be necessary to protect the rights and articles affected by the agreement. It is true, of course, as the Appellate Division has said, that if he was under no duty to try to market designs or to place certificates of indorsement, his promise to account for profits or take out copyrights would be valueless.

But in determining the intention of the parties, the promise has a value. It helps to enforce the conclusion that the plaintiff had some duties. His promise to pay the defendant one-half of the profits and revenues resulting from the exclusive agency and to render accounts monthly was a promise to use reasonable efforts to bring profits and revenues into existence.

For this conclusion the authorities are ample. *Wilson v. Mechanical Orguinette Co.*, 170 N. Y. 542, 63 N. E. 550; *Phoenix Hermetic Co. v. Filtrine Mfg. Co., supra*; *Jacquin v. Boutard*, 89 Hun, 437, 35 N. Y. Supp. 496; Id., 157 N. Y. 686, 51 N. E. 1091; *Moran v. Standard Oil Co., supra*; *City of N. Y. v. Paoli*, 202 N. Y. 18, 94 N. E. 1077; *McIntyre v. Belcher*, 14 C. B. [N. S.] 654; *Devonald v. Rosser & Sons,* 2 K. B. 728 (1906); *W. G. Taylor Co. v. Bannerman, supra*; *Mueller v. Mineral Spring Co., supra*; *Baker Transfer Co. v. Merchants' R. & I. Mfg. Co.*, 1 App. Dov. 507, 37 N. Y. Supp. 276.

The judgment of the Appellate Division should be reversed, and the order of the Special Term affirmed, with costs in the Appellate Division and in this court.

NOTES AND QUESTIONS

1. **Wood's Consideration.** Consider these questions: 1) whether or not Wood and Lucy formed a valid contract; 2) whether or not Wood and Lucy made valid promises; 3) whether or not there was a promise for a promise, and 4) whether or not there was "mutuality of obligation" between the parties. Which was the central question in *Wood v. Lucy*?

2. **Wood v. Lucy, Consideration, and the Illusory Promise Doctrine.** Was there an illusory promise in *Wood v. Lucy*? If so, who was the author? Wood? Lady Duff-Gordon? In *Magruder Quarry & Co., L.L.C. v. Briscoe*, 83 S.W.3d 647, 650–51 (Mo. Ct. App. 2002), the Missouri court presented the following analysis:

   > [O]n appeal, [the Briscoes] contend that the trial court erred in holding the lease was null and void due to a lack of mutuality of obligation. Briscoes argue the lease agreement was not invalid because the promise to pay rent in the amount of eighteen cents per ton of rock sold from the quarry during the preceding month was not an illusory promise in that they, as

lessees, were legally obligated to exercise good faith and use reasonable efforts to mine and sell the rock.

Magruder argues that the lease was null and void because it did not obligate the Briscoes to do anything, or in other words, that it was within their power not to mine any rock, thereby relieving them of any duty to pay rent to Magruder. Magruder contends the lease is invalid due to a lack of consideration rendering the promise illusory.

The phrase "illusory promise" means "words in promissory form that promise nothing." CORBIN ON CONTRACTS § 5.28. An illusory promise is not a promise at all and cannot act as consideration; therefore no contract is formed. The tendency of the law, however, is to uphold the contract by finding the promise was not illusory when it appears that the parties intended a contract. "Frequently a court will find an apparently illusory promise to be accompanied by an implied promise to use 'best efforts' or 'reasonable efforts.'" Consequently, an implied obligation to use good faith is enough to avoid finding a contract null and void due to an illusory promise. Such is the case here.

Justice Cardozo—in his famed opinion of *Wood v. Lucy, Lady Duff-Gordon*—articulated the theory of implied covenants of good faith and reasonable efforts. 118 N.E. 214, 215 (N.Y. 1917). Cardozo stated that even though the plaintiff did not promise in so many words to use reasonable efforts to market defendant's designs, "such a promise is fairly to be implied. ... A promise may be lacking, and yet the whole writing may be 'instinct with an obligation,' imperfectly expressed. If that is so, there is [an enforceable] contract." In Missouri, the covenants of good faith and fair dealing are implied in every contract. *Home Shopping Club, Inc. v. Roberts Broadcasting Co.*, 989 S.W.2d 174,179 (Mo. App. 1998). ... Although the lease does not in express terms provide that Briscoes must mine and sell the limestone, such an obligation must be implied. In fact, Briscoes did mine and sell the rock and paid Magruder rent pursuant to the terms of the lease for almost one year before Magruder claimed the contract was void.

3. **"Exclusive Dealing Contracts".** In *Wood v. Lucy*, Justice Cardozo found: "[Duff-Gordon] gave an exclusive privilege. She was to have no right for at least a year to place her own indorsements or market her own designs except through the agency of [Wood]. The acceptance of the exclusive agency was an assumption of its duties." Here, it is sufficient to know that the parties formed an "exclusive dealings" contract. Section 2-306 of the UCC governs the

formation, interpretation, and enforcement of exclusive dealings, output, and requirements contracts involving the sale of goods. In PART II of this text, these concepts are discussed more fully.

D. Pleas: "Want of Consideration" and "Failure of Consideration"

Batsakis v. Demotsis
226 S.W.2d 673
(Tex. Civ. App.—El Paso 1949)

George Batsakis sued Eugenia The. Demotsis to recover amount alleged to be due on instrument executed by the parties when they were residents of Greece.

McGill, Justice. This is an appeal from a judgment of the 57th judicial District Court of Bexar County. Appellant was plaintiff and appellee was defendant in the trial court. The parties will be so designated.

[George Batsakis] sued [Eugenia Demotsis] to recover $2,000 with interest at the rate of 8% per annum from April 2, 1942, alleged to be due on the following instrument, being a translation from the original, which is written in the Greek language:

> Peiraeus
>
> April 2, 1942
>
> Mr. George Batsakis
>
> Konstantinou Diadohou #7
>
> Peiraeus
>
> Mr. Batsakis:
>
> I state by my present (letter) that I received today from you the amount of two thousand dollars ($2,000.00) of United States of America money, which I borrowed from you for the support of my family during these difficult days and because it is impossible for me to transfer dollars of my own from America.
>
> The above amount I accept with the expressed promise that I will return to you again in American dollars either at the end of the present war or even before in the event that you might be able to find a way to collect them (dollars) from my representative in America to whom I shall write and give him an order relative to this You understand until the final execution (payment) to the above amount an eight per cent interest will be added and paid together with the principal.
>
> I thank you and I remain yours with respects.

The recipient,

(Signed) Eugenia The. Demotsis.

Trial to the court without the intervention of a jury resulted in a judgment in favor of plaintiff for $750.00 principal, and interest at the rate of 8% per annum from April 2, 1942 to the date of judgment, totaling $1163.83, with interest thereon at the rate of 8% per annum until paid. Plaintiff has perfected his appeal.

The court sustained certain special exceptions of plaintiff to defendant's first amended original answer on which the case was tried, and struck therefrom paragraphs II, III and V. Defendant excepted to such action of the court, but has not cross-assigned error here. The answer, stripped of such paragraphs, consisted of a general denial contained in paragraph I thereof, and of paragraph IV, which is as follows:

> IV. That under the circumstances alleged in Paragraph II of this answer, the consideration upon which said written instrument sued upon by plaintiff herein is founded, is wanting and has failed to the extent of $1975.00, and defendant pleads specially under the verification hereinafter made the want and failure of consideration stated, and now tenders, as defendant has heretofore tendered to plaintiff, $25.00 as the value of the loan of money received by defendant from plaintiff, together with interest thereon.
>
> Further, in connection with this plea of want and failure of consideration defendant alleges that she at no time received from plaintiff himself or from anyone for plaintiff any money or thing of value other than, as hereinbefore alleged, the original loan of 500,000 drachmae. That at the time of the loan by plaintiff to defendant of said 500,000 drachmae the value of 500,000 drachmae in the Kingdom of Greece in dollars of money of the United States of America, was $25.00, and also at said time the value of 500,000 drachmae of Greek money in the United States of America in dollars was $25.00 of money of the United States of America. The plea of want and failure of consideration is verified by defendant as follows.

The allegations in paragraph II which were stricken, referred to in paragraph IV, were that the instrument sued on was signed and delivered in the Kingdom of Greece on or about April 2, 1942, at which time both plaintiff and defendant were residents of and residing in the Kingdom of Greece, and

> *Plaintiff [sic]* (emphasis ours) avers that on or about April 2, 1942 she owned money States of America, but was then and there States of America, but was then and there in the Kingdom of Greece in straitened financial circumstances

> due to the conditions produced by World War II and could not make use of her money and property and credit existing in the United States of America. That in the circumstances the plaintiff agreed to and did lend to defendant the sum of 500,000 drachmae, which at that time, on or about April 2, 1942, had the value of $25.00 in money of the United States of America. That the said plaintiff, knowing defendant's financial distress and desire to return to the United States of America, exacted of her the written instrument plaintiff sues upon, which was a promise by her to pay to him the sum of $2,000.00 of United States of America money.'

Plaintiff specially excepted to paragraph IV because the allegations thereof were insufficient to allege either want of consideration or failure of consideration, in that it affirmatively appears therefrom that defendant received what was agreed to be delivered to her, and that plaintiff breached no agreement. The court overruled this exception, and such action is assigned as error. Error is also assigned because of the court's failure to enter judgment for the whole unpaid balance of the principal of the instrument with interest as therein provided.

Defendant testified that she did receive 500,000 drachmas from plaintiff. It is not clear whether she received all the 500,000 drachmas or only a portion of them before she signed the instrument in question. Her testimony clearly shows that the understanding of the parties was that plaintiff would give her the 500,000 drachmas if she would sign the instrument. She testified:

> Q. … who suggested the figure of $2,000.00?
>
> A. That was how he asked me from the beginning. He said he will give me five hundred thousand drachmas provided I signed that I would pay him $2,000.00 American money.

The transaction amounted to a sale by plaintiff of the 500,000 drachmas in consideration of the execution of the instrument sued on, by defendant. It is not contended that the drachmas had no value. Indeed, the judgment indicates that the trial court placed a value of $750.00 on them or on the other consideration which plaintiff gave defendant for the instrument if he believed plaintiff's testimony. Therefore the plea of want of consideration was unavailing. A plea of want of consideration amounts to a contention that the instrument never became a valid obligation in the first place. *National Bank of Commerce v. Williams*, 125 Tex. 619, 84 S.W.2d 691.

Mere inadequacy of consideration will not void a contract. 10 TEX. JUR., CONTRACTS, § 89, at 150; *Chastain v. Texas Christian Missionary Society*, Tex. Civ. App., 78 S.W.2d 728, loc. cit. 731(3), wr. ref.

Nor was the plea of failure of consideration availing. Defendant got exactly what she contracted for according to her own testimony. The court should have rendered judgment in favor of plaintiff against defendant for the principal sum of $2,000.00 evidenced by the instrument sued on, with interest as therein provided. We construe the provision relating to interest as providing for interest at the rate of 8% per annum. The judgment is reformed so as to award appellant a recovery against appellee of $2,000.00 with interest thereon at the rate of 8% per annum from April 2, 1942. Such judgment will bear interest at the rate of 8% per annum until paid on $2,000.00 thereof and on the balance interest at the rate of 6% per annum. As so reformed, the judgment is affirmed.

Reformed and affirmed.

NOTES AND QUESTIONS

1. **Plea of Want of Consideration and the Requisite "Mutuality of Obligation"**. *See Cheung-Loon, LLC v. Cergon, Inc.*, 2012 WL 1678105, *7 (Tex. App.—Dallas May 15, 2012) ("We first note that a *want or lack of consideration* is different from a failure of consideration. A lack of consideration occurs when a contract, *at its inception*, does not impose obligations on both parties. Without *a mutuality of obligation*, a contract is unenforceable. In contrast, a failure of consideration occurs when, because of some supervening cause arising after the contract is formed, the promised performance fails.") (emphasis added).

2. **Plea of Failure of Consideration and the Requisite "Mutuality of Obligation" or "Mutual Promises".** *See Teter v. Glass Onion, Inc.*, 723 F. Supp. 2d 1138, 1159 (W.D. Mo. 2010) ("Consideration is found where both parties have *obligated* themselves by *mutual promises* that impose some legal duty or liability on each promisor. 'If, on the other hand, plaintiffs have not bound themselves to such an obligation by a promise on their part, ... there is a *failure of consideration*.") (emphasis added).

3. **The "Mutuality Doctrine" and Its Problems**. A review of the Ohio court's analysis in *Helle v. Landmark, Inc.*, 472 N.E.2d 765, 776–77 (Ohio Ct. App. 1984) explains why the "mutuality of obligation" concept clouds principles of contract law and generates a considerable amount of confusion:

In the case *sub judice*, the trial court found that lack of mutuality of obligation, and the related doctrine of illusory promise, precluded the creation of an *enforceable* contract. ... Stripped to its essence, the concept of "mutuality of obligation" expresses the idea that "both parties to the contract must be bound or neither is bound." However, this formulation applies only to an analysis of *bilateral contracts*, in which reciprocal promises are exchanged. Unilateral contracts, almost by definition, are not amenable to the "mutuality" doctrine. *See* 1 RESTATEMENT OF CONTRACTS § 79, at 203

"The modern decisional tendency is against lending the aid of courts to defeat contracts on technical grounds of want of mutuality." *Texas Gas Utilities Co. v. Barrett*, 460 S.W.2d 409, 412 (Tex. 1970). As a contract defense, the mutuality doctrine has become a faltering rampart to which a litigant retreats at his own peril. Under contemporary analysis of unilateral contracts, the "mutuality" doctrine crumbles of its own weight.

Hence, recent authority portends a decisive shift to a more radical (i.e., more fundamental) approach. This approach treats the "mutuality of obligation" doctrine as requiring only a *quid pro quo*. Thus understood, a unilateral contract lacks "mutuality" only when there is *a failure of consideration*. *See* 1 RESTATEMENT OF CONTRACTS § 79, at 200 ("If the requirement of consideration is met, there is no additional requirement of ... 'mutuality of obligation.'"). *See also Toussaint v. Blue Cross & Blue Shield of Michigan*, 292 N.W.2d 880, 885 (Mich. 1980) ("The *enforceability of a contract* depends ... on consideration and not mutuality of obligation. The proper inquiry is whether the employee has given consideration for the employer's promise of ... [benefit]."); and, *Pine River State Bank v. Mettille*, (Minn. 1983), 333 N.W.2d 622, 629 (Minn. 1983) ("[T]he concept of mutuality [of obligation] in contract law has been widely discredited.")

In the case of a unilateral contract, as here, the promisor's offer is accepted by the promisee's performance rather than by a return promise to perform. Consequently, when the promisee's performance is executed, *enforceable obligations arise* without more. Under this analysis, ... [the] appellants' continued employment—as the bargained-for-consideration—rendered the contract to pay severance benefits enforceable, regardless of "mutuality" or a lack thereof.

E. Past Consideration and Moral Consideration

This chapter has devoted a lot of paper and ink—distinguishing bargained-for consideration from a "mere gratuity," discussing major differences between the bargained-for-exchange and promissory-estoppel doctrines, outlining the dissimilarities between "want of consideration" and "failure of consideration" pleas, and explaining the distinctions between "adequate consideration" and "legally sufficient consideration." In light of the numerous and complex "consideration" rules, why not dispense with all of them and craft two simple rules? We would call the first principle Rule A, or the "first-party beneficiary rule." It would read:

> If JR performs for or delivers a benefit to MO without MO's consent, JR has formed an implied-in-law contract or promise with MO. Therefore, as a matter of law, MO must compensate JR within a timely manner.

Quite simply, Rule A would force MO to compensate JR when MO is the direct beneficiary of JR's non-negotiated benefits or performance. On the other hand, the second rule would impose a different burden on MO when MO is an *indirect* beneficiary of JR's performance or benefits. Rule B or the "third-party beneficiary rule" would state:

> If MO and AL have an interdependent relationship—familial, fiduciary, or financial—and JR performs for or delivers a benefit to AL with or without MO's consent, MO has a moral obligation to compensate JR. As a matter of law, MO must compensate JR within a timely manner.

Again, under Rules A and B, the bargained-for-exchange, promissory-estoppel, change-of-position, and detrimental-reliance doctrines would expire immediately. Now, assume that we renamed Rule A "past consideration" and Rule B "moral obligation." Are Rules A and B fair? Are they efficient and likely to reduce litigation costs?

Explaining the past-consideration doctrine, one commentator wrote:

> Events which occur prior to the making of the promise and not with the purpose of inducing the promise in exchange are viewed as "past consideration" and are the legal equivalent of "no consideration. ... The promisor is making his promise because those events occurred, but he is not making his promise in order to get them. There is no "bargaining" [and] no saying[:] "[I]f you will do this for me I will do that for you."
> 1 A. CORBIN, CORBIN ON CONTRACTS § 210 (1963)

Some courts, however, have invoked the "doctrine of moral obligation" to enforce some promises, which are nothing more than past consideration. The former doctrine is an exception to the latter. *See Manwill v. Oyler*, 361 P.2d 177, 178 (Utah 1961). Briefly stated, some courts apply the "moral obligation" exception if a party rendered services, with an expectation that a first- or third-party beneficiary would eventually pay for the non-negotiated services.

Do you see any hidden or unintended consequences if state supreme courts abandoned all bargained-for-exchange and promissory-estoppel rules and applied only the modified "past consideration" doctrine—Rule A—and the current "moral obligation" doctrine? As you read the next two cases, try to make *arguments against* the universal application of the "past consideration" doctrine and *arguments for* the general application of the "moral obligation" doctrine.

1. Past Consideration Doctrine

DeMentas v. Estate of Tallas
764 P.2d 628
(Utah Ct. App. 1988)

Orme, Judge. Jack Tallas came to the United States, as an immigrant from Greece, in 1914. He lived in Salt Lake City for nearly seventy years, residing at Little America Hotel during the last years of his life. Tallas achieved considerable success in business, primarily as an insurance agent and landlord. Over a period of fourteen years, Peter Dementas, who was a close personal friend of Tallas, rendered at least some assistance to Tallas.

On December 18, 1982, Tallas met with Dementas and dictated a memorandum to him, in Greek, stating that he owed Dementas $50,000 for his help over the years for such things as picking up his mail, driving him to the grocery store, and assisting with the management of Tallas's rental properties. Tallas also indicated in the memorandum that he would change his will to make Dementas an "heir for the sum of $50,000."

Tallas kept the Greek document, retyped it in English, notarized the English version with his own notary seal, and, three days later, delivered the documents to Dementas. Tallas died on February 4, 1983, without changing his will to include Dementas as an "heir." He left a substantial estate. Dementas filed a timely claim for $50,000 with Tallas's estate, pursuant to UTAH CODE ANN. § 75–3–803 (1978). A copy of the memorandum given to him by Tallas was attached to the claim. The estate denied the claim and Dementas brought this action to recover $50,000.

In its pretrial order, the trial court disposed of the issues of *quantum meruit*; a contract to make, change or modify a will; and gift *causa mortis*. The court found, as a matter of law, that the memorandum was at best "an acknowledgment of a previously existing debt resulting from the performance of a previously existing oral contract," and the case proceeded to trial. Following trial, in which the court heard extensive testimony from witnesses and received numerous exhibits, the court concluded that the memorandum was executed by Tallas free from fraud, duress, or undue influence.

However, the court did not find the memorandum to constitute an enforceable contract. Rather, the court found that the memorandum was an expression of Tallas's appreciation for services gratuitously performed by Dementas. The court concluded that the memorandum, both in its Greek and English versions, showed that Tallas intended—at some time in the future—to include Dementas in his will or to otherwise compensate him, but that Tallas failed to complete the transaction prior to his death. The court also ruled that Dementas's "account stated" theory was barred since no such claim was articulated in the notice of claim filed with the estate. Alternatively, the court concluded no "account stated" had been proven.

* * *

The English version of the memorandum, as translated and revised by Tallas, reads exactly as follows:

> Peter K. Dementas, is my best friend I have in this country and since he came to the United States he treats me like a father and I think of him as my own son. I visit his house and have dinner with his family twice a week. He takes me in his car grocery shopping. He drives me to the doctor and has also takes me every week to Bingham to pick up my mail, collect the rents and manage my properties. For all the services Peter has given me all these years, for the use of his automobile, for the money he spent on gasoline and his time, I owe to him the amount of $50,000 (Fifty Thousand Dollars.) I have already mentioned Peter in my will for all the services and love he has offered me during all these years and I will shortly change my will to include him as my heir.
>
> Salt Lake City, Utah
>
> December 18, 1982
>
> Jack G. Tallas

* * *

CONSIDERATION

"A generally accepted definition of consideration is that a legal detriment has been bargained for and exchanged for a promise." *Miller v. Miller*, 664 P.2d 39, 40–41 (Wyo. 1983). "The mere fact that one man promises something to another creates no legal duty and makes no legal remedy available in case of non-performance." 1 A. CORBIN, CORBIN

ON CONTRACTS § 110 (1963). "[A] performance or a returned promise must be bargained for." *Miller v. Miller*, 664 P.2d at 41 (citing RESTATEMENT (SECOND) OF CONTRACTS § 71 at 172 (1981)).

In determining whether consideration to support a personal service contract exists, the focus is not whether the amount promised represents the fair market value for the services rendered. On the contrary, "[a]s a general rule it is settled that any detriment no matter how economically inadequate will support a promise." J. CALAMARI & J. PERILLO, CONTRACTS § 55 at 107 (1970). *See Gasser v. Horne*, 557 P.2d 154, 155 (Utah 1976) ("It has further been held that there is consideration whenever a promisor receives a benefit or where promisee suffers a detriment, however slight.").

Thus, while the estate introduced extensive testimony as to whether the services Dementas claimed to have rendered were actually performed, the court expressly admitted this testimony only insofar as it bore on Dementas's credibility and not to prove that the services were worth less than the amount Tallas promised to pay. While the testimony suggested that Dementas did not actually perform all the services he claimed to have rendered, this testimony had no relevance to the question of whether there was consideration for Tallas's promise since the testimony suggested Dementas did at least some work. In this regard, the court correctly stated: "If Tallas thought it was worth 50,000 bucks to get one ride to Bingham, that's Tallas' decision. ... The only thing you can't do is take it with you."

* * *

PAST CONSIDERATION

Even though the testimony showed that Dementas rendered at least some services for Tallas, the subsequent promise by Tallas to pay $50,000 for services already performed by Dementas is not a promise supported by legal consideration. Events which occur prior to the making of the promise and not with the purpose of inducing the promise in exchange are viewed as "past consideration" and are the legal equivalent of "no consideration." 1 A. CORBIN, CORBIN ON CONTRACTS § 210 (1963). This is so because "[t]he promisor is making his promise because those events occurred, but he is not making his promise in order to get them. There is no 'bargaining'; no saying that if you will do this for me I will do that for you." *See also County of Clark v. Bonanza No. 1*, 615 P.2d 939, 943 (Nev. 1980) ("A benefit conferred or detriment incurred in the past is not adequate consideration for a present bargain.").

This rule can surely work unfair results and has accordingly been criticized and the object of legislation. *See* J. CALAMARI AND J. PERILLO, CONTRACTS §§ 54, 96 (1970). Some courts have sought to enforce promises supported only by past consideration by invoking a "moral obligation" notion to make at least some of these promises enforceable. *See Manwill v. Oyler*, 361 P.2d 177, 178–79 (Utah 1961). Although the "moral obligation" exception has not been embraced in Utah, other courts apply the exception in cases where services rendered in the past were rendered with the expectation of payment rather than gratuitously.

Even if the "moral obligation" doctrine applied in Utah, Dementas would not prevail. The trial court found that the services rendered by Dementas to Tallas were not rendered with the expectation of being compensated, but were performed gratuitously. That finding has not been shown to be erroneous.

* * *

CONCLUSION

Dementas failed to prove there was any valid consideration for Tallas's promise to pay $50,000. Even if the "moral obligation" exception applied in Utah, the court found that the services Dementas performed were rendered without the expectation of payment. ... We acknowledge, as have other courts in disregarding contracts for lack of consideration, that "[appellant] will probably remain convinced [he] should be paid. Nevertheless, [he] failed to meet [his] burden of proof" and "this court will not find a contract where one has not been proved to exist." *Miller v. Miller*, 664 P.2d 39, 43 (Wyo. 1983).

The judgment appealed from is affirmed. ...

2. Moral Obligation Doctrine

Mills v. Wyman
20 Mass. (3 Pick.) 207
(Mass. 1825)

This was an action of *assumpsit* brought to recover a compensation for the board, nursing, &c., of Levi Wyman, son of the defendant (Seth Wyman), from the 5th to the 20th of February, 1821. The plaintiff (Daniel Mills) then lived at Hartford, in Connecticut; the defendant, at Shrewsbury, in this county. Levi Wyman, at the time when the services were rendered, was about 25 years of age, and had long ceased to be a member of his father's family. He was on his return from a voyage at sea, and being suddenly taken sick at Hartford, and being poor and in distress, was relieved by the plaintiff in the manner and to the extent above stated.

On the 24th of February, after all the expenses had been incurred, the defendant wrote a letter to the plaintiff, promising to pay him such expenses. There was no consideration for this promise, except what grew out of the relation which subsisted between Levi Wyman and the defendant. … [Judge] Howe—whom the cause was tried in the Court of Common Pleas—thinking this not sufficient to support the action, directed a nonsuit. To this direction the plaintiff filed exceptions.

The opinion of the Court was read, as drawn up by Parker, C. J.

General rules of law established for the protection and security of honest and fair-minded men, who may inconsiderately make promises without any equivalent, will sometimes screen men of a different character from engagements which they are bound in *foro conscientiæ* to perform. This is a defect inherent in all human systems of legislation. The rule that a mere verbal promise, without any consideration, cannot be enforced by action, is universal in its application, and cannot be departed from to suit particular cases in which a refusal to perform such a promise may be disgraceful.

The promise declared on in this case appears to have been made without any legal consideration. The kindness and services towards the sick son of the defendant were not bestowed at his request. The son was in no respect under the care of the defendant. He was twenty-five years old, and had long left his father's family. On his return from a foreign country, he fell sick among strangers, and the plaintiff acted the part of the good Samaritan, giving him shelter and comfort until he died. The defendant, his father, on being informed of this event, influenced by a transient feeling of gratitude, promises in writing to pay the plaintiff for the expenses he had incurred. But he has determined to break this promise, and is willing to have his case appear on record as a strong example of particular injustice sometimes necessarily resulting from the operation of general rules.

It is said a moral obligation is a sufficient consideration to support an express promise; and some authorities lay down the rule thus broadly; but upon examination of the cases we are satisfied that the universality of the rule cannot be supported, and that there must have been some preexisting obligation, which has become inoperative by positive law, to form a basis for an effective promise. The cases of debts barred by the statute of limitations, of debts incurred by infants, of debts of bankrupts, are generally put for illustration of the rule. Express promises founded on such preexisting equitable obligations may be enforced; there is a good consideration for them; they merely remove an impediment created by law to the recovery of debts honestly due, but which public policy protects the debtors from being compelled to pay.

In all these cases there was originally a *quid pro quo*; and according to the principles of natural justice the party receiving ought to pay; but the legislature has said he shall not be coerced; then comes the promise to pay the debt that is barred, the promise of the man to pay the debt of the infant, of the discharged bankrupt to restore to his creditor what by the law he had lost. In all these cases there is a moral obligation founded upon an antecedent valuable consideration. These promises therefore have a sound legal basis. They are not promises to pay something for nothing; not naked pacts; but the voluntary revival or creation of obligation which before existed in natural law, but which had been dispensed with, not for the benefit of the party obliged solely, but principally for the public convenience.

If moral obligation, in its fullest sense, is a good substratum for an express promise, it is not easy to perceive why it is not equally good to support an implied promise. What a man ought to do, generally he ought to be made to do, whether he promise or refuse. But the law of society has left most of such obligations to the interior forum, as the tribunal of conscience has been aptly called. Is there not a moral obligation upon every son who has become affluent by means of the education and advantages bestowed upon him by his father, to relieve that father from pecuniary embarrassment, to promote his comfort and happiness, and even to share with him his riches, if thereby he will be made happy?

And yet such a son may, with impunity, leave such a father in any degree of penury above that which will expose the community in which he dwells, to the danger of being obliged to preserve him from absolute want. Is not a wealthy father under strong moral obligation to advance the interest of an obedient, well-disposed son, to furnish him with the means of acquiring and maintaining a becoming rank in life, to rescue him from the horrors of debt incurred by misfortune? Yet the law will uphold him in any degree of parsimony, short of that which would reduce his son to the necessity of seeking public charity. ... The general position, that moral obligation is a sufficient consideration for an express promise, is to be limited in its application, to cases where at some time or other a good or valuable consideration has existed.

A legal obligation is always a sufficient consideration to support either an express or an implied promise; such as an infant's debt for necessaries, or a father's promise to pay for the support and education of his minor children. But when the child shall have attained to manhood, and shall have become his own agent in the world's business, the debts he in curs, whatever may be their nature, create no obligation upon the father; and it seems to follow, that his promise founded upon such a debt has no legally binding force.

The cases of instruments under seal and certain mercantile contracts, in which considerations need not be proved, do not contradict the principles above suggested. The first import a consideration in themselves, and the second belong to a branch of the mercantile law, which has found it necessary to disregard the point of consideration in respect to instruments negotiable in their nature and essential to the interests of commerce.

Instead of citing a multiplicity of cases to support the positions I have taken, I will only refer to a very able review of all the cases in the note in 3 Bos. & Pul. 249. The opinions of the judges had been variant for a long course of years upon this subject, but there seems to be no case in which it was nakedly decided, that a promise to pay the debt of a son of full age, not living with his father, though the debt were incurred by sickness which ended in the death of the son, without a previous request by the father proved or presumed, could be enforced by action.

It has been attempted to show a legal obligation on the part of the defendant by virtue of our statute, which compels lineal kindred in the ascending or descending line to support such of their poor relations as are likely to become chargeable to the town where they have their settlement. But it is a sufficient answer to this position that such legal obligation does not exist except in the very cases provided for in the statute, and never until the party charged has been adjudged to be of sufficient ability thereto.

We do not know from the report any of the facts which are necessary to create such an obligation. Whether the deceased had a legal settlement in this commonwealth at the time of his death, whether he was likely to become chargeable had he lived, whether the defendant was of sufficient ability, are essential facts to be adjudicated by the court to which is given jurisdiction on this subject. The legal liability does not arise until these facts have all been ascertained by judgment, after hearing the party intended to be charged. …

For the foregoing reasons we are all of opinion that the nonsuit directed by the Court of Common Pleas was right, and that judgment be entered thereon for costs for the defendant.

NOTES AND QUESTIONS

1. **Statutory Exception to the Common-Law "Past Consideration" Doctrine.** In *Cy Gruberg v. McCarthy*, 289 A.D.2d 915, 735 N.Y.S.2d 638 (N.Y. App. Div. 2001), Gruberg loaned Robert Sanzi $55,000. After an erratic payment history, Robert stopped making payments. Gruberg met with Robert's wife—Ann Marie Sanzi McCarthy—to discuss Robert's default. At the conclusion of their meeting, McCarthy signed a handwritten document that Gruberg drafted. In part, the agreement read:

   I, Ann Marie Sanzi, agree to include my name to legal documents, as wife of Robert Sanzi, and assume financial

> responsibility, for debts incurred on October 7 and October 30, 1985 in two separate loans ... [totaling] $55,000." ... These loans are due and fully payable, with any accrued interest, on October 30, 1995 to [C.Y. Gruberg].

Robert died and McCarthy continued to make interest payments for a year. Eventually, she stopped. Citing the written agreement, Gruberg sued to collect the balance. McCarthy argued that the "past consideration" doctrine precluded the court's enforcing the written guarantee. The appellate court disagreed, citing NEW YORK'S GENERAL OBLIGATIONS LAW §§ 5-701 and 5-1105. That statute reads:

> A promise in writing and signed by the promisor ... shall not be denied effect as a valid contractual obligation on the ground that consideration for the promise is past or executed, if the consideration is expressed in the writing and is proved to have been given or performed and would be a valid consideration but for the time when it was given or performed. GENERAL OBLIGATIONS LAW § 5–1105.

2. **The "Moral Obligation" Doctrine's Perceived Flaw**. In *Manwill v. Oyler*, 361 P.2d 177, 178 (Utah 1961), Justice Crockett suggested the "moral obligation" doctrine contains a logical flaw and stated:

> The difficulty we see with the doctrine is that if a mere moral—as distinguished from a legal—obligation were recognized as valid consideration for a contract that would practically erode to the vanishing point the necessity for finding a consideration. This is so ... because in nearly all circumstances where a promise is made, there is some moral aspect of the situation which provides the motivation for making the promise even if it is to make an outright gift. And second, if we are dealing with moral concepts, the making of a promise itself creates a moral obligation to perform it. It seems obvious that if a contract to be legally enforceable need be anything other than a naked promise, something more than mere moral consideration is necessary.

3. **Consideration and the "Good Samaritan" Rule.** In *Mills v. Wyman*, the learned judge concluded: "[Daniel Mills] acted the part of the good Samaritan, giving [Levi Wyman] shelter and comfort until [Levi] died." Generalizing to all situations, it appears that any "kind" or "compassionate" person—who delivers a benefit, goods, or services to another person—has no legitimate expectation to receive any reimbursement or remuneration. So why do hospitals send bills to persons who were unconscious when they received treatment in an emergency ward?

4. **The "Good Samaritan Doctrine" as an Affirmative Defense to Tort Liability.** In Texas, the Good Samaritan statute provides an affirmative defense against ordinary negligence for persons who administer emergency care, under specified circumstances. TEX. CIV. PRAC. & REM. CODE § 74.001. The Legislature amended the statute, effective September 1, 2003. Acts of June 1, 2003, 78th Leg., R.S., ch. 204, § 10.01, 2003 Tex. Gen. Laws 204. *See also McIntyre v. Ramirez*, 109 S.W.3d 741, 747–48 (Tex. 2003) (declaring that the Good Samaritan statute was enacted to protect persons who respond to an emergency absent a preexisting relationship or duty to respond).

SECTION FOUR: MODIFIED CONTRACTS, THE PREEXISTING DUTY RULE, AND PROOF OF "NEW" CONSIDERATION

Frequently, contracting parties amend or modify their agreements. The reasons are numerous and diverse. Some familiar reasons are 1) the parties face unexpected and adverse market conditions; 2) the parties are precluded from completely financing a planned venture; 3) the financial constraints of new governmental regulations require a modification; 4) one party cannot find enough skilled workers to complete the original undertaking; and 5) one party cannot secure all of the necessary goods, services, leases, easements, or rights to complete a project.

Quite often, when parties modify or try to modify marital, settlement, or debt-forgiveness agreements, dissatisfaction and lawsuits ensue. And the issues presented in courts are: 1) whether a modification was valid; 2) whether consideration supported a valid modified agreement; and 3) whether the consideration was "new" or simply a preexisting duty. The cases and materials in this section cover these questions.

A. The Modification of Marital Contracts

Kuder v. Schroeder
430 S.E.2d 271
(N.C. Ct. App. 1993)

Wells, Judge.... Plaintiff and defendant were married in March of 1978. One child was born to their marriage in June of 1984. After plaintiff and defendant were married, they entered into an oral agreement that plaintiff would forego her career as a veterinarian and would work as a teacher in a local community college to support their family in order that defendant might pursue his undergraduate education at the

University of North Carolina in Chapel Hill. Defendant agreed that upon the completion of his undergraduate studies, he would provide the family's total support, so that plaintiff could then give up her employment and devote her full time to being a wife and mother.

Pursuant to this agreement, plaintiff did work and provide the sole support for their family. Plaintiff and defendant subsequently amended or extended their agreement to allow defendant to obtain a master's degree and a law degree. Following his graduation from law school, defendant was unable to earn sufficient income to fully support the family, but in December of 1989, defendant obtained a position with a law firm which provided him with sufficient income to fully support the family. Three months later—in April of 1990—defendant told plaintiff he no longer loved her and that there was no hope for their marriage; whereupon, the parties separated.

Plaintiff contends that the oral agreement asserted by her in her complaint is a valid and binding contract, entitling her to damages for its breach. Taking plaintiff's allegations as true, we are sympathetic to her apparent dilemma, and certainly would not condone defendant's apparent knavish ingratitude, but we do not find support in the law of this State for such a claim and therefore hold that the trial court correctly dismissed plaintiff's claims.

Under the law of this State, there is a personal duty of each spouse to support the other, a duty arising from the marital relationship, and carrying with it the corollary right to support from the other spouse. *See N.C. Baptist Hospitals v. Harris*, 354 S.E.2d 471 (N.C. 1987). So long as the coverture endures, this duty of support may not be abrogated or modified by the agreement of the parties to a marriage. *See Ritchie v. White*, 35 S.E.2d 414 (N.C. 1945). *See also generally* Lee, N.C. FAMILY LAW, §§ 16.4 and 183 (4th ed. 1980).

Plaintiff's reliance on our decision in *Suggs v. Norris*, 364 S.E.2d 159 (N.C. App.), *cert. denied*, 370 S.E.2d 236 (N.C. 1988) is misplaced. In that case, we sanctioned a claim for remuneration for services performed in a business (farming) enterprise by a person who was cohabiting with, but not married to, a deceased cohabitor. The facts and ruling in that case are in no sense relevant to the facts and issues presented in the case now before us.

For the reasons stated, the trial court's order must be and is affirmed.

* * *

Greene Judge, dissenting.

I agree with the majority, but for a different reason, that the trial court correctly dismissed plaintiff's breach of contract action. I, however, would reverse the trial court's dismissal of plaintiff's claim for unjust enrichment.

I reiterate the allegations of plaintiff's complaint in order to provide a fuller appreciation of the facts at issue. Plaintiff and defendant were married on 17 March 1978, in Sanford, North Carolina. On 19 June 1984, the parties' only child was born. During the entire course of the marriage, plaintiff, a veterinarian, worked as a teacher at a local community college. She provided total financial support for the family.

Upon their marriage, plaintiff and defendant agreed that plaintiff would remain in her teaching position in order to ensure a steady source of income for the family while defendant returned to school full-time to complete his undergraduate education at the University of North Carolina. Plaintiff also agreed that she would have only one child while defendant was in school. In return, defendant agreed that he would provide the family's total financial support upon the completion of his undergraduate studies, at which time plaintiff could achieve her goal of becoming a full-time wife and mother. Pursuant to this agreement, plaintiff taught and provided the family's sole source of income, including the income for defendant's education, with the expectation that she would soon be able to remain at home and raise a family.

Defendant obtained his undergraduate degree as planned; however, defendant decided upon graduation that he wanted to earn a Master's degree as well. The parties decided to extend their original agreement for a period which would allow defendant to achieve this goal. After two years, however, defendant discontinued his efforts to obtain a Master's degree and decided instead to enroll in law school at UNC. Again, the parties extended their original agreement in order to allow defendant to complete law school. Plaintiff continued to work and provide all of the family's income. Defendant continued to devote his time to completing his education.

Upon graduation from law school, defendant told plaintiff that, instead of entering the private practice of law, he wanted to start his own legal research business. The parties, plaintiff reluctantly, once more extended their original agreement, with plaintiff continuing to work in order to ensure a steady income for the family until defendant's business became profitable. Plaintiff, who by this time had reached the age of forty, also agreed to forego having more children. In his first two years of self-employment, defendant failed to earn enough money to fully support the family.

In December, 1989, defendant obtained a position with a law firm in Charlotte, North Carolina, with a starting salary of approximately $38,000.00 per year. For the first time during eleven years of marriage, defendant was able to provide total financial support for the family. Three months later, however, in April, 1990, defendant told plaintiff that he no longer loved her and that there was no hope for their marriage, and the parties separated.

BREACH OF CONTRACT

I agree with the majority that arising out of the marital relationship there is the equal duty of each spouse to support the other spouse, and that a spouse may not recover for support provided in the discharge of the duties imposed by the marital status. It has long been observed by our Courts, however, that a husband and wife are free to contract for the performance of services or the rendering of support outside those duties. *See Dorsett v. Dorsett*, 111 S.E. 541, 542 (N.C. 1922) (wife entitled to compensation where, pursuant to an agreement with her husband, she renders services outside the home); *accord Ritchie v. White*, 35 S.E.2d 414, 417 (N.C. 1945); **see also** N.C.G.S. § 52-10 (1991) (contracts between husband and wife not inconsistent with public policy are valid). In my opinion, the type of support furnished by plaintiff in the instant case is outside the scope of the marital duty of support as recognized by our Courts. Therefore, plaintiff and defendant were not precluded from entering, as husband and wife, into the agreement at issue.

Even assuming, as the majority apparently does, that plaintiff's contribution to defendant's educational endeavors falls within her spousal duty of support, I question the continued validity of the rule that the duty of support arising out of the marital relationship cannot be modified by the agreement of the parties. Our Legislature currently recognizes the validity of contracts which modify or abrogate the marital duty of support, provided that such contracts are entered into before marriage and are in contemplation of marriage, or are entered into upon separation of the parties. *See* N.C.G.S. § 52B-1 et seq. (1987); N.C.G.S. § 52-10.1 (1991).

Parties are also permitted before, during, or after marriage to provide in a written agreement for distribution of marital property in a manner deemed by the parties to be equitable. N.C.G.S. § 50-20(d) (Supp. 1992). Moreover, our Courts recognize the validity of an agreement of the type at issue provided that the parties to such agreement are unmarried cohabiting partners. *See Suggs v. Norris*, 364 S.E.2d 159 (N.C.), *cert. denied*, 370 S.E.2d 236 (N.C. 1988) (citing *Marvin v. Marvin*, 557 P.2d 106 (Cal. 1976)).

I find it incongruous that, given a cohabiting partner on the one hand and a spouse on the other hand, both of whom pursuant to an agreement provide total financial support for their partner in order for that partner to obtain a degree, an advanced degree, or a professional license with the expectation that both parties would benefit therefrom, upon the dissolution of the relationship, the cohabiting partner is entitled to compensation for such contribution to the educational achievements of his partner, but a spouse who made the same contribution is not. I am at a loss to understand the "public policy" supporting such a rule.

In the instant case, I agree with the majority that the trial court properly dismissed plaintiff's claim for breach of contract, but for a different reason. It is a basic principle of contract law that, even if the parties intend to contract, an agreement which is not reasonably certain as to its material terms is indefinite and will not be—because it cannot be—enforced by our Courts. ... Generally, "material terms" include such items as subject matter, price, payment terms, quantity, quality, duration, time and place of performance, and so forth.

A review of the allegations in plaintiff's amended complaint relating to the terms of her alleged express oral contract with defendant, taken as true, reveals the agreement's pervasive and fatal lack of definiteness. Among other things, plaintiff fails to allege that the parties agreed on any specific time period during which defendant was to complete his various educational efforts and plaintiff was to begin her pursuit as a full-time wife and mother. Nor is there any mention of the intended duration of plaintiff's role as full-time wife and mother.

In addition, the parties never agreed on what amount of financial support plaintiff was obligated to provide for the parties' living expenses while defendant was in school or for defendant's educational expenses. Likewise, the complaint fails to allege the amount of financial support defendant was expected to provide once the parties switched breadwinner roles. Therefore, I would affirm the trial court's order dismissing this claim. *See Pyeatte v. Pyeatte*, 661 P.2d 196 (Ariz. App. 1983). Even though plaintiff's contract claim was properly dismissed, however, I believe that the trial court erred in dismissing plaintiff's claim for unjust enrichment, an issue which the majority fails to address. ...

WYNN, Judge, concurring. ... I concur fully in the majority opinion and write separately to point out that the law provides different protection for married couples and unmarried cohabitants, and to address the issue of unjust enrichment, on which the dissenting opinion invites comment.

First, the dissent submits that there is something incongruous in allowing an unmarried but cohabiting partner to enter into a valid contract regarding the support of the other partner, but not affording a married partner this same privilege. The marital relationship is bestowed special protections by the laws of North Carolina, protections that a cohabiting partner cannot claim. These include, for example: the right to have property held as tenants by the entireties, N.C. GEN. STAT. § 39-13.6 (1984); the right, upon the death of one's spouse, to dissent from an unfavorable bequest in the deceased's will, in favor of a larger portion of the estate, N.C. GEN. STAT. § 30-1 (1992); an entitlement to a year's allowance upon the death of one's spouse, N.C. GEN. STAT. § 30-15 (1992); and numerous rights arising from the dissolution of the marital relationship that are not available to a cohabiting partner when his or her relationship comes to an end. *See generally* N.C. GEN. STAT. Chapter 50 (1987, Supp. 1992).

Quite simply, the rules are different for married couples. *See Ritchie v. White*, 453, 35 S.E.2d 414, 416 (N.C. 1945) (the moment the marriage relation comes into existence certain rights and duties spring into being). The dissent chooses to focus on one aspect of the law which does not grant a married person the same privilege as an otherwise similarly situated unmarried cohabitant in an effort to illustrate that the married couple is unduly restrained by our laws. The fact that the law does not allow a married couple to contract regarding spousal support, however, is not indicative of a general trend in the law to deprive married individuals of otherwise valid legal rights.

NOTES AND QUESTIONS

1. **General Rule—Varied, Modified, Waived, or Annulled Written Contracts.** In *Fast v. Kahan*, 481 P.2d 958, 691 (Kan. 1971), the Kansas Supreme Court declared:

   > It is well settled that the terms of a written contract may be varied, modified, waived, annulled or wholly set aside by any subsequently executed contract, whether such subsequently executed contract be in parol or in writing. One party to a contract cannot unilaterally change the terms thereof. Modification requires the assent of all the parties to the contract. Their mutual assent is as much a requisite in effecting a modification as it is in the initial creation of a contract. Mutual assent may not only be shown by an express agreement, but also may be implied from the circumstances and conduct of the parties. In either case, however, there must be a meeting of the minds with respect to the proposed modification.

2. **General Rule—"New Consideration" Must Support a Modified Contract**. Again, consideration may be a benefit for a promisor or a detriment to the promisee. But generally, an agreement to modify a contract must be supported by independent consideration or "new consideration." *See Block v. Fedak*, 499 P.2d 1052, 1054 (Kan. 1972).

3. **Exception—"New Consideration" Not Required to Enforce a Modified Contract**. As we have discovered, proof of "new consideration" is generally required to enforce a modified contract. *See Recker v. Gustafson*, 279 N.W.2d 744, 759 (Iowa 1979).

However, proof of "new consideration" is not always necessary. IOWA CODE § 554.2209(1) (1999) reads: "An agreement modifying a contract within this Article needs no consideration to be binding." Furthermore, parties do not always anticipate all circumstances which may affect or undermine their contractual agreements. Consequently, their contract must be modified. If a modification is "fair and equitable" in light of new realities, a modified contract may be enforced even if "new" consideration is absent. *See Quigley v. Wilson*, 474 N.W.2d 277, 280 (Iowa Ct. App. 1991).

4. **Exception Under the RESTATEMENT (SECOND) OF CONTRACTS § 89 (1981)**. It reads:

   A promise modifying a duty under a contract not fully performed on either side is binding

   (a) if the modification is fair and equitable in view of circumstances not anticipated by the parties when the contract was made; or

   (b) to the extent provided by statute; or

   (c) to the extent that justice requires enforcement in view of material change of position in reliance on the promise.

5. **The Preexisting Duty Rule and Modified Contracts.** Generally, a preexisting duty may not serve as "new consideration" for either a modified contract or an entirely new contractual agreement between the parties. *See California Grocers Assn. v. Bank of America*, 22 Cal. App. 4th 205, 219 (Cal. Ct. App. 1994) ("[The general rule in California is] that consideration cannot consist of the promise to perform a preexisting duty owed to a third person.").

PROBLEM

Black Enterprise Magazine (BEM) asked James Vanderzee—the renowned photographer—to take pictures of Roy Hargrove. Hargrove is the celebrated American jazz trumpeter who has two Grammy Awards. BEM decided to write an extensive article about Hargrove and they wanted pictures of the trumpeter while he visited his birthplace in Waco, Texas. Vanderzee took 100 photos. BEM used several; however, all photos remained Vanderzee's property. In the course of events, Essence Magazine decided to write an article about Roy Hargrove. Learning about Vanderzee's photos, an Essence agent telephoned Vanderzee and they discussed the photos. The agent instructed Vanderzee to send all of the "Hargrove negatives" to Essence's photo editors. Vanderzee accepted the offer. The parties also agreed that Essence would "pay the space rate for any photos that were used in the article: $250/picture up to page, $600/picture up to ¼ page, $900/picture up to ½ page, $1200/picture up to 1/8 page, $2750/picture up to a full picture, and $3500 for [a] full cover." Vanderzee agreed. In fact, "he was ecstatic."

For unknown reasons, Essence did not publish the "Hargrove Story." Furthermore, Essence did not use Vanderzee's photos and did not return the negatives. Ultimately, Vanderzee filed a breach-of-contract action against Essence. According to Vanderzee, Essence breached the following written contract—"Delivery Memorandum of Understanding"—which accompanied the negatives. It reads in pertinent part:

> The negatives and transparencies (hereafter "photographs") may be held for fifteen (15) days. Unless a longer period of time is requested and granted by James Vanderzee (hereinafter "JV") in writing, a late fee of twenty dollars ($20.00) per week for each transparency or negative and thirty dollars ($30.00) per week for each color print will be charged commencing the 15th day and continuing until the items' return. …
>
> The monetary damage for loss or damage of an original transparency or negative shall be determined by the value of each individual photograph. Recipient agrees, however, that the reasonable minimum value of such lost or damaged photograph shall be no less than twenty-five hundred dollars ($2500). JV agrees to deliver the goods herein only upon the express covenant and understanding by Recipient … that the terms contained in this Paragraph "4" are material to this agreement. Recipient assumes full liability for its employees, agents, assigns, messengers and freelance researchers for the Loss, damage or misuse of the photographs.

James Vanderzee argued that the Delivery Memo was a valid contract and Essence was liable for the unreturned negatives. In response, Essence argued that Delivery Memo is unenforceable, either as an original written contract, or as a modification of the "initial oral, over-the-telephone contract." Is the Memo a written confirmation of an existing oral contract? Is the Memo a modification of the oral contract? Assume that the Memo is a modification. Is it enforceable?

B. Contract Modification, Consideration, and the Preexisting Duty Doctrine

Alaska Packers' Ass'n v. Domenico 117 F. 99 (9th Cir. 1909)

Oss, Circuit Judge. The libel in this case was based upon a contract alleged to have been entered into between the libelants and the appellant corporation on the 22d day of May, 1900, at Pyramid Harbor, Alaska, by which it is claimed the appellant promised to pay each of the libelants, among other things, the sum of $100 for services rendered and to be rendered. In its answer the respondent denied the execution, on its part, of the contract sued upon, averred that it was without consideration, and for a third defense alleged that the work performed by the libelants for it was performed under other and different contracts than that sued on, and that, prior to the filing of the libel, each of the libelants was paid by the respondent the full amount due him thereunder, in consideration of which each of them executed a full release of all his claims and demands against the respondent.

The evidence shows without conflict that on March 26, 1900, at the city and county of San Francisco, the libelants entered into a written contract with the appellants, whereby they agreed to go from San Francisco to Pyramid Harbor, Alaska, and return, on board such vessel as might be designated by the appellant, and to work for the appellant during the fishing season of 1900, at Pyramid Harbor, as sailors and fishermen, agreeing to do "regular ship's duty, both up and down, discharging and loading; and to do any other work whatsoever when requested to do so by the captain or agent of the Alaska Packers' Association." By the terms of this agreement, the appellant was to pay each of the libelants $50 for the season, and two cents for each red salmon in the catching of which he took part.

On the 15th day of April 1900, 21 of the libelants signed shipping articles by which they shipped as seamen on the *Two Brothers*, a vessel chartered by the appellant for the voyage between San Francisco and Pyramid Harbor, and also bound themselves to perform the same work for the appellant provided for by the previous contract of March 26th; the appellant agreeing to pay them therefor the sum of $60 for the season, and two cents each for each red salmon in the catching of which they should respectively take part.

Under these contracts, the libelants sailed on board the *Two Brothers* for Pyramid Harbor, where the appellants had about $150,000 invested in a salmon cannery. The libelants arrived there early in April of the year mentioned, and began to unload the vessel and fit up the cannery. A few days thereafter, to wit, May 19th, they stopped work in a body, and demanded of the company's superintendent there in charge $100 for services in operating the vessel to and from Pyramid Harbor, instead of the sums stipulated for in and by the contracts; stating that unless they were paid this additional wage they would stop work entirely, and return to San Francisco.

The evidence showed, and the court below found, that it was impossible for the appellant to get other men to take the places of the libelants, the place being remote, the season short and just opening; so that, after endeavoring for several days without success to induce the libelants to proceed with their work in accordance with their contracts, the company's superintendent, on the 22d day of May, so far yielded to their demands as to instruct his clerk to copy the contracts executed in San Francisco, including the words "Alaska Packers' Association" at the end, substituting, for the $50 and $60 payments, respectively, of those contracts.

[T]he sum of $100, which document, so prepared, was signed by the libelants before a shipping commissioner whom they had requested to be brought from Northeast Point; the superintendent, however, testifying that he at the time told the libelants that he was without authority to enter into any such contract, or to in any way alter the contracts made between them and the company in San Francisco.

Upon the return of the libelants to San Francisco at the close of the fishing season, they demanded pay in accordance with the terms of the alleged contract of May 22d, when the company denied its validity, and refused to pay other than as provided for by the contracts of March 26th and April 5th, respectively.

Some of the libelants, at least, consulted counsel, and, after receiving his advice, those of them who had signed the shipping articles before the shipping commissioner at San Francisco went before that officer, and received the amount due them thereunder, executing in consideration thereof a release in full, and the others paid at the office of the company, also receipting in full for their demands.

On the trial in the court below, the libelants undertook to show that the fishing nets provided by the respondent were defective, and that it was on that account that they demanded increased wages. On that point, the evidence was substantially conflicting, and the finding of the court was against the libelants the court saying:

> The contention of libelants is that the nets provided them were rotten and unserviceable is not sustained by the evidence. The defendants' interest required that libelants should be provided with every facility necessary to their success as fishermen, for on such success depended the profits defendant would be able to realize that season from its packing plant, and the large capital invested therein. In view of this

> self-evident fact, it is highly improbable that the defendant gave libelants rotten and unserviceable nets with which to fish. It follows from this finding that libelants were not justified in refusing performance of their original contract. 112 Fed. 554.

The evidence being sharply conflicting in respect to these facts, the conclusions of the court, who heard and saw the witnesses, will not be disturbed.

The real questions in the case as brought here are questions of law, and, in the view that we take of the case, it will be necessary to consider but one of those. Assuming that the appellant's superintendent at Pyramid Harbor was authorized to make the alleged contract of May 22d, and that he executed it on behalf of the appellant, was it supported by a sufficient consideration?

From the foregoing statement of the case, it will have been seen that the libelants agreed in writing, for certain stated compensation, to render their services to the appellant in remote waters where the season for conducting fishing operations is extremely short, and in which enterprise the appellant had a large amount of money invested; and, after having entered upon the discharge of their contract, and at a time when it was impossible for the appellant to secure other men in their places, the libelants, without any valid cause, absolutely refused to continue the services they were under contract to perform unless the appellant would consent to pay them more money.

Consent to such a demand, under such circumstances, if given, was, in our opinion, without consideration, for the reason that it was based solely upon the libelants' agreement to render the exact services, and none other, that they were already under contract to render. The case shows that they willfully and arbitrarily broke that obligation. As a matter of course, they were liable to the appellant in damages, and it is quite probable, as suggested by the court below in its opinion, that they may have been unable to respond in damages. But we are unable to agree with the conclusions there drawn, from these facts, in these words:

> Under such circumstances, it would be strange, indeed, if the law would not permit the defendant to waive the damages caused by the libelants' breach, and enter into the contract sued upon,—a contract mutually beneficial to all the parties thereto, in that it gave to the libelants reasonable compensation for their labor, and enabled the defendant to employ to advantage the large capital it had invested in its canning and fishing plant.

Certainly, it cannot be justly held, upon the record in this case, that there was any voluntary waiver on the part of the appellant of the breach of the original contract. The company itself knew nothing of such breach until the expedition returned to San Francisco, and the testimony is uncontradicted that its superintendent at Pyramid Harbor, who, it is claimed, made on its behalf the contract sued on, distinctly informed the libelants that he had no power to alter the original or to make a new contract, and it would, of course, follow that, if he had no power to change the original, he would have no authority to waive any rights thereunder. The circumstances of the present case bring it, we think, directly within the sound and just observations of the supreme court of Minnesota in the case of *King v. Railway Co.*, 61 Minn. 482, 63 N.W. 1105:

> No astute reasoning can change the plain fact that the party who refuses to perform, and thereby coerces a promise from the other party to the contract to pay him an increased compensation for doing that which he is legally bound to do, takes an unjustifiable advantage of the necessities of the other party. Surely it would be a travesty on justice to hold that the party so making the promise for extra pay was estopped from asserting that the promise was without consideration. A party cannot lay the foundation of an estoppel by his own wrong, where the promise is simply a repetition of a subsisting legal promise. There can be no consideration for the promise of the other party, and there is no warrant for inferring that the parties have voluntarily rescinded or modified their contract. The promise cannot be legally enforced, although the other party has completed his contract in reliance upon it.

* * *

The Supreme Court of Vermont in … *Cobb v. Cowdery*, 40 Vt. 25, 94 Am. Dec. 370 … held that:

> A promise by a party to do what he is bound in law to do is not an illegal consideration, but is the same as no consideration at all, and is merely void; in other words, it is insufficient, but not illegal. Thus, if the master of a ship promise his crew an addition to their fixed wages in consideration for and as an incitement to, their extraordinary exertions during a storm, or in any other emergency of the voyage, this promise is *nudum pactum*; the voluntary performance of an act which it was before legally incumbent on the party to perform being in law an insufficient consideration; and so it would be in any other case where the only consideration for the promise of one party was the promise of the other party to do, or his actual doing, something which he was previously bound in law to do.

The Massachusetts cases cited by the court below in support of its judgment commence with the case of Munroe v. Perkins, 9 Pick. 305, 20 Am. Dec. 475, which really seems to be the foundation of all of the cases in support of that view. In that case, the plaintiff had agreed in writing to erect a building for the defendants. Finding his contract a losing one, he had concluded to abandon it, and resumed work on the oral contract of the defendants that, if he would do so, they would pay him what the work was worth without regard to the terms of the original contract. The court said that whether the oral contract was without consideration. ...

It results from the views above expressed that the judgment must be reversed, and the cause remanded, with directions to the court below to enter judgment for the respondent, with costs. It is so ordered.

NOTES AND QUESTIONS

1. **Shipping Articles and Proof of Consideration**. In *Alaska Packers*, the Ninth Circuit found: "On the 15th day of April 1900, 21 of the libelants signed shipping articles by which they shipped as seamen on the *Two Brothers*." What are "shipping articles"?

2. **Shipping Articles, Pre-Voyage Contracts, Preexisting Duty, and Seamen's Compensation**. When the *Two Brothers* vessel sailed in 1900, the 1790 Act of Congress governed the employment and compensation of seaman. The relevant sections of the Act appear below. Did the master or commander of the *Two Brothers* violate federal law? Assuming that a violation occurred, should Alaska Packers have been estopped from challenging the validity of the allegedly modified contract and from raising the preexisting duty defense?

3. **Collective-Bargaining Agreements, Strikes, and the Preexisting Duty Rule**. Does the common-law preexisting duty doctrine prevent players in the National Football League from striking and demanding more money? May professional baseball, basketball, football, and hockey players stop working and force the owners to pay "increased compensation for doing that which [they are] legally bound to do"?

4. **Federal Labor Laws, Collective-Bargaining Agreements, and Workers' Right to Strike.** Consider the Supreme Court's ruling and observations in *Amalgamated Ass'n of Street Elec. Ry. & Motor Coach Employees of America, Division 998 v. Wisconsin Employment Relations Bd.*, 340 U.S. 383, 389 (1951):

We have recently examined the extent to which Congress has regulated peaceful strikes for higher wages in industries affecting commerce. *International Union of United Auto Workers v. O'Brien*, 339 U.S. 454 (1950). We noted that Congress, in § 7 of the NATIONAL LABOR RELATIONS ACT OF 1935 (49 Stat. 449, 29 U.S.C. §§ 151 et seq., 29 U.S.C.A. §151 et seq), as amended by the LABOR MANAGEMENT RELATIONS ACT OF 1947 (61 Stat. 136, 29 U.S.C (Supp. III) § 141 et seq., 29 U.S.C.A. § 141 et seq)—expressly safeguarded for employees in such industries the "right ... to engage in ... concerted activities for the purpose of collective bargaining or other mutual aid or protection,"—e.g., "to strike." *See* Section 7 of both acts, 29 U.S.C. (Supp. III) § 157, 29 U.S.C.A. § 157; §§ 23 and 13, 29 U.S.C. (Supp. III) §§ 152(3), 163, 29 U.S.C.A. §§152(3), 163; S. Rep. No. 573, 74th Cong., 1st Sess. 8–9 (1935); House Conf. Rep. No. 510, 80th Cong., 1st Sess. 38 (1947); and, H.R. Rep. No. 245, 80th Cong., 1st Sess. 26 (1947).

We also listed the qualifications and regulations which Congress itself has imposed upon its guarantee of the right to strike—including requirements that notice be given prior to any strike upon termination of a contract, prohibitions on strikes for certain objectives declared unlawful by Congress, and special procedures for certain strikes which might create national emergencies. *See* Section 8(d) of the 1947 Act, 29 U.S.C. (Supp. III) § 158(d), 29 U.S.C.A. §§ 158(d). Petitioners in both cases had complied with all notice requirements before strike action was taken. Section 8(b)(4) of the 1947 Act, 29 U.S.C. (Supp. III) § 158(b)(4), 29 U.S.C.A. § 158(b)(4). *See also* § 10(j, l), 29 U.S.C. (Supp. III) § 160(j, l), 29 U.S.C.A. § 160(j, l), empowering and directing the N.L.R.B. to obtain injunctive relief against such unlawful strikes, and Sections 206–210 of the 1947 Act, 29 U.S.C. (Supp. III) §§ 176–180, 29 U.S.C.A. §§176–180.

Upon review of these federal legislative provisions, we held, 339 U.S. at page 457 In the "Declaration of Policy" of the Labor Management Relations Act of 1947, Congress stated: 'It is the purpose and policy of this Act, in order to promote the full flow of commerce, to prescribe the legitimate rights of both employees and employers in their relations affecting commerce. ..." 29 U.S.C. (Supp. III) § 141(b), 29 U.S.C.A. §141(b).

The "Findings and Policies" of the National Labor Relations Act provides, inter alia:

It is hereby declared to be the policy of the United States to eliminate the causes of certain substantial obstructions to the free flow of commerce and to mitigate and eliminate these obstructions when they have occurred by encouraging the practice and procedure of collective bargaining and by protecting the exercise by workers of full freedom of association, self-organization, and designation of representatives of their own choosing, for the purpose of negotiating the terms and conditions of their employment or other mutual aid or protection." 49 Stat. 449, 29 U.S.C. (Supp. III) § 151, 29 U.S.C.A. §§ 151.

ACT OF CONGRESS OF JULY 20, 1790, 1 STAT. 131
AN ACT THE GOVERNMENT AND REGULATION OF SEAMEN IN THE MERCHANTS SERVICE

Master and Seamen to Execute a Shipping Agreement

Section 1. Be it enacted by the Senate and House of Representatives of the United States of America in Congress assembled, That from and after the first day of December next, every master or commander of any ship or vessel bound from a port in the United States to any foreign port, or of any ship or vessel of the burthen of fifty tons or upwards, bound from a port in one state to a port in any other than an adjoining state, ***shall, before he proceed on such voyage, make an agreement in writing or in print, with every seaman or mariner on board such ship or vessel*** (except such as shall be apprentice or servant to himself or owners) declaring the voyage or voyages, term or terms of time, for which such seaman or mariner shall be shipped.

And if any master or commander of such ship or vessel shall carry out any seaman or mariner (except apprentices or servants as aforesaid) without such contract or agreement being first made and signed by the seamen and mariners, ***such master or commander shall pay to every such seaman or mariner the highest price or wages which shall have been given at the port or place where such seaman or mariner shall have been shipped***, for a similar voyage, within three months next before the time of such shipping: ***Provided such seaman or mariner shall perform such voyage***: or if not, then for such time as he shall continue to do duty on board such ship or vessel; and shall moreover forfeit twenty dollars for every such seaman or mariner, one half to the use of the person prosecuting for the same, the other half to the use of the United States: and such seaman or mariner, not having signed such contract, shall not be bound by the regulations, nor subject to the penalties and forfeitures contained in this act.

SECTION 2. And be it [further] enacted, That ***at the foot of every such contract, there shall be a memorandum in writing, of the day and the hour on which such seaman or mariner, who shall so ship and subscribe, shall render themselves on board, to begin the voyage agreed upon***. And if any such seaman or mariner shall neglect to render himself on board the ship or vessel, for which he has shipped, at the time mentioned in such memorandum, and if the master, commander, or other officer of the ship or vessel, shall, on the day on which such neglect happened, make an entry in the log-book of such ship or vessel, of the name of such seaman or mariner, and shall in like manner note the time that he so neglected to render himself (after the time appointed); every such seaman or mariner shall forfeit for every hour which he shall so neglect to render himself, one day's pay, according to the rate of wages agreed upon, to be deducted out of his wages.

And if any such seaman or mariner shall wholly neglect to render himself on board of such ship or vessel, or having rendered himself on board, shall afterwards desert and escape, so that the ship or vessel proceed to sea without him, every such seaman or mariner shall forfeit and pay to the master, owner or consignee of the said ship or vessel, a sum equal to that which shall have been paid to him by advance at the time of signing the contract, over and besides the sum so advanced, both of which sums shall be recoverable in any court, or before any justice or justices of any state, city, town or county within the United States, which, by the laws thereof, have cognizance of debts of equal value, against such seaman or mariner, or his surety or sureties, in case he shall have given surety to proceed the voyage. …

SECTION 5. And be it [further] enacted, That if any seaman or mariner, who shall have subscribed such contract as is herein before described, shall absent himself from on board the ship or vessel in which he shall so have shipped, without leave of the master or officer commanding on board; and the mate, or other officer having charge of the log-book, shall make an entry therein of the name of such seaman or mariner, on the day on which he shall so absent himself, and if such seaman or mariner shall return to his duty within forty-eight hours, such seaman or mariner shall forfeit three days pay for every day which he shall so absent himself, to be deducted out of his wages; but if any seaman or mariner shall absent himself for more than forty-eight hours at one time, he shall forfeit all the wages due to him, and all his goods and chattels which were on board the said ship or vessel, or in any store where they may have been lodged at the time of his desertion, to the use of the owners of the ship or vessel, and moreover shall be liable to pay to him or them all damages which he or they may sustain by being obliged to hire other seamen or mariners in his or their place, and such damages shall be recovered with costs, in any court or before any justice or justices having jurisdiction of the recovery of debts to the value of ten dollars or upwards.

SECTION 6. And be it [further] enacted, When, and at what port entitled to demand his wages. That every seaman or mariner shall be entitled to demand and receive from the master or commander of the ship or vessel to which they belong, one third part of the wages which shall be due to him at every port where such ship or vessel shall unlade and deliver her cargo before the voyage be ended, unless the contrary be expressly stipulated in the contract: and as soon as the voyage is ended, and the cargo or ballast be fully discharged at the last port of delivery, every seaman or ***mariner shall be entitled to the wages which shall be than due according to his contract; and if such wages shall not be paid within ten days after such discharge, or if any dispute shall arise between the master and seamen or mariners touching the said wages, it shall be lawful for the judge of the district where the said ship or vessel shall be***, or in case his residence be more than three miles from the place, or of his absence from the place of his residence, then, for any judge or justice of the peace, to summon the master of such ship or vessel to appear before him, to show cause why process should not issue against such ship or vessel, her tackle, furniture and apparel, according to the course of admiralty courts, to answer for the said wages:

[A]nd if the master shall neglect to appear, or appearing, shall not show that the wages are paid, or otherwise satisfied or forfeited, and if the matter in dispute shall not be forthwith settled, in such case the judge or justice shall certify to the clerk of the court of the district, ***that there is sufficient cause of complaint whereon to found admiralty process,*** and thereupon the clerk of such court shall issue process against the said ship or vessel, and the suit shall be proceeded on in the said court, and final judgment be given according to the course of admiralty courts in such cases used; and in such suit all the seamen or mariners. (having cause of complaint of the like kind against the same ship or vessel) shall be joined as complainants***; and it shall be incumbent on the master or commander to produce the contract and log-book***, if required, to ascertain any matters in dispute; otherwise the complainants shall be permitted to state the contents thereof, and the proof of the contrary shall lie on the master or commander[.]

[B]ut nothing herein contained shall prevent any seaman or mariner from having or **maintaining any action at common law** for the recovery of his wages, or from immediate process out of any court having admiralty jurisdiction, wherever any ship or vessel may be found, in case she shall have left the port of delivery where her voyage ended, before payment of the wages, or in case she shall be about to proceed to sea before the end of the ten days next after the delivery of her cargo or ballast.

C. Contract Disputes, Settlement Agreements, Consideration, and the Preexisting Duty Rule

Contract disputes are quite prevalent. However, in most instances, neither party to a contract wants to terminate the agreement completely or go to court to litigate a dispute. To avoid those ends, the parties fashion settlement agreements. But it is important to stress: Settlement contracts evolve from disputes over rights and obligations under an original contract. And, in most instances, a settlement is a "new" contract that modifies original contractual rights, expectations, and obligations. To be sure, traditional principles of contracts govern the formation, interpretation, and enforcement of settlement contracts. Consequently, an important question often arises: whether proof of "new" consideration is required to enforce a settlement agreement. Or the question may be fashioned this way: May a preexisting duty serve as consideration, if one wants to enforce a valid settlement agreement?

Green v. Millman Bros., Inc.
151 N.W.2d 860
(Mich. Ct. App. 1967)

Lesinski, Chief Judge. Defendant Millman Brothers, Inc., a Michigan corporation, appeals from a decision of the common pleas court for the city of Detroit, in favor of plaintiffs Abe Green, Rose Green and Henry S. Alper. The plaintiffs are the owners and operators of the Wonderland Shopping Center in the city of Livonia, Michigan.

The dispute arose out of a written lease agreement between the plaintiffs—as landlords—and the defendant, as tenant. The lease was entered into on July 8, 1958, for a term of 20 years to commence April 1, 1960. The annual rental of $12,250.08 was payable in monthly installments of $1,020.84 in advance—the first day of each month. A provision for additional rent to be paid on gross sales is not here involved.

The defendant paid the stipulated monthly rental from April 1, 1960, until February of 1963. In 1962, and 1963, the president of the defendant corporation had several conversations with Henry S. Alper, the general manager of the shopping center, relative to a reduction in the annual rent. No agreement was reached until April, 1963, when an oral understanding was arrived at whereby the monthly rental was to be reduced by $150 commencing March 1, 1963. The defendant contends that the reduction in monthly rental was for the remaining term of the lease; however, the plaintiffs deny this and assert that the reduction was for one year only.

Based on the oral agreement, defendant issued a check dated April 1, 1963—in payment of the reduced monthly rental. Defendant continued such payments until February, 1966, for a total of 36 checks. The reverse side of the checks bear a notation indicating that each check was for the rent of a given month and year. The checks were accepted and cashed by the plaintiffs.

Several months after the expiration of the one year period, for which they admit the rent was reduced, the plaintiffs made demands for deficiency of $150 per month. Such demands were denied by the defendant.

On February 21, 1966, the plaintiffs brought suit to recover alleged accumulated deficiencies covering the period from March, 1964, to February, 1966—totaling $3,600. The defendant filed an appearance and answer in the lower court alleging that the oral agreement for reduction of rent was not for one year—as the plaintiffs contended—but for the balance of the lease; that the delivery of the checks to the plaintiffs and the subsequent cashing by them operated as an estoppel to prevent the recovery of any deficiency for the period in dispute; and that the receipt of the checks at the reduced rental was an accord and satisfaction of defendant's obligation during the period that such checks were received and deposited.

The trial court sustained plaintiffs' right to recovery and entered a judgment against the defendant in the amount of $3,600. It is from this decision that the defendant brings the present appeal.

In its first assignment of error, the defendant contends that the trial court erred in deciding that the oral agreement in dispute was not supported by consideration. Defendant contends that its continued tenancy—after indicating its desire to vacate—supplied the consideration for the subsequent oral agreement for reduced rental.

To decide defendant's first argument on appeal, it is necessary to consider C.L.1948, § 566.1 (STAT. ANN. 1953 REV. § 26.978(1)):

> An agreement hereafter made to change or modify, or to discharge in whole or in part, any contract, obligation, or lease, or any mortgage or other security interest in personal or real property, shall not be invalid because of the absence of consideration: *Provided,* That the agreement changing, modifying, or discharging such contract, obligation, lease, mortgage or security interest shall not be valid or binding unless it shall be in writing and signed by the party against whom it is sought to enforce the change, modification, or discharge.

From a reading of this statute, it is clear that it does not apply to an oral modification of a written lease agreement. The question then for this Court is whether the subsequent oral modification was supported by consideration.

The performance of a pre-existing duty or legal obligation is generally held not to be sufficient consideration for a return promise. 17 AM.JUR.2D, CONTRACTS, § 119 at 465, reads: "The general rule is that a promise to do that which the promisor is legally bound to do, or the performance of an existing legal obligation, does not constitute consideration, or sufficient consideration, for a contract." *Also see Puett v. Walker,* 50 N.W.2d 740 (Mich. 1952).

The defendant claims that its continued occupancy formed the consideration for the oral agreement for reduced rental. In support of its claim the defendant directs our attention to *Minor-Dietiker v. Mary Jane Stores of Michigan, Inc.*, 141 N.W.2d 342 (Mich. App. 1966). There, as here, the disputed question was an oral agreement that called for a reduction of stipulated rental price in a prior written lease. This Court's holding in *Minor-Dietiker, supra*, is not applicable to the fact situation presented by the instant case.

In *Minor-Dietiker, supra*, although the lessee had covenanted to pay stipulated rentals during the term of the lease, it had not made a covenant to remain in actual occupancy. Therefore, the lessee's subsequent refraining from vacating, at the behest of the lessor, formed the necessary consideration for the oral agreement to reduce the monthly rental. The lessee in agreeing to remain in the premises was forbearing from doing that which it had every legal right to do, even though it might have had a continuing liability for the payment of rent.

Cases in this State which make a distinction between a covenant to pay rent and occupy the premises and a covenant which relates only to the payment of rent are sparse. This Court, however, deems it a valid distinction. Where the covenant is twofold, to pay rent and to occupy, the subsequent agreement to remain in occupancy cannot form the consideration for an oral agreement to reduce rental because the lessee is already obligated contractually to remain. However, if the covenant is to pay the stipulated rental only, the decision of the lessee to remain in occupancy may be a distinct advantage to the lessor and would provide the necessary consideration for an agreement to reduce the rental. *See Copper v. Fretnoransky*, 16 N.Y.S. 866 (1892); *Ten Eyck v. Sleeper*, 67 N.W. 1026 (Minn. 1896).

In the instant case the defendant covenanted not only to pay the stipulated rental but also to "operate 100% of the leased premises during the entire term of this lease." Consequently the defendant's agreement to remain in possession of the premises did not supply the consideration for the subsequent oral agreement for reduced rental. *See* 5A CORBIN, CONTRACTS, § 1249.

It is necessary to distinguish the instant case from those where the lessee experiences unforeseeable conditions or hardship and as a consequence of concessions as to rental, agrees to continue occupancy and meet the new difficulties. The failure of the location under lease here to be productive of a volume of business such as would produce a profit was not such an extraordinary or unforeseen condition as would fall within the ambit of the aforementioned exception.

For this Court to hold that the failure to carry out a party's threat to breach a contract in writing—barring unforeseen or extraordinary circumstances—is valid consideration for oral concessions made by the other party to prevent such breach, would destroy the stability of written contracts in this State. ...

It is the decision of this Court, based upon the aforementioned considerations, that the result reached by the trial court was correct.

Affirmed.

NOTES AND QUESTIONS

1. **Consideration and Significant Modification of Contracts—RESTATEMENT (SECOND) OF CONTRACTS.** Many of today's courts allow parties to modify and enforce contracts without worrying about proving consideration. Those tribunals have embraced the language in the RESTATEMENT (SECOND) OF CONTRACTS § 89. That section reads:

   A promise modifying a duty under a contract not fully performed on either side is binding

   (a) if the modification is fair and equitable in view of circumstances not anticipated by the parties when the contract was made; or

   (b) to the extent provided by statute; or

   (c) to the extent that justice requires enforcement in view of material change of position in reliance on the promise.

2. **Synopsis—Law of Settlements.** In *Cross v. District Court In and For First Judicial Dist.* 643 P.2d 39, 41 (Colo. 1982), the Colorado Supreme Court reiterated accepted rules:

   A compromise and settlement is, in effect, a contract to end judicial proceedings. *H. W. Houston Constr. Co. v. District Court, Colo.*, 632 P.2d 563 (Colo. 1981). As we said in *Houston*, "In order for a settlement to be binding and enforceable, there

> must be a 'meeting of the minds' as to the terms and conditions of the compromise and settlement." In addition, as we have stated on numerous occasions, an attorney does not have the authority to compromise and settle the claim of his client without the knowledge or consent of his client. *Radosevich v. Pegues*, 292 P.2d 741 (Colo. 1956). ... It is also well established that an attorney who is clothed with no other authority than that arising from his employment as attorney has no implied authority by virtue of his general retainer to compromise and settle a claim of his client.

PROBLEM

Bianca Serna sells tractors. Her inventory fluctuates between 300–350 tractors each month. To cover her inventory, she purchased a commercial liability insurance contract from a subsidiary of American Insurance General (AIG). Under the terms of the policy, AIG promised "to pay all legitimate claims promptly." The contract also stated: 1) "The owner of this policy must pay the premium(s) on time"; 2) "If the owner of the policy does pay the premium(s) on time, the owner will have a 30-day grace period to pay the premium(s)"; and 3) "During the 30-day grace period, coverage for all 'covered vehicles' will not terminate." The vehicle insurance contract required Serna to pay $7,856.00 every six months.

Serna and AIG have had a 10-year relationship. Three years ago, on two occasions, Serna forgot to pay the premiums on time or during the grace periods. Still, AIG processed her claims—two weeks beyond the grace period—and paid insurance proceeds when hail and lightening destroyed some of Serna's inventory. A year ago, an unexplained fire destroyed 25 tractors in Serna's inventory. When the fire occurred, the $7,856 premium had not been paid and the grace period had expired six days earlier. Still, Serna filed a $1.5 million notice-of-loss claim with AIG. The insurer rejected the claim. Serna filed a $1.8 million breach-of-contract lawsuit against AIG. Shortly thereafter, both Serna and AIG filed motions for summary judgment.

However, before the federal district court considered the respective motions, Serna and AIG settled the $1.8 million breach-of-contract lawsuit. Under the terms of the settlement agreement, Serna "promised to pay the outstanding $7,856 premium." AIG promised "to process Bianca Serna's notice-of-loss claim immediately and pay any and all legitimate claims." Serna paid the outstanding premium. As of two months ago, AIG still had not processed the fire-loss claim or paid any proceeds to cover the losses. Therefore, five days ago, Serna sued AIG again, alleging that AIG breached the settlement agreement. AIG filed a declaratory judgment action, asking the court to declare the following: Serna's failure to give "new" consideration precludes the enforcement of the settlement agreement. Should the federal district judge grant or deny AIG's request for declaratory relief? Explain.

CHAPTER FOUR

Breach and Non-Performance of Stand-Alone and Contractual Promises

If one reads court opinions carefully, one finds courts' discussions regarding "bargained-for obligations," "bargained-for exchange of obligations," "binding obligations," "contractual obligations," "promissory obligations," "legal obligations," "performance obligations," and "performance-based obligations." Understandably, one might conclude: There are numerous and different classes of obligations. But, in truth, these are only different labels, describing the stand-alone and contractual promises outlined in chapters 1 and 2. On the other hand, nonperformance of contractual and stand-alone promises appears in various forms. Or stated in a different way, stand-alone and contractual promises can be breached in a variety of ways.

But, it is important to stress: Every nonperformance of a promise does not guarantee complainants' receiving compensation for every resulting personal, financial, or property injury. Under the common law, some breached promises and contracts are inconsequential. They do not produce injuries or losses. Then again, under certain circumstances, complainants may receive damages even before a breach or one's failure to perform occurs. This chapter discusses some of the ways that parties might breach stand-alone promises and contracts. In addition, the chapter outlines the legal standard for determining whether breach-of-promise evidence is legally and factually sufficient or insufficient.

SECTION ONE: ANTICIPATORY BREACH OF PROMISES AND CONTRACTS

Consider these brief facts. Joshua Patton is a photographer and the sole proprietor of Patton's Orbital Imaging. Cooperstown Sports is the owner, operator, and manager of a youth baseball camp. Fifteen months ago, Patton and Cooperstown consummated a five-year contract. Under the agreement, Patton secured the "exclusive rights to provide photographic services to Cooperstown's customers." Among other provisions, the exclusive-dealing contract stated: "If termination of this agreement is required for any reason, either party must submit a written conformation to the other party 90 days before the termination." Yesterday, Cooperstown sent a letter to Patton, announcing that Cooperstown would terminate the exclusive-dealing contract "within 100 days." May Patton commence a breach-of-contract action within 48 hours? Did Cooperstown breach the contract yesterday? Was Patton injured yesterday?

Hochster v. De La Tour
2 E. & B. 678 (Queen's Bench)
118 Eng. Rep. 922 (1853)

On the trial, before Erie J., at the London sittings in last Easter Term, it appeared that plaintiff was a courier, who, in April, 1852, was engaged by defendant to accompany him on a tour, to commence on 1st June 1852, on the terms mentioned in the declaration. On the 11th May 1852, defendant wrote to plaintiff that he had changed his mind, and declined his services. He refused to make him any compensation. The action was commenced on 22d May. The plaintiff, between the commencement of the action and the 1st June, obtained an engagement with Lord Ashburton, on equally good terms, but not commencing till 4th July. The defendant's counsel objected that there could be no breach of the contract before the 1st of June. The learned Judge was of a contrary opinion, but reserved leave to enter a nonsuit on this objection. The other questions were left to the jury, who found for plaintiff. ...

LORD CAMPBELL C.J.

On this motion in arrest of judgment, the question arises, Whether, if there be an agreement between *A* and *B*, whereby *B* engages to employ *A* on and from a future day for a given period of time, to travel with him into a foreign country as a courier, and to start with him in that capacity on that day, *A* being to receive a monthly salary during the continuance of such service, *B* may, before the day, refuse to perform the agreement and break and renounce it, so as to entitle *A* before the day to commence an action against *B* to recover damages for breach of the agreement; *A* having been ready and willing to perform it, till it was broken and renounced by *B*. The defendant's counsel very powerfully contended that, if the plaintiff was not contented to dissolve the contract, and to abandon all remedy upon it, he was bound to remain ready and willing to perform it till the day when the actual employment as courier in the service of the defendant was to begin; and that there could be no breach of the agreement, before that day, to give a right of action.

But it cannot be laid down as a universal rule that, where by agreement an act is to be done on a future day, no action can be brought for a breach of the agreement till the day for doing the act has arrived. If a man promises to marry a woman on a future day, and before that day marries another woman, he is instantly liable to an action for breach of promise of marriage; *Short v. Stone* (8 Q. B. 358). If a man contracts to execute a lease on and from a future day for a certain term, and, before that day, executes a lease to another for the same term, he may be immediately sued for breaking the contract; *Ford v. Tiley* (6 B. & C. 325). So, if a man contracts to sell and deliver specific goods on a future day, and before the day he sells and delivers them to another, he is immediately liable to an action at the suit of the person with whom he first contracted to sell and deliver them. *Bowdell v. Parsons* (10 East 359).

One reason alleged in support of such an action is, that the defendant has, before the day, rendered it impossible for him to perform the contract at the day: but this does not necessarily follow; for, prior to the day fixed for doing the act, the first wife may have died, a surrender of the lease executed might be obtained, and the defendant might have repurchased the goods so as to be in a situation to sell and deliver them to the plaintiff. Another reason may be, that, where there is a contract to do an act on a future day, there is a relation constituted between the parties in the meantime by the contract, and that they impliedly promise that in the meantime neither will do anything to the prejudice of the other inconsistent with that relation. As an example, a man and woman engaged to marry are affianced to one another during the period between the time of the engagement and the celebration of the marriage.

In this very case, of traveller and courier, from the day of the hiring till the day when the employment was to begin, they were engaged to each other; and it seems to be a breach of an implied contract if either of them renounces the engagement. This reasoning seems in accordance with the unanimous decision of the Exchequer Chamber in *Elderton v. Emmens*, which we have followed in subsequent cases in this Court.

The declaration in the present case, in alleging a breach, states a great deal more than a passing intention on the part of the defendant which he may repent of, and could only be proved by evidence that he had utterly renounced the contract, or done some act which rendered it impossible for him to perform it. If the plaintiff has no remedy for breach of the contract unless he treats the contract as in force, and acts upon it down to the 1st June 1852, it follows that, till then, he must enter into no employment which will interfere with his promise "to start with the defendant on such travels on the day and year," and that he must then be properly equipped in all respects as a courier for a three months' tour on the continent of Europe.

But it is surely much more rational, and more for the benefit of both parties, that, after the renunciation of the agreement by the defendant, the plaintiff should be at liberty to consider himself absolved from any future performance of it, retaining his right to sue for any damage he has suffered from the breach of it. Thus, instead of remaining idle and laying out money in preparations which must be useless, he is at liberty to seek service under another employer, which would go in mitigation of the damages to which he would otherwise be entitled for a breach of the contract. It seems strange that the defendant, after renouncing the contract, and absolutely declaring that he will never act under it, should be permitted to object that faith is given to his assertion, and that an opportunity is not left to him of changing his mind.

If the plaintiff is barred of any remedy by entering into an engagement inconsistent with starting as a courier with the defendant on the 1st June, he is prejudiced by putting faith in the defendant's assertion: and it would be more consonant with principle, if the defendant were precluded from saying that he had not broken the contract when he declared that he entirely renounced it. Suppose that the defendant, at the time of his renunciation, had embarked on a voyage for Australia, so as to render it physically impossible for him to employ the plaintiff as a courier on the continent of Europe in the months of June, July and August 1852. According to decided cases, the action might have been brought before the 1st June; but the renunciation may have been founded on other facts, to be given in evidence, which would equally have rendered the defendant's performance of the contract impossible.

The man who wrongfully renounces a contract into which he has deliberately entered cannot justly complain if he is immediately sued for a compensation in damages by the man whom he has injured; and it seems reasonable to allow an option to the injured party, either to sue immediately, or to wait till the time when the act was to be done, still holding it as prospectively binding for the exercise of this option, which may be advantageous to the innocent party, and cannot be prejudicial to the wrongdoer.

An argument against the action before the 1st of June is urged from the difficulty of calculating the damages; but this argument is equally strong against an action before the 1st of September, when the three months would expire. In either case, the jury in assessing the damages would be justified in looking to all that had happened, or was likely to happen, to increase or mitigate the loss of the plaintiff down to the day of trial.

We do not find any decision contrary to the view we are taking. … If it should be held that, upon a contract to do an act on a future day, a renunciation of the contract by one party dispenses with a condition to be performed in the meantime by the other, there seems no reason for requiring that other to wait till the day arrives before seeking his remedy by action: and the only ground on which the condition can be dispensed with seems to be, that the renunciation may be treated as a breach of the contract.

Upon the whole, we think that the declaration in this case is sufficient. It gives us great satisfaction to reflect that, the question being on the record, our opinion may be reviewed in a Court of Error. In the meantime we must give judgment for the plaintiff.

Judgment for plaintiff.

NOTES AND QUESTIONS

1. **The Restatement of Contracts—Effect of Prospective Non-Performance.** Consider the following language which appears in RESTATEMENT (SECOND) OF CONTRACTS § 253 (1981):

   (1) Where an obligor repudiates a duty before he has committed a breach by non-performance and before he has received all of the agreed exchange for it, his repudiation alone gives rise to a claim for damages for total breach.

   (2) Where performances are to be exchanged under an exchange of promises, one party's repudiation of a duty to render performance discharges the other party's remaining duties to render performance.

   COMMENT a. *Breach*. An obligee under a contract is ordinarily entitled to the protection of his expectation that the obligor will perform. For this reason, a repudiation by the obligor under § 250 or § 251 generally gives rise to a claim for damages for total breach even though it is not accompanied or preceded by a breach by non-performance. Such a repudiation is sometimes elliptically called an "anticipatory breach."

2. **Anticipatory Breach and the Legal Sufficiency of Evidence.** Stated simply, "[a]n anticipatory repudiation is a breach of contract giving rise to a claim for damages and also excusing the necessity for the non-breaching party to tender performance."

United California Bank v. Prudential Ins. Co., 681 P.2d 390, 435 (Ariz. Ct. App. 1983). When a promisor declares that s/he will not perform under the terms of the contract, an anticipatory repudiation occurs and the injured party may immediately commence a breach-of-contract action. *Cambridge Co., Ltd. v. Telsat, Inc.*, 2008 WL 649582, *3 (Ohio App. [9 Dist.] 2008). Or, evidence is sufficient if a promisor requests a cancellation of the contract or a change in the terms of the contract, as long as the repudiation is expressed clearly and unequivocally. *McDonald v. Bedford Datsun*, 59 Ohio App.3d 38, 40 (Ohio Ct. App. 1989). Indirect inferences are not sufficient. *Sentinel Consumer Prod. Inc. v. Mills, Hall, Wallborn & Assoc., Inc.*, 110 Ohio App.3d 211, 213–215 (Ohio Ct. App. 1996). On the other hand, anticipatory repudiation of a contract has been found where the promisor engaged in overt action which indicated that the promisor will not continue to perform. *See, e.g., Farmers Comm. Co. v. Burks*, 130 Ohio App.3d 158, 173 (Ohio Ct. App. 1998).

3. **Anticipatory Breach and the Injured Party's Options and Burden.** In *Lucente v. International Bus. Machines Corp.,* 310 F.3d 243, 258 (2d Cir. 2002), the Court of Appeals for the Second Circuit wrote:

> [When confronted with an anticipatory repudiation], the non-repudiating party has two mutually exclusive options. He may a) elect to treat the repudiation as an anticipatory breach and seek damages for breach of contract, thereby terminating the contractual relation between the parties, or b) he may continue to treat the contract as valid and await the designated time for performance before bringing suit. ... The non-repudiating party must, however, make an affirmative election. He cannot at the same time treat the contract as broken and subsisting, for [o]ne course of action excludes the other.

Assuming that the aggrieved party commences a breach-of-contract action, the party must establish several elements: 1) a valid contract that imposed obligations on the parties, 2) proof that performance was not required when the breach occurred, 3) evidence of the defendant's refusing to perform in the future under the terms of the contract, 4) causation—cause in fact and proximate cause, and 5) damages. *McDonald v. Bedford Datsun*, 59 Ohio App.3d 38, 40 (Ohio Ct. App. 1989).

Furthermore, to secure damages in an anticipatory-breach-of-contract action, the non-breaching party must prove that she had the ability to perform under the contract. *County of Solano v. Vallejo Redev. Agency*, 75 Cal. App. 4th 1262, 1275–76 (Cal. Ct. App. 1999). Also, a non-breaching party may not recover damages without establishing that—but for the breach—he was ready, willing, and able to perform under the terms of the contract. 1 WITKIN SUMMARY OF CALIFORNIA LAW § 862 (10th ed. 2005).

4. **Additional Types of Nonperformance**. As stated earlier, nonperformance appears in different forms. The following examples are fairly common:

   Failure to Deliver Goods—*Pfeifle v. Chemoil Corp.*, 73 Fed. Appx. 720, 722 (5th Cir. 2003) ("The 'goods' promised were the options at the price fixed in the employment agreement; the breach occurred when the employer failed to deliver the promised goods on the date the employee sought to exercise the options."), and *In re Kiki, Ltd.*, 35 B.R. 175, 177 (Bankr. D. Haw. 1983) (failure to deliver shares of stock pursuant to settlement agreement was a material breach).

   Failure to Deliver Legal Documents—*Smith v. Smith*, 820 So. 2d 64, 72 (Ala. 2001) ("the jury implicitly concluded that Paul was not, in fact, required under the contract to sign the closing documents, and that, when Frances signed the closing documents and tendered her down payment, she fulfilled her contractual obligations. The defendants' failure to deliver the deed to her amounted to a breach of contract. The jury's findings are supported by the evidence, and, therefore, we affirm the trial court's judgment in favor of Frances on the breach-of-contract claims and counterclaims").

   Failure to Render Services—*Dixey v. A.H. Woods Productions Co.,* 154 N.Y.S. 49, 53 (N.Y. App. Div. 1915) ("[T]hese provisions indicate that the words 'when services are rendered' were intended by the parties to mean no more than the due performance of the contract of employment by the employed. ... [Therefore], when the defendant agreed to pay plaintiff for services rendered, the right to receive compensation was not limited to actual public appearances, but extended as well to so much of the contract period within which plaintiff was ready, willing, and able to perform the services contracted for. ... Nor can it be argued successfully that defendant had a right to terminate this period at will.")

   Foot Dragging—*Community Builders, Inc. v. Indian Motocycle Assoc., Inc.*, 692 N.E.2d 964, 978–79 (Mass. App. Ct. 1998) (after defendant engaged in willful effort to impair plaintiff's right to be paid under the contract, the court found that defendant's conduct amounted to "foot dragging.").

   Nonpayment—*ARP Films, Inc. v. Marvel Entertainment Group, Inc.*, 952 F.2d 643, 649 (2d Cir. 1991) ("[F]ailure to tender payment is generally deemed a material breach of a contract."); and *REI Transport, Inc. v. C.H. Robinson Worldwide, Inc.*, 519 F.3d 693, 698 (7th Cir. 2008) ("Nonpayment is a material breach of a contract unless the withholding party has a valid excuse.").

Repudiation—*Microsoft Corp. v. Motorola, Inc.*, 864 F.Supp. 2d 1023, 1036 (W.D. Wash. 2012) ("[A]lthough Motorola cites no legal standard for repudiation, repudiation is closely related with the doctrine of anticipatory breach. An anticipatory breach occurs when one of the parties to a bilateral contract either expressly or impliedly repudiates the contract prior to the time for performance").

Unilateral Adjustments—*Angell v. Don Jones Ins. Agency Inc.,* 620 So.2d 1012, 1013–14 (Fla. Dist. Ct. App. 1993) ("Below, [the employee] alleged that [the employer] breached the employment contract by unilaterally reducing [her] annual base salary. [The employer] does not dispute its actions but urges that the "Base Salary" clause of the "Producer Compensation Plan" contemplates just such a unilateral downward adjustment … any time after the first eighteen months of [the employee's] employment. While the trial judge agreed with [the employer's] interpretation of that contract provision, we do not. … The contract does not … provide for a unilateral downward adjustment of base salary and, in making such a unilateral downward adjustment, [the employer] breached the terms of the contract.").

Unreasonable Delays and Extensions—*Stocker v. Cochran's Decorative Curbing Inc.*, 2010 WL 1328539, *7 (Ohio Ct. App. Mar. 30, 2010) ("[W]e generally presume that the contract [must] be performed within a reasonable time. An unreasonable delay in performance may constitute a material breach of the contract. To determine whether a party has breached a contract through unreasonable delay, the trier of fact must consider the circumstances contemplated by the parties at the time the contract was executed, and the circumstances surrounding performance"), citing 23 WILLISTON, CONTRACTS § 63:18 (4 Ed. 2000) at 487–488

SECTION TWO: BREACH OF PROMISES AND CONTRACTS

A. The "Material Breach" and "Substantial Performance" Doctrines

Consider this reasonable assumption: When parties form contracts, they expect and want each other to perform as promised. But we know parties breach contractual as well as stand-alone promises quite frequently. Why? To be sure, most breaches are unintentional and unexpected. On the other hand, some rational and intelligent parties make contracts for "deceptive" reasons, planning and expecting to breach the agreements without performing fully. Certainly, there are many competing reasons to explain why members of the latter group allow deceptive motives to influence their behaviors. But one reason is paramount. Deceptive—but otherwise intelligent, knowledgeable, and rational—people know: They will not be penalized legally, if their planned nonperformance or intentional inadequate performances are inconsequential.

So, this leads to the fundamental question: What is the legal standard for determining a "material breach"? In *Richard v. Deutsche Bank Nat. Trust Co.*, 2012 WL 1082602, *3 n.2 (D. Or. Mar. 30, 2012), the federal district embraced this rule: "Substantial performance is the antithesis of material breach; if it is determined that a breach is material ... it follows that substantial performance has not been rendered" citing 15 R. LORD WILLISTON ON CONTRACTS § 44:55 (4th ed. 2000). However, in *General Motors Corp. v. New A.C. Chevrolet, Inc.*, 263 F.3d 296, 317 n. 8 (3rd Cir. 2001), the Court of Appeals for the Third Circuit stated: "Substantial performance is performance without a material breach." And, in *1.9 Little York, Ltd. v. Allice Trading Inc.*, 2012 WL 897776, *6 (Tex. App.—Houston [1st Dist.] 2012), the Texas Court of Appeals in Houston declared: "Substantial performance is a doctrine that allows *breaching* parties who have substantially completed their obligations *to recover* on a contract." Are those rules crystal clear? Does the "material breach doctrine" have a sound and uncomplicated foundation? As you read the cases in this part, try to answer these questions.

Another Attic, Ltd. v. Plains Builders, Inc.
2010 WL 4941694
(Tex. App.—Amarillo 2010)

Per curiam. Appellant, Another Attic, Ltd. (Another Attic)—a limited liability partnership—appeals from a judgment rendered in favor of Appellees, Plains Builders, Inc. (Plains Builders), Wendy White—as Independent Executrix of the Estate of G. Tim White, formerly d/b/a White Associates Architecture (White)—and Chavez Concrete

Company (Chavez), in a contract dispute lawsuit arising out of a written contract. ...

FACTUAL BACKGROUND

In 2004, Plains Builders and Another Attic executed a written contract for the construction of a mini-storage facility in Plainview, Texas. Plains Builders subcontracted the architect-related work to White and the concrete work to Chavez. Construction began in May of that year; however, towards the end of construction, disputes arose about the work being performed by Plains Builders. By a letter dated October 8, 2004, Another Attic directed Plains Builders to cease work, which it did. Plains Builders contended that—at the time it was ordered off the project—Another Attic owed it $57,938 under the terms of the contract. According to Plains Builders, this sum was calculated by deducting from the full contract price, the sum of the amounts already paid plus the value of work that was not performed by Plains Builders due to Another Attic's termination of the contract.

Another Attic refused to pay this sum and on February 4, 2005, Plains Builders filed a suit for breach of contract for failure to pay, declaratory judgment as to substantial completion, and enforcement of its statutory mechanic's and materialmen's lien. Asserting lack of substantial completion, Another Attic filed multiple counterclaims against Plains Builders, as well as a third-party claim against two of the subcontractors—the architect, White—and the concrete provider, Chavez. Another Attic contended the work performed was so defective the alleged deficiencies could not be remedied without having the entire facility torn down and rebuilt. Another Attic also contended that certain provisions of the contract were ambiguous.

On April 5, 2008, the trial court submitted the dispute to a jury based upon thirteen questions. The first two questions dealt with the issue of contract liability, as it pertained to the dispute between Another Attic and Plains Builders. As submitted to the jury, questions one and two, together with the jury's verdict, provided as follows:

> QUESTION NO. 1
>
> Did ANOTHER ATTIC fail to comply with the construction contract?
>
> You are instructed that a "failure to comply" is an unjustified failure or refusal of one of the parties to the contract to perform all or part of what is promised in the contract. Failure to comply by Another Attic would be excused by a previous failure by Plains Builders to comply with a material obligation of the same agreement. A failure to comply must be material. A "failure to comply" becomes material when it

deprives the injured party of any substantial benefit which the injured party could reasonably have anticipated. The less the non-breaching party is deprived of expected benefit, the less material the breach.

Answer "Yes" or "No"

Answer: *Yes*

QUESTION NO. 2

Did PLAINS BUILDERS fail to comply with the construction contract?

You are instructed that a "failure to comply" is an unjustified failure or refusal of one of the parties to the contract to perform all or part of what is promised in the contract. Failure to comply by Plains Builders would be excused by a previous failure by Another Attic to comply with a material obligation of the same agreement. A "failure to comply" must be material. A "failure to comply" becomes material when it deprives the injured party of any substantial benefit which the injured party could have [sic] reasonably have anticipated. The less the non-breaching party is deprived of expected benefits, the less material the breach.

Answer "Yes" or "No"

Answer: *No*

Another Attic did not object to the submission of these liability questions or the corresponding instructions in any respect material to this appeal. By these issues the jury was asked to determine whether Another Attic and/or Plains Builders materially breached the contract. Simply stated, the jury decided that Another Attic did—excusing Plains Builders from further performance—and that Plains Builders did not (thereby rejecting Another Attic's defective construction claims).

Having found that Another Attic had breached the contract ... and that Plains Builders had not ..., the jury concluded that as a result thereof, Plains Builders had been damaged in the sum of $57,938. ... The jury also found that neither White, nor Chavez, had negligently damaged Another Attic. Due to their conditional submission, the remaining jury questions were unanswered. Following cross-motions for judgment, on July 15, 2008, the trial court entered judgment that Plains Builders recover of and from Another Attic the sum of $57,938, plus attorney's fees, pre-judgment interest and costs of court, together with foreclosure of its mechanic's and materialmen's lien. The judgment further provided that Another Attic take nothing as to White and Chavez and that it recover costs of court from Another Attic.

SUBSTANTIAL PERFORMANCE VERSUS EXCUSED PERFORMANCE

A considerable portion of Another Attic's arguments is predicated on the premise that Plains Builders' theory of recovery was based upon the equitable doctrine of substantial performance. At trial and on appeal, Another Attic has pursued a theory that defects in the construction of the mini-storage facility were so material they could not be remedied without the entire facility being torn down and rebuilt. Another Attic posits that because substantial performance requires that any defects be remediable without doing material damage to the structure, there can be no substantial performance as a matter of law. Plains Builders counters this argument by contending that "this is not a substantial performance case," or, alternatively, that the defects that could not be remediated without doing material damage to the structure, if any, were immaterial. Plains Builders further contends that this is a suit for "breach of contract, *quantum meruit* and unjust enrichment."

In an ordinary contract case, a party who has materially breached a contract cannot maintain a suit on the contract for its breach by the other party to the contract. *Gulf Pipe Line Co. v. Nearen*, 138 S.W.2d 1065, 1068 (Tex. 1940). However, in the area of construction contracts, this strict rule has been relaxed by the equitable doctrine of substantial performance which allows a breaching party who has "substantially completed" a construction contract to sue for the recovery of damages under that contract rather than being relegated to a cause of action based on breach of contract and quantum meruit. *See Dobbins v. Redden*, 785 S.W.2d 377, 378 (Tex. 1990); and, *Vance v. My Apartment Steak House of San Antonio, Inc.*, 677 S.W.2d 480, 481 (Tex. 1984).

By definition, the doctrine recognizes that the contractor has breached his obligations under the contract; and, accordingly, his recovery is decreased by the cost of remedying those defects or omissions for which he is responsible. The doctrine also assumes that, if there is substantial performance by the contractor, any breach by the contractor is immaterial. *R.B. Hardy & Sons, Inc. v. Hoyer Global (USA), Inc.*, 2010 WL 2305753 (Tex. App.—Houston [1st Dist.] June 10, 2010, pet. filed).

Substantial performance is not, however, the exclusive theory upon which a contractor can pursue recovery in a dispute concerning a construction contract where that contractor has not completed full performance of the contract. Under the doctrine of repudiation, a party's further performance under a contract is excused if the opposing party has repudiated the contract. *Burford v. Pounders*, 199 S.W.2d 141, 144–45 (Tex. 1947). A repudiation occurs when a party absolutely repudiates the obligation—without just excuse—and the other party is damaged by the repudiation. *Consumer Portfolio Servs. v. Obregon*, 2010 Tex. App. Lexis 8835, at *11–12, (Tex. App.—Corpus Christi Nov. 4, 2010, no pet. h.). Furthermore, in those situations where the other party to the contract has materially breached the contract, the contractor's failure to complete full performance may be excused. *Mustang Pipeline Co. v. Driver Pipeline Co.*, 134 S.W.3d 195, 198 (Tex. 2004)

In cases where a contractor has not fully performed his obligations under the contract, neither the doctrine of substantial performance nor the doctrine of excused performance permits the breaching contractor to recover the full consideration provided for in the contract. Where the theory of recovery has been substantial performance, courts have limited the amount recoverable by the contractor to "the contract price, less the reasonable cost of remedying the defects or omissions in such a way as to make the building conform to the contract." *Atkinson v. Jackson Bros.*, 270 S.W. 848, 851 (Tex. Comm'n App. 1925, holding approved).

Where a contractor has failed to complete a construction contract because full performance has been excused due to a material breach or repudiation of the contract by the owner, courts have limited the amount recoverable by the contractor to the damages suffered by reason of the breach of contract. *Dankowski v. Cremona*, 352 S.W.2d 334, 336 (Tex. App.—Eastland 1961, writ ref'd n.r.e.). Equity requires that the contractor recover that amount of money which would place the contractor in a position equivalent to that which he would have occupied if there had been no breach, and the contract had been fully performed. In such situations, the contractor is entitled to recover the value of his work had the contract been completed, i.e., the contract price, less the value of any work not completed due to the builder's repudiation or material breach. *Dill v. Helms,* 468 S.W.2d 608, 611 (Tex. App.—Waco 1971, writ ref'd n.r.e.).

Issue One

By its first issue, Another Attic contends the trial court erred by denying its motion for instructed verdict and motion for judgment non obstante veredicto because there was no substantial completion as a matter of law. ... [T]he jury questions submitted track the Texas Pattern Jury Charge recommended for a breach of contract case. Comm. On Pattern Jury Charges, State Bar of Tex., Texas Pattern Jury Charges—Business, Consumer, Insurance & Employment PJC 101.2 (2008). The instructions following the submission of questions one and two also roughly follow the instructions contained in PJC 101.22 pertaining to excused performance due to a material breach of contract. Neither question asked the jury to make a finding on the issue of "substantial performance."

Nevertheless, Another Attic contends the trial court erred in denying its motion for judgment non obstante veredicto because various defects impaired the structure as a whole, preventing a finding of substantial performance as a matter of law. However, under the theory of liability submitted to the jury, substantial performance was not a vital fact. Having chosen to submit the issue to the jury as a straight breach of contract case, Another Attic cannot now complain that the trial court erred in somehow not applying a theory of recovery not presented to the jury.

As stated above, the liability issue was submitted to the jury by asking two basic questions: 1) did Another Attic fail to comply with the contract, and 2) did Plains Builders fail to comply with the contract? In this case, the jury was presented with evidence pertaining to alleged defects or omissions in seven particular areas: 1) the location of steel in the concrete, 2) the adequacy of the concrete finish work, 3) whether a cross walk was in violation of the Texas Accessibility Standards, 4) whether a portion of the finished building lies within a 100–year flood plain, 5) whether the appropriate insulation was installed, 6) the installation of a security gate, and 7) completion of landscaping. The jury was presented with evidence from both lay witnesses and experts concerning the existence and materiality of each of these alleged defects. The jury was also presented with testimony concerning the value of the work not performed.

As the issue was framed, based on the evidence presented, the jury could have reasonably concluded that: 1) the alleged defects were not material, 2) Another Attic was not justified in repudiating the contract, 3) Another Attic's termination of the contract was a material breach of its obligations under the contract, 4) Plains Builders was thus prevented from completing the remainder of its obligations under the contract, 5) Another Attic's breach excused Plains Builders from further performance, and 6) Plains Builders had allowed an appropriate credit for work not completed. Accordingly, the record contains legally sufficient evidence to support the jury's liability findings. Issue one is overruled.

Issues Two Through Four—Legally and Factually Sufficient Evidence

By its next three issues, Another Attic essentially contends the trial court erred by either submitting questions one and two, or by accepting the jury's verdict thereto because the findings are not supported by legally or factually sufficient evidence. As stated above, we have already found that the evidence supporting the jury's liability findings is legally sufficient.

An assertion that the evidence is factually insufficient to support a fact finding means that the evidence supporting the finding is so weak or the evidence to the contrary is so overwhelming that the answer should be set aside and a new trial ordered. *Garza v. Alviar*, 395 S.W.2d 821, 823 (Tex. 1965). In reviewing factual sufficiency, the reviewing court must consider, examine, and weigh all of the evidence in the record. *Maritime Overseas Corp. v. Ellis*, 971 S.W.2d 402, 406–07 (Tex. 1998), cert. denied, 525 U.S. 1017 (1998). In doing so, the court no longer considers the evidence in the light most favorable to the jury's finding; instead, the court considers and weighs all the evidence and sets aside the disputed finding only if it is so contrary to the great weight and preponderance of the evidence as to be clearly wrong and unjust. *Gooch v. American Sling* Co., 902 S.W.2d 181, 183–84 (Tex. App. Fort Worth 1995, no writ).

Having reviewed the evidence in the light most favorable to the judgment, we cannot say that reasonable and fair-minded people could not have reached the verdict in question. Furthermore, having reviewed the evidence in a neutral light, we cannot say that the disputed findings are so contrary to the great weight and preponderance of the evidence as to be clearly wrong or unjust. Accordingly, we conclude the evidence was both legally and factually sufficient to support the jury's affirmative finding as to Another Attic's breach and its negative finding as to Plains Builders breach. Issues two, three, and four are overruled.

ISSUE FIVE—LEGAL SUFFICIENCY AND MEASURE OF DAMAGES

By its fifth issue, Another Attic contests the legal sufficiency of the jury's determination of damages. Specifically, Another Attic contends there was no evidence regarding the cost of remediating the "admitted defects." Another Attic contends that when a contractor seeks recovery on a substantial performance theory, the contractor has the burden to prove the reasonable cost of remedying the defects or omissions necessary to constitute complete performance. Again, Another Attic's argument is erroneously predicated on the assumption that Plains Builders' theory of recovery was based upon the equitable doctrine of substantial performance.

Where, as here, the jury found that Plains Builders did not breach its contractual obligation in any material fashion; Plains Builders did not have the burden to prove the reasonable cost of remediating any alleged defects. Plains Builders was entitled to recover the full unpaid contract price, less the value of any work not completed due to Another Attic's initial breach of contract by wrongfully preventing full performance. Because evidence was presented concerning the value of work not completed, Plains Builders met its burden to establish its damages under the theory of recovery presented. Issue five is overruled. …

CONCLUSION

Having overruled issues one through seven and having modified the judgment to reduce the recovery of attorney's fees pursuant to issue eight; the judgment of the trial court is affirmed as modified.

NOTES AND QUESTIONS

1. **Comparative Analysis—The Material Breach Doctrine Versus the Substantial Performance Doctrine.** Judge Benjamin Cardozo's well-known contract-law decision—*Jacob & Youngs v. Kent*, 230 N.Y. 239 (N.Y. 1921)—is frequently cited because he discusses the difference between the material breach doctrine and the equitable doctrine of substantial performance. In pertinent part, Judge Cardozo wrote:

    The [contractor] built a country residence for the [homeowner] at a cost of upwards of $77,000, and now sues to recover a balance of $3,483.46, remaining unpaid. The work of construction ceased … and the [homeowner] … began to occupy the dwelling. There was no complaint of defective performance until [later]. One of the specifications for the plumbing work provides that "all wrought iron pipe must be well galvanized, lap welded pipe of the grade known as 'standard pipe' of Reading manufacture." The [homeowners] learned … that some of the pipe, instead of being made in Reading, was the product of other factories. The [contractor] was accordingly directed by the architect to do the work anew. … The [contractor] left the work untouched, and asked for a certificate that the final payment was due. Refusal of the certificate was followed by this suit.

    The evidence sustains a finding that the omission of the prescribed brand of pipe was neither fraudulent nor willful. It was the result of the oversight and inattention of the [contractor's] subcontractor. … The [contractor] tried to show that the brands installed, though made by other manufacturers, were the same in quality, in appearance, in market value and in cost as the brand stated in the contract—that they were, indeed, the same thing, though manufactured in another place. The evidence was excluded, and a verdict directed for the [homeowner]. We think the evidence, if admitted, would have supplied some basis for the *inference that the defect was insignificant in its relation to the project*.

* * *

The decisions in this state commit us to the liberal view, which is making its way ... in jurisdictions slow to welcome it. *Where the line is to be drawn between the important and the trivial cannot be settled by a formula.* ... The question is one of degree, to be answered, if there is doubt, by the triers of the facts and, if the inferences are certain, by the judges of the law. We must weigh the purpose to be served, the desire to be gratified, the excuse for deviation from the letter, the cruelty of enforced adherence.

* * *

In the circumstances of this case, we think the measure of the allowance is not the cost of replacement, which would be great, but the difference in value, which would be either nominal or nothing. ... The measure of allowance is not the cost of reconstruction. "There may be omissions ... which could not afterwards be supplied exactly as called for by the contract without taking down the building to its foundations, and at the same time the omission may not affect the value of the building for use or otherwise, except so slightly as to be hardly appreciable." *Oberlies v. Bullinger*, 132 N.Y. 598, 601; 2 WILLISTON ON CONTRACTS, § 805 at 1541). The rule—that gives a remedy in cases of *substantial performance*, with compensation for defects of trivial or inappreciable importance—has been developed by the courts as an instrument of justice. The measure of the allowance must be shaped to the same end. The [intermediate court's] order should be affirmed, and judgment absolute directed in favor of the [contractor]. ... (Emphasis added.)

2. **Restatement (Second) of Contracts § 241 (1981).** In determining whether a failure to render or to offer performance is material, the following circumstances are significant:

(a) the extent to which the injured party will be deprived of the benefit which he reasonably expected;

(b) the extent to which the injured party can be adequately compensated for the part of that benefit of which he will be deprived;

(c) the extent to which the party failing to perform or to offer to perform will suffer forfeiture;

(d) the likelihood that the party failing to perform or to offer to perform will cure his failure, taking account of all the circumstances including any reasonable assurances; and

(e) the extent to which the behavior of the party failing to perform or to offer to perform comports with standards of good faith and fair dealing.

3. **Definition—"Material Breach"**. Ohio courts embrace the following definition: "A 'material breach of a contract' is a fundamental failure to perform, which defeats the essential purpose of the contract or makes it impossible for the other party to perform." *Marion Family YMCA v. Hensel*, 178 Ohio App. 3d 140, 142–43 (Ohio Ct. App. 2008) (citing WILLISTON ON CONTRACTS, Chapter § 63:3).

4. **The Equitable Doctrine of Substantial Performance**. It is equally true that "default by a party who has substantially performed does not relieve the other party from performance." *Kersh v. Montgomery Dev. Ctr.*, 35 Ohio App. 3d 61, 62 (Ohio Ct. App. 1987).

5. **Material Breach and Discharged Obligations**. "A fundamental principle of contract law is that when one party to a contract commits a material breach of that contract, the other party is discharged or excused from any obligation to perform." *Hernandez v. Gulf Group Lloyds*, 875 S.W.2d 691, 692 (Tex. 1994). *See also United States for the Use and Benefit of James Cape & Sons v. American Home Assurance Co.*, 2004 WL 3119029, at *7 (N.D. Ill. 2004) (stressing that under Illinois law, one party's material breach of a contract discharges the other party from performing its obligations under the contract), citing *Kel-Keef Enterprises, Inc. v. Quality Components Corp.*, 738 N.E.2d 524, 527 (Ill. Ct. App. 2000).

6. **Material Breach and Damages Awards**. "A party who has materially breached a contract is not entitled to damages stemming from the other party's later material breach of the same contract." *McClain v. Kimbrough Constr. Co., Inc.*, 806 S.W.2d 194, 199 (Tenn. Ct. App. 1990).

SECTION THREE: BREACH OF IMPLIED COVENANTS AND JUDGE-MADE DUTIES OF GOOD FAITH AND FAIR DEALING

In the immediately preceding Notes & Questions section, an excerpt from Judge Benjamin Cardozo's opinion—in *Jacob & Youngs v. Kent*, 230 N.Y. 239 (N.Y. 1921)—appears. To repeat, applying the equitable doctrine of substantial performance, Cardozo and the court's majority ruled in favor of the contractor, finding that his breach was immaterial. But, Justice McLaughlin dissented and wrote:

> I dissent. The [contractor] did not perform its contract. Its failure to do so was either intentional or due to gross neglect which, under the uncontradicted facts, amounted to the same thing. ... Under [the] contract [the contractor] obligated itself to use in the plumbing only pipe—between 2,000 and 2,500 feet—made by the Reading Manufacturing Company. ... I am of the opinion the trial court was right in directing a verdict for the [homeowner]. The [contractor] agreed that all the pipe used should be of the Reading Manufacturing Company. Only about two-fifths of it ... was of that kind. ...
>
> The question of substantial performance of a contract ... depends in no small degree upon the *good faith* of the contractor. If the [contractor] had intended to, and had complied with the terms of the contract—except as to minor omissions, due to inadvertence, then he might be allowed to recover the contract price, less the amount necessary to fully compensate the [homeowner] for damages caused by such omissions. But that is not this case. It installed between 2,000 and 2,500 feet of pipe, of which only 1,000 feet at most complied with the contract. No explanation was given why pipe called for by the contract was not used, nor [was] any effort made to show what it would cost to remove the pipe of other manufacturers and install that of the Reading Manufacturing Company.
>
> The [homeowner] had a right to contract for what he wanted. He had a right before making payment to get what the contract called for. It is no answer to this suggestion to say that the pipe put in was just as good as that made by the Reading Manufacturing Company, or that the difference in value between such pipe and the pipe made by the Reading Manufacturing Company would be either "nominal or nothing." [The homeowner] contracted for pipe made by the Reading Manufacturing Company. What his reason was for requiring this kind of pipe is of no importance. He wanted that and was entitled to it. It may have been a mere whim on his part, but even so, he had a right to this kind of pipe, regardless of whether some other kind, according to the opinion of the contractor or experts, would have been "just as good, better, or done just as well." He agreed to pay only upon condition that the pipe installed were made by that company and he ought not to be compelled to pay unless that condition be performed.

Consider a slightly modified version of Justice McLaughlin's sound observation: Performance of a contract depends in no small degree upon the *good faith* of the performers. Unquestionably, contracting parties must perform according to the *express* terms and conditions in valid contracts. But, depending on the jurisdiction, contracting parties also have an *implied* contractual obligation or a judge-made, *imposed* obligation to perform in good faith and to deal fairly with each other. Even more importantly, if one party breaches or deviates from an implied or imposed good-faith-and-fair-dealing standard, the injured party may sue to secure various damages and equitable remedies. This section discusses the pertinent procedural and substantive rules.

A. "Breach of an Implied Covenant of Good Faith and Fair Dealing"

Gruenberg v. Aetna Ins. Co.
510 P.2d 1032
(Cal. 1973)

Sullivan, Justice. ... On and after April 7, 1969, plaintiff was the owner of a cocktail lounge and restaurant business in Los Angeles known as the Brass Rail. The business premises were insured against fire loss in the aggregate sum of $35,000 by the three defendant insurers—Aetna Insurance Company (Aetna), Yosemite Insurance Company (Yosemite), and American Home Assurance Company (American). In the early hours of the morning of November 9, 1969, a fire occurred at the Brass Rail. Plaintiff was notified and immediately went to the scene. While there, he became involved in an argument with a member of the arson detail of the Los Angeles Fire Department and was placed under arrest.

On November 10, 1969, defendant insurers—upon being informed of the fire—engaged the services of defendant P. E. Brown and Company (Brown). Carl Busching, a claims adjuster employed by Brown, went to the Brass Rail to investigate the fire and inspect the premises. While he was there, he stated to an arson investigator of the Los Angeles Fire Department that plaintiff had excessive coverage under his fire insurance policies. Eventually the premises were locked and nothing was removed until November 14, 1969, when Busching authorized the removal of the rubble and debris. About November 13, 1969, plaintiff was charged in a felony complaint with the crimes of arson (PEN. CODE § 448a) and defrauding an insurer (PEN. CODE § 548). A preliminary hearing was set for January 12, 1970.

Defendant insurance companies also retained defendant law firm Cummins, White, Briedenbach & Alphson (Cummins) to represent them in the matter of plaintiff's claim of fire loss. On November 25, 1969, defendant Donald Ricketts—an attorney-employee of Cummins—demanded in writing that plaintiff appear at the offices of said firm on

December 12, 1969, to submit to an examination under oath and to produce certain documents. On November 26, 1969, plaintiff's attorney responded by letter to Ricketts explaining that he had advised plaintiff not to make any statements concerning the fire loss while criminal charges were pending.

The letter also requested that the insurers waive the requirement of an examination until the criminal charges lodged against plaintiff were concluded. Ricketts refused the request and warned that failure to appear for the examination would void coverage under the policies. On December 16, 1969, Ricketts—on behalf of the Cummins law firm—advised plaintiff's attorney in writing that defendant insurers were denying liability under the policies because of plaintiff's failure to submit to an examination under oath and to produce documents.

On January 12, 1970, a preliminary hearing was held on the complaint charging plaintiff with arson and defrauding an insurer. Busching appeared as a witness for the prosecution and restated his belief that plaintiff had excessive fire insurance coverage for his business. The charges were dismissed by the magistrate for lack of probable cause. On January 26, 1970, plaintiff's attorney advised defendant insurers that plaintiff was now prepared to submit himself for an examination. However, the insurers reaffirmed their position that they were denying liability because of plaintiff's failure to appear.

According to the allegations of the complaint, all defendants—other than the insurance company defendants—were the agents and employees of the three defendant companies and were acting within the scope of such agency and employment when the acts attributed to them were committed. It was further alleged:

> [T]he defendants and each of them joined together and acted in concert to falsely imply that the plaintiff had a motive to deliberately set fire to and burn down his place of business [and that] [t]he purpose of the defendants in creating such false implication was to establish a grounds (sic) upon which the defendant Insurers could avoid paying the amounts due to plaintiff under the policies of insurance issued by the defendant Insurers.
>
> To carry out their purpose, defendants "conducted themselves in the following manner": (a) defendant Busching stated to an arson investigator that plaintiff had acquired excessive fire insurance coverage; (b) defendant insurers demanded that plaintiff submit to an examination under oath and to produce certain documents "in order to enable them to secure further evidence to support the false implication that plaintiff was guilty of arson"; and (c) defendant Busching—appearing as a witness for the People at the preliminary hearing on

> the felony complaint reaffirmed his statement made to the arson investigator. As a "direct and proximate result of the outrageous conduct and bad faith of the defendants," plaintiff suffered "severe economic damage," "severe emotional upset and distress," loss of earnings and various special damages.

Plaintiff sought both compensatory and punitive damages. Defendants filed general demurrers to the complaint which were sustained with leave to amend. Plaintiff elected to stand on his complaint and an order of dismissal was entered. This appeal followed.

* * *

Plaintiff contends that he has stated sufficient facts to constitute a cause of action in tort against defendants for breach of an implied duty of good faith and fair dealing. The duty of an insurer to deal fairly and in good faith with its insured is governed by our decisions in *Crisci v. Security Ins. Co.* 426 P.2d 173 (Cal. 1967), and *Comunale v. Traders & General Ins. Co.*, 328 P.2d 198 (Cal. 1958). We explained that this duty—the breach of which sounds in both contract and tort—is imposed because "'[t]here is an implied covenant of good faith and fair dealing in every contract (including insurance policies) that neither party will do anything which will injure the right of the other to receive the benefits of the agreement. Therefore, "an insurer … who refuses to accept a reasonable settlement within the policy limits in violation of its duty to consider in good faith the interest of the insured in settlement, is liable for the entire judgment against the insured even if it exceeds the policy limits."

Thus in *Comunale* and *Crisci*, we made it clear that "[l]iability is imposed (on the insurer) not for a bad faith breach of contract but for failure to meet the duty to accept reasonable settlements, a duty included within the implied covenant of good faith and fair dealing." *Crisci, supra,* 426 P.2d at p. 177. In those two cases, we considered the duty of the insurer to act in good faith and fairly in handling the claims of third persons against the insured—described as a "duty to accept reasonable settlements."

[I]n the case before us, we consider the duty of an insurer to act in good faith and fairly in handling the claim of an insured—namely a duty not to withhold unreasonably payments due under a policy. These are merely two different aspects of the same duty. That responsibility is not the requirement mandated by the terms of the policy itself—to defend, settle, or pay. It is the obligation, deemed to be imposed by the law, under which the insurer must act fairly and in good faith in discharging its contractual responsibilities. Where in so doing, it fails to deal fairly and in good faith with its insured by refusing—without proper cause—to compensate its insured for a loss covered by the policy, such conduct may give rise to a cause of action in tort for breach of an implied covenant of good faith and fair dealing.

Thus, in *Richardson v. Employers Liab. Assur. Corp.*, 102 Cal. Rptr. 547, 552 (1972), where the insurer refused to indemnify its insured for a loss covered by the uninsured motorist provision of an automobile liability policy, the court had this to say:

> In every insurance policy there is implied by law a covenant of good faith and fair dealing. This implied obligation requires an insurer to deal in good faith and fairly with its insured in handling an insured's claim against it. Here, Employers deliberately, willfully and in bad faith withheld payment of the Richardson claim months after it knew the claim to be completely valid; it forced an arbitration hearing on a claim against which it already knew that it had no defense; even after the award was made, it instructed its local office to attempt "to make the best possible settlement," and forced plaintiffs to resort to litigation to have the award judicially confirmed. This conduct toward its own insured was unconscionable, and constituted a tortious breach of contract. The duty violated—that of dealing fairly and in good faith with the other party to a contract of insurance—is a duty imposed by law, not one arising from the terms of the contract itself. In other words, this duty of dealing fairly and in good faith is nonconsensual in origin rather than consensual. Breach of this duty is a tort.

In *Fletcher v. Western National Life Ins. Co.*, 89 Cal. Rptr. 78 (1970), an insurer was held liable in tort for damages caused by the insurer's refusal to indemnify its insured under a disability policy. Although the action was brought on the theory of intentional infliction of emotional distress, the court explained that the insurer's conduct might also be viewed as a violation of its implied obligation of good faith and fair dealing. The insurer—refusing to pay its insured under the injury provision of the policy, which set forth a maximum liability period of 30 years—insisted on payment under the sickness provision of the policy, having a two-year maximum period, even though its own investigation established that plaintiff's disability was caused by injury. It sought to avoid liability under the policy, at first by claiming that the insured had made a material misrepresentation in the application for insurance and later by urging the insured to agree to a settlement for an amount far less than the insurer's potential liability.

In response, the *Fletcher* court observed:

> An insurer owes to its insured an implied-in-law duty of good faith and fair dealing that it will do nothing to deprive the insured of the benefits of the policy. Included within this

> duty in the case of a liability insurance policy is the duty to act reasonably and in good faith to settle claims against the insured by a third person. The violation of that duty sounds in tort notwithstanding that it may also constitute a breach of contract. We think that, similarly, the implied-in-law duty of good faith and fair dealing imposes upon a disability insurer a duty not to threaten to withhold or actually withhold payments, maliciously and without probable cause, for the purpose of injuring its insured by depriving him of the benefits of the policy. We think that, as in *Crisci*, the violation of that duty sounds in tort notwithstanding that it also constitutes a breach of contract.

It is manifest that a common legal principle underlies all of the foregoing decisions; namely, that in every insurance contract there is an implied covenant of good faith and fair dealing. The duty to so act is imminent in the contract whether the company is attending to the claims of third persons against the insured or the claims of the insured itself. Accordingly, when the insurer unreasonably and in bad faith withholds payment of the claim of its insured, it is subject to liability in tort.

In the case at bench, plaintiff has alleged in essence that defendants wilfully and maliciously entered into a scheme to deprive him of the benefits of the fire policies in that they encouraged criminal charges by falsely implying that he had a motive to commit arson, and in that, knowing plaintiff would not appear for an examination during the pendency of criminal charges against him, they used his failure to appear as a pretense for denying liability under the policies.

We conclude therefore that while the complaint is far from a model pleading, it does allege in substance a breach on the part of defendant insurance companies of their duty of good faith and fair dealing which they owed plaintiff. We emphasize that we are passing only upon the sufficiency of these allegations which of course must be sustained by proper proof.

With regard to the defendants other than the three insurance companies, we reach a different result. Plaintiff alleges that Brown—the insurance adjusting firm, and its employee, Busching, and Cummins, the law firm, and its employee, Ricketts—were the agents and employees of defendant insurers and of each other and were acting within the scope of that agency and employment when they committed the acts attributed to them. However, plaintiff contends that these non-insurer defendants breached only the duty of good faith and fair dealing; therefore, we need not consider the possibility that they may have committed another tort in their respective capacities as total strangers to the contracts of insurance.

Obviously, the non-insurer defendants were not parties to the agreements for insurance; therefore, they are not, as such, subject to an implied duty of good faith and fair dealing. Moreover, as agents and employees of the defendant insurers, they cannot be held accountable on a theory of conspiracy. ... Accordingly, the judgment of dismissal in favor of the non-insurer defendants must be affirmed.

* * *

Defendants' duty, as we have explained, arises from a contractual relationship existing between the parties. This duty has been characterized as an "implied covenant" that "neither party will do anything which will injure the right of the other to receive the benefits of the agreement." While it might be argued that defendants would be excused from their contractual duties (e.g., obligation to indemnify) if plaintiff breached his obligations under the policies, we do not think that plaintiff's alleged breach excuses defendants from their duty, implied by law, of good faith and fair dealing. In other words, the insurer's duty is unconditional and independent of the performance of plaintiff's contractual obligations.

* * *

We conclude, therefore, that the duty of good faith and fair dealing on the part of defendant insurance companies is an absolute one. At the same time, we do not say that the parties cannot define, by the terms of the contract, their respective obligations and duties. We say merely that no matter how those duties are stated, the non-performance by one party of its contractual duties cannot excuse a breach of the duty of good faith and fair dealing by the other party while the contract between them is in effect and not rescinded.

* * *

In summary, we conclude that plaintiff has stated facts sufficient to constitute a cause of action in tort against defendant insurance companies for breach of their implied duty of good faith and fair dealing; that plaintiff's failure to appear at the office of the insurers' counsel in order to submit to an examination under oath and to produce certain documents, as appearing from the allegations of the complaint, is not fatal to the statement of such cause of action; and that plaintiff has stated facts sufficient for the recovery of damages for mental distress whether or not these facts constitute "extreme" or "outrageous" conduct. On the other hand, since the remaining defendants were not subject to the implied duty arising from the contractual relationship, we conclude that the complaint does not state sufficient facts to constitute a cause of action against them and that the judgment of dismissal in their favor was proper.

As to defendants Aetna Insurance Company, Yosemite Insurance Company and American Home Assurance Company, the judgment is reversed and the cause is remanded to the trial court with directions to overrule the demurrers and to allow said defendants a reasonable time within which to answer. As to the remaining defendants, the judgment is affirmed.

B. "Breach of the Common Law Duty of Good Faith and Fair Dealing"

Natividad v. Alexsis, Inc.
875 S.W.2d 695
(Tex. 1994)

Gonzalez, Justice. Rosa Natividad was injured twice within a year while in the course of her employment with Revco D.S., Inc. She filed a workers' compensation claim for each injury. Both claims were settled. On February 24, 1989, Natividad filed suit alleging various causes of action arising from the handling of her workers' compensation claims by Revco, National Union Fire Insurance Company of Pittsburgh, AIG Risk Management, Alexsis, Inc., and William Steen. National Union was Revco's workers' compensation carrier. National Union contracted to have AIG provide all the services under the policy. AIG contracted with Alexsis, Inc. for claims adjusting services under the policy. William Steen, a claims adjuster, was an employee of Alexsis, Inc.

Natividad settled with National Union, AIG, and Revco, and dismissed them from the suit. Natividad's Fifth Amended Petition asserted the following causes of action against Alexsis, Inc. and Steen: 1) breach of the duty of good faith and fair dealing; 2) fraud; 3) economic duress, oppression and outrage; 4) negligent infliction of emotional distress; and, 5) extreme and outrageous conduct which caused severe emotional distress as set forth in SECTION 46 of the SECOND RESTATEMENT OF TORTS.

Alexsis, Inc. and Steen moved for summary judgment on the grounds that they did not owe a duty of good faith and fair dealing to Natividad and that Natividad could not recover for her emotional distress. The trial court rendered a take-nothing summary judgment in favor of the defendants.

The court of appeals reversed the summary judgment in part. Although there were no pleadings and evidence to support the theory, the court of appeals held that Natividad was a third-party beneficiary of a contract between Alexsis, Inc. and National Union, and that Alexsis, Inc. owed Natividad a duty of good faith and fair dealing. However, the court of appeals held that Steen did not owe a duty of good faith and fair dealing because "[h]e did not issue an insurance policy and did not contract with the carrier … to provide any adjusting services." …

On appeal to this court, Natividad argues that the court of appeals erred in holding that Steen did not owe Natividad a duty of good faith and fair dealing. By cross-application, Alexsis, Inc. and Steen argue that because the duty of good faith and fair dealing must be based on a contract between the parties, neither Alexsis, Inc. nor Steen owed Natividad this duty. …

DUTY OF GOOD FAITH AND FAIR DEALING

Rosa Natividad asks this court to extend the common-law duty of good faith and fair dealing which we first recognized in *Arnold v. National County Mutual Fire Insurance Company*, 725 S.W.2d 165 (Tex. 1987), to bind entities and individuals in the insurance industry that are not in contractual privity with the claimant. Because the existence of a contract—vesting the insurer with "exclusive control over the evaluation, processing, and denial of claims," that gives rise to a "special relationship"—is a necessary element of the duty of good faith and fair dealing, we decline to do so.

Since its inception, the duty of good faith and fair dealing has only been applied to protect parties who have a special relationship based on trust or unequal bargaining power. In the insurance context, this special relationship arises out of "the parties' unequal bargaining power and the nature of insurance contracts which would allow unscrupulous insurers to take advantage of their insureds." *Viles v. Security Nat'l Ins. Co.*, 788 S.W.2d 566 (Tex. 1990); *Aranda v. Insurance Co. of N. Am.*, 748 S.W.2d 210 (Tex. 1988); *Chitsey v. National Lloyds Ins. Co.*, 738 S.W.2d 641 (Tex. 1987).

This court in *Arnold* stated: While this court has declined to impose an implied covenant of good faith and fair dealing in every contract, we have recognized that a duty of good faith and fair dealing may arise as a result of a special relationship between the parties governed or created by a contract. *Arnold*, 725 S.W.2d at 167; *See also English v. Fischer*, 660 S.W.2d 521, 524 (Tex. 1983) (Spears, J. concurring) ("I would note … that Texas courts have read a duty of good faith and fair dealing into many types of contractually based transactions.")

When this court applied the duty of good faith and fair dealing to the workers' compensation relationship in *Aranda*, 748 S.W.2d at 212, we continued to focus on the special relationship created by the contractual relationship of the parties: the employer, the employee, and the insurance carrier. We stated:

> The Workers' Compensation Act sets forth a compensation scheme that is based on a three-party agreement entered into by the employer, the employee, and the compensation carrier. … As between the compensation carrier and the employee, there

> is a promise for a promise: the carrier agrees to compensate the employee for injuries sustained in the course of employment, and the employee agrees to relinquish his common law rights against his employer. The employee is thus a party to the contract and therefore entitled to recover in that capacity.
>
> The contract between a compensation carrier and an employee creates the same type of special relationship that arises under other insurance contracts. The duty of good faith and fair dealing emanates from the special relationship between the parties and not from the terms of the contract, therefore its breach gives rise to tort damages and not simply to contractual liability. However, the "special relationship" exists only because the insured and the insurer are parties to a contract that is the result of unequal bargaining power, and by its nature allows unscrupulous insurers to take advantage of their insureds. Without such a contract there would be no "special relationship" and hence, no duty of good faith and fair dealing.

The court of appeals and the Dissent look to *Scott Wetzel Services, Inc. v. Johnson*, 821 P.2d 804 (Colo. 1991), to support extending the duty of good faith and fair dealing to the agents of insurance carriers. Their reliance on this case is misplaced. In *Wetzel*, 821 P.2d at 812, the court imposed a duty of good faith based on policy goals contained in that state's compensation act. In contrast, as set out above, we have always recognized that in an insurance context, the duty of good faith and fair dealing arises only when there is a contract giving rise to a "special relationship."

In the present case, there is no special relationship between Natividad and either Alexsis, Inc. or Steen. Natividad is not a party to a contract with Alexsis, Inc. or Steen. Natividad's contractual privity is only with her employer and National Union. Natividad is owed a duty of good faith and fair dealing from National Union. This duty is non-delegable. When the insurance carrier has contracted with agents or contractors for the performance of claims handling services, the carrier remains liable for actions by those agents or contractors that breach the duty of good faith and fair dealing owed to the insured by the carrier.

Natividad was entitled to and did recover from National Union for actions by its employees, agents or contractors that breached the duty of good faith and fair dealing owed to Natividad by National Union. Alexsis, Inc. and Steen—because they were not parties to a contract with Natividad giving rise to a "special relationship"—owed Natividad no duty of good faith and fair dealing.

Thus, the court of appeals was correct in affirming the trial court's summary judgment as to Natividad's claim for breach of the duty of good faith and fair dealing against Steen. The court of appeals erred, however, in reversing the trial court's summary judgment as to Natividad's claim for breach of the duty of good faith and fair dealing against Alexsis, Inc. ...

Conclusion

There is no need to extend the duty of good faith and fair dealing—owed by insurance carriers to their insureds—to include agents or contractors of the insurance carrier. Insurance carriers are liable for actions of their agents or contractors that breach the duty of good faith and fair dealing. We reverse the judgment of the court of appeals and render judgment that Rosa Natividad take nothing in her suit against defendants Alexsis, Inc. and William Steen.

Notes and Questions

1. **Distinguishing a Contract's Implied Covenant of Good Faith and Fair Dealing from a Common Law Duty of Good Faith and Fair Dealing.** In *Gruenberg*, Justice Sullivan wrote: "There is an implied covenant of good faith and fair dealing in every contract." And the majority of state supreme courts have embraced that rule. *See, e.g.*, *Cantwell v. City of Boise*, 191 P.3d 205, 213 (Idaho 2008) ("Idaho law recognizes a cause of action for breach of an implied covenant of good faith and fair dealing); *In re Hennepin Cnty. 1986 Recycling Bond Litig.*, 540 N.W.2d 494, 502 (Minn. 1995) ("Under Minnesota law, every contract includes an implied covenant of good faith and fair dealing ..."); and *Wood v. N.J. Mfrs. Ins. Co.*, 206 N.J. 562, 577 (N.J. 2011) ("[E]very contract in New Jersey contains an implied covenant of good faith and fair dealing[, t]hat is, neither party shall do anything which will have the effect of destroying or injuring the right of the other party to receive the fruits of the contract[.]"). On the other hand, in *Natividad*, Justice Gonzalez wrote: "[T]his court has declined to *impose* an implied covenant of good faith and fair dealing in every contract. ... [But] we have recognized that a duty of good faith and fair dealing may arise as a result of a special relationship between the parties governed or *created by a contract.*" What is the major distinction between the two doctrines?

2. **Blurred Distinction Between a Breach of a Covenant in a Contract and a Breach of Duty Arising from a Contractual Relationship**. Does the dissenting opinion in *Natividad* raise an

important point? Justice Gammage—joined by Justices Hightower, Doggett and Spector—wrote:

> I dissent from the majority's holding that the duty of good faith and fair dealing does not extend to both National Union and its adjusting company, Alexsis. This court has never held that privity between the parties is a necessary talisman giving rise to the duty of good faith and fair dealing. *See e.g. Manges v. Guerra*, 673 S.W.2d 180 (1984). There, we held that the special relationship between an executive mineral rights owner and the nonexecutive owners gave rise to the duty of utmost good faith. The contract in that case, however, was between Manges and the Guerra partnership, not the individual nonexecutive owners. Manges, 673 S.W.2d at 181.
>
> The duty of good faith and fair dealing "emanates not from the terms of the insurance contract, but from an obligation imposed in law 'as a result of a special relationship between the parties governed or created by a contract.'" *Viles v. Security National Ins. Co.*, 788 S.W.2d 566, 567 (Tex. 1990). Here, although there is no contract between Natividad and the insurance company's agent, Alexsis, there is a contract whereby Alexsis promised to handle the claims of Revco employees in accordance with the terms of the policy issued by National Union. Consequently, when Alexsis directly dealt with Natividad the relationship was governed by the workers' compensation insurance contract.
>
> Moreover, this court—unlike other jurisdictions which require privity—has declined to base the duty on an implied covenant in contract. *Arnold v. Nat. County Mut. Fire Ins. Co.,* 725 S.W.2d 165, 167 (Tex. 1987), citing *English v. Fischer*, 660 S.W.2d 521, 522 (Tex. 1983); cf. *Gruenberg v. Aetna Ins. Co.*, 510 P.2d 1032 (Cal. 1973). By its decision today to require contractual privity, the majority blurs the distinction between the *breach of a covenant in contract* and the *breach of a duty arising from a relationship*, ironically a distinction Justice Gonzalez, the author of the majority opinion, earlier felt worthy of note. *See Chitsey v. National Lloyds Ins. Co.*, 738 S.W.2d 641, 643 n. 1 (1987).
>
> In addition, … [i]n Aranda, we recognized a legal fiction by holding that the insured employee is party to a tripartite agreement and exchanges a "promise for a promise" with the employer's insurance carrier. *Aranda v. Insurance Co. of N. America*, 748 S.W.2d 210, 212 (Tex. 1988). When the carrier delegates his duty to fulfill that promise, the employee necessarily becomes a third party beneficiary under the delegation

contract, here between National Union and AIG. Under the majority's holding, however, Natividad would not even have a cause of action against AIG, the entity which steps directly into the carrier's contractual relationship. ... Because I believe you must punish the actor to curb the actions, I respectfully dissent. National Union and Alexsis have the duty of good faith and fair dealing, whether the power derives from a contract with the insured or through a delegation of duties under the same contract.

3. **Good Faith, Fair Dealing, and Fulfilling Contracting Parties' Reasonable Expectations.** In *Magnan v. Anaconda Industries, Inc.*, 193 Conn. 558, 567 (Conn. 1984), the Supreme Court of Connecticut addressed the essential purpose of the implied covenant of good faith and fair dealing: "[It is] a rule of construction designed to fulfill the reasonable expectations of the contracting parties as they presumably intended. The principle, therefore, cannot be applied to achieve a result contrary to the clearly expressed terms of a contract, unless, possibly, those terms are contrary to public policy."

4. **Proving a Cause of Action Based on a Breach of a Covenant of Good Faith and Fair Dealing.** *See, e.g., New Breed Logistics, Inc. v. CT INDY, NH TT, LLC,* 2011 WL 4909116 (Conn. Super. Ct. Sept. 22, 2011) ("An action for breach of the covenant of good faith and fair dealing requires proof of three essential elements: (1) that the plaintiff and the defendant were parties to a contract under which the plaintiff reasonably expected to receive certain benefits; (2) that the defendant engaged in conduct that injured the plaintiff's right to receive benefits it reasonably expected to receive under the contract; and (3) that when committing the acts by which it injured the plaintiff's right to receive under the contract, the defendant was acting in bad faith.").

Section Three: Breach of Contractual Warranties

Along with judge-made covenants and duties of good faith and fair dealing, negotiated and boilerplate contracts often contain express warranties. Furthermore, various implied warranties are generally attached to construction, manufacturing, insurance, real estate, landlord–tenant, and goods-and-services contracts. But what is a warranty? And what is the difference between a warranty and a covenant or a promise? To be sure, these are important questions. On the other hand, the numerous competing answers are not so clear.

To illustrate, consider these definitions: 1) "A warranty is a contractual term concerning some aspect of the sale—such as title to the goods, or their quality or quantity." *Windham at Carmel Mountain Ranch Assn. v. Superior Court*, 109 Cal. App. 4th 1162, 1168 (Cal. Ct. App. 2003); 2) "[A warranty is] an assurance by one party to a contract of the existence of a fact upon which the other party may rely. ... [I]t amounts to a promise to indemnify the promisee for any loss if the fact warranted proves untrue. ... [A] warranty is not a promise of performance, but a statement of present fact." *First Bank of the Americas v. Motor Car Funding, Inc.*, 690 N.Y.S.2d 17, 21 (N.Y. App. Div. 1999); 3) "A warranty is defined as an affirmation of fact or promise by the seller of items possessing certain characteristics." *Alpine Climate Control, Inc. v. DJ's, Inc.*, 78 P.3d 685, 690 (Wyo. 2003); and 4) "A warranty is an agreement—collateral to the sale of goods or service—by which the seller undertakes to vouch for the condition or quality of the goods sold or service provided. Even though a warranty is a part of a sales contract, it is an independent subsidiary promise, collateral to the main object of the contract, the breach of which gives rise to a cause of action for damages." *Glockzin v. Rhea*, 760 S.W.2d 665, 669 (Tex. App.—Hous. [1st Dist.] 1988).

Moreover, under section 2-313 of the UCC , each of the following acts creates an express warranty: 1) an affirmation of fact or promise made by the seller to the buyer relating to the goods that becomes the basis of the bargain, 2) a description of the goods that becomes part of the basis of the bargain, and 3) a sample or model made part of the basis of the bargain. Perhaps, Judge Doherty's statement—in *Malpass v. Callahan Const. Inc.*, 2001 WL 1772695, *2 (C.C. Va. Oct. 30, 2001)—provides the most cogent explanation. He stated:

> [A] claim for breach of warranty is nothing more than a claim that certain specific express warranties were contained in the oral contract, and that certain warranties arose from that contract by operation of law. Proof at trial of the terms of the oral agreement would answer the question as to whether or not these warranties exist. The argument that the warranties are subsumed by the contract ignores the difference between contract claims and warranty claims. "A good deal of confusion has arisen in many cases on this subject [warranty], from the unfortunate use made of the word warranty. Two things which have been confounded together. A warranty is an express or implied statement of something which the party undertakes shall be part of a contract; and though part of the contract, yet collateral to the express object of it." *Mason v. Chappell*, 56 Va. 572, 585 (1860). While a contract may be made and completed, its collateral warranty—which is nothing more than a promise that a particular proposition of fact related to

> the contract is true—may not yet be resolved. The law allows a suit for breach of warranty, just as it allows a suit for breach of contract. The two can exist simultaneously.

Of course, as Judge Doherty stressed, there are "breach-of-contract claims" and "breach-of-warranty claims." And, to be sure, a claim or an allegation is not a legal theory of recovery. Therefore, when a party wants to litigate a breach-of-warranty claim and secure damages, which cause of action or theory of recovery should appear in the party's complaint? Should the action commence under the law of contract, tort law, or warranty law?

As William Prosser observed more than a half-century ago, it is difficult to answer the latter question categorically. Prosser concluded that an "implied warranty" was "a freak hybrid born of the illicit intercourse of tort and contract." William L. Prosser, *The Assault upon the Citadel (Strict Liability to the Consumer)*, 69 Yale L.J. 1099, 1126 (1960). Of course, Prosser's widely quoted and prototypically imaginative passage takes second place to Karl Llewellyn's all-encompassing metaphor: "True. A warranty is 'a bastard.'" But more importantly, a warranty's tort and contract 'parents' are engaged in a battle. Therefore, it would be wrong for mother-tort to submit to 'over-domination by an illegitimate contract father.'" Karl Llewellyn, *On Warranty of Quality, and Society: II*, 37 COLUM. L. REV. 341, 402 (1937). Today, depending on the jurisdiction, a "breach of warranty claim" may commence under one or a combination of three *common-law* theories of recovery: contract principles, tort law, and the law of warranty.

A. Breach of an Express Warranty

In *Stuart v. Wilkins*, 99 Eng. Rep. 15, 16 (K.B. 1778), Lord Mansfield reiterated the law: "A warranty extends to all faults known and unknown to the seller; ... [and] there must either be an express warranty of soundness, or fraud in the seller, in order to maintain an action." Nearly thirty-five year later, a different King's Bench court expanded the rule: "If an express warranty [is] given, the seller will be liable for any latent defect, according to the old law [of] warranties. But if there [is not a] warranty and the seller sells the thing—as he believes it to be—without fraud, ... the law will [not] imply that he sold it on any other terms than what passed in fact." *Parkinson v. Lee*, 102 Eng. Rep. 389, 392 (K.B. 1802).

Later, in *Curtis v. Hannay*, 170 Eng. Rep. 546, 546 (1800) Lord Eldon restated the measure of damages for a breach of warranty: "I take it to be clear law, that if a person purchases a horse that is warranted, and it afterwards turns out that the horse was unsound at the time of warranty, the buyer may—if he pleases—keep the horse and bring an action on the warranty. ... [H]e will have a right to recover the difference between the value of a sound horse, and one with such defects." *See also Caswell v. Coare*, 127 Eng. Rep. 954, 954 (Com. Pl. 1809) (concluding that if a warranty is false, the buyer has a remedy against the seller to recover damages. But as soon as the unsoundness is discovered, the buyer should immediately tender the horse to the seller, for otherwise he will not be entitled to recover for the keep.).

To be sure, those English law principles are still sound, and state supreme courts in America have adopted each one in various forms. But, if one reads carefully, it appears that those rules govern the disposition of legal disputes only when sellers of goods and services breach express warranties. Do American courts apply different rules to resolve a breach-of-an-express-warranty conflict when aggrieved consumers commence actions against, say, construction companies or manufacturers? A partial answer appears in the next case.

Jones v. Centex Homes
2012 WL 877561
(Ohio 2012)

Pfeifer, J. Appellants Paul Jones and Latosha Sanders purchased a new house from appellee—Centex Homes—in 2004. After moving into their new home, they discovered that their computers, cordless telephones, and televisions did not operate properly. They alleged that metal joists in the house are magnetized and are causing the problems.

Apparently, efforts to resolve the problem were unavailing, because they filed suit against Centex Homes, alleging various causes of action, including breach of contract, breach of express and implied warranties, negligence, and failure to perform in a workmanlike manner. On April 30, 2008, that case was consolidated with a nearly identical case filed by Eric and Ginger Estep, who are also appellants in this case. Centex Homes moved for summary judgment, arguing that appellants had waived all warranties—whether express or implied—except the specific limited warranty that Centex Homes provided in the sales agreements.

The trial court agreed and granted the motion for summary judgment, finding "as a matter of law that the Limited Home Warranty is not unconscionable." On appeal, the court of appeals affirmed the trial court's judgment, stating: [W]e find no error with the trial court's determination that both the sale agreement and the limited warranty adequately explained in "numerous places that the Limited Home Warranty covers all defects in materials and workmanship and that there are no other warranties either expressed or implied." We granted appellants' discretionary appeal.

ANALYSIS

A. The Duty to Construct a House in a Workmanlike Manner

The duty to construct a house in a workmanlike manner has been imposed by law on all home builders in Ohio since at least 1966. In *Mitchem v. Johnson*, 218 N.E.2d 594 (Ohio 1966), home buyers sought compensation for water damage resulting from their houses having been built in a low portion of a lot with surface-water problems and without a foundation drainage system. Notwithstanding the fact that no warranty covered the alleged defect, we concluded that the home buyers were entitled to recover damages if they could establish that the home builder had not constructed the house in a workmanlike manner, stating:

> A duty is imposed by law upon a builder-vendor of a real-property structure to construct the same in a workmanlike manner and to employ such care and skill in the choice of materials and work as will be commensurate with the gravity of the risk involved in protecting the structure against faults and hazards, including those inherent in its site. If the violation of that duty proximately causes a defect hidden from revelation by an inspection reasonably available to the vendee, the vendor is answerable to the vendee for the resulting damages.

In determining that a duty to construct a house in a workmanlike manner exists, the court plowed the wide fertile plain between two extreme concepts: *caveat emptor* and strict liability. Without expressly saying so, the court appears to have determined that it would be unfair for it to apply either of these standards. The court also stated that "[t]he requirement of workmanlike performance is no more than that which the law imposes upon the builder of a structure on land owned by another, unless, of course, a higher duty may be fairly implied from the terms of the contract itself." citing 17A CORPUS JURIS SECUNDUM, CONTRACTS § 515, at 851. The court specifically stated that an implied warranty was not being imposed.

In *Ins. Co. of N. Am. v. Bonnie Built Homes*, 64 Ohio St.2d 269, 270–271 (1980), we stated that the "duty of the builder-vendor to build a structure in a workmanlike manner is a duty arising out of the contract of sale and not out of a general duty owed to the public at large," and held that the duty to construct a house in a workmanlike manner did not extend to subsequent buyers of the house. Just three years later, we recanted. In *McMillan v. Brune–Harpenau–Torbeck Builders*, Inc., 8 Ohio St.3d 3, 4 (1983), we overruled *Bonnie Built*, stating, "No sound policy reasons exist to prevent the extension of this duty to all subsequent vendees as well." Our decision was grounded in two policy considerations: "extension of the duty of care in the real property context follows the trend of strong legal precedent in the area of products liability" and "[i]mproved workmanship and accountability are promoted by an expansion of the scope of the duty."

Between *Bonnie Built* and *McMillan*, we further explored the ramifications of the duty to construct in a workmanlike manner in *Velotta v. Leo Petronzio Landscaping, Inc.*, 433 N.E.2d 147 (Ohio 1982). The court clearly differentiated an *implied warranty of suitability*, which in effect would hold a builder strictly liable for defects in the structure, from the *duty to construct in a workmanlike manner*, which essentially holds a builder liable only for negligence. Id. at 377–378, 433 N.E.2d 147. We concluded that although the obligation to construct in a workmanlike manner may arise from a contract, the cause of action is not based on contract but on a duty imposed by law. Thus, we held that the duty applied in *Velotta*, even though no oral or written warranties had been offered or agreed to. In fact, the house had been sold "as is."

We conclude that in Ohio, a duty to construct houses in a workmanlike manner using ordinary care is imposed by law on all home builders.

B. Can a Home Buyer Waive His Right to Enforce the Home Builder's Duty to Construct the House in a Workmanlike Manner?

Appellants and Centex Homes agree that the purchase contracts associated with this case contain provisions that waive all implied warranties. In place of whatever implied warranties might otherwise be in effect, Centex Homes offered a detailed limited warranty. Although we see no legal impediment to such an arrangement, that issue is not squarely before us. We are called upon only to determine whether a home buyer can waive his right to enforce the builder's legal duty to construct the house in a workmanlike manner using ordinary care.

At oral argument, Centex Homes repeatedly referred to the requirement that a home builder construct a house in a workmanlike manner as an "implied warranty," while appellants repeatedly referred to it as a "duty." In *Mitchem*, we referred to the requirement as a "duty," but we also said that it was an "implied term of the sale" that the builder would complete the house in a workmanlike manner. *Mitchem*, 7 Ohio St.2d at 73. ... It is clear, based on the discussion above, that we concluded that the requirement is not an implied warranty, but instead is a duty imposed by law.

To determine whether a home buyer can waive his right to enforce this duty, we again turn to *Mitchem* and *Velotta*. In *Mitchem*, we stated that all persons must "measure their conduct by that of the ordinarily prudent person under all the circumstances, which include the risk of harm from the natural and probable consequences of that conduct." Having enunciated this general rule, we stated that it applied to home builders. In *Velotta*, we stated that the duty owed by a builder-vendor "is the duty imposed by law on all persons to exercise ordinary care." *Velotta*, 69 Ohio St.2d at 378. And we held that the duty applied even though the house had been sold "as is" and there had been no express or implied warranties.

We conclude that the duty to construct a house in a workmanlike manner—using ordinary care—is the baseline standard that Ohio home buyers can expect builders to meet. The duty does not require builders to be perfect, but it does establish a standard of care below which builders may not fall without being subject to liability, even if a contract with the home buyer purports to relieve the builder of that duty. Accordingly, we conclude that a home builder's duty to construct a house in a workmanlike manner using ordinary care is a duty imposed by law, and a home buyer's right to enforce that duty cannot be waived.

CONCLUSION

We reverse the judgment of the court of appeals and remand the cause to the court of common pleas for a trial on appellants' tort claims that Centex Homes breached its duty to construct their homes in a workmanlike manner using ordinary care. The various other issues decided by the trial court and the court of appeals are unaffected by our opinion.

Judgment reversed and cause remanded.

NOTES AND QUESTIONS

1. **A Breach-of-Warranty Action Sounds in Both Contract and Tort.** *See Reid v. Eckerds Drugs, Inc.*, 253 S.E.2d 344, 347 (N.C. 1979) ("It is now generally acknowledged that the action for breach of warranty is an offspring of mixed parentage, aspects of it sounding in both tort and contract, but following strictly the rules and precedents of neither."); and, *Mitchell v. Pearson Enterprises*, 697 P.2d 240, 247 (Utah 1985) ("An action for breach of warranty may sound in either contract or tort.").

2. **A Breach-of-Warranty Action Sounds Only in Contract**. *See Fried v. Freeman*, 176 S.E.2d 458, 460 (Ga. Ct. App. 1970) ("An action for mere breach of warranty unmixed with fraud sounds in contract, not tort"), and *Rucker v. Hagar et al.*, 230 P. 70, 71 (Kan. 1924) ("Warranty sounds in contract ... and liability predicated on breach of warranty is contract and not tort liability.").

3. **A Breach-of-Warranty Action Sounds Only in Tort.** *See Iacono v. Anderson Concrete Corp.*, 326 N.E.2d 267, 270 n.1 (Ohio 1975) ("This court has recognized that, historically, an action grounded on breach of warranty sounded in tort rather than contract. It is a mistaken notion that use of the term 'warranty' always carried the implication of a contractual relationship."), and *Humber v. Morton,* 426 S.W.2d 554, 556 (Tex. 1968) (under Texas law, breach of implied warranties of merchantability and fitness for a particular purpose sound in tort and not in contract.).

4. **Whether a Breach-of-Warranty Action Sounds in Contract or Tort Depends**. *See Evans Laboratories, Inc. v. Roberts*, 423 S.W.2d 271, 272 (Ark. 1968) ("Whether a suit for breach of warranty sounds in contract or in tort depends upon the nature of the suit, the nature and extent of the warranty, and the effect or results of the breach."), and *Gazija v. Nicholas Jerns Co.,* 543 P.2d 338, 340 (Wash. 1975) ("Whether an action sounds in contract or tort is determined from the pleadings and complaint as a whole and the evidence relied upon, not by particular words and allegations, the form adopted by the pleader, what the pleader calls it, or the understanding of counsel or the trial court.").

5. **Breach-of-an-Express-Warranty Action: Establishing a Prima Case Using Different Elements**. In Minnesota, an action for breach of express warranty requires a complainant to establish three elements: 1) the existence of a warranty ; 2) a breach of the warranty; and 3) a causal link between the breach and the harm. *Peterson v. Bendix Home Sys., Inc.*, 318 N.W.2d 50, 52–53 (Minn. 1982). On the other hand, under New Jersey law, a breach-of-an-express-warranty action has four elements: 1) proof a contract between the parties; 2) proof of a breach of contract; 3) proof of damages flowing from the breach; and 4) proof that complainant performed her contractual obligations. *Hemy v. Perdue Farms, Inc.*, 2011 WL 6002463, *23 (D.N.J. Nov. 30, 2011). Furthermore, in Texas, a plaintiff must prove six elements to establish a breach-of-an-express-warranty action: 1) the defendant sold services to the plaintiff; 2) the defendant made a representation to the plaintiff about the characteristics of the services by affirmation of fact, by promise, or by description; 3) the representation became part of the basis of the bargain; 4) the defendant breached the warranty; 5) the plaintiff notified the defendant of the breach; and 6) the plaintiff suffered injury. *See Paragon General Contractors, Inc. v. Larco Const., Inc.,* 227 S.W.3d 876, 886 (Tex. App. Ct.—Dallas

2007), citing *Sw. Bell Tel. Co. v. FDP Corp.*, 811 S.W.2d 572, 576–77 & n. 3 (Tex. 1991) (embracing some of the UCC's elements).

B. Breach of an Implied Warranty

To repeat, depending on the jurisdiction and contracting parties' undertaking, one or a combination of implied warranties may attach to a contract. Some names are 1) an "implied warranty of merchantability," 2) an "implied warranty of fitness for a particular purpose," 3) an "implied warranty of workmanship," 4) an "implied warranty of good and workmanlike service," 5) an "implied warranty of workmanlike performance," 6) an "implied warranty of the plans and specifications," 7) an "implied warranty of the adequacy of specifications," 8) an "implied warranty of design," 9) an "implied warranty of eviction," 10) a "statutory, implied warranty of title," 11) an "implied warranty of suitability," and 12) an "implied warranty of habitability."

When implied warranties are breached, they also generate a considerable amount of conflict over whether complainants may commence an action that sounds in tort or in contract. Compare *American Medical Electronics, Inc. v. Korn*, 819 S.W.2d 573, 576 (Tex. App.—Dallas 1991, writ denied) (declaring that cause of action—framed as a breach of an implied warranty in an oral contract—sounds in tort), with *Garcia v. Edgewater Hosp.*, 613 N.E.2d 1243, 1249 (Ill. Ct. App. 1993) (reaffirming that a breach of an implied warranty of merchantability sounds in contract law, not tort law). Consider the case below: It explains in part why one court forced contracting parties to litigate their implied-warranty dispute under contract principles.

Pugh v. Holmes
405 A.2d 897
(Pa. 1979)

Larsen, Justice. Eloise Holmes, appellee, had been—pursuant to an oral month-to-month lease—renting a residential dwelling in Chambersburg in Franklin County at the rate of $60.00 per month from November, 1971 until recently. Her landlord, appellant J. C. Pugh, instituted two separate landlord-tenant actions against appellee before a justice of the peace—the first resulting in a judgment for unpaid rent (for the period from September, 1975 through June, 1976) and the second resulting in a judgment for unpaid rent (for the period from June, 1976 through August, 1976) and for possession of the premises.

Following Mrs. Holmes' appeals to the Court of Common Pleas of Franklin County, appellant filed separate complaints—the first seeking unpaid rent and the second seeking both unpaid rent and possession. In both actions, appellee filed answers asserting a defense of the landlord's alleged breach of an implied warranty of habitability. Additionally, in the second action, appellee asserted a setoff due in an amount which she claimed she had spent to repair a broken lock after having given appellant notice and a reasonable opportunity to repair the lock. Appellee also filed a counterclaim for the cost of repairing other allegedly defective conditions of which she had given appellant notice. Appellant filed preliminary objections to the answer and counterclaim which the Court of Common Pleas sustained finding that appellee's answer failed to set forth a legal defense to the landlord's actions, and that the counterclaim failed to set forth a legal cause of action.

On appeal, the Superior Court, by opinion of President Judge Jacobs, reversed and remanded. The Superior Court abolished the doctrine of caveat emptor as applied to residential leases and held that a warranty of habitability by the landlord will be implied in all such leases—which implied warrant would be mutually dependent upon the tenant's obligation to pay rent. … [T]his Court granted appellant's petition for allowance of appeal.

I. Doctrine of Caveat Emptor Abolished/Implied Warranty of Habitability Adopted

The doctrine of caveat emptor comported with the needs of the society in which it developed. However, we find that the doctrine of caveat emptor has outlived its usefulness and must be abolished, and that, in order to keep in step with the realities of modern day leasing, it is appropriate to adopt an implied warranty of habitability in residential leases. The rule of caveat emptor—as applied to landlord-tenant relationships—developed in England in the sixteenth century and was adopted in the nineteenth century as the law of this Commonwealth in *Moore v. Weber*, 71 Pa. 429 (Pa. 1872). *Moore* held:

> The rule here, as in other cases, is caveat emptor. The lessee's eyes are his bargain. He is bound to examine the premises he rents, and secure himself by covenants to repair. In the primarily agrarian society in which the doctrine developed, the law viewed the lease transaction as a conveyance of land for a term, and the focal interest in the conveyance was the land. [A]ny shelters or structures existing on the land were "incidental" concerns. The rent was viewed as "coming out of the land" itself, not from the dwelling or the dweller. The feudal landlord "had no obligations to the tenant other than those made expressly, and the tenant's obligation to pay rent was independent of the landlord's (covenants). … The doctrine of caveat emptor was fully applicable. The tenant's only protections were to inspect the premises before taking

> possession or to extract express warranties from the landlord. It was assumed that landlords and tenants held equal bargaining power in arranging their rental agreements, and that the agrarian tenant had the ability to inspect the dwelling adequately and to make simple repairs in the buildings which possessed no modern conveniences such as indoor plumbing or electrical wiring.
>
> As agrarian society declined and population centers shifted from rural to urban areas, the common law concepts of landlord-tenant relationships did not change. Despite the facts that the primary purpose of the urban leasing arrangement was housing and not land and that the tenant could neither adequately inspect nor repair urban dwelling units, landlords still were not held to any implied warranties in the places they rented and tenants leased dwellings at their own risk.

As stated by appellee, "times have changed. So has the law." Today, the doctrine of the implied warranty of habitability has attained majority status in the United States, the doctrine having been embraced by the appellate courts and/or the legislatures of some 40 state jurisdictions and the District of Columbia. The warranty recognizes that the modern tenant is not interested in land, but rather bargains for a dwelling house suitable for habitation.

"Functionally viewed, the modern apartment dweller is a consumer of housing services. The contemporary leasing of residences envisions one person (landlord) exchanging for periodic payments (rent) a bundle of goods and services, rights and obligations. The now classic description of this economic reality appears in *Javins v. First National Realty Corp.*, 428 F.2d 1071, 1074 (D.C. Cir. 1970). When American city dwellers both rich and poor, seek "shelter today, they seek a well-known package of goods and services a package which includes not merely walls and ceilings, but also adequate heat, light and ventilation, serviceable plumbing facilities, secure windows and doors, proper sanitation, and proper maintenance." *Commonwealth v. Monumental Properties, Inc.*, 329 A.2d 812, 820–21 (Pa. 1974) (holding that Unfair Trade Practices and Consumer Protection Law are applicable to residential leases.)

Moreover, prospective tenants today can have vastly inferior bargaining power compared with the landlord, as was recognized in *Reitmeyer v. Sprecher*, 243 A.2d 395, 398 (Pa. 1968). In *Reitmeyer* this court stated:

> Stark necessity very often forces a tenant into occupancy of premises far from desirable and in a defective state of repair. The acute housing shortage mandates that the average prospective tenant accede to the demands of the prospective landlord as to conditions of rental, which, under ordinary conditions with housing available, the average tenant would not

> and should not accept. No longer does the average prospective tenant occupy a free bargaining status and no longer do the average landlord-to-be and tenant-to-be negotiate a lease on an "arm's length" basis.

The Superior Court correctly observed that to join the trend toward an implied warranty of habitability would not be a complete and sudden break with the past, but would be the "next step in the law which has been developing in the Commonwealth for a number of years." Pennsylvania courts have held that a tenant's obligation to pay rent was mutually dependent on express covenants of a landlord to repair and that a material breach of the landlord's covenant to repair relieved a tenant from his obligation to pay rent. *McDanel v. Mack Realty Company*,172 A. 97 (Pa. 1934). In *Reitmeyer v. Sprecher, supra*, recognizing the contractual nature of modern leasing and the severe housing shortage resulting in unequal bargaining power, this court adopted § 357 of the RESTATEMENT (SECOND) OF TORTS and imposed liability on a landlord who had breached a covenant to repair a dangerous condition on the premises, which breach resulted in injury to the tenant.

In *Elderkin v. Gaster*, 288 A.2d 771, 776 (Pa. 1972), we abolished caveat emptor and adopted an implied warranty of habitability in sales of new homes to buyers by vendors/builders. In *Elderkin* we noted "caveat emptor developed when the buyer and seller were in an equal bargaining position and they could readily be expected to protect themselves in the deed. ... 'The caveat emptor rule as applied to new houses is an anachronism patently out of harmony with modern home buying practices.'" ...

Given the foregoing considerations and authority, we affirm the Superior Court's holding that a lease is in the nature of a contract and is to be controlled by principles of contract law. The covenants and warranties in the lease are mutually dependent; the tenant's obligation to pay rent and the landlord's obligation imposed by the implied warranty of habitability to provide and maintain habitable premises are, therefore, dependent and a material breach of one of these obligations will relieve the obligation of the other so long as the breach continues.

* * *

III. BREACH OF THE IMPLIED WARRANTY OF HABITABILITY

Appellant also asserts that the Superior Court erred by failing to establish definite standards by which habitability can be measured and breach of the warranty ascertained. We disagree the parameters of the warranty were adequately defined by the Superior Court. "The implied warranty is designed to insure that a landlord will provide facilities and services vital to the life, health, and safety of the tenant and to the use of the premises for residential purposes." *Pugh v. Holmes*, 384 A.2d at 1240. This warranty is applicable both at the beginning of the lease and throughout its duration.

In order to constitute a breach of the warranty the defect must be of a nature and kind which will prevent the use of the dwelling for its intended purpose to provide premises fit for habitation by its dwellers. At a minimum, this means the premises must be safe and sanitary of course, there is no obligation on the part of the landlord to supply a perfect or aesthetically pleasing dwelling. "Materiality of the breach is a question of fact to be decided by the trier of fact on a case-by-case basis." Several factors (not exclusive) are listed by the Superior Court as considerations in determining materiality, including the existence of housing code violations and the nature, seriousness and duration of the defect.

We believe these standards fully capable of guiding the fact finder in his determination of materiality of the breach. Further, these standards are flexible enough to allow the gradual development of the habitability doctrine in the best common law tradition. This finds support in *Elderkin v. Gaster, supra*, wherein we declined to establish rigid standards for determining habitability and its breach in the builder/vendor vendee context. … [I]nstead, [we] defined habitability in terms of "contemporary community standards" and breach of the warranty as whether the defect prevented the use of the dwelling for the purposes intended habitation. In that case, we held that lack of a potable water supply to the home prevented its use as habitation and, accordingly, found the implied warranty of habitability to have been breached.

Additionally, we agree with the Superior Court[:] … [T]o assert a breach of the implied warranty of habitability, a tenant must prove he or she gave notice to the landlord of the defect or condition, that he (the landlord) had a reasonable opportunity to make the necessary repairs, and that he failed to do so.

Appellant would require that a determination of breach of the implied warranty be dependent upon proof of violations of the local housing codes. We decline to accept this argument as it would unnecessarily restrict the determination of breach. The Supreme Court of Massachusetts was asked to define their implied warranty of habitability by reference to a housing code of statewide applicability, but declined to do so. In *Boston Housing Authority v. Hemingway*, 293 N.E.2d 831, 844, n 16 (Mass. 1973) that court stated:

> The State Sanitary Code minimum standards of fitness for human habitation and any relevant local health regulations provide the trial court with the threshold requirements that all housing must meet. Proof of any violation of these regulations would usually constitute compelling evidence that the apartment was not in habitable condition, regardless of whether

> the evidence was sufficient proof of a constructive eviction under our old case law. However, the protection afforded by the implied warranty or (sic) habitability does not necessarily coincide with the Code's requirements. There may be instances where conditions not covered by the Code regulations render the apartment uninhabitable. Although we have eliminated the defense of constructive eviction in favor of a warranty of habitability defense, a fact situation, which would have demonstrated a constructive eviction, would now be sufficient proof of a material breach of the warranty of habitability, regardless of whether a sanitary code violation existed or not.

Other courts have likewise concluded that the existence of housing code violations is only one of several evidentiary considerations that enter into the materiality of the breach issue—e. g., *Foisy v. Wyman*, 515 P.2d 160 (Wash. 1973); *King v. Moorehead*, 495 S.W.2d 65 (Mo. App. 1973); *Mease v. Fox*, 200 N.W.2d 791 (Iowa 1972). This reasoning is even more persuasive in Pennsylvania where there is no statewide housing code and where many municipalities have not promulgated local housing regulations.

In this case, appellee alleged ten specific defective conditions including a leaky roof, lack of hot water, leaking toilet and pipes, cockroach infestation and hazardous floors and steps. If proven on remand, these conditions would substantially prevent the use of the premises as a habitable dwelling place and could justify a finding by the trier of fact that a breach of the implied warranty of habitability had occurred.

IV. REMEDIES FOR BREACH OF IMPLIED WARRANTY OF HABITABILITY

As the adoption today of the implied warranty of habitability creates new legal rights and obligations, it is essential for this court to outline and clarify some of the available remedies and the manner in which these remedies are to be implemented. The tenant may vacate the premises where the landlord materially breaches the implied warranty of habitability we have held analogously where the landlord materially breaches express covenants to repair or to maintain the leasehold in a habitable state. See *McDanel v. Mack Realty Co., supra,* 172 A. 97. Surrender of possession by the tenant would terminate his obligation to pay rent under the lease. *Lemle v. Breeden*, 462 P.2d 470 (Haw. 1969).

Where the tenant remains in possession and the landlord sues for possession for unpaid rent, the implied warranty of habitability may be asserted as a defense. Virtually all courts addressing the issue of breach of this warranty as a defense concur with this view. *See e. g., Rome v. Walker*, 196 N.W.2d 850 (Mich. App. 1972); *Fritz v. Warthen*, 213 N.W.2d 339 (Minn. 1973); and RESTATEMENT (SECOND) OF PROPERTY,

LANDLORD AND TENANT, § 11.1 (Rent Abatement). If the landlord totally breached the implied warranty of habitability, the tenant's obligation to pay rent would be abated in full the action for possession would fail because there would be no unpaid rent.

If the landlord had not breached the warranty at all, no part of the tenant's obligation to pay rent would be abated and the landlord would be entitled to a judgment for possession and for unpaid rent. If there had been a partial breach of the warranty, the obligation to pay rent would be abated in part only. In such case, a judgment for possession must be denied if the tenant agrees to pay that portion of the rent not abated; if the tenant refuses to pay the partial rent due, a judgment granting possession would be ordered.

* * *

Finally, since the lease is a contract, other traditional contract remedies such as specific performance are available to enforce the implied warranty of habitability. As with other contracts, however, specific performance is an equitable remedy not available as a matter of course but only in unique situations. 11 S. WILLISTON, CONTRACTS § 1418A (3d ed. 1968)

* * *

Accordingly, on remand, if breach of the implied warranty of habitability is proven, the trial court is to apply the "percentage reduction in use" formula to determine the percentage by which the use and enjoyment of the premises had been diminished.

For the foregoing reasons, we overrule all cases inconsistent with this opinion, affirm the order of the Superior Court with the aforementioned modifications, and remand to the Court of Common Pleas of Franklin County for proceedings consonant with this opinion.

NOTES AND QUESTIONS

1. **Implied Warranty of Particular Quality or Fineness.** In *Gardiner v. Gray,* 171 Eng. Rep. 46, 47 (1815), the defendant sold twelve bags of allegedly "waste silk" at 10s. 6d. per pound. When it arrived, the buyer discovered that the quality of the silk could not be sold under the "waste silk" label. Writing for the court, Lord Ellenborough concluded:

    [T]he plaintiff cannot recover on the count alleging that the silk should correspond with the sample. The written contract containing no such stipulation, I cannot allow it to be superadded by parol testimony. This was not a sale by sample. The sample was not produced as a warranty that the bulk corresponded with it, but to enable the purchaser to form a reasonable judgment of the commodity. I am of opinion, however, that under such circumstances, the purchaser has a right to expect a saleable article answering the description in the contract. Without any particular warranty, this is an implied term in every such contract. Where there is no opportunity to inspect the commodity, the maxim of *caveat emptor* does not apply. He cannot without a warranty insist that it shall be of any particular quality or fineness; but the intention of both parties must be taken to be, that it shall be saleable in the market under the denomination mentioned in the contract between them. The purchaser cannot be supposed to buy goods to lay them on a dunghill.

2. **Breach-of-an-Implied-Warranty-of-Merchantability Action**. In *Para-Chem Southern, Inc. v. Sandstone Products, Inc.*, 2009 WL 276507, *14 (Tex. App.—Houston [1st Dist.] Feb. 5, 2009, pet. denied), the Texas Appellate Court in Houston stated that a plaintiff who files a breach of implied warranty of merchantability action must prove that 1) a product was defective for its purpose; 2) the alleged defect existed when the product left the defendant's possession; and 3) the alleged defect proximately caused the injuries and damages.

3. **Breach-of-an-Implied-Warranty-of-Good-Workmanship Action**. *See Cocke v. White*, 697 S.W.2d 739, 743 (Tex. App.—Corpus Christi 1985, writ ref'd n.r.e.) ("The elements that a plaintiff must prove [in a breach of implied warranty claim] are 1) the implied warranty of good workmanship, 2) the breach thereof and 3) that such breach was the proximate cause of the plaintiff's damages.").

4. **Breach-of-an-Implied-Warranty Action in Tort**. *See Smith v. E. R. Squibb & Sons, Inc.*, 273 N.W.2d 476, 479–80 (Mich. 1979) ("A manufacturer of a prescription drug has a legal duty to warn the medical profession, not the patient, of any risks inherent in the use of the drug which the manufacturer knows or should know to exist. ... Breach of implied warranty, on the other hand, is established when plaintiff proves that a product defect attributable to the manufacturer has a causal relationship to plaintiff's injuries. ... The distinction between the elements of negligence and breach of implied warranty is that in the former plaintiff must prove that the defect was caused by the manufacturer's negligence, whereas under the warranty theory, plaintiff need only establish that the defect was attributable to the manufacturer, regardless of the amount of care utilized by the manufacturer.").

CHAPTER FIVE

Proof of Causation, Damages, and Other Remedies

Once more, a plaintiff must prove that a defendant materially breached a stand-alone or a contractual promise. And after satisfying that requirement, the plaintiff then must prove that the breached promise, or a contractual term or condition caused one or a combination of the following events: a bodily injury, mental anguish or emotional distress, lost or destroyed tangible or intangible property, a missed financial or beneficial opportunity, business interruption, lost profits, or some other adverse outcome. Also, the plaintiff must establish that defendant's material breach or non-performance caused or generated damages. This chapter is devoted to discussing common-law theories of causation, damages as well as other common-law and equitable remedies.

Section One: Common-Law Theories of Causation

Under the common law's theory of causation, a plaintiff has two burdens: 1) to prove that defendant's breach was the "cause in fact" and 2) to prove that defendant's breach was the "legal cause" or "proximate cause" of plaintiff's loss and damages. But what are "cause in fact" and "proximate cause"? Have state supreme courts crafted competing definitions of the terms? Is "cause in fact" synonymous with "scientific cause"? The following cases and material present answers to these and related questions.

A. Establishing the Cause in Fact of Losses and Injuries

Ruminations on Cause-in-Fact
9 Stan. L. Rev. 60 (1956)
Wex S. Malone

THE PROCESS OF DETERMINING CAUSE-IN-FACT

A cause is not a fact in the sense that its existence can be established merely through the production of testimony. Although evidentiary data must supply the raw material upon which a finding of cause or no-cause will be based, yet something must first be done with this data by the trier, be he judge or juryman. He must refer the facts presented by the testimony to some judging capacity within himself before he can venture the conclusion that a cause exists. He must arrange the events established by the evidence into a relationship of some kind and he must satisfy himself that the relationship can properly be labeled "cause." The most that can be said is that the trier is making a deduction from evidentiary facts. This operation is not self-performing. It calls into play a variety of intellectual functions that are peculiar to the trier as an individual. It is these that play the decisive role in reaching an answer and it is clear that they are no integral part of the raw fact data upon which the operation is being performed.

Doubtless the above observation holds true to some extent, not only for cause, but for the entire phenomenon of proof. Raw evidence requires interpretation. It must be referred to the experience of the trier before it can acquire meaning. The extent to which the past experience and the judging personality of the trier will be brought into play depends to a large extent upon what is being proved. Very little of a trier's experience background, for example, is required in order to induce him to agree that an automobile tire presented in evidence is "different" from other tires. Somewhat more is required to tell him that the tire is "old," and a goodly amount of his capacity to reach conclusions must be brought into play before he can announce that the tire is "bad," that it is "unfit for use" or that its presence on a vehicle indicates negligence on the part of a car owner. Furthermore, it is noteworthy that in passing from one of these determinations to another we have moved almost imperceptibly from matters of "fact" to matters of "judgment" or "evaluation."

Even more important, the evaluation which the trier will make of the new fact data will necessarily be affected by the purpose he is seeking to serve. This is particularly true of cause, which, as we have seen, is merely an acceptable deduction from evidential facts. All deductions are drawn purposively—that is to say, they are drawn for a reason. A moment's reflection will show that this is true. A car is being driven in haste by an irresponsible youngster along a road which has recently been covered with large loose gravel. A wheel picks up a piece of rock and hurls it into the face of a pedestrian. The comments that this incident may evoke from each of several bystanders will differ.

A neighbor of the youthful driver may attribute the accident to the indifference of the child's parents, who ought not to allow him to drive. This, she will say, is the cause of the injury. A critical road engineer may see the cause of the accident in terms of improper road construction. A teacher of physics might be inspired to use the same incident as an illustration of the impact of a given speed upon an object of certain weight and dimensions. This, he observes, is the cause of the phenomenon. Each observer has put the term "cause" to the use that interests him. Each has drawn upon his own background in varying degrees and each has brought into play different parts of his judging capacity. No single one of these attributions of cause can be said to be more valid than any other, for each observer is using the term for his own purpose.

This same observation is applicable in the court room. Where a doctor and a judge both seek to answer the same question of simple cause, the answers given may be different because their respective interpretations of cause are colored by the purpose to which each puts that word. An elderly worker with a heart ailment of long standing happens to drop dead while engaged in some trivial task for his employer. A medical expert is likely to testify with assurance that the exertion was not a cause of the death. He may explain that the heart was spent and that there was nothing about the work being done that could account for the tragedy. He finds that the relationship between the two events is not sufficiently close to justify him in characterizing it as a cause and effect relationship. ...

Those factors that have proved useful in the resolution of legal disputes, rather than for the purposes of medicine, will dominate the deliberations of the judge. He likely will be impressed by the law's desire to throw its protection around the susceptible and aged worker as well as the one who is in sound health. His judicial experience in other areas of compensation law has made him aware of the fact that the point of contact between job and injury need not be a close one for the purposes served by this statute. He appreciates the fact that workmen's compensation serves as a compromise vehicle which meets only in part the real needs of the worker or widow. Furthermore, he is aware of the traditional uncertainty of the mind of medical science, and he well knows that judges cannot escape the responsibility of taking prompt and final action upon such approximations of truth as can be made available in the courtroom.

Much misunderstanding between lawyers and physicians could be obviated if members of both professions would realize that "simple" causation is not merely an abstract issue of fact and that the resolution of the cause problem depends largely upon the purpose for which cause is to be used. What is a cause for the judge need not be a cause for the physician. It is through the process of selecting what is to be regarded as a cause for the purpose of resolving a legal dispute that considerations of policy exert their influence in deciding an issue of cause-in-fact. ...

From this it is clear that the process is basically one of conjecture, for facts almost never represent themselves in identical patterns. All that can be said with any assurance is that the facts introduced in evidence call to mind or suggest sequences between events which have been previously observed, or that the facts in evidence bring into play generalities which we have derived from previous observations—such as fire causes burn—and which we regard as being more or less dependable. Furthermore, even though the habit of expecting certain consequences to follow certain antecedents is projected toward a new situation, we are still not in a position to announce that a cause and effect relation has been established. ... In an effort to lend some sense of definiteness and finality to the process described above, the courts have evolved several tests, the most frequently used of which is the "but-for" test.

1) Cause-in-Fact and the "But-For" Test

Caro Associates II, LLC v. Best Buy Co., Inc.
2012 WL 762304
(D.N.J. 2012)

Wigenton, District Judge. [Best Buy Inc. and Best Buy LP (collectively Best Buy or Defendants), and Caro Associates II, LLC (Caro or Plaintiff) were before the federal district court.] ...

FACTUAL AND PROCEDURAL HISTORY

In May 2000, Best Buy leased a warehouse located at 75 Carter Drive in Edison, New Jersey, from Plaintiff ("property" or "warehouse"). Caro and Best Buy executed a Lease Agreement ("original lease"). On May 31, 2000, Best Buy, Inc. entered into an "Assignment and Assumption of Lease" agreement with Best Buy LP. Pursuant to the assignment agreement, Best Buy, Inc., transferred all of its rights and interests under the original lease to Best Buy LP, and Best Buy LP assumed the performance of all obligations and liabilities.

Article 15.01 of the original lease required Defendants to "take good care of the Demised Premises, the fixtures and appurtenances therein, and shall not do, suffer, or permit any waste ... [as well as] keep and maintain all interior portions of the Demised Premises." Additionally, under Article 22.01, Best Buy was required to restore the property to the "condition existing" at the time tenancy commenced with respect to certain alterations.

Subsequently, on October 13, 2004, Caro and Best Buy executed the Second Amendment to the Lease ("second amended lease") extending the lease to May 31, 2009. In addition to extending the lease, Paragraph 4(a) of the second amended lease titled "Tenant Improvements" required Best Buy to make certain improvements and renovations to the property. However, under Paragraph 4(g) of the second amended lease, Defendants were not required to remove the improvements they made pursuant to the second amended lease at the end of tenancy.

Pursuant to Paragraph 4(a) of the second amended lease, Best Buy performed several improvements to the warehouse. Of significance are two of such improvements. First, Best Buy sought to paint black and yellow lines over the floors of the warehouse ("striping") because that is the system it employs to mark aisles and exit paths as well as indicate where each product type should be stored. Defendants, with the assistance of Plaintiff's architect, Phil Harris (Harris), prepared specifications and drawings for the various improvements and alterations they wanted to perform at the warehouse.

Defendants, consistent with Paragraph 4(a) of the second amended lease, provided Caro with the specifications of its intended improvements. The striping was included on the blueprints provided to Plaintiff for renovation review and approval. Although the landlord, Jack Sutton (Sutton), could not recall if Best Buy provided him with the specifications for the work it performed, he testified that "Caro was aware of all of the work [Defendants] did in conjunction with" the second amended lease. Second, Best Buy removed bathrooms from the property to expand the service area. The bathrooms were also included in the specifications Best Buy provided to Plaintiff for review.

On August 29, 2007, Best Buy accelerated the termination of the lease to May 31, 2008. Subsequently, on November 21, 2007, the parties entered into the Third Amendment to Lease and extended the lease to August 31, 2008. On August 31, 2008, Defendants vacated the warehouse without removing the striping or restoring the bathrooms. As part of Defendants' notice-and-termination obligations, Defendants coordinated with Plaintiff regarding any remaining work and repairs Best Buy needed to complete before vacating the property. On May

29, 2008, Randall Patzke (Patzke), Defendants' senior project manager, conducted a walk-through of the warehouse with Sutton, and Caro's caretaker—Magdy Keriakos. During the walk-through, Sutton identified repairs Best Buy had to complete. Notably, Plaintiff did not ask Defendants to remove the striping.

In addition, according to Patzke, during the walk-through, Sutton informed him that Caro intended to sell the property in an "as is" condition to Credit Suisse; therefore, Caro would accept $45,000 from Best Buy in lieu of Best Buy['s] completing the necessary repairs. As a result, on September 9, 2008, in response to an email from Sutton detailing the repairs Best Buy had to complete, Dan Manning (Manning)—Defendants' employee—wrote:

> I know during our phone conversation that you had a rough estimate of about $400,000 for repairs. Randy did state to you last week that we are willing to go outside this issue and issue a check for the amount $45,000 to resolve all these issues. If ownership accepts this, then I can get a check issued, if not, then we will require the repairs to be done and invoice Best Buy for reimbursement. If you accept the one[-]time payment of $45,000 to resolve these issues, I will complete this and get a check to you as owner.

Subsequently, Sutton replied: "To the extent that you wish a formal document, please forward the same for review of our attorneys. Otherwise[,] please forward the check for $45,000 [.]" Ultimately, Defendants did not tender the $45,000 check because they did not receive a signed release from Caro.

However, on November 1, 2008, Plaintiff and Credit Suisse were unable to reach an agreement on the sale of the property. As a result, in December 2008, Plaintiff retained Jones Lang LaSalle Brokerage, Inc., (JLL) to market and lease the warehouse. Shortly thereafter, JLL advised Plaintiff that the striping deterred potential tenants from renting the warehouse. JLL, therefore, recommended that Caro remove the striping. Plaintiff retained Questmark Flooring Systems (Questmark) to remove the striping and repair the warehouse floor.

On December 16, 2008, Plaintiff sent Defendants a demand letter with repairs and estimates. Plaintiff sought $861,607.55 in damages. The damages included: $237,000 for repairing the warehouse floor; $487,000 for repair and restoration of the exterior parking lot; $4,884.55 for replacement of exterior sign; $26,835 for replacement of three unit heaters and six drinking fountains; $18,150 for repair and replacement of railings and steel bollards; $32,203 for replacement of the restrooms; $7,150 for replacement of a fence; $15,200 to repair the roof drains; $7,600 to paint the office; $13,585 to replace the carpet; and $12,000 for electrical repairs. (Id. at 2–3.)

In February 2009, Questmark commenced repairs on the warehouse floor using a high finish in accordance with Sutton's request. Questmark projected that the repairs would and could be completed between thirty to forty-five days. However, Questmark did not complete the repairs until July 2009. Gregory Wagner (Wagner), Questmark's Project Manager, proffers the following to explain why the project lasted five months: "What we found out, as we started the project, was that they … weren't in the need for us to finish quickly. They were very—take your time with it. You know … there's no rush on it." Wagner also testified that the high finish improved the warehouse floor because it gave the floor characteristics it did not possess before.

On January 23, 2009, Plaintiff initiated this action in the Superior Court of New Jersey Court of New Jersey, Middlesex County alleging breach of contract and waste. On March 2, 2009, Defendants removed the action to the United States District Court for the District of New Jersey.

In July 2009, Plaintiff rented half of the warehouse to Amster. Even though Questmark removed the striping and repaired the floor of the warehouse with a high-shine polish, Caro had yet to rent the easterly portion of the property as of February 2, 2010. …

CARO AND BEST BUY'S MOTIONS FOR SUMMARY JUDGMENT ON LOST RENT CLAIM

Both Plaintiff and Defendants move for summary judgment on Plaintiff's lost rent claim. Caro maintains that pursuant to Article 22.01 of the original lease, Best Buy was required to remove the striping after it vacated the property. Plaintiff maintains that as a result of Best Buy's failure to remove the striping it was unable to rent the property. Consequently, Caro is seeking lost rent from December 2008 to July 2009. Yet, Defendants assert that Plaintiff's reliance on Article 22.01 is misplaced because the striping was done pursuant to Paragraph 4(a) of the second amended lease, which did not require Best Buy to remove the striping.

To sustain a breach of contract claim, Plaintiff must establish: "(1) a contract between the parties; (2) a breach of that contract; (3) damages flowing therefrom; and (4) that [Plaintiff] performed its own contractual obligations." *Frederico v. Home Depot*, 507 F.3d 188, 203 (3d Cir. 2007).

Without determining if Defendants' failure to remove the striping constitutes a breach, this court concludes Plaintiff has failed to establish that it was unable to rent the property solely as a result of Best Buy's failure to remove the striping. The New Jersey Supreme Court explained the contract principle of damages causation as follows:

> The wrong done and the injury sustained must bear to each other the relation of cause and effect; and the damages … to be recoverable, must be the natural and proximate consequence of the act complained of. *Sheet Metal Workers Int'l Ass'n Local Union No. 27 v. E.P. Donnelly, Inc.*, 2010 U.S. Dist. Lexis 21160, *10–11, 2010 WL 905616 (D.N.J. Mar. 9, 2010). *See also Merchants Ins. Co of N.H., Inc. v. 3 R Painting & Contracting Co., Inc.*, 2009 U.S. Dist. Lexis 84615, *13, 2009 WL 3030126 (D.N.J. Sept. 16, 2009) ("Under New Jersey law, a plaintiff must prove that defendant's breach of contract was both a *but for* cause as well as a proximate cause of the damages—that is, that defendant's breach was a '*substantial factor*' in causing the damages.") (Emphasis added).

Caro bases its lost rent claim on JLL's November 2008 report. At the time JLL prepared the report, it had shown the property to "between ten and twenty" potential tenants. The report concluded "that the property was not marketable due to the condition of the warehouse floors. The primary concern was the 'staking plan' which had been painted onto the floors. These black and yellow lines made showings, to prospective tenants and buyers alike, difficult."

Nevertheless, other evidence indicates that the striping is not the only reason Caro was unable to rent the property until July 2009. Perhaps the most telling is that even though the striping had been removed, Caro had only rented fifty percent of the property as of February 2010. In addition, Steven Beyda (Beyda), the author of the report testified that not all of the ten to twenty potential tenants lost interest as a result of the striping. Beyda also stated that he could only remember two potential tenants who specifically indicated that they were not interested in the property as a result of the striping.

Additionally, Beyda acknowledged in November 2008, the time Caro began its efforts to rent the property, the country was in "one of the worst recessions in recent history," and as a result it would take longer to rent the property, irrespective of the property's condition. Caro's expert, Anthony Rinaldi (Rinaldi), also testified that the economic downturn in late 2008 had a negative impact on the real estate market. According to Rinaldi, the real estate market was "downhill" meaning that less activity, less transactions. Rinaldi also testified that the state of the economy "extended absorption time[,]" the time it took to rent property. In addition to the economic downturn, Sutton acknowledged that "[i]t … takes time to find a tenant[,] especially, for a large property because "not every tenant needs that much space."

Furthermore, Caro terminated its contract with JLL because Sutton was dissatisfied with JLL's services. According to Beyda, Sutton believed JLL was "not spending enough money" to market the property.

Hence, JLL's performance and efforts towards marketing the property are additional factors that may have contributed to Caro's inability to rent the property.

Moreover, Beyda testified that between February 2009 and October 2009, Caro received proposals to rent the warehouse from companies such as Pitney Bowes, Prime Source, MGM, and Super Winn but Caro rejected them. Caro maintains that one of the reasons it rejected these offers is that the potential tenants only sought "to rent a minimal amount of space ... making the Premises less marketable to larger tenants who would otherwise seek to rent the entire warehouse." This Court finds this argument unpersuasive because the current tenant, Amstar, only rents fifty percent of the property. The other fifty percent of the property remains vacant.

Similarly, Caro's assertion that it rejected some of the potential tenants because the monthly rent they offered was below market value is unavailing. Caro's expert testified that the economy resulted in "softer prices." Rinaldi clarified that "softer prices" meant that "prices ... [went] down." Additionally, around this period, landlords offered concessions such as "free rent to induce [tenants] to move in ... [for] a month or two or three."

Proof of damages is essential to a breach of contract claim, *Gazaro v. The Diocese of Erie*, 80 F. App'x. 202, 206 (3d Cir. 2003), and Caro has the burden of proof as to that element. *Video Pipeline, Inc. v. Buena Vista Home Entm't, Inc.*, 275 F.Supp.2d 543, 566 (D.N.J. 2003). Overall, this court concludes that Plaintiff has "fail[ed] to make a showing sufficient to establish the existence of an element essential to [its] case, and on which ... [it has] the burden of proof[.]" Consequently, Best Buy is entitled to summary judgment on this claim. ...

CONCLUSION

For the reasons stated above, Best Buy's motion for summary judgment is granted in part, ... and Caro's motion for partial summary judgment is denied.

---

2) Cause in Fact and the "Substantial Factor" Test

Fowler v. Campbell
612 N.E.2d 596
(Ind. Ct. App. 1993)

NAJAM, JUDGE. This is an appeal from an action for breach of a contract to install a septic system. Elesmolee Fowler d/b/a Fowler Construction (Fowler) appeals from a judgment in favor of Michael G. Campbell and

Diane K. Campbell (Campbells). ... The Campbells owned property on the lakefront of Lamb Lake in Johnson County. On March 2, 1988, the Campbells and Fowler executed a contract (Contract) for Fowler to build a custom built house for the Campbells on this property (House), which included a septic system.

As lot owners on Lamb Lake, the Campbells were members of the Lamb Lake Estates Lot Owners Association (Association) and were bound by the Association's rules and regulations. Those rules and regulations required that the Association's Architectural Control Committee (Committee) review and approve plans for a septic system and that the Committee inspect and approve the system during installation. The Johnson County Department of Health (Department) imposed similar requirements.

Before their Contract with Fowler was executed, the Campbells had consulted with the Committee and with the Department regarding their plans for the House and septic system (Plans). The Campbells employed a professional, Robert Etter of MAJ Civil Engineering (MAJ), who prepared a plot plan and a septic system design, and the Campbells then submitted these Plans to the Department and to the Committee for approval. The Committee did not approve the original plot plan as submitted. After making field measurements, the Committee revised the Plans by making changes in the location of the finger system to accommodate the actual distances and topography. The revised plot plan was signed by the Campbells and approved by the Committee on October 28, 1987.

The Department issued a septic system installation permit to the Campbells, dated November 6, 1987. The permit approved "minimum requirements" and installation "as shown on engineered plot." Thus, the permit incorporated by reference the Plans which MAJ had prepared. The Association approved the Plans for the House and septic system on December 12, 1987.

The Contract stated that the Campbells would furnish the Plans, that the House would be built according to the Plans and that Fowler would furnish a "complete septic system according to Johnson County Health Dept. and Lamb Lake Association." The Contract provided that "[a]ll materials and labor will be furnished by Fowler Construction to meet building codes of Johnson County and Lamb Lake Association."

During installation, the Association and the Department inspected the septic system to make certain that the system satisfied their requirements. With the apparent approval of the Committee—but not of MAJ or the Campbells, Fowler moved the septic tank from below the House toward the lake, where it was located on the plot plan, to an entirely different location up on the hill. No further changes in the septic system's design were approved by the Committee. After the septic system was completely installed, the Department made a final inspection so that an occupancy permit could be issued. Upon the final inspection at the Campbells' property, the Association returned the Campbells' $500 performance deposit.

It was shortly after Fowler completed construction of the House and within thirty (30) days after the Campbells had moved into the House on April 1, 1989, that the first sewage water back-up occurred. Fowler testified that he discovered cloths, plastic bags, and other debris in the septic pump which had caused it to lock up and to cease pumping. Fowler advised the Campbells that the septic pump had been damaged because of the debris which was introduced into the system. Fowler cleaned out the pump and it began functioning again.

Several weeks later, another back-up occurred. Again, Fowler found debris in the septic pump. He notified the Campbells that these objects placed in the septic system were preventing it from functioning properly. Fowler told the Campbells that the septic pump was damaged and that a new one should be installed.

A third back-up occurred beginning in June of 1989. Also, during the summer months, sewage seeped out of the finger system onto the Campbells' driveway and yard. Fowler again visited the property, and on that visit Fowler took members of the Association and Department with him to observe the septic system's condition. The septic pump had again stopped working because foreign objects had become clogged in it. The Department official who accompanied Fowler to the Campbells' home told the Campbells that the problems they were having were not caused by any deficiency in the septic system's design, but rather were "due to the apparent misuse of the system."

The Campbells contend that it was not until after this third back-up that they first learned, in October of 1989, that the septic system had not been installed according to the original Plans. Thereafter, Fowler installed a new septic pump, another 1,000 gallon septic tank and a warning light at a cost of $2,200.00, and the Campbells agreed to this new installation although they paid nothing for it. After the new pump was installed, no further sewage water back-ups occurred in the Campbells' home, although sewage water continued to seep through the fingers of the septic system onto the Campbells' driveway and yard. The warning light stayed on continuously, and in November of 1989, the pump again stopped working. When the Campbells uncovered the pump station, sewage ran out of the pump, down their yard, and into the lake. The Campbells claim that they tried again to contact Fowler but that he never responded.

During the winter of 1989–1990, the pump was not working. In May of 1990, the Campbells hired Jack Justice, a licensed electrician (Justice), who examined the pump and found numerous electrical code violations. Justice found that sewage water had entered the pump housing and "burnt the pump up." Justice replaced the pump and rewired the pump station. The Campbells paid Justice $1,249.57 for his labor and materials in making these repairs.

On May 9, 1990, the Campbells filed a complaint for breach of contract against Fowler. After a bench trial, on October 15, 1991, the trial court entered judgment in favor of the Campbells and awarded them $12,199.57 in damages. This appeal followed. We will state other relevant facts in our discussion of the issues. ...

The judgment below turns on two essential findings: that Fowler breached the Contract when he did not install the septic system according to the Plans and that the Campbells suffered damages attributable to Fowler's alleged breach.

ISSUE ONE: BREACH OF CONTRACT

Fowler first contends that he did not breach the Contract because he installed a septic system which complied with the regulations of both the Association and the Department, as required under the Contract. We disagree.

The essential elements of a breach of contract action are the existence of a contract, the defendant's breach thereof, and damages. *Peterson v. Culver Educational Foundation*, 402 N.E.2d 448, 461 (Ind. App. 1980). Here, the parties agree there was a contract but disagree whether Fowler breached the Contract in his installation of the septic system and whether the breach, if any, caused the damages which the Campbells claim.

The Contract contained two provisions which must be reconciled. In its introductory paragraph, the Contract provided that, "House will be built according to plans." More specifically, in numbered Paragraph 5., the Contract also provided that Fowler would, "Complete septic system according to Johnson County Health Dept. and Lamb Lake Association." We believe the term "House" means not only the house itself but also its necessary appurtenances, including the septic system. ... Paragraph 5 does not stand alone but imposes an additional requirement with respect to the septic system.

Under the rules of contract construction, the provisions of a contract are to be construed together, *See Equimart Ltd. v. Epperly*, 545 N.E.2d 595, 598 (Ind. App. 1989), and specific terms control over general terms. *See BeerMart, Inc. v. Stroh Brewery Co.* 804 F.2d 409, 411 (7th Cir. 1986) (construing Indiana law). Where the parties have agreed to a specific term, an apparently inconsistent general statement must yield to the more specific term. Thus, to the extent that Fowler modified the Plans in order to secure approval from the Department and the Association, as required under the Contract, there was no breach of contract.

However, in our review of this question, we make a distinction between those modifications in the Plans which were actually required and those which Fowler made unilaterally and which may have been approved, but which were not required, by the Association and the Department. The fact that the Association and the Department may have approved the septic system as it was installed does not insulate Fowler from a breach of contract claim. While Fowler's compliance with the requirements of the Association and the Department was necessary, such compliance was in itself insufficient to satisfy Fowler's entire contractual obligation to the Campbells with respect to the septic system.

After comparing the septic system specifications contained in the Plans with the actual work completed, the evidence in the Record clearly demonstrates that, even when the modifications which the Association requested during installation are taken into account, Fowler did not install the septic system pursuant to the Plans, and he thereby breached the Contract. The specifications for the septic system called for a 1,500 gallon septic tank, a pump station with a storage chamber capacity of 250 gallons, and a pump set to pump 100 gallons per cycle. The Plans also precisely delineated the location of the septic tank.

The evidence shows, and Fowler admits, that he did not comply with these specifications when installing the septic system. It is uncontroverted that Fowler installed a 1,000 gallon septic tank, a pump station with a storage capacity of only 50 to 55 gallons and a pump capable of pumping only 55 gallons per cycle. Fowler could not explain why these capacities varied from the Plans, although he did explain that the location of the finger system and of the septic tank itself differed from the original Plans because of requirements imposed by the Association, which had approved these two variations.

Fowler failed to install the septic tank, pump station and pump according to the Plans and specifications, and the trial court specifically found that the Campbells did not consent to any of these changes. At common law, under general contract principles, the slightest breach of the contract, no matter how trivial or unintended, may be the basis for an action for breach of contract. *Miller Brewing Co. v. Best Beers of Bloomington, Inc.* 608 N.E.2d 975, 980 (Ind. 1993). Here, the evidence shows that Fowler's failure to follow the Plans cannot be attributed entirely to requirements imposed by the Department or the Association and that more than a slight or incidental breach occurred. Thus, we conclude that the Campbells have shown that Fowler breached the Contract.

ISSUE TWO: CAUSATION

Fowler next contends that there is no evidence of probative value linking the alleged breach of contract to the damages awarded. Fowler further contends that because foreign material was introduced into the septic system, it was not a deviation from the Plans, but the foreign material which caused the septic system to back up and damage the Campbells' home. Fowler argues, in effect, that even if a breach occurred, there was no causal relationship between the breach and the damages which the Campbells claim to have suffered.

In order to recover on a breach of contract claim, the alleged breach must be a cause in fact of the plaintiff's loss. For a cause in fact to be a legal cause, it must have been a substantial factor in bringing about the harm. *Krauss v. Greenbarg* 137 F.2d 569, 572 (3rd Cir. 1943), cert. denied, 320 U.S. 791. While there may be other contributing causes and more than one factor operating, the trier of fact may determine that one cause predominates over another in bringing about the harm. *Cf. Huey v. Milligan*, 175 N.E.2d 698, 703 (Ind. 1961) (actor's negligent conduct is "legal cause" of harm to another if his conduct is substantial factor in bringing about harm).

The principle of legal causation in contracts is similar to that in negligence. However, in a breach of contract action, where an injury arising from the breach may have resulted from multiple causes, Indiana does not recognize comparative causation. The test of causation in common law contract actions is not whether the breach was the only cause, or whether other causes may have contributed, but whether the breach was a substantial factor in bringing about the harm. *Greenbarg*, 137 F.2d at 572.

While the Campbells' misuse contributed to the sewage water back-ups from their septic system, the record supports the trial court's conclusion that Fowler's failure to install the septic system according to the Plans was a substantial factor in bringing about the Campbells' damages, which is all that is required. Thus, we are not persuaded by Fowler's challenge to the trial court's finding that the breach caused the damages.

There is sufficient evidence of probative value in the record to conclude that Fowler's unauthorized modifications contributed to the sewage water back-ups which occurred in the House. There is also evidence in the record that the Campbells abused the septic system. However, the only question we may consider on appeal is whether the trial court, as the trier of fact, made a permissible deduction of causation from other established facts. *Lewis by Lewis v. Bonahoom*, 583 N.E.2d 175, 178 (Ind. App., 1991). Fowler made unauthorized modifications to the Plans which altered the capacity of the septic system, and the septic system failed. From those established facts, the trial court deduced that

Fowler's breach of contract contributed to the sewage water back-ups which occurred in the House, a reasonable inference.

The reasonableness of an inference is determined by whether the inferred fact is a probable hypothesis from the proven facts and circumstances in light of common knowledge and experience. *Puckett v. McKinney* , 373 N.E.2d 909, 912 (Ind. App. 1978); *DeMichaeli & Associates v. Sanders*, 340 N.E.2d 796, 803 (Ind. App. 1976). An unreasonable inference yields an arbitrary or capricious result based on speculation, guess, surmise, conjecture or mere possibility. On appeal we may not substitute our own judgment on the question whether the inference drawn is a right one or whether a different inference would be better supported but must determine whether the inference is unreasonable as a matter of law.

Thus, within the scope of appellate review, where the evidence permits conflicting inferences, we must affirm unless we are left with a definite and firm conviction that the inference was unreasonable and that a mistake was made by the trial court. *See Searcy v. Searcy*, 583 N.E.2d 1216, 1220 (Ind. App. 1991). We cannot say that the trial court's inference was unreasonable, and we find no such mistake. We conclude that the evidence supports the finding of a causal relationship between the breach and the damages claimed. ...

CONCLUSION

Fowler breached the Contract, the trial court construed the Contract as written, and the trial court properly awarded damages. The judgment is in all things affirmed.

NOTES AND QUESTIONS

1. **Same Cause-in-Fact Theory of Causation for Both Breach-of-Contract and Negligence Actions**. It is extremely important to stress a point that appears in the *Fowler* opinion: "In order to recover on a breach of contract claim, the alleged breach must be a cause in fact of the plaintiff's loss. ... *The principle of legal causation in contracts is similar to that in negligence*."

2. **Cause in Fact and the "Greatly Multiplies" Test**. Consider the following excerpt which appears in WILLIAM PROSSER, LAW OF TORTS § 41, at 242 (4th ed. 1971):

   The fact of causation is incapable of mathematical proof, since no man can say with absolute certainty what would

> have occurred if the defendant had acted otherwise. Proof of what we call the relation of cause and effect—that of necessary antecedent and inevitable consequence—can be nothing more than "the projection of our habit of expecting certain consequents to follow certain antecedents merely because we had observed these sequences on previous occasions." If as a matter of ordinary experience a particular act or omission might be expected—under the circumstances—to produce a particular result, and that result in fact has followed, the conclusion may be permissible that the causal relation exists. ... Thus it is everyday experience that unlighted stairs create a danger that someone will fall. Such a condition *"greatly multiplies* the chances of accident, and is of a character naturally leading to its occurrence." When a [person] tumbles down the steps, it is a reasonable conclusion that it is *more likely than not* that the bad lighting has played a substantial part in the fall. When a child is drowned in a swimming pool, no one can say with certainty that a lifeguard would have saved him; but the experience of the community permits the conclusion that the absence of the guard played a significant part in the drowning. (Emphasis added.)

Some courts have embraced the rule: A breach of promise or a breach of duty is the cause in fact of a complainant's injury and damages if the breach "greatly multiplies" the likelihood of those events. *See Purcell v. Zimbelman*, 500 P.2d 335, 342–43 (Ariz. Ct. App. 1972), and *Bettencourt v. Pride Well Service, Inc.*, 735 P.2d 722, 728–29 (Wyo. 1987).

3. **Employing the Hybrid "Ease of Association" Test to Establish Both "Cause in Fact" and "Proximate Cause"**. In *Hill v. Lundin & Associates, Inc.,* 256 So.2d 620, 622 (La. 1972), the Louisiana Supreme Court adopted an ease of association test, "which asks how easily the risk of harm can be associated with the rule which was breached." Later, in *Roberts v. Benoit*, 605 So.2d 1032 (La. 1991), the supreme court discussed the ease of association test more fully and stated:

> CAUSE IN FACT
>
> [T]he first inquiry is whether the sheriff's conduct ... was a cause in fact of plaintiff's injuries. ... In reviewing these factual findings, we are mindful of the Louisiana tradition of giving great deference to the findings of the trier of fact, jury or judge We, nonetheless, must determine whether the plaintiff has met his burden of establishing a factual, causal

relationship between the defendant's actions and his injuries, i.e., a cause in fact.

Cause in fact is generally a "but for" inquiry; if the plaintiff probably would have not sustained the injuries but for the defendant's substandard conduct, such conduct is a cause in fact. Stated differently, the inquiry is "[d]id the defendant contribute to the plaintiff's harm or is the defendant a cause of the plaintiff's harm?"

An alternative method for determining cause in fact—which is generally used when multiple causes are present—is the "substantial factor" test. Under this test, cause in fact is found to exist when the defendant's conduct was a "substantial factor" in bringing about plaintiff's harm. *Dixie Drive It Yourself System v. American Beverage* Co., 137 So.2d 298 (La. 1962). Under either method, it is irrelevant in determining cause in fact whether the defendant's actions were "lawful, unlawful, intentional, unintentional, negligent or non-negligent." Rather, the cause in fact inquiry is a neutral one, free of the entanglements of policy considerations—morality, culpability or responsibility—involved in the duty-risk analysis. *Shelton v. Aetna Casualty & Surety Co.*, 334 So.2d 406, 409 (La. 1976).

We recognized the very limited scope of the cause in fact inquiry in *Hill v. Lundin & Associates, Inc.*, 256 So.2d 620, 622 (La. 1972). There, we held that to the extent the defendant's actions had something to do with the injury [of] the plaintiff …, the test of a factual, causal relationship is met. …

SCOPE OF PROTECTION OF DUTY

There is no "rule" for determining the scope of the duty. Regardless if stated in terms of proximate cause, legal cause, or duty, the scope of the duty inquiry is ultimately a question of policy as to whether the particular risk falls within the scope of the duty. … All rules of conduct … are designed to protect some persons under some circumstances against some risks. Seldom does a rule protect every victim against every risk that may befall him, merely because it is shown that the violation of the rule played a part in producing the injury. The task of defining the proper reach or thrust of a rule in its policy aspects is one that must be undertaken by the court in each case as it arises. … In short, the scope of protection inquiry asks "whether the enunciated rule or principle of law extends to or is intended to protect this plaintiff from this type of harm arising in this manner." …

> In determining the limitation to be placed on liability for a defendant's substandard conduct—i.e., whether there is a duty-risk relationship—we have found the proper inquiry to be how easily the risk of injury to plaintiff can be associated with the duty sought to be enforced. *Hill, supra*. Restated, the ease of association inquiry is simply: "How easily does one associate the plaintiff's complained-of harm with the defendant's conduct? ... Although ease of association encompasses the idea of foreseeability, it is not based on foreseeability alone." Absent an ease of association between the duty breached and the damages sustained, we have found legal fault lacking. *Hill, supra*; *Sibley v. Gifford Hill and Co., Inc.*, 475 So.2d 315, 319 (La. 1985). ...
>
> When ... a combination of causes exists, we have employed the following approach for defining the scope of protection: The keys for the solution of the issue of responsibility when there is more than one cause-in-fact of damages are (1) a determination of the exact risk or risks anticipated by imposition of the legal duty which has been breached and (2) the legal or policy considerations which grant excuses from certain circumstances which follow an act of negligence. This requires, under the facts and the law of each case and the attendant exigencies, a jurisprudential determination which will implement and make effective our broad codal provisions concerning those who should respond in damages for their faults.

B. Establishing the Proximate Cause of Losses, Injuries, and Damages

In *Blair v. Property Management Consultants*, 531 N.E.2d 752 (Ohio Ct. App. 1987), the Ohio Appellate Court reported the following pertinent and chilling facts:

> Felita Blair wanted an apartment. A vacant unit was located in her aunt's building. Thomas and Margaret Luebbe owned the building. Lawrence Osky, doing business as Property Management Consultants, managed the complex. Virgil Broach was the caretaker. Blair visited the building and inspected the basement apartment. During the inspection, she noticed that the windows in the apartment were three feet above ground level. She also discovered that the windows did not have locks. At trial, Blair's testimony was clear: She asked Broach to secure the windows with locks and he agreed to do so. In light of that assurance, Blair agreed to rent the basement apartment on a month-to-month basis.

> However, when Blair moved into the apartment, she discovered that Broach had secured the windows with sticks instead of locks. Still, Blair remained in the basement apartment. Shortly thereafter, a male intruder entered the apartment. Blair and her children were sleeping. The intruder raped Blair. In the course of events, Blair filed a breach-of-contract action, alleging that Lawrence Osky and Property Management Consultants (PMC) failed to secure her apartment windows with locks. She sought various damages.

Assume that the jury finds these facts: 1) PMC and Blair formed a valid, month-to-month lease agreement; 2) Blair paid good consideration; 3) PMC materially breached the contract; 4) PMC's breach was the cause in fact of Blair's injuries; and 5) PMC's breach was the cause in fact of Blair's damages. But, in the end, the jury concludes that PMC is not liable for the consequences that followed in the wake of its nonperformance and broken contractual promise. What could possibly explain that arguably "unsettling" outcome? Does the analysis in the next celebrated case provide an intelligible or convincing answer?

1) Proximate Cause and "Foreseeability" Doctrines

Hadley v. Baxendale
9 Exch. 341
156 Eng. Rep. 145 (1854)

At the trial before Crompton, J., at the last Gloucester Assizes, it appeared that the plaintiffs carried on an extensive business as millers at Gloucester; and that, on the 11th of May, their mill was stopped by a breakage of the crank shaft by which the mill was worked. The steam-engine was manufactured by Messrs. Joyce & Co., the engineers, at Greenwich, and it became necessary to send the shaft as a pattern for a new one to Greenwich. The fracture was discovered on the 12th, and on the 13th the plaintiffs sent one of their servants to the office of the defendants, who are the well-known carriers trading under the name of Pickford & Co., for the purpose of having the shaft carried to Greenwich.

The plaintiffs' servant told the clerk that the mill was stopped, and that the shaft must be sent immediately; and in answer to the inquiry when the shaft would be taken, the answer was, that if it was sent up by twelve o'clock any day, it would be delivered at Greenwich on the following day. On the following day the shaft was taken by the defendants, before noon, for the purpose of being conveyed to Greenwich, and the sum of £ 2, 4s. was paid for its carriage for the whole distance; at the same time the defendants' clerk was told that a special entry, if required, should be made to hasten its delivery.

The delivery of the shaft at Greenwich was delayed by some neglect; and the consequence was, that the plaintiffs did not receive the new shaft for several days after they would otherwise have done, and the working of their mill was thereby delayed, and they thereby lost the profits they would otherwise have received.

On the part of the defendants, it was objected that these damages were too remote, and that the defendants were not liable with respect to them. The learned Judge left the case generally to the jury, who found a verdict with £ 25 damages beyond the amount paid into Court.

Whateley, in last Michaelmas Term, obtained a rule nisi for a new trial on the ground of misdirection. ...

ALDERSON, B. We think that there ought to be a new trial in this case; but, in so doing, we deem it to be expedient and necessary to state explicitly the rule which the Judge, at the next trial, ought, in our opinion, to direct the jury to be governed by when they estimate the damages.

It is, indeed, of the last importance that we should do this; for, if the jury are left without any definite rule to guide them, it will in such cases as these, manifestly lead to the greatest injustice. The Courts have done this on several occasions; and, in *Balke v. Midland Railway Company*, 18 Q.B. 93, the Court granted a new trial on this very ground, that the rule had not been definitely laid down to the jury by the learned Judge at Nisi Prius. ...

Now we think the proper rule in such a case as the present is this—Where two parties have made a contract which one of them has broken, the damages which the other party ought to receive in respect of such breach of contract should be such as may fairly and reasonably be considered either arising naturally, i.e., according to the usual course of things, from such breach of contract itself, or such as may reasonably be supposed to have been in the contemplation of both parties, at the time they made the contract, as the probable result of the breach of it.

Now, if the special circumstances under which the contract was actually made were communicated by the plaintiffs to the defendants, and thus known to both parties, the damages resulting from the breach of such a contract, which they would reasonably contemplate, would be the amount of injury which would ordinarily follow from a breach of contract under these special circumstances so known and communicated.

But, on the other hand, if these special circumstances were wholly unknown to the party breaking the contract, he, at the most, could only be supposed to have had in his contemplation the amount of injury which would arise generally, and in the great multitude of cases not affected by any special circumstances, from such a breach of contract. For, had the special circumstances been known, the parties might have specially provided for the breach of contract by special terms as to the damages in that case; and of this advantage it would be very unjust to deprive them.

Now the above principles are those by which we think the jury ought to be guided in estimating the damages arising out of any breach of contract.

It is said, that other cases such as breaches of contract in the non-payment of money, or in the not making a good title to land, are to be treated as exceptions from this, and as governed by a conventional rule. But as, in such cases, both parties must be supposed to be cognizant of that well-known rule, these cases may, we think, be more properly classed under the rule above enunciated as to cases under known special circumstances, because there both parties may reasonably be presumed to contemplate the estimation of the amount of damages according to the conventional rule.

Now, in the present case, if we are to apply the principles above laid down, we find that the only circumstances here communicated by the plaintiffs to the defendants at the time the contract were made, were, that the article to be carried was the broken shaft of a mill, and that the plaintiffs were the millers of that mill. But how do these circumstances shew reasonably that the profits of the mill must be stopped by an unreasonable delay in the delivery of the broken shaft by the carrier to the third person?

Suppose the plaintiffs had another shaft in their possession put up or putting up at the time, and that they only wished to send back the broken shaft to the engineer who made it; it is clear that this would be quite consistent with the above circumstances, and yet the unreasonable delay in the delivery would have no effect upon the intermediate profits of the mill. Or, again, suppose that, at the time of the delivery to the carrier, the machinery of the mill had been in other respects defective, then, also, the same results would follow.

Here it is true that the shaft was actually sent back to serve as a model for a new one, and that the want of a new one was the only cause of the stoppage of the mill, and that the loss of profits really arose from not sending down the new shaft in proper time, and that this arose from the delay in delivering the broken one to serve as a model. But it is obvious that, in the great multitude of cases of millers sending off broken shafts to third persons by a carrier under ordinary circumstances, such consequences would not, in all probability, have occurred; and these special circumstances were here never communicated by the plaintiffs to the defendants.

It follows, therefore, that the loss of profits here cannot reasonably be considered such a consequence of the breach of contract as could have been fairly and reasonably contemplated by both the parties when they made this contract. For such loss would neither have flowed naturally from the breach of this contract in the great multitude of such cases occurring under ordinary circumstances, nor were the special circumstances, which, perhaps, would have made it a reasonable and natural consequence of such breach of contract, communicated to or known by the defendants.

The Judge ought, therefore, to have told the jury, that, upon the facts then before them, they ought not to take the loss of profits into consideration at all in estimating the damages. There must therefore be a new trial in this case.

Rule absolute.

NOTES AND QUESTIONS

1. **Proximate Cause, Foreseeability, and Limitation on a Negligent Defendant's Liability**. *Palsgraf v. Long Island Railroad Company* 162 N.E. 99, 100–01 (N.Y. 1928) is a "law of tort" case. In its *dicta*, the theories of proximate cause and foreseeability are articulated. But, one finds considerable conflicts—among courts which decide tort-based disputes—over the precise definition of proximate cause or legal cause. Generally, those courts have embraced two primary tests to establish proximate cause. The tort-law, "foreseeability" theory states: A negligent defendant is not liable for his conduct unless the consequences of defendant's negligence were reasonably foreseeable. *St. Louis, S. F. & T. R. Co. v. Green*, 37 S.W.2d 123, 125 (Tex. Com. App. 1931) ("The trial court defined 'proximate cause' as follows: 'Proximate cause, as used in this charge, is the cause which in a natural and continuous sequence, unbroken by any new cause, produces an event that without which the event would not have happened.' The definition given is clearly erroneous under repeated decisions in this state in omitting foreseeableness or anticipation of the injury, such element being an essential one, where proximate cause is an issuable fact."). Also, plaintiff has the burden of proof. On the other hand, many jurisdictions do not require a plaintiff to prove that a particular injury or process was foreseeable. The "natural and probable consequences" test is the second method for establishing tort-related proximate cause. Under this latter theory, a defendant is liable for all of the natural and probable consequences of her conduct. *Milwaukee & St. P. R. Co. v. Kellogg*, 94 U.S. 469, 475 (1877) ("In order to warrant a finding that negligence, or an act not amounting to wanton wrong, is the proximate cause of an injury, it must appear that the injury was the natural and probable consequence of the negligence or wrongful act, and

that it ought to have been foreseen in the light of the attending circumstances.").

2. **Proximate Cause, Foreseeability, and Limitation on a Defendant's Liability After a Breach of Contract.** In *Hadley v. Baxendale*, the English court outlined the standard for establishing proximate cause in a breach-of-contract action. To be sure, the *Hadley* proximate-cause test is considerably more stringent than the tort-based standard that appears in *Palsgraf*'s dicta. Writing for the *Hadley* court, Baron Alderson concluded: "Where two parties have made a contract which one of them has broken, the damages which the other party ought to receive … should be such as … may reasonably be supposed to have been in the contemplation of both parties, at the time they made the contract. …" 156 Eng. Rep. at 151. *See also Nat'l Hills Shopping Ctr. v. Ins. Co. of N. Am.*, 308 F. Supp. 248, 251 (S.D. Ga. 1970) (concluding that the breach-of-contract, proximate cause ruler is stricter than the tort-based standard because "the probable and natural consequences of the breach must have been foreseeable at the time the contract was entered into."), and E. FARNSWORTH, CONTRACTS § 12.14, at 876–77 (1982) (observing that the concept of foreseeability in contract law is a more severe limitation than the requirement of "proximate cause" in tort.).

3. **Restatement (Second) of Contracts § 351.** The authors of the RESTATEMENT also adopted the view: Generally, a contracting party must be cognizant of foreseeable risks during the contract-formation stage. Respecting proximate cause, foreseeability, and limitations on breach-of-contract liability, the authors wrote:

> 1) Damages are not recoverable for loss that the party in breach did not have reason to foresee as a probable result of the breach when the contract was made.
>
> 2) Loss may be foreseeable as a probable result of a breach because it follows from the breach
>
> (a) in the ordinary course of events, or
>
> (b) as a result of special circumstances, beyond the ordinary course of events, that the party in breach had reason to know.
>
> 3) A court may limit damages for foreseeable loss by excluding recovery for loss of profits, by allowing recovery only for loss incurred in reliance, or otherwise if it concludes that in the circumstances justice so requires in order to avoid disproportionate compensation.

4. **The Erosion of Hadley's "Strict" Foreseeability–Proximate-Cause Standard**. *Hadley*'s strict proximate cause standard has been waning increasingly in both American and English courts. To illustrate, in *Hector Martinez & Co. v. Southern Pacific Transportation Co.*, 606 F.2d 106, 110 (5th Cir. 1979), the Fifth Circuit Court of Appeals stated: "[A complainant] need only demonstrate that his harm was not so remote as to make it unforeseeable at the time of contracting." And in *Koufos v. C. Czarnikow, Ltd.*, 1 A.C. 350 (H.L. 1969), the House of Lords approved three less stringent standards—the "real danger," the "serious possibility," and the "liable to result" tests.

2) "Proximate Cause Consists of Two Separate Elements"

Scott v. Countrywide Home Loans, Inc.
2006 WL 1689424
(Mich. Ct. App. 2006)

PER CURIAM. Plaintiff owned a home on which Countrywide Home Loans (CHL) held a mortgage. Plaintiff fell behind on the mortgage payments and moved out of the house, leaving personal property and debris behind. Six months later, CHL hired DIY, Inc. to winterize and secure the property. When DIY employees arrived, they found a side door unlocked. After winterizing the house and making note of the contents, they secured the doors and windows and left.

Plaintiff returned, gaining access to the house through an unlocked window, and found that some property was missing. CHL later hired DIY to remove hazardous material and exterior debris from the premises. When DIY employees returned, they found that the padlock on the front door of the house had been cut, and a padlock on the garage door had been opened and removed. There were obvious signs that someone had been inside the house and the garage. When the employees completed their work, they resecured the doors and left.

Plaintiff returned again and found even more property missing. Plaintiff seeks to hold defendants liable for the missing personalty. The trial court ruled that there was insufficient evidence that defendants took the missing items.

The trial court's ruling on a motion for summary disposition is reviewed de novo. *Kefgen v. Davidson*, 241 Mich. App 611, 616 (2000). A motion brought under MCR 2.116(C)(10) tests the factual support for a claim. In ruling on such a motion, the trial court must consider not only the pleadings, but also depositions, affidavits, admissions and other documentary evidence, MCR 2.116(G)(5), and must give the benefit of any reasonable doubt to the nonmoving party, being liberal in finding a genuine issue of material fact. If the moving party satisfies its burden of identifying undisputed facts that entitle it to judgment, summary disposition is properly granted unless the opposing party presents evidence of the existence of a material factual dispute. *Smith v. Globe Life Ins. Co*, 460 Mich. 446, 455 (1999).

The disputed issue is that of causation. Proximate cause consists of two separate elements: 1) *cause in fact*, which requires a showing that *but for* the defendant's conduct, the plaintiff would not have been injured, and 2) *legal* or *proximate cause*, which involves examination of the *foreseeability* of consequences and whether a defendant should be held legally responsible for those consequences. *Skinner v. Square D Co.,* 445 Mich. 153, 162–163 (1994).

The cause in fact element generally requires a showing that "but for" the defendant's actions, the plaintiff's injury would not have occurred. "Generally, an act or omission is a cause in fact of an injury only if the injury could not have occurred without (or "but for") that act or omission. While a plaintiff need not prove that an act or omission was the sole catalyst for his injuries, he must introduce evidence permitting the jury to conclude that the act or omission was a cause." *Craig v. Oakwood Hosp.*, 471 Mich. 67, 87 (2004)

It is important to bear in mind that a plaintiff cannot satisfy this burden by showing only that the defendant may have caused his injuries. Our case law requires more than a mere possibility or a plausible explanation. Rather, a plaintiff establishes that the defendant's conduct was a cause in fact of his injuries only if he "set[s] forth specific facts that would support a reasonable inference of a logical sequence of cause and effect." A valid theory of causation, therefore, must be based on facts in evidence. And while "[t]he evidence need not negate all other possible causes," this court has consistently required that the evidence "exclude other reasonable hypotheses with a fair amount of certainty." *Id.* at 87–88

In this case, plaintiff discovered items were missing from the house between DIY's first and second visit. But, there is no evidence that DIY's employees took anything during that first visit. Further, it is undisputed that the side door had been left unlocked, thus allowing access to anyone before DIY first entered. ... [T]here is a presumption in the absence of direct evidence to the contrary that a person acts in accordance with the law[.] *See Bauman v. Grand Trunk W R Co.*, 376 Mich. 675, 689 (1965). [Therefore], plaintiff argues that it cannot be inferred that a third person would have entered and taken the property given that such action involves illegal conduct. The same presumption, however, operates in favor of defendants as well. Thus, absent evidence that the missing items were in fact in the house on the first day DIY's employees entered the premises and were gone immediately after they left, it cannot be inferred from the employees' mere presence that they took the missing items.

Plaintiff discovered that more items were missing after DIY's second visit. Evidence that DIY employees found that one padlock had been cut and the enclosed porch had been ransacked was sufficient to rebut any presumption of legality and create an inference that third persons had entered illegally. Plaintiff's claim that it could be inferred that a DIY employee had taken her property because he had taken property from other jobs must be rejected because it violates MRE 404(b)(1). Because plaintiff did not, with one exception, present any facts which permit a reasonable inference that DIY's employees took the missing property, the trial court did not err in concluding that there was insufficient evidence of causation. ...

We affirm in part, reverse in part, and remand for further proceedings consistent with this opinion.

NOTES AND QUESTIONS

1. **Texas's Law—Tort-Based Actions and Proof of Proximate Cause**. In *Marathon Corp. v. Pitzner*, 106 S.W.3d 724, 727 (Tex. 2003), the Texas Supreme Court repeated its explanation of "proximate cause." The court wrote:

   > The components of proximate cause are *cause in fact* and *foreseeability*. *Doe v. Boys Clubs of Greater Dallas, Inc.*, 907 S.W.2d 472, 477 (Tex. 1995). The test for *cause in fact*, or "*but for causation*," is whether the act or omission was *a substantial factor* in causing the injury "without which the harm would not have occurred." *Id.* A finding of *cause in fact* "may be based on either direct or circumstantial evidence." *Havner v. E-Z Mart Stores, Inc.*, 825 S.W.2d 456, 459 (Tex. 1992). "[But it] cannot be supported by mere conjecture, guess, or speculation." *Boys Clubs*, 907 S.W.2d at 477 (emphasis added).

2. The Michigan and Texas supreme courts have embraced the same proximate-cause rule. Is that rule exceptionally clear? Under Texas and Michigan laws, what is a "substantial factor"? What is "but for causation"?

3) The Dominant or Efficient Proximate Cause of Losses and Injuries

Shirey v. Tri-State Ins. Co.
274 P.2d 386
(Okl. 1954)

WELCH, JUSTICE. Essie Shirey, as plaintiff, seeks in this action to recover on an automobile insurance policy, insuring against the peril of windstorm, damage to her automobile alleged to have been sustained as a result of a windstorm. The policy excludes from coverage damage sustained to the automobile caused by collision or upset. Defendant answered by general and special denial. It specifically denied that the damage to plaintiff's automobile, if any, was caused by windstorm, but alleged that it was caused by collision and upset.

At the conclusion of plaintiff's evidence on motion of defendant the trial court directed a verdict in its favor, and a verdict was returned accordingly. Plaintiff's motion for new trial was overruled and judgment was entered on the verdict denying plaintiff recovery. Plaintiff appeals and assigns this ruling as error.

Plaintiff relies for recovery on paragraph D of the policy which provides:

> COVERAGE D. Comprehensive loss of or damage to the automobile except by collision or upset: to pay for any direct and accidental loss of or damage to the automobile, hereinafter called loss, except loss caused by collision of the automobile with another object, or by the upset of the automobile, or by collision of the automobile with a vehicle to which it is attached. Breakage of glass and the loss caused by missiles, falling objects, fire, theft, explosion, earthquake, windstorm, hail, water, flood, vandalism, riot or civil commotion, shall not be deemed loss caused by collision of upset.

The evidence offered by plaintiff is substantially as follows: On the morning of February 13, 1951, J. F. Shirey—husband of plaintiff—and grandson left Shawnee, Oklahoma, in an automobile en route to Oklahoma City, Oklahoma. It was sleeting some on that day and the roads were icy in spots. The wind was blowing hard. It was a terrific wind, an unusual wind, a wind of such force and velocity as is rarely seen in this country short of tornadoes or cyclones. One could scarcely stand up and walk against the wind.

J. F. Shirey, driver of the automobile, testified that about 8:30 A.M. of that day—while driving on the East Reno road at a point close to Oklahoma City—the wind blew his automobile from the north side to the south side of the road and turned it sideways across the road. The force of the wind blew it over the icy road into a borrow ditch against an embankment causing it to upset and damage the automobile. Defendant offered no evidence.

Defendant contends plaintiff's evidence was insufficient to establish that the damage to the automobile was caused by windstorm, but shows that it was caused by collision and upset. Defendant asserts that in order for plaintiff to recover it is necessary for her to establish that the force of the wind—in and of itself without aid of other causes—caused the damage to the automobile. ... [I]n support of this contention cites *Clark v. Fidelity and Guaranty Co., City Ct.*, 39 N.Y.S.2d 377 (1943); *Matthews v. Shelby Mutual Plate Glass & Casualty Co.*, 46 N.E.2d 473 (Ohio App. 1939).

In each of these cases it appears that a windstorm blew the car of the plaintiff against some object causing damage to the car, and the courts in each of these cases held that it was not the windstorm that caused the damage, but that the damage was caused by collision with some other object which character of loss was excluded from coverage under the policy. There cases, however, are contrary to the weight of authority as well as contrary to our own decisions.

The cases generally hold that in an action to recover damages on an insurance policy insuring property against the peril of windstorms excluding from coverage other causes, the insured may recover if the windstorm was the efficient and proximate cause of the damages to the property insured, and it is immaterial that the damage may have been incidentally and indirectly contributed to by other causes expressly excluded from coverage.

In *Pennsylvania Fire Insurance Co. v. Sikes*, 197 Okl. 137 (1946), the court said:

> Where an insurance contract on household goods and a motor vehicle covers loss and damage by windstorm, expressly excluding damage by flood waters, and the personal property insured thereby is blown into a flooded street by the force of wind alone, and upon recovery from flood waters is found to be broken and water soaked, the aggregate damage may be said to be windstorm damage in the purview of the contract, in the absence of a clear showing that the contracting parties intended to exclude such damage which might be expected to follow as the result of the displacement of the property by the wind.

In *Fireman's Ins. Co. of New Jersey v. Weatherman*, 193 S.W.2d 247 (Tex. Civ. App. 1946), the court held: "In action on windstorm policy for damage to automobile which was driven off the highway against a telephone post and completely wrecked, whether damage to automobile was proximately caused by windstorm was for jury." In that case it appeared insured brought an action to recover damage to his automobile on an insurance policy insuring the automobile against the peril of windstorm. The policy excluded from coverage damage caused by collision or upset.

The evidence showed that while [the] insured was driving his automobile along a highway he encountered a windstorm which carried his automobile from the highway against a telephone pole completely destroying the automobile. Insurer defended on the ground that the damage to the automobile was not caused by windstorm, but was caused by collision with the telephone pole, and that no recovery could be had because loss or damage to the automobile caused by collision was excluded from coverage, and at the close of the evidence requested the court to direct a verdict in its favor.

The request was denied and the ruling was sustained on appeal. The court said:

> In appellant's motion for an instructed verdict, the contention is made that the loss or damage to the automobile was caused by collision with another object, to wit, a telephone post, which character of loss was excluded by the terms of the policy. ... The jury found that the loss was caused by a windstorm. It would be idle to contend that the loss would have occurred without the windstorm. As shown by the undisputed evidence, the wind first blew the rear of the car off the pavement to the south, then suddenly reversed the direction of the car northward, blowing the occupants therefrom, and hurled the automobile across the bar pit and into the telephone post with such force as completely to wreck it. The fact that an obstruction interrupted the mad course of said automobile was purely incidental. The windstorm was the sole, inducing and efficient cause of the collision, and the facts bring the loss within the terms of the policy.

In *Clouse v. St. Paul Fire & Marine Insurance Co.*, 40 N.W.2d 820 (Neb. 1950), the court held:

> A policy against loss or damage caused by lightning to the property insured usually covers all known effects of electricity coming under the general head of lightning, and includes all loss or damage which results as a direct and natural consequence of the lightning, notwithstanding other incidental agencies may be instrumental in adding to the loss or damage. ... In determining the cause of a loss for the purpose of fixing insurance liability, when evidence of concurring causes of the damage appears, the proximate cause to which the loss is to be attributed is the dominant, the efficient one that sets the other causes in operation; and causes which are incidental

> are not proximate, though they may be nearer in time and place to the loss.

See also Providence Washington Insurance Co. v. Cooper, 223 S.W.2d 329 (Tex. Civ. App. 1949); *Anderson v. Connecticut Fire Ins. Co.*, 43 N.W.2d 807 (Minn. 1950); and, *Marks v. Lumbermen's Ins. Co. of Philadelphia*, 49 A.2d 855 (Pa. Super. 1946).

Defendant's contention that plaintiff cannot recover under the policy unless she establishes that the damage to her automobile was caused by the windstorm in and of itself, unaided by other causes, cannot be sustained. It is further contended by defendant that no expert evidence has been offered tending to show the velocity of the wind on that day, and that the evidence is therefore insufficient to show that a windstorm existed. We do not agree. The evidence shows that the wind was of sufficient force and velocity to blow the car from one side of the street to the other, and thence into the borrow ditch and is sufficient to establish that a windstorm existed. In *Fidelity-Phenix Fire Ins. Co. of New York v. Board of Education of Town of Rosedale*, 204 P.2d 982, 983 (Okl. 1948), this court held:

> Under policy insuring against perils of windstorm, a "windstorm," in absence of any more specific definition, must be taken to be a wind of such extraordinary force and violence as to be thereby capable of damaging insured property.

In that case after holding that an ordinary gust of wind, no matter how prolonged, is not a windstorm, further said:

> We think the correct standard and applicable to the instant situation is stated in *Gerhard v. Travelers Fire Ins. Co.*, 18 N.W.2d 336, 337 (Wis. 1945), as follows: "In the absence of definition or limitation in the policy, we think that a windstorm must be taken to be a wind of sufficient violence to be capable of damaging the insured property either by its own unaided action or by projecting some object against it. ... If defendant wishes to adopt some scale which establishes the velocity of wind necessary for a windstorm, or if it desires to limit its liability beyond the point that we have indicated, it should incorporate its proposed standard in the policy by clear terms and such ambiguities as are left in this policy should be resolved against it."

The evidence is sufficient to have authorized the jury to find that the windstorm was the proximate cause of the injury and damage to plaintiff's automobile and sufficient to have authorized a verdict in her favor.

Judgment reversed, with directions to grant plaintiff a new trial.

NOTES AND QUESTIONS

1. **Distinguishing "Proximate Consequences" from "Remote Consequences"**. In *Hadley v. Baxendale*, defendants Baxendale and Ors—who operated as a common carrier under the name Pickford & Company—raised this defense: Hadley's "damages were too remote"; therefore, Pickford & Company "were not liable." What is the definition of "remote" in *Hadley*? Is it the opposite of "proximate"? What are the definitions of "proximate" and "remote" in *Shirey*?

2. **Proximate Cause and the Definition of Coverage Under Property Insurance Contracts.** In *de Laurentis v. United Services Auto. Ass'n,* 162 S.W.3d 714, 722–23 (Tex. App.—Houston [14th Dist.] 2005), the Texas Appellate Court stressed the following:

    The HOB–T policy is a named-perils policy that covers "physical loss to the property ... caused by a named peril." It is helpful to our analysis to characterize the perils contributing to the loss and to determine which perils are covered and which are excluded. The accidental discharge, leakage, or overflow of water from within an air conditioning system is a named peril. Because the HOB–T policy is a named-perils policy, all perils not specifically included in the policy are excluded from coverage. If there is a single guiding principle that governs our interpretation of the insurance policy, it is to give effect to the parties' intent as expressed in the policy's plain language. *See Forbau v. Aetna Life Ins. Co.*, 876 S.W.2d 132, 133 (Tex. 1994).

    The HOB–T policy does not define the terms "physical loss" or "caused by" so we look to the plain meaning of these undefined terms. "Loss" signifies "the act of losing or the thing lost; it is not a word of limited, hard and fast meaning and has been synonymous with or equivalent to, 'damage'..." BLACK'S LAW DICTIONARY at 945 (6th ed. 1990). ... "Caused" is defined as "to serve as cause or occasion of: bring into existence: make," and "cause" is defined as "something that occasions or effects a result: ... something that ... produces a phenomenon." WEBSTER'S THIRD NEW INT'L DICT. at 356. Applying the plain meaning of the policy language, we conclude that the policy covers tangible damage to the Policyholder's personal property by water leaking from an air conditioning unit. Such water leaks can produce mold damage—a tangible loss to the Policyholder's personal property. Therefore, the policy's plain language, when read in context, giving effect to all contractual provisions, is unambiguous and requires payment for mold damage caused by a leaking air conditioning unit. ...

In *Travelers Indem. Co. v. Jarrett*, 369 S.W.2d 653 (Tex. App.—Waco 1963, no writ), the court stated: Where insurance against property damage is only against "direct" loss by lightning it has been said the quoted term means "immediate" or "proximate," as distinguished from remote or incidental causes. But a provision insuring against "loss or damage caused by lightning" renders the insurer liable for all known effects of lightning, "and includes all loss or damage which results as a direct and natural consequence of the lightning, notwithstanding other incidental agencies may be incidental in adding to the loss or damage." *Id.* at 655 Thus, Texas courts have determined that a physical loss, as opposed to a direct physical loss, includes the natural consequences of the named peril.

3. **Breach of Property-Insurance Contracts—Distinguishing "Efficient Proximate Cause" from the Tort-Based Foreseeability Test.** In *Garvey v. State Farm Fire & Casualty Company*, 770 P.2d 704, 710 (Cal. 1989), the Supreme Court of California observed:

Property insurance ... is unconcerned with establishing negligence or otherwise assessing tort liability. ... "Property insurance ... is an agreement, a contract, in which the insurer agrees to indemnify the insured in the event that the insured property suffers a covered loss. Coverage, in turn, is commonly provided by reference to causation, e.g., "loss caused by ..." certain enumerated perils. The term 'perils' in traditional property insurance parlance refers to fortuitous, active, physical forces such as lightning, wind, and explosion, which bring about the loss. Thus, the "cause" of loss in the context of a property insurance contract is totally different from that in a liability policy. This distinction is critical to the resolution of losses involving multiple causes. Frequently property losses occur which involve more than one peril that might be considered legally significant. If one of the causes (perils) arguably falls within the coverage grant—commonly either because it is specifically insured (as in a named peril policy) or not specifically excepted or excluded (as in an "all risks" policy)—disputes over coverage can arise. The task becomes one of identifying the most important cause of the loss and attributing the loss to that cause."

On the other hand, the right to coverage in the third-party liability insurance context draws on traditional tort concepts of fault, proximate cause and duty. This liability analysis differs substantially from the coverage analysis in the property insurance context, which draws on the relationship between perils that are either covered or excluded in the contract. In liability insurance, by insuring for personal liability, and agreeing to cover the insured for his … negligence, the insurer agrees to cover the insured for a broader spectrum of risks.

SECTION TWO: MEASURES OF DAMAGES FOR ONE'S NON-PERFORMANCE

In *Hadley v. Baxendale*, Baron Alderson stated at least three rules which allow a plaintiff to receive damages in a breach-of-contract action. A plaintiff may recover if he proves one, a combination, or all of the following: 1) the damages arose "naturally—according to the usual course of things—from [the] breach of contract itself"; 2) the damages are the "probable result of the breach" and both parties contemplated the likelihood of such damages when they were crafting the contract; and 3) "special circumstances"—which were within both parties' knowledge and discussed during the formation of the contract—caused the damages.

As discussed more fully in the following cases, it is generally accepted that the second and third rules allow a complainant to secure "consequential" and "liquidated" damages, respectively. But, what types of damages are recoverable under the first rule—contract damages, expectation damages, actual damages? Furthermore, assuming that we have correctly identified the list of recoverable damages, there is an even more pressing question: How are they calculated? Or asked slightly differently, are there multiple ways to measure or calculate say, breach-of-warranty damages or compensatory damages? Do measures of damages vary across jurisdictions? The remainder of this chapter will address these questions and discuss various equitable remedies.

A. "Contract," "Compensatory," or "Actual" Damages

Mead v. Johnson Group, Inc.
615 S.W.2d 685
(Tex. 1981)

DENTON, JUSTICE. This is a suit to recover damages for breach of contract. … Evadine Mead, plaintiff, was formerly the owner of Century 21/Associated Real Estate in Austin, Texas. On December 19, 1975, she entered into a written contract with John W. "Bull" Johnson and The Johnson Group, Inc., defendants, for the sale of her business (Johnson).

Johnson agreed to: 1) pay Mead $3,000, 2) assume payment of a Small Business Administration (SBA) loan, 3) pay in full all business and trade-related debts owed by Century 21/Associated Real Estate by March 1, 1976, 4) pay Mead fifty percent commission on all sales which she generated, and, 5) pay Mead a fifteen percent override on all commissions paid to other agents and employees.

Mead agreed to: 1) convey to Johnson her interest in all assets of the business, and, 2) continue to work for Johnson for three years from the contract date and not compete within this three-year period. Mead conveyed her interest and Johnson paid her $3,000. Mead began to work for Johnson, but was not paid any commissions or overrides. On March 24, 1976, Mead terminated her employment and began to compete with Johnson.

Mead filed suit against Johnson in April 1976 alleging that the defendants had failed to: 1) assume the SBA loan, 2) pay all business and trade-related debts, and, 3) pay commissions and overrides as agreed. Johnson answered and counterclaimed alleging that Mead had breached her employment contract and agreement not to compete. Larson Equipment Company—lessor of the real estate office—intervened to recover unpaid rent.

Trial was before a jury which entered a verdict for the plaintiff. The trial court rendered judgment: 1) denying Johnson's counterclaim on the grounds that no damage occurred because of Mead's breach, 2) awarding Larson Equipment Company $1,600 damages against Mead for unpaid rent, and, 3) awarding Mead: a) $3,000 damages for injury to her credit reputation, b) $9,733.37 damages for Johnson's failure to assume and pay the balance of the SBA loan, c) $7,420.70 damages for Johnson's failure to pay all business and trade-related debts owed by Century 21/Associated Real Estate on March 1, 1976, d) $1,999.20 for unpaid commissions, e) $232.26 for unpaid overrides, and f) $2,950.00 for attorneys' fees.

The judgment ordered Mead to pay the balance due on the SBA loan and the unpaid creditors of Century 21/Associated Real Estate if, and only if, she recovers the judgment against Johnson. In the event Mead is paid by Johnson the trial court further directed that she indemnify Johnson for such payment.

The court of civil appeals reformed the judgment of the trial court and affirmed. The court deleted the award of damages for loss of credit, for failure to assume the SBA loan, for failure to pay business and trade-related debts, and the order that Mead conditionally pay the loan and debts. The court further reformed the judgment to award Mead recovery over against Johnson for the rent owed to Larson Equipment Company. The court of civil appeals held, as a matter of law that actual damages are not recoverable for loss of credit. We disagree.

In an action for breach of contract, actual damages may be recovered when loss is the natural, probable, and foreseeable consequence of the defendant's conduct. See e.g., *Texas P. Ry. Co. v. Nicholson*, 61 Tex. 491, 496 (1884); *Jones v. George*, 61 Tex. 345, 354–355 (1884); *Humble Oil & Refining Co. v. Wood*, 292 S.W. 200, 201 (Tex. Comm'n App. 1927).

The leading case on foreseeability of contract damages is *Hadley v. Baxendale*, 9 Exch. 341, 354 (1854) in which the English court wrote:

> Where two parties have made a contract which one of them has broken, the damages which the other party ought to receive in respect of such breach of contract should be such as may fairly and reasonably be considered either arising naturally; *i.e.,* according to the usual course of things, from such breach of contract itself, or such as may reasonably be supposed to have been in the contemplation of both parties at the time they made the contract as the probable result of the breach.

This is the rule in the majority of American jurisdictions and is recognized by the RESTATEMENT (SECOND) OF CONTRACTS § 351—UNFORESEEABILITY AND RELATED LIMITATIONS ON DAMAGES:

> 1) Damages are not recoverable for loss that the party in breach did not have reason to foresee as a probable result of the breach when the contract was made.
>
> 2) Loss may be foreseeable as a probable result of a breach because it follows from the breach
>
> (a) in the ordinary course of events, or
>
> (b) as a consequence of general or particular requirements of the other party that the party in breach had reason to know.
>
> 3) Even if the party in breach had reason to foresee the loss as a probable result of his breach when the contract was made, a court may limit damages by excluding recovery for loss of profits, by allowing recovery only for loss incurred in reliance, or otherwise if it concludes that in the circumstances justice so requires.

Prior Texas cases have held that loss of credit or injury to credit reputation is too speculative or remote to constitute an element of actual damages. In *Trawick v. Martin-Brown Co.*, 14 S.W. 564, 566 (Tex. 1890), this court wrote that loss of credit may be considered in determining exemplary damages, but not actual damages. *See Wallace v. Finberg*, 46 Tex. 35, 47 (1876). *Trawick* was a tort action for wrongful attachment in which the court determined the plaintiff's loss of credit was too speculative or remote to constitute an element of actual damages. *Trawick v. Martin-Brown Co. supra*, 14 S.W. at 566.

There are several other cases on wrongful attachment which have denied recovery of actual damages for loss of credit relying on *Trawick*. *Kauffman v. Armstrong*, 11 S.W. 1048, 1049 (Tex. 1889); *Security State Bank & Trust v. Craighead*, 440 S.W.2d 701, 710 (Tex. Civ. App. San Antonio 1969, writ ref'd n. r. e.); *First Nat. Bank of Littlefield v. Cooper*, 12 S.W.2d 271, 274 (Tex. Civ. App. Amarillo 1928, writ ref'd). *See also Mayer v. Duke*, 10 S.W. 565, 569 (Tex. 1889); *Wallace v. Finberg, supra* at 47.

The only contract case involving loss of credit is *Sterling Projects, Inc. v. Fields*, 530 S.W.2d 602 (Tex. Civ. App. Waco 1975, no writ). This was a suit for breach of a construction contract in which a subcontractor sought to recover damages from the general contractor for loss of credit and business reputation. The court of civil appeals, in reliance on the wrongful attachment cases noted above, held that loss of credit was not recoverable as actual damages. *Id*. at 605.

The Uniform Commercial Code allows recovery of actual damages for loss of credit resulting from wrongful dishonor of a check. Tex. Bus. & Com. Code Ann. § 4.402, Comment 3 (UCC). Under section 4.402, a bank's liability is limited to actual damages proved when dishonor occurs through the bank's mistake. *Id.* Actual damages may include consequential damages such as for loss of credit. *Id. See First Nat. Bank of Bellaire v. Hubbs*, 566 S.W.2d 375, 378 (Tex. Civ. App. Houston [1st Dist.] 1978, no writ); *Northshore Bank v. Palmer*, 525 S.W.2d 718, 720 (Tex. Civ. App. Houston [14th Dist.) 1975, writ ref'd n. r. e.). *But cf. State Nat. Bank of Iowa Park v. Rogers*, 89 S.W.2d 825, 826 (Tex. Civ. App. Fort Worth 1936, no writ) (pre UCC case). Comment 2 to section 4.402 describes the liability of the bank as sounding both in contract and in tort.

The rule of *Wallace v. Finberg, supra* and *Trawick v. Martin-Brown Co., supra*, is not an absolute bar to recovery of actual damages for loss of credit resulting from breach of contract. The prior cases held that loss of credit was too speculative or remote to be an element of actual damages. Before the Great Depression of the 1930's, most commercial transactions were for cash. Since then, use of consumer credit has increased tremendously. Today, very few major purchases are transacted in cash; but rather, reliance upon long-term mortgages, installment contracts, charge accounts, and credit cards is commonplace. Good credit rating is essential in today's economy.

The 1980 SUPPLEMENT TO CORBIN ON CONTRACTS states: "[T]here is no good reason why damage to credit rating should not be compensable in contract." 2 CORBIN, CONTRACTS § 1007 (Kaufman Supp. 1980). Recognition that loss of credit may be a foreseeable result of breach of contract is in line with the realities of today's economy.

To recover for loss of credit, as with any element of contract damage, it must be proved that the injury was the natural, probable, and foreseeable consequence of the breach of contract or there are no actual damages. *See Hadley v. Baxendale, supra*, at 354; RESTATEMENT (SECOND) OF CONTRACTS § 365 (Tent. Draft 1979). This is not a departure from the general rule of contract damages, but only recognition of an element of damages if proven.

We hold that actual damages for loss of credit or injury to credit reputation in an action for breach of contract may be recovered when there is evidence that loss of credit was a natural, probable, and foreseeable consequence of the defendant's breach.

The jury found that Johnson's failure to assume the SBA loan and to pay the trade and business-related debts of Century 21/Associated Real Estate was the proximate cause of Mead's loss of credit. Johnson contends there is no evidence to support the jury's finding of proximate cause. In deciding a "no evidence" point, which is a question of law, we consider only that evidence and reasonable inferences therefrom which viewed in its most favorable light supports the jury finding and we must reject all evidence or inferences contrary to the finding. *McClure v. Allied Stores of Texas, Inc.*, 608 S.W.2d 901, 904 (Tex. 1980); *East Texas Theatres, Inc. v. Rutledge*, 453 S.W.2d 466, 467 (Tex. 1970); *Garza v. Alviar*, 395 S.W.2d 821, 823 (Tex. 1965).

The record indicates that after March 24, 1976, Mead was refused a loan at Oak Hill National Bank, lost her credit with Exxon, had her account closed at several stores including J. C. Penney's, Sears, Montgomery Wards, and Yarings. She was also denied credit by Master Charge, BankAmericard, Carte Blanc, Waterloo Leasing, Lamar Leasing, Joske's, Handy Dan, and Bank of Austin. When viewed in its most favorable light, this is some evidence to support the jury finding of proximate cause. We accordingly hold that the trial court correctly awarded Mead actual damages for loss of credit.

The court of civil appeals held that Mead could acquire a right of action against Johnson for the balance of the SBA loan and the business and trade-related debts assumed by the defendants only by first paying the loan and debts. We disagree.

In so holding, the court followed the rule announced in *Gunst v. Pelham*, 12 S.W. 233, 234 (Tex. 1889), a case involving a mortgage on real property. In *Gunst*, Johnson purchased a tract of land from Pelham assuming an existing indebtedness. He conveyed the land to Gunst who later defaulted. Pelham sued Johnson and Gunst. This court held that Johnson was primarily liable on the mortgage and Pelham could acquire a right of action against Johnson only by first paying the mortgage. *Id.* 12 S.W. at 233. *Accord Talley v. Howsley*, 176 S.W.2d 158, 159

(Tex. 1944); *French v. May*, 484 S.W.2d 420, 424 (Tex. Civ. App. Corpus Christi 1972, writ ref'd n. r. e.).

The *Gunst* rule also has been applied to actions for breach of indemnity contracts. A party complaining of breach of an indemnity contract must pay the debt in controversy before he is entitled to recover from a breaching surety. *Latimer v. Texas & N. O. Ry. Co.*, 56 S.W.2d 933, 935 (Tex. Civ. App. Beaumont 1933, writ ref'd); *Meier v. Service Corp. of the Nat. Ass'n of Credit Men*, 129 S.W.2d 690, 692 (Tex. Civ. App. Dallas 1939, writ dism'd judgmt. cor.); *First State Bank of Pardise v. Wallace*, 161 S.W. 957, 959 (Tex. Civ. App. Fort Worth 1913, writ ref'd).

The present case involves neither a mortgage nor an indemnity contract, but rather a contract for the sale of a business. This court has written, albeit dictum, that in a suit to recover damages on a written contract the promisee is not required first to pay the debt in order to maintain the cause of action. *Smith v. Nesbitt*, 230 S.W. 976, 977–978 (Tex. 1921). In a suit similar to the instant case involving the sale of business and assumption of existing debts, it was held the contract created a direct obligation from the promisor to the promisee and did not require that the promisee first pay the debts in order to recover. *Cohen v. Simpson*, 32 S.W. 59, 61 (Tex. Civ. App. 1895, writ dism'd). *See also Smith v. Smith*, 595 S.W.2d 631, 632 (Tex. Civ. App. Fort Worth 1980, no writ).

There are other cases in which Texas courts have permitted recovery for expenses incurred without first requiring payment by the plaintiff. *See, e. g., Triton Oil & Gas Corp. v. E. W. Moran Drilling Co.*, 509 S.W.2d 678, 686 (Tex. Civ. App. Fort Worth 1974, writ ref'd n. r. e.) (materials and services in drilling contract); *Taylor v. Mark*, 376 S.W.2d 927, 928 (Tex. Civ. App. Waco 1964, writ ref'd n. r. e.) (materials in a construction contract); *San Antonio & A. P. Ry. Co. v. Moore*, 31 Tex. Civ. App. 371, 72 S.W. 226, 228 (1903, writ ref'd) (medical expenses).

This court noted in *Smith v. Nesbitt, supra*, 230 S.W. at 978, that proper orders directing the promisee to apply the recovery to payment of the debt would prevent double recovery. Here, the trial court so ordered. Johnson received valuable assets from Mead from which he has profited. He breached the contract, yet is relieved of the obligation to perform that which he agreed to do pay the SBA loan and business debts. To permit this result is inequitable and allows Johnson to be unjustly enriched. We hold that Mead is not required first to pay the loan and debts assumed under the contract.

Johnson urges several other points by way of conditional application. First, he contends the court of civil appeals erred in holding Mead could recover the amount of unpaid rent owing to Larson Equipment Company. The courts properly allowed this recovery for the same reason we held that Mead could recover the balance of the loan and debts. Second, Johnson argues that it was error to award Mead commissions and overrides because her breach excused performance by the defendants.

The record indicates that Johnson breached the contract to pay the balance of the loan and debts on March 1, 1976. Mead was in compliance with the contract until March 24, 1976. A party in default on a contract is not relieved by a subsequent breach by the other party. *Whittenburg v. Groves*, 208 S.W. 901, 904 (Tex. Comm'n App. 1919, judgmt. adopted). Default by one party excuses performance by the other party. *See, e. g., Glass v. Anderson*, 596 S.W.2d 507, 511 (Tex. 1980); *Lewis v. River Oaks Capital Corp.*, 466 S.W.2d 348, 352 (Tex. Civ. App. Houston (1st Dist.) 1971, writ ref'd n. r. e.); *Battles v. Adams*, 415 S.W.2d 479, 484 (Tex. Civ. App. Austin 1967, writ ref'd n.r.e.). Third, Johnson contends it was error to award Mead attorneys' fees. The award of attorneys' fees was proper. Article 2226, TEX. REV. CIV. STAT. ANN., permits recovery of attorneys' fees in suits founded upon written contracts. Johnson's conditional points of error are overruled.

The judgment of the court of civil appeals is reversed insofar as it denied recovery of actual damages for loss of credit and judgment is rendered that Mead recover for loss of credit in accordance with the judgment of the trial court. That portion of the judgment of the court of civil appeals denying Mead recovery for the balance of the SBA loan and the business and trade-related debts is reversed.

Judgment is rendered for Mead against Johnson for the balance of the SBA loan and the amount of the trade and business-related debts, and if paid, Johnson is entitled to indemnity for the amount paid. In all other respects, the judgment of the court of civil appeals is affirmed.

NOTES AND QUESTIONS

1. **The Search for a Precise Label—"Contract Damages," "Actual Damages," or "Compensatory Damages".** In *Mead*, Justice Denton wrote: 1) "In an action for breach of contract, *actual damages* may be recovered when loss is the natural, probable, and foreseeable consequence of the defendant's conduct," and 2) "The leading case on *foreseeability of contract damages* is *Hadley v. Baxendale*, 9 Exch. 341, 354 (1854)." In addition, the following excerpt appears in *Southern Elec. Services, Inc. v. City of Houston*, 355 S.W.3d 319, 324 (Tex. App.—Houston [1st Dist.] 2011): "To recover *compensatory damages*, the plaintiff must prove that he suffered some pecuniary loss as a result of the breach. Such losses must be the natural, probable, and foreseeable consequence of the defendant's conduct."—citing *Mead v. Johnson Group, Inc.*, 615

S.W.2d 685, 687 (Tex. 1981), citing *Hadley v. Baxendale*, 9 Exch. 341, 354 (1854). Therefore, under Texas law, the three terms—contract, compensatory, and actual damages—are synonymous.

2. **The Purpose and Types of Compensatory Damages**. Under the *Hadley* rule, a plaintiff may recover compensatory damages when her loss is "the natural, probable, and foreseeable consequence" of the defendant's breach of contract. But what is the purpose of compensatory damages? A review of caselaw reveals two purposes:

a) "Reliance damages" are awarded to make a plaintiff whole—to return the promisee to the position he occupied before entering into the contract. *See e.g., MCI Communications Services, Inc. v. F.D.I.C.*, 808 F.Supp.2d 24, 30 (D.D.C. 2011) ("The D.C. Circuit has ... held that "reliance damages"—which are intended to make a contracting party whole after a breach—are recoverable. ... These damages give the plaintiff 'the repayment of his expenditures in preparing to perform and in part performance,' and put him 'in as good a position as he was in before the promise was made. ... The fact that reliance damages are backward-looking does not destroy their pedigree as a species of compensatory relief.'"), citing *Nashville Lodging Co. v. Resolution Trust Corp.*, 59 F.3d 236, 245–46 (D.C. Cir. 1995).

b) "Expectancy damages" are designed to place a non-repudiating party in the position it would have held had the contract been performed. *RSB Bedford Associates LLC v. Ricky's Williamsburg, Inc.*, 2012 WL 1699844, *2 (N.Y. Sup.). *See also Curley v. Allstate Ins. Co.*, 289 F.Supp.2d 614, 621 (E.D. Pa. 2003) ("When [a] non-breaching party elects to sue on [a] contract, ordinary contract rules limit compensatory damages to his expectancy interest ..."); *525 Main Street Corp. v. Eagle Roofing Co.*, 34 N.J. 251, 254 (1961) (The purpose of compensatory damages is "to put the injured party in as good a position as he would have had if performance had been rendered as promised."); and *In re Grace*, 2008 WL1766752, *5 (Bkrtcy. D.N.M. 2008) ("[I]t is never the purpose of compensatory damages to put the plaintiff in a better position than he or she had been in before the injury."), citing *McNeill v. Burlington Resource Oil & Gas Co.*, 153 P.3d 46, 55 (Ct. App. 2006).

3. **The Purpose and Types of Compensatory Damages Under Texas Law**. Consider the following excerpt from the decision in

Geis v. Colina Del Rio, LP, 362 S.W.3d 100, 112 (Tex. App.—San Antonio 2011):

> Breach of contract damages are generally designed to protect three interests: a restitution interest, a reliance interest, and an expectation interest. *O'Farrill Avila v. Gonzalez*, 974 S.W.2d 237, 247 (Tex. App.—San Antonio 1998, pet. denied).
>
> The purpose of reliance damages is to restore the status quo at the time before the contract was made. *Hart v. Moore*, 952 S.W.2d 90, 97 (Tex. App.—Amarillo 1997, pet. denied). On the other hand, the purpose of expectancy damages is to restore the non-breaching party to the same economic position that it would have been in had the contract not been breached. *Qaddura v. Indo-European Foods, Inc.,* 141 S.W.3d 882, 888–89 (Tex. App.—Dallas 2004, pet denied).
>
> Reliance damages are similar to out-of-pocket damages. *Hart*, 952 S.W.2d at 97. Out-of-pocket damages measure the difference between the value the buyer has paid and the value of what he has received. *Arthur Andersen & Co. v. Perry Equip. Corp.*, 945 S.W.2d 812, 817 (Tex. 1997); *Brown Found. Repair & Consulting, Inc. v. Henderson*, 719 S.W.2d 229, 231 (Tex. App.—Dallas 1986, no writ) ("Damages may be established by proving the amount paid for repairs and the entire lack of value thereof").
>
> Expectancy damages are similar to benefit-of-the-bargain damages. *See Qaddura*, 141 S.W.3d at 888–89. Benefit-of-the-bargain damages measure the difference between the value as represented and the value received. *Perry*, 945 S.W.2d at 817.

Are the reliance and expectancy damages rules in Note 2 identical to the ones in Note 3? And do the measure-of-damages rules in Note 3 comport with those discussed in the following sections?

B. Measuring "Expectancy Damages"

1) Mixed Breach-of-Contract and Statutory Actions and Types of Expenditures Comprising Expectancy Damages

Mays v. Pierce
203 S.W.3d 564
(Tex. App.—Houston [14th Dist.] 2006)

EVA M. GUZMAN, JUSTICE. [Edward Eugene Mays and Traci Bailey were doing business as Pro-Tech Restoration (Pro-Tech)]. On December 6,

2001, Connie Pierce and Edward Mays (Mays) signed a work order/contract for Pro-Tech to perform work on Pierce's home. The scope of the work was described as "mold & water remediation/restoration of contents & structure." The contract also provided:

> It is understood that payment for the above services will be paid from Insurance Company Proceeds and Pro-Techs [sic] name is to be on all checks. ... Billing will be made directly to the Insurance Company, however if payment is not made it will be the responsibility of the insured."

Pro-Tech then arranged for mold testing. On December 17, 2001, Mays told Pierce, based on the results of the test, her house contained toxic mold, the mold was dangerous, and she and her daughter had to leave the house "with the clothes on their back[s]," and move into a motel. Pierce and her daughter did so.

By mid-January 2002, Pro-Tech had submitted a bid to Farmers Insurance—Pierce's insurance company—for the costs to remediate and rebuild the house. The bid included a room-by-room "Building Est.," which contained itemized costs of remediation totaling $15,841.81, together with a room-by-room estimate of the costs for reconstruction totaling $9,647.37 before depreciation and $7,142.51 after depreciation. Farmers calculated a net claim of $24,905.50, after depreciation, for the full cost to remediate and reconstruct the house and to conduct post-remediation testing.

Pro-Tech sent a facsimile copy of these documents to Michael Pierce. According to the Pierces, this claim was for mold remediation, post-remediation testing, and rebuilding the house. Pro-Tech separately submitted a bid of $12,296.00 for contents remediation, which, according to Farmers' documents, included two months of storage through April 11, 2002. None of the bids estimated costs for packing and removing the contents of the house.

In January and February 2002, Pierce received checks from Farmers in the amounts of $24,905.50, $4,216.00, and $7,940.83. She gave the first two checks totaling $29,121.50 to Pro-Tech and kept the third check. According to Pierce, the first two checks represented partial payment for the mold remediation of the house, the contents, and the rebuilding of the house, and the third check represented additional rebuilding costs.

In early 2002, Pro-Tech placed toxic warning signs on the exterior of the house and removed carpet, cabinets, sheetrock, appliances, and the air conditioner. Pro-Tech virtually emptied the living area of the house of its contents, moving some items into off-site storage and placing others, such as toilets, bathtubs, appliances, clothing, and household items in the garage. Pro-Tech left the job on March 3, 2002—without rebuilding the house, remediating its contents, or furnishing a post-remediation certificate showing the house had been cleared of mold. No evidence was presented that Pro-Tech informed Pierce it was stopping work on the project at that time. Pro-Tech did not return Pierce's house key until July 2002. In July 2002, Pierce hired another company to test her house for mold. The test cost $875.00. The results indicated the house still contained toxic mold.

Farmers paid Pierce's living expenses through April 2002. Because her house was still not habitable, Pierce moved her contents from Pro-Tech's off-site storage facility to a different facility in July. She incurred $360.00 in moving expenses and $822.00 in storage fees during the time required to make her house suitable for living. Pierce later discovered some of the property stored off-site had been damaged or destroyed. Pierce testified that she was unable to salvage any of the property Pro-Tech had moved to the garage, and she opined the "fair value" of the damaged or destroyed items in the garage was $8,226.00. Finally, Pierce believed a credit card had been taken from her house or property at some time during the period when Pro-Tech had custody of the house and property. She reported $126.36 of fraudulent charges on the card.

Pierce subsequently sold the home to her former husband for $5,000 and sued Pro-Tech, alleging breach of contract, misrepresentations and unconscionable actions under the Deceptive Trade Practices Act (DTPA), and conversion based on unauthorized use of the credit card.

Trial was to the bench. Mays testified Pro-Tech was paid for remediation and was never paid to rebuild the house or remediate its contents. He further testified that, if Pro-Tech had been paid to restore the contents and structure, it would have done so. The trial court rendered judgment in favor of Pierce, awarding her actual damages of $43,678.50, additional DTPA damages of $43.678.50, attorneys' fees, and pre- and post-judgment interest. Pro-Tech filed a motion for new trial, which was denied by operation of law. *See* Tex. R. Civ. P. 329b(c).

II. ISSUE PRESENTED

In a single issue, Pro-Tech contends (1) there is no evidence, or alternatively factually insufficient evidence, to establish liability for Pierce's DTPA claims; (2) the evidence is legally, or alternatively factually, insufficient to support Pierce's breach-of-contract claims; (3) no evidence, or alternatively, factually insufficient evidence, supports the theft/conversion claim; and (4) there is no evidence, or alternatively, factually insufficient evidence, to support any of the damages sought by, or awarded to, Pierce.

IV. DISCUSSION

A. Pierce's DTPA Claims

Pierce alleged both an unconscionable action or course of action in violation of TEX. BUS. & COM. CODE ANN. § 17.50(a)(3) (Vernon 2002) and false, misleading, or deceptive acts or practices in violation of TEX. BUS. & COM. CODE ANN. §§ 17.46(b)(5) and (7) (Vernon 2002). The two claims are distinct and either basis will support recovery. To recover under either theory, however, a plaintiff must establish more than a mere breach of contract. *See Riddick v. Quail Harbor Condo. Ass'n*, 7 S.W.3d 663, 670 (Tex. App.—Houston [14th Dist.] 1999, no pet.) (stating that a simple breach-of-contract claim is neither a DTPA violation nor an unconscionable act).

Pro-Tech argues Pierce's evidence of her DTPA claims is insufficient because: 1) Pierce failed to establish any of the alleged misrepresentations that serve as the basis of her DTPA claims; 2) there is no evidence to support any unconscionable action or course of action by Pro-Tech; 3) Pierce failed to establish any reliance or causation in relation to her DTPA claims; 4) Pierce's claims are essentially contractual claims, precluding liability under the DTPA; and 5) there is no evidence, or factually insufficient evidence, to support any implied finding Pro-Tech's alleged conduct was knowing or intentional under the DTPA. We discuss Pierce's two DTPA claims separately.

1. Unconscionable Action or Course of Action

"Unconscionable action or course of action" means an act or practice which, to a consumer's detriment, takes advantage of the lack of knowledge, ability, experience, or capacity of the consumer to a grossly unfair degree." TEX. BUS. & COM. CODE ANN. § 17.45(5) (Vernon 2002). A court examines the entire transaction to determine whether a defendant took advantage of a consumer to a grossly unfair degree. *See Chastain v. Koonce*, 700 S.W.2d 579, 583 (Tex. 1985). A plaintiff need not prove reliance to establish a claim based on unconscionability. *Compare* TEX. BUS. & COM. CODE ANN. § 17.50(a)(1)(B) (requiring a claimant to demonstrate reliance in order to maintain an action for a "laundry list" violation), *with* TEX. BUS. & COM. CODE ANN. § 17.50(a)(3) (omitting the reliance requirement). The plaintiff also need not prove specific representations. *See Teague v. Bandy*, 793 S.W.2d 50, 54 (Tex. App.—Austin 1990, writ denied) ("A consumer may maintain a DTPA cause of action for unconscionable conduct even if the seller made no specific misrepresentations.") ...

Pierce presented no evidence that Pro-Tech misrepresented the presence of mold or its risks, and Pierce does not contend it was unnecessary for her family to leave the home. Second, Pro-Tech's actions in "ripping up the home" were performed pursuant to the contract and to Pro-Tech's representations to Pierce and her insurer that it was necessary to remove carpeting, air conditioning, cabinetry, fixtures, sheetrock, etc. Again, Pierce does not contend these measures were unnecessary. Pierce's third contention merely alleges breach of contract. ... Because the evidence is so weak that it creates only a suspicion of Pro-Tech's lack of intent to perform, we conclude the evidence is legally insufficient to support Pierce's claim of an unconscionable action or course of action.

2. False, Misleading, or Deceptive Acts or Practices

Pierce states an additional or alternative DTPA claim pursuant to TEX. BUS. & COM. CODE ANN. § 17.46(b)(5), (7). These subsections provide that false, misleading, or deceptive acts or practices include:

> (5) representing that goods or services have sponsorship, approval, characteristics, ingredients, uses, benefits, or quantities which they do not have or that a person has a sponsorship, approval, status, affiliation, or connection which he does not. ...
>
> (7) representing that goods or services are of a particular standard, quality, or grade, or that goods are of a particular style or model, if they are of another. ... TEX. BUS. & COM. CODE ANN. § 17.46(b)(5), (7).

In her claim under section 17.46(b), Pierce relied on evidence of the following representations: 1) Pro-Tech would, in a timely manner, remove the toxic mold and would restore the contents and structure as set forth in the work order/contract, and 2) Pro-Tech would provide a certificate showing the house had been retested and was safe. The only evidence of such representations is the contract itself and bids prepared by Pro-Tech after entering into the contract. The bids include the costs of post-remediation testing and the costs of storing Pierce's personal property for two to three months.

Pro-Tech contends Pierce's § 17.46(b) claim constitutes nothing more than a breach-of-contract claim. The determination of whether a breach of contract rises to the level of a misrepresentation sufficient to trigger the DTPA is a fact-driven inquiry. *Chilton Ins. v. Pate & Pate Enter., Inc.*, 930 S.W.2d 877, 890 (Tex. App.—San Antonio 1996, writ denied). Whether the facts, once ascertained, constitute a DTPA misrepresentation is a question of law. *Id.*

Here, Pierce did not show she was harmed by Pro-Tech's representations, but only showed harm caused by Pro-Tech's failure to perform. *See Crawford v. Ace Sign, Inc.*, 917 S.W.2d 12, 14–15 (Tex. 1996) (per curiam) (holding no DTPA violation when statements of Yellow Pages representative did not cause any harm, but, instead, failure to run advertisement actually caused plaintiff's lost profits). Pierce contends Pro-Tech never intended to restore the house or remediate its contents, but as discussed previously, we conclude the evidence of Pro-Tech's intent is legally insufficient.

Accordingly, we hold Pro-Tech's failure to perform as represented does not rise above a breach-of-contract claim, and therefore is not actionable under the DTPA. *See id.* Having concluded there is legally insufficient evidence to support Pierce's DTPA claims, we sustain Pro-Tech's issue to the extent Pro-Tech challenges the sufficiency of the evidence to support those claims. Accordingly, we reverse that portion of the judgment awarding additional DTPA damages of $43,678.50 and render judgment that Pierce takes nothing on her DTPA claims.

B. Pierce's Breach-of-Contract Claim

The elements of a breach-of-contract action are 1) the existence of a valid contract, 2) performance or tendered performance by the plaintiff, 3) breach of the contract by the defendant, and 4) damages sustained by the plaintiff as a result of the breach. *Frost Nat'l Bank v. Burge*, 29 S.W.3d 580, 593 (Tex. App.—Houston [14th Dist.] 2000, no pet.). A breach occurs when a party fails or refuses to do something he has promised to do. *See Townewest Homeowners Ass'n v. Warner Comm'n Inc.*, 826 S.W.2d 638, 640 (Tex. App.—Houston [14th Dist.] 1992, no writ).

Pro-Tech argues Pierce's evidence of her breach-of-contract claim is insufficient because Pierce failed to 1) offer any competent evidence to establish Pro-Tech failed to perform mold remediation services, 2) establish any contractual duties regarding potential physical damage to the residence or contents, and 3) establish any contractual duty for Pro-Tech to rebuild or remodel her residence. In her petition, Pierce alleged Pro-Tech breached the contract "when Pro-Tech Restoration failed to complete the services of mold remediation, thus leaving the house uninhabitable and the contents unusable. Pro-Tech Restoration further breached the contract described in this petition when they [sic] caused damage to Connie Pierce's house and the contents of the house." At trial, Pierce asserted Pro-Tech had contracted to rebuild or restore her house and the contents after it completed remediation, but never did so.

1. Restoration of the Structure and Remediation of Contents

It is undisputed that Pro-Tech ceased work on Pierce's house on March 3, 2002, but did not return the key until July 2002. At the time Pro-Tech left, it had placed biohazard warning signs on the exterior of the house, removed carpet, cabinets, appliances, sheetrock, and the air conditioner, and virtually emptied the living area of the house of its contents, moving some items into off-site storage and placing others items in the garage. It is also undisputed that Pro-Tech did not rebuild the house or remediate the contents.

Additionally, there was testimony indicating Pro-Tech did not provide Pierce with a certificate showing the house had been retested and was clear of toxic mold. Thus, the issue in this case is not what Pro-Tech did or failed to do, but rather the scope of what Pro-Tech promised to do. By the terms of the contract/work order, Pro-Tech described the "scope of the work to be performed" as "mold & water remediation/restoration of contents & structure." Thus, the contract between Pierce and Pro-Tech unambiguously included remediation of the home's contents and restoration of the structure.

Moreover, Pro-Tech prepared a set of documents under the heading of "Estimates and Tests." These documents included a bid Pro-Tech submitted to Farmers for the dwelling, including a room-by-room estimate of the itemized costs for remediation and a separate room-by-room estimate of the itemized costs of reconstruction. These documents also listed the cost for post-remediation testing. Based on these figures, Farmers calculated a net claim for the dwelling, including mold remediation, post-remediation testing, and rebuilding the house. Pro-Tech also submitted a separate bid for remediation of the contents.

We conclude there is legally sufficient evidence that Pro-Tech breached the terms of the work order/contract when it failed to remediate the contents of Pierce's home and restore the structure. We also conclude there is legally sufficient evidence that Pro-Tech breached a promise to Pierce when it did not provide a certificate showing the house had been retested for mold.

2. Mold Remediation

Pro-Tech also argues the evidence is insufficient to support a finding of breach of contract because Pierce presented no evidence Pro-Tech failed to perform mold remediation. With this argument, Pro-Tech attempts to isolate the promise to perform mold remediation from the remaining promises in the contract and insurance bids. As discussed above, the contract contemplated that Pro-Tech would return Pierce's house and its contents to her in a remediated and restored state. Pro-Tech's argument is therefore contrary to the general principle of contract construction that requires a court to examine the entire agreement in an effort to harmonize and give effect to all provisions of the contract so that none will be rendered meaningless. *See MCI Telecomms. Corp. v. Tex. Utils. Elec. Co.*, 995 S.W.2d 647, 652 (Tex. 1999).

3. Damage to House and Contents

In response to Pierce's contention that Pro-Tech breached the contract by damaging Pierce's house and its contents, Pro-Tech points to a hold-harmless clause in the work order/contract; however, Pro-Tech did not plead release as an affirmative defense. *See* TEX. R. CIV. P. 94 (stating party shall set forth affirmatively release and any other matter constituting an avoidance or affirmative defense); *Cole v. Johnson*, 157 S.W.3d 856, 862 (Tex. App.—Fort Worth 2005, no pet.) (stating hold-harmless agreement is synonymous with release).

In summary, we hold the evidence is legally sufficient to support the trial court's implied finding that Pro-Tech promised to perform mold remediation, post-remediation testing, and to remediate the home's contents and rebuild the structure, but did not do so. Accordingly, we overrule Pro-Tech's issue to the extent it challenges the sufficiency of the evidence on Pierce's breach-of-contract claim.

C. Pierce's Conversion Claim

Appellants challenge the legal and factual sufficiency of the evidence to support Pierce's claim for conversion. Pierce does not respond to this argument on appeal.

Conversion is defined as the wrongful exercise of dominion and control over another's property in denial of or inconsistent with the owner's rights. *Green Int'l, Inc. v. Solis*, 951 S.W.2d 384, 391 (Tex. 1997). Here, Pierce alleges Pro-Tech converted one of her credit cards, pointing to unauthorized purchases on the account; however, Pierce presented no evidence that the amounts were charged by Edward or Traci Mays or by anyone under Pro-Tech's control. Accordingly, we sustain Pro-Tech's issue to the extent it challenges the sufficiency of the evidence on Pierce's conversion claim.

D. The Challenges to Damages

Pro-Tech presents the following five arguments regarding the trial court's award of damages: 1) the evidence is legally, or alternatively factually, insufficient to support any award based on mental anguish; 2) Pierce failed to offer competent evidence to establish any recoverable measure of damage available under the DTPA or her breach-of-contract claims; 3) Pierce failed to offer competent evidence to permit the recovery of out-of-pocket expenses; 4) Pierce failed to offer competent evidence to recover the value of her personal property; and 5) Pierce is not entitled to the recovery of attorneys' fees or additional DTPA damages.

The trial court rendered judgment in Pierce's favor and awarded actual damages of $43,678.50—without specifying the claim or claims on which Pierce prevailed or the proven damages. Having concluded that Pierce presented sufficient evidence to support liability only on her breach-of-contract claim, we address the sufficiency of Pierce's evidence to support damages for that claim.

The ultimate goal in measuring damages for a breach-of-contract claim is to provide just compensation for any loss or damage actually sustained as a result of the breach. *Walden v. Affiliated Computer Servs., Inc.*, 97 S.W.3d 303, 328 (Tex. App.—Houston [14th Dist.] 2003, pet. denied). The normal measure of damages in a breach-of-contract case is the benefit-of-the-bargain measure, the purpose of which is to restore the injured party to the economic position it would have been in had the contract been performed. *SAVA Gumarska in Kemijska Industria D.D. v. Advanced Polymer Scis., Inc.*, 128 S.W.3d 304, 317 n. 6 (Tex. App.—Dallas 2004, no pet.).

Nevertheless, as the Seventh Court of Appeals explained in the context of discussing whether damages for misrepresentation and breach of contract constitute double recovery:

> The theories of recovery for misrepresentation include out-of-pocket expenses or loss of the benefit of the bargain. The recovery of out-of-pocket expenses compensates one for actual loss due to another's representation while a benefit-of-the-bargain recovery allows the recovery of what an individual might reasonably have expected to recover as the result of another's representation. In contract law, theories of recovery for a breach of contract include reliance or expectancy damages.
>
> Reliance damages—similar to out-of-pocket recovery—reimburse one for expenditures made towards the execution of the contract in order to restore the status quo before the contract. Expectancy damages—similar to benefit-of-the-bargain recoveries—award damages for the reasonably expected value of the contract. Thus, the theories of recovery for both tortious misrepresentation and breach of contract are similar and necessarily involve the same type of damages. *Hart v. Moore*, 952 S.W.2d 90, 97 (Tex. App.—Amarillo 1997, pet. denied).

In the present case, Pierce's total request for actual damages—whether arising from Pro-Tech's breach of contract or from its actions allegedly violating the DTPA—consists of the following:

> $29,121.50—total amount Farmers Insurance paid to Pro-Tech
>
> 8,226.00—damage to property stored in garage
>
> 822.00—additional storage fees
>
> 875.00—post-remediation inspection report
>
> 360.00—moving expenses
>
> 15,000.00—additional living expenses (6 months @ $2,500/month)

$54,404.50—total actual breach of contract/DTPA damages requested

The trial court's award of $43,678.50 was therefore $10,726.00 less than Pierce's requested DTPA/breach-of-contract damages.

A trial court has discretion to award damages within the range of the evidence presented at trial. *City of Houston v. Harris County Outdoor Adver. Ass'n*, 879 S.W.2d 322, 334 (Tex. App.—Houston [14th Dist.] 1994, writ denied). With this precept in mind, we turn to Pro-Tech's specific arguments challenging the sufficiency of the evidence to support the award of actual damages.

1. Mental Anguish Damages

Pro-Tech first challenges the sufficiency of the evidence to support an award of mental anguish damages. Although Pierce pleaded for mental anguish damages, at trial she did not refer to or request any amount for mental anguish damages. Thus, Pro-Tech's challenge to the sufficiency of the evidence to support mental anguish damages is without merit.

2. Recovery of Amounts Farmers Paid to Pro-Tech

Pro-Tech's second argument appears directed at damages compensating Pierce for the sums she, through her insurer, paid to Pro-Tech. Pro-Tech argues, regardless of whether one applies a benefit-of-the-bargain measure of damages or an out-of-pocket measure of damages, Pierce failed to prove the value of the services she actually received. *See Leyendecker & Assocs., Inc. v. Wechter*, 683 S.W.2d 369, 373 (Tex. 1984) (defining benefit-of-the-bargain and out-of-pocket damages in context of DTPA case). We disagree.

The trial court could have found that Pro-Tech's services were of zero value. Pierce presented the following evidence supporting that interpretation: 1) testimony and photographs showing that Pro-Tech left Pierce's house virtually empty of its contents, essentially gutted except for the wiring and some sheetrock; 2) testimony that Pro-Tech had removed and not replaced the air conditioner; 3) testimony that Pro-Tech had not provided Pierce with a certificate showing the house had been cleared of mold, and when Pierce tried to find someone else to rebuild, there were still biohazard signs on the house; 4) testimony that Mays did not return Pierce's key until July 2002; and 5) documentation of the results of an inspection done in July 2002, showing the house contained toxic mold as of that date.

Pro-Tech, however, contends Pierce's evidence is legally insufficient because 1) Pierce did not provide competent evidence that Pro-Tech had not performed remediation and Pierce failed to plead or prove Pro-Tech had contracted to rebuild; 2) Pierce offered no evidence to establish the reasonable value of the services Pro-Tech performed; and

3) to the extent Pierce relied on completion costs, the amounts charged by or paid to Pro-Tech constitutes no evidence of the reasonableness of those costs. Again, we disagree.

Regarding Pro-Tech's first and second points, we have construed the contract as requiring Pro-Tech to provide both remediation and restoration. Because Pro-Tech left Pierce's house in the condition that it did, the trial court could have reasonably found that any work Pro-Tech may have performed was of zero value. Regarding Pro-Tech's third point, there is nothing in Pierce's argument to the trial court to suggest she characterized reimbursement for the sums Farmers had paid Pro-Tech as completion costs.

3. Out-of-Pocket Expenses

Pro-Tech next complains about Pierce's evidence of her out-of-pocket expenses for moving her stored items to a second facility, additional storage fees, an inspection report, and additional living expenses. Pierce presented her own testimony regarding her expenses for the first two items, her testimony and a receipt for the third item, and testimony and insurance documents showing what Farmers had paid for Pierce's living expenses during the period covered by her claim.

Pro-Tech challenges the legal sufficiency of this evidence solely on the ground that Pierce purportedly did not establish that her expenses were reasonable and necessary. In support of this argument, Pro-Tech cites *Mustang Pipeline Co., Inc. v. Driver Pipeline Co., Inc.*, 134 S.W.3d 195, 200–01 (Tex. 2004), which, in turn cites *Dallas Ry. Terminal Co. v. Gossett*, 294 S.W.2d 377, 382–83 (Tex. 1956).

In *Mustang Pipeline*, the Texas Supreme Court observed that Mustang's expert "was careful to limit his opinion solely to what it cost [a second company] to complete the contract, and not whether that contracted amount was a reasonable cost to build a pipeline." *Mustang Pipeline*, 134 S.W.3d at 201. The court also pointed to evidence indicating that the amount may not have been reasonable under the circumstances. *See id*. In *Gossett*, the Texas Supreme Court observed that "the amount of the charges [was] the only evidence in the record which might throw any light on the reasonable value of the services rendered." *Gossett*, 294 S.W.2d at 382.

Here, Pierce's evidence included not only testimony and documentation of her out-of-pocket expenses for storage, inspection, and additional living expenses, but also evidence of what Farmers had been willing to pay for similar categories of expenses. Additionally, Mays testified that the cost for packing and moving the contents of Pierce's home exceeded $12,000.00. Thus, there is some evidence of the reasonableness of Pierce's out-of-pocket expenses (i.e., $822 total for additional storage, $360 for moving expenses, $875 for the July 2002 inspection, and $2,500 per month for additional living expenses).

4. Damage to Personal Property

Pro-Tech also challenges the legal sufficiency of Pierce's evidence that she incurred $8,226 in damages to her stored personal property. Specifically, Pro-Tech contends 1) although Pierce testified about the "fair value" of the property, she did not testify about the fair market value; 2) she did not tie her estimate of value to the location where the damages occurred; and 3) she did not distinguish between the damaged property and the destroyed property.

Because we have determined that the categories of actual damages previously discussed are supported by sufficient evidence, and because these categories of damages exceed the trial court's award, we do not reach this argument. We overrule Pro-Tech's issue to the extent it challenges the sufficiency of the evidence of actual damages.

5. DTPA Additional Damages and Attorneys' Fees

Finally, Pro-Tech argues Pierce is not entitled additional DTPA damages or the recovery of attorneys' fees. As discussed above, we reverse the part of the judgment awarding Pierce DTPA damages; however, we have concluded there is sufficient evidence to support Pierce's breach-of-contract claim and the award of actual damages for that claim. Here, Pierce may recover reasonable attorneys' fees for that claim. See TEX. CIV. PRAC. & REM. CODE ANN. § 38.001 (Vernon 1997) (stating person may recover reasonable attorneys' fees in addition to the amount of valid claim if claim is for an oral or written contract). Pro-Tech does not challenge the reasonableness of Pierce's attorneys' fees, but only Pierce's entitlement to them. We overrule Pro-Tech's issue to the extent it challenges the award of attorneys' fees.

CONCLUSION

Having concluded Pierce's allegations do not rise above a breach-of-contract claim, we reverse the part of the judgment awarding Pierce additional DTPA damages and render judgment that Pierce takes nothing on her DTPA claim. Having concluded Pierce presented sufficient evidence to establish her breach-of-contract claim and actual damages, we affirm the remainder of the judgment awarding actual damages, attorneys' fees, and pre- and post-judgment interest.

2) Mixed Breach-of-Warranty and Breach-of-Contract Actions— Types of Expenses and Costs Comprising Expectancy Damages

Hawkins v. McGee
146 A. 641
(N.H. 1929)

BRANCH, J. The operation in question consisted in the removal of a considerable quantity of scar tissue from the palm of the plaintiff's right hand and the grafting of skin taken from the plaintiff's chest in place thereof. The scar tissue was the result of a severe burn caused by contact with an electric wire, which the plaintiff received about nine years before the time of the transactions here involved.

There was evidence to the effect that before the operation was performed the plaintiff and his father went to the defendant's office, and that the defendant, in answer to the question, "How long will the boy be in the hospital?" replied, "Three or four days, not over four; then the boy can go home and it will be just a few days when he will go back to work with a good hand." Clearly this and other testimony to the same effect would not justify a finding that the doctor contracted to complete the hospital treatment in three or four days or that the plaintiff would be able to go back to work within a few days thereafter. The above statements could only be construed as expressions of opinion or predictions as to the probable duration of the treatment and plaintiff's resulting disability, and the fact that these estimates were exceeded would impose no contractual liability upon the defendant.

The only substantial basis for the plaintiff's claim is the testimony that the defendant also said before the operation was decided upon, "I will guarantee to make the hand a hundred per cent perfect hand or a hundred per cent good hand." The plaintiff was present when these words were alleged to have been spoken, and, if they are to be taken at their face value, it seems obvious that proof of their utterance would establish the giving of a warranty in accordance with his contention.

The defendant argues, however, that, even if these words were uttered by him, no reasonable man would understand that they were used with the intention of entering "into any contractual relation whatever," and that they could reasonably be understood only "as his expression in strong language that he believed and expected that as a result of the operation he would give the plaintiff a very good hand."

It may be conceded, as the defendant contends, that, before the question of the making of a contract should be submitted to a jury, there is a preliminary question of law for the trial court to pass upon—*i. e.* "whether the words could possibly have the meaning imputed to them by the party who founds his case upon a certain interpretation[.]" [B]ut it cannot be held that the trial court decided this question erroneously in the present case. It is unnecessary to determine at this time whether the argument of the defendant, based upon "common knowledge of the uncertainty which attends all surgical operations," and the improbability that a surgeon would ever contract to make a damaged part of the human body "one hundred per cent perfect," would, in the absence of countervailing considerations, be regarded as conclusive, for there were other factors in the present case which tended to support the contention of the plaintiff.

There was evidence that the defendant repeatedly solicited from the plaintiff's father the opportunity to perform this operation, and the theory was advanced by plaintiff's counsel in cross-examination of defendant that he sought an opportunity to "experiment on skin grafting," in which he had had little previous experience. If the jury accepted this part of plaintiff's contention, there would be a reasonable basis for the further conclusion that, if defendant spoke the words attributed to him, he did so with the intention that they should be accepted at their face value, as an inducement for the granting of consent to the operation by the plaintiff and his father, and there was ample evidence that they were so accepted by them. The question of the making of the alleged contract was properly submitted to the jury.

The substance of the charge to the jury on the question of damages appears in the following quotation: "If you find the plaintiff entitled to anything, he is entitled to recover for what pain and suffering he has been made to endure and for what injury he has sustained over and above what injury he had before." To this instruction the defendant reasonably excepted. By it, the jury was permitted to consider two elements of damage: 1) Pain and suffering due to the operation; and 2) positive ill effects of the operation upon the plaintiff's hand. Authority for any specific rule of damages in cases of this kind seems to be lacking, but, when tested by general principle and by analogy, it appears that the foregoing instruction was erroneous.

"By 'damages,' as that term is used in the law of contracts, is intended compensation for a breach, measured in the terms of the contract." *Davis v. New England Cotton Yarn Co.*, 92 A. 732, 733 (N.H. 1914). The purpose of the law is "to put the plaintiff in as good a position as he would have been in had the defendant kept his contract." 3 WILLISTON CONT. § 1338; *Hardie-Tynes Mfg. Co. v. Easton Cotton Oil Co.*, 63 S. E. 676, 677–78 (N.C. 1909). The measure of recovery "is based upon what the defendant should have given the plaintiff, not what the plaintiff has given the defendant or otherwise expended." 3 Williston Cont. § 1341. "The only losses that can be said fairly to come within the terms of a contract are such as the parties must have had in mind when the contract was made, or such as they either knew or ought to have known would probably result from a failure to comply with its terms." *Davis v.*

New England Cotton Yarn Co., 92 A. 732, 733 (N.H. 1914) and *Hurd v. Dunsmore*, 63 N. H. 171 (1884)

The present case is closely analogous to one in which a machine is built for a certain purpose and warranted to do certain work. In such cases, the usual rule of damages for breach of warranty in the sale of chattels is applied, and it is held that the measure of damages is the difference between the value of the machine—if it had corresponded with the warranty and its actual value—together with such incidental losses as the parties knew, or ought to have known, would probably result from a failure to comply with its terms. *Hooper v. Story*, 155 N. Y. 171, 175 (1898); *Adams Hardware Co. v. Wimbish*, 78 So. 902 (Ala. 1918); *Isaacs v. Jackson, etc., Co.*, 193 P. 1081 (Kan. 1920); *Paducah Hosiery Mills Co. v. Proctor*, 276 S. W. 803 (Ky. 1925); *Pioneer Co. v. McCurdy*, 186 N. W. 776 (Minn. 1922); *Christian, etc., Co. v. Goodman*, 96 So. 692 (Miss. 1923); *Hardie, etc., Co. v. Easton, etc., Co.*, 63 S. E. 676 (N.C. 1909); *York Mfg. Co. v. Chelten, etc., Co.*, 123 A. 327 (Pa. 1924); *General Motors, etc., Co. v. Shepard Co.*, 129 A. 825 R. I. 1925); *Cavanagh v. Stevens Co.*, 123 N. W. 681 S.D. 1909; and *Foutty v. Chalmax Co.*, 128 S. E. 389 (W.Va. 1925).

The rule thus applied is well settled in this state. "As a general rule, the measure of the vendee's damages is the difference between the value of the goods as they would have been if the warranty as to quality had been true, and the actual value at the time of the sale, including gains prevented and losses sustained, and such other damages as could be reasonably anticipated by the parties as likely to be caused by the vendor's failure to keep his agreement, and could not by reasonable care on the part of the vendee have been avoided." *Union Bank v. Blanchard*, 18 A. 90, 91 (N. H. 1889); *Hurd v. Dunsmore, supra*; *Noyes v. Blodgett*, 58 N. H. 502 (1878); P. L. ch. 166, § 69, subd. 7.

We therefore conclude that the true measure of the plaintiff's damage in the present case is the difference between the value to him of a perfect hand or a good hand, such as the jury found the defendant promised him, and the value of his hand in its present condition, including any incidental consequences fairly within the contemplation of the parties when they made their contract. 1 SUTHERLAND, DAMAGES (4th Ed.) § 92. Damages not thus limited, although naturally resulting, are not to be given.

The extent of the plaintiff's suffering does not measure this difference in value. The pain necessarily incident to a serious surgical operation was a part of the contribution which the plaintiff was willing to make to his joint undertaking with the defendant to produce a good hand. It was a legal detriment suffered by him which constituted a part of the consideration given by him for the contract. It represented a part of the price which he was willing to pay for a good hand, but it furnished no test of the value of a good hand or the difference between the value of the hand which the defendant promised and the one which resulted from the operation.

It was also erroneous and misleading to submit to the jury as a separate element of damage any change for the worse in the condition of the plaintiff's hand resulting from the operation, although this error was probably more prejudicial to the plaintiff than to the defendant. Any such ill effect of the operation would be included under the true rule of damages set forth above, but damages might properly be assessed for the defendant's failure to improve the condition of the hand, even if there were no evidence that its condition was made worse as a result of the operation.

It must be assumed that the trial court, in setting aside the verdict, undertook to apply the same rule of damages which he had previously given to the jury, and, since this rule was erroneous, it is unnecessary for us to consider whether there was any evidence to justify his finding that all damages awarded by the jury above $500 were excessive.

Defendant's requests for instructions were loosely drawn, and were properly denied. A considerable number of issues of fact were raised by the evidence, and it would have been extremely misleading to instruct the jury in accordance with defendant's request No. 2, that "the only issue on which you have to pass is whether or not there was a special contract between the plaintiff and the defendant to produce a perfect hand."

Equally inaccurate was defendant's request No. 5, which reads as follows: "You would have to find, in order to hold the defendant liable in this case, that Dr. McGee and the plaintiff both understood that the doctor was guaranteeing a perfect result from this operation." If the defendant said that he would guarantee a perfect result, and the plaintiff relied upon that promise, any mental reservations which he may have had are immaterial. The standard by which his conduct is to be judged is not internal, but external. *Woburn Bank v. Woods,* 77 N. H. 172 (1914); *McConnell v. Lamontagne*, 82 N. H. 423, 425 (1926); *Eleftherion v. Great Falls Mfg. Co.* 84 N. H. 32 (1929)

Defendant's request No. 7 was as follows: "If you should get so far as to find that there was a special contract guaranteeing a perfect result, you would still have to find for the defendant unless you also found that a further operation would not correct the disability claimed by the plaintiff." In view of the testimony that the defendant had refused to perform a further operation, it would clearly have been erroneous to give this instruction. The evidence would have justified a verdict for an amount sufficient to cover the cost of such an operation, even if the theory underlying this request were correct. It is unlikely that the questions now presented in regard to the argument of plaintiff's counsel will arise at another trial, and therefore they have not been considered. New trial.

3) Post-Breach Market Conditions and the Measure of Damages

Under *Hadley v. Baxendale*, the rule is clear: If a party breaches a contract, the non-breaching party may receive damages for injury, property loss, or lost profits. However, there is a proviso: The injuries or losses must have been foreseeable when the parties were forming the contract. In addition, another general principle has evolved: Damages for lost profits must be calculated, using information about a market's conditions or financial projections when the offending party initially breached the contract.

But assume that a market's financial conditions deteriorate or improve substantially while the parties litigate their differences. Should the calculation of damages be based on "changed market conditions"? Sometimes, it takes years before a jury or judge issues a pro-plaintiff verdict. What are the arguments for and against allowing a trier of fact to weigh improved or depressed post-breach market conditions when calculating lost-profits damages? Consider the analysis and answer in the next case.

CR-RSC Tower I, LLC v. RSC Tower I, LLC
32 A.3d 456
(Md. Ct. App. 2011)

EYLER, JAMES R., J. [In this breach-of-contract action, CR–RSC Tower I, LLC are lessors/appellants. RSC Tower I, LLC are lessees/appellees.] Lessors own a 53-acre tract of land in Montgomery County. On June 16, 2004, lessors as landlords entered into two 90-year ground leases with lessees as tenants. Lessees are partially owned and controlled by the Penrose Group, a real estate development company. One lease was for approximately three acres, and the other lease was for approximately two acres, together with easements to use certain common areas in the rest of the tract. The parties executed a "DECLARATION OF EASEMENTS AND RELATED AGREEMENTS" on June 16, 2004. At that time, the parties contemplated that lessors would develop the portion of the tract not subject to the ground leases. Indeed, in 2003, the owners of the entire tract, lessors' assignors, and Penrose Development Company, LLC entered into a Development Services Agreement. ... [Under the latter], Penrose Development Company, LLC agreed to act as a consultant to the owners in connection with development of the tract.

Pursuant to the terms of the ground leases between the parties herein, each [lessee] agreed to construct an apartment building (hereinafter Tower I and Tower II) on its respective site. After construction and initial rental, the parties contemplated that lessees would sell the buildings. The parties projected that construction on Tower II would begin approximately two years after construction of Tower I. The leases contained provisions obligating the parties to cooperate with each other in the development of the apartment buildings and the rest of the tract.

After executing the leases, in late 2004 and early 2005, the parties modified their agreements to permit development of condominium buildings, a hotel, and spa rather than apartments (the "Canyon Ranch project"). The parties executed several agreements in furtherance of the Canyon Ranch project, but in September 2006, the parties abandoned the project and entered into a termination agreement. Lessees then obtained county approval to revert to the original plan to build apartments. Lessees also arranged financing with Northwestern Mutual Life Insurance Company (NML) to construct Tower I.

In late September, lessees requested lessors to execute estoppel certificates in which lessors would represent that lessees were not in default under the ground leases. The project's financing terms required that lessees provide such estoppel certificates and the leases required lessors to execute such certificates to the lessees. Specifically, paragraph 14.6 in both leases provided:

> ESTOPPEL CERTIFICATE. Each party agrees from time to time, upon no less than fifteen (15) days' prior written request of the other, to execute, acknowledge, and deliver to the other a statement in writing certifying (i) that this Lease is unmodified and in full force and effect (or, if there have been any modifications, that the same is in full force and effect as modified and stating the modifications), (ii) the Lease Commencement Date and Fixed Rent Commencement Date, (iii) the then current amount of the Fixed Rent, (iv) the dates to which the Fixed Rent and Additional Rent has been paid, (v) to such party's knowledge, whether there exists any uncured default by the other party and, if so, the nature of such default, and (vi) such other matters relating to this Lease as the party requesting the statement may reasonably require. Any such statement delivered pursuant to this Section 14.6 may be relied upon by any prospective purchaser or mortgagee or any prospective holder of a sublease from Tenant or any prospective assignee of any such holder of a mortgage or sublease.

Lessors disagreed with the language in the proposed certificates. The parties attempted to reach agreement on the language, were unable to do so, and lessors did not execute the certificates. Lessors also initiated proceedings to challenge the county's approval of lessees' site plans and building permits.

On November 8, 2006, lessees filed suit against lessors FN1 in the Circuit Court for Montgomery County, alleging that lessors had breached the leases, and seeking declaratory and injunctive relief (the 2006 action), which would require lessors to perform their obligations under the leases. On January 16, 2007, the court issued a preliminary injunction, ordering lessors to deliver executed estoppel certificates to lessees. On January 26, 2007, lessees filed a motion for summary judgment.

On April 4, 2007, the court entered summary judgment in favor of lessees. The court, inter alia, ruled that lessors breached their obligations under the ground leases; the breaches prohibited lessees from obtaining financing; and lessees could not obtain equity investment or financing without a final order in their favor. The court ordered lessors to specifically perform their obligations under the leases, extended the term and certain due dates in the leases, and suspended payments required by lessees pending the entry of a final non-appealable order. [Several additional motions were submitted and appealed. A new trial was ordered].

On March 1 through 10, 2010, the case was tried before a jury. In lessees' words:

> [A]mong other things, [lessees] demonstrated that, in reliance on the ground leases and its bargained-for development rights, [they] had incurred nearly $23 million in out-of-pocket expenses—$16,770,134 in connection with Phase I and $6,226,518 in connection with Phase II. [Lessees] also introduced the contemporaneous financial analyses that it and [NML] had conducted at the time of [lessors'] breaches as to the Apartment Project's projected profits, along with the testimony of real estate experts supporting those financial analyses. Based on that evidence and the testimony of expert forensic accountants, [lessees] argued that [they] had suffered lost profits—after the return of its out-of-pocket expenses—in excess of $28 million ($18,082,103 in Phase I and $10,491,313 in Phase II.)

At the close of lessees' case, lessors' moved for judgment in their favor on the grounds that lessees 1) had failed to prove lost profits or reliance damages with reasonable certainty, 2) had failed to prove that any damages were caused by lessors' breach of the leases; 3) had failed to establish third party beneficiary status or any basis for joint and several liability, 4) could not use the implied covenant of good faith and fair dealing to impose additional contract obligations on lessors, and 5) had not introduced any evidence to show that any breaches subsequent to April 4, 2007 had caused damages. The court denied lessors'/appellants' motion for judgment. ...

The jury found that each appellant had breached the ground leases after the court's April 4, 2007 order and that each appellee was entitled to enforce the other's ground lease either as a third party beneficiary or a "third-party entitled to the benefit of a covenant running with the land." The jury awarded damages against lessors/appellants in the total amount of $36,350,239.00. On April 9, 2010, after the entry of final judgment, appellants noted an appeal. ...

Lessors/appellants charge that the evidence presented at trial was not legally sufficient to prove lost profits damages with reasonable certainty. Lessors argue that 1) the circuit court erred in excluding evidence of post-breach actual market conditions, and 2) lessees' December 2006 market projections were too speculative to support an award, particularly because the claims were based on collateral, and not direct, lost profits.

Post-Breach Market Conditions

As mentioned above, lessees' claim for lost profits was based on market projections as of December 2006, the time of lessors' initial breach. While this case was on appeal to this court from the summary judgment entered in the 2006 action, the real-estate market deteriorated significantly, thus making the project unfeasible. Before trial in early 2010, lessees moved in limine to exclude evidence of post-breach actual market conditions, and the court granted it. In opposition to the motion, lessors argued that because Tower I was projected to not be fully leased until 2010 and Tower II was projected to not be fully leased until 2012, actual market conditions in that time frame were relevant and would show that, had the apartment buildings been built as planned, lessees would not have made a profit because of changed market conditions. Lessees reasoned that the law provides that damages are measured as of the time of breach, and therefore, evidence of post-breach market conditions was inadmissible.

"[T]he admission of evidence is committed to the considerable and sound discretion of the trial court." *Merzbacher v. State*, 346 Md. 391, 404 (1997). In reviewing a motion in limine, "we are generally loath to reverse a trial court" unless the evidence was plainly improperly admitted or excluded under law, "or there is a clear showing of an abuse of discretion." *Id.* at 404–405

Damages for breach of contract generally include "expectancy" damages. The traditional rule is that expectancy damages—which include lost profits—are measured at the time of the breach. *Republic Ins. Co. v. Prince George's County*, 92 Md. App. 528, 533 (1992). *See also Beard v. S/E Joint Venture*, 321 Md. 126, 141(1990) ("As we have seen, the ordinary rule for computing loss of the bargain damages is to value the property at the time of breach"). Frequently, later events such as "fluctuations in value after the breach" are irrelevant for damage determinations. *Republic Ins. Co.*, 92 Md. App. at 533

While the Court of Appeals has stated and applied the general rule, there are very few appellate cases in Maryland in which the courts have applied the general rule to claims for direct lost profits, when the issue was contested, and seemingly none that have applied it to claims for collateral lost profits. Direct lost profits result "immediately from the performance of the contract broken." CORBIN, CONTRACTS, § 1020 (1951). Collateral lost profits result from the loss of "other contracts collateral to the one broken," to which the defendant was not a party. *Id.*

In *M & R Contractors,* 215 Md. 340 (1958), the Court of Appeals stated that the plaintiff's direct lost profits damages for a breach of contract should be measured "under the circumstances that existed at the time of the breach." *Id.* at 349 (quoting CORBIN, CONTRACTS, § 1094 (1951)). *M & R Contractors* favorably cited a leading American case on lost profits damages, *Masterton v. Mayor of Brooklyn*, in which the court held that lost profits "damages are to be settled and ascertained according to the existing state of the market at the time the cause of action arose, and not at the time fixed for full performance." 7 Hill 61, 71 (N.Y. Sup. Ct. 1845).

A possible explanation as to why there are no Maryland cases which address whether the traditional rule measuring contract damages at the time of the breach should apply to collateral lost profits cases is because, until relatively recently, collateral lost profits damages were considered too speculative to be awarded. The Court of Appeals and this Court first approved the recovery of collateral lost profits damages in the late 1970s, and then only in cases in which the plaintiff proved that collateral contracts had already been entered into at the time of the breach. *See Impala Platinum, Ltd. v. Impala Sales, Inc.,* 283 Md. 296, 389 A.2d 887 (1978); *John D. Copanos & Sons, Inc. v. McDade Rigging & Steel Erection Co.*, 43 Md. App. 204, 403 A.2d 402 (1979); *Sergeant Co. v. Clifton Building Corp.*, 47 Md. App. 307, 423 A.2d 257 (1981). *See also Hoang v. Hewitt Ave. Assocs.*, 177 Md. App. 562, 597–604, 936 A.2d 915 (2007) (discussing the history of collateral lost profits damages cases in Maryland).

Only in 2007 did this Court first uphold an award of collateral lost profits damages in a case in which there were no existing collateral contracts at the time of breach. *See Hoang*, 177 Md. App. at 609, 936 A.2d 915 (stating that "[t]he cases do not hold, however, that such evidence is necessary to the recovery of collateral lost profits, i.e., that without evidence of third party contracts in hand when the contract at issue is made, collateral lost profits are not recoverable"). *Hoang* involved a breach of contract for the sale of real estate.

In *Hoang*, the use or non-use of post-breach market conditions was not addressed, but this court referred to expert testimony regarding "the prices the finished town houses would have fetched on the real estate market as it existed at the relevant time" helped prove collateral lost profits damages with reasonable certainty. *Id.* at 610–11, 936 A.2d

915. That expert testified on the basis of projections of the real estate market, as the trial took place in 2004 and early 2005 and the town houses were not slated to be completed until the summer of 2007. *Id.* at 571, 936 A.2d 915. Thus, the Court of Appeals and this court have not directly addressed whether it is proper to award collateral lost profits damages on the basis of otherwise reasonable projections at the time of the breach without consideration of post breach market conditions.

Other jurisdictions have differed on whether lost profit contract damages should be measured at the time of the breach. The Supreme Court touched on this issue in a breach of contract action for failure to execute applications for a patent. *Sinclair Refining Co. v. Jenkins Petroleum Process Co.*, 289 U.S. 689, 697–98 (1933). The Court noted that determining the market value for a patent at the time of breach is difficult because "[a] patent is a thing unique." *Id.* at 697. Instead, the Court reasoned that in order to determine the value of the patent at the time of the breach, and thus to determine damages, experts can testify based on the "state of the art, the character of the improvement, and the probable increase of efficiency or saving of expense" if "the trial follows quickly after the issue of the patent." *Id.* at 698.

The Court went on to say that "a different situation is presented if years have gone by before the evidence is offered." In that case, the Court reasoned that "[e]xperience is then available to correct uncertain prophecy. Here is a book of wisdom that courts may not neglect. We find no rule of law that sets a clasp upon its pages, and forbids us to look within." *Id.* at 698.

The Court explained that "[t]o correct uncertain prophecies in [breach of contract or tort cases] is not to charge the offender with elements of value non-existent at the time of his offense" but rather "it is to bring out and expose to light the elements of value that were there from the beginning." *Id. See also Advent Sys. Ltd. v. Unisys Corp.*, 925 F.2d 670 (3rd Cir. 1991) (holding that lost profits damages were not established with reasonable certainty when a damages expert testified, after the damages period had expired, as to projections made at the time of the breach that were significantly higher than actual market value during the period in question); Sun Ins. *Marketing Network, Inc. v. AIG Life Insurance Co.,* 254 F.Supp.2d 1239 (M.D. Fla. 2003) (actual market conditions should be considered when the time period during which damages were projected had already expired).

In contrast, the United States Court of Appeals for the District of Columbia Circuit held that evidence of favorable post-breach market conditions is inadmissible to show increased direct lost profits. *J.D. Hedin Constr. Co. v. F.S. Bowen Elec. Co.*, 273 F.2d 511, 513 (D.C. Cir. 1960). *J.D. Hedin* concerned the breach of a sub-contract under a construction contract. The trial court admitted plaintiff's evidence of post-breach market conditions that showed increased lost profits due to diminished costs of performance. The United States Circuit Court of Appeals for the District of Columbia found that the trial court committed reversible error because "[s]uch costs are to be estimated as nearly as may be according to 'the circumstances that existed at the time of breach'" and should not reflect "events which occurred after the contract was executed, and after its breach." *Id.* (citing CORBIN, CONTRACTS, § 1094 (1951)).

Similarly, the Arizona Court of Appeals upheld a finding of lost profits for a development project based upon projections made at the time of the breach. *Rhue v. Dawson*, 173 Ariz. 220, 841 P.2d 215 (Ariz. Ct. App. 1992). *Rhue* concerned a partnership dispute where the defendant attempted to introduce evidence that the real estate market deteriorated after his breach in order to show that he should not have to pay the value of partnership property at the time of the breach. *Id.* at 230, 841 P.2d 215. The court in *Rhue* specifically held that the fact that the real estate market deteriorated after the defendant's breach was irrelevant and violated the "general contract rule" that measures damages at the time of the breach. *Id.* The Court stated that measuring damages at the date of the breach is "sound policy" because "[t]he adverse consequences of a controlling partner's delays and decisions which prevent the partnership from realizing the profits should be at that partner's risk, not at the risk of the ousted, innocent partner." Id. at 230–31.

Citing 22 AM.JUR.2D DAMAGES § 78 (2011), lessors argue that the general rule that contract damages are measured at the time of the breach does not apply to "anticipated profits or to other expectancy damages that, absent the breach, would have accrued on an ongoing basis over the course of the contract." We note that the case cited in AM.JUR. for that proposition, *Energy Capital Corp. v. United States*, merely reduced to present value the damages that would have arisen after the date of judgment ("future lost profits"). 302 F.3d 1314, 1330 (Fed. Cir. 2002). The court did not apply this principle to hold that the amount of lost profits should be determined by market value at some date later than at the time of the breach.

However, citing *Energy Capital Corp.*, the United States Court of Appeals for the Federal Circuit recently held that the trial court did not abuse its discretion by considering post-breach evidence in order to determine direct lost profits damages. *Anchor Sav. Bank, FSB v. United States*, 597 F.3d 1356 (Fed. Cir. 2010). The court in *Anchor*, citing and relying upon other Federal Circuit decisions, reasoned that the general rule favoring the measurement of damages at the time of the breach should not apply to profits that would have accrued over the course of a contract because it "may not result in the most accurate assessment of expectancy damages." *Id.* at 1369 (quoting *Fifth Third Bank v. United States*, 518 F.3d 1368, 1377 (Fed. Cir. 2008)).

In that case, the plaintiffs recovered damages based on the sale of assets it otherwise would not have sold but for the defendants' breach. The assets would have accrued profits over time, so the court admitted post-breach evidence to determine the amount of lost profits. The court stated that a court can consider post-breach evidence "in order to place the non-breaching party in as good a position as he would have been had the contract been performed." *Id.* at 1370 (quoting *Fifth Third Bank v. United States*, 518 F.3d 1368, 1377 (Fed. Cir. 2008)).

Maryland cases have been consistent with the principle set forth in AM.JUR., although they do not cite to it directly. The Court of Appeals in *Macke Co. v. Pizza of Gaithersburg, Inc.*, 259 Md. 479, 492, 270 A.2d 645 (1970), stated that actual experience after the breach could be used in measuring direct lost profits. In *Macke Co.*, on December 30, 1966, Macke Co. placed vending machines at certain locations pursuant to contracts with an automatically renewable term of one year. The owner of the premises was to be paid a percentage of gross revenue realized from the machines. In January and February, 1968, the owner of the premises terminated the contracts. Macke Co. sued for breach of contract.

The trial court found that the owners breached the contracts but that Macke Co. failed to prove damages with reasonable certainty. *Id.* at 482, 270 A.2d 645. At trial, Macke Co. had attempted to prove damages by putting in evidence gross sales figures for the month of January, 1968 at the locations in question. *Id.* at 489–490, 270 A.2d 645. Even though an extrapolation for the rest of 1968 was in existence, Macke Co. did not introduce any evidence projecting losses for the rest of 1968. *Id.* at 490, 270 A.2d 645. Macke Co. also called one of the defendants to testify, who stated that he received a certain amount of money from the machines in 1967. Id.

Based on that testimony, Macke Co. submitted to the court an extrapolation of 1967 figures to show a projection of profits lost in 1968. *Id.* The court concluded that the trial court erred when it concluded that damages could not be proved and remanded for the trial court to reconsider the issue of damages. *Id.* at 491. The court stated that instead of relying on the two varying projections based on past performance in 1967 and January 1968, the trial court could consider whether the defendants had obtained other vending machines, and if so, it could consider the actual experience with those machines during 1968. *Id.* at 492. The court noted that the defendants' actual earnings during the time period in question would be a "more appropriate measure of damages" than the projections, particularly in light of evidence that factors potentially affecting the vending machines' earnings had changed from 1967 to 1968. ...

Under the current state of Maryland law, the general principle is that breach of contract damages are measured at the time of the breach. We see no distinction, relevant to this issue, between direct and collateral lost profits. Thus, the circuit court did not abuse its discretion in barring evidence of post-breach market conditions.

C. Measuring "Reliance Damages" in Mixed Breach-of-Contract and Tort-Based Actions

Sullivan v. O'Connor
296 N.E.2d 183
(Mass. 1973)

Kaplan, Justice. The plaintiff patient secured a jury verdict of $13,500 against the defendant surgeon for breach of contract in respect to an operation upon the plaintiff's nose. The substituted consolidated bill of exceptions presents questions about the correctness of the judge's instructions on the issue of damages.

The declaration was in two counts. In the first count, the plaintiff alleged that she, as patient, entered into a contract with the defendant, a surgeon, wherein the defendant promised to perform plastic surgery on her nose and thereby to enhance her beauty and improve her appearance; that he performed the surgery but failed to achieve the promised result; rather the result of the surgery was to disfigure and deform her nose, to cause her pain in body and mind, and to subject her to other damage and expense. The second count, based on the same transaction, was in the conventional form for malpractice, charging that the defendant had been guilty of negligence in performing the surgery. Answering, the defendant entered a general denial.

On the plaintiff's demand, the case was tried by jury. At the close of the evidence, the judge put to the jury, as special questions, the issues of liability under the two counts, and instructed them accordingly. The jury returned a verdict for the plaintiff on the contract count, and for the defendant on the negligence count. The judge then instructed the jury on the issue of damages.

As background to the instructions and the parties' exceptions, we mention certain facts as the jury could find them. The plaintiff was a professional entertainer, and this was known to the defendant. The agreement was as alleged in the declaration. More particularly, judging from exhibits, the plaintiff's nose had been straight, but long and prominent; the defendant undertook by two operations to reduce its prominence and somewhat to shorten it, thus making it more pleasing in relation to the plaintiff's other features. Actually the plaintiff was obliged to undergo three operations, and her appearance was worsened. Her nose now had a concave line to about the midpoint, at which it became bulbous; viewed frontally, the nose from bridge to midpoint was flattened and broadened, and the two sides of the tip had lost symmetry. This configuration evidently could not be improved by further surgery. The plaintiff did not demonstrate, however, that her change of appearance had resulted in loss of employment. Payments by the plaintiff covering the defendant's fee and hospital expenses were stipulated at $622.65.

The judge instructed the jury, first, that the plaintiff was entitled to recover her out-of-pocket expenses incident to the operations. Second, she could recover the damages flowing directly, naturally, proximately, and foreseeably from the defendant's breach of promise. These would comprehend damages for any disfigurement of the plaintiff's nose—that is, any change of appearance for the worse—including the effects of the consciousness of such disfigurement on the plaintiff's mind, and in this connection the jury should consider the nature of the plaintiff's profession. Also consequent upon the defendant's breach, and compensable, were the pain and suffering involved in the third operation, but not in the first two. As there was no proof that any loss of earnings by the plaintiff resulted from the breach, that element should not enter into the calculation of damages.

By his exceptions the defendant contends that the judge erred in allowing the jury to take into account anything but the plaintiff's out-of-pocket expenses (presumably at the stipulated amount). The defendant excepted to the judge's refusal of his request for a general charge to that effect, and, more specifically, to the judge's refusal of a charge that the plaintiff could not recover for pain and suffering connected with the third operation or for impairment of the plaintiff's appearance and associated mental distress.

The plaintiff on her part excepted to the judge's refusal of a request to charge that the plaintiff could recover the difference in value between the nose as promised and the nose as it appeared after the operations. However, the plaintiff in her brief expressly waives this exception and others made by her in case this court overrules the defendant's exceptions; thus she would be content to hold the jury's verdict in her favor.

We conclude that the defendant's exceptions should be overruled.

It has been suggested on occasion that agreements between patients and physicians by which the physician undertakes to effect a cure or to bring about a given result should be declared unenforceable on grounds of public policy. *See Guilmet v. Campbell*, 385 Mich. 57, 76, 188 N.W.2d 601 (dissenting opinion). But there are many decisions recognizing and enforcing such contracts, see annotation, 43 A.L.R.3d 1221, 1225, 1229–1233, and the law of Massachusetts has treated them as valid, although we have had no decision meeting head on the contention that they should be denied legal sanction. These causes of action are, however, considered a little suspect, and thus we find courts straining sometimes to read the pleadings as sounding only in tort for negligence, and not in contract for breach of promise, despite sedulous efforts by the pleaders to pursue the latter theory. *See Gault v. Sideman*, 42 Ill.App.2d 96, 191 N.E.2d 436; annotation, *supra*, at 1225, 1238–1244.

It is not hard to see why the courts should be unenthusiastic or skeptical about the contract theory. Considering the uncertainties of medical science and the variations in the physical and psychological conditions of individual patients, doctors can seldom in good faith promise specific results. Therefore, it is unlikely that physicians of even average integrity will in fact make such promises. Statements of opinion by the physician with some optimistic coloring are a different thing, and may indeed have therapeutic value. But patients may transform such statements into firm promises in their own minds, especially when they have been disappointed in the event, and testify in that sense to sympathetic juries.

If actions for breach of promise can be readily maintained, doctors, so it is said, will be frightened into practising "defensive medicine." On the other hand, if these actions were outlawed, leaving only the possibility of suits for malpractice, there is fear that the public might be exposed to the enticements of charlatans, and confidence in the profession might ultimately be shaken. The law has taken the middle of the road position of allowing actions based on alleged contract, but insisting on clear proof. Instructions to the jury may well stress this requirement and point to tests of truth, such as the complexity or difficulty of an operation as bearing on the probability that a given result was promised. See annotation, 43 A.L.R.3d 1225, 1225–1227.

If an action on the basis of contract is allowed, we have next the question of the measure of damages to be applied where liability is found. Some cases have taken the simple view that the promise by the physician is to be treated like an ordinary commercial promise, and accordingly that the successful plaintiff is entitled to a standard measure of recovery for breach of contract: "compensatory" ("expectancy") damages—an amount intended to put the plaintiff in the position he would be in if the contract had been performed, or, presumably, at the plaintiff's election [and] "restitution" damages—an amount corresponding to any benefit conferred by the plaintiff upon the defendant in the performance of the contract disrupted by the defendant's breach. *See* RESTATEMENT: CONTRACTS § 329 and comment a, §§ 347, 384(1).

Thus in *Hawkins v. McGee*, 146 A. 641 (N.H. 1929), the defendant doctor was taken to have promised the plaintiff to convert his damaged hand by means of an operation into a good or perfect hand, but the doctor so operated as to damage the hand still further. The court, following the usual expectancy formula, would have asked the jury to estimate and award to the plaintiff the difference between the value of a good or perfect hand, as promised, and the value of the hand after the operation. (The same formula would apply, although the dollar result would be less, if the operation had neither worsened nor improved the condition of the hand.) If the plaintiff had not yet paid the doctor his fee, that amount would be deducted from the recovery. There could be no recovery for the pain and suffering of the operation, since that detriment would have been incurred even if the operation had been successful; one can say that this detriment was not 'caused' by the breach.

But where the plaintiff by reason of the operation was put to more pain that he would have had to endure, had the doctor performed as promised, he should be compensated for that difference as a proper part of his expectancy recovery. It may be noted that on an alternative count for malpractice the plaintiff in the *Hawkins* case had been nonsuited; but on ordinary principles this could not affect the contract claim, for it is hardly a defence to a breach of contract that the promisor acted innocently and without negligence. The New Hampshire court further refined the *Hawkins* analysis in *McQuaid v. Michou*, 85 N.H. 299, 157 A. 881, all in the direction of treating the patient-physician cases on the ordinary footing of expectancy. *See McGee v. United States Fid. & Guar. Co.*, 53 F.2d 953 (1st Cir.) (later development in the *Hawkins* case); *Cloutier v. Kasheta*, 105 N.H. 262, 197 A.2d 627; *Lakeman v. LaFrance*, 102 N.H. 300, 305, 156 A.2d 123.

Other cases ... without distinctly repudiating the *Hawkins* type of analysis, have indicated that a different and generally more lenient measure of damages is to be applied in patient-physician actions based on breach of alleged special agreements to effect a cure, attain a stated result, or employ a given medical method. This measure is expressed in somewhat variant ways, but the substance is that the plaintiff is to recover any expenditures made by him and for other detriment (usually not specifically described in the opinions) following proximately and foreseeably upon the defendant's failure to carry out his promise.

This, be it noted, is not a "restitution" measure, for it is not limited to restoration of the benefit conferred on the defendant (the fee paid) but includes other expenditures, for example, amounts paid for medicine and nurses; so also it would seem according to its logic to take in damages for any worsening of the plaintiff's condition due to the breach. Nor is it an 'expectancy' measure, for it does not appear to contemplate recovery of the whole difference in value between the condition as promised and the condition actually resulting from the treatment. Rather the tendency of the formulation is to put the plaintiff back in the position he occupied just before the parties entered upon the agreement, to compensate him for the detriments he suffered in reliance upon the agreement. ...

For breach of the patient-physician agreements under consideration, a recovery limited to restitution seems plainly too meager, if the agreements are to be enforced at all. On the other hand, an expectancy recovery may well be excessive. The factors, already mentioned, which have made the cause of action somewhat suspect, also suggest moderation as to the breadth of the recovery that should be permitted. Where, as in the case at bar and in a number of the reported cases, the doctor has been absolved of negligence by the trier, an expectancy measure may be thought harsh. We should recall here that the fee paid by the patient to the doctor for the alleged promise would usually be quite disproportionate to the putative expectancy recovery. ...

There is much to be said, then, for applying a reliance measure to the present facts, and we have only to add that our cases are not unreceptive to the use of that formula in special situations. We have, however, had no previous occasion to apply it to patient-physician cases.

The question of recovery on a reliance basis for pain and suffering or mental distress requires further attention. We find expressions in the decisions that pain and suffering (or the like) are simply not compensable in actions for breach of contract. The defendant seemingly espouses this proposition in the present case. True, if the buyer under a contract for the purchase of a lot of merchandise, in suing for the seller's breach, should claim damages for mental anguish caused by his disappointment in the transaction, he would not succeed; he would be told, perhaps, that the asserted psychological injury was not fairly foreseeable by the defendant as a probable consequence of the breach of such a business contract. *See* RESTATEMENT: CONTRACTS, § 341, and comment a. But there is no general rule barring such items of damage in actions for breach of contract.

It is all a question of the subject matter and background of the contract, and when the contract calls for an operation on the person of the plaintiff, psychological as well as physical injury may be expected to figure somewhere in the recovery, depending on the particular circumstances. ... These remarks seem unduly sweeping. Suffering or distress resulting from the breach going beyond that which was envisaged by the treatment as agreed, should be compensable on the same ground as the worsening of the patient's condition because of the breach. Indeed it can be argued that the very suffering or distress "contracted for"—that which would have been incurred if the treatment achieved the promised result—should also be compensable. ... For that suffering is "wasted" if the treatment fails. Otherwise stated, compensation for this waste is arguably required in order to complete the restoration of the status *quo ante*.

In the light of the foregoing discussion, all the defendant's exceptions fail: the plaintiff was not confined to the recovery of her out-of-pocket expenditures; she was entitled to recover also for the worsening of her condition, and for the pain and suffering and mental distress involved in the third operation. These items were compensable on either an expectancy or a reliance view.

We might have been required to elect between the two views if the pain and suffering connected with the first two operations contemplated by the agreement, or the whole difference in value between the present and the promised conditions, were being claimed as elements of damage. But the plaintiff waives her possible claim to the former element, and to so much of the latter as represents the difference in value between the promised condition and the condition before the operations.

Plaintiff's exceptions waived. Defendant's exceptions overruled.

NOTES AND QUESTIONS

1. **Breach of Construction Contracts and Measure of Damages.** In *American Standard, Inc. v. Schectman*, 80 A.D.2d 318; 439 N.Y.S.2d 529 (N.Y. App. Div. 1981), a demolition and excavating contractor failed to grade completely certain foundations and other subsurface structures on property as promised in a contract of conveyance. The plaintiff sued. The jury charge stated that the cost of completion—an expert's estimate of $110,500—rather than the diminution in the value of the property was the measure of damage. Defendant argued that the trial court's charge unjustly permitted the plaintiffs to reap a windfall. More specifically, the defendant argued that his breach of contract was immaterial because 1) "it [made] no difference in the value of the property whether the old foundations [were] at grade or one foot below grade," 2) "the plaintiffs succeeded in selling the property for $183,000—only $3,000 less than its full fair market value," and 3) the proper measure of damage should be the diminution in value. Affirming the trial court's ruling, the Supreme Court of New York's appellate division held:

    The general rule of damages for breach of a construction contract is that the injured party may recover those damages which are the direct, natural and immediate consequence of the breach and which can reasonably be said to have been in the contemplation of the parties when the contract was made. *See Hadley v. Baxendale*, 9 Exch. 341. In the usual case where the contractor's performance has been defective or incomplete, the reasonable cost of replacement or completion is the measure. When, however, there has been a substantial performance of the contract made in good faith but defects exist, the correction of which would result in economic waste, courts have measured the damages as the difference between the value of the property as constructed and the value if performance had been properly completed. …

The "economic waste" of the type which calls for application of the "diminution in value" rule generally entails defects in construction which are irremediable or which may not be repaired without a substantial tearing down of the structure. … Where, however, the breach is of a covenant which is only incidental to the main purpose of the contract and completion would be disproportionately costly, courts have applied the diminution in value measure even where no destruction of the work is entailed. *See, e. g., Peevyhouse v. Garland Coal & Min. Co.*, 382 P.2d 109 (Okla. 1962), holding that diminution in value is the proper measure where defendant—the lessee of plaintiff's lands under a coal mining lease—failed to perform costly remedial and restorative work on the land at the termination of the lease. The court distinguished the "building and construction" cases and noted that the breach was of a covenant incidental to the main purpose of the contract which was the recovery of coal from the premises to the benefit of both parties[.]

It is also a general rule in building and construction cases, … that a contractor who would ask the court to apply the diminution of value measure "as an instrument of justice" must not have breached the contract intentionally and must show substantial performance made in good faith.

In the case before us, plaintiffs chose to accept—as part of the consideration for the promised conveyance of their valuable plant and machines to defendant—his agreement to grade the property as specified and to remove the foundations, piers and other structures to a depth of one foot below grade to prepare the property for sale. It cannot be said that the grading and the removal of the structures were incidental to plaintiffs' purpose of "achieving a reasonably attractive vacant plot for resale." Nor can defendant maintain that the damages which would naturally flow from his failure to do the grading and removal work and which could reasonably be said to have been in the contemplation of the parties when the contract was made would not be the reasonable cost of completion. *See Hadley v. Baxendale, supra*

That the fulfillment of defendant's promise would—contrary to plaintiffs' apparent expectations—add little or nothing to the sale value of the property does not excuse the default. … Defendant's completed performance would not have involved undoing what in good faith was done improperly but only doing what was promised and left undone. That the burdens of performance were heavier than anticipated and the cost of completion disproportionate to the end to be obtained does not, without more, alter the rule that the measure of plaintiffs' damage is the cost of completion. … The judgment and order should be affirmed.

2. **English Courts' Common-Law Measures of Damages—Breach of Contract and Warranties.** The following English cases state a variety of equations for calculating damages awards. Are they similar to the equations which appear under Article 2 of the Uniform Commercial Code §§§ §2-313, 2-314, 2-315? (See the breach-of-warranties discussion in PART II, CHAPTER 10 of this casebook.)

   - *Simons v. Patchett*, 119 English Reports 1357 (1857)—This is an action for breach of an implied warranty. The defendant purchased a ship in the name of R. from plaintiff. "It appeared … that, R. having refused to adopt defendant's contract, plaintiff resold the ship at a less price than the contract price. The resale was taken to be reasonably made for the best price that could be obtained: and it was taken that R. was perfectly solvent. A verdict for the plaintiff being taken for *the difference between the contract price and that (price) obtained on the resale*."
   - *Randall v. Raper*, 120 Eng. Rep. 438, 440 (1858)—"The damage ought to be such as—according to the usual course of things—would arise naturally from the breach of the contract between the plaintiffs and the defendant, or such as might reasonably be supposed to have been contemplated between the parties to the contract. *See Hadley v. Baxendale*, 156 Eng. Rep. 145, 151 (1854). … In an action for breach of contract to deliver goods at a specified time, *the measure of the damages is the difference between the contract price and either the market price at the time specified*. … Or, if the purchaser have sold over, the price at which he has so sold. … [B]ut the anticipated profits—which such purchaser's vendee might have made—cannot be taken into account; *Peterson v Ayre* (13 Com. B. 353). That is the rule upon which the present defendant insists."

- *Dingle v. Hare*, 141 Eng. Rep. 770 (1859)—"In an action for a breach of warranty on the sale of goods which the buyer has sold again (resale), ... *the proper measure of damages [is] the difference between the real market value at the time of the sale and the contract price*."
- *De Mattos v. Gibson*, 70 Eng. Rep. 669, 671 (1860)—"[I] t is settled that the loss of possible contingent profits is too remote an injury to be taken as the *measure of damages*." *See Hadley v. Baxendale*, 9 Exch. 341; SEDGWICK ON THE MEASURE OF DAMAGES, at 78, 111.
- *Boswell v. Kilborn*, 15 Moore 309, 15 Eng. Rep. 511, 514 (1862) —"This was an executory contract. [N] o specific hops were bought and sold; and therefore no property in any particular five tons of hops ever passed to the Appellant. Neither by the English nor the French law could the Appellant be held liable. By the English law the full price of the goods was not recoverable, for the goods specified were never tendered; and the Appellant, in any circumstances, could only be liable for damages. ... *[T]he proper measure of which would be the difference between the contract price and the market price on the day on which the contract was broken*."

D. Measuring Liquidated, Predetermined, or Stipulated Damages

The following is a fair conclusion: Parties who design and negotiate the terms and conditions in contracts are rational beings. In most instances, they form contracts to generate wealth and positive outcomes. Yet, they understand that "special circumstances" might prevent them from fulfilling their contractual obligations. Consequently, realizing that uncontrollable circumstances might force them to breach a contract, the parties insert a liquidated-damages clause in the contract. Under the terms of that provision, the parties agree to pay a "stipulated" amount of money or liquidated damages if either breaches the contract.

In *Willert v. Russo*, 2009 WL 1532376, *4 (Conn. Super. Ct. May 4, 2009), the court stressed the following points:

> Enforcement of liquidated damages clause is subject to well established legal criteria. First, Connecticut recognizes the right of parties to agree to liquidated damages in the form of forfeiture of a deposit or a portion thereof for breach of an

> agreement to purchase real estate. *See Ritucci v. Brandt*, 57 A.2d 728 (Conn. 1948). Second, a liquidated damage clause in a contract will be upheld if the following requisite conditions are met: 1) The damage which was expected as a result of the breach of contract was uncertain in amount or difficult to prove; 2) there was an intent on the part of the parties to liquidate the damages in advance; 3) the amount stipulated was reasonable. *Norwalk Door Closer Co. v. Eagle Lock & Screw Co.*, 153 Conn. 681, 686 (1966), and *HH East Parcel, LLC v. Handy & Harman, Inc.*, 47 A.2d 916 (Conn. 2008)

Regarding the purpose of stipulated damages, other courts have stated: A liquidated-damages clause allows a non-breaching party to receive agreed-upon, predetermined damages when actual damages may be difficult to ascertain. *Karimi v. 401 North Wabash Venture, LLC*, 952 N.E.2d 1278, 1287 (Ill. Ct. App. 2011); the purpose of liquidated damages is to allow the parties to avoid the cost, difficulty, and delay of proving damages. *Radisson Hotels Intern., Inc. v. Majestic Towers, Inc.* 488 F.Supp.2d 953, 963 (C.D. Cal. 2007); and the "typical" liquidated damages provision allows a non-breaching party to receive a stated sum of money without having to prove actual damages. *Gaddis v. Stardust Hills Owners Ass'n, Inc.*, 804 N.E.2d 231, 236 (Ind. Ct. App. 2004).

Yet, some liquidated-damages provisions might not be valid. More specifically, some clauses might be nothing more than "penalty clauses," which are illegal. Courts have fashioned tests to determine whether liquidated-damages clauses are enforceable. Consider the discussions in the following cases.

1) Establishing Predetermined, Liquidated, or Stipulated Damages Under Hadley v. Baxendale*'s "Special Circumstances" Rule*

E & B Specialties Co., Inc. v. Phillips
523 P.2d 1357
(N.M. 1974)

STEPHENSON, JUSTICE. Suit was brought in the District Court of Bernalillo County by plaintiff-appellant (E & B) to recover the amount due under a contract between the parties. Defendant-appellee (Phillips) counterclaimed. The case was tried [before] the court without a jury and judgment was entered in favor of Phillips on the counterclaim after allowing a setoff. ... E & B appeals.

E & B's complaint alleged that it had subcontracted with Phillips to perform certain masonry work which was required to repair the central heating plant at Kirtland Air Force Base, such repair being the subject of a contract between Phillips and the United States Government. E

& B alleged that it had substantially performed its obligations under the subcontract, but that Phillips had refused to pay it for its services, and prayed for judgment. Phillips answered, denying the material allegations of the complaint, and counterclaimed for damages. The counterclaim alleged that E & B had failed to perform its obligations under the subcontract and that, as a result, the Government had made an assessment for liquidated damages against Phillips in the sum of $2,450, provision being made for such assessment in the prime contract.

The trial court in its findings of fact found the execution of the prime contract and the subcontract. It then found:

> 6. That plaintiff negligently failed to perform its obligations under the subcontract, and, as a result, the United States Government invoked the penalty provisions provided for in said contract.
>
> 7. That, as a result of plaintiff's negligent performance and failing to complete performance within the time limits of the contract, defendant was assessed $2,450 for liquidated damages under the penalty provisions of his contract.
>
> 8. That defendant is entitled to the sum of $2,450.00 from plaintiff for failure to perform its obligation under the sub-contract.

[The trial court] concluded that Phillips was entitled to judgment against E & B in the sum of $2,450 on his counterclaim. It is undisputed that E & B was entitled to $1,600 on its complaint.

E & B argues that there was no substantial evidence that it was at fault in its performance of the subcontract. We have no hesitation in holding that there is substantial evidence to support the court's finding of "negligence" on the part of E & B which we take to be a determination that it failed and neglected to perform the subcontract within a reasonable time.

The real issue in the case centers on damages. E & B argues that there was no substantial evidence of any damages, but the chief thrust of its argument is that the court erred in accepting the liquidated damages apparently assessed under the prime contract as the measure of damages to be applied to the subcontract.

We first review the evidence on this subject. It is rather sparse. The subcontract is before us. It provides neither a completion date nor for liquidated damages. The prime contract was neither offered nor introduced into evidence. It was not mentioned in the subcontract. We are uninformed as to its content even as to its amount. The prime contract was not furnished to E & B, and there is no evidence it had knowledge of the completion date or of any liquidated damage or penalty provisions which the prime contract may have contained.

The totality of the evidence regarding damages and their amount can be summarized by testimony emanating from Mr. Sinkew, the Government's representative in respect to this project. He said that the brickwork which E & B was to perform was rejected on September 9, 1970. After recounting change orders which had extended the contract completion date to September 8, 1970, and ultimate acceptance by the Government on December 18 of that year, he testified as follows:

> Q. December 18th, excuse me, and at that time did they terminate the penalty provisions?
>
> A. That's correct.
>
> Q. And how much did the government assess against Mr. Phillips for penalty?
>
> A. $ 2,450
>
> Q. Mr. Sinkew, I want to ask you, do you think you have the technical ability as well as the capacity to state to the court why this job was delayed as long as it was?
>
> A. In my opinion it was delayed due to the brick work, the fire brick work or refractory work.

New Mexico follows the general rule of foreseeability in measuring damages for breach of contract. *See Mitchell v. Intermountain Casualty Company*, 364 P.2d 856 (N.M. 1961); *Lommori v. Milner Hotels*, 319 P.2d 949 (N.M. 1957); and *Price v. Van Lint*, 120 P.2d 611 (N.M. 1941).

The leading case most often quoted for the rule is *Hadley v. Baxendale*, 9 Exch. 341, 156 Eng. Rep. 145 (1854). In that case it was said:

> Where two parties have made a contract which one of them has broken, the damages which the other party ought to receive in respect of such breach of contract should be such as may fairly and reasonably be considered either arising naturally, *i.e.,* according to the usual course of things, from such breach of contract itself, or such as may reasonably be supposed to have been in the contemplation of both parties, at the time they made the contract, as the probable result of the breach of it.
>
> Now, if the special circumstances under which the contract was actually made were communicated by the plaintiffs to the defendants, and thus known to both parties, the damages resulting from the breach of such contract which they would reasonably contemplate, would be the amount of injury which would ordinarily follow from a breach of contract under those special circumstances so known and communicated.

> But, on the other hand, if these special circumstances were wholly unknown to the party breaking the contract, he, at the most, could only be supposed to have had in his contemplation the amount of injury which would arise generally, and in the great multitude of cases not affected by any special circumstances, from such a breach of contract.

We consider the liquidated damages provisions—which were apparently included in the prime contract—to be "special circumstances" within the meaning of *Hadley v. Baxendale*. Thus damages which resulted from those special circumstances were recoverable only if they were communicated to or known by both parties at the time they entered into the subcontract. 22 AM. JUR. 2D, DAMAGES § 56. The basis for this rule is simply that:

> Parties, when they enter into contracts, may well be presumed to contemplate the ordinary and natural incidents and consequences of performance or non-performance; but they are not supposed to know the condition of each other's affairs, nor to take into consideration any existing or contemplated transactions, not communicated nor known, with other persons.
>
> Few persons would enter into contracts of any considerable extent as to subject matter or time if they should thereby incidentally assume the responsibility of carrying out, or be held legally affected by, other arrangements over which they have no control and the existence of which are (sic) unknown to them. 1 SUTHERLAND ON DAMAGES § 47 at 182 (4th Ed.) and, *Macchia v. Megow*, 355 Pa. 565, 50 A.2d 314 (1947).

Here, there is no evidence upon which the trial court could have correctly decided that the damages suffered by Phillips were foreseeable by E & B.

We hold, therefore, that the trial court erred in awarding the liquidated damages assessed Phillips by the Government as the measure of damages for Phillips' counterclaim against E & B. There is no reasonable relationship between the work E & B contracted to do and the amount of damages Phillips was assessed under its separate contract with the Government and this amount should not govern as between Phillips and E & B unless it was adopted by them as the measure of damages for any breach of their agreement. *See United States v. Foster Construction (Panama) S.A.*, 456 F.2d 250 (5th Cir. 1972).

The judgment entered upon the counterclaim is reversed. The trial court is directed to set aside its judgment and enter judgment for E & B in the sum of $1600. It is so ordered.

2) *Differentiating Liquidated-Damages and Penalty Clauses*

Days Inn Worldwide, Inc. v. Satyam Shivam Associates, LLC
2008 WL 3287234
(N.J. Super. App. Div. 2008)

PER CURIAM. This is a breach of contract action, arising out of defendant's Satyam Shivan Associates, LLC—a limited liability company d/b/a Days Inn Kingsland (SSA)—default under a guest lodge licensing agreement (Agreement) with plaintiff Days Inn Worldwide, Inc. SSA and the individual defendant guarantors of the Agreement—Manish Saraswat, Mahesh C. Saraswat, and Manju Saraswat (collectively, the defendants)—appeal from the June 8, 2007 order of the Law Division, which granted plaintiff partial summary judgment in the amount of $726,005.55.

On February 16, 1998, plaintiff entered into the Agreement with SSA for the operation of a Days Inn guest lodging facility located in Kingsland, Georgia (the Facility) for a term of fifteen years. The Agreement required SSA to periodically pay plaintiff "recurring fees," which primarily consisted of royalty fees and basic reservation system user fees. The royalty fee is equal to 6.5% of the gross room revenues earned at the Facility, and the basic reservation system user fee is equal to 2.3% of gross room revenues. SSA was required to report the amount of gross room revenue to plaintiff.

Pursuant to the Agreement, SSA agreed to maintain accurate financial information, including books, records, and accounts, relating to the gross room revenues of the Facility and agreed to allow plaintiff to examine and audit the accounts. Under Section 11.4 of the Agreement, plaintiff could suspend the Facility from its reservation system for any default under the Agreement, although during such suspension, all reservation fees would continue to accrue.

Section 11.2 of the Agreement permitted plaintiff, on notice to SSA, to terminate the Agreement, for various reasons: including SSA's 1) failure to pay amounts due under the Agreement, 2) failure to remedy any other default of its obligations or warranties under the Agreement within thirty (30) days after receipt of written notice specifying one or more defaults under the Agreement, and 3) receipt of two or more notices of default under the Agreement in any one-year period, whether or not the defaults were cured.

Pursuant to Section 11.2, SSA agreed that in the event of a termination of the Agreement, it would pay liquidated damages to plaintiff in an amount not less than the product of $2,000 multiplied by the number of guest rooms at the Facility. Interest would be payable on any past due amounts at the rate of 1.5% per month, or the maximum rate permitted by law, whichever is less. Under Section 17.4, the parties agreed that if either party instituted legal proceedings to enforce its rights under the Agreement, the non-prevailing party would "pay all costs and expenses, including reasonable attorneys' fees, incurred by the prevailing party to enforce the Agreement or collect amounts owed under this Agreement."

On January 26, 2004, plaintiff and SSA entered into an Addendum to the Agreement for Satellite Connectivity Services (Addendum). Section 13(a) of the Addendum provided that plaintiff could terminate the Addendum if SSA defaulted under the Agreement. Section 13(c) of the Addendum provided that in the event of termination of the Addendum, SSA would pay liquidated damages to plaintiff in the amount of $1,000 within ten days following the date of termination.

Defendants Manish Saraswat, Mahesh C. Saraswat, and Manju Saraswat—jointly and severally—guaranteed SSA's obligations under the Agreement (the Guaranty). Pursuant to the terms of the Guaranty, the individual defendants agreed that on SSA's default, they would immediately make all payments and perform all other obligations required under the Agreement.

SSA failed to properly report the gross room revenues, and repeatedly failed to timely pay the recurring fees as required by the Agreement. On October 11, 2004, plaintiff conducted an audit of the Facility's accounts. On November 11, 2004, plaintiff sent SSA a letter advising that an audit assessment of $234,013.03 was due because of discrepancies revealed during the audit, that is, "differences between revenues transmitted through [plaintiff's reservation system] and the amounts reported to [plaintiff]. By letters dated February 9, 2005, July 22, 2005, and December 1, 2005, plaintiff advised SSA that 1) it was in breach of the Agreement for failing to pay the recurring fees, 2) it had thirty days within which to cure the default, and 3) if the default was not cured, then the Agreement might be terminated. Defendants failed to cure the default.

On March 15, 2006, plaintiff sent defendants a letter—terminating the Agreement and Addendum, as "a result of your failure to cure your default under the Agreement, due to your failure to meet your financial obligations." The letter further advised defendants that they were to: 1) immediately discontinue the use of plaintiff's trade name, service mark, signs, and advertisements, indicating that the guest lodge facility operated as a Days Inn; 2) pay plaintiff $241,000 liquidated damages for premature termination of the Agreement and Addendum; and 3) pay plaintiff all outstanding recurring fees through the date of termination, which, as of March 8, 2006, was estimated at $340,092.10. Defendants failed to pay the amounts due.

On July 6, 2005, plaintiff filed its complaint, seeking monetary and equitable relief alleging defendants defaulted under the Agreement, the Addendum, and the Guaranty. On March 27, 2006, the trial court entered default judgment against defendants in the amount of $341,440.83—representing $336,299.93 in recurring fees, $1,096.30 in costs of suit, and $4,044.60 in attorneys' fees. ...

On June 8, 2007, the trial court granted the motion as to all counts of the amended complaint ... and awarded plaintiff damages in the amount of $726,005.55—representing $388,931.20 in recurring fees (including interest), $32,823.00 in attorneys' fees, $3,836.15 in costs of suit, $241,000 in liquidated damages, and $59,415.37 in interest on the liquidated damage award.

On appeal, defendants argue: ...

> POINT II. SUMMARY JUDGMENT WAS INAPPROPRIATELY ENTERED BECAUSE THERE EXISTS GENUINE ISSUES OF MATERIAL FACT AS TO THE AMOUNT OF DAMAGES.
>
> A. THE TRIAL COURT ERRONEOUSLY INTERPRETED AND APPLIED THE LIQUIDATED DAMAGE PROVISIONS OF THE PARTIES' CONTRACT IN AWARDING $240,000 IN POST-TERMINATION DAMAGES ...
>
> C. THE TRIAL COURT IMPROPERLY AWARDED INTEREST ON LIQUIDATED DAMAGES. ...

We have considered defendants' arguments in light of the record and applicable law. Except for the arguments discussed below, none of defendants' contentions are of sufficient merit to warrant discussion in a written opinion.

In POINT II-A, defendants argue that the trial court erred in awarding plaintiff $240,000 in post-termination liquidated damages under the Agreement. Defendants contend that the trial court's "conclusion that the aforesaid liquidated damages provision is enforceable and not a penalty constitutes a gross misapplication of the law." Defendants assert that there existed a "genuine issue of material fact as to the reasonableness" of the liquidated damages. We disagree.

"The purpose of a stipulated damages clause is not to compel the promissor to perform, but to compensate the promisee for non-performance." *Wasserman's, Inc. v. Twp. of Middletown*, 137 N.J. 238, 254 (1994). "Enforceable stipulated damages clauses are referred to as 'liquidated damages,' while unenforceable provisions are labeled 'penalties.'" *MetLife Capital Fin. Corp. v. Wash. Ave. Assocs.*, L.P., 159 N.J. 484, 493 (1999) (quoting *Wasserman's, Inc., supra*, 137 N.J. at 248). "Liquidated damages [are] the sum a party to a contract agrees to pay if he breaks some promise, ... arrived at by a good faith effort to estimate in advance the actual damage that will probably ensue from the breach, is legally recoverable as agreed damages if the breach occurs." *Westmount Country Club v. Kameny*, 82 N.J.Super. 200, 205 (App. Div. 1964). However, "[a] penalty is the sum a party agrees to pay in the event of a breach, but which is fixed, not as a pre-estimate of probable actual damages, but as a punishment, the threat of which is designed to prevent the breach." *Id.*

Courts favor enforcement of liquidated damage clauses because of principles of judicial economy and freedom of contract. *MetLife, supra*, 159 N.J. at 504. In determining whether a stipulated damage clause is enforceable as a valid liquidated damage clause or unenforceable as a penalty, we are guided by the test of whether the stipulated damage clause "is reasonable under the totality of the circumstances." *MetLife, supra*, 159 N.J. at 495 (quoting *Wasserman's Inc., supra*, 137 N.J. at 249). "The reasonableness test is applied either at the time the contract is made or when it is breached." *Id.* at 502.

Here, the liquidated damage clause contained in section 12.1 of the Agreement provides in pertinent part:

> If we terminate the License ... you will pay us within 30 days following the date of termination, as Liquidated Damages, an amount equal to ... [nothing] less than the product of $2,000.00 multiplied by the number of guest rooms in the Facility. ...

In support of its motion for summary judgment, plaintiff submitted a certification from Valerie Capers-Workman, Vice President of plaintiff's Franchise Administration, stating in relevant part:

> Pursuant to Section 12.1 of the Agreement, SSA agreed that it would pay liquidated damages to [plaintiff] in an amount that would be no less than the product of $2,000 multiplied by the number of guest rooms at the Facility. (i.e. $2,000 x 120 = $240,000).
>
> This dollar amount is based on the system-wide average revenue earned by [plaintiff] on a per-room annual basis, as determined periodically by the information set forth in [plaintiff]'s Uniform Franchise Offering Circular. Due to the nature of the transient lodging business, revenue can fluctuate drastically from month to month depending upon factors such as the national, regional and local economy, the travel patterns of vacationers, the entry or withdrawal of competitors from the market and the effort, skill and resources of the licensee.

Based on the variables pertaining to the operation of a guest lodging facility and the formula agreed on by the parties for the purpose of determining the amount of liquidated damages, we are satisfied that the trial court correctly determined that the liquidated damages provision represented a reasonable estimate of future damages caused by termination of the Agreement, and that actual damages would have been difficult to estimate.

Defendants argue in POINT II-C that the trial court erroneously awarded plaintiff interest on the $241,000 in stipulated damages. We agree.

Plaintiff sought, and the trial court awarded, interest on the stipulated damage award at the rate of 1.5% per month from March 15, 2006, the date of termination of the Agreement, to June 8, 2007, the return date of the summary judgment motion. We are satisfied that the Agreement did not require SSA to pay such interest. The only provision in the Agreement requiring payment of interest on amounts due was Section 7.3. That section states that "[i]nterest is payable when you receive our invoice on any past due amount payable to us under this Agreement at the rate of 1.5% per month ... accruing from the due date until the amount is paid."

Defendants received a letter dated March 15, 2006, providing defendants with a "formal notice of termination" and explaining how "the termination of the Agreement [was] effective as of March 15, 2006." More importantly, the letter informed defendants that they "must ... pay Liquidated Damages of $240,000 as specified in the Agreement [and] ... pay Liquidated Damages of $1,000 for early termination of the Addendum to the Agreement. ..."

Section 12.1 provided that if plaintiff terminates the Agreement, that defendants would have "30 days following the date of termination" to pay the liquidated damages. Also, under Section 13(c) of the "Satellite Connectivity Services Addendum," defendants had to pay Addendum liquidated damages "within 10 days following the date of termination." Defendants received the termination notice on March 15, 2006. Under the aforementioned provisions, the Addendum liquidated damages and the Agreement liquidated damages would not have become due until March 25, 2006, and April 14, 2006, respectively.

The record is devoid of any evidence that plaintiff sent SSA invoices after March 15, 2006. Accordingly, pursuant to section 7.3 of the Agreement, which provides that, "[i]nterest is payable when you receive our invoice on any past due amount," defendants did not owe interest on the liquidated damages, because they never received an invoice on any "past due amount" of liquidated damages. ...

We affirm in part; reverse in part; and remand the matter to the trial court to ... enter an amended judgment in accordance with this opinion. We do not retain jurisdiction.

NOTES AND QUESTIONS

1. **The Efficacy of Using Key Words and Phrases to Distinguish a Penalty Clause from a Liquidated-Damages Clause.** Often, contracting parties insert the word "penalty" or the phrase "stipulated damages" in a contract—expecting that the plain meaning of those terms will clearly indicate the parties' intentions. But, in the end, courts interpret contracts. Therefore, the parties' use of certain words is not determinative in and of itself. The inserted words and phrases may or may not establish an enforceable liquidated-damages provision or an unenforceable penalty clause. Stated succinctly, courts do not necessarily give conclusive effect to the contracting parties' words or phrases—"liquidated damages," "penalties," or "forfeitures." *See Taylor v. Sanders*, 557 P.2d 1017, 1020 (Mont. 1976). To underscore this point, consider an excerpt from the opinion in *Crawford v. Heatwole & Hedrick*, 66 S.E. 46, 47 (Va. 1909): "No form of words has been regarded as controlling. But the fundamental rule, so often announced, is that the construction of these stipulations depends, in each case, upon the intent of the parties, as evidenced by the entire agreement construed in the light of the circumstances under which it was made."

2. **Liquidated Damages and the Gross Disproportionate Test.** In *Harbours Condominium Ass'n, Inc. v. Hudson*, 852 N.E.2d 985, 993 (Ind. Ct. App. 2006), the appellate court stated: "We acknowledge some contradiction within the rules that define how to distinguish liquidated damages from a penalty." But consider the Virginia Supreme Court's explanation in *Crawford v. Heatwole & Hedrick*, 66 S.E. 46, 47 (Va. 1909):

   > [I]n order to show that the sum stipulated in an agreement as liquidated damages is not "grossly disproportionate" to the loss, the party seeking to enforce the liquidated damages provision must demonstrate some proportionality between the loss and the sum established as liquidated damages. Thus, a party who seeks to enforce a liquidated damages clause need not prove actual damages but may be required to show a correlation between the liquidated damages and actual damages in order to assure that a sum charged may fairly be attributed to the breach.

3. **Remote or Consequential Damages.** Generally, under the principle of *Hadley v. Baxendale*, consequential damages may be recovered only if the breaching party expected—when the contract was being formed—that a breach would likely produce damages

as a result of the breach. *But see Bill Parker & Assocs. v. Rahr*, 456 S.E.2d 221, 224 (Ga. Ct. App. 1995) (general and special tort damages may be recovered in a breach of contract action if they are not too remote or consequential).

E. Proving Exemplary, Punitive, or Treble Damages

In some quarters, some persons still embrace an unfounded belief: Under the common law, the freedom to contract is sacrosanct and absolute. *Cf. Manufactured Housing Communities of Washington v. State*, 13 P.3d 183, 224 (Wash. 2000). However, in *Chicago, B. & Q.R. Co. v. McGuire*, 219 U.S. 549, 566 (1911), the United States Supreme Court explained the right-to-contract principle:

> [F]reedom of contract is a qualified, and not an absolute, right. There is no absolute freedom to do as one wills or to contract as one chooses. The guaranty of liberty does not withdraw from legislative supervision that wide department of activity which consists of the making of contracts, or deny to government the power to provide restrictive safeguards. Liberty implies the absence of arbitrary restraint, not immunity from reasonable regulations and prohibitions imposed in the interests of the community.

On the other hand, in civil-law countries, one finds fewer restrictions on persons' right to form contracts and subject themselves to all sorts of "strange," "novel," or "offensive" obligations. For example, in most civil-law societies, parties may insert penalty or punitive-damages clauses into their negotiated or standardized contracts, and civil-law judges will enforce them. *See* Aristides N. Hatzis, *Having the Cake and Eating It Too: Efficient Penalty Clauses in Common and Civil Contract Law*, 22 Int'l Rev. L. & Econ. 381, 383 (2002) (reporting that in most civil-law European countries, liquidated-damages and penalty clauses are readily enforced when they are not extravagant or pure-gambling clauses).

In addition, the legislature and judiciary in Puerto Rico have embraced the civil-law traditions of continental Europe. *See Arthur Young & Co. v. Vega III*, 1994 WL 909262 (P.R. May 24, 1994) ("[W]e must bear in mind that freedom of contract prevails in our jurisdiction. This means that the kinds of agreements contracting parties may reach are only limited by their imagination, and that the will of the parties is the supreme law between them. But, 'freedom of private contracting is not unrestrictive.'"), quoting *Hernández v. Méndez & Assoc. Dev. Corp.*, 105 D.P.R. 149, 153 (P.R. 1976). Consequently, in Puerto Rico, courts take a more forgiving view of penalty provisions in contracts. To illustrate, in

Simonet v. Igaravidez, 90 P.R.R. 1, 8 (P.R. 1964), the Supreme Court of Puerto Rico stated:

> [T]he verbal formula which is employed in the contract is not what provides normally the key. The functions which the penal clause generally fulfills must first be specified and its impact must be scrutinized in each specific case. We have expressed ourselves before with respect to the functions of the penal clause upon stating that the two most important functions of a penal clause are to guarantee the performance of an obligation ... and to serve as liquidator of the damage—to evaluate in advance the damages which may be caused to the creditor by the improper nonperformance of the obligation.

As reported earlier, under the common law, penalty clauses in contracts are generally void as against public policy. *See Freedman v. Rector*, 37 Cal. 2d 16, 21–22 (Cal. 1951), and Frank v. Jansen, 226 N.W.2d 739, 743 (Minn. 1975) (reiterating that a penalty clause is usually unenforceable). However, the Montana Supreme Court's observation is worth restating: "[A] penalty clause is *prima facie* void and to come within the exception, facts must be alleged and proven from which the court can say the liquidated damages clause is valid because the damages are by the nature of the case extremely difficult or impracticable to fix." *Morgen & Oswood Const. Co., Inc. v. Big Sky of Montana, Inc.*, 557 P.2d 1017, 1019 (Mont. 1976).

There is another general rule: Punitive or exemplary damages are not recoverable in a breach-of-contract action. *See Fluorine on Call, Ltd. v. Fluorogas Ltd.*, 380 F.3d 849 (5th Cir. 2004) and *Boorhem-Fields, Inc. v. Burlington Northern R. Co.,* 884 S.W.2d 530 (Tex. App.—Texarkana 1994). But there is an exception to this rule: If a plaintiff establishes that an independent malicious or oppressive tort accompanied the breach of contract, the non-breaching party may secure punitive damages. *See Transportation Ins. Co. v. Moriel*, 879 S.W.2d 10 (Tex. 1994).

A comparison of the civil and common-law rules generates these questions: Why do common-law courts prevent contracting parties from inserting penalty clauses in contracts? Are the reasons sound? Why do punitive or exemplary damages spawn so much judicial hostility? Are the answers and analyses in the following cases intelligible and convincing?

1. Generally Impermissible Punitive Damages for Breach of Contract

Hibschman Pontiac, Inc. v. Batchelor
362 N.E.2d 845
(Ind. 1977)

GIVAN, CHIEF JUSTICE. James B. Batchelor brought an action for breach of contract and oppressive conduct by Hibschman Pontiac, Inc. and General Motors Corporation. A trial before a jury resulted in a verdict for Batchelor and against Hibschman Pontiac and General Motors Corporation in the amount of $1,500.00. Further, the jury assessed punitive damages against Hibschman Pontiac, Inc. in the amount of $15,000.00. The Court of Appeals, Third District, reversed the grant of punitive damages. Batchelor now petitions for transfer.

The record reveals the following evidence: Prior to buying the Pontiac GTO automobile involved in this case, Batchelor inquired of the salesman, the service manager and the vice president as to the quality of Hibschman Pontiac's service department, as it was important that any deficiencies in the car be corrected. The salesman and the service manager responded that the service department at Hibschman Pontiac was above average. Jim Hibschman, the vice president, assured him that he would personally see that any difficulties would be corrected. Batchelor stated that he relied on the statements of the three men and ordered a 1969 GTO Pontiac automobile.

When Batchelor picked up his new car he discovered several problems with it. As requested by the service manager of Hibschman Pontiac, Batchelor made a list of his complaints and brought the car in for repair a few days later. The service manager attached the list to a work order but did not list the deficiencies on the work order. Later the manager called Batchelor and said that the car was ready. When he picked up the car Batchelor noticed that several items on the list had not been touched. Batchelor testified that there were many occasions when he took the car to Hibschman Pontiac for repairs and the service manager told him that the defects had been fixed when in fact they were not fixed. Batchelor testified that the service manager knew the defects were not corrected, but represented to him that the defects were corrected. Batchelor stated that he relied on the service manager's statements and took the car on several trips, only to have it break down. Some of the deficiencies resulted in abnormal wear of the car and breakdowns after the warranty period had expired.

Batchelor testified that he had taken the car in for repairs five times before he had owned it a month but that the defects had not been corrected. Batchelor had taken the car in 12 times during the warranty period for overnight repair and at least 20 times in all during the period. During the warranty period Batchelor lost use of the car approximately 45 days while it was at Hibschman Pontiac.

Batchelor had appealed to Jim Hibschman on several occasions to take care of his car. Hibschman replied that he realized the repairs were not affected properly but that Hibschman Pontiac would "do everything to get you happy." On another occasion Jim Hibschman responded they had done all they could with the car but that Batchelor was just a particular, habitual complainer whom they could not satisfy and 'I would rather you would just leave and not come back. We are going to have to write you off as a bad customer.'

On several occasions Batchelor attempted to see Dan Shaules, an area service representative from Pontiac Division, about the car but was kept waiting so long that he had to leave without seeing him. Batchelor did see Shaules in Buchanan, Michigan, when he took the car to an authorized Pontiac dealer there after the warranty had expired. Shaules inspected the car and told Batchelor to return the car to Hibschman Pontiac for repairs.

Hugh Haverstock, the owner of the garage where several of the deficiencies where corrected after the expiration of the warranty, testified that Batchelor was a good customer and paid his bills. He stated that an average transmission man could have corrected the problem with the transmission and that a problem with the timing chain was discovered and corrected when a tune up lasted only 800 miles. Haverstock stated that the difference in value of the car without defects and with the defects it had was approximately $1,500.00. Haverstock testified that when a person complains about problems with cars that have not been fixed by dealerships, word gets out and others do not want to work on the cars.

Arnold Miexel, the service manager for Hibschman Pontiac during the time in question, testified that his representation to Batchelor regarding Hibschman Pontiac service department was based on the fact that the mechanics were factory trained and that he had received no complaints regarding their work. He further stated that he could not check the work of the mechanics. Miexel testified that if their work was unsatisfactory it was done over but no work order was written for it. He stated that it was possible Batchelor made complaints about the car, but the defects were not corrected. The warranty expired and, as a consequence, later work was not considered under warranty.

Dan Shaules testified that Miexel was an average service manager. He testified that not all of the deficiencies in the car were corrected properly. He further stated that if any defects in the car were brought to their attention within the warranty period, items would be corrected if necessary after the warranty had expired.

Appellant first argues that there was insufficient evidence to permit the issue of punitive damages to go to the jury and that the court should have rendered a directed verdict on the issue of punitive damages on behalf of Hibschman Pontiac. This Court has recently dealt with the question of punitive damages in a contract action. In *Vernon Fire & Casualty Ins. Co. v. Sharp,* 349 N.E.2d 173 (Ind. 1976), the majority restated the general provision that punitive damages are not recoverable in contract actions and went on to state exceptions to this rule. Where the conduct of a party, in breaching his contract, independently establishes the elements of a common law tort, punitive damages may be awarded for the tort.

Punitive damages may be awarded in addition to compensatory damages "whenever the elements of fraud, malice, gross negligence or oppression mingle in the controversy." *Vernon Fire & Casualty Ins. Co. v. Sharp, supra*, 349 N.E.2d 173 at 180. Further, where a separate tort accompanies the breach or the elements of tort mingle with the breach, it must appear that the public interest will be served by the deterrent effect of the punitive damages. *Vernon Fire & Casualty Ins. Co. v. Sharp, supra.*

Appellant urges that the evidence presented does not indicate tortious conduct of any sort on its part. While a reasonable inference could be made from the evidence that appellant merely attempted to fulfill its contract and to do no more than that contract required, it is also reasonable to infer that Hibschman Pontiac acted tortiously and in willful disregard of the right of Batchelor. This court has often stated the maxim that it will not reweigh the evidence nor determine the credibility of witnesses, but will sustain a verdict if there is any evidence of probative value to support it.

A corporation can act only through its agents, and their acts, when done within the scope of their authority, are attributable to the corporation. Here, the jury could reasonably have found elements of fraud, malice, gross negligence or oppression mingled into the breach of warranty. The evidence showed that requested repairs were not satisfactorily completed although covered by the warranty and capable of correction. Some of these defects were clearly breaches of warranty. Paint was bubbled, the radio never worked properly, the hood and bumper were twisted and misaligned, the universal joints failed, the transmission linkage was improperly adjusted, the timing chain was defective causing improper tune-ups and the carburetor was defective, among other things.

Batchelor took the car to the defendant with a list of defects on numerous occasions and picked up the car when told it was "all ready to go." It was reasonable to infer that the defendant's service manager represented repairs to have been made when he knew that the work had not been done and that in reliance on his representations, Batchelor drove the car on trips and had breakdowns. Before purchasing the car Batchelor was given special representations on the excellence of Hibschman's service department, and the jury could find that Batchelor relied on these in buying the car from the defendant. After having brought the car in on numerous occasions, Batchelor was told by Jim Hibschman, "I would rather you would just leave and not come back. We are going to have to write you off as a bad customer."

And he was told by one of Hibschman's mechanics that, "If you don't get on them and get this fixed, they will screw you around and you will never get it done." From these statements the jury could infer that the defendant was attempting to avoid making certain repairs by concealing them during the period of the warranty. Batchelor gave the defendant numerous opportunities to repair the car and the defendant did not do so; instead he tried to convince Batchelor that the problems were not with the car, but rather with Batchelor. We are of the opinion that in this case the jury could have found there was cogent proof to establish malice, fraud, gross negligence and oppressive conduct.

Although fraudulent conduct was not alleged in the complaint, evidence on the subject was admitted. Any inconsistency between the pleadings and proof will be resolved in favor of the proof at trial. Thus there was probative evidence supporting the claim for punitive damages. The trial court did not err in denying a directed verdict as to that issue.

Appellant next presents a collective argument for three issues: whether there was sufficient evidence to support an award for punitive damages in the amount of $15,000; whether the award of $15,000 punitive damages bears a reasonable relationship to the actual damages; and whether punitive damages of $15,000 is excessive in this case.

Appellant here urges that there was no evidence presented concerning its worth or ability to pay. In *Physicians Mutual Ins. Co. v. Savage*, 296 N.E.2d 165 (Ind. App. 1973), the Court of Appeals held that the assessment of punitive damages in the amount of $50,000 "was not excessive when considered in relation to the evidence available to the trial court." The opinion noted that included in the evidence was a statement of net worth of the defendant. In *Manning v. Lynn Immke Buick, Inc.*, 276 N.E.2d 253 (Ohio App. 1971), the court held that where punitive damages are to be assessed, the wealth of the defendant may be shown so that the jury will assess damages that will punish him. Such a rule is based on the theory that it will take a greater amount of penalty to dissuade a rich person than a poor person from oppressive conduct. However there appears to be no requirement that evidence of worth be submitted in cases of punitive damages.

Indiana has followed a rule that punitive damages in a proper case may be assessed by the jury within their sound discretion guided by proper instructions given by the court. There is no rule that the amount of punitive damages must be within a certain ratio to compensatory damages, although in the case of *Bangert v. Hubbard*, 126 N.E.2d 778 (Ind. App. 1955)—a malicious prosecution suit, the court held that punitive damages of $10,500, being 105 times the compensatory damages, was so excessive as to indicate that the verdict was given under the influence of passion and prejudice. ...

In the case at bar, although it was within the province of the jury to assess punitive damages, the amount in this case is so high as to violate the "first blush" rule as set out in *City of Indianapolis v. Stockes*, 105 N.E. 477 (Ind. 1914): "Damages are not [to be] considered excessive unless at first blush they appear to be outrageous and excessive or it is apparent that some improper element was taken into account by the jury in determining the amount."

For the above reasons transfer is granted and the cause is remanded to the trial court with instruction to order a remittitur of $7,500 of the punitive damages. In the event the remittitur is not made, the trial court shall order a new trial. The trial court is in all other matters affirmed.

2. Freedom to Contract Includes the Right to Impose Breach-of-Contract Penalties

Lake River Corp. v. Carborundum Co.
769 F.2d 1284
(7th Cir. 1985)

POSNER, CIRCUIT JUDGE. This diversity suit between Lake River Corporation and Carborundum Company requires us to consider questions of Illinois commercial law, and in particular to explore the fuzzy line between penalty clauses and liquidated-damages clauses.

Carborundum manufactures "Ferro Carbo," an abrasive powder used in making steel. To serve its midwestern customers better, Carborundum made a contract with Lake River by which the latter agreed to provide distribution services in its warehouse in Illinois. Lake River would receive Ferro Carbo in bulk from Carborundum, "bag" it, and ship the bagged product to Carborundum's customers. The Ferro Carbo would remain Carborundum's property until delivered to the customers.

Carborundum insisted that Lake River install a new bagging system to handle the contract. In order to be sure of being able to recover the cost of the new system—$89,000—and make a profit of 20 percent of the contract price, Lake River insisted on the following minimum-quantity guarantee:

> In consideration of the special equipment [i.e., the new bagging system] to be acquired and furnished by LAKE-RIVER for handling the product, CARBORUNDUM shall, during the initial three-year term of this Agreement, ship to LAKE-RIVER for bagging a minimum quantity of [22,500 tons]. If, at the end of the three-year term, this minimum quantity shall not have been shipped, LAKE-RIVER shall invoice CARBORUNDUM at the then prevailing rates for the difference between the quantity bagged and the minimum guaranteed.

If Carborundum had shipped the full minimum quantity that it guaranteed, it would have owed Lake River roughly $533,000 under the contract.

After the contract was signed in 1979, the demand for domestic steel, and with it the demand for Ferro Carbo, plummeted; and Carborundum failed to ship the guaranteed amount. When the contract expired late in 1982, Carborundum had shipped only 12,000 of the 22,500 tons it had guaranteed. Lake River had bagged the 12,000 tons and had billed Carborundum for this bagging, and Carborundum had paid. … [B]ut by virtue of the formula in the minimum-guarantee clause, Carborundum still owed Lake River $241,000—the contract price of $533,000 if the full amount of Ferro Carbo had been shipped, minus what Carborundum had paid for the bagging of the quantity it had shipped.

When Lake River demanded payment of this amount, Carborundum refused, on the ground that the formula imposed a penalty. At the time, Lake River had in its warehouse 500 tons of bagged Ferro Carbo—having a market value of $269,000—which it refused to release unless Carborundum paid the $241,000 due under the formula. Lake River did offer to sell the bagged product and place the proceeds in escrow until its dispute with Carborundum over the enforceability of the formula was resolved. [B]ut Carborundum rejected the offer and trucked in bagged Ferro Carbo from the East to serve its customers in Illinois, at an additional cost of $31,000.

Lake River brought this suit for $241,000, which it claims as liquidated damages. Carborundum counterclaimed for the value of the bagged Ferro Carbo when Lake River impounded it and the additional cost of serving the customers affected by the impounding. The theory of the counterclaim is that the impounding was a conversion, and not as Lake River contends the assertion of a lien. The district judge—after a bench trial—gave judgment for both parties. Carborundum ended up roughly $42,000 to the good: $269,000 + $31,000—$241,000—$17,000, the last figure representing prejudgment interest on Lake River's damages. (We have rounded off all dollar figures to the nearest thousand.) Both parties have appealed. …

The hardest issue in the case is whether the formula in the minimum-guarantee clause imposes a penalty for breach of contract or is merely an effort to liquidate damages. Deep as the hostility to penalty clauses runs in the common law, ... we still might be inclined to question, if we thought ourselves free to do so, whether a modern court should refuse to enforce a penalty clause where the signator is a substantial corporation, well able to avoid improvident commitments.

Penalty clauses provide an earnest of performance. ... On the other side it can be pointed out that by raising the cost of a breach of contract to the contract breaker, a penalty clause increases the risk to his other creditors; increases—what is the same thing and more, because bankruptcy imposes "deadweight" social costs—the risk of bankruptcy; and could amplify the business cycle by increasing the number of bankruptcies in bad times, which is when contracts are most likely to be broken. But since little effort is made to prevent businessmen from assuming risks, these reasons are no better than makeweights.

A better argument is that a penalty clause may discourage efficient as well as inefficient breaches of contract. Suppose a breach would cost the promisee $12,000 in actual damages but would yield the promisor $20,000 in additional profits. Then there would be a net social gain from breach. After being fully compensated for his loss the promisee would be no worse off than if the contract had been performed, while the promisor would be better off by $8,000. But now suppose the contract contains a penalty clause under which the promisor if he breaks his promise must pay the promisee $25,000. The promisor will be discouraged from breaking the contract, since $25,000, the penalty, is greater than $20,000, the profits of the breach; and a transaction that would have increased value will be forgone.

On this view, since compensatory damages should be sufficient to deter inefficient breaches (that is, breaches that cost the victim more than the gain to the contract breaker), penal damages could have no effect other than to deter some efficient breaches. But this overlooks the earlier point that the willingness to agree to a penalty clause is a way of making the promisor and his promise credible and may therefore be essential to inducing some value-maximizing contracts to be made. It also overlooks the more important point that the parties (always assuming they are fully competent) will, in deciding whether to include a penalty clause in their contract, weigh the gains against the costs—costs that include the possibility of discouraging an efficient breach somewhere down the road, and will include the clause only if the benefits exceed those costs as well as all other costs.

On this view the refusal to enforce penalty clauses is (at best) paternalistic; and it seems odd that courts should display parental solicitude for large corporations. But however this may be, we must be on guard to avoid importing our own ideas of sound public policy into an area where our proper judicial role is more than usually deferential. The responsibility for making innovations in the common law of Illinois rests with the courts of Illinois, and not with the federal courts in Illinois. And like every other state, Illinois—untroubled by academic skepticism of the wisdom of refusing to enforce penalty clauses against sophisticated promisors—continues steadfastly to insist on the distinction between penalties and liquidated damages. *See, e.g., Bauer v. Sawyer*, 134 N.E.2d 329, 333–34 (Ill. 1956).

To be valid under Illinois law a liquidation of damages must be a reasonable estimate at the time of contracting of the likely damages from breach, and the need for estimation at that time must be shown by reference to the likely difficulty of measuring the actual damages from a breach of contract after the breach occurs. If damages would be easy to determine then, or if the estimate greatly exceeds a reasonable upper estimate of what the damages are likely to be, it is a penalty. See, e.g., *M.I.G. Investments, Inc. v. Marsala*, 414 N.E.2d 1381, 1386 (Ill. App. 1981).

The distinction between a penalty and liquidated damages is not an easy one to draw in practice; but we are required to draw it and can give only limited weight to the district court's determination. Whether a provision for damages is a penalty clause or a liquidated-damages clause is a question of law rather than fact; and unlike some courts of appeals, we do not treat a determination by a federal district judge of an issue of state law as if it were a finding of fact, and reverse only if persuaded that clear error has occurred, though we give his determination respectful consideration.

Mindful that Illinois courts resolve doubtful cases in favor of classification as a penalty, we conclude that the damage formula in this case is a penalty and not a liquidation of damages, because it is designed always to assure Lake River more than its actual damages. The formula—full contract price minus the amount already invoiced to Carborundum—is invariant to the gravity of the breach.

When a contract specifies a single sum in damages for any and all breaches even though it is apparent that all are not of the same gravity, the specification is not a reasonable effort to estimate damages; and when in addition the fixed sum greatly exceeds the actual damages likely to be inflicted by a minor breach, its character as a penalty becomes unmistakable. This case is within the gravitational field of these principles even though the minimum-guarantee clause does not fix a single sum as damages.

NOTES AND QUESTIONS

1. **Establishing that Punitive Damages Are Warranted.** Once more, under an exception to the general rule, punitive damages are available "where the breach of contract is accompanied by a connected, but independent tort involving fraud, malice or oppression." *See Goldfarb v. Robb Report, Inc.*, 101 Ohio App.3d 134, 140 (Ohio Ct. App. 1995). However, to secure a punitive-damages award, a plaintiff must prove that a) the defendant breached the contract, b) the defendant committed a connected tort independently of that breach, and c) the defendant's tortious conduct was fraudulent, malicious, or oppressive in nature. *Id. See also Moskovitz v. Mt. Sinai Med. Ctr.*, 69 Ohio St.3d 638, 651 (Ohio 1994) ("The purpose of punitive damages is not to compensate a plaintiff, but to punish and deter certain conduct.").

2. **Proving "Excessive Punitive Damages" and the Efficacy of the "First Blush" Test.** In *Batchelor*, the Indiana Supreme Court applied a so-called "first blush" test to determine whether a punitive-damages award is excessive. What are the elements of that test? What does a defendant have to prove to secure a remittitur? Is the test sound? Justice DeBruler penned the following passage in a concurring opinion:

   > I agree that the punitive damage award of $15,000 was excessive, and that remittitur of $7,500 is reasonable. However, I doubt the efficacy of the standard enunciated by the majority for the review of punitive damages awards, the "first blush" rule. This rule is vague and contains no objective standards for the evaluation of such awards in view of their purpose, the deterrence of tortious conduct, and the danger to be guarded against, awards motivated by vindictiveness and prejudice. I believe that we should undertake to define a standard of review of punitive damages which imposes objective limitations upon such damages.

3. **Proving "Excessive Punitive Damages" Using the Degree of Reprehensibility Test.** In *State Farm Mutual Automobile Insurance Co. v. Campbell*, 538 U.S. 408, 418 (2003), the Supreme Court fashioned the "degree of reprehensibility test." To determine whether an award of punitive damages is excessive, courts must weigh three factors: "(a) the degree of reprehensibility of the defendant's misconduct; (b) the disparity between the actual or potential harm suffered by the plaintiff and the punitive damages award; and (c) the difference between the punitive damages

awarded by the jury and the civil penalties authorized or imposed in comparable cases."

SECTION THREE: REMEDIES UNDER EQUITABLE AND OTHER ACTIONS

Here, some earlier observations are worth repeating. Constitutions, statutes, or regulations have abolished multiple forms of actions in most jurisdictions. Instead, states have embraced a single form of civil action. But, it is important to stress, legal and equitable actions were merged only for *procedural purposes*. The merger did not abolish the distinctions between common law and equitable actions. *Steelvest, Inc. v. Scansteel Serv. Ctr., Inc.*, 908 S.W.2d 104, 108 (Ky. 1995). The inherent distinctions between legal and equitable *principles* and *forms of relief* remain.

Again, in equitable actions, a court has "the inherent power to adjust equity between the parties without rigid adherence to any determined form and may shape the remedy to meet the demands of justice." *Estate of Cantonia v. Sindel*, 684 S.W.2d 592, 595 (Mo. Ct. App. 1985). Also, when legal and equitable actions are filed in a single lawsuit, each action retains its own identity as legal or equitable for purposes of the applicable standard of review on appeal. *Corley v. Ott*, 485 S.E.2d 97, 99 (S.C. 1997).

Assume that contracting parties filed a lawsuit, which presents multiple actions in law—breach-of-contract, breach-of-warranty and breach-of-promise actions. In that same lawsuit, the parties may also file an action in equity to secure equitable relief. In fact, the parties may file multiple actions in equity. This section discusses some of the equitable actions that contracting parties may commence in stand-alone lawsuits as well as in breach-of-contract lawsuits.

A. Declaratory Judgment Actions

1) Single-Action Lawsuits

Woodhouse v. Farmers Union Mut. Ins. Co.
785 P.2d 192
(Mont. 1990)

SHEEHY, JUSTICE. Plaintiff Patricia Woodhouse (Woodhouse) brought suit, seeking a declaratory judgment that the loss of her personal property by fire be covered by her insurer, Farmers Union Mutual Insurance Company. Defendant (Farmers) counterclaimed, seeking a declaratory judgment excluding coverage for the loss. The issue raised by appellant Farmers is: whether the district court erred in its determination that Farmers is obligated to provide coverage for an insured whose co-insured destroyed the property by arson.

Patricia and Alan Woodhouse were divorced on September 24, 1986. Alan Woodhouse was awarded the trailer house the parties had acquired during the marriage. The trailer house and its contents were insured by Farmers, with Patricia and Alan named as the insureds on the policy.

Following the divorce, Patricia Woodhouse left many items of personal property in the dwelling due to lack of storage space elsewhere. On January 5, 1987, Alan Woodhouse intentionally set fire to the trailer house, and committed suicide within the burning dwelling. The dwelling was totally consumed by the fire.

Patricia Woodhouse submitted a claim to Farmers Insurance for the value of her personal goods lost in the fire. Farmers denied the claim on the basis that coverage was excluded because the loss was intentionally caused by an insured party.

Farmers maintains that this is a clear contract case. They submit that the "intentional loss" exclusion of the Woodhouse insurance policy acts to deny coverage in this situation. The provision reads as follows:

> We do not insure for loss caused directly or indirectly by ... [an] Intentional Loss, meaning any loss arising out of any act committed: (1) by or at the direction of an insured; and (2) with the intent to cause a loss.

Arson by an insured, Farmers maintains, is not, therefore, an insured risk. Alan Woodhouse was an insured party who clearly committed an intentional loss. Patricia Woodhouse is a named coinsured party and is therefore bound to the contractual provisions of the policy.

Farmers cites several cases for the premise that clear and unambiguous language of the contract controls. In *Amick v. State Farm Fire and Casualty Company*, 862 F.2d 704 (8th Cir. 1988), the court stated:

> The court sees no injustice in requiring the company to pay only those risks it insured, where, as here, the coverages are spelled out in clear and unambiguous language. *Bryan v. Employers National Insurance*, 742 S.W.2d 557, 577 (Ark. 1988). An innocent co-partner [may] not recover under a policy where arson was committed by a partner because the language of the policy specifically barred recovery. *West Bend Mutual Insurance Co. v. Salemi*, 511 N.E.2d 785, 789 (Ill. App. 1987). ... The key factor is whether the policy provision barring recovery by an innocent co-insured is clear and unambiguous.

Farmers cites the exclusion clause contained in the policy noted in *Spezialetti v. Pacific Employers Insurance Co.*, 759 F.2d 1139 (3rd Cir.

1985), which reads: "[The] insurance shall not apply to loss or damage … [resulting from] any dishonest act or omission by any insured." The court in *Spezialetti* denied the innocent spouse's claim for insurance proceeds, based on the exclusionary language.

Finally, Farmers takes issue with the district court's reliance on *Kulubis v. Texas Farm Bureau Underwriters Insurance Co.*, 706 S.W.2d 953 (Tex. 1986) for the proposition that an insurer's obligations under such insurance policies are "several and not joint, the wrongful acts of one coinsured cannot be imputed to another as a basis for denying coverage." This, Farmers states, unfairly places the burden of proving the innocence of the non-acting spouse on the insurer. Farmers contends that *Kulubis* is bad policy, stating that:

> The law should assiduously seek … to avoid holding out any incentive to such actions [as arson] and should be diligent to assure that it permits no benefits to be derived from them by their perpetrators. We conclude that it would be a strange rule indeed that guaranteed the would-be arsonist a minimum of one-half of the insured value of his building … even were he found guilty of the act, as long as he arranged matters so that the insurance company could not prove that he had let his spouse in on the scheme.

In summary, Farmers contends that the lower court erred by not ruling that the language of the exclusionary clause barred coverage. They maintain that the "clear and unambiguous" policy language of not covering intentional loss applies in the case of arson. All insured parties are thereby denied coverage. To hold otherwise would negate clear contractual provisions and create potentially harmful precedent.

Woodhouse contends that of the several jurisdictions that have considered this same question, the majority have ruled that the innocent coinsured should recover. Woodhouse states that equity and public policy considerations, the basis of many of these rulings, should also apply in the case at bar. Woodhouse cites *Hoyt v. New Hampshire Fire Insurance Co.*, 29 A.2d 121 (N.H. 1942), as one of the first such cases tending to allow the co-insured to recover. In *Hoyt*, the court reasoned that an ordinary person "not versed in the nice distinctions of insurance law" would naturally assume their individual interests covered by the insurance policy. The insurer argued in that case, as in the present, that the policy was a contract and the terms were clear and enforceable. The court in *Hoyt* ruled that as a matter of equity and of public policy, the wrongs of one individual should not be imputed to another. The test, the court stated, was not how the insurer construed the policy language, but what a reasonable person in the position of the insured would have understood it to mean.

Some courts have focused on the language of the policy to make their determination. Woodhouse cites *Hildebrand v. Holyoke Mutual Fire Insurance*, 386 A.2d 329 (Me. 1978), where the court scrutinized the term "insured." The insurer argued, as does Farmers, that the word "insured" included all named insureds. The policy excluded coverage if the loss was caused by an "insured." The court determined that the definition of "insured," when a claim is denied, must be limited to include only the insureds who intentionally cause the loss.

Although the results are undeniably harsh for Patricia Woodhouse, the clear meaning of the contract must govern here. We concur with Farmers that this is, plainly and simply, a contract case. The provision clearly and unequivocally states that a loss caused by an intentional act of an insured party bars coverage. Alan Woodhouse was clearly an "insured," and his act was clearly intentional. Accordingly, we find that the loss was not covered, and reverse the decision of the district court.

NOTES AND QUESTIONS

1. **Declaratory Judgment Actions Under State Law**. The TEXAS UNIFORM DECLARATORY JUDGMENTS ACT—TEX. CIV. PRAC. & REM. CODE ANN. § 37.003—gives Texas courts the power to make declarations and award declaratory relief. It reads:

   POWER OF COURTS TO RENDER JUDGMENT—FORM AND EFFECT

   (a) A court of record within its jurisdiction has power to declare rights, status, and other legal relations whether or not further relief is or could be claimed. An action or proceeding is not open to objection on the ground that a declaratory judgment or decree is prayed for.

   (b) The declaration may be either affirmative or negative in form and effect, and the declaration has the force and effect of a final judgment or decree.

   (c) The enumerations in Sections 37.004 and 37.005 do not limit or restrict the exercise of the general powers conferred in this section in any proceeding in which declaratory relief is sought and a judgment or decree will terminate the controversy or remove an uncertainty.

2. **Declaratory Judgment Actions Under the Federal Law**. THE DECLARATORY JUDGMENT ACT, 28 U.S.C. § 2201(a) reads in pertinent part:

> In a case of actual controversy within its jurisdiction, any court of the United States, upon the filing of an appropriate pleading, may declare the rights and other legal relations of any interested party seeking such declaration, whether or not further relief is or could be sought. Any such declaration shall have the force and effect of a final judgment or decree and shall be reviewable as such.

3. **Employing Traditional Rules of Contract Interpretation to Award or Deny Declaratory Relief.** In *Woodhouse*, the Montana Supreme Court concluded: "Although the results are undeniably harsh for Patricia Woodhouse, the clear meaning of the contract must govern here. We concur with Farmers that this is, plainly and simply, a contract case." Although failing to state the precise name, the court was citing language that appears in a major doctrine that courts employ to construe and interpret contracts. *See e.g., Davis v. Beling,* 2012 WL 2154552,*13 (Nev. June 14, 2012) ("In general, a district court may not award 'attorney fees ... unless authorized to do so by a statute, rule or contract.' Parties are free to provide for attorney fees by express contractual provisions. The objective in interpreting an attorney fees provision, as with all contracts, 'is to discern the intent of the contracting parties. ... [T]raditional rules of contract interpretation [are employed] to accomplish that result. ... Therefore, the initial focus is on whether the language of the contract is clear and unambiguous; if it is, the contract will be enforced as written."), citing *Ellison v. C.S.A.A.*, 797 P.2d 975, 977 (Nev. 1990), and *Cline v. Rocky Mountain, Inc.*, 998 P.2d 946, 949 (Wyo. 2000). *See also Boyer v. U.S. Fidelity & Guaranty Co.* 274 P. 57, 59 (Ca. 1929) (holding that "insurance policies are governed by the same general rules which pertain to all contracts. There must be a meeting of the minds.").

4. **Employing the Doctrine of Reasonable Expectation to Award or Deny Declaratory Relief.** The insured consumer in *Woodhouse* cited several cases and argued that "equity and public policy considerations" should determine whether the insured or insurer should receive declaratory relief. Why? An "ordinary person"—who is "not versed in the nice distinctions of insurance law"—would "naturally assume" his individual interests are covered under an insurance policy. The insured consumer was citing the "reasonable expectation doctrine." *See State Farm Fire & Cas. Co. v. Slade*, 747 So.2d 293, 311 (Ala. 1999) (embracing the view that the "objectively reasonable expectations of applicants and intended beneficiaries regarding the terms of insurance contracts will be honored"), and *Hazen Paper Co. v. U.S. Fidelity and Guar. Co.*, 555 N.E.2d 576, 583 (Mass. 1990) (declaring that "what an

objectively reasonable insured ... expect[s] to be covered" under an insurance contract must be conisdered).

---

2) Mixed-Actions Lawsuit

Lidawi v. Progressive County Mut. Ins. Co.
112 S.W.3d 725
(Tex. App.—Houston [14th Dist.] 2003)

JOHN S. ANDERSON, JUSTICE. In this case arising from denial of an insurance claim based on the insured's non-cooperation, we address an issue of first impression: whether clauses in an insurance contract requiring the insured to cooperate in the investigation of a claim and to submit to an examination under oath (EUO) permit the insurance company to require separate, segregated examinations of the insureds. ...

Appellants Mohammad Lidawi and Zeina Mohamad—who are husband and wife—represent they are victims of an accident in which someone failed to stop at a stop sign, striking the left side of appellants' automobile as appellants passed through the intersection. According to appellants, the driver then drove away without providing any identifying information. Appellants filed a claim with their insurer, Progressive County Mutual Insurance Company, the appellee. Appellants' policy provides in part: "A person seeking any coverage must ... [c]ooperate with us in the investigation ... of any claim." The policy also provides, "A person seeking any coverage must ... [w]hen required by us ... submit to examination under oath."

On or after February 9, 2001, Progressive Claims Inspector David Tews took a recorded statement from Lidawi regarding the accident. Progressive also inspected appellants' automobile. This inspection revealed damage from multiple impacts involving several incidents. Additionally, the impacts left paint transfer marks that did not match Lidawi's description of the vehicle causing the accident. Based on the discrepancies between the physical damage and Lidawi's statement, Tews hired an engineer to investigate the damage. The engineer also concluded the damage was not consistent with Lidawi's statement.

On March 14, 2001, Tews sent letters to appellants and their attorney, Michael Engelhart, requesting appellants submit to an EUO. The letter did not refer to separate examinations. On April 11, 2001, Engelhart, appellants, and an interpreter met Tews and another Progressive representative at Engelhart's office. When Progressive insisted the EUOs be conducted separately, Engelhart insisted each appellant be permitted to be in the room when the other was examined because "they are husband and wife, and are both claimants and insured under the policy." Progressive refused, and Tews left without taking the examination. ...

Appellants then sued Progressive for breach of contract and also sought a declaratory judgment regarding their rights and duties under the policy, specifically the duty of cooperation, the requirement of separate examinations, and the insurer's waiver of examination. Progressive counterclaimed for a declaratory judgment 1) that its request for separate examinations was consistent with the cooperation obligations of the contract, appellant's failure to cooperate constituted a breach of the policy, and Progressive therefore properly denied the claim; and 2) by failing to cooperate and refusing separate examinations, appellants failed to meet all conditions precedent to recovery on their suit.

Both parties moved for summary judgment. Appellants moved for traditional summary judgment on their claims and a partial no-evidence summary judgment on Progressive's request for declaratory judgment that appellants failed to satisfy a condition precedent to the lawsuit. Progressive moved for traditional summary judgment. The trial court rendered [summary and declaratory judgment in favor of Progressive]. ...

ANALYSIS OF POINT OF ERROR

POINT OF ERROR: Are appellants entitled to summary judgment on their affirmative claims for breach of contract and declaratory judgment because the insurance policy does not entitle Progressive to separate, segregated EUOs?

[A]ppellants argue the insurance policy does not entitle Progressive to conduct separate, segregated EUOs of the insureds. Insurance policies are controlled by rules of interpretation applicable to contracts generally. *Nat'l Union Fire Ins. Co. v. CBI Indus., Inc.*, 907 S.W.2d 517, 520 (Tex. 1995). In construing the written contract, our primary concern is to ascertain the true intent of the parties as expressed in the contract. When the written contract is so worded it may be given a definite or certain legal meaning, the contract is not ambiguous and parol evidence cannot be admitted to create an ambiguity.

If, however, the language of a policy is subject to two or more reasonable interpretations, the language is ambiguous. "Whether a contract is ambiguous is a question of law for the court to decide by looking at the contract." A court may consider the parties' interpretations only when the court first determines the policy is ambiguous. Only if a court decides a policy is ambiguous may the court construe its language in favor of providing coverage for the insured. *See State Farm Life Ins. Co. v. Beaston*, 907 S.W.2d 430, 433 (Tex. 1995).

Ambiguity in contract language, however, is not to be confused with silence. Ambiguity results when the intention of the parties is expressed in language susceptible of more than one meaning. *Med. Towers, Ltd. v. St. Luke's Episcopal Hosp.*, 750 S.W.2d 820, 822 (Tex. App.—Houston [14th Dist.] 1988, writ denied). In contrast, when a contract is silent, the question is not one of interpreting the language but rather one of determining its effect.

Neither party seriously argues the policy is ambiguous. Appellants contend the policy is clear in not requiring separate examinations. They contend the policy is not silent because it contains a clause pertaining to examinations under oath. The policy provides: "A person seeking any coverage must ... [c]ooperate with us in the investigation ... of any claim." The policy also provides, "A person seeking any coverage must ... [w]hen required by us ... submit to examination under oath." Use of the singular strongly suggests any examination of "a person" may proceed separately from that of any other person. Nevertheless, we conclude the policy is silent regarding the manner in which the EUO is to be conducted.

When a contract is silent on an issue, Texas courts will infer reasonable terms. *See Med. Towers*, 750 S.W.2d at 822–24 (concluding that the lease agreement was silent as to method of appraisal required; and inferring comparable sales approach the proper method for determining value of property using accepted rules of construction). Texas courts will also supply missing terms when necessary to effectuate the purposes of the parties under the agreement. *O'Farrill v. Gonzalez*, 974 S.W.2d 237, 244 (Tex. App.—San Antonio, 1998, pet. denied).

As a United States District Court has explained regarding insurance policies:

> [T]he court must tread carefully when ascribing implicit obligations on the contracting parties. The court should not venture beyond construing the contract to effectuate the manifest intentions of the parties. The court must determine what the parties bargained for when they agreed to the terms of the cooperation clause.
>
> The [insureds] bargained for the right to make an honest claim under the policy and to receive compensation with a minimum of inconvenience. In return, [the insurer] bargained for a reasonable means to ascertain the truth surrounding a claim. The cooperation clause embodies [the insurer's] right to uncover the probability of truth from the [insureds].

The court must bear these interests in mind when construing the cooperation clause. Where the precise details of an agreement have not been defined by the parties, the court should assume the parties implicitly intended the agreement to operate in a reasonable manner.

For example, courts routinely deem contracts to require performance within a reasonable time where the parties did not explicitly set any deadlines. The cooperation clause, therefore, should be deemed to allow [the insurer] to take reasonable steps to ascertain the truth of the claims. *State Farm Fire & Cas. Co. v. Tan*, 691 F.Supp. 1271, 1273 (S.D. Cal. 1988)

See also Shelter Ins. Cos. v. Spence, 656 S.W.2d 36, 38 (Tenn. Ct. App. 1983) (viewing as relevant and material the obtaining of true and accurate information about the type and extent of damage to insured premises and its contents and observing the parties conceded determination of true facts is principal purpose of taking sworn statements).

Like the *Spence* court, we conclude "more accurate factual statements could likely be taken in any set of circumstances where multiple parties are involved, if such statements were taken separately." *Spence*, 656 S.W.2d at 38. *See also Tan*, 691 F.Supp. at 1273 (stating "[u]ndoubtedly, separate examinations would greatly enhance [the insurer's] ability to discover the true facts and to assess the veracity of the [insureds'] claims"). Accordingly, we infer a reasonable term permitting Progressive to require separate, segregated EOUs of its insureds.

Appellants, however, cite this court to three cases in which courts from other jurisdictions have declined to infer such a provision: *United States Fid. & Guar. Co. v. Welch*, 854 F.2d 459 (11th Cir. 1988); *Ahmadi v. Allstate Ins. Co.*, 22 P.3d 576 (Colo. Ct. App. 2001); and *United States Fid. & Guar. Co. v. Hill*, 722 S.W.2d 609 (Mo. Ct. App. 1986). ... We conclude the better rationale is to be found in *Spence* and *Tan*. In the face of silence regarding the manner in which an insurer is to conduct an EUO, we infer a reasonable term allowing the insurer to require separate, segregated examinations.

We overrule appellant's point of error one. We affirm that part of the trial court's judgment declaring, "The Standard Texas Personal Auto Policy permits Progressive to require separate examinations under oath from Lidawi and Mohamad." ...

Nevertheless, we ... decline to conclude Progressive is presently entitled to summary judgment in its favor and dismissal of appellants' lawsuit. Depending on how the policy is written, an insurer's proper remedy to enforce a condition precedent is abatement rather than barring the claim. *See State Farm Gen. Ins. Co. v. Lawlis*, 773 S.W.2d 948, 949 (Tex. App.—Beaumont 1989, no writ), citing *Humphrey v. Nat'l Fire Ins. Co.*, 231 S.W. 750 (Tex. Com. App. 1921).

Furthermore, like Progressive, appellants had no means, other than insisting on their position, of protecting what they believed, based on case law from outside Texas, to be their rights under the policy. The summary judgment proof does not contain any parts of the policy dealing with the ramifications of non-compliance with the cooperation and examination clauses, particularly under circumstances such as those presented here. Accordingly, we reverse that part of the judgment granting final summary judgment in favor of Progressive and dismissing appellants' lawsuit for the reason they failed to comply with a condition precedent.

In addition, because we are today deciding an issue of first impression, the case has not been fully developed consistent with that law. *See Bayway Servs., Inc. v. Ameri-Build Constr., L.C.*, 106 S.W.3d 156, 161 (Tex. App.—Houston [1st Dist.] no pet.) (stating, "As long as there is a probability that a case has for any reason not been fully developed, an appellate court has the discretion to remand rather than render a decision").

Accordingly, we remand to the trial court to afford appellants the opportunity of complying with the requirement of separate, segregated EUOs as a condition precedent to their lawsuit. ...

NOTES AND QUESTIONS

1. **Employing the Doctrine of Ambiguity to Award or Deny Declaratory Relief**. In *Aetna Casualty & Surety Co. v. Cartmel*, 100 So. 802, 803 (Fla. 1924), the Florida Supreme Court declared that ambiguities in insurance contracts "must be liberally construed in favor of the insured." *See also Trombly v. Blue Cross / Blue Shield of New Hampshire-Vermont*, 423 A.2d 980, 985 (N.H. 1980) (adopting the proposition that an ambiguous insurance policy will be construed in favor of the insured and against the insurer, but only where there is ambiguity in the contract), and *Mazzilli v. Accident & Casualty Insurance Co. of Winterthur*, 170 A.2d 800, 803 (N. J. 1961) (concluding that "if the controlling language will support two meanings, one favorable to the insurer, and the other favorable to the insured, the interpretation sustaining coverage must be applied.").

2. **General Rules of Contract Construction Versus the Doctrine of Ambiguity**. In *Grain Dealers Mutual Insurance Company v. McKee*, 943 S.W.2d 455, 458 (Tex. 1997), the Texas Supreme Court wrote:

   [The] named insured's president and sole shareholder sought declaratory judgment that business automobile insurance policy covered his child for uninsured motorist (UM), underinsured motorist (UIM), and personal injury protection (PIP) benefits for injuries sustained while passenger in vehicle that was not covered auto. The 37th District Court, Bexar County, Don McManus, J., granted summary judgment finding daughter to be insured under policy. Following severance and abatement of remaining issues, insurer appealed. The Court of Appeals, Chapa, C.J., 911 S.W.2d 775, affirmed. On application for writ of error, the Supreme Court, Abbott, J., held that child could not be family member of named insured and, therefore, was not insured under the policy. Reversed.

The general rules of contract construction govern insurance policy interpretation. *State Farm Life Ins. Co. v. Beaston*, 907 S.W.2d 430, 433 (Tex. 1995); *Forbau v. Aetna Life Ins. Co.*, 876 S.W.2d 132, 133 (Tex. 1994). "Whether a contract is ambiguous is a question of law that must be decided by examining the contract as a whole in light of the circumstances present when the contract was entered." *Columbia Gas Transmission Corp. v. New Ulm Gas, Ltd.*, 940 S.W.2d. 587 (Tex. 1996); *National Union Fire Ins. Co. v. CBI Indus., Inc.*, 907 S.W.2d 517, 520 (Tex. 1995). A contract is unambiguous as a matter of law if it can be given a definite or certain legal meaning. *Columbia Gas*, 940 S.W.2d at 589; *CBI*, 907 S.W.2d at 520. Conversely, if an insurance contract is subject to more than one reasonable interpretation, the contract is ambiguous and the interpretation that most favors coverage for the insured will be adopted. *Kelly Associates., Ltd. v. Aetna Cas. & Sur. Co.*, 681 S.W.2d 593, 596 (Tex. 1984).

Therefore, we must discern whether there is more than one reasonable interpretation of the UM/UIM and PIP endorsements. In making this determination, we note that an ambiguity does not arise simply because the parties advance conflicting interpretations of the contract. *Columbia Gas*, 940 S.W.2d at 589. McKee's status as president and sole shareholder of the named insured Future Investments, combined with the "family member" language in the PIP and UM/UIM, does not create an ambiguity. There is no *reasonable interpretation of the policy* that can construe McKee as the "you" to whom the covered family members are linked in the endorsements. McKee, unambiguously, is not the named insured under the policy, and his status as president and sole shareholder does not equate him with the insured company. Under Texas law, a corporation is an entity separate from its shareholders.

B. Actions for Specific Performance

1) Contracts for Personal Services and Specific Performance

In re Mary Clark, Woman of Colour
1 Blackf. 122
(Ind. 1821)

HOLMAN, J. In obedience to a writ of habeas corpus, issued by the Knox Circuit Court, G. W. Johnson brought before that Court the body of Mary Clark (a woman of color), said to be illegally detained by him; and assigned as the cause of her detention, that she was his servant by indenture, executed at Vincennes, in this State, on the 24th of October, 1816: which indenture is set out in the return, regularly executed and acknowledged, by which the said Mary (being a free woman) voluntarily bound herself to serve him as an indented servant and house maid for 20 years. This cause of detention was deemed sufficient by the Circuit Court, and said Mary remanded to the custody of the said Johnson. She has appealed to this Court.

This application of Mary Clark to be discharged from her state of servitude, clearly evinces that the service she renders to the obligee is involuntary; and the Constitution, having determined that there shall be no involuntary servitude in this State, seems at the first view to settle this case in favor of the appellant. But a question still remains, whether her service, although involuntary in fact, shall not be considered voluntary by operation of law, being performed under an indenture voluntarily executed. This indenture is a writing obligatory.

The clause in the 7th section of the 11th article of the Constitution—that provides that no indenture hereafter executed by any Negro or mulatto without the bounds of this State shall be of any validity within this State—has no bearing on it. An indenture executed by a Negro or mulatto out of this State is by virtue of this provision, absolutely void; and can be set up neither as a demand for the services therein specified, nor as a remuneration in damages for a non-performance.

But the Constitution, having confirmed the liberty of all our citizens, has considered them as possessing equal right and ability to contract, and, without any reference to the color of the contracting parties, has given equal validity to all their contracts when executed within the State.

We shall, therefore, discard all distinctions that might be drawn from the color of the appellant, and consider this indenture as a writing obligatory, and test it, in all its bearings, by the principles that are applicable to all cases of a similar nature. It is a covenant for personal service, and the obligee requires a specific performance.

It may be laid down as a general rule, that neither the common law nor the statutes in force in this State recognize the coercion of a specific performance of contracts. The principal, if not the only exceptions to this general rule, are statutory provisions, few, if any, of which are applicable to this State, and none of them has any bearing on this case. Apprentices are compellable to a specific performance of the articles of apprenticeship, but their case rests on principles of a different nature. They are not considered as performing a contract of their own, but acting in conformity to the will of those whose right and duty it was to exact obedience from them.

That right and duty existed by nature in the parent, and are, by legal regulations, transferrable to the master during the minority of the child: and when transferred, either by the parent, or those who stand in loco parentis, the duty of obedience arises, and is enforced on the ground of parental authority, and not on the principle of a specific performance of contracts, and cannot be urged as an exception to the general rule, that the coercion of a specific performance of contracts is not contemplated in law. The case of soldiers and sailors depends on national policy, and cannot be used in the elucidation of matters of private right.

There are some covenants that may be specially enforced in equity; but they are of a very different nature from the contract before us. They are mostly covenants for the conveyance of real estate, and in no case have any relation to the person. But if the law were silent, the policy of enforcing a specific performance of a covenant of this nature, would settle this question.

Whenever contracting parties disagree about the performance of their contract, and a Court of justice of necessity interposes to settle their different rights, their feelings become irritated against each other, and the losing party feels mortified and degraded in being compelled to perform for the other what he had previously refused, and the more especially if that performance will place him frequently in the presence or under the direction of his adversary. But this state of degradation, this irritation of feeling, could be in no other case so manifestly experienced, as in the case of a common servant, where the master would have a continual right of command, and the servant be compelled to a continual obedience.

Many covenants, the breaches of which are only remunerated in damages, might be specially performed, either by a third person at a distance from the adversary, or in a short space of time. But a covenant for service, if performed at all, must be performed under the eye of the master; and might, as in the case before us, require a number of years. Such a performance, if enforced by law, would produce a state of servitude as degrading and demoralizing in its consequences, as a state of absolute slavery; and if enforced under a government like ours, which acknowledges a personal equality, it would be productive of a state of feeling more discordant and irritating than slavery itself.

Consequently, if all other contracts were specifically enforced by law, it would be impolitic to extend the principle to contracts for personal service. Very dissimilar is the case of apprentices. They are minors, and for the want of discretion, are necessarily under the control of parents, guardians, or masters; and obedience is exacted from them, whether considered as children, wards, or apprentices. They are incapable of regulating their own conduct, and are subjected by nature and by law to the government of others; and that government, instead of humbling and debasing the mind, has a tendency to give it a regular direction, and a suitable energy for future usefulness.

But it is not the master who in this case applies for legal aid. He has not appealed to a Court of justice to obtain a specific performance of this indenture. All he asks from the constituted authorities is, that they would withhold their assistance from his servant. Does this alter the case in his favor? Is it more consistent with good policy, that a man possessing the power, should be left to enforce a specific performance of a contract in his own behalf, than that the officers of justice, on a full consideration of his case, should enforce it for him? These questions are not only easily answered in the negative, but their reverse is unquestionably true.

Deplorable indeed would be the state of society, if the obligee in every contract had a right to seize the person of the obligor, and force him to comply with his undertaking. In contracts for personal service, the exercise of such a right would be most alarming in its consequences. If a man, contracting to labor for another a day, a month, a year, or a series of years, were liable to be taken by his adversary, and compelled to perform the labor, it would either put a stop to all such contracts, or produce in their performance a state of domination in the one party, and abject humiliation in the other.

We may, therefore, unhesitatingly conclude that when the law will not directly coerce a specific performance, it will not leave a party to exercise the law of the strong, and coerce it in his own behalf. A state of servitude thus produced, either by direct or permissive coercion, would not be considered voluntary either in fact or in law. It presents a case where legal intendment can have no operation.

While the appellant remained in the service of the obligee without complaint, the law presumes that her service was voluntarily performed; but her application to the Circuit Court to be discharged from the custody of her master, establishes the fact that she is willing to serve no longer; and, while this state of the will appears, the law cannot, by any possibility of intendment, presume that her service is voluntary.

The case of an apprentice presents a different state of things. The minor is considered as having no legal will. He has neither the power nor the right of choosing, whether he will obey or disobey the commands of his master. The law, therefore, on account of the immaturity of his will, cannot presume that any of his services are involuntarily performed.

The appellant in this case is of legal age to regulate her own conduct; she has a right to the exercise of volition; and, having declared her will in respect to the present service, the law has no intendment that can contradict that declaration. We must take the fact as it appears, and declare the law accordingly. The fact then is, that the appellant is in a state of involuntary servitude; and we are bound by the constitution, the supreme law of the land, to discharge her therefrom.

Per Curiam.

NOTES AND QUESTIONS

1. **Specific-Performance Awards for Personal Services—General Rule**. In *Mary Clark*, the learned judge concluded that the ethnicity of each party was not relevant. Instead, the judge viewed the indenture as an obligatory writing. Before deciding whether to compel specific performance of personal services, the judge tells us that he would apply specific-performance *principles*. Are those rules clearly stated in the opinion? As the judge reported, the general rule is exceptionally clear: "Specific performance is not available to enforce a contract for personal services." *Rhodes v. Designer Distribution Services, LLC,* 2012 WL 642434,*4 (Nev. Fen. 24, 2012). *See also* RESTATEMENT (FIRST) OF CONTRACTS § 379: "A promise to render personal service or supervision will not be specifically enforced by an affirmative decree." What justifies the rule? Courts generally believe that "mischief [is] likely to result from an enforced continuance of [a] relationship after it has become personally obnoxious to one of the parties. ... Consequently, to protect the "the interests of society," a disinterested contracting party should not be compel to perform personal services for another party's benefit. *Holstein v. Crescent Communities, Inc.,* 2003 WL 22077778, *3 (Ohio Ct. App. 2003).

2. **Specific-Performance Awards for Personal Services—Exceptions to the General Rule**. Specific performance has been awarded under some circumstances where services have a unique and peculiar value. For example, consider the principles which appear in *American Broadcasting Companies, Inc. v. Wolf,* 430 N.Y.S.2d 275, 284 (N.Y. App. Div. 1980):

   No cogent reason is shown to break with precedent and to order an unwilling party to perform services of a personal

> nature. ... Of course, if the services to be rendered are of an unusual or unique nature, then the situation is more clearly one in which an adequate remedy at law does not exist. In such cases a rule—generally traced to the English case of *Lumley v. Wagner*, 42 Eng. Rep. 687 (1852)—has developed. Where a contract for such unique services contains a negative covenant by the one who is to render the services that he will not render like services for anyone else during the contract term, equity will enjoin the breach of this negative covenant, if no adequate remedy at law is available and the contract is fair and reasonable.

The Alabama Supreme Court's analysis in *Roquemore & Hall v. Mitchell*, 52 So. 423, 424 (Ala. 1910) is also instructional:

> Courts of equity will not undertake to enforce the specific performance of a contract for personal services which are material or mechanical, and not peculiar or individual; but where the contract stipulates for special, unique, or extraordinary services, or where the services to be rendered are purely intellectual and individual in their character, the courts will grant an injunction in aid of specific performance.

2) Commercial Goods and Services Contracts and Specific Performance

Campbell Soup Co. v. Wentz
172 F.2d 80
(3rd Cir. 1949)

Goodrich, Circuit Judge. The transactions which raise the issues may be briefly summarized. On June 21, 1947, Campbell Soup Company (Campbell)—a New Jersey corporation—entered into a written contract with George B. Wentz and Harry T. Wentz, who are Pennsylvania farmers, for delivery by the Wentzes to Campbell of all the Chantenay red cored carrots to be grown on fifteen acres of the Wentz farm during the 1947 season. Where the contract was entered into does not appear. The contract provides, however, for delivery of the carrots at the Campbell plant in Camden, New Jersey. The prices specified in the contract ranged from $23 to $30 per ton according to the time of delivery. The contract price for January 1948 was $30 a ton.

The Wentzes harvested approximately 100 tons of carrots from the fifteen acres covered by the contract. Early in January 1948, they told a Campbell representative that they would not deliver their carrots at the contract price. The market price at that time was at least $90 per ton, and Chantenay red cored carrots were virtually unobtainable.

The Wentzes then sold approximately 62 tons of their carrots to the defendant Lojeski, a neighboring farmer. Lojeski resold about 58 tons on the open market, approximately half to Campbell and the balance to other purchasers.

On January 9, 1948, Campbell, suspecting that Lojeski was selling it "contract carrots," refused to purchase any more, and instituted these suits against the Wentz brothers and Lojeski to enjoin further sale of the contract carrots to others, and to compel specific performance of the contract. The trial court denied equitable relief. We agree with the result reached, but on a different ground from that relied upon by the District Court.

The case has been presented by both sides as though *Erie Railroad v. Tompkins*, 304 U.S. 64 (1938) and *Klaxon Company v. Stentor Electric Manufacturing Co., Inc.*, 313 U.S. 487 (1941) had never been decided. We are not advised as to the place of the contract, although as we have pointed out in other cases: The Pennsylvania conflict of laws rule, which binds us here, refers matters concerning the validity and extent of obligation of the contract to the place of making.

In this instance, however, the absence of data on which to base a rule of reference does not preclude the decision of the case. We have said several times in this circuit that the question of the form of relief is a matter for a federal court to decide. But neither federal decisions nor the law of New Jersey or Pennsylvania as expressed in the Uniform Sales Act differ upon this point. A party may have specific performance of a contract for the sale of chattels if the legal remedy is inadequate. Inadequacy of the legal remedy is necessarily a matter to be determined by an examination of the facts in each particular instance.

We think that on the question of adequacy of the legal remedy the case is one appropriate for specific performance. It was expressly found that at the time of the trial it was "virtually impossible to obtain Chantenay carrots in the open market." This Chantenay carrot is one which the plaintiff uses in large quantities, furnishing the seed to the growers with whom it makes contracts. It was not claimed that in nutritive value it is any better than other types of carrots. Its blunt shape makes it easier to handle in processing. And its color and texture differ from other varieties. The color is brighter than other carrots.

The trial court found that the plaintiff failed to establish what proportion of its carrots is used for the production of soup stock and what proportion is used as identifiable physical ingredients in its soups. We do not think lack of proof on that point is material. It did appear that the plaintiff uses carrots in fifteen of its twenty-one soups. It also appeared that it uses these Chantenay carrots diced in some of them and that the appearance is uniform. The preservation of uniformity in appearance in a food article marketed throughout the country and sold under the manufacturer's name is a matter of considerable commercial significance and one which is properly considered in determining whether a substitute ingredient is just as good as the original.

The trial court concluded that the plaintiff had failed to establish that the carrots, "judged by objective standards," are unique goods. This we think is not a pure fact conclusion like a finding that Chantenay carrots are of uniform color. It is either a conclusion of law or of mixed fact and law and we are bound to exercise our independent judgment upon it. That the test for specific performance is not necessarily "objective" is shown by the many cases in which equity has given it to enforce contracts for articles—family heirlooms and the like—the value of which was personal to the plaintiff. *See Burr v. Bloomsburg*, 101 N.J. Eq. 615 (1927); *Sloane v. Clauss*, 1901, 64 Ohio St. 125 (1901); and, 5 WILLISTON, CONTRACTS § 1419 n. 6 (Rev. ed. 1937).

Judged by the general standards applicable to determining the adequacy of the legal remedy, we think that on this point the case is a proper one for equitable relief. *See* RESTATEMENT OF CONTRACTS § 361 (1932); 5 WILLISTON, CONTRACTS § 1419 (Rev. ed. 1937); and, 1 POMEROY, EQUITY JURISPRUDENCE § 221b (5th ed. 1941). There is considerable authority—old and new—showing liberality in the granting of an equitable remedy.

We see no reason why a court should be reluctant to grant specific relief when it can be given without supervision of the court or other time-consuming processes against one who has deliberately broken his agreement. Here the goods of the special type contracted for were unavailable on the open market, the plaintiff had contracted for them long ahead in anticipation of its needs, and had built up a general reputation for its products as part of which reputation uniform appearance was important. We think if this were all that was involved in the case specific performance should have been granted.

The reason that we shall affirm instead of reversing with an order for specific performance is found in the contract itself. We think it is too hard a bargain and too one-sided an agreement to entitle the plaintiff to relief in a court of conscience. For each individual grower the agreement is made by filling in names and quantity and price on a printed form furnished by the buyer. This form has quite obviously been drawn by skilful draftsmen with the buyer's interests in mind.

Paragraph 2 provides for the manner of delivery. Carrots are to have their stalks cut off and be in clean sanitary bags or other containers approved by Campbell. This paragraph concludes with a statement that Campbell's determination of conformance with specifications shall be conclusive.

The defendants attack this provision as unconscionable. We do not think that it is, standing by itself. We think that the provision is comparable to the promise to perform to the satisfaction of another and that Campbell would be held liable if it refused carrots which did in fact conform to the specifications.

The next paragraph allows Campbell to refuse carrots in excess of twelve tons to the acre. The next contains a covenant by the grower that he will not sell carrots to anyone else except the carrots rejected by Campbell nor will he permit anyone else to grow carrots on his land. Paragraph 10 provides liquidated damages to the extent of $50 per acre for any breach by the grower. There is no provision for liquidated or any other damages for breach of contract by Campbell.

The provision of the contract which we think is the hardest is paragraph 9, set out in the margin:

> Grower shall not be obligated to deliver any Carrots which he is unable to harvest or deliver, nor shall Campbell be obligated to receive or pay for any Carrots which it is unable to inspect, grade, receive, handle, use or pack at or ship in processed form from its plants in Camden (1) because of any circumstance beyond the control of Grower or Campbell, as the case may be, or (2) because of any labor disturbance, work stoppage, slow-down, or strike involving any of Campbell's employees. Campbell shall not be liable for any delay in receiving Carrots due to any of the above contingencies. During periods when Campbell is unable to receive Grower's Carrots, Grower may with Campbell's written consent, dispose of his Carrots elsewhere. Grower may not, however, sell or otherwise dispose of any Carrots which he is unable to deliver to Campbell.

It will be noted that Campbell is excused from accepting carrots under certain circumstances. But even under such circumstances the grower, while he cannot say Campbell is liable for failure to take the carrots, is not permitted to sell them elsewhere unless Campbell agrees. This is the kind of provision which the late Francis H. Bohlen would call "carrying a good joke too far." What the grower may do with his product under the circumstances set out is not clear. He has covenanted not to store it anywhere except on his own farm and also not to sell to anybody else.

We are not suggesting that the contract is illegal. Nor are we suggesting any excuse for the grower in this case who has deliberately broken an agreement entered into with Campbell. We do think, however, that a party who has offered and succeeded in getting an agreement as tough as this one is, should not come to a chancellor and ask court help in the enforcement of its terms. That equity does not enforce unconscionable bargains is too well established to require elaborate citation. 4 Pomeroy, Equity Jurisprudence § 1405a (5th ed. 1941); and, 5 Williston, Contracts § 1425 (Rev. ed. 1937).

The plaintiff argues that the provisions of the contract are separable. We agree that they are, but do not think that decisions separating out certain provisions from illegal contracts are in point here. As already said, we do not suggest that this contract is illegal. All we say is that the sum total of its provisions drives too hard a bargain for a court of conscience to assist.

This disposition of the problem makes unnecessary further discussion of the separate liability of Lojeski, who was not a party to the contract, but who purchased some of the carrots from the Wentzes. The judgments will be affirmed.

NOTES AND QUESTIONS

1. **Establishing Specific-Performance Awards—The Applicability of the "Objective" and "Subjective" Standard Tests.** In *Campbell Soup*, the Third Circuit declared: "[T]he test for specific performance is not *necessarily* 'objective.'" The implication is clear: Sometimes courts sitting in equity will employ both "objective" and "subjective" tests to determine whether or not to grant specific-performance awards. Consider the court's conclusion in *Patel v. Liebermensch*, 197 P.3d 177, 183 (Cal. 2008) ("The mere state of mind of the parties is not the object of inquiry. The terms of the contract are determinable by an external, not by an internal standard or by what has been termed the objective rather than the subjective test. Measured by any reasonable standard there is here mutual assent to a contract which is sufficiently certain so that the court was within its power in decreeing specific performance."). The court's analysis in *L & L Auto Distributors and Suppliers Inc. v. Auto Collection, Inc.*, 2009 WL 1652852, *9 (N.Y. App. Div. June 12, 2009) is also worth considering:

   Plaintiffs' fourth cause of action for a "turnover," however, actually seeks an order requiring defendants to account for and deliver the particular cars that they paid for, or, in the alternative, that any transfer of the cars be declared invalid and fraudulent and that title and ownership of the cars be turned over to them as the rightful owners. In support of this claim, plaintiffs allege that the majority of the cars are high-end luxury brand cars, such as Mercedes Benz and Lexus. Plaintiffs further allege that such luxury cars are in high demand and short supply, and that they are very difficult to purchase, especially for export. Plaintiffs state that for many of these cars, the waiting lists to obtain new cars are unacceptably long, and can be three months or longer. Plaintiffs claim that this long replacement period to obtain new cars, as opposed to the specific cars which they already bought and paid for, will cripple and possibly destroy their businesses. The motor vehicles at issue, however, are new cars and not unique, antique, or one-of-a-kind vehicles. Plaintiffs are not entitled to specific performance of the sale of this vehicle; rather, it can be fully compensated by way of monetary damages.

2. **The Doctrine of Unclean Hands, Undue Hardship, and Specific-Performance Awards**. Here, it is important to stress some new and previously stated principles: a) "Specific performance is an equitable remedy and the power of equity is as broad as equity and justice require." *Buteau v. Biggar*, 409 N.Y.S.2d 451, 453 (N.Y. App. Div. 1978); b) A party's right to specific performance is not automatic, therefore a party who wants a specific-performance award must come to court with clean hands. *Pecorella v. The Greater Buffalo Press, Inc.*, 486 N.Y.S.2d 562, 563 (N.Y. App. Div. 1985); c) A court has broad discretion to determine whether or not to award specific performance. *Bander v. Grossman*, 611 N.Y.S.2d 985, 989 (N.Y. App. Div. 1994); d) A court may not grant specific performance if the offending party would experience unreasonable hardship or if injustice would occur. *Concert Radio Inc. v. GAF Corp.*, 488 N.Y.S.2d 696, 699 (N.Y. App. Div. 1985); e) To determine whether unreasonable hardship exists, a court must weigh defendant's detriment and plaintiff's reward in the wake of a specifically enforced contract. *Id.* at 699–700; and f) If defendant's hardship is disproportionate to plaintiff's reward, a court must deny specific performance. *Bander*, 611 N.Y.S.2d at 989.

3. **Specific-Performance Awards for "Intangible" Assets.** Regarding the specific enforcement of contracts for the sale of goods or "tangible" property, the rules are settled: a) A court's decision to grant or deny specific performance is a matter of judicial discretion. *Dunham v. Hogan*, 56 A.2d 550, 551 (Me. 1948); b) Courts will not grant a specific-performance award unless the contractual terms are sufficiently clear to allow a court to fashion an appropriate order. *Jenkins Petroleum Process Co. v. Sinclair Refining Co.*, 32 F.2d 252, 257 (1st Cir. 1928); c) If there is an adequate remedy at law, courts may not specifically enforce a contract. *McIntyre v. Plummer Associates*, 375 A.2d 1083, 1084 (Me. 1977); d) Contracts for the sale of realty may be specifically enforced. *Forbes v. Wells Beach Casino, Inc.*, 307 A.2d 210, 220 (Me. 1973); and e) Under certain conditions, courts will specifically enforce personalty contracts. *Northeast Investment Co., Inc. v. Leisure Living Communities, Inc.*, 351 A.2d 845, 855–56 (Me. 1976) (specific performance was appropriate to enforce an oral contract to purchase stock, where the stock had

no readily ascertainable market value, was not easily obtainable elsewhere, and was of special interest to the buyer).

But, may courts specifically enforce "intangible assets" contracts? In *Triple-A Baseball Club Associates v. Northeastern Baseball, Inc.*, 832 F.2d 214, 223–224 (1st Cir. 1987), the seller of a Double-A franchise wanted specific enforcement of a provision in a contract. Allegedly, the controversial clause allowed him to transfer to a Triple-A franchise. Consider the First Circuit's truncated analysis and conclusion:

> We have been unable to find any Maine case deciding whether specific performance is appropriate with respect to the sale of a franchise. The few courts that have addressed this issue have all decided that specific performance was appropriate. ... In *DeBauge Brothers, Inc. v. Whitsitt*, 512 P.2d 487, 489 (Kan. 1973), the Supreme Court of Kansas explained its holding in favor of specific performance ... [by stressing that franchises] are by their very nature unique and exclusive, which is the source of their value to the possessor. Similarly, a Florida court has stated: Sale of businesses including franchises and good will have frequently been the subject of specific enforcement in equity. *Hogan v. Norfleet*, 113 So.2d 437, 439 (Fla. Dist. Ct. App. 1959). ... We think the facts of this case bring it well within the ambit of the rules requiring specific performance. The contract's terms are unambiguous; there is no problem in drafting a clear order. ... The same factors that impelled specific performance of the sale of corporate stock in *Northeast Invest. Co., Inc. v. Leisure Liv. Com., Inc.*, 351 A.2d at 855–56, are present here: the Triple-A franchise has no readily ascertainable market value, it cannot be easily obtained from other sources, and it is of special interest to NBI. There can be no doubt that what NBI sought, a Triple-A franchise, was unique.

C. "Unjust Enrichment" and an Action for *Quantum Meruit*

Consider the following facts. Nadine is the seasoned owner and operator of a real estate brokerage firm. Festus is a manager; he works for Nexus-App Corporation. Festus called Nadine and reported that Nexus wanted to lease commercial office space in Dallas. Nadine compiled a list of various properties. Empire Ventures owns Centre Plaza, which was on the list. Festus expressed an interest in Centre Plaza and he encouraged Nadine to determine if Centre Plaza met several unique requirements. Nadine contacted Empire. Shortly thereafter, Empire faxed a proposal to Nadine and she relayed the proposal to Festus. In fact, during a four-month period, Nadine negotiated terms and conditions on behalf of Festus and Empire—relaying numerous additional proposals and counterproposals between the parties.

At the beginning of the fifth month, both parties stopped contacting Nadine. She "was in the dark." She repeatedly called Empire's agents, trying to determine the state of the negotiations with Festus. Three weeks later, she learned that Nexus-App Corporation and Empire Ventures had signed a 5-year lease agreement. Immediately, Nadine contacted the CEO of Empire and asked: "Will my brokerage firm receive our full commission, as we were instrumental in bringing the deal to fruition?" Empire's CEO said: "Don't worry about it. You are fine. You are protected." That same day, Nadine sent a letter and an invoice for $51,000 to Empire. The letter encouraged the CEO to pay the full commission. The CEO never responded to the letter and never paid the commission. Nadine filed a lawsuit.

Does Nadine have an enforceable breach-of-contract claim? Does she have an enforceable breach-of-promise claim? She performed before a promise was made. At best, that performance was "past consideration." Can she establish any bargained-for-exchange consideration? Was her performance a gift? Is Empire obligated to pay any amount of money for Nadine's services? In this section, the cases and notes provide answers.

1) The Absence of an Express Employment Contract and the Application of the Quantum Meruit Doctrine in English Courts

Alfred v. Marquis of Fitzjames
3 Espinasse 3,
170 Eng. Rep. 518 (1799)

Assumpsit for servant's wages. The plaintiff proved his employment as a servant in the family of the defendant, and relied on a *quantum meruit*—for the time he had served.

It appeared in evidence that the plaintiff came over from Martinique with the Duchess of Fitzjames, then Mademoiselle Le Brun. His father and mother had been slaves on an estate belonging to her in that island. He had entered into her service in Martinique and continued to serve her after her marriage. [A]nd the Duke found him with necessaries of every description.

There was no contract for any hiring for wages; but a witness said that the Marquis had been heard to promise to pay him wages.

Lord Kenyon asked Mr. Erskine, counsel for the defendant, if he objected to the demand *in toto*. Mr. Erskine said he did—That the contract was not a contract for any wages in Martinique and had so continued in this country [England] without any variation.

Lord Kenyon said he was prepared to give a decided opinion[:] That up to the time of the promise to pay wages—which the witness had said the defendant had made—the plaintiff had no title to recover, as there was no original contract of service for wages.

2) The Absence of Express Employment Contracts and the Application of the Quantum Meruit Doctrine in American Courts

Livingston v. Ackeston
5 Cow. 531 1826 WL 2035
(N.Y. Sup. Ct. 1826)

The action below was assumpsit for work and labor by Ackeston against Livingston. ... Ackeston, a black man, worked for Livingston from the spring of 1819 till June, 1820, when he sold him to one Benn. ... Livingston had bought [Ackeston from] one Ham, as a slave or servant, at $200 ... and ... he was to serve till he was 28 years old. ... [Livingston] became dissatisfied and procured Benn to purchase [Ackeston from] Livingston. ... Ackeston was born of black parents, who kept house and acted for themselves as long ago as 1798, in which year he was born. The parents had before been slaves to one Dings. Ham had also bought Ackeston as a servant till he was 28. He was sold to Livingston at 16 years and 4 months old.

The counsel for the defendant below moved for a nonsuit, on the ground that there was no contract to pay wages, and none could be implied, between the parties. But the motion was overruled.

Where one bought the time of a Negro till he should be 28 years old, both he and the Negro supposing the latter to be bound to serve till that time, it was held that, though the Negro was in fact free, yet he could not maintain an action for his services. D. B. Tallmadge, for [Livingston], cited ... *Alfred v. Marquis of Fitzjames*, 3 Esp. Rep. 3.

The plaintiff knew and admitted that the defendant had purchased his time until he was 28 years of age; that he paid 200 dollars for it; that he was entitled to his services. He procured another person to purchase the unexpired term of his services, from the defendant; thereby admitting the defendant's right to sell it. The law, under such circumstances, cannot raise an implied assumpsit.

The case of *Alfred v. Fitzjames,* 3 Esp. Rep. 4 is precisely in point. It appeared, in that case, that the plaintiff, a colored man, came over from Martinique with the dutchess of Fitz James, having been born a slave on an estate belonging to her in that Island. There was no contract of hiring for wages; but a witness said the marquis had been heard to promise him wages. Lord Kenyon ruled, that up to the time of the promise to pay wages, the plaintiff could not recover, as there was no original contract of service for wages.

Judgment reversed.

3) Special Contracts and the Application of the Quantum Meruit Doctrine in American Courts

Britton v. Turner
6 N.H. 481
(N.H. 1834)

Assumpsit for work and labour performed by the plaintiff, in the service of the defendant, from March 9th, 1831, to December 27, 1831. The declaration contained the common counts, and among them a count in *quantum meruit*, for the labor, averring it to be worth one hundred dollars. At the trial in the C.C. Pleas, the plaintiff proved the performance of the labor as set forth in the declaration.

The defence was that it was performed under a special contract—that the plaintiff agreed to work one year, from sometime in March, 1831 to March 1832, and that the defendant was to pay him for said year's labor the sum of one hundred and twenty dollars; and the defendant offered evidence tending to show that such was the contract under which the work was done. Evidence was also offered to show that the plaintiff left the defendant's service without his consent, and it was contended by the defendant that the plaintiff had no good cause for not continuing in his employment. There was no evidence offered of any damage arising from the plaintiff's departure, farther than was to be inferred from his non-fulfilment of the entire contract.

The court instructed the jury, that if they were satisfied from the evidence that the labor was performed, under a contract to labor a year, for the sum of one hundred and twenty dollars, and if they were satisfied that the plaintiff labored only the time specified in the declaration, and then left the defendant's service, against his consent, and without any good cause, yet the plaintiff was entitled to recover, under his *quantum meruit* count, as much as the labor he performed was reasonably worth, and under this direction the jury gave a verdict for the plaintiff for the sum of $95.

The defendant excepted to the instructions thus given to the jury. …

Parker, J. It may be assumed, that the labor performed by the plaintiff, and for which he seeks to recover a compensation in this action, was commenced under a special contract to labor for the defendant the term of one year, for the sum of one hundred and twenty dollars, and that the plaintiff has labored but a portion of that time, and has voluntarily failed to complete the entire contract. It is clear, then, that he is not entitled to recover upon the contract itself, because the service, which was to entitle him to the sum agreed upon, has never been performed. But the question arises, can the plaintiff, under these circumstances, recover a reasonable sum for the service he has actually performed, under the count in *quantum meruit*. Upon this, and questions of a similar nature, the decisions to be found in the books are not easily reconciled.

It has been held, upon contracts of this kind for labor to be performed at a specified price, that the party who voluntarily fails to fulfil the contract by performing the whole labor contracted for, is not entitled to recover any thing for the labor actually performed, however much he may have done towards the performance, and this has been considered the settled rule of law upon this subject. ... That such rule in its operation may be very unequal, not to say unjust, is apparent.

A party who contracts to perform certain specified labor, and who breaks his contract in the first instance, without any attempt to perform it, can only be made liable to pay the damages which the other party has sustained by reason of such nonperformance, which in many instances may be trifling—whereas a party who in good faith has entered upon the performance of his contract, and nearly completed it, and then abandoned the further performance—although the other party has had the full benefit of all that has been done, and has perhaps sustained no actual damage—is in fact subjected to a loss of all which has been performed, in the nature of damages for the non-fulfilment of the remainder, upon the technical rule, that the contract must be fully performed in order to [obtain] a recovery of any part of the compensation.

By the operation of this rule, then, the party who attempts performance may be placed in a much worse situation than he who wholly disregards his contract, and the other party may receive much more, by the breach of the contract, than the injury which he has sustained by such breach, and more than he could be entitled to were he seeking to recover damages by an action.

The case before us presents an illustration. Had the plaintiff in this case never entered upon the performance of his contract, the damage could not probably have been greater than some small expense and trouble incurred in procuring another to do the labor which he had contracted to perform. But having entered upon the performance, and labored nine and a half months, the value of which labor to the defendant as found by the jury is $95[.] [I]f the defendant can succeed in this defence, he in fact receives nearly five sixths of the value of a whole year's labor, by reason of the breach of contract by the plaintiff a sum not only utterly disproportionate to any probable, not to say possible damage which could have resulted from the neglect of the plaintiff to continue the remaining two and an half months, but altogether beyond any damage which could have been recovered by the defendant, had the plaintiff done nothing towards the fulfilment of his contract. …

There are other cases, however, in which principles have been adopted leading to a different result. It is said, that where a party contracts to perform certain work, and to furnish materials, as, for instance, to build a house, and the work is done, but with some variations from the mode prescribed by the contract, yet if the other party has the benefit of the labor and materials he should be bound to pay so much as they are reasonable. …

Those cases are not to be distinguished, in principle, from the present, unless it be in the circumstance, that where the party has contracted to furnish materials, and do certain labor, as to build a house in a specified manner, if it is not done according to the contract, the party for whom it is built may refuse to receive it—elect to take no benefit from what has been performed—and therefore if he does receive, he shall be bound to pay the value—whereas in a contract for labor, merely, from day to day, the party is continually receiving the benefit of the contract under an expectation that it will be fulfilled, and cannot, upon the breach of it, have an election to refuse to receive what has been done, and thus discharge himself from payment. But we think this difference in the nature of the contracts does not justify the application of a different rule in relation to them.

The party who contracts for labor merely, for a certain period, does so with full knowledge that he must, from the nature of the case, be accepting part performance from day to day, if the other party commences the performance, and with knowledge also that the other may eventually fail of completing the entire term. If under such circumstances he actually receives a benefit from the labor performed, over and above the damage occasioned by the failure to complete, there is as much reason why he should pay the reasonable worth of what has thus been done for his benefit, as there is when he enters and occupies the house which has been built for him, but not according to the stipulations of the contract, and which he perhaps enters, not because he is satisfied with what has been done, but because circumstances compel him to accept it such as it is, that he should pay for the value of the house. …

It is as "hard upon the plaintiff to preclude him from recovering at all, because he has failed as to part of his entire undertaking," where his contract is to labor for a certain period, as it can be in any other description of contract, provided the defendant has received a benefit and value from the labor actually performed.

We hold then, that where a party undertakes to pay upon a special contract for the performance of labor, or the furnishing of materials, he is not to be charged upon such special agreement until the money is earned according to the terms of it, and where the parties have made an express contract the law will not imply and raise a contract different from that which the parties have entered into, except upon some farther transaction between the parties.

In case of a failure to perform such special contract, by the default of the party contracting to do the service, if the money is not due by the terms of the special agreement he is not entitled to recover for his labor, or for the materials furnished, unless the other party receives what has been done, or furnished, and upon the whole case derives a benefit from it.

But if, where a contract is made of such a character, a party actually receives labor, or materials, and thereby derives a benefit and advantage, over and above the damage which has resulted from the breach of the contract by the other party, the labor actually done, and the value received, furnish a new consideration, and the law thereupon raises a promise to pay to the extent of the reasonable worth of such excess. This may be considered as making a new case, one not within the original agreement, and the party is entitled to "recover on his new case, for the work done, not as agreed, but yet accepted by the defendant." ...

In fact we think the technical reasoning, that the performance of the whole labor is a condition precedent, and the right to recover any thing dependent upon it—that the contract being entire there can be no apportionment—and that there being an express contract no other can be implied, even upon the subsequent performance of service—is not properly applicable to this species of contract, where a beneficial service has been actually performed; for we have abundant reason to believe, that the general understanding of the community is, that the hired laborer shall be entitled to compensation for the service actually performed, though he do not continue the entire term contracted for, and such contracts must be presumed to be made with reference to that understanding, unless an express stipulation shows the contrary. ...

It is easy, if parties so choose, to provide by an express agreement that nothing shall be earned, if the laborer leaves his employer without having performed the whole service contemplated, and then there can be no pretense for a recovery if he voluntarily deserts the service before the expiration of the time. The amount, however, for which the employer ought to be charged, where the laborer abandons his contract, is only the reasonable worth, or the amount of advantage he receives upon the whole transaction ... and, in estimating the value of the labor, the contract price for the service cannot be exceeded. ...

This rule, by binding the employer to pay the value of the service he actually receives, and the laborer to answer in damages where he does not complete the entire contract, will leave no temptation to the former to drive the laborer from his service, near the close of his term, by ill treatment, in order to escape from payment; nor to the latter to desert his service before the stipulated time, without a sufficient reason; and it will in most instances settle the whole controversy in one action, and prevent a multiplicity of suits and cross actions. ...

The defendant sets up a mere breach of the contract in defence of the action, but this cannot avail him. He does not appear to have offered evidence to show that he was damnified by such breach, or to have asked that a deduction should be made upon that account. The direction to the jury was therefore correct, that the plaintiff was entitled to recover as much as the labor performed was reasonably worth, and the jury appear to have allowed a pro rata compensation, for the time which the plaintiff labored in the defendant's service. ...

Judgment on the verdict.

NOTES AND QUESTIONS

1. **The Purpose of the *Quantum Meruit* Doctrine**. *Quantum meruit* is "generally awarded when one party confers some benefit upon another without receiving just compensation for the reasonable value of the services rendered." *Aultman Hosp. Assn. v. Community Mut. Ins. Co.*, 46 Ohio St.3d 51, 55 (Ohio 1989). Therefore, the purpose of the remedy is to prevent an offending party from becoming unjustly enriched.

2. **Whether or Not Proof of an Express Contract Is a Prerequisite for a *Quantum Meruit* Award**. In *Alfred v. Marquis of Fitzjames*, Lord Kenyon concluded that Alfred could not recover under the doctrine of *quantum meruit* because he could not produce an "original contract of service for wages." And citing Lord Kenyon's rule, the New York Supreme Court concluded in *Livingston v. Ackeston* that "the law, under such circumstances, [could] raise an implied assumpsit." Therefore, in the hypothetical conflict between Nadine—the real estate broker—and Empire Ventures, Nadine would not prevail under the principles stated in *Alfred* and *Livingston*. But consider what appears in THE LECTRIC LAW LIBRARY'S LEXICON ON QUANTUM MERUIT:

   Quantum Meruit means "as much as he has deserved." When a person employs another to do work for him—*without any agreement as to his compensation,* the law *implies a promise* from, the employer to the workman that he will pay him for his services, as much as he may deserve or merit. In such case, the plaintiff may suggest in his declaration that the defendant promised to pay him as much as he reasonably deserved, and then aver that his trouble was worth such a sum of money, which the defendant has omitted to pay. This is called an assumpsit on a *quantum meruit*. When there is an *express contract for a stipulated amount* and mode of compensation for services, the plaintiff cannot abandon the contract and resort to an action for a *quantum meruit* on an implied assumpsit.

3. ***Quantum Meruit*, Quasi-Contracts, Contracts Implied in Law, and Legal Fictions**. An equitable action for *quantum meruit* is different from, say, a breach of an-implied-in-law contract action. But both doctrines are bases on legal fictions. The court in *City of Indianapolis v. Twin Lakes Enter., Inc.*, 568 N.E.2d 1073, 1078 (Ind. Ct. App. 1991) informs the reader that *quantum meruit* is a legal fiction and that it is "a breach of contract remedy available to an innocent party to recover the value of services performed under the contract." It "seeks to provide the injured party with the fair value of work and services rendered and thus prevent the unjust enrichment of another." *Id.* Similar doctrines—quasi-contract, contract-implied-in-law, or constructive-contract—share the same purpose as *quantum meruit*. By operation of law and equitable principles, these doctrines permit a remedy where "no contract exists in fact but where justice nevertheless warrants a recovery under the circumstance as though there had been a promise." *Id. See also Legros v. Tarr*, 44 Ohio St.3d 1, 7–8 (1989) (stressing that *quantum meruit* is not based on contract-implied-in-law principles. Instead, it evolves by operation of law.).

4. **General Rules—The Extent of Plaintiff's Recovery Under the Doctrine of *Quantum Meruit***. First, it is important to repeat: An action for *quantum meruit* involves courts' applying equitable principles to the facts and circumstances. *Natl. City Bank v. Fleming*, 2 Ohio App.3d 50, 57–58 (Ohio Ct. App. 1981). Consequently, the amount which a party may recover under the theory of *quantum meruit* is subject to a double limitation: 1) a plaintiff may not recover more than the actual value of the services rendered for defendant—including the value of materials and fair profit and 2) a plaintiff may not recover an amount that exceeds defendant's unjust enrichment. *Sonkin & Melena Co., L.P.A. v. Zaransky*, 83 Ohio App.3d 169, 176 (Ohio Ct. App. 1992).

CHAPTER SIX

Common-Law Affirmative Defenses

A careful reading of the cases in CHAPTERS 1–5 reveals that defendants defend themselves in various ways. For example, after plaintiffs file breach-of-promise, breach-of-contract, and breach-of-warranty actions, some defendants answer the lawsuits by asserting general and specific denials. *See Petty v. Clark*, 129 P.2d 568, 571 (Utah 1942) ("A specific denial ... specifically points out and denies a particular allegation. ... A general denial, without attempting to point out particular allegations, denies every material allegation in the complaint which it will be necessary for the plaintiff to prove in order to recover.").

However, the aggregate of the remaining defendants answer and raise affirmative defenses like those listed in *City and County of San Francisco v. O'Flynn*, 2012 WL 968059, *10 n. 8 (Cal. Ct. App. Mar. 22, 2012). The *O'Flynn* court reports:

> In his first amended answer to the City's first amended complaint, O'Flynn raised the following affirmative defenses to the breach of contract claim: "no breach of contract"; "failure to join necessary and/or indispensable parties"; "cannot ascertain whether [the] agreement is written, oral or implied"; "enforcement is barred by the statute of limitations"; "enforcement is barred by statute of frauds"; "lack of consideration"; "no contract"; "enforcement is barred by modification, alteration and change of terms"; "contract is unlawful"; "contract

> is contrary to policy of express law"; "contract is contrary to good morals"; "plaintiff [breached] fiduciary and confidential duties"; "intentional misrepresentation"; "negligent misrepresentation"; "concealment or suppression of facts"; "constructive fraud"; "fraud in the execution"; "nonperformance ... by plaintiff"; "damages sought violate the rule against penalties"; "setoff"; "plaintiff has not suffered damages or injury"; "violation of the ... sales act"; "latches"; and "mistake."

Still, some fairly important affirmative defenses do not appear on the *O'Flynn* list and are not discussed in the prior chapters. Furthermore, the *O'Flynn* report contains several major common-law defenses that are not discussed in CHAPTERS 1–5. This chapter, therefore, is devoted to discussing those key defenses.

SECTION ONE: STATUTE-OF-FRAUDS DEFENSE

In 1677, the Parliament of England enacted, "AN ACT FOR PREVENTION OF FRAUDS AND PERJURIES." 29 Car. 2, c. 3 (1677). Today, in most jurisdictions, that act is commonly referred to as the "Statute of Frauds" or the English Statute of Frauds of 1677. The statute's stated purpose was to prohibit fraud and perjury when contracting parties clashed over the enforceability of oral contracts. Although the English Statute of Frauds has been repealed, nearly every state has enacted a statute that contains language that is substantially similar to language that appears in the original act. *See Kiely v. St. Germain*, 670 P.2d 764, 768 (Colo. 1983). More specifically, the repealed Statute of Frauds contained two "model" or highly relevant provisions—sections four and seventeen. Section four read:

> And be it further enacted by the authority aforesaid, That from and after the said four and twentieth day of June no action shall be brought (1) whereby to charge any executor or administrator upon any special promise, to answer damages out of his own estate, (2) or whereby to charge the defendant upon any special promise to answer for the debt, default or miscarriages of another person; (3) or to charge any person upon any agreement made upon consideration of marriage; (4) or upon any contract or sale of lands, tenements, or hereditaments, or any interest in or concerning them; (5) or upon any agreement that is not to be performed within the space of one year from the making thereof; (6) unless the agreement upon which such action shall be brought, or some memorandum or note thereof, shall be in writing, and signed by the party to

> be charged therewith, or some other person thereunto by him lawfully authorized.

Section seventeen stated:

> And be it further enacted by the authority aforesaid, That from and after the said four and twentieth day of June no contract for the sale of any goods, wares and merchandizes, for the price of ten pounds sterling or upwards, shall be allowed to be good, except the buyer shall accept part of the goods so sold, and actually receive the same, or give something in earnest to bind the bargain, or in part payment, or that some note or memorandum in writing of the said bargain be made and signed by the parties to be charged by such contract, or their agents thereto lawfully authorized.

Generally, legislatures in the United States used the English Statute of Frauds § 4 to fashion their own statutes. And the drafters of the Uniform Commercial Code used the Statute of Frauds § 17 to craft section 2-201 of the UCC.

To repeat, the title of the English statute clearly states its purpose—to prevent frauds and perjuries. When English common law was changed to allow parties to enforce oral contracts, widespread perjury became a major problem. *C. R. Klewin, Inc. v. Flagship Properties, Inc.*, 600 A.2d 772, 775 (Conn. 1991). Quite simply, lies and untruths became prevalent because English law allowed jurors to use their personal knowledge rather than probative evidence to decide breach-of-contract controversies. The statute of frauds changed that procedure by requiring a plaintiff to produce a written and signed contract.

In modern times, *legislatures* have advanced at least three reasons to justify the continued use of statutes of frauds: 1) The statute is an effective evidentiary weapon to combat perjury; 2) Its cautionary effect forces the parties to understand and appreciate the significance of their agreement; and 3) It is a channeling device that distinguishes enforceable contracts from unenforceable contracts. *See Wior v. Anchor Industries, Inc.*, 669 N.E.2d 172, 174 (Ind. 1996). Nevertheless, *some courts* have created exceptions to the general rule. Do the exceptions to the general rule increase the likelihood of perjury and fraudulent statements? Then again, other courts have refused to undermine legislative intent and avoid "weakening" the statute of frauds. Consequently, there are conflicting rulings. As you read the next two cases and notes, try to answer this question: Is possible to harmonize the conflicting positions?

A. Oral Contracts, the Statute-of-Frauds Defense, and the Material Benefit Rule

Boone v. Coe
154 S.W. 900
(Ky. 1913)

CLAY, C. Plaintiffs, W. H. Boone and J. T. Coe, brought this action against defendant, J. F. Coe, to recover certain damages, alleged to have resulted from defendant's breach of a parol contract of lease for one year to commence at a future date. It appears from the petition that the defendant was the owner of a large and valuable farm in Ford County, Tex. Plaintiffs were farmers and were living with their families in Monroe County, Ky. In the fall of 1909 defendant made a verbal contract with plaintiffs, whereby he rented to them his farm in Texas for a period of 12 months, to commence from the date of plaintiffs' arrival at defendant's farm.

Defendant agreed that if plaintiffs would leave their said homes and businesses in Kentucky, and with their families, horses, and wagons, move to defendant's farm in Texas, and take charge of, manage, and cultivate same in wheat, corn, and cotton for the 12 months next following plaintiffs' arrival at said farm, the defendant would have a dwelling completed on said farm and ready for occupancy upon their arrival, which dwelling plaintiffs would occupy as a residence during the period of said tenancy. Defendant also agreed that he would furnish necessary material at a convenient place on said farm out of which to erect a good and commodious stock and grain barn, to be used by plaintiffs.

The petition further alleges that plaintiffs were to cultivate certain portions of the farm, and were to receive certain portions of the crops raised, and that plaintiffs, in conformity with their said agreement, did move from Kentucky to the farm in Texas, and carried with them their families, wagons, horses, and camping outfit, and in going to Texas they traveled for a period of 55 days. It is also charged that defendant broke his contract, in that he failed to have ready and completed on the farm a dwelling house in which plaintiffs and their families could move, and also failed to furnish the necessary material for the erection of a suitable barn; that on December 6th defendant refused to permit plaintiffs to occupy the house and premises, and failed and refused to permit them to cultivate the land or any part thereof; that on the ___ day of December, 1909, they started for their home in Kentucky, and arrived there after traveling for a period of 4 days.

It is charged that plaintiffs spent in going to Texas, in cash, the sum of $150; that the loss of time to plaintiffs and their teams in making the trip to Texas was reasonably worth $8 a day for a period of 55 days, or the sum of $440; that the loss of time to them and their teams during the period they remained in Texas was $8 a day for 22 days, or $176; that they paid out in actual cash for transportation for themselves, families, and teams from Texas to Kentucky the sum of $211.80; that the loss of time to them and their teams in making the last-named trip was reasonably worth the sum of $100; that in abandoning and giving up their homes and businesses in Kentucky they had been damaged in the sum of $150, making a total damage of $1,387.80, for which judgment was asked. Defendant's demurrer to the petition was sustained and the petition dismissed. Plaintiffs appeal.

Under the rule in force in this state the statute of frauds relates to the remedy or mode of procedure, and not to the validity of the contract. Though the land is located in Texas, the parol contract of lease was made here, and here it is sought to enforce it. If unenforceable under our statute, it cannot be enforced here. If the statute requires the contract to be in writing, and the petition does not allege it to be in writing, defense may be presented by demurrer.

The statute of frauds—§ 470, subsections 6 and 7, KENTUCKY STATUTES—provides as follows:

> No action shall be brought to charge any person: 6) Upon any contract for the sale of real estate, or any lease thereof, for longer term than one year; nor 7) Upon any agreement which is not to be performed within one year from the making thereof, unless the promise, contract, agreement, representation, assurance, or ratification, or some memorandum or note thereof, be in writing, and signed by the party to be charged therewith, or by his authorized agent; but the consideration need not be expressed in the writing; it may be proved when necessary, or disproved by parol or other evidence.

A parol lease of land for one year, to commence at a future date, is within the statute. *Greenwood v. Strother*, 91 Ky. 482, 16 S. W. 138, 13 Ky. Law Rep. 33. The question sharply presented is: May plaintiffs recover for expenses incurred and time lost on the faith of a contract that is unenforceable under the statute of frauds? …

[I]t is the general rule that damages cannot be recovered for violation of a contract within the statute of frauds. … To this general rule there are certain well-recognized exceptions. … [In] a number of other cases, it has been held that, where services have been rendered during the life of another, on the promise that the person rendering the service should receive at the death of the person served a legacy, and the contract so made is within the statute of frauds, a reasonable compensation may be recovered for the services actually rendered. It has also been held that the vendee of land under a parol contract is entitled to recover any portion of the purchase money he may have paid, and is also entitled to compensation for improvements. …

And under a contract for personal services, within the statute an action may be maintained on a *quantum meruit*. ... The doctrine of these cases proceeds upon the theory that the defendant has actually received some benefits from the acts of part performance; and the law therefore implies a promise to pay. In 29 AM. & ENG. ENCY. 836, the rule is thus stated:

> Although part performance by one of the parties to a contract within the statute of frauds will not, at law, entitle such party to recover upon the contract itself, he may nevertheless recover for money paid by him, or property delivered, or services rendered in accordance with and upon the faith of the contract. The law will raise an implied promise on the part of the other party to pay for what has been done in the way of part performance. But this right of recovery is not absolute. The plaintiff is entitled to compensation only under such circumstances as would warrant a recovery in case there was no express contract; and hence it must appear that the defendant has actually received, or will receive, some benefit from the acts of part performance. It is immaterial that the plaintiff may have suffered a loss because he is unable to enforce his contract.

In BROWN ON STATUTE OF FRAUDS, § 118a, the rule is announced in the following language:

> The rule that, where one person pays money or performs services for another upon a contract void under the statute of frauds, he may recover the money upon a count for money paid, or recover for the services upon a *quantum meruit*, applies only to cases where the defendant has received and holds the money paid or the benefit of the services rendered. It does not apply to cases of money paid by the plaintiff to a third person in execution of a verbal contract between the plaintiff and defendant, such as by the statute of frauds must be in writing. ...

In the case under consideration, the plaintiffs merely sustained a loss. Defendant received no benefit. Had he received a benefit, the law would imply an obligation to pay therefor. Having received no benefit, no obligation to pay is implied. The statute says that the contract of defendant made with plaintiffs is unenforceable. Defendant therefore had the legal right to decline to carry it out. To require him to pay plaintiffs for losses and expenses incurred on the faith of the contract, without any benefit accruing to him, would, in effect, uphold a contract upon which the statute expressly declares no action shall be brought.

The statute was enacted for the purpose of preventing frauds and perjuries. That it is a valuable statute is shown by the fact that similar statutes are in force in practically all, if not all, of the states of the Union. Being a valuable statute, the purpose of the lawmakers in its enactment should not be defeated by permitting recoveries in cases to which its provisions were intended to apply.

The contrary rule was announced by this court in the case of *McDaniel v. Hutcherson*, 124 S. W. 384 (Ky. 1910). There the plaintiff lived in the state of Illinois. The defendant owned a farm in Mercer County, Ky. The defendant agreed with plaintiff that if plaintiff and his family would come to Kentucky and live with defendant the defendant would furnish the plaintiff a home during defendant's life, and upon his death would give plaintiff his farm. It was held that, although the contract was within the statute of frauds, plaintiff could recover his reasonable expenses in moving to Kentucky, and reasonable compensation for loss sustained in giving up his business elsewhere. Upon reconsideration of the question involved, we conclude that the doctrine announced in that case is not in accord with the weight of authority, and should be no longer adhered to. It is therefore overruled.

Judgment affirmed.

NOTES AND QUESTIONS

1. **Texas Rule of Civil Procedure 94—Pleadings of Defendant.**

   The rule reads:

   AFFIRMATIVE DEFENSES

   In pleading to a preceding pleading, a party shall set forth affirmatively accord and satisfaction, arbitration and award, assumption of risk, contributory negligence, discharge in bankruptcy, duress, estoppel, failure of consideration, fraud, illegality, injury by fellow servant, laches, license, payment, release, res judicata, statute of frauds, statute of limitations, waiver, and any other matter constituting an avoidance or affirmative defense. Where the suit is on an insurance contract which insures against certain general hazards, but contains other provisions limiting such general liability, the party suing on such contract shall never be required to allege that the loss was not due to a risk or cause coming within any of the exceptions specified in the contract, nor shall the insurer be allowed to raise such issue unless it shall specifically allege that the loss was due to a risk or cause coming within a particular exception to the general liability; provided that nothing herein shall be construed to change the burden of proof on such issue as it now exists.

2. **English Statute of Frauds and the Puzzling Purpose of the One-Year Provision**. Section 4 of the Statute of Frauds states that a contract or a related memorandum must be in writing if it takes the parties more than a year to perform their contractual obligations. Why did the English Parliament embrace a one-year rule rather than a rule based on the contract price? Why did Parliament force parties to put "simple" agreements in writing, if performance could not occur within twelve months? Is the one-year rule sound? Some jurists and commentators say no. *See, e.g.* 2 FARNSWORTH, § 6.4, at 130–131. He writes:

    The one-year provision is ill-contrived if it is based on the tendency of memory to fail and of evidence to go stale with the passage of time. The one-year period does not run from the time that the contract is made to the time for proof that it was made, but from the time that the contract was made to the time for completion of performance. If an oral contract that cannot be performed within a year is broken the day after it making, the provision applies though the terms of the contract are fresh in the minds of the parties. But if an oral contract that can be performed within a year is broken and suit is not brought until nearly six years (the usual statute of limitations for contract actions) after the breach, the provision does not apply, even though the terms of the contract are no longer fresh in the minds of the parties.

    The one-year provision is equally ill-contrived if it is an attempt to separate significant contracts of long duration, for which writings should be required, from less significant contracts of short duration, for which writings are unnecessary. The one-year period does not run from the time for commencement of performance to the time for completion of performance, but from the time that the contract is made to the time for completion of performance.

3. **Statute-of-Frauds Defense and the Enforcement of Orally Modified Contracts.** Does the statute of frauds prevent the enforcement of an orally modified provision in a contract? In *Bamberger Co. v. Certified Productions*, 48 P.2d 489, 490–91 (Utah 1935), the Supreme Court of Utah addressed that question this way:

    The defendant corporation set up as an answer to both causes of action that there were supplemental agreements which modified the original lease, and that such supplemental agreements in reference to the covenants and conditions which plaintiffs claim were broken were acted upon by the corporate defendant, and that it materially changed its position in reliance upon them. Nothing is said in either defense as to the supplemental agreements or modifications being in writing.

The lease, being for a period of ten years, was governed by the statute of frauds (Rev. St. 1933, 33-5-3). … [W]hile the answer was silent as to the character of the modification, both sides treated it as being oral and a motion to strike as hereunder set forth was argued as if it had been pleaded as oral. … The parties first divide on the question as to whether an oral modification of an agreement required to be in writing by the statute of frauds can be set up as a defense, granted it is shown in addition that the defendant had acted on said oral modification and had performed in accordance therewith and materially changed its position by reason thereof.

Many cases have been cited to the effect that such oral modification may be enforced where the modification or new agreement has been executed, or where the particular part of the original agreement changed or modified is not one required to be by the statute of frauds in writing, or where the party seeking to avoid the oral agreement has received material benefit therefrom, or where the situation is such as to work an estoppel of the party seeking to avoid the effect of the agreement, or where such modification constitutes a waiver of the original terms of the contract.

At the outset, it may be said that there is no question but that parties may orally modify an agreement in writing where the original contract is not required by the statute of frauds to be in writing, at least where there is consideration for such modification. We make no statement concerning the case where the original contract is not required to be in writing, but the matter covered by the modification is in reference to a subject covered by the statute of frauds. A different question presents itself when the original contract is required by the statute of frauds to be in writing.

As a broad general doctrine, it may be announced that a contract required by the statute of frauds to be in writing cannot be modified by a subsequent oral agreement. At the moment the principle is thus announced, it is immediately subject to many and varied exceptions. The first great division comes between executory and executed modifications. Even where the contract is still executory and specific performance is asked, or where an action is brought, on the contract as originally written, for failure to perform and the modification is set up as a defense to the alleged failure, or where the action is brought upon the original contract with its oral modifications as the basis of the suit and defense to the action is made on the ground that such contract was not wholly in writing, the courts have recognized the validity of the oral modifications in certain cases.

The rule that there can be no oral modification of a contract required by the statute of frauds to be in writing has been most rigidly enforced in England where, as a general rule, even an oral modification permitting an extension of time in which to perform has been held invalid. Most of the courts of this country hold, as a general rule, that an oral modification of a contract required by the statute of frauds to be in writing will not be permitted. Exceptions have been made by some courts where the matter in the original contract which has been modified was not such matter as was required to be in writing. Other courts have made a supposed distinction between matters relating to performance, permitting such matters to be modified. This would appear to be a difficult line to draw because most of the provisions of the contract are to be performed. …

It is claimed by the corporate defendant in this case that the modified part of the contract was by it performed. Consequently we may proceed immediately to a consideration as to whether an oral modification which has been acted upon is valid. Here again, there is a division of authority. The note in A. L. R. cites in the United States, California, Illinois, Kansas, Minnesota, Mississippi, Nebraska, New York, North Carolina, Ohio, Oregon, Pennsylvania, Washington, and Wisconsin, as states in which it has been held that where an agreement as modified has been acted upon the rights of the parties are to be determined by the modified agreement.

As stated by Mr. Justice Cardozo, then justice of the Court of Appeals of New York, in *Imperator Realty Co. v. Tull*, 228 N. Y. 447, 127 N. E. 263, 266: "Sometimes the resulting disability has been characterized as an estoppel, sometimes as a waiver. … We need not go into the question of the accuracy of the description. … The truth is that we are facing a principle more nearly ultimate than either waiver or estoppel, one with roots in the yet larger principle that no one shall be permitted to found any claim upon his own inequity or take advantage of his own wrong. … The statute of frauds was not intended to offer an asylum of escape from that fundamental principle of justice."

We accept this principle. If a party has changed his position by performing an oral modification so that it would be inequitable to permit the other party to found a claim upon the original agreement as unmodified or defeat the former's claim by setting up a defense that performance was not according to the written contract, after he has induced or consented to the former going forward, the modified agreement should be held valid.

B. Oral Contracts, the Statute-of-Frauds Defense, and the Doctrine of Estoppel

McIntosh v. Murphy
469 P.2d 177
(Haw. 1970)

Levinson, Justice. This case involves an oral employment contract which allegedly violates the provision of the Statute of Frauds requiring "any agreement that is not to be performed within one year from the making thereof" to be in writing in order to be enforceable. HRS § 656-1(5). In this action the plaintiff-employee Dick McIntosh seeks to recover damages from his employer, George Murphy and Murphy Motors, Ltd., for the breach of an alleged one-year oral employment contract.

While the facts are in sharp conflict, it appears that defendant George Murphy was in southern California during March, 1964 interviewing prospective management personnel for his Chevrolet-Oldsmobile dealerships in Hawaii. He interviewed the plaintiff twice during that time.

The position of sales manager for one of the dealerships was fully discussed but no contract was entered into. In April, 1964 the plaintiff received a call from the general manager of Murphy Motors informing him of possible employment within thirty days if he was still available. The plaintiff indicated his continued interest and informed the manager that he would be available.

Later in April, the plaintiff sent Murphy a telegram to the effect that he would arrive in Honolulu on Sunday, April 26, 1964. Murphy then telephoned McIntosh on Saturday, April 25, 1964 to notify him that the job of assistant sales manager was open and work would begin on the following Monday, April 27, 1964. At that time McIntosh expressed surprise at the change in job title from sales manager to assistant sales manager but reconfirmed the fact that he was arriving in Honolulu the next day, Sunday. McIntosh arrived on Sunday, April 26, 1964 and began work on the following day, Monday, April 27, 1964.

As a consequence of his decision to work for Murphy, McIntosh moved some of his belongings from the mainland to Hawaii, sold other possessions, leased an apartment in Honolulu and obviously forwent any other employment opportunities. In short, the plaintiff did all those things which were incidental to changing one's residence permanently from Los Angeles to Honolulu, a distance of approximately 2200 miles. McIntosh continued working for Murphy until July 16, 1964, approximately two and one-half months, at which time he was discharged on the grounds that he was unable to close deals with prospective customers and could not train the salesmen.

At the conclusion of the trial, the defense moved for a directed verdict arguing that the oral employment agreement was in violation of the Statute of Frauds, there being no written memorandum or note thereof. The trial court ruled that as a matter of law the contract did not come within the Statute, reasoning that Murphy bargained for acceptance by the actual commencement of performance by McIntosh, so that McIntosh was not bound by a contract until he came to work on Monday, April 27, 1964. Therefore, assuming that the contract was for a year's employment, it was performable within a year exactly to the day and no writing was required for it to be enforceable.

Alternatively, the court ruled that if the agreement was made final by the telephone call between the parties on Saturday, April 25, 1964, then that part of the weekend which remained would not be counted in calculating the year, thus taking the contract out of the Statute of Frauds. With commendable candor, the trial judge gave as the motivating force for the decision his desire to avoid a mechanical and unjust application of the Statute.

The case went to the jury on the following questions: 1) whether the contract was for a year's duration or was performable on a trial basis, thus making it terminable at the will of either party; 2) whether the plaintiff was discharged for just cause; and 3) if he was not discharged for just cause, what damages were due the plaintiff. The jury returned a verdict for the plaintiff in the sum of $12,103.40. The defendants appeal to this court on four principal grounds, three of which we find to be without merit. The remaining ground of appeal is whether the plaintiff can maintain an action on the alleged oral employment contract in light of the prohibition of the Statute of Frauds making unenforceable an oral contract that is not to be performed within one year.

I. TIME OF ACCEPTANCE OF THE EMPLOYMENT AGREEMENT

The defendants contend that the trial court erred in refusing to give an instruction to the jury that if the employment agreement was made more than one day before the plaintiff began performance, there could be no recovery by the plaintiff. The reason given was that a contract not to be performed within one year from its making is unenforceable if not in writing.

The defendants are correct in their argument that the time of acceptance of an offer is a question of fact for the jury to decide. But the trial court alternatively decided that even if the offer was accepted on the Saturday prior to the commencement of performance, the intervening Sunday and part of Saturday would not be counted in computing the year for the purposes of the Statute of Frauds. The judge stated that Sunday was a non-working day and only a fraction of Saturday was left which he would not count. In any event, there is no need to discuss the relative merits of either ruling since we base our decision in this case on the doctrine of equitable estoppel which was properly briefed and argued by both parties before this court, although not presented to the trial court.

II. Enforcement by Virtue of Action in Reliance on the Oral Contract

In determining whether a rule of law can be fashioned and applied to a situation where an oral contract admittedly violates a strict interpretation of the Statute of Frauds, it is necessary to review the Statute itself together with its historical and modern functions. The Statute of Frauds, which requires that certain contracts be in writing in order to be legally enforceable, had its inception in the days of Charles II of England. Hawaii's version of the Statute is found in HRS § 656-1 and is substantially the same as the original English Statute of Frauds.

The first English Statute was enacted almost 300 years ago to prevent "many fraudulent practices, which are commonly endeavored to be upheld by perjury and subornation of perjury.". 29 Car. 2, c. 3 (1677). Certainly, there were compelling reasons in those days for such a law. At the time of enactment in England, the jury system was quite unreliable, rules of evidence were few, and the complaining party was disqualified as a witness so he could neither testify on direct-examination nor, more importantly, be cross-examined. The aforementioned structural and evidentiary limitations on our system of justice no longer exist.

Retention of the Statute today has nevertheless been justified on at least three grounds: 1) the Statute still serves an evidentiary function thereby lessening the danger of perjured testimony (the original rationale); 2) the requirement of a writing has a cautionary effect which causes reflection by the parties on the importance of the agreement; and 3) the writing is an easy way to distinguish enforceable contracts from those which are not, thus channeling certain transactions into written form.

In spite of whatever utility the Statute of Frauds may still have, its applicability has been drastically limited by judicial construction over the years in order to mitigate the harshness of a mechanical application. Furthermore, learned writers continue to disparage the Statute regarding it as "a statute for promoting fraud" and a "legal anachronism."

Another method of judicial circumvention of the Statute of Frauds has grown out of the exercise of the equity powers of the courts. Such judicially imposed limitations or exceptions involved the traditional dispensing power of the equity courts to mitigate the "harsh" rule of law. When courts have enforced an oral contract in spite of the Statute, they have utilized the legal labels of "part performance" or "equitable estoppel" in granting relief. Both doctrines are said to be based on the concept of estoppel, which operates to avoid unconscionable injury. 3 WILLISTON, CONTRACTS § 533A at 791 (Jaeger ed. 1960); *Monarco v. Lo Greco*, 35 Cal.2d 621, 220 P.2d 737 (1950).

Part performance has long been recognized in Hawaii as an equitable doctrine justifying the enforcement of an oral agreement for the conveyance of an interest in land where there has been substantial reliance by the party seeking to enforce the contract. *Perreira v. Perreira*, 447 P.2d 667 (Haw. 1968) (agreement to grant life estate); *Vierra v. Shipman*, 26 Haw. 369 (1922) (agreement to devise land); *Yee Hop v. Young Sak Cho*, 25 Haw. 494 (1920) (oral lease of real property). Other courts have enforced oral contracts (including employment contracts) which failed to satisfy the section of the Statute making unenforceable an agreement not to be performed within a year of its making. This has occurred where the conduct of the parties gave rise to an estoppel to assert the Statute. *Oxley v. Ralston Purina Co.*, 349 F.2d 328 (6th Cir. 1965) (equitable estoppel); *Alaska Airlines, Inc. v. Stephenson*, 217 F.2d 295 (9th Cir. 1954) ("promissory estoppel"); *Seymour v. Oelrichs*, 106 P. 88 (Cal. 1909) (equitable estoppel).

It is appropriate for modern courts to cast aside the raiments of conceptualism which cloak the true policies underlying the reasoning behind the many decisions enforcing contracts that violate the Statute of Frauds. There is certainly no need to resort to legal rubrics or meticulous legal formulas when better explanations are available. The policy behind enforcing an oral agreement which violated the Statute of Frauds, as a policy of avoiding unconscionable injury, was well set out by the California Supreme Court. In *Monarco v. Lo Greco*, 220 P.2d 737, 739 (Cal. 1950), a case which involved an action to enforce an oral contract for the conveyance of land on the grounds of 20 years performance by the promisee, the court said:

> The doctrine of estoppel to assert the statute of frauds has been consistently applied by the courts of this state to prevent fraud that would result from refusal to enforce oral

> contracts in certain circumstances. Such fraud may inhere in the unconscionable injury that would result from denying enforcement of the contract after one party has been induced by the other seriously to change his position in reliance on the contract.

In seeking to frame a workable test which is flexible enough to cover diverse factual situations and also provide some reviewable standards, we find very persuasive the RESTATEMENT (SECOND) OF CONTRACTS § 217A. That section specifically covers those situations where there has been reliance on an oral contract which falls within the Statute of Frauds. Section 217A states:

> (1) A promise which the promisor should reasonably expect to induce action or forbearance on the part of the promisee or a third person and which does induce the action or forbearance is enforceable notwithstanding the Statute of Frauds if injustice can be avoided only by enforcement of the promise. The remedy granted for breach is to be limited as justice requires.
>
> (2) In determining whether injustice can be avoided only by enforcement of the promise, the following circumstances are significant: (a) the availability and adequacy of other remedies, particularly cancellation and restitution; (b) the definite and substantial character of the action or forbearance in relation to the remedy sought; (c) the extent to which the action or forbearance corroborates evidence of the making and terms of the promise, or the making and terms are otherwise established by clear and convincing evidence; (d) the reasonableness of the action or forbearance; (e) the extent to which the action or forbearance was foreseeable by the promisor.

We think that the approach taken in the RESTATEMENT is the proper method of giving the trial court the necessary latitude to relieve a party of the hardships of the Statute of Frauds. Other courts have used similar approaches in dealing with oral employment contracts upon which an employee had seriously relied. This is to be preferred over having the trial court bend over backwards to take the contract out of the Statute of Frauds. In the present case, the trial court admitted just this inclination and forthrightly followed it.

There is no dispute that the action of the plaintiff in moving 2200 miles from Los Angeles to Hawaii was foreseeable by the defendant. In fact, it was required to perform his duties. Injustice can only be avoided by the enforcement of the contract and the granting of money damages. No other remedy is adequate. The plaintiff found himself residing in Hawaii without a job.

It is also clear that a contract of some kind did exist. The plaintiff performed the contract for two and one-half months receiving $3,484.60

for his services. The exact length of the contract, whether terminable at will as urged by the defendant, or for a year from the time when the plaintiff started working, was up to the jury to decide.

In sum, the trial court might have found that enforcement of the contract was warranted by virtue of the plaintiff's reliance on the defendant's promise. Naturally, each case turns on its own facts. Certainly there is considerable discretion for a court to implement the true policy behind the Statute of Frauds, which is to prevent fraud or any other type of unconscionable injury. We therefore affirm the judgment of the trial court on the ground that the plaintiff's reliance was such that injustice could only be avoided by enforcement of the contract.

Affirmed.

NOTES AND QUESTIONS

1. **An Exception to the Statute of Frauds Rule—The "Unconscionable Injury" Rule**. In *McIntosh*, the Hawaii Supreme Court embraced the RESTATEMENT'S "unconscionable injury rule" and decided in favor of the plaintiff. How does a complaining party prove an "unconscionable injury"? Or what was the McIntosh court's methodology for establishing that the plaintiff had an unconscionable injury? Is the test or methodology intelligible?

2. **Texas Statute of Frauds.** The Texas "statute of frauds" is found in Tex. Bus. & Com. Code § 26.01. Outlining when a promise or an agreement must be in writing, it reads:

   (a) A promise or agreement described in Subsection (b) of this section is not enforceable unless the promise or agreement, or a memorandum of it, is (1) in writing; and (2) signed by the person to be charged with the promise or agreement or by someone lawfully authorized to sign for him.

   (b) Subsection (a) of this section applies to:

   (1) a promise by an executor or administrator to answer out of his own estate for any debt or damage due from his testator or intestate;

   (2) a promise by one person to answer for the debt, default, or miscarriage of another person;

   (3) an agreement made on consideration of marriage or on consideration of nonmarital conjugal cohabitation;

(4) a contract for the sale of real estate;

(5) a lease of real estate for a term longer than one year;

(6) an agreement which is not to be performed within one year from the date of making the agreement;

(7) a promise or agreement to pay a commission for the sale or purchase of: (A) an oil or gas mining lease; (B) an oil or gas royalty; (C) minerals; or (D) a mineral interest; and

(8) an agreement, promise, contract, or warranty of cure relating to medical care or results thereof made by a physician or health care provider as defined in Section 74.001, Civil Practice and Remedies Code. This section shall not apply to pharmacists.

3. **Enforcement of Oral and Employment-at-Will Contracts, and the Statute-of-Frauds Defense.** The majority in *McIntosh* acknowledged the possibility that an employment-at-will contract governed the employer and employee's rights and obligations. As evidence, Justice Levinson wrote: "The exact length of the contract—whether terminable at will as urged by the defendant or for a year from the time when the plaintiff started working—was up to the jury to decide." Therefore, since Hawaii is an employment-at-will state, why did the court apply the unconscionable-injury rule or the estoppel doctrine, which creates an exception to the statute-of-frauds defense? Is the estoppel doctrine also an exception to the employment-at-will doctrine?

4. **Enforcement of Oral Employment-at-Will Contracts, and the Statute-of-Frauds Defense in Texas**. In *Petkunas v. Virtual Village, Inc.* 2001 WL 664999, *2 (Tex. App.—Dallas, 2001, pet. denied), the Texas Court of Appeals in Dallas addressed the questions raised in Note 3. Consider that court's observations and review of settled rules, which appear in the following bullets:

   - The employment-at-will doctrine permits either the employer or employee to terminate the employment relationship at any time with or without cause. *See Goodyear Tire & Rubber Co. v. Portilla,* 879 S.W.2d 47, 48, n. 1 (Tex. 1994).
   - The at-will employment presumption may only be rebutted by an agreement specifically limiting in a "meaningful and special way" the employer's right to terminate at will. *Massey v. Houston Baptist Univ.,* 902 S.W.2d 81, 83 (Tex. App.—Houston [1st Dist.] 1995, writ denied).

- At-will employment may be modified by an oral agreement. *Morgan v. Jack Brown Cleaners, Inc.*, 764 S.W.2d 825, 826 (Tex. App.—Austin 1989, writ denied).
- When the oral agreement cannot be performed within one year, however, it will be unenforceable under the statute of frauds. *See Schroeder v. Texas Iron Works, Inc.*, 813 S.W.2d 483, 489 (Tex. 1991).
- Whether a contract falls within the statute of frauds is a question of law. *Bratcher v. Dozier*, 346 S.W.2d 795, 796 (Tex. 1961).
- The statute of frauds applies only to those employment contracts that *must* last longer than one year. *Morgan*, 764 S .W.2d at 827.
- If there is any possibility the contract can be performed within one year, the statute of frauds does not apply and the oral agreement is enforceable.

SECTION TWO: AFFIRMATIVE DEFENSES ARISING UNDER THE "DOCTRINE OF UTMOST GOOD FAITH"

Owen v. Homan, 42 Eng. Rep. 307, 414–15 (1850) involved a dispute between parties—creditor and debtor—who executed a suretyship. And, in that case, English Law Lord Truro discussed the viability of certain affirmative defenses under the doctrine of utmost good faith. Although he did not clearly identify or label his theory, Lord Truro stated:

> I must … consider the true character of the case. The first ground of defence is that the securities were all obtained by fraud, that is, by *misrepresentation* and by *a suppression of material facts* relative to the transactions between the plaintiffs and the principal debtors; and that the plaintiffs were in collusion with [a third party], who made such misrepresentation and was guilty of such suppression. I am not aware that either … textbooks or the decisions distinctly define the extent of the [creditor's] obligation and responsibility [when a suretyship is created]. … [However, the] cases which are reported have generally arisen out of transactions in which there has been personal communication between the creditor and surety; and the clear law deducible from those decisions is that the creditor must *make a full, fair and honest communication of every circumstance* calculated to influence the discretion of the surety in entering into the required obligation.

> Lord Cranworth—while sitting as Lord Commissioner—observed that ... special injunctions are very much governed by the same principles which govern insurances, where the *assured is bound to give to the underwriter all the information in his power to enable him to estimate the character of the risk he is invited to undertake*. ... In the case of ... insurance, however, communication necessarily takes place between the assured or his agent (which is the same thing) and the insurer. ...

Five years later, the court in *Newton v. Chorlton*, 61 Eng. Rep. 749 (1856) reiterated Lord Truro's conclusions and stated the law succinctly: "[When] parties enter into a contract of suretyship, all the parties agree there shall be the *utmost good faith* between them, that the situation of the creditor and of the principal debtor *should be perfectly made known to all the sureties*, and therefore the creditor is conceived to have made known to them—whether he does so or not in fact, every security which he possesses, and the existing position of the parties at the time the contract is entered into."

Under the terms of a reinsurance contract or a Reinsurance Treaty, a reinsurer promises to indemnify a reinsured for a "covered" loss. Of course, in England, the law of marine insurance predates the ASSURANCE ACT OF 1601, 43 Eliz. c. 12 (1601). And as early as the 1500's, English courts recognized the principle that reinsurance is "an honorable engagement" and gentlemen's handshake may secure a reinsurance agreement. Quite simply, courts declared that a reinsurer and a reinsured are "partners." *Commercial Union Ins. Co. v. Seven Provinces Ins. Co., Ltd.*, 9 F.Supp.2d 49, 69 (D. Mass. 1998). And, the traditional principle of utmost good faith (*uberrima fides*) governs reinsurance relationships.

Regarding the plausible affirmative defenses that a reinsurer might raise under the doctrine of utmost good faith, the New Supreme Court wrote the following in *Matter of Liquidation of Union Indem. Ins. Co. of New York*, 674 N.E.2d 313, 319–20 (N.Y. 1996):

> The phrase *uberrimae fidei*—translation, "of the utmost good faith"—has long been used to characterize the core duty accompanying reinsurance contracts. Encompassed within this duty is a basic obligation of a reinsured to *disclose* to potential reinsurers all *"material facts"* regarding the original risk of loss, and failure to do so renders a reinsurance agreement voidable or rescindable. Material facts are those likely to influence the decisions of underwriters; facts which, had they been revealed by the reinsured, would have either prevented a reinsurer from issuing a policy or prompted a reinsurer to issue it at a higher premium. A reinsured need

> not possess a specific intent to *conceal* information from a reinsurer to make a contract voidable, rather "an innocent failure to *disclose* a *material fact* is sufficient." Additionally, "[t]here is no principle of imputed knowledge of facts *material to the risk* that the reinsurer is asked to assume."

Although the affirmative defenses—misrepresentation, concealment, and nondisclosure—evolved largely from the doctrine of utmost good faith, all types of defendants use these defenses to defend themselves in all types of actions involving a breach of promise, breach of warranty, and breach of contract. As you read the courts' opinions that follow, consider this question: Do courts employ a universal standard to define "materiality"—a "material fact," a "material nondisclosure," and a "material misrepresentation"?

A. Misrepresentation Defense

Hampton v. Sandy Cowen Agency, Inc.
739 P.2d 1331
(Ariz. Ct. App. 1987)

VERMORE, PRESIDING JUDGE. On September 24, 1984, appellee—Brian Hampton—entered into an employment contract with appellant, Sandy Cowen Agency, Inc. One term of that contract provided that if Hampton's employment was terminated, he would receive three months' severance pay. In March 1985, he was terminated without severance pay. He then brought a breach of contract action. At this point, appellant learned for the first time of what it believed to be material misrepresentations made by Hampton at the time of employment. It sought, on this basis, to rescind its contract with Hampton. It appeals from a summary judgment against it on the rescission defense and in favor of Hampton on the contract claim.

The misrepresentations alleged are that Hampton failed to list on his resume his recent employment with a Phoenix company (he was fired after two months) and that he was accustomed to making between $40,000 and $50,000 a year (his income tax returns showed income substantially below that). Appellee argued below, alternatively, that any such misrepresentations were immaterial and that, in any event, they could not defeat his contract action because they were not known to appellant at the time the contract was breached.

Hampton's resume stated that from 1978 to present he had been self-employed. Appellant contemplated hiring him to develop new business for the agency. In this context, we believe both alleged misrepresentations could be material. By saying he was self-employed from 1978 to 1984, Hampton misled appellant into believing that he had not been employed by others. He thus prevented her from learning of the bad opinion one employer had of him. A primary purpose of a resume is to learn of prior employment so that the opinions of those employers can be canvassed.

With respect to his claimed earnings, such a claim by a self-employed person directly relates to his ability to garner business, the very purpose for which appellant wished to hire him. We find almost incomprehensible the assertion that had appellee told the truth—"In my last employment I was fired five months ago after being employed for two months and I have averaged earnings of $10,000 a year being self-employed"—appellant nonetheless as a matter of law would have hired him at a base salary of $36,000 a year. *See* RESTATEMENT (SECOND) OF CONTRACTS § 164 (1979).

With respect to the argument that appellant cannot now assert a claim for rescission because the grounds for it were not known at the time of the breach, we believe it fully answered by RESTATEMENT (SECOND) OF CONTRACTS § 385 (1979). Comment (a) states that one has no duty to perform a contract that he has the power to avoid "even if he is ignorant of his power of avoidance and believes that his refusal or failure is a breach."

The judgment is reversed and the matter remanded for trial of the claim and defense.

B. Fraudulent Non-Disclosure Defense

Hollinger v. Mutual Benefit Life Ins. Co.
541 P.2d 128
(Colo. Ct. App. 1975)

RULAND, JUDGE. Plaintiff, Sherry Hollinger, as beneficiary, initiated this action to recover the proceeds under a life insurance policy issued by defendant—Mutual Benefit Life Insurance Company—to her deceased husband. Mutual refused payment on the grounds, inter alia, that false and incomplete answers had been provided by decedent on the insurance application. After a jury verdict for plaintiff, the trial court granted Mutual's motion for judgment notwithstanding the verdict. Plaintiff appeals the judgment for Mutual. ...

The facts material to this appeal are not disputed. Decedent was a military academy graduate and subsequent to his service in the armed forces, he was engaged for a time as a salesman for IBM Corporation in Chicago. Beginning in August 1971, decedent was employed as a trainee life insurance salesman by Mutual in Colorado Springs, and the policy at issue here was purchased in connection with this employment on November 10, 1971.

Insofar as material, the following questions were included in the application for insurance:

> 4. For what have you consulted, or been attended by, a physician, surgeon, psychiatrist, or other practitioner during the past 7 years? ...
>
> 15. Have you ever had or been told that you had or received treatment for ... e) frequent headaches, paralysis, dizzy spells, loss of consciousness, epilepsy, nervous breakdown, or mental disorder?

In answering these questions, the application form required the insured to provide detailed information, including the name of the attending physician, for each instance listed. The answer to question 4 on decedent's application reflected only that he had been treated for acute viral influenza. The answer to number 15(e) was negative.

The application contained the following statement above decedent's signature: "The undersigned represents that the foregoing statements are true and complete, and that every occasion and instance as to each item answered 'yes' has been disclosed."

The answers to the above-quoted questions were written on decedent's application by Mutual's examining physician on the basis of a medical history obtained from decedent and prior to decedent's signing the application. This doctor testified that although he might sometimes omit from an application information given him by an applicant, including information relating to marital and job problems, if an applicant indicated that he had consulted a psychiatrist, for whatever reason, he would always include that information on the application.

While living in Chicago and over a period of approximately two months in the spring and summer of 1971, decedent consulted a psychiatrist. The psychiatrist testified that the decedent first consulted him after an apparent suicide attempt, that he had seen decedent on 11 occasions, and that decedent was suffering from "anxiety depression." According to the psychiatrist, decedent was advised of the diagnosis, and the psychiatrist recommended that decedent seek further treatment when he moved to Colorado Springs. Decedent's last visit to the psychiatrist occurred less than four months before he signed the application for life insurance.

Mutual's medical director testified that if decedent's application had indicated his psychiatric consultation, or affirmative answers to question 15(e), the insurance policy would not have been issued without further inquiry. Also, if the medical information revealed in the psychiatrist's testimony had been available to Mutual, the policy would not have been issued. In the course of the trial, Mutual made timely motions for a directed verdict asserting that the evidence clearly established fraud by the decedent in answering various questions on the application.

Following denial of Mutual's motion, and relative to Mutual's defense of fraud, the trial court instructed the jury, inter alia, on the elements of fraud as they are delineated in *Morrison v. Goodspeed*, 68 P.2d 458 (Colo. 1937)—including the requirement that the jury must find not only that decedent knowingly provided false information on the application, but also that he did so with the intent to deceive Mutual. The jury found for plaintiff.

In granting Mutual's motion for judgment notwithstanding the verdict, the trial court concluded that the rule of law announced in *Germania Life Insurance Co. v. Klein*, 137 P. 73 (Colo. App. 1913) was applicable to the facts of this case and that, therefore, it was not necessary for Mutual to establish an intent to deceive. Since it was not disputed that decedent possessed the ability to understand and the knowledge to answer correctly the questions concerning his psychiatric consultations, that the answers were incomplete and false, and that accurate answers to these questions were material to the issuance of the policy, the court concluded that judgment should enter for Mutual. In reaching this conclusion, the trial court determined that the holding of this court in *Gomogda v. Prudential Insurance Co.*, 501 P.2d 756 (Colo. App. 1972) was not controlling here.

Plaintiff contends that the trial court's ruling was erroneous, asserting that *Gomogda* modified the rule in *Germania* to require that in every case where the applicant has made false statements material to the risk, the insurer must prove an intent to deceive. We disagree. *Gomogda* merely clarified the rule in *Germania*. ... *Gomogda* does not operate to alter the *Germania* rule that where the evidence conclusively shows that the applicant has knowingly made false statements material to the risk undertaken by the insurer, the insurance policy can be avoided.

In the case at bar, plaintiff does not contend that decedent was unaware that he had recently consulted a psychiatrist. It is also not disputed that the information withheld by decedent was material to the insurance risk. Further, plaintiff's contention that decedent may have attached no significance to his psychiatric consultations is immaterial. Hence, we agree with the trial court that the jury should not have been instructed relative to decedent's intent to deceive Mutual, and the trial court was correct in granting Mutual's motion. ...

Judgment affirmed.

NOTES AND QUESTIONS

1. **Restatement (Second) of Contracts § 164 (1979).** This restatement outlines "when a misrepresentation makes a contract voidable." It reads:

   (1) If a party's manifestation of assent is induced by either a fraudulent or a material misrepresentation by the other party upon which the recipient is justified in relying, the contract is voidable by the recipient.

   (2) If a party's manifestation of assent is induced by either a fraudulent or a material misrepresentation by one who is not a party to the transaction upon which the recipient is justified in relying, the contract is voidable by the recipient, unless the other party to the transaction in good faith and without reason to know of the misrepresentation either gives value or relies materially on the transaction.

2. **Restatement (Second) of Contracts § 385 (1979).** This restatement clarifies the effect of one's power to avoid a contract, which is a defense. It reads:

   (1) Unless an offer to restore performance received is a condition of avoidance, a party has no duty of performance while his power of avoidance exists.

   (2) If an offer to restore performance received is a condition of avoidance, a duty to pay damages is terminated by such an offer made before the power of avoidance is lost.

3. **Restatement (Second) of Contracts § 161 (1981).** Section 161 states that "person's non-disclosure of a fact known to him is equivalent to an assertion that the fact does not exist in the following cases only":

   (a) where he knows that disclosure of the fact is necessary to prevent some previous assertion from being a misrepresentation or from being fraudulent or material.

   (b) where he knows that disclosure of the fact would correct a mistake of the other party as to a basic assumption on which that party is making the contract and if non-disclosure of the fact amounts to a failure to act in good faith and in accordance with reasonable standards of fair dealing.

   (c) where he knows that disclosure of the fact would correct a mistake of the other party as to the contents or effect of a writing, evidencing or embodying an agreement in whole or in part.

(d) where the other person is entitled to know the fact because of a relation of trust and confidence between them.

4. **The Defense of Concealment and "Materiality" Under Colorado Law.** The Supreme Court of Colorado presented an extensive analysis in *Connecticut Fire Ins. Co. v. Colorado Leasing, Min. & Mill. Co.*, 116 P. 154, 157 (Colo. 1911):

> The defendant claims that inasmuch as these matters, which it says were concealed, were material, the court should have instructed for it. The defendant loses sight of a very important fact in this case, and that is that no inquiry was made of the plaintiff about the matters alleged to have been concealed, and that no written application was made for this insurance. "Concealment is the designed and intentional withholding of any fact, material to the risk, which the assured in honesty and good faith ought to communicate." *Clark v. Ins. Co.*, 40 N. H. 333 (1860). ...
>
> [A] concealment involves, not only the materiality of the fact withheld and which ought to have been communicated, but also the design and intention of the insured in withholding it, and, of course, the condition in the policy must be construed in the light of this definition of a concealment with which it is concerned. If an inquiry is made about a material fact and that fact is not disclosed upon such inquiry, it is very likely that the person questioned intended to withhold it; but, if no inquiry is made, the intention to withhold the fact is not so plain. Hence the authorities make a distinction between cases where inquiry is made and cases in which no inquiry is made. The rule is stated in WOOD ON INSURANCE § 388: "When no inquiries are made, the intention of the assured becomes material, and, to avoid the policy, they must find, not only that the matter was material, but also that it was intentionally fraudulently concealed."
>
> [Thus] in the circumstances of this case, it is not alone the materiality of the facts which were withheld that was to be found, but also whether ... the plaintiff intentionally and fraudulently withheld them. The materiality of these facts was not fixed by any writing, as is often the case in insurance, but it must be drawn from circumstances. ... [Also] the fraudulent intent of the insured [must] be drawn. It is said in 1 MAY ON INSURANCE, § 195, that, where the materiality is to be inferred from circumstances and not upon the construction of some writing, it is a question for the jury. How much more would the fraudulent intent of the insured in withholding these facts be for the jury? It was not for the court to say as a matter of

law that the facts alleged to have been concealed were material, and that the insured had intentionally and fraudulently withheld them, and hence no error was committed in refusing to instruct the jury to return a verdict for the defendant so far as such concealments were concerned.

5. **The Test of Materiality Under Texas Law**. Quite frankly, Texas courts have stated the law of materiality in a variety of ways. *See Labbe v. Corbett*, 6 S. W. 808, 811 (Tex. 1888) (declaring that the test of materiality is whether the misrepresentation induce the insurer to accept the risk); *Inter-Ocean Insurance Co. v. Ross*, 315 S.W.2d 71, 74 (Tex. Civ. App.—Fort Worth 1958) ("The test of materiality is said to be whether knowledge of the true facts would have influenced a prudent insurer in determining whether to accept the risk, or in fixing the amount of premiums. 'If the applicant makes statements that are material, which are untrue, it will avoid the policy, unless the company knew that those identical statements were untrue.' ... [I]t is not necessary to prove that a false representation was intentionally made for the purpose of deceiving the insurer."); and *Kiel v. Texas Employers Ins. Ass'n*, 679 S.W.2d 656, 659 (Tex. App.—Houston [1st Dist.] 1984) ("TEX. R. EVID. 401(a) defines the test for "materiality" as whether the evidence rationally relates to any controlling fact issue in dispute.").

SECTION THREE: BREACH-OF-CONDITION DEFENSE

When parties bind themselves under negotiated and standardized contracts, they often attach conditions, limitations, qualifications, or "subject to" clauses. Some conditions modify or clarify rights and obligations before an undertaking or performance starts. Other conditions put limitations on the parties' respective contractual duties or privileges after performance has commenced. The former qualifications or limitations are called "conditions precedent" and the latter are labeled "conditions subsequent."

To be sure, both promisors and promisees breach conditions-precedent and conditions-subsequent clauses. But are the respective, remedial consequences identical after promisors and promisees breach "subject to" clauses? At least one federal court concluded that the respective contracting parties' breaches produced different consequences. Consider the case *In re Dibiase* 270 B.R. 673,686–87 (Bkrtcy. W.D. Tex. 2001). Attempting to distinguish conditions precedent from conditions subsequent and citing C. Wright & A. Miller, 5 Fed. Pract. & Proc.2d, § 1304 at 687 (West 1990), the bankruptcy judge stated:

> *Failure* of a condition precedent means that the defending party is relieved of the duty of ever having to perform in the first place—the benefit of the contract never arises. The occurrence of a condition subsequent means that the defending party is relieved of an otherwise pre-existing duty—the benefit of the contract is lost. With conditions precedent, it is the *plaintiff* that must plead the occurrence of the condition precedent, or face a motion to dismiss for failure to state a claim. With conditions subsequent, it is the defendant that must plead the occurrence of the condition subsequent as an affirmative defense. (emphasis in original).

But Rule 9(c) of the Federal Rules of Civil Procedure simply reads in pertinent part: "In pleading conditions precedent, it suffices to allege generally that all conditions precedent have occurred or been performed. But when denying that a condition precedent has occurred or been performed, a party must do so with particularity." Quite simply, Rule 9(c) is neither plaintiff- nor defendant-specific. As the following cases illustrate, a defendant may defend against a breach-of-contract action by proving with "particularity" that a plaintiff breached either a condition precedent or a condition subsequent. However, the crucial question is this one: Do state supreme courts require defendants to prove more than a breach of condition with particularity? Must defendants also prove "prejudice"?

A. Legal Defenses Premise on a Breach of Conditions Precedent

Lewis v. Foxworth
170 S.W.3d 900
(Tex. App.—Dallas 2005)

Opinion by Justice Morris. This is an appeal from a jury verdict awarding Jack Foxworth—as attorney-in-fact for Walter L. Foxworth and Warren H. Foxworth—damages for breach of a contract for the sale of real estate. Harold Ray Lewis contends the trial court erred in granting judgment against him because the evidence shows he was excused from performing under the contract. The Foxworths respond that Lewis's performance was not excused and his failure to close the sale was a breach of the contract entitling them to recover $50,000 in earnest money on deposit with the title company. …

I.

In November 2002, Walter and Warren Foxworth as sellers, and Harold Ray Lewis as buyer, executed a contract for the sale of approximately 450 acres of land in Grayson County, Texas. Under the contract, Lewis agreed to pay the Foxworths $1,675,000 in cash for the property. Lewis further agreed to deposit $50,000 in earnest money in an interest bearing escrow account with the title company. In return, the Foxworths agreed to deliver possession of the property to Lewis upon closing. The sale of the property was scheduled to close on January 15, 2003. The contract specified that, in the event Lewis failed to close the sale, the Foxworths were entitled to the earnest money on deposit with the title company as their sole remedy.

In addition to setting forth the payment and delivery obligations, the contract also contained a section entitled "Special Provisions." Under the Special Provisions section, the contract stated:

> Both Seller and Purchaser agree that there are items of Personal Property which will be removed from the Property and that all fixtures which are attached to the Property will remain with the Property, said fixtures including, but not limited to fences, working pens, gates, chutes, water well fixtures, and tanks.

It is undisputed that the Foxworths removed personal items from the property before the sale was due to close. As of the date of the scheduled closing, however, some personal property remained on the land. Lewis did not close the sale on January 15 as required by the contract.

On January 17, 2003, two days after the closing was supposed to occur, the Foxworths sent Lewis a letter stating they were willing to extend the time for closing to 3:00 p.m. on January 21, 2003. The Foxworths also informed Lewis that if he failed to tender the remaining funds by that time, they would exercise their right to recover the earnest money and terminate the agreement.

Lewis did not tender the money on January 21 and the Foxworths informed Lewis by letter dated January 22 that they were terminating the agreement. When the Foxworths attempted to recover the earnest money from the title company, the title company refused to turn over the funds without a signed release from Lewis. The Foxworths sent two requests to Lewis asking him to sign the necessary release but received no reply. The Foxworths then brought this suit alleging breach of contract and seeking recovery of the $50,000 earnest money as damages pursuant to the terms of the contract.

In response to the Foxworths' claim for breach of contract, Lewis asserted various affirmative defenses including excuse, failure of conditions precedent, anticipatory breach, and failure of consideration.

All of the affirmative defenses were based upon Lewis's assertion that the Foxworths failed to remove their personal items from the property before the closing date as required under the contract. The Foxworths moved for summary judgment arguing that Lewis's affirmative defenses were without merit and they were entitled to the earnest money as a matter of law. The trial court declined to grant the Foxworths' summary judgment on their breach of contract claim but granted them a partial summary judgment on Lewis's affirmative defenses of failure of conditions precedent and failure of consideration. Lewis does not challenge on appeal the trial court's decision to grant summary judgment on those defenses.

The breach of contract claim against Lewis was tried to a jury. The jury charge asked the jury to determine whether Lewis failed to comply with his agreement to purchase the land and whether that failure was excused. The charge instructed the jury that Lewis's failure to comply would be excused if, before Lewis was required to perform, the Foxworths either failed to comply with a material obligation of the contract or repudiated the contract. The charge defined "repudiation" as an indication by a party to the contract—either by his words or actions—that he is not going to fulfill his obligations under the contract in the future "showing a fixed intention to abandon, renounce, and refuse to perform the agreement." The jury found that Lewis failed to comply with the contract and his failure was not excused.

Lewis moved for a judgment notwithstanding the verdict. The trial court denied the motion and granted judgment in favor of the Foxworths, awarding them the $50,000 earnest money as well as attorney's fees. Lewis then filed a motion for new trial arguing the evidence was insufficient to support the jury's finding that his failure to comply with the contract was not excused. The trial court denied the motion for new trial. This appeal ensued.

II.

In his sole point of error, Lewis contends the evidence is legally and factually insufficient to support the jury's finding that he was not excused from complying with his contractual obligation to purchase the Foxworths' property. Lewis argues the evidence conclusively shows the Foxworths failed to comply with the "Special Provisions" section of the contract requiring them to remove their personal items from the property and that their failure excused his performance under the contract. We disagree.

When a party challenges the legal sufficiency of the evidence supporting an adverse finding on an issue on which he bore the burden of proof, he must demonstrate on appeal that the evidence establishes, as a matter of law, all vital facts in support of the issue. *Dow Chemical*

Co. v. Francis, 46 S.W.3d 237, 241 (Tex. 2001). In reviewing the legal sufficiency of the evidence, we view the evidence in the light favorable to the verdict, crediting favorable evidence if reasonable jurors could and disregarding contrary evidence unless reasonable jurors could not. *See City of Keller v. Wilson*, 168 S.W.3d 802, 807 (Tex. 2005).

When a party challenges the factual sufficiency of the evidence supporting an adverse finding on which he bore the burden of proof, he must demonstrate that the adverse finding is against the great weight and preponderance of the evidence. In conducting a factual sufficiency review, we consider all the evidence and set aside the verdict only if it is so contrary to the overwhelming weight of the evidence as to be clearly wrong and unjust. *See Plas–Tex, Inc. v. U.S. Steel Corp.*, 772 S.W.2d 442, 445 (Tex. 1989); *Cain v. Bain*, 709 S.W.2d 175, 176 (Tex. 1986) (per curiam).

At trial, the Foxworths testified they removed the personal items they wanted from the property several days before the sale to Lewis was scheduled to close. Lewis does not dispute the Foxworths removed some of their personal items from the property. It is Lewis's contention, however, that the contract required the Foxworths to remove all their personal property from the land before the sale closed and their failure to do so was either a material breach or a repudiation of the contract. Lewis's argument contradicts the plain language of the contract.

In construing a written contract, the primary concern of the court is to ascertain the true intentions of the parties as expressed in the instrument. The parties' intent must be taken from the contract itself, not from the parties' present interpretation, and the contract must be enforced as it is written. We may neither rewrite the contract nor add to its language. *See American Mfrs. Mut. Ins. Co. v. Schaefer*, 124 S.W.3d 154, 162 (Tex. 2003).

The contract at issue states that "[b]oth Seller and Purchaser agree that there are items of Personal Property which will be removed from the Property. ..." The evidence presented at trial clearly shows that items of personal property were removed from the property and, therefore, the requirements of the provision were met. For the contract to require the Foxworths to remove all personal items from the property before the property was transferred to Lewis, the contract would have to be rewritten to state that "both Seller and Purchaser agree that all items of Personal Property will be removed from the Property by the Seller before closing."

The contract language is clearly not as expansive as Lewis would have us read it. Lewis agreed to the terms and provisions of the contract as it was written, and we cannot now change those provisions simply because Lewis believes something more was needed.

Lewis urges us to construe the contract strictly against the Foxworths because they were the drafters of the agreement. But the doctrine of *contra proferentem* is applied only when construing an ambiguous contract. *See Evergreen Nat. Indem. Co. v. Tan It All, Inc.*, 111 S.W.3d 669, 675 (Tex. App.—Austin 2003, no pet.). At no point have the parties urged, nor did the trial court find, that the contract at issue was ambiguous. Lewis, in fact, strenuously argues on appeal that the contract is unambiguous. The plain language of the contract provides for the removal of personal items from the property, and the evidence shows unequivocally that this was done. Accordingly, the evidence is both legally and factually sufficient to support the jury's finding that Lewis had no excuse for his failure to close on the sale.

Even if the evidence did not support a finding that the requirements of the special provision were met, the evidence is both legally and factually sufficient to support the jury's finding that any failure by the Foxworths to remove all personal items from the property was neither a material breach nor a repudiation of the contract excusing Lewis from performing under the agreement. The evidence shows that Lewis never contacted the Foxworths before either of the scheduled closings to communicate his dissatisfaction with the condition of the property. Furthermore, the Foxworths presented evidence that Lewis made an agreement with the foreman of the property allowing the foreman to keep some personal property on the land. Although the jury charge did not define the term "material obligation," the jury could have concluded from the above evidence that any obligation the Foxworths may have had to remove personal items from the property was not a material obligation of the contract. In addition, the Foxworths clearly demonstrated their desire to go forward with the sale when they informed Lewis by letter of their willingness to extend the date of the closing to give Lewis another opportunity to perform.

Accordingly, the Foxworths did not demonstrate, either by their words or their actions, an intention to abandon, renounce, or refuse to perform the agreement. Absent either a breach of a material obligation or a repudiation of the agreement, Lewis had no excuse for his failure to comply with the terms of the agreement. Based on the foregoing, we conclude the evidence is legally and factually sufficient to support the jury's finding. We resolve Lewis's sole issue against him.

We affirm the trial court's judgment.

B. Legal Defenses Premise on a Breach of Conditions Subsequent

Hanover Fire Ins. Co. v. Pruitt
2 S.E.2d 123
(Ga. Ct. App. 1939)

GUERRY, JUDGE. This is a suit on a fire insurance policy because of the destruction by fire of a certain stock of goods covered by the policy sued on. The petition alleged that the policy was in force ... [and] alleged the destruction of the stock of goods covered by the policy because of fire. ... [Plaintiff submitted] proofs of loss and the failure to pay. The defendant admitted that it issued the policy sued on and says said policy contained this provision: "If a building or any part thereof falls, except as a result of fire, all insurance by this policy shall immediately cease." ... "[A]bout 8:40 o'clock on the morning of April 6, 1936 and prior to the occurrence of any fire on the premises described in said policy, a tornado or violent windstorm occurred at or about said premises, which said tornado or windstorm then and there immediately caused a part of the building described in said policy to fall." "Defendant avers that the falling of said building or a part thereof occurred prior to the fire alleged to have occurred in plaintiff's petition."

We shall not go into any detailed description of the evidence with reference to the frightful tornado which struck Gainesville, Georgia, that day. It disclosed without dispute that the stock of goods insured was located in a four story brick building; that during the progress of the tornado the building was demolished and was immediately on fire and the remains were destroyed by fire. The main question which was for determination of the jury was whether the fire started before the building fell or whether after it fell. Under the decision of this court in an identical contract it is held that if the fire began after the fall of the building there could be no recovery on the policy. *Nalley v. Hanover Fire Insurance Co.*, 193 S.E. 619 (Ga. App. 1937)

We think it is also well settled that if the fire started before the fall of the building but the destruction was not complete before the fall, a recovery may be had. If the fire after the fall was the continuation of the fire in progress before the building fell a recovery may be had on the policy. A careful reading of the very voluminous brief of the evidence without recounting it convinces us that the circumstances detailed did not preponderate to such an extent as to demand a finding either that the fire began before or after the building was demolished.

The plaintiff in error—defendant in the court below—says in its brief: "The plaintiff's theory was that there was a strong wind prior to the tornado, which blew out the plate glass windows, and this strong wind blew down the [red hot] stove pipes and overturned the stove located on the first floor (of the four story building) spreading the fire to the stock of merchandise prior to the collapse of the building." It is contended that there was no evidence to support this theory except the fact "that there was a strong wind which blew out the front plate glass of the plaintiff's windows some few seconds before the tornado struck." It is further contended that the plaintiff in the court below insisted that it could be inferred from this circumstantial evidence that this wind was strong enough to overturn the stove and thus spread the fire to the stock of goods before the tornado demolished the building.

Plaintiff in error says first in its brief, "There was no evidence to support the verdict for the plaintiffs and a finding that plaintiffs' stock of goods caught fire prior to the falling of a material portion of plaintiffs' building." Did the burden rest upon the plaintiff to show this fact or was the burden on the defendant to show the converse, that is, that the building did not catch on fire until after it fell? An answer to this question decides this feature of the case.

In the present case, it is undisputed that there was a valid policy in effect insuring plaintiffs' stock of goods against loss by fire. It is also undisputed that plaintiffs' insured property was destroyed by fire. The condition in the policy that no liability under the policy was to exist in the event the building fell before the fire was a condition subsequent. It is a condition subsequent, analogous to a provision that the policy is void if the title to the building or property insured be not in the plaintiff. In *Morris v. Imperial Ins. Co.,* 32 S.E. 595 (Ga. 1899), it was said: "Where, to a suit upon a policy of fire insurance, the defense is interposed that at the time the policy was taken out by the insured he was not the owner of the property thereby covered, the burden of satisfactorily establishing this contention rests upon the defendant, notwithstanding it may be incumbent upon the plaintiff, in order to make out a *prima facie* case, to show that the property in question, alleged to have been destroyed by fire, belonged to him at the time the same was burned." ...

We think the plaintiff made out a *prima facie case* when it introduced the policy sued on, which on its face in effect showed a loss by fire, the amount of the loss and proper demand and refusal. This proof fully measured up to the allegations contained in the petition and nothing else appearing would have entitled the plaintiff to a verdict. The defendant pleaded a breach of a condition subsequent. The question therefore for determination is not whether the plaintiff has shown that the fire began before the building fell, but whether or not the defendant has established that the building fell before the fire began.

The burden or the duty of going forward with the evidence was upon the defendant to show the breach of this condition subsequent, just as would have been his duty in case his plea had been that title to the building was not in plaintiff at the time of the issuance of the policy or that it was vacant at the time of the fire, or that the risk had been increased by hazard named in the policy, or that there was other insurance on the same property. The defendant has the burden of proving an affirmative defense, to wit, that the building fell before it caught on fire.

We are not able to say that the evidence "conclusively shows that the collapse of the building, caused by the tornado, preceded the fire." As was said by this court in *Georgia Ry. & El. Co. v. Harris*, 57 S.E. 1076 (Ga. App. 1907): "Where a plaintiff in a civil case supports his action solely by circumstantial evidence, before he is authorized to have a verdict in his favor the testimony must be such as to reasonably establish the theory relied upon, and to preponderate to that theory rather than to any other reasonable hypothesis."

When the plaintiff had introduced his evidence in this case, unless such evidence itself established the fact that the building fell before the fire started, he would be entitled to a verdict. We do not believe the evidence in this case, which was entirely circumstantial as to when the fire started, was sufficient to establish the defendant's contention that the building collapsed before the fire began. On the other hand, had the burden been upon the plaintiff to establish that the fire began before the building fell, we think it would have failed. Applying the rule quoted in [another] case, we think the evidence failed to preponderate to the theory that the building fell before the fire began, rather than to the theory the fire caught from the stove which may have overturned before the fall of the building.

We agree with counsel for plaintiff in error that if the burden was on the plaintiff in the court below to establish the time when the fire began, its theory would be based on a succession of inferences. Likewise we think the burden which was on the defendant as to that matter was only established by a succession of inferences. Counsel are agreed that if the fire began before the collapse of the building because of the tornado, plaintiff is entitled to recover. ...

Complaint is made as to the following charge of the court:

> I charge you that the falling building clause, as contained in this policy, or contract of fire insurance, will not void this policy, or relieve the defendant company of liability, if a fragmentary or minute portion of the material in the insured building should fall. Before the defendant company would be relieved, under this stipulation or condition in the contract of fire insurance, in this case, the burden is upon the defendant company to show that some functional or material portion of the building fell prior to the fire—the falling of which destroyed its distinctive character, that is, its distinctive character as a building. ...

Plaintiff in error insists that it was incumbent on the insured to prove "that the damage occurred at a time when the contract of insurance was in force and effect." The policy insured against loss by fire occurring within the dates named in the policy. The evidence demanded a finding that the fire occurred within those dates. The fact that there was a condition subsequent which would avoid the policy was an affirmative defense set up by insurer.

While there is no plea of confession and avoidance in this case which would give to defendant the right to open and conclude because there is a general denial of plaintiff's petition, it does not alter the fact that when plaintiff has made out a *prima facie* case by the introduction of the policy and proof that loss has occurred by reason of the hazard insured against and the extent of the loss, that defendant must either disprove these contentions established by evidence or establish an affirmative defense. If the evidence for the defendant does not negative the evidence for the plaintiff except that it tends to support its affirmative defense, the plaintiff has carried the burden resting on him and the burden of establishing the affirmative defense filed shifts to defendant.

If he fails to carry this burden, the plaintiff is entitled to recover. Besides the general issue the defense interposed was an affirmative defense, to wit, that the building fell before the fire began, which was a condition subsequent. Code, § 38-103, provides that "The burden of proof generally lies upon the party asserting or affirming a fact and to the existence of whose case or defense [italics ours] the proof of such fact is essential."

The colloquy between counsel and the motion for mistrial based thereon was properly overruled, especially in view of the instruction of the court at the time. ... We do not think the remarks of counsel in view of what had been argued by counsel for the opposite party, even if it be conceded that they were prejudicial which we do not concede, would require the grant of a new trial. ...

We have read with care the 46 grounds of the amended motion and have discussed those to which the plaintiff in error in his brief has devoted most attention. For no reason assigned do we think the court erred in overruling the motion for new trial.

Judgment affirmed.

Notes and Questions

1. **Breach-of-Conditions Clauses and the Prejudice Doctrine.** In *Lewis*, the court declared that the Foxworths did not materially breach the conditions-precedent provision. Therefore, Lewis's

nonperformance under the contract could not be excused. However, under some circumstances, a defendant's nonperformance may still not be excused even if a plaintiff materially breaches a conditions-precedent or a conditions-subsequent clause. Some courts require a defendant to prove that a plaintiff's material breach of a condition prejudiced the defendant's interests or rights—which, in turn, precluded the defendant from performing. *See International Ins. Co. v. RSR Corp.*, 148 Fed. Appx. 226, 230 (5th Cir. 2005) ("Under Texas law, which is applicable to this diversity case, insurance policies are contracts which are subject to the applicable rules of Texas contract law. ... The Texas Supreme Court and this court—sitting in diversity and applying the substantive law of Texas—have found that in some cases an insurer must demonstrate that it was prejudiced by the insured's breach of a condition in order to be excused from performance, but in other cases prejudice is presumed and the insurer is not required to show prejudice."). *Compare Hanson Production Co. v. American Ins. Co.,* 108 F.3d 627, 628 (5th Cir. 1997) (holding that an insurer must show prejudice) and *Hernandez v. Gulf Group Lloyds*, 875 S.W.2d 691, 692 (Tex. 1994) (same), *with Federal Ins. Co. v. CompUSA, Inc.,* 319 F.3d 746, 754 (5th Cir. 2003) (finding that the insurer was not required to show prejudice) and *Matador Petroleum Corp. v. St. Paul Surplus Lines Ins. Co.*, 174 F.3d 653, 658–59 (5th Cir. 1999) (same).

2. **Contract Interpretation Redux and the Doctrine of Contra Proferentem.** Stated simply, the doctrine of ambiguity requires a court to interpret ambiguous words and phrases in a contract against the drafter of the contract. This is the general rule. But the *Lewis* court applied the minority rule and refused to apply the doctrine and construe the conditions-precedent clause against the drafters—the Foxworths. The court found no ambiguous language in the clause. In some jurisdictions, an ambiguity exists if the parties simply disagree about the meaning of a word or phrase. As the *Lewis* decision reaffirmed, under Texas law, an ambiguity exists only if a court finds one.

SECTION FOUR: THE DOCTRINE OF MISTAKE

Mistake in the Formation and Performance of a Contract
11 Columbia L. Rev. 197 (1911)
Roland R. Foulke

The law relating to mistake is in a state of great confusion, and several different views have been entertained as to the cause of the difficulty. Mr. Pollock says that the difficulty is mainly verbal, and arises from three causes: 1) confusion of proximate with remote causes of legal consequences, 2) the assertion of propositions as general rules which ought to be taken with reference only to particular effects of mistake in particular classes of cases, and 3) omission to assign an exact meaning to the term "ignorance of law." Mr. Kerr is of the opinions that the difficulty has been increased by the fact that no clear and sharp line has been drawn between mistakes in fact and mistakes in law. …

The notion of a mistake has always been confined to a mistake with reference to a past or present fact. … The cases of mistake as to the future are generally discussed under the heading of impossibility of performance. … A mistake may occur through ignorance, negligence, forgetfulness, heedlessness, surprise, confusion, accident, etc. The law … rarely takes account of any of the mental states accompanying the mistake. It is the tendency of many judges and writers to confuse the accompanying state of mind with mistake. …

The subject of mistake was originally, and is still, considered as a heading of equitable relief. When a mistake was made, the Chancellor was called upon to exercise his powerful jurisdiction to relieve the parties from the consequences, and the common law afforded little opportunity for such relief. …

Furthermore, the distinction between a mistake of law and a mistake of fact is as elusive and difficult to draw as is the distinction between law and fact themselves. Since no one has been able to state with any clearness the principle upon which the distinction proceeds or to furnish any test by which it can be applied, … the decided cases are in hopeless confusion when studied with the distinction in mind, there seem to be a few good reasons for discarding it altogether. … [As] far as mistake in the formation and performance of a contract is concerned, the distinction we have just referred to is totally immaterial. If we distinguish between mistakes of law and mistakes of fact, the cases resolve themselves into hopeless confusion. If the distinction is disregarded, the cases can be arranged with very little conflict under a few well-settled principles … under the following headings: 1) mistake in the formation of a contract, 2) mistake in reducing the contract to writing, and 3) mistake in the performance of the contract. …

Mistake entering into the formation of the contract may be divided into three headings: 1) such mistake as will prevent the formation of the contract, 2) such mistake as will not prevent the formation of the contract, but may or may not be a ground of relieving one party or the other from its burden, and 3) such mistake as will neither prevent formation nor be any ground for relief to the party making the mistake. Mistake, furthermore, is of two kinds, unilateral and mutual. By unilateral mistake is meant a mistake made by one party to the contract; and by mutual mistake is meant a mistake made by both parties to the contract.

The case of mutual mistake is to be subdivided into 1) the case where the parties do not agree in the terms of the offer and acceptance, and there is, therefore, no contract formed, and 2) the case where the terms of the offer and acceptance agree, but the parties in that agreement both make the same mistake. The first instance of mistake prevents the formation of the contract, and the second does not prevent the formation, but may or may not be ground for relieving the parties from the burden of the obligation. …

[Regarding a misunderstanding], we must distinguish several cases: 1) where the offer and acceptance apparently agree but there is a latent ambiguity because of which the minds of the parties do not meet, 2) where the offer and acceptance do not agree on their face—the case of a bilateral contract, and 3) where the offeree performs or attempts to perform upon a misapprehension of the terms of the offer—the case of a unilateral contract. …

It is commonly said that the mistake must be as to the subject matter or as to some intrinsic fact. This principle, however, does not assist us, because it does not tell us what is the subject matter or what is an intrinsic fact. It further fails to distinguish between 1) mistake involving impossibility of performance, 2) mistake involving the principle of unjust enrichment, 3) the question of relieving one party from the burden of the contract because of mistake, and 4) the question of permitting one party to recover a performance on the ground of failure of performance on the other side. This question of mutual mistake in formation is the most difficult part of the whole subject, and it is probably not possible at the present time to offer any more definite conclusion on the matter.

Roland Foulke penned his doctrine-of-mistake article more than one hundred years ago. Yet most of the less-than-intelligible and conflicting rulings that are discussed in the article persist today. Certainly, as Foulke reiterated in the last paragraph of his article, contracting parties make various types of mistakes. However, in this section, the reader will find cases that address only one question: whether a unilateral or a mutual mistake excuses a defendant's non-performance of contractual obligations. As you read the cases, be extremely mindful of the problems that Foulke highlighted in his article.

A. The Doctrine of Mutual Mistake

Federated Guaranty Life Ins. Co. v. Painter 360 So.2d 309 (Ala. 1978)

Beatty, Justice. Federated Guaranty Life Insurance Company appeals from a judgment in favor of the plaintiff, Painter, which reformed an employment contract between them and also granted incidental relief in the form of money damages for a breach of that contract as reformed.

Dennis E. Painter was first employed in September, 1965 as an agent by the defendant's predecessor, Cotton States Life Insurance Company. On June 9, 1969, he was promoted to the position of general agent—having been recruited by William Lanford, agency vice-president for the company. He signed a standard general agent's contract form.

This contract consisted of several parts, among them being a schedule which set forth the commissions to be received by a general agent according to plan of insurance and the first, second, and third through tenth years in which premiums were paid. It also listed the percentage the service fee to be allowed the general agent based upon renewal premiums paid during the third through tenth policy years, and the service fee allowed him after that period of time. For example, the schedule of commissions on a whole-life policy with 20 or more annual premiums is shown as follows: …

> Renewal Rights: if this Agreement is terminated by the Company or by the Agent or should the Agent die while this Agreement is in force or become totally disabled from its performance he, or in case of his death, his heirs or legal representatives shall, except as hereinafter provided in Paragraphs A, B and C, receive renewal commissions that accrue under the provisions of this Agreement relating to compensation, if any, less a service fee of 3% of each premium. In the event of termination of this Agreement, other than by death or disability, the maximum period during which renewal commissions shall accrue under the terms hereof shall not exceed an additional period equal to the period which the Agent has been under contract with the Company prior to such termination, provided the Agent has been under contract at least three (3) years from the date of the contract. At which time this vested portion of the contract is retroactive to the original date of contract.

> A. Renewal commissions shall not be payable after the termination of this Agreement if the Agent has misappropriated or failed to account for any of the Company's funds.
>
> B. If, after this Agreement is terminated, the Agent writes a new policy with another company to replace any policy in this Company, the Agent shall thereby forfeit all rights of this Agreement and renewal commissions shall not be payable thereafter.
>
> C. After the termination of this Agreement renewal commissions shall cease to be payable at the end of any calendar year during which renewal commissions received by or credited to the Agent average less than $25.00 per month.

It is important to observe, as the testimony also explained, that the commission schedule and the renewal rights clause dealt with different "service fees." In the former, the service fee is an amount paid to the general agent for servicing the policy, an amount in addition to the earned commission. The "service fee" referred to in the renewal rights clause, however, is a charge against the agent's commissions he is to receive following termination of his employment contract by death, total disability, or otherwise by either party.

Approximately one year after executing his contract, Painter realized that the word "premium," as it appears in the renewal rights clause, should have been "commissions." He went to Lanford who told him that it would be changed in his contract to three per cent of the commission. In fact, the provision was not changed. Subsequently both Painter and Lanford left the employ of the company which later merged with Federated Guaranty and retained that name. Ultimately Painter brought an action against Federated for breach of contract in failing to pay the full commissions to which he was entitled. That action ended in a mistrial. Then Painter amended his complaint to request a reformation and incidental relief. That suit was heard by the trial court without a jury. Reformation was granted as requested.

The defendant's contention on appeal is that there was no clear, convincing and satisfactory evidence before the trial court proving that the written agreement executed by the parties did not reflect their intention at the time it was executed. In short, it maintains that there was absent in the trial court a sufficient showing of mutual mistake on which to base a reformation.

The right to have a court revise a written contract which through mutual mistake does not express the parties' intention has been recognized by statute since the Code of Alabama 1923, § 6825; Tit. 9, § 59, Alabama Code of 1940 (Recomp. 1958). Because there is a presumption which arises from the instrument itself that supports it as the true agreement, our Court has cautiously placed the burden upon the reform seeker to prove his case by clear, convincing and satisfactory evidence. The quality of such evidence has been variously described, denoting the seriousness with which this court has looked upon such a claim and its concomitant regard for the integrity of the written instrument.

Thus we see expressions of Mr. Pomeroy adopted by this court in *Hammer v. Lange*, 174 Ala. 337, 340 (1911): "The authorities all require that the parol evidence of the mistake and of the alleged modification must be most clear and convincing in the language of some judges, 'the strongest possible' or else the mistake must be admitted by the opposite party; the resulting proof must be established beyond a reasonable doubt. 2 POM. EQ. JUR. § 859 at 1515 (3rd Ed.). [A]nd that opinion added:

> This court has said: "To authorize the reformation of a contract which has been reduced to writing and signed, the proof must be clear, exact, and satisfactory—that the writing does not truly express the intention of the parties that on which their minds had agreed; and second, what it was the parties intended the writing should express." ... Also: "If the proof is uncertain in any material respect, it will be held insufficient; and, while the courts may feel a great wrong has been done, they cannot grant relief by reason of uncertainty."

That description of the burden assumed by a plaintiff seeking reformation conforms to a principle applied in an earlier case, *Page v. Whatley*, 50 So. 116, 117 (Ala. 1909): "Equity grants reformation of deeds only when error certainly appears, and never upon a mere probability or a mere preponderance of evidence." Thus, as the court recognized in *Holland Blow Stave Co. v. Barclay*, 69 So. 118 (Ala. 1915), again citing Pomeroy: "[T]he only authority in the court is to reform the contract so as to express that which the parties agreed on. It cannot make a new contract for the parties, nor establish that as a contract between them, which it is supposed they would have made, if they had understood the facts."

Since the plaintiff's basis for reformation is grounded upon a mutual mistake of the parties, he had the burden of proving by such evidence as would meet those tests that there had been a meeting of the parties' minds on his version of their contract at the time that contract was made. *Behan v. Friedman*, 119 So. 20 (Ala. 1928).

In his testimony Lanford described the life commission schedule and explained its computations, together with the application of a general agent's rights to renewal premiums. He explained that variances existed among companies pertaining to vested renewal rights, and that one of his responsibilities was to convince general agents of the advantages of these benefits over those of other companies. This particular provision was a part of the original contract existing when he became agency vice-president of the company. He testified that its effect as written (to allow the company to retain a larger sum for servicing the policy after the agent had terminated the employment agreement than the company would retain if it took that service fee from each commission) was first shown to him by a general agent named Carl.

Lanford's testimony established that Carl complained to him that the three per cent service fee deducted from renewal commissions would amount to more than the agent would earn in service fee commissions, and to an amount over fifty per cent of his renewal commission in the third through tenth years. Lanford's response to Carl and to Painter shortly thereafter, was that the provision would be interpreted as *three per cent of commission* rather than *three per cent of premium*.

Lanford's testimony also disclosed a variance in the terms of the vested renewal section of some of the agency contracts, for he changed the Carl contract from ten per cent of the renewal commission to three per cent. The Carl contract, he explained, had for some reason shown a "ten per cent override" as opposed to a "three per cent renewal commission on vested renewal." (An override, in insurance parlance, is an additional amount of commission based upon what an agent produces). The problem regarding the three per cent service charge on commission was also raised by an agent named Worsham, and Lanford executed a contract with him allowing the percentage of renewal commissions specified in the agency agreement less a service fee of three per cent of each commission.

In addition, he and Mr. Boozer (company president) negotiated a new contract with an agent named Kubiszyn which involved changes in his commission schedule. He also referred to a memorandum he sent to Mr. Watkinson, another agent, pointing out that the three per cent service fee would be charged on commission. With regard to Painter's contract, his recollection was that he told Painter that (the clause in question) would be changed in his contract. "[I]t was not my intent," he testified, "that we take three per cent of the premium. ..."

Painter himself testified that he signed the general agent contract forms, but he did not question Mr. Lanford about their contents. He did not, in fact, discuss any details other than the fact that the commissions were different from those he had earned as an agent, and his right to employ agents. It was about a year later when he learned from George Carl about the three per cent charge. When he mentioned it to Mr. Lanford, he was told by him that it was supposed to be three per cent of commission and not premiums, and that "it was going to be three per cent of commission, that it would be changed when contracts were reprinted." On cross-examination he acknowledged a present awareness of the provision in his contract that all changes had to be in writing, but that Lanford had told him that the provision was not effective.

Taken as a whole, this evidence falls short of clearly establishing what Painter and Lanford agreed upon at the time the contract was made. It comes much closer to establishing what they would have agreed upon had they both considered the terms of the contract at the time it was executed and the implications it would have upon future eligibility for net renewal premiums.

What the evidence does show is that Painter entertained no intent at all upon that subject at the time the contract was executed. His intent was to sign a written contract which he had not read, the only terms of which discussed at that time being the commissions and the authority to employ agents. In fact, it is clear that Painter gave no thought to the question of vested renewal rights until a year after the contract had been executed. This hardly comports to a purpose, at the time of signing, to agree to a percentage of a service fee applied to commissions, and thus cannot support an inference that he made a mistake at that time, that is, that he misunderstood the terms, or made a wrong judgment. Painter could not have misunderstood the terms unless he attempted to acquaint himself with them, nor could he have made a wrong judgment unless he had considered the alternatives at the time of execution. ...

Considering the entire record favorably to the plaintiff, nevertheless it appears to prove a later intention of the parties rather than an intention of the parties at the time they contracted. There is an absence of that clear, convincing and satisfactory evidence which is required to overcome the presumption attending the deliberately written word, that most clear evidence which removes uncertainty about the parties' meaning. The evidence is equivocal, and being so it could not justify—on the ground of a mistake by both parties—the reformation decreed by the trial court which changed the words "of each premium" to the words "of each commission." It follows that the decree of the circuit court must be reversed and the case remanded, and it is so ordered.

Reversed and remanded.

B. The Doctrine of Unilateral Mistake

James T. Taylor & Son, Inc. v. Arlington Independent School District
335 S.W.2d 371
(Tex. 1960)

HAMILTON, JUSTICE. ... The School District had decided to build a Junior High School building and had called for competitive bids from various contractors for the construction. James Taylor submitted a bid, together with a performance bond, as was required, and his bid of $534,175 was the lowest of nine bids submitted. The School District, within a few minutes after the bids were opened, accepted the bid of Taylor. His bond, furnished by Seaboard Surety Company, provided that it would be null and void if the contract to build the building was subsequently executed by him; otherwise the obligors would pay the difference between the Taylor bid and the bid finally accepted. In addition to the total amount of the estimates, an amount of 6% was to be added by Taylor as anticipated profit margin. When this was done an error of $100,000 occurred due to a failure to carry a digit.

The error was not discovered until the morning after the School District had accepted the Taylor bid, when notice of such mistake was promptly given to the School District. Taylor refused to execute the tendered construction contract, and when the contract was returned unexecuted the Board awarded the contract to the next lowest bidder, Bock Construction Company. No readvertisement or additional expense was involved for the School District. Suit was instituted by the School District to recover on the bond the amount of the difference between the Bock bid and the Taylor bid, an amount of $36,278.

In reversing and remanding the summary judgment granted by the trial court to the petitioner, the Court of Civil Appeals held that on a new trial Taylor must prove by clear and convincing evidence that the unilateral mistake made by petitioner was not due to Taylor's negligence, and that the School District knew or had reason to know that Taylor had made a mistake prior to its acceptance of the bid. The holding of the Court of Civil Appeals is that Taylor is liable unless he proves these points. Taylor's points of error assert that equitable relief is not barred by ordinary negligence, but only by gross negligence or bad faith, and that it was not necessary that the School District know or have reason to know of the error prior to acceptance of the bid before rescission can be granted.

On the question of equitable relief by way of rescission, we have concluded that we cannot agree with the Court of Civil Appeals in holding that before petitioner is entitled to relief he must show by clear and convincing evidence that the unilateral mistake was not due to his own negligence and that the School District either knew or should have known of the mistake before accepting his bid. We think the great weight of authority is against the law as announced by the Court of Civil Appeals.

Most of the cases and legal writers affirm the proposition that equitable relief will be granted against a unilateral mistake when the conditions of remediable mistake are present. These conditions generally are: 1) the mistake is of so great a consequence that to enforce the contract as made would be unconscionable; 2) the mistake relates to a material feature of the contract; 3) the mistake must have been made regardless of the exercise of ordinary care; and 4) the parties can be placed in status quo in the equity sense, *i. e.*, rescission must not result in prejudice to the other party except for the loss of his bargain. There may be other circumstances which will govern or influence the extension of relief, such as the acts and extent of knowledge of the parties. ...

It is said in 43 AMERICAN JURISPRUDENCE, PUBLIC WORKS AND CONTRACTS § 63 at 805:

> As a general rule, equitable relief will be granted a bidder for a public contract where he has made a material mistake of fact in the bid which he submitted, and upon the discovery of that mistake acts promptly in informing the public authorities and requesting withdrawal of his bid or opportunity to rectify his mistake, particularly where he does so before any formal contract is entered into.

It seems to us to be well settled that even after acceptance of a bid, but before the execution of the contract contemplated by the parties, a bidder for a public contract who makes a remediable mistake in his bid may, by giving notice thereof before material change of position to the detriment of the offeree, obtain rescission of the bid or relief against its enforcement.

In applying the rules that should govern the granting of equitable relief for remediable mistake, the principal difficulty with which we are confronted is determining the effect of negligence on the part of one claiming equitable relief for his ... mistake. Of course, the very word "mistake" itself may connote some degree of negligence, and when the cases speak of an honest mistake and one made without negligence, it is difficult to determine just what kind of negligence is meant. In a footnote on page 794 of 52 A.L.R.2d, it is stated:

> The term "negligence," or its equivalent, in this connection generally means ordinary negligence, which will not necessarily bar granting equitable relief. Otherwise qualified, it generally means carelessness or lack of good faith in calculation which violates a positive duty in making up a bid, so as to amount to gross negligence, or wilful negligence, when it takes on a sinister meaning and will furnish cause, if established, for holding a mistake of the offending bidder to be one not remediable in equity. It is thus distinguished from a clerical or inadvertent error in handling items of a bid, either through setting them down or transcription.

In the case of *Dixon v. Morgan*, 285 S.W. 558 (Tenn. 1926), the court points out that only culpable negligence will preclude relief, and for negligence to be culpable it must be due to the failure to perform some duty, that it is not a failure of duty to one's self, but to another, that constitutes culpable negligence, and that a mistake in the computation of the cost of construction work in order to make a bid therefor does not indicate such culpable negligence as will preclude equitable aid to rescind the contract where to sustain it would give the other party an unconscionable advantage.

In the case of *Board of Regents of Murray State Normal School v. Cole,* 273 S.W. 508 (Ky. 1925), the contractor by mistake omitted a $22,000 item in submitting his bid, and it was there held that he was entitled to have the contract rescinded, the court saying that there was no doubt the contractor had made an honest mistake and it did not appear that he was guilty of culpable negligence. It was such an error as any businessman might make.

In *Barlow v. Jones*, 87 A. 649 (N.J. Ch. 1913), it was held the contractor was entitled to have his bid for public work cancelled where in making up his bid he had inadvertently omitted an item of $28,000. It appeared that he was in ill health and subjected to considerable pressure at the time, and under the circumstances the court said the mistake was one which might be made by a careful man, and certainly one which could not be characterized as gross negligence.

Several of the appellate courts of this state have had occasion to comment on this question. The *State v. Scholz Bros.,* 4 S.W.2d 661 (Tex. Civ. App. 1928) case indicates that any negligence will prevent rescission. However, in that case it appears that the elements of remediable mistake probably were not present. From the court's opinion it appears that the mistake may have resulted only in the contractor's not making a profit on his contract. Furthermore, it appears that the contractor, after his bid had been accepted, had signed the principal contract before notifying the owner of the mistake. In the *Warren v. Osborne*, 154 S.W.2d 944 (Tex. Civ. App. 1941) case, reformation was granted where one party had knowledge of the other's mistake. The court, in allowing reformation, though the party seeking it had been found negligent in the mistake, said: "The term 'mistake' involves some element of negligence which may or may not be excusable under the circumstances." ...

We think the authorities, both from this state and from other jurisdictions, clearly indicate that in cases of this kind ordinary negligence will not necessarily bar the granting of equitable relief. Generally, it is only when negligence amounts to such carelessness or lack of good faith in calculation which violates a positive duty in making up a bid, taking into consideration the nature of the transaction and the position of the opposite contracting party, that equitable relief will be denied.

We think that ... the facts—as testified to by Hicks, Taylor's estimator relating how the error was made and under the circumstances in which it was made—do not indicate such negligence as would bar Taylor from equitable relief. He says that he was severely limited as to time, and that it was necessary to compile the bids of many subcontractors, which were being received almost up to the deadline when the bid was to be submitted. He was rushed to get the estimate completed in time for submission. The work sheets, consisting of eight pages, were made a part of his deposition. From an examination of them it appears that the completed estimate as prepared by Hicks showed the cost to the contractor to be $598,326.86. ... While these facts, if true, would not necessarily bar equitable relief where the elements of remediable mistake are present, still we think that the trial court's summary judgment should not have been granted, for the reason that the record shows that the only witness testifying with reference to the error was Hicks, who was an interested witness.

The general rule is that the testimony of an interested witness does no more than raise a fact issue to be determined by the jury. While there are exceptions to the rule, it seems settled that when testimony comes from an interested party and is of such a nature that it cannot be readily contradicted if untrue, an issue relating to the credibility of the witness is presented. Further, the petitioner Taylor did not appear before the Board in his request for withdrawal of his bid, nor did he file an affidavit or submit his deposition in support of his motion for summary judgment, nor excuse his failure to do so. Consequently, it cannot be said as a matter of law that he did not know of the error, and on the issue of whether a mistake was in fact made, we think the court should, under the circumstances, have had the benefit of his testimony before granting him the equitable relief which he seeks. We therefore conclude that there was an issue of fact to be determined by the jury as to whether a mistake was in fact made.

Of course each of the elements of the test applicable to a remediable, unilateral mistake is a fact issue to be submitted to a jury unless it can be resolved by the court under the undisputed evidence. As we have heretofore said, the question of negligence gives us the most difficulty. We have said that every negligence will not necessarily bar equitable relief in a case of this kind. It follows, therefore, that the trial court, guided by the principles herein stated, should determine from the facts and circumstances under which the mistake was made whether there is raised such issue of negligence that should be submitted to the jury.

If there is raised an issue of fact as to whether the mistake was the result of such carelessness or lack of good faith in calculation which violates the positive legal duty in making a bid, then the court should inquire whether such mistake was wholly caused by the failure to exercise at least that minimum degree of care which a public authority in the position of the School District may reasonably expect all of its bidders to exercise in the light of the circumstances of the transaction and the practice of the trade.

Although we remand the case for different reasons than those set out by the Court of Civil Appeals in its opinion, its judgment remanding the cause for a new trial is affirmed.

NOTES AND QUESTIONS

1. **Remedying a Mutual Mistake Under the Restatement (Second) of Contracts § 152**. This restatement describes the remedy when *both parties* are mistaken about the terms in an agreement. It states:

   (1) Where a mistake of both parties at the time a contract was made as to a basic assumption on which the contract was made has a material effect on the agreed exchange of performances, the contract is voidable by the adversely affected party unless he bears the risk of the mistake under the rule stated in § 154.

   (2) In determining whether the mistake has a material effect on the agreed exchange of performances, account is taken of any relief by way of reformation, restitution, or otherwise.

2. **Remedying a Unilateral Mistake Under the Restatement (Second) of Contracts § 153**. This restatement reads:

   Where a mistake of one party at the time a contract was made as to a basic assumption on which he made the contract has a material effect on the agreed exchange of performances that is adverse to him, the contract is voidable by him if he does not bear the risk of the mistake under the rule stated in § 154, and (a) the effect of the mistake is such that enforcement of the contract would be unconscionable, or (b) the other party had reason to know of the mistake or his fault caused the mistake.

3. **The Doctrine of Reformation**. Reformation is a remedy. And a contracting party may reform a contract when antecedent immaterial expressions—during the preliminary stage of a contract's formation—become a part of the contract. *See Cerberus Intern., Ltd. v. Apollo Management, L.P.,* 794 A.2d 1141, 1152 n. 40 (Del. Supr., 2002) (citing Arthur Linton Corbin et al., CORBIN ON CONTRACTS § 614 (2001)). A court sitting in equity has the power to reform a contract to reflect the parties "real agreement." *Colvocoresses v. W.S. Wasserman Co.*, 28 A.2d 588, 589 (Del. Ch. 1942). But the law is clear: A court will not order a reformation unless a specific

prior contractual understanding exists between the parties and it conflicts with the terms of the written agreement. The prior understanding "provides a comparative standard" that tells the court of equity "exactly what terms to insert in the contract rather than ... creating a contract for the parties." *Collins v. Burke*, 418 A.2d 999, 1002 (Del. 1980).

4. **An Action for Reformation and the Doctrines of Mistake.** The doctrines of mutual and unilateral mistake allow an aggrieved party to reform a contract. Again, under the doctrine of mutual mistake, the aggrieved party must show that both parties were mistaken about certain material terms in the written agreement. Under the doctrine of unilateral mistake, the complaining party must prove that he was mistaken and that the other party was cognizant of the mistake and remained silent. In *Cerberus Intern., Ltd. v. Apollo Management, L.P.*, 794 A.2d 1141, 1151–52 (Del. 2002), the court added the following: "Regardless of which doctrine is used, the plaintiff must show by clear and convincing evidence that the parties came to a specific prior understanding that differed materially from the written agreement. ... The clear and convincing evidentiary standard is 'an intermediate evidentiary standard, higher than mere preponderance, but lower than proof beyond a reasonable doubt.'" *Id.* (quoting *In re Tavel*, 661 A.2d 1061, 1070 n. 5 (Del. 1995)

5. **An Action for Reformation and Standing Requirements Under the Restatement (Second) of Contracts § 155, Comment (e).** The following comment discloses who has standing to commence an action for reformation. It reads:

   > Reformation may be granted at the request of any party to the contract, including an intended beneficiary, or of a party's successor in interest. In contrast to the rules for avoidance stated in §§ 152 and 153, the party seeking relief need not show that the mistake has resulted in an inequality that adversely affects him. A party may, for example, seek and be granted reformation even though it makes his own performance more onerous when, absent reformation, the agreement would be unenforceable for lack of consideration or where the agreement would be voidable by the other party. A court will, however, deny reformation where the effect of the mistake is trivial.

6. **Reformation and Remedying a Mistake Under the Restatement (Second) of Contracts § 155.** This restatement

outlines when a mutual mistake involving written expressions justifies a reformation. It reads:

> Where a writing that evidences or embodies an agreement in whole or in part fails to express the agreement because of a mistake of both parties as to the contents or effect of the writing, the court may at the request of a party reform the writing to express the agreement, except to the extent that rights of third parties such as good faith purchasers for value will be unfairly affected.

SECTION FIVE: THE DOCTRINES OF IMPOSSIBILITY, IMPRACTICABILITY, AND FRUSTRATION OF PURPOSE

Consider RESTATEMENT (SECOND) CONTRACTS § 266. It reads:

EXISTING IMPRACTICABILITY OR FRUSTRATION

> (1) Where, at the time a contract is made, a party's performance under it is impracticable without his fault because of a fact of which he has no reason to know and the non-existence of which is a basic assumption on which the contract is made, no duty to render that performance arises, unless the language or circumstances indicate the contrary.
>
> (2) Where, at the time a contract is made, a party's principal purpose is substantially frustrated without his fault by a fact of which he has no reason to know and the non-existence of which is a basic assumption on which the contract is made, no duty of that party to render performance arises, unless the language or circumstances indicate the contrary.

Now, consider the impossibility of performance doctrine. A concise statement of the doctrine appears in 17 AM.JUR.2D ON CONTRACTS § 655 and it states:

> Impossibility of performance may be classified as original impossibility or supervening impossibility. Original impossibility is impossibility of performance existing at the time the contract was made, so that the contract was to do something, that was impossible from the outset, while supervening impossibility exists when the subject matter of the contract for which the parties bargained is no longer in existence or is no longer capable of being performed due to an unforeseen supervening act, for which the promisor is not responsible.

Generally, the authors of both treatises would force a defendant to overcome an arguably substantial legal barrier: Before a court excuses a defendant's non-performance, a defendant must prove that his contractual undertaking was frustrated, impracticable, or impossible "at the time the contract was made." But, as discussed in an earlier chapter, many negotiated contracts are fashioned over a long period of time. Therefore, it is difficult for one to pinpoint precisely the date or hour when "the contract was made."

Do state supreme courts embrace this rule without any restrictions? What is the test for establishing when a "contract was made"? Also, a bargained-for performance can be impracticable, impossible, or frustrated in fact as well as in law. Must a defendant prove the former or latter? Furthermore, what must be impossible or impracticable—the defendant's unique performance or a particular task?

A. Impossibility of Performance Doctrine

1) Employing the Impossibility Doctrine Defensively to Excuse Non-Performance

Opera Company of Boston, Inc. v. Wolf Trap Foundation for Performing Arts 817 F.2d 1094 (4th Cir. 1987)

DONALD RUSSELL, CIRCUIT JUDGE: This is a breach of contract suit by the plaintiff to recover the agreed payment from the defendant for four operatic performances at the Filene Center in The Wolf Trap Park. The plaintiff asserts it was prepared, able and willing to perform as agreed but that it was prevented from giving one of the performances because of cancellation by the defendant of the performance on the ground it considered the performance impossible as a result of an electrical storm which terminated power to the pavillion during the time this performance was to be given. The court found against defendant's claim of cancellation of the performance because of an unexpected occurrence and granted judgment in favor of plaintiff. Defendant has appealed.

I.

The parties in this suit are the The Opera Company of Boston, Inc., an operatic organization recognized both nationally and internationally. The defendant—The Wolf Trap Foundation for the Performing Arts—is an organization for the advancement of the performing arts headquartered at Vienna, Virginia, and as such sponsors at the Filene Center in the Wolf Trap Park operatic performances and similar artistic programs. The Filene Center is located in the Wolf Trap National

Park and is a part of the various facilities maintained and controlled by the National Park Service. …

This suit between the parties arises under a contract between the plaintiff The Opera Company of Boston, Inc. (Opera Company) and the defendant, The Wolf Trap Foundation for the Performing Arts (Wolf Trap). … [T]he Opera Company for its part agreed to give four "fully staged orchestrally accompanied [operatic] performances to the normally recognized standards" of the Opera Company on the nights of June 12, 13, 14 and 15, 1980 at the Filene Center. For this the Opera Company was to be paid by Wolf Trap $272,000 payable under a schedule providing for payment of $20,000 at the signing of the contract and a further $40,000 on April 1, 1980, with the balance payable in four equal installments before the rise of the curtain on each performance. Wolf Trap … was obliged to make the above payments and also to furnish the place of performance including an undertaking "to provide lighting equipment as shall be specified by the Opera Company of Boston's lighting designer."

Both parties to the contract performed apparently all their obligations under the contract through the operatic performance on June 14. These performances had been fully sold as well as had the remaining performance on June 15. During this final day, the weather was described as hot and humid, with rain throughout the day. Sometime between 6:00 and 6:30 p.m. a severe thunderstorm arose causing an electrical power outage. As a result all electrical service in the Park, in its roadways, parking area, pathways and auditorium were out. … [S]ome 3,000 people were in the Park for the performance; 3,500 more were expected before 8:00 p.m. when the performance was to begin.

The Park Service recommended the immediate cancellation of the performance and advised Wolf Trap if the performance were not cancelled, it disclaimed any responsibility for the safety of the people who were to attend as well as those who were to perform. … Since the performance was cancelled, Wolf Trap failed to make the final payment under the contract to the Opera Company. Five years after the cancellation, the Opera Company filed this suit to recover the balance due under the contract. Wolf Trap defended on the ground that performance by it of its obligation under the contract was excused under the doctrine of impossibility of performance. The basis for this defense was that the final performance by the Opera Company for which payment was claimed had been cancelled because a performance was impracticable as a result of the power outage.

II.

The district judge began his oral opinion granting judgment in favor of the plaintiff by noting that the parties had stipulated the contract in question, a memorandum detailing the occurrence at the Park on the evening of June 15 by ... an official of Wolf Trap, and the amount in issue. ... The single question on appeal is whether this dismissal of Wolf Trap's defense of impossibility of performance was proper. The resolution of this issue requires a review of the doctrine of impossibility. We proceed first to that review.

III.

The doctrine of impossibility of performance as an excuse or defense for a breach of contract was for long smothered under a declared commitment to the principle of sanctity of contracts. This rationale for constrained application of the doctrine was expressed by the United States Supreme Court in *Dermott v. Jones* (2 Wall.), 69 U.S. 1, 8 (1864):

> The principle which controlled the decision of the cases referred to rests upon a solid foundation of reason and justice. It regards the sanctity of contracts. It requires parties to do what they have agreed to do. If unexpected impediments lie in the way, and a loss must ensue, it leaves the loss where the contract places it. If the parties have made no provision for a dispensation, the rule of law gives none. It does not allow a contract fairly made to be annulled, and it does not permit to be interpolated what the parties themselves have not stipulated.

The growth of commercial activity in the nineteenth century, however, made this rigidity of the doctrine of impossibility both "economically and socially unworkable." ... [I]n *Taylor v. Caldwell*, 122 Eng. Rep. 309, 324 (1863), the English courts recognized these changed conditions and, relying largely on civil law precedents, relaxed the constraints on the doctrine. ...

It based such relaxation on the theory of an implied condition arising without express condition in the contract itself. ... [T]he United States Supreme Court in its decision in *Dermott v. Jones*, ... adopted the reasoning and the restatement of the doctrine of impossibility as enunciated in *Taylor v. Caldwell* in its decision in *The Tornado*, 108 U.S. 342, 351(1883). In that case the Court said:

> In *Taylor v. Caldwell*, 3 Best & Smith, 826, it is laid down as a rule, that, "in contracts in which the performance depends on the continued existence of a given person or thing, a condition is implied, that the impossibility of performance arising from the perishing of the person or thing shall excuse the performance." The reason given for the rule is, that without "any express stipulation that the destruction of the person or thing shall excuse the performance," "that excuse is by law implied, because, from the nature of the contract, it is apparent that

> the parties contracted on the basis of the continued existence of the particular person or chattel." ...

Lawson in his THE PRINCIPLES OF THE AMERICAN LAW OF CONTRACTS AT LAW AND IN EQUITY, § 425 at p. 465 (F.H. Thomas Law Book Co., St. Louis, 1893), stated as the prevalent American rule in this regard:

> Where the contract relates to the use or possession or any dealing with specific things in which the performance necessarily depends on the existence of the particular thing, the condition is implied by the law that the impossibility arising from the perishing or destruction of the thing, without default in the party, shall excuse the performance, because, from the nature of the contract, it is apparent that the parties contracted on the basis of the continued existence of the subject of the contract.

This relaxed rule for the application of the doctrine of impossibility of performance was adopted by the Supreme Court of Virginia. ... [I]n *Housing Authority, etc. v. East Tenn. L. & P. Co.*, 31 S.E.2d 273, 276 (Va. 1944), the court, observing that "[t]he tendency of the law is towards an enlargement of the defense, ..." said:

> It is, however, fairly well settled that where impossibility is due to domestic law, to the death or illness of one who by the terms of the contract was to do an act requiring his personal performance, or to the fortuitous destruction or change in the character of something to which the contract related, or which by the terms of the contract was made a necessary means of performance, the promisor will be excused, unless he either expressly agreed in the contract to assume the risk of performance, whether possible or not, or the impossibility was due to his fault. ...

[T]he United States Supreme Court in *Texas Co. v. Hogarth Shipping Co.,* 256 U.S. 619, 629–30 (1921) declared:

> [W]here parties enter into a contract on the assumption that some particular thing essential to its performance will continue to exist and be available for the purpose and neither agrees to be responsible for its continued existence and availability, the contract must be regarded as subject to an implied condition that, if before the time for performance and without the default of either party the particular thing ceases to exist or be available for the purpose, the contract shall be dissolved and the parties excused from performing it. ...

Increasingly, though, commentators and text writers were uncomfortable with the implied condition rationale for the new doctrine of impossibility of performance. In 6 CORBIN ON CONTRACTS § 1331, at 360

(1962 ed.), the author puts his objection to the implied condition theory strongly and rephrased the rationale for the doctrine thus:

> Though it has been constantly said by high authority, including Lord Sumner, that the explanation of the rule is to be found in the theory that it depends on an implied condition of the contract, that is really no explanation. It only pushes back the problem a single stage. It leaves the question what is the reason for implying a term. Nor can I reconcile that theory with the view that the result does not depend on what the parties might, or would as hard bargainers, have agreed. The doctrine is invented by the court in order to supplement the defects of the actual contract. The parties did not anticipate fully and completely, if at all, or provide for what actually happened. ...

The modern doctrine of impossibility or impracticability ... has been formulated in § 265 of the RESTATEMENT (SECOND) OF CONTRACTS in these words:

> Where, after a contract is made, a party's principal purpose is substantially frustrated without his fault by the occurrence of an event the non-occurrence of which was a basic assumption on which the contract was made, his remaining duties to render performance are discharged, unless the language or the circumstances indicate the contrary.

Supplementing this statement of the doctrine, the RESTATEMENT in § 263 defines the event the "non-occurrence of which [may be] a basic assumption on which the contract was made":

> If, ... the existence of a specific thing is necessary for the performance of a duty ... its failure to come into existence or its destruction or deterioration makes performance impracticable, [is an event] ... "the non-occurrence of which was a basic assumption on which the contract was made. ..."

[W]e accept as the correct statement of the modern and prevailing doctrine of impossibility of performance as a defense to a breach of contract to be essentially as equitable in character ... Manifestly the first fact to be established in making out this modern defense of impossibility or impracticability of performance is the existence of an "occurrence of an event, the non-occurrence of which was a basic assumption on which the contract was made."

And, in determining the existence of such occurrence, it is necessary to have in mind the RESTATEMENT's definition of an "occurrence" in this context as that which, because of the "destruction, or such deterioration" of a "specific thing necessary for the performance" of the contract "makes performance impracticable." The occurrence ... must be unexpected but it does not necessarily have to have been unforeseeable. A requirement of absolute non-foreseeability as a condition to the application of the doctrine would be so logically inconsistent that in effect it would nullify the doctrine. …

The second fact to be determined in the proposed application of the doctrine is that the frustration of performance was substantial. To satisfy this requirement "[t]he frustration must be so severe that it is not fairly to be regarded as within the risks [the obligor] assumed under the contract." Comment a, § 265 of RESTATEMENT (SECOND) OF CONTRACTS. And, finally, the defendant asserting the defense must establish that performance was impossible as that term has been defined in the refinements of the doctrine.

In summary, then, a party relying on the defense of impossibility of performance must establish (1) the unexpected occurrence of an intervening act, (2) such occurrence was of such a character that its non-occurrence was a basic assumption of the agreement of the parties, and (3) that occurrence made performance impracticable. When all those facts are established the defense is made out.

IV.

Applying the law as above stated to the facts of this case, we conclude, as did the district judge, that the existence of electric power was necessary for the satisfactory performance by the Opera Company on the night of June 15. While he seems to conclude that public safety was the main consideration on which the cancellation was based, he found that the power outage was the reason assigned for cancellation, and in that connection he found it to be questionable that "a generator could [have been] set up to provide additional light for the theater itself (when power from the utility company became unavailable) and still provide adequate light for the people who had to move backstage."

Such findings meet the requirement of RESTATEMENT (SECOND) ON CONTRACTS § 263 for an event, the "non-occurrence of which was a basic assumption on which the contract was made" and accordingly satisfies the definition of an impracticability which will relieve the obligor of his duty to perform as declared in section 265 of such RESTATEMENT (which we have accepted as the proper present statement of the doctrine of impossibility of performance as a defense to a breach of contract suit). Moreover, the facts as found make out impracticability of performance under the phraseology of the doctrine of impossibility in the Virginia case of *Housing Authority, supra*. The district judge, however, refused to sustain the defense because he held that if the contingency that occurred was one that could have been foreseen reliance on the doctrine of impossibility as a defense to a breach of contract suit is absolutely barred. As we have said, this is not the modern rule and he found that the power outage was foreseeable. In this the district judge erred. ...

CONCLUSION

The judgment herein must, therefore, be vacated and the action remanded to the district court to make findings, based on a statement of reasons, whether the possible foreseeability of the power failure in this case was of that degree of reasonable likelihood as to make improper the assertion by Wolf Trap of the defense of impossibility of performance.

The judgment of the district court is reversed, and the action is remanded with instructions.

2) Employing the Impossibility Doctrine Offensively to Reform a Contract

Silsbe v. Houston Levee Indus. Park, LLC
165 S.W.3d 260
(Tenn. Ct. App. 2004)

HOLLY M. KIRBY, J. delivered the opinion of the court. ... This is a contract case. On December 21, 2001, the parties entered into a contract granting the plaintiff an option to purchase real property. The plaintiff was required to exercise his option by 5:00 p.m., January 21, 2002, either by delivering written notice by that date to the defendant corporation, or by mailing written notification, postmarked no later than January 21, 2002. At the time the contract was executed, the parties were unaware that January 21st was a national holiday recognizing Martin Luther King, Jr.

On January 21, 2002, the plaintiff attempted to hand-deliver written notification of his intent to exercise the option, found no one at the defendant's office at the time and mistakenly assumed the office was closed because of the holiday. On January 22, the plaintiff hand-delivered written notice to the defendant. The defendant maintained that the option had expired. The plaintiff filed this lawsuit, seeking a declaratory judgment that the January 22 notice was timely and that the defendant was obligated to sell him the property pursuant to the option contract. After a trial, the trial court held in favor of the defendant, finding that the option had expired. The plaintiff appeals, arguing impossibility of performance and mutual mistake. ...

Plaintiff/Appellant Danny Silsbe (Silsbe) and Defendant/Appellee Houston Levee Industrial Park, LLC (Houston Levee) entered into a contract granting Silsbe the option to purchase from Houston Levee two certain parcels of real estate in Shelby County. The contract was negotiated on Houston Levee's behalf by its sole owner and registered agent, Ray Mattingly. The contract, executed on December 21, 2001, provided:

> [Houston Levee] does hereby give and grant to [Silsbe], the right to purchase said above described parcel of real estate, at any time, from this date until 5:00 P.M. (CST), January 21, 2002. ... If [Silsbe] exercises this option, [Silsbe] shall give [Houston Levee] written notice of his intention by the aforesaid date, said notice to be delivered in person or mailed by certified mail, return receipt requested, postmarked on or prior to the date herein specified, to the address of [Houston Levee]. ...

Both parties understood that Silsbe's notice of intent to exercise the option was to be given to Mattingly. Toward that end, Mattingly provided Silsbe with several telephone numbers, including his cell phone numbers, for Silsbe to contact him. At the time the contract was executed, both parties were unaware that they had set the deadline on the national holiday honoring Martin Luther King, Jr.

On January 21, 2002, neither Mattingly nor his agents received any notice that Silsbe had decided to exercise the option. On January 22, 2002, however, there was a flurry of activity designed to communicate Silsbe's intent to exercise the option. Silsbe hand-delivered a handwritten notice of intent to exercise the option to Mattingly's office assistant, Lisa Haddick (Haddick). Silsbe also telephoned both Mattingly and Houston Levee's attorney to tell them he wanted to exercise the option. Silsbe had his attorney fax a copy of the written notice to Houston Levee's attorney. The next day, Houston Levee's attorney notified Silsbe's attorney that the option had not been timely exercised and that Mattingly declined to extend the option.

On January 29, 2002, Silsbe filed this lawsuit, seeking a declaratory judgment that the notice provided to Houston Levee on January 22 was timely and that Houston Levee was therefore obligated to sell him the real property that was the subject of the option. In his complaint, Silsbe alleged in part that it had been impossible for him to provide notice by 5:00 p.m. on January 21, 2002, because January 21st was Martin Luther King, Jr. Day. He asked the trial court to construe the option contract in such a manner that the notice delivered to Haddick on January 22 would be deemed timely.

The trial was held on November 4, 2002. Silsbe testified at the trial. Silsbe described his attempts to deliver notice of his intent to exercise the option on January 21, 2002, in accordance with the terms of the contract. He testified that he called Mattingly's office that morning, and the telephone was answered by a recording. He did not leave a message. Later, at approximately 11:30 a.m., Silsbe went to Mattingly's office to hand deliver a type-written notice of his intent to exercise the option. He said, however, that the building was quiet and the door to Mattingly's office was closed. Although the door to Mattingly's office had a mail slot, Silsbe did not leave his typed notice or any other writing at the office. When asked whether he saw the mail slot in Mattingly's office door, Silsbe vacillated as to whether he saw the mail slot in the door, or saw it and did not recognize it as something in which he could have dropped the notice. Silsbe, however, steadfastly maintained in his testimony that, in any event, he would not have left the notice in the mail slot, because he was trying to hand deliver the document in accordance with the terms of the contract. ...

Haddick—Mattingly's administrative assistant of ten years—testified at the trial. She said that Mattingly's office was open on January 21, 2002, Martin Luther King, Jr. Day, and that Mattingly had told her to expect something from Silsbe either by mail or by hand-delivery from Silsbe himself. She testified that the office regularly opens at 8:30 a.m. and closes at 5:00 p.m. The office staff takes its lunch break every day from either 11:30 a.m. to 12:30 p.m. or 12:30 p.m. to 1:30 p.m. ... Haddick testified that, on January 21, 2002, the staff did not deviate from its normal practice of leaving for lunch at either 11:30 or 12:30 or from placing the clock sign on the door. If the staff is out of the office or the phone lines are busy, Haddick said, a caller has the option of leaving a message. She said that, on January 21, 2002, no such message was left by Silsbe.

At the conclusion of the trial, the parties submitted proposed findings of fact and conclusions of law. In his proposed findings and conclusions, Silsbe asserted that it was impossible to satisfy the terms of the option contract due to the Martin Luther King, Jr. holiday, the fact that Mattingly was out of town, and the difficulties he encountered in attempting to deliver notice to Mattingly's office on January 21, 2002. Silsbe argued that the parties did not intend for the option contract deadline to fall on a legal holiday, and contended that, when the contract was executed, the parties were unaware that January 21 was a national holiday. ... The trial court then held, "The fact that [the deadline] given to exercise the option, January 21, 2002, was a legal holiday, does not extend the time required for acceptance." ... The trial court therefore concluded that the option had expired. From that order, Silsbe now appeals.

On appeal, Silsbe argues that the trial court should have reformed the contract to set the option deadline on January 22, 2002. First, Silsbe asserts that, because 1) the mail could not be postmarked on January 21, 2002, due to the holiday, 2) Mattingly was unavailable to personally receive the notification, and 3) Silsbe was unable to make delivery at Silsbe's office, this amounts to impossibility of performance which justifies reforming the contract. Next, Silsbe argues that the contract should be reformed based on mutual mistake, because the parties were unaware that the day the option expired fell on Martin Luther King, Jr. Day. He notes that the contract contemplates that Silsbe would provide written notice on the deadline for exercising the option. Therefore, he contends, because the parties knew Mattingly would be out of town on January 21, 2002, the parties could not have intended for the deadline to fall on a national holiday, because this foreclosed both methods for Silsbe to exercise his option… .

It is well settled that an option is only enforceable as a contract when it is exercised by an unqualified, absolute, unconditional, unambiguous acceptance, without reservation, and in accordance with the terms of the option. *See Pinney v. Tarpley*, 686 S.W.2d 574, 580 (Tenn. Ct. App. 1984). It is also well settled that an optionee's method of acceptance may be limited by the optionor's specifications for notification. *See Dobson & Johnson, Inc., v. Waldron*, 47 Tenn. App. 121, 336 S.W.2d 313, 317 (1960). If an option contract specifies a certain manner in which the option must be exercised, the optionee must exercise the option according to those terms. *See Hall v. Crocker*, 241 S.W.2d 548, 549 (Tenn. 1951).

We first address Silsbe's argument that it was impossible for him to exercise his option on the deadline. In Tennessee, the doctrine of impossibility of performance is usually employed defensively, excusing nonperformance of a contract, rather than offensively, in order to reform a contract. Moreover, the doctrine of impossibility of performance is not applicable where performance becomes impossible due to factors which should have been foreseen and provided against. Silsbe has cited no Tennessee case applying the doctrine of impossibility of performance to an option contract, nor has our research revealed any such Tennessee cases.

Instead, Silsbe cites a case from the Supreme Court of Michigan, *O'Toole & Nedeau Co. v. Boelkins*, 235 N.W. 820 (Mich. 1931), in support of his "offensive" application of the doctrine to an option contract. O'Toole, however, has no application to the case at bar. In *O'Toole*, the plaintiffs attempted to exercise a real estate option by the deadline. The defendants learned that the plaintiffs intended to exercise the option and failed to appear to accept plaintiffs' tender. The *O'Toole* court found for the plaintiffs, holding that their failure to provide tender was excused because their attempt to do so "operate[d] as proof[ ] of readiness to perform" and "the tender [was] prevented through the contrivance of the persons to whom it should [have been] made."

In the present case, unlike *O'Toole*, there is no proof that Mattingly tried to avoid Silsbe. To the contrary, at the time the parties entered into the option, both were aware that Mattingly would be out of the city on January 21. Because of this, Mattingly gave Silsbe several phone numbers at which he could be reached on that day. The evidence does not preponderate against the trial court's finding that Mattingly's office was open on January 21, and that Mattingly's assistant was there to accept written notice on Mattingly's behalf. On January 21, 2002, Silsbe did not deliver written notice to Mattingly's assistant, leave a voice mail message at Mattingly's office, drop his typed notice in Mattingly's office mail slot, contact Mattingly on his mobile phone, or leave notice with Houston Levee's attorney.

Here, Silsbe simply has not shown that it was impossible for him to exercise the option in accordance with the contract. As noted by the trial court, Silsbe could have provided notice at any time from December 21, 2001 to January 21, 2002. Silsbe cannot rely on the fact that Mattingly was out of town on January 21, because Silsbe was aware that Mattingly would be out of town on that date at the time the contract was written. Silsbe was provided with a myriad of avenues for contacting Mattingly, even if he waited until the January 21 deadline, including hand-delivering a written notice to Mattingly's office, but he failed to do so. This argument is without merit.

We next address Silsbe's argument that reformation of the contract is warranted in light of the parties' mutual mistake in not being aware that the deadline for exercising the option fell on a national holiday. A written instrument may be reformed on the ground of mutual mistake when the mistake "is an act which would not have been done, or an omission which would not have occurred, but from ignorance, forgetfulness, inadvertence, mental incompetence, surprise, misplaced confidence, or imposition. ..." *Williams v. Botts,* 3 S.W.3d 508, 509–10 (Tenn. Ct. App. 1999). However, "[i]nattention, as distinguished from mistake, is no ground for reformation." Since the purpose of the doctrine is to permit the writing to fully and accurately reflect the parties' agreement, courts will not rewrite a contract "where the written instrument is drawn exactly as it was intended." Courts are to take into consideration the surrounding circumstances and any other factors which shed light on the parties' intentions. *City of Memphis ex rel. State v. Moore*, 818 S.W.2d 13, 16 (Tenn. Ct. App. 1991).

In this case, the trial court expressly found that the parties to the contract intended to grant Silsbe one month from the date of the contract in which to exercise his option, and the evidence does not preponderate against this finding. The contract was executed on December 21, 2001, and the option expired on January 21, 2002. Thus, the option contract was written in accordance with the parties' intentions. The fact that the parties were unaware that the last day of the option period fell on Martin Luther King, Jr. Day did not preclude Silsbe from exercising his option, and any "mistake" by the parties about this fact does not warrant reformation of the contract.

Therefore, we must conclude that the trial court did not err in finding that Silsbe failed to timely exercise the option and in declining to reform the contract as sought by Silsbe. ... The decision of the trial court is affirmed.

NOTES AND QUESTIONS

1. **Proving Impossibility of Performance—Objective Versus Subjective Test.** The *Opera* court identified the elements that a defendant must prove to construct a sound impossibility-of-performance defense. Is it a subjective or an objective standard? The court in *YPI 180 N. LaSalle Owner, LLC v. 180 N. LaSalle II, LLC*, 403 Ill. App. 3d 1, 7 (Ill. App. Ct. 2010) declared: The doctrine of legal impossibility or impossible performance excuses performance of a contract only when performance is rendered objectively impossible either because the subject matter is destroyed or by operation of law.

2. **Proof of an Impossible Task or Defendant's Inability to Perform?** "[I]t is the task itself which must be impossible—it is not enough that the particular promisor is unable to perform the task if it would be possible for a different promisor to perform." *State v. Chacon*, 198 P.3d 749, 752 (Idaho Ct. App. 2008). *See also Haessly v. Safeco Title Ins. Co. of Idaho*, 825 P.2d 1119, 1121 (Idaho 1992) ("The doctrine of impossibility operates to excuse performance when the bargained-for performance is no longer in existence or is no longer capable of being performed due to the unforeseen, supervening act of a third party.").

3. **Competing Standards for Establishing an Impossibility-of-Performance Defense**. Reconsider the three-prong standard that the court fashioned in *Opera*. Now, consider the Idaho Supreme Court's declaration in *Kessler v. Tortoise Dev., Inc.*, 937 P.2d 417, 420 (Idaho 1997): "In order to prove impossibility: (1) a contingency must occur; (2) performance must be impossible, not just more difficult or more expensive; and (3) the nonoccurrence of the contingency must be a basic assumption of the agreement." Obviously, the tests in *Kessler* and *Opera* are different. Can they be harmonized?

B. Impracticability of Performance Doctrine

The following statements appear in the *Opera* opinion: 1) "Manifestly the first fact to be established in making out this modern defense of *impossibility or impracticability* of performance is the existence of an 'occurrence of an event, the non-occurrence of which was a basic assumption on which the contract was made'"; and 2) "a party relying on the *defense of impossibility* of performance must establish "that [an] occurrence made performance *impracticable*." Is there a bright-line test which truly distinguishes the two doctrines? Does the analysis in the next case remove the confusion?

Luminous Neon, Inc. v. Parscale
836 P.2d 1201
(Kan. Ct. App. 1992)

BRAZIL, PRESIDING JUDGE. Rita M. Parscale and Rawhide Enterprises of Kansas, Inc. (Parscale) appeal from the district court's grant of summary judgment in favor of Luminous Neon, Inc. Luminous Neon filed suit against Parscale, seeking liquidated damages in accordance with a lease between the parties. On appeal, Parscale contends that the liquidated damages clause constitutes a penalty and is consequently unenforceable, the doctrine of impracticability should release her from the lease, and Luminous Neon has been unjustly enriched by the court's ruling.

The facts are not largely in dispute. Parscale leased two custom-designed outdoor advertising signs from Luminous Neon. Parscale used the signs for her recently opened restaurant business in Topeka. Under the terms of the lease, Parscale paid $191.75 plus tax per month. The lease expired after five years. Sometime after Parscale leased the signs, the City of Topeka commenced construction on 21st Street that limited access to Parscale's business. That construction had an adverse effect upon Parscale's business, and the enterprise was subsequently closed. Parscale stopped making payments on the signs after making a total of 19 payments.

Under the liquidated damages clause of the lease, Parscale was liable to Luminous Neon for damages equal to 80 percent of the remaining payments due. That 80 percent represented Luminous Neon's expenses incurred in manufacturing, financing, and installing the signs, as well as profit. The 20 percent of the remaining payments that was not included as liquidated damages was for maintenance and service expenses that will not be incurred due to Parscale's breach.

Forty-one monthly payments of $191.75 remained due and payable, resulting in liquidated damages—including tax—of $6,651.04. Luminous Neon removed the signs from Parscale's business following her request to do so. The removal added another $300 for a total of

$6,951.04. The district court granted Luminous Neon's motion for summary judgment and awarded the company $6,951.04.

Parscale contends the court erred in granting summary judgment because a material fact existed relating to the liquidated damages claim of Luminous Neon. She argues that Luminous Neon's offer, made at the outset of negotiations between the parties, to sell the sign for $5,600 plus tax reveals that the liquidated damages were unreasonable. …

Parscale challenges, in a variety of ways, the reasonableness of the liquidated damages. The contention that only the original sale price of the signs constitutes reasonable damages is not persuasive. There are advantages and disadvantages to be weighed when one considers leasing rather than purchasing an item. However, when one chooses to lease an item and then breaches that lease, it is unreasonable to believe damages should be based upon values attendant to a purchase of that item.

By leasing rather than purchasing, Parscale avoided financing charges, insurance, repair, and maintenance expenses. Luminous Neon agreed to maintain the signs during the term of the lease. The general rule is that courts will "refuse to enforce a liquidated damage provision which fixes damages in an amount grossly disproportionate to the harm actually sustained or likely to be sustained, and under certain circumstances indicative of gross disproportion," such a provision will be deemed a penalty. 22 AM.JUR.2D, DAMAGES § 701 at 758. … There is, however, case law from other jurisdictions that supports the manner in which liquidated damages were determined in this case. … Luminous Neon custom designed the signs specifically for Parscale, and, notwithstanding her argument to the contrary, we are not persuaded that the signs are of particular value to Luminous Neon. Moreover, the trial court awarded the signs to Parscale.

The district court properly ruled as a matter of law that the liquidated damages were appropriate. The damage clause of the lease was not a penalty, and the award did not unjustly enrich Luminous Neon. Because there was no dispute regarding any material issue of fact, the court's entry of summary judgment should not be disturbed.

Next, Parscale contends that the doctrine of impracticability of performance applies to this case and consequently she should be excused from her obligations under the lease. Specifically, Parscale asserts that she should be excused from the lease because the City of Topeka closed 21st Street for construction, which made access to Parscale's business difficult. Her business suffered as a consequence, and she was eventually forced to close the establishment.

"Whether a party should be excused from its obligations under a contract because of impossibility or impracticability of performance is a question of law." *Sunflower Electric Coop., Inc. v. Tomlinson Oil Co.*,

638 P.2d 963 (Kan. App. 1981). ... As a general rule, difficulty or improbability of accomplishment without financial loss will not release a party from a contract. Though compliance may become a hardship, that will not excuse a party from contractual obligations that are possible and lawful. *See* 17A AM.JUR.2D, CONTRACTS § 669.

This court has held:

> To excuse performance, impracticability must be objective as opposed to subjective. When one agrees to perform an act possible in itself, he will be liable for a breach thereof although contingencies not foreseen by him arise which make it difficult, or even beyond his power, to perform and which might have been foreseen and provided against in the contract." *Sunflower Electric Coop., Inc. v. Tomlinson Oil Co.*, 7 Kan. App. 2d 131.

This court has also noted that a distinction exists between impracticability that is subjective and that which is objective: subjective impracticability being, "I cannot do it"; objective impracticability being, "the thing cannot be done." 7 Kan. App. 2d at 139. Only objective impracticability may serve to relieve a party of his or her obligation.

The present case is one of subjective impracticability. Parscale could no longer afford to operate her business due to road construction or some other reason. It is not sufficient merely that the business suffered. *See also White Lakes Shopping Center, Inc. v. Jefferson Standard Life Ins. Co.*, 490 P.2d 609 (Kan. 1971) (Where the alleged impossibility was that more financing was needed for a construction project than had previously been agreed to in a loan commitment, the impossibility was subjective.) and, *Wichita Properties v. Lanterman*, 633 P.2d 1154 (Kan. App. 1981) (Inability to obtain liquor license from the state was subjective impossibility to perform.).

In addition, it cannot be said that road construction within Topeka is an unforeseeable event. Certainly, Parscale was aware that such an eventuality might take place. It was incumbent upon Parscale to safeguard her position in the terms of the lease. If impossibility existed in this case, it was subjective only. The district court's grant of summary judgment was appropriate. Affirmed.

C. Frustration of Purpose Doctrine

Huber v. Farmers Union Service Ass'n of North Dakota
787 N.W.2d 268
(N.D. 2010)

MARING, JUSTICE. Farmers Union Service Association of North Dakota (Farmers Union) appeals from a judgment awarding Duane Huber $34,534 plus interest, costs and disbursements in Huber's breach of contract action to recover his retirement benefits. We conclude the district court did not err in its interpretation of the contracts between the parties and in holding the contracts were not unlawful and void as a matter of law. …

Huber was a licensed insurance agent in North Dakota who began selling insurance for National Farmers Union Property and Casualty Company and Farmers Union Mutual Insurance Company in 1975. Under the local agent's agreements Huber signed, Farmers Union acted as the general agent for these companies. The local agent's agreement with National Farmers Union Property and Casualty Company provided in part:

> 6. Termination: (a) The parties hereto agree that each party hereto without assigning cause may terminate this Agreement at any time upon written notice mailed certified or registered, postage fully paid, to the other parties at the address shown in this Agreement at least thirty (30) days before the date of termination. Upon termination LOCAL AGENT shall be paid all commission earnings and bonuses currently due and unpaid less any obligations due INSURER, or GENERAL AGENT, and thereafter LOCAL AGENT shall have no further interest in the contracts or policies of INSURER or commission earnings thereof and bonuses thereon whether sold by him during or before the life of this Agreement. …

The local agent's agreement with Farmers Union Mutual Insurance Company similarly provided in part:

> 14. The parties hereto agree that any party hereto may terminate this contract at any time upon written notice mailed certified or registered, postage fully paid, to the other parties at the address shown above at least thirty (30) days before date of termination. Upon termination LOCAL AGENT shall be paid all earned commissions currently due and unpaid less any obligations due INSURER or GENERAL AGENT and thereafter shall have no further interest in the policies or contracts of INSURER or commission thereon whether sold by him during or before the life of this contract. …

Each local agent's agreement contained an identical agent's annuity benefit attachment. The agent's annuity benefit attachments provided that the companies would pay "an annuity benefit as described herein on the total combined commissions earned on paid-for premiums written or serviced by Local Agent for [the companies] during each calendar year, subject to the conditions and limitations stated herein, …" The annuity benefits payable were to be applied by the companies "to the purchase of a deferred to age 65 annuity contract for LOCAL AGENT or to fund LOCAL AGENT'S Internal Revenue Service qualified retirement plan. …" One of the conditions and limitations provided in the attachments was that "[t]he annuity benefits hereunder shall be payable only if this LOCAL AGENT'S Agreement and Attachment are in effect on the last day of the applicable calendar year, unless earlier terminated by death of LOCAL AGENT."

On November 27, 2002, a federal district court jury found Huber guilty of felony charges involving money laundering, fraud, making false statements, and tax related crimes. Huber was sentenced to five years in prison and ultimately ordered to forfeit $3.9 million. These convictions were not related to Huber's work as an insurance agent. On December 2, 2002, the North Dakota Insurance Commissioner, based on Huber's federal court convictions, issued a cease and desist order preventing Huber "from soliciting, transacting, or otherwise engaging in the business of insurance." The cease and desist order further provided that if Huber failed to request a hearing "within 30 days," the cease and desist order would become "permanent." Huber requested a hearing.

On December 5, 2002, the general manager of Farmers Union sent Huber a letter which stated in part:

> This is to notify you of the termination of your local agent's agreement with the Farmers Union Companies along with any other appointments secured through Farmers Union Service Association, Ltd.
>
> This termination is based on, but not limited to, events that are in violation of the contract, culminating with the recent "cease and desist" order from the North Dakota Insurance Department. Without a North Dakota insurance license, you will not be able to perform the functions required of a Farmers Union insurance agent.

On December 10, 2002, the federal district court issued an order freezing Huber's accounts and assets. On July 1, 2003, Huber entered into a consent order with the Insurance Commissioner that allowed his insurance agent license to be revoked. In a letter dated September 21, 2004, Farmers Union informed the United States Attorney that it was holding $253,869.11 in "unremitted earned commissions" belonging to Huber, and in November 2005, Farmers Union issued a check to the federal government for that amount. These funds did not include the annuity benefit of $34,534 based on Huber's production for calendar year 2002. The federal court order freezing Huber's assets was lifted in March 2006.

After Farmers Union refused to pay him his annuity benefit for calendar year 2002, Huber brought this breach of contract action against Farmers Union to recover the annuity benefit of $34,534. Farmers Union argued its contractual obligations to Huber were extinguished as a matter of law upon his federal court convictions for felony fraud and upon the Insurance Commissioner's issuance of the cease and desist order. Farmers Union also argued Huber was not entitled to the annuity benefit because his local agent's agreements were terminated on December 5, 2002, and therefore those agreements were not in effect on the last day of the calendar year.

Through a series of summary judgment rulings, the district court rejected Farmers Union's arguments. The court held Farmers Union was obligated to pay Huber the $34,534 annuity benefit because the parties' agreements required 30 days' notice before termination, Huber was not given notice of termination until early December 2002, so the 30 days did not expire until early January 2003. The court held, consequently, the local agent's agreements remained in effect on the last day of 2002, entitling Huber to the annuity benefits under the parties' agreements. The court awarded Huber $34,534 plus interest, costs and disbursements. This award included prejudgment interest dating from January 1, 2003, because, the court reasoned, Farmers Union "had the beneficial use of the funds for any purposes of its business" at that time.

II

Farmers Union argues the district court erred in holding its contractual obligations to Huber were not extinguished as a matter of law upon his felony fraud conviction and upon the Insurance Commissioner's issuance of the cease-and-desist order. ... Farmers Union argues its obligations to Huber under the local agent's agreements were extinguished under the doctrines of frustration of purpose and impossibility of performance because the "sole purpose" of the agreements was to allow Huber to act as an insurance agent, and after the federal court convictions and the cease and desist order, Huber could no longer act as an insurance agent. The district court ruled the cease and desist order was "temporary in nature," and "temporary impossibility of performance or temporary frustration of purpose of the contract does not discharge the contractual obligations of a contracting party."

Even if we assume the district court ascribed the wrong reason for the result it reached, this court will not reverse if the result is the same under the correct law and reasoning. There is a much more fundamental reason why neither doctrine applies in this case. In *Red River Wings, Inc. v. Hoot, Inc.*, 751 N.W.2d 206 (N.D. 2008), this court explained:

> [T]he doctrine of frustration of purpose [and] the doctrine of impossibility ... are closely related. Frustration of purpose "occurs when 'after a contract is made, a party's principal purpose is substantially frustrated without his fault by the occurrence of an event the non-occurrence of which was a basic assumption on which the contract was made.'" The doctrine of

> impossibility or impracticality is similarly described as "[w] here, after a contract is made, a party's performance is made impracticable without his fault by the occurrence of an event the non-occurrence of which was a basic assumption on which the contract was made, his duty to render that performance is discharged, unless the language or the circumstances indicate the contrary." Neither doctrine applies if either the frustration or the impossibility is caused by a party to the contract.

The principle that the doctrines of frustration of purpose and impossibility of performance do not apply if the frustration or impossibility is caused by one of the contracting parties is explained in the RESTATEMENT (SECOND) OF CONTRACTS (1981). Illustration 5 to Comment a of RESTATEMENT (SECOND) OF CONTRACTS § 264 (1981) (relating to prevention of performance by governmental regulation or order) states:

> 5. *A* and *B* make a contract under which *A* is to employ *B* for a year. *B* is unable to complete his performance because he is arrested and imprisoned for a burglary that he has committed. Because his inability was due to his own fault, *B's* duty to work for a year is not discharged, and *B* is liable to *A* for breach of contract.

Comment d to RESTATEMENT (SECOND) OF CONTRACTS § 261 (1981) (relating to discharge by supervening impracticability) states:

> d. Impracticability. Events that come within the rule stated in this Section are generally due either to "acts of God" or to acts of third parties. If the event that prevents the obligor's performance is caused by the obligee, it will ordinarily amount to a breach by the latter and the situation will be governed by the rules stated in Chapter 10, without regard to this Section. *See* Illustrations 4–7 to § 237. If the event is due to the fault of the obligor himself, this Section does not apply. As used here "fault" may include not only "willful" wrongs, but such other types of conduct as that amounting to breach of contract or to negligence.

In this case, Farmers Union argues the frustration or impossibility was caused by Huber, a party to the local agent's agreements. Therefore, we conclude the district court did not err in ruling that neither doctrine applies. ... The judgment is affirmed.

NOTES AND QUESTIONS

1. **Frustration of Venture Doctrine and Alias Names**. The Wyoming Supreme Court discussed the frustration of venture doctrine and its various names in *Downing v. Stiles,* 635 P.2d 808, 811 (Wyo. 1981). The court stated:

   The doctrine of "commercial frustration" or "frustration of the venture" or "discharge of commercial contract by supervening frustration" in the law of contracts "has been said to be a relatively modern one." 17A C.J.S. CONTRACTS § 463(2)(b). It grew out of the so-called coronation cases initiated *in Krell v. Henry*, 2 K.B. 740 (1903) wherein a defendant was excused from payment for use of an apartment from which to view the coronation proceedings of King Edward VII because the proceedings were cancelled when the king became ill. … The general principle underlying the doctrine of commercial frustration is that where the purpose of a contract is completely frustrated and rendered impossible of performance by a supervening event or circumstance, the contract will be discharged. The doctrine is predicated on the premise of giving relief in a situation where the parties could not provide themselves, by the terms of the contract, against the happening of subsequent events, so, if the intervening or supervening event was reasonably foreseeable, or was controllable by the parties, they may not invoke the principles of the doctrine as a defense to escape their obligations. It applies to executory contracts alone." 17A C.J.S. CONTRACTS § 463(2)(b) at 620–621.

2. **Distinguishing the Commercial Frustration and Impossibility Doctrines**. In *Downing v. Stiles,* 635 P.2d 808, 811 (Wyo. 1981), the court states that the doctrine of commercial frustration "is akin to the doctrine of impossibility of performance of a contract, and the two doctrines are often treated under the same heading in encyclopedias and textbooks." (citing 18 WILLISTON ON CONTRACTS (3rd ed.) § 1946, et seq.; 6 CORBIN ON CONTRACTS § 1353, et seq., 17A C.J.S. CONTRACTS § 462(2); and, 17 AM.JUR.2D CONTRACTS § 400, et seq. However, the generally recognized distinction between the two doctrines lies in the inability to literally perform (impossibility) and the impracticability to perform (commercial frustration)." (citing 17 AM. JUR. 2D CONTRACTS § 401; and, 17A C.J.S. CONTRACTS § 463).

3. **Frustration of Venture Doctrine Applied to Disputes Involving Marine-Insurance Contracts.** A still timely discussion of the frustration of venture doctrine appears in *Recent*

Cases—Insurance Clause Excepting Loss or Frustration of Venture by Government Restraint Held Inapplicable to Constructive Loss of Goods, 55 Harv. L. Rev. 686, 686–87 (1942). In relevant part, the author reported:

> In the summer of 1939, a British owner insured goods for a voyage from South America to China in the German steamship *Minden*. Although the policy covered war risks, it contained the standard Lloyd's frustration clause—relieving the underwriter of liability for claims "based upon loss of, or frustration of, the insured voyage or venture caused by arrests, restraints or detainments of kings, princes, peoples. …" When hostilities became imminent, the master of the *Minden* deviated from his course and put into Rio. After war was declared, he sailed for Germany, finally scuttling the vessel in the presence of a British warship. All these actions were in accordance with the orders of the German Government. The owner sought to recover for the loss of the cargo, but the King's Bench Division sustained the underwriter's contention that liability was precluded by the frustration clause. This judgment was reversed by the Court of Appeal, and the underwriter appealed to the House of Lords. Held: [T]he owner could recover since the claim was based not upon a frustration of the venture but upon a constructive loss of the goods occurring at the latest when the *Minden* left Rio. Appeal dismissed. *Rickards v. Forestal Land, Timber & Railways Co.*, 3 All Eng. 62 (H. L. 1941). …
>
> The frustration clause—couched in the archaic phraseology of marine insurance—was adopted following a decision in the last war, establishing … that a policy on cargo covers a loss of the venture although the goods are safe and, … that a legal prohibition evoked by a declaration of war constitutes a "restraint of princes" even without presence of force. … The intention of the underwriters in introducing the frustration clause may well have been to escape generally the indirect war risks which this allocated to them rather than to avoid only liability[.]
>
> Since the frustration clause, unlike the basic provisions, had not acquired an established meaning from judicial construction, their Lordships relied to some extent on a literal interpretation of "voyage or venture" to exclude goods, although "loss of, or frustration of, the insured voyage or venture" might have been construed to contemplate two distinct factual situations—where the venture including the goods is lost and where the venture is frustrated but the goods remain intact.

> ... The holding that the deviation was involuntary because of the German orders is questionable, since in any case the master probably would have entered a neutral port to avoid capture, and his instructions made discretionary the return to Germany from a place of safety. Since this was a test case to secure an interpretation of the frustration clause, their Lordships placed their holding on the ground of a constructive loss, although they might have relied on the actual loss by scuttling.

SECTION SIX: THE COMMON-LAW PAROL EVIDENCE RULE

The statute-of-frauds defense was discussed in an earlier chapter. And, among several general rules and exceptions, we learned that an oral contract must be in writing if contracting parties cannot perform the undertaking within one year. We also learned that state legislatures and courts advance competing reasons for requiring parties to fashion a written contract if it takes the parties more than a year to perform. They are: 1) A written contract helps a court to fulfill the parties' intent by protecting against fraud and undue influence, and by providing probative evidence of their intent; 2) A written contract allows a court to resolve contractual disputes more efficiently, without guessing or trying to determine what the parties intended twelve months earlier; and 3) A thoughtful, well-constructed and written contract is an intelligible barrier that engenders protectionism and prevents unscrupulous parties from exploiting the legal system.

In addition, for many jurists and commentators, a written contract is a sacred instrument. Consequently, it must be protected forever at all cost. *See* Joseph M. Perillo, CALAMARI AND PERILLO ON CONTRACTS § 13.1, at 445 (6th ed. 2009) ("The harsh traditional common law rule was '*pacta sunt servanda*;' promises must be kept though the heavens fall."). Moreover, as we have learned, the doctrines of impossibility, impracticality of performance, frustration of purpose, and similar manifestations of force majeure impose virtually insurmountable hurdles for defendants. Without doubt, the sanctity of written contracts is the celebrated and guiding principle that lies behind those legal doctrines. *See* Nagla Nassar, SANCTITY OF CONTRACTS REVISITED 205–215 (1999); and, *Silverman v. Charmac*, 414 So.2d 892, 894 (Ala. 1982) ("This court has not recognized the defense of impossibility or impracticability. 'Where one by his contract undertakes an obligation which is absolute, he is required to perform within the terms of the contract or answer in damages, despite an act of God, unexpected difficulty, or hardship, because these contingencies could have been provided against by his contract.'").

The parol evidence rule dovetails the latter points and reinforces the notion that written contracts are sacred. Some commentators, however, have asserted that the parol evidence rule has too many exceptions; therefore, courts' ever-increasing creative applications of the rule have undermined the sanctity of written contracts. For example, in Mark O. Morris and Elizabeth Evensen's article entitled, *What's Happening to the Parol Evidence Rule? More Holes in the Dike*, 67 DEF. COUNS. J. 209, 209 (2000), they assert:

> Sanctity of contract has been a hallmark of American commerce. One of the guardians of this sanctity has been the parol evidence rule, which was developed to prevent contracting parties from trying to offer evidence to vary the terms of an unambiguous contract. Unfortunately, creative lawyers have persuaded some courts to effectively abandon the rule. The result is creating uncertainty in contractual relationships, turning contract interpretation into a sophomoric exercise that undermines expectations of certainty.

The parol evidence rule essentially forbids a court's considering parties' prior or contemporaneous writings or oral statements in a breach-of-contract dispute, if those written or oral statements contradict the parties' final, written contract. This section discusses the parol evidence rule and its exceptions. As you read the cases and notes, try to determine whether Morris and Evensen's concern is legitimate or simply overstatement.

A. Parol Evidence Rule and Totally Integrated Written Contracts

Mitchill v. Lath
160 N.E. 646
(N.Y. 1928)

ANDREWS, J. In the fall of 1923 the Laths owned a farm. This they wished to sell. Across the road, on land belonging to Lieutenant Governor Lunn, they had an icehouse which they might remove. Mrs. Mitchill looked over the land with a view to its purchase. She found the icehouse objectionable. Thereupon "the defendants orally promised and agreed, for and in consideration of the purchase of their farm by the plaintiff, to remove the said icehouse in the spring of 1924." Relying upon this promise, she made a written contract to buy the property for $8,400 for cash and mortgage and containing various provisions usual in such papers. Later receiving a deed, she entered into possession, and has spent considerable sums in improving the property for use as a summer residence. The defendants have not fulfilled their promise as to the icehouse, and do not intend to do so. We are not dealing, however, with their moral delinquencies. The question before us is whether their oral agreement may be enforced in a court of equity.

This requires a discussion of the parol evidence rule—a rule of law which defines the limits of the contract to be construed. It is more than a rule of evidence, and oral testimony, even if admitted, will not control the written contract. It applies, however, to attempts to modify such a contract by parol. It does not affect a parol collateral contract distinct from and independent of the written agreement. It is, at times, troublesome to draw the line.

Williston, in his work on CONTRACTS § 637 points out the difficulty. "Two entirely distinct contracts," he says, "each for a separate consideration, may be made at the same time, and will be distinct legally. Where, however, one agreement is entered into wholly or partly in consideration of the simultaneous agreement to enter into another, the transactions are necessarily bound together. ... Then if one of the agreements is oral and the other in writing, the problem arises whether the bond is sufficiently close to prevent proof of the oral agreement." That is the situation here. It is claimed that the defendants are called upon to do more than is required by their written contract in connection with the sale as to which it deals.

The principal may be clear, but it can be given effect by no mechanical rule. As so often happens it is a matter of degree, for, as Prof. Williston also says, where a contract contains several promises on each side, it is not difficult to put any one of them in the form of a collateral agreement. If this were enough, written contracts might always be modified by parol. Not from, but substance, is the test.

In applying this test, the policy of our courts is to be considered. We have believed that the purpose behind the rule was a wise one, not easily to be abandoned. Notwithstanding injustice here and there, on the whole it works for good. Old precedents and principles are not to be lightly cast aside, unless it is certain that they are an obstruction under present conditions. New York has been less open to arguments that would modify this particular rule, than some jurisdictions elsewhere. Thus in *Eighmie v. Taylor*, 98 N. Y. 288, it was held that a parol warranty might not be shown, although no warranties were contained in the writing.

Under our decisions before such an oral agreement as the present is received to vary the written contract, at least three conditions must exist: (1) The agreement must in form be a collateral one; (2) it must not contradict express or implied provisions of the written contract; (3) it must be one that parties would not ordinarily be expected to embody in the writing, or, put in another way, an inspection of the written contract, read in the light of surrounding circumstances, must not indicate that the writing appears "to contain the engagements of the parties, and to define the object and measure the extent of such engagement." Or, again, it must not be so clearly connected with the principal transaction as to be part and parcel of it.

The respondent does not satisfy the third of these requirements. It may be, not the second. We have a written contract for the purchase and sale of land. The buyer is to pay $8,400 in the way described. She is also to pay her portion of any rents, interest on mortgages, insurance premiums, and water meter charges. She may have a survey made of the premises. On their part, the sellers are to give a full covenant deed of the premises as described, or as they may be described by the surveyor, if the survey is had, executed, and acknowledged at their own expense; they sell the personal property on the farm and represent they own it; they agree that all amounts paid them on the contract and the expense of examining the title shall be a lien on the property; they assume the risk of loss or damage by fire until the deed is delivered; and they agree to pay the broker his commissions. Are they to do more? Or is such a claim inconsistent with these precise provisions? It could not be shown that the plaintiff was to pay $500 additional. Is it also implied that the defendants are not to do anything unexpressed in the writing?

That we need not decide. At least, however, an inspection of this contract shows a full and complete agreement, setting forth in detail the obligations of each party. On reading it, one would conclude that the reciprocal obligations of the parties were fully detailed. Nor would his opinion alter if he knew the surrounding circumstances. The presence of the icehouse, even the knowledge that Mrs. Mitchill thought it objectionable, would not lead to the belief that a separate agreement existed with regard to it. Were such an agreement made it would seem most natural that the inquirer should find it in the contract. Collateral in form it is found to be, but it is closely related to the subject dealt with in the written agreement—so closely that we hold it may not be proved. Where the line between the competent and the incompetent is narrow the citation of authorities is of slight use. Each represents the judgment of the court on the precise facts before it. How closely bound to the contract is the supposed collateral agreement is the decisive factor in each case. …

We do not ignore the fact that authorities may be found that would seem to support the contention of the appellant. Such are *Erskine v. Adeane,* L. R. 8 Ch. App. 756 (1873), and *Morgan v. Griffith*, L. R. 6 Exch. 70 (1871), where—although there was a written lease—a collateral agreement of the landlord to reduce the game was admitted. In this state, *Wilson v. Deen* might lead to the contrary result. Neither are they approved in New Jersey. Nor in view of later cases in this court can *Batterman v. Pierce*, 3 Hill, 171, be considered an authority. A line of cases in Massachusetts, of which *Durkin v. Cobleigh*, 156 Mass. 108, 30 N. E. 474 is an example, have to do with collateral contracts made before a deed is given. But the fixed form of a deed makes it inappropriate to insert collateral agreements, however closely connected with the sale. This may be cause for an exception. Here we deal with the contract on the basis of which the deed to Mrs. Mitchill was given subsequently, and we confine ourselves to the question whether its terms may be modified.

Finally there is the case of *Chapin v. Dobson*, 78 N. Y. 74, 76 (1879). This is acknowledged to be on the border line and is rarely cited except to be distinguished. Assuming the premises, however, the court was clearly right. There was nothing on the face of the written contract, it said, to show that it intended to express the entire agreement. And there was a finding, sustained by evidence, that there was an entire contract, only part of which was reduced to writing. This being so, the contract as made might be proved.

It is argued that what we have said is not applicable to the case as presented. The collateral agreement was made with the plaintiff. The contract of sale was with her husband, and no assignment of it from him appears. Yet the deed was given to her. It is evident that here was a transaction in which she was the principal from beginning to end. We must treat the contract as if in form, as it was in fact, made by her.

Our conclusion is that the judgment of the Appellate Division and that of the Special Term should be reversed and the complaint dismissed, with costs in all courts.

B. Merger or Integration Clauses and the Parol Evidence Rule Exceptions

UAW-GM Human Resource Center v. KSL Recreation Corp.
579 N.W.2d 411
(Mich. Ct. App. 1998)

MARKMAN, PRESIDING JUDGE. In December 1993, plaintiff entered into a contract with Carol Management Corporation (CMC) for the use of its property—Doral Resort and Country Club—for a convention scheduled in October 1994. The "letter of agreement" included a merger clause that stated that such agreement constituted "a merger of all proposals, negotiations and representations with reference to the subject matter and provisions." The letter of agreement did not contain any provision requiring that Doral Resort employees be union-represented. However, plaintiff contends in its appellate brief that it signed the letter of agreement in reliance on an "independent, collateral promise to provide [plaintiff] with a union-represented hotel."

Plaintiff provided the affidavits of Herschel Nix, plaintiff's agent, and Barbara Roush, CMC's agent, who negotiated the contract. In his affidavit, Nix states that during the contract negotiation he and Roush discussed plaintiff's requirement that the hotel employees be union-represented and that Roush agreed to this requirement. In her affidavit, Roush states that "prior to and at the time" the contract at issue was negotiated she "was well aware" of plaintiff's requirement that the hotel employees be union-represented and that "that there is no doubt that I agreed on behalf of the Doral Resort to provide a union hotel." The letter of agreement also included a liquidated damages clause in the event plaintiff canceled the reservation "for any reason other than the following: Acts of God, Government Regulation, Disaster, Civil Disorders or other emergencies making it illegal to hold the meeting/convention."

Later in December 1993, the hotel was sold to defendants, who subsequently replaced the resort's union employees with a nonunionized work force. In June 1994, when plaintiff learned that the hotel no longer had union employees, it canceled the contract and demanded a refund of its down payment. Defendants refused to refund the down payment, retaining it as a portion of the liquidated damages allegedly owed to them pursuant to the contract. Plaintiff filed suit for return of the down payment and asserted claims of breach of contract, conversion of the deposit, and fraud. Defendants filed a counterclaim and moved for summary disposition and enforcement of the liquidated damages clause. Plaintiff filed a cross-motion for summary disposition. The trial court granted plaintiff's motion for summary disposition regarding the breach of contract count on the basis of its determination that there was a separate agreement requiring that the hotel employees be union-represented. It also granted plaintiff's motion for summary disposition on the conversion and fraud counts. …

Merger Clause

Defendants claim that the trial court erred in granting plaintiff's motion for summary disposition and in denying defendants' motion for summary disposition. Regarding the breach of contract count, they specifically contend that parol evidence of a separate agreement providing that the hotel would have union employees at the time of the convention was inadmissible because the letter of agreement included an express merger clause.

We begin by reiterating the basic rules regarding contract interpretation. "The primary goal in the construction or interpretation of any contract is to honor the intent of the parties." *Rasheed v. Chrysler Corp.*, 445 Mich. 109, 127, n. 28 (1994). "We must look for the intent of the parties in the words used in the instrument. This court does not have the right to make a different contract for the parties or to look to extrinsic testimony to determine their intent when the words used by them are clear and unambiguous and have a definite meaning." *Michigan Chandelier Co. v. Morse*, 297 Mich. 41, 49 (1941).

In *Port Huron Ed. Ass'n v. Port Huron Area School Dist.*, 452 Mich. 309, 323 (1996), the court stated:

> The initial question whether contract language is ambiguous is a question of law. If the contract language is clear and unambiguous, its meaning is a question of law. Where the contract language is unclear or susceptible to multiple meanings, interpretation becomes a question of fact.

A contract is ambiguous if "its words may reasonably be understood in different ways." Courts are not to create ambiguity where none exists. "Contractual language is construed according to its plain and ordinary meaning, and technical or constrained constructions. If the meaning of an agreement is ambiguous or unclear, the trier of fact is to determine the intent of the parties."

The parol evidence rule may be summarized as follows: "Parol evidence of contract negotiations, or of prior or contemporaneous agreements that contradict or vary the written contract, is not admissible to vary the terms of a contract which is clear and unambiguous." This rule recognizes that in "[b]ack of nearly every written instrument lies a parol agreement, merged therein." *Lee State Bank v. McElheny*, 227 Mich. 322, 327 (1924). "The practical justification for the rule lies in the stability that it gives to written contracts; for otherwise either party might avoid his obligation by testifying that a contemporaneous oral agreement released him from the duties that he had simultaneously assumed in writing." 4 WILLISTON, CONTRACTS, § 631. ...

However, parol evidence of prior or contemporaneous agreements or negotiations is admissible on the threshold question whether a written contract is an integrated instrument that is a complete expression of the parties' agreement. *NAG Enterprises, Inc. v. All State Industries, Inc.*, 407 Mich. 407, 410–411 (1979). The NAG court noted four exceptions to the parol evidence rule, stating that extrinsic evidence is admissible to show (1) that the writing was a sham, not intended to create legal relations, (2) that the contract has no efficacy or effect because of fraud, illegality, or mistake, (3) that the parties did not integrate their agreement or assent to it as the final embodiment of their understanding, or (4) that the agreement was only partially integrated because essential elements were not reduced to writing. Importantly, ... NAG [did not involve] a contract with an explicit integration clause.

The first issue before us is whether parol evidence is admissible with regard to the threshold question of integration even when the written agreement includes an explicit merger or integration clause. In other words, the issue is whether NAG applies to allow parol evidence regarding this threshold issue when a contract includes an explicit merger clause. While this issue is one of first impression, its answer turns on well-established principles of contract law.

4 WILLISTON ON CONTRACTS § 633 at 1014 and 3 CORBIN ON CONTRACTS § 578 at 402–411 offer specific guidance regarding this issue. ... [B] oth Corbin and Williston indicate that an explicit integration clause is conclusive and that parol evidence is not admissible to determine whether a contract is integrated when a written contract contains such a clause. In the context of an explicit integration clause, Corbin recognizes exceptions to the barring of parol evidence only for fraud (or other grounds sufficient to set aside a contract) and for the rare situation when the written document is obviously incomplete "on its face" and, therefore, parol evidence is necessary "for the filling of gaps."

The conclusion that parol evidence is not admissible to show that a written agreement is not integrated when the agreement itself includes an integration clause is consistent with the general contract principles of honoring parties' agreements as expressed in their written contracts and not creating ambiguities where none exist. This conclusion accords respect to the rules that the parties themselves have set forth to resolve controversies arising under the contract. The parties are bound by the contract because they have chosen to be so bound.

Further, and most fundamentally, if parol evidence were admissible with regard to the threshold issue whether the written agreement was integrated despite the existence of an integration clause, there would be little distinction between contracts that include an integration clause and those that do not. When the parties choose to include an integration clause, they clearly indicate that the written agreement is integrated; accordingly, there is no longer any "threshold issue" whether the agreement is integrated and, correspondingly, no need to resort to parol evidence to resolve this issue.

Thus NAG, which allows resort to parol evidence to resolve this "threshold issue," does not control when a contract includes a valid merger clause. 3 CORBIN, CONTRACTS, § 577 at 401 states in pertinent part:

> A finding that the parties had assented to a writing as the complete integration of their then existing agreement is necessarily a finding that there is no simultaneous oral addition. On such a finding of fact, we are no longer required to decide whether proof of simultaneous oral agreement is admissible, for we have just found that there was no such oral agreement.

The conclusion that parol evidence is not admissible regarding this "threshold issue" when there is an explicit integration clause honors the parties' decision to include such a clause in their written agreement.

It gives effect to their decision to establish a written agreement as the exclusive basis for determining their intentions concerning the subject matter of the contract.

This rule is especially compelling in cases such as the present one, where defendants—successor corporations—assumed performance of another corporation's obligations under a letter of agreement. Because defendants were not parties to the negotiations resulting in the letter of agreement, they would obviously be unaware of any oral representations made by CMC's agent to plaintiff's agent in the course of those negotiations. Defendants assumed CMC's obligations under the letter of agreement, which included an explicit merger clause. Defendants could not reasonably have been expected to discuss with every party to every contract with CMC whether any parol agreements existed that would place further burdens upon defendants in the context of a contract with an explicit merger clause.

Under these circumstances, it would be fundamentally unfair to hold defendants to oral representations allegedly made by CMC's agent. Of the participants involved in this controversy, defendants are clearly the least blameworthy and the least able to protect themselves. Unlike plaintiff, which could have addressed its concerns by including appropriate language in the contract, and unlike CMC, which allegedly agreed to carry out obligations not included within the contract, defendants did nothing more than rely upon the express language of the instant contract, to wit, that the letter of agreement represented the full understanding between plaintiff and CMC. We believe that defendants acted reasonably in their reliance and that the contract should be interpreted in accordance with its express provisions. ...

We are aware of two Michigan decisions suggesting that parol evidence may, under some circumstances, be admissible to vary the terms of a written agreement despite the existence of an integration clause, *Central Transport, Inc. v. Fruehauf Corp.*, 139 Mich. App. 536 (1984), and *Van Pembrook v. Zero Mfg. Co.*, 146 Mich. App. 87, 98 (1985). We have reviewed these decisions with great interest because they seem to be contrary to Corbin, Williston, and the Supreme Court's statements regarding the matter. With respect to *Fruehauf*, we conclude that while the decision does contain some rather opaque language, it is consistent with the rule set forth above. With respect to *Van Pembrook*, we conclude that it suggests that parol evidence may be used to vary the terms of a written agreement despite the existence of an integration clause, and we accordingly decline to follow *Van Pembrook*. ...

Parol evidence generally may be considered to determine whether fraud occurred under the second exception to the parol evidence rule discussed in *NAG*, supra at 410–411. However, a contract with a merger clause nullifies all antecedent claims. In our view, this includes any collateral agreements that were allegedly an inducement for entering into the contract. In the context of a contract that included a merger clause, parol evidence regarding false representations in a collateral agreement that induced the plaintiff to enter into the contract would vary the terms of the contract. The *Van Pembrook court*, in our judgment, erred in finding otherwise. Its decision failed to discuss or accord any meaning to the merger clause that the parties freely chose to include in their contract. Accordingly, we believe that Van Pembrook was wrongly decided.

For these reasons, we hold that when the parties include an integration clause in their written contract, it is conclusive and parol evidence is not admissible to show that the agreement is not integrated except in cases of fraud that invalidate the integration clause or where an agreement is obviously incomplete "on its face" and, therefore, parol evidence is necessary for the "filling of gaps." ...

Reversed and remanded for proceedings consistent with this opinion.

NOTES AND QUESTIONS

1. **Parol Evidence Rule and the Contradiction of Integrated Terms.** RESTATEMENT (SECOND) OF CONTRACTS § 215 reads: "Except as stated in the preceding Section, where there is a binding agreement, either completely or partially integrated, evidence of prior or contemporaneous agreements or negotiations is not admissible in evidence to contradict a term of the writing."

2. **Parol Evidence Rule and Consistent Additional Terms.** RESTATEMENT (SECOND) OF CONTRACTS § 216 reads:

   (1) Evidence of a consistent additional term is admissible to supplement an integrated agreement unless the court finds that the agreement was completely integrated.

   (2) An agreement is not completely integrated if the writing omits a consistent additional agreed term which is

   (a) agreed to for separate consideration, or

   (b) such a term as in the circumstances might naturally be omitted from the writing.

3. **Collateral-and-Consistent Exception.** *See Houston Exploration Co. v. Wellington Underwriting Agencies, Ltd.*, 352 S.W.3d 462, 469 (Tex. 2011) ("The parol evidence rule applies when parties have a valid, integrated written agreement, and precludes enforcement

of prior or contemporaneous agreements."), and *David J. Sacks, P.C. v. Haden,* 266 S.W.3d 447, 451 (Tex. 2008) (discussing the collateral-and-consistent exception to the parol evidence rule).

4. **Ambiguity, Duress, Fraud, Illegality, Mistake, and Undue Influence Exceptions.** The Indiana Supreme Court reiterated the settled principle in *Sees v. Bank One, Indiana*, 839 N.E.2d 154, 161 (Ind. 2005): Under the parol evidence rule, a party to a contract is precluded from presenting evidence of prior or contemporaneous oral agreements or other extrinsic evidence to vary or contradict the terms in a written contract. Furthermore, if a contract contains an integration clause that states the contract is a complete, final, and accurate expression of all the parties' agreements, evidence of a prior or contemporaneous statement or negotiation may not add to or contradict the terms of the agreement. *Hinkel v. Sataria Distrib. & Packaging, Inc.*, 920 N.E.2d 766, 769 (Ind. Ct. App. 2010). The parol evidence rule, however, does not apply when evidence establishes that fraud, mistake, ambiguity, illegality, duress, or undue influence has tainted the written contract. *People's Bank & Trust Co. v. Price,* 714 N.E.2d 712, 717 (Ind. Ct. App. 1999).

5. **Parol Evidence Rule and Exceptions Under the Restatement.** The RESTATEMENT (SECOND) OF CONTRACTS § 214 outlines several exceptions to the parol evidence rule and it states:

   > Agreements and negotiations prior to or contemporaneous with the adoption of a writing are admissible in evidence to establish
   >
   > (a) that the writing is or is not an integrated agreement;
   >
   > (b) that the integrated agreement, if any, is completely or partially integrated;
   >
   > (c) the meaning of the writing, whether or not integrated;
   >
   > (d) illegality, fraud, duress, mistake, lack of consideration, or other invalidating cause;
   >
   > (e) ground for granting or denying rescission, reformation, specific performance, or other remedy.

SECTION SEVEN: MITIGATION-OF-DAMAGES DOCTRINE

A cursory search of major newspapers reveals that civil litigants have adopted an intelligent, commonsensical, and efficient strategy to cut litigation costs: Litigants settle more than 90 percent of their disputes before juries deliver a verdict or before a court enters a judgment. Among the remaining disputes, one finds many defendants employing an even more effective tactic to reduce their defense costs: Rather than issuing an array of general denials and trying to prove an arsenal of affirmative defenses, each defendant simply admits that his action or inaction produced plaintiff's personal injury or property loss. So, how does a defendant defend himself against a plaintiff's claims and causes? The defendant simply asserts that the plaintiff should not receive the requested damages, because the plaintiff failed to mitigate her damages or losses.

To illustrate, consider the brief facts and civil dispute in *Brockman v. Webber*, 2000 WL 210421, *1 (Iowa App. 2000). John Webber and Tracy Brockman's cars collided. Tracy Brockman was injured. She filed a negligence action against Webber, asking the jury to award certain damages. Webber conceded that he caused the accident. However, he presented only one affirmative defense. Webber asserted that Tracy failed to mitigate her damages. What was Tracy's inaction? She failed to lose weight as part of her treatment program. The jury embraced Webber's mitigation-of-damages defense and returned a favorable verdict on behalf of Webber. The jury found that Tracy was fifty percent comparatively negligent for her financial losses because she did not follow her physician's orders and lose weight.

The dispute in *Hurwitz v. Kohm*, 594 S.W.2d 643, 644–646 n.1 (Mo. Ct. App. 1980) presents an even more instructive example. Jeanette Hurwitz and Evelyn Floret were lessors and the owners of real estate. William Kohm, dba Advertising Matrix Company, was the lessee. All three were parties to a commercial-lease agreement. In the course of events, Kohm breached the contract. The lessors sued. Kohm conceded that he had breached the lease. But he raised a single affirmative defense: He insisted that the lessors failed to make reasonable efforts to mitigate their damages. The trial court awarded damages—an amount equal to the rent due under the lease as monthly installments, plus interest. Kohm appealed and lost. But, the important point is this one: By raising a single affirmative defense, Kohm reduced his litigation costs substantially.

So what explains Webber's success and Kohm's lack of success? Did the latter defendant fail to establish an effective mitigation-of-damages defense? What is the mitigation-of-damages doctrine? Must a non-breaching party use all legitimate means and efforts to reduce or mitigate his loss or damages? Must an injured party mitigate damages by allowing a defendant or a breaching party to correct or undo the harm or injury? This section presents cases and materials that address these questions.

A. Mitigation of Damages Doctrine and Non-Breaching Parties' Obligations

Alamo Community College District v. Miller
274 S.W.3d 779
(Tex. App.—San Antonio 2008)

CATHERINE STONE, JUSTICE. This case concerns Alamo Community College District's breach of a settlement agreement with a tenured San Antonio College professor, Dr. William Miller, following Miller's termination from his employment. The trial court awarded Miller \$487,237.57 in damages and ordered the Alamo Community College District (ACCD) to reinstate Miller to his position at the college (SAC). Both ACCD and Miller appeal the trial court's judgment. ...

MILLER'S TERMINATION

Miller joined SAC's faculty in 1965 and eventually became a tenured chemistry professor. In 1996, when Miller was working in SAC's Distance Education Department, a female coworker, Rosario Duque, accused Miller of engaging in inappropriate sexual conduct. Miller's conduct caused Duque to feel depressed and miss work, and she decided to report Miller to SAC's executive vice president, Robert Zeigler. Although Duque reported Miller's conduct to Ziegler, Duque asked Zeigler not to confront Miller about her allegations. Zeigler honored Duque's request, but reassigned Miller and Duque to positions elsewhere within SAC.

After Miller was reassigned to SAC's Chemistry Department, Cynthia Bello, one of Miller's female coworkers, accused Miller of engaging in inappropriate sexual behavior in 2001. Bello stated Miller's behavior made her miss work because she did not want to have contact with Miller. Bello reported Miller's behavior to her superiors, and Ziegler and Vern Loland, SAC's president at the time, initiated an investigation into the matter. Upon the conclusion of Ziegler and Loland's investigation, Miller was given the opportunity to retire from his position at SAC. When Miller refused to retire by the deadline provided to him, ACCD terminated Miller for his improper sexual behavior during the course of his employment.

THE SETTLEMENT AGREEMENT

Miller filed suit in federal court, alleging ACCD terminated him from SAC without due process. Miller and ACCD reached a settlement agreement, agreeing that Miller would be given an opportunity to challenge his dismissal before a faculty hearing panel as required by district policy. ... The agreement also provided that ACCD would pay Miller $150,000 for attorney's fees and that Miller would waive his right to sue ACCD for any reason related to his termination, except for a breach of the parties' settlement agreement.

The Faculty Hearing Panel

A faculty hearing panel was convened pursuant to the terms of the parties' settlement agreement. Following the testimony of Miller's accusers, Bello and Duque, the Faculty Hearing Panel issued its "findings, conclusions, and recommendations concerning the termination of [Miller]." ...

The Faculty Hearing Panel concluded ACCD had failed to follow its own policies in terminating Miller. The Faculty Hearing Panel also concluded that Miller's conduct constituted "inappropriate behavior" in violation of ACCD's sexual harassment policy (Policy DHA (Local)) because his "actions created hostile and adverse employment environments and caused suffering to the employees in question." ... Pursuant to the parties' settlement agreement, Judge Meyers reviewed the Faculty Hearing Panel's findings and determination and concluded the Panel's findings and determination were supported by substantial evidence. ... The Board of Trustees concluded that "[w]hen the panel's fact findings are applied to the proper interpretation of Board-approved College Policy, then the decision to terminate Dr. Miller should be upheld."

The Breach of Contract Suit

Miller filed suit against ACCD in federal court following the Board of Trustees's decision to uphold his termination, for, among other things, breach of the parties' 2005 settlement agreement. The district court dismissed Miller's claims, explaining that Miller's breach of settlement claim belonged in state court, while Miller's other claims were barred by the terms of the parties' settlement agreement. Miller subsequently refiled his breach of settlement claim against ACCD in state court, seeking an order of reinstatement, stipulated damages in the amount of $487,237.57, two years additional salary and benefits, and attorney's fees.

Both Miller and ACCD moved for summary judgment on the issue of whether ACCD had breached the parties' 2005 settlement agreement. The trial court granted summary judgment in Miller's favor and denied ACCD's summary judgment motion. Miller next moved for a final summary judgment. The trial court granted Miller's motion with respect to his request for reinstatement and $487,237.57 in stipulated damages. However, the trial court denied Miller's motion with respect to his request for two years additional salary and benefits and attorney's fees. The trial court later considered, and granted, ACCD's motion for summary judgment on Miller's attorney fee's claim.

The trial court proceeded to conduct a bench trial on Miller's request for additional salary and benefits for the 2005–06 and 2006–07 academic years. The trial court awarded Miller zero damages on his claim, and the court entered a final judgment ordering Miller's reinstatement and awarding Miller $487,237.57 in stipulated damages. The trial court issued findings of fact and conclusions of law following its ruling. Both Miller and ACCD appeal the trial court's judgment. ...

MILLER'S CROSS APPEAL

In his cross appeal, Miller challenges the trial court's conclusion that his failure to mitigate his damages bars him from recovering two additional years of lost wages and benefits. We review a trial court's conclusions of law to determine their correctness based upon the facts. *Citizens Nat'l Bank v. City of Rhome*, 201 S.W.3d 254, 256 (Tex. App.—Fort Worth 2006, no pet.). A trial court's conclusions of law are reviewed *de novo*, and we will not reverse them unless they are erroneous as a matter of law. *See State v. Heal*, 917 S.W.2d 6, 9 (Tex. 1996) and, *Tex. Dep't of Public Safety v. Stockton*, 53 S.W.3d 421, 423 (Tex. App.—San Antonio 2001, pet. denied).

In Texas, a wrongfully discharged employee must exercise reasonable diligence to mitigate damages by pursuing other employment, *Gorges Foodservice, Inc. v. Huerta*, 964 S.W.2d 656, 669 (Tex. App.—Corpus Christi 1997, pet. withdrawn), or else the employee is barred from recovering those losses that could have been avoided. *Pinson v. Red Arrow Freight Lines, Inc.*, 801 S.W.2d 14, 15 (Tex. App.—Austin 1990, no writ). The duty to mitigate damages arises only if it can be done with "trifling expense or with reasonable exertions." *Walker v. Salt Flat Water Co.*, 96 S.W.2d 231, 232 (Tex. 1936). The burden is on the defendant to show that an employee did not use ordinary care in reducing or avoiding his damages. *Hygeia Dairy Co. v. Gonzalez*, 994 S.W.2d 220, 224 (Tex. App.—San Antonio 1999, no pet.).

Here, the record from the bench trial on Miller's claim for additional lost wages and benefits shows that while Miller was prepared to return to work following the Faculty Hearing Panel's decision, ACCD did not allow him to return to work. As a result of ACCD's decision not to reinstate him, Miller lost wages and benefits for the 2005–06 and 2006–07 academic years. The record shows that had ACCD allowed Miller to return to work, he would have received $123,708 in wages and benefits for the 2005–06 academic year and $128,834 in wages and benefits for the 2006–07 academic year.

At trial, Miller admitted that following the Board of Trustee's decision, he made no attempt to secure a teaching position substantially similar to the one he held at SAC. He did testify, however, that he searched the classified ads for teaching positions following his termination. Miller stated that he earned $12,582.70 working for a friend's construction company during the 2005–06 academic year. Miller further testified Schreiner University contacted him to teach part-time during the 2006–07 academic year and that he earned $13,333.00 through such employment.

Miller's employment expert—Merrill Jones—testified that allegations of sexual harassment would be a "major red flag" to a prospective employer. Jones stated that an allegation of sexual harassment is "very stigmatizing" because employers generally take "a zero tolerance to sexual harassment." He noted colleges will typically search the internet for information about a potential employee. Jones stated that when he searched the internet for information on Miller, reports of Miller's sexual harassment were readily available.

Zeigler also testified at trial. Zeigler testified that an allegation of sexual harassment would be a "red flag" if he were considering a job applicant. He testified that an allegation of sexual harassment is a "serious charge," and that Miller's termination for sexual harassment "would make employment difficult" for him. Zeigler agreed that Miller's termination for sexual harassment "substantially foreclosed other comparable employment opportunities" for Miller.

Following a bench trial, the trial court denied Miller's claim for two years of additional wages and benefits. The court entered the following findings of fact and conclusions of law in support of its ruling:

FINDINGS OF FACT

1. …

2. From the time of his termination in the spring of 2001 until the time of trial, Miller made no effort to seek employment substantially similar to his position with ACCD.

3. In Miller's case, substantially similar employment would have included a teaching position at a public or private secondary school or institution of higher education …

4. With an exception noted below, Miller's only employment since the spring of 2001 has consisted of jobs building retaining walls

and boat docks, sodding yards, moving equipment, and building bathrooms. …

5. This employment was not actively sought by Miller, but was offered to him without substantial effort on his part.

6. This employment was not substantially similar to Miller's job with ACCD.

7. In August 2006, Miller began teaching part-time at Schreiner University.

8. Miller did not seek this position; the university contacted him.

9. In light of its part-time nature, this employment was not substantially similar to Miller's job with ACCD.

10. Miller has failed to exercise reasonable diligence to seek and maintain employment substantially similar to his job with ACCD.

11. Miller has failed to prove that he could not have secured other employment through reasonable diligence.

12. Miller has failed to prove the amounts he might have earned through the exercise of reasonable diligence. …

CONCLUSIONS OF LAW

1. A terminated employee has a duty, for a reasonable time after his discharge, to seek and accept employment substantially similar to his previous job.

2. After a reasonable time and a reasonable and diligent effort, a terminated employee who has been unable to obtain substantially similar employment has a duty to seek and accept any work for which he is qualified.

3. If a terminated employee fails to exercise reasonable diligence to mitigate his damages, any amounts he might have earned through such diligence must be offset against the damages resulting from his termination.

4. Once a terminated employee's failure to exercise reasonable diligence has been established by the employer, the burden shifts to

the employee to show the amounts he could have earned through the exercise of reasonable diligence.

5. Miller's failure to exercise reasonable diligence and his failure to prove whether he could have obtained other employment through the exercise of reasonable diligence and the amounts he could have earned through such exercise constitute a failure to mitigate damages, which bars his recovery of damages beyond the stipulated damage[s] set forth in the parties' Settlement Agreement dated April 13, 2005.

Miller requested additional findings of fact and amended conclusions of law from the trial court. The trial court made the following additional findings of fact and amended conclusions of law:

ADDITIONAL FINDINGS OF FACT

1. The newspaper articles reporting that Dr. Miller had been terminated by ACCD based on allegations of sexual harassment made any attempts by Dr. Miller to seek same or similar employment virtually impossible.

2. ACCD's termination of Dr. Miller based on allegations of sexual harassment and the publicity of the sexual harassment allegations has foreclosed other comparable employment opportunities for Dr. Miller.

3. If ACCD had reinstated Dr. Miller for the 2005–2006 academic year, which includes summer employment, Dr. Miller's salary and benefits would have totaled $123,708.49.

4. If ACCD had reinstated Dr. Miller for the 2006–2007 academic year, which includes summer employment, Dr. Miller's salary and benefits would have totaled $128,833.75. …

AMENDED CONCLUSIONS OF LAW

1. Because failure to mitigate is an affirmative defense, the employer bears the burden of proving lack of diligence on the part of the employee and the amount by which the employee's damages were increased by his failure to mitigate.

2. The general rule as to the correct measure of damages for wrongful discharge of an employee is the present cash value of the contract

> to the employee if it had not been breached, less any amounts that the employee should, through the exercise of reasonable diligence, have been able to earn through other employment.

After reviewing the fact findings and conclusions of law made by the trial court, we believe the trial court correctly concluded that Miller cannot recover additional lost wages and benefits for the 2005–06 and 2006–07 academic years due to his failure to mitigate his damages. The trial court recognized that Miller was obligated to "seek and accept any work for which he [was] qualified" once it was determined that he could not secure employment substantially similar to his position with SAC. *See Kramer v. Wolf Cigar Stores Co.*, 91 S.W. 775, 777 (Tex. 1906) (holding that a terminated employee has a duty, at least for a reasonable time after his or her discharge, to seek employment comparable to his or her previous job; however, after that time, employee is obligated to seek and accept any work for which he or she is qualified).

Although the trial court found that Miller took positions working construction and teaching part-time, the court determined that Miller nonetheless failed to exercise reasonable diligence following his termination. The record supports the trial court's conclusion, as the record indicates that Miller did not actively seek any employment opportunities following his termination from SAC. The record shows Miller's friend gave him his position working construction, while Schreiner University contacted him about its open part-time teaching position. Given Miller's lack of reasonable diligence to secure other employment for which he was fit following his termination from SAC, we cannot say the trial court's conclusion that Miller failed to mitigate his damages is erroneous as a matter of law. Miller's cross issue is therefore overruled.

Based on the foregoing, we affirm the trial court's judgment in all respects.

B. Mitigation of Damages Doctrine and Breaching Parties' Subsequent Offers of Performance

Kendall v. Dunn
76 S.E. 454
(W.Va. 1912)

ROBINSON, J. Plaintiff—forty-two years old and no doubt comely—sued defendant, seventy-six years old and well-to-do, for forty thousand dollars damages because he did not keep his promise to marry her. She recovered, through the verdict of a jury, a judgment against him for $2,408.33. A reversal and new trial are sought.

The verdict is by no means contrary to the evidence. The promise is admitted by defendant in his testimony; the breach is proved by the testimony of plaintiff and by facts and circumstances which corroborate her testimony in that regard. The jury was fully warranted in finding that defendant broke his promise to marry plaintiff. They were the judges of the amount of compensation that she should have for the injury. ... The brief on behalf of defendant is devoted wholly to [a] complaint in regard to instructions. No other points are relied on in the argument. ... Let us now, as briefly as may be, notice these objections.

In plaintiff's first instruction the jury were told that if they found from the evidence that a contract was made between the parties whereby defendant promised to marry plaintiff, and that defendant broke the contract and refused to comply with his promise, then the plaintiff was entitled to recover, and they might so find. The instruction then proceeds:

> In ascertaining, determining and assessing plaintiff's damages, not to exceed the amount sued for, the jury should take into consideration the financial circumstances of the defendant; his social position, and all the rights and privileges that plaintiff would have acquired pecuniarily and socially if the defendant had performed his contract; the worldly advantage of a marriage which would have given her a permanent home and an advantageous establishment; the injuries and wounds to plaintiff's feelings, affection and pride, the disappointment, humiliation, mortification, contempt, pain and distress of mind she suffered at the loss of the marriage, and the station in life plaintiff would have occupied as a result of her marriage; injury to her future prospects of marriage; injury to her reputation, moral or physical, resulting from the defendant's refusal to perform his promise.

It is submitted that this instruction is wrong—that in assessing the damages the jury could take into consideration only "injured feelings, anxiety of mind, wounded pride, or blighted affections." But under the facts and circumstances proved in this case, and the reasonable inferences arising therefrom, this instruction was a proper one except in a particular of mere surplusage as to which we shall speak. The case called for a consideration of the elements of damages named in the instruction, except in that one particular. The law warrants a consideration of such elements in a case like this one. 2 SEDGWICK ON DAMAGES §§ 638, 638a, 638b, 639a, 641 (Ninth Edition); 3 SUTHERLAND ON DAMAGES §§ 986–988 (Third Edition).

Our attention is directed to the use of the phrase "injury to her reputation, moral or physical." This phrase has been before used in a breach of promise case. *Goddard v. Westcott*, 46 N. W. 242 (Mich. 1890).

However, in that case there was evidence on which to base injury to the plaintiff's physical reputation. There it was claimed the defendant, as an excuse for the breach, had circulated statements accusing the plaintiff of physical disease. It is not so in this case; for the only injury to plaintiff's reputation which the jury could find is that which they might say naturally arose from the notoriety of the broken engagement. The words "or physical" were not in place.

As trial judges, we would not have used them; but it would be going far to reverse the judgment merely because the instruction contained them, when the facts and circumstances in evidence did justify a consideration of injury to her moral reputation. The instruction did not bind the jury to a consideration of injury to physical reputation, for in that regard it is in the disjunctive. The words used "or physical," are quite different from "and physical." We shall not assume that they carried weight to the jury in the face of the fact that no injury to physical reputation was proved or could be inferred from the evidence. In the ordinary reasoning of intelligent jurors, these words as applied in this case would be considered as mere surplusage. On the whole case, we clearly see that the use of these words of surplusage did not mislead the jury. We must not be prone to reverse on slight grounds.

Another objection urged as to the instruction is that it precludes the consideration of anything mitigative of the damages. It does not do so. Besides, if the evidence warranted a theory of mitigation, defendant could have asked an instruction on that subject. He asked none on that score. But the court did deal with the subject of mitigation, as we shall presently show, in such a way that defendant's rights in that particular were by no means prejudiced.

For a clear disposition of the objections made to another of the instructions given at plaintiff's instance, we must set out the whole of it, as follows:

> The court instructs the jury that if they believe from the evidence in this case, that plaintiff Mattie B. Kendall and the defendant L. B. Dunn entered into a contract whereby the said defendant L. B. Dunn contracted with and promised to marry the plaintiff, Mattie B. Kendall, as alleged by her, and that said defendant refused to marry plaintiff prior to the institution of this action, it was an absolute repudiation of the contract; and that plaintiff was justified in treating it as having been violated and suing for damages for the breach thereof. That plaintiff was no longer bound to perform the contract after refusal of performance, by the defendant, and that a subsequent offer of performance, by the defendant after the plaintiff (the injured party) had signified her intention to terminate it, constitutes no defence to this action for

> the breach of said contract. That said offer after this action was brought, is not ground for mitigation of damages. And the jury should find for the plaintiff such damages as they adjudge right not exceeding the amount sued for.

This instruction is objected to because it told the jury that an offer by defendant to perform—made after defendant broke the contract and after plaintiff, because of the breach, had signified her intention to terminate the contract—was no defense to the action. It is said that this statement of the law is contrary to the holding in *Connolly v. Bollinger*, 67 S. E. 71 (W.Va. 1910), which asserts that such a subsequent offer of performance "does not bar recovery." It is argued that there is a great difference between "constitutes no defense to the action" and "does not bar recovery"—that the former phrase precludes mitigation of damages. ...

The word "defense" is used in the sense of "bar." The use of the word "defense" instead of the word "bar" in the instruction before us could not be understood to eliminate from the consideration of the jury any question of mitigating the damages because of a renewed offer to marry before the suit was instituted. In the very next sentence, the jury was told that an offer to renew and perform would not mitigate the damages if made after the suit was brought. Were not the jury thereby virtually told that mitigation could be considered as to an offer made *before* the suit was brought?

The instruction in effect told them that mitigation of damages on account of an offer to renew and perform was limited to such an offer made *before* the suit was instituted. It did not totally bar a consideration of mitigation of damages on account of such an offer, as is contended. We have had doubt as to whether the instruction left to the jury a question as to which the evidence was conflicting. Did it allow the jury to find whether the offer to renew and perform was made *before* or *after* the suit was brought? Or, did it assume and tell the jury that the subsequent offer was made after the institution of the suit?

After mature reflection, we are of opinion that the instruction sufficiently submitted to the jury this controverted question. The evidence plainly proved an offer to perform made subsequent to the breach. The only controversy in relation to that offer was whether it was made before or after suit brought. The instruction did, we think, contemplate a determination of this question by the jury. It did not directly assert that the offer was made at any particular time. It did say "that said offer after this suit was brought is not ground for mitigation of damages." But this is only one way of saying "that said offer if made after this suit was brought is not ground for mitigation of damages." In the light of the case before them, the jury could not reasonably have interpreted it otherwise.

Then was the instruction sound in law? We may readily approve it in that regard except as to the proposition that an offer to marry subsequent to the breach but after suit is brought is not ground to mitigate the damages. As we have stated, this indirectly asserts that damages may be mitigated by an offer before suit is brought. May the damages be mitigated by an offer to renew and perform? And if so, is mitigation on this score limited to such an offer made before the bringing of the suit?

An eminent authority says: "An offer of the defendant, after breach, to marry the plaintiff may be shown as bearing on the amount of damages. This is perhaps not properly mitigation of damages. ... Under certain circumstances the offer will not mitigate the damages; as where the defendant by his misconduct has made an acceptance of the offer impossible." 2 SEDGWICK ON DAMAGES § 641c. Another says: "It is doubtful if any hard-and-fast rule can be laid down on this proposition. The facts and circumstances of the whole case will determine whether such evidence is to be received or rejected." 3 SUTHERLAND ON DAMAGES § 990 (Third Edition). ...

We conclude that the jury may—when the circumstances warrant—take into consideration in assessing the damages proof of an offer to renew and perform made prior to the beginning of a suit on the breach. But we cannot sanction the mitigating of damages by an offer to renew and perform after suit brought. It is clearly against the well-established general principle that evidence of facts occurring after the beginning of suit cannot be given in aggravation or mitigation of damages. In a breach of promise case, Judge Lucas referred to this principle, saying: "The general rule, however, in all such cases, is that no evidence can be given of any fact having a tendency to aggravate or diminish the damages, which has occurred after the commencement of the suit." *Dent v. Pickens*, 12 S. E. 698 (W.Va. 1890). ...

Finding no error to the prejudice of defendant, we affirm the judgment.

NOTES AND QUESTIONS

1. **Mitigation of Damages in Actions Sounding in Tort and Contract.** Generally, if a party's wrongful or negligent act injures another party via a tort or a breach of contract, the injured party must exercise reasonable care and diligence to avoid loss or to minimize or lessen the resulting damage. The injured party may not recover damages, to the extent that his damages are the result of his failure to exercise care and diligence. *Cook & Nichols, Inc.*

v. Peat, Marwick, Mitchell & Co., 480 S.W.2d 542, 545 (Tenn. Ct. App. 1971).

2. **Mitigation of Damages and the Reasonable Standard of Care**. The law is clear: When determining whether an injured party has fulfilled its duty to mitigate damages, a court must determine "whether the method … employed to avoid consequential injury was reasonable under the circumstances existing at the time." *Action Ads, Inc. v. William B. Tanner Co., Inc.*, 592 S.W.2d 572, 575 (Tenn. Ct. App. 1979). Perhaps, the court's analysis in *Tampa Electric Company v. Nashville Coal Company*, 214 F. Supp. 647 (M.D. Tenn. 1963) presents a more succinct discussion of the duty-to-mitigate rule:

> The critical factor in determining fulfillment of a plaintiff's duty to mitigate is whether the method which he employed to avoid consequential injury was reasonable under the circumstances existing at the time.
>
> The rule with respect to the mitigation of damages may not be invoked by a contract breaker "as a basis for hypercritical examination of the conduct of the injured party, or merely for the purpose of showing that the injured person might have taken steps which seemed wiser or would have been more advantageous to the defaulter." *In re Kellett Aircraft Corp.*, 186 F.2d 197, 198–199 (3d Cir. 1950).
>
> As stated in McCORMICK, DAMAGES § 35 (1935), "a wide latitude of discretion must be allowed to the person who by another's wrong has been forced into a predicament where he is faced with a probability of injury or loss. Only the conduct of a reasonable man is required of him." …

3. **Mitigation of Damages, "Undue Burden," and "Duty to Use All Proper Means to Reduce Losses and Damages".** To be sure, the mitigation of damages doctrine does not require an injured party to mitigate damages if mitigation would create an undue burden. *Cummins v. Brodie*, 667 S.W.2d 759, 766 (Tenn. Ct. App. 1983). On the other hand, some courts embrace the principle stated in *Anderson-Gregory Co., Inc. v. Lea*, 370 S.W.2d 934 (Tenn. Ct. App. 1963): In a breach-of-contract action, a defendant may establish plaintiff's failure to mitigate damages by proving that plaintiff did not use all proper means and efforts to prevent or reduce plaintiff's loss or injury.

CHAPTER SEVEN

Third Parties' Contractual Rights, Obligations, and Remedies

Early on in their first-year civil procedures course, law students learn that a person must have standing to commence a lawsuit. And that rule applies if the action sounds in tort, in contract, or under state or federal statutes. However, a person can establish standing if she satisfies the "real party in interest" test. The Supreme Court of Nebraska outlined the purpose and general parameters of the test in *Countryside Co-op. v. Harry A. Koch Co.* 790 N.W.2d 873, 881 (Neb. 2010):

> Neb. Rev. Stat. § 25–301 (2008) provides that '[e]very action shall be prosecuted in the name of the real party in interest. ...' The purpose of the statute is to prevent the prosecution of actions by persons who have no right, title, or interest in the cause. The statute also discourages harassing litigation and keeps litigation within certain bounds in the interest of sound public policy. The focus of the real party in interest inquiry is whether the party has standing to sue due to some real interest in the cause of action, or a legal or equitable right, title, or interest in the subject matter of the controversy. The purpose of the inquiry is to determine whether the party has a legally protectable interest or right in the controversy that would benefit by the relief to be granted.

Without a doubt, a person qualifies as a real party in interest if he is a party to a contract. Or stated slightly differently, a person has standing to bring a breach-of-contract action if he proves that he has privity of contract. BLACK'S LAW DICTIONARY (9th ed. 2009) defines privity of contract as "[t]he relationship between the parties to a contract, allowing them to sue each other but preventing a third party from doing so." On the other hand, third-party complainants or non-contracting parties generally do not have privity of contract. Consequently, they do not have standing to enforce, terminate, reform, or rescind a contract between a promisor and a promisee. *Cf. Sousa v. Town of Coventry*, 774 A.2d 812, 815 n.4 (R.I. 2001) ("[T]here is no support for the proposition that ... an individual—who is not a party to a contract—may assert the rights of one of the contracting parties in order to void a contract or have it declared unenforceable.").

There are, however, a few exceptions to the latter rule. As discussed in an earlier chapter, agents are third parties. But even more importantly, they may form contracts and commence breach-of-contract actions on behalf of principals. To establish an agency, the agent or principal must prove: 1) the agent acts on the principal's behalf; 2) the agent accepted the undertaking; and 3) the parties mutually understand that the principal controls the undertaking. The party that raises an agency theory has the burden to prove an agency. But the law is clear: Direct evidence of an agent's authority is not necessary. Courts may reasonably infer an agency from the circumstances of the case. Also, parties' intention to create a principal-agent relationship may be implied in law or in fact. *See Scott v. Purcell*, 415 A.2d 56, 60–62 n.8 (Pa. 1980).

Furthermore, non-contracting parties may acquire contractual rights and duties under several additional common-law doctrines: third-party beneficiary doctrine, doctrine of assignment, and the judgment-creditor rule. Consequently, a third party that satisfies the requirements under these doctrines have standing to file breach-of-contract actions on behalf of themselves and other real parties in interest. *See, e.g., Allan v. Nersesova*, 307 S.W.3d 564, 567 (Tex. App.—Dallas 2010, no pet.) ("To have standing to bring suit for breach of contract, the plaintiff must either be in privity of contract with the defendant or a third party beneficiary.").

The doctrines of non-delegable duty and novation also govern the enforcement of third parties' rights and obligations under various contracts. Therefore, this chapter is devoted to discussing these various third-party doctrines along with their advantages and limitations.

A. Third-Party Beneficiary Doctrine and Contractual Rights

Valley Landscape Company, Inc. v. Rolland
237 S.E.2d 120
(Va. 1977)

HARRISON, JUSTICE. Old Dominion University (ODU or owner) filed an action against Valley Landscape Company, Inc. (Valley or contractor) and its surety, alleging the breach of a construction contract. Valley filed a third party motion for judgment against Peter G. Rolland (Rolland or architect). Rolland filed a demurrer which was sustained by the trial court. ... Valley has appealed this judgment on the ground that its motion sufficiently alleged that it was entitled to recover as a third-party beneficiary of a contract between ODU and Rolland.

Valley, a landscaping contractor, was awarded a contract by ODU to construct the mall improvement project at the college's Norfolk campus. Rolland was the landscape architect employed by ODU to provide plans and specifications for, and to supervise the construction of, this project. Prior to completion, Valley ceased performance and terminated its contract with ODU. Thereafter, ODU employed another contractor to complete the work and instituted an action to recover $400,000 damages from Valley and the surety on the payment and performance bond given by the contractor. Valley then attempted to add Rolland as a third-party defendant to the action. ...

Valley bases its right to recover against Rolland on the theory that it was a third-party beneficiary of the contract between Rolland and ODU. The only paragraph of the amended motion for judgment which addresses this question is paragraph 4, which states: "4. That certain *provisions* of (Rolland's) contract with (ODU) were for the benefit of the general contractor."

The amended motion does not set forth any such "provisions", and the contract between ODU and Rolland was not made a part of the record. While ODU contracted with the architect Rolland to draw plans and specifications and to make periodic site inspections, their contract was made prior to the employment by ODU of a contractor to build the project. It was a separate and independent construction contract that was thereafter made by ODU and Valley.

The right to sue as a third-party beneficiary is governed by Code § 55-22, which provides, in relevant part, that:

> [I]f a covenant or promise be made for the benefit, in whole or in part, of a person with whom it is not made, or with whom it is made jointly with others, such person, whether named in the instrument or not, may maintain in his own name any action thereon which he might maintain in case it had been

> made with him only and the consideration had moved from him to the party making such covenant or promise.

Valley concedes that in order to maintain an action under this section "it must be shown that the contract was intended at least in part to benefit the non-contracting party."

The question whether a building contractor is a third-party beneficiary of a contract between the architect and the owner is one of first impression for this court. Nonetheless, we have on numerous occasions applied the third-party beneficiary doctrine, and we are guided by certain well established principles. "The third party beneficiary doctrine is subject to the limitation that the third party must show that the parties to the contract clearly and definitely intended it to confer a benefit upon him." *Professional Realty v. Bender*, 222 S.E.2d 810, 812 (Va. 1976). "A clear intent to benefit the third person must appear to enable him to sue on the contract; incidental beneficiaries cannot maintain an action thereon." *N.-P. Newspapers v. Stott*, 156 S.E.2d 610, 612 (Va. 1967).

Consonant with these principles is the rule that the third-party beneficiary statute "has no application unless the party sought to be held liable has assumed an obligation for the benefit of a third party. The statute does not purport to create a contract when no contract exists." *Burton v. Chesapeake Box, etc., Corp.*, 57 S.E.2d 904, 909 (Va. 1950).

Appellant argues that the conclusionary allegation, that "certain provisions" of the architect's contract with ODU "were for the benefit of" Valley, was sufficient to meet the above standards. Appellant also contended in oral argument that the standard owner-architect contract gives rise to a third-party beneficiary contract in favor of the contractor.

On the other hand, Rolland contends that facts must be alleged in a motion for judgment which tend to prove that the architect and owner, in reaching their agreement, intended to bestow a direct benefit upon the contractor. It is a matter of common knowledge that any contract for construction is usually of incidental benefit to numerous persons. However, the crucial question in this case is whether the standard owner-architectural contract, without any special provisions inuring to the direct benefit of the contractor, is intended to, and directly benefits, the contractor.

Architects are employed to design a project of a kind, type and style desired by the owner. They draw plans to accomplish this object and once the plans are agreed upon, the owner customarily employs the architect to monitor the performance by the builder. The purpose of this employment is to assure that the owner will get a finished product in accordance with the plans which he has approved. The duty of the architect is to protect the owner to the end that the quality of the workmanship that goes into the project, and the kind and quality of the materials that are used, will be in accordance with the plans and specifications upon which the owner and architect have agreed.

These undertakings by the architect are not designed to protect and enhance the profit or any other interest of the contractor. The fact that a contractor will benefit and profit from plans that are carefully and professionally drawn, and from specifications that are clear and precise, is an incidental benefit that accrues to the contractor. But it is not the benefit that is primarily envisioned by the architect and the owner. The reason is obvious when the adverse interests of the parties are considered. The owner employs an architect, to a degree, to protect himself from the contractor.

Numerous out-of-state and federal decisions have considered the third-party beneficiary doctrine as it applies to the owner-architect-contractor relationship. In *A. R. Moyer, Inc. v. Graham*, 285 So.2d 397 (Fla. 1973), one of the questions certified to the court was whether a general contractor could be a third-party beneficiary of a contract between the owner and the supervising architect where the general contractor, under his contract with the owner, was obligated to construct the project in accordance with the architect's plans and specifications. The court observed that whether a contract was intended for the benefit of a third person was generally regarded as one of construction and that the intention of the parties is determined by the terms of the contract as a whole. There, the court did not have before it the owner-architect contract, since it was not made a part of the record. The court, nevertheless, concluded:

> Our review of the law suggests to us that supervision generally is undertaken for the benefit of the owner to insure that the construction is proceeding in compliance with the plans and specifications approved by the owner. In general terms, a contractor is an incidental beneficiary absent clear intent manifested in the owner-architect contract to the contrary. Exceptions may exist possibly, such as in supervision to insure compliance with safety regulations which would be for the benefit of third party construction workers; however, no exceptions are apparent in the third question as posed. The theory that a supervising architect acts as agent for the owner also militates against a third party beneficiary approach. 285 So.2d at 403.

Appellant says that the above cited case is not applicable for the reason that it "speaks in general terms of the usual relationship between the owner, the builder and the architect. The facts of the case at bar take it out of any such 'general rule.'" We disagree. We have heretofore pointed out that the allegations of Valley's motion for judgment are general, and the provisions relied upon are those found in the standard owner-architect agreement. As in *A. R. Moyer, Inc.*, the owner-architect contract is not before the court. If this court can only speak in "general terms," as did the Florida court, appellant is therefore in no position to complain. ...

A review of the authorities makes it clear that it is not sufficient that Valley would be incidentally benefited by a proper performance of duties on the part of the architect. We find no allegation of facts in Valley's third-party motion for judgment from which we could draw a conclusion that the owner-architect agreement was "clearly and definitely intended" and made to bestow a direct benefit on Valley.

Under Rule 3:10, a defendant can bring in a third-party defendant only for the purpose of passing through to the third-party defendant all or part of the liability which might be imposed on the defendant by the plaintiff as the result of the conduct of the third-party defendant. Rule 3:10 is the state counterpart of RULE 14 OF THE FEDERAL RULES OF CIVIL PROCEDURE. In the discussion of when a third-party action is proper, 6 WRIGHT & MILLER, FEDERAL PRACTICE AND PROCEDURE § 1446, at 245–50 (1971), states:

> Rule 14(a) authorizes defendant to bring into a lawsuit any person "not a party to the action who is or may be liable to him for all or part of the plaintiff's claim against him." This language does not compel defendant to bring third parties into the litigation; rather, it simply permits the addition of anyone who meets the standard set forth in the rule. In many instances tactical considerations will lead a party to pursue an independent action against a possible third-party defendant rather than resorting to impleader.
>
> A third-party claim may be asserted under Rule 14(a) only when the third party's liability is in some way dependent on the outcome of the main claim or when the third party is secondarily liable to defendant. The secondary or derivative liability notion is central and it is irrelevant whether the basis of the third-party claim is indemnity, subrogation, contribution, express or implied warranty, or some other theory. But impleader is proper only when a right to relief exists under the applicable substantive law.

The allegations of Valley's motion for judgment do not show that Rolland was potentially liable for all or a part of ODU's claims against Valley and therefore are not sufficient to state a case against Rolland. A third-party motion for judgment is not proper under the circumstances.

The judgment of the lower court will be affirmed.

NOTES AND QUESTIONS

1. **Contractual Rights of Intended and Incidental Beneficiaries.** RESTATEMENT (SECOND) OF CONTRACTS § 302 reads:

   (1) Unless otherwise agreed between promisor and promisee, a beneficiary of a promise is an intended beneficiary if recognition of a right to performance in the beneficiary is appropriate to effectuate the intention of the parties and either

   (a) the performance of the promise will satisfy an obligation of the promisee to pay money to the beneficiary; or

   (b) the circumstances indicate that the promisee intends to give the beneficiary the benefit of the promised performance.

   (2) An incidental beneficiary is a beneficiary who is not an intended beneficiary.

2. **Intended Beneficiary's Contractual Right to Enforce a Contractual Duty.** RESTATEMENT (SECOND) OF CONTRACTS § 304 reads: "A promise in a contract creates a duty in the promisor to any intended beneficiary to perform the promise, and the intended beneficiary may enforce the duty."

3. **Third-Party Beneficiary and Privity of Contract.** "A person may enforce a contract as third-party beneficiary if the contract indicates that he or she was either specifically intended by the contracting parties to benefit from the contract or is a member of the class the parties intended to benefit." *Milwaukee Area Technical College v. Frontier Adjusters of Milwaukee*, 752 N.W.2d 396, 404 (Wis. Ct. App. 2008). "Traditionally, third-party beneficiaries can enforce the terms of a contract, but they are not considered to be in privity of contract, and therefore they are not in a position to actively negotiate the contract's terms. *City of Santa Fe v. Travelers Cas. & Sur. Co.,* 228 P.3d 483, 486 (N.M. 2010). "Although courts stop short of declaring an intended third-party beneficiary to be in privity of contract, such a party is accorded traditional contract remedies with respect to the bargain intended for his or her benefit." *Leyba v. Whitley*, 907 P.2d 172, 175 (N. M. 1995).

4. **Third-Party Beneficiary's Knowledge and Assent**. The beneficiary does not have to assent to the contract or even have knowledge of the contract. *Rodgers v. Reinking*, 217 N.W. 441, 444 (Iowa 1928).

B. Judgment Creditors as Third-Party Beneficiaries Under a Statute

Hand v. Farmers Insurance Exchange
23 Cal. App. 4th 1847
(Cal. Ct. App. 1994)

FUKUTO, ASSOCIATE JUSTICE. … The principal, novel issue presented is whether a cause of action in tort for breach of the implied covenant of good faith and fair dealing may lie in favor of a judgment creditor who has become a third party beneficiary of the insurance policy by operation of section 11580, on account of the insurer's bad faith refusal to pay the judgment. In light of *Murphy v. Allstate Ins. Co.* 553 P.2d 584 (Cal. 1976) (*Murphy*), we have concluded that such a cause of action may be stated in the limited circumstances presented by this case, involving a "third party claimant" who is also a judgment creditor of the insured, presently entitled to recover her judgment from the insurer "on the policy" (§ 11580). …

FACTS

On December 3, 1983, plaintiff—Danelle Hand—was injured when the car in which she was riding was rear-ended by one driven by Angela Dubel. Dubel's vehicle was insured by Farmers Insurance Exchange and Truck Insurance Exchange (collectively Farmers), under a policy issued to First Interstate Bank, as trustee for numerous trusts, including the Henry Mudd Trust (the trust). Dubel's vehicle was an asset of the trust, and she was listed as the car's driver on an insurance broker's certificate prepared to identify insured vehicles. The policy provided $500,000 coverage per accident.

According to plaintiff's second amended complaint, beginning in early 1984 various claims personnel of Farmers informed plaintiff's counsel that Dubel was covered under the policy, up to $500,000. In 1984 plaintiff sued Dubel, along with Mudd, the declarant of the trust, in superior court. Farmers allegedly provided for Dubel's defense. In answers to interrogatories countersigned by counsel furnished by Farmers, Dubel stated she was covered by the policy, for $500,000.

During the years before trial in 1990, Dubel's several counsel allegedly reiterated these representations, and made settlement offers to plaintiff ranging from $20,000 to $190,000. At a pretrial settlement conference, a Farmers claims adjuster offered $100,000. All of these offers were made on Farmers' behalf. Plaintiff's case was tried in mid-1990. The jury awarded her $234,681, against both Dubel and Mudd. The court added to the verdict prejudgment interest under Civil Code section 3291, together with costs.

After the judgment had become final, Farmers refused plaintiff's demand to pay it. Five months after the verdict, Farmers informed plaintiff for the first time that it believed it was obligated on behalf of Dubel only for $15,000, on the theory that she had been only a "permissive user" of the trust vehicle, and as such was entitled to only $15,000 coverage, under Insurance Code section 11580.1.

Plaintiff commenced this action against Farmers in June 1991. She sought first to recover, under section 11580, the amounts owing on the judgment against Dubel and Mudd. In addition, as relevant here, plaintiff asserted two purported tort causes of action. As restated in the second amended complaint, plaintiff's claim for "Bad Faith Deprivation of a Protected Property Interest" alleged that Farmers' denial that its policy covered and obligated it to pay plaintiff's judgment against Dubel in excess of $15,000 was made with knowledge or reckless disregard of its untruth, with knowledge of plaintiff's financial needs, and for the purposes of avoiding Farmers' obligation to plaintiff, depriving her of her property interest in the insurance policy (created by section 11850), and injuring her emotionally, physically, and financially.

Plaintiff further alleged a claim for intentional infliction of emotional distress (IIED), which incorporated the preceding allegations and further alleged Farmers knew that its conduct would interfere with plaintiff's physical and financial rehabilitation and would cause her emotional distress. On both causes of action, plaintiff prayed for general, special, and punitive damages.

The trial court granted plaintiff's motion for summary adjudication of her first cause of action, to recover the entire judgment from Farmers. Contrary to Farmers' assertions, the court held not only that Farmers' coverage of a permissive user was not limited by the policy or Insurance Code section 11580.1, but also that Dubel had been fully covered as a named insured under the policy.

Farmers then moved for summary adjudication that plaintiff's remaining causes of action were without merit. The trial court granted this motion also. Although it had previously overruled a demurrer to the bad faith cause of action (in a prior amended complaint), the court now reversed itself, and ruled that a duty of good faith and fair dealing could not be "grafted onto th[e] relationship" created by section 11580 between a judgment creditor and the insurer. The court further held that the failure to pay or to settle could not form the basis for an IIED claim.

The court thereafter entered judgment awarding plaintiff $398,128.89 on account of her judgment against Dubel and Mudd. This sum included various items of interest. Farmers thereafter paid $346,936.22 of the judgment, reserving certain elements of interest it contested, and appealed from the judgment with respect to them. Plaintiff appealed from the judgment insofar as it disallowed her tort causes of action, and with reference to certain discovery orders. Plaintiff's counsel joined in the appeal as to discovery sanctions assessed against them as well as plaintiff. Farmers has not appealed from the determination that it is fully liable to plaintiff on the policy for the prior judgment. ...

I. THE BAD-FAITH CLAIM

The covenant of good faith and fair dealing, implied by law in every contract including insurance policies, "imposes on each contracting party the duty to refrain from doing anything which would render performance of the contract impossible by any act of his own, [and] also the duty to do everything that the contract presupposes that he will do to accomplish its purpose." "The precise nature and extent of the duty imposed by such an implied promise will depend on the contractual purposes." *Egan v. Mutual of Omaha Ins. Co.*, 24 Cal.3d 809, 818 (1979).

In the context of the contractual relationship between a liability insurer and its insured, the implied covenant has been held to require the insurer to accept a reasonable settlement offer when it is likely that the judgment will exceed policy limits. In the context of a casualty or disability policy, including the uninsured motorist coverage of an automobile policy, the covenant has been held to require that the insurer not unreasonably and in bad faith withhold payment of the insured's claim or benefits. In both contexts, breach of the covenant's respective duties by the insurer has been held actionable in tort—permitting recovery of consequential damages (such as emotional distress) and punitive damages—because of the absolute and relative status of insurers, who perform a sensitive, quasi-public service, undertaking to safeguard their insureds against calamities, and who also enjoy a superior bargaining position.

Generally—by definition—the implied covenant runs in favor of the other contracting party, and hence it is generally perceived as axiomatic that a "third party claimant" may not bring an action for breach of the covenant or its duties. Thus, an ordinary accident claimant is categorically disqualified, regardless of the insurer's conduct, from invoking or suing upon the insurer's good faith duty to settle the claim within policy limits. ...

Yet exceptions have arisen, with respect to third party beneficiaries of insurance contracts in whose favor the implied covenant and its duties have been held to run. Thus, in *Northwestern Mut. Ins. Co. v. Farmers' Ins. Group,* 143 Cal. Rptr. 415 (1978), a permissive user of a truck—not a party to the policy—was held to have possessed a bad-faith claim against the owner's insurer for failure to settle, because he had been an insured under the terms of the policy, and therefore was an express third party beneficiary, entitled to enforce the contract (CIV. CODE, § 1559), including the implied covenant insofar as it ran for his benefit. Because he stood in the same relationship with the insurer under the policy as the named insured, and would be benefited by performance of the duty to settle, he was entitled to sue for its breach.

In *Northwestern Mutual, supra*, the third party beneficiary held the status of an insured under the policy. In the present case, plaintiff cannot claim that status: rather, she encountered Farmers, in the first instance, as a third party claimant for damages from Farmers' non-party insured, Dubel. The significance of this distinction was explored by the Supreme Court in the case that is most relevant to our decision, *Murphy, supra*, 553 P.2d 584.

Like this case, *Murphy* involved a judgment creditor claimant, empowered to sue the insurer by section 11580. She sought to invoke the good-faith duty to settle, and its remedy of insurer liability for the entire judgment notwithstanding policy limits. The high court, in a unanimous opinion by Justice Clark, determined the resulting issues as follows.

First, the court reaffirmed the good faith duty to settle, and that its breach qualified an insured for tort relief. On the other hand, the duty to settle had been implied to protect the insured, and it did not directly benefit the injured claimant. Although the insured could have assigned the cause of action for breach of the covenant to the claimant, that had not happened here.

Second, the court considered the plaintiff's status by virtue of section 11580. Citing a substantial line of cases, the court straightforwardly declared that the section "makes the judgment creditor a third party beneficiary of the insurance contract between the insurer and the insured." *Murphy, supra*, 17 Cal.3d at 943) This meant that the adjudicated claimant could enforce those contractual promises made directly for him or her. And in this connection, the court added, "the implied covenant of good faith and fair dealing has become a contract 'term' within the meaning of section 11580. ..."

However, the court concluded the *Murphy* plaintiff could not maintain her cause of action for breach of the implied covenant, because, once again, the duty to settle that she sought to enforce was not one imposed for her benefit. "A third party [beneficiary] should not be permitted to enforce covenants made not for his benefit, but rather for others"; to allow it would confer an unintended "bonus" beyond the contractual benefits intended. *Murphy, supra*, 17 Cal.3d at p. 944. "Allstate having paid plaintiff the policy limits, she has already received all benefit contemplated by the policy."

Although *Murphy* has since been cited for the general proposition that "third party claimants" may not raise claims of breach of the covenant of good faith, the decision plainly has both a narrower import and a broader one, with respect to the present case. First, Murphy reiterates and establishes that, by virtue of section 11580, a judgment creditor of an insured enjoys third party beneficiary status and rights under the policy, and in this respect stands distinct from those "third party claimants" who have not achieved that status.

Second, *Murphy* validates the principle stated in such cases as *Northwestern Mutual, supra*, 143 Cal. Rptr. 415, that a third party beneficiary—in particular one so situated by virtue of section 11580—may enforce implied contractual covenants, including the covenant of good faith, to the extent that those covenants or their duties run in its favor. Conversely, *Murphy* disallows such a beneficiary from claiming the benefits of a duty under the implied covenant that was not implied or posited to protect its interests under the contract.

The critical question thus left pregnant but unresolved by *Murphy, supra*, 553 P.2d 584, is whether an unreasonable, bad-faith refusal to pay a judgment creditor claimant the entire amount of the judgment, after it becomes final, implicates some recognizable duty of good faith by the insurer under its policy, which was intended to benefit such a third party beneficiary. We believe so.

Although the policy in this case does not appear in the record, it may safely be inferred that it included "the usual promise to pay 'on behalf of the insured … all sums which the insured shall become legally obligated to pay as damages because of bodily injury or property damage. …" There can be no doubt that, pursuant to this express policy undertaking, the implied covenant of good faith and fair dealing imposes a duty not to withhold in bad faith payment of damages which the insured has become obligated by judgment to pay. Certainly with respect to the insured, "The duty to so act is immanent in the contract whether the company is attending to the claims of third persons against the insured or the claims of the insured itself. Accordingly, when the insurer unreasonably and in bad faith withholds payment of the claim of its insured, it is subject to liability in tort."

Moreover, unlike the duty to settle that was at issue in *Murphy, supra*, the duty not to withhold in bad faith payment of adjudicated claims runs not only in favor of the insured but also in favor of a judgment creditor such as plaintiff here. Section 11580 operates as part of a larger body of California law that seeks to assure that accident victims will be securely compensated through automobile policies.

"The public policy expressed in the Financial Responsibility and related laws requires that we construe statutes applicable to automobile liability insurance policies, as well as contractual provisions in those policies, in light of its purpose to protect those who may be injured by the use of automobiles." Accordingly, the insurer's policy duty to pay adjudicated liabilities is in place as much to protect adjudicated injured parties from uncompensated loss as to protect the insured from personal financial disaster.

To this end, once having secured a final judgment for damages, the plaintiff becomes a third party beneficiary of the policy, entitled to recover on the judgment on the policy. At that point the insurer's duty to pay runs contractually to the plaintiff as well as the insured. And the plaintiff having also become a beneficiary of the covenant of good faith, the duty to exercise good faith in not withholding adjudicated damages necessarily is owing to the plaintiff also.

Farmers argues that this conclusion ignores and conflicts with section 11580, in that the statute in terms provides the judgment creditor only a right of action against the insurer, not a right to payment without suit. … Farmers' broader argument that the rights of the class enabled by section 11580 extend no further than its bare terms is fallacious, for several reasons.

First, section 11580 cannot be read to create merely a judicial remedy, without an underlying right; and it is clear from the history of the statute that its purpose and effect was to create a right in the insurance contract. Indeed, as a matter of public policy, duties beyond those specifically set forth in section 11580 have been imposed on insurers for the benefit of statutory creditors.

Second, judgment creditors granted a right of action by the statute have been repeatedly and definitively held to be third party beneficiaries of the policy. *Murphy, supra*. And, as explained in *Murphy*, these beneficiaries are entitled to performance, without suit, of implied covenants and duties imposed to secure their benefits, just as they are not entitled to invoke duties unnecessary, or in addition, to their receiving "all intended benefit. …"

Farmers finally contends that if plaintiff is entitled to a right of action under the implied covenant, it should be construed as only contractual, not tortious, because plaintiff did not enjoy the special relationship with Farmers that is necessary to give rise to a good faith duty actionable in tort. Once more, we respectfully disagree.

As Farmers notes, the "special relationship" indispensable to a bad faith action in tort has only been perceived between insurers and insureds. However, if this is a peculiar relationship, its elements also appear in the relationship between an insurer and its contractual and statutory third party beneficiary obligee. The obligor is the same "purveyor of a vital service labeled quasi-public in nature." The plaintiff looks to the insurer for recompense from external calamity. …

Therefore, just as is the case with other, insureds' bad faith causes of action against insurers, the present cause of action for bad faith nonpayment of a finally adjudicated claim may sound in tort as well as contract. We have reached the conclusion that plaintiff's bad faith cause of action does state a cause of action. ... The leading authority for that proposition appears to be *Murphy*, *supra*, 132 Cal. Rptr. 424. Yet, as explained, ... *Murphy* actually and inexorably drives the conclusion that, with respect to the specific good faith duty to pay adjudicated claims, a judgment creditor like plaintiff, under section 11580, enjoys the contractual status, rights, and posture that vest such a cause of action. Accordingly, summary adjudication of plaintiff's bad faith cause of action should not have been granted.

The judgment is reversed with respect to the cause of action for bad faith. In all other respects, the judgment is affirmed.

NOTES AND QUESTIONS

1. **Breach-of-Contract Actions and Third-Party Claimants as "Intermeddlers"**. The Supreme Court of California emphasized the following principles in *Murphy v. Allstate Ins. Co.*, 553 P.2d 584 (Cal. 1976):

   A third party should not be permitted to enforce covenants made not for his benefit, but rather for others. He is not a contracting party; his right to performance is predicated on the contracting parties' intent to benefit him. *Lucas v. Hamm*, 56 Cal.2d 583, 590–91 (1961); 4 CORBIN, CONTRACTS §§ 775–777 at 8–28 (1951); and 2 WILLISTON, CONTRACTS § 356A at 835–42 (1959). As to any provision made not for his benefit but for the benefit of the contracting parties or for other third parties, he becomes an intermeddler.

   Permitting a third party to enforce a covenant made solely to benefit others would lead to the anomaly of granting him a bonus after his receiving all intended benefit. Because, as we have seen, the duty to settle is intended to benefit the insured and not the injured claimant, third party beneficiary doctrine does not furnish a basis for the latter to recover.

2. **Third-Party Actions and Judgment Creditors' Statutory Rights**. In *Murphy*, the California Supreme Court also stressed the following:

   INSURANCE CODE § 11580 lists provisions to be included in every liability insurance policy issued or delivered in this state. Subdivision (b), ... subpart (2) makes the judgment creditor a third party beneficiary of the insurance contract between

> the insurer and the insured. A third party beneficiary may enforce a contract expressly made for his benefit. (CIV. CODE § 1559.) And although the contract may not have been made to benefit him alone, he may enforce those promises directly made for him.
>
> The injured claimant's rights under the statute may extend beyond third party beneficiary principles. In *Barrera v. State Farm Mut. Automobile Ins. Co.*, 456 P.2d 674 (Cal. 1969), this court held that Insurance Code § 11580 must be read in light of the FINANCIAL RESPONSIBILITY LAW and that its underlying policy providing benefits to injured parties may not be limited by third party beneficiary law. ...

3. **Judgment Creditors' Direct Writ-of-Execution Actions Against Judgment Debtors.** In *Murphy*, the California Supreme Court stated:

> CODE OF CIVIL PROCEDURE §§ 714–723 provide for supplemental proceedings for a **judgment creditor** when his writ of execution against the judgment debtor has been returned unsatisfied. Section 719 states that in supplemental proceedings, property of the judgment debtor may be ordered applied toward satisfaction of the judgment, provided that no such order may be made as to property or money in the hands of another who also claims an interest in the property adverse to the judgment debtor or who denies the debt. ... "Since ... the purpose of these statutory proceedings supplementary to execution is the same as that of the original creditors' bill in equity—namely, to enable the creditor to reach property which could not otherwise be made to contribute to the payment of the judgment, the statutory proceedings should be given an operation at least as broad as that of the creditor's bill." *Travis Glass Co. v. Ibbetson*, (1921) 186 Cal. 724, 727 (1921).

B. Assignment Contracts and Third-Party Rights, Obligations, Claims, and Causes of Actions

The general rules governing the enforcement of assignment contracts are settled and fairly clear: "A party may assign to another a contractual right to collect payment, including the right to sue to enforce the right. But an assignment must be in writing in order for the contractual right to be enforceable by the assignee. ... Further, the writing must identify the assignor and assignee." *Wirth v. Cach, LLC,* 685 S.E.2d 433, 434–35 (Ga. Ct. App. 2009). A non-contracting party may commence a breach-of-contract action against a party to a contract if the other party to the contract assigns his interests to the non-contracting or third party. *Travelers Indem. Co. v. Mahiai*, 76 Pa. D. & C.4th 34, 46 (Pa. Com. Pl. 2005).

In addition, to established privity of contract or standing to sue, the third party must prove that the defendant was a party to an enforceable contract with the party who assigned the cause of action to the third-party plaintiff. *Redmon v. Griffith*, 202 S.W.3d 225, 239 (Tex. App.—Tyler 2006). Of course, an assignee steps into the shoes of its assignor. However, an assignee does not acquire rights which are greater than the rights that the assignor possessed when the assignment contract was fashioned. *Carlund Corp. v. Crown Ctr. Redevelopment*, 849 S.W.2d 647, 650–51 (Mo. App. W.D. 1993).

On the other hand, even a cursory search of caselaw reveals heated discussions and conflict surrounding the construction and enforcement of assignment contracts. The following questions generate some of those debates: 1) whether courts must apply an objective or a subjective standard to establish a party's status as an "assignee"; 2) whether parties must always construct assignment contracts like parties fashion all contracts; and 3) whether proof of sufficient consideration is a prerequisite before courts will enforce assignment contracts. General answers to these and related questions appear in the following cases and notes.

1) Duty to Prove One's Status as an "Assignee"

Brown Bark, II, LP v. Bay Area Floorcovering & Design, Inc.
2011 WL 2140368
(Mich. Ct. App. 2011)

PER CURIAM. Plaintiff appeals … the judgment of no cause for action entered by the trial court following a bench trial. Plaintiff specifically challenges the trial court's determination that it had failed to establish both the existence of a valid assignment of the defaulted loan at issue and its damages with reasonable certainty. …

This action centers around a small business loan obtained by defendant Bay Area Floorcovering & Design (BAFD) from National City Bank of Michigan/Illinois. Defendant Gregory Gromaski—BAFD's president—personally guaranteed the loan. No payments were made on the line of credit from June 2006 through December 2006. In December 2007, plaintiff Brown Bark II, L.C. purchased a block of loans from National City, ostensibly including the loan at issue here.

Plaintiff commenced this lawsuit, alleging that it was entitled to recover money owed related to the loan as the assignee of the loan. To prove its assignee status, plaintiff relied on a half-page document, which purported to be an Allonge. An "allonge" is "[a] piece of paper annexed to a bill of exchange or promissory note, on which to write endorsements for which there is no room on the instrument itself." Black's Law Dictionary (4th ed). ... [The Allonge] stated:

Allonge to the Business Credit Line and Security Agreement Dated August 5, 2002, in the Original Principal Amount of Twenty-Five Thousand Dollars ($25,000), and Made by and Between Bay Area Floorcovering & Design, Inc. (Borrower) and Gregory Gromaski (Guarantor) and National City Bank, Successor by Merger to National City Bank of Michigan/Illinois

> Pay to the order of Brown Bark II, L.P. without recourse, warranty or representation except as specifically contained in a certain Agreement for Purchase and Sale of Loan Accounts, dated December 3, 2007 by and between National City Bank and Brown Bark II, L.P.

Plaintiff argues this document was sufficient to establish a valid assignment and the trial court's finding to the contrary constituted reversible error. We disagree.

Following a bench trial, a trial court's findings of fact are reviewed for clear error and its conclusions of law are reviewed *de novo*. *Glen Lake–Crystal River Watershed Riparians v. Glen Lake Ass'n*, 264 Mich. App. 523, 531 (2004). A determination related to an assignment is a question of fact. *See Keyes v. Scharer*, 14 Mich.App. 68, 74–75 (1968).

An assignment is defined as a transfer or making over to another of the whole of any property, real or personal, in possession or in action, or any estate or right therein. To constitute a valid assignment there must be a perfected transaction between the parties which is intended to vest in the assignee a present right in the thing assigned. *Weston v. Dowty,* 163 Mich.App. 238, 242 (1987). "[A]n assignee stands in the shoes of the assignor and acquires the same rights as the assignor possessed." *Prof Rehab. Assoc. v. State Farm Mut. Auto. Ins. Co.*, 228 Mich. App. 167, 177 (1998).

An assignment requires no particular form of words; rather, the assignor must simply "manifest an intent to transfer and must not retain any control or any power of revocation." *Burkhardt v. Bailey*, 260 Mich.App. 636, 654–655 (2004). Stated differently, even a poorly drafted written instrument can create a valid assignment so long as it clearly reflects the necessary intent on the part of the assignor. However, "Michigan's version of the statute of frauds [still] requires that an assignment of 'things in action' be 'in writing and signed with an authorized signature by the party to be charged with the agreement, contract, or promise.'" *Id.* at 654, quoting MCL 566.132(f).

Burkhardt provided the following definition of "thing in action": A "chose in action" is a "right to personal things of which the owner has not the possession, but merely a right of action for their possession." *City of Holland v. Fillmore Twp.*, 363 Mich. 38, 43(1961), quoting BLACK'S LAW DICTIONARY (4th ed) at 305. A "thing in action" is synonymous with a "chose in action." *See Powers v. Fisher*, 279 Mich. 442, 448–449 (1937). *See also* BALLENTINE'S LAW DICTIONARY (3d ed), defining "chose in action" as "the right of a creditor to be paid; a right not reduced to possession but recoverable by bringing and maintaining an action," and "thing in action" as the "same as chose in action."

In the instant case, while the ALLONGE was presented as evidence at trial, it was not attached to the note; nor did plaintiff introduce the agreement referenced in the ALLONGE as evidence, citing privilege as its reason for failing to do so. Because the trial court did not have an opportunity to review the referenced agreement, and consequently could not determine what limitations might exist, the trier of fact could not reasonably conclude the half-page document constituted documentation of National City Bank's intent to transfer all of its rights related to the defaulted loan without any power of revocation.

In addition, plaintiff's representative conceded that James Hrebenar—the person who purportedly signed the ALLONGE on behalf of National City Bank—was actually an employee of plaintiff's affiliate. Plaintiff presented no evidence, either of an actual signed power of attorney or testimony by Hrebenar or a representative of National City Bank, to support the assertion that Hrebenar had been authorized to act as an attorney-in-fact on National City Bank's behalf. In light of the foregoing facts, we cannot conclude that the trial court clearly erred in finding that plaintiff had failed to prove the existence of a valid assignment.

In light of our conclusion that plaintiff failed to establish a valid assignment in its favor, it is not necessary to address whether the trial court correctly found that plaintiff failed to meet its burden to establish damages with reasonable certainty.

Affirmed.

NOTES AND QUESTIONS

1. **General Rule—Doctrine of Assignment in Texas and in Other Jurisdictions**. Consider the Supreme Court of Texas's analysis which appears in *State Farm Fire and Cas. Co. v. Gandy*, 925 S.W.2d 696, 706–07 (Tex. 1996):

In Texas, the merger of law and equity allowed assigned rights to be enforced as fully as they would have been in chancery court. Only five days after the Congress of the Republic of Texas adopted the common law—(current version at TEX. CIV. PRAC. & REM. CODE § 5.001), it provided by statute for assignment of both negotiable and non-negotiable written instruments, Act approved Jan. 25, 1840, 4th Cong., R.S., §§ 1–4, 1840 REPUBLIC OF TEXAS LAWS 144, 144–146, reprinted in 2 H.P.N. GAMMEL, LAWS OF TEXAS 318, 318–320 (1898) (formerly at Tex. REV. CIV. STAT. ANN. ARTS. 568–571 (Vernon 1935)). But even contract rights not covered by the statute could be assigned.

In some jurisdictions the rule expanded to include claims *ex delicto* as well as *ex contractu*. An 1895 Texas statute provided that personal injury claims survived to the heirs and legal representatives of the injured party. (current version at TEX. CIV. PRAC. & REM. CODE § 71.021). On the theory that assignability of a chose in action depended on whether it survived the owner's death, personal injury claims thus became assignable in Texas. This is not true in every state.

Practicalities of the modern world have made free alienation of choses in action the general rule, but they have not entirely dispelled the common law's reservations to alienability, or displaced the role of equity or policy in shaping the rule. Even today, the general rule is that a contractual assignment may be "inoperative on grounds of public policy." RESTATEMENT (SECOND) OF CONTRACTS § 317(2)(b) (1981). The RESTATEMENT notes numerous limitations on alienation of choses in action.

2. **Earlier Common-Law Rules Against Assigning All Claims or Causes of Action.** The Texas Supreme Court presented the following pertinent historical information in *State Farm Fire and Cas. Co. v. Gandy,* 925 S.W.2d 696, 705 (Tex. 1996):

Alienability of choses in action has its roots in equity, not law. At early common law, a chose in action could not be assigned. 6A C.J.S. ASSIGNMENTS § 6 (1975). ... Two principal bases have been suggested for the rule. One is that the rule precluded litigation like that already prohibited by champerty and maintenance. An early proponent of this explanation was the great Lord Coke, who declared "the aversion of the 'sages and founders of our law' to the 'multiplying of contentions and suits'" *Lampet's Case*, 77 Eng. Rep. 994, 997 (K.B. 1613). The second basis offered for the rule is that the common law regarded rights as personal. ... A claim or cause of action was part of a right of redress that was personal to the holder by virtue of the injury suffered and thus incapable of transfer. To separate a cause of action from a particular plaintiff's right of redress was to risk unjust prosecution of claims. A right or obligation could not be enforced apart from its context without risking distortion.

3. **Modern-Day Rules Against Assigning Certain Claims or Causes of Action**. The Texas Supreme Court also reaffirmed the following doctrine-of-assignment principles in *Gandy,* 925 S.W.2d at 707–11:

> As early as the fifteenth century the common-law rule against alienability of choses in action began to give way to the demand of commerce that assigned debts be enforceable. ... Little by little, the common law's resistance to alienability of choses in action was weakening, and by the eighteenth century it had collapsed. ... This court has held an assignment of a chose in action invalid in at least four instances. Each is based on the historical reservations to such assignments. ... In *Zuniga v. Groce, Locke & Hebdon*, 878 S.W.2d 313, 314 (Tex. App.—San Antonio 1994, writ ref'd), we considered "whether a client may assign his cause of action for legal malpractice arising out of litigation." ... Noting that legal malpractice claims are not assignable in most jurisdictions, ... [w]e concluded that the disadvantages to assignments of legal malpractice claims clearly outweighed the advantages. ... Accordingly, we held that Bauer's assignment of its cause of action to Zuniga was invalid.
>
> In *Elbaor v. Smith*, 845 S.W.2d 240, 247–50 (Tex. 1992), we held that Mary Carter agreements are void as against public policy. A Mary Carter agreement is any settlement arrangement between the plaintiff and some of the defendants in a case by which the settling defendants agree to pay the plaintiff a certain amount of money and to participate in the trial against the nonsettling defendants, and the plaintiff agrees to release the settling defendants from liability and, if the judgment against a nonsettling defendant is large enough, to repay the settlement amount. In effect, the plaintiff assigns the settling defendants part of plaintiff's claim against the nonsettling defendants. ... We concluded that the Mary Carter agreement was "an unwise and champertous device." ... Thus, we declare them void as violative of sound public policy.
>
> In *International Proteins Corp. v. Ralston–Purina Co.,* 744 S.W.2d 932, 934–35 (Tex. 1988), we held that a tortfeasor cannot take an assignment of a plaintiff's claim as part of

a settlement agreement with the plaintiff and prosecute that claim against a joint tortfeasor. ... We held that "[a]s a general rule a cause of action may be assigned, but it is contrary to public policy to permit a joint tortfeasor the right to purchase a cause of action from a plaintiff to whose injury the tortfeasor contributed." ... We are mindful of the general rule that a cause of action for damages for personal injuries may be sold or assigned. Our holding in the present case is an exception to this general rule. A settling defendant who is jointly responsible for personal injuries to a common plaintiff may not preserve contribution rights either by obtaining a complete release for all other parties allegedly responsible or by obtaining assignment of the plaintiff's entire claim. ... In essence, we concluded that the assignments in these cases were invalid and conveyed no viable rights to the assignees. ... Finally, in *Trevino v. Turcotte*, 564 S.W.2d 682 (Tex. 1978), we held an assignment of interests in an estate invalid. ... Although we observed that interests in estates are freely assignable, and that assigned interests enable assignees to contest wills, we held the assignments [based on the unique facts in *Trevino* were] invalid. The assignments distorted their real positions.

2) Assignment Contracts and Proof of Consideration

S. Yamamoto v. Puget Sound Lumber Co.
146 P. 861
(Wash. 1915)

FULLERTON, J. On March 19, 1913, fire destroyed a Japanese lodging house, situated in the city of Tacoma, and with it certain personal property of the Japanese tenants and their several lodgers. The individuals suffering the losses assigned their claims for damages to S. Yamamoto, who brought the present action against the Puget Sound Lumber Company to recover the value of the property destroyed. In his complaint the plaintiff alleged that the fire which destroyed the property escaped from an open burner which the lumber company carelessly and negligently maintained at its sawmill. The amount of the demand in the complaint was $6,918.48. The jury returned a general verdict in favor of the assignee for $2,350. From a judgment entered on the verdict, the lumber company appeals.

The appellant first assigns that the court erred in refusing to grant its motion for nonsuit made at the conclusion of the plaintiff's evidence in chief, and later in refusing to sustain its motion for judgment notwithstanding the verdict; the chief contention being that the evidence was insufficient to justify the conclusion that the fire originated from the open burner. But, without specially reviewing the record, we think the most that can be said is that there was a sharp conflict in the evidence on the question, and that the jury could well have found for the other side. Under these circumstances, the verdict is conclusive on us here. It is the peculiar province of the jury to judge of the weight and sufficiency of the evidence, and their findings on conflicting evidence are conclusive on the appellate court, even though that court may be convinced that the evidence preponderates the other way.

The case before us differs from the case of *Imeson v. Tacoma R. & P. Co.*, 42 Wash. 74, 84 Pac. 624, cited and relied upon by the appellant. In the first place, the case cited, having been tried by the court by below sitting without a jury, was reviewable in this court on its facts; and, in the second place, there was no direct evidence that the fire concerning the losses for which recovery was sought originated from a cause for which the defendant would have been liable; in fact, the court construed the evidence as pointing rather to the contrary conclusion. Here there was direct evidence tracing the fire from the open burner maintained by the defendant to the burned building, which contained the articles of personal property destroyed in its burning. …

It is contended, however, that certain of the causes of action were not proven; that there was no proof that the claims of H. Ando, T. Doho or J. Terao had been assigned to the plaintiffs; that the complaint alleged that certain of the property destroyed was the property of T. Tamari, whereas the proofs showed that it was, in fact, the property of A. Tamari; that on certain of the claims, particularly those of T. Hashimoto and A. Tamari, there were no proofs of value at the time they were destroyed; and that no consideration was shown for any of the assignments.

As to the objection of a want of consideration for the assignments, there was no need of any express consideration. The assignments being in writing, the assignee became vested with the legal title to the claims assigned, and could maintain an action thereon in his own name, notwithstanding each assignor may have retained an interest in his particular claim. REM. & BAL. CODE § 191.

As to the contention that there were no proofs of the assignments of the claims of H. Ando, T. Doho, and J. Terao to the respondent, we find that the names of all of these persons appear on the written assignment introduced in evidence, and that T. Doho and J. Terao severally testified that he had made such an assignment of his claim. H. Ando seems not to have so testified, but he was permitted, without objection, to testify to the goods lost by him in the fire, and as to their value, and a list of his goods is included in the typewritten list submitted to the jury by stipulation of the counsel as an exhibit to aid their memory when making up their verdict.

More than this, the assignment itself was put in evidence without objection, on the ground that it had not been properly authenticated. Under these circumstances the court and jury had a right to assume that the loss of this particular claimant was a subject for consideration, and, conceding there was a default in the technical proofs, we think the appellant now estopped to claim an advantage from it. ... The judgment is affirmed.

NOTES AND QUESTIONS

1. **Statutory Rule—Assignment Contracts and Proof of Consideration**. MCKINNEY'S CONSOLIDATED LAWS OF NEW YORK ANNOTATED § 5-1107 outlines the effects of no consideration on the enforcement of an assignment contract. It reads: "An assignment shall not be denied the effect of irrevocably transferring the assignor's rights because of the absence of consideration, if such assignment is in writing and signed by the assignor, or by his agent."

2. **Common-Law Rule—Assignment Contracts and Proof of Consideration**. The Pennsylvania court addressed an important common-law question in *Ertel v. McCloskey*, 74 A.2d 652, 654 (Pa. Super. Ct. 1950): whether an assignee must prove sufficient consideration before a court enforces an assignment contract. The following excerpt appears in *Ertel*:

   > [T]he defense of lack of consideration was not available, since the assignment was under seal and evidences the signer's intention "to be legally bound." Nor was the defense available to McCloskey. The debtor may not question the motive or purpose underlying the assignment, or set up lack of consideration as a defense. Since a chose in action may be the subject of a gift, no consideration is necessary to the validity of an assignment. 6 C.J.S., ASSIGNMENTS § 132.

3. **Assignment Contracts and Holders in Due Course**. Negotiable instruments may be assigned like all contracts. Generally, a holder in due course is a party who has received rights under a negotiable instrument. On the other hand, there is an important distinction between an assignee and a holder of, say, a promissory note. Consider the discussion in *Lorain Ready Mixed Concrete & Builders Supply, Inc. v. Wheeler*, 1984 WL 6146, *1 (Ohio Ct. App. May 2, 1984). "At issue in [*Lorain*] is whether Lorain Ready Mixed

was a holder in due course or an assignee to the note. The distinction is relevant because a holder in due course takes the note free from the defense of a failure of consideration, while an assignee is subject to this defense." In *Carius v. Ohio Contract Purchase Co.*, 30 Ohio App. 57, 62–63 (Ohio Ct. App. 1928), the court of appeals explained the distinction as follows:

> The word "assign" has a definite and distinct meaning, and a transfer of a contract by assignment is quite different from a transfer of a contract for the payment of money only by indorsement—in other words, a promissory note. That a promissory note—that could otherwise be transferred by indorsement—need not be so transferred, but may be transferred by assignment, is unquestionably the law, and the books are filled with such cases. ... Now what are an assignee's rights under a contract, whether it [is] negotiable paper or any other contract? Why, manifestly he stands in the shoes of the assignor. He has the same title that the assignor had, no better, no worse, and if the assignor could not recover, neither can the assignee. ...

C. Doctrines of Non-Delegable Duty and Novation

Unquestionably, the doctrine of assignment and the third-party beneficiary doctrine create third-party contractual rights and obligations. But even more importantly, those principles govern whether or not third parties may enforce various agreements without establishing privity of contract. To a lesser extent, third parties' interests, rights, and/or obligations are also implicated in any discussion or analysis involving the doctrines of non-delegable duty and novation. Two brief examples should help to prove the point.

First, consider these brief facts. The owner of a small commercial building and an applicant formed a one-year lease. In the contract, the landlord promised that he would "personally patrol the premises every day between 12:01 a.m. and 6:01 a.m." Relying on that promise, the applicant/tenant signed the lease and occupied the commercial unit. Two months later, the owner stopped patrolling the premises and hired ABT Security—delegating the duty to patrol the building to the "top-notched and highly experienced security firm." In the course of events, the tenant's store was burglarized one evening when ABT's agents failed to patrol the building.

Now contemplate the second hypothetical, which is a slight modification of the facts in the first example. A landlord and a tenant formed a one-year lease. In the contract, the landlord promised that he would "personally patrol the premises every day between 12:01 a.m. and 6:01 a.m." Relying on that promise, the tenant signed the lease and occupied the commercial unit. Two months later, the owner realized that his health would not permit him to patrol the building. Therefore, the landlord approached the tenant and inquired whether the tenant would condone ABT Security's accepting the duty to patrol the building. The tenant said yes. A week later, the landlord, tenant, and ABT formed a new contract—a novation. A month later, the tenant's business was burglarized one evening when ABT's agents failed to patrol the building.

In light of the facts in both examples, weigh these questions: Which party had a contractual duty to patrol the building? Which party is severally liable under the doctrines of non-delegable duty and novation doctrines—the landlord or third-party security firm? Which party has the burden to prove that a non-delegable contractual duty was breached? Which party has the burden to prove that the novation was breached? Must the tenant establish liability under the original lease, the novation, or both? As you read the cases and notes appearing below, determine whether novation and the non-delegable duty doctrines are truly independent principles or essentially a single, multi-prong doctrine.

1. Doctrine of Non-Delegable Duty

General Building Contractors Association, Inc. v. Pennsylvania
458 U.S. 375
(1982)

JUSTICE REHNQUIST DELIVERED THE OPINION OF THE COURT. Respondents, the Commonwealth of Pennsylvania and the representatives of a class of racial minorities who are skilled or seek work as operating engineers in the construction industry in Eastern Pennsylvania and Delaware, commenced this action under a variety of federal statutes protecting civil rights, including 42 U.S.C. § 1981. The complaint sought to redress racial discrimination in the operation of an exclusive hiring hall established in contracts between Local 542 of the International Union of Operating Engineers and construction industry employers doing business within the Union's jurisdiction. Respondents also alleged discrimination in the operation of an apprenticeship program established by Local 542 and several construction trade associations.

Named as defendants were Local 542, the trade associations, the organization charged with administering the trade's apprenticeship program, and a class of approximately 1,400 construction industry employers. Petitioners, the defendant contractors and trade associations, seek review of a judgment granting an injunction against them. The questions we resolve are whether liability under 42 U.S.C. § 1981 requires proof of discriminatory intent and whether, absent such proof, liability can nevertheless be imposed vicariously on the employers and trade associations for the discriminatory conduct of the Union.

I

The hiring hall system that is the focus of this litigation originated in a collective-bargaining agreement negotiated in 1961 by Local 542 and four construction-trade associations in the Philadelphia area, three of whom are petitioners in this Court. The agreement was concluded only after a 10-week strike prompted by the resistance of the trade associations to the Union's demand for an exclusive hiring hall. Under the terms of the agreement, the Union was to maintain lists of operating engineers, or would-be engineers, classified according to the extent of their recent construction experience.

Signatory employers were contractually obligated to hire operating engineers only from among those referred by the Union from its current lists. Workers affiliated with the Union were barred from seeking work with those employers except through Union referrals. Thus, the collective-bargaining agreement effectively channeled all employment opportunities through the hiring hall. Since 1961 this requirement has been a constant feature of contracts negotiated with Local 542 by the trade associations, as well as of contracts signed with the Union by employers who were not represented by one of those associations in collective bargaining.

Among the means of gaining access to the Union's referral lists is an apprenticeship program established in 1965 by Local 542 and the trade associations. The program, which involves classroom and field training, is administered by the Joint Apprenticeship and Training Committee (JATC), a body of trustees half of whom are appointed by the Union and half by the trade associations. While enrolled in the program, apprentices are referred by the Union for unskilled construction work. Graduates of the program become journeymen operating engineers and are referred for heavy equipment jobs.

This action was filed in 1971 by the Commonwealth of Pennsylvania and 12 black plaintiffs representing a proposed class of minority group members residing within the jurisdiction of Local 542. The complaint charged that the Union and the JATC had violated numerous state and federal laws prohibiting employment discrimination, including TITLE VII OF THE CIVIL RIGHTS ACT of 1964, 78 Stat. 253, as amended, 42 U.S.C. § 2000e *et seq.* (1976), and 42 U.S.C. § 1981. The complaint alleged that these defendants had engaged in a pattern and practice of racial discrimination, by systematically denying access to the Union's referral lists, and by arbitrarily skewing referrals in favor of white workers, limiting most minority workers who did gain access to the hiring hall to jobs of short hours and low pay. The contractor employers and trade associations were also named as defendants, although the complaint did not allege a Title VII cause of action against them. ...

The District Court's opinion in the liability phase of the trial is lengthy. For our purposes, however, the relevant findings and conclusions can be summarized briefly. First, the court found that the hiring hall system established by collective bargaining was neutral on its face. Indeed, after May 1, 1971, the contracts contained a provision expressly prohibiting employment discrimination on the basis of race, religion, color, or national origin. But the court found that Local 542, in administering the system, "practiced a pattern of intentional discrimination and that union practices in the overall operation of a hiring hall for operating engineers created substantial racial disparities." ... On the basis of these findings, the District Court held that Local 542 and the JATC had violated Title VII, both because they intentionally discriminated and because they enforced practices that resulted in a disparate racial impact. ...

Turning to petitioners' liability under § 1981, the court found that the plaintiffs had failed to prove "that the associations or contractors viewed simply as a class were actually aware of the union discrimination," and had failed to show "intent to discriminate by the employers as a class." Nevertheless, the court held the employers and the associations liable under § 1981 for the purpose of imposing an injunctive remedy "as a result of their contractual relationship to and use of a hiring hall system which in practice effectuated intentional discrimination, whether or not the employers and associations knew or should have known [of the Union's conduct]."

In light of its disposition, the court found it unnecessary to address other causes of action alleged by the plaintiffs. Following an appeal authorized by 28 U.S.C. § 1292(b), the Court of Appeals for the Third Circuit, sitting en banc, affirmed the judgment of liability against petitioners by an equally divided vote. We granted certiorari. ...

III

The District Court held petitioners liable under § 1981 notwithstanding its finding that the plaintiffs had failed to prove intent to discriminate on the part of the employers and associations as a class. In light of our holding that § 1981 can be violated only by intentional discrimination, the District Court's judgment can stand only if liability under § 1981 can properly rest on some ground other than the discriminatory motivation of the petitioners themselves. Both the District Court and respondents have relied on such grounds, but we find them unconvincing.

A

The District Court reasoned that liability could be vicariously imposed upon the employers and associations, based upon the intentional discrimination practiced by Local 542 in its operation of the hiring hall. The court's theory was that petitioners had delegated to the "union hiring hall" the authority to select workers as "the agent for two principals—the union and the contractors, with their respective associations." Since the hiring hall came into existence only through the agreement of petitioners, and since the exclusive hiring hall was the means by which "the intentional discrimination of the union was able to work its way broadly into the common workforce of operating engineers," the court concluded that "[t]he acts of the union therefore justify imposition of responsibility upon those employers participating in the original delegation." The effect of this holding, as the court recognized, was to impose a "duty to see that discrimination does not take place in the selection of one's workforce," regardless of where the discrimination originates.

As applied to the petitioner associations, the District Court's theory is flawed on its own terms. The doctrine of respondeat superior, as traditionally conceived and as understood by the District Court, enables the imposition of liability on a principal for the tortious acts of his agent and, in the more common case, on the master for the wrongful acts of his servant. See RESTATEMENT (SECOND) OF AGENCY §§ 215–216, 219 (1958) (RESTATEMENT). ... "Agency is the fiduciary relation which results from the manifestation of consent by one person to another that the other shall act on his behalf and subject to his control, and consent by the other so to act." RESTATEMENT § 1. A master-servant relationship is a form of agency in which the master employs the servant as "an agent to perform service in his affairs" and "controls or has the right to control the physical conduct of the other in the performance of the service."

Local 542, in its operation of the hiring hall, simply performed no function as the agent or servant of the associations. The record demonstrates that the associations themselves do not hire operating engineers, and never have. Their primary purpose is to represent certain employers in contract negotiations with the Union. Even if the doctrine of respondeat superior were broadly applicable to suits based on § 1981, therefore, it would not support the imposition of liability on a defendant based on the acts of a party with whom it had no agency or employment relationship. ...

B

The District Court also justified its result by concluding that § 1981 imposes a "nondelegable duty" on petitioners "to see that discrimination does not take place in the selection of [their] workforce." The concept of a nondelegable duty imposes upon the principal not merely an obligation to exercise care in his own activities, but to answer for the well-being of those persons to whom the duty runs. *See* RESTATEMENT § 214. The duty is not discharged by using care in delegating it to an independent contractor. Consequently, the doctrine creates an exception to the common-law rule that a principal normally will not be liable for the tortious conduct of an independent contractor. So understood, a nondelegable duty is an affirmative obligation to ensure the protection of the person to whom the duty runs.

In a sense, to characterize such a duty as "nondelegable" is merely to restate the duty. Thus, in this litigation the question is not whether the employers and associations are free to delegate their duty to abide by § 1981, for whatever duty the statute imposes, they are bound to adhere to it. The question is what duty does § 1981 impose. More precisely, does § 1981 impose a duty to refrain from intentionally denying blacks the right to contract on the same basis as whites or does it impose an affirmative obligation to ensure that blacks enjoy such a right?

The language of the statute does not speak in terms of duties. It merely declares specific rights held by "[a]ll persons within the jurisdiction of the United States." We are confident that the Thirty-ninth Congress meant to do no more than prohibit the employers and associations in these cases from intentionally depriving black workers of the rights enumerated in the statute, including the equal right to contract. It did not intend to make them the guarantors of the workers' rights as against third parties who would infringe them.

Our earlier holding that § 1981 reaches only intentional discrimination virtually compels this conclusion. It would be anomalous to hold that § 1981 could be violated only by intentional discrimination and then to find this requirement satisfied by proof that the individual plaintiffs did not enjoy "the same right … to make and enforce contracts … as is enjoyed by white citizens" and that the defendants merely failed to ensure that the plaintiffs enjoyed employment opportunities equivalent to that of whites. Such a result would be particularly inappropriate in the case of the associations, who are not engaged in the construction business, do not employ operating engineers, and consequently did not delegate to the Union any hiring functions which they otherwise would have performed themselves. Neither the District Court nor respondents identify anything in the language or legislative history of the statute to support a contrary conclusion. …

The judgment of the Court of Appeals is reversed, and the case is remanded for proceedings consistent with this opinion. It is so ordered.

JUSTICE MARSHALL, WITH WHOM JUSTICE BRENNAN JOINS, DISSENTING.

Today the Court reaches out and decides that 42 U.S.C. § 1981 requires proof of an intent to discriminate—an issue that is not at all necessary to the disposition of these cases. Because I find no support for the majority's resolution of this issue, and because I disagree with its disposition of these cases even if proof of intent should ordinarily be required, I respectfully dissent.

I

The question whether intent generally should be required in § 1981 actions is at most tangentially related to these cases. There was unquestionably intentional discrimination on the part of both the union (Local 542) and the Joint Apprenticeship and Training Committee (JATC), a body composed of officials from the union and the petitioner contracting associations, which jointly administered the apprenticeship and training program. As a result, the only question that the Court need address today is whether limited injunctive liability may be vicariously imposed upon an employer when the person or entity to whom it delegates a large portion of its hiring decisions intentionally discriminates on the basis of race. However, because the majority has chosen to reach first the more general question whether proof of intent is a prerequisite to recovery in a § 1981 action, I likewise will address this issue first.

Section 1981 provides in unqualified terms:

> All persons within the jurisdiction of the United States shall have the same right in every State and Territory to make and enforce contracts, to sue, be parties, give evidence, and to the full and equal benefit of all laws and proceedings for the security of persons and property as is enjoyed by white citizens. ..." 42 U.S.C. § 1981.

The plain language does not contain or suggest an intent requirement. A violation of § 1981 is not expressly conditioned on the motivation or intent of any person. The language focuses on the effects of discrimination on the protected class, and not on the intent of the person engaging in discriminatory conduct. Nothing in the statutory language implies that a right denied because of sheer insensitivity, or a pattern of conduct that disproportionately burdens the protected class of persons, is entitled to any less protection than one denied because of racial animus. ...

The purposes behind § 1981, and the profound national policy of blotting out all vestiges of racial discrimination, are no less frustrated when equal opportunities are denied through cleverly masked or merely insensitive practices, where proof of actual intent is nearly impossible to obtain, than when instances of intentional discrimination escape unremedied. For this reason, I cannot accept the Court's glib and unrealistic view that requiring proof of intent in § 1981 actions does not frustrate that statute's purpose of protecting against the devastating effects of racial discrimination in employment.

II

Even if I agreed with the Court that intent must be proved in a § 1981 action, I could not agree with its conclusion that the petitioner contracting associations should be immunized, even from injunctive liability, for the intentional discrimination practiced by the union hall to which they delegated a major portion of their hiring decisions. Under § 1981, minorities have an unqualified right to enter into employment contracts on the same basis as white persons. It is undisputed that in these cases, the respondent class was denied this right through intentional discrimination. The fact that the associations chose to delegate a large part of the hiring process to the local union hiring hall, which then engaged in intentional discrimination, does not alter the fact that respondents were denied the right to enter into employment contracts with the associations on the same basis as white persons.

At the very least, § 1981 imposes on employers the obligation to make employment decisions free from racial considerations. The hiring decisions made by the contracting associations in these cases were fraught with racial discrimination. Solely because of their race, hundreds of minority operating engineers were totally excluded from the industry and could not enter into employment contracts with any employer. Those minorities allowed into the industry suffered discrimination in referrals, and thus they too were denied the same right as white persons to contract with the contracting associations. Not one of the petitioner contracting associations has ever claimed, nor could they, that minorities had the same right as white operating engineers to contract for employment.

Instead, the contracting associations attempt to hide behind the veil of ignorance, shifting their responsibility under § 1981 to the very entity which they chose to assist them in making hiring decisions. The suggestion that an employer's responsibility under § 1981 depends upon its own choice of a hiring agent finds no support in the statute, nor does any other source of law authorize the circumvention of § 1981 that the contracting associations seek here. Their obligation to make employment contracts free from racial discrimination is a nondelegable one: [I]t does not disappear when, as is often the case, the actual employer designates a particular agent to assist in the hiring process. In my view, the fact that the discriminating entity here is a union hiring hall, and not a person or corporation which has a traditional agent-principal relationship with the employer, does not alter this analysis. *Cf. Morrison-Knudsen Co. v. NLRB*, 275 F.2d 914 (2d Cir. 1960) (An employer cannot escape liability for discrimination against nonunion members by the union hiring hall to which it turns over the task of supplying men for employment).

The majority does not really analyze the question whether petitioners should be held injunctively liable because § 1981 imposes upon them a nondelegable duty. Instead the majority argues that, because it has held that § 1981 is intended only to reach intentional discrimination, the statute cannot make employers "guarantors of the workers' rights as against third parties who would infringe them." This argument does not withstand analysis. The majority does not assert that employers may escape liability under § 1981 by delegating their hiring decisions to a third-party agent. Indeed, in light of the importance attached to the rights § 1981 is intended to safeguard, the duty to abide by this statute must be nondelegable, as the majority apparently recognizes.

Instead, the majority argues that because § 1981 imposes only the duty to refrain from intentional discrimination in hiring, it somehow automatically follows that this duty could not have been violated in this case. However, it was precisely this duty that was violated here. The District Court found, and this Court does not disagree, that the entity to whom the petitioner associations effectively delegated their hiring decisions intentionally discriminated against the respondent class on the basis of race in making these decisions. Even under the Court's own narrow view of the scope of the duty imposed by § 1981, then, the duty was unquestionably violated in these cases.

The majority obfuscates the issue by suggesting that the District Court imposed upon the contracting associations an obligation to seek out and eliminate discrimination by unrelated third parties wherever it may occur. In reality, the District Court did nothing more than impose limited injunctive liability upon the associations for violating their nondelegable duty under § 1981 when the union hiring hall, which effectively made hiring decisions for the associations, engaged in intentional discrimination on the basis of race in making these decisions.

By immunizing the employer from the injunctive relief necessary to remedy the intentional discrimination practiced by those through whom the employer makes its hiring decisions, the Court removes the person most necessary to accord full relief—the entity with whom the aggrieved persons will ultimately make a contract. I believe that the District Court appropriately rejected the petitioners' argument when it explained: "With intensity some employers urge that they agreed to the exclusive hiring hall system solely as a matter of economic survival at the end of a destructive ten week strike when the union would not compromise for any other hiring alternative. Yet economic pressures, however strong and harmful they might be, do not create immunity for employers, at least not in [the injunctive] liability phase." 469 F.Supp., at 338.

Section 1981 provides Negroes "the same right" to make contracts as white persons enjoy. In the present cases, this unqualified right was violated, and the violation is made no more palatable because the persons who actually made the hiring decisions and referrals, and not the employer itself, engaged in intentional discrimination. The devastating violation of their rights under § 1981 remains the same and will go at least partially unremedied when the person with whom the ultimate employment contract must be made is immunized from even injunctive relief. I cannot impute to the Congress which enacted § 1981 the intention to reach such an inequitable and nonsensical result. Accordingly, I must dissent.

NOTES AND QUESTIONS

1. **"Non-Delegable Duty"—Its Definition and Origin.**" [T]here is no general rule [regarding] what constitutes a non-delegable duty. Rather, the determination 'necessarily entails a sui generis inquiry, since the conclusion ultimately rests on policy considerations.'" *Rangolan v. County of Nassau*, 749 N.E.2d 178, 183 (N.Y. 2001). However, it is universally recognized that a non-delegable duty may arise from a contract, one's voluntary assumption, a statute, or the common law. *Damron v. C.R. Anthony Co.*, 586 S.W.2d 907, 913–914 (Tex. Civ. App.—Amarillo 1979) ("[T] here are certain non-delegable duties that exist, whether created by contract, voluntary assumption or public policy, and when a person assumes one of those duties that person remains accountable for its performance regardless of the means used to effectuate the performance.").

2. **Special Relationships and Non-Delegable Duties.** A non-delegable duty may evolve from a special relationship. In *Guideone America Ins. Co., Inc. v. Shore Ins. Agency, Inc.* 259 P.3d 864, 870 (Okla. Ct. App. 2011), the court stated:

A "special relationship" exists between an insurer and its insured stemming from the quasi-public nature of insurance, the unequal bargaining power between the insurer and insured, and the potential for an insurer to unscrupulously exert that power at a time when the insured is particularly vulnerable. ... The special relationship creates a nondelegable duty of good faith and fair dealing on the part of the insurer. This duty is nondelegable so that insurers cannot escape liability by delegating tasks to third parties.

3. **Agency Doctrine and the Principal's Special Relationship with a Third Party**. The RESTATEMENT (THIRD) OF AGENCY § 7.05(2) (2006) reads: "When a principal has a special relationship with another person, the principal owes that person a duty of reasonable care with regard to risks arising out of the relationship, including the risk that agents of the principal will harm the person with whom the principal has such a special relationship."

4. **Agency Doctrine and Master's Liability for Agent's Nonperformance of a Duty**. The RESTATEMENT (SECOND) OF AGENCY § 214 states: "A master or other principal who is under a duty to provide protection for or to have care used to protect others or their property and who confides the performance of such duty to a servant or other person is subject to liability to such others for harm caused to them by the failure of such agent to perform the duty."

5. **Non-Delegable Duties Under State and Federal Statutes.** Without doubt, statutes often create non-delegable duties. But only a judge has authority to declare whether or not a particular statute creates a non-delegable duty. In *General Building Contractors Association*, the federal district judge interpreted § 1981 and declared that Congress *impliedly* created a non-delegable *duty*. The dissenters agreed. The Court's majority, however, declared that § 1981 only established *expressly* a federal *right*. Is it possible for a statute to create a right without also creating an implied duty? Are rights and duties simply the opposite sides of the same coins?

6. **Non-Delegable Duty Doctrine and the Independent Contractor Rule**. Generally, under the common-law, an employer is not liable for an independent contractor's tortious conduct. The doctrine of non-delegable duty, however, is an exception to that rule. Under the doctrine of non-delegable duty, a party may contract away the performance of a non-delegable duty. However, a party may not contract away legal responsibility for an injury arising from the failure to perform a non-delegable duty. *Bouziden*

v. Alfalfa Elec. Coop., Inc., 16 P.3d 450, 455 (Okla. 2000) ("The independent-contractor rule of non-liability has been eroded by well-recognized exceptions. One exception is that an employer who performs work through an independent contractor is liable for damages to third persons caused by the negligence of the independent contractor where the employer owes a non-delegable contractual or defined legal duty to the injured party."). The exception is based on the theory that certain employer's duties are extremely vital or important for the general welfare of the community; therefore, the employer may not escape liability by delegating performance to another. *Majorowicz v. Allied Mut. Ins. Co.*, 569 N.W.2d 472, 476 (Wis. Ct. App. 1997).

2. Doctrine of Novation

Rosenbergs v. Son, Inc.
491 N.W.2d 71
(N.D. 1992)

ERICKSTAD, CHIEF JUSTICE. Harold Rosenberg and Gladys E. Rosenberg (Rosenbergs) appeal two district-court decisions granting summary judgment in favor of Son, Inc. and Mary Pratt. ... On February 8, 1980, Pratt entered into a contract for the sale of a business with the Rosenbergs, agreeing to purchase the Rosenbergs' Dairy Queen located in the City Center Mall in Grand Forks. The terms of the sales contract for the franchise, inventory, and equipment were a purchase price totaling $62,000, a $10,000 down payment, and $52,000 due in quarterly payments at 10 percent interest over a 15-year-period. The sales contract also contained a provision denying the buyer a right to prepayment for the first five years of the contract.

Mary Pratt assigned her rights and delegated her duties under the sales contract to Son, Inc., on October 1, 1982. The assignment agreement contained a "CONSENT TO ASSIGNMENT" clause which was signed by the Rosenbergs on October 14, 1982. The assignment agreement also included a "save harmless" clause in which Son, Inc., promised to indemnify Pratt. Subsequent to this transaction, Mary Pratt moved to Arizona and had no further knowledge of, or involvement with, the Dairy Queen business. Also following the assignment, the Dairy Queen was moved from the City Center Mall to the corner of DeMers and North Fifth Street in Grand Forks.

The sales contract was then assigned by Son, Inc., to Merit, Corporation (Merit) on June 1, 1984. This assignment agreement did not contain a consent clause for the Rosenbergs to sign. However, the Rosenbergs had knowledge of the assignment and apparently acquiesced. They accepted a large prepayment from Merit, reducing the principal balance due to $25,000. Following this assignment, Merit pledged the inventory and equipment of the Dairy Queen as collateral for a loan from Valley Bank and Trust of Grand Forks.

Payments from Merit to the Rosenbergs continued until June of 1988, at which time the payments ceased, leaving an unpaid principal balance of $17,326.24 plus interest. The Rosenbergs attempted collection of the balance from Merit, but the collection efforts were precluded when Merit filed bankruptcy. The business assets pledged as collateral for the loan from Valley Bank and Trust of Grand Forks were repossessed. The Rosenbergs brought this action for collection of the outstanding debt against Son, Inc., and Mary Pratt.

The trial court denied a summary judgment motion by the Rosenbergs. ... Several months later, Pratt and Son, Inc., renewed their summary judgment motions. The trial court granted Pratt's motion on December 2, 1991, and granted Son, Inc.'s motion on January 10, 1992, dismissing the Rosenbergs' claims against both parties. ... We disagree with the trial court's analysis and decision to grant summary judgment.

It is a well-established principle in the law of contracts that a contracting party cannot escape its liability on the contract by merely assigning its duties and rights under the contract to a third party. This principle is codified in N.D.C.C. § 41-02-17(1):

> DELEGATION OF PERFORMANCE—ASSIGNMENT OF RIGHTS
>
> A party may perform his duty through a delegate unless otherwise agreed or unless the other party has a substantial interest in having his original promisor perform or control the acts required by the contract. No delegation of performance relieves the party delegating of any duty to perform or any liability for breach.

Professor Corbin explained this point succinctly in his treatise on contract law:

> An assignment is an expression of intention by the assignor that his duty shall immediately pass to the assignee. Many a debtor wishes that by such an expression he could get rid of his debts. Any debtor can express such an intention, but it is not operative to produce such a hoped-for result. It does not cause society to relax its compulsion against him and direct it toward the assignee as his substitute. In spite of such an 'assignment,' the debtor's duty remains absolutely unchanged. The performance required by a duty can often be delegated; but by such a delegation the duty itself is not escaped. 4 CORBIN ON CONTRACTS § 866 at 452.

This rule of law applies to all categories of contracts, including contracts for the sale or lease of real property, service contracts, and contracts for the sale of goods, which is present in the facts of this case.

"In the case of a contract for the sale of goods, the assignment and delegation may be by the buyer as well as by the seller. The buyer's assignment of his right to the goods and his delegation of the duty to pay the price are both effective; but he himself remains bound to pay the price just as before. If the assignee contracts with the assignor to pay the price, the seller can maintain suit for the price against the assignee also, as a creditor beneficiary of the assumption contract; the seller has merely obtained a new and additional security." 4 Corbin on Contracts § 866 at 454–455.

Thus, when Pratt entered into the "assignment agreement" with Son, Inc., a simple assignment alone was insufficient to release her from any further liability on the contract. *See Jedco Development Co., Inc. v. Bertsch*, 441 N.W.2d 664 (N.D. 1989) (lessee is not relieved of this obligation to pay rent merely because he had assigned lease with lessor's consent absent a novation); *Brooks v. Hayes*, 133 Wis.2d 228, 395 N.W.2d 167 (1986) (party delegating duties under contract is not relieved of responsibility for fulfilling an obligation or liability in the event of a breach). *See also* Restatement (Second) of Contracts § 318; 6A C.J.S. Assignments § 97 at 753; and, 6 Am.Jur.2d Assignments § 110.

It is not, however, a legal impossibility for a contracting party to rid itself of an obligation under a contract. It may seek the approval of the other original party for release, and substitute a new party in its place. In such an instance, the transaction is no longer called an assignment; instead, it is called a novation. There are three statutes applicable to novation in the present case. The first statute defines the concept of novation: "Novation Defined. Novation is the substitution of a new obligation for an existing one." N.D.C.C. § 9-13-08. The second statute explains how a novation is created: "Novation-Created by Contract. Novation is made by contract and is subject to all the rules concerning contracts in general." N.D.C.C. § 9-13-09.

The third and final statute points out the various methods for making a novation:

> How Novation Made
>
> Novation is made by the substitution of: 1) A new obligation between the same parties with intent to extinguish the old obligation; 2) A new debtor in the place of the old one with intent to release the latter; or 3) A new creditor in place of the old one with intent to transfer the rights of the latter to the former. N.D.C.C. § 9-13-10.

If a novation occurs in this manner, it must be clear from the terms of the agreement that a novation is intended by all parties involved. "An obligor is discharged by the substitution of a new obligor only if the contract so provides or if the obligee makes a binding manifestation of assent, forming a novation." Restatement (Second) of Contracts § 318 cmt. d. Therefore, both original parties to the contract must intend and mutually assent to the discharge of the obligor from any further liability on the original contract. *See Schmitt v. Berwick Township*, 488 N.W.2d 398 (N.D. 1992) and, *Butler v. Roberts*, 437 N.W.2d 839 (N.D. 1989).

It is evident from the express language of the assignment agreement between Pratt and Son, Inc., that only an assignment was intended, not a novation. The agreement made no mention of discharging Pratt from any further liability on the contract. To the contrary, the latter part of the agreement contained an indemnity clause holding Pratt harmless in the event of a breach by Son, Inc. Thus, it is apparent that Pratt contemplated being held ultimately responsible for performance of the obligation.

Furthermore, the agreement was between Pratt and Son, Inc.; they were the parties signing the agreement, not the Rosenbergs. An agreement between Pratt and Son, Inc., cannot unilaterally affect the Rosenbergs' rights under the contract. ... The question of whether or not there has been a novation is a question of fact, as decided by this court in *Herb Hill Ins., Inc. v. Radtke*, 380 N.W.2d 651. ... The trial court should not have granted summary judgment on the basis of guaranty law.

First of all, guaranty law does not apply to contract assignments without more. Further, there are questions of fact remaining as to the result of the changes in the contract. These issues were not addressed by the trial court. In reversing and remanding in *Jedco*, we said:

> We cannot determine as a matter of law that the assignment was intended to be a novation which resulted in a release of [the assignor's] liability under the lease. Because there are different inferences to be drawn from the undisputed facts, reasonable persons could draw more than one conclusion in this case. Therefore, the summary judgment is reversed and the case is remanded for further proceedings. 441 N.W.2d at 668.

We must do the same in this case. Thus, we reverse the summary judgment and remand for further proceedings.

NOTES AND QUESTIONS

1. **A Novation Is an Affirmative Defense**. A novation is created when a new valid contract extinguishes a previous valid obligation. Under the new contract, new parties or a new undertaking is substituted with the consent of all parties. And there must be proof of valid consideration. *Sheet Metal Workers Natl. Pension Fund v. Bryden House Ltd. Partnership*, 130 (Ohio Ct. App. 1998).

2. **Distinguishing Assignment of Rights from Delegation of Duties.** Consider the court's observation in *Rosenbergs*:

> The term "assign" is normally associated with a party's rights under a contract (i.e., getting paid, receiving goods); whereas the term "delegate" is associated with a party's duties under a contract (i.e., making a payment, performing a service). However, it is a common practice to call the assigning of rights and delegating of duties merely an "assignment of contract." This is especially true when language such as "all right, title and interest" is used. This was the exact language contained in the assignment agreement between Pratt and Son, Inc., and also in the assignment agreement between Son, Inc., and Merit, Corporation. ...
>
> An assignment of "the contract" or of "all my rights under the contract" or an assignment in similar general terms is an assignment of rights and unless the language or the circumstances—as in an assignment for security—indicate the contrary, it is a delegation of performance of the duties of the assignor and its acceptance by the assignee constitutes a promise by him to perform those duties. This promise is enforceable by either the assignor or the other party to the original contract." (Footnote 1)

Part 2

The Formation and Enforcement of Contracts Under Article II of the Uniform Commercial Code

INTRODUCTION

The Uniform Commercial Code and the Codification of Contract Laws

As discussed in Part I, common-law rules govern the construction, interpretation, and enforcement of all contracts—including the sale-of-goods contracts. For the most part, in both England and the United States, those rules have protected contracting parties' various interests extremely well for hundreds of years. To a large extent, the rigidity or exactness of common-law rules explain their general capacity to resolve contractual disputes, even though English and American courts have crafted many exceptions to those principles.

In addition, common-law principles of contract have helped to settle disputes and "keep the peace" between "battling" contracting parties, because many doctrines require litigants to prove clearly defined elements. And if plaintiffs and defendants fail to prove *every* element, there are dire consequences: The former will be effectively precluded from proving a specific theory of recovery and securing various remedies. And the latter will be liable, since they failed to fashion certain affirmative defenses.

On the other hand, some legal scholars have questioned the contract doctrines' allegedly beneficial effects. After state supreme courts in the United States adopted reasonably settled English principles of contract law, conflicting judicial interpretations and applications of those principles evolved. In the wake, state supreme courts created even more exceptions to general rules. And contracting parties—who resided in different states, but who fashioned interstate, sale-of-goods contracts—found themselves having to navigate ever-meandering rivers of conflicting, unpredictable, and unintelligible rules. Consequently, something had to be done to arrest the trade-and-commerce class from the "chaos."

Citing numerous primary and secondary legal sources, Lawrence Schlam discussed the general problem and the earlier remedial actions to solve it in *Federalism and the Question of Uniform Laws: The Case of Third Party Custody "Standing" Provisions*, 15 N.Y.U. J. Legis. & Pub. Pol'y 157, 183–84 (2010):

> The "Uniform Law Movement" began in the latter part of the nineteenth century when prominent leaders of the legal profession argued that there was confusion or "uncertainty and complexity" in the common law among the states. Many academics took the view that there was a need for a national common law. This growing sense, at least in some quarters, that significant problems resulted from inter-state doctrinal inconsistencies resulted in the formation of the National Conference of Commissioners on Uniform State Laws (NCCUSL) in 1892, and the American Law Institute (ALI) in 1923. ... The NCCUSL has drafted uniform codes on a variety of matters, the most well-known being the Uniform Commercial Code (UCC).

Furthermore, during the mid-twentieth century, international trade and commerce grew astronomically. Contracting parties—who resided in different countries, but who fashioned international sale-of-goods contracts—also found themselves having to negotiate oceans of conflicting and unpredictable rules of commerce and sales. Again, affirmative action was required to "remove complicated and diverse bodies of legal shackles from the throats" of persons who formed international sale-of-goods contracts. To help solve this problem, an international body developed a set of rules entitled, THE UNITED NATIONS CONFERENCE ON CONTRACTS FOR THE INTERNATIONAL SALE OF GOODS, Apr. 10, 1980, 19 I.L.M. 668 (CISG or Convention).

In PART II of this first-year casebook, Article 2 of the Uniform Commercial Code is discussed. The discussion, however, will be truncated; the reason is not complicated. The greater majority of law schools devote an entire upper-level Sales I or Sales II course to covering all sections of Article 2. Quite clearly, such a review is precluded in a first-year contracts course. Nevertheless, some major and controversial sections of Article 2 are discussed in the part of the text. But first, some additional introductory remarks about the UCC and the CISG are warranted before discussing the theories of recovery and affirmative defenses that litigants might raise under Article 2.

A. The Uniform Commercial Code's Purpose and Article 2

To repeat, NCCUSL and ALI crafted Article 2 of the UCC in the 1940s. However, the UCC's stated purposes appear in § 1-103(a). It reads: "[The Uniform Commercial Code] must be liberally construed and applied to promote its underlying purposes and policies, which are: (1) to simplify, clarify, and modernize the law governing commercial transactions; (2) to permit the continued expansion of commercial practices through custom, usage, and agreement of the parties; and (3) to make uniform the law among the various jurisdictions."

As of this writing, each state has adopted the UCC in whole or in part. Some states, however, have not embraced the most recent version of the UCC. In fact, many states have amended various "uniform" provisions in Article 2. Thus, the following telling development should not be surprising: A cursory search of law-related databases reveals that significantly more Article 2 disputes are litigated annually than any other UCC-related controversy. What caused this development? There are competing explanations.

First, ambiguous language in Article 2's subsections explains in part contracting parties' greater propensity to litigate disputes under the article. To illustrate, consider the language in U.C.C. § 2-204(1). It reads in pertinent part: "A contract for sale of goods may be made in *any manner* sufficient to show agreement." Consider also U.C.C. § 2-311(1): "An agreement for sale which is otherwise sufficiently definite to be a contract *is not made invalid by the fact that it leaves particulars of performance to be specified* by one of the parties. Any such specification must be made in *good faith* and within limits set by commercial *reasonableness*." Put simply, the italicized words and phrases are sufficiently indefinite, causing contracting parties to litigate the meaning of those terms. In response, fifty-plus state courts' interpretations vary and generate all sorts of contradictory explanations and declarations of contractual rights and obligations. And the consequences are predictable—substantial numbers of conflicting judicial rulings.

Second, UCC rules generally and most of Article 2's rules are "default" rules. The proposed or revised U.C.C. § 1-302 (a) is reasonably clear: "Except as otherwise provided ... elsewhere ..., the effect of provisions of [the Uniform Commercial Code] may be varied by agreement." Stated simply, the "default" rules were constructed fairly loosely—without defining all material terms—to achieve two additional ends: 1) to resolve contracting parties' specific or unique disputes and 2) to reduce the need to amend the UCC frequently. Therefore, since contracting parties may alter the rules when creating their agreements, the parties are significantly more likely to find themselves in courts more frequently, litigating breach-of-contract disputes under Article 2. Consequently, even more judicial conflicts and unsettled rules will follow. To be sure, these latter, and unintended, consequences will undermine considerably one of the UCC's stated purposes: "[T]o simplify, clarify, and modernize the law governing commercial transactions."

B. The United Nations Convention on Contracts for the International Sale of Goods and Its Stated Purpose

The drafters of the Convention adopted uniform rules to govern contracts involving the international sale of goods. Although the rules had to take into account the countries' various social, economic, and legal systems, CISG's stated purpose is simple: "[To remove] legal barriers in international trade and promote the development of international trade." CISG, MAR. 2, 1987, S. TREATY DOC. NO. 98–9, 1489 U.N.T.S. 3, at pmbl.

After the Convention adopted the rules, CISG has governed every international sale-of-goods contract that has been written in North America, generally, and in the United States specifically. The U.S. and the majority of its key trading partners quickly adopted CISG after its enactment in 1980. *See* Christopher Sheaffer, *The Failure of the United Nations Convention on Contracts for the International Sale of Goods and a Proposal for a New Uniform Global Code in International Sales Law*, 15 CARDOZO J. INT'L & COMP. L. 461, 478 n. 98 (2007).

Certain sale-of-goods and sale-of-services contracts are excluded from CISG's enforcement tentacles: (a) goods bought for personal, family, or household use; (b) goods bought by auction; (c) goods acquired on execution or otherwise by authority of law; (d) sales of stock, shares, investment securities, negotiable instruments, or money; (e) sales of ships, vessels, hovercraft, or aircraft; and (f) sales of electricity. CISG, at ART. 2. The international statute also exempts sales contracts in "which the preponderant part of the obligations of the party who furnishes the goods consists in the supply of labour or services." CISG, at ART. 3(2).

Even more importantly, CISG governs only sale-of-goods contracts that involve "international transaction." ARTICLE 1 reads:

> (1) This Convention applies to contracts of sale of goods between parties whose places of business are in different States:
>
> (a) when the States are Contracting States; or
>
> (b) when the rules of private international law lead to the application of the law of a Contracting State.
>
> (2) The fact that the parties have their places of business in different States is to be disregarded whenever this fact does not appear either from the contract or from any dealings

> between, or from information disclosed by, the parties at any time before or at the conclusion of the contract.
>
> (3) Neither the nationality of the parties nor the civil or commercial character of the parties or of the contract is to be taken into consideration in determining the application of this Convention.

Without doubt, international trade has increased substantially since CISG's adoption. Moreover, if one considers the number of nations that have embraced the sale-of-goods rules, CISG is one of the United Nations'most successful international conventions. Presently, seventy-eight nations are signatory members. (See Note 3 below.) On the other hand, some commentators have raised questions: 1) whether or not CISG has truly promoted international trade and 2) whether or not CISG's laws have governed the thousands of international sale-of-goods contracts that have been crafted in the United States. Consequently, several proposals to abandon or revise CISG have been proffered. *See* Philip Hackney, *Is the United Nations Convention on the International Sale of Goods Achieving Uniformity?*, 61 LA. L. REV. 473 (2001).

C. The Grand Debate: Whether or Not the UCC and CISG Are "Mirror Images" of Each Other

As we have learned, both the UCC and CISG are statutes that govern sale-of-goods contracts' formation, interpretation, and enforcement. But even more interesting, it seems that CISG's drafters used key provisions of the UCC-Article 2 to structure the international statute. To illustrate, compare the following four clauses—focusing carefully on the italicized words and phrases:

UCC § 2-313(2)(c)—Express Warranties by Description and Sample

> Express warranties by the seller to the immediate buyer are created as follows: ... Any *sample or model* that is made part of the basis of the bargain creates an express warranty that the whole of the *goods shall conform to the sample or model*.

UCC § 2-315—Implied Warranty: Fitness for Particular Purpose

> Where the seller *at the time of contracting* has reason to know any *particular purpose* for which the goods are required and that the buyer is *relying on* the seller's skill or judgment to select or furnish suitable goods, there is unless excluded or modified under the next section an implied warranty that the *goods shall be fit for such purpose*.

UCC § 2-503 (1)—Manner of Seller's Tender of Delivery

Tender of delivery requires that the seller put and hold *conforming goods* at the buyer's disposition and give the buyer any notification reasonably necessary to enable him to take delivery. The *manner, time and place for tender are determined by the agreement* and this Article, and in particular

(a) tender must be at a reasonable hour, and if it is of goods they must be kept available for the period reasonably necessary to enable the buyer to take possession; but,

(b) *unless otherwise agreed* the buyer must furnish facilities reasonably suited to the receipt of the goods.

CISG, Art. 35—Conformity of the Goods

(1) The seller must deliver goods which are of *the quantity, quality and description required by the contract* and which are contained or packaged in the manner *required by the contract*.

(2) *Except where the parties have agreed otherwise*, the *goods do not conform* with the contract unless they:

(a) are *fit for the purposes* for which goods of the *same description* would ordinarily be used;

(b) are *fit for any particular purpose* expressly or impliedly made known to the seller at the time of the conclusion of the contract, except where the circumstances show that the buyer *did not rely*, or that it was unreasonable for him *to rely*, on the seller's skill and judgement;

(c) possess the qualities of goods which the seller has held out to the buyer as *a sample or model*;

(d) are contained or packaged in the manner usual for such goods or, where there is no such manner, in a manner adequate to preserve and protect the goods.

(3) The seller is not liable under subparagraphs (a) to (d) of the preceding paragraph for *any lack of conformity* of the goods if at the time of the conclusion of the contract the buyer knew or could not have been unaware of such *lack of conformity*.

Clearly, identical "material" words and phrases appear in UCC Article 2 as well as in the CISG. But are the interpretations and implications of those words and phrases in the two statutes identical? Consider a second comparison, which includes three relatively shorter provisions:

UCC § 2-504—Shipment by Seller

> Where the seller is required or authorized to send the goods to the buyer and the contract does not require him to deliver them *at a particular destination*, then unless otherwise agreed he must
>
> (a) *put the goods in the possession of such a carrier* and make such a contract for their transportation as may be reasonable having regard to the nature of the goods and other circumstances of the case; and
>
> (b) obtain and promptly *deliver or tender in due form any document necessary to enable the buyer to obtain possession* of the goods or otherwise required by the agreement or by usage of trade; and
>
> (c) promptly notify the buyer of the shipment.

Delivery of the Goods and Handing Over of Documents

> CISG, ART. 30—The seller must *deliver the goods, hand over any documents relating to them* and transfer the property in the goods, *as required by the contract* and this Convention.
>
> CISG, ART. 31—If the seller is not bound to deliver the goods *at any other particular place*, his obligation to deliver consists:
>
> (a) if the contract of sale involves carriage of the goods—in *handing the goods over to the first carrier* for transmission to the buyer;
>
> (b) if, in cases not within the preceding subparagraph, the contract relates to specific goods, or unidentified goods to be drawn from a specific stock or to be manufactured or produced, and at the time of the conclusion of the contract the parties knew that the goods were at, or were to be manufactured or produced *at a particular place*—in placing the goods at the buyer's disposal at that place;
>
> (c) in other cases—in placing the goods at the buyer's disposal at the place where the seller had his place of business at the time of the conclusion of the contract.

Are these latter UCC and CISG clauses mirror images of each other? The mirror-images question has generated a grand debate. One commentator has suggested that the two statutes are fairly similar or substantially equivalent. In *Facing the Truth: Seeing the Convention on Contracts for the International Sale of Goods as an Obstacle to a Uniform Law of International Sales*, 32 Cornell Int'l L.J. 273, 280 (1999), James E. Bailey wrote:

> Despite the CISG's applicability to every international contract for the sale of goods in North America as well as for most contracts involving the major trading partners of the United States, many U.S. businesses, lawyers and courts have yet to realize *that contracts they assume are governed by the UCC are actually governed by the CISG*. The dearth of U.S. case law concerning the CISG—despite its ten years of applicability to the majority of U.S. international sales transactions—is itself evidence of the lack of awareness of the CISG in the United States. … [T]o date, only fifteen federal court opinions and two state court opinions have cited the CISG. While other reasons may contribute to this lack of awareness, the treaty's character under U.S. law as a self-executing treaty is probably the main reason U.S. parties are unaware of its existence. Hence, as it currently exists under U.S. law, the CISG does not bring uniformity to the law of international sales but instead fosters disharmony based on ignorance. (emphasis added).

But, Franco Ferrari presents a counter view in his article entitled, *The Relationship Between the UCC and the CISG and the Construction of Uniform Law*, 29 Loy. L.A. L. Rev. 1021, 1022–1024 (1996):

> [T]he assertion that the UCC's and CISG's basic concepts of good faith and trade usages are similar in approach and content … are misleading. Although the UCC has greatly influenced the CISG, it is impossible and even perilous to assert that the aforementioned sets of rules are similar in content, or, even worse, that they "are sufficiently compatible to support claims of overall consistency." An awareness of the UCC's influence might aid in understanding the CISG, especially with respect to issues which the Convention's legislative history demonstrates this influence. It is, however, impermissible and dangerous to assert that the concepts of the CISG and the UCC are analogous. The comparison is dangerous because it makes one believe—erroneously—that the concepts of the CISG correspond to those of the UCC and can therefore be interpreted in light of the UCC. But this is impermissible since a similar approach conflicts with the principle, expressly laid down in Article 7(1) of the CISG, that the CISG and its concepts must be interpreted in light of its international character and the need to promote uniformity in its application.

Comparing Article 2 and CISG provisions, other commentators embrace an intermediary interpretation. They argue UCC rules must be considered or applied only if CISG rules clearly evolved from the common law. To illustrate, consider the italicized words and phrases in the following international statute:

CISG, Art. 74—Damages

> *Damages* for breach of contract by one party consist of a sum equal to the loss, including loss of profit, suffered by the other party *as a consequence of the breach*. Such damages may not exceed the loss which the party in *breach foresaw* or ought to *have foreseen at the time of the conclusion of the contract*, in the light of the facts and matters of which he then *knew or ought to have known*, as a possible *consequence of the breach* of contract.

Commentators—who embrace the intermediary approach—correctly observe that the damages rule appearing in Article 74 of the CISG mirrors precisely the "foreseeability test" which was established in *Hadley v. Baxendale*, 156 Eng. Rep. 145 (L.R. Exch. 1854). And, as discussed more fully in a later chapter in PART II, UCC Article 2 also incorporates *Hadley*. In fact, section 2-715(2)(a) reads: "Consequential damages resulting from the seller's breach include ... any loss resulting from *general or particular requirements* and needs of which the seller at the time of contracting had *reason to know* and which *could not reasonably* be prevented by cover or otherwise."

What have federal courts contributed to the debate? Some courts think the respective provisions in UCC Article 2 and in CISG are substantially equivalent. In *Raw Materials Inc. v. Manfred Forberich GmbH & Co.*, No. 03 C 1154, 2004 WL 1535839, at *3 (N.D. Ill. 2004), the federal district court concluded that "case law interpreting analogous provisions of Article 2 of the Uniform Commercial Code ... may also inform a court where the language of the relevant CISG provisions tracks that of the UCC." *Id.* at *3 (quoting *Delchi Carrier SpA v. Rotorex Corp.*, 71 F.3d 1024, 1028 (2d Cir. 1995); *Chicago Prime Packers, Inc. v. Northam Food Trading Co.*, No. 01-4447, 2004 WL 1166628 (N.D. Ill. 2003)).

Conversely, in *MCC-Marble Ceramic Center Inc. v. Ceramica Nuova D'Agostino*, 144 F.3d 1384, 1391 (11th Cir. 1998), the Eleventh Circuit Court of Appeals stressed: "Courts applying the CISG cannot ... upset the parties' reliance on the Convention by substituting familiar principles of domestic law when the Convention requires a different result. We may only achieve the directives of good faith and uniformity in contracts under the CISG by interpreting and applying the plain language of [the] article ... as written[.]")

The author will not contribute to this extremely heated debate. But, the dispute is significant and it is likely to persist for many years, even beyond first-year law students' tenure in law school. The important point, however, is this one: International sale-of-goods contracts are spiraling upward. Inevitably, some contracting parties will clash—complaining about breached contracts, nonperformance, and partial performances. Consequently, deciding whether UCC's Article 2, CISG, or both statutes should govern the resolution of international sale-of-goods disputes is likely to be continuing and challenging questions of law for state and federal courts in the United States.

NOTES AND QUESTIONS

1. **Regulation and Sale-of-Goods Contracts in England.** Alexandre A. Montagu penned the article entitled, *Intellectual Property: Tectonic Shifts in the Legal Landscape*, 16 J. TECH. L. & POL'Y 1, *5–6 (2011). Citing multiple authorities, the author reported:

   > The SALE OF GOODS ACT was originally enacted by the English Parliament in 1893. It regulates the purchase and sale of goods by contract. After the passage of the SALE OF GOODS ACT, the most important laws affecting the economy were part of a body of law known as Commercial Law. Commercial Law regulates commerce, defined as the manufacture, sale, and delivery of goods. In the twentieth century, commerce could not have been imaginable without the SALE OF GOODS ACT and its equivalents in other jurisdictions such as the UNIFORM COMMERCIAL CODE in the United States. What did business-people do prior to 1893? They lived with unsettled laws and the concomitant confusion brought about in a society that is evolving from one dominant, economic system to another.
   >
   > Discussing the SALE OF GOODS BILL before Parliament, Lord Chalmers stated: "What the fate of the measure may be I do not know; but I venture to think it would be beneficial to the trading community if the Bill were to become law. Even if no substantial amendments in the law were introduced, numerous more or less debatable points could be settled. It needs no argument to prove that in matters of this kind legislation is cheaper and speedier than litigation. Again, men of business as a rule are more concerned with the certainty of the law than the nicety of its application. If they know what the law is they can regulate their conduct with regard to it beforehand.

2. **The National Conference of Commissioners on Uniform State Laws, the American Law Institute, Model Codes, and the Uniform Commerce Code**. Citing a long list of sources, Lawrence Schlam reported the following information in

Federalism and the Question of Uniform Laws: The Case of Third Party Custody "Standing" Provisions, 15 N.Y.U. J. Legis. & Pub. Pol'y 157, 183–84 (2010): "Over the years, the National Conference of Commissioners on Uniform State Laws (NCCUSL) has expanded its scope of activity but has remained dedicated to the formation and promulgation of model codes within non-regulatory areas. Among the founders and early leaders of the American Law Institute (ALI) were some of the country's most prominent legal minds. William Draper Lewis, the first director of the ALI, characterized its goal at its founding in 1923 as follows:

> There existed then a growing feeling among the members of the legal profession [that they owed] a duty to the public to improve the administration of justice. Many lawyers felt that the growing indigestible mass of decisions threatened the continuance of our common law system. The ALI, therefore, generally sought only to clarify and summarize existing law. The NCCUSL, on the other hand, drafted codes for states to either adopt directly or with minimal changes.
>
> The first set of ALI restatements, drafted between 1923 and 1944, spoke to subjects such as agency, contracts, and torts. These areas were chosen because the founding committee concluded that uncertainty in the law should first be addressed through subjects with apparent interstate consequences. In 1952, however, the ALI expanded its function to more closely resemble that of the NCCUSL. It drafted model and uniform codes, such as the joint effort between both entities that resulted in the UCC.

3. **Countries Adopting the 1980 United Nations Convention on Contracts for the International Sale of Goods.** Immediately preceding the publication of this text, seventy-nine countries had adopted the Convention or CISG. The signatory countries are: Albania, Argentina, Armenia, Australia, Austria, Belarus, Belgium, Benin, Bosnia and Herzegovina, Bulgaria, Burundi, Canada, Chile, China, Colombia, Croatia, Cuba, Cyprus, Czech Republic, Denmark, Dominican Republic, Ecuador, Egypt, El Salvador, Estonia, Finland, France, Gabon, Georgia, Germany, Ghana, Greece, Guinea, Honduras, Hungary, Iceland, Iraq, Israel, Italy, Japan, Kyrgyzstan, Latvia, Lebanon, Lesotho, Liberia, Lithuania, Luxembourg, Mauritania, Mexico, Moldova, Montenegro, Netherlands, New Zealand, Norway, Paraguay, Peru, Poland, Republic of Korea, Romania, Russian Federation, Saint Vincent and the Grenadines, San Marino, Serbia, Singapore, Slovakia, Slovenia, Spain, Sweden, Switzerland, Syrian Arab Republic, the former Yugoslav Republic of Macedonia, Turkey,

Uganda, Ukraine, United States of America, Uruguay, Uzbekistan, Venezuela (Bolivarian Republic of), and Zambia. U.N. COMMISSION ON INTERNATIONAL TRADE LAW, STATUS, 1980 UNITED NATIONS CONVENTION ON CONTRACTS FOR THE INTERNATIONAL SALE OF GOODS, available at *http://www.uncitral.org/uncitral/en/uncitral_texts/sale_goods/1980CISG.html* (last visited March 13, 2013).

4. **The Ratification of the CISG in the United States.** Consider again James E. Bailey's article entitled, *Facing the Truth: Seeing the Convention on Contracts for the International Sale of Goods as an Obstacle to a Uniform Law of International Sales*, 32 Cornell Int'l L.J. 273, 282–83 (1999). Describing the CISG's enactment in the United States, the commentator wrote:

   [T]he CISG became federal law without any changes, without the addition of individual section numbers, and without being included in the various indices of the U.S. Code. Essentially, the CISG was simply dumped, without introduction or comment, into the APPENDIX to TITLE 15 of the U.S. CODE. The effect is that one cannot find the CISG in the U.S. Code unless one already knows it exists and where it is located. Further, since none of the provisions of the CISG are contained in the indices to the U.S. Code, the individual subjects regulated by the CISG cannot be discovered through traditional legal research methods.

5. **Signatory Countries and CISG's Opt-Out Provisions.** Under the Convention, countries have an option. When ratifying the CISG, each country may declare that certain portions of the Convention do not apply to contracts that are formed in the ratifying country. The United States and many other countries have exercised that option. What has been the effect? Certainly, opinions vary among commentators and jurists in the United States and elsewhere. But, one researcher has discovered: "The Convention's allowance for reservations to various aspects of the CISG both decreases uniformity and increases the likelihood of confusion regarding the application of the CISG." *See* James E. Bailey, *Facing the Truth: Seeing the Convention on Contracts for the International Sale of Goods as an Obstacle to a Uniform Law of International Sales*, 32 Cornell Int'l L.J. 273, 274–75 (1999).

D. Goods-and-Services Contracts, Article 2 Actions, and the Predominant Purpose Test

Ponder this hypothetical. A consumer visits Lowe's Home Improvement store. He purchases a highly efficient, LG front-loader washer. The appliance has a small, highly sophisticated computer. He pays $1,124 for the product. Two weeks after Lowe's agents delivered the washer, two of twenty software programs begin giving "faulty" instructions. For example, when the consumer instructs the washer to spin at a certain speed, the washer spins at a higher or lower speed. Additionally, when the washer begins the first cycle, it dispenses a liquid water softener immediately, but not liquid detergent.

The consumer contacts Lowe's and reports the "software glitch." The consumer also instructs Lowe's to send an agent "to service the washer." Lowe's responds, stressing that the washer is "not broken." In the end, Lowe's refuses "to service the washer." The consumer sues Lowe's under UCC Article 2 for breach of contract, asking for $459.34 in actual damages. Lowe's files an answer. Citing UCC §§ 2-102, 2-105(1), and 2-106(1), the seller raises a single affirmative defense: "Article 2 of the UCC applies only to transactions in 'goods.' A lawsuit involving a service-related claim is not actionable under the UCC." Is the seller's defense sound? The next case and notes that follow provide competing answers.

Lohman v. Wagner
862 A.2d 1042
(Md. Ct. App. 2004)

MEREDITH, J. This case involves a suit for an alleged breach of contract concerning the sale of weaner pigs. The term "weaner pigs" refers to young pigs in the developmental stage from the time of their birth until they are weaned from their mothers at a weight of seven to fourteen pounds, after which they are known as "feeder pigs" until they reach a weight of 50 pounds. Appellant, Charles D. Lohman, trading as Lohman Farms, filed a complaint in the Circuit Court for Washington County against Appellees, John C. Wagner and Joyce E. Wagner, trading as Swine Services.

The complaint alleged the breach of a "Weaner Pig Purchase Agreement" between the parties. After a three-day bench trial, the trial judge entered judgment for the defendants. The trial court found … that the alleged agreement was not enforceable against the Wagners. Lohman appealed. …

BACKGROUND

Prior to 1998, Lohman operated a "farrow to finish" pig-raising operation at his farm in Washington County. A "farrow to finish" pig operation involves the breeding, gestation, and raising of pigs to a weight of 50 pounds so that they can be transferred to a finishing floor, where they continue to mature until they reach a market weight of 250 to 300 pounds.

Lohman knew John Wagner because of Wagner's longtime involvement in various aspects of the pork industry. In approximately December 1997, Lohman contacted Wagner and asked if Wagner knew of any business opportunities for Lohman. Wagner responded that Lohman's timing was good because Wagner was in the process of putting together a network of pork producers and buyers. Lohman and Wagner met numerous times and had a number of telephone conversations concerning Lohman becoming a weaner pig producer for the pork network being proposed by Wagner.

By January 1998, Lohman had decided he wanted to convert his farrow to finish operation into a weaner pig facility. This would entail remodeling his building to provide for more gestation space, reducing his feeder-pig inventory, and increasing the number of sows he maintained. Lohman began the conversion process by selling his feeder pigs.

In May or June 1998, Lohman began selling weaner pigs to Wagner even though Lohman had not yet remodeled his barn to accommodate an operation that was exclusively devoted to producing weaner pigs. Wagner's pork network was still not in place.

In July 1998, Lohman sought financing from First National Bank of Mercersburg to fund the remodeling of his facility. Wagner testified that Lohman contacted him at home on a Friday or Saturday night in July, and that Lohman had asked Wagner to give him a sample copy of a weaner pig purchase agreement that the pork network would be using. According to Wagner, he did not have any sample agreements for the weaner pig operation at that time because Wagner's contemplated network of pork purchasers was still not ready to enter into contracts. Lohman told Wagner that he was meeting with his banker the next day and needed something to show his banker. Wagner testified as follows:

> He [Lohman] called me at home. ... And said he needed something to show to his banker that he was trying to get financing for the remodeling. And I didn't have anything, but ... I found an old one ... from one of my files and ... I think my wife actually retyped it and put together what we were calling a sample or a draft of what, what it would look like when we were ready to put a true network agreement together. ...

> There seemed to be some urgency ... so we put one together and faxed it to Mr. Lohman.

There were several blank lines in the document that Wagner faxed to Lohman, but Wagner nevertheless had signed the document on the signature line for the purchaser. The fax cover sheet said: "Dear Charlie, I trust this will help you in securing financing as we had discussed."

Wagner testified that after he faxed the document to Lohman, "I never saw it again and really wasn't expecting to see it because it was simply a draft or a sample." When asked if he had intended the faxed sample of a weaner pig purchase agreement to be a contract with Lohman, Wagner testified, "It was strictly a sample or a draft of what we were going to be using. ... No this was not the contract."

Lohman admitted that he filled in several blanks on the document he received from Wagner. Most significantly, there was a blank line for the number of pigs to be supplied and purchased under the agreement. The document as faxed by Wagner read: "Producer agrees to .... supply approximately _______ weaner pigs weekly." Without having any further communications with Wagner, Lohman inserted the quantity "300" as the approximate number of weaner pigs to be supplied weekly. Although Lohman signed his copy of the agreement as "Producer" and faxed a copy to his bank, it was undisputed that he never sent Wagner a copy of the agreement containing his handwritten alterations.

Lohman became a producer exclusively of weaner pigs in July 1998 and continued shipping weaner pigs to Wagner at $28 per head. This price was consistent with the pricing schedule contained in the weaner pig purchase agreement that Wagner had faxed to Lohman.

Lohman shipped weaner pigs to Wagner at $28 per head until October 1998, when Lohman received a telephone call from Wagner about a price decrease. Wagner said he needed to reduce the price to $18 per head because of an extreme drop in market prices for pork. When Lohman responded that this price reduction would probably put him out of business, Wagner told Lohman he would see what he could do, but Wagner never offered to pay Lohman any higher price after October 1998.

Lohman continued selling pigs to Wagner at $18 per head until March 1999, when Lohman wound down his business. During this time, Lohman attempted to find another buyer for his pigs, but was unable to do so. Lohman acknowledged that prior to filing suit he never told Wagner he believed Wagner breached their agreement. Wagner's pork network never came into being. Lohman filed a one-count complaint against the Wagners, alleging breach of contract and seeking damages.

GOODS AND SERVICES

Lohman asserts that the trial court erred in finding the Maryland Uniform Commercial Code applies to the alleged contract in this case. Lohman contends the agreement with Wagner was a contract for the provision of services, not a contract for the sale of goods, and therefore, the UCC does not apply. Lohman argues that the language of the agreement "was carefully crafted to avoid a sales transaction" by requiring the "Producer" (Lohman) to furnish housing facilities, labor, utilities, and production supplies in producing and raising weaner pigs.

Additionally, Lohman notes that the agreement gave Wagner the authority to access Lohman's facility and to oversee various aspects of breeding and raising the pigs. Lohman contends the agreement is therefore one for the provision of services by him, and not a contract for the sale of weaner pigs.

In *DeGroft v. Lancaster Silo Co., Inc.*, 72 Md. App. 154, 164 (1987), this court recognized that "Section 2-102 of the UCC provides: 'Unless the context otherwise requires,' the UCC applies to 'transactions in goods,' a term which has been said to be broader than the sale of goods." "Goods" are defined in § 2-105(1), which states:

> "Goods" means all things (including specially manufactured goods) which are movable at the time of identification to the contract for sale other than the money in which the price is to be paid, investment securities (Title 8) and things in action. "Goods", also includes the unborn young of animals and growing crops and other identified things attached to realty as described in the section on goods to be severed from realty (§ 2-107). Md. Code Commercial Law Art. (C.L.) § 2-105(1).

The Official Comment to § 2-105 further states:

> The young of animals are also included expressly in this definition since they, too, are frequently intended for sale and may be contracted for before birth. The period of gestation of domestic animals is such that the provisions of the section on identification can apply as in the case of crops to be planted. C.L. § 2-105(1).

The definition of the goods that are subject to Article 2 of the UCC covers young animals and even the unborn young of animals. The definition of goods would cover the weaner pigs that were raised by Lohman.

Other courts have found that contracts for the sale of pigs are governed by the UCC. *See, e.g., Purina Mills, L.L.C. v. Less*, 295 F.Supp.2d 1017, 1031 (N.D. Iowa 2003) (weanling pigs are goods); *Flanagan v. Consolidated Nutrition, L.C.*, 627 N.W.2d 573, 577 (Iowa Ct. App. 2001) (because the definition of "goods" encompasses livestock, Article

2 governs a contract to buy and sell pigs). *See also Embryo Progeny Assoc. v. Lovana Farms*, 203 Ga. App. 447, 448 (1992) (sales of animals found to be transactions in goods).

Lohman is correct that the alleged weaner pig purchase agreement involves providing certain services. However, as the trial court correctly observed, the UCC may apply to contracts involving both services and the delivery of goods. These hybrid or mixed sales and services contracts were discussed by the Court of Appeals in *Burton v. Artery Co., Inc.,* 279 Md. 94 (1977), where the court adopted the test used in *Bonebrake v. Cox*, 499 F.2d 951 (8th Cir.1974), to assess the UCC's applicability to mixed contracts by analyzing the predominant purpose of the agreement.

Burton involved a contract for the sale and installation of trees, shrubs, and sod. The court explained that the fact that the contract required substantial amounts of labor as well as sales of goods did not remove the contract from the purview of the Uniform Commercial Code. *Burton*, 279 Md. at 108 (quoting *Bonebrake*, 499 F.2d at 959). The *Bonebrake* test requires examining the contract to determine its main purpose. The court said in *Bonebrake*:

> [T]he cases presenting mixed contracts of this type are legion. The test for inclusion or exclusion is not whether they are mixed, but, granting that they are mixed, whether their predominant factor, their thrust, their purpose, reasonably stated, is the rendition of service, with goods incidentally involved (e.g., contract with artist for painting) or is a transaction of sale, with labor incidentally involved (e.g., installation of a water heater in a bathroom). 499 F.2d at 960.

Applying this test, the *Bonebrake* court found that a contract involving the delivery and installation of used bowling equipment was primarily a "goods" contract and was governed by the UCC even though it involved a substantial amount of services. In *Burton*, the Court of Appeals expressly adopted the *Bonebrake* analysis, stating:

> We adopt the criteria enunciated in *Bonebrake*. We have already concluded that the trees, shrubs, and sod are goods. Burton is a nurseryman. He is engaged, therefore, in selling trees and shrubs. If he also grows sod, then he is engaged in the business of selling sod. The number of trees and shrubs—and the substantial amount of sod here involved—make this contract much more nearly analogous to the installation of a water heater in a bathroom than to a contract with an artist for a painting. Thus, the predominant factor here, the thrust, the purpose, reasonably stated, is a transaction of sale with labor incidentally involved. 279 Md. at 114–15, 367 A.2d 935.

This court has applied the *Burton-Bonebrake* test when faced with analyzing mixed contracts involving sales of goods and services. *See, e.g., DeGroft v. Lancaster Silo Co., Inc.*, 72 Md. App. 154, 164 (1987) (genuine issue of material fact existed as to whether contract involving the sale and construction of a silo was predominantly a sales or service contract); and *Snyder v. Herbert Greenbaum & Assoc., Inc.*, 38 Md. App. 144, 147–48 (1977) (primary thrust of contract was the sale rather than the installation of carpet). *Cf. Chlan v. KDI Sylvan Pools, Inc.*, 53 Md. App. 236, 240 (1982) (contract for the sale and installation of a concrete in-ground swimming pool not subject to UCC).

In *DeGroft*, 72 Md. App., at 168, this court recognized that "[c]ourts have generally looked principally to the language of the parties' agreement and the circumstances surrounding its making in determining the predominant thrust of the transaction." Moreover, "[i]n analyzing the parties' agreement, it is appropriate to look to the terminology used therein to determine whether it is peculiar to sales or service contracts." *Id.* at 168.

In this case, the trial court expressly applied the *Bonebrake* analysis to the alleged contract and concluded that the predominant purpose of the document captioned "Weaner Pig Purchase Agreement" was a sale of goods. The court stated:

> Applying the *Bonebrake* test to the instant contract, the court finds that the Weaner Pig Purchase Agreement is a mixed contract, but that its predominant thrust and purpose is the sale of weaner pigs to Wagner. ... The court therefore concludes that the principal purpose under the Weaner Pig Purchase Agreement was the sale of pigs with the provision of housing facilities and labor being incidental to those sales. Therefore, the UCC applies to the entire contract.

The evidence supports the trial court's conclusion that although the agreement called for Lohman to provide certain services, those services were all incidental to the eventual delivery of the specified pigs and did not constitute the main thrust or predominant purpose of the agreement. The predominant purpose of the agreement was the purchase and sale of young pigs. Therefore, the alleged agreement is governed by the UCC. ...

Judgment affirmed.

NOTES AND QUESTIONS

1. **Mixed-Claims Actions Under UCC Article 2.** Does Article 2 cover breach-of-contract disputes involving "hybrid" claims? In

Golden v. Den-Mat Corp., 276 P.3d 773, 791 (Kan. Ct. App. 2012), the Appellate Court of Kansas presents a short and intelligible answer:

> In UCC parlance, those transactions involving goods and services are commonly known as mixed or hybrid contracts. The UCC does not address mixed contracts as such. So, courts have created common-law rules to determine if those transactions should be treated as sales of goods covered under the UCC or service contracts outside the Code's regulation. Some 30 years ago, the Kansas Supreme Court adopted the "predominant purpose" test for classifying mixed contracts. *Care Display, Inc. v. Didde-Glaser, Inc.*, 225 Kan. 232, 238–39 (1979)
>
> The predominant purpose test has become the commonly accepted, if not the near universal, standard. As the name suggests, the test attempts to discern the principal nature of the transaction: Is the buyer seeking services to which the goods are incidental, or is the buyer acquiring goods to which the services are auxiliary? ... The *Bonebrake v. Cox*, 499 F.2d 951, 960 (8th Cir. 1974) case, on which *Care Display* relied, has come to be viewed as the archetypal statement of the predominant purpose test. ... The predominant purpose test, however, is not especially predictive in the abstract. It looks at and depends upon the factual circumstances of the transaction being litigated. *Care Display*, 225 Kan. at 238 ("[E]ach case must be determined on an individual basis [,] and ... broad statements of principles are of little assistance in deciding a particular [case].").

2. **Predominant Purpose Test—Question of Law or Question of Fact?** In *Bruel and Kjaer v. Village of Bensenville,* 969 N.E.2d 445, 450 (Ill. Ct. App. 2012), the court penned the following:

> A contract for services is not a transaction in goods and is not covered by Article 2 of the UCC. Where a contract mixes the sale of goods and the provision of services, the applicability of Article 2 of the UCC is determined by the "predominant purpose" test. Under this test, if the contract is predominantly for goods and only incidentally for services, Article 2 of the UCC will apply. If the contract is predominantly for services and only incidentally for goods, Article 2 of the UCC will not apply. Further, the determination of the predominant purpose of a contract is usually a question of fact. Nevertheless, the predominant purpose of a contract is also susceptible to determination as a matter of law.

Other courts, however, are split over whether the predominant purpose of a mixed contract is a question of law for a court, or a question of fact for a jury. *See Higgins v. Lauritzen*, 209 Mich. App. 266, 269–70 (Mich. Ct. App. 1995) (a question of fact); *Valley Farmers' Elevator v. Lindsay Bros.*, 398 N.W.2d 553, 556 (Minn.1987) (generally a question of law); *MBH, Inc. v. John Otte Oil & Propane*, 15 Neb. App. 341, 348 (Neb. Ct. App. 2007) ("whether goods or nongoods predominate a contract is generally a question of law"); *Quality Roofing v. Hoffmann-La Roche*, 302 N.J.Super. 163, 166 (N.J. Super. Ct. App.1997) (a question of fact).

3. **Component Part Test.** A minority of jurisdictions divides mixed goods-and-services contracts into their component parts and apply Article 2 solely to the transaction for the sale of goods. *See Foster v. Colorado Radio Corp.*, 381 F.2d 222, 226 (10th Cir. 1967).

UNIFORM COMMERCIAL CODE

§ 2-102. Scope; Certain Security and Other Transactions Excluded from This Article.

Unless the context otherwise requires, this Article applies to transactions in goods; it does not apply to any transaction which although in the form of an unconditional contract to sell or present sale is intended to operate only as a security transaction nor does this Article impair or repeal any statute regulating sales to consumers, farmers or other specified classes of buyers.

§ 2-103. Definitions and Index of Definitions.

> (k) "Goods" means all things that are movable at the time of identification to a contract for sale. The term includes future goods, specially manufactured goods, the unborn young of animals, growing crops, and other identified things attached to realty as described in § 2-107. The term does not include information, the money in which the price is to be paid, investment securities under Article 8, the subject matter of foreign exchange transactions, or choses in action.

§ 2-105. Definitions: Transferability; "Future" Goods; "Lot"; "Commercial Unit"

> (1) Goods must be both existing and identified before any interest in them may pass. Goods that are not both existing and identified are "future" goods. A purported present sale of future goods or of any interest therein operates as a contract to sell.

(2) There may be a sale of a part interest in existing identified goods.

(3) An undivided share in an identified bulk of fungible goods is sufficiently identified to be sold although the quantity of the bulk is not determined. Any agreed proportion of the bulk or any quantity thereof agreed upon by number, weight, or other measure may to the extent of the seller's interest in the bulk be sold to the buyer that then becomes an owner in common.

§ 2-106. Definitions: "Contract"; "Agreement"; "Contract for Sale"; "Sale"

(1) In this Article unless the context otherwise requires "contract" and "agreement" are limited to those relating to the present or future sale of goods. "Contract for sale" includes both a present sale of goods and a contract to sell goods at a future time. A "sale" consists in the passing of title from the seller to the buyer for a price (§ 2-401). A "present sale" means a sale which is accomplished by the making of the contract.

(2) There may be a sale of a part interest in existing identified goods.

(3) An undivided share in an identified bulk of fungible goods is sufficiently identified to be sold although the quantity of the bulk is not determined. Any agreed proportion of such a bulk or any quantity thereof agreed upon by number, weight or other measure may to the extent of the seller's interest in the bulk be sold to the buyer who then becomes an owner in common.

§ 2-106. Definitions: "Contract"; "Agreement"; "Contract for Sale"; ...

(1) In this Article unless the context otherwise requires "contract" and "agreement" are limited to those relating to the present or future sale of goods. "Contract for sale" includes both a present sale of goods and a contract to sell goods at a future time. A "sale" consists in the passing of title from the seller to the buyer for a price (Section 2-401). A "present sale" means a sale which is accomplished by the making of the contract.

CHAPTER EIGHT

ARTICLE 2 CAUSE OF ACTION AND PLAINTIFF'S BURDEN—PROOF OF A VALID CONTRACT

The discussion in CHAPTER 2 disclosed an extremely important rule: Under the common law, a plaintiff must establish an intelligent and sound *prima facie* case to increase his likelihood of prevailing in a breach-of-contract action. More specifically, in a court of law, the plaintiff must prove several elements: 1) the plaintiff and defendant formed a "valid" contract; 2) both parties exchanged "sufficient" consideration; 3) the defendant breached the contractual promise or another provision in the contract; 4) defendant's breach was the cause in fact of plaintiff's injury and damages; 5) defendant's breach was the proximate cause of plaintiff's injury and damages; and 6) monetary damages.

To repeat, UCC Article 2 governs the formation, interpretation, and enforcement of sale-of-goods contracts. And if a complaint files a breach-of-contract action under Article 2, he also must establish a *prima facie* case. Actually, the plaintiff must prove the six (6) general elements listed above. *Cf. Thomas v. Louisiana-Pacific Corp.*, 246 F.R.D. 505, 515 (D.S.C. 2007) ("[A] court must examine the elements of plaintiffs' *prima facie* case and determine the extent to which those facts also prove the claims of the absent class members. ... [U]nless modified by contract, a buyer must give a seller seasonable notice of the breach. Failure to do so precludes maintaining an action for breach of an Article 2 warranty ... [under] the Uniform Commercial Code.").

But there is a proviso: UCC Article 2 relaxes considerably the standard for establishing a *prima facie* case. As discussed more fully in this and other chapters in PART II, the level of *prima facie* evidence required to prove a valid sale-of-goods contract or a breach of contract is substantially lower under Article 2 than under the common law.

CHAPTER 2 discusses a complainant's duty to prove a "valid" contract. And in that chapter the author stressed: One's burden to prove a "valid" contractual agreement is arguably the toughest common-law requirement that one must satisfy in a breach-of-contract action. Again, the reason is simple. Under settled common-law principles, a plaintiff must present *prima facie* evidence of several sub-elements to prove a "valid" contract: 1) evidence of the parties' mutual intent to bind themselves to the "undertaking"; 2) proof of one party's offer; 3) proof of the other party's acceptance; 4) proof of the parties' meeting of the minds regarding the "undertaking"; 5) proof of each party's consent to the terms of the contract; 6) execution of the contract; and 7) the "delivery" of the contract. *See Prime Products, Inc. v. S.S.I. Plastics, Inc.*, 97 S.W.3d 631, 636 (Tex. App.—Houston [1st Dist.] 2002, pet. denied).

To be sure, under UCC Article 2, a plaintiff must also prove that he and defendant consummated a "valid" sale-of-goods contract. In fact, Article 2 contains several rules regarding "offers" and "acceptances." But, as discussed more completely below, the Uniform Commercial Code does not require a plaintiff to prove a valid sales agreement by presenting probative evidence of the remaining sub-elements.

SECTION ONE. TYPES OF SALES CONTRACTS AND THEIR ENFORCEABILITY UNDER ARTICLE 2

In PART I, we learned that contracts appear in several flavors: 1) express oral contracts, 2) express written contracts, 3) contracts implied in law, and 4) contracts implied in facts. But even more importantly, we also learned that common-law principles of contracts govern the interpretation and enforcement of all contracts—express and implied, services and goods, construction and real estate, employment and financial, as well as other forms. But, to repeat, UCC Article 2 governs the construction, interpretation, and enforcement of sale-of-goods contracts.

Without doubt, under UCC § 2-201(1), a party may enforce an oral or a written sale-of-goods contract. A proviso, however, states: If the value of the contract is greater than $500, the agreement must be in writing. On the other hand, whether or not Article 2 covers the formation and enforcement of implied-in-fact and implied-in-law contracts has been frequently litigated. Put simply, there is no provision in UCC Article 2 that states categorically that breach-of-implied-contract actions may commence under the statute. But consider UCC § 2-204(1). It reads: "A contract for sale of goods may be made in any manner sufficient to show agreement, including conduct by both parties which recognizes the existence of such a contract."

Interpreting the language in section 2-204(1) of the UCC, state and federal courts have reached fairly similar conclusions: 1) "Under both the U.C.C. and Oregon common law, a contract may be implied-in-fact from the parties' conduct and have the same legal effect as an express contract." *George Packing Co., Inc. v. FMC Technologies, Inc.*, 2011 WL 7082545, *6 (D. Or. Sep. 20, 2011); 2) "Under Illinois law, 'an implied-in-fact contract is a true contract, containing all necessary elements of a binding agreement; it differs from other contracts only in that it has not been committed to writing or stated orally in express terms, but rather is inferred from the conduct of the parties in the milieu in which they dealt.' The Illinois Uniform Commercial Code—810 ILCS 5/2–204—also allows for contracts implied-in-fact." *Control Solutions LLC v. Oshkosh Corp.*, 2012 WL 3096678, *7 (N.D. Ill., July 27, 2012), quoting *AEI Music Network, Inc. v. Business Computers, Inc.*, 290 F.3d 952, 956 (7th Cir. 2002); and, 3) The UCC Article 2 "encompasses implied-in-law sales contracts." *In H. Russell Taylor's Fire Prevention Service, Inc. v. Coca Cola Bottling Corp.*, 160 Cal. Rptr. 411, 419 (Cal. Ct. App. 1979).

Section 1-305 of the UCC requires a court to award statutory remedies—including declaratory relief—liberally. Therefore, providing liberal interpretations of sections 2-204(1), 2-204(3), and 2–207(3), the federal district judge wrote an informative analysis in *Quaker State Mushroom Co., Inc. v. Dominick's Finer Foods, Inc., of Illinois,* 635 F. Supp. 1281, 1285 (N.D. Ill. May 22, 1986) (emphasis added):

> Having rejected both sides' theories, we are left with the problem of how to properly analyze the above facts. It is clear that the parties intended to have a contract, acted as if they had a contract, but had not agreed upon a price for the goods. The UCC has several provisions which are relevant to such a situation. Conduct by the parties which recognizes the existence of a contract may sometimes suffice to create the contract. ... If the parties act in a way which recognizes the existence of a contract, one may exist even though the writings of the parties do not otherwise establish a contract; the terms of such a contract are those upon which the writing agrees, along with *other terms implied by law* under the UCC. From these provisions, it is possible to conclude that the parties had an enforceable contract, since their *conduct* in many ways recognized the existence of one. Sellers usually do not ship and buyers do not receive goods unless they think they have struck a deal.

UNIFORM COMMERCIAL CODE

U.C.C. § 1-305. REMEDIES TO BE LIBERALLY ADMINISTERED

(a) The remedies provided by [the Uniform Commercial Code] must be liberally administered to the end that the aggrieved party may be put in as good a position as if the other party had fully performed but neither consequential or special damages nor penal damages may be had except as specifically provided in [the Uniform Commercial Code] or by other rule of law.

(b) Any right or obligation declared by [the Uniform Commercial Code] is enforceable by action unless the provision declaring it specifies a different and limited effect.

U.C.C. § 2-104. DEFINITIONS: "MERCHANT" AND "BETWEEN MERCHANTS"

(1) "Merchant" means a person who deals in goods of the kind or otherwise by his occupation holds himself out as having knowledge or skill peculiar to the practices or goods involved in the transaction or to whom such knowledge or skill may be attributed by his employment of an agent or broker or other intermediary who by his occupation holds himself out as having such knowledge or skill. ...

(3) "Between merchants" means in any transaction with respect to which both parties are chargeable with the knowledge or skill of merchants.

U.C.C. § 2-201. FORMAL REQUIREMENTS; STATUTE OF FRAUDS

(1) Except as otherwise provided in this section a contract for the sale of goods for the price of $500 or more is not enforceable by way of action or defense unless there is some writing sufficient to indicate that a contract for sale has been made between the parties and signed by the party against whom enforcement is sought or by his authorized agent or broker. A writing is not insufficient because it omits or incorrectly states a term agreed upon but the contract is not enforceable under this paragraph beyond the quantity of goods shown in such writing.

(2) Between merchants if within a reasonable time a writing in confirmation of the contract and sufficient against the sender is received and the party receiving it has reason to know its contents, it satisfies the requirements of subsection (1) against such party unless written notice of objection to its contents is given within 10 days after it is received.

(3) A contract which does not satisfy the requirements of subsection (1) but which is valid in other respects is enforceable

(a) if the goods are to be specially manufactured for the buyer and are not suitable for sale to others in the ordinary course of the seller's business and the seller, before notice of repudiation is received and under circumstances which reasonably indicate that the goods are for the buyer, has made either a substantial beginning of their manufacture or commitments for their procurement; or

(b) if the party against whom enforcement is sought admits in his pleading, testimony or otherwise in court that a contract for sale was made, but the contract is not enforceable under this provision beyond the quantity of goods admitted; or

(c) with respect to goods for which payment has been made and accepted or which have been received and accepted (§ 2-606).

U.C.C. § 2-204. FORMATION IN GENERAL

(1) A contract for sale of goods may be made in any manner sufficient to show agreement, including conduct by both parties which recognizes the existence of such a contract.

(2) An agreement sufficient to constitute a contract for sale may be found even though the moment of its making is undetermined.

(3) Even though one or more terms are left open a contract for sale does not fail for indefiniteness if the parties have intended to make a contract and there is a reasonably certain basis for giving an appropriate remedy.

SECTION TWO. THE FORMATION OF A SALES CONTRACT UNDER ARTICLE 2

Again, like a complainant's general obligation under the common law, Article 2 of the Uniform Commercial Code requires a plaintiff to prove the existence of a valid contract. But, unlike the common-law burden, a plaintiff's burden under the UCC is much lighter because section 2-204(1) is clear: A sale-of-goods contract "may be made in any manner" that is "sufficient to produce an agreement."

Basically, in a sale-of-goods contract, "the *essential terms* are quantity, price, and time and manner of delivery." *Judal Indus. v. Welsbach Elec. Corp.*, 138 A.D.2d 573, 573 (N.Y. App. Div. 1988) (emphasis added). But even more importantly, under UCC Article 2, an *enforceable* contract can never emerge if either party to a contract fails to *embrace* those material terms. Consequently, when disputes about essential terms arise, a rebuttable presumption also arises: The parties did not intend to form an enforceable sales contract. Therefore, in a breach-of-contract action, a UCC plaintiff must present probative evidence of three important sub-elements—the parties' intent to form a sales contract, one party's offer, and the other party's acceptance.

A. Proof of the Parties' Intent to Be Bound

Under the UCC and the common law, one finds a universal principle that governs the formation of a valid contract: Specific *manifestations of commitment* are necessary to establish a contractual agreement. Consequently, parties' future intentions do not qualify as "clear and unambiguous" manifestations of their intent to form a contract. *Brown v. American Ecology Corp*. 1997 U.S. App. LEXIS 15518, *2 (6th Cir. 1997). In some jurisdictions, this doctrine is called the *manifestation of mutual assent*.

In *Quality Truck and Auto Sales, Inc. v. Yassine,* 730 So.2d 1164, 1168–69 (Ala. 1999), the Alabama Supreme Court discussed an Article 2 plaintiff's burden to prove that the parties had a mutual intent to form a sale-of-goods contract:

> Generally, "any conduct of one party—from which the other may reasonably draw the inference of a promise—is effective in law as such." Courts generally accept the "objective theory" of contracts, which determines the existence of a contract based on "the external or objective appearance of the parties' intentions as manifested by their actions. [A] contract for [the] sale of goods may be made in any manner sufficient to show agreement, including conduct by both parties that recognizes the existence of such a contract." 67 AM.JUR.2D SALES § 129 (1985) (discussing contracts under the Uniform Commercial Code). In keeping with the general rule, this court has held: "The existence *vel non* of a contract is determined by reference to the reasonable meaning of the parties' external and objective manifestations of mutual assent. Conduct of one party from which the other may reasonably draw the inference of assent to an agreement is effective as acceptance." (citations omitted).

Again, one prong of the "mutual assent" principle must be stressed: "A manifestation of mutual assent may be inferred wholly or partly from ... the conduct of the parties." *Hy-Vee Food Stores, Inc. v. Minn. Dep't of Health*, 705 N.W.2d 181, 186 (Minn. 2005).

Now, assume that two parties discussed regularly a specific transaction over the telephone and in various e-mails, faxes, and text messages.

Also assume that the parties exchanged purchase orders, memoranda, and other "essential" documents. Still, under UCC Article 2, the buyers and sellers may freely exchange their documents, ideas, words, and the proposal without incurring any contractual obligations. The law, however, is clear: Unless and until there is evidence of the parties' objective manifestation of mutual assent, an essential requirement for a valid contract has not been satisfied. In some jurisdictions, this requirement is called a "meeting of the minds." *Audio Visual Associates, Inc. v. Sharp Electronics Corp.*, 210 F.3d 254, 258 (4th Cir. 2000).

B. Proof of an Offer

UCC Article 2 does not define "offer." Therefore, when courts resolve Article 2 disputes, they normally review and embrace the common law to guide their analyses, findings, and judgments. Most state supreme courts have adopted RESTATEMENT (SECOND) OF CONTRACTS § 24 (1981), which reads: "An offer is the manifestation of willingness to enter into a bargain, so made as to justify another person in understanding that his assent to that bargain is invited and will conclude it." But the RESTATEMENT (SECOND) OF CONTRACTS § 26 (1981) creates an exception, which state courts have also embraced: "A manifestation of willingness to enter into a bargain is not an offer if the person to whom it is addressed knows or has reason to know that the person making it does not intend to conclude a bargain until he has made a further manifestation of assent."

To be sure, whether a communication is, say, a price quotation or an offer to contract depends upon the intention of the offeror. Therefore, to decide whether an offer has been presented, courts generally comb the specific facts and circumstances surrounding each case. *See Nickel v. Theresa Farmers Coop. Ass'n*, 20 N.W.2d 117, 118–19 (Wis. 1945), and *Kraft Foods N. America, Inc. v. Banner Eng'g & Sales, Inc.*, 446 F.Supp.2d 551, 569 (E.D. Va. 2006) (stressing that the expressed intention of the offeror determines whether an offer inviting acceptance has been made).

Under the UCC, an offer is only one of several manifestations of parties' intention to contract. Furthermore, parties typically have only minimal difficulty establishing whether or not a verbal or written exchange is an "offer to contract." And the reason is not complicated: When parties attempt to prove that an offer was made and accepted, the UCC tolerates "probative" evidence that contains "a good deal of incompleteness and even contradiction." *See Architectural Metal Sys., Inc. v. Consol. Sys., Inc.*, 58 F.3d 1227, 1230 (7th Cir. 1995), and WHITE AND SUMMERS, UNIFORM COMMERCIAL CODE §§ 1–2 at 4–5 (4th Ed. 1995) (noting that Article 2 of the UCC makes contracts easier to form by reducing the required formalities).

On the other hand, UCC § 2-205 is entitled "firm offers." And, as discussed above, the UCC embraces the common law's "manifestation of mutual assent" doctrine to determine whether a communication is an offer. Also under the common law, an offer may be revoked, withdrawn, or modified. But courts generally have not addressed this question: whether section 2-205 allows parties to use "incomplete" and "contradictory" evidence to revoke or modify a merchant's firm offer.

Under TEX. BUS. & COM. CODE § 2.104(a), a merchant is "a person who deals in goods of the kind or otherwise by his occupation holds himself out as having knowledge or skill peculiar to the practices or goods involved in the transaction or to whom such knowledge or skill may be attributed by his employment of an agent or broker or other intermediary who by his occupation holds himself out as having such knowledge or skill."

The Texas Supreme Court presented a valuable discussion of section 2-205 and related issues in *1464-Eight, Ltd. v. Joppich*, 154 S.W.3d 101, 113 (Tex. 2004):

> [T]he Uniform Commercial Code's "firm offer" rule [was] adopted verbatim in Texas in 1966. *See* TEX. BUS. & COM. CODE § 2.205. Section 2.205 eliminates the consideration requirement for some option agreements by sanctioning "firm offers"—enforceable option contracts without any consideration. Under the U.C.C., a "firm offer" is enforceable if it is in writing, states that it is irrevocable, and is signed by the offeror, who is a merchant. "Firm offers" are "not revocable, for lack of consideration" during the stated time—or, if no time is stated, a reasonable time—not to exceed three months. Section 2.205 applies only to transactions in goods, however. §§ 2.102, 2.205.
>
> The U.C.C. "firm offer" rule was promulgated to give the business community a means of making options binding even without consideration. 1 WILLIAM D. HAWKLAND, UNIFORM COMMERCIAL CODE SERIES § 2–205:1(1998) (noting that pre-Code law permitted a businessperson to revoke an offer in spite of a promise not to do so if the promise to keep the offer open was not supported by consideration and "[t]he commercial community needed legislation to make firm offers efficacious"). Despite eliminating the consideration requirement, § 2.205 does not seem to have spawned much litigation—having been mentioned in just five published decisions since the Texas Legislature adopted it thirty-eight years ago. Given Texas's apparently favorable experience

with § 2.205, it seems logical to expand its principles to other types of option contracts.

UNIFORM COMMERCIAL CODE

U.C.C. § 2-205. FIRM OFFERS

An offer by a merchant to buy or sell goods in a signed writing which by its terms gives assurance that it will be held open is not revocable, for lack of consideration, during the time stated or if no time is stated for a reasonable time, but in no event may such period of irrevocability exceed three months; but any such term of assurance on a form supplied by the offeree must be separately signed by the offeror.

U.C.C. § 2-206. OFFER AND ACCEPTANCE IN FORMATION OF CONTRACT

(1) Unless otherwise unambiguously indicated by the language or circumstances

(a) an offer to make a contract shall be construed as inviting acceptance in any manner and by any medium reasonable in the circumstances;

(b) an order or other offer to buy goods for prompt or current shipment shall be construed as inviting acceptance either by a prompt promise to ship or by the prompt or current shipment of conforming or non-conforming goods, but such a shipment of non-conforming goods does not constitute an acceptance if the seller seasonably notifies the buyer that the shipment is offered only as an accommodation to the buyer.

(2) Where the beginning of a requested performance is a reasonable mode of acceptance an offeror who is not notified of acceptance within a reasonable time may treat the offer as having lapsed before acceptance.

C. Proof of an Acceptance

1) Brief Review: Common-Law Rules of Acceptance

CHAPTER 2 outlines and discusses the methods of accepting an offer under the common law. Therefore, another exhaustive discussion of those common-law principles will not be repeated in this section. A brief review of the most pertinent common-law rules, however, is warranted. First, to determine whether a verbal statement or a standardized form is an acceptance of an offer, courts generally look beyond a party's words and employ a "totality of the circumstances" test before reaching a declaration. *Challenge Machinery Co. v. Mattison Machine Works*, 138 Mich. App 15, 21 (Mich. Ct. App. 1984). Second, if one manifests an intention to bind himself to another party's stated terms and conditions, the former party's acceptance is sufficient to create the first three prongs of a valid contract. *Kloian v. Domino's Pizza, LLC*, 273 Mich. App 449, 453 (Mich. Ct. App. 2006).

Generally, under the common law, a party must have at least two minimum qualifications to accept an offer: 1) a party must have knowledge or be cognizant of the offer and 2) the party must be the offeror's intended recipient. Quite simply, an *offer* may not be assigned. On the other hand, an *option* may be assigned.

Furthermore, the common law prescribes several methods of accepting an offer. If an offeree *begins* to perform, that is evidence of an acceptance. Certainly, an offeree's actual, ongoing performance is *prima facie* evidence of an acceptance. However, under some circumstances, an offeree must inform the offeror that the offeree is performing. In addition, an offeree's promise to perform is evidence of an acceptance. Moreover, under the so-called mail box rule, an acceptance of an offer occurs if an offeree has been "invited" to accept an offer by mail, text messaging, e-mail, or fax. Therefore, when a letter or writing has been "posted," *prima facie* evidence of an acceptance is established.

There are two additional methods of accepting an offer under the common law. Assume a consumer visits Footlocker's website and submits an order—an offer—for four pairs of "Michael Jordan basketball shoes." Footlocker sends the "wrong pairs of shoes." In this illustration, the consumer is the *offeror*. And Footlocker is the *offeree*. So, the general rules state: 1) Footlocker—the offeree—accepted the consumer/offeror's offer and 2) Footlocker—the offeree—breached the contract. Finally, under the common law, silence is not *prima facie* evidence of an acceptance. But, there is an exception to that general rule: Silence is a legitimate way to accept an offer only if an offeree clearly embraces that method. Typically, courts review an offeree's conduct as well as written and spoken words to reach a conclusion.

2) Rules of Acceptance Under UCC § 2-206

At this point, a proposition is worth repeating: Generally, the Uniform Commercial Code departs considerably from common law rules, which require "strict conformance." But consider this exception: Section 2-206(1)(a) provides that *an offer must unambiguously* state whether a special mode of acceptance is required. However, "[b]arring such an explicit and clear stipulation in the offer, the offeree may adopt any 'reasonable manner of acceptance.'" *Extrusion Painting, Inc. v. Awnings Unlimited, Inc.*, 37 F.Supp 2d 985, 993 (E.D Mich. 1999).

Under section 2-206, contracting parties frequently litigate various questions. Two of those questions are: When did the parties form the contract? What are the material terms in the contracts? *Rogers v. Dell Computer Corp.*, 138 P.3d 826, 832 (Okla. 2005). Generally, subsection 2-206(1) answers the first question. It provides in relevant part: "Unless otherwise unambiguously indicated by the language or circumstances ... an order or other offer to buy goods for prompt or current shipment shall be construed as inviting acceptance ... by a prompt promise to ship."

Also, law students and even seasoned jurists fail to appreciate another important point: Under § 2-206(1), *the buyer is the offeror* and *the seller is the offeree*. To underscore this point, consider the facts and rulings in *Kahn Lucas Lancaster, Inc. v. Lark Int'l Ltd.*, 1997 WL 458785 (S.D.N.Y. Aug. 11, 1997) (*Kahn Lucas II*). Kahn Lucas is a New York corporation, engaged in the business of selling children's clothing. Lark is a Hong Kong corporation and the agent for clothing buyers in the United States. In early 1995, Kahn Lucas—the buyer—submitted two purchase orders to Lark. The goods were finished fleece garments. They were imported from the Philippines and sold to Sears. Among several questions, the prevailing one was whether the parties consummated an agreement in writing.

Section 2-206(1)(b) states that "an order or other offer to buy goods for prompt or current shipment shall be construed as *inviting acceptance* either by *a prompt promise to ship* or by the *prompt or current shipment* of conforming or non-conforming goods." Citing that statute, the federal district court concluded that "the purchase orders were offers to buy, which Lark accepted when it performed." *Kahn Lucas II*, 1997 WL 458785, at *6. The buyer/offeror's purchase orders stated that an acceptance of the goods would occur if: 1) Lark failed to object within ten days, 2) all or a part of the goods were delivered, or 3) evidence of Lark's manifesting assent was present.

The federal judge stressed: "Lark accepted the offer embodied in the purchase orders by ordering the goods from the manufacturers, overseeing production, complying with the other terms of the letters of credit, and arranging for the shipment of the goods." Other courts have reached similar conclusions. *See, e.g. Avila Group, Inc. v. Norma J. of California,* 426 F.Supp. 537, 542–43 (S.D.N.Y. 1977) (citing § 2-206(1)(b) and holding that a partial shipment of goods was acceptance of the "offer" which was embodied in purchase order).

Certainly, section 2-206 generates other legal questions. Of course, a serious discussion of each issue is precluded in this text. There is, however, one issue that requires some comments. The dispute in *Kahn Lucas II* reached the Court of Appeals for the Second Circuit. *See Kahn Lucas Lancaster, Inc. v. Lark Intern. Ltd.*, 186 F.3d 210 (2nd Cir. 1999)

(*Kahn Lucas III*). Put simply, the question was whether section 2-206 of the UCC or an article under the CISG would resolve the controversy.

Although it did not generate the disagreement in *Kahn Lucas*, Article 18 of the CISG governs the formation of international sale-of-goods contracts. More specifically, Article 18 outlines rules about offers and acceptances. It reads:

> (1) A statement made by or other conduct of the offeree indicating assent to an offer is an acceptance. Silence or inactivity does not in itself amount to acceptance.
>
> (2) An acceptance of an offer becomes effective at the moment the indication of assent reaches the offeror. An acceptance is not effective if the indication of assent does not reach the offeror within the time he has fixed or, if no time is fixed, within a reasonable time, due account being taken of the circumstances of the transaction, including the rapidity of the means of communication employed by the offeror. An oral offer must be accepted immediately unless the circumstances indicate otherwise.
>
> (3) However, if, by virtue of the offer or as a result of practices which the parties have established between themselves or of usage, the offeree may indicate assent by performing an act, such as one relating to the dispatch of the goods or payment of the price, without notice to the offeror, the acceptance is effective at the moment the act is performed, provided that the act is performed within the period of time laid down in the preceding paragraph.

Comparing the respective and arguably "substantially equivalent" statutes under the UCC and the CISG, del Pilar Perales Viscasillas wrote the following insightful observation in *Contract Conclusion Under CISG,* 16 J. LAW AND COM. 315 (1997):

> [T]he general rule for contract conclusion is "at the moment when an acceptance of an offer becomes effective." ... The recognition of silence or inaction as potentially effective acceptance under article 18(1) demonstrates the unimportance of communication. Although silence and inaction are not applicable to any of the other classic theories such as the Dispatch or Mail Box rules, silence and inaction may effect contract conclusion under CISG. ... Silence or inaction are considered effective confirmations of contract conclusion if a certain length of time has passed. The offeror is given an option to confirm a late or modified acceptance through silence or inaction, thereby concluding the contract. ...

Article 18(3) covers the situations in which the practices already established between the parties or the usages authorize the offeree to accept by acts of performance without communicating acceptance expressly to the offeror. In this case, the contract is concluded when the offeree performs the act specified in the practice or usage. Notwithstanding the clear language of article 18(3), some scholars still believe that such an acceptance needs to be expressly communicated to be effective. …

UCC § 2-206(1)(a) corresponds to article 18(1) of the CISG insofar as the manner of acceptance is left up to the parties. Similarly, UCC § 2-206(1)(b) parallels article 18(3) of the CISG because performance is a valid manner of acceptance. Nevertheless, there is a difference between UCC § 2-206 and article 18 of the CISG. When the acceptance is made through performance under article 18(3) of the CISG, there is no need to communicate that acceptance; but, under the UCC, the performance must be communicated when the period of time for the delivery of the goods is lengthy.

UNIFORM COMMERCIAL CODE

U.C.C. § 2-206. OFFER AND ACCEPTANCE IN FORMATION OF CONTRACT

(1) Unless otherwise unambiguously indicated by the language or circumstances

(a) an offer to make a contract shall be construed as inviting acceptance in any manner and by any medium reasonable in the circumstances;

(b) an order or other offer to buy goods for prompt or current shipment shall be construed as inviting acceptance either by a prompt promise to ship or by the prompt or current shipment of conforming or non-conforming goods, but such a shipment of non-conforming goods does not constitute an acceptance if the seller seasonably notifies the buyer that the shipment is offered only as an accommodation to the buyer.

(2) Where the beginning of a requested performance is a reasonable mode of acceptance an offeror who is not notified of acceptance within a reasonable time may treat the offer as having lapsed before acceptance.

---

3) Additional "Material" Terms and Rules of Acceptance Under § 2-207

Again, under the common-law "mirror image rule," an offer and an acceptance must be mirror images of each other. If an offeree deletes any term or condition in an offer, the offeree rejects rather than accepts the offer. Also, under the common law, an offeree presents a counteroffer or rejects an offer if she attaches "additional" terms to an offer. A conditional acceptance operates the same way as a counteroffer: It terminates the offer and becomes a new offer.

But, section 2-207(2) rejects the mirror-image rule and states that "additional or different terms [must] be construed as proposals for [an] addition to the contract." In addition, if both parties are merchants, the general statutory rule states: Additional terms become part of the contract. U.C.C. § 2-207(2). There are, however, two important exceptions to the general rule: 1) an additional term does not become a part of a contract if the offeror and offeree are merchants, and the additional term "materially" changes the offer. U.C.C. § 2-207(2)(b), and 2) an ultimate contract between merchants will not contain an additional term if the offeror objects to the change, U.C.C. § 2-207(2)(c). On the other hand, if the offeror and offeree are a consumer and a merchant, an additional term becomes a proposal; consequently, it may be separately accepted or rejected.

Certainly, standing alone, the rules in section 2-207 of the UCC do not appear to be terribly complicated. This is a reasonable conclusion—even though courts apply one set of unique rules to resolve disputes between two merchants, and employ a different set of principles to settle conflicts between a consumer and a merchant. Yet, for reasons discussed in the next two cases, section 2-207 produces arguably more legal disputes and litigation than any other section in Article 2 of the UCC.

Reilly Foam Corporation v. Rubbermaid Corporation
206 F. Supp. 2d 643
(E.D. Pa. 2002)

SCHILLER, DISTRICT JUDGE.

I. INTRODUCTION

A dispute between Plaintiff Reilly Foam Corporation (Reilly Foam) and Defendant Rubbermaid Corporation (Rubbermaid) over a contract for sponges results in the court doing the mopping-up. Reilly Foam alleges that it contracted to supply Rubbermaid with its requirements for certain sponges for assembly into mops sold to Target stores. Reilly Foam alleges that rather than obtaining sponges solely from Reilly

Foam, Rubbermaid continued to obtain sponges from another supplier and failed to make set minimum purchases. Rubbermaid denies that the contract created between the parties called for Reilly Foam to be its exclusive supplier. … The water here is murkier than both parties believe. …

II. BACKGROUND

Reilly Foam manufactures custom-order sponges and other foam products. Defendant Rubbermaid manufactures home products, including mops nationwide. Before its agreement with Reilly Foam, Rubbermaid obtained sponges for its mop products from a company known as Tek Pak, a competitor of Reilly Foam.

In 1997, Rubbermaid launched its "Tidal Wave Project" to introduce new and improved sponge mops into the marketplace. The new sponge mops were named for a wave pattern which would be cut into the sponges. There were to be two basic designs for the Tidal Wave mops: a butterfly sponge and a roller sponge. The butterfly sponge mop included a mechanism which folded in half like the wings of a butterfly in order to wring out water. The roller sponge would be squeezed by a roller mechanism.

Target Stores agreed to stock cobalt blue and yellow laminate versions of the Tidal Wave sponge mop line at its stores nationwide. Rubbermaid initially sought to obtain sponges for the mops from Tek Pak. However, Tek Pak could not make timely deliveries of sponges to meet Target's needs. Rubbermaid contacted Reilly Foam on March 4, 1999 to determine if it could fulfill Rubbermaid's need for sponges. Rubbermaid's immediate objective with Reilly Foam was to satisfy Target's current demand. Reilly Foam submitted a price quotation to Rubbermaid on March 8, 1999 for Pattern Butterfly sponges and Pattern Roller Mop sponges on an expedited basis. Reilly Foam then manufactured and delivered the sponges.

Between March 8 and March 30, the parties discussed a longer-term relationship in which Reilly Foam would supply sponges for Rubbermaid's Tidal Wave Project. But the parties now vigorously dispute what the terms of the relationship were. According to Joseph Reilly of Reilly Foam, his company was to be the exclusive supplier of Butterfly and Roller Mop sponges with a Tidal Wave design. Rubbermaid was to purchase a minimum of 300,000 Butterfly, 300,000 Roller Mop, and 300,000 yellow ester Tidal Wave sponges each year. Rubbermaid also submitted written estimates to Reilly Foam of its requirements for Butterfly and Roller Mop sponges. Reilly Foam needed to retool its equipment and to license technology from a corporation named Foamex to produce the sponges with a "tidal wave" effect carved into their bottoms. Reilly Foam expressed concern that its profits on the contract permit it to recoup its costs.

On March 26, 1999, Reilly Foam forwarded a letter to Tony Ferrante of Rubbermaid signed by Joseph Reilly. The letter read:

> This letter details the proposal that we briefly spoke about last evening. This includes the two laminates that we are currently working on, the roller mop and the butterfly mop. There are other products that we are familiar with through Kendo/New Knight, which would be the brown large celled ester, the pattern yellow ester and the yellow ether and white scrubmate. All of these are priced on the ensuing quotation.
>
> Our proposal is that Rubbermaid Cleaning Products commit to two million pieces of product under the sub-heading Other Affected Products. There would be a surcharge of $.015 per part in an effort to amortize the cost of tooling for the wave pattern. The two million products would need to be taken over a two year period. We would also require a commitment for all of the butterfly and roller mop laminates that include the Rubbermaid Cleaning Products design.
>
> I have also spoken to Foamex and they have agreed to run their "sample" tool for the short term until the production tool is complete, which would be approximately eight weeks. Please keep in mind that this is a proprietary pattern and we would need your design should this project move forward.
>
> Finally, we appreciate the opportunity and understand the price sensitive nature of your products. Reilly Foam Corporation has made various concessions to keep this program moving forward. Tony, after reviewing the quotation and the conditions of this letter, please respond through a letter stating Rubbermaid Cleaning Products intentions. I look forward to your response.
>
> /s/ Joseph G. Reilly

Accompanying the letter was a list of products, prices, and quantities on Reilly Foam letterhead. ... Tony Ferrante responded by letter on March 30, 1999. The letter, addressed to "Joe" Reilly, read in relevant part:

> This letter is to serve as Rubbermaid's commitment and authorization to procure tooling so that Reilly Foam will be in a position to make sponge products with Rubbermaid's patent pending Tidal Wave™ design. I understand that $.015 will be added to the cost of the sponge purchase price until we have made purchases of 2 million sponges, thereby covering the

> tooling cost of $30,000. Referencing the attached quotation, our commitment is as follows:
>
> 1. Any sponge mop product produced by New Knight, Inc., on behalf of Rubbermaid Home Products, will source the sponge component from Reilly Foam. This includes the current product offering, as referenced in your quotation, as well as any future new products that New Knight will produce for us.
>
> 2. Should any cost savings arise from productivity improvements, Rubbermaid is entitled to share in those benefits. ...
>
> Best Regards,
>
> /s/ Tony Ferrante
>
> Product Manager
>
> Rubbermaid Home Products

New Knight, an independent corporation, assembled mops on behalf of Rubbermaid. Attached to his letter was Reilly Foam's price list, marked "Approved" and signed by Mr. Ferrante. Shortly thereafter, Rubbermaid supplied Reilly Foam with a forecast of how many sponges of each variety it would need.

Following the exchange of letters, Rubbermaid instructed New Knight to purchase sponges solely from Reilly Foam. New Knight complied and used Reilly Foam as its exclusive source of sponges until New Knight entered bankruptcy in August 2001. Rubbermaid itself made purchases of sponges listed under the "other affected products" category. At the same time, Rubbermaid continued to purchase sponges from Tek Pak for use in the Tidal Wave line of mops. Moreover, Rubbermaid did not purchase two million sponges within the two-year window which Reilly Foam sought.

Reilly Foam contends that Rubbermaid has breached the contract by failing to use Reilly Foam as Rubbermaid's exclusive supplier for the Tidal Wave Project (including roller mop and butterfly mop sponges) and making purchases from Plaintiff's competitors, by failing to purchase the minimum annual quantities of sponges in the "other affected products category" set forth in the price list which Joseph Reilly sent on March 26, 1999, and by failing to purchase two million "other affected sponges" within two years with a $0.015 surcharge.

III. DISCUSSION OF CROSS-MOTIONS FOR SUMMARY JUDGMENT

CHOICE OF LAW

Reilly Foam contends that Pennsylvania law applies to all claims in this action. In its briefs, Rubbermaid has relied heavily on PENNSYLVANIA'S UNIFORM COMMERCIAL CODE, 13 PENN. CONS. STAT. ANN. § 1101 et seq. (Pa. U.C.C.). ... Because I ordered the parties to brief the court on the choice of law question and Rubbermaid has not done so, I deem it to have waived any recourse to Ohio law. The parties agree that Article 2 of the Pa. U.C.C. governs the sales contract at issue.

CONTRACT CLAIM

Plaintiff alleges that the March 26 letter was a contractual offer, which Rubbermaid accepted through its March 30 correspondence. Under the contract's terms, Reilly Foam became Rubbermaid's exclusive supplier of sponges for the Tidal Wave project. Rubbermaid was to purchase at minimum two million sponges of "other affected products" within two years of execution of the contract. Of the sponges in the category of "Other Affected Products," Rubbermaid was to annually purchase 340,000 Brown Sponges, 350,000 Yellow Ester Sponges with Wave Pattern, and 300,000 Yellow Ether to White Scrubmate Sponges.

Rubbermaid, in turn, argues that Reilly Foam's March 26 letter was merely a price quote, and [that its terms] are not part of the contract. Alternatively, Rubbermaid argues that the March 30 letter from Mr. Ferrante demonstrates that Rubbermaid did not accept all the terms contained in the March 26 letter, and certain key terms must be excluded under the "knockout rule."

1. Whether the March 26, 1999 Letter Was an Offer Within the Meaning of Pa. UCC 2206

The parties first dispute whether the March 26, 1999 correspondence was merely a price quote or an "offer" within the meaning of the Pa.U.C.C. The Pa.U.C.C. does not expressly define "offer," but it has been defined based on common law principles as "the manifestation of willingness to enter into a bargain, so made as to justify another person in understanding that his assent to that bargain is invited and will conclude it." *Bergquist Co. v. Sunroc Corp.*, 777 F. Supp. 1236, 1248 (E.D. Pa. 1991). Documents reflecting preliminary negotiations between the parties do not evince an enforceable contract. *See ATACS Corp. v. Trans World Communs.*, 155 F.3d 659, 666 (3d Cir. 1998).

In the U.C.C. context, courts have encountered difficulty determining whether a document that quotes a seller's prices constitutes an offer. Generally, price quotes are not considered an offer, but rather "mere invitations to enter into negotiations or to submit offers." *Cf. Dean Foods Co. v. Brancel*, 187 F.3d 609, 619 (7th Cir. 1999) (price quote commonly deemed invitation to offer rather than offer even if directed at particular customer). The buyer's purchase order—which sets such terms as product choice, quantity, price, and terms of delivery—is usually the offer. *See Audio Visual Assocs. v. Sharp Elec. Corp.*, 210 F.3d 254, 259 (4th Cir. 2000).

However, some price quotes are sufficiently detailed to be deemed offers, which turns a subsequent document from a buyer containing a positive response into an acceptance. *See White Consol. Indus., Inc. v. McGill Mfg. Co.*, 165 F.3d 1185, 1190-91 (8th Cir. 1999) (holding price quotation may constitute offer if it sets forth sufficient detail and contract can be formed by acceptance of its terms). ... What transforms a quotation into an offer cannot be neatly defined; it depends on the manifestation of intent by the seller and the "unique facts and circumstances of each case." *Rich Prods. Corp. v. Kemutec, Inc.*, 66 F.Supp.2d 937, 956 (E.D. Wis. 1999). As is the case with a purported offer under the common law, the seller "must intend that the contract exist upon acceptance of the offer; that is, it must reasonably appear from the price quotation that assent to that quotation is all that is needed to ripen the offer into a contract." *Bergquist*, 777 F.Supp. at 1249.

Reviewing Reilly Foam's March 26 correspondence and its treatment by Rubbermaid, both parties treated the price quote as an offer and not merely a price quote. First, the March 26 letter did not merely list price. The letter refers to itself as a "proposal" in its opening paragraph. The attached list also includes a number of specific terms including the identification of products, their quantities, the licensing of needed technology, and details for the special manufacture of the sponges. Rubbermaid treated the letter as an offer at least with respect to quantities and prices of "other affected products." Mr. Ferrante's March 30 response merely noted that the terms states on the price list were "approved" and stated in his letter that the $0.015 surcharge for the first two million sponges purchased was acceptable.

While it may have been desirable to include additional terms in the March 26, 1999 letter to clarify its status as an offer, contract formation depends on the manifestation of intent by the parties to be bound rather than the presence or absence of specific terms. See ATACS Corp., 155 F.3d at 667. Moreover, Joseph Reilly's March 26 letter described the price list as a quotation, no such appellation is given to the letter itself. In any event, a party's description of a document as a price quote or offer is not determinative. The Court finds the March 26 correspondence contains sufficient detail and is deemed an offer as a matter of law.

2. Effect of Different Terms in Rubbermaid's March 30 Acceptance

Once Reilly Foam's March 26 letter is deemed an offer, there can be no doubt that Rubbermaid's March 30 response accepted it. *See* Pa.U.C.C. § 2207(a) (expression of acceptance operates to form contract even if it states additional or different terms). Rubbermaid does argue that its March 30, 1999 letter was not an acceptance but a rejection and counteroffer because it constituted a conditional acceptance. However, to be deemed a rejection due to conditional acceptance, the offeree must do more than allude to preferred terms. It must make its acceptance "expressly ... conditional on assent to the additional or added terms." Pa.U.C.C. § 2207(a).

In other words, it must demonstrate an unwillingness to proceed with the transaction unless its conditions are met. *See Step-Saver Data Sys., Inc. v. Wyse Tech.*, 939 F.2d 91, 102 (3d Cir. 1991); *Reaction Molding Techs., Inc. v. Gen. Elec. Co.*, 588 F.Supp. 1280, 1289 (E.D. Pa. 1984) (strictly construing clauses claiming to make acceptance expressly conditional). Rubbermaid's March 30 letter evinces a willingness to proceed with the transaction and therefore cannot be deemed a rejection or counteroffer.

However, Rubbermaid argues that even if the March 26 letter is deemed an offer, its March 30 acceptance contained a number of different terms which modified the contract under the Pa.U.C.C.'s purported "knockout rule." Reilly Foam retorts that the court should not follow the knockout rule and permit the terms of its offer to govern. If the knockout rule does apply, it argues, Rubbermaid's acceptance did not contain any different terms.

a. Rubbermaid's March 30 Acceptance Contains Different Terms

Pointing to Mr. Ferrante's writing "approved" on the list accompanying the March 26 letter, Reilly Foam first contends that Rubbermaid accepted all terms on the price list in their entirety without modification. Therefore, Mr. Ferrante's "hidden intent" to impose additional or different terms should not be enforced. As a general matter, Reilly Foam is correct; undisclosed intentions cannot be considered terms of a contract. *See Ingrassia Constr. Co. v. Walsh*, 337 Pa.Super. 58, 486 A.2d 478, 483 (1984).

Mr. Ferrante did not "hide" his intentions, however; he stated a number of new terms quite clearly in his letter of March 30. In particular, he attempted to do three things: restrict Rubbermaid's commitment to two million sponges, permitting Reilly Foam to recoup its tooling cost of $30,000; ensure that New Knight would purchase its sponges from

Reilly Foam; and provide that Rubbermaid would share in any cost savings from productivity improvements.

Although Reilly Foam seeks to dismiss the letter as mere "correspondence" without any effect on the contract terms, the court is bound to read both documents of March 30—Ferrante's letter and the approved list—together. Reilly Foam's March 26 correspondence specifically invited Rubbermaid to respond by letter. It would be incongruous for Reilly Foam to now ignore that letter after Rubbermaid complied with its instructions. As part of the contract, the documents should be read as a whole, with the aim of construing conflicting clauses together, if possible. *See Brown v. Cooke*, 707 A.2d 231, 233 (Pa. Super. Ct. 1998).

Reilly Foam notes that, in part, Mr. Ferrante has accepted and concluded purchase contracts with a mere notation of approval on a price quote. Thus, he should be deemed to have approved and accepted Reilly Foam's offer. The Court need not speculate as to Mr. Ferrante's intentions based solely on the single word "approved" on a price list in other cases or the instant one. Mr. Ferrante's letter expresses an intent to impose new terms on the contract.

b. Terms of the Contract

If Reilly Foam's March 26 letter operates as an offer and Rubbermaid's March 30 correspondence acts as an acceptance, the court is left with the task of determining the terms of the agreement between these merchants under Pa.U.C.C. § 2207, commonly called the "Battle of the Forms" provision.

SECTION 2207

Frequently, businessmen do not set forth all of the terms of their agreements in a single, comprehensive document. Rather, deals are made on the basis of conversations and letters exchanged between the parties. Ultimately, one party reduces the terms of a proposed deal to writing, which is deemed an offer. Under the common law, a document qualifying as an offer could only be "accepted" by a second document expressing acceptance on terms identical to the offer. *See Slaymaker v. Irwin*, 4 Whart. 369, 380-81 (Pa. 1839); *Joseph v. Richardson,* 2 Pa. Super. 208, 212-14 (Pa. Super. Ct. 1896).

The rule changed with the enactment of the Battle of the Forms provision of the Pa.U.C.C., which permits an expression of acceptance to operate as an acceptance even if it contains additional or different terms. *See* Pa.U.C.C. § 2207(a). The additional terms become part of the contract unless: (1) the offer expressly limits acceptance to the terms of the offer; (2) the inserted term materially alters the offer; or (3) notification of objection to the inserted terms has been given or is given within a reasonable time. Pa.U.C.C. § 2207(b)(1)–(3). For the sake of consistency, all citations to the U.C.C. use Pennsylvania's format. Section 2207 is the equivalent to § 2-207 in the original version promulgated by the American Law Institute and the National Conference of Commissioners of Uniform States Laws. Section 2207(b) corresponds to § 2-207(2).

The fate of different terms is less clear. Section 2207(b) does not directly address different terms in an acceptance, and the question remains: if the offer is accepted on different terms, should the terms of the offer control or should the acceptance be followed, or should the conflicting terms cancel each other out, to be replaced by gap fillers provided by the U.C.C.? The question has divided courts and scholars.

One approach considers any expression of acceptance with differing terms as actually a rejection and counter-offer. Thus, the terms outlined in the acceptance would govern. *See Roto-Lith, Ltd. v. F.P. Bartlett & Co.*, 297 F.2d 497 (1st Cir. 1962), overruled by *Ionics, Inc. v. Elmwood Sensors, Inc.,* 110 F.3d 184, 187 (1st Cir. 1997). This view has been widely discredited as a revival of the common law rule, and the Court is not aware of any jurisdiction in which it is currently in force.

The minority view permits the terms of the offer to control. Because there is no rational distinction between additional terms and different terms, both are handled under § 2207(b). For support, advocates of this position point to Official Comment 3: "Whether or not additional or different terms will become part of the agreement depends upon the provisions of subsection [b]." *See Steiner v. Mobil Oil Corp.*, 569 P.2d 751, 759-60 n. 5 (Cal. 1977) and *Mead Corp. v. McNally-Pittsburg Mfg. Corp.*, 654 F.2d 1197, 1204 & n. 11 (6th Cir. 1981) (implicitly assuming, without holding, that different terms in acceptance would be subject to analysis under Ohio's version of § 2207(b). ...

The final approach, held by a majority of courts, is now known as the "knockout rule." Under this approach, terms of the contract include those upon which the parties agreed and gap fillers provided by the U.C.C. provisions. This approach recognizes as ... the fundamental tenet behind U.C.C. § 2207: to repudiate the "mirror-image" rule of the common law. One should not be able to dictate the terms of the contract merely because one sent the offer. Indeed, the knockout rule recognizes that merchants are frequently willing to proceed with a transaction even though all terms have not been assented to. It would be inequitable to lend greater force to one party's preferred terms than the other's.

As one court recently explained, "An approach other than the knockout rule for conflicting terms would result in ... any offeror ... always prevailing on its terms solely because it sent the first form. That is not a desirable result, particularly when the parties have not negotiated for the challenged clause." *Richardson v. Union Carbide Indus. Gases, Inc.*, 790 A.2d 962, 968 (N.J. Super. Ct. App. Div. 2002). Support for this view is also found in the Official U.C.C. Comments:

> Where clauses on confirming forms sent by both parties conflict each party must be assumed to object to a clause of the other conflicting with one on the confirmation sent by himself. As a result the requirement that there be notice of objection which is found in subsection [b] is satisfied and the conflicting terms do not become a part of the contract. The contract then consists of the terms originally expressly agreed to, terms on which the confirmations agree, and terms supplied by this Act, including subsection [b]. U.C.C. § 2207 cmt. 6.

Advocates of the knockout rule interpret Comment 6 to require the cancellation of terms in both parties' documents that conflict with one another, whether the terms are in confirmation notices or in the offer and acceptance themselves. A majority of courts now favor this approach. (citations omitted).

The court's task today is to predict how the Pennsylvania Supreme Court would rule if confronted with the issue. ... The Pennsylvania Supreme Court has never addressed the issue. ... The Tenth Circuit has predicted that the Pennsylvania Supreme Court would opt for the knockout rule. In light of the superior policy reasons behind the knockout rule, its fit with the text of the statute, and the vast majority of jurisdictions adopting it, I concur with the Tenth Circuit and conclude that the Pennsylvania Supreme Court would adopt the knockout rule. ...

V. Conclusion

In summary, Rubbermaid has breached the contract in failing: (1) to make minimum annual purchases of "other affected products" as set forth on the March 26 price list; (2) to purchase two million sponges under the "other affected products" category with a $0.015 surcharge within two years of the contract date. Reilly Foam must prove at trial the extent of its damages. ... Plaintiff's motion for partial summary is granted in part. ...

Notes and Questions

1. **The Knockout Rule**. Consider the Kentucky court's explanation of the knockout doctrine in *General Steel Corp. v. Collins*, 196 S.W.3d 18, 21 (Ky. Ct. App. 2006):

> [Under the] common law the disparity between the fine-print terms in the parties' forms would have prevented the consummation of a contract when these forms are exchanged. ... [However, a] court may conclude that the parties have formed a contract even where the acceptance of the offer contains terms additional to or different from those stated in the offer. As long as the parties demonstrate their mutual assent to the essential terms of an agreement, a written contract is deemed to exist. ... A majority of jurisdictions holds that the conflicting terms between an offer ... and [an] acceptance are properly subject to the "knockout" rule. Where the terms of the offer and acceptance are clearly at odds, they cancel out one another, and neither becomes a part of the contract.

2. **A Listing of Jurisdictions Adopting the Knockout Rule**. A majority of court apply the "knockout rule" to resolve UCC § 2-207 disputes. *See JOM, Inc. v. Adell Plastics, Inc.*, 193 F.3d 47, 54 (1st Cir. 1999) (ascribing knockout rule to law of Maine and Maryland); *Ionics v. Elmwood Sensors, Inc.*, 110 F.3d 184, 189 (1st Cir. 1997) (applying Massachusetts law); *Northrop Corp. v. Litronic Indus.*, 29 F.3d 1173, 1178 (7th Cir. 1994) (describing this approach as "majority rule" and predicting Illinois would adopt it); *Daitom, Inc. v. Pennwalt Corp.*, 741 F.2d 1569, 1578–79 (10th Cir. 1984) (applying Pennsylvania law); *Westinghouse Elec. Corp. v. Nielsons, Inc.*, 647 F.Supp. 896 (D. Colo. 1986) (applying Colorado law); *Owens-Corning Fiberglas Corp. v. Sonic Dev. Corp.*, 546 F.Supp. 533 (D. Kan. 1982) (applying Kansas law); *Armco Steel Corp. v. Isaacson Structural Steel Co.*, 611 P.2d 507, 518 & n. 30 (Ala. 1980); *Southern Idaho Pipe & Steel Co. v. Cal-Cut Pipe & Supply, Inc.*, 98 Idaho 495, 567 P.2d 1246, 1254–55 (Idaho 1977); *Uniroyal, Inc. v. Chambers Gasket & Mfg. Co.*, 177 Ind. App. 508, 380 N.E.2d 571, 578 (Ind. Ct. App. 1978); *S. C. Gray, Inc. v. Ford Motor Co.*, 92 Mich. App. 789, 286 N.W.2d 34 (Mich. Ct. App. 1979); *St. Paul Structural Steel Co. v. ABI Contracting, Inc.*, 364 N.W.2d 83 (N.D. 1985) (applying Minnesota law); *Richardson v. Union Carbide Industrial Gases, Inc.* 790 A.2d 962, 968 (N.J. Super. Ct. App. Div. 2002) (applying New Jersey law); *Gardner Zemke Co. v. Dunham Bush, Inc.*, 850 P.2d 319, 325–26 (N.M. 1993); *Lory Fabrics, Inc. v. Dress Rehearsal, Inc.*, 434 N.Y.S.2d 359, 363 (N.Y. App. Div. 1980); *Superior Boiler Works v. R.J. Sanders, Inc.*, 711 A.2d 628, 635 (R.I. 1998); and, *Hartwig Farms, Inc. v. Pacific Gamble Robinson Co.*, 28 Wash. App. 539, 625 P.2d 171 (Wash. Ct. App. 1981).

3. **The Last Shot Doctrine.** In *Step-Saver Data Sys., Inc. v. Wyse Tech.*, 939 F.2d 91, 99 (3rd Cir. 1991), the Court of Appeals for the Third Circuit explained the doctrine:

> Under the common law of sales, and to some extent still for contracts outside the UCC, an acceptance that varied any term of the offer operated as a rejection of the offer, and simultaneously made a counteroffer. This common law formality was known as the mirror image rule, because the terms of the acceptance had to mirror the terms of the offer to be effective. If the offeror proceeded with the contract despite the differing terms of the supposed acceptance, he would, by his performance, constructively accept the terms of the 'counteroffer,' and be bound by its terms. As a result of these rules, the terms of the party who sent the last form, typically the seller, would become the terms of the parties' contract. This result was known as the 'last shot rule.' ... The UCC, in § 2-207, reject[s] this approach."

4) Multiple Offers and Acceptances: The "Battle of Forms" Under § 2-207

Ionics, Inc. v. Elmwood Sensors, Inc.
110 F.3d 184
(1st Cir. 1997)

TORRUELLA, CHIEF JUDGE. Ionics, Inc. (Ionics) purchased thermostats from Elmwood Sensors, Inc. (Elmwood) for installation in water dispensers manufactured by the former. Several of the dispensers subsequently caused fires which allegedly resulted from defects in the sensors. Ionics filed suit against Elmwood in order to recover costs incurred in the wake of the fires. Before trial, the district court denied Elmwood's motion for partial summary judgment. The District Court of Massachusetts subsequently certified to this court "the question whether, in the circumstances of this case, § 2-207 of M.G.L. c. 106 has been properly applied." Order of the district court, November 6, 1995.

I. STANDARD OF REVIEW

We review the grant or denial of summary judgment de novo. *See Borschow Hosp. & Medical Supplies v. Cesar Castillo, Inc.*, 96 F.3d 10, 14 (1st Cir. 1996).

II. BACKGROUND

The facts of the case are not in dispute. Elmwood manufactures and sells thermostats. Ionics makes hot and cold water dispensers, which it leases to its customers. On three separate occasions, Ionics purchased thermostats from Elmwood for use in its water dispensers. Every time Ionics made a purchase of thermostats from Elmwood, it sent the latter a purchase order form which contained, in small type, various "conditions." Of the 20 conditions on the order form, two are of particular relevance:

> 18. Remedies—The remedies provided Buyer herein shall be cumulative, and in addition to any other remedies provided by law or equity. A waiver of a breach of any provision hereof shall not constitute a waiver of any other breach. The laws of the state shown in Buyer's address printed on the masthead of this order shall apply in the construction hereof.
>
> 19. Acceptance—Acceptance by the Seller of this order shall be upon the terms and conditions set forth in items 1 to 17 inclusive, and elsewhere in this order. Said order can be so accepted only on the exact terms herein and set forth. No terms which are in any manner additional to or different from those herein set forth shall become a part of, alter or in any way control the terms and conditions herein set forth.

Near the time when Ionics placed its first order, it sent Elmwood a letter that it sends to all of its new suppliers. The letter states, in part:

> The information preprinted, written and/or typed on our purchase order is especially important to us. Should you take exception to this information, please clearly express any reservations to us in writing. If you do not, we will assume that you have agreed to the specified terms and that you will fulfill your obligations according to our purchase order. If necessary, we will change your invoice and pay your invoice according to our purchase order.

Following receipt of each order, Elmwood prepared and sent an "Acknowledgment" form containing the following language in small type:

> THIS WILL ACKNOWLEDGE RECEIPT OF BUYER'S ORDER AND STATE SELLER'S WILLINGNESS TO SELL THE GOODS ORDERED BUT ONLY UPON THE TERMS AND CONDITIONS SET FORTH HEREIN AND ON THE REVERSE SIDE HEREOF AS A COUNTEROFFER. BUYER SHALL BE DEEMED TO HAVE ACCEPTED SUCH COUNTEROFFER UNLESS IT IS REJECTED IN WRITING WITHIN TEN (10) DAYS OF THE RECEIPT HEREOF, AND ALL SUBSEQUENT ACTION SHALL BE PURSUANT TO THE TERMS AND CONDITIONS OF THIS COUNTEROFFER ONLY; ANY ADDITIONAL OR DIFFERENT TERMS ARE HEREBY OBJECTED TO AND SHALL NOT BE BINDING UPON THE PARTIES UNLESS SPECIFICALLY AGREED TO IN WRITING BY SELLER.

Although this passage refers to a "counteroffer," we wish to emphasize that this language is not controlling. The form on which the language appears is labeled an "Acknowledgment" and the language comes under a heading that reads "Notice of Receipt of Order." The form, taken as a whole, appears to contemplate an order's confirmation rather than an order's rejection in the form of a counteroffer.

It is undisputed that the Acknowledgment was received prior to the arrival of the shipment of goods. Although the district court, in its ruling on the summary judgment motion, states that "with each shipment of thermostats, Elmwood included an Acknowledgment Form," Order of the District Court, August 23, 1995, this statement cannot reasonably be taken as a finding in support of the claim that the Acknowledgment and the shipment arrived together.

First, in its certification order, the court states that "[t]he purchaser, after receiving the Acknowledgment, accepted delivery of the goods without objection." Order Pursuant to 28 U.S.C. § 1292(b), Nov. 6, 1995 (emphasis added). This language is clearer and more precise than the previous statement and suggests that the former was simply a poor choice of phrasing. Furthermore, Ionics has not disputed the arrival time of the Acknowledgment. In its Memorandum in Support of Defendant's Motion for Partial Summary Judgment Elmwood stated, under the heading of "Statements of Undisputed Facts," that "for each of the three orders, Ionics received the Acknowledgment prior to receiving the shipment of thermostats." Memorandum in Support of Defendant's Motion for Partial Summary Judgment, at 3.

In its own memorandum, Ionics argued that there existed disputed issues of material fact, but did not contradict Elmwood's claim regarding the arrival of the Acknowledgment Form. Furthermore, in its appellate brief, Ionics does not argue that the time of arrival of the Acknowledgment Form is in dispute. Ionics repeats language from the district court's summary judgment ruling that "with each shipment of thermostats, Elmwood included an Acknowledgment Form," but does not argue that the issue is in dispute or confront the language in Elmwood's brief which states that "[i]t is undisputed that for each of the three orders, Ionics received the Acknowledgment prior to receiving the shipment of thermostats."

As we have noted, the Acknowledgment Form expressed Elmwood's willingness to sell thermostats on "terms and conditions" that the Form indicated were listed on the reverse side. Among the terms and conditions listed on the back was the following:

> 9. Warranty—All Goods Manufactured By Elmwood Sensors, Inc. Are Guaranteed To Be Free Of Defects In Material And Workmanship For A Period Of Ninety (90) Days After Receipt Of Such Goods By Buyer Or Eighteen Months From The Date

> OF MANUFACTURER [SIC] (AS EVIDENCED BY THE MANUFACTURER'S DATE CODE), WHICHEVER SHALL BE LONGER. THERE IS NO IMPLIED WARRANTY OF MERCHANTABILITY AND NO OTHER WARRANTY, EXPRESSED OR IMPLIED, EXCEPT SUCH AS IS EXPRESSLY SET FORTH HEREIN. SELLER WILL NOT BE LIABLE FOR ANY GENERAL, CONSEQUENTIAL OR INCIDENTAL DAMAGES, INCLUDING WITHOUT LIMITATION ANY DAMAGES FROM LOSS OF PROFITS, FROM ANY BREACH OF WARRANTY OR FOR NEGLIGENCE, SELLER'S LIABILITY AND BUYER'S EXCLUSIVE REMEDY BEING EXPRESSLY LIMITED TO THE REPAIR OF DEFECTIVE GOODS F.O.B. THE SHIPPING POINT INDICATED ON THE FACE HEREOF OR THE REPAYMENT OF THE PURCHASE PRICE UPON THE RETURN OF THE GOODS OR THE GRANTING OF A REASONABLE ALLOWANCE ON ACCOUNT OF ANY DEFECTS, AS SELLER MAY ELECT.

Neither party disputes that they entered into a valid contract and neither disputes the quantity of thermostats purchased, the price paid, or the manner and time of delivery. The only issue in dispute is the extent of Elmwood's liability.

In summary, Ionics' order included language stating that the contract would be governed exclusively by the terms included on the purchase order and that all remedies available under state law would be available to Ionics. In a subsequent letter, Ionics added that Elmwood must indicate any objections to these conditions in writing. Elmwood, in turn, sent Ionics an Acknowledgment stating that the contract was governed exclusively by the terms in the Acknowledgment, and Ionics was given ten days to reject this "counteroffer." Among the terms included in the Acknowledgment is a limitation on Elmwood's liability. As the district court stated, "the terms are diametrically opposed to each other on the issue of whether all warranties implied by law were reserved or waived."

We face, therefore, a battle of the forms. This is purely a question of law. The dispute turns on whether the contract is governed by the language after the comma in § 2-207(1) of the Uniform Commercial Code, according to the rule laid down by this court in *Roto-Lith, Ltd. v. F.P. Bartlett* & Co., 297 F.2d 497 (1st Cir. 1962), or whether it is governed by subsection (3) of the Code provision, as enacted by both MASSACHUSETTS, MASS. GEN. L. CH. 106, § 2-207 (1990 and 1996 Supp.), and Rhode Island, R.I. Gen. Laws § 6A-2-207 (1992). We find the rule of *Roto-Lith* to be in conflict with the purposes of section 2-207 and, accordingly, we overrule *Roto-Lith* and find that subsection (3) governs the contract. Analyzing the case under section 2-207, we conclude that Ionics defeats Elmwood's motion for partial summary judgment.

III. LEGAL ANALYSIS

Our analysis begins with the statute. Section 2-207 reads as follows:

§ 2-207. Additional Terms in Acceptance or Confirmation

(1) A definite and seasonable expression of acceptance or a written confirmation which is sent within a reasonable time operates as an acceptance even though it states terms additional to or different from those offered or agreed upon, unless acceptance is expressly made conditional on assent to the additional or different terms.

(2) The additional or different terms are to be construed as proposals for addition to the contract. Between merchants such terms become part of the contract unless:

(a) the offer expressly limits acceptance to the terms of the offer;

(b) they materially alter it; or

(c) notification of objection to them has already been given or is given within a reasonable time after notice of them is received.

(3) Conduct by both parties which recognizes the existence of a contract is sufficient to establish a contract for sale although the writings of the parties do not otherwise establish a contract. In such case the terms of the particular contract consist of those terms on which the writings of the parties agree, together with any supplementary terms incorporated under any other provisions of this chapter. Mass. Gen. L. ch. 106, § 2-207 (1990 and 1996 Supp.).

In *Roto-Lith*, Roto-Lith sent a purchase order to Bartlett, who responded with an acknowledgment that included language purporting to limit Bartlett's liability. Roto-Lith did not object. *Roto-Lith*, 297 F.2d at 498-99. This court held that "a response which states a condition materially altering the obligation solely to the disadvantage of the offeror is an 'acceptance ... expressly ... conditional on assent to the additional ... terms.'" This holding took the case outside of § 2-207 by applying the exception after the comma in subsection (1).

The court then reverted to common law and concluded that Roto-Lith "accepted the goods with knowledge of the conditions specified in the acknowledgment [and thereby] became bound." Id. at 500. In other words, the *Roto-Lith* court concluded that the defendant's acceptance was conditional on assent, by the buyer, to the new terms and, therefore, constituted a counter offer rather than an acceptance. When Roto-Lith accepted the goods with knowledge of Bartlett's conditions, it accepted the counteroffer and Bartlett's terms governed the contract.

Elmwood argues that *Roto-Lith* governs the instant appeal, implying that the terms of Elmwood's acknowledgment govern. Ionics claims that the instant case is distinguishable because in *Roto-Lith* "the seller's language limiting warranties implied at law was proposed as an addition to, but was not in conflict with, the explicit terms of the buyer's form. [In the instant case] the explicit terms of the parties' forms conflict with and reject each other."

We do not believe that Ionics' position sufficiently distinguishes *Roto-Lith*. It would be artificial to enforce language that conflicts with background legal rules while refusing to enforce language that conflicts with the express terms of the contract. Every contract is assumed to incorporate the existing legal norms that are in place. It is not required that every contract explicitly spell out the governing law of the jurisdiction. Allowing later forms to govern with respect to deviations from the background rules but not deviations from the terms in the contract would imply that only the terms in the contract could be relied upon.

Aside from being an artificial and arbitrary distinction, such a standard would, no doubt, lead parties to include more of the background rules in their initial forms, making forms longer and more complicated. Longer forms would be more difficult and time consuming to read-implying that even fewer forms would be read than under the existing rules. It is the failure of firms to read their forms that has brought this case before us, and we do not wish to engender more of this type of litigation.

Our inquiry, however, is not complete. Having found that we cannot distinguish this case from *Roto-Lith*, we turn to the UNIFORM COMMERCIAL CODE, quoted above. A plain language reading of § 2-207 suggests that subsection (3) governs the instant case. Ionics sent an initial offer to which Elmwood responded with its "ACKNOWLEDGMENT." Thereafter, the conduct of the parties established the existence of a contract as required by § 2-207(3).

Furthermore, the case before us is squarely addressed in comment 6, which states:

> 6. If no answer is received within a reasonable time after additional terms are proposed, it is both fair and commercially sound to assume that their inclusion has been assented to. Where clauses on confirming forms sent by both parties conflict[,] each party must be assumed to object to a clause of the other conflicting with one on the confirmation sent by himself. As a result [,] the requirement that there be notice of objection which is found in subsection (2) [of § 2-207] is satisfied and the conflicting terms do not become part of the

> contract. The contract then consists of the terms originally expressly agreed to, terms on which the confirmations agree, and terms supplied by this ACT. MASS. GEN. L. CH. 106, § 2-207, UNIFORM COMMERCIAL CODE COMMENT 6.

This Comment addresses precisely the facts of the instant case. Any attempt at distinguishing the case before us from § 2-207 strikes us as disingenuous. We are faced, therefore, with a contradiction between a clear precedent of this court, *Roto-Lith*—which suggests that the language after the comma in subsection (1) govern—and the clear dictates of the UNIFORM COMMERCIAL CODE, which indicate that subsection (3) governs. It is our view that the two cannot coexist and the case at bar offers a graphic illustration of the conflict.

We have, therefore, no choice but to overrule our previous decision in *Roto-Lith, Ltd. v. F.P. Bartlett & Co.*, 297 F.2d 497 (1st Cir. 1962). Our decision brings this circuit in line with the majority view on the subject and puts to rest a case that has provoked considerable criticism from courts and commentators and alike.

We hold, consistent with § 2-207 and Official Comment 6, that where the terms in two forms are contradictory, each party is assumed to object to the other party's conflicting clause. As a result, mere acceptance of the goods by the buyer is insufficient to infer consent to the seller's terms under the language of subsection (1). Nor do such terms become part of the contract under subsection (2) because notification of objection has been given by the conflicting forms. *See* § 2-207(2)(c).

The alternative result, advocated by Elmwood and consistent with *Roto-Lith*, would undermine the role of § 2-207. Elmwood suggests that "a seller's expressly conditional acknowledgment constitutes a counteroffer where it materially alters the terms proposed by the buyer, and the seller's terms govern the contract between the parties when the buyer accepts and pays for the goods." Under this view, section 2-207 would no longer apply to cases in which forms have been exchanged and subsequent disputes reveal that the forms are contradictory. That is, the last form would always govern.

The purpose of § 2-207, as stated in *Roto-Lith*, "was to modify the strict principle that a response not precisely in accordance with the offer was a rejection and a counteroffer." *Roto-Lith*, 297 F.2d at 500. *See also Dorton v. Collins & Aikman Corp.*, 453 F.2d 1161, 1165-66 (6th Cir. 1972) (stating that § 2-207 "was intended to alter the 'ribbon-matching' or 'mirror' rule of common law, under which the terms of an acceptance or confirmation were required to be identical to the terms of the offer"). Under the holding advocated by Elmwood, virtually any response that added to or altered the terms of the offer would be a rejection and a counteroffer. We do not think that such a result is consistent with the intent of § 2-207 and we believe it to be expressly contradicted by Comment 6.

Applied to this case, our holding leads to the conclusion that the contract is governed by § 2-207(3). Section 2-207(1) is inapplicable because Elmwood's acknowledgment is conditional on assent to the additional terms. The additional terms do not become a part of the contract under § 2-207(2) because notification of objection to conflicting terms was given on the order form and because the new terms materially alter those in the offer. Finally, the conduct of the parties demonstrates the existence of a contract, as required by § 2-207(3). Thus, section 2-207(3) applies and the terms of the contract are to be determined in accordance with that subsection.

We conclude, therefore, that § 2-207(3) prevails and "the terms of the particular contract consist of those terms on which the writings of the parties agree, together with any supplementary terms incorporated under any other provisions of this chapter." MASS. GEN. L. CH. 106, § 2-207(3).

The reality of modern commercial dealings, as this case demonstrates, is that not all participants read their forms. To uphold Elmwood's view would not only fly in the face of Official Comment 6 to § 2-207 of the UNIFORM COMMERCIAL CODE, and the overall purpose of that section, it would also fly in the face of good sense. The sender of the last form—in the instant case, the seller—could insert virtually any conditions it chooses into the contract, including conditions contrary to those in the initial form. The final form, therefore, would give its sender the power to re-write the contract.

Under our holding today, we at least ensure that a party will not be held to terms that are directly contrary to the terms it has included in its own form. Rather than assuming that a failure to object to the offeree's conflicting terms indicates offeror's assent to those terms, we shall make the more reasonable inference that each party continues to object to the other's contradictory terms. We think it too much to grant the second form the power to contradict and override the terms in the first form.

IV. CONCLUSION

For the reasons stated herein, the district court's order denying Elmwood's motion for partial summary judgment is affirmed and the case is remanded to the district court for further proceedings.

NOTES AND QUESTIONS

1. **Texas Commercial Code and the Rejection of Common-Law "Mirror Image Rule".** TEXAS. BUS. & COM. CODE § 2.207 rejects the common law "mirror image" rule and allows a contract to be formed even though the parties' exchanged documents contain varying terms. However, the formation is subject to the following qualifications: 1) the offer may not expressly limit an acceptance of the terms in the offer; 2) the varying terms may not materially alter the contract; or 3) neither party objects to the varying terms.

2. **UCC § 2-207 and the "Mirror Image Rule"**. Under the common law, the failure of a responding document to mirror the terms of an offer precludes the formation of a contract. Section 2-207 of the UCC does not completely eliminate the rule. Instead, it merely "alters" the "mirror-image" rule by providing that the inclusion of additional or different terms would not prevent an acceptance from being operative, unless the other party's assent to those additional or different terms made the acceptance conditional. *Challenge Machinery Co. v. Mattison Machine Works*, 138 Mich. App 15, 22 (Mich. Ct. App. 1984), citing MCL 440.2207(1).

3. **UCC § 2-207 and "Dickered" Terms.** Dickered terms are unique rather than the usual unbargained-for terms in a contract. Unique price, quality, quantity, or delivery terms are good examples. WHITE & SUMMERS, UNIFORM COMMERCIAL CODE § 33 (2000). State and federal courts have considered whether or not the common-law "mirror-image rule" governs the interpretation and enforcement of "dickered terms." They generally conclude: A counteroffer is any response that changes or modifies the price or any dickered term in an offer. Consequently, the common-law mirror-image rule also applies to "dickered terms." *See, e.g., Gage Prods. Co. v. Henkel Corp.*, 393 F.3d 629, 637–638 (6th Cir. 2004) and *Gen. Electric Co. v. G. Siempelkamp GmbH & Co.*, 29 F.3d 1095, 1098–1099 (6th Cir. 1994). On the other hand, courts have also embraced this view: Section 2-207 is designed to determine which non-negotiated terms are included in a contract. Therefore, the statute does not exclude specifically negotiated terms or dickered terms. *Gen Electric Co.*, 29 F.3d at 1099, quoting *Olefins Trading, Inc. v. Han Yang Chem. Corp.*, 9 F.3d 282, 287–88 (3rd Cir. 1993).

4. **UCC § 2-207, the Parties' Conduct, and "Complete Performance"**. Under § 2-207(3), both parties' conduct is sufficient to establish a contract for sale. *See American Parts Co. v. American Arbitration Assoc.*, 8 Mich. App 156, 176 (Mich. Ct.

App. 1967). Shipping goods, sending and accepting receipts, and making payments—those provide sufficient evidence and allow a court to declare that the parties formed a contract. *See Audio Visual Assocs. v. Sharp Electronics Corp.*, 210 F.3d 254, 260 (4th Cir. 2000), and *Avedon Engineering, Inc. v. Seatex,* 126 F.3d 1279, 1284 n. 10 (10th Cir. 1997). But note: Under section 2-207(3) of the UCC, evidence of the parties' complete performance is not required to establish the existence of a valid sale-of-goods contract under the plain language of the code. *Audio Visual Assocs.*, 210 F3d at 260; *Apex Oil Co. v. Vanguard Oil & Service Co., Inc.*, 760 F.2d 417 (2d Cir. 1985); and *Glasstech, Inc. v. Chicago Blower Corp.*, 675 F. Supp. 2d 752 (N.D. Ohio 2009).

CHAPTER NINE

Proof and Enforcement of Warranties Under the Uniform Commercial Code

In chapters 1 and 2, stand-alone and contractual promises were discussed, respectively. And, we learned that a complainant may commence a *breach-of-promise action* or a *breach-of-contract action* to secure damages for a breach-of-promise *claim*. Like contractual promises, warranties appear regularly in negotiated and standardized contracts. But quite often, sellers of goods and services fashion various warranties—along with limitations and exceptions—and insert these provisions in an independent or a stand-alone instrument. The document may be entitled, "Warranty Agreement," or "Limited Warranty."

In addition, a fairly large section of Chapter 4 was devoted to discussing breach-of-warranty claims and actions under the common law. The cases and notes appearing in that chapter reveal that a breach-of-warranty action may commence or "sound" under a variety of common-law theories: (1) under rules of contract—*See Rucker v. Hagar et al.*, 230 P. 70, 71 (Kan. 1924) ("Warranty sounds in contract ... and liability predicated on breach of warranty is contract and not tort liability."); (2) under tort principles—*See Iacono v. Anderson Concrete Corp.*, 326 N.E.2d 267, 270 n.1 (Ohio 1975) ("This court has recognized that, historically, an action grounded on breach of warranty sounded in tort rather than contract. It is a mistaken notion that use of the term 'warranty' always carried the implication of a contractual relationship."); (3) under both tort and contract principles—*See Reid v. Eckerds Drugs, Inc.*, 253 S.E.2d 344, 347 (N.C. Ct. App. 1979) ("It is now generally acknowledged that the action for breach of warranty is an offspring of mixed parentage, aspects of it sounding in both tort and contract, but following strictly the rules and precedents of neither."); or (4) under warranty law—*See Young v. Great Atl. & Pac. Tea Co.*, 15 F. Supp. 1018, 1018–19 (C.C.W.D. Pa. 1936) (declaring that a husband who bit into a mouse was a proper plaintiff under warranty law, even though wife had purchased the product).

To be sure, common-law breach-of-warranty rules are extensive and complicated. But even more problematic for litigants, the application of common law rules generates a considerable number of conflicting summary judgments, declaratory judgments, and jury verdicts in breach-of-warranty trials across states. A straightforward reason explains much of the confusion: Some state courts apply only contract principles to adjudicate breach-of-warranty actions. In other jurisdictions, courts employ only tort doctrines to resolve breach-of-warranty claims. Still, a few other courts allow warranty actions to commence under all three bodies of law. Therefore, given the large and entangled web of breach-of-warranty rules and conflicting judicial decisions under the common law, many contracting parties use the UCC's "uniform" rules to litigate breach-of-warranty disputes.

Again, an observation that appears in Chapter 4 is worth repeating here. Using common-law principles, parties to a contract may litigate numerous breach-of-warranty claims: (1) "breach of an express warranty"; (2) "breach of an implied warranty of merchantability"; (3) "breach of an implied warranty of fitness for a particular purpose"; (4) "breach of an implied warranty of workmanship"; (5) "breach of an implied warranty of good and workmanlike service"; (6) "breach of an implied warranty of workmanlike performance"; (7) "breach of an implied warranty of plans and specifications"; (8) "breach of an implied warranty regarding the adequacy of specifications"; (9) "breach of an implied warranty of design"; (10) "breach of an implied warranty of eviction"; (11) "breach of a statutory implied warranty of title"; (12) "breach an of an implied warranty of suitability"; and (13) "breach of an implied warranty of habitability."

On the other hand, under the UCC, parties to a sale-of-goods contract are restricted to litigating breach-of-warranty disputes that only involve one or a combination of the following warranties: an express warranty, an implied warranty of merchantability, and an implied warranty of fitness for a particular purpose. This chapter presents federal and state court cases illustrating the interpretation, application, and enforcement of UCC Article 2 breach-of-warranty rules.

SECTION ONE. ESTABLISHING PRIMA FACIE EVIDENCE OF VARIOUS WARRANTIES UNDER ARTICLE 2

A. Proof of an Express Warranty under § 2-313

With the exception of a few states, most states have adopted section 2-313 of the UCC verbatim. Tex. Bus. & Com. Code § 2-313 reads:

EXPRESS WARRANTIES BY AFFIRMATION, PROMISE, DESCRIPTION, SAMPLE

(a) Express warranties by the seller are created as follows:

(1) Any affirmation of fact or promise made by the seller to the buyer which relates to the goods and becomes part of the basis of the bargain creates an express warranty that the goods shall conform to the affirmation or promise.

(2) Any description of the goods which is made part of the basis of the bargain creates an express warranty that the goods shall conform to the description.

(3) Any sample or model which is made part of the basis of the bargain creates an express warranty that the whole of the goods shall conform to the sample or model.

(b) It is not necessary to the creation of an express warranty that the seller use formal words such as "warrant" or "guarantee" or that he have a specific intention to make a warranty, but an affirmation merely of the value of the goods or a statement purporting to be merely the seller's opinion or commendation of the goods does not create a warranty.

In section 2-313(a)(1)(2)(3), the phrase "basis of the bargain" appears. Stated simply, a number of litigated, substantive questions have evolved from that language, producing conflicting judicial rulings. Some of the more pressing questions have been: (1) whether the "basis of the bargain" test requires a buyer/plaintiff to prove that she relied on the seller's inaccurate affirmations or promises; (2) whether a seller's disclosure of false facts and a buyer's full knowledge and acceptance of those facts preclude the buyer from securing breach-of-warranty damages under section 2-313(a); and (3) whether a buyer's "common knowledge" of a seller's false promises or a third party's disclosure of a seller's false facts to a buyer precludes the buyer from securing damages under section 2-313(a). Answers to these salient questions appear in the next case.

Rogath v. Siebenmann
129 F.3d 261
(2nd Cir. 1997)

MCLAUGHLIN, CIRCUIT JUDGE. This case revolves around a painting, entitled "Self Portrait," supposedly painted in 1972 by a well-known English artist, Francis Bacon. In July 1993, defendant Werner Siebenmann sold the Painting to plaintiff David Rogath for $570,000. In the Bill of Sale, Siebenmann described the provenance of the Painting and warranted that he was the sole owner of the Painting, that it was authentic, and that he was not aware of any challenge to its authenticity.

Problems arose three months later when Rogath sold the Painting to Acquavella Contemporary Art, Inc., in New York, for $950,000. Acquavella learned of a challenge to the Painting's authenticity and, on November 1, 1993, requested that Rogath refund the $950,000 and take back the Painting. Rogath did so, and then sued Siebenmann in the Southern District of New York for breach of contract, breach of warranty and fraud.

Rogath moved for partial summary judgment on the breach of warranty claims, and the district court granted his motion. The court concluded that (1) Siebenmann was unsure of the provenance of the Painting when he sold it to Rogath; (2) he was not the sole owner of the Painting; and (3) when he sold the Painting to Rogath he already knew of a challenge to the Painting's authenticity by the Marlborough Fine Art Gallery in London. The court awarded Rogath $950,000 in damages, the price at which he had sold it to Acquavella. The court dismissed, *sua sponte*, Rogath's remaining claims for fraud and breach of contract "in light of the full recovery on the warranties granted herein." ... Siebenmann appeals the grant of partial summary judgment. ...

DISCUSSION

Siebenmann concedes that his promises and representations set forth in the Bill of Sale constitute warranties under New York law. He claims, however, that Rogath was fully aware when he bought the Painting that questions of authenticity and provenance had already been raised regarding the Painting. He maintains that, under New York law, Rogath therefore cannot rest claims for breach of warranty on the representations made in the Bill of Sale. ...

A. BREACH OF WARRANTY UNDER NEW YORK LAW

The Bill of Sale provides:

> In order to induce David Rogath to make the purchase, Seller ... make[s] the following warranties, representations and

> covenants to and with the Buyer. (1) That the Seller is the sole and absolute owner of the painting and has full right and authority to sell and transfer same; having acquired title as described in a copy of the Statement of Provenance signed by Seller annexed hereto and incorporated herein; [and] that the Seller has no knowledge of any challenge to Seller's title and authenticity of the Painting. …

Because the Bill of Sale was a contract for the sale of goods, Rogath's breach of warranty claims are governed by Article 2 of the Uniform Commercial Code (UCC). *See* N.Y.U.C.C. § 2-102 (McKinney 1993). Section 2-313 of the UCC provides that "[a]ny description of the goods which is made part of the basis of the bargain creates an express warranty that the goods shall conform to the description." N.Y.U.C.C. § 2-313(1)(b) (McKinney 1993).

Whether the "basis of the bargain" requirement implies that the buyer must rely on the seller's statements to recover and what the nature of that reliance requirement is are unsettled questions. Not surprisingly, this same confusion haunted the New York courts for a time. *See Ainger v. Michigan Gen. Corp.*, 632 F.2d 1025, 1026 n. 1 (2d Cir. 1980); *CPC Int'l, Inc. v. McKesson Corp.*, 513 N.Y.S.2d 319, 322 (N.Y. 1987). Some courts reasoned that the buyer must have relied upon the accuracy of the seller's affirmations or promises in order to recover. Other courts paid lip service to a "reliance" requirement, but found that the requirement was met if the buyer relied on the seller's promise as part of "the basis of the bargain" in entering into the contract; the buyer need not show that he relied on the truthfulness of the warranties.

Finally, some courts reasoned that there is a "reliance" requirement only when there is a dispute as to whether a warranty was in fact given by the seller. These courts concluded that no reliance of any kind is required "where the existence of an express warranty in a contract is conceded by both parties." *CPC Int'l*, 513 N.Y.S.2d at 322; *Ainger*, 476 F.Supp. at 1226–27. In these cases, the buyer need establish only a breach of the warranty.

In 1990 New York's Court of Appeals dispelled much of the confusion when it squarely adopted the "basis of the bargain" description of the reliance required to recover for breach of an express warranty. In *CBS Inc. v. Ziff-Davis Publishing Co.*, 553 N.E.2d 997 (N.Y. 1990), the court concluded that "[t]his view of 'reliance'—*i.e.*, as requiring no more than reliance on the express warranty as being a part of the bargain between the parties—reflects the prevailing perception of an action for breach of express warranty as one that is no longer grounded in tort, but essentially in contract." 553 N.E.2d at 1001. The court reasoned that "[t]he critical question is not whether the buyer believed in the truth of the warranted information … but whether [he] believed [he] was purchasing the [seller's] promise [as to its truth]." 553 N.E.2d at 1000–1001.

CBS was not decided on the basis of the UCC, probably because the sale of the magazine business at issue did not constitute the sale of goods. Nevertheless, the court relied heavily on UCC authorities, expressly noting that "analogy to the Uniform Commercial Code is 'instructive'." 553 N.E.2d at 1002 n. 4.

In 1992, in a case also involving the sale of a business, we followed the New York Court of Appeals and delineated fine factual distinctions in the *law of warranties*: a court must evaluate both the extent and the source of the buyer's knowledge about the truth of what the seller is warranting. "Where a buyer closes on a contract in the full knowledge and acceptance of facts disclosed by the seller which would constitute a breach of warranty under the terms of the contract, the buyer should be foreclosed from later asserting the breach. In that situation, unless the buyer expressly preserves his rights under the warranties ..., we think the buyer has waived the breach." *Galli v. Metz*, 973 F.2d 145, 151 (2d Cir. 1992). The buyer may preserve his rights by expressly stating that disputes regarding the accuracy of the seller's warranties are unresolved, and that by signing the agreement the buyer does not waive any rights to enforce the terms of the agreement.

On the other hand, if the seller is not the source of the buyer's knowledge, *e.g.,* if it is merely "common knowledge" that the facts warranted are false, or the buyer has been informed of the falsity of the facts by some third party, the buyer may prevail in his claim for breach of warranty. In these cases, it is not unrealistic to assume that the buyer purchased the seller's warranty "as insurance against any future claims," and that is why he insisted on the inclusion of the warranties in the bill of sale. *Cipollone v. Liggett Group, Inc.,* 893 F.2d 541, 568 n. 31 (3d Cir. 1990).

In short, where the seller discloses up front the inaccuracy of certain of his warranties, it cannot be said that the buyer—absent the express preservation of his rights—believed he was purchasing the seller's promise as to the truth of the warranties. Accordingly, what the buyer knew and, most importantly, whether he got that knowledge from the seller are the critical questions.

1. What Siebenmann Knew

Here, as the district court pointed out, Siebenmann—the seller—produced no evidence to contradict Rogath's evidence that Siebenmann knew of the cloud that hung over the Painting's authenticity before he sold it to Rogath. Siebenmann admits that he was told that the Marlborough Gallery was troubled by certain peculiarities of the Painting—including shiny black paint (as opposed to the matte black that Bacon apparently preferred) and the use of pink paint (which Bacon evidently did not use)—that suggested that Bacon was not the painter.

Siebenmann also admits that Julian Barran, a London art dealer, had earlier refused to buy the Painting because of doubts harbored by the Marlborough Gallery. Moreover, there was uncontroverted evidence that, on a prior occasion, Siebenmann's attempted sale of the Painting to a client of Robert Peter Miller—the owner of an art gallery in New York—was aborted when (1) Miller learned that the Marlborough had concerns about the Painting's authenticity, and (2) David Sylvester, a British art critic, advised Miller not to proceed with the purchase because of the Marlborough objection and because Sylvester himself was not sure of the authenticity of the Painting. Finally, Siebenmann does not deny that in June 1993 he received a fax from Anita Goldstein, an art dealer in Zurich, Switzerland, stating that "everybody is afraid of the authenticity" of the Painting.

2. What Siebenmann Told Rogath: Reasonable Inferences

In an affidavit in opposition to Rogath's motion for partial summary judgment, Siebenmann stated that "I spoke directly with David Rogath about the controversy created by the Marlborough Gallery towards this painting." He also said that, in a phone conversation with Rogath on July 13, 1993, "I specifically mentioned Marlborough Gallery and the 'problems' or the 'controversy' that it had produced for this painting. ... Mr. Rogath brushed aside the Marlborough Gallery controversy. He told me he had experienced difficulties with this particular gallery in the past and did not consider them to be especially reputable." In his deposition, Siebenmann added that he told Rogath on the phone "that I had problems with the Marlborough Gallery."

Siebenmann also filed an affidavit from Ronald Alley, the curator of the Tate Gallery in London, England, and the author of a survey of Bacon's work as well as several other writings about Bacon. Alley stated:

> I was phoned by Mr. David Rogath, hitherto unknown to me, who said that he was thinking of buying the painting and asked whether it was correct that I had seen it and thought it to be authentic. My reply, to the best of my recollection, can be summarized as follows: "It is a picture which did not pass through Marlborough Fine Art and is said to have a provenance which sounds quite plausible but is more or less impossible to check. Both Ms. Beston of Marlborough Fine Art and David Sylvester say they don't think it is by Bacon, but Sylvester knows it only from a photograph. I flew to Geneva for the day to look at it in a warehouse and felt convinced it was genuine."

For his part, Rogath denied that he was aware of any challenges to the authenticity or provenance of the Painting before entering into the Bill of Sale. He stated in his affidavit:

> During our telephone conversation, Mr. Siebenmann did not tell me that the Marlborough Gallery had "questioned" or "reserved judgment" about the Painting, or had caused any "problems" or "controversy" concerning the Painting. He said nothing at all like that during the conversation. Neither did Mr. Alley, in our subsequent conversation, refer to any such matters. He certainly did not tell me that Ms. Beston and Mr. Sylvester "don't think it is by Bacon." In fact, I spoke with Mr. Alley after the inauthenticity of the Painting had become known to me. ... Had either Mr. Siebenmann or Mr. Alley hinted to me that the Painting was of questioned authenticity, it would have been a "red flag" for me, as I had no desire to spend some $600,000 dollars to purchase a painting the authenticity of which was in dispute.

Here, the Bill of Sale states that the warranties induced Rogath to buy the Painting, but Rogath did not "expressly preserve his rights" under the Bill of Sale, as required by *Galli*. See 973 F.2d at 150. Accordingly, exactly what Siebenmann told Rogath is clearly crucial. On the other hand, what Alley may have told Rogath about the authenticity and provenance of the Painting is immaterial. Only if the seller, Siebenmann himself, informed Rogath of doubts about the provenance or challenges to authenticity will Rogath be deemed to have waived any claims for breach of warranty arising from the written representations appearing in the Bill of Sale. *See Galli*, 973 F.2d at 151.

As Rogath emphasizes, Siebenmann nowhere specifically alleges that he informed Rogath of his doubts about the authenticity and provenance of the Painting. He merely alluded to the "controversy" or "problems" with the Marlborough Gallery. Still, Siebenmann's testimony, however ambiguous, may justify the inference that Rogath knew more than he now claims to have known when he entered into the Bill of Sale.

At the very least, there is indisputable ambiguity in the affidavits about the pivotal exchange between Rogath and Siebenmann. We are satisfied that genuine issues of fact persist. In this posture, we must draw all reasonable inferences in Siebenmann's favor. Accordingly, as regards the Marlborough challenge, summary judgment on Rogath's claims for breach of the warranties of provenance and no challenges to authenticity is inappropriate.

3. What Sylvester Said

Sylvester's doubts about the Painting also cannot justify summary judgment for Rogath, but for different reasons. Siebenmann was aware that "Sylvester advised Miller not to proceed with the purchase of the Painting because of the 'Marlborough objection and that he wasn't sure himself of the authenticity of the painting.'" Siebenmann did not claim to have disclosed to Rogath Sylvester's statement. Indeed, in his affidavit opposing Rogath's summary judgment motion, Siebenmann stated that he did not consider Sylvester's doubts to be a challenge. Siebenmann's nondisclosure could constitute a breach of warranty—but only if Sylvester's statement was a "challenge" to authenticity. We conclude that the question of whether Sylvester's statement constituted a challenge poses factual issues for trial.

A contractual term is ambiguous where it may be ascribed "conflicting reasonable interpretations." *Mellon Bank, N.A. v. United Bank Corp. of N.Y.*, 31 F.3d 113, 116 (2d Cir. 1994). "As a general matter, we have held that when a contract is ambiguous, its interpretation becomes a question of fact and summary judgment is inappropriate." *Id.*

Although the parties apparently agree as to what Sylvester said, reasonable minds could differ as to whether what he said constituted a challenge apart from the Marlborough challenge. Sylvester's recommendation that the buyer not proceed "because of the Marlborough objection" could reasonably be interpreted as merely advice to heed the Marlborough challenge. Further, a rational juror could interpret the statement that "[Sylvester] wasn't sure" as evincing an ambivalence on the part of Sylvester that did not rise to the level of a challenge, especially given that Sylvester himself had not seen the Painting, but only photographs of it.

In this context, moreover, the term may well be a specialized one. It is hardly clear as a matter of law that "challenge" includes every mention by one person of the fact that a challenge has been made by another person (or, for example, that it would include Anita Goldstein's statement that "everybody is afraid of the authenticity" of the Painting). Nor is it clear as a matter of law whether the term "challenge" would include an expression of uncertainty by someone who had never seen the painting in question. If Siebenmann proffers art-industry or other evidence as to the meaning of this ambiguous contract term, its meaning will be a question for the jury at trial. *See In Time Prods., Ltd. v. Toy Biz, Inc.*, 38 F.3d 660, 665 (2d Cir. 1994)

B. No Alternate Basis for the Damages Award

The district court also concluded that Siebenmann breached the warranty of ownership of the Painting. The court did not specify, however, whether this breach contributed to the collapse of the resale to Acquavella. Was there a cause and effect relationship? We cannot say, based on the evidence before us, that the breach of this warranty resulted in the failed Acquavella sale and caused Rogath's damages.

It appears from the record that Acquavella was more concerned over whether Bacon was the painter than whether Siebenmann was the owner of the Painting. In aborting the sale, Acquavella sent to Rogath a copy of a fax from Valerie Beston, the managing director of the Marlborough Gallery, in which Beston opines at the outset of her letter that the Painting is an "outright fake." There is also some evidence that the Acquavella may have been concerned with the provenance of the Painting. In her letter, Beston goes on to describe the provenance as "dubious." There is no evidence, however, that Acquavella's concern about Siebenmann's title to the Painting fueled the failed sale. …

CONCLUSION

The order granting Rogath's motion for partial summary judgment is vacated, and the case is remanded to the district court for disposition not inconsistent with this opinion.

NOTES AND QUESTIONS

1. **Breach of an Express Warranty Action Under UCC § 2-313.** "To recover money damages under the theory of express warranty in Texas, one must prove: (1) an affirmation of fact or promise made by the seller to the buyer relating to the goods; (2) such affirmation of fact or promise became a part of the basis of the bargain; (3) that the injured party, in making the purchase, relied on the representations, affirmations of fact, or promises; (4) that the goods sold by the seller failed to comply with the promises or affirmations of fact made by the seller; (5) that the buyer, because of such failure, was financially injured; and (6) that such failure to comply was a proximate cause of the financial injury suffered by the buyer. *See* Sec. 2.313, TEXAS BUSINESS AND COMMERCE CODE AND THE UNIFORM COMMERCIAL CODE Comment following Sec. 2.313." *General Supply & Equipment Co., Inc. v. Phillips*, 490 S.W.2d 913, 917 (Tex. Civ. App.—Tyler 1972, writ ref'd n.r.e.)

2. **Establishing Proof of Reliance Under UCC § 2-313**. As the Second Circuit stresses in *Rogath*, courts are divided over whether a buyer/plaintiff must build a *prima facie* case under section 2-311 by providing evidence of the buyer's reliance on the seller's promises, descriptions, or statement of facts. In *Compaq*

Computer Corp. v. Lapray, 135 S.W.3d 657, 675 (Tex. 2004), the Supreme Court of Texas discussed the conflict:

> Section 2-313 of the UCC addresses the creation of express warranties. That section incorporates a reliance element, providing that a seller's statement that is "part of the basis of the bargain" creates an express warranty. U.C.C. § 2-313. This provision has been adopted verbatim by all states except Maine, Michigan, and South Carolina, which adopted the section with minor changes. Although the official comments to section 2-313 provide that "no particular reliance on such statements need be shown in order to weave them into the fabric of the agreement," U.C.C. § 2-313 cmt. 3 (1989), it appears that this suggestion is not uniformly followed. Like the notice requirement, state courts have interpreted this reliance element differently. *See McManus v. Fleetwood Enters., Inc.,* 320 F.3d 545, 550 (5th Cir. 2003) ("There is a split of authority [over whether [the "basis of the bargain"] wording ... is meant to dispense with the common law's requirement of reliance in express warranty cases.") ...
>
> Some courts have concluded that reliance by a buyer on a seller's statements (even those contained in a warranty) remains an essential element of a breach of express warranty claim under the basis of the bargain test as set forth in the UCC. ... Other courts hold that under the UCC, reliance is no longer required and a buyer may recover on an express warranty even if the buyer never actually received a copy of the warranty and was unaware of its existence. (citations omitted). Still other states have not decided whether reliance is required, nor what the "basis of the bargain" actually means. ...
>
> Under Texas law, we have said: "Reliance is ... not only relevant to, but an element of proof of, plaintiffs' claims of breach of express warranty (to a certain extent). ..." In *American Tobacco Co. v. Grinnell*, 951 S.W.2d 420, 436 (Tex. 1997), we held: "[A]n express warranty claim also requires a form of reliance. The Uniform Commercial Code provides that an express warranty is created when "[a]ny affirmation of fact or promise [is] made by the seller to the buyer which relates to the goods and becomes part of the basis of the bargain." TEX. BUS. & COM. CODE § 2.313(a)(1) (emphasis added). "Basis of the bargain" loosely reflects the common-law express warranty requirement of reliance.

3. **Proof of Reliance Under UCC § 2-313—Before or After the Sale of Goods?** The Supreme Court of Texas also discussed a corollary reliance-related conflict *Lapray* at 675:

Another difference among states is the timing of reliance and, specifically, whether warranties not relied on prior to the sale can form the basis of an express warranty claim. *Compare Downie v. Abex Corp.*, 741 F.2d 1235, 1238 n. 1, 1240 (10th Cir. 1984) (under both Utah and California law, UCC "clearly contemplates that warranties made after the sale may become a basis of the bargain"), and *Autzen v. John C. Taylor Lumber Sales, Inc.*, 572 P.2d 1322, 1326 (Or. 1977) (post-sale survey of a used boat can create an express warranty if it "induce[d] and [was] intended by the Seller to induce Buyer's satisfaction with the agreement just made"), *with DiIenno v. Libbey Glass Div., Owens–Ill., Inc.*, 668 F. Supp. 373, 376 (D. De. 1987) (express warranty claim failed where there was no evidence plaintiff saw the warranty before making her purchase), *Ciba–Geigy Corp. v. Alter*, 834 S.W.2d 136, 147 (Ark. 1992) (breach of express warranty claim failed when plaintiff did not recall reading the express warranty before making his purchase), *Schmaltz v. Nissen*, 431 N.W.2d 657, 661 (S.D. 1988) (language on seed bags could not have been basis of the bargain, when purchasers did not read the language until after the sale was completed), *Cuthbertson v. Clark Equip. Co.*, 448 A.2d 315 (Me. 1982) (owner's manual not seen prior to sale could not be part of "basis of the bargain"), and *Anderson v. Heron Eng'g Co.*, 198 Colo. 391, 604 P.2d 674, 676 (1979) (brochure must have been seen or relied on at time of purchase).

4. **Breach of Express Warranty Actions and Attorney's Fees Under UCC § 2-313.** Consider the Texas Supreme Court's analysis in *Medical City Dallas, Ltd. v. Carlisle Corp.*, 251 S.W.3d 55, 59 (Tex. 2008):

The Uniform Commercial Code (UCC) governs Medical City's express warranty claim. Because the transaction here involved a sale of goods, the Uniform Commercial Code (UCC)—as adopted in TEXAS' BUSINESS AND COMMERCE CODE—applies. *See* TEX. BUS. & COM. CODE §§ 2.101–.725 and § 2.313. However, the UCC sections and comments dealing with remedies for breach of warranty, adopted verbatim in Texas, are silent on the issue of attorney's fees. *See, e.g.,* TEX. BUS. & COM. CODE §§ 2.714–2.715 and cmt. (providing for consequential damages to a buyer in a breach of warranty action, but failing to indicate in the comment whether attorney's fees are considered either consequential or incidental damages). ... [B]ecause Texas' UCC provisions and the parties' warranties are silent on the issue, section 38.001 of the Civil Practice and Remedies Code provides the only basis for an award of attorney's fees

> here. We thus examine the nature of the claim to determine whether an express warranty claim is a suit based on an oral or written contract. …
>
> [B]reach of warranty and breach of contract are distinct causes of action with separate remedies. *See, e.g.,* TEX. BUS. & COM. CODE §§ 2.711, 2.714 (providing remedies for breach of contract and breach of warranty respectively). We held as much in *Southwestern Bell Telephone Co. v. FDP Corp.*, 811 S.W.2d 572, 576 (Tex. 1991), when we stated that "[t]he UCC recognizes that breach of contract and breach of warranty are not the same cause of action." But while an express warranty is a distinct claim, it is nonetheless a part of the basis of a bargain and is contractual in nature. *See* TEX. BUS. & COM. CODE § 2.313(a) ("Any affirmation of fact or promise made by the seller to the buyer which relates to the goods and becomes part of the basis of the bargain creates an express warranty that the goods shall conform to the affirmation or promise.") … An express warranty is the result of a negotiated exchange and is a "creature of contract." *See, e.g., U.S. Pipe & Foundry Co. v. City of Waco*, 108 S.W.2d 432, 434 (Tex. 1937), and 18 WILLISTON ON CONTRACTS § 52:45. …
>
> Moreover, the damages recoverable here support our conclusion that the claim is based in contract. … It is not surprising, then, that we have previously suggested that attorney's fees are recoverable when an express warranty is breached. *See PPG Indus., Inc. v. JMB/Houston Ctrs. Partners L.P.*, 146 S.W.3d 79, 92 (Tex. 2004). … The only cases to hold that breach of express warranty is not founded on contract for the purposes of an award of attorney's fees are unpersuasive. To the extent these cases are inconsistent with our holding today, they are disapproved.

B. Proof of an Implied Warranty of Merchantability Under § 2-314

Again, common-law courts have created, interpreted, and enforced multiple types of implied warranties. Article 2 of the Uniform Commercial Code, however, has codified only two of those. By operation of law, an implied warranty of merchantability attaches to the sale-of-goods contracts. Section 2-314 outlines a complex web of rules which govern the interpretation and enforcement of implied warranties of merchantability under the UCC. That section reads:

§ 2-314. Implied Warranty: Merchantability; Usage of Trade

(1) Unless excluded or modified (Section 2-316), a warranty that the goods shall be merchantable is implied in a contract for their sale if the seller is a merchant with respect to goods of that kind. Under this section the serving for value of food or drink to be consumed either on the premises or elsewhere is a sale.

(2) Goods to be merchantable must be at least such as

(a) pass without objection in the trade under the contract description; *and*

(b) in the case of fungible goods, are of fair average quality within the description; *and*

(c) are fit for the ordinary purposes for which such goods are used; *and*

(d) run, within the variations permitted by the agreement, of even kind, quality and quantity within each unit and among all units involved; *and*

(e) are adequately contained, packaged, and labeled as the agreement may require; *and*

(f) conform to the promise or affirmations of fact made on the container or label if any.

(3) Unless excluded or modified (Section 2-316) other implied warranties may arise from course of dealing or usage of trade.

Reading section 2-314 extremely carefully, one discovers immediately that the language in section 2-314(1) presents a more-than-academic question: whether a buyer or seller must provide *prima facie* evidence of an implied warranty of merchantability in a breach-of-warranty action? The answer is not straightforward. The general rule does not require proof, since a warranty of merchantability is implied in law. On the other hand, the language in section 2-314(1) contains several provisos, which color or create exceptions to the general rule. First, an implied warranty of merchantability is implied in law only if a "seller is a merchant." Consequently, a buyer might have to prove that the defendant is a merchant before successfully establishing a *prima facie* case and receiving breach-of-warranty damages. Second, section 2-316(2) allows parties to a sale-of-goods contract to exclude or modify implied warranties of merchantability. Later in this chapter, such exclusions and modifications are discussed more fully.

Although the rules in section 2-314 are generally easy to understand, some of the words and phrases are not. In section 2-314(2), the drafters fashioned an exceedingly complicated definition of "merchantability"—inserting the conjunction "and" in multiple places. For example, to be "merchantable," goods must satisfy six criteria—each containing highly ambiguous terms. Section 2-314(2)(a) states that goods which are described in the contract must "*pass without objection* in the trade." Also, under section 2-314(2)(b) goods must be of "*fair average quality* within the description" if they are "fungible goods."

Furthermore, Comment 6—which accompanies section 2-314—adds to the confusion. It states that the statutory definition of "merchantability" is not exhaustive, leaving open the possibility that other factors may be included in the definition. Courts, however, have been generally clear about one issue: Under section 2-314(1)(2), the term "merchantable" does not mean "perfect." *Nassau Suffolk White Trucks, Inc. v. Twin County Transit Mix Corp.*, 403 N.Y.S.2d. 322, 325 (N.Y. App. Div. 1978). In *Hannon v Original Gunite Aquatech Pools, Inc.*, 434 N.E.2d 611, 616 (Mass. 1982), the Massachusetts Supreme Court declared the following principle emphatically: "There is no implied warranty that the goods shall be of the best or even a very high quality."

Just as important, the common-law warranty of fitness and quality as well as section 2-314(2)(c) of the UCC require goods to be reasonably fit for their ordinary purposes. *Matulunas v. Baker*, 569 S.W.2d 791, 795 (Mo. Ct. App. 1978). But, the UCC does not provide an exceptionally clear definition of "fit for the ordinary purposes." Consequently, over the years, large numbers of litigants have asked courts to give favorable pro-buyers and pro-sellers interpretations of that phrase. The next cases illustrate how two courts determined whether certain goods were statutorily "fit" for their intended use.

1. "Goods Fit for an Ordinary Purpose"

Flippo v. Mode O'Day Frock Shops of Hollywood
449 S.W.2d 692
(Ark. 1970)

HARRIS, CHIEF JUSTICE. This litigation in occasioned by a spider bite. Gladys Flippo, appellant herein, went into a ladies clothing store in Batesville, operated by Rosie Goforth, and known as Mode O'Day Frock Shops of Hollywood. Mrs. Flippo tried on two pairs of pants, of slacks, which were shown to her by Mrs. Goforth. The first pair proved to be too small, and according to appellant's evidence, when Mrs. Flippo put on the second pair, she suddenly felt a burning sensation on her thigh; she immediately removed the pants, shook them, and a spider fell to the floor which was then stepped upon. An examination of her thigh revealed a reddened area, which progressively grew worse. Mrs. Flippo was subsequently hospitalized for approximately 30 days. According to her physician, the injury was caused by the bite of a brown recluse spider.

Suit for damages was instituted against Mode O'Day Frock Shops and Rosie Goforth, the complaint asserting three grounds for recovery, first that a pair of slacks in a defective condition (by reason of the presence of a poisonous spider), and unreasonably dangerous was sold to appellant; second, that both appellees were guilty of several acts of negligence, and third, that there was an implied warranty that the slacks were fit for the purpose for which they were purchased, though actually not fit, because of the poisonous spider concealed therein.

On trial, the court refused requested instructions offered by appellant on theories of implied warranty, and strict tort liability, and instructed the jury only on the issue of appellees' alleged negligence as the proximate cause of the injury. The jury returned a verdict for both appellees, and judgment was entered accordingly. From the judgment so entered, appellant brings this appeal, not however, appellant from the finding of no negligence; instead, the appeal is based entirely upon the court's refusal to submit the case upon implied warranty and strict tort liability theories.

Accordingly, for reversal, it is first urged that "there was sufficient evidence to justify a finding that Mrs. Flippo was injured by goods unfit for their intended use, supplied by a merchant with respect to goods of that kind, and therefore the trial court erred in refusing to instruct upon the law of implied warranty of merchantability."

It might be said at the outset that appellant has filed a very thorough and comprehensive brief in support of the positions taken; however, we are unable to agree with the views presented under the circumstances of this case. As pointed out by appellant, there was ample evidence to support a finding that Mrs. Flippo suffered a bite by a brown recluse spider concealed on the slacks furnished her by Mrs. Goforth (it is not conceded by appellees that the bite occurred in this manner). Appellant says: "If that be true, then appellant submits that such an article of clothing is not reasonably fit for use as an article of clothing and is thus not merchantable."

It is contended that appellees were bound by the implied warranty of merchantability imposed by Ark. Stat. Ann. § 85-2-314 (Add. 1961), this statute providing that, in order to be merchantable, the goods must, inter alia, be fit for the ordinary purposes for which such goods are used. Appellant argues that an article of clothing which conceals a venomous creature is certainly unfit for use, and therefore at the time the slacks were handed to Mrs. Flippo, the garment was unfit for the use for which it was intended, and there was accordingly a breach of the implied warranty of merchantability under either the statute or common law.

We cannot agree that the law of implied warranty of merchantability is applicable to a case of this nature. The pair of pants itself was fit for the ordinary purposes for which stretch pants are used; there was nothing wrong from a manufacturing standpoint. In fact, the evidence reflects that Mrs. Flippo bought this particular pair after being bitten, and she has worn and laundered them since the accident. There is absolutely no evidence that the goods were defective in any manner. It is, of course, readily apparent that the spider was not a part of the product, and there is no evidence that either the manufacturer or retailer had any control of the spider, or caused it to be in the pants.

Mrs. Goforth testified that the Mode O'Day company had six or eight factories, and that she received the clothing on consignment, the goods belonging to the company until sold. She said that the company products have an identifying tag sewn in; that occasionally, the parent company purchases items from other companies. The witness stated that the pants tried on by Mrs. Flippo did not have a Mode O'Day tag, and were manufactured by some other company.

Mrs. Goforth said she receives the shipments once a week in pasteboard cartons sealed with tape, and that upon receiving the cartons, she immediately opens them, places the garments on plastic hangers, and hangs them out. The cartons are delivered by truck line, and the witness stated that the slacks in question had been in the store for some time in excess of 20 days.

The evidence reflected that Mrs. Flippo had, at some previous time, been in the business of raising chickens, and owned a chicken house. She said that she had seen spiders in this chicken house, though not at the time chickens were being raised. It is suggested by appellees that she could have brought the spider into the store with her.

Irrespective of whether the spider attached itself to the garment in Kansas City, or in Batesville, it was not a part of the garment. The three cases cited by appellant as authority for the common law implied warranty of merchantability, all deal with a defective product, which is not the situation in the present litigation. Perhaps our position can best be made clear by simply stating that the spider was not a part of the manufactured article, and the injury to Mrs. Flippo was caused by the spider—and not the product. We find no cause of action under either the statute or the common law.

Nor can we agree that the trial court erred in refusing to instruct the jury upon the principles of strict tort liability. In RESTATEMENT (SECOND), TORTS § 402A, which deals with products that are defective, and thus made unreasonably dangerous to the user or consumer, we find:

> (1) One who sells any product in a defective condition unreasonably dangerous to the user or consumer or to his property is subject to liability for physical harm thereby caused to the ultimate user or consumer, or to his property, if
>
> (a) the seller is engaged in the business of selling such a product, and

> (b) it is expected to and does reach the user or consumer without substantial change in the condition in which it is sold. …

It is at once obvious that the product sold in the instant case was a pair of slacks, and the slacks were not in a defective condition; nor were they unreasonably dangerous; in fact, they were not dangerous at all; still further, the slacks did not cause any physical harm to Mrs. Flippo. Without elaboration, it is at once apparent that subheadings (a) and (b) are not applicable to this litigation, for no one can really contend that the spider was a part of the product, nor can anyone do more than guess at when the spider attached itself to the slacks.

Appellant points out that the lack of privity between a plaintiff and defendant is no longer a defense in any action brought against a manufacturer or seller of goods to recover damages for breach of warranty, or for negligence "if the plaintiff was a person whom the manufacturer or seller might reasonably have expected to use, consume, or be affected by the goods." *See* Ark. Stat. Ann. § 85-2-318.1. This court had already held that the doctrine of privity should not be a shield against a breach of warranty action when the suit was instituted by an employee of the original purchaser. *See Delta Oxygen Company v. Scott*, 383 S.W.2d 885 (Ark. 1964).

She asserts that it is now entirely logical for this court to adopt the rule of strict tort liability. In cases involving the sale and use of alleged defective products, we have pointed out that there must be substantial evidence of negligence, such negligence being a proximate cause of the injuries sustained before recovery will be permitted. *See, inter alia, Kapp v. Bob Sullivan Chevrolet Company*, 234 Ark. 395, 353 S.W.2d 5; *Ford Motor Company v. Fish*, 232 Ark. 270, 335 S.W.2d 713. In one case, *Chapman Chemical Company v. Taylor et al.*, 215 Ark. 630, 222 S.W.2d 820, we applied the rule of strict liability to the use of the substance, 2-4-D, stating:

> If one casts into the air a substance which he knows may do damage to others, and in some circumstances will certainly do so, principles of elementary justice, as well as the best public policy require that he know how far the substance will carry or be conveyed through the air and what damage it will do in the path of its journey, and if he releases such a substance either from ignorance of, or in indifference to the damage that may be done, the rule of strict liability should be applied.

Were we inclined to a more liberal view of the theory of strict tort liability, it would not be applied in this case, for we have no hesitancy in stating that the facts in the instant litigation do not support the submission of the case on that theory. This case was properly submitted upon the issue of negligence, and it would have been improper for the court to have given the instructions sought by appellant. Affirmed.

2. *"Unfit Goods for an Ordinary Purpose"*

Martel v. Duffy-Mott Corporation
166 N.W.2d 541
(Mich. Ct. App. 1968)

Levin, Presiding Judge. The plaintiffs appeal a directed verdict granted at the conclusion of their proofs. The complaint charged the defendant—Duffy-Mott Corporation—with both negligence and breach of implied warranty of merchantability. On appeal the plaintiffs rely solely on the statutory implied warranty that to be merchantable goods must be fit for the ordinary purposes for which they are used. M.C.L.A. § 440.2314(2)(c).

Edwina Martel served her sons—Brian, 8, and Gary, 10—Mott's applesauce as part of their meal. Brian mixed his applesauce with the rest of his food and consumed a sizeable portion of the mixture. Gary ate the applesauce separately and after a spoonful or 2 reported to his mother that the applesauce tasted funny. She tasted and smelled the applesauce—at the trial she and Gary testified that it both tasted and smelled bad—and immediately telephoned the poison control center at Children's Hospital which, on the basis of her description of the applesauce, instructed her to take the children and remaining applesauce to the nearest hospital. When she arrived the applesauce was examined by hospital personnel who decided to and did pump the children's stomachs. Mrs. Martel was advised to watch the children carefully that night for certain symptoms. These symptoms did not appear and no other ill effects were suffered.

There was testimony the children were apprehensive on the way to the hospital although neither Mrs. Martel nor her sons knew of the imminent stomach pumping until after they reached the hospital. Mrs. Martel conceded the children may have gagged because of excitement or fright and not necessarily because of a deleterious substance in the applesauce. On the way to the hospital the boys said they were having a hard time breathing and asked to open the windows. Later they were chilled and asked that the windows be closed.

The boys testified that stomach pumping involves having a tube put through one's nose and swallowing it; the pumping then commences and is a very unpleasant experience. There was also testimony that prior to this incident, applesauce was one of the favorites of the boys and was served 3 or 4 times a week, but since the incident they have refused to eat applesauce at all and even shy away from apples. When asked about their apprehensions, one of the boys stated, "I don't seem to trust it anymore" and the other said, "I don't want to get my stomach pumped again." The trial judge ruled that the plaintiffs had failed to establish a *prima facie* case:

> The court must first find that there was sufficient testimony upon which reasonable minds might differ, that there is some testimony from which individuals might legitimately infer that the applesauce contained a deleterious matter; secondly, because of the deleterious matter the minors no longer like applesauce. This, in effect, as the court sees it, is basing an inference upon an inference, which is not sufficient to go to a jury.

We reverse and remand for a new trial.

When Michigan adopted the Uniform Commercial Code it enacted the following implied warranty of merchantability for transactions in goods: "'Goods to be merchantable must be at least such as ... are fit for the ordinary purposes for which such goods are used." M.C.L.A. § 440.2314(2)(c). The language of this implied warranty parallels prior law. *See* C.L.1948, § 440.15 and authorities hereafter cited. The trial court erroneously assumed that food is necessarily "fit for the ordinary purposes" if it is not deleterious. There was indeed no evidence that the applesauce contained any deleterious substance. However, it was not therefore to be regarded as merchantable as a matter of law.

The statements in some of the cases that the implied warranty insures that food is "free from foreign, poisonous or deleterious substances" were entirely appropriate on the facts of those cases. Still earlier statements can be found to the effect that there is an implied warranty of "wholesomeness in the sale of provisions for direct consumption" and that they be "fit for food." Be that as it may, it is now settled in this and other jurisdictions, that factors other than those concerned exclusively with the safety of the product may be important in determining a product's merchantability and that recovery may be allowed on the basis of breach of implied warranty of merchantability for damage other than personal injuries. *Spence v. Three Rivers Builders & Masonry Supply*, 353 Mich. 120, 126 (1958).

In this case there was testimony—by persons well experienced in eating applesauce—that the applesauce tasted and smelled bad. From such direct testimony, the jury would have been justified in concluding that the applesauce did in fact taste and smell bad and was inedible. We also note that the hospital personnel, on the basis of their examination of the applesauce, decided to pump the boys' stomachs. If the applesauce was inedible, it was not fit for the ordinary purposes for which it is used.

If the jury were to find that the applesauce was inedible, it could also properly conclude the applesauce so found to be inedible caused the boys to gag and to have their stomachs pumped, whether the precise cause of the gagging was excitement, fright or microbes and irrespective of whether the hospital attendants' decision to pump was well-advised or a mistake in judgment. We are not prepared to say that what is alleged to have occurred was not a proximate consequence of the experiences described. Whether the defendant's breach was a material element and a substantial factor in bringing about the alleged injuries is a question for the trier of fact. It is, of course, open to the defendant to suggest an alternative theory of causation.

Concern has been expressed that if recovery is allowed solely on the basis of a plaintiff's testimony that a manufacturer's food tasted bad or smelled bad, the "floodgates" will have been opened to countless spurious claims. When that occurs, if it does, they can be closed. In the meantime, there is no good reason why in the food area we should so limit the implied warranty that food is merchantable even if inedible as long as not deleterious, when as to every other commodity we apply the "fit for the ordinary purpose for which used" test without a showing that the lack of fitness represents a peril of physical harm.

Nor does any reason appear why biological or laboratory proof should be required as part of plaintiff's case. Accused persons have been convicted and sentenced to serve long terms on one eyewitness's identification testimony even though the witness's view may have been fleeting, the witness was excited at the time of the incident, or there were other doubt engendering circumstances. A witness may make a mistake in identifying a person because of bad eyesight, ineptitude or preconceived notions—he may lie. In a case such as this one, a witness may mistakenly identify a food substance because he has an uneducated palate, or at the time is subject to some systematical disturbance he too may lie.

It is the business of juries to determine the credibility of witnesses, to sift out the conflicting claims and to decide the disputed issues. If they go too far afield, it is the trial judge's and our responsibility to correct error. We should not deny recovery of just claims because of fear we cannot recognize and exclude the malingerer. We have also concluded that, if upon the new trial we have ordered, the jury finds the applesauce unfit for consumption, this is a "proper case" under M.C.L.A. § 440.2714(3), 2715(2)(b) for allowance of "consequential damages," including "injury to person or property."

It is a close question whether the plaintiffs should be permitted to recover as part of their consequential damages for past and future loss of enjoyment of applesauce. Applesauce is but one of a large variety of desserts, most of which other desserts can, no doubt, we take judicial notice, fill the gastronomical void created when plaintiffs lost their taste for applesauce. Plaintiffs do not claim permanent injury or loss of taste or appetite in general, or loss of ability to consume or enjoy a basic nutriment or variety of food substances. We could well draw a line—no recovery for loss of enjoyment of applesauce and put a label on it: the claimed damages are "remote," "uncertain," "conjectural," etc. But we decline to do so.

More and more of the food sold to the public come in cans, frozen, prepared, and even precooked ready to eat. Whole meals can be bought all prepared, ready or almost ready to go on the table. We do not think it a sensible use of the time of the profession or of the bench to construct a body of law as to which foods are of such importance that loss of enjoyment is compensable and those which, as a matter of law, are not of that rank. We think it sounder to permit a plaintiff who can convince a jury that the food product he consumed was inedible and in consequence he no longer enjoys eating it, to recover damages, including damages for loss of enjoyment, if he can additionally convince the jury that a true loss was suffered and that it should add a dollar amount therefor. In some cases loss of enjoyment may be real and substantial, an injury not to be made light of.

We see no need to create rules of law in a narrow area that the good sense of the average jury can handle with greater dispatch and probably sounder results. If a recovery seems disproportionate, the corrective remedies for excessive verdicts are available.

Reversed. Remanded for a new trial. ...

NOTES AND QUESTIONS

1. **Establishing a Prima Facie Case Under UCC 2-314.** To establish a breach of implied warranty of merchantability in North Carolina, a plaintiff must prove the following elements: (1) an implied warranty of merchantability attached to the sale and purchase of certain goods; (2) the goods were defective at the time of sale; (3) the defective goods caused the buyer's injury and loss; and (4) damages were suffered as a result. *DeWitt v. Eveready Battery Co., Inc.*, 565 S.E.2d 140, 147 (N.C. 2002). On the other hand, to prevail in a breach of warranty of merchantability action in Delaware, a plaintiff must prove: "(1) that a merchant sold the goods; (2) which were defective at the time of sale; (3) causing injury to the ultimate consumer; (4) the proximate cause of which was the defective nature of the goods; and (5) that the seller received notice of the injury." *Reybold Group, Inc. v. Chemprobe Tech., Inc.*, 721 A.2d 1267, 1269 (Del. 1998).

2. **Standards for Determining Whether or Not Restaurant Food Is Merchantable Under UCC 2-314**. In *Hochberg v.*

O'Donnell's Restaurant, Inc., 272 A.2d 846, 847–48 (D.C. Cir. 1971), the court of appeals presented this analysis:

> It is apparent that we have before us the question of what test should be applied under the doctrine of implied warranty where an injury is incurred by a patron from an object in food served him in a restaurant. Under the Uniform Commercial Code-Sale—D.C. Code 1967, § 28:2-314—there is an implied warranty that food sold and consumed on a premises or elsewhere is "fit for the ordinary purposes for which such goods are used." ... Both parties agree there is a split in the authorities throughout the country [over] what test should be applied where an injury is suffered from an object in food or drink consumed in a restaurant. Some courts hold there is no breach of implied warranty on the part of a restaurant if the object in the food causing the injury was "natural" to the food served. On the other hand, if the object was "foreign" to the food there may be a recovery. This has come to be known as the "foreign-natural" test. On the other side are authorities which hold that ... the test is what should reasonably be expected by the consumer to be in the food served to him. This is known as the "reasonable expectation" test.

3. **Cause of Action and Proof of a "Defect".** Proof of a defect is an essential element of a claim for breach of warranty of merchantability. In *Brink v. Ethicon, Inc.*, 2003 WL 23277272, at *2 (Del. Super. Ct. Dec. 9, 2003), the court stated: "It is clear [that] 'some evidence of the existence of a defect at the time of delivery is an essential element of a cause of action.'" What is the test? Consider the court's answer in *DiIenno v. Libbey Glass Div., Owens–Illinois, Inc.*, 668 F. Supp. 373, 377 (C.C.D. Del. 1987): "A defect may take the form of a design defect, where an entire product line is designed improperly, or a manufacturing defect, where a product line is properly designed but a particular item was manufactured incorrectly." But, consider the federal district court's discussion of Vermont law in *Moffitt v. Icynene, Inc.*, 407 F. Supp. 2d 591, 599 (C.C.D. Vt. 2005): "The warranty of merchantability under the UCC is equivalent to strict product liability. Vermont has adopted the strict product liability principles found in RESTATEMENT (SECOND) OF TORTS § 402A. Hence, establishing a breach of this warranty requires showing a defect in the product and causation. ... [T]he product defect must have existed when the product left the defendant's control."

C. Proof of an Implied Warranty of Fitness for a Particular Purpose

Section 2-315 of the UCC codifies common-law rules regarding the enforcement of an implied warranty of fitness for a particular purpose. The statute reads:

> Where the seller at the time of contracting has reason to know any particular purpose for which the goods are required and that the buyer is relying on the seller's skill or judgment to select or furnish suitable goods, there is unless excluded or modified under the next section an implied warranty that the goods shall be fit for such purpose.

Although section 2-315 is comparatively a short statute, it contains multiple important words and phrases. First, it creates arguably an exceptionally heavy burden for a disgruntled buyer. To be successful in court, the buyer must prove a key element: The defendant/seller knew—when the parties *were fashioning the sale-of-goods contract*—that the buyer was purchasing goods for a *particular purpose*. Why would this requirement create a substantial load for the buyer? Remembering the "battle of forms" discussion, buyers and sellers normally exchange forms—purchase orders and acknowledgments. Therefore, in light of the competing language in the respective forms, a buyer's attempting to establish precisely when the contract was created is not a simple task.

Furthermore, section 2-315 presents another hurdle for the buyer: Proving that a seller had *knowledge* of the buyer's particular needs—*when the contract was being created*—can be a problem. If a buyer does not craft an intelligent and informative, say, purchase order which discloses the buyer's particular needs, the buyer's likelihood of prevailing diminishes considerably. But even more problematic for the buyer, he must prove that he was *relying on the seller's skill or judgment*. Put simply, the buyer must prove reliance. Yet, buyers as well as sellers prevail under section 2-315. How do they win and lose lawsuits involving breach of implied warranty of fitness for a particular purpose? The following cases provide some insight.

1. "Goods Must Be Fit for a Particular Purpose"

Rubin v. Marshall Field & Company
597 N.E.2d 688
(Ill. Ct. App. 1992)

JUSTICE MCCORMICK DELIVERED THE OPINION OF THE COURT: Plaintiff, Cynthia Rubin, sued defendants, Marshall Field & Company (Fields) and Princess Marcella Borghese, Inc., (Princess Marcella) for injuries caused by cosmetics that defendants marketed. A jury awarded plaintiff damages for breach of implied warranty of fitness for a particular purpose and for violation of the Illinois Consumer Fraud Act. Defendants appeal from the judgment entered on the verdict and from the trial court's award of attorney fees.

On April 5, 1986, plaintiff purchased instant eye makeup remover distributed by Princess Marcella from Fields. That night she used the product to remove her eye makeup. Her eyelids and the skin around her eyes turned red, became taut and rough and started to sting. She washed the skin repeatedly and kept a cold washrag on her eyes all night. Two days later, when the burning did not subside, she called an ophthalmologist, and she went to see him the next day. He told her that she had contact dermatitis and he prescribed an ointment.

A few weeks later, because the burning and roughness of her eyelids persisted, plaintiff decided to see Dr. Katherine Wier, a dermatologist. Dr. Wier prescribed a similar ointment and told plaintiff that the chemical which was causing the burning would remain in her system for three or four months. The stinging subsided, but plaintiff could not wear eye makeup again regularly until summer 1987. When she tried to wear makeup again before that, her eyelids turned bright red and began swelling upon removal of the makeup.

In March 1988, plaintiff filed her four-count complaint. In December 1989, she amended her complaint to six counts, charging defendants in count I with violation of the Illinois Consumer Fraud and Deceptive Business Practices Act (Ill. Rev. Stat. 1985, ch. 121 1/2, par. 261 *et seq.*) She also sought to recover for her personal injuries on theories of breach of express warranty (count II); breach of implied warranty (count III); strict products liability (count IV); negligence (count V); and common law fraud (count VI). Defendants did not object to the amendment of the complaint or to trial by jury on any count of the complaint.

At trial plaintiff testified that when she went to Fields on April 5, 1986, she was not especially shopping for cosmetics. While browsing she got into a conversation with Julianna Reiner, a sales clerk, and she told Reiner that she used Vaseline to remove her eye makeup. Reiner said Vaseline could clog her eye ducts and cause cataracts or other permanent eye damage. Reiner recommended Princess Marcella Borghese Instant Eye Make-Up Remover. Plaintiff asked if the product was safe and Reiner showed her the box, which said "recommended for all skin types." Reiner said, "If it wouldn't be safe for you, it wouldn't say this on the box." Relying on Reiner's representations, plaintiff purchased the product.

Defendants admit that Reiner was an agent for both defendants when she sold plaintiff the product. Reiner testified that she had no specific recollection of the transaction, but she never said anything about adverse effects of other products, and she "never use[d] the word [V]aseline, ever."

Dr. Wier testified that eyelid skin and genital skin is the most sensitive skin on the body, and very fair skin—like plaintiff's—is easily irritated. Dr. Wier could say with medical certainty that the makeup remover caused plaintiff's reaction, which was probably a primary irritant reaction compounded by an allergic reaction. Dr. Wier testified in her deposition that although the distinction is sometimes difficult to draw, an irritant reaction is an immediate skin reaction, like burning, which the irritant would cause on almost anyone's skin, while an allergic reaction is usually delayed and occurs only in persons with the allergy. She classified plaintiff's reaction as a primary irritant reaction because of the speed with which the reaction occurred. The detergent in the makeup remover was probably the irritant, opening the pores and allowing other chemicals, to which plaintiff was allergic, to penetrate the skin. She believed that some other people whose skin was as fair as plaintiff's would react adversely to the product, and "a few might have a similar disastrous reaction."

On cross-examination, Dr. Wier admitted that the detergent in the eye makeup remover was also used in at least three other products, including baby shampoo. She considered the eye makeup remover fairly safe.

Revlon, Inc.—which owns Princess Marcella—manufactured the eye makeup remover. Dr. Earl Brauer, vice-president of medical affairs for Revlon Research, testified that he tested the product plaintiff returned to defendants and found that it included only the proper chemicals with nothing extraneous added. He used the returned product in a skin patch test on 105 individuals chosen to represent the general population, and three had some reaction. He concluded that the product did not contain any irritant. He monitors personal injury complaints for Revlon products, and with more than 50,000 units of the eye makeup remover manufactured since 1978, plaintiff is the first consumer to complain of adverse effects. He said that she must have had an idiosyncratic allergic reaction because the product does not contain any irritants.

Dr. Brauer admitted that if the concentration of the detergent were increased sufficiently, it could possibly become an irritant, but he doubted that it would act as such even in high concentrations. He had never heard of Vaseline causing cataracts or similar problems to the eye. He agreed with Dr. Wier's conclusion that plaintiff's injuries were a reaction to the eye makeup remover.

Defendants moved for directed verdicts on all counts. Based on Dr. Wier's testimony that the product was fairly safe, the court granted the motion as to the strict product liability count. Plaintiff then withdrew the negligence count. The court denied the motion as to all other counts. The jury found for defendants on the express warranty and common law fraud counts, but it found for plaintiff on the implied warranty and Consumer Fraud Act counts. The jury awarded plaintiff damages of $1,250. … Defendants filed a post-trial motion for a new trial, arguing that plaintiff failed to prove a defect in the product and a pattern of deceptive practices. At oral argument on the motion, defendants also contended that plaintiffs had not shown an intent to deceive. The court denied the motion.

IMPLIED WARRANTY OF FITNESS FOR A PARTICULAR PURPOSE

Defendants argue that this court should reverse the judgment for plaintiff on the cause of action for breach of implied warranty because plaintiff did not prove that there was any defect in the makeup remover, and because the evidence showed that her reaction to the product was idiosyncratic. The UNIFORM COMMERCIAL CODE, ILL. REV. STAT. 1985, ch. 26, § 2-315, provides:

> Where the seller at the time of contracting has reason to know any particular purpose for which the goods are required and that the buyer is relying on the seller's skill or judgment to select or furnish suitable goods, there is unless excluded or modified under the next section an implied warranty that the goods shall be fit for such purpose.

Therefore, under the statute, plaintiff needed to prove (1) a sale of goods; (2) before the sale the seller had reason to know (a) a particular purpose for which plaintiff bought the goods, and (b) that she was relying on the seller's skill to select goods suitable for that purpose; and (3) the goods were not suitable for that particular purpose. The action is in contract, not tort, based on the implicit promises "derived from the interplay of a transaction's factual circumstances with the foreseeable expectations of a buyer … who is protected by law in those expectations." *Collins Co. v. Carboline Co.*, 125 Ill.2d 498, 508 (1988).

Some cases have added a requirement that plaintiff prove the product was defective. None of these cases makes reference to the UCC. The reasoning of these cases has been criticized. Anderson, in his commentary to the UCC, said:

> It is unfortunate that the warranty law has been so influenced by the tort law. With respect to negligence and strict tort, it is logical to require that there be a defect in the goods. In the case of warranty, it should be sufficient to impose liability that there has been a breach of warranty. In many cases, the breach of warranty consists of the presence of a defect that prevents the goods from being used. In other cases, the breach consists merely of failing to conform to the contract's standard. For example, when the seller delivers a red table

> instead of the green table required by the contract there is clearly a breach of warranty. Yet the red table was not defective in any intelligent sense of the word merely because it did not conform to the contract. ...
>
> Many of the cases seek to make a quantitative distinction as to how dangerous a product must be in order to be classified as "defective." Yet there is not a warranty in the [Uniform Commercial] Code that could not be broken by a perfectly made product. Conformity to the standard, satisfaction of the minimum criteria of the warranty of merchantability, [and] fitness for the particular purpose of the buyer are the criteria for determining whether warranties have been satisfied. Conversely, there is a breach of warranty by proof that these criteria have not been satisfied. Failures to satisfy the criteria are the significant matters without regard to whether the goods are 'defective' or without a flaw.
>
> The need for defining a defect becomes unnecessary insofar as warranty law is concerned if the matter is approached from the aspect of conformity or nonconformity, rather than in terms of whether there is a defect. The presence of a defect should be regarded as merely evidence of the fact that the goods are in such a condition that some warranty has been broken. If all the circumstances lead to the conclusion that the goods do not conform, there is a breach of warranty. It is unnecessary to determine whether what made them not conform is to be labeled a 'defect.' 3 ANDERSON, UNIFORM COMMERCIAL CODE, § 2-314:56, at 163 (3d ed. 1983), quoted in *Malawy v. Richards Manufacturing Co.*, 150 Ill.App.3d 549, 559–60 (1986).

We agree with Anderson and the appellate court in *Malawy*. Plaintiff's proof of breach of implied warranty was complete when she showed that defendants' agent implicitly warranted that the product would be safe for her skin in particular, and it was not suitable for that particular use. She did not need to prove in addition that the product was defective.

Defendants contend that they proved that plaintiff's reaction was idiosyncratic, and this provides an absolute defense to the implied warranty action. In *Stanton v. Sears Roebuck & Co.*, 312 Ill. App. 496, 501 (1942), the court said: "It can hardly be said that a vendor ... would be liable for a breach of an implied warranty solely because of the harmful effect due to a buyer's individual idiosyncrasy." ... Following *Stanton*, the court in *Presbrey v. Gillette Co.*, 105 Ill.App.3d 1082, 1091–92 (1982), found that the idiosyncratic consumer is generally barred from recovery under theories of strict liability, negligence or breach of warranty.

The court further held that "the rule of nonliability has been relaxed by some courts where the defendant has breached an express warranty of safety to the ultimate consumer." *Presbrey*, 105 Ill.App.3d at 1094. The court found that the evidence in that case could not support such a theory. Under *Stanton* and *Presbrey*, it appears that if plaintiff had no evidence of warranty beyond the fact that defendants offered the product for sale, her cause of action for breach of warranty would be defeated by proof that her reaction was idiosyncratic.

Plaintiff has presented considerable evidence beyond the sale itself to show that the warranty implied by defendants' acts in this case was far more specific. Plaintiff testified that after defendants' agent, Reiner, recommended the product, she asked whether the product would be safe for her. Reiner pointed to the box, which said "recommended for all skin types," and said "if it wouldn't be safe for you, it wouldn't say this on the box." Reiner could see plaintiff's skin and she knew of plaintiff's concern about the safety of the product for use on that skin. Under these specific factual circumstances, it is reasonable to infer a warranty that the product would not harm plaintiff's skin.

While an idiosyncratic reaction may provide a defense in most implied warranty cases, in which the warranty is only that most people could use the product for the general purpose for which it was made, idiosyncrasy is not a defense when the warranty implied by the circumstances of the transaction is more specific, as it was in this case. *See Malawy*, 150 Ill. App.3d at 560. Therefore, we affirm the finding of liability, and the award of $1,250 in damages on the implied warranty count. …

For the reasons stated above, we affirm the judgment entered on the jury verdict finding defendants liable for breach of implied warranty, we vacate the judgment on the Consumer Fraud Act count and the award of attorney fees, and we remand for a determination of defendants' liability for Consumer Fraud and appropriate attorney fees.

Affirmed in part, vacated in part, and remanded with directions.

2. "Seller Must Have Knowledge of Buyer's Particular Purpose"

Ford Motor Company v. General Accident Insurance Company
779 A.2d 362
(Md. 2001)

HARRELL, JUDGE. On 5 August 1995, International Motors, Inc.—trading as Montrose Towing (Montrose or Respondent)—purchased a tow truck from Elzenheimer Chevrolet. The tow truck had been created by Elzenheimer by adding necessary components to a 1995 Ford F-350 base chassis cab truck that Elzenheimer had purchased from a Ford dealership. Respondent insured the truck with General Accident Insurance Company (General Accident). On 19 August 1997, the tow truck caught fire as its operator was about to tow a vehicle. As a result of the fire, General Accident determined that the truck was a total loss and paid Montrose for its value. General Accident then sought reimbursement from Ford Motor Company (Ford or Petitioner), the manufacturer of the chassis cab truck, but Ford refused.

On 5 May 1998, General Accident, on behalf of Respondent, filed a subrogation claim against Ford in the Circuit Court for Montgomery County alleging negligence, breach of warranty, and strict liability based on a manufacturing defect. The trial court, after a bench trial, entered judgment in favor of Ford on all claims. General Accident appealed. The Court of Special Appeals affirmed the Circuit Court's judgment in favor of Ford on the express warranty, negligence, and strict liability claims, but vacated that part of the Circuit's Court's judgment with regards to claims of breach of the implied warranty of merchantability and the implied warranty of fitness for a particular purpose. We granted Petitioner's petition for writ of certiorari. …

I.

On 15 March 1995, Ford sold a 1995 F-350 chassis cab truck it had manufactured to Homer Skelton Ford, Inc., a Ford dealership in Olive Branch, Mississippi. The truck came with an express "bumper to bumper" warranty that provided, in pertinent part:

> Chassis cab trucks are sold with the anticipation that they can be, and usually are, modified into a tow truck, dump truck, garbage truck, or any one of many other acceptable uses through the addition of the required equipment. Authorized Ford Motor Company dealers will repair, replace or adjust all parts on your vehicle (except tires) that are defective in factory-supplied materials or workmanship for 3 years or 36,000 miles (whichever occurs first). WARRANTY INFORMATION BOOKLET FOR 1995-MODEL FORD AND MERCURY CARS AND LIGHT TRUCKS 5 (1995).

The "bumper to bumper" warranty did not cover, in pertinent part, "alteration, misuse, or damage caused by accident" or consequential or incidental damages.

On 16 May 1995, Elzenheimer Chevrolet—located in the State of New York—purchased the truck from Homer Skelton Ford and converted it into a tow truck. To convert the chassis cab into a tow truck, Elzenheimer Chevrolet added, among other things, a towing bar, boom-tow sling, a light illumination bar on top of the pre-existing lights along the body of the truck, a strobe light in the grill, a two-way radio mounted to the dash board, a three-switch electrical panel inside the passenger cab, and a power take-off with controls on the transmission hump. On 5 August 1995, Montrose purchased the truck, as yet unused as a tow truck, from Elzenheimer and insured it with General Accident.

On 19 August 1997, the truck—now with 27,600 miles on the odometer—caught fire while its operator, Greg Blum, a Montrose employee, was preparing to tow another vehicle. Mr. Blum had responded to a routine call to Dulles Airport in Virginia to tow a limousine, which had been struck on the driver's side door by a shuttle bus. When Mr. Blum arrived, he observed that the door to the limousine was stuck in the open position. Before the vehicle could be towed safely, the door of the limousine needed to be closed. It took approximately fifteen minutes to secure the door. While working on closing the car door, Mr. Blum kept the engine of the tow truck running. This was necessary apparently because the engine must be running in order to use the power take-off to tow a vehicle. He reentered the driver's compartment of the tow truck to back the truck up to begin the actual hook-up and towing.

When Mr. Blum reentered the tow truck to begin the towing process, he noticed steam or smoke coming from under the hood of the vehicle. He checked the engine temperature gauge, but it registered normal. When Mr. Blum looked up from the gauge, he noticed flames coming from under the hood of the vehicle on the passenger side. After pulling the hood release located under the driver's side of the dashboard, he exited the cab and proceeded to the rear of the truck to retrieve a fire extinguisher. When he went to the front of the truck with the extinguisher and attempted to lift the engine hood, he found the hood too hot to touch. He aimed the fire extinguisher towards the flames and completely discharged the extinguisher.

The truck was deemed a total loss. General Accident paid Montrose for its value, stipulated to be $23,880.21. General Accident, the subrogated insurer, thereafter wrote to Ford seeking reimbursement. Ford initially responded that it needed to inspect the vehicle. General Accident voluntarily made the vehicle available to Mr. Samuel, an inspector employed by Ford. After Mr. Samuel inspected the vehicle and reported, Ford denied the claim.

On 5 May 1998, General Accident, on behalf of its insured, Montrose, filed a subrogation claim against Ford in the Circuit Court for Montgomery County. General Accident thereafter filed two amended complaints, the last of which alleged claims for negligence, breach of warranty, and strict liability based on a manufacturing defect. The Second Amended Complaint states, in pertinent part: Plaintiff sues Defendant for negligence for failing to exercise reasonable care in manufacturing a product which caused damage to the Defendant's vehicle, for breach of warranty for selling a product which cause property damage and also for strict liability in tort. ... The Defendants placed a defective product on the market which caused property damage and which created a substantial and unreasonable risk of death and personal injury.

A one-day bench trial was held on 24 June 1999. At trial, General Accident abandoned its claim of a manufacturing defect, claiming instead that a design defect in the Ford vehicle caused the fire. General Accident, it is supposed, proceeded to trial under claims of negligence, express warranty, implied warranty of merchantability, implied warranty of fitness for a particular purpose, and strict liability. ... The MARYLAND CODE, COMMERCIAL LAW ARTICLE § 2-314(1) (1975) states that an implied warranty of fitness for a particular purpose exists:

> Where the seller at the time of contracting has reason to know any particular purpose for which the goods are required and that the buyer is relying on the seller's skill or judgment to select or furnish suitable goods, there is unless excluded or modified under the next section an implied warranty that the goods shall be fit for such purpose.

The second question under review in the present case asks us to consider whether the issue of implied warranty of fitness for a particular purpose was preserved properly at trial. ...

III. IMPLIED WARRANTY OF FITNESS FOR A PARTICULAR PURPOSE

Sufficient Evidence

Petitioner alternatively argues that there was insufficient evidence to support a claim of implied warranty of fitness for a particular purpose. The Court of Special Appeals determined that, as to the implied warranty of fitness for a particular purpose, § 2-315, Respondent did not have to prove a defect in order to prevail under this theory. The intermediate appellate court surmised:

> Ford manufactures chassis cabs with knowledge that they will be modified in some form or another. Ford was aware that Elzenheimer had, in the past, purchased Ford chassis cabs for the purpose of turning them into tow trucks. Thus, Ford impliedly warranted that the truck would be fit for usage as a tow truck.

Here, the evidence showed that Ford breached its implied warranty of fitness for a particular purpose when (1) General [Accident]'s insured was using the truck as a tow truck, and (2) the truck unexpectedly caught on fire. The circuit court was persuaded that the fire started in the engine compartment of the truck while the truck was idling. The truck was being used "normally" at that time, and trucks do not normally catch on fire while idling. It is our view that the Court of

Special Appeals improperly analyzed what the required elements of the implied warranty of fitness for a particular purpose are.

The Elements of § 2-315

An implied warranty of fitness for a particular purpose is conceded generally to have three affirmative elements:

(1) The seller must have reason to know the buyer's particular purpose.

(2) The seller must have reason to know that the buyer is relying on the seller's skill or judgment to furnish appropriate goods.

(3) The buyer must, in fact, rely upon the seller's skill or judgment.

According to the Official Comment to § 2-315, a particular purpose means:

> A "particular purpose" differs from the ordinary purpose for which the goods are used in that it envisages a specific use by the buyer which is peculiar to the nature of his business whereas the ordinary purposes for which goods are used are those envisaged in the concept of merchantability and go to uses which are customarily made of the goods in question. For example, shoes are generally used for the purpose of walking upon ordinary ground, but a seller may know that a particular pair was selected to be used for climbing mountains. MD. CODE (1975, 1997 REPL. VOL.), COMM. LAW ART. § 2-315, COMMENT 2.

Explained in another manner, the particular purpose "must be distinguishable from the normal use of the goods"; "[t]he purpose must be peculiar to the buyer as distinguished from the ordinary or general use to which the goods would be put by the ordinary buyer. ... A 'particular purpose' under Section 2-315 contemplates a specific use of the good that is peculiar to the nature of the buyer's business, while an 'ordinary purpose' refers to use customarily made of the goods." *Berkeley Pump Co. v. Reed-Joseph Land Co.,* 279 Ark. 384 (1983).

In addition to the particular purpose requirement, a party asserting a claim under § 2-315 must establish that the seller had reason to know, at the time of sale, that the purchaser had that particular use of the good in mind and that the purchaser was relying on the seller's expertise to select an appropriate product for that purpose. The need to establish specific knowledge on the part of the seller often may create a near requirement of direct dealing, if not actual privity. *See Wood Products, Inc. v. CMI Corp.*, 651 F.Supp. 641, 649 (D. Md. 1986) (seeking to apply Maryland law and stating that "[p]rivity is ... required in an action for breach of express warranty or an implied warranty of fitness for a particular purpose in which only economic loss is claimed"). It is often impossible for a seller to learn of a particular purpose of a buyer, and for a buyer to rely upon a seller to select the right product, without some direct dealing between such buyer and seller. As one treatise has explained:

> The warranty of fitness theory is usually not available against a remote manufacturer, who would have no reason to know of any special use to which the buyer would put the goods, even though the dealer could be liable. In other words, the absence of vertical privity removes the elements necessary to support the warranty of fitness. On this ground, the warranty of fitness sharply contrasts with the warranty of merchantability, which involves an inherent defect in the goods that existed before they left the hands of the manufacturer. Barkley Clark & Christopher Smith, THE LAW OF PRODUCT WARRANTIES, ¶ 6.03[1], at S6-12 (Supp. 1999).

Clark and Smith also noted:

> Vertical privity would almost always be a bar against a plaintiff suing a remote link in the chain of distribution for breach of the implied warranty of fitness for a particular purpose under Section 2-315. Under this Section, a cause of action requires (1) the seller's "reason to know" the buyer's special use of the goods, and (2) the buyer's reliance upon the seller's expertise. By its very nature, [the implied warranty of fitness for a particular purpose] is a warranty embracing adjoining links in the chain. Since breach does not normally involve any inherent defect in goods, but instead arises out of the unique relationship between immediate buyer and seller, suit based upon the warranty of fitness would rarely be brought against a remote defendant. If it were brought, the warranty of fitness would probably be dashed due to the absence of vertical privity or the absence of the requisite elements to support the theory. In short, the vertical privity defense and the warranty of fitness do not fit together in any rational way. Clark & Smith, *supra*, ¶ 10.03, at 10–17 (1984).

This sentiment is echoed by Anderson: The elements of knowledge of the seller of the buyer's particular need and of the buyer's reliance on the seller's skill and judgment may suggest the existence of direct dealings between the seller and the buyer. This in turn would suggest that privity of contract is present and, conversely, that the lack of privity would tend to negate the existence of knowledge on the part of the seller or reliance on the part of the buyer. Ronald Anderson, 3A UNIFORM COMMERCIAL CODE, § 2-315:93, at 55 (1995).

Under the circumstances of the present case, a problem of proof of knowledge exists. Neither Elzenheimer Chevrolet—which transformed the cab chassis truck into a tow truck—nor Respondent was the direct purchaser of the original product from Petitioner. Because neither was the direct purchaser of the truck, it becomes more difficult to prove that Ford knew or had reason to know, when first selling the truck to Homer Skelton Ford, Inc., that Respondent would buy the converted vehicle from Elzenheimer and would use it as a tow truck, or that anyone in the chain of purchasers was relying on Ford to provide an appropriate product for that ultimate use.

Respondent responds to the privity argument by stating: "Contrary to [Petitioner's] assertions, there is no need for a showing of privity under § 2-315. Plaintiff needs to prove that the buyer had a particular purpose known to seller. ... Indeed § 2-318 of the UCC even extends warranty protection to some third parties." It is correct that the plaintiff only needs to prove that the buyer had a particular purpose known to seller, and that privity itself is not a required element that must be shown independently. The problem here is that, given the intermediate chain of owners, there was no proof that Ford had knowledge that the chassis cab in question would be purchased ultimately for use as a tow truck.

The only basis for the asserted breach of the implied warranty of fitness in this case is that Ford knew the chassis cab could be converted into a tow truck and the vehicle, so converted, caught fire while idling. This basis is insufficient, as is the Court of Special Appeals' assertion that Petitioner knew that (a) chassis cabs "will be modified in some form or another," and (b) "that Elzenheimer had, in the past, purchased Ford chassis cabs for the purpose of turning them into tow trucks." The Court of Special Appeals incorrectly determined that the particular purpose for which the tow truck was purchased was towing and that the mere happening of the fire while the tow truck was in ordinary operation constituted a breach of the warranty of fitness for the particular purpose of towing.

As far as the record of this case reveals, the customary and ordinary uses of a chassis cab after modification are not particular uses as contemplated by § 2-315, but rather are the ordinary uses of such a product. When Petitioner sold the truck to Homer Skelton Ford, Petitioner was unaware specifically how the chassis cab would be used, though it was aware of several configurations to which such trucks had been converted historically. Petitioner's expert, Mr. Elhert, testified at trial: "[Ford] did not know when this truck was shipped what it was going to be used for. It could have been used in a variety of applications. That is why we build a chassis cab."

Additionally, ... Petitioner—in an interrogatory read at trial—stated: "Ford states that it sold the subject vehicle as an incomplete chassis cab with the anticipation that it would be or could be modified into a tow truck, dump truck, garbage truck, or any one of many other acceptable uses." Petitioner sold the chassis cab to a dealership in Mississippi, which dealer in turn sold the chassis cab (unaltered) to Elzenheimer Chevrolet, which converted it into a tow truck. There is no evidence that General Accident's insured articulated to Petitioner what particular purpose it had in mind for the chassis cab and no evidence that General Accident's insured sought to use the vehicle for other than one of its ordinary purposes. ...

We conclude that there is no basis in law or fact to find any particular purpose in the present case, let alone that Petitioner had knowledge of such a purpose on Montrose's part. Because of this determination, we do not need to consider the remaining elements of § 2-315. The implied warranty of fitness for a particular purpose is inapplicable to the present case. Moreover, the chassis cab was being used for its ordinary purpose, rather than a particular purpose. Accordingly, we reverse the decision of the Court of Special Appeals and remand the case with direction to affirm the trial court's judgment.

Judgment of the Court of Special Appeals reversed; case remanded ... with directions to affirm the judgment of the Circuit Court for Montgomery County. ...

NOTES AND QUESTIONS

1. **Horizontal and Vertical Privity, and Standing to Sue Under UCC 2-315.** Consider the Washington Supreme Court's analysis and holding in *Tex Enterprises, Inc. v. Brockway Standard, Inc.* 66 P.3d 625, 628–29 (Wash. 2003):

   [L]ack of privity has historically been a defense to claims of breach of warranty. There are two types of plaintiffs for whom lack of privity has been a concern. A "'horizontal' non-privity plaintiff" is not a buyer of the product in question, but is one who consumes or is affected by the goods. The "'vertical' non-privity plaintiff" is a buyer who is in the distributive chain, but who did not buy the product directly from the defendant. Tex is a vertical nonprivity plaintiff.

   By adopting alternative A of section 2-318 of The American Law Institute, Uniform Commercial Code 1972 Official Text, the Washington Legislature chose to eliminate the privity requirement for horizontal nonprivity plaintiffs under certain circumstances. ... UCC comment 3 to section 2-318, as adopted in Washington, notes that this provision is silent

> with regard to vertical privity. ... Thus, questions regarding the extension of warranties to vertical nonprivity plaintiffs are left to the courts. ... [T]he plain language of both RCW 62A.2-314 and 2-315 requires that implied warranties only arise out of contractual relationships. RCW 62A.2-314 states that the warranty that goods shall be merchantable is "implied in a contract for their sale." Similarly, RCW 62A.2-315 explains that the implied warranty of fitness for a particular purpose arises based on the seller's understanding "at the time of contracting." This language can be contrasted with RCW 62A.2-313 (express warranties), the language of which does not refer to an underlying "contract." Thus, the plain meaning of this statutory language forecloses application of implied warranties where there is no underlying contract to which the purchaser is a party or an intended third-party beneficiary.

2. **Establishing a Prima Facie Case Under UCC 2-315.** In *Divis v. Clarklift of Nebraska, Inc.*, 256 Neb. 384, 590 N.W.2d 696, 702 (Neb. 1999), the Supreme Court of Nebraska presented a "global" rule:

> To maintain a warranty action, several factors must be proved: (1) The plaintiff must prove the defendant made a warranty, express or implied, under §§ 2-313, 2-314, or 2-315; (2) the plaintiff must prove the goods did not comply with the warranty, *i.e.*, the goods were defective at the time of the sale; (3) the plaintiff must prove the injury was caused, proximately and in fact, by the defective nature of the goods; and (4) the plaintiff must prove damages.

3. **Court's Embellished Test for Finding an Implied Warranty of Fitness for a Particular Purpose**. In *Norcold, Inc. v. Gateway Supply Co.*, 798 N.E.2d 618, 625–26 (Ohio Ct. App. 2003), the court outlined the parameters of the test, which require evidence of the following: "(1) that the seller knew ... the buyer's particular purpose, (2) that the seller had reason to know that the buyer was relying on the seller's skill or judgment to furnish or select the appropriate goods, and (3) that the buyer relied upon the seller's skill or judgment. Additionally, the buyer's expertise or potentially superior knowledge with regard to the goods sold is a relevant factor to weigh into the reliance analysis."

4. **Attributes of a "Particular Purpose".** Quoting Comment 2 that accompanies UCC § 2-315, the Massachusetts Supreme court wrote the following statement in *Hannon v. Original Gunite Aquatech Pools, Inc.*, 385 Mass. 813, 821 (Mass. 1982): "A

'particular purpose' differs from the ordinary purpose for which the goods are used in that it envisages a specific use by the buyer which is peculiar to the nature of his business whereas the ordinary purposes for which goods are used are those envisaged in the concept of merchantability and go to uses which are customarily made of the goods in question."

UNIFORM COMMERCIAL CODE

§ 2-316. Exclusion or Modification of Warranties.

(1) Words or conduct relevant to the creation of an express warranty and words or conduct tending to negate or limit warranty shall be construed wherever reasonable as consistent with each other; but subject to the provisions of this Article on parol or extrinsic evidence (Section 2-202) negation or limitation is inoperative to the extent that such construction is unreasonable.

(2) Subject to subsection (3), to exclude or modify the implied warranty of merchantability or any part of it the language must mention merchantability and in case of a writing must be conspicuous, and to exclude or modify any implied warranty of fitness the exclusion must be by a writing and conspicuous. Language to exclude all implied warranties of fitness is sufficient if it states, for example, that "There are no warranties which extend beyond the description on the face hereof."

(3) Notwithstanding subsection (2)

(a) unless the circumstances indicate otherwise, all implied warranties are excluded by expressions like "as is", "with all faults" or other language which in common understanding calls the buyer's attention to the exclusion of warranties and makes plain that there is no implied warranty; and

(b) when the buyer before entering into the contract has examined the goods or the sample or model as fully as he desired or has refused to examine the goods there is no implied warranty with regard to defects which an examination ought in the circumstances to have revealed to him; and

(c) an implied warranty can also be excluded or modified by course of dealing or course of performance or usage of trade.

(4) Remedies for breach of warranty can be limited in accordance with the provisions of this Article on liquidation or limitation of damages and on contractual modification of remedy (Sections 2-718 and 2-719).

SECTION TWO. BREACH-OF-WARRANTY CLAIMS AND STATUTORY DEFENSES

To reiterate, warranties of merchantability and fitness for a particular purpose are implied in law and this general principle has been codified in Article 2 of the UCC. Consequently, those warranties impose various obligations and restrictions on sellers of goods and services. Still, under Article 2, sellers may disclaim and exclude implied warranties. Also, under certain conditions, sellers may limit or eliminate completely their liabilities after breaching an implied warranty. More specifically, a seller may raise this defense: During the formation of the sales agreement, circumstances surrounding the transaction sufficiently informed the buyer that, say, an implied warranty of merchantability would not be enforced or allow the seller to escape liability for failing to perform certain acts. UCC § 2-316, cmt 6 (1977).

Additionally, section 2-316(3)(a) allows a seller to place limitations on implied warranties by inserting phrases like "AS IS" and "WITH ALL FAULTS" into a sales contract. Those and similar expressions—which an ordinary layperson should understand intuitively—are inserted to inform the buyer that all implied warranties are excluded. Furthermore, a buyer's conduct may provide probative evidence of the seller's decision to disclaim, modify, exclude, or attach limitations to an implied warranty. Under section 2-316(3)(b), a disclaimer or modification is valid if: (1) a buyer examines the goods before consummating the sales contract; (2) a buyer studies samples or models of the products before accepting the terms and conditions in the sales contract; or (3) a buyer ignores a seller's demand and refuses to examine the goods before the parties execute the sales agreement.

As one might predict, some juries and judges return verdicts against sellers who allegedly breach implied warranties under Article 2. And in those cases, one finds little or any probative evidence of disclaimers, exclusions, "AS IS" language, or modifications. Other triers of facts, however, have decided against sellers when the sales agreements clearly disclaim or exclude implied warranties. Several cases are presented in this section. A comparison of the conflicts, legal analyses, and decisions in those cases will help the reader to appreciate an important point: Disclaiming, modifying, or excluding implied warranties may or may not help sellers to escape liability under the UCC.

A. Warranty Disclaimers

Hauter v. Zogarts
120 Cal. Rptr. 681
(Cal. 1975)

TOBRINER, J. After the jury found for defendants in this products liability case, the trial court granted plaintiff's motion for judgment notwithstanding the verdict. Defendants appeal, claiming that substantial evidence supports the jury's verdict. ...

THE FACTS

Defendants are Rudy C. Zogarts, who does business as House of Zog (manufacturer) and Miles Kimball Company (seller). Defendants manufacture and sell the "Golfing Gizmo" (Gizmo), a training device designed to aid unskilled golfers improve their games. Defendants' catalogue states that the Gizmo is a "completely equipped backyard driving range." In 1966, Louise Hauter purchased a Gizmo from the catalogue and gave it to Fred Hauter, her 13½-year-old son, as a Christmas present.

The Gizmo is a simple device consisting of two metal pegs, two cords—one elastic, one cotton—and a regulation golf ball. After the pegs are driven into the ground approximately 25 inches apart, the elastic cord is looped over them. The cotton cord, measuring 21 feet in length, ties to the middle of the elastic cord. The ball is attached to the end of the cotton cord. When the cords are extended, the Gizmo resembles the shape of a large letter "T," with the ball resting at the base.

The user stands by the ball in order to hit his practice shots. The instructions state that when hit correctly, the ball will fly out and spring back near the point of impact; if the ball returns to the left, it indicates a right-hander's "slice"; a shot returning to the right indicates a right-hander's "hook." If the ball is "topped," it does not return and must be retrieved by the player. The label on the shipping carton and the cover of the instruction booklet urge players to "drive the ball with full power" and further state: "Completely Safe Ball Will Not Hit Player."

On July 14, 1967, Fred Hauter was seriously injured while using defendants' product. Thereafter, plaintiffs filed the instant suit on his behalf, claiming false representation, breach of express and implied warranties and strict liability in tort.

Fred Hauter testified at trial that prior to his injury, he had practiced golf 10 to 20 times at driving ranges and had played several rounds of golf. His father instructed him in the correct use of the Gizmo. Fred had read the printed instructions that accompany the product and had used the Gizmo about a dozen times. Before the accident, Fred set up the Gizmo in his front yard according to the printed instructions. The area was free of objects that might have caused the ball to ricochet, and no other persons were nearby. Fred then took his normal swing with a seven-iron. The last thing he remembers was extreme pain and dizziness. After a period of unconsciousness, he staggered into the house and told his mother that he had been hit on the head by the ball. He suffered brain damage and, in one doctor's opinion, is currently an epileptic.

George Peters, a safety engineer and an expert on the analysis and reconstruction of accidents, testified for plaintiffs. In Peters' opinion, Fred Hauter had hit underneath the ball and had caught the cord with his golf club, thus drawing the cord upwards and toward him on his follow-through. The ball looped over the club producing a "bolo" effect and struck Fred on the left temple. Peters, an expert on the cause of accidents, concluded that the Gizmo is a "major hazard."

Ray Catan, a professional golfer, also testified for plaintiffs. He added that even if the club had hit the lower part of the ball, the same result probably would have occurred. He personally tested the Gizmo, intentionally hitting low shots, and found that his club became entangled in the cord, bringing the ball back toward him as he completed his swing. Describing Fred Hauter as a beginner, Catan stated that since such a golfer's swing usually is very erratic, he rarely hits the ball solidly. Defendants did not dispute plaintiffs' version of the accident. The manufacturer merely stated that he bought the rights to manufacture and distribute the Gizmo from a former professional golfer in 1962 and that the product had been on the market since that time.

Following a unanimous jury verdict for defendants on each cause of action, the trial judge granted plaintiffs' motion for judgment notwithstanding the verdict and plaintiffs' alternative motion for a new trial. Defendants have limited their appeal to the order granting judgment notwithstanding the verdict. ...

THE ANALYSIS

3. As a matter of law, plaintiffs should recover on their cause of action for false representation.

Plaintiffs' claim of false representation relies on common law tort principles reflected in section 402B of THE RESTATEMENT SECOND OF TORTS. Section 402B provides:

> One engaged in the business of selling chattels who, by advertising, labels, or otherwise, makes to the public a misrepresentation of a material fact concerning the character or quality of a chattel sold by him is subject to liability for physical harm to a consumer of the chattel caused by justifiable reliance upon the misrepresentation, even though"(a) it is not made fraudulently or negligently, and"(b) the consumer has not bought the chattel from or entered into any contractual relation with the seller. *See also* Civ. Code, § 1572.

For plaintiffs to recover under this section, defendants' statement "Completely Safe Ball Will Not Hit Player" must be a misrepresentation of material fact upon which plaintiffs justifiably relied. The fact that Fred Hauter did not purchase the Gizmo and hence is not in "privity" with defendants does not bar his claim of false representation. Section 402B eliminates the privity requirement and affords protection to all injured consumers. REST. 2D TORTS, 402B, com. i.

If defendants' assertion of safety is merely a statement of opinion—mere "puffing"—they cannot be held liable for its falsity. Defendants' statement is so broad, however, that it properly falls within the ambit of section 402B. The assertion that the Gizmo is completely safe, that the ball will not hit the player, does not indicate the seller's subjective opinion about the merits of his product but rather factually describes an important characteristic of the product. Courts have consistently held similar promises of safety to be representations of fact. *See, e.g., McCormack v. Hankscraft Co.*, 154 N.W.2d 488 (Minn. 1967) (vaporizer called "safe" and "practically foolproof"); *Spiegel v. Saks 34th St.*, 252 N.Y.S.2d 852 (1964) (representation that cosmetic was "safe"); and, *Pritchard v. Liggett & Myers Tobacco Company,* 295 F.2d 292, 301(3d Cir. 1961) (representation that cigarettes "can cause no ills") (concurring opinion). These decisions evidence the trend toward narrowing the scope of "puffing" and expanding the liability that flows from broad statements of manufacturers as to the quality of their products.FN6

Courts have come to construe unqualified statements such as the instant one liberally in favor of injured consumers. Furthermore, the illustrations in the RESTATEMENT indicate that the assertion "Completely Safe Ball Will Not Hit Player" constitutes a factual representation. Defendants' statement parallels that of an automobile dealer who asserts that the windshield of a car is "shatterproof" or that of a manufacturer who guarantees his product is "safe" if used as directed.

Moreover, the materiality of defendants' representation can hardly be questioned; anyone learning to play golf naturally searches for a product that enables him to learn safely. Fred Hauter's testimony that he was impressed with the safety of the item demonstrates the importance of defendants' statement. That Fred's injury occurred while he used the Gizmo as instructed proves the inaccuracy of the assertion on the carton.

Defendants, however, maintain that plaintiffs' reliance upon the assurance of safety is not justifiable. Alluding to the danger inherent to the sport, defendants argue that the Gizmo is a "completely safe" training device only when the ball is hit squarely. Defendants repeatedly state that an improperly hit golf shot exposes the player, as well as others nearby, to a serious risk of harm; they point to testimony recounting how an experienced player once hit a shot so poorly that the ball flew between his legs. As a result, contend defendants, plaintiffs cannot reasonably expect the Gizmo to be "completely safe" under all circumstances, particularly those in which the player hits beneath the ball.

Defendants' argument does not withstand analysis. Fred Hauter was not "playing golf." He was home on his front lawn learning to play the game with the aid of defendants' supposedly danger-free training device. By practicing in an open, isolated area apart from other golfers and free of objects off which a poorly hit shot could ricochet, Fred Hauter eliminated most of the dangers present during a normal round of play. Moreover, even though certain dangers are inherent in playing golf, the risk that the golfer's own ball will wrap itself around his club and strike the golfer on the follow-through is not among those dangers. Fred Hauter's injury stemmed from a risk inherent in defendants' product, not a risk inherent in the game of golf.

Additionally, defendants' analysis would render their representation of safety illusory. Were we to adopt their analysis, the words "Completely Safe Ball Will Not Hit Player" would afford protection to consumers only in relatively infrequent instances in which the "duffers" using the Gizmo managed to hit the ball solidly. Yet defendants' instructions supplied with the Gizmo clearly indicate that defendants anticipated the users of their product would "hook," "slice" and "top" the ball. They expected their customers to commit the errors that normally plague beginning golfers. Thus, when they declared their product "completely safe," the only reasonable inference is that the Gizmo was a safe training device for all golfers regardless of ability and regardless of how squarely they hit the ball.

Although defendants claim they did not intend their statement to cover situations such as the one at bar, subjective intent is irrelevant. The question is not what a seller intended, but what the consumer reasonably believed. The rule "is one of strict liability for physical harm to the consumer, resulting from a misrepresentation of the character or quality of the chattel sold, even though the misrepresentation is an innocent one, and not made fraudulently or negligently." (REST. 2D TORTS, § 402B, com. a.) We conclude that Fred Hauter reasonably believed he could use the Gizmo with safety and agree with the trial court that plaintiffs established all the elements of a cause of action for misrepresentation.

4. Defendants breached their express warranty that the Golfing Gizmo ball was "completely safe" and would "not hit player," as well as their implied warranty of merchantability.

As an alternative cause of action, plaintiffs claim that defendants breached both an express warranty and an implied warranty of merchantability. The fact that Fred Hauter is not in privity with defendants does not bar recovery. Privity is not required for an action based upon an express warranty. *Seely v. White Motor Co.*, 403 P.2d 145 (Cal. 1965). Although privity appears to remain a requirement for actions based upon the implied warranty of merchantability, Fred Hauter comes within a well-recognized exception to the rule: he is a member of the purchaser's family. (*Cf. Peterson v. Lamb Rubber Co.,* 54 Cal.2d 339, 347–348 (1960).

In analyzing these claims, we confront for the first time the California Uniform Commercial Code provisions relating to warranties. (CAL. U. COM. CODE, §§ 2313, 2314, and 2316.) The crucial issue here is not whether defendants created a warranty—as explained below, they clearly did. Rather, the bone of contention is whether they can escape liability by impliedly limiting the scope of their promise.

We first treat the claim for breach of express warranty, which is governed by California Commercial Code section 2313. The key under this section is that the seller's statements—whether fact or opinion—must become "part of the basis of the bargain." The basis of the bargain requirement represents a significant change in the law of warranties. Whereas plaintiffs in the past have had to prove their reliance upon specific promises made by the seller, the Uniform Commercial Code requires no such proof. According to official comment 3 to the Uniform Commercial Code following section 2313, "no particular reliance ... need be shown in order to weave [the seller's affirmations of fact] into the fabric of the agreement. Rather, any fact which is to take such affirmations, once made, out of the agreement requires clear affirmative proof." ...

We are not called upon in this case to resolve the reliance issue. The parties do not discuss the changes wrought by the Uniform Commercial Code, and plaintiffs are fully able to meet their burden regardless of which test we employ. Fred Hauter's testimony shows that he read and relied upon defendants' representation; he was impressed by "something on the cover dealing with the safety of the item." More importantly, defendants presented no evidence which could remove their assurance of safety from the basis of the bargain. The trial court properly concluded, therefore, that defendants expressly warranted the safety of their product and are liable for Fred Hauter's injuries which resulted from a breach of that warranty.

The trial court also held for plaintiffs on the theory of breach of an implied warranty of merchantability. Unlike express warranties, which are basically contractual in nature, the implied warranty of merchantability arises by operation of law. 2 WITKIN, SUMMARY OF CAL. LAW (8th ed. 1973) § 63, p. 1138.) "Into every mercantile contract of sale the law inserts a warranty that the goods sold are merchantable, the assumption being that the parties themselves, had they thought of it, would specifically have so agreed." Consequently, defendants' liability for an implied warranty does not depend upon any specific conduct or promise on their part, but instead turns upon whether their product is merchantable under the code.

Merchantability has several meanings, two of which are relevant to the instant case: The product must "[c]onform to the promises or affirmations of fact made on the container or label"—CAL. U. COM. CODE, § 2314, subd. (2)(f))—and must be "fit for the ordinary purposes for which such goods are used." CAL. U. COM. CODE, § 2314 (2)(c). The Gizmo fails in both respects. As already explained, it does not live up to the statement on the carton that it is "Completely Safe Ball Will Not Hit Player." Furthermore, as explained below, the evidence shows that the Gizmo is not fit for the ordinary purposes for which such goods are normally used.

The Gizmo is designed and marketed for a particular class of golfers—"duffers"—who desire to improve their technique. Such players rarely hit the ball solidly. When they do, testified the golf pro, "It would be sort of a mistake, really." The safety expert classed the Gizmo as a major safety hazard. Furthermore, defendants admit that when a person using the Gizmo hits beneath the ball as Fred Hauter apparently did, he stands a substantial chance of seriously injuring himself. Defense counsel stated to the jury: "It is obvious if you miss the ball and you come along, you touch the cord, that you could possibly get [the ball] either in the head or some other part of your person, and there is no way in the world that I am going to be able to show that couldn't happen to any of us here. ..."

Defendants nevertheless seek to avoid liability by limiting the scope of their warranties. They claim that the box containing the Gizmo and the instructions pertaining to its use clarified that the product was "completely safe" only when its user hit the ball properly. They point to no language expressing such a limitation but instead claim that a drawing in the instructions depicting a golfer "correctly" using their product implies the limitation.

As we explained above in discussing the false representation claim, defendants' argument is wholly without merit. Furthermore, they fail to meet the stern requirements of California Uniform Commercial Code section 2316 which governs disclaimer and modification of warranties. Section 2316 provides:

> (1) Words or conduct relevant to the creation of an express warranty and words or conduct tending to negate or limit warranty shall be construed wherever reasonable as consistent with each other; but subject to the provisions of this division on parol or extrinsic evidence (Section 2202) negation or limitation is inoperative to the extent that such construction is unreasonable.
>
> ...
>
> (3) [T]o exclude or modify the implied warranty of merchantability or any part of it the language must mention merchantability and in case of a writing must be conspicuous, and to exclude or modify any implied warranty of fitness the exclusion must be by a writing and conspicuous.

Although section 2316 has drawn criticism for its vagueness, its purpose is clear. No warranty, express or implied, can be modified or disclaimed unless a seller clearly limits his liability. *Greenspun v. American Adhesives, Inc.*, 320 F.Supp. 442, 444 (E.D. Pa. 1970). ... Because a disclaimer or modification is inconsistent with an express warranty, words of disclaimer or modification give way to words of warranty unless some clear agreement between the parties dictates the contrary relationship. *Wilson Trading Corp. v. David Ferguson, Ltd.*, 23 N.Y.2d 398, 405 (1968). At the very least, section 2316 allows limitation of warranties only by means of words that clearly communicate that a particular risk falls on the buyer. Moreover, any disclaimer or modification must be strictly construed against the seller. Although the parties are free to write their own contract, the consumer must be placed on fair notice of any disclaimer or modification of a warranty and must freely agree to the seller's terms. "A unilateral nonwarranty cannot be tacked onto a contract containing a warranty." *Klein v. Asgrow Seed Co.*, 246 Cal.App.2d 87, 97 (1966).

In the instant case, defendants do not point to any language or conduct on their part negating their warranties. They refer only to a drawing on the box and to the notion that golf is a dangerous game; based on that meager foundation, they attempt to limit their explicit promise of safety. Such a showing does not pass muster under the code, which requires clear language from anyone seeking to avoid warranty liability. We conclude, therefore, that the trial court properly granted plaintiffs judgment notwithstanding the verdict with regard to the warranty causes of action. ...

We affirm the order of the trial court granting judgment notwithstanding the verdict and remand the case to the trial court for the purpose of ascertaining damages.

B. Inconspicuous and Post-Sale Disclaimers

Bowdoin v. Showell Growers, Inc.
817 F.2d 1543
(11th Cir. 1987)

WISDOM, SENIOR CIRCUIT JUDGE: This appeal raises a single question: whether the defendants effectively disclaimed the implied warranties of fitness and merchantability with respect to a high pressure spray rig that caused injuries to the plaintiffs. The district court concluded that a disclaimer found in the instruction manual that accompanied the spray rig when it was delivered to the purchaser was conspicuous and therefore effective. We disagree. Even assuming that the disclaimer was otherwise conspicuous, it was delivered to the purchaser after the sale. Such a post-sale disclaimer is not effective because it did not form a part of the basis of the bargain between the parties to the sale. The decision of the district court is therefore reversed.

FACTS

At the time this controversy arose, the plaintiffs in this action, Rachel and Billy Bowdoin, raised chickens in Sampson, Alabama, for Showell Growers, Inc., a Maryland corporation. Under their contract with Showell Growers, the Bowdoins were required once a year to give a thorough cleaning to their chicken house and the chicken coop pallets. To aid them in this annual task, Showell Growers lent the Bowdoins a high pressure spray rig. In December 1980, Mrs. Bowdoin was using the spray rig to clean the pallets when an article of her clothing caught in the safety shield covering the spray rig's power takeoff shaft. Mrs. Bowdoin was pulled into the shaft and suffered severe injuries.

The spray rig in question was manufactured by FMC Corporation, an Illinois corporation. The safety shield and drive shaft component was manufactured for FMC by NEAPCO, Inc., a Pennsylvania corporation. Showell purchased the spray rig from FMC through an FMC dealer, Brushy Mountain Co-op of Moravian Falls, North Carolina. Two weeks after the sale, the spray rig was shipped to Brushy Mountain and then delivered to Showell Growers. An instruction manual was included with the spray rig when it was delivered to Showell Growers. The last page of the instruction manual included a purported warranty disclaimer, which stated: "The foregoing warranty is expressly in lieu of any and all other warranties, express, implied, statutory or otherwise (including, but without limitation, the implied warranties of merchantability and fitness for a particular purpose). ..."

Usually, FMC required its dealer and the purchaser to complete an "agriculture delivery report" before a sale. The report contains a disclaimer of the implied warranties of fitness and merchantability. The purchaser is required to read the report and sign it, acknowledging that he has read the warranty information. The report is then returned to FMC. The record shows that no agriculture delivery report was completed in connection with the purchase by Showell Growers.

In 1982, the Bowdoins filed a diversity action against Showell Growers and FMC in the United States District Court for the Northern District of Florida. The Bowdoins later added NEAPCO as a defendant. The Bowdoins sought to recover on a number of counts including one count alleging breach by FMC and NEAPCO of the implied warranties of fitness and merchantability. FMC and NEAPCO moved for summary judgment on this count. The district court concluded that the law of Alabama applied to the warranty claims and that under Alabama law, FMC and NEAPCO had effectively disclaimed the implied warranties with the disclaimer in the instruction manual. The district court, therefore, granted summary judgment in favor of FMC and NEAPCO, and dismissed with prejudice the Bowdoins' implied warranties claims. The Bowdoins now appeal that ruling.

The sole issue on appeal is whether the district court correctly determined that FMC and NEAPCO had effectively disclaimed the implied warranties. The Bowdoins contend that the district court's ruling in favor of FMC and NEAPCO is erroneous for several reasons: (1) the disclaimer was not part of the bargain and is therefore ineffective; (2) the disclaimer is not conspicuous as required under Alabama law; (3) the spray rig comes within the classification of "consumer goods" and therefore a manufacturer cannot disclaim implied warranties; (4) the disclaimer is unconscionable; and (5) even if the disclaimer is effective as to FMC, it is ineffective as to NEAPCO, which manufactured the drive shaft and safety shield component. ...

DISCUSSION

Under the Uniform Commercial Code as adopted by Alabama and virtually every other state, a manufacturer may disclaim the implied warranties of merchantability and fitness provided that the disclaimer is in writing and conspicuous, and provided that the disclaimer is part of the parties' bargain. ALA. CODE § 7-2-316(2) (1984). If a disclaimer was conspicuous to the purchaser before the sale, a court will generally hold the disclaimer effective based on the assumption that the disclaimer formed a part of the basis of the bargain. If, however, the disclaimer was not presented to the purchaser before the sale, the court will hold such a disclaimer ineffective because it did not form a part of the basis of the bargain. R. Anderson, 3 UNIFORM COMMERCIAL CODE § 2-316:25 at 342.

We turn now to determine whether the FMC disclaimer was a part of the basis of the bargain. The parties agree that for purposes of this analysis, the Bowdoins stand in the shoes of Showell Growers. The question therefore is whether the disclaimer is effective as to Showell Growers. We conclude that it is not. Showell Growers purchased the spray rig at least two weeks before it was delivered. When the rig was delivered, an instruction manual was enclosed; and in that instruction manual is the disclaimer upon which FMC and NEAPCO rely. The disclaimer was never brought to Showell's attention.

Such a post-sale disclaimer is ineffective. *See Tiger Motor Co. v. McMurtry*, 224 So.2d 638 (Ala. 1969). "By definition, a disclaimer that appears for the first time after the sale in something supplied by the seller is not a part of the basis of the bargain and therefore is not binding on the buyer. Thus, the buyer is not bound by the disclaimer to which he had never agreed at the time of the sale and which first appears in the manufacturer's manual delivered to the buyer with the goods [or] the manufacturer's printed material, brochure, or warranty booklet that accompanies the goods. ..." R. Anderson, 3 UNIFORM COMMERCIAL CODE § 2-316:32 at 345.

The leading Alabama decision on disclaimers of implied warranties is in harmony with this position. In *Tiger Motor Co. v. McMurtry*, the Alabama Supreme Court addressed the validity of a disclaimer of implied warranties with respect to an automobile. The evidence showed that the day after the sale took place, the automobile was delivered to the purchaser along with the disclaimer. The evidence also showed that the disclaimer was never called to the purchaser's attention before the sale. The court concluded that the disclaimer was ineffective. *Tiger Motor,* 224 So.2d at 642–44. Decisions of other courts construing the same provisions of the Uniform Commercial Code have also concluded that a post-sale disclaimer is not effective. (Citations omitted).

FMC attempts to distinguish these cases on three grounds. First, FMC argues that unlike the purchasers involved in most of the cases, who were, for the most part, individual consumers, Showell Growers is a sophisticated commercial enterprise. But FMC has not offered and we have not found a post-sale disclaimer case in which such a distinction was material. Indeed, several of the cases in other states did involve commercial transactions between sophisticated commercial enterprises or businessmen, and the results reached were not affected: Courts consistently held that post-sale disclaimers were ineffective.

FMC next argues that here the post-sale disclaimer was effective because it was conspicuous. Specifically, FMC asserts that the cases which have held post-sale disclaimers ineffective involved "egregious facts involving the combination of the failure of a disclaimer to be conspicuous and its appearance subsequent to the parties' transaction." FMC's argument is, however, wrong on both the facts and the law. Several of the cases holding post-sale disclaimers ineffective did not even mention whether the disclaimer was otherwise conspicuous.

And the cases to which FMC is apparently referring typically involved not one disclaimer but two: one in the sales contract and the other in a document delivered after the sale, such as an instruction manual or a warranty. In those cases, the courts held both disclaimers ineffective: the disclaimer in the sales contract because it was in small print and therefore not conspicuous, and the post-sale disclaimer because it was not a part of the basis of the bargain. In these cases, as in the cases involving only a post-sale disclaimer, the courts generally did not discuss whether the disclaimer was otherwise conspicuous.

The absence of such a discussion is not surprising, because as a general rule the conspicuousness of a post-sale disclaimer is immaterial. By definition, a post-sale disclaimer is not conspicuous in the full sense of that term because the reasonable person against whom it is intended to operate could not have noticed it before the consummation of the transaction. A post-sale disclaimer is therefore not effective merely because it was otherwise conspicuous. *See* Ala. Code § 7-1-201(10) (1984) (defining the term "conspicuous" as being such that "a reasonable person against whom it is to operate ought to have noticed it"). *See also Flory v. Silvercrest Indus., Inc.*, 633 P.2d 424, 427 (Ariz. App. 1980) (post-sale disclaimer cannot be conspicuous), *aff'd in part, vacated in part*, 633 P.2d 383 (Ariz. 1981); and, *Marion Power Shovel Co. v. Huntsman*, 437 S.W.2d 784, 787 (Ark. 1969) (same).

Finally, FMC argues that its post-sale disclaimer is effective because of prior dealings with Showell Growers that put Showell on notice that FMC's practice was to disclaim implied warranties with respect to high pressure spray rigs. Showell Growers had previously purchased an FMC spray rig similar to the one that caused Mrs. Bowdoin's injuries. The instruction manual accompanying the first spray rig contained a disclaimer of implied warranties, and according to one Showell employee, that instruction manual appeared to be identical to the one accompanying the spray rig in question. From this, FMC argues that Showell was on notice that FMC was disclaiming the implied warranties with respect to the second spray rig.

This argument misses the point. Even assuming that the mere similar appearance of two instruction manuals could put a purchaser on notice that a disclaimer in the first would also be found in the second,

FMC's argument fails for the same reason its argument that a post-sale disclaimer can be effective if it was otherwise conspicuous failed. A disclaimer must be conspicuous before the sale, for only then will the law presume that the disclaimer was part of the bargain. In this case, Showell Growers did not receive the second instruction manual until after the second sale was consummated. The disclaimer in that instruction manual was therefore without significance. This is not less true merely because earlier Showell had received a similar instruction manual. Until it received the second instruction manual, it could not know what it would look like or what it would contain.

Similarly, mere acceptance by Showell of the spray rig and the instruction manual is insufficient to show that Showell assented to a modification of the original bargain. FMC did not present Showell with a modification and then offer Showell an opportunity knowingly to accept or reject that modification. *See Gold Kist, Inc. v. Citizens and Southern Nat. Bank of South Carolina,* 333 S.E.2d 67, 71 (S.C. App. 1985) ("An agreement to modify can only be found, however, if the evidence reveals that the buyer acquired knowledge of the offered modification and had an opportunity to object to it."). *See also Monsanto Agricultural Prods. Co. v. Edenfield*, 426 So.2d 574 (Fla. Ct. App. 1982) (modification found where label on product clearly stated that the manufacturer disclaimed all implied warranties and that if the purchaser did not wish to keep the product given that disclaimer, he could return it for a full refund).

Although we express no opinion as to whether *Monsanto Agricultural Products, Co.* represents a correct statement of the law in Alabama, we note that it is consistent with the result we reach today because unlike the label involved in *Monsanto Agricultural Products Co.*, the disclaimer in the instruction manual that accompanied the spray rig did not offer the purchaser an opportunity to return the product if that purchaser did not wish to accept the disclaimer.

Conclusion

We conclude that the post-sale disclaimer of implied warranties found in the instruction manual that accompanied the FMC spray rig is ineffective because it did not form a part of the basis of the bargain. The decision of the district court is therefore reversed, and the district court is instructed to reinstate the Bowdoins' breach of implied warranties of fitness and merchantability claims against FMC and NEAPCO.

C. Exclusions Using "As Is" Clauses

Wilke v. Woodhouse Ford, Inc.
774 N.W.2d 370
(Neb. 2009)

McCORMACK, J.

I. NATURE OF CASE

Elizabeth A. Wilke and her husband—Mark Wilke—purchased a van from Woodhouse Ford, Inc. (Woodhouse). That same day, Elizabeth was injured when their 3-year-old daughter allegedly pulled the gearshift out of park, allowing the van to roll over Elizabeth's foot and leg, causing her to fall and hit her head on a concrete driveway. The Wilkes testified that the key was out of the ignition at the time of the accident. The van was purchased that day from Woodhouse. Woodhouse sold the van to the Wilkes "as is" and disclaimed all implied warranties. The Wilkes brought suit against Woodhouse alleging two alternative theories: negligence and breach of implied warranty of merchantability. The district court entered summary judgment in favor of Woodhouse, and the Wilkes appealed. ...

II. BACKGROUND

The Wilkes purchased a used 2002 Ford Econoline cargo van from Woodhouse on September 18, 2004. Mark is not a trained mechanic and has only a basic knowledge of mechanics. Before purchasing the van, Mark started the van's engine but did not test-drive the van. Mark felt that test-driving the van or inspecting it further was unnecessary because he had purchased "good vehicles from Woodhouse before."

The purchase agreement stated that the van was used and purchased "As Is" and "WITHOUT ANY WARRANTY" in bold type. The agreement further provided in a smaller font, "DEALER HEREBY EXPRESSLY DISCLAIMS ALL WARRANTIES, EXPRESS OR IMPLIED, INCLUDING ANY IMPLIED WARRANTIES OF MERCHANTABILITY OR FITNESS FOR A PARTICULAR PURPOSE. ..." Both the Wilkes and the Woodhouse salesman signed the purchase agreement. There is no evidence that Woodhouse made any representations to the Wilkes regarding the condition or quality of the van.

Immediately after purchasing the van, the Wilkes drove directly to the home of their friend, approximately a 30- to 45-minute drive from the dealership. Elizabeth and her daughter drove in the family vehicle, and Mark followed in the new van. Upon arriving, Mark pulled the van into the driveway, which was slightly sloped, and parked. Mark did not apply the emergency brake after he parked the van. The Wilkes both remembered Mark taking the key out of the ignition and putting it in his pocket after parking the van. Mark testified that he had no doubt that he took the key out of the ignition. And Elizabeth testified in her deposition that she did not hear any chimes or buzzers indicating that the key had been left in the ignition.

After parking the van, the Wilkes and their daughter went inside for approximately 30 minutes. They then went back outside to show their friend the new van. Mark opened the driver's-side door and the two doors in the back of the van. Elizabeth testified that she was standing directly behind the van and that Mark was sitting at the end of the van with their daughter on his lap. At some point, the daughter got down from Mark's lap and stood beside Elizabeth. Elizabeth testified that she turned her head to talk to their friend for a moment and that when she was turning back to look at Mark, she saw her daughter climbing into the driver's seat. Elizabeth immediately screamed for her daughter to get down, and Elizabeth ran around to the driver's side of the van.

Elizabeth testified that as she approached the side of the van, she saw her daughter with her left hand on the steering wheel and her right hand on the gearshift. According to Elizabeth, her daughter's legs were tucked underneath her and she was on her knees. Before getting to the driver's side, Elizabeth heard a "clunk," and then the van started rolling backward. Elizabeth explained that her daughter grabbed the gearshift to pull herself up to come to Elizabeth, but that Elizabeth shoved her back into the van to make sure she would not fall out as the van rolled backward.

As the van rolled backward, Elizabeth was hit by the door and her right foot got caught under the van's tire. The force caused her to fall backward onto the pavement and hit her head. According to Elizabeth, the left front tire rolled over her right foot and thigh. The tire missed her shoulder, but her shirt was pinned under the tire.

Once the van started to roll, Mark turned and saw his daughter in the front seat. Mark entered the van through the open back doors, pushed open the separator cage, and "dove for the brake pedal with [his] hand." The van stopped rolling at that point. Mark testified that he noticed his daughter was in the front seat after he realized the van was moving and that she was on the seat either on her knees or standing. Mark also testified that he did not know which gear the van was in as it rolled over Elizabeth but that he knew the gearshift was not "aligned with the P." After stopping the van, Mark moved the van to release Elizabeth's shirt. Elizabeth was taken by ambulance to a hospital.

The deputy sheriff's report regarding the accident states: "Vehicle 1 Was Discovered To Have A Defective Shift Lever That Was Able To Be Shifted Out Of Park Mode Without Depressing Brake Pedal." The report does not explain or provide any details as to whether the key was in the ignition or how the defective gearshift was discovered.

Donald Jeffers, an automotive engineering consultant and the Wilkes' expert witness, conducted an investigation of the accident and prepared a report on his findings. In making his findings, Jeffers examined the State of Nebraska investigator's motor vehicle accident report, color prints of photographs of the accident scene, transcripts of depositions and telephone interviews, Ford engineering drawings and shop manuals, the Federal Motor Vehicle Safety Standards, and Elizabeth's medical report.

In his report, Jeffers summarized parts of the telephone interview transcripts. According to Jeffers' report, the police officer who responded to the call to the 911 emergency dispatch service testified in his telephone interview that "'[he] got in the driver's side and moved the shift lever, which shouldn't have moved, and it went into neutral and drive out of park without stepping on the brake pedal.'" According to the Federal Motor Vehicle Safety Standards relied upon by Jeffers, vehicles which have an automatic transmission with a "park" position must "'prevent removal of the key unless the transmission or transmission shift lever is locked in "park" as the direct result of removing the key.'" The purpose of this feature is "'to reduce the incidence of crashes resulting from the rollaway of parked vehicles with automatic transmissions as a result of children moving the shift mechanism out of the "park" position.'"

After the accident, Elizabeth's father took the van to Woodhouse for the first of two repairs. The record does not contain a repair order regarding the first repair. However, it appears as though Woodhouse adjusted the linkage on the gearshift because it was not going into park completely. According to Mark, the transmission continued to shift out of park without the key in the ignition after the first Woodhouse repair. Mark explained that he and Elizabeth's father tested it by pulling the gearshift without his foot on the brake and that the gearshift would go into any gear that he put it into. Woodhouse came and picked up the van a second time for repairs.

Matthew Eschliman is a Woodhouse employee, and portions of his deposition testimony were included in the record. Eschliman's deposition testimony indicates that there was excessive play in the gearshift. Specifically, Eschliman stated, "You could move the lever up and down excessively but not actually physically get it out of gear." Eschliman testified that although there was free play in the gearshift, the transmission would not shift from park to reverse without the key in the ignition. It is unclear from the record whether this observation was made before the first repair or the second repair.

The record suggests that Dustin Oppliger was the Woodhouse technician who actually repaired the van. Part of Oppliger's deposition was also included in the record. Oppliger testified that he checked the van before he made any repairs to see whether the gearshift would move. When asked if the gearshift had "free play from park to drive," Oppliger stated, "I wouldn't really call it free play. The shifter had free play, but not the actual linkage. You could feel the free play but you couldn't—there was no strength there." Oppliger also testified that he parked the van on a steep hill and tried to pull the gearshift out of park but was unable to get the gearshift to shift out of park. In other words, Oppliger was allegedly unable to duplicate the problem. Even though the Woodhouse employees reportedly could not shift the van out of park without the key in the ignition and the brake depressed, Oppliger replaced the bushings and adjusted the shifter cable.

The repair order concerning the second repair states:

> CUSTOMER REPORTS: WHEN KEY IS OUT OF IGNITION THE TRANS WILL COME OUT OF GEAR ENOUGH TO ROLL FREELY. CHECK AND ADVISE. CAUSED BY ADJUSTED THE SHIFTER CABLE, R & I THE STEERING COLUMN & DISASSEMBLED THE SHIFT SHAFT, REPLACED THE BARINGS & RETEST.

The repair order also contains handwritten notes, which state:

> ADJUST SHIFTER CABLE. R & R STEERING COLUMN. DISASSEMBLE FOUND SHIFT SHAFT. BUSHINGS WORN OUT. REPLACED THEM. INSPECT SHIFT LOCKOUT MECHANISM. NOTHING WORN ON THAT. REASSEMBLE AND CHECK. WORKS GOOD.

After the second repair, a Woodhouse employee brought the van back to Mark, and Mark testified that when the van was brought back the second time, he could not get the gearshift to come out of park without the key in the ignition and the brake pedal depressed. In other words, according to Mark, the gearshift on the van worked properly after the second repair.

Based on his review and investigation, Jeffers concluded that "[t] hree separate failure modes caused and contributed" to the accident. According to Jeffers' report, the brake shift interlock system failed, the transmission shift cable was misadjusted, and the key shift interlock failed or malfunctioned. Jeffers did not make any determinations regarding whether the defect in the gearshift could have been discovered by a reasonable inspection.

It is undisputed that the van was not inspected by Woodhouse employees prior to the Wilkes' purchase. Eschliman explained in his deposition testimony that because of the high volume of vehicles traded in, there are times when the service department does not inspect used vehicles before they are resold. Oppliger testified similarly.

He explained that Woodhouse gets "too many vehicles in that we can't keep up on inspecting every one of them." There is no indication in the record that Woodhouse was aware prior to the accident that the gearshift on the van was defective.

The Wilkes filed a petition, which was later amended, against Ford Motor Company and Woodhouse seeking damages for Elizabeth's injuries. Ford Motor Company has been dismissed, without prejudice, and is not a party in this appeal. The petition contains three theories of recovery, only two of which involve Woodhouse. In count II of the petition, the Wilkes allege that Woodhouse knew or should have known that the defective condition of the van would pose an unreasonable and foreseeable danger to its customer or, alternatively, that Woodhouse knew or should have known that the van was defective when it was sold and that such negligence was the proximate cause of Elizabeth's injuries. In count III of the petition, the Wilkes allege that Woodhouse impliedly warranted, pursuant to NEB. U.C.C. § 2-314 (Reissue 2001), the van was merchantable and that Woodhouse breached that implied warranty. The district court granted Woodhouse's motion for summary judgment, and the Wilkes appeal.

III. ASSIGNMENTS OF ERROR

The Wilkes allege that the district court erred (1) as a matter of law in holding that no genuine issue of material fact exists and in granting summary judgment to Woodhouse and (2) in determining that used-car dealers can exclude through "As Is" clauses an implied warranty of safety that involves the vehicle's inherently dangerous defects, because such exclusions violate public policy. ...

V. ANALYSIS

This case presents two issues: (1) whether a car dealer can exclude through the use of an "As Is" clause the implied warranty of merchantability, and (2) whether a car dealer has a duty to inspect used vehicles for safety defects prior to selling the vehicle.

1. IMPLIED WARRANTY OF MERCHANTABILITY

The Wilkes' breach of warranty claim arises from the law of sales as codified in the Uniform Commercial Code (U.C.C.). *See* NEB. U.C.C. §§ 2-101 to 2-725 (Reissue 2001). Historically, a warranty is an undertaking or assertion by the seller that the thing sold is as represented. *See Erskine v. Swanson*, 64 N.W. 216 (Neb. 1895). Under the U.C.C., warranties relating to goods sold can be either express or implied. *See* §§ 2-313 and 2-315. [Section 2-314 reads]:

> (1) Unless excluded or modified (section 2-316), a warranty that the goods shall be merchantable is implied in a contract for their sale if the seller is a merchant with respect to goods of that kind. ...
>
> (2) Goods to be merchantable must be at least such as ... (c) are fit for the ordinary purposes for which such goods are used[.]

The Wilkes contend that Woodhouse breached this express warranty of merchantability with respect to the van it sold to them. As noted in the statutory language defining an implied warranty of merchantability, it exists "unless excluded or modified." U.C.C. § 2-315. Section 2-316(3)(a) provides:

> [U]nless the circumstances indicate otherwise, all implied warranties are excluded by expressions like 'as is', 'with all faults' or other language which in common understanding calls the buyer's attention to the exclusion of warranties and makes plain that there is no implied warranty.

The purchase agreement evidencing the sale of the van from Woodhouse to the Wilkes included a conspicuous statement that it was sold "as is," "without any warranty either expressed or implied," and further stated that Woodhouse was disclaiming any implied warranty of merchantability. This language met the requirements of § 2-316(2) and (3)(a) for excluding an implied warranty of merchantability.

The Wilkes argue, however, that exclusion of an implied warranty of merchantability with respect to a safety defect would violate public policy and therefore should not be enforced by a court. In support of their argument, the Wilkes cite to general propositions defining public policy as restrictions on the freedom to contract in order to prevent acts injurious to the public. *See New Light Co. v. Wells Fargo Alarm Servs.*, 525 N.W.2d 25 (Neb. 1994). But, we have also explained that it is the function of the Legislature, through the enactment of statutes, to declare what is the law and public policy of this state. *See State v. Barranco*, 769 N.W.2d 343 (Neb. 2009). And our Legislature has provided, in § 2-316, that the implied warranty of merchantability may be disclaimed or excluded.

The provisions of the U.C.C. which permit a seller to exclude warranties make no exception for warranties relating to the safety of the product. We conclude that the use of an "as is" clause to exclude the implied warranty of merchantability cannot be against the public policy of this state when it mirrors the statutory requirements specifically allowing for such exclusion. *See, Continental Western Ins. Co. v. Conn*, 262 Neb. 147, 629 N.W.2d 494 (Neb. 2001)

Section 2-316 is the Legislature's clear expression of the public policy of this state. Therefore, the purchase agreement effectively disclaimed and excluded any implied or express warranties for the vehicle. As such, the district court properly entered summary judgment in favor of Woodhouse for the Wilkes' cause of action for breach of the implied warranty of merchantability. …

VI. CONCLUSION

We conclude that Woodhouse effectively disclaimed all implied warranties, including the warranty of merchantability. But we also conclude that commercial dealers of used vehicles have a duty to exercise reasonable care to discover any existing safety defects that are patent or discoverable in the exercise of reasonable care or through reasonable inspection. Because there are genuine issues of material fact as to whether Woodhouse breached its duty of care and, if so, whether Woodhouse's breach was the proximate cause of Elizabeth's injuries, we conclude that the district court incorrectly granted summary judgment in favor of Woodhouse on the Wilkes' negligence claim. We affirm the grant of summary judgment in favor of Woodhouse on count III and reverse the judgment of the district court granting summary judgment in favor of Woodhouse on count II.

Affirmed in part, and in part reversed.

NOTES AND QUESTIONS

1. **Federal Statutory Breach-of-Warranty Actions**. Generally, the Magnuson-Moss Warranty—Federal Trade Commission Improvement Act, 15 U.S.C. § 2310—creates rights and remedies for disgruntled consumers who raise breach-of-warranty claims. More specifically, § 2310(d) reads:

   CIVIL ACTION BY CONSUMER FOR DAMAGES

   (1) Subject to subsections (a)(3) and (e) of this section, a consumer who is damaged by the failure of a supplier, warrantor, or service contractor to comply with any obligation under this chapter, or under a written warranty, implied warranty, or service contract, may bring suit for damages and other legal and equitable relief—

(A) in any court of competent jurisdiction in any State or the District of Columbia; or

(B) in an appropriate district court of the United States, subject to paragraph (3) of this subsection.

(2) If a consumer finally prevails in any action brought under paragraph (1) of this subsection, he may be allowed by the court to recover as part of the judgment a sum equal to the aggregate amount of cost and expenses (including attorneys' fees based on actual time expended) determined by the court to have been reasonably incurred by the plaintiff for or in connection with the commencement and prosecution of such action, unless the court in its discretion shall determine that such an award of attorneys' fees would be inappropriate.

2. **Federal Statutory Definition of a "Consumer"**. The Magnuson-Moss Act, 15 U.S.C. § 2301(3) reads:

The term "consumer" means a buyer (other than for purposes of resale) of any consumer product, any person to whom such product is transferred during the duration of an implied or written warranty (or service contract) applicable to the product, and any other person who is entitled by the terms of such warranty (or service contract) or under applicable State law to enforce against the warrantor (or service contractor) the obligations of the warranty (or service contract).

3. **Federal Statutory Definition of a "Written Warranty."** The Magnuson-Moss Act § 2301(6) defines a "written warranty" as follows:

The term "written warranty" means—

(A) any written affirmation of fact or written promise made in connection with the sale of a consumer product by a supplier to a buyer which relates to the nature of the material or workmanship and affirms or promises that such material or workmanship is defect free or will meet a specified level of performance over a specified period of time, or

(B) any undertaking in writing in connection with the sale by a supplier of a consumer product to refund, repair, replace, or take other remedial action with respect to such product in the event that such product fails to meet the specifications set forth in the undertaking, which written affirmation, promise, or undertaking becomes part of the basis of the bargain between a supplier and a buyer for purposes other than resale of such product.

4. ***Federal Statutory Restrictions on Warranty Disclaimers, Modifications, and Limitations***. Under the Magnuson–Moss Warranty Act, 15 U.S.C. § 2308(a), "[n]o supplier may disclaim or modify ... any implied warranty to a consumer with respect to such consumer product if (1) such supplier makes any written warranty to the consumer with respect to such consumer product, or (2) at the time of sale, or within 90 days thereafter, such supplier enters into a service contract with the consumer which applies to such consumer product." On the other hand, under § 2308(b), "implied warranties may be limited in duration to the duration of a written warranty of reasonable duration, if such limitation is conscionable and is set forth in clear and unmistakable language and prominently displayed on the face of the warranty." To underscore that, §§ 2308(a) and (b) preempt pertinent states laws, and § 2308(c) of Magnuson-Moss reads: "A disclaimer, modification, or limitation made in violation of this section shall be ineffective for purposes of this chapter and State law." Clearly, § 2308 conflicts with common-law, implied-warranty rules as well as with the language in UCC § 2-314 and § 2-315.

5. **Disclaimers Under the UCC and the Conspicuous-Disclosure Rule.** Section 1-201(10) of the UCC defines "conspicuous" this way: "so written that a reasonable person against whom it is to operate ought to have noticed it." The following factors can influence whether or not a disclaimer is conspicuous: (1) The color, width, height, hue, and style of a disclaimer's lettering or font; (2) the disclaimer's location in the contract; (3) whether or not the disclaimer appears in a block; and (4) whether or not the disclaimer has a heading. 73 A.L.R. 3d 248.

CHAPTER TEN

Proof of Consideration Under Article 2 of the Uniform Commercial Code

Reconsider the some general rules. Under section 2-204 of the UCC, an agreement between a buyer and a seller may be made in any manner. But there is a proviso: The selected methodology must establish sufficiently the parties' intent to mutually embrace the contractual terms. In fact, the parties' conduct may be enough to prove the existence of a valid sale-of-goods contract. Section 2-204(1) of the UCC. Therefore, since the UCC does not codify many of the "draconian" common-law rules, proof of only a few terms is required to establish a valid contract under the commercial statute: "In a contract for a sale of goods, the essential terms are quantity, price, and time and manner of delivery." *Judal Indus. v. Welsbach Elec. Corp.*, 138 A.D.2d 573, 573, 526 N.Y.S.2d 154 (1988).

On the other hand, to recover breach-of-contract damages under both the common law and Article 2, a buyer or seller must establish a *prima facie* case. Again, the plaintiff must prove: 1) the existence of a contract, 2) consideration, 3) a breach of the contract, 4) causation, and 5) damages. *See, e.g., Palmetto Partners, L.P. v. AJW Qualified Partners, LLC*, 83 A.D.3d 804, 806, 921 N.Y.S.2d 260 (2011). Focusing on a plaintiff's burden to prove consideration in an Article 2, breach-of-contract lawsuit, a state court judge cited multiple primary sources and presented a highly relevant discussion in *Petroleum Traders Corp. v. Hillsborough County*. The judge wrote:

> The UCC governs contracts for the sale of goods. The UCC displaces the common law to the extent it is inconsistent therewith. *See Burtman v. Tech. Chems. & Prods., Inc.*, 724 So.2d 672, 676 (Fla. Dist. Ct. App. 1999) (stating that the principles of law and equity shall supplement the provisions of the UCC unless displaced by particular provisions of it). However, unless a code provision dictates otherwise, the general law of contracts is applicable. One fundamental principle of contract law *not displaced by the UCC is that a promise is not enforceable unless it is supported by consideration*. *Petroleum Traders Corp. v. Hillsborough County*, 2008 WL 4570318,at *4 (C.C.M.D. Fla. 2008) (emphasis added).

In *Potamkin New York, LP v. Gem Auto Brokers Inc.*, a federal district court judge reinforced the state court's ruling in *Petroleum Traders*. The *Potamkin* court wrote:

> Under New York's Uniform Commercial Code, which governs contracts for the sale of goods such as automobiles, an order to purchase goods constitutes an offer to buy such goods, which the seller may accept by timely shipping such goods to the ordering party. *See* N.Y.U.C.C. § 2-206(1)(b). ... Gem placed various orders to buy automobiles from plaintiffs, and plaintiffs shipped the automobiles Gem ordered. Each shipment by plaintiffs constituted an acceptance of the corresponding offer, mutual assent to the purchase order's terms, and a showing of an intent to be bound by the agreement. *Consideration supports the agreements* by virtue of *plaintiffs' delivery of automobiles in exchange for Gem's promises to pay money* for the automobiles. *Potamkin New York, LP v. Gem Auto Brokers Inc.*, No. 8:06-CV-2289-T-TBM, 2012 WL 1898896, at *2–3 (C.C.S.D.N.Y. Oct. 14, 2012) (emphasis added).

Since an Article 2 plaintiff must also prove consideration, courts have had to address the following common law-related questions: (1) whether or not a plaintiff must establish "sufficient" consideration under Article 2 of the UCC; (2) whether or not a plaintiff's preexisting duty may serve as "new" consideration to modify a sale-of-goods contract under Article 2; (3) whether or not the UCC covers both "one-shot" and "relational" transactions; (4) whether or not contracting parties may modify requirements and output contracts under the UCC without exchanging "new" consideration; and (5) whether or not the parties' failure to exchange consideration during the formation of a contract—under the UCC—prevents a seller or buyer from enforcing the terms of a sales contract in a court of law. The cases and materials in this chapter provide answers to these and several related questions.

A. Multiple Methods of Proving Consideration Under Article 2

Security National Bank of Sioux City, Iowa v. Abbott Laboratories
2012 WL 327863
(C.C. N.D. Iowa)

DONALD E. O'BRIEN, SENIOR DISTRICT JUDGE. ... This matter is before the court due to the unfortunate infection of a newborn, J.M.K., with Enterobacter sakazakii meningitis, resulting in severe brain damage. On March 16, 2011, [the] court appointed conservator for J.M.K.—The Security National Bank of Sioux City, Iowa (Plaintiff)—filed an amended complaint alleging eleven separate causes of action against Abbott Laboratories (Defendant). ... This matter is currently before the court on Defendant's motion to dismiss the amended complaint and Defendant's motion to dismiss Plaintiff's second amended complaint pursuant to Federal Rules of Civil Procedure 12(b)(6) and 9(b).

I. Factual Allegations

Plaintiff arranged its factual allegations so that general allegations are first presented and only then followed by other allegations related to their specific causes of action. For simplicity, this court will present Plaintiff's factual allegations in a similar manner.

A. General Allegations

J.M.K. was born at the St. Luke's Regional Medical Center in Sioux City, Iowa, on April 14, 2008. J.M.K. was a full-term, healthy new born. Upon discharge from the hospital, "J.M.K.'s mother was given an unsolicited gift bag" containing Similac powder infant formula (PIF) and "liquid infant formula also manufactured by [Defendant]." The gift bag was provided due to an "agreement wherein [Defendant] supplied gift bags to the hospital containing Similac PIF in exchange for consideration from the hospital."

From April 17, 2008, to April 24, 2008, J.M.K.'s mother fed J.M.K. only the liquid infant formula. When the liquid infant formula ran out, J.M.K.'s mother began feeding J.M.K. the Similac PIF. J.M.K. was 10 days old at this time. Prior to preparing the PIF, "J.M.K.'s mother boiled the water, utensils, bottles and all bottle parts she used with the PIF" and "prepared the PIF in her kitchen" in compliance with Defendant's product label recommendations.

"On April 24, 2008, after being fed the Similac PIF, J.M.K. began showing signs of a possible infection and J.M.K.'s mother took her to the emergency department at St. Luke's Regional Medical Center of Sioux City. ..." Two days later, J.M.K. was flown to the Children's Hospital and Medical Center in Omaha, Nebraska, where she "was admitted and diagnosed with neonatal Enterobacter sakazakii meningitis," resulting "in severe brain damage. ..." Subsequently, the Federal Drug Administration (FDA) tested for and did not find Enterobacter sakazakii in the kitchen where J.M.K.'s PIF was prepared, suggesting an alternate source of contamination.

From J.M.K.'s date of birth through the time she suffered her injuries, J.M.K. was a neonate, "an infant younger than 28 days. Plaintiff contends Defendant's Similac PIF was not and is not "reasonably safe for ... neonates, whether or not the neonate is full term and whether or not the neonate is healthy. ... The only known cause of neonatal Enterobacter sakazakii meningitis is food-borne ingestion," and "PIF is the only known source of neonatal Enterobacter sakazakii meningitis." The Center for Disease Control has associated PIF with every documented case of neonatal Enterobacter sakazakii except one." In the one exception, "it is believed that the infant may have been fed its twin's PIF because of an admitted crib card switch resulting in misidentification." ...

From the above alleged facts, Plaintiff concludes the "source of bacteria that caused J.M.K.'s neonatal Enterobacter sakazakii meningitis was Defendant's Similac PIF;" and Enterobacter sakazakii originated in Defendant's "facilities, and/or [Defendant's] finished product PIF prior to distribution, and/or PIF consumed [by J.M.K.] prior to the diagnosis of Enterobacter sakazakii infection." Plaintiff intends to demonstrate the source of the Enterobacter sakazakii that infected J.M.K. by matching its DNA with "isolate found in [Defendant's] factory, manufacturing equipment, raw materials, finished product (before or after distribution) or with one found in another baby following ingestion of [Defendant's] PIF. ..."

B. Specific Allegations

Plaintiff asserts seven causes of action: (1) manufacturing defects, (2) design defects, (3) failure to warn, (4) breach of express warranties, (5) breach of implied warranty of fitness for a particular purpose, (6) breach of implied warranty of merchantability, and (7) fraud. ...

3. Breach of Express Warranty

Plaintiff alleges Defendant has made several express warranties over the years. For instance, the product J.M.K.'s parents received from the hospital was accompanied by a "label that expressly warranted that its product was beneficial and safe for infants, including neonates." Defendant also expressly states that its "formula is microbiologically safe on its website" and that "infant formula is the only safe, nutritious, and recommended alternative to breastfeeding." On December 23, 2008, Defendant "issued a press release stating that its infant formulas were completely safe." Defendant also advertises that its products nurture and fortify the immune systems of infants.

Plaintiff contends J.M.K.'s parents fed J.M.K. PIF in reliance on Defendant's express warranties; specifically, Defendant's warranty that its "PIF is both safe and beneficial for neonates with normal immune systems." Since the PIF did not conform to Defendant's express warranties, they breached those warranties. Finally, the making and breaching of their express warranties amounted to "willful and wanton disregard for J.M.K.'s rights or safety."

4. Implied Warranty of Fitness for a Particular Purpose

Plaintiff alleges Defendant knew their product was used to feed babies, and their sale, advertising, and distribution of their PIF included an implied warranty that their product "was beneficial and safe for infants." Further, Defendant "had reason to know J.M.K. was relying on its skill or judgment to furnish the PIF." For instance, their advertising indicates their product was designed for healthy balance, and "[m] oms can count on Similac for trusted nutrition and the formula that's right for their babies." However, according to Plaintiff, the PIF was not fit for its particular purpose, and this failure "was a cause of J.M.K.'s damage." Further, Plaintiff contends Defendant's breach of the implied warranty of fitness for a particular purpose amounted to "willful and wanton disregard of J.M.K.'s rights or safety."

5. Implied Warranty of Merchantability

Plaintiff alleges Defendant "was a merchant at the time the PIF was distributed to J.M.K. The PIF Defendant distributed to J.M.K. was not merchantable in that it was not in fair average quality because it contained Enterobacter sakazakii," and Defendant's failure to provide a merchantable product "was a cause of J.M.K.'s damage." Finally, Defendant's breach of the implied warranty of merchantability was a "willful and wanton disregard of J.M.K.'s safety." ...

III. LAW AND ANALYSIS

A. Legal Standard

Rule 12(b)(6) provides that a defendant may assert a defense for "failure to state a claim upon which relief can be granted." Fed.R.Civ.P. 12(b)(6). Rule 8(a)(2) requires a plaintiff to plead "a short plain statement of the claim showing" they are "entitled to relief." F.R.C.P. 8(a)(2). Rule 8(e) requires courts to construe pleadings "so as to do justice." Fed.R.Civ.P. 8(e). ...

E. Warranty Claims

Plaintiff asserts three warranty causes of action: (1) breach of express warranties, (2) breach of the implied warranty of fitness for a particular purpose, and (3) breach of the implied warranty of merchantability. Prior to determining whether Plaintiff has properly alleged a cause of action for its three warranty claims, this court must decide a threshold issue, *i.e.*, whether there was a sale of goods, which is necessary for a warranty, express or implied, to be created.

1. Whether There Was a Sale of Goods

Iowa breach of warranty claims are based in the Iowa Uniform Commercial Code, Chapter 554, Article 2—Sales (IUCC). All three of the warranty claims Plaintiff asserts expressly require a "seller," and, therefore, implicitly require a sale of goods. Iowa Code §§ 554.2313, 554.2314, 554.2315. Far from arbitrary, this requirement separates commercial transactions for economic gain from benevolent donations. Sound policy dictates that donations [must] be encouraged, and unsound business practices [must] be discouraged. Warranty law imposes duties on individuals and companies motivated by economic gain in relation to their implicit and explicit representations which induce buyers to purchase their goods.

As previously noted, Plaintiff alleges Defendant "supplied gift bags to the hospital containing Similac PIF in exchange for consideration from the hospital. *See* BLACK'S LAW DICTIONARY (9th ed. 2009) (defining "consideration" as being "an act, a forbearance, or a return promise … bargained for and received by a promisor from a promisee."). The question is whether Plaintiff's allegation of goods "in exchange for consideration" constitutes a sale under the IUCC.

In its reply brief, the Defendant claims that Plaintiff's allegation is a "legal conclusion." While the difference between legal conclusions and facts are often difficult to distinguish, and an allegation that consideration was given may constitute a conclusion in a contract case, in these circumstances, the allegation is more factual than legal in nature. The Plaintiff is clearly saying that the Defendant received something in exchange for the product it usually sells for money, even if that something was nothing more than enhanced good will among the hospital's customers.

Though at times unclear, Defendant's contention seems to hinge on the popular notion that a sale is the exchange of goods for currency. Plaintiff's Complaint does not specify whether the hospital's consideration given for Defendant's PIF was actual currency. Regardless, after reviewing relevant case law and relevant sections of the IUCC, this court is convinced Plaintiff has sufficiently alleged Defendant sold the goods to the hospital as contemplated under the IUCC.

A sale of goods under the IUCC does not require the exchange of goods for currency but includes other types of consideration. Section 554.2102 provides [that] the scope of Article 2 covers "transactions in goods," which is broad enough to incorporate non-cash consideration. *See* BLACK'S LAW DICTIONARY (9th ed. 2009) (defining a "business transaction" as an "action that affects the actor's financial or economic interest"). Furthermore, § 554.2304 provides [that] a "price can be made payable in money or otherwise." Though this "otherwise" is not explained, this court thinks it is obvious it is intended to include various, non-currency consideration.

Finally, in *Johnson County v. Guernsey Ass'n of Johnson*, 232 N.W.2d 84, 86 (Iowa 1975), the Iowa Supreme court ruled the IUCC definition of a sale was "[p]ractically the same definition" as found in a former Iowa Code § 192A.1(9), dealing with the marketing of dairy products. In that section, a sale was defined as "any commercial transfer for consideration, exchange, barter, gift, or offer for sale and distribution in any manner or by any means." Clearly, under this definition, Plaintiff's allegation constitutes a sale as contemplated by the IUCC.

Defendant implies the definition of sale at § 554.2106 of the IUCC defeats Plaintiff's warranty claims, but this court fails to comprehend how. Section 554.2106 provides: A "'sale' consists in the passing of title from the seller to the buyer. ..." Section 554.2401 provides that "title passes to the buyer at the time and place at which the seller completes the seller's performance with reference to the physical delivery of the goods." Clearly, assuming Defendant received some type of consideration for providing its product to the hospital, as alleged by Plaintiff and as is likely considering the Defendant and the hospital are businesses, rather than charities, title passed to the hospital upon Defendant's delivery of the PIF and a sale was consummated.

Even assuming a sale of goods under the IUCC involves the exchange of goods for currency, Plaintiff's allegation of an exchange of goods for consideration is sufficient. Absent the cooperation of the hospital or Defendant, Plaintiff has no means to verify the nature of the consideration given by the hospital. When considering a motion to dismiss for failure to state a claim, a court must take into account a plaintiff's "limited access to crucial information." *U.S.A. v. Dico*, 2011 WL 677448 (S.D. Iowa 2011). When a fact is in the control of defendant(s) but can be reasonably inferred from a plaintiff's allegations, specific allegations are not necessary. *See Braden v. Wal-Mart Stores, Inc.*, 588 F.3d 585, 598 (8th Cir. 2009) ("If plaintiffs cannot state a claim without pleading facts which tend systematically to be in the sole possession of defendants, the remedial scheme ... will fail, and crucial rights ... will suffer."). Therefore, even assuming a sale requires an exchange of currency, which it does not, it is reasonable to infer the hospital paid cash for the Similac PIF, and Plaintiff's allegation is sufficient.

Defendant also argues that, because Plaintiff alleges J.M.K.'s parents received an unsolicited gift bag, there was no sale. Defendant's argument confuses the issue. The question is not whether there was a sale between the hospital and J.M.K.'s parents but whether there was a sale between Defendant and the hospital. Section 554.2318 of the IUCC unambiguously provides that a "seller's warranty whether express or implied extends to any person who may reasonably be expected to use, consume or be affected by the goods and who is injured by breach of the warranty." Thus, assuming Defendant sold the PIF to the hospital, as alleged by Plaintiff, any and all warranties associated with that sale extended to J.M.K.'s parents, who were reasonably expected to use the product.

Defendant further argues Plaintiff, in order to state a warranty claim under Iowa law, must allege title passed from buyer to seller but failed to do so. As with many of its arguments, Defendant fails to cite a single case stating that such an allegation is necessary and instead relies on inapplicable case law. Plaintiff's allegation that Defendant gave the hospital its Similac PIF in exchange for consideration, as explained above, is another manner of saying that title passed from Defendant to the hospital. Defendant would have Plaintiff allege the same thing under every conceivable variation in the English language, something clearly not contemplated under notice pleading.

Finally, in its reply, Defendant argues Similac PIF was exchanged for services, or, specifically, "the distribution of the infant formula gift bags," and, since the "provision of services ... is not subject to the" IUCC, there can be no warranty claims. Defendant specifically notes: "If anything, the Complaint suggests that the 'consideration' was exchanged for Abbott's services in distributing infant formula gift bags." If taken literally, this argument would make little sense.

First, Plaintiff alleges the goods were exchanged for consideration, not that consideration was exchanged for services. Second, Defendant did not distribute the gift bags, the hospital did. Given these facts, this court has decided to cast Defendant's argument in its best light. Defendant asks this court to assume something Plaintiff does not allege, which would be inappropriate in a motion to dismiss. This Court has no reason to and refuses to presume a certain type of consideration was given. ...

In a motion to dismiss, a court may not draw inferences in the moving parties favor. [Also], Defendant's argument distorts the purpose of the IUCC. "'Goods' means all things ... which are movable. ..." Iowa Code § 554.2105(1). Similac PIF is movable and constitutes a good. The price paid for goods, as previously noted, "can be made payable in money or otherwise," including services. Iowa Code § 554.2304. If, as alleged, Defendant exchanged goods for a price, they are subject to the duties imposed under the IUCC. If the hospital's consideration given in fact consisted of distributing Similac PIF, the hospital is a seller of services and could not be held liable under IUCC warranty claims.

In short, a single transaction may constitute both a sale of goods and a sale of services; in which case, one party is subject to the warranty provisions of the IUCC and one party is not. How a seller of goods is paid has nothing to do with the policy underlying warranty causes of action; again, warranty law imposes duties on individuals and companies motivated by economic gain in relation to their implicit and explicit representations which induce buyer to purchase their goods. In conclusion, Plaintiff properly alleged there was a sale of goods between Defendant and the hospital and any warranties created by such an alleged sale passed on to J.M.K. However, various warranties identified in the IUCC are not automatically created once there is a sale of goods; each requires an additional set of circumstances to apply.

The remainder of this section will determine whether Plaintiff properly alleges sufficient facts to show an express warranty, an implied warranty of fitness for a particular purpose and an implied warranty of merchantability were actually created; and, if so, if Plaintiff properly alleges they were breached.

IV. SUMMARY

Defendant's motion to dismiss is denied in part and granted in part. … In relation to Plaintiff's manufacturing defect, design defect, inadequate warning, breach of express warranty, breach of implied warranty of merchantability, and fraud claims, Defendant's motion to dismiss is denied. In relation to Plaintiff's implied warranty of fitness for a particular purpose claim, Defendant's motion is granted. …

UNIFORM COMMERCIAL CODE

§ 2-306. OUTPUT, REQUIREMENTS AND EXCLUSIVE DEALINGS

(1) A term which measures the quantity by the output of the seller or the requirements of the buyer means such actual output or requirements as may occur in good faith, except that no quantity unreasonably disproportionate to any stated estimate or in the absence of a stated estimate to any normal or otherwise comparable prior output or requirements may be tendered or demanded.

(2) A lawful agreement by either the seller or the buyer for exclusive dealing in the kind of goods concerned imposes

unless otherwise agreed an obligation by the seller to use best efforts to supply the goods and by the buyer to use best efforts to promote their sale.

B. Proof of Consideration and the Enforcement of Requirements and Output Contracts Under Section 2-306 of the UCC

Courts of law and equity recognize a distinction between "one-shot transactions" and long-term or ongoing contractual relationships. *Kerry Steel, Inc. v. Paragon Industries, Inc.*, 106 F.3d 147, 151 (6th Cir. 1997). To be sure, the distinction is an important one. When buyers and sellers form long-term agreements, the parties soon discover that uncertainties as well as unspecified future acts and conditions determine whether or not the parties can reasonably fulfill their respective promises and obligations. By definition, ongoing contractual agreements are indeterminate agreements. Consequently, parties must learn to expect and adapt to uncertainties, changing circumstances and, even, nuanced expectations, conditions, limitations, and obligations.

In contrast, negotiated, one-shot agreements are more precise. The price, quantity, and quality of goods—plus any concomitant services—are stated clearly in the contract. Furthermore, buyers' and sellers' respective obligations are more definite in a one-shot transaction. In fact, parties make a concerted effort to eliminate any or all ambiguities surrounding the transaction. Even more relevant, one-shot obligations must be performed fully and the transaction must terminate by a certain date. *McCarthy v. Azure*, 22 F.3d 351, 357 (1st Cir. 1994).

But the reader should be aware: In the Sixth Circuit, the law of the panels is not settled. Quite simply, the justices have not been able to describe definitively the unique attributes of a one-shot transaction and a long-term contractual relationship. *Compare Kerry Steel*, 106 F.3d at 151 (declaring that parties' contract was "nothing more than an isolated transaction," since there was "no indication in the record that the parties intended to create an ongoing relationship") and *LAK, Inc. v. Deer Creek Enterprises*, 885 F.2d 1293, 1303 (6th Cir. 1989) (holding that the defendant did not form an "ongoing," "far-reaching," "continuous," or "substantial" relationship with a party in another state), *with CompuServe, Inc. v. Patterson*, 89 F.3d 1257, 1265 (6th Cir. 1996) (finding evidence of an "ongoing marketing relationship" between the parties over three years), *and Cole v. Mileti*, 133 F.3d 433, 436 (6th Cir. 1998) (finding a continuing obligation between parties who had negotiated and executed a contract via telephone calls and letters).

Also, in at least one state, an intrajurisdictional split exists over whether a consumer statute applies to both one-shot and ongoing transactional relationships. *See Waverly Properties, LLC v. KMG Waverly*, LLC, 824 F.Supp. 2d 547, 566 (C.C.S.D.N.Y. 2011) ("New York courts have split on whether the purchase of a condominium unit is the sort of "consumer-oriented" transaction to which the statute was intended to apply, or more closely resembles the complex, single-shot transactions that fall outside the statute's purview.").

Without doubt, the Uniform Commercial Code is an enacted "consumer" statute and it governs the creation, interpretation, and enforcement of both one-shot and long-term sale-of-goods contracts. Actually, section 2-306 of the UCC regulates the formation and enforcement of two types of long-term agreements—requirements and output contracts. And depending on the terms, these latter agreements might also be "exclusive dealing contracts." But as discussed above, long-term agreements—like requirements and output contracts—have indefinite terms regarding the quantity of goods that will be exchanged between sellers and buyers. Therefore, the doctrine of "good faith" is the test that courts apply to determine if the parties have satisfied their respective long-term contractual obligations.

Consider two questions while reading the following cases. May contracting parties modify ongoing requirements and output contracts under the UCC without exchanging "new" consideration? Is "good faith" consideration under section 2-306 and "sufficient consideration" under the common law essentially synonymous? The analyses in the following cases will help you to answer these questions.

1. Distinguishing Requirements and Output Contracts Under § 2-306

Griffith v. Clear Lakes Trout Company, Inc.
200 P.3d 1162
(Idaho 2009)

BURDICK, JUSTICE. This is the second appeal of a commercial sales contract dispute between Appellants/Cross-Respondents Rodney and Carla Griffith, individually and d/b/a Boswell Farms (the Griffiths), and Respondent/Cross-Appellant Clear Lakes Trout Co., Inc. (Clear Lakes). ...

I. FACTUAL AND PROCEDURAL BACKGROUND

In September 1998, Clear Lakes—which operates a fish hatchery—executed a six-year contract with the Griffiths, trout growers. ... Clear Lakes agreed to sell the Griffiths sufficient quantities of small trout to enable the Griffiths to grow "up to two million pounds live weight" each year. ... [T]he Griffiths agreed to sell [the trout] back to Clear Lakes once the trout grew to "market size." The parties performed satisfactorily under the agreement for the first three years; however, after September 11, 2001, the market for trout changed significantly as Clear Lakes' customers began to demand larger fish. As Clear Lakes' resale market began to dry up, it started taking trout deliveries from the Griffiths much later and in smaller loads, leaving the Griffiths with overcrowded ponds and a tightened cash flow.

By 2002, the Griffiths were experiencing financial difficulty due to the slowdown in volume. Clear Lakes promised to work better with the Griffiths in the future, and also agreed to extend the terms of the contract for one year to 2005. However, the contract was terminated near the end of the fifth year in August 2003.

In September 2003, the Griffiths filed suit, alleging Clear Lakes had breached the contract by refusing to accept and purchase back in a timely manner the trout that the Griffiths had grown to market size. The district court agreed with the Griffiths and found that Clear Lakes was in breach of the parties' output contract. The district court awarded the Griffiths $446,099.80 for increased costs and lost profits from years four and five of the contract; however, the court refused to grant lost profits for the remaining years—six and seven—finding that the potential for raising additional fish was too speculative to support an award of damages. ...

In *Griffith v. Clear Lakes Trout Co., Inc.* (*Griffith I*), 152 P.3d 604 (Idaho 2007), the Griffiths cross-appealed from the district court's denial of damages for contract years six and seven. This court held that although damages would be difficult to ascertain, the Griffiths were entitled to damages for the remaining two years of the contract. As such, the court remanded the case to the district court with instructions to calculate damages for contract years six and seven. ...

On remand, the district court relied upon the evidence presented at trial regarding damages for years six and seven. Rather than using the Griffiths' output figures from years two and three of the contract as the Griffiths requested, the district court used the Griffiths' average output from years four and five to determine what the Griffiths' output would have been during years six and seven had the contract been carried out in its entirety. ... Based on the court's calculation table, it determined that the Griffiths were entitled to an additional $266,294.24 in damages for contract years six and seven. ...

The Griffiths appeal the amount of damages awarded to them by the district court for contract years six and seven, arguing their average output figure from years two and three, rather than years four and five, was the proper measure of damage. Clear Lakes crossed appealed, arguing the district court erred in awarding the Griffiths attorney fees after remand pursuant to their contingency fee agreement, rather than on an hourly basis. Both parties seek attorney fees on appeal.

II. Discussion

A. Damages for Contract Years Six and Seven

2. Clear Lakes' failure to contest the district court's conclusion that the parties entered into an output contract does not prevent this court from considering whether the parties entered into an output contract on appeal.

First, the Griffiths argue the district court's ruling that the parties entered into an output contract is binding. After trial, the district court concluded—as a matter of law—that the parties entered into an output contract. Although Clear Lakes initially disputed that the agreement was an output contract at the trial court level, it failed to challenge the district court's ruling on either appeal. As such, the Griffiths argue that the district court's ruling is final and cannot be considered by this court on appeal. We disagree. ...

Here, the Griffiths assert that one of the issues surrounding contract damages is whether the district court erred as a matter of law in reducing the Griffiths' output based on Clear Lakes' market decline. ... This issue statement is broken down into two sub issue statements, which are: 1) "The court should not have reduced [the Griffiths'] output because Clear Lakes' market to sell fish declined," and 2) "The court should not rely on Griffith's output in years where Griffith's output was reduced due to Clear Lakes' breach of contract."

In order to address this issue, we must first determine what type of contract is involved. For example, Clear Lakes' market decline would be irrelevant to the district court's determination of damages if the agreement were strictly an output contract, whereas the market decline would be a relevant consideration in an output/requirements contract. Therefore, we conclude that whether an output contract is involved to be a subsidiary issue in the case

3. This court did not state that the parties entered into an output contract in Griffith I.

In addition, the Griffiths argue that this court already acknowledged that the parties entered into an output contract on the first appeal and, therefore, the issue has been resolved and cannot be contested on the second appeal. However, in *Griffith I*, this court merely addressed the Griffiths' argument that the contract's quantity was certain as a matter of law because it was an output contract. Although we went on to reverse the district court on the issue of contract damages for years six and seven, this court did not provide a definitive reason for doing so. Specifically, this court stated: "While damages may be difficult to determine it is clear that the Clear Lakes breach deprived Griffith of the opportunity to complete performance of the contract for the remaining years and that losses for those years occurred." Thus, we never held that the parties entered into an output contract in *Griffith I*.

4. The district court erred in concluding as a matter of law that the parties entered into an output contract.

After trial, the district court concluded as a matter of law that the parties entered into an output contract. In an output contract, the seller determines quantity. I.C. § 28-2-306(1). Yet, the district court also concluded that Clear Lakes—the buyer to the contract—was the party who determined quantity. Specifically, the district court stated:

> Clear Lakes argues that the agreement is not an output contract because Clear Lakes controlled the amount of fingerlings sold to the Griffiths. Nevertheless, the agreement required Clear Lakes to purchase all of the Griffiths' output, up to two million pounds of trout. As the "party who will determine quantity," Clear Lakes is bound to exercise good faith in managing the output contract.

The district court quoted language from comment 2 to section 2-306 of the Uniform Commercial Code, which states:

> Under this Article, a contract for output or requirements is not too indefinite since it is held to mean the actual good faith output or requirements of the particular party. Nor does such a contract lack mutuality of obligation since, under this section, the party who will determine quantity is required to operate his plant or conduct his business in good faith and according to commercial standards of fair dealing in the trade so that his output or requirements will approximate a reasonably foreseeable figure.

When reviewing a trial court's decision after a bench trial, our review is limited to ascertaining "whether the evidence supports the findings of fact, and whether the findings of fact support the conclusions of law." *Griffith I*, 152 P.3d at 608, quoting *Idaho Forest Indus., Inc. v. Hayden Lake Watershed Imp. Dist.*, 17 P.3d 260, 263 (Idaho 2000). "[I]f the findings of fact are supported by substantial and competent evidence, even if the evidence is conflicting, this court will not disturb those findings." *Griffith I*, 152 P.3d at 608. Conclusions of law, however, are reviewed under a different standard. "[T]his court is not bound by the legal conclusions of the trial court, but may draw its own conclusions from the facts presented." *Id.*

The entirety of comment 2 to U.C.C. § 2-306 clarifies that the drafters did not mean to imply that either party to an output contract could determine quantity when they said "the party who will determine quantity." The drafters merely chose this language for the sake of simplicity. Rather than saying "the seller in an output contract and the buyer in a requirements contract," the drafters decided to refer to both parties through a single phrase as "the party who will determine quantity." Thus, contrary to the district court's conclusion, the buyer to an output contract cannot determine quantity.

What the district court really determined was that the parties entered into an output/requirements contract—an output contract subject to the buyer's requirements. Other courts have recognized that parties may enter into a contract that falls within the definitions of both an output and a requirements contract under U.C.C. § 2-306. *See Northern Nat. Gas Co. v. Conoco, Inc.*, 986 S.W.2d 603 (Tex. 1998). By using the phrase "buyer's requirements," we are referring to the requirements of a buyer to an output contract.

Here, the parties agreed that Clear Lakes would sell the Griffiths sufficient quantities of small trout to enable the Griffiths to grow up to two million pounds of market size trout per year, and Clear Lakes would repurchase the trout once they reached market size. The whole purpose of this arrangement was for the Griffiths to profit from raising the trout to market size, and for Clear Lakes to profit from reselling the market size trout. Since Clear Lakes controlled the Griffiths' production, it reasonably follows that it would not have sold more small trout to the Griffiths than it thought it could later resell once the fish reached market size. Otherwise, from an economic standpoint, it would make no sense for Clear Lakes to enter into such an agreement. As such, the quantity of fish under the agreement was not only subject to the Griffiths' good faith output of market size trout, up to the stated maximum of two million pounds, but was also subject to Clear Lakes' good faith requirements for trout in its resale market. Therefore, we hold that the parties entered into an output/requirements contract.

5. The contract does not contain a stated estimate of "two million pounds."

The Griffiths assert that the contract has a stated estimate of "two million pounds" of trout per year. As such, the Griffiths argue that 1,390,454 pounds of fish—which was the quantity the district court used to measure the Griffiths' prior output—is unreasonably disproportionate to the contract's stated estimate of two million pounds of fish. Although the Griffiths argue the contract language estimates the Griffiths' output at "two million pounds," the full language of the contract states that Clear Lakes was to provide enough fingerlings to the Griffiths to enable them to grow "up to two million pounds live weight for each year under the agreement." Based on this language, the district court found that Clear Lakes was not contractually obligated to deliver enough small trout to equal at least two million pounds of market size trout.

Idaho Code § 28-2-306(1), which governs output contracts, states in pertinent part:

> A term which measures the quantity by the output of the seller ... means such actual output ... as may occur in good faith, except that no quantity unreasonably disproportionate to any stated estimate or in the absence of a stated estimate to any normal or otherwise comparable prior output ... may be tendered or demanded.

Comment 3 to I.C. § 28-2-306 goes on to state:

> If an estimate of output or requirements is included in the agreement, no quantity unreasonably disproportionate to it may be tendered or demanded. Any minimum or maximum set by the agreement shows a clear limit on the intended elasticity. In similar fashion, the agreed estimate is to be regarded as a center around which the parties intend the variation to occur.

Upon reading I.C. § 28-2-306(1) in conjunction with comment 3, it is clear that a stated estimate is treated differently than a stated maximum in determining damages for an output contract. A stated maximum sets an upper limit on what the parties intend the elasticity of the seller's output to be, whereas a stated estimate is the basis from which contract damages are to be centered around. Here, the two million pound provision was prefaced by the words "up to." Thus, two million pounds merely serves as a maximum amount of trout that Clear Lakes was obligated to purchase under the agreement, rather than, as the Griffiths argue, the center from which the parties intended output variation to occur. As such, we hold that there is no stated estimate in the contract.

6. Clear Lakes' market decline during years four and five of the contract was relevant to the district court's determination of damages for years six and seven.

The Griffiths also argue that Clear Lakes' requirements from years four and five of the contract were irrelevant to the district court's determination of damages for years six and seven. If the parties' agreement was merely an output contract, then the Griffiths would be correct. In an output contract, the quantity of goods to be delivered under the contract is governed by the seller's good faith output. I.C. § 28-2-306(1); 77A C.J.S. Sales § 306 (2008).

However, as set forth above, this agreement was an output contract subject to the buyer's requirements. Courts' recognizing output/requirements contracts have found that parties to such contracts undertake the risk that their counterparts to the contract may make good faith variations. As the Texas Supreme Court explained in *Northern Natural Gas Co. v. Conoco, Inc.*, 986 S.W.2d 603, 608 (Tex. 1998):

> Nothing requires the seller in an output contract to have any output, and nothing requires the buyer in a requirements contract to have requirements. On the other hand, parties to output/requirements contracts are required to exercise good faith in determining outputs or requirements, as well as accept the concomitant risk that their counterparts to the contract may make good faith variations, even to the extent of liquidating or discontinuing the business.

Here, Clear Lakes controlled the Griffiths' production; thus, by entering into the contract, the Griffiths undertook the risk that Clear Lakes could reduce the quantity of trout it sold to the Griffiths based on its good faith requirements for trout in the resale market. As such, the district court properly considered Clear lakes' market decline in its determination of damages.

7. The district court properly exercised its discretion in using the Griffiths' average production figure from contract years four and five as the measure of damage for contract years six and seven. ...

Finally, the Griffiths assert their average production figure from years two and three of the contract—the years in which Clear Lakes was not in breach—was the proper measure of damage. During years two and three (from September 1999 through September 2001), the Griffiths produced an estimated 1,870,577 pounds of trout per year. After September 11, 2001, however, the market for trout changed significantly as Clear Lakes' customers began to demand larger size fish. Once Clear Lakes' resale market began to dry up, it started decreasing the number of small trout it provided to the Griffiths. As a result, the Griffiths' average output declined to 1,390,454 pounds of fish per year over contract years four and five.

The district court exercised discretion in using the Griffiths' average production figure from contract years four and five as the measure of damage for years six and seven. Idaho Code § 28-2-306(1) sets forth that in the absence of a stated estimate, the quantity term for an output contract is to be measured by "any normal or otherwise comparable prior output." Here, contract years two and three were unaffected by the decline in Clear Lakes' resale market, which, as set forth above, was a relevant consideration to the district court's calculation of damages. Thus, the production figures from years four and five reflect a more comparable prior output to what the Griffiths' production would have been during years six and seven than years two and three had the contract been carried out in its entirety.

Therefore, we hold that the district court did not err in utilizing the Griffiths' average output figure from years four and five as the proper measure of damage. ... [However, without] more precise reasoning from the district court we are unable to evaluate whether the court abused its discretion. ... [W]e remand the case to the district court for a clear explanation as to its treatment of the effects of Clear Lakes' breach during contract years four and five in its calculation of damages for years six and seven.

III. CONCLUSION

We vacate the district court's award of damages for contract years six and seven and remand with instructions for the district court to make a finding as outlined above. ...

NOTES AND QUESTIONS

1. **Attributes of a Requirements Contract.** Generally, under the terms of a requirements contract, a seller promises to supply all the specific goods or services which the buyer may need during a certain period and for an agreed price. In exchange, the buyer promises to purchase his required goods or services exclusively from the seller. *Propane Indus., Inc. v. Gen. Motors Corp.*, 429 F.Supp. 214, 219 (C.C.W.D. Mo. 1977). *See also Tenn. Valley Auth. v. Imperial Prof'l Coatings*, 599 F.Supp. 436, 438 (C.C.E.D. Tenn. 1984) ("A requirements contract is a contract in which the purchaser agrees to buy all of its needs of a specified material from a particular supplier, and the supplier agrees, in turn, to fill all of the purchaser's needs during the period of the contract."). Essentially, a requirements contract is fashioned to give a buyer an assured source of supply—for a certain period—without compelling the buyer to purchase a specified quantity of goods. Consequently, this allows the buyer to meet consumers' fluctuating demands. In fact, courts have allowed buyers to reduce or eliminate the requirements orders if bona fide decreases in demands occur. *Tenn. Valley Auth.*, 599 F. Supp. at 438–39.

2. **"Good Faith" Output/Requirements Contracts Under § 2-303**. Again, to reiterate, the Idaho Supreme Court declared in *Griffith*, "[P]arties may enter into a contract that falls within the definitions of both an output and a requirements contract under UCC § 2-306." The Texas Supreme Court implicitly embraced the

same principle in *Northern Natural Gas Co. v. Conoco, Inc.*, 986 S.W.2d 603, 608 (Tex. 1998), writing:

> Conoco argues that this court should impose a good-faith obligation on Northern because the Agreement is an output/requirements contract, and a party should not be able to cease business and thereby cancel such a contract unless the cessation is in good faith. Several jurisdictions have applied this principle to service contracts as well as to sales contracts. Indeed, the seminal case that first enunciated the common-law requirement that changes in the quantity of output/requirements services be in good faith was a contract for services, not sales. *See Wood v. Lucy, Lady Duff-Gordon*, 222 N.Y. 88, 118 N.E. 214, 215 (1917).
>
> Nothing requires the seller in an output contract to have any output, and nothing requires the buyer in a requirements contract to have requirements. On the other hand, parties to output/requirements contracts are required to exercise good faith in determining outputs or requirements, as well as accept the concomitant risk that their counterparts to the contract may make good faith variations, even to the extent of liquidating or discontinuing the business. We agree with Conoco that a party who seeks to avoid performance of an output contract by having no output—or of a requirements contract by having no requirements—may not do so in bad faith.

2. Proving "Good Faith" and "Mutuality of Obligation" Under § 2-306

Structural Polymer Group, Ltd. v. Zoltek Corporation
543 F.3d 987
(8th Cir. 2008)

COLLOTON, CIRCUIT JUDGE. A jury awarded Structural Polymer Group and Structural Polymer Systems (SP) $36,044,895 in lost profits from Zoltek Corporation for breach of a requirements contract for the sale of carbon fiber. The district court reduced the award to $21,138,518—finding the remainder of the award duplicative. Zoltek appeals the district court's denial of its motion for a new trial and motion for judgment as a matter of law. Structural Polymer cross-appeals the district court's modification of the jury's damages award.

I.

Zoltek is a Missouri corporation that manufactures and sells carbon fiber. SP are British corporations that manufacture a strong, lightweight building material produced using carbon fiber called "prepreg." Prepreg is made by weaving carbon fiber into textile-like sheets and then impregnating the sheets with liquid resin. The prepreg sheets are then sold to builders who can mold them into different shapes for a variety of applications. Used in this way, prepreg is a common substitute for fiberglass. One common application for prepreg is the manufacture of wind energy turbine blades.

The parties entered into a Supply Agreement in November 2000. Under the disputed agreement, Zoltek promised to manufacture and sell to SP all of SP's requirements—between November 6, 2000, and December 31, 2010—for "Large Filament Count Carbon Fibers (Carbon Fibers) as defined by PANEX 33 specifications," at "then-current market price." SP, in turn, promised to "obtain their total requirements for suitable quality—in the reasonable opinion of [SP]—Carbon Fibers from [Zoltek]," the volume not to exceed "the amount actually purchased by [SP] in the preceding Contract Year plus one million (1,000,000) pounds."

"Large Filament Count" or large-tow carbon fiber contains 48,000 or more filaments per bundle. "Small-tow" carbon fiber, by contrast, contains ... commonly 24,000 or fewer filaments per bundle. Small-tow is more expensive to produce, but superior in quality. When the Supply Agreement was formed, most manufacturers used small-tow carbon fiber. The purpose of the agreement was to develop a new market for large-tow fiber as a less expensive alternative to small-tow fiber in the wind-energy industry.

Before April 2002, Zoltek produced a large-tow carbon fiber product called Panex 33. SP purchased 28,219.17 and 20,943.91 pounds of Panex 33 from Zoltek under the Supply Agreement in 2000 and 2001, respectively. SP placed an order for 1,763.70 pounds of Panex 33 in 2002, but returned it due to alleged quality defects. In April 2002, Zoltek stopped manufacturing Panex 33, and started making a large-tow carbon fiber product called Panex 35. SP ordered no Panex 33 or 35 in 2003. SP ordered and received 548,935 pounds of Panex 35 in 2004. The dispute in this case centers on two orders that SP placed with Zoltek in 2005 and 2006 that were never filled. SP ordered 1,480,138 pounds of Panex 35 in 2005, and claims that it was entitled to 2,480,138 pounds of Panex 35 in 2006.

On February 22, 2005, SP sued Zoltek for breach of contract alleging lost profits through December 31, 2006, and future lost profits through December 31, 2010. ... On November 29, 2006, a jury awarded SP lost profits ... through December 31, 2006, but declined to award SP future lost profits. The district court ... [gave] SP a final sum of $21,138,518. Zoltek filed motions ... and the district court denied both motions. Zoltek appeals the district court's denial of those motions. SP cross-appeals the district court's vacation of the jury's award under Count II of the complaint. ...

II.

We first consider Zoltek's objection to the district court's resolution of arguments concerning mutuality of obligation. Zoltek urged that the Supply Agreement was "unenforceable as a requirements contract due to a lack of mutuality," which is in essence an argument that SP failed to show that the Supply Agreement was supported by valid consideration. *See* Restatement (Second) of Contracts § 79 (1981) ("If the requirement of consideration is met, there is no additional requirement of ... 'mutuality of obligation.'"); and, *USA Chem, Inc. v. Lewis*, 557 S.W.2d 15, 24 (Mo. Ct. App. 1977). We conclude that whether or not Zoltek's contention should not have been characterized as an affirmative defense, the district court correctly ruled in the alternative that the Supply Agreement contained mutuality as a matter of law.

SP contends that our decision in *Overholt Crop Ins. Serv. Co. v. Travis*, 941 F.2d 1361, 1368 (8th Cir. 1991), establishes that "lack of consideration" is an affirmative defense that is waived if not raised in an answer. *Overholt* held that it was unnecessary to reach the merits of an argument that certain restrictive covenants in a contract were "void for lack of consideration," because the defendants "waived this affirmative defense by failing to raise it in their answer, and by failing to identify any relevant exceptions to this general rule." *See* Fed.R.Civ.P. 8(c), at 1368.

Zoltek counters with our statement in *First Union Nat'l Bank v. Pictet Overseas Trust Corp.*, 477 F.3d 616, 621–22 (8th Cir. 2007), that whether a contention "is an affirmative defense is a question of state law," and with Missouri authority that distinguishes between "failure of consideration," which is an affirmative defense applicable where consideration that once existed becomes worthless or non-existent, and "lack of consideration," which is an element of the claim that cannot be waived through failure to plead. *Ennis v. McLaggan*, 608 S.W.2d 557, 561 (Mo. Ct. App. 1980).

Assuming for the sake of argument that Zoltek's argument regarding lack of consideration need not be pleaded as an affirmative defense, we agree with the district court that the Supply Agreement was supported by adequate consideration as a matter of law. Under Missouri law, "whether consideration is sufficient to establish a contract is normally a question of law for the court and not a question of fact for the jury." *Allison v. Agribank, FCB*, 949 S.W.2d 182, 188 (Mo. Ct. App. 1997). Missouri law long has followed a rule that "[w]hen a party relies upon a writing or a number of writings to establish a contract, it is unquestionably the province of the court to determine from the writing or writings whether or not a contract was entered into." *Nelson v. Cal Hirsch & Sons' Iron & Rail Co.*, 77 S.W. 590, 594 (Mo. App. 1903).

Zoltek advances three reasons why the contract lacked mutuality of obligation. All three are based on an allegation that SP's requirements under the agreement are "hopelessly manipulable" and determined by SP's subjective preferences, rather than by objective criteria outside of SP's control. Specifically, Zoltek argues that "SP could at all times order or not order Zoltek fiber as it wanted" because (1) SP had zero requirements for large-tow fiber when the contract was formed, (2) the price protection clause gave SP the option "to purchase carbon fibers from other producers" whenever SP wanted to, and (3) SP was free to buy small-tow fiber, which Zoltek alleges is "interchangeable" with large-tow fiber, in place of large-tow whenever it pleased.

First, we disagree with Zoltek that the Supply Agreement lacks mutuality if SP had zero requirements for large-tow fiber when the contract was formed. A duty of good faith is implied in requirements contracts under Missouri law. See MO. REV. STAT. § 400.2-306(1) (1994); and, *Home Shopping Club, Inc. v. Roberts Broad. Co.*, 989 S.W.2d 174, 179 (Mo. Ct. App. 1998). … [T]his "implied obligation of good faith is enough to avoid finding a contract null and void due to an illusory promise." *Magruder Quarry & Co., v. Briscoe*, 83 S.W.3d 647, 650–51 (Mo. Ct. App. 2002).

The Supply Agreement bound SP to order product from Zoltek in good faith, and if SP failed to purchase anything from Zoltek during the term of the agreement, then the contract allowed Zoltek to allege that SP acted in bad faith by failing to make purchases. An assertion of bad faith, however, is an argument that SP breached the agreement, not that the agreement lacked mutuality or consideration in the first place. The district court's ruling on Zoltek's proposed defense did not foreclose it from arguing to the jury that SP breached the agreement.

Second, we disagree with Zoltek that the price protection clause in the contract made SP's obligation illusory. The price protection clause gave Zoltek a right of first refusal to sell large-tow carbon fiber to SP for the same price as offered by a third party seller. If Zoltek offered to match the price offered by another supplier, then SP was obligated to purchase from Zoltek. We think the Missouri courts are likely to agree with the observation in a leading treatise that this mechanism does not render the contract illusory:

> The seller may not promise to meet such prices, but the seller may be given the option of doing so. If the seller meets such

> prices, the buyer must buy of the seller or not at all. If the seller does not meet such prices, the buyer has the privilege of buying elsewhere. Such promises are not illusory and the contract is valid. Arthur Linton Corbin, et al., 2-6 CORBIN ON CONTRACTS § 6.8.

Zoltek's authorities do not persuade us to the contrary. They demonstrate only that if SP had an unfettered option to purchase from another supplier during the term of the contract, then this option would destroy the exclusivity of the arrangement, and demonstrate lack of consideration. *In re Modern Dairy of Champaign, Inc.*, 171 F.3d 1106, 1108 (7th Cir. 1999); *Harvey v. Fearless Farris Wholesale, Inc.*, 589 F.2d 451, 459 (9th Cir. 1978). The inclusion in the Supply Agreement of a right of first refusal for Zoltek to retain its exclusive right to supply SP—so long as it matched a market price offered by another supplier—is sufficient to create mutuality of obligation and consideration.

Third, we do not agree with Zoltek that if small-tow and large-tow fiber are "interchangeable," then the Supply Agreement lacked mutuality. There was a good deal of evidence at trial that small-tow and large-tow fiber are distinct products, with different qualities and applications. But assuming for the sake of argument that a jury could find that small-tow and large-tow fibers are in fact "interchangeable," as Zoltek contends, the authorities cited by Zoltek do not establish that the Supply Agreement is void for lack of mutuality.

These cases illustrate, rather, that when a buyer contracts to purchase its requirements for a product from a particular seller, but then—without a "good faith" basis to do so—purchases an interchangeable product from a third party instead, the buyer may have breached the requirements contract. *Fike Corp. v. Great Lakes Chemical Corp.*, 332 F.3d 520, 524 (8th Cir. 2003); *Empire Gas Corp. v. American Bakeries Co.*, 840 F.2d 1333, 1339–41 (7th Cir. 1988). Zoltek was free to argue on this basis that SP's purchase of small-tow fiber from parties other than Zoltek was a breach of the agreement to purchase large-tow fiber exclusively from Zoltek. But the jury found that SP performed its obligations under the contract. SP's obligation to purchase in good faith all of its requirements for large-tow fiber exclusively from Zoltek was sufficient consideration to make the contract valid.

For these reasons, we agree with the district court's alternative holding that "on the face of the agreement, there is mutuality of obligation and, therefore, consideration." Therefore, any error in characterizing lack of consideration as an affirmative defense or in denying Zoltek's motion to amend its complaint did not prejudice Zoltek. ...

For these reasons, the judgment of the district court is affirmed.

NOTES AND QUESTIONS

1. **Distinguishing Section 2-306 Requirements and Output Contracts from Section 2-612 Installment Contracts.** In *Ho Myung Moolsan, Co. Ltd. v. Manitou Mineral Water,* Inc., 2010 WL 4892646, at *1, *3-4 (S.D.N.Y.), the federal district judge wrote:

   Plaintiff—Ho Myung Moolsan (Moolsan), a South Korean mineral water reseller—brought this breach of contract action against defendant Manitou Mineral Water (Manitou), a mineral water manufacturer based out of Colorado and New York. ... Under the contract, defendant agreed to sell a distribution right for its mineral water to plaintiff for $500,000 and agreed to sell mineral water to plaintiff at $1 per one-liter bottle. Plaintiff also made an advance payment of $1 million for mineral water inventory. The contract was to run for five years. After the first year, plaintiff was required to make minimum yearly orders of $1 million worth of water. Plaintiff was additionally required to place its orders, in writing, normally 3 months in advance. And payment on orders was also to be made in advance. Plaintiff argued that this writing constituted an output contract while defendant argued it was an installment contract.

   Generally, a contract is void under the Uniform Commercial Code if it does not specify a quantity term. N.Y.U.C.C. 2-201 cmt. 1. A minimum quantity term, like the $1 million minimum for years two-through-five in the contract in question in this case, is satisfactory. *Corning Inc. v. VWR Int'l, Inc.*, 2007 WL 841780, at *6 (W.D.N.Y. 2007), citing *Nora Beverages, Inc. v. Perrier Group of America, Inc.*, 164 F.3d 736, 749 (2d Cir. 1998). When a contract contains a quantity term but allows for delivery in separate lots separately accepted, it is an installment contract. N.Y.U.C.C. 2-612(1).

   A breach of the entire contract occurs only when a non-conformity or default with respect to one or more installments substantially impairs the value of the whole contract. N.Y.U.C.C. 2-612(3). This standard for determining breach differs from that for single-lot contracts in that, for the latter, if the goods or the tender of delivery fail in any way to conform to the contract, a breach has occurred and a buyer may reject the goods and cease performing under the contract. N.Y.U.C.C. 2-601. Additionally, a breach of an individual installment occurs when the default in question substantially reduces or impairs the value, to the buyer, of that shipment. *Arkla*

Energy Resources v. Roye Realty Developing Corp., 9 F.3d 855, 862–63 (10th Cir. 1993). ...

[T]he definition of an installment contract includes coverage of installment deliveries tacitly authorized by the circumstances or by the option of either party. N.Y.U.C.C. 2-612 cmt. 1. Each delivery of a separate lot need not even be separately paid for. N.Y.U.C.C. 2-612 N.Y. annot. 1. Additionally, a contract that: provides that deliveries are to be made only at times authorized and chosen by the buyer, without specifying the times for delivery, may also properly be treated as an installment contract under the Code ... since the uncertainty of when and if the buyer will request delivery does not change the essential character of the contract.

15 Williston on Contracts 45:2 (4th ed. 2010). Finally, the lack of a regular shipment schedule does not preclude a contracts characterization as an installment contract. Contracts that lack quantity terms but instead specify quantity based on the output of a seller, on the other hand, are also valid. N.Y.U.C.C. 2-306(1)

An output contract is one that measures quantity by the output of the seller ... as may occur in good faith, except that no quantity unreasonably disproportionate to any ... normal or otherwise comparable prior output ... may be tendered or demanded. 3 Williston on Contracts 7:12 (4th ed. 2010) ([A]greements by a seller to sell all the goods or services he may produce to a buyer in exchange for the buyers agreement to purchase them are known as output contracts. Because the quantity term of an output contract varies, the test to determine breach centers on the parties' good faith in producing or accepting amounts of the product in question.) *See* N.Y.U.C.C. 2-306 cmt. 3. ... The contract here is a hybrid installment-requirements contract.

2. **Exclusive Dealing Contracts and Section 2-306 Codification of the Common Law.** In *CQ Intern. Co., Inc. v. Rochem Intern., Inc., USA*, 2010 WL 2292162, *9 (D. Mass.), the federal district court presented the following analysis:

Although CQ's contract with Huizhou Successor was a mixed contract for both goods (Clozapine) and services (assistance with obtaining FDA approval and complying with U.S. laws), the parties agree that Massachusetts's version of Article 2 of the Uniform Commercial Code (U.C.C.)—which applies only to "transactions in goods"—governs the contract. Mass. Gen. Laws ch. 106, § 2-102. ... *See also Specialty Beverages, L.L.C.*

v. Pabst Brewing Co., 537 F.3d 1165, 1174 (10th Cir. 2008) (noting that the majority of courts that have addressed the issue have concluded that "Article 2 governs distribution agreements because the sale of goods is the predominant factor"). Under the U.C.C., CQ's agreement to serve as the exclusive distributor of Huizhou Successor's Clozapine carried with it an implied obligation to use its best efforts to promote the sale of Huizhou Successor's product. *See* MASS. GEN. LAWS CH. 106, § 2-306(2). This rule codifies the common-law principle that a party who contracts to serve as another's exclusive agent implicitly promises to make reasonably strenuous efforts to further the principal's interests. *See Wood v. Lucy, Lady Duff-Gordon*, 118 N.E. 214, 214–15 (N.Y. 1917).

C. Consideration, Preexisting Duty, and Modification of Contracts Under Section 2-209

In CHAPTER 3, the modification of contracts is discussed and multiple reasons are presented to explain contracting parties' propensities to amend their agreements. Here, a reexamination of those reasons will not appear. It is sufficient to repeat that a host of foreseeable and unforeseeable financial, economic, political, environmental, social, legal, and regulatory constraints force parties to modify their goods and services contracts. Also, as stated earlier, contacting parties often litigate the common-law question: whether "new" consideration must support a valid, modified agreement. Or, stated differently, the question becomes: whether a preexisting contractual duty may serve as sufficient consideration to enforce a modified contract.

Again, under the common law, the general rule is clear: A preexisting duty may not serve as consideration for a modified agreement. *See, e.g. Block v. Fedak*, 499 P.2d 1052, 1054 (Kan. 1972) (concluding that proof of independent consideration or "new consideration" is required to enforce a modified agreement). Some courts, however, have fashioned a common-law exception to the rule: A modified contract may be enforced without evidence of any "new" consideration, if a modification is "fair and equitable" in light of new realities. *See Quigley v. Wilson*, 474 N.W.2d 277, 280 (Iowa Ct. App. 1991).

In very recent years, an increasing number of courts and commentators have stressed that the common-law, preexisting-duty rule is outdated and pointless. *See e.g.*, Robert A. Hillman, *Contract Modification in Iowa-Recker v. Gustafson and the Resurrection of the Preexisting Duty Doctrine*, 65 Iowa L. Rev. 343 (1980) (questioning whether the preexisting-duty rule is warranted in Iowa); Corneill A. Stephens, *Abandoning the Pre-Existing Duty Rule: Eliminating the Unnecessary*,

8 Hous. Bus. & Tax L.J. 355 (2008) (asserting that the preexisting-duty rule is outdated); 2 JOSEPH M. PERILLO & HELEN H. BENDER, CORBIN ON CONTRACTS § 7.1, at 342 (rev. ed. 1995) ("The pre-existing duty rule is undergoing a slow erosion and, as a general rule, is destined to be overturned."); and, FARNSWORTH ON CONTRACTS § 4.22, at 528–29 n. 3 (listing judicial decisions which question the rule).

But consider UCC § 2-209. It reads:

§ 2-209. Modification, Rescission and Waiver

> (1) An agreement modifying a contract within this Article needs no consideration to be binding.
>
> (2) A signed agreement which excludes modification or rescission except by a signed writing cannot be otherwise modified or rescinded, but except as between merchants such a requirement on a form supplied by the merchant must be separately signed by the other party.
>
> (3) The requirements of the statute of frauds section of this Article (Section 2-201) must be satisfied if the contract as modified is within its provisions.
>
> (4) Although an attempt at modification or rescission does not satisfy the requirements of subsection (2) or (3) it can operate as a waiver.
>
> (5) A party who has made a waiver affecting an executory portion of the contract may retract the waiver by reasonable notification received by the other party that strict performance will be required of any term waived, unless the retraction would be unjust in view of a material change of position in reliance on the waiver.

Clearly, the UCC completely eliminates the pre-existing-duty rule. To enforce a "good faith," modified sale-of-goods contract, a party does not have to produce evidence of "new" consideration. Section 2-209(1) of the UCC reads: "An agreement modifying a contract within this Article needs no consideration to be binding." *See also, In re Laibe Corp.*, 307 S.W.3d 314, 317 (Tex. 2010) ("[U]nder the Uniform Commercial Code, an agreement modifying a contract for the sale of goods requires no new consideration to be binding.") (citing TEX. BUS. & COM. CODE § 2.209(a); *Sociedad Aeronautica De Santander S.A. v. Weber*, 2010 WL 2803044, *7 (D. Mont.) ("Unlike a modification under Montana's common law of contracts, "[a]n agreement modifying a contract under [the UCC's sale-of-goods provision] needs no consideration to be binding."), citing MONT. CODE ANN. § 30-2-209(1)).

D. Consideration and the Enforcement of Option Contracts Under Sections 2-205 and 2-306

At this point, a mini review of some previously stated principles is warranted. Again, under the common law, sufficient consideration is necessary to form an enforceable contract. In fact, a myriad of acceptable actions and inactions for another's benefit may serve as consideration. *TMA Fund, Inc. v. Biever*, 380 F. Supp. 1248, 1253 (C.C.E.D. Pa. 1974). But more importantly, consideration must be mutual. Both an offeror and an offeree must do something for the other's benefit. 17A AM. JUR. 2D CONTRACTS § 129 (2006). Otherwise, the contract will not be enforced, because a party failed to produce evidence of a bargained-for-exchange, or detrimental reliance on a contractual promise. *Cf. Roth Steel Products v. Sharon Steel Corp.*, 705 F.2d 134, 144–45, n. 22 (6th Cir. 1983).

To be sure, requirements and output agreements are contracts. They create legal duty—requiring buyers and sellers to perform their negotiated obligations. On the other hand, under section 2-306 of the UCC, requirements and output contracts may be enforced without proof of sufficient consideration. Simply put, evidence of a party's "good faith" performance is enough to enforce a valid requirements or output contract. *Cf. General Motors Corp. v. Paramount Metal Products Co.*, 90 F.Supp.2d 861 (C.C.E.D. Mich. 2000). And, as stated above, proof of consideration is not required to enforce a modified contract under section 2-209(1) of the UCC.

Furthermore, like contracts generally, requirements and output contracts may contain an option clause. Under the common law, for even nominal consideration, an option provision in a requirements contract gives a purchaser a right—an option—to purchase goods, services, as well as other tangible and intangible property interests for a specified period. BLACK'S LAW DICTIONARY (9th ed. 2009). Even more importantly, an option clause in a requirements or an output contract creates a completely new and separate agreement entitled, "Option Contract." *Cf. In re Wheeling-Pittsburgh Steel Corp.*, 360 B.R. 632, 639 (Bankr.N.D. Ohio 2006) ("At common law, a [contractual] promise to keep an offer open is known as an option contract.")

But consider section 2-205, which is entitled "Firm Offers." The entire statute reads:

> An offer by a merchant to buy or sell goods in a signed writing which by its terms gives assurance that it will be held open is not revocable, for lack of consideration, during the time stated or if no time is stated for a reasonable time, but in no event may such period of irrevocability exceed three months; but any such term of assurance on a form supplied by the offeree must be separately signed by the offeror.

Section 1-103(b) of the Uniform Commercial Code provides in pertinent part: Unless otherwise displaced by particular provisions of the UCC, "the principals of law and equity ... shall supplement their provisions." For sure, section 2-205 does not displace common-law option-contract rules. But, a careful reading of the "firm offer" language in section 2-205 reveals that it neither completely rejects nor totally codifies general common-law principles, those which govern the formation and enforcement of option contracts. To help understand the seemingly contradictory rule in the statute, consider Justice Hutchinson's concurring opinion and analysis in *Bethlehem Steel Corp. v. Litton Indus., Inc.*, 488 A.2d 581, 600 (Pa. 1985). He wrote:

> An option agreement—although it may seem to have only the characteristics of an offer—is nevertheless a contract. As a contract, the option agreement requires contract formalities including consideration. In cases involving the sale of goods, the U.C.C. has modified the common law of offer and acceptance by creating what it calls firm offers in § 2-205, 13 Pa. C. S. § 2205, which bind the offeror, in a limited sense, without consideration. Such an offer, if it states that it will be held open for a definite time—not in excess of a statutorily limited period—does not fail for lack of consideration, *i.e.* it is not revocable during the period set up to the statutory limit.
>
> This Code section limits the time a firm offer can be held irrevocable to three months. Option contracts, however, are not governed by 13 Pa. C. S. § 2205. The firm offer—which § 2-205 makes irrevocable for a limited time—is sometimes loosely called an "option," but it has a different character than the option contract recognized at common law. The Code discloses no legislative intent to eliminate the option contract, with its requirement of consideration. Hence, [it is necessary to distinguish an "option"]—which is in reality a firm offer—[from an] option contract.

Still, it is important to stress five salient points: 1) section 2-306 of the UCC governs the formation and enforcement of requirements and output contracts involving the sale of goods; 2) section 2-306 does not contain language that prevents parties from inserting "option clauses" in sale-of-goods requirements and output agreements; 3) an option contract is a separate contract—under which a promisor agrees to limit his power to revoke an offer for a prescribed period of time. 17A AM. JUR. 2D CONTRACTS § 53 (2006); 4) section 2-306 does not contain language that prohibits the use of option contracts in relation to sale-of-goods requirements and output contracts; and 5) sufficient consideration is required to enforce an option contract.

In *Bethlehem Steel*, the court embraced the view: Section 2-205 does not govern the creation and enforcement of option contracts. Does section 2-306 govern the construction and interpretation of option contracts, which evolve from sale-of-goods contracts? Do sale-of-goods, requirements and output contracts qualify as true, "enforceable" option contracts—since section 2-306 does not require evidence of any "new" consideration? Does Article 2 apply to option contracts? The excellent analysis in the next case provides answers to these questions.

Merritt-Campbell, Inc. v. RxP Products, Inc.
164 F.3d 957
(5th Cir. 1999)

Reynaldo G. Garza, Circuit Judge:

I. Factual and Procedural Background

In August, 1995, Carl Merritt (Merritt) telephoned RxP and talked to its President—Don Woodward (Woodward)—about selling a fuel additive known as "RxP Gas Kicker" as a private label product. Woodward referred Merritt to RxP's National Sales Manager, James Potts (Potts). On August 19, 1995, Potts met with Merritt. During the next few weeks, the parties had numerous discussions relating to the potential private label arrangement. On September 18, 1995, Merritt-Campbell, Inc. (M-C) was incorporated by Merritt and Harvey Campbell (Campbell).

On September 28, 1995, Merritt gave Potts a proposed agreement which Potts faxed to Woodward the following day. Woodward made changes to the proposal, signed it, and returned it to Potts to be signed by M-C. On October 3, 1995, Merritt signed the agreement on behalf of M-C. The agreement in its entirety states:

> This agreement is made on this 28th day of September, 1995, between RxP Products, Inc., hereafter referred to as RxP, and Merritt-Campbell, Incorporated, hereinafter referred to as Merritt-Campbell. In consideration of the sum of ten dollars ($10.00), the receipt of which is acknowledged, RxP agrees to sell to Merritt-Campbell the product marketed as "RxP Gas Kicker" under the following terms:
>
> 1. RxP guarantees the following price to Merritt-Campbell for a period of five (5) years from the date of first order.
>
> a. RxP Gas Kicker bottled in 2.5 ounce quantities—$1.25 per bottle (excluding labels).
>
> b. RxP Gas Kicker in 55 gallon drum quantity—$1,280,00 (sic) per drum.

> Said pricing may be increased only in the case of documented price increases to RxP for raw materials.
>
> 2. RxP will bottle RxP Gas Kicker in either green or black bottles, as provided as samples, upon request for Merritt-Campbell.
>
> 3. RxP guarantees shipment within fourteen (14) days from receipt of order from Merritt-Campbell.
>
> 4. Both RxP and Merritt-Campbell agree unconditionally to maintain confidentiality regarding the relationship between the two companies. This confidentiality includes, but is not limited to, any disclosure of the source product market by RxP and Merritt-Campbell. The scope of this confidentiality includes, but is not limited to, any director, officer, employee, or agent of both RxP and Merritt-Campbell.
>
> 5. It is understood by RxP that it is the intention of Merritt-Campbell to market the product heretofore referred to as "RxP Gas Kicker" under a private label.

On November 9, 1995, Merritt presented to Potts a purchase order for 25,000 bottles of product with 60-day credit terms. Potts refused the purchase order because it contained credit terms. On April 8, 1996, RxP received a second order and a cashier's check from M-C for a total of 8,016 bottles of RxP Gas Kicker. RxP refused the order and returned the cashier's check to M-C uncashed.

On May 17, 1996, M-C filed suit against RxP in the United States District Court for the Northern District of Texas. M-C claimed that RxP breached a requirements contract entered into by RxP and M-C in September of 1995. M-C claimed that the contract entitled it to purchase from RxP quantities of RxP Gas Kicker. M-C described the contract as one for the sale of goods and acknowledged that it was governed by the Uniform Commercial Code (UCC). M-C sought specific performance and in the alternative, damages in the sum of $2,020,000.

RxP counterclaimed seeking a declaration that the agreement was not an enforceable contract. RxP also pleaded the affirmative defenses of failure to satisfy the statute of frauds, failure of consideration, failure to satisfy conditions precedent, repudiation by M-C, failure to provide adequate assurance of performance, and failure by M-C to perform in a commercially reasonable manner. ...

On June 30, 1997, the magistrate judge granted RxP's motion with respect to damages holding that M-C was not entitled to recover damages for lost profits. The judge denied RxP's motion with respect to the enforceability of the contract between RxP and M-C. Without a motion before him the magistrate judge held that the contract was not one for the sale of goods. The court characterized the agreement as an option contract and held that option contracts are not subject to the UCC or the statute of frauds. The court also held that the agreement was potentially enforceable as an option contract.

A jury trial was scheduled for July 21, 1997. On July 14, 1997, the parties filed their pretrial order, which was approved and signed by the magistrate judge. The issues included: (1) whether the agreement is an enforceable contract; (2) whether the agreement is unenforceable because it lacks a quantity term; (3) whether the parties intended to form an option contract; (4) whether option contracts for the sale of goods are subject to the UCC; (5) whether the September 1995 agreement was intended to be the entire agreement between the parties; and (6) whether an option contract lacking numerous terms, including a quantity term, is capable of specific performance.

On July 21, 1997, the magistrate judge announced that a trial would not be held and that the parties would not be allowed to present evidence concerning the contested issues. On September 9, 1997, the judge held that the agreement entered into by the parties is an option contract whereby M-C purchased from RxP, for consideration of $10.00, the right to purchase RxP Gas Kicker for a specified price over five years from the date of first order. The magistrate judge also held that the option contract was not one for the sale of goods and was not subject to §§ 2.102, 2.106(a) and 2.201 of the TEXAS BUSINESS AND COMMERCIAL CODE. The magistrate judge also held that the option contract represented the full and complete agreement between RxP and M-C and could not be supplemented by evidence of additional terms. The judge awarded M-C specific performance of the contract and attorney's fees that amounted to $32,156.25. On October 2, 1997, RxP filed a timely appeal to this court. On October 10, 1997, M-C cross appealed. …

III. DISCUSSION

There are four issues that are presented before this court: (1) whether the magistrate judge was correct in holding that the agreement was an option contract not for the sale of goods and therefore not subject to the UCC; (2) whether RxP received proper notice of the magistrate judge's granting sua sponte summary judgment; (3) whether attorneys' fees were properly awarded; and (4) whether lost profits were properly denied. We will only address the first issue because we hold that the magistrate judge was incorrect in ruling that the TEXAS BUSINESS AND COMMERCIAL CODE does not apply to this case.

M-C asserts that the agreement is a valid and unambiguous enforceable contract. First, it supports the trial court's finding that the agreement is an enforceable option contract not governed by the UCC. In addition, M-C argues that the writing is an enforceable requirements contract governed by the UCC. Finally, M-C argues that the agreement is a valid distributorship agreement governed by the UCC.

RxP argues that option contracts are governed by the UCC. In the case at bar, however, the written agreement between M-C and RxP created an unenforceable option contract because it failed to satisfy the UCC statute of frauds by failing to state a quantity term. RxP argues that a quantity term is essential to form a valid option contract and therefore the writing is unenforceable. RxP ardently argues that the lower court's ruling, that option contracts are not governed by the UCC, is erroneous and unsupported by case law.

TEXAS BUSINESS AND COMMERCIAL CODE

Chapter 2 of the UCC applies to all transactions in goods. TEX. BUS. & COM. CODE ANN. § 2.102. A contract for the sale of goods includes "both a present sale of goods and a contract to sell goods at a future time." TEX. BUS. & COM. CODE ANN. § 2.106(a). Therefore, rights of parties are not effected by whether the transaction is one for a present sale of goods or a contract relating to the future.

The UCC unequivocally states that a contract involving the sale of goods is not enforceable without a quantity term. *See* TEX. BUS. & COM. CODE ANN. § 2.201. Thus, the only term that must appear in a writing to support an enforceable contract for the sale of goods is the quantity term. TEX. BUS. & COM. CODE ANN. § 2.201cmt. 1. Section 2.201(a) states:

> Except as otherwise provided in this section a contract for the sale of goods for the price of $500 or more is not enforceable by way of action or defense unless there is some writing sufficient to indicate that a contract for sale has been made between the parties and signed by the party against whom enforcement is sought or by his authorized agent or broker. A writing is not insufficient because it omits or incorrectly states a term agreed upon but the contract is not enforceable under this paragraph beyond the quantity of goods shown in such writing.

However, a contract which fails to satisfy the requirements of section 2.201(a) but which is valid in other respects is enforceable pursuant to section 2.201(c):

> (1) if the goods are to be specially manufactured for the buyer and are not suitable for sale to others in the ordinary course of the seller's business and the seller, before notice of repudiation is received and under circumstances which reasonably indicate that the goods are for the buyer, has made either a substantial beginning of their manufacture or commitments for their procurement; or

> (2) if the party against whom enforcement is sought admits in his pleading, testimony or otherwise in court that a contract for sale was made, but the contract is not enforceable under this provision beyond the quantity of goods admitted.

M-C maintains that although the agreement lacks a quantity term, it still does not violate the statute of frauds because the agreement is within the exception for specifically manufactured goods under 2.201(c)(1). Although M-C's contention may have merit, this issue was not raised in the magistrate court and therefore is waived. ... In addition, RxP maintains that the evidence merely confirms that the parties were working toward an anticipated business relationship and does not confirm the existence of a contract. After reviewing the record we find that RxP's references to the agreement did not constitute an admission under 2.201(c)(2). Therefore, this section is inapplicable to the facts of this case. Thus, because a quantity term was not sufficiently stated in the agreement we hold that the statute of frauds is not satisfied.

CHARACTERIZATION OF THE AGREEMENT

We will not address whether the agreement is a valid distributorship agreement because M-C failed to a present this issue before the magistrate court. Consequently, M-C has waived that issue. It is clearly established that the UCC applies to both option and requirements contracts. *See W.H. McCrory & Co., Inc. v. Contractors Equipment and Supply Co.*, 691 S.W.2d 717 (Tex. App.—Austin 1985, writ ref'd n.r.e) (holding that an option contract to purchase a forklift must satisfy the statute of frauds); and, *Eastern Dental Corp. v. Isaac Masel Co., Inc.*, 502 F.Supp. 1354 (E.D. Pa. 1980) (applying the statute of frauds requirement of a quantity term to requirements contracts). Therefore, the classification of the agreement as an option or requirements contract is irrelevant. This is because either characterization will result in the agreement violating the statute of frauds because the agreement fails to state a quantity term. Nevertheless, this court classifies the agreement as an option contract.

The agreement cannot be characterized as a requirements contract. An essential element of a requirements contract is the promise of the buyer to purchase exclusively from the seller either the buyer's entire requirements or up to a specified amount. *Mid-South Packers, Inc. v. Shoney's, Inc.,* 761 F.2d 1117, 1120 (5th Cir. 1985). Without such a promise by the buyer, a requirements contract fails for lack of consideration. *Id.* at 1121. A requirements contract is a contract that, although it does not establish the amount that a buyer must purchase from the seller, prohibits the buyer from purchasing from other sellers. *See Cardiovascular Services, Inc. v. West Houston Health Care Group, Inc.*, 1995 WL 523615 (Tex. App.—Hous. [1 Dist.] 1995). In this case, however, the agreement's language fails to contain a promise of exclusivity or demonstrate in any fashion that M-C was restricted from purchasing from other sellers.

In addition, in output and requirements contracts, the quantity of goods to be delivered under the contract is determined by the good faith output or requirements of the parties. This does not mean, however, that the statute of frauds' requirement of a quantity term is obviated since the inclusion of a quantity term is a mandatory requirement under the UCC. While the quantity term in requirements contracts need not be numerically stated, there must be some writing which indicates that the quantity to be delivered under the contract is a party's requirements or output. "The writing must specify the quantity of goods to be sold. ... For a requirements contract, the quantity to be specified is 'a party's requirements.'" *Omega Engineering, Inc. v. Eastman Kodak Co.*, 908 F.Supp. 1084, 1090 (D. Conn. 1995). The language in the agreement does not specify a quantity of M-C's requirements or RxP's output. Thus, we find that the correct classification of the agreement cannot be as a requirements contract.

We hold that the agreement is properly characterized as an option contract. An option contract has two components: 1) the underlying contract which is not binding until accepted; and 2) the covenant to hold open to the optionee the opportunity to accept. *Casa El Sol—Acapulco, S.A. v. Fontenot*, 919 S.W.2d 709, 717 n. 9 (Tex. App.—Houston. [14 Dist.] 1996). "The purpose of a purchase option is to give the optionee the right to purchase, at his election, within an agreed period, at a named price, which presumably was considered satisfactory by the optionor in case the option should be exercised at any time during the option term." *Maxwell v. Lake*, 674 S.W.2d 795, 798 (Tex. App.—Dallas, 1984).

To be binding, an option contract must: (1) be signed by the offeror; (2) recite a purported consideration for making the offer; and (3) propose an exchange on fair terms within a reasonable time. RESTATEMENT (SECOND) OF CONTRACTS § 87 (1979). We find that the agreement should be classified as an option contract because it was (1) was signed by RxP, the offeror; (2) the agreement states a consideration of the sum of ten dollars for making the offer; and (3) M-C had the option to purchase RxP Gas Kicker for five years from the date of the first order at the price of $1.25 per 2.5 ounce bottles and $1,280 per drum. We find these terms to be fair and within a reasonable time. Therefore, we conclude that the correct classification of the agreement is an option contract.

Although we agree with the magistrate judge in his conclusion that the agreement was properly characterized as an option contract, we find that there is no authority to support the proposition that the UCC does not apply to option contracts. The magistrate judge incorrectly cites *Sinclair Refining Co. v. Allbritton*, 218 S.W.2d 185 (Tex. 1949), in support of his holding. As RxP notes, the UCC became effective in Texas as of June 30, 1966, but *Sinclair* was decided almost eighteen years before that date. *Sinclair* involved a dispute between a lessee and lessor over a purchase option clause in an oil and gas lease and is not applicable to our case.

Furthermore, Texas courts apply the UCC when dealing with option contracts. The Austin Court of Appeals held that an option to purchase a forklift was unenforceable because it failed to satisfy the statute of frauds. *W.H. McCrory & Co., Inc.*, 691 S.W.2d at 721. The option, which was connected to an equipment lease, was characterized as a contract for the sale of goods. The court held that the contract did not comply with TEXAS BUSINESS AND COMMERCIAL CODE § 2.201. *Id.* at 719–720. … Also, UCC § 2-201 has been held applicable to an alleged option contract involving the sale of an airplane. *McCollum Aviation, Inc. v. CIM Associates, Inc.*, 446 F.Supp. 511, 513 (S.D. Fla. 1978).

IV. CONCLUSION

Although this court would classify the agreement between RxP and M-C as an option contract, the agreement fails to sufficiently state a quantity term and therefore does not satisfy the statute of frauds. Thus, there is no valid and enforceable contract between M-C and RxP. Accordingly, this court concludes that the magistrate judge's decision is incorrect and is hereby reversed and rendered.

UNIFORM COMMERCIAL CODE

§ 1-306. Waiver or Renunciation of Claim or Right After Breach

A claim or right arising out of an alleged breach may be discharged in whole or in part without consideration by agreement of the aggrieved party in an authenticated record.

CHAPTER ELEVEN

Breach of Sale-of-Goods and Delivery Contracts Under Article 2

Chapter 4 outlines various ways that contracting parties breach contracts under the common law—failing to deliver goods, failing to render services, unreasonably delaying the delivery of goods or services, failing to deliver legal documents, failing to pay for goods and services, repudiating a negotiated contract, unilaterally extending or shortening the performance deadline, unilaterally modifying or readjusting contractual terms and conditions, and "foot dragging." Similarly, under Article 2 of the UCC, sale-of-goods contracts may also be breached in numerous ways. Moreover, under the common law and in most jurisdictions, an *implied covenant* of good faith and fair dealing is associated with every contract. But, section 1-203 of the UCC *imposes* a general obligation of good faith on buyers and sellers; therefore, sellers and buyers' potential to breach sale-of-goods contracts also increases in numerous other ways.

Furthermore, under the common law, there are no unique or different rules that govern, say, a party's failure to deliver a product, and a party's failure to deliver a completely unblemished product. In addition, when a seller or a buyer breaches a contract, courts do not apply two different sets of common-law rules to determine whether a seller or a buyer is liable. Instead, courts apply a single body of common-law rules to reach a conclusion.

On the other hand, Article 2 provides separate rules for sellers and buyers who breach sale-of-goods contracts. Additionally, the UCC outlines different sets of remedial rules that courts must apply when sellers and buyers, respectively, are complainants. Furthermore, it is common for buyers and sellers to form independent delivery contracts when sales contracts are being fashioned. Put simply, "shipment" and "destination" agreements describe the methods and places, respectively, for delivering goods to buyers. Fairly often, sellers or their agents breach delivery contracts. And once more, one finds Article 2 providing separate sets of rules to determine whether or not a seller is liable for breaching a "shipment" or a "destination" contract.

Also, sometimes parties delegate their contractual obligations to third parties, without securing the other contracting party's informed consent or permission. Furthermore, a delegation of performance may occur with or without one's assigning a contract. In effect, when a party delegates a contractual duty without permission, the party breaches the contract. Under the common law, the doctrine of novation gives a breaching party an effective defense. The doctrine of assignment may also allow a defendant to escape liability. Article 2 has codified the doctrines of novation and assignment. But the UCC's rules are not, if you will, mirror images of the common-law rules.

Finally, when a seller or buyer files a breach-of-contract action under Article 2, the party must establish a *prima facie* case. Proving that a defendant breached a sale-of-goods contract or a "delivery contract" satisfies one of several requirements. This chapter presents cases and materials, outlining how a plaintiff should establish a breach-of-contract action under Article 2. Additionally, where warranted, brief comparisons of plaintiffs' respective burdens of proof under the common law and the UCC are discussed in this chapter.

UNIFORM COMMERCIAL CODE

§ 2-106. DEFINITIONS: "CONTRACT"; "AGREEMENT"; "CONTRACT FOR SALE"; "SALE"; "PRESENT SALE"; "CONFORMING" TO CONTRACT; "TERMINATION"; "CANCELLATION"

> (1) In this Article unless the context otherwise requires "contract" and "agreement" are limited to those relating to the present or future sale of goods. "Contract for sale" includes both a present sale of goods and a contract to sell goods at a future time. A "sale" consists in the passing of title from the seller to the buyer for a price (Section 2-401). A "present sale" means a sale which is accomplished by the making of the contract.

(2) Goods or conduct including any part of a performance are "conforming" or conform to the contract when they are in accordance with the obligations under the contract.

(3) "Termination" occurs when either party pursuant to a power created by agreement or law puts an end to the contract otherwise than for its breach. On "termination" all obligations which are still executory on both sides are discharged but any right based on prior breach or performance survives.

(4) "Cancellation" occurs when either party puts an end to the contract for breach by the other and its effect is the same as that of "termination" except that the cancelling party also retains any remedy for breach of the whole contract or any unperformed balance.

SECTION ONE: BREACH OF SALE-OF-GOODS CONTRACTS

A. The Perfect Tender Rule Under § 2-601

Under the common law, the doctrine of material breach is an affirmative defense in a breach-of-contract action. *Compass Bank v. MFP Fin. Servs.*, 152 S.W.3d 844, 852 (Tex. App.—Dallas 2005, pet. denied). A "material breach" is a party's failure to perform a fundamental obligation under a contract, which "defeats an essential purpose of the contract." *Mathews v. PHH Mortg. Corp.*, 724 S.E.2d 196, 200 (Va. 2012). The general principle is quite simple: When a contracting party materially breaches a contract, "the other party is discharged or excused from further performance." *Mustang Pipeline Co. v. Driver Pipeline Co.*, 134 S.W.3d 195, 196 (Tex. 2004).

The doctrine of substantial performance, however, is an exception to the material breach doctrine. *See Richard v. Deutsche Bank Nat. Trust Co.*, 2012 WL 1082602, *3 n.2 (C.C.D. Or.) ("Substantial performance is the antithesis of material breach; if it is determined that a breach is material ... it follows that substantial performance has not been rendered"), citing 15 R. LORD WILLISTON ON CONTRACTS § 44:55 (4th ed. 2000). Quite simply, under the doctrine of substantial performance, breaching parties—who have substantially performed their contractual obligations—may recover contract damages. *Tips v. Hartland Developers, Inc.*, 961 S.W.2d 618, 623 (Tex. App.—San Antonio 1998, no pet.).

The drafters of the UCC, however, replaced the common-law doctrines of material breach and substantial performance with the "perfect tender" rule. Section 2-601(1) of the UCC states that "if ... goods or the tender of delivery fail in *any respect* to conform to the contract," the buyer may reject the goods. Conformity does not mean substantial performance; it means complete performance. *Printing Ctr., Inc. v. Supermind Publ'g Co.*, 669 S.W.2d 779, 783 (Tex. App.—Houston [14th Dist.] 1984, no writ). In fact, courts stress: The perfect tender rule subjects sellers to "a very high level of conformity"; the rule allows buyers to "reject a seller's tender for any trivial defect, whether it be in the quality of the goods, the timing of the performance, or the manner of delivery." *Midwest Mobile Diagnostic Imaging v. Dynamics Corp.*, 965 F. Supp. 1003, 1011 (C.C.W.D. Mich. 1997). Or stated slightly differently, if the tender of the goods differs from the terms of the contract in any way, the seller *breaches the contract* and the buyer is released from its duty to accept the goods.

A buyer accepts goods by signifying that the goods conform by taking the goods anyway—section 2-606(1)(a), or by doing an act inconsistent with the seller's ownership—section 2-606(1)(c). The buyer who accepts the goods must pay the contract price for them, even if the goods are nonconforming. U.C.C. § 2-607(1). *See also, Cayuga Press of Ithaca Inc. v. Lithografiks Inc.*, 211 A.D.2d 908, 910, 621 N.Y.S.2d 187 (N.Y. App. Div. 1995).

In addition, the UCC establishes strict procedural requirements for an effective and rightful rejection: It must occur within a reasonable period of time of delivery or tender, and the buyer must seasonably notify the seller of the rejection. "Rejection of the goods must be within a reasonable period of time after their delivery or tender. It is ineffective unless the buyer seasonably notifies the seller." U.C.C. § 2-602(1). However, consistent with the obligation of good faith that is part of every commercial contract, section 1-203 of the UCC states that a buyer's rejection of the goods must be made in good faith. *Hubbard v. UTZ Quality Foods, Inc.,* 903 F. Supp. 444, 451 (C.C. W.D.N.Y. 1995); *Clark v. Zaid, Inc.*, 263 Md. 127, 282 A.2d 483 (Md. 1971). And, if a buyer "rightfully rejects" the goods, the buyer may cancel the contract, and seek a remedy for the breach. U.C.C. § 2-711(1).

Contrarily, if a buyer fails to make an effective rejection, the buyer will be deemed to have accepted the goods. U.C.C. § 2-606(1)(b). Or stated another way, "[i]f the seller has made a tender which in all respects conforms to the contract, the buyer has a positive duty to accept and [a] failure to do so constitutes a 'wrongful rejection' which gives the seller immediate remedies for breach." U.C.C. § 2-602 cmt. 3; U.C.C. § 2-602(3).

Of course, a buyer who makes a "rightful rejection" of the goods has a "duty" to hold the goods with reasonable care—for a sufficient period of time—until the seller secures the goods. U.C.C. § 2-602(2)(b). A merchant buyer may have additional duties under section 2-603. Conversely, if a seller fail to gives instructions—within a reasonable period of time—after the buyer rejects the goods, the buyer may store the goods for the seller's account," and take other actions. Such actions will not be evidence of acceptance or conversion. U.C.C. § 2-604. The buyer's remedy then for any nonconformity is to seek damages for the seller's breach. U.C.C. § 2-714.

But it is important to stress: Section 2-508—which affords sellers a right to cure any nonconformity—tempers the perfect tender rule. *See Midwest Mobile Diagnostic Imaging v. Dynamics Corp.*, 965 F. Supp. 1003, 1011 (C.C.W.D. Mich. 1997) ("To avoid injustice, the Code limits the buyer's correlative right to cancel the contract under § 2-508. ... Thus, § 2-508's right to cure serves to temper the buyer's expansive right to reject under a single delivery contract.").

The judicial opinions appearing below expand the discussion of these statutory principles. As you read each case, determine if the court reverts to applying some common-law principles to reach each conclusion.

Uniform Commercial Code

§ 2-601. BUYER'S RIGHTS ON IMPROPER DELIVERY

Subject to the provisions of this Article on breach in installment contracts (Section 2-612) and unless otherwise agreed under the sections on contractual limitations of remedy (Sections 2-718 and 2-719), if the goods or the tender of delivery fail in any respect to conform to the contract, the buyer may

(a) reject the whole; or

(b) accept the whole; or

(c) accept any commercial unit or units and reject the rest.

§ 2-602. MANNER AND EFFECT OF RIGHTFUL REJECTION

(1) Rejection of goods must be within a reasonable time after their delivery or tender. It is ineffective unless the buyer seasonably notifies the seller.

(2) Subject to the provisions of the two following sections on rejected goods (Sections 2-603 and 2-604),

(a) after rejection any exercise of ownership by the buyer with respect to any commercial unit is wrongful as against the seller; and

(b) if the buyer has before rejection taken physical possession of goods in which he does not have a security interest under the provisions of this Article (subsection

(3) of Section 2-711), he is under a duty after rejection to hold them with reasonable care at the seller's disposition for a time sufficient to permit the seller to remove them; but

(c) the buyer has no further obligations with regard to goods rightfully rejected.

(3) The seller's rights with respect to goods wrongfully rejected are governed by the provisions of this Article on Seller's remedies in general (Section 2-703).

§ 2-603. MERCHANT BUYER'S DUTIES AS TO RIGHTFULLY REJECTED GOODS

(1) Subject to any security interest in the buyer (subsection (3) of Section 2-711), when the seller has no agent or place of business at the market of rejection a merchant buyer is under a duty after rejection of goods in his possession or control to follow any reasonable instructions received from the seller with respect to the goods and in the absence of such instructions to make reasonable efforts to sell them for the seller's account if they are perishable or threaten to decline in value speedily. Instructions are not reasonable if on demand indemnity for expenses is not forthcoming.

(2) When the buyer sells goods under subsection (1), he is entitled to reimbursement from the seller or out of the proceeds for reasonable expenses of caring for and selling them, and if the expenses include no selling commission then to such commission as is usual in the trade or if there is none to a reasonable sum not exceeding ten per cent on the gross proceeds.

(3) In complying with this section the buyer is held only to good faith and good faith conduct hereunder is neither acceptance nor conversion nor the basis of an action for damages.

§ 2-604. BUYER'S OPTIONS AS TO SALVAGE OF RIGHTFULLY REJECTED GOODS

Subject to the provisions of the immediately preceding section on perishables if the seller gives no instructions within a reasonable time after notification of rejection the buyer may store the rejected goods for the seller's account or reship them to him or resell them for the seller's account with reimbursement as provided in the preceding section. Such action is not acceptance or conversion.

B. Breach of Contract: Buyer's Rights Under § 2-601 Before Accepting Goods

Ramirez v. Autosport 440 A.2d 1345 (N.J. 1982)

POLLOCK, J. This case raises several issues under the Uniform Commercial Code (the Code and UCC) concerning whether a buyer may reject a tender of goods with minor defects and whether a seller may cure the defects. We consider also the remedies available to the buyer, including cancellation of the contract. The main issue is whether plaintiffs, Mr. and Mrs. Ramirez, could reject the tender by defendant, Autosport, of a camper van with minor defects and cancel the contract for the purchase of the van.

The trial court ruled that Mr. and Mrs. Ramirez rightfully rejected the van and awarded them the fair market value of their trade-in van. The Appellate Division affirmed in a brief *per curiam* decision which, like the trial court opinion, was unreported. ...

I

Following a mobile home show at the Meadowlands Sports Complex, Mr. and Mrs. Ramirez visited Autosport's showroom in Somerville. On July 20, 1978 the Ramirezes and Donald Graff, a salesman for Autosport, agreed on the sale of a new camper and the trade-in of the van owned by Mr. and Mrs. Ramirez. Autosport and the Ramirezes signed a simple contract reflecting a $14,100 purchase price for the new van with a $4,700 trade-in allowance for the Ramirez van, which Mr. and Mrs. Ramirez left with Autosport. After further allowance for taxes, title, and documentary fees, the net price was $9,902. Because Autosport needed two weeks to prepare the new van, the contract provided for delivery on or about August 3, 1978.

On that date, Mr. and Mrs. Ramirez returned with their checks to Autosport to pick up the new van. Graff was not there so Mr. White, another salesman, met them. Inspection disclosed several defects in the van. The paint was scratched, both the electric and sewer hookups were missing, and the hubcaps were not installed. White advised the Ramirezes not to accept the camper because it was not ready.

Mr. and Mrs. Ramirez wanted the van for a summer vacation and called Graff several times. Each time Graff told them it was not ready for delivery. Finally, Graff called to notify them that the camper was ready. On August 14, Mr. and Mrs. Ramirez went to Autosport to accept delivery, but workers were still touching up the outside paint. Also, the camper windows were open, and the dining area cushions were soaking wet. Mr. and Mrs. Ramirez could not use the camper in that condition, but Mr. Leis, Autosport's manager, suggested that they take the van and that Autosport would replace the cushions later. Mrs. Ramirez counteroffered to accept the van if they could withhold $2,000, but Leis agreed to no more than $250, which she refused. Leis then agreed to replace the cushions and to call them when the van was ready.

On August 15, 1978, Autosport transferred title to the van to Mr. and Mrs. Ramirez—a fact unknown to them until the summer of 1979. Between August 15 and September 1, 1978, Mrs. Ramirez called Graff several times urging him to complete the preparation of the van, but Graff constantly advised her that the van was not ready. He finally informed her that they could pick it up on September 1. When Mr. and Mrs. Ramirez went to the showroom on September 1, Graff asked them to wait. And wait they did—for one and a half hours. No one from Autosport came forward to talk with them, and the Ramirezes left in disgust.

On October 5, 1978 Mr. and Mrs. Ramirez went to Autosport with an attorney friend. Although the parties disagreed on what occurred, the general topic was whether they should proceed with the deal or Autosport should return to the Ramirezes their trade-in van. Mrs. Ramirez claimed they rejected the new van and requested the return of their trade-in. Mr. Lustig—the owner of Autosport—thought, however, that the deal could be salvaged if the parties could agree on the dollar amount of a credit for the Ramirezes. Mr. and Mrs. Ramirez never took possession of the new van and repeated their request for the return of their trade-in.

Later in October, however, Autosport sold the trade-in to an innocent third party for $4,995. Autosport claimed that the Ramirezes' van had a book value of $3,200 and claimed further that it spent $1,159.62 to repair their van. By subtracting the total of those two figures, $4,159.62, from the $4,995.00 sale price, Autosport claimed a $600-700 profit on the sale. On November 20, 1978 the Ramirezes sued Autosport seeking, among other things, rescission of the contract. Autosport counterclaimed for breach of contract.

II

Our initial inquiry is whether a consumer may reject defective goods that do not conform to the contract of sale. The basic issue is whether under the UCC—adopted in New Jersey as N.J.S.A. 12A:1-101 *et seq.*—a seller has the duty to deliver goods that conform precisely to the contract. We conclude that the seller is under such a duty to make a "perfect tender" and that a buyer has the right to reject goods that do not conform to the contract. That conclusion, however, does not resolve the entire dispute between buyer and seller. A more complete answer requires a brief statement of the history of the mutual obligations of buyers and sellers of commercial goods.

In the nineteenth century, sellers were required to deliver goods that complied exactly with the sales agreement. *See Filley v. Pope*, 115 U.S. 213, 220 (1885) (buyer not obliged to accept otherwise conforming scrap iron shipped to New Orleans from Leith, rather than Glasgow, Scotland, as required by contract); *Columbian Iron Works & Dry-Dock Co. v. Douglas*, 34 A. 1118, 1120–1121 (Md. 1896) (buyer who agreed to purchase steel scrap from United States cruisers not obliged to take any other kind of scrap). That rule, known as the "perfect tender" rule, remained part of the law of sales well into the twentieth century. By the 1920's the doctrine was so entrenched in the law that Judge Learned Hand declared "[T]here is no room in commercial contracts for the doctrine of substantial performance." *Mitsubishi Goshi Kaisha v. J. Aron & Co., Inc.*, 16 F.2d 185, 186 (2 Cir. 1926).

The harshness of the rule led courts to seek to ameliorate its effect and to bring the law of sales in closer harmony with the law of contracts, which allows rescission only for material breaches. Nevertheless, a variation of the perfect tender rule appeared in the Uniform Sales Act. N.J.S.A. 46:30-75 (purchasers permitted to reject goods or rescind contracts for any breach of warranty); N.J.S.A. 46:30-18 to -21 (warranties extended to include all the seller's obligations to the goods). The chief objection to the continuation of the perfect tender rule was that buyers in a declining market would reject goods for minor nonconformities and force the loss on surprised sellers. *See* N.J.S.A. 12A:2-508, New Jersey Study Comment 3.

To the extent that a buyer can reject goods for any nonconformity, the UCC retains the perfect tender rule. Section 2-106 states that goods conform to a contract "when they are in accordance with the obligations under the contract". N.J.S.A. 12A:2-106. Section 2-601 authorizes a buyer to reject goods if they "or the tender of delivery fail in any respect to conform to the contract". N.J.S.A. 12A:2-601. The Code, however, mitigates the harshness of the perfect tender rule and balances the interests of buyer and seller. The Code achieves that result through its provisions for revocation of acceptance and cure. N.J.S.A. 12A:2-608, § 2-508.

Initially, the rights of the parties vary depending on whether the rejection occurs before or after acceptance of the goods. Before acceptance, the buyer may reject goods for any nonconformity. N.J.S.A. 12A:2-601. Because of the seller's right to cure, however, the buyer's rejection does not necessarily discharge the contract. N.J.S.A. 12A:2-508. Within the time set for performance in the contract, the seller's right to cure is unconditional. Some authorities recommend granting a breaching party a right to cure in all contracts, not merely those for the sale of goods. RESTATEMENT (SECOND), CONTRACTS, CH. 10, especially §§ 237 and 241. Underlying the right to cure in both kinds of contracts is the recognition that parties should be encouraged to communicate with each other and to resolve their own problems.

The rights of the parties also vary if rejection occurs after the time set for performance. After expiration of that time, the seller has a further reasonable time to cure if he believed reasonably that the goods would be acceptable with or without a money allowance. N.J.S.A. 12A:2-508(2). The determination of what constitutes a further reasonable time depends on the surrounding circumstances, which include the change of position by and the amount of inconvenience to the buyer. N.J.S.A. 12A:2-508, Official Comment 3. Those circumstances also include the length of time needed by the seller to correct the nonconformity and his ability to salvage the goods by resale to others. *See* RESTATEMENT (SECOND), CONTRACTS, § 241 comment (d). Thus, the Code balances the buyer's right to reject nonconforming goods with a "second chance" for the seller to conform the goods to the contract under certain limited circumstances. N.J.S.A. 12A:2-508, New Jersey Study Comment 1.

After acceptance, the Code strikes a different balance: the buyer may revoke acceptance only if the nonconformity substantially impairs the value of the goods to him. N.J.S.A. 12A:2-608. *See Herbstman v. Eastman Kodak Co.*, 68 N.J. 1, 9 (1975). This provision protects the seller from revocation for trivial defects. It also prevents the buyer from taking undue advantage of the seller by allowing goods to depreciate and then returning them because of asserted minor defects. Because this case involves rejection of goods, we need not decide whether a seller has a right to cure substantial defects that justify revocation of acceptance. *See Pavesi v. Ford Motor Co.*, 155 N.J. Super. 373, 378, 382 A.2d 954 (App. Div. 1978) (right to cure after acceptance limited to trivial defects). ... Other courts agree that the buyer has a right of rejection for any nonconformity, but that the seller has a countervailing right to cure within a reasonable time. *Marine Mart Inc. v. Pearce*, 480 S.W.2d 133, 137 (Ark. 1972). ...

A further problem, however, is identifying the remedy available to a buyer who rejects goods with insubstantial defects that the seller fails to cure within a reasonable time. The Code provides expressly that when "the buyer rightfully rejects, then with respect to the goods involved, the buyer may cancel." N.J.S.A. 12A:2-711. "Cancellation" occurs when either party puts an end to the contract for breach by the other. N.J.S.A. 12A:2-106(4). Nonetheless, some confusion exists whether the equitable remedy of rescission survives under the Code. *Compare Ventura v. Ford Motor Corp.*, 173 N.J. Super. 501, 503 (Ch. Div. 1980) (rescission under UCC) *and Pavesi v. Ford Motor Corp.*, 155 N.J. Super. at 377 (equitable remedies still available since not specifically superceded, § 1-103) *with*

Edelstein v. Toyota Motors Dist., 176 N.J.Super. 57, 63–64 (App. Div. 1980) (under UCC rescission is revocation of acceptance) *and Sudol v. Rudy Papa Motors*, 175 N.J. Super. 238, 241–242 (D. Ct. 1980) (under UCC, rescission no longer exists as such).

The Code eschews the word "rescission" and substitutes the terms "cancellation", "revocation of acceptance", and "rightful rejection". N.J.S.A. 12A:2-106(4); 2-608; and 2-711 & Official Comment 1. Although neither "rejection" nor "revocation of acceptance" is defined in the Code, rejection includes both the buyer's refusal to accept or keep delivered goods and his notification to the seller that he will not keep them. Revocation of acceptance is like rejection, but occurs after the buyer has accepted the goods. Nonetheless, revocation of acceptance is intended to provide the same relief as rescission of a contract of sale of goods. N.J.S.A. 12A:2-608 Official Comment 1; N.J. Study Comment 2. In brief, revocation is tantamount to rescission. *See Herbstman v. Eastman Kodak Co.*, supra, 68 N.J. at 9. *Accord, Peckham v. Larsen Chevrolet-Buick-Oldsmobile, Inc.,* 587 P.2d 816, 818 (Idaho 1978) (rescission and revocation of acceptance amount to the same thing). …

Although the complaint requested rescission of the contract, plaintiffs actually sought not only the end of their contractual obligations, but also restoration to their pre-contractual position. That request incorporated the equitable doctrine of restitution, the purpose of which is to restore plaintiff to as good a position as he occupied before the contract. In UCC parlance, plaintiffs' request was for the cancellation of the contract and recovery of the price paid. N.J.S.A. 12A:2-106(4), 2-711.

General contract law permits rescission only for material breaches, and the Code restates "materiality" in terms of "substantial impairment". *See Herbstman v. Eastman Kodak Co.*, supra, 68 N.J. at 9. The Code permits a buyer who rightfully rejects goods to cancel a contract of sale. N.J.S.A. 12A:2-711. Because a buyer may reject goods with insubstantial defects, he also may cancel the contract if those defects remain uncured. Otherwise, a seller's failure to cure minor defects would compel a buyer to accept imperfect goods and collect for any loss caused by the nonconformity. N.J.S.A. 12A:2-714.

Although the Code permits cancellation by rejection for minor defects, it permits revocation of acceptance only for substantial impairments. That distinction is consistent with other Code provisions that depend on whether the buyer has accepted the goods. Acceptance creates liability in the buyer for the price, N.J.S.A. 12A:2-709(1), and precludes rejection. N.J.S.A. 12A:2-607(2); N.J.S.A. 12A:2-606, New Jersey Study Comment 1. Also, once a buyer accepts goods, he has the burden to prove any defect. N.J.S.A. 12A:2-607(4). By contrast, where goods are rejected for not conforming to the contract, the burden is on the seller to prove that the nonconformity was corrected. *Miron v. Yonkers Raceway, Inc.*, 400 F.2d 112, 119 (2nd Cir. 1968).

Underlying the Code provisions is the recognition of the revolutionary change in business practices in this century. The purchase of goods is no longer a simple transaction in which a buyer purchases individually-made goods from a seller in a face-to-face transaction. Our economy depends on a complex system for the manufacture, distribution, and sale of goods, a system in which manufacturers and consumers rarely meet. Faceless manufacturers mass-produce goods for unknown consumers who purchase those goods from merchants exercising little or no control over the quality of their production. In an age of assembly lines, we are accustomed to cars with scratches, television sets without knobs and other products with all kinds of defects. Buyers no longer expect a "perfect tender". If a merchant sells defective goods, the reasonable expectation of the parties is that the buyer will return those goods and that the seller will repair or replace them.

Recognizing this commercial reality, the Code permits a seller to cure imperfect tenders. Should the seller fail to cure the defects—whether substantial or not—the balance shifts again in favor of the buyer, who has the right to cancel or seek damages. N.J.S.A. 12A:2-711. In general, economic considerations would induce sellers to cure minor defects. Assuming the seller does not cure, however, the buyer should be permitted to exercise his remedies under N.J.S.A. 12A:2-711. The Code remedies for consumers are to be liberally construed, and the buyer should have the option of cancelling if the seller does not provide conforming goods. See N.J.S.A. 12A:1-106. To summarize, the UCC preserves the perfect tender rule to the extent of permitting a buyer to reject goods for any nonconformity. Nonetheless, that rejection does not automatically terminate the contract. A seller may still effect a cure and preclude unfair rejection and cancellation by the buyer. N.J.S.A. 12A:2-508, Official Comment 2; N.J.S.A. 12A:2-711, Official Comment 1.

III

The trial court found that Mr. and Mrs. Ramirez had rejected the van within a reasonable time under N.J.S.A. 12A:2-602. The court found that on August 3, 1978 Autosport's salesman advised the Ramirezes not to accept the van and that on August 14, they rejected delivery and Autosport agreed to replace the cushions. Those findings are supported by substantial credible evidence, and we sustain them. Although the trial court did not find whether Autosport cured the defects within a reasonable time, we find that Autosport did not effect a cure. Clearly the van was not ready for delivery during August, 1978 when Mr. and Mrs. Ramirez rejected it, and Autosport had the burden of proving that it had corrected the defects. Although the Ramirezes gave Autosport ample time to correct the defects, Autosport did not demonstrate that the van conformed to the contract on September 1. In fact, on that date, when Mr. and Mrs. Ramirez returned at Autosport's invitation, all they received was discourtesy.

On the assumption that substantial impairment is necessary only when a purchaser seeks to revoke acceptance under N.J.S.A. 12A:2-608, the trial court correctly refrained from deciding whether the defects substantially impaired the van. The court properly concluded that plaintiffs were entitled to "rescind"—*i.e.,* to "cancel"—the contract.

Because Autosport had sold the trade-in to an innocent third party, the trial court determined that the Ramirezes were entitled not to the return of the trade-in, but to its fair market value, which the court set at the contract price of $4,700. A buyer who rightfully rejects goods and cancels the contract may, among other possible remedies, recover so much of the purchase price as has been paid. N.J.S.A. 12A:2-711. The Code, however, does not define "pay" and does not require payment to be made in cash.

A common method of partial payment for vans, cars, boats and other items of personal property is by a "trade-in." When concerned with used vans and the like, the trade-in market is an acceptable, and perhaps the most appropriate, market in which to measure damages. It is the market in which the parties dealt; by their voluntary act they have established the value of the traded-in article. *See Frantz Equipment Co. v. Anderson*, 37 N.J. 420, 431–432 (1962) (in computing purchaser's damages for alleged breach of uniform conditional sales law, trade-in value of tractor was appropriate measure). In other circumstances, a measure of damages other than the trade-in value might be appropriate. *See Chemical Bank v. Miller Yacht Sales*, 173 N.J. Super. 90, 103 (App. Div. 1980) (in determining value of security interest in boat, court rejected both book value and contract trade-in value and adopted resale value as appropriate measure of damages).

The ultimate issue is determining the fair market value of the trade-in. This court has defined fair market value as "the price at which the property would change hands between a willing buyer and a willing seller when the former is not under any compulsion to buy and the latter is not under any compulsion to sell, both parties having reasonable knowledge of relevant facts." *In re Estate of Romnes*, 79 N.J. 139, 144 (1978). Although the value of the trade-in van as set forth in the sales contract was not the only possible standard, it is an appropriate measure of fair market value.

For the preceding reasons, we affirm the judgment of the Appellate Division.

UNIFORM COMMERCIAL CODE

§ 2-508. CURE BY SELLER OF IMPROPER TENDER OR DELIVERY; REPLACEMENT

(1) Where any tender or delivery by the seller is rejected because non-conforming and the time for performance has not yet expired, the seller may seasonably notify the buyer of his intention to cure and may then within the contract time make a conforming delivery.

(2) Where the buyer rejects a non-conforming tender which the seller had reasonable grounds to believe would be acceptable with or without money allowance the seller may if he seasonably notifies the buyer have a further reasonable time to substitute a conforming tender.

§ 2-605. WAIVER OF BUYER'S OBJECTIONS BY FAILURE TO PARTICULARIZE

(1) The buyer's failure to state in connection with rejection a particular defect which is ascertainable by reasonable inspection precludes him from relying on the unstated defect to justify rejection or to establish breach

(a) where the seller could have cured it if stated seasonably; or

(b) between merchants when the seller has after rejection made a request in writing for a full and final written statement of all defects on which the buyer proposes to rely.

(2) Payment against documents made without reservation of rights precludes recovery of the payment for defects apparent in the documents.

§ 2-606. WHAT CONSTITUTES ACCEPTANCE OF GOODS

(1) Acceptance of goods occurs when the buyer

(a) after a reasonable opportunity to inspect the goods signifies to the seller that the goods are conforming or that he will take or retain them in spite of their non-conformity; or

(b) fails to make an effective rejection (subsection (1) of Section 2-602), but such acceptance does not occur until the buyer has had a reasonable opportunity to inspect them; or

(c) does any act inconsistent with the seller's ownership; but if such act is wrongful as against the seller it is an acceptance only if ratified by him.

(2) Acceptance of a part of any commercial unit is acceptance of that entire unit.

C. Breach of Contract: Buyer's Rights and Obligations Under § 2-607 After Accepting Goods

Golden v. Den-Mat Corporation
276 P.3d 773
(Kan. Ct. App. 2012)

ATCHESON, J. Plaintiff Brenda Golden purchased dental veneers—porcelain overlays meant to improve the appearance of teeth—that Defendant Den-Mat manufactured and marketed and Defendant Dr. Carissa M. Gill, a dentist, put in place. Golden contends the veneers became discolored and stained despite representations from Den-Mat and Dr. Gill that they would retain their appearance. So she sued them in Sedgwick County District Court on the grounds the veneers breached implied warranties applicable to goods sold under Article 2—Sales of the UNIFORM COMMERCIAL CODE (UCC), K.S.A. 84-2-101 *et seq.*, and the transaction entailed deceptive acts and practices and improper limitations of those warranties in violation of the KANSAS CONSUMER PROTECTION ACT (KCPA), K.S.A. 50-623 *et seq.* The district court granted summary judgment to Den-Mat and Dr. Gill. Golden has timely appealed. ...

FACTUAL AND PROCEDURAL HISTORY

Because the district court entered summary judgment against Plaintiff Golden, we review the facts in the light most favorable to her. So our narrative presents the events that way. Before turning to that recitation, we note that Defendants Den-Mat Corporation, Cerinate Corporation, and Den-Mat Holdings, LLC appear to be united in interest and are represented by the same counsel. Neither the facts, as we understand them, nor the legal issues on appeal require we distinguish among those defendants. We refer to them collectively as Den-Mat.

In late 2004, Golden wanted to replace the veneers on her teeth with new ones that would give her smile what she described as a "super white" appearance. Veneers are synthetic panels cemented to the front of a person's teeth, thereby covering discoloration or other imperfections in the natural dentition. Golden saw a magazine advertisement for Cerinate veneers, a proprietary product Den-Mat manufactures. In response to her telephone call to the number in the advertisement, Den-Mat sent Golden a brochure describing the Cerinate veneers as "thin porcelain shields ... bonded to the front of" the teeth "to create dramatic changes in your smile."

The brochure touted "long-term clinical research" showing the Cerinate veneers would last up to 16 years "with no discoloration" and "100% retention." The brochure also explained that the porcelain veneers "are stronger and more durable" than comparable products made from plastic. According to the brochure, "[s]ometimes plastic composites stain and discolor with age, whereas, Cerinate Veneers maintain their beautiful luster and vitality." The brochure referred several times to the durability of the veneers and promoted the "strong, patented adhesive" used to attach them. The brochure, however, contained no unequivocal statement that the veneers would not come loose or crack.

Golden decided to get the Cerinate veneers and contacted Den-Mat for a dentist in the Wichita area. Den-Mat supplied Golden with Dr. Gill's name and contact information as the nearest professional authorized to apply Cerinate veneers. Dr. Gill worked in Wellington, some 35 miles south of Golden's home. Golden first met with Dr. Gill on November 8, 2004, and they discussed Golden's desire for "really white" teeth. Golden wanted the whitest veneers Den-Mat produced. Golden showed Dr. Gill the Den-Mat brochure and specifically asked about the durability of the veneers and the potential for discoloration. ... Apparently without referring specifically to the Cerinate veneers, Dr. Gill assured Golden that porcelain would not discolor. Dr. Gill recalled telling Golden that the whitest veneers might not be the best choice cosmetically because they could look artificial rather than natural. But Golden was adamant she wanted the whitest shade.

Dr. Gill removed the old veneers, took impressions of Golden's teeth, and ordered the new veneers from Den-Mat. On January 10, 2005, Dr. Gill attached the Cerinate veneers to Golden's upper teeth. At the end of that visit, Dr. Gill gave Golden a written warranty for the veneers. The document is entitled "FIVE YEAR LIMITED WARRANTY" and states the Cerinate porcelain is "warranted against defects in workmanship and materials for a period of five (5) years from delivery date." The warranty covers the "repair or replacement" of the veneers but expressly excludes the costs for "removal or reinsertion," any cash refund, and consequential damages such as lost wages or pain and suffering. The warranty card states in small print that it "is in lieu of all other warranties, whether expressed or implied." The warranty card was filled in with Golden's name and address. Dr. Gill signed the card and a certification that the veneers had been applied using Den-Mat's bonding cement and appropriate preparation techniques.

Golden later testified in her deposition that she felt the veneers seemed darker or less white as soon as they had been affixed to her teeth. Nonetheless, Golden returned to Dr. Gill 3 weeks later and had the remaining veneers applied to her lower teeth. By then, one of the upper veneers had come loose and another appeared to have a crack in it. Dr. Gill ordered replacement veneers and later applied them; she did not charge Golden for that work. Golden paid $9,875.25 for the Cerinate veneers. The payment was made to Dr. Gill. The record on appeal is unclear as to whether Golden made a single payment or paid a portion of the cost as a deposit. The record does not indicate when Golden tendered any payments. Neither a bill nor an invoice has been included among the evidentiary materials.

Another veneer came off about 6 months later. Dr. Gill reapplied the veneer, again at no cost to Golden. In late March 2007, another veneer came off. Dr. Gill ordered a replacement veneer from Den-Mat. The replacement veneer was considerably whiter than the veneers Golden already had. On April 23, 2007, Dr. Gill spoke with a Den-Mat representative who said it was possible that Golden's veneers had become stained or had darkened over time. Dr. Gill recounted the conversation to Golden the same day.

Later on April 23, 2007, Golden wrote a letter to Dr. Gill expressing her dissatisfaction with the veneers and her belief they had developed "a gray cast" in the 15 months since they were placed on her teeth. Golden asked for Dr. Gill's help in obtaining a new set of veneers from Den-Mat at no cost. Dr. Gill's staff noted the letter in her office chart a week later. Den-Mat declined to replace Golden's veneers.

In the first part of 2008, Golden went to her regular dentist to have the Cerinate veneers removed from her upper teeth and replaced with a similar product from another manufacturer. The replacements cost about $4,500. In the summary judgment materials, Golden submitted a close-up photograph of her teeth after the upper veneers had been replaced. In the photograph, the lower teeth, with the Cerinate veneers, are noticeably duller than the replacement veneers and seem to have what could be stains.

On January 9, 2008, Golden filed a petition against the Den-Mat entities and Dr. Gill alleging breach of express warranties regarding the veneers and breach of implied warranties of merchantability and fitness for a particular purpose. ... Golden alleged the veneers had become stained and discolored and some of them came off or cracked. Den-Mat and Dr. Gill duly filed separate answers denying liability. The parties conducted significant discovery. In the final pretrial order, Golden sought to recover the cost of the Cerinate veneers; the cost of the replacement veneers she got in 2008; and $5,000 for lost time, inconvenience, and pain and suffering. Den-Mat and Dr. Gill filed separate motions for summary judgment with supporting memorandums and exhibits. Golden responded. The district court requested and received additional briefing on issues related to sales under the UCC.

The district court granted summary judgment to the defendants on all of Golden's claims. ... Golden has timely appealed. ...

LEGAL ISSUES

Statutes of Limitation and UCC Notice

The defendants asserted and the district court relied on multiple statute of limitations arguments to defeat Golden's claims. The district court recast Golden's statutory claims against both defendants under the UCC and her claims against Dr. Gill under the KCPA as common-law torts and granted summary judgment because, so treated, they were filed outside the governing limitations period. The district court also ruled that the KCPA claims against Den-Mat were filed after the 3-year statute of limitations had run.

Both Dr. Gill and Den-Mat additionally argue that Golden failed to give timely notice under the UCC that the veneers failed to perform as warranted and, therefore, those claims should be barred. *See* K.S.A. 84-2-607(3)(a). While not strictly a statute of limitations, the requirement for timely notice that goods sold fail to conform to the contract creates a condition precedent for bringing suit under Article 2 of the UCC and, thus, would be applicable here. The district court erred in granting summary judgment on the grounds that Golden's suit was filed after the governing statutes of limitation had expired or that the notice of breach was untimely for UCC purposes.

Before turning to those issues, we settle some procedural skirmishing between Golden and the defendants. Dr. Gill argues that Golden did not assert UCC claims in her petition. And Golden argues the defendants failed to properly preserve their statute of limitations defenses. Neither side presents a convincing procedural bar.

Golden did not specifically cite the UCC in her petition. But a plaintiff is not required to categorize causes of action or cite statutory or common-law bases for the suit. *See Berry v. National Medical Services, Inc.*, 41 Kan.App.2d 612 (2009), aff'd on other grounds 292 Kan. 917, 257 P.3d 287 (2011). A plaintiff must simply set forth "a short and plain statement of the claim showing that the pleader is entitled to relief," coupled with a demand for appropriate relief. K.S.A. 60-208(a).

In her petition, Golden alleged misrepresentations about the Cerinate veneers, her reliance on those misrepresentations in purchasing the veneers, and their failure to maintain their appearance. She also characterized the veneers as "goods," the term used to describe items subject to Article 2 of the UCC, citing K.S.A. 84-2-101 *et seq. See* K.S.A. 84-2-102 (Article 2 applies to "transactions in goods"); K.S.A. 84-2-105(1) (defining goods). She alleged breaches of an express warranty and of warranties of merchantability and fitness for a particular purpose. Those allegations satisfy the notice requirements of an opening pleading. The legal theories may, but need not, be expressly identified in the petition; they can be fleshed out during the discovery process. Here, the UCC claims were plainly included in the final pretrial order. *See* K.S.A. 60-216. And the parties had full opportunity to address those claims on summary judgment. *See Nelson v. Nelson*, 288 Kan. 570, 584 (2009). The UCC claims are properly in the case. ...

Statute of Limitations on UCC Claims and Untimely Notice of Breach

The UCC contains a 4-year statute of limitations for contract claims based on the sale of goods under Article 2 of the Code. K.S.A. 84-2-725(1) ("An action for breach of contract for sale must be commenced within four years after the cause of action has accrued."). The UCC provides that the cause of action accrues when the breach occurs. The injured party need not know of the breach to trigger the limitations period. K.S.A. 84-2-725(2). Of particular importance here, given the facts, a breach of a contractual warranty under the UCC "occurs when tender of delivery is made." K.S.A. 84-2-725(2). If the warranty includes a promise of future performance of the goods, a breach does not occur until the recipient discovers or should have discovered the deficient performance. K.S.A. 84-2-725(2). Consistent with those statutes, the Kansas Supreme Court has recognized the limitation period for a breach of warranty typically begins running when the goods are delivered or installed. *Atlas Industries, Inc. v. National Cash Register Co.*, 216 Kan. 213, 221(1975). That reflects the general rule.

Here, the veneers were delivered under the contract on January 10, 2005, when Dr. Gill applied them to Golden's upper teeth. The 4-year limitations period began to run then at the earliest. Golden filed suit on January 9, 2008, well within the limitations period in K.S.A. 84-2-725(1), (2). Assuming the UCC otherwise applies to the transaction, an issue we take up later, Golden asserted those claims against Den-Mat and Dr. Gill within the limitations period.

But Den-Mat and Dr. Gill also argued to the district court that Golden failed to provide timely notice that the veneers performed in a way that breached the sales contract and, therefore, her UCC claims should be dismissed as a matter of law. The notice requirement appears in K.S.A. 84-2-607(a)(3). The district court accepted that argument as an alternative basis for granting summary judgment on the UCC claims. The district court erred in doing so.

As we have indicated, Article 2 of the UCC governs the sale of goods and, thus, essentially reflects a codification of contract principles to be applied to transactions within its scope. *See* K.S.A. 84-2-101, Kansas

Comment 1 (1996); K.S.A. 84-2-102. If the buyer of goods covered under the UCC "discovers or should have discovered" a breach of the contract after accepting the goods, the buyer "must within a reasonable time" notify the seller. K.S.A. 84-2-607(3)(a). A failure to give timely notice, as required in K.S.A. 84-2-607(3)(a), bars the buyer from any remedy. K.S.A. 84-2-607(3)(a).

The purpose, in part, is to allow a seller a chance to look into the transaction and correct any deficiency, thereby giving the parties an opportunity to avert potentially expensive, time-consuming litigation. *See* K.S.A. 84-2-607, Kansas Comment 2 (1996); *Smith v. Stewart*, 233 Kan. 904, 909 (1983). The notification also permits the seller to prepare for negotiation or litigation, as by gathering and preserving documents and other evidentiary materials relevant to the transaction.

Den-Mat and Dr. Gill argued that Golden failed to give timely notice of the problems with the veneers. They point to the letter Golden sent to Dr. Gill in late April 2007 as the first notification she was dissatisfied with the veneers and believed the sales contract had been breached. Assuming the letter to be the first notice of potential breach, Golden made her position known about 27 months after the veneers were delivered and applied and some 20 months before the UCC limitations period would have expired. Neither Den-Mat nor Dr. Gill suggests the delay compromised any defenses they might have had to the suit or otherwise resulted in the loss of evidence. They do not claim they might have been able to negotiate a resolution without litigation had Golden given notice sooner—suit was not filed for another 8 months after Dr. Gill received the letter.

Basically, Den-Mat and Dr. Gill contend that Golden's 27-month delay in giving notice was unreasonable as a matter of law under K.S.A. 84-2-607(3)(a). The district court apparently accepted that rationale. We do not. The statute requires notice within "a reasonable time." In turn, the UCC expressly recognizes that a reasonable time for acting "depends on the nature, purpose and circumstances" of the required or contemplated action. K.S.A. 84-1-204(2). The Kansas Comment to K.S.A. 84-2-607 points out that the courts do not apply the notice-of-breach obligation as stringently in cases involving consumers as in those between commercial entities. And, according to the Comment, a relaxed notice requirement is particularly appropriate when the consumer-buyer's delay neither prevented remediation of the breach nor prejudiced the seller in defending against the suit. K.S.A. 84-2-607, Kansas Comment 2 (1996).

The Kansas Supreme Court took that approach in *Smith*, recognizing that the reasonableness of the notice from a consumer-buyer under K.S.A. 84-2-607(3)(a) should be assessed "[u]nder the totality of the circumstances" rather than with "blind adherence to the generally appropriate 'condition precedent' concept," especially when any claimed delay compromised none of the purposes to be furthered through timely notification. *See Smith*, 233 Kan. at 914. The court pointed out that the notice requirement aims "'to defeat commercial bad faith, not to deprive a good faith consumer of his remedy.'" 233 Kan. at 914, quoting Official UCC Comment 4 to K.S.A. 84-2-607.

Other courts have taken the same view. *Wal-Mart v. Wheeler*, 262 Ga. App. 607, 611(2003); *Fitl v. Strek*, 269 Neb. 51, 54–56 (2005) (2-year delay in giving notice of breach after consumer sale not unreasonable under Nebraska UCC 2-607); *Maybank v. Kresge Co.,* 302 N.C. 129, 135–36 (1981) (3-year delay by consumer in giving notice of breach in sale of goods under UCC is not unreasonable as a matter of law on facts presented); and, *Hays v. General Elec. Co.*, 151 F.Supp.2d 1001, 1012–13 (N.D. Ill. 2001) (In a case between commercial entities, the court recognizes that timeliness of notification under UCC 2-607 typically presents a jury question, especially if the buyer communicates before filing suit and without causing demonstrable prejudice to the seller.).

The circumstances here preclude a finding as a matter of law that Golden's letter amounted to untimely notice under K.S.A. 84-2-607(3)(a). Given Golden's status as a consumer and the lack of claimed prejudice from Den-Mat and Dr. Gill, the timeliness of the notice is a matter of fair debate and, hence, a question for the jury. The courts commonly consider determinations of reasonable time under 2-607(3)(a) and under the UCC generally to be within the province of the factfinder. *La Villa Fair v. Lewis Carpet Mills, Inc.*, 219 Kan. 395, 401–03 (1976) (rejection of goods within reasonable time under K.S.A. 84-2-602(1) question for factfinder); *Inter-Americas Ins. Corp. v. Imaging Solutions Co.*, 39 Kan. App.2d 875, 885–86 (2008) (reasonable time under UCC "usually a question of fact for the jury"); *Sherkate Sahami Khass Rapol v. Henry R. Jahn & Son*, 701 F.2d 1049, 1051 (2d Cir. 1983) (rejection of goods under New York UCC 2-602). This is such a case. Whether Golden provided notice of breach within a reasonable time under K.S.A. 84-2-607(3)(a) should have been left for the jury. …

Application of UCC

Dr. Gill has fired a veritable broadside at the substance of the UCC claims Golden has asserted. Despite the numerous arguments Dr. Gill asserts, we do not find any that would support summary judgment on the factual record in this case. We address the points sequentially.

UCC Coverage

Dr. Gill contends there was "no transaction in goods" between her and Golden and, therefore, the UCC does not apply. Beneath that overstatement of the circumstances lurks an actual controversy that should be left for the jury. As we have said, Article 2 of the UCC regulates the sale of goods. The UCC defines goods expansively as meaning "all things (including specially manufactured goods) which are movable at the time of identification to the contract for sale," except for the money to be paid under the contract for the goods, investment securities, and legal rights to things or property. K.S.A. 84-2-105(1).

Goods—the Cerinate veneers—were plainly involved in and integral to the transaction involving Golden and Dr. Gill, as we have already indicated. Golden met with Dr. Gill, as Den-Mat's recommended dentist, and ordered the veneers through her. Dr. Gill received the veneers and then applied them to Golden's teeth. Golden paid Dr. Gill. But a sale does not come within the scope of the UCC merely because the contract includes the transfer of goods. Many contracts also entail services associated with the goods. The arrangement here was of that sort, and Dr. Gill provided services essential for Golden's use of the veneers. In UCC parlance, those transactions involving goods and services are commonly known as mixed or hybrid contracts.

The UCC does not address mixed contracts as such. So courts have created common-law rules to determine if those transactions should be treated as sales of goods covered under the UCC or service contracts outside the Code's regulation. Some 30 years ago, the Kansas Supreme Court adopted the "predominant purpose" test for classifying mixed contracts. *Care Display, Inc. v. Didde-Glaser, Inc.*, 225 Kan. 232, 238–39 (1979). The predominant purpose test has become the commonly accepted, if not the near universal, standard.

As the name suggests, the test attempts to discern the principal nature of the transaction: Is the buyer seeking services to which the goods are incidental, or is the buyer acquiring goods to which the services are auxiliary? *Care Display*, 225 Kan. at 238 ("The test for inclusion or exclusion [of mixed contracts under the UCC] is ... whether their predominant factor, their thrust, their purpose, reasonably stated, is the rendition of service, with goods incidentally involved ... or is a transaction of sale, with labor incidentally involved," quoting *Bonebrake v. Cox*, 499 F.2d 951, 960 8th Cir. 1974). ... Having concluded the predominant purpose of a mixed contract to be a question of fact, we turn to whether the transaction here, nonetheless, must be considered one principally for services rather than goods based on the summary judgment record. If so, the UCC would be inapplicable, as Dr. Gill argues.

Unlike most medical or dental procedures, Golden's acquisition of the veneers was purely for cosmetic purposes. She was not seeking treatment for some illness or injury. The transaction was materially different from, for example, a dentist filling a cavity. In that instance, the patient or buyer has a malady, perhaps a painful one, and seeks a cure from the dentist. The dentist may drill and fill the cavity, though there might be other treatment options, such as installing a crown or pulling the offending tooth. The patient has received services in the form of a diagnosis, a recommended course of care, and actual treatment.

The patient has also received whatever material the dentist used to fill the cavity. The filling itself would likely be a form of goods under the UCC, and the contract between the patient and dentist would be a mixed one. But the services would plainly seem to predominate. The patient wanted treatment for the cavity and principally sought diagnostic and therapeutic services from the dentist to accomplish that purpose. The patient had no particular interest in what the dentist used to fill the cavity and likely left the decision to the dentist's professional judgment. We think that would be true of the vast majority of transactions between a patient and a healthcare provider for treatment of illness or injury in which there were a single contract.

Golden, however, suffered from no malady and sought no professional diagnosis or treatment. She simply wanted whiter teeth and sought replacements for the veneers she had been wearing. Golden had received information from Den-Mat containing representations about the characteristics of its Cerinate veneers making them appear to be a satisfactory choice. Although disputed in the record, there is evidence Golden shared that information with Dr. Gill and received some assurance from her as to the accuracy of a critical characteristic—the veneers, being made of porcelain, would not stain or dull over time. Golden then purchased Den-Mat's Cerinate veneers through Dr. Gill, who applied them to Golden's teeth.

Viewing the record favorably to Golden, as we must in considering her opposition to summary judgment, she did not go to Dr. Gill with a problem—dull or aesthetically unappealing teeth—for which she wanted a professional consultation about various corrective options. Golden wanted Cerinate veneers and understood from Den-Mat that Dr. Gill could provide and apply that product. To be sure, Dr. Gill also provided services in that she removed the existing veneers, sized and ordered the Cerinate veneers, and applied the new veneers to Golden's teeth. But a jury could fairly conclude Golden wanted the veneers, while the services were simply part of the means of accomplishing that purpose. That would be consistent with the notion that but for the buyer's acquisition of the goods, the services would have been unnecessary, making the contract predominately one for the goods, as the Kansas Supreme Court has suggested.

The predominance of the veneers as goods also seems plausible and, thus, within a jury's reasonable consideration when the transaction is compared with orthodontics, another form of dentistry often used for largely cosmetic purposes. To straighten the patient's teeth, the orthodontist applies braces and other devices, often over an extended time period. The goods, those devices, are an integral part of the process. But the orthodontist makes a professional judgment about the types of braces to achieve the ultimate purpose of realigning the patient's teeth. Again, the contract is a mixed one for goods and services. But the patient's purpose is not the acquisition of braces but of straight teeth. The braces are temporary appliances, used by the orthodontist, for achieving that end. In those circumstances, the orthodontist's services would seem to predominate over the goods.

The same degree of professional skill and judgment is lacking here in that Golden essentially selected the goods independently, though she sought affirmation of that selection from both Dr. Gill and representatives of Den-Mat regarding particular characteristics of the goods. And, unlike braces, the veneers themselves, once applied, provided the desired cosmetic result. The result continued only so long as the veneers remained in place and performed as Golden understood they would.

Finally, nothing in the record evidence shows Dr. Gill contracted separately with Golden for professional services apart from the purchase of the veneers. The parties do not argue there were separate or distinct contracts for the veneers, on the one hand, and Dr. Gill's services, on the other. The transaction was unitary, combining goods and services. Likewise, there is no evidence Golden was charged separately for the veneers and for Dr. Gill's services or that the services were even broken out as a distinct component or cost in the contract or in any billing. ...

In short, the record evidence fails to support a finding as a matter of law for Dr. Gill that the transaction with Golden was one in which acquisition and use of services predominated over the purchase of goods so that the UCC would not apply. Summary judgment could not be granted to Dr. Gill on the UCC claims on that basis or on any KCPA claims dependent upon an exclusion or dilution of otherwise applicable UCC warranties.

CONCLUSION

The judgment for Den-Mat and Dr. Gill is reversed ... and remanded for further proceedings, including trial. Golden may proceed with her claims for breach of express warranty, for breach of implied warranty of merchantability under K.S.A. 84-2-314, for breach of implied warranty of fitness for a particular purpose under K.S.A. 84-2-315, for deceptive acts and practices under K.S.A. 50-626, and for improper limitation of implied warranties under K.S.A. 50-639.

Affirmed in part, reversed in part, and remanded with directions.

UNIFORM COMMERCIAL CODE

§ 2-607. EFFECT OF ACCEPTANCE; NOTICE OF BREACH; BURDEN OF ESTABLISHING BREACH AFTER ACCEPTANCE; NOTICE OF CLAIM OR LITIGATION TO PERSON ANSWERABLE OVER

(1) The buyer must pay at the contract rate for any goods accepted.

(2) Acceptance of goods by the buyer precludes rejection of the goods accepted and if made with knowledge of a nonconformity cannot be revoked because of it unless the acceptance was on the reasonable assumption that the non-conformity would be seasonably cured but acceptance does not of itself impair any other remedy provided by this Article for non-conformity.

(3) Where a tender has been accepted

(a) the buyer must within a reasonable time after he discovers or should have discovered any breach notify the seller of breach or be barred from any remedy; and

(b) if the claim is one for infringement or the like (subsection (3) of Section 2-312) and the buyer is sued as a result of such a breach he must so notify the seller within a reasonable time after he receives notice of the litigation or be barred from any remedy over for liability established by the litigation.

(4) The burden is on the buyer to establish any breach with respect to the goods accepted.

(5) Where the buyer is sued for breach of a warranty or other obligation for which his seller is answerable over

(a) he may give his seller written notice of the litigation. If the notice states that the seller may come in and defend and that if the seller does not do so he will be bound in any action against him by his buyer by any determination of fact common to the two litigations, then unless the seller after seasonable receipt of the notice does come in and defend he is so bound.

(b) if the claim is one for infringement or the like (subsection (3) of Section 2-312) the original seller may demand in writing that his buyer turn over to him control of the litigation including settlement or else be barred from any remedy over and if he also agrees to bear all expense and to satisfy any adverse judgment, then unless the buyer after seasonable receipt of the demand does turn over control the buyer is so barred.

(6) The provisions of subsections (3), (4) and (5) apply to any obligation of a buyer to hold the seller harmless against infringement or the like (subsection (3) of Section 2-312).

§ 2-608. REVOCATION OF ACCEPTANCE IN WHOLE OR IN PART

(1) The buyer may revoke his acceptance of a lot or commercial unit whose non-conformity substantially impairs its value to him if he has accepted it

(a) on the reasonable assumption that its non-conformity would be cured and it has not been seasonably cured; or

(b) without discovery of such non-conformity if his acceptance was reasonably induced either by the difficulty of discovery before acceptance or by the seller's assurances.

(2) Revocation of acceptance must occur within a reasonable time after the buyer discovers or should have discovered the ground for it and before any substantial change in condition of the goods which is not caused by their own defects. It is not effective until the buyer notifies the seller of it.

(3) A buyer who so revokes has the same rights and duties with regard to the goods involved as if he had rejected them.

§ 2-609. RIGHT TO ADEQUATE ASSURANCE OF PERFORMANCE

(1) A contract for sale imposes an obligation on each party that the other's expectation of receiving due performance will not be impaired. When reasonable grounds for insecurity arise with respect to the performance of either party the other may in writing demand adequate assurance of due performance and until he receives such assurance may if commercially reasonable suspend any performance for which he has not already received the agreed return.

(2) Between merchants the reasonableness of grounds for insecurity and the adequacy of any assurance offered shall be determined according to commercial standards.

(3) Acceptance of any improper delivery or payment does not prejudice the aggrieved party's right to demand adequate assurance of future performance.

(4) After receipt of a justified demand failure to provide within a reasonable time not exceeding thirty days such assurance of due performance as is adequate under the circumstances of the particular case is a repudiation of the contract.

§ 2-612. "INSTALLMENT CONTRACT"; BREACH

(1) An "installment contract" is one which requires or authorizes the delivery of goods in separate lots to be separately accepted, even though the contract contains a clause "each delivery is a separate contract" or its equivalent.

(2) The buyer may reject any installment which is non-conforming if the non-conformity substantially impairs the value of that installment and cannot be cured or if the non-conformity is a defect in the required documents; but if the non-conformity does not fall within subsection (3) and the seller gives adequate assurance of its cure the buyer must accept that installment.

(3) Whenever non-conformity or default with respect to one or more installments substantially impairs the value of the whole contract there is a breach of the whole. But the aggrieved party reinstates the contract if he accepts a non-conforming installment without seasonably notifying of cancellation or if he brings an action with respect only to past installments or demands performance as to future installments.

§ 2-614. SUBSTITUTED PERFORMANCE

(1) Where without fault of either party the agreed berthing, loading, or unloading facilities fail or an agreed type of carrier becomes unavailable or the agreed manner of delivery otherwise becomes commercially impracticable but a commercially reasonable substitute is available, such substitute performance must be tendered and accepted.

(2) If the agreed means or manner of payment fails because of domestic or foreign governmental regulation, the seller may withhold or stop delivery unless the buyer provides a means or manner of payment which is commercially a substantial equivalent. If delivery has already been taken, payment by the means or in the manner provided by the regulation discharges the buyer's obligation unless the regulation is discriminatory, oppressive or predatory.

SECTION TWO: ANTICIPATORY BREACH OR REPUDIATION OF SALE CONTRACTS UNDER ARTICLE 2

Here, a brief review of a few common-law principles—those appearing in Chapter 4—is warranted. First, the doctrine of repudiation and the doctrine of anticipatory breach are closely related. *Microsoft Corp. v. Motorola, Inc.*, 2012 WL 2030098, *9 (W.D. Wash. 2012). Under the doctrine of anticipatory breach, a non-repudiating party to a contract may escape his obligation to perform and secure damages for a "total breach," if the other party wrongfully repudiates a contract before beginning to perform. Courts apply slightly different standards, however, to determine when a contract was repudiated.

In New York, repudiation occurs when "the repudiating party has indicated an unqualified and [a] clear refusal to perform." *De Lorenzo v. Bac Agency, Inc.*, 256 A.D.2d 906, 908, 681 N.Y.S.2d 846 (N.Y. App. Div. 1998). On the other hand, under West Virginia law, contractual repudiation occurs when a party's statement positively, absolutely, or unequivocally renounces a contract. *Mollohan v. Black Rock Contracting, Inc.*, 235 S.E.2d 813, 816 (W.Va. 1977). And, in the Second Circuit, repudiation occurs "when a party manifests an intent not to perform, either by words or by deeds." *Aetna Cas. and Sur. Co. v. Aniero Concrete Co.*, 404 F.3d 566, 587 (2d Cir. 2005).

But, the common law is settled regarding one issue: The doctrine of anticipatory breach may not be considered or applied when interpreting and enforcing unilateral contracts, or payment-of-money contracts. *Roehm v. Horst*, 178 U.S. 1, 17 (1900). In addition, whether a contracting party has repudiated or abandoned a contract is generally a question of fact under the common law. *DiFolco v. MSNBC Cable LLC*, 622 F.3d 104, 112 (2d Cir. 2010).

Article 2 of the Uniform Commercial Code codifies the closely connected, common-law doctrines of repudiation and anticipatory breach. Under section 2-610, a nonbreaching party may "resort to any remedy for breach," if the other party repudiates a contract and declares that he will not perform future, contractual obligations. Of course, a nonbreaching party may attempt to persuade the breaching party to retract his repudiation. *Gaglia v. Kichner*, 317 N.J. Super. 292, 299, 721 A.2d 1028 (N.J. Super. Ct. App. Div. 1999). Section 2-611(2) reads: "Retraction may be by any method which clearly indicates to the aggrieved party that the repudiating party intends to perform." Like many UCC provisions, these two sections have generated some controversy. Therefore, this part of the text presents illustrations of how courts have addressed conflicts involving sections 2-610 and 2-611.

A. Proving an Anticipatory Breach Under § 2-610

Cabot Corp. v. Lucent Technologies, Inc.
836 N.E.2d 349
(Mass. App. Ct. 2005)

Cabot Corporation (Cabot) filed a three-count complaint in the Superior Court against Lucent Technologies (Lucent) and OFS Fitel, LLC (OFS)—Lucent's assignee—claiming that Lucent and OFS violated a supply agreement (contract) for the purchase of certain material used in the production of glass tubes and optical fiber products. ... After argument, a Superior Court judge issued a memorandum of decision in which she allowed Lucent and OFS' joint motion for summary judgment, denied their counterclaim for declaratory relief because there was no controversy, and allowed Cabot's motion for summary judgment on the counterclaim but denied it on the termination claim. Cabot appealed.

BACKGROUND

On or about June 2, 2000, Cabot entered into a contract with Lucent pursuant to which Cabot agreed to manufacture and Lucent agreed to purchase certain minimum annual quantities of Cabot's silica dispersion products (material). The term of the contract was from July 1, 2000, until September 30, 2002. For the final year of the contract, the parties agreed that Lucent would buy, and Cabot would sell, a minimum of 890,000 and a maximum of 1,336,000 wet pounds of material. Lucent was required to provide Cabot with a twelve-month forecast for material on a quarterly basis.

The contract contained a provision establishing an early termination fee of $3,000,000, reduced to $2,500,000 if Lucent terminated within six months of the end of the contract term. It also stated that "construction, interpretation and performance of this Agreement and all transactions under it shall be governed by the laws of the State of New York." Finally, it specified that all notices made pursuant to the contract "shall be in writing and shall be given or made by telegram, tested telex, confirmed facsimile or similar communication or by certified or registered mail, or express courier service." On or about November 16, 2001, Lucent assigned the contract to OFS.

During the first two years of the contract, Lucent/OFS purchased significantly more than the minimum quantities specified in the contract. Production, purchase, and sale of the material under the contract ceased at some time after December 21, 2001. On December 21, 2001, Lucent informed Cabot—by phone and email—that it predicted no need for any material for most, and possibly all, of the first quarter of 2002. Such forecasts were required under the contract, but were not binding on Lucent; they were only intended to give Cabot advance notice of the amount of material to prepare for future orders.

A conversation took place on January 25, 2002—between a Lucent employee, Walter Simmons, and Valdemir Prodocimo, a Cabot employee. Simmons informed Prodocimo that Lucent/OFS was contemplating suspending its operations at a Georgia facility, and therefore would no longer require "production quantities" of material. Simmons was aware that there was a termination provision in the contract, but did not expressly mention terminating the contract during the call.

According to the record ..., Cabot contends that OFS terminated the contract during this conversation. Cabot ceased all contract related activity on January 25, 2002. ... After consulting an attorney, Simmons sent a letter to Prodocimo on February 21, 2002, stating:

> The purpose of this letter is to inform you that after extensive evaluation and review, OFS has decided to suspend operations ... at the Norcross, Georgia facility. It is our current plan to continue with Research and Development activities ... using Material. However, our production quantities from Cabot Corporation related to CONTRACT AT21990008 will no longer be required. Cabot is an extremely valuable and important supplier to OFS and it is unfortunate that the business conditions have necessitated this decision. We sincerely appreciate Cabot's ongoing support and the positive nature of our business relationship. We look forward to discussing this matter at your earliest convenience.

Another letter written by Simmons dated June 17, in response to a May 14 letter, attempted to clarify OFS's position regarding the contract. Regarding the February letter, it states:

> There is no mention of termination in this letter. ... [N]owhere is it stated in the letter that OFS will no longer place any orders with Cabot under the contract. ... I concluded my letter not by stating that I wanted to terminate the contract, but that I looked forward to discussing [the matter].

The letter also referred to telephone conversations prior to March 22, during which neither party "raised the topic of contract termination or termination charges." It further stated, "Cabot's position that OFS has terminated the contract is unfounded and Cabot's request for a termination fee is unwarranted and unacceptable. As further proof that the contract is not terminated, OFS will be placing an order ... for Material under the contract before its normal expiration on September 30, 2002."

Cabot's August 13, 2002, letter to OFS disputed these claims and maintained that OFS terminated the contract on January 25, 2002, as confirmed by the February 21 letter. The August letter states, "in light of your unequivocal communications Cabot stopped all production of the material." Cabot asserted that since the Norcross facility "continues to be shut down, [OFS's] July 26, 2002 [purchase order] serves no meaningful purpose except to enable you to argue that the Contract has not been terminated." The purchase order was never filled.

DISCUSSION

"An order granting or denying summary judgment will be upheld if the trial judge ruled on undisputed material facts and his ruling was correct as a matter of law." *Commonwealth v. One 1987 Mercury Cougar Automobile*, 413 Mass. 534, 536 (1992). We begin our discussion by observing that the decision of the Superior Court judge is thorough and well-reasoned, and we base our decision on substantially the same analysis.

1. Termination by OFS

The parties do not dispute that, under the plain language of the contract, the option to terminate belonged to OFS. Section 14—the termination clause—permitted OFS to terminate the contract in circumstances of commercial infeasibility, but did not require it to do so. The contract also set out specific procedures such termination was to follow. Substantially for the reasons stated by the judge, we agree that neither the January 25, 2002, telephone call nor the February 21, 2002, letter satisfied the contract's requirements for termination. Cabot's attempt to establish OFS's termination by relying on the general notice provisions of the NEW YORK UNIFORM COMMERCIAL CODE (U.C.C.) is unavailing, where the undisputed facts plainly demonstrate that the contract's express notice provisions were not met.

2. Repudiation by OFS

In the alternative, Cabot argues that OFS's communications constituted an anticipatory repudiation of the contract. When a party to a contract repudiates the contract, substantially impairing its value, New York law permits the other party to suspend its own performance and initiate an action for breach. N.Y.U.C.C. § 2-610 (McKinney 2004). Section 2-610 provides:

> When either party repudiates the contract with respect to a performance not yet due the loss of which will substantially impair the value of the contract to the other, the aggrieved party may (a) for a commercially reasonable time await performance by the repudiating party; or (b) resort to any remedy for breach (Section 2-703 or Section 2-711), even though he has notified the repudiating party that he would await the latter's performance and has urged retraction; and (c) in either case suspend his own performance or proceed in accordance with the provisions of this Article on the seller's right to identify goods to the contract notwithstanding breach or to salvage unfinished goods (Section 2-704).

In applying the statute, we look to see whether there was "an overt communication of intention or an action which renders performance impossible or demonstrates a clear determination not to continue with performance." N.Y.U.C.C. § 2-610, comment 1. Cabot, in its blue brief, and the judge, in her memorandum of decision, reference the N.Y.U.C.C., as effective 2004, and we therefore do the same.

As to the first prong of the analysis, Cabot points to the OFS's suspending of certain operations at the Norcross, Georgia, facility as proof that OFS's performance would be impossible. But the undisputed facts established that OFS's communications regarding that facility did not necessarily render performance impossible. As the judge observed, the contract required that the material be shipped to the Norcross plant, but OFS had another facility—at Murray Hill, New Jersey—that conceivably could have utilized the material.

We therefore look to the second prong, that is, whether OFS's communications demonstrated a clear determination not to continue with performance under the contract. New York cases—in describing the kind of overt communication that would evince the requisite determination not to continue—have required one that is unequivocal, definite and final. *Rachmani Corp. v. 9 E. 96th St. Apartment Corp.*, 211 A.D.2d 262, 267 (N.Y. 1995) ("there must be a definite and final communication of the intention to forego performance"); *D'Abreau v. Smith*, 240 A.D.2d 616, 617 (N.Y. 1997) ("definite and final communication evincing an intention to forego performance under the contract"); *Canali U.S.A., Inc. v. Solow Bldg. Co.*, 292 A.D.2d 170, 171 (N.Y. 2002) ("definite and final communication" necessary); *Coney Island Exhaust, Inc. v. Mobil Oil Corp.*, 304 A.D.2d 706, 707 (N.Y. 2003) ("unequivocal, definite and final repudiation").

Certainly, statements from one party to the other that their agreement "was over" and that the parties "had no contract"—followed by letters reiterating the same—satisfied the U.C.C.'s requirement. *See Record Club of America, Inc. v. United Artists Records, Inc.*, 643 F.Supp. 925, 936 (S.D.N.Y. 1986). *See also Cary Oil Co. v. MG Ref. & Mktg., Inc.*, 90 F.Supp.2d 401, 411 (S.D.N.Y. 2000) (letters to customers purporting to confirm agreement to cancel contracts and relieve both sides from any further obligations thereunder could only be interpreted as anticipatory repudiation).

However, a party's expression of doubt—as to whether it would perform according to the contract, prior to the time when performance became due—was not necessarily repudiation, at least not as matter of law. *See O'Shanter Resources, Inc. v. Niagara Mohawk Power Corp.*, 915 F.Supp. 560, 567–568 (W.D.N.Y. 1996) (genuine issue of fact as to whether inconsistent statements about wanting to negotiate a new contract, while not explicitly stating that the existing contract would not be honored, constituted an unequivocal repudiation). *See also Scavenger, Inc. v. GT Interactive Software Corp.*, 289 A.D.2d 58, 59 (N.Y. 2001) (written communication that included an opportunity to cure was not an "unequivocal repudiation" of the parties' contract).

OFS's communications to Cabot, while not optimistic, nevertheless fall short of an unequivocal, definite, and final indication that it was abandoning the contract. In the February 21, 2002, letter, OFS suggested that additional orders of the material would be forthcoming, but would not be in the quantities previously called for or forecasted. The written statement further referenced Cabot as an "extremely valued and important supplier to OFS," in the present tense, and expressed the desire for further discussions "at your earliest convenience." As the judge observed, these communications—while perhaps ambiguous as to OFS's intentions—fell short of the unequivocal, definite, and final repudiation that New York cases require. *See O'Shanter Resources, Inc. v. Niagara Mohawk Power Corp.*, 915 F.Supp. at 567–568 (question of fact whether Niagara Mohawk repudiated, given its continuing performance, its recognition of the parties' contractual relationship, and its desire for further negotiations).

Cabot argues that OFS's statement in its February 21 letter that "production quantities" would "no longer be required," was tantamount to repudiation. In Cabot's view, the reduction in quantities to be ordered by OFS translated into an intention not to continue with performance, because the minimum quantity for the fiscal year—ending September 30, 2002—would not be met. But the U.C.C. expressly requires that, in order to qualify as an anticipatory repudiation, the performance repudiated must "substantially impair the value of the contract" to the other party. N.Y.U.C.C. § 2-610.

As the judge pointed out, by February 21, 2002, OFS's total orders—since the contract's inception—had already exceeded the minimum quantity requirements for the entire contract term. This was due largely to the fact that OFS's orders had exceeded the annual maximum quantity for the previous year. Thus, while OFS's orders for the contract's final year appeared in jeopardy, its total purchases from Cabot had already satisfied the contract's overall minimum requirements. *Compare Pitcher v. Benderson-Wainberg Assocs. II Ltd. Partnership*, 277 A.D.2d 586, 587–588 (N.Y. 2000) (tenant's letter, notifying landlord that it was going out of business and seeking to negotiate a lease termination after one year into a five and one-half-year lease, constituted anticipatory repudiation as matter of law).

Thus, Cabot has not shown that a reduction in orders for the contract's final year would substantially impair the contract's value, so as to evince a clear determination on OFS's part not to perform. *See e.g., Cary Oil Co. v. MG Ref. & Mktg., Inc.*, 90 F.Supp.2d at 410–411 (action that threatened financial stability of supplier, thereby threatening its ability to deliver the product, was held susceptible of varying interpretations and did not evince a clear determination not to perform under the contract). In any event, as the judge rightly concluded, any question or ambiguity as to whether OFS, by its communications, intended to abandon performance should not have prompted Cabot to assume the worst.

In such instances [and] in accordance with the U.C.C., Cabot could have sought clarification from OFS. In this manner, Cabot could have avoided liability for its own repudiation. N.Y.U.C.C. § 2-609(1). *See Norcon Power Partners Ltd. Partnership v. Niagara Mohawk Power Corp.*, 92 N.Y.2d 458, 464–466 (1998). Section 2-609(1) provides, in relevant part:

> When reasonable grounds for insecurity arise—with respect to the performance of either party—the other may in writing demand adequate assurance of due performance and until he receives such assurance may if commercially reasonable suspend any performance for which he has not already received the agreed return.

3. Repudiation by Cabot

Having concluded—without demanding assurances—that OFS had violated the contract, Cabot elected to terminate the contract and cease performance under it. We agree with the arguments made by OFS in its brief ... that Cabot did make a positive and unequivocal announcement that the contract was terminated. Cabot has shown no genuine issue of fact as to its termination of the contract as of July 2002 to preclude summary judgment in favor of OFS. Under New York law, the "test for an anticipatory repudiation is an objective one and good faith is immaterial." *Record Club of America, Inc. v. United Artists Records, Inc.*, 643 F.Supp. at 939.

Therefore, even if Cabot were acting in good faith, having reasonably believed that OFS had repudiated the contract, such belief would not excuse its own repudiation. We agree with the Superior Court judge's determination that after Cabot repudiated the contract, at the latest by refusing to fill the July 2002 purchase order under the contract, OFS was discharged of all remaining obligations.

CONCLUSION

For the reasons stated in the appellee's brief, and in the well-reasoned Superior Court's decision, we conclude that OFS neither terminated nor repudiated its contract with Cabot. Instead, Cabot repudiated the contract after misconstruing and failing to clarify OFS's communications.

Judgment affirmed.

Uniform Commercial Code

§ 2-609. Right to Adequate Assurance of Performance

(1) A contract for sale imposes an obligation on each party that the other's expectation of receiving due performance will not be impaired. When reasonable grounds for insecurity arise with respect to the performance of either party the other may in writing demand adequate assurance of due performance and until he receives such assurance may if commercially reasonable suspend any performance for which he has not already received the agreed return.

(2) Between merchants the reasonableness of grounds for insecurity and the adequacy of any assurance offered shall be determined according to commercial standards.

(3) Acceptance of any improper delivery or payment does not prejudice the aggrieved party's right to demand adequate assurance of future performance.

(4) After receipt of a justified demand failure to provide within a reasonable time not exceeding thirty days such assurance of due performance as is adequate under the circumstances of the particular case is a repudiation of the contract.

§ 2-610. Anticipatory Repudiation

When either party repudiates the contract with respect to a performance not yet due the loss of which will substantially impair the value of the contract to the other, the aggrieved party may

(a) for a commercially reasonable time await performance by the repudiating party; or

(b) resort to any remedy for breach (Section 2-703 or Section 2-711), even though he has notified the repudiating party that he would await the latter's performance and has urged retraction; and

(c) in either case suspend his own performance or proceed in accordance with the provisions of this Article on the seller's right to identify goods to the contract notwithstanding breach or to salvage unfinished goods (Section 2-704).

B. Proving a Retraction of an Anticipatory Breach Under § 2-611

Red River Commodities, Inc. v. Eidsness
459 N.W.2d 811
(N.D. 1990)

MESCHKE, JUSTICE. Red River Commodities, Inc. (RRC) sued George Eidsness for breach of his contracts to grow and to deliver sunflowers. The trial court awarded RRC judgment for $33,760.50. George appealed.

While wintering in Arizona in early 1988, North Dakota farmer—George Eidsness—agreed by telephone to grow and to sell 350,000 pounds of confection sunflowers to RRC at a floor price of 11.25 cents per pound. In George's absence, one of his sons signed "Confection Sunflower Production" contracts for George. Contract No. 217, signed on February 15, 1988, was for 200,000 pounds, and Contract No. 224, signed on March 4, 1988, was for 150,000 pounds. Later in the spring, George obtained sunflower seed from RRC for planting as the contracts stipulated: "The Grower agrees to purchase his seed requirements from RRC or its designated contracting representatives."

In June, George discovered that one field of sunflowers was severely weed infested. At George's request, a representative of RRC inspected the field on June 11, confirmed that George could destroy 121 acres, and prepared a handwritten letter to RRC for George's signature. The letter referred to contract No. 217 and said:

> This letter is to inform you that I have destroyed approximately 121 acres of my contracted confection sunflowers due to a severe infestation of kochia and pigeongrass. This notification is to comply with item No. 8 of the contract.

Besides weeds, drought also reduced George's crop yield. George did not deliver any sunflowers to RRC from his 1988 crop. In mid-December 1988, RRC learned that George was selling sunflowers to a competitor at 22 cents per pound. RRC promptly sued George for anticipatory breach and also wrote George urging him to perform his contracts. George failed to deliver any sunflowers to RRC.

After trial without a jury, the trial court found that George had not signed Contracts 217 and 224, that "he did receive the benefits of same" without objecting to them, and that "he endorsed and ratified same." The trial court also found that George produced sufficient sunflowers to meet his contracts with RRC "but instead sold the product to a competitor. ..." After adjusting contracted amounts proportionately for the destroyed 121 acres, the trial court held that George "was obligated to deliver 229,000 pounds" and "failed to deliver any product whatsoever. ..."

Finding that RRC purchased replacements, the trial court held that George was liable to RRC for the difference between the cost of cover at 26 cents per pound and the contract price of 11.25 cents per pound. The trial court awarded damages of $33,776.50 to RRC based on 14.75 cents for each of 229,000 pounds undelivered. George appealed various questions:

1. Did he contract to deliver 350,000 pounds?
2. Was he obligated to deliver 229,000 pounds?
3. Was RRC notified of low yields?
4. Was evidence wrongly excluded that RRC knew about his low yields?
5. Did he breach the contracts?
6. Did RRC "cover" reasonably?
7. Was RRC liable for his sunflower storage?

CONTRACTS

Farmers' agreements to grow and deliver grain in the future are commonly called "forward contracts." Because crops are the chief source of income for farmers, forward-crop contracts furnish economic protection to farmers. Forward contracts protect farmers from future price declines and ensure payment of production expenses. Correspondingly, forward contracts protect grain dealers from future price increases and ensure adequate supplies. *See Allenberg Cotton Co., Inc. v. Pittman*, 419 U.S. 20, 26–27 (1974); *Merrill Lynch, Pierce, Fenner & Smith, Inc. v. Curran*, 456 U.S. 353, 357–59 (1982). Forward-crop contracts are commercially important, even though unanticipated occurrences and price fluctuations sometimes upset expectations.

The UNIFORM COMMERCIAL CODE chapter on Sales applies to transactions in goods, including growing crops. NDCC § 41-02-02 (UCC § 2-102); NDCC § 41-02-05(2) (UCC § 2-105). NORTH DAKOTA CENTURY CODE § 41-02-07(2) (UCC § 2-107) declares that a contract for the sale of growing crops can be a present sale before severance of the crop from the land. *See Remmick v. Mills*, 165 N.W.2d 61, 67 (N.D. 1968) (Growing alfalfa is "goods" under UCC); *Breden v. Johnson*, 56 N.D. 921, 219 N.W. 946 (1928) (Growing hay is "goods" within earlier Uniform Sales Act.). We are guided by the UNIFORM COMMERCIAL CODE.

George concedes that he orally agreed to grow and deliver sunflowers to RRC. Still, George contends that the trial court misinterpreted the facts and misapplied the law to his agreements. George insists that he only agreed to grow 300 acres of sunflowers, not 350 acres, and to deliver the quantity actually produced, not 350,000 pounds. Because loss of the weedy 121 acres reduced his commitment, George urges that his net obligation was to grow 179 acres, not 229 acres. In the second part of this argument, George urges that he was only obligated to deliver actual production from those acres, not a fixed number of pounds.

The statute of frauds in the Uniform Commercial Code, NDCC § 41-02-08 (UCC § 2-201), makes a contract for the sale of goods for a price of $500 or more—when not signed by the party or his authorized agent—enforceable only if that party admits the contract. "[But,] the contract is not enforceable ... beyond the quantity of goods admitted." Under this statute, George argues that he was only bound to grow 300 acres. Although George admitted his oral agreements, he denied signing the written contracts and denied authorizing his son to do so for him. In his testimony, George admitted one oral agreement to grow "200 acres," and equivocated about the extent of his second oral agreement. George testified, "I thought I had said another hundred and I may have said 150, I don't know if I was wrong or not on that." George acknowledged buying seed for planting from RRC for "right around 300 acres," but later he conceded that "I was supposed to seed 350, yeah."

In addition, by dealing with RRC's representative to destroy a weedy field and by writing RRC to reduce his contract commitments, George confirmed the written contracts. *See Askew v. Joachim Memorial Home*, 234 N.W.2d 226, 237 (N.D. 1975). "A contract for sale of goods may be made in any manner sufficient to show agreement, including conduct by both parties which recognizes the existence of such a contract." NDCC § 41-02-11(1) (UCC § 2-204). *See also* NDCC § 41-02-14(3) (UCC § 2-207). We conclude that there was sufficient evidence for the trial court to find that George ratified the written contracts. Those written contracts obligated George, as "The Grower" to "plant a minimum of [350] acres to cover [350,000] contracted lbs."

In the second part of his contract argument, George urges that the trial court misinterpreted the contracts as requiring delivery of a fixed quantity rather than the quantity actually produced on the acreage agreed. George argues that the contracts should be interpreted as obligating him to deliver the quantity produced on the acreage agreed, not to deliver an agreed number of pounds. George testified that he harvested about 80,000 pounds from the acreage that he planted for RRC, although he harvested over 330,000 pounds from the entire 640 acres that he planted to sunflowers in 1988. According to George, the contracts only obligated him to deliver the 80,000 pounds actually produced from the 179 acres that he intended for RRC. ...

George did not submit any evidence that he had notified RRC of "a legal description" of acres planted for RRC as prescribed by paragraph 6 of the contracts. George did not describe how he designated particular acreage for RRC out of the 640 acres of growing sunflowers without so notifying RRC. The trial court determined, as a matter of fact, that the contracts obligated George to deliver 229,000 pounds and that he "produced sufficient sunflowers to meet [his] contracts with" RRC. George produced over 330,000 pounds of sunflowers.

A contract must be construed as a whole, and every clause, sentence, and provision should be given effect if reasonably practicable. See NDCC § 9-07-06, and *Heupel, Inc. v. Schuch*, 453 N.W.2d 776 (N.D. 1990). We believe that the trial court fairly determined that these contracts—construed as a whole—obligated George to deliver 229,000 pounds after adjusting proportionately for the decreased pounds from the 121 acres destroyed. Accordingly, we affirm the trial court's finding that the contracts obligated George to deliver 229,000 pounds of confection sunflowers to RRC.

BREACH AND RETRACTION OF REPUDIATION

The trial court determined that George breached the contracts "by failing to give the proper notice of low production or the inability to satisfy the contracts" as called for by the excuse clause in the contracts. Paragraph 8 of each contract said:

> Fire, strikes, accidents, acts of God and public enemy, or other causes beyond the control of the parties hereto, shall excuse them from the performance of this contract. Should said events occur, either party is to notify the other within 10 days of the event by Certified Mail. Grower shall be obligated to notify RRC and the contracting representative identified below. Excuse from performance of this contract is dependent upon delivery of this notice.

George challenges the trial court's finding that RRC was not notified of drought effects as "without substantial evidentiary support." Except for the weedy field, George does not claim that he personally notified RRC of any other excuse. Nonetheless, George contends that RRC had actual knowledge of his low production through a report from its representative—Richard Frith—the same representative of RRC who inspected and authorized destruction of the weedy acreage. Because RRC knew that George's production per acre was insufficient to fill his commitments, George claims that he was excused from delivering except for what he grew on his 229 acre commitment. RRC's representative, Richard Frith, testified:

> I contacted all of the growers that I worked with in October of 1988. And at that time, I determined from each one of them[,] and [George] was one ... that I contacted[,] as to how much he had in the bin when he was done harvesting. How much he felt he had in the bin and those figures were submitted to Red River.

George also complains that the trial court did not allow into evidence Frith's written report to RRC about low production by growers, which may have evidenced the extent of RRC's knowledge about George's reduced crop yields. George relies upon this testimony and the excluded report as actual notice to RRC about his low production. George argues that "RRC's actual notice supersedes any requirement under the contract to give notice" by certified mail. According to George, "RRC in fact did have notice and George cannot be found to have breached the contract by failing to send a document personally by certified mail."

In an appropriate case, this argument might have worth. *See Red River Commodities, Inc. v. Kelby Eidsness*, 459 N.W.2d 805 (N.D. 1990). But, this argument does not help George in this case. The trial court determined that George "produced sufficient sunflowers to meet [his] contracts with [RRC] but instead sold the product to a competitor" and "failed to deliver any product whatsoever" to RRC. The contracts stipulated: "The Grower agrees ... not to contract said acreage to third party. In such case this occurs grower is obligated without excuse to deliver the total lbs. stated in the contract."

George did not deliver any sunflowers to RRC and sold substantial amounts to a competitor. "The obligation of the seller is to transfer and deliver. ..." NDCC § 41-02-18 (UCC § 2-301). The trial court was entitled to view George's anticipatory breach and nondelivery as a breach of the contracts in their entirety. When RRC sued George for anticipatory breach, RRC also wrote and asked him to perform. George testified at trial that he still had 80,000 pounds on hand for delivery if he was obligated to deliver; but he gave no acceptable reason for why he did not deliver that amount promptly after RRC's action against him.

The burden was then on George to immediately retract his repudiation and to perform. NDCC § 41-02-73 (UCC § 2-610) (Anticipatory repudiation); 41-02-74 (UCC § 2-611) (Retraction of anticipatory repudiation). *See* NDCC § 41-02-72(4) (UCC § 2-609) ("After receipt of a justified demand, failure to provide within a reasonable time—not exceeding thirty days, such assurance of due performance as is adequate under the circumstances of the particular case—is a repudiation of the contract.") *See Glatt v. Bank of Kirkwood Plaza*, 383 N.W.2d 473, 479 (N.D. 1986) and, *Sawyer Farmers' Cooperative Association v. Linke*, 231 N.W.2d 791, 795 (N.D. 1975) ("The contract was breached by the repudiation alone, and the effect of the breach was never nullified by a seasonable retraction of the repudiation.").

After being sued for his anticipatory breach in selling sunflowers elsewhere, George made no effort to perform, even partially, and made no "seasonable retraction" of his anticipatory repudiation. In effect, the trial court determined that George breached the whole of the contracts. A default in an installment contract—which substantially impairs the value of the whole contract—is a breach of the whole contract. NDCC § 41-02-75(3) (UCC § 2-612). An anticipatory repudiation, "which will substantially impair the value of the contract," authorizes the aggrieved party to "[r]esort to any remedy for breach." NDCC § 41-02-73.

North Dakota Century Code §41-02-90(1) (UCC § 2-711) says that "[w]here the seller fails to make delivery or repudiates ..., then with respect to any goods involved, and with respect to the whole if the breach goes to the whole contract (§ 41-02-75), the buyer may ... a. 'Cover' and have damages under the next section as to all the goods affected whether or not they have been identified to the contract; ..." We conclude that the trial court reasonably found that RRC was entitled to damages for George's breach of the whole of the contracts because he "failed to deliver any product whatsoever."

We affirm.

Uniform Commercial Code

§ 2-611. Retraction of Anticipatory Repudiation

(1) Until the repudiating party's next performance is due he can retract his repudiation unless the aggrieved party has since the repudiation cancelled or materially changed his position or otherwise indicated that he considers the repudiation final.

(2) Retraction may be by any method which clearly indicates to the aggrieved party that the repudiating party intends to perform, but must include any assurance justifiably demanded under the provisions of this Article (Section 2-609).

(3) Retraction reinstates the repudiating party's rights under the contract with due excuse and allowance to the aggrieved party for any delay occasioned by the repudiation.

SECTION THREE: BREACH OF DELIVERY CONTRACTS UNDER ARTICLE 2

Many delivery-of-goods contracts apportion the risk of loss during transport. Or stated differently, shipment contracts state whether the seller, carrier, or buyer will bear some or all of the loss, if goods are destroyed or lost while being transported from the seller to the buyer. In fact, the Uniform Commercial Code clearly provides that parties have discretion to allocate the risk of loss in an express agreement. UCC § 2.509(4). Also, the UCC invites lawyers who draft contracts for the sale of goods to include clauses that specifically allocate the risk of loss between buyers and sellers. *See* JAMES J. WHITE & ROBERT S. SUMMERS, UNIFORM COMMERCIAL CODE § 5-1, at 332 (5th ed. 2006).

In addition, several sections of the UCC instruct sellers and buyers how to allocate risks of losses if and when the parties fail to craft delivery-of-goods contracts. *See* UCC §§ 2-319, 2-503, 2-504, 2-509, 2-510. Generally, under the UCC, a seller must bear the risk of loss when the parties have specified "F.O.B. the place of shipment" and the goods have been shipped. Section 2-319(1)(a) requires a seller to ship goods to a buyer as prescribed in section 2-504 and bear the expense and risk of putting them into the possession of the carrier.

The UCC also states that a seller will bear the risk of a loss, when the contracting parties specify "F.O.B. the place of destination." More specifically, section 2-319(1)(b) requires a seller to transport goods to a certain place and ensure their safe delivery in a manner provided in section 2-503. *See also*, JAMES J. WHITE & ROBERT S. SUMMERS, UNIFORM COMMERCIAL CODE § 5-2, at 339 (5th ed. 2006) ("[W]hen the contract reads 'F.O.B. buyer's place of business,' both [§§ 2-319(1)(b) and 2-509(1)(b)] make it clear that the risk does not pass to the buyer until the goods are tendered to the buyer at the place of destination.").

Arguably, these and other UCC shipment-of-goods provisions are not difficult to understand. Yet, since the UCC's enactment, various words and phrases in sections 2-319, 2-503, 2-504, 2-509, and 2-510 have generated conflicts between sellers and buyers. Specifically, those statutory provisions continue to spurn disputes over whether a seller or a buyer is comparatively or entirely liable for: (1) a partially or totally destroyed shipment of goods, or (2) a breach of a shipment-of-goods contract. The cases in this part illustrate how some courts have addressed and resolved these shipment-of-goods disputes.

A. Breach of Destination and Shipment Contracts Under the UCC

Princesse D'Isenbourg et Cie Ltd. v. Kinder Caviar, Inc.
2011 WL 720194
(C.C.E.D. Ky.)

DANNY C. REEVES, DISTRICT JUDGE. This matter is pending for consideration of the Motion for Summary Judgment filed by Plaintiff Princesse D'Isenbourg Et Cie Ltd. (Isenbourg). …

I. BACKGROUND

The facts in this case are generally undisputed. Defendant Kinder Caviar, Inc. is a producer and exporter of caviar located in Owenton, Kentucky. Isenbourg is a purveyor of fine wines and gourmet foods located in London, England. In the Fall of 2008, Isenbourg and Kinder negotiated a transaction whereby Isenbourg would purchase a large amount of caviar to be imported into the United Kingdom (Caviar Purchase Agreement). On October 20, 2008, the deal was memorialized by a one-page invoice (Invoice).

The Invoice contained the essential terms of the transaction. Isenbourg was to purchase 550.80 pounds of paddlefish caviar at a price of $235 per pound. The total sale amount was $129,438. The "Terms" provided were: "wire transfer upon receipt of invoice." Importantly for the case at hand, the Invoice stated that the caviar would be shipped to Isenbourg's place of business and provided the address: "2 Bard Road, London, W10 6TP." Upon receipt of the Invoice, Isenbourg paid Kinder the full purchase price via wire transfer.

Kinder received the payment on November 3, 2008 and began preparations to ship the caviar to the United Kingdom. The exportation of paddlefish caviar is subject to the CONVENTION ON INTERNATIONAL TRADE IN ENDANGERED SPECIES OF WILD FAUNA AND FLORA (CITES). Under CITES, caviar may be traded internationally, but it must meet certain requirements and certifications. To meet one of these requirements, Kinder had to apply for an export permit from the United States Fish and Wildlife Service. CITES also requires import permits and specific labels from the importing country. Kinder asserts that, while it was obtaining the required export permits, Isenbourg acquired the necessary CITES import documents from the UK.

In addition to CITES requirements, food products imported into the UK are also subject to European Union food health and safety regulations. *See* COMMISSION REGULATION 853/2004, art. 5, 2004 O. J. (L139) 55(EC). One of the EU regulations requires a shipment to be accompanied by a document known as an "EU HEALTH CERTIFICATE" which is issued by the United States government. In this case, the certificate was issued by the United States Food and Drug Administration (FDA). For the shipment in question, the FDA issued a two-page health certificate on two separate pieces of paper.

During the period prior to shipment, Tony Leung of Isenbourg and Joyce Kinder of Kinder Caviar communicated concerning the shipment requirements. On October 27, 2008, Leung sent Joyce Kinder an e-mail concerning shipping procedures. The e-mail contained a "check-list" which outlined a number of requirements and documents needed for successful importation. Joyce Kinder asserts that she used this e-mail—along with information from her two prior experiences shipping caviar to foreign countries—to prepare the shipment. In February 2009, Kinder shipped the caviar from Louisville, Kentucky, bound for Heathrow Airport in London, England.

When the shipment arrived in the United Kingdom, it was stopped by customs officials at its point of entry in London. On February 20, 2009, the officials from the United Kingdom Environment and Consumer Protection Port Health Division in the London Borough of Hillingdon (Hillingdon) sent a letter to Isenbourg's import agent, DHL Global Forwarding. In the letter, Hillingdon explained that the shipment was refused entry for two reasons: (1) the identification mark on the boxes did not "indicate the approval number of the establishment of origin, as required by Article 5 (and detailed in Annex II, Section I) of Regulation (EC) No 853/2004[;]" and (2) the health certificate was on two sheets of paper, rather than on a single sheet as required. The letter provided information on appealing the decision and further ordered that the caviar be shipped out of the EU within 60 days or it would be destroyed.

Isenbourg notified Kinder of the customs problem. It recommended that the caviar be shipped back to Kinder to be re-labeled in a compliant manner. But Kinder attempted to avoid the time and expense accompanying re-importation. Kinder enlisted the assistance of a number of officials and experts. Kinder was eventually able to cure the health certificate issue, but not the labeling issue. Kinder prepared new labels and sent them to Hillingdon, but they were not accepted. Until this point, the caviar had remained in the possession of United Kingdom customs agents.

On April 4, 2009, Isenbourg directed DHL to return the caviar back to Kinder. Kinder arranged to receive the shipment; the caviar arrived back in the United States; and Kinder took possession. Kinder claims that certain original documents were not returned with the caviar. So, Kinder was unable to apply for re-export permits for a number of weeks. Kinder also asserts that the caviar was damaged when it was returned. According to Kinder, the condition of the boxes and packing materials inside each box and cooler suggested that the shipment had thawed and then had been re-frozen. Kinder informed Isenbourg of the damage to caviar. Isenbourg had obtained insurance coverage on the shipment. So, Kinder filed an insurance claim with the cargo carrier—United Airlines. Because United has not paid that claim, Kinder has joined them as a third-party defendant in this suit.

Kinder maintains possession of the caviar. Kinder considers the caviar to "belong" to Isenbourg, but Isenbourg has informed Kinder that it no longer wishes to receive the caviar. Isenbourg claims that it was forced to purchase replacement caviar from other vendors to meet its contractual obligations. The cost of the replacement caviar was significantly higher than the original purchase price (220,025 Euros).

The final conflict between the parties concerns an alleged agreement for Kinder to purchase caviar tins from Isenbourg (Caviar Tin Agreement). According to Isenbourg, Kinder agreed to purchase 1,300 empty caviar tins from it for the purchase price of 1,476 Euros. Isenbourg has produced an invoice which it claims memorialized this agreement, but Kinder denies ever having seen the invoice. Kinder asserts that the two parties agreed that Kinder would distribute the tins on Isenbourg's behalf, rather than purchase the tins outright. On February 13, 2009, Isenbourg informed Kinder that it had shipped the caviar tins to the United States. Kinder is in possession of the caviar tins, but has not returned any payment to Isenbourg.

II. ANALYSIS

Choice of Law

The interpretation and construction of a contract is a matter of law. *Detroit Radiant Prods. Co. v. BSH Home Appliances Corp.*, 473 F.3d 623, 627 (6th Cir. 2007). Because the events in this case transpired between the United Kingdom and the United States, the threshold question is what law governs the alleged contract. As a federal court sitting in diversity, this court applies the choice of law rules of the state in which it sits. *Klaxon Co. v. Stentor Elec. Mfg. Co.*, 313 U.S. 487 (1941). ... The parties agree that Kentucky has the most significant relationship with the transaction in question and that Kentucky law should apply. ... Kentucky has adopted Article 2 of the UNIFORM COMMERCIAL CODE (UCC) to govern contracts for the sale of goods. KY. REV. STAT. ANN. (KRS) § 355.2.

However, despite indicating that Kentucky contract law applies, Isenbourg argues that the UCC should not apply. [Record No. 59, p. 2 n. 1 ("Plaintiff and Defendant are citizens of different countries. The UCC has no applicability with regard to foreign citizens.") The court finds that this contention is without merit.[a] The UCC has been adopted in Kentucky with respect to the sale of goods such as those in issue in this case. Therefore, since the choice of law rules dictate that Kentucky law should apply, the UCC governs the contract at issue.[b]

Breach of Caviar Purchase Contract

The contract in this case is very simple. It includes a price term, a quantity term, short instructions on payment and timing, and the following language: "SHIP TO: PRINCESSE D'ISENBOURG ET CIE LIMITED, 2 BARD ROAD, LONDON, W10 6TP." Thus, the ultimate question before the Court is which party bore the responsibility for delivery of the caviar and ensuring that the shipment met UK Customs and CITES requirements? The answer is the seller: Kinder Caviar.

The UCC describes the general obligations of the parties in § 2-301: "The obligation of the seller is to transfer and deliver and that of the buyer is to accept and pay in accordance with the contract." KRS § 355.2-301. Thus, absent a contrary provision, delivery is the seller's responsibility. The Invoice contained no provisions concerning the matter, so delivery is Kinder's responsibility. Therefore, the question this court must answer is whether Kinder satisfied its obligation to deliver.

The UCC defines delivery obligations in two types of contracts: shipment contracts and destination contracts. *See Permalum Window & Awning Mfg. Co. v. Permalum Window Mfg. Corp.*, 412 S.W.2d 863, 867 (Ky. App. 1967). Under destination contracts, delivery is complete when the goods reach a particular, identified destination such as the

---

a The court recognizes that contracts for the sale of goods between citizens of different countries are, in some cases, governed by the Convention for the International Sale of Goods (CISG) rather than the UCC. Typically, when a contract is signed between two international parties and one of the parties is a resident of a country that is a signatory to the CISG (Contracting State), the contract is governed by the CISG. *See* CISG art. 1(1)(b). However, when it ratified the CISG, the United States declared a reservation that its courts would not be bound by Article 1(1)(b). Ralph H. Folsom, 1 INTERNATIONAL BUSINESS TRANSACTIONS § 1.4 (3d ed.). In United States courts, the CISG is not applicable "when a contract is between parties having places of business in different states and only one state is a Contracting State." *Id.* While the United States is a Contracting State, the United Kingdom is not. *See id.* "Thus, a contract of sale between a United States party and another party in a non-Contracting State [such as the United Kingdom], will not be governed by CISG, even though United States law is applicable under usual choice-of-law rules." *Id.* "Instead of CISG, United States law for domestic sales transactions would govern, which means the Uniform Commercial Code (UCC) is applicable in forty-nine states." *Id.*

b Because one of the purposes of the UCC is "to make uniform the law among the various jurisdictions," non-Kentucky cases that interpret parallel UCC provisions are also persuasive. *Star Bank v. Parnell*, 992 S.W.2d 189, 192 (Ky. Ct. App. 1998).

buyer's place of business. Shipment contracts, however, only require the seller to "put the goods in the possession of such a carrier and make such a contract for their transportation as may be reasonable having regard to the nature of the goods and other circumstance of the case." KRS § 355.2-504(a). Whether the contract is a shipment or destination contract can be important in determining both the seller's delivery obligation, and when the risk of loss passes from seller to buyer. *See* KRS § 355.2-509.

The only provision in the Invoice concerning delivery is the following language: "SHIP TO: PRINCESSE D'ISENBOURG ET CIE LIMITED, 2 BARD ROAD, LONDON, W10 6TP." Kinder argues that the contract language is ambiguous concerning delivery responsibility and, therefore, summary judgment is inappropriate. Isenbourg, on the other hand, contends that "the Caviar Agreement Invoice—drafted by Kinder, including this particular provision—clearly indicates that the caviar was to be shipped to Isenbourg at its place of business." In other words, Isenbourg argues that the invoice was a destination contract.[c]

In reality, however, the court need not decide whether the Invoice was a shipment or destination contract because Kinder breached its obligation under either designation. If, as Isenbourg argues, the Caviar Agreement was a destination contract, Kinder would have had the duty to ensure that the goods reached the particular location of delivery—Isenbourg's place of business—in a manner that enabled the buyer to take possession. KRS § 355.2-503(1), (3). There is no dispute that the goods never reached Isenbourg's place of business. The caviar never physically reached "2 BARD ROAD, LONDON, W10 6TP" nor did it even reach the United Kingdom in a manner that would have allowed Isenbourg to accept it. A United Kingdom corporation cannot take possession of an import that does not pass customs.

Conversely, if the court interpreted the Caviar Agreement as a shipment contract, Kinder still failed to meet its obligation. Section 2-504 of the UCC defines the seller's obligation in shipping contracts. Unless otherwise agreed, the seller must

> (a) put the goods in the possession of such a carrier and make such a contract for their transportation as may be reasonable having regard to the nature of the goods and other circumstances of the case; and
>
> (b) obtain and promptly deliver or tender in due form any document necessary to enable the buyer to obtain possession

c Contrary to Isenbourg's assertion, other courts have explained that ship-to addresses "have no significance in determining whether a contract is a shipment or destination contract." *Electric Regulator Corp. v. Sterling Extruder Corp.*, 280 F. Supp. 550, 557–58 (D. Conn. 1968).

> of the goods or otherwise required by the agreement or by usage of trade; and
>
> (c) promptly notify the buyer of the shipment. KRS § 355.2-504 .

Comment 3 to this section explains:

> In the absence of agreement, the provision of this Article on options and co-operation respecting performance gives the seller the choice of any reasonable carrier, routing and other arrangements. Whether or not the shipment is at the buyer's expense the seller must see to any arrangements, reasonable in the circumstances, such as refrigeration, watering of livestock, protection against cold, the sending along of any necessary help, selection of specialized cars and the like for paragraph (a) is intended to cover all necessary arrangements whether made by contract with the carrier or otherwise.

Under this section, the seller bears responsibility for shipping arrangements. While the actual shipment is done by carrier, the seller must provide all necessary documents and provide for other needs such as refrigeration or sending along additional assistance. Essentially, when the seller provides the goods to the carrier, it must be properly arranged so as to be able to reach their final destination.

When Kinder provided the caviar to the carrier, it was not in a condition that would allow it to reach Isenbourg. The customs paperwork was not in proper order. Customs paperwork falls within "any document necessary to enable the buyer to obtain possession." Had the proper documents been included and the proper labels attached, the goods would have reached Isenbourg. As previously stated, the seller bears the responsibility to provide the necessary documents and make the proper arrangements for the shipment to reach its destination. *See* KRS § 355.2-504. And Kinder did not do so in this case. Consequently, even if the Caviar Purchase Agreement is construed as a shipment contract, Kinder breached the agreement by not making adequate arrangements for the carrier to successfully deliver the goods. Therefore, any dispute whether the Caviar Agreement was a shipment or destination contract is immaterial, because in either instance Kinder failed to meet its delivery obligation.

This holding is also supported by simple logic. At all times prior to shipping, Kinder maintained possession of the caviar. Kinder made all the arrangements for shipping and contracted with the common carrier. Kinder presumably labeled the packages and provided all the import and customs documents to the carrier. It would not be logical to place the burden of those arrangements—or ensuring the proper completion of those arrangements—on the trans-Atlantic buyer who never touched the shipment. In summary, Kinder failed to meet its delivery obligation under the contract. Kinder breached an essential term of the contract and, therefore, is liable to Isenbourg for the resulting damages.

When a seller fails to deliver under a contract for the sale of goods, UCC § 2-713 provides the measure of damages: the difference between the market price at the time when the buyer learned of the breach and the contract price, plus any incidental and consequential damages, but less the expenses saved in consequence of the breach. KRS § 355.2-713. Additionally, when the buyer has already paid for the goods, the buyer may also recover "so much of the price as has been paid." KRS § 355.2-711(1). Isenbourg has established the price paid, $129,438.00, but has not provided proof of the market price at the time of breach, see KRS § 355.2-723, or other incidental or consequential damages. Therefore, the court will grant summary judgment to Isenbourg on Count 1 of the Complaint—breach of the Caviar Purchase Agreement—but it cannot award damages based on the current state of the record.

Caviar Tin Agreement

The next concerns whether Kinder also breached the Caviar Tin Agreement. Isenbourg claims that the companies made an agreement, that Isenbourg shipped the tins to Kinder, and that Kinder has not paid pursuant to the parties' agreement. Isenbourg produced an invoice it claims memorialized this agreement. However, Kinder claims that the two companies reached an entirely different agreement regarding the tins and that it never received the invoice Isenbourg produced. In essence, the parties dispute both the terms of the agreement and whether the contract, as memorialized by the invoice, ever existed. Thus, there are disputes regarding issues of both formation and interpretation.

Contract formation is a question of fact. *See McMurty v. Botts*, 2006 U.S. Dist. LEXIS 54402, at *12 (W.D. Ky.) (distinguishing scope of employment from formation of a contract, the latter of which would be a question of fact); *Ankle & Foot Care Ctrs. v. Infocure Sys.*, 164 F.Supp.2d 953, 958 (N.D. Ohio 2001) ("Whether or not a contract exists is a question of fact."). In this case, the parties present different versions of the facts supporting formation.

An oral contract can be memorialized by sending a confirmatory memo. See KRS § 355.2-201. Consequently, Isenbourg points to the Caviar Tin Invoice as confirmation of what the oral agreement contained. However, a confirmatory memo will only bind the parties if it "is received and the party receiving it has reason to know of its contents." Kinder has established a genuine issue of material fact regarding whether the Caviar Tin Agreement was ever received. As a result, the court cannot accept its contents as evidence of an oral agreement. Isenbourg has failed to show that there is "no genuine dispute" as to the existence of a contract for sale of caviar tins. Fed.R.Civ.P. 56. Therefore, the Court will deny summary judgment on Count 2. ...

III. CONCLUSION

With respect to the Caviar Purchase Agreement, Kinder failed to meet its delivery obligations. Kinder breached the Caviar Purchase Agreement by failing to deliver or ship the goods in a proper manner. While the court will grant summary judgment on Count 1 of Isenbourg's Complaint and hold Kinder liable under the Caviar Purchase Agreement, Isenbourg still must prove the amount of damages resulting from the breach. Additionally, factual disputes exist concerning the formation and substance of the Caviar Tin Agreement. Therefore, summary judgment will be denied as to Count 2. Finally, summary judgment will be denied regarding Count 3, unjust enrichment.

Accordingly, it is hereby ordered that Plaintiff Princesse D'Isenbourg et Cie Ltd.'s Motion for Summary Judgment is granted as to Kinder's liability on Count 1 of the Complaint, but denied regarding damages under this count. The motion for summary judgment is denied as to Counts 2 and 3.

UNIFORM COMMERCIAL CODE

§ 2-319. F.O.B. AND F.A.S. TERMS

(1) Unless otherwise agreed the term F.O.B. (which means "free on board") at a named place, even though used only in connection with the stated price, is a delivery term under which

(a) when the term is F.O.B. the place of shipment, the seller must at that place ship the goods in the manner provided in this Article (Section 2-504) and bear the expense and risk of putting them into the possession of the carrier; or

(b) when the term is F.O.B. the place of destination, the seller must at his own expense and risk transport the goods to that place and there tender delivery of them in the manner provided in this Article (Section 2-503);

(c) when under either (a) or (b) the term is also F.O.B. vessel, car or other vehicle, the seller must in addition at his own expense and risk load the goods on board. If the term is F.O.B. vessel the buyer must name the vessel and in an appropriate case the seller must comply with the provisions of this Article on the form of bill of lading (Section 2-323).

(2) Unless otherwise agreed the term F.A.S. vessel (which means "free alongside") at a named port, even though used only in connection with the stated price, is a delivery term under which the seller must

(a) at his own expense and risk deliver the goods alongside the vessel in the manner usual in that port or on a dock designated and provided by the buyer; and

(b) obtain and tender a receipt for the goods in exchange for which the carrier is under a duty to issue a bill of lading.

(3) Unless otherwise agreed in any case falling within subsection (1)(a) or (c) or subsection (2) the buyer must seasonably give any needed instructions for making delivery, including when the term is F.A.S. or F.O.B. the loading berth of the vessel and in an appropriate case its name and sailing date. The seller may treat the failure of needed instructions as a failure of cooperation under this Article (Section 2-311). He may also at his option move the goods in any reasonable manner preparatory to delivery or shipment.

(4) Under the term F.O.B. vessel or F.A.S. unless otherwise agreed the buyer must make payment against tender of the required documents and the seller may not tender nor the buyer demand delivery of the goods in substitution for the documents.

§ 2-503. MANNER OF SELLER'S TENDER OF DELIVERY

(1) Tender of delivery requires that the seller put and hold conforming goods at the buyer's disposition and give the buyer any notification reasonably necessary to enable him to take delivery. The manner, time and place for tender are determined by the agreement and this Article, and in particular

(a) tender must be at a reasonable hour, and if it is of goods they must be kept available for the period reasonably necessary to enable the buyer to take possession; but

(b) unless otherwise agreed the buyer must furnish facilities reasonably suited to the receipt of the goods.

(2) Where the case is within the next section respecting shipment tender requires that the seller comply with its provisions.

(3) Where the seller is required to deliver at a particular destination tender requires that he comply with subsection

(1) and also in any appropriate case tender documents as described in subsections (4) and (5) of this section.

(4) Where goods are in the possession of a bailee and are to be delivered without being moved

(a) tender requires that the seller either tender a negotiable document of title covering such goods or procure acknowledgment by the bailee of the buyer's right to possession of the goods; but

(b) tender to the buyer of a non-negotiable document of title or of a record directing the bailee to deliver is sufficient tender unless the buyer seasonably objects, and except as otherwise provided in Article 9 receipt by the bailee of notification of the buyer's rights fixes those rights as against the bailee and all third persons; but risk of loss of the goods and of any failure by the bailee to honor the non-negotiable document of title or to obey the direction remains on the seller until the buyer has had a reasonable time to present the document or direction, and a refusal by the bailee to honor the document or to obey the direction defeats the tender.

(5) Where the contract requires the seller to deliver documents

(a) he must tender all such documents in correct form, except as provided in this Article with respect to bills of lading in a set (subsection 2-323); and

(b) tender through customary banking channels is sufficient and dishonor of a draft accompanying or associated with the documents constitutes non-acceptance or rejection.

§ 2-504. SHIPMENT BY SELLER

Where the seller is required or authorized to send the goods to the buyer and the contract does not require him to deliver them at a particular destination, then unless otherwise agreed he must

(a) put the goods in the possession of such a carrier and make such a contract for their transportation as may be reasonable having regard to the nature of the goods and other circumstances of the case; and

(b) obtain and promptly deliver or tender in due form any document necessary to enable the buyer to obtain possession of the goods or otherwise required by the agreement or by usage of trade; and

(c) promptly notify the buyer of the shipment.

Failure to notify the buyer under paragraph (c) or to make a proper contract under paragraph (a) is a ground for rejection only if material delay or loss ensues.

§ 2-509. RISK OF LOSS IN THE ABSENCE OF BREACH

(1) Where the contract requires or authorizes the seller to ship the goods by carrier

(a) if it does not require him to deliver them at a particular destination, the risk of loss passes to the buyer when the goods are duly delivered to the carrier even though the shipment is under reservation (Section 2-505); but

(b) if it does require him to deliver them at a particular destination and the goods are there duly tendered while in the possession of the carrier, the risk of loss passes to the buyer when the goods are there duly so tendered as to enable the buyer to take delivery.

(2) Where the goods are held by a bailee to be delivered without being moved, the risk of loss passes to the buyer

(a) on his receipt of possession or control of a negotiable document of title covering the goods; or

(b) on acknowledgment by the bailee of the buyer's right to possession of the goods; or

(c) after his receipt of possession or control of a non-negotiable document of title or other direction to deliver in a record, as provided in subsection (4)(b) of Section 2-503.

(3) In any case not within subsection (1) or (2), the risk of loss passes to the buyer on his receipt of the goods if the seller is a merchant; otherwise the risk passes to the buyer on tender of delivery.

(4) The provisions of this section are subject to contrary agreement of the parties and to the provisions of this Article on sale on approval (Section 2-327) and on effect of breach on risk of loss (Section 2-510).

B. Breach of C.I.F. Shipment Contracts Under the UCC and Payment of Insurance Proceeds

William D. Branson, Ltd. v. Tropical Shipping & Const. Co., Ltd.
598 F. Supp. 680
(C.C.D.C. Fla. 1984)

GONZALEZ, DISTRICT JUDGE. This cause has come before the court upon the defendant's motion for summary judgment. ... The starting point for the court's analysis is section 672.2-320, Florida Statutes. FLA. STAT. ANN. § 672.2-320 (West 1966). Section 672.2-320 provides in pertinent part:

> (1) The term C.I.F. means that the price includes in a lump sum the cost of the goods and the insurance and freight to the named destination. ...
>
> (2) Unless otherwise agreed and even though used only in connection with the stated price and destination, the term C.I.F. destination or its equivalent requires the seller at his own expense and risk to:
>
> (a) Put the goods into the possession of a carrier at the port for shipment and obtain a negotiable bill or bills of lading covering the entire transportation to the named destination; and
>
> (b) Load the goods and obtain a receipt from the carrier (which may be contained in the bill of lading) showing that the freight has been paid or provided for; and
>
> (c) Obtain a policy or certificate of insurance, including any war risk insurance, of a kind and on terms then current at the port of shipment in the usual amount, in the currency of the contract, shown to cover the same goods covered by the bill of lading and providing for payment of loss to the order of the buyer or for the account of whom it may concern; but the seller may add to the price the amount of the premium for any such war risk insurance; and
>
> (d) Prepare an invoice of goods and procure any other documents required to effect shipment or to comply with the contract; and
>
> (e) Forward and tender with commercial promptness all the documents in due form and with any indorsement necessary to perfect the buyer's rights.
>
> ...

> (4) Under the term C.I.F. ... unless otherwise agreed the buyer must make payment against the tender of the required documents and the seller may not tender nor the buyer demand delivery of the goods in substitution for the documents.

The contract in question provided for the shipment of tomatoes *C.I.F. Bridgetown, Barbados*. Upon arrival in Bridgetown, the buyer inspected the tomatoes and found them to be spoiled. Finding the shipment unsatisfactory, the buyer shipped the tomatoes back to the seller-shipper, William D. Branson, Ltd. (Branson, Ltd.). The question now is whether Branson, Ltd. has an action for the price of the tomatoes against the common carrier—Tropical Shipping & Construction Co. (Tropical).

Tropical maintains that Branson, Ltd. is not a proper plaintiff in this action. As Tropical construes section 672.2-320, the buyer in Bridgetown is the party who must sue for the price of the tomatoes. All other facts being undisputed, Tropical would be correct—for title and risk of loss under a C.I.F. shipment contract passes to the buyer upon shipment if the seller has properly performed all his obligations with respect to the goods. *See Sig M. Glukstad, Inc. v. Lineas Aereas Paraguayas*, 619 F.2d 457, 459 (5th Cir. 1980); FLA. STAT. ANN. § 672.2-320 comments 1, 16 (West 1966).

The buyer would be the proper plaintiff if he had indeed accepted the goods. However, two facts militate against this conclusion. First, a representative of plaintiff—Mr. Charles William Branson—testified in his deposition that the buyer did not pay for the tomatoes. Second, the tomatoes themselves were not only condemned by the Ministry of Health of Barbados, but were deemed unsalvageable by the United States Department of Agriculture (USDA) and dumped.

Generally, the buyer must make payment against tender of the required documents in order to entitle and enable him to receive the goods. FLA. STAT. ANN. § 672.2-320 comment 1 (West 1966). The contract may provide that the buyer has no right to inspect the goods prior to payment or acceptance of the documents. FLA. STAT. ANN. §§ 672.2-320 comment 1, 672.2-512 (West 1966). In this case, however, the contract, pleadings, interrogatories and depositions indicate that payment was to await arrival of the tomatoes. In this latter situation, inspection before payment is proper since the goods are then "available for inspection." FLA. STAT. ANN. § 672.2-513 comment 5 (West 1966).

The significance of the foregoing is that under the facts as construed in the plaintiff's favor, it appears that the buyer never accepted the shipment of tomatoes from the seller because he found them to be substantially nonconforming. The buyer's shipment of the tomatoes back to the seller is further evidence of the buyer's non-acceptance; and the seller's decision to call in the USDA and dump the tomatoes is consistent with the seller's continued dominion and control over the goods. Even section 672.2-320 recognizes the soundness of this conclusion: "The buyer must pay before inspection and assert his remedy against the seller afterward unless the nonconformity of the goods amounts to a real failure of consideration. ..." FLA. STAT. ANN. § 672.2-320 comment 12 (West 1966).

In summary, contrary to the defendant's protestations to the contrary, the buyer does not have an action against the common carrier for the price of the tomatoes. The more important question, however, is whether the seller—Branson, Ltd.—can maintain the instant action against Tropical?

The court finds that Branson, Ltd. is not a proper plaintiff in this action. Plaintiff's representative Charles William Branson testified in his deposition that Branson, Ltd.'s insurance company paid the seller in full for the total cost of the tomatoes. The insurance payment included Branson, Ltd.'s "cost factor" and "profit" for the sale to the buyer. The seller's collection of the insurance proceeds was proper because it had never relinquished title to the tomatoes. Although the insurance stipulated by the C.I.F. term is for the buyer's benefit, the facts of this case suggest that the buyer neither accepted nor enjoyed the benefits of the bargain. Because plaintiff has been made whole by its insurance company, it is abundantly clear that Branson, Ltd. no longer has an action for damages against the common carrier, Tropical.

The gravamen of plaintiff's complaint was that [Tropical's] vessel arrived at the port of destination where it and the Defendant made delivery of the said shipment ... [which was] seriously injured and impaired in value. ... Without deciding the merits, it appears that if any person has an action against Tropical, it is Branson's insurance company, which conceivably has a subrogation claim against the common carrier.

Simply because Tropical is not being sued by the real party in interest is not sufficient reason to dismiss this case outright. Rule 17(a), FED.R.CIV.P. provides that "[n]o action may be dismissed on the ground that it is not prosecuted in the name of the real party in interest until a reasonable time has been allowed after objection for ratification of commencement of the action by, or joinder or substitution of, the real party in interest. ..." Thus, although the court grants defendant's motion for summary judgment, plaintiff shall have twenty days from entry of this order to join or substitute the real party in interest.

UNIFORM COMMERCIAL CODE

§ 2-320. C.I.F. AND C. & F. TERMS

(1) The term C.I.F. means that the price includes in a lump sum the cost of the goods and the insurance and freight to the named destination. The term C.& F. or C.F. means that the price so includes cost and freight to the named destination.

(2) Unless otherwise agreed and even though used only in connection with the stated price and destination, the term C.I.F. destination or its equivalent requires the seller at his own expense and risk to

(a) put the goods into the possession of a carrier at the port for shipment and obtain a negotiable bill or bills of lading covering the entire transportation to the named destination; and

(b) load the goods and obtain a receipt from the carrier (which may be contained in the bill of lading) showing that the freight has been paid or provided for; and

(c) obtain a policy or certificate of insurance, including any war risk insurance, of a kind and on terms then current at the port of shipment in the usual amount, in the currency of the contract, shown to cover the same goods covered by the bill of lading and providing for payment of loss to the order of the buyer or for the account of whom it may concern; but the seller may add to the price the amount of the premium for any such war risk insurance; and

(d) prepare an invoice of the goods and procure any other documents required to effect shipment or to comply with the contract; and

(e) forward and tender with commercial promptness all the documents in due form and with any indorsement necessary to perfect the buyer's rights.

(3) Unless otherwise agreed the term C. & F. or its equivalent has the same effect and imposes upon the seller the same obligations and risks as a C.I.F. term except the obligation as to insurance.

(4) Under the term C.I.F. or C. & F. unless otherwise agreed the buyer must make payment against tender of the required documents and the seller may not tender nor the buyer demand delivery of the goods in substitution for the documents.

§ 2-505. SELLER'S SHIPMENT UNDER RESERVATION

(1) Where the seller has identified goods to the contract by or before shipment:

(a) his procurement of a negotiable bill of lading to his own order or otherwise reserves in him a security interest in the goods. His procurement of the bill to the order of a financing agency or of the buyer indicates in addition only the seller's expectation of transferring that interest to the person named.

(b) a non-negotiable bill of lading to himself or his nominee reserves possession of the goods as security but except in a case of conditional delivery (subsection 2-507) a non-negotiable bill of lading naming the buyer as consignee reserves no security interest even though the seller retains possession or control of the bill of lading.

(2) When shipment by the seller with reservation of a security interest is in violation of the contract for sale it constitutes an improper contract for transportation within the preceding section but impairs neither the rights given to the buyer by shipment and identification of the goods to the contract nor the seller's powers as a holder of a negotiable document of title.

SECTION FOUR: BREACH OF SALES CONTRACT AND THE DOCTRINES OF NOVATION AND ASSIGNMENT UNDER THE UCC

A. Novation and Delegation of Performance Under § 2-210(1)

Novelis Corporation v. Anheuser-Busch, Inc.
559 F.Supp.2d 877
(C.C.N.D. Ohio 2008)

SARA LIOI, DISTRICT JUDGE. This matter comes before the court upon the motion of Defendant Anheuser-Busch, Inc. (A-B) for summary judgment. ...

I. FACTUAL AND PROCEDURAL HISTORY

This is a contract dispute. The agreement at issue began in 1987, and set forth the terms by which Plaintiff Novelis Corp. (Novelis) sold aluminum can sheet to A-B. In June of 2004, the parties amended their prior agreement, and the terms of the amended agreement (Agreement) govern the dispute in this case. The Agreement governs the parties' relationship from 2005 through 2009—which included the sale of approximately 587 million pounds of aluminum in 2005, 635 million pounds in 2006, and 659 million pounds in 2007.

The Agreement provides for a variable price for aluminum can sheet based on a "metal" and a "conversion" component. The metal component of the formula is subject to a price ceiling, such that it is variable only up to the ceiling rate. The parties thus allocated the risk of aluminum prices rising to A-B, so long as prices remained under 85 cents per pound. If such prices did rise above the price ceiling, the burden of the risk shifted to Novelis.

The Agreement also contains a provision (b.10 provision), which provides as follows:

> If during the Term of this Agreement, either party believes that market conditions have changed structurally up or down, in such a manner which causes the current pricing mechanisms to no longer be appropriate, A-B and [Novelis] will meet to discuss a new pricing mechanism with the continued intent to provide competitive pricing to A-B, including without limitation, providing A-B the Contract Discount set forth above. It is the intent of the parties, however, that if the parties, in each party's sole discretion, are unable to reach a mutually acceptable modification to this Agreement, this Agreement as amended shall remain in full force and effect until the expiration or earlier termination hereof.

Novelis invoked the b.10 provision in early 2006 by notifying A-B that Novelis believed a structural change in the market had resulted in a dramatic increase in aluminum prices, thereby rendering a need for modification to the Agreement's pricing mechanism. Novelis alleged that a combination of the rise in energy prices, speculation by hedge funds and other investors, and dramatically increased demand for aluminum from China and other developing countries prompted an unforeseen structural change in the market. Representatives from both parties met in person on January 13, February 22, April 13, May 8, May 10, June 16, June 19, and July 3, 2006. They also held teleconferences on December 15 and 22, 2005, a date in early January 2006, April 18 or 19, May 3, June 1, June 13, and June 20, 2006.

Despite this multitude of meetings and discussions, the parties did not reach an agreement. Novelis at one point proposed that it begin supplying A-B solely with used beverage cans (UBC), which would significantly reduce Novelis's losses, but also cause A-B to lose approximately $78 million annually. A-B studied the proposal and advised Novelis during subsequent meetings that A-B was reluctant to adopt it. A-B representatives, in turn, raised the possibility of increasing the price ceiling to help Novelis receive a higher price while also extending the ceiling's temporal duration to provide A-B with the accordant price stability over a longer period. Novelis rejected this offer and indicated that they "were not interested in a ceiling of any sort." A-B also indicated to Novelis during the meetings that its negotiations were complicated by the fact that it sold aluminum to Pepsi, a fact of which Novelis was aware when the Agreement was drafted.

Novelis then brought this suit, claiming in part that A-B breached its contractual duty pursuant to the b.10 provision to "meet to discuss a new pricing mechanism with the continued intent to provide competitive pricing to A-B" in good faith. The Amended Complaint claimed breaches of multiple different provisions as set forth below, as well as mutual mistake, commercial impracticability, and unjust enrichment. The court granted A-B's motion to dismiss the mutual mistake, commercial impracticability and unjust enrichment claims, and the parties proceeded through discovery. A-B has now filed a motion for summary judgment on the remaining claims, which is ripe for the court's determination.

II. LAW & ANALYSIS

B. Breach of b.10 Provision

In Count I, Novelis claims that A-B breached its obligation to meet and discuss a new pricing mechanism in good faith pursuant to the b.10 provision. The Agreement provides that it shall be governed by New York law, which includes the regulation of sales of goods under the Uniform Commercial Code. Under New York law, the ultimate goal of contract interpretation is to construe agreements "in accord with the parties' intent." *Eternity Global Master Fund Ltd. v. Morgan Guaranty Trust Co.*, 375 F.3d 168, 177 (2nd Cir. 2004). To establish a claim for breach of contract, a plaintiff must establish "(1) the existence of an agreement, (2) adequate performance of the contract by the plaintiff, (3) breach of contract by the defendant, and (4) damages." *Id.*

Every contract governed by New York law includes an obligation of good faith in its performance. N.Y. U.C.C. § 1-203; *Readco, Inc. v. Marine Midland Bank*, 81 F.3d 295, 300 (2nd Cir. 1996). A breach of the covenant of good faith is considered to be a breach of the underlying contract. *See Wolff v. Rare Medium*, 210 F.Supp.2d 490, 497 (S.D.N.Y. 2002). A breach of the implied duty of good faith does not substitute for an unsustainable breach of contract action. The duty of good faith also "does not create obligations that go beyond those intended and stated in the language of the contract." *Gordon v. Nationwide Mut. Ins. Co.*, 285 N.E.2d 849, 854 (N.Y.1972) ("Bad faith requires an extraordinary showing of a disingenuous or dishonest failure to carry out a contract.") As such, for purposes of the Agreement, the implied duty of good faith is imposed upon the contractual requirement that the parties meet to discuss a new pricing mechanism with the continued intent to provide competitive pricing to A-B.

In order to interpret the b.10 provision and assess Novelis's claims of breach thereof, the Court first must establish the contours of the provision. The provision does not require an actual structural change in the market to activate the parties' duties. Instead, one party need only believe that the market has changed structurally. Here, there is no question that Novelis believed a structural change occurred, and that the duty was therefore triggered. *Eternity Global*, 375 F.3d at 177 (2nd Cir. 2004) (agreements "must be enforced according to the plain meaning of [their] terms."). As such, A-B was required to "meet to discuss a new pricing mechanism with the continued intent to provide competitive pricing to A-B" in good faith.

An obligation to meet to discuss is an even lighter burden than an obligation to negotiate. "Discuss" is defined as "to investigate or examine by argument; to sift the considerations for and against; to debate." OXFORD ENGLISH DICTIONARY (2d ed.1989). In contrast, to "negotiate" is "[t]o hold communication or conference (with another) for the purpose of arranging some matter by mutual agreement; to discuss a matter with a view to some compromise or settlement." Id. Thus, while "negotiate" includes a connotation of "compromise or settlement," which could imply a need to give concessions, "discuss" merely includes investigating or examining by argument.

In addition, the parties expressly agreed in the b.10 provision that "if the parties, in each party's sole discretion, are unable to reach a mutually acceptable modification to this Agreement, this Agreement as amended shall remain in full force and effect until the expiration or earlier termination hereof," so any argument that A-B was required to agree to a certain alteration to the Agreement directly contradicts the Agreement's terms. *See Greenfield v. Philles Records, Inc.*, 98 N.Y.2d 562, 569 (2002) ("[I]f the agreement on its face is reasonably susceptible of only one meaning, a court is not free to alter the contract to reflect its personal notions of fairness and equity").

Consequently, the only question for the court with regard to Count I is whether the evidence viewed in a light most favorable to Novelis would allow a reasonable jury to find that A-B breached its contractual duty under the b.10 provision to meet to discuss a new pricing mechanism in good faith. The court finds that it does not.

"In commercial transactions, the question is not what is fair but what comports with the contract. An obligation to bargain in good faith differs from an obligation to make concessions, as it differs from a fiduciary duty." *PSI Energy v. Exxon Coal USA*, 17 F.3d 969, 974 (7th Cir. 1994) (Easterbrook, J. discussing the U.C.C.'s implied duty of good faith). The undisputed evidence shows that A-B met face-to-face eight times with Novelis and held multiple teleconferences to discuss the pricing mechanism. A-B representatives traveled to meet Novelis, took detailed notes, and engaged in discussions regarding the intricacies of Novelis's problems with the current pricing structure, its objections to further price ceilings, A-B's proposal to raise and extend the price ceiling, possible remedies from Novelis's predecessor corporation, and Novelis's proposal to replace the Agreement's pricing mechanism by providing A-B 100% used beverage cans (UBC).

In addition, Novelis President Kevin Greenawalt admitted that A-B representatives were engaged and acted in good faith during a meeting he attended. Novelis representative Andrew King conceded that A-B dealt with Novelis in good faith at a meeting in which he participated. Indeed, one of Novelis's negotiators testified that "we were kind of having discussions, and, you know, [A-B representatives Cliff Segal and Bob Golden] and [Novelis representative Tom Walpole] and myself would go back and forth in the meetings, talk about various options and opportunities and, you know, we white boarded a few different things."

King also testified that A-B representative Bob Golden was at the board leading discussions regarding the specific figures involved in potential deals. Novelis would have this Court find that A-B's conduct over this period of more than six months was a huge charade, where it never intended to even consider any alteration to the contract whatsoever. Taking the evidence in a light most favorable to Novelis, the record does not support such a contention. ...

Novelis faults A-B for its failure to agree to a complete overhaul of the contract terms. The parties' intent, however, as illustrated by the Agreement's terms, provided that if "in each party's sole discretion," they were "unable to reach a mutually acceptable modification to [the] Agreement," then the Agreement was to remain "in full force and effect" until its expiration or termination. New York law provides that where an agreement specifically contemplates financial risk allocation and grants discretion to choose to accept or deny a proposal, it is appropriate for the court to determine that a party has not acted in bad faith as a matter of law. *Halpern Dev. Venture v. Bd. of Trustees*, 247 A.D.2d 584, 584–585 (N.Y.A.D. 2 Dept. 1998). ...

A-B's consideration and rejection of Novelis' offer to provide only UBC to A-B, an offer that would have subjected A-B to losses totaling hundreds of millions of dollars, does not demonstrate a lack of good faith. Novelis took a hard line stance that no price ceilings could be considered. A-B, in turn, expressed reluctance to depart completely from the price ceiling. This does not illustrate a lack of intent to provide competitive pricing to A-B or a lack of good faith on the part of A-B. ... Further, because the b.10 provision only required A-B to meet to discuss a new pricing mechanism, not to agree to a new pricing mechanism, the fact that A-B rejected the UBC proposal is not at all probative of the issue. …

D. Breach of Anti-Assignment Provision

In Count V of the First Amended Complaint, Novelis claims that A-B breached the Agreement by delegating to Pepsi its duty to meet and discuss under the b.10 provision. The relevant portion of the Agreement provides, "Neither A-B nor [Novelis] shall have any right, without the prior written approval of the other party which approval shall not be unreasonably withheld, to (i) assign or delegate, in whole or in part, any of its rights, duties or obligations hereunder."

In arguing that a delegation occurred, Novelis relies upon the contract between Pepsi and A-B and upon testimony that A-B representatives told Novelis representatives they could not change the Agreement without Pepsi's consent. Under New York law, a "delegation involves the appointment of another to perform one's duties." *Inter Impex S.A.E. v. Comtrade Corp.*, 2004 WL 2793213, at *3, (S.D.N.Y. Dec. 6, 2004) (quoting *Contemporary Mission, Inc. v. Famous Music Corp.*, 557 F.2d 918, 924 (2d Cir. 1977)). *See also* N.Y. U.C.C. 2-210(1) (to "delegate" is to perform one's duty under a contract through another).

Novelis does not offer any evidence that A-B appointed, or even asked, Pepsi to negotiate in its place. Pepsi executives did not attend the b.10 discussions with Novelis. The undisputed evidence shows that A-B offered a proposal that included concessions despite the fact that Pepsi had not offered its approval of any changes to A-B's contract with Novelis. The undisputed evidence also shows that Pepsi representatives never attempted to restrict A-B's discussions with Novelis. Consequently, Novelis's reliance upon evidence that A-B executives discussed the situation concerning Novelis with Pepsi has little or no probative value in discerning whether A-B delegated its duty to meet and discuss.

Novelis further claims that A-B's contract with Pepsi provides evidence that A-B improperly delegated its duties under the Agreement's b.10 provision. A-B's contract with Pepsi states that "as AB is actively considering a new purchase commitment to a Cansheet supplier, it will discuss with Pepsi the price mechanism, the volume, warranty and the other terms and conditions applicable to such commitment. … A-B may not enter into any commitment that does not satisfy the Acceptable Criteria [separately provided] without the prior approval of Pepsi, which shall not be unreasonably withheld." This provision's explicit terms limit its application to a "new purchase commitment" considered by A-B.

In the case at hand, Novelis has not produced evidence that a "new purchase commitment" ever was considered. Instead, what was contemplated was a modification of the existing agreement. The parties discussed altering the pricing mechanism or adopting a situation where Novelis provided all of the aluminum A-B required in the form of UBC. Neither would have constituted a "new purchase commitment" which would have triggered A-B's duty to receive Pepsi's approval. Further, at the time the parties entered into their agreement, Novelis was aware of A-B's relationship with Pepsi, and that relationship benefited Novelis by creating a greater demand for its product.

The terms of the Agreement itself, which allow for the disclosure of confidential information to Pepsi, illustrate conclusively that the parties did not intend the general anti-assignment/delegation provision in the contract to preclude A-B's discussions with Pepsi regarding changes in A-B's ability to supply Pepsi. *See Viacom Int'l Inc. v. Tandem Prods., Inc.*, 526 F.2d 593, 596 (2nd Cir. 1975) (contract's anti-assignment provision did not forbid agreement with third party where undisputed evidence showed that plaintiff knew of defendant's intention to assign a portion of its rights at time of contract). Ultimately, when construed in a light most favorable to Novelis, the evidence does not support a claim for a breach of the anti-delegation provision. Summary judgment on Count V is, therefore, warranted. ...

III. CONCLUSION

For all of the foregoing reasons, Defendant's motion for summary judgment is granted in its entirety. This case is closed. It is so ordered.

B. Breach of Assignments Contracts Under § 2-210(2)

MacWilliams v. BP Products North America Inc.
2010 WL 4860629
(C.C.D.N.J. Nov. 23, 2010)

KUGLER, DISTRICT JUDGE. This matter arises out of several fuel supply agreements between Plaintiff Frank MacWilliams and Defendant BP Products North America Inc. (BP). ... Plaintiff claims that BP breached agreements and violated the Petroleum Marketing Practices Act (PMPA), 15 U.S.C. § 2801, et seq., by assigning the agreements to a third-party that immediately raised fuel prices and terminated a monthly rebate program. This matter comes before the court pursuant to BP's motion for summary judgment dismissing the Amended Complaint. ...

I. BACKGROUND

Plaintiff owns and operates two New Jersey gasoline service stations known as "Edgewater Park Amoco" and "Mac's Amoco." In December 2000, Plaintiff entered into Dealer Supply Agreements (DSAs) with BP's predecessor-in-interest—Amoco Oil Company (Amoco). The original DSAs had five-year terms. In 2005, BP renewed the DSAs for an additional five years. The renewed DSAs gave Plaintiff the option of terminating the contracts before their expiration by paying a $30,000 early termination fee for each station.

The DSAs governed many aspects of the franchise relationship, including the supply of fuel. They required BP to supply BP-branded gasoline and petroleum products to Plaintiff's gas stations. According to the DSAs, BP set the price for fuel at the "dealer buying price ... in effect for [Plaintiff's] pricing area." But BP could "change prices for all products at any time." The DSAs also provided that BP may assign its rights under the agreements and that the assignee may change fuel prices. Section 3(b) of the agreements provided: "If this Agreement is assigned by [BP] to a [BP] jobber or other party, the price to be paid by [Plaintiff] for motor fuel and other products hereunder will be as established by said jobber or other party." The DSAs further required Plaintiff to provide a security deposit in the amount of $80,000, which he paid in the form of letters of credit ($60,000) and cash ($20,000).

In separate writings executed [when the DSAs were fashioned], Plaintiff and Amoco agreed that Plaintiff would be entitled to End-of-Month Volume Allowances (EOM Agreements). The EOM Agreements required Amoco (and later BP) to pay Plaintiff a certain amount per gallon of gasoline that Plaintiff sold at his gas stations. The more gasoline Plaintiff sold, the greater the per-gallon allowance. The EOM Agreements contained a provision authorizing BP to unilaterally cancel the End-of-Month Volume Allowances "at any time." If BP terminated the allowances, the agreements required BP to give Plaintiff a 30-day written notice.

Plaintiff's gas stations prospered under its arrangement with Amoco and BP. Plaintiff attributes his success to a strategy of aggressive gasoline pricing whereby he offered gasoline to the consuming public at the lowest price available for name-brand gasoline. According to Plaintiff, he could not afford to offer this pricing without BP's payments under the EOM Agreements.

Plaintiff's troubles with BP began in August 2008 when BP advised him that it had assigned the DSAs to third-party jobber Ocean Petroleum, LLC (Ocean). According to a declaration from BP's Northeast Regional Sales Manager—Jeffrey C. Burrell, BP also advised Plaintiff ... "that it was exercising its rights under the EOM Agreements to cancel the EOM Program, as BP typically does when assigning supply contracts to third parties." BP does not contend, nor submit any evidence, that it gave Plaintiff written notice regarding termination of the EOM Program.

Plaintiff asserts in his declaration that "BP never provided Plaintiff with the required written notice that the EOM allowances would be cancelled." Plaintiff admits, however, that in August 2008 Ocean notified him that it was terminating the End-of-Month Volume Allowances. Plaintiff provides no evidence regarding when payments under the EOM Agreements actually ended. Plaintiff did not consent to BP's assignment of the DSAs to Ocean or the termination of the End-of-Month Allowances.

Upon learning that BP assigned the DSAs to Ocean, Plaintiff told BP that he did not wish to receive fuel from Ocean. Plaintiff claims that "[i]n virtually all cases in which BP has assigned supply contracts to Ocean, including mine, Ocean has engaged in unfair and inequitable conduct with the dealers—such as terminating EOM allowances [and] threatening to charge dealers up to twenty cents a gallon over the rack rate if the dealer did not enter into ten year supply agreements rather than standard five year agreements."

Thus, rather than accept fuel from Ocean under the DSAs and the EOM Agreements, which allowed Ocean to raise fuel prices and terminate the allowance program, Plaintiff chose to negotiate a supply contract with another BP jobber—Arfa Enterprises, Inc. (Arfa). Plaintiff claims that "Ocean insisted that [he] and [Arfa] pay it $200,000 so that [Plaintiff] could be relieved of the contractual obligations that BP has assigned to Ocean, and Arfa and [Plaintiff] did so, under duress." Plaintiff also claims that he tried to terminate the DSAs by paying BP the $30,000 early termination fee, but BP refused to accept the fee or the termination.

After Plaintiff secured Arfa as his fuel supplier and paid Ocean to be released from the DSAs, he requested that BP return his security deposit. BP returned the $60,000 in letters of credit; but, according to Mr. Burrell, BP had already transferred the $20,000 cash deposit to Ocean as part of its assignment of the DSAs. Plaintiff states in his declaration that when he asked Ocean for the deposit, Ocean told him to "get it from BP."

Plaintiff filed his Complaint against BP in April 2009. The Complaint alleged that BP's assignment of the DSAs to Ocean and the termination of the EOM Agreements constituted a constructive termination of Plaintiff's franchise in violation of the PMPA. The Complaint also asserted a common law contract claim based on BP's termination of the EOM Agreements and refusal to return Plaintiff's cash deposit. In lieu of filing an Answer, BP moved to dismiss the Complaint. On February

3, 2010, this court granted BP's motion to dismiss Plaintiff's PMPA claim under Rule 12(b)(6).

The court held that because the DSAs and the EOM Agreements allowed the franchisor to set fuel prices and to terminate the EOM Agreements, Plaintiff could not argue that his franchise was constructively terminated by either a price increase or termination of the EOM Agreements. The court denied BP's motion in so far as it sought to dismiss Plaintiff's breach of contract claim based on the return of Plaintiff's security deposit, but granted BP's motion in so far as it sought to dismiss Plaintiff's breach of contract claim based on BP's termination of the EOM Agreements. The court nevertheless granted Plaintiff ten days to amend his Complaint to allege facts sufficient to establish a contractual right to continued receipt of the End-of-Month Volume Allowances.

Plaintiff timely filed an Amended Complaint on February 12, 2010. The Amended Complaint alleges that BP made oral representations to him that the EOM Agreements "would remain in existence." BP also allegedly told Plaintiff that if the EOM Agreements were terminated, Plaintiff "would be permitted to terminate its [DSAs]." In reliance on those oral representations and the expected income from the End-of-Month Volume Allowances, Plaintiff claims to have spent approximately $750,000 in capital improvements to his service stations. The Amended Complaint reasserts claims for constructive discharge of the franchise in violation of the PMPA and breach of contract based on BP's "conduct in terminating the Agreements." BP now moves for summary judgment regarding all of Plaintiff's claims. ...

III. DISCUSSION

Plaintiff opposes BP's motion for summary judgment based on four breach-of-contract theories. The Court addresses each of Plaintiff's theories in turn.

A. Assignment of the DSAs

Plaintiff first claims that BP's assignment of the DSAs to Ocean was invalid because the UNIFORM COMMERCIAL CODE (UCC) prohibits assignments that "increase materially the burden or risk imposed on" the other party. N.J.S.A. 12A:2-210 (adopting § 2-210 of the UCC).

The parties do not dispute, and this court previously ruled, that the fuel supply contracts between the parties are governed by New Jersey's version of the UCC, N.J.S.A. 12A:2-210, *et seq. See MacWilliams*, 2010 U.S. Dist. LEXIS 8967, at *16. The UCC provides that "unless otherwise agreed, all rights of either [party] ... can be assigned except where the assignment would materially change the duty of the other party, or increase materially the burden or risk imposed on him by his contract, or impair materially his chance of obtaining return performance." N.J.S.A. 12A:2-210.

The DSAs do not prohibit, and in fact provide, that BP may assign its rights to a third-party. Plaintiff nevertheless argues that Ocean's threatened price increases and termination of the EOM Agreements imposed an increased risk and impaired Plaintiff's chance of obtaining the bargained for return. Plaintiff's argument is unavailing.

First, the DSAs did not fix or guarantee Plaintiff's fuel price. In fact, the DSAs expressly permitted BP to "change prices for all products at any time." Moreover, the DSAs provided: "If this Agreement is assigned by [BP] to a Supplier jobber or other party, the price to be paid by [Plaintiff] for motor fuel and other products hereunder will be established by said jobber or other party." Thus, Plaintiff cannot argue that Ocean's threatened price increases would "materially increase his burden" under the DSAs because the DSAs expressly allowed for price increases. Second, Plaintiff cannot argue that Ocean's termination of the EOM Agreements materially affected his burdens and risks because the EOM Agreements expressly permitted BP to terminate the End-of-Month Volume Allowances "at any time."

In short, BP's assignment to Ocean was not invalid under the UCC because the assignment created no new risks or burdens. *See Beachler v. Amoco Oil Co.*, 112 F.3d 902, 908 (7th Cir. 1997) (analyzing assignment of fuel supply contract under UCC § 2-210 and concluding that assignment was valid notwithstanding assignee-supplier's price increase because contract expressly allowed for price increase); *Clark v. BP Oil Co.*, 137 F.3d 386, 393–94 (6th Cir. 1998) (holding that "open price term" in fuel supply contract estopped plaintiff from arguing that assignee's price increase amounted to "material change in the risks and burdens imposed on him" under UCC § 2-210). Therefore, Plaintiff's breach-of-contract theory based on BP's assignment to Ocean fails, and BP is entitled to summary judgment regarding this claim. ...

D. Plaintiff's Security Deposit

Plaintiff's final breach-of-contract theory is that BP breached the DSAs by failing to return his $20,000 cash deposit once the DSAs were terminated. BP claims that it did not breach the DSAs because it transferred the $20,000 to Ocean when it assigned Ocean its rights under the agreements.

As noted above, a breach-of-contract claim under New Jersey law requires proof of three elements: "a valid contract, defective performance by the defendant, and resulting damages." In general, an assignment of contractual rights "does not discharge the original [promisor], but merely transfers the duty to the assignee as an additional obligor."

Fusco v. Union City, 618 A.2d 914, 916–17 (N.J. Sup. Ct. App. Div. 1993), citing 15 WILLISTON ON CONTRACTS § 1867A (3d ed. 1972). "A party 'cannot relieve himself of the obligations of a contract without the consent of the obligee.'" *Id.*, quoting *Riley v. New Rapids Carpet Center*, 294 A.2d 7, 10 (N.J. 1972). "There must be a 'clear and definite intention on the part of all concerned' that it is the purpose of the agreement to substitute a new debtor for the old one." *Id.*, quoting *Tolland v. Lista*, 134 A.2d 601, 603–04 (N.J. Sup. Ct. App. Div. 1957).

Here, Plaintiff not did consent to BP's assignment of the DSAs to Ocean. Thus, although the assignment made Ocean an additional obligor under the DSAs, it did not release BP from any of its obligations. Consequently, the fact that BP transferred Plaintiff's deposit to Ocean is irrelevant because BP remains liable to Plaintiff under the DSAs if Ocean holds the deposit in violation of the agreements. BP's motion for summary judgment is therefore denied regarding this claim.

IV. CONCLUSION

For the reasons discussed above, BP's motion for summary judgment is granted regarding Plaintiff's PMPA claim. BP's motion for summary judgment regarding Plaintiff's breach-of-contract claims is denied to the extent BP seeks to dismiss Plaintiff's claim based on his unreturned $20,000 deposit. Summary judgment is granted regarding Plaintiff's remaining breach-of-contract claims.

UNIFORM COMMERCIAL CODE

§ 2-210. DELEGATION OF PERFORMANCE; ASSIGNMENT OF RIGHTS

(1) A party may perform his duty through a delegate unless otherwise agreed or unless the other party has a substantial interest in having his original promisor perform or control the acts required by the contract. No delegation of performance relieves the party delegating of any duty to perform or any liability for breach.

(2) Except as otherwise provided in Section 9-406, unless otherwise agreed, all rights of either seller or buyer can be assigned except where the assignment would materially change the duty of the other party, or increase materially the burden or risk imposed on him by his contract, or impair materially his chance of obtaining return performance. A right to damages for breach of the whole contract or a right arising out of

the assignor's due performance of his entire obligation can be assigned despite agreement otherwise.

(3) The creation, attachment, perfection, or enforcement of a security interest in the seller's interest under a contract is not a transfer that materially changes the duty of or increases materially the burden or risk imposed on the buyer or impairs materially the buyer's chance of obtaining return performance within the purview of subsection (2) unless, and then only to the extent that, enforcement actually results in a delegation of material performance of the seller. Even in that event, the creation, attachment, perfection, and enforcement of the security interest remain effective, but

(i) the seller is liable to the buyer for damages caused by the delegation to the extent that the damages could not reasonably be prevented by the buyer, and

(ii) a court having jurisdiction may grant other appropriate relief, including cancellation of the contract for sale or an injunction against enforcement of the security interest or consummation of the enforcement.

(4) Unless the circumstances indicate the contrary a prohibition of assignment of "the contract" is to be construed as barring only the delegation to the assignee of the assignor's performance.

(5) An assignment of "the contract" or of "all my rights under the contract" or an assignment in similar general terms is an assignment of rights and unless the language or the circumstances (as in an assignment for security) indicate the contrary, it is a delegation of performance of the duties of the assignor and its acceptance by the assignee constitutes a promise by him to perform those duties. This promise is enforceable by either the assignor or the other party to the original contract.

(6) The other party may treat any assignment which delegates performance as creating reasonable grounds for insecurity and may without prejudice to his rights against the assignor demand assurances from the assignee (Section 2-609).

NOTES AND QUESTIONS

1. **Dearth of Decisions Interpreting the Delegation of Performance Doctrine Under UCC § 2-210(1).** Consider the court's observations, analysis, and conclusion in *Sunoco, Inc. (R*

& M) v. MX Wholesale Fuel Corp., 565 F.Supp.2d 572, 579–80 (C.C.D.N.J. 2008):

Sunoco argues that Monmouth is an obligor pursuant to Section 2-210(1) of the UCC, as codified at N.J.S.A. 12A:2-210(1). N.J.S.A. 12A:2-210(1) states: "A party may perform his duty through a delegate unless otherwise agreed or unless the other party has a substantial interest in having his original promisor perform or control the acts required by the contract. No delegation of performance relieves the party delegating of any duty to perform or any liability for breach." Monmouth does not address the applicability of N.J.S.A. 12A:2-210(1).

There is also a dearth of opinions interpreting this particular section. Only two cases were found by the court that cite to this section of the statute, but neither of them address the scope of liability retained by the assignor under § 12A:2-210(1). *In Florham Park Chevron, Inc. v. Chevron U.S.A.*, 1990 WL 61787, at *6, *8 n. 5 (D.N.J. May 9, 1990), the court acknowledged that New Jersey has adopted section 2-210 of the UCC and that N.J.S.A. § 12A:2-210(1)-(2) is applicable to the sale of motor fuels. In the second case, *Sawhney v. Mobil Oil Corp.*, 970 F.Supp. 366 (D.N.J.1997), the only reference to N.J.S.A. § 12A:2-210(1) was the court's statement in dicta that "[t]o be sure, Mobil's delegation of its contractual duties does not relieve it of its duty to perform under the franchise agreement, or its liability to plaintiff in case of a breach." That case, however, was reversed in an unpublished opinion by the Third Circuit. *See Sawhney v. Mobil Oil Corp.*, 173 F.3d 421 (3d Cir. Dec. 11, 1998).

In the Third Circuit's opinion, the court acknowledged that the Petroleum Marketing Practices Act does not expressly permit nor prohibit assignment of franchise agreements and held that state law governs the legality of such assignments. *See Sawhney*, at 5. Although the Third Circuit did not specifically address the lower court's reference to N.J.S.A. § 12A:2-210(1), it did state that under subsection (2) of that statute, that New Jersey law permits assignments "unless otherwise agreed."

Therefore, although there is no case law interpreting the scope of liability retained by the assignor under § 12A:2-210(1), *Florham Park* and *Sawhney* provide that franchise contracts concerning the sale of motor fuel are governed by state law concerning assignments and by applicable U.C.C. provisions. ...

> [B]ased on the clear language of the statute, we find that N.J.S.A. § 12A:2-210(1) is applicable and that Monmouth is not relieved of its duty to perform or its liability for breach. Under N.J.S.A. § 12A:2-210(1), a party may delegate performance under the contract to another party, but cannot delegate its duty to perform or its liability for breach. For example, here, Monmouth could delegate to MX its right to purchase and sell Coastal gas, but could not under N.J.S.A. § 12A:2-210(1) delegate to MX its duties or liabilities, such as Monmouth's contractual duty to pay Coastal, or Coastal's successors, for the gas.
>
> There is no language in the contract expressing an intent by the parties to relieve Monmouth of its duties under N.J.S.A. § 12A:2-210(1), or an intent to relieve Monmouth of its duty to perform or liability for breach. Rather, the language in the contract appears to express an intent that the parties were to remain bound under the provisions of N.J.S.A. § 12A:2-210(1). Thus, without an express intent by the parties to relieve Monmouth of its duty to perform or its liability for breach, the provisions in N.J.S.A. § 12A:2-210(1) apply and Monmouth remains liable under the terms of the contract.

2. **An Exception to the Assignability of Warranty Claims Under UCC § 2-210(2).** In *Kaiser Aluminum & Chemical Corp. v. Ingersoll-Rand Co.*, 519 F. Supp. 60, 73 (C.C.D.C. Ga. 1981), the federal district court wrote:

> The settlement agreement between Kaiser and Weatherly clearly purports to assign Weatherly's supplier and vendor warranties to Kaiser. Kaiser argues that such an assignment is expressly permitted by Georgia Code Annotated § 109A-2-210(2). ... However, it has long been the law in Georgia that a warranty may not be assigned. "In a sale of personal property, the warranty is not negotiable or assignable and does not run with the article sold." *Smith v. Williams*, 117 Ga. 782, 45 S.E. 394 (1903). This language was reaffirmed in 1974 after Georgia's adoption of the UNIFORM COMMERCIAL CODE. *Stewart v. Gainesville Glass Co.*, 131 Ga. App. 747 (1974).
>
> In *Stewart*, the purchaser of a house sued the manufacturer of insulating glass. The glass was defective in that moisture and dust collected between the sheets of glass obscuring the view. The defect was in direct violation of an express ten-year warranty which was given by the manufacturer to the first buyer. No injury to other property or to a person was involved. The Georgia Court of Appeals in *Stewart* clearly upheld the privity requirement in a warranty action, whether the warranty was

express or implied. The court stated: "No principle is in sight which would … invest the new party with any right whatever as against the manufacturers or first vendors. Further, in a sale of personal property the warranty is not negotiable or assignable, and does not run with the article sold. … Here we deal with an express warranty, rather than an implied warranty, and it would appear that the privity requirement applies with even more force." *Stewart*, 131 Ga. App. at 752.

CHAPTER TWELVE

Proof of Causation and Damages Under Article 2 of the Uniform Commercial Code

As discussed in Chapter 11, a complainant who files a breach-of-contract action under Article 2 must establish that a defendant breached a sale-of-goods contract. And, like a plaintiff who commences a breach-of-contract action under the common law, an Article 2 plaintiff must also prove that a defendant's breach caused one or several of the following outcomes: loss of goods, a partial or total destruction of purchased goods, business-interruption losses, loss of sales, loss of profits, or some other adverse financial event.

But, Article 2 of the UCC differs from the common law in a major respect: The UCC provides two sets of different rules that govern the award of damages and equitable remedies after a contracting party breaches a sale-of-goods contract. Under Article 2, courts must apply one set of rules when the plaintiff is a buyer. Additionally, a second set of rules must be applied when the complainant is a seller.

Furthermore, an Article 2 plaintiff must establish that a defendant's non-performance caused various damages. However, whether or not courts should apply common-law theories of causation to establish liability under the UCC is a persistent question. As discussed below, some courts have concluded that the UCC codifies common-law principles. This chapter is devoted to discussing theories of causation, measure-of-damages rules, as well as equitable doctrines, which govern the resolution of contract disputes under Article 2.

SECTION ONE: PROOF OF CAUSATION AND THE APPLICABILITY OF COMMON-LAW THEORIES UNDER ARTICLE 2

A. Situations Requiring Proof of Cause in Fact and Proximate Cause Under the UCC

Under the common law, complainants must prove that defendants' breach of contract was the "cause in fact" and "proximate cause" of the complainants' losses and damages. On the other hand, depending on the types of breaches or nonperformance, complainants may or may not be required to prove those elements under Article 2 of the UCC. For example, in *Hope v. Nissan North America, Inc.*, 353 S.W.3d 68, 90–92 (Mo. Ct. App. 2011) the court required a class of complainants to prove cause in fact and proximate cause. The *Hope* court wrote:

> Section 2-314 of the U.C.C. creates an implied warranty of merchantability, which warrants that goods must be at least "fit for the ordinary purposes for which such goods are used." ... To prove a claim for breach of implied warranty of merchantability in Missouri, a plaintiff must show: (1) that a merchant sold goods, (2) which were not "merchantable" at the time of the sale, (3) injury and damages to the plaintiff or his property (4) which were *caused proximately or in fact* by the defective nature of the goods, and (5) notice to the seller of the injury. *Ragland Mills, Inc. v. General Motors Corp.*, 763 S.W.2d 357, 360 (Mo. App. 1989). ... [Here, the plaintiffs] claim that a purchase of FX Vehicles, *ipso facto*, caused an economic loss. We find no authority, in Missouri or otherwise, for this proposition. ... Because it appears a majority of the putative class members ... have no breach of implied warranty claim, the action in reality becomes hundreds or thousands of individual claims. Class membership would require ... individual inquiries into the extent of damage sustained, whether the alleged defect was the cause in fact or proximate cause of the damage sustained. ... The overwhelming requirement of individual determinations is fatal to a showing of predominance of common questions. As a result, we find the trial court abused its discretion in certifying a class for the breach of implied warranty of merchantability claim under Rule 52.08(b)(3).

Other courts have embraced the rulings in *Hope* and *Ragland* as well. *See Taylor v. Ramsay-Gerding Const. Co.*, 226 P.3d 45, 55 (Or. Ct. App. 2010), and *Sparks v. Total Body Essential Nutrition, Inc.*, 27 So.3d 489, 492 (Ala. 2009) ("Alabama's UNIFORM COMMERCIAL CODE is equally attentive to the plaintiff's burden of establishing proximate cause.").

Furthermore, section 2-715(2)(b) reads in relevant part: "Consequential damages resulting from the seller's breach include ... [i]njury to person or property proximately resulting from any breach of warranty." And OFFICIAL COMMENT 13 of section 2-314 reads in pertinent part: "In an action based on breach of warranty, it is of course necessary to show not only the existence of the warranty but the fact that the warranty was broken and that *the breach of the warranty was the proximate cause of the loss* sustained."

B. Relaxing the Proof-of-Causation Requirement Under the UCC

To repeat, under the UCC, some circumstances may eliminate a complainant's burden to prove proximate cause. OFFICIAL COMMENT 8 discusses an exception to the proximate-cause rule under section 2-316. It reads in pertinent part:

> Under paragraph (b) of subsection (3) warranties may be excluded or modified by the circumstances where the buyer examines the goods or a sample or model of them before entering into the contract. "Examination" as used in this paragraph is not synonymous with inspection before acceptance or at any other time after the contract has been made. It goes rather to the nature of the responsibility assumed by the seller at the time of the making of the contract. Of course if the buyer discovers the defect and uses the goods anyway, or if he unreasonably fails to examine the goods before he uses them, resulting injuries may be found to result from his own action rather than proximately from a breach of warranty.

In addition, OFFICIAL COMMENT 5 provides a brief explanation of a proximate-cause exception under section 2-715(2)(b). The comment states:

> Subsection (2)(b) states the usual rule as to breach of warranty allowing recovery for injuries "proximately" resulting from the breach. Where the injury involved follows the use of goods without discovery of the defect causing the damage, the question of "proximate" cause turns on whether it was reasonable for the buyer to use the goods without such inspection as would have revealed the defects. If it was not reasonable for him to do so, or if he did in fact discover the defect prior to his use, the injury would not proximately result from the breach of warranty.

How have courts interpreted and applied the proximate-cause exception? Is the exception essentially a comparative-fault or comparative-negligence scheme under Article 2? Consider the Texas Supreme

Court's analysis and explanation in *JCW Electronics, Inc. v. Garza*, 257 S.W.3d 701, 706–707 (Tex. 2008):

> [A]rticle 2 does not undertake a comprehensive fault scheme. ... [Section 2-715(2)(b)] merely provides that a party may recover ... for "injury to person or property proximately resulting from any breach of warranty." Although a UCC COMMENT 5 indicates that the buyer's conduct may affect the recovery of consequential damages under an implied warranty cause of action, Article 2 does not apportion liability under these circumstances. ... "[T]he question of 'proximate' cause turns on whether it was reasonable for the buyer to use the goods without such inspection as would have revealed the defects." ... *See Signal Oil & Gas Co. v. Universal Oil Prods.*, 572 S.W.2d 320, 329 (Tex. 1978) (finding that where both the unsuitable product and the buyer's negligence are found to be proximate causes of the damage in an implied warranty claim, "the buyer may not recover consequential damages to the extent that the buyer's negligence or fault was a concurring proximate cause of such damages").

There is more. Proof of proximate cause is not mandatory under section 2-608(1)(a) of the UCC. Quite simply, a buyer may "revoke his acceptance" of the non-conforming goods—thereby significantly reducing or eliminating the likelihood of a buyer's experiencing a loss or an injury. Or stated differently, a buyer's rejecting non-conforming goods and returning them to the seller would eliminate the buyer's need to sue for damages. Even more importantly, a rejection of non-conforming goods would remove the buyer's burden to prove the proximate cause of an injury and damages. As a matter of law, a buyer establishes all elements of a breach-of-contract action if the buyer commences an action under section 2-608. *See Scoti Zahner, Inc. v. City of Fredericksburg, Texas*, 2000 WL 277317, *3 (Tex. App.—San Antonio).

But assume that a buyer failed to "revoke an acceptance" of non-conforming goods. Is the buyer liable for failing to pay the contract price? Must a seller commence a breach-of-contract action and prove that the buyer's breach was the cause in fact and proximate cause of the seller's damages? Does section 2-608 create a right of action for a seller to collect damages, or does it create an affirmative defense for a seller? The next case illustrates how one court addressed these and related questions.

Viking Packaging Technologies, Inc. v. Vassallo Foods, Inc.
804 N.W.2d 507
(Wis. App. 2011)

KESSLER, J. Vassallo Foods, Inc. *d/b/a* Country Pasta (Country Pasta) appeals the trial court's judgment in favor of Viking Packaging Technologies, Inc. (Viking) and an order dismissing its counterclaims. Country Pasta contends that the trial court erred in granting judgment in favor of Viking and in dismissing its counterclaims. ... Country Pasta alternatively argues that if a determination is made that it did accept the packaging system, it revoked the acceptance. ...

BACKGROUND

Viking commenced this action against Country Pasta seeking damages in the amount of $34,110.22 for unpaid products and services provided by Viking under its contract with Country Pasta to provide Country Pasta with a product packaging system. Country Pasta—located in Polson, Montana—is in the business of making noodles. Viking is a Wisconsin corporation and manufactures, fabricates, and services industrial packaging equipment. In 2006, Gary Ivory—the production manager at Country Pasta—contacted Robb Leonhard—one of the owners of Viking—to discuss a quotation for a more automatic pasta bagging system.

Specifically, Country Pasta wanted a system in which the pasta bags would be weighed more accurately and in which the bags would be closed or tied more automatically. Ivory provided Leonhard with a sample of Country Pasta's product in the bag it was using at the time and indicated what he wanted the product to look like. Leonhard then sent Ivory photographs of a bag of Country Pasta's product with a tin-tie on it and stated "this is basically what your look is going to be." Viking included the photographs on the second page of the quotation.

On July 13, 2007, Country Pasta accepted Viking's quotation to purchase a pasta packaging system. The quotation provided pricing for a packaging system consisting of a Viking M400 bagger (bagger), a Weigh Right PMB-3 Net Weigh filling machine (scale), a tin-tie applicator and its transition conveyor. The quotation shows photos of the equipment and of Country Pasta bags closed with a tin-tie. The items related to the tin-tie applicator were priced at $47,173. The total purchase price for the product packaging system was $178,074.

The quotation, found by the trial court to be a contract, called for a "checkout," or a pre-shipment inspection, by Country Pasta "prior to shipment." In April 2008, Country Pasta sent Ivory and Scott Knutson to Viking's facility in Kohler, Wisconsin to perform the checkout of the packaging system. Viking demonstrated the operation for Country

Pasta's employees. The tin-ties on the finished bags did not regularly close up during this demonstration; however, Viking worked on the packaging system, and told Country Pasta that the system was "working better." Country Pasta approved the shipment and the packaging system was delivered to Country Pasta before June 17, 2008. Ivory helped unpack and set up the equipment; he did not notice any defects.

The contract provided that "if requested by the customer, [Viking] will provide a service technician for installation of the quoted equipment." The contract did not include free installation, but estimated that two days of installation and training for Country Pasta employees would cost $3,373. The contract also provided that "[a]n installation will be considered complete when all systems purchased from [Viking] perform per the Product Performance Specifications." "Product Performance Specifications" are not defined in the contract.

From June 17, 2008, through June 25, 2008, Viking technician Tim Parrish worked on installing the equipment and training Country Pasta's employees in Montana. During this visit, Parrish discovered that Country Pasta workers would drop or tap bags full of pasta on a table in order to settle the noodles to allow for a twist tie to be applied to the bag. Parrish made adjustments to the machinery, including adding a shelf to assist in the settling of the noodles. Despite these efforts, the tin-tie applicator was not functioning properly at the time he left. Viking and Country Pasta agreed to split the cost of a second visit by Parrish.

Parrish returned to Country Pasta in July 2008 with Steve Almberg—a representative from Weigh Right, the manufacturer of the scale. Parrish and Almberg improved the operation of the scale and bagger by making modifications to Country Pasta's equipment feeding the scale and bagger. Almberg discovered the scale was not being operated correctly because it had no automatic control; however, there were no actual problems with the scale itself. …

On December 4, 2008, five months after delivery of the packaging system, and four months after Parrish's final visit, Kellogg sent an email to Viking stating that Country Pasta wanted a refund for the tin-tie applicator and the associated conveyor in the amount of $47,173. At that time, Country Pasta had outstanding invoices due to Viking in the amount of $34,110.22. Viking brought suit against Country Pasta, seeking the outstanding amount. Country Pasta counterclaimed, alleging breach of contract. Country Pasta's first objection to the Viking invoices was made in its answer to Viking's complaint.

After a trial to the court, judgment for money damages was entered in favor of Viking on its contract claim against Country Pasta. In addition, an order was entered dismissing Country Pasta's counterclaim alleging breach of contract by Viking, and alleging Country Pasta's revocation of acceptance of the tin-tie applicator and conveyor. Country Pasta now appeals.

Discussion

Country Pasta contends that the trial court erred in granting judgment in favor of Viking and in dismissing its counterclaims because: (1) Viking breached the contract by failing to complete installation of the packaging system; (2) Country Pasta did not accept the tin-tie applicator; and (3) if Country Pasta did accept the packaging system, it revoked acceptance. We disagree. …

II. Breach of Contract

Country Pasta contends that Viking breached its contract by failing to complete installation of the entire packaging system because the tin-tie applicator did not consistently put tin-ties on its pasta bags in accordance with the product performance specifications mentioned in the contract. Country Pasta asserts that because the tin-tie applicator would not consistently apply the tin-ties to Country Pasta's product, "a component of the system did not perform according to the product performance specifications." Although Country Pasta makes no complaint about the performance of the bagger, the scale, or their related conveyors, it argues that Viking failed to complete "installation of the entire packaging system" and therefore breached its obligations under the contract.

The contract required Viking to install the packaging system, if and only if, Country Pasta requested that service and agreed to pay for that service at the rates set out in the contract. The trial court found that the parties agreed to two visits by a Viking technician—Parrish. After Parrish told Country Pasta at the end of his second visit in July 2008, that the tin-tie applicator would not work with its product, Kellogg never requested further installation or other work by Viking. Kellogg never asked to have the applicator replaced, nor did he identify any defective or broken parts. All of these alternatives were available to Country Pasta under the contract. …

Country Pasta has not established that the packaging system as a whole, or the tin-tie applicator specifically, failed to meet any identifiable "product performance specifications." Country Pasta failed to establish a breach of contract by Viking. The trial court properly dismissed Country Pasta's counterclaim based on breach of contract.

III. ACCEPTANCE

Country Pasta argues that the trial court erred in finding that County Pasta accepted the tin-tie applicator and its related conveyor because without a complete installation, Country Pasta never had a reasonable opportunity to inspect the packaging system. Installation was required under the contract only if requested by Country Pasta. The predominant purpose of the contract was the sale of the packaging system. Consequently, WIS. STAT. CH. 402, relating to sale of goods, applies to this transaction.

WISCONSIN STAT. § 402.606(1) describes buyer conduct which establishes the acceptance of goods. The full text of WIS. STAT. § 402.606 provides:

> (1) Acceptance of goods occurs when the buyer:
>
> (a) After a reasonable opportunity to inspect the goods signifies to the seller that the goods are conforming or that the buyer will take or retain them in spite of their nonconformity; or
>
> (b) Fails to make an effective rejection (§ 402.602(1)), but such acceptance does not occur until the buyer has had a reasonable opportunity to inspect them; or
>
> (c) Does any act inconsistent with the seller's ownership; but if such act is wrongful as against the seller it is an acceptance only if ratified by the seller.
>
> (2) Acceptance of a part of any commercial unit is acceptance of that entire unit.

Acceptance occurs when the buyer: (1) "signifies to the seller" that the goods are nonconforming, but will be retained in spite of the failing; (2) when goods are not rejected after a reasonable opportunity to inspect them; or (3) when the buyer does anything inconsistent with the seller's ownership. As our supreme court explained in *Gerner v. Vasby*, 75 Wis.2d 660, 668 (1977):

> Acceptance is the unilateral act of the buyer alone, or of his representative; it requires no action or expression on the part of the seller. Acceptance within the meaning of the statute is an expression of assent by the buyer to become the owner of specific goods as the subject matter of the contract made by him with the seller.

WISCONSIN STAT. § 402.606(2) provides that "[a]cceptance of a part of any commercial unit is acceptance of that entire unit." A "commercial unit" is defined by WIS. STAT. § 402.105(1)(a) as:

> a unit of goods as by commercial usage is a single whole for purposes of sale and division of which materially impairs its

> character or value on the market or in use. A commercial unit may be a single article (as a machine) or a set of articles (as a suite of furniture or an assortment of sizes) or a quantity (as a bale, gross, or carload) or any other unit treated in use or in the relevant market as a single whole.

Accordingly, we must first determine whether the contract involved the packaging system as "a single whole," or as the separate purchase of the bagger, scale, tin-tie applicator and some conveyors, before determining whether Country Pasta accepted the packaging system. The purchase of a "packaging system" composed of multiple single machines is very similar in concept to the statutory example of "a suite of furniture or an assortment of sizes." Both the hypothetical suite of furniture and the packaging system would be materially impaired in their value to the user if parts (a chair, a tin-tie applicator) were removed from the whole. ...

We conclude that Viking quoted, and Country Pasta ordered and received, an integrated packaging system. By the time Parrish left Montana in July 2008, Country Pasta was dissatisfied only with the performance of the tin-tie applicator. The other machines comprising the packaging system apparently functioned satisfactorily. Country Pasta expressed no intent to return the bagger, the scale, or the other equipment related to the operation of those machines. Earlier, after its "checkout" of the system and knowledge that there had been problems with the tin-tie applicator, Country Pasta approved of the shipment of the packaging system. No defective or broken parts were identified when Country Pasta unpacked and set up the machines. Country Pasta employees participated in installation and training sessions.

Ultimately, Kellogg was informed that the tin-tie applicator would not work with Country Pasta's product, yet he retained the applicator for an additional four or five months before making a complaint. Country Pasta had a reasonable opportunity to inspect the system. It accepted the system as a whole, as it did not wish to return any equipment other than the tin-tie applicator. By retaining all of the items in the contract, Country Pasta treated the packaging system in a way that was inconsistent with the seller's ownership.

This conduct constitutes acceptance of goods pursuant to WIS. STAT. § 402.606(1)(c). *See Dunck Tank Works, Inc. v. Sutherland*, 236 Wis. 83, 85–87 (1940) (keeping and using storage tanks when buyer ordered pressurized tanks is inconsistent with seller's ownership); *Fox v. Wilkinson*, 133 Wis. 337, 341–42 (1907) (use of an engine after giving notice that the engine was unacceptable is inconsistent with the seller's interest); and *J.B. Bradford Piano Co. v. Baal*, 166 Wis. 134, 136 (1917). (By retaining a piano for three months with the knowledge of the defects, and by making payments, the buyer waived the defects.)

The only conduct in this record that might arguably be considered a notice of rejection is an email dated December 4, 2008—from Kellogg to Viking—demanding a refund of the cost of the tin-tie applicator. To reject goods, however, WIS. STAT. § 402.602(1) FN6 requires that the rejection occur within a reasonable time after delivery, and the rejection only becomes effective when the buyer "seasonably notifies the seller." Kellogg's email was sent four months after Parrish's second visit to Montana, in which Parrish indicated that the tin-tie applicator would not work with Country Pasta's product. Country Pasta never rejected the commercial unit.

IV. REVOCATION OF ACCEPTANCE

Country Pasta finally argues that if it accepted the packaging system, it was done with the assumption that "Viking was continuing to work on a solution to fix the tin-tie applicator" after Parrish left Montana in July 2008. Country Pasta argues that it revoked acceptance upon Kellogg's realization that "Viking was not going to provide a solution." We are not persuaded.

WISCONSIN STAT. § 402.608(1)(a) and (2) describe the revocation of the acceptance of goods. The full text of WIS. STAT. § 402.608 provides:

> (1) The buyer may revoke the buyer's acceptance of a lot or commercial unit whose nonconformity substantially impairs its value to the buyer if the buyer has accepted it:
>
> (a) On the reasonable assumption that its nonconformity would be cured and it has not been seasonably cured; or
>
> (b) Without discovery of such nonconformity if the buyer's acceptance was reasonably induced either by the difficulty of discovery before acceptance or by the seller's assurances.
>
> (2) Revocation of acceptance must occur within a reasonable time after the buyer discovers or should have discovered the ground for it and before any substantial change in condition of the goods which is not caused by their own defects. It is not effective until the buyer notifies the seller of it.
>
> (3) A buyer who so revokes has the same rights and duties with regard to the goods involved as if the buyer had rejected them.

The buyer may revoke acceptance "of a lot or commercial unit whose nonconformity substantially impairs its value to the buyer" when the buyer has accepted the goods "[o]n the reasonable assumption that its nonconformity would be cured and it has not been seasonably cured."

WIS. STAT. § 402.608(1)(a). The revocation must occur "within a reasonable time after the buyer discovers ... the ground [for revocation] and ... is not effective until the buyer notifies the seller" of the revocation. WIS. STAT. § 402.608(2). Ordinarily, what constitutes a reasonable time is a question of fact for the factfinder.

Country Pasta knew when its technicians did their "checkout" of the tin-tie applicator in Viking's plant that the machine did not function satisfactorily on Country Pasta bags. When all of the machines arrived in Montana in June 2008, and were installed in the Country Pasta plant, Country Pasta could see that the problem had not been fixed. Parrish came to instruct employees and assist with installation. Country Pasta knew that Parrish had not been able to fix the problem when he left in June because Country Pasta agreed to pay for half of his cost to return and try again.

Country Pasta knew in July 2008 that the problem it perceived with the tin-tie applicator continued because Parrish told Country Pasta the machine would not work on Country Pasta's product. Because the seller's agent made repeated repairs to a machine at the buyer's request and the machine still did not work as the contract required, the buyer knew, or should have known that the machine would not do good work, and could not be made to do good work. *See Walter A. Wood Mowing & Reaping Mach. Co. v. Calvert*, 89 Wis. 640, 643–45 (1895).

The trial court found that when Parrish "told [Country Pasta's] employees that the tin-tie applicator would not work, that certainly ... was an indication ... that there was not going to be additional work done." The trial court also found that "there was no evidence presented at trial as to any further discussion of [additional work]." Thereafter, as the trial court found, Country Pasta "could not reasonably assume that the nonconformity of the machinery would be cured." These findings make revocation under WIS. STAT. § 402.608(1)(a) and (2) unavailable to Country Pasta.

CONCLUSION

We conclude that Country Pasta accepted the packaging system when it was delivered to the Country Pasta plant and Country Pasta noted no defects in the equipment. *See* WIS. STAT. § 402.606. Thereafter, Viking twice responded to Country Pasta's requests for installation assistance. When Viking told Country Pasta the tin-tie applicator could not be made to perform as Country Pasta wished, Country Pasta never requested further assistance from Viking and thus could not have reasonably believed Viking was making further efforts to resolve the problem.

Country Pasta made no effort at any time to revoke its earlier acceptance of the entire package under WIS. STAT. § 402.606(1)(c). Instead, four or five months after Country Pasta was told that the tin-tie applicator could not be made to perform to Country Pasta's satisfaction, Country Pasta attempted to revoke its acceptance of only that part of the commercial unit. Such partial revocation of acceptance of a commercial unit is barred under WIS. STAT. § 402.608(1)(a) and (2). Viking did not breach this contract and Country Pasta's counterclaims were properly dismissed.

Judgment and order affirmed.

SECTION TWO: THEORIES OF CAUSATION, DAMAGES, AND OTHER REMEDIES FOR NON-PERFORMANCE UNDER ARTICLE 2 OF THE UCC

A. The UCC and Competing Theories of Causation

Again, to satisfy one element of a complainant's *prima facie* case, the plaintiff must prove that a breached contract was the cause of a loss. But that burden is very different from requiring a complainant to select a legally sufficient methodology or theory of causation to prove the connection between a breach and a loss. Put simply, under the common law, one finds multiple theories of causation. And a plaintiff's *theory of recovery* usually dictates the *theory of causation* that a jury or judge must apply.

Theories of causation appear in various flavors. First, among principles of insurance law, one finds the "efficient proximate cause" and "dominant efficient cause" doctrines. Under the latter, a property insurer is liable for a loss, if a "covered peril" or a "risk insured against" is the dominant efficient cause of the loss. *See Fidelity Southern Fire Ins. Co. v. Crow*, 390 S.W.2d 788, 793 (Tex. Civ. App.—Waco 1965). Similarly, under the former doctrine, an insurer is liable for a property loss if a "covered risk is the predominant or efficient proximate cause of the loss. *See Garvey v. State Farm Fire & Casualty Company*, 770 P.2d 704, 707 (Ca. 1989).

Second, among tort-based principles, one finds the foreseeability doctrine. *See Palsgraf v. Long Island R. Co.*, 162 N.E. 99, 103 (N.Y. 1928) ("Everyone owes to the world at large the duty of refraining from those acts that may unreasonably threaten the safety of others.") (Andrews, J., dissenting). In *Doe v. Boys Clubs of Greater Dallas, Inc.*, 907 S.W.2d 472, 477–78 (Tex. 1995), the Texas Supreme Court explained the tort-based foreseeability doctrine, citing in part the RESTATEMENT (SECOND) OF TORTS § 435(2) (1965). The court stated:

> The components of proximate cause are cause in fact and foreseeability. These elements cannot be established by mere conjecture, guess, or speculation. ... The test for cause in fact is whether the negligent "act or omission was a substantial factor in bringing about injury," without which the harm would not have occurred. ... Foreseeability, the other aspect of proximate cause, requires that a person of ordinary intelligence should have anticipated the danger created by a negligent act or omission. ... It asks whether the injury "might reasonably have been contemplated" as a result of the defendant's conduct. Foreseeability requires more than someone, viewing the facts in retrospect, theorizing an extraordinary sequence of events whereby the defendant's conduct brings about the injury.

Third, as discussed in CHAPTER 5, an English court fashioned a contract-based foreseeability test in *Hadley v. Baxendale,* 9 Exch. 341, 354 (1854). Once more, the *Hadley* foreseeability doctrine is substantially stricter than the *Palsgraf* doctrine. In *Hadley*, Baron Alderson concluded: "Where two parties have made a contract which one of them has broken, the damages which the other party ought to receive ... should be such as ... may reasonably be supposed to have been in the contemplation of both parties, at the time they made the contract. ..." 156 Eng. Rep. at 151. It is worth repeating, however, that the application of the *Hadley* strict foreseeability test has been disappearing in American courts. For example, in *Hector Martinez & Co. v. Southern Pacific Transportation Co.*, 606 F.2d 106, 110 (5th Cir. 1979), the Court of Appeals for the Fifth Circuit declared: "[A complainant] need only demonstrate that his harm was not so remote as to make it unforeseeable at the time of contracting."

To repeat, under certain situations, Article 2 also requires a plaintiff to prove causation. Therefore, the following questions are warranted: Does the UCC require a complaining party to use a UCC-specific theory of causation to establish the connection between a breach of a sales contract and damages? Are UCC and common-law theories of causation different? Several courts have addressed these important questions.

For example, in J. WIGHT AND S. SUMMERS, HANDBOOK OF THE LAW UNDER THE UNIFORM COMMERCIAL CODE 396–397 (1980), the authors concluded:

> To sum up what we have said about consequential damages, 2-715(2) codifies the more liberal reading of *Hadley v. Baxendale*. Most of the courts have recognized that a seller is liable for all damages resulting from his breach if they arise from circumstances that the seller knew about or had reason to know about, even if he did not consciously assume the risk of such liability. The plaintiff can recover lost profits if the

> seller had reason to know at the time of contracting that if he breached the contract the plaintiff would be deprived of those profits. But subsection (2) imposes two restrictions on the recovery of consequential damages in addition to the foreseeability requirement: they must be reasonably ascertainable, and the plaintiff cannot recover for losses he reasonably could have prevented. While damages for injuries to person and property may be recovered under 2-715(2)(b) even if they were not foreseeable, the requirement that injuries proximately result from a breach of warranty probably embraces the mitigation restriction.
>
> Section 2-715(2) is remarkably brief in light of its impact; whether or not consequential damages are allowed can mean the difference between a fifty-cent and a million-dollar damages award. For example, if a defective fifty-cent bolt snaps, it may cause the deaths of thirty children riding a school bus or the break-down for several months of a giant generator needed to operate a factory. The consequential damages provisions provide the only Code remedy that can come close to fully compensating plaintiffs in these cases. Because of the brevity and significance of 2-715, it is important to remember that it draws on over a century of common law development, which began with *Hadley v. Baxendale*.

In *Massey-Ferguson, Inc. v. Evans,* 406 So.2d 15, 19–20 (Miss. 1981), the Supreme Court of Mississippi embraced Wight and S. Summers' analysis and applied the *Hadley* foreseeability test or theory of causation to the facts. The court concluded:

> Section 75-2-715(2)(a) defines consequential damages as follows: "any loss resulting from general or particular requirements and needs of which the seller at the time of contracting had reason to know and which could not reasonably be prevented by cover or otherwise. ..." This section has been interpreted to allow a plaintiff to recover lost profits if the seller has reason to know at the time of contracting that if he breached the contract, the plaintiff would be deprived of those profits. The subsection also imposes two restrictions in addition to foreseeability. The damages must be reasonably ascertainable and the plaintiff cannot recover from losses he reasonably could have prevented.

Also, in *Cricket Alley Corp. v. Data Terminal Sys.,* 732 P.2d 719, 724–25 (Kan. 1987), the Kansas Supreme Court cited the Official UCC COMMENT 3 to K.S.A. 84-2-715. It reads in pertinent part:

> In the absence of excuse under the section on merchant's excuse by failure of presupposed conditions, the seller is liable

> for consequential damages in all cases where he had reason to know of the buyer's general or particular requirements at the time of contracting. It is not necessary that there be a conscious acceptance of an insurer's liability on the seller's part, nor is his obligation for consequential damages limited to cases in which he fails to use due effort in good faith.
>
> Particular needs of the buyer must generally be made known to the seller while general needs must rarely be made known to charge the seller with knowledge."

Embracing the analysis in COMMENT 3, the *Cricket Alley* court reached a conclusion—very similar to the court's conclusion in *Massey-Ferguson*:

> In this action plaintiff sought consequential and incidental damages. DTS contends that, as a matter of law, plaintiff was not entitled to recover any consequential damages and consideration of same should not have been submitted to the jury. The parties concede K.S.A. 84-2-714 and 2-715 constitute the applicable law. ... The consequential damages consist of increased labor costs attributable to the failure of the DTS cash registers to communicate with the Wang computer. DTS contends that it did not know the general or particular requirements and needs of plaintiff's business at the time the express warranties were made and, hence, has no liability under K.S.A. 84-2-715(2)(a) for consequential damages.
>
> DTS concedes that K.S.A. 84-2-715(2)(a) is "simply a codification" of the old tests contained in *Hadley v. Baxendale*, 9 Ex. 341, 156 Eng. Rep. 145 (1854). Computerized cash registers are manufactured for use in retail business establishments. DTS sought to attract retail merchants to their products by advertising in trade magazines and the setting up of a major display of their wares at a national convention of the National Retail Merchants Association where it employed a number of persons to be on hand to answer questions of the convention delegates concerning its products. ... The submission of data from the cash registers to the mainline computer on sales, payrolls, inventory, etc. is a common feature of such equipment and the failure of the cash registers to do so would foreseeably create additional labor costs for the afflicted retail merchants. The additional labor costs sought by plaintiff, herein, as consequential damages are not attributable to any unique features of plaintiff's business. We conclude that consequential damages as an element of plaintiff's damages were properly submitted to the jury herein.

B. In a Nutshell: Breach-of-Contract and Breach-of-Warranty Damages Under the Common Law

Once more, *Hadley v. Baxendale* present rules, which determine when triers of fact must award breach-of-contract as well as breach-of-warranty damages. Generally, a complainant may recover if the plaintiff proves: 1) the damages arose naturally or according to the usual course of things from the breach of contract; 2) the damages are the "probable result of the breach" and the contracting parties contemplated the likelihood of such damages when fashioning the agreement; and 3) "special circumstances"—which were discussed during the formation of the contract—caused the damages.

More specifically, under *Hadley*, a plaintiff may recover contract, compensatory, or actual damages when a loss is "the natural, probable, and foreseeable consequence" of a defendant's breach. Quite simply, compensatory damages appear in two flavors. "Reliance damages" are awarded to make a plaintiff whole—to return the plaintiff to the position that he occupied before entering into the contract and before a breach. *See MCI Communications Services, Inc. v. F.D.I.C.*, 808 F. Supp. 2d 24, 30 (C.C.D.D.C. 2011). Under the common law, reliance damages are essentially out-of-pocket damages—the difference between the value of the buyer's consideration and the value of the goods or services that the buyer received. *Arthur Andersen & Co. v. Perry Equip. Corp.*, 945 S.W.2d 812, 817 (Tex. 1997).

Conversely, "expectancy damages" are designed to put a nonbreaching party in a position that the party would have occupied if the contract had been performed. *RSB Bedford Associates LLC v. Ricky's Williamsburg, Inc.*, 2012 WL 1699844, *2 (N.Y. Sup. Ct. May 9, 2012). Expectancy damages are similar to benefit-of-the-bargain damages. *See Qaddura v. Indo-European Foods, Inc.,* 141 S.W.3d 882, 888–89 (Tex. App.—Dallas 2004, pet denied). Under the common law, a trier of fact determines benefit-of-the-bargain damages by computing the difference between the represented value of goods and the value of the goods received. *Arthur Andersen & Co.*, 945 S.W.2d at 816.

Furthermore, under *Hadley*, a complainant may receive consequential or "special" damages. They "result naturally, but not necessarily from the defendant's wrongful acts." *Arthur Andersen & Co.*, 945 S.W.2d at 816. *See also, Frunzi v. Paoli Services, Inc.*, 2012 WL 2691164,*8 (Del. Super. Ct. July 6, 2012) ("Consequential damages are those that result 'naturally but not necessarily from the wrongful act, because they require the existence of some other contract or relationship.' Consequential damages are not recoverable unless they are foreseeable and are traceable to the wrongful act and result from it.").

Additionally, a party may secure incidental damages, which are "reasonable expenses incident to the breach." *Caplin v. Laser Center of*

Northeastern Connecticut, LLC, 2011 WL 4089579, *4 (Conn. Super. Ct. July 6, 2011). *See also West Virginia American Water Co. v. Nagy*, 2011 WL 8583425, *4 (W.Va.) (reaffirming that incidental damages also include compensation for humiliation, embarrassment, emotional and mental distress, and loss of personal dignity.) Finally, liquidated damages are the amount money that a party agrees to pay for breaching a contract, based on a good-faith estimate of actual damages. *Wasserman's, Inc. v. Twp. of Middletown*, 137 N.J. 238, 248–49 (N.J. 1994).

As discussed above, Article 2 of the UCC codifies *Hadley*. However, stressing an even earlier observation, the common law does not contain separate sets of damages rules for buyers and sellers. On the other hand, discrete remedies and damages provisions appear in Article 2 for buyers and sellers, respectively. Therefore, one might ask: Are consequential and incidental damages calculated differently for buyers and sellers under the UCC? Is the computation of, say, consequential damages under Article 2 comparable to the measure of damages under the common law? Are the common-law and UCC's definitions of consequential damages identical?

The latter two questions are quite important. And to underscore this assertion, consider the Kansas Court of Appeals' analysis in *Hochman v. American Family Ins. Co.*, 673 P.2d 1200, 1202–03 (Kan. Ct. App. 1984):

> Neither party to this action has addressed the applicability of *Schatz Distributing Co. v. Olivetti Corp. of America,* 647 P.2d 820 (Kan. App. 1982) to the issue before us. It would appear this case is the only Kansas authority addressing whether interest can be allowed as compensatory damages in breach of contract actions. *Schatz* involved the breach of a U.C.C. warranty in the sale of a computer. When the breach was discovered, plaintiff was paying for the computer through a financing scheme arranged by defendant with a third party. ... [The] plaintiff requested—as consequential damages—the amount it had paid in interest. After examining other breach-of-warranty cases, we [concluded that the interest was] recoverable as consequential damages. The decision was based on the U.C.C.'s definition of consequential damages—which includes "any loss resulting from general or particular requirements and needs ... which the seller at the time of contracting had reason to know."
>
> Although the U.C.C. does not apply to the case at bar, the common-law rule of consequential damages is not very different from that of the U.C.C. The common-law rule may be stated thus: damages recoverable for breach of contract are limited to those which may fairly be considered as arising, in the usual course of things, from the breach itself, or as may

> reasonably be assumed to have been within the contemplation of both parties as the probable result of the breach. ... [A]s the official U.C.C. Comment to K.S.A. § 84-2-715 observes, [the common-law rule] is actually more "liberal" in its scope of recovery than its counterpart in the U.C.C.

As the *Hochman* court stressed, the respective UCC and common-law damages rules are not mirror images of each other. Depending on conditions or circumstances, common-law damages awards might be more "liberal" or "conservative" than damages awards under the UCC. However, in the following sections, selected cases illustrate how courts apply different sets of rules to grant or deny buyers and sellers' respective requests for consequential and incidental damages under the UCC. It is also important to stress: When sellers deliver nonconforming goods to buyers or fail to deliver conforming goods to buyers, the UCC outlines different rules for awarding buyers' damages. Likewise, when buyers accept *or* fail to accept conforming goods, different sets of UCC rules apply to determine sellers' damages.

In addition, pay close attention to the equations that courts employ to compute various damages awards for sellers and buyers, respectively. Are there significant differences between the two sets of UCC equations? Are the UCC formulas substantially equivalent to the measures of consequential and incidental damages under the common law?

C. Buyer's Damages Awards Under the UCC

1. Seller Has the Goods and Seller Breaches Contract

NHF Hog Marketing, Inc. v. Pork-Martin, LLP
811 N.W.2d 116
(Minn. Ct. App. 2012)

PETERSON, JUDGE. Appellant NHF Hog Marketing Inc. is a hog-marketing business, and respondent Pork-Martin LLP is a business that owns and finishes hogs. In November 2005, NHF entered into a master hog-procurement contract (master contract) with third-party J.B.S. Swift, under which NHF agreed to deliver approximately 750,000 hogs to Swift each year from January 2006 through December 2010. The master contract required that the hogs come from designated production facilities specified in the contract and that the hogs meet specified quality requirements. The contract provided that NHF would be paid a base price equal to market price, subject to adjustments if the market price per carcass hundred weight fluctuated above or below a specified range. To meet the requirements of the master contract, NHF entered into contracts with operators of designated production facilities, including Pork-Martin.

In January 2006, NHF and Pork-Martin entered into a hog-procurement contract, under which Pork-Martin agreed to deliver 2,333 market-weight hogs per month to NHF. The price terms of the hog-procurement contract and the master contract were the same, except that Pork-Martin was paid $0.33 less per carcass hundred weight than NHF received from Swift. The $0.33 difference between the price that NHF paid Pork-Martin and the price that NHF received from Swift was NHF's commission for negotiating and coordinating Pork-Martin's delivery of hogs to Swift. In May 2008, the market price for hogs increased, and Pork-Martin stopped delivering hogs under the hog-procurement contract and sold its hogs to another buyer.

NHF brought this breach-of-contract action against Pork-Martin, seeking damages equal to the difference between the hog-procurement-contract price and the market price at the time the hogs were to have been delivered to Swift. NHF sought total damages of $439,844.95. Of this amount, $396,647.45 was for damages incurred by Swift under the master contract due to Pork-Martin's failure to deliver hogs. This amount is the difference between the market price on the day the hogs were to be delivered to Swift and the sale price under the master contract; it is the additional amount that Swift would have had to pay to buy hogs when Pork-Martin failed to deliver. The remaining $43,197.50 in damages sought was for the commission that NHF lost when Pork-Martin failed to deliver and no sale occurred.

The case was tried to the court. At the time of trial, Swift had not started any action against NHF to enforce the terms of the master contract, and NHF presented no evidence indicating that Swift was likely to insist on performance. The district court awarded NHF $43,197.50 in damages. This appeal followed.

ISSUE

Did the district court err in limiting NHF's damages to its lost commission?

ANALYSIS

This court reviews issues of statutory construction *de novo*. Uniform laws are interpreted "to effect their general purpose to make uniform the laws of those states which enact them." MINN. STAT. § 645.22 (2010). Accordingly, "we give great weight to other states' interpretations of a uniform law." *Johnson v. Murray*, 648 N.W.2d 664, 670 (Minn. 2002).

NHF argues that, under the Uniform Commercial Code (U.C.C.), in addition to its lost commission, it is entitled to damages in the amount of the difference between the master-contract price and the market price at the time Pork-Martin failed to deliver the hogs. The U.C.C. states:

> (1) Subject to the provisions of this article with respect to proof of market price (section 336.2-723), the measure of damages for nondelivery or repudiation by the seller is the difference between the market price at the time when the buyer learned of the breach and the contract price together with any incidental and consequential damages provided in this article (section 336.2-715), but less expenses saved in consequence of the seller's breach.
>
> (2) Market price is to be determined as of the place for tender or, in cases of rejection after arrival or revocation of acceptance, as of the place of arrival. MINN. STAT. § 336.2-713 (2010).

Minnesota's appellate courts have not addressed whether a buyer is entitled to market-differential damages under this statute when those damages exceed actual damages. Courts in other jurisdictions are divided on the issue. *See Allied Canners & Packers, Inc. v. Victor Packing Co.*, 162 Cal.App.3d 905, 912 (1984) (noting division). One view is that U.C.C. § 2-713, codified in Minnesota as section 336.2-713, is a statutory liquidated-damages provision and, therefore, damages should not be limited to a plaintiff's actual economic loss.

The other view, which is urged by Pork-Martin, is that a buyer's damages should be limited to actual damages. This view is consistent with the U.C.C. policy that remedies provided by the Uniform Commercial Code must be liberally administered to the end that the aggrieved party may be put in as good a position as if the other party had fully performed but neither consequential or special damages nor penal damages may be had except as specifically provided in the Uniform Commercial Code or by other rule of law. MINN. STAT. § 336.1-305 (2010).

Pork-Martin's position was adopted in *H-W-H Cattle Co. v. Schroeder,* 767 F.2d 437 (8th Cir. 1985). In *H-W-H*, the buyer contracted to buy cattle from the seller and resell them to a third party. *H-W-H*, 767 F.2d at 438. The market price of cattle increased, the seller breached the contract, and the buyer sought damages under U.C.C. § 2-713 as codified in Iowa, and corresponding to MINN. STAT. § 336.2-713. The United States Court of Appeals for the Eighth Circuit upheld the district court's award of lost-profits damages, stating that adopting the buyer's position would result in a windfall to the buyer and violate the general principle of remedies underlying the statutory provision corresponding to MINN. STAT. § 336.1-305.

NHF argues that *H-W-H* is distinguishable because the issue in *H-W-H* was whether the parties modified the contract to allow for a later delivery date. In *H-W-H*, the price of cattle increased during the spring and then fell to the contract price during the fall. Although the district court found that the parties modified the contract to allow for a later delivery date, the Eighth Circuit did not address that issue. The court stated, "Because we affirm the district court's judgment on the basis of restricting its recovery to its expectancy interest in lost commission, we find it unnecessary to review whether the parties modified the delivery date of the contract." *Id.* at 440.

The position taken by *H-W-H* and *Allied* is favored by commentators James J. White and Robert S. Summers ... [who] state:

> Courts should take care to apply the *Allied* and *H-W-H* limitation narrowly. First, it should be applied only when the defendant proves that the plaintiff's expected resale profit was less than the 2-713 differential; we would not impose the burden of proving the negative on the plaintiff as part of its case in chief. Second, in any case in which the buyer's resale purchaser will likely insist upon performance, the buyer's damages should not be limited to the buyer's expected resale profit, for in that case the buyer will be liable in damages to its own purchaser equal to the difference between the buyer's resale contract price and the market price (or will have to cover at market price in order to make delivery). ...
>
> We recognize that the prospect of a reduction in damages may have some impact upon a seller's willingness to perform, and may make the security of a buyer's expectations somewhat smaller than would otherwise be the case. Arguably, too, our position will unjustly enrich an occasional seller and may also make the trial more complicated. Even so, we think our overall position is more faithful to the idea that the contract plaintiff should recover only his lost expectancy. That idea is deeply entrenched in Anglo-American common law and is adopted in section 1-305 of Revised Article One and its predecessor section 1-106 of the Uniform Commercial Code. Limiting the plaintiff to expectation damages also preserves the possibility of what economists call efficient breach, an idea endorsed by one of your authors[a].

We are persuaded that the position adopted in *H-W-H* and *Allied* and favored by White and Summers is the better approach. The damages awarded by the district court put NHF in as good a position as if Pork-Martin had fully performed. We, therefore, hold that a buyer's damages under MINN. STAT. § 336.2-713 are limited to the buyer's actual

---

a James J. White & Robert S. Summers, Uniform Commercial Code § 6-4, at 413–14 (5th ed. 2006).

damages when the breaching seller shows that the buyer's expected resale profit was less than market-differential damages and the buyer fails to show a likelihood that the resale purchaser will enforce the resale contract.

DECISION

Because NHF's actual damages were limited to its lost commission and there was no showing of a likelihood of enforcement of the master contract, the district court properly awarded NHF damages of $43,197.50 for its lost commission.

Affirmed.

UNIFORM COMMERCIAL CODE

§ 2-711. BUYER'S REMEDIES IN GENERAL; BUYER'S SECURITY INTEREST IN REJECTED GOODS

(1) Where the seller fails to make delivery or repudiates or the buyer rightfully rejects or justifiably revokes acceptance then with respect to any goods involved, and with respect to the whole if the breach goes to the whole contract (Section 2-612), the buyer may cancel and whether or not he has done so may in addition to recovering so much of the price as has been paid

(a) "cover" and have damages under the next section as to all the goods affected whether or not they have been identified to the contract; or

(b) recover damages for non-delivery as provided in this Article (Section 2-713).

(2) Where the seller fails to deliver or repudiates the buyer may also

(a) if the goods have been identified recover them as provided in this Article (Section 2-502); or

(b) in a proper case obtain specific performance or replevy the goods as provided in this Article (Section 2-716).

(3) On rightful rejection or justifiable revocation of acceptance a buyer has a security interest in goods in his possession or control for any payments made on their price and any expenses reasonably incurred in their inspection, receipt,

transportation, care and custody and may hold such goods and resell them in like manner as an aggrieved seller (§ 2-706).

§ 2-712. "COVER"; BUYER'S PROCUREMENT OF SUBSTITUTE GOODS

(1) After a breach within the preceding section the buyer may "cover" by making in good faith and without unreasonable delay any reasonable purchase of or contract to purchase goods in substitution for those due from the seller.

(2) The buyer may recover from the seller as damages the difference between the cost of cover and the contract price together with any incidental or consequential damages as hereinafter defined (Section 2-715), but less expenses saved in consequence of the seller's breach.

(3) Failure of the buyer to effect cover within this section does not bar him from any other remedy.

§ 2-713. BUYER'S DAMAGES FOR NON-DELIVERY OR REPUDIATION

(1) Subject to the provisions of this Article with respect to proof of market price (Section 2-723), the measure of damages for non-delivery or repudiation by the seller is the difference between the market price at the time when the buyer learned of the breach and the contract price together with any incidental and consequential damages provided in this Article (Section 2-715), but less expenses saved in consequence of the seller's breach.

(2) Market price is to be determined as of the place for tender or, in cases of rejection after arrival or revocation of acceptance, as of the place of arrival.

2. Buyer Has the Goods and Seller Breaches the Contract

General Supply & Equipment Company, Inc. v. Phillips
490 S.W.2d 913
(Tex. Civ. App. 1972)

MOORE, JUSTICE. ... Appellant, General Supply and Equipment Company, Inc., was engaged in the business of selling greenhouse covering products—known as P.V.C. panels or polyvinyl-chloride. Appellee, Harry S. Phillips, owned and operated four large greenhouses in Smith County, Texas, and was engaged in the business of growing and selling plants. ... [But he] was principally in the business of growing "'mums"—chrysanthemum. The appellant mailed out certain advertising material to greenhouse owners to promote sales of its P.V.C. paneling product.

The advertising material invited inquiries concerning P.V.C. paneling. Phillips received some of the material containing the following statements:

> How are you planning to cover your plants this year ... with single season polyethylene ... two or three season P.V.C. soft ag film ... Or five to seven year rigid corrugated PVC panels? Finest Quality—Import PVC Rigid Plastic Panels from World-Famous Mitsubishi, 1¼ and 2½ Corrugations, 26 , 28 wide 8 , 10 , 12 long. Tests show no deteriaration (sic) in 5 years of normal use. Because of the tremendous increase in the use of P.V.C. Panels and Film, and the uncertainty of shipping schedules in the Far East, we must know your requirements for summer and fall construction now to guarantee delivery. From Japan ... a land where floral and agricultural growing skills are legendary ... comes a modern material that meets all requirements of greenhouse construction ... perfectly. Light in weight, easy to handle, easy to work. It's tough and virtually indestructible; provides maximum protection. And its light stability is exceptional. It won't turn black or discolor ... even after years of exposure.

Another advertisement from the appellant stated its P.V.C. paneling would "not burn, rot, rust or mildew." After numerous conversations, a representative of appellant traveled to appellee's place of business offering construction and operation suggestions and thereafter appellee purchased the P.V.C. paneling. It is undisputed that the paneling darkened and turned black within a period of approximately two years after it was installed on the greenhouses. As a result the mums failed to grow and the blooms failed to mature, thereby causing appellee substantial damages.

The primary question presented by appellant's points one through seven is whether appellant made any affirmations of fact or promises to appellee relating to the paneling amounting to an express warranty or whether the representations were merely appellant's opinion or commendation of the goods and the value thereof. In this connection appellant urges that there is no evidence to support the jury's finding of an express warranty and that the jury's finding that the statements made by appellant were not mere statements of opinion is against the overwhelming weight and preponderance of the evidence. The points appear to be without merit and are overruled.

Section 2.313 of the TEXAS BUSINESS AND COMMERCE CODE (U.C.C.) provides that "any affirmation of fact or promise made by the seller to the buyer which relates to the goods and becomes part of the basis of the bargain" is an express warranty. To recover money damages under the theory of express warranty in Texas, one must prove: (1) an affirmation of fact or promise made by the seller to the buyer relating to the goods; (2) such affirmation of fact or promise became a part of the basis of the bargain; (3) that the injured party, in making the purchase, relied on the representations, affirmations of fact or promises; (4) that the goods sold by the seller failed to comply with the promises or affirmations of fact made by the seller; (5) that the buyer, because of such failure, was financially injured; and (6) that such failure to comply was a proximate cause of the financial injury suffered by the buyer.

The test for whether a given representation is a "warranty" or a mere expression of opinion is: did the seller assume to assert a fact of which the buyer is ignorant, or did he merely express a judgment about a thing as to which they may each be expected to have an opinion. *Wedding v. Duncan*, 310 Ky. 374, 220 S.W.2d 564 (1969).

As we view the record, the appellant made more than one affirmation of fact to appellee relating to the quality of the panels: (1) that "tests show no deterioration in 5 years of normal use," (2) "It won't turn black or discolor ... even after years of exposure," and (3) it "will not burn, rot, rust or mildew." The record shows that appellee had no knowledge of any of these facts. It is without dispute that the panels commenced turning dark after about two years' use causing a diminution of light in the greenhouses.

Whether the retailer or his agent affirmed a fact or made a promise concerning the product amounting to a warranty is usually a question of fact for the jury. *Lindroth v. Walgreen Co.*, 407 Ill. 121, 94 N.Ed.2d 847 (1950). When viewed in a light most favorable to the verdict, we think the jury's answer ... is amply supported by the evidence. After a careful review of all the evidence we find that we are unable to agree with appellant's contention that the statements and representations of appellant amounted to nothing more than a mere expression of opinion. Consequently we cannot agree with appellant's contention that [the finding] is against the overwhelming weight and preponderance of the evidence. ...

[A]ppellant challenged the judgment on the ground that there is no evidence to support the jury's finding that appellant's failure to comply with the express warranty proximately caused appellee financial injury as found by the jury. ... Appellee testified that two years after the roof had been installed, the plants began to "stretch" or reach up for more light. The stems became thin. The leaves were too far apart and the blooms were small. He attributed this condition to a lack of light transmission through the panels. He testified that this was caused by the panels becoming clouded and dark.

Ben Browning—the County Agent of Smith County—testified he observed the panels and found them to be turning dark. He testified that light was a critical factor in the growing of flowers, and there was a shortage of light coming through the roof and as a result the plants were not getting enough light. Appellee testified that "due to the lack of light the mums failed to mature properly, [and] … those that reached the flower stage were small in size which adversely affected the sale's price and other plants failed to bloom and became worthless."

Ordinarily, the issue of proximate cause is a question of fact for the determination of the jury. 40 Tex.Jur.2d, § 165, at 708. The issue of proximate cause may be proved by circumstantial evidence. *Hopson v. Gulf Oil Corp.*, 237 S.W.2d 352 (Tex. 1951). When viewed in a light most favorable to the verdict, we are convinced that there was ample evidence raising the issue of proximate cause.

All other points brought forward by appellant challenging the judgment fixing liability on appellant based upon the findings of a breach of an express warranty have been considered and found to be without merit and are overruled. In view of the foregoing conclusion, it will not be necessary to discuss other points challenging the judgment decreeing liability for breach of an implied warranty. Rule 434, Texas Rules of Civil Procedure. Suffice it to say, we have reviewed the record and have concluded that there is adequate evidence to sustain the jury's verdict finding that appellee's damage was proximately caused by a breach of both an express warranty and an implied warranty of fitness.

[Also,] … appellant complains of the submission of Special Issue No. 18 on the ground that the issue did not constitute a proper measure of damages. He also complains of the submission of the issue and the jury's finding because he contends that a diminution in market value of the greenhouses was not in the contemplation of the parties at the time of the sale of the goods. The question … which we [confront] is what damages are recoverable by appellee for appellant's breach of warranty.

The applicable statutes are § 2.714(b)-(c), and § 2.715 of the UNIFORM COMMERCIAL CODE, VERNON'S ANNOTATED TEXAS STATUTES. Sec. 2.714 provides in part:

> (b) The measure of damages for breach of warranty is the difference at the time and place of acceptance between the value of the goods accepted and the value they would have had if they had been as warranted, unless special circumstances show proximate damages of a different amount.
>
> (c) In a proper case any incidental and consequential damages under the next section may also be recovered.

Sec. 2.715—Buyer's Incidental and Consequential Damages—reads in pertinent part:

> (a) Incidental damages resulting from the seller's breach include … any other reasonable expense incident to the delay or other breach.

(b) Consequential damages resulting from the seller's breach include

(1) any loss resulting from general or particular requirements and needs of which the seller at the time of contracting had reason to know and which could not reasonably be prevented by cover or otherwise; and

(2) injury to person or property proximately resulting from any breach of warranty.

In the instant case, the ordinary measure of damages for breach of warranty stated in 2.714(b) is not applicable because of special circumstances showing proximate damages of a different amount. The proximate damages in this case consist of incidental and consequential damages as provided by § 2.715. Subsection (a) of § 2.715 is intended to provide reimbursement for the buyer who incurs reasonable expenses incident to the breach of warranty. ... [T]he trial court seems to have assumed that incidental damages included a diminution in market value of the greenhouses. Under the record before us, we do not believe this constituted a proper measure of damages.

When appellee decided to put a new roof on his greenhouses in the fall of 1966, he took off the old roofing on greenhouse No. 2 and replaced it with the P.V.C. paneling purchased from appellant. In the spring of 1967 he replaced the roof on house No. 4. The roofing on houses Nos. 1 and 3 was replaced with P.V.C. panels purchased from appellant sometime in the fall of 1967 or early spring of 1968. After discovering the P.V.C. paneling to be defective, appellee put a new roof on houses Nos. 2 and 4 in October, 1969. Appellee did not replace the defective P.V.C. paneling on houses Nos. 1 and 3, prior to the time he sold all four greenhouses on July 24, 1970. It is without dispute that the roofs on the two greenhouses were replaced without structural damages to the greenhouses.

While the diminution in market value is evidence of damages, it is generally understood that the measure of damages is the cost of repair. *Bowman Steel Corp. v. Lumbermens Mutual Casualty Co.*, 364 F.2d 246 (3rd Cir. 1966); *Winandy Greenhouse Construction, Inc. v. Graham Wholesale Floral, Inc.*, 456 S.W.2d 470 (Tex.Civ.App., Ft. Worth, 1970). We sustain appellant's contention that the diminution in cash market value in this instance is not the proper measure of damages, especially since the evidence shows that the defective paneling was replaced without material damage to the structure. It occurs to us that the incidental damages involved here would be the reasonable cost of replacing the defective paneling with equal quality as that represented by appellant, less the salvage value, if any, of the defective paneling. Therefore, we think the trial court erred [by] ... allowing a recovery based upon the jury finding. ...

[A]ppellant urges that there is no evidence to support the jury's answer ... wherein the jury found that appellee's actual business loss—including lost profits—was $145,322.00. In this connection appellant urges that the testimony as to lost profits was so conjectural and speculative that it amounted to no evidence of probative force establishing damages for lost profits.

Section 2.715(b) provides that the buyer is also entitled to consequential damages resulting from the seller's breach of warranty. This includes loss of profits. Damages for lost profits, however, must not be so indefinite as to be conjectural. Anderson, UNIFORM COMMERCIAL CODE, Sec. 2-715:4. Where the buyer can show "a reasonably definite pattern of sales to customers which they would have made but the buyer did not make them because his customers were dissatisfied with the buyer's product because of a defect traceable to the seller's breach of warranty, the buyer is entitled to recover for loss of profits from the seller in his action for breach of warranty." Anderson, UNIFORM COMMERCIAL CODE, SECOND EDITION, § 2-715:26, at 478–479; *Lewis v. Mobil Oil Corp.*, 438 F.2d 500 (8th Cir. 1971).

In a Committee Comment 4 to § 2.715 of our UNIFORM COMMERCIAL CODE we find:

> The burden of proving the extent of loss incurred by way of consequential damage is on the buyer, but the section on liberal administration of remedies rejects any doctrine of certainty which requires almost mathematical precision in the proof of loss. Loss may be determined in any manner which is reasonable under the circumstances.

The loss of profits in this instance rests solely upon appellee's assumption that if the four greenhouses were fully planted in chrysanthemums, and if they produced flowers as expected, he would have expected to make a profit of $30,240.00 a year. His estimate was based solely upon his own projection that he could grow a crop of "mums every fourteen weeks" and that he would "make a net profit of five cents for each mum sold." As we view the record there is no evidence whatever to support appellee's estimate as to net profits. His testimony clearly shows that he had never made a profit out of mums and that his projections were merely what he thought he should make under the most favorable conditions.

The record shows that in addition to growing mums, appellee also raised other plants in the greenhouses. While he admits he kept no separate set of records on the profits or losses from the sale of the 'mums, his sole and only claim for loss of profits is based upon the losses he contends he sustained on the mums. He does not contend he sustained losses on any of the other plants. According to the testimony of his accountant, the greenhouse business for the fiscal year ending in June, 1967, suffered a loss of $6,882.00; for the year ending in 1968 the business had a profit of $203.41; for the year ending in 1969, the business sustained a loss of $23,817.51 and for the year ending in June, 1970, the business sustained a loss of $53,537.32. The greenhouses were sold on July 24, 1970.

Appellee seeks to uphold the jury's finding of lost profits by arguing that the evidence shows a loss of profit in the amount of $30,240.00 per year. He therefore says that since the panels were warranted for six years the proof was more than ample to sustain the jury's finding of $145,322.00. We do not agree.

The generally accepted rule is that where it is shown that a loss of profit is a natural and probable consequence of the act or omission complained of and that amount is shown with sufficient certainty, there may be a recovery therefor; but anticipated profits cannot be recovered where they are dependent upon uncertain and changing conditions—such as market fluctuations or a change of business, or where there is no evidence from which they may be intelligently estimated. Evidence to establish profits must not be uncertain or speculative. It is not necessary that profits should be susceptible of exact calculation; it is sufficient that there be data from which they may be ascertained with a reasonable degree of certainty and exactness. *Southwest Battery Corporation v. Owen*, 115 S.W.2d 1097 (Tex. 1938). ...

While we believe the evidence was sufficient to show a loss of at least some profits, we think the case was tried and submitted on the wrong theory of damages. As we view the record, the proper measure of damages for lost profits in this instance [is] the difference between the reasonable market value of each crop of mums as actually raised and sold and the reasonable market value of the crop which would have been produced and sold had the P.V.C. paneling been as warranted. *Hoopes v. East*, 19 Tex. Civ. App. 531, 48 S.W. 764 (1898). ... This measure of damages would include lost profits and would also allow for a fluctuation in the market price. ...

Under the record before us, we are of the opinion that the ends of justice would be better served by reversing and remanding for a new trial rather than reversing and rendering.

Reversed and remanded.

Uniform Commercial Code

§ 2-714. Buyer's Damages for Breach in Regard to Accepted Goods

(1) Where the buyer has accepted goods and given notification (subsection (3) of Section 2-607) he may recover as damages

for any non-conformity of tender the loss resulting in the ordinary course of events from the seller's breach as determined in any manner which is reasonable.

(2) The measure of damages for breach of warranty is the difference at the time and place of acceptance between the value of the goods accepted and the value they would have had if they had been as warranted, unless special circumstances show proximate damages of a different amount.

(3) In a proper case any incidental and consequential damages under the next section may also be recovered.

§ 2-715. BUYER'S INCIDENTAL AND CONSEQUENTIAL DAMAGES

(1) Incidental damages resulting from the seller's breach include expenses reasonably incurred in inspection, receipt, transportation and care and custody of goods rightfully rejected, any commercially reasonable charges, expenses or commissions in connection with effecting cover and any other reasonable expense incident to the delay or other breach.

(2) Consequential damages resulting from the seller's breach include

(a) any loss resulting from general or particular requirements and needs of which the seller at the time of contracting had reason to know and which could not reasonably be prevented by cover or otherwise; and

(b) injury to person or property proximately resulting from any breach of warranty.

D. Seller's Damages Awards Under the UCC

1. Buyer Has the Goods and Buyer Breaches the Contract

Morris Graphics, Inc. v. Casey Printing, Inc.
2000 WL 34019592
(C.C.D.R.I. 2000)

TORRES, CHIEF J. Morris Graphics, Inc. brought this action to recover the balance allegedly due on the purchase price for a used printing press that it sold to Casey Printing, Inc. Casey has counter-claimed for the expenses it allegedly incurred to bring the press up to the standard specified in the contract. The matter was tried before this court sitting without a jury. My findings of fact and conclusions of law are as follows.

FINDINGS OF FACT

On August 5, 1997, Morris Graphics, Inc. and Casey Printing, Inc. entered into a Conditional Sales Contract and Security Agreement (Agreement)—wherein Morris agreed to sell and Casey agreed to buy one used Komori printing press L540 III Serial Number 435 with various attachments described in Exhibit A to the Agreement. The Agreement required Morris Graphics to refurbish the press and defined "refurbished" to mean "cleaned, painted as needed, inspected and parts replaced as needed." The Agreement also required Morris to install the press at Casey's shop in King City, California.

Casey was required to provide—at its sole cost—a "suitable foundation, adequate floor conditions, construction, exhaust ducting for the press or its component parts, and/or electrical wiring required, as well as labor and materials (for carpentry, plumbing, masonry, etc.) necessary to remove obstructions, and/or locate the Equipment and any outside labor not authorized in writing by [Morris]."

Installation by Morris Graphics was defined to mean that the press must: 1) produce commercially acceptable printing at its normal speed; 2) accurately register at its normal speed; and 3) be successfully tested. The Agreement contained a "Limited Warranty" provision under which Morris warranted that—at the completion of installation and testing—the press would produce commercially acceptable printing and accurate register at its normal speed on suitable paper. The warranty terminated when installation and testing were completed.

The purchase price was $600,000 for the press plus $50,000 for labor, freight and installation costs. The Agreement required Casey to pay $25,000 to Morris upon the signing of the agreement, and an additional $525,000 prior to shipment. The remaining $100,000 was to be paid upon completion of installation.

The Agreement has a choice-of-law clause, providing that all rights and obligations under the contract shall be governed by the laws of the State of Rhode Island. On September 5, 1997, Bill and Richard Casey—the principals in Casey Printing—visited Morris's place of business in Rhode Island and examined the press. At that time, the press had been disassembled for shipping and some parts had been packed in boxes. Consequently, the Caseys were unable to see the press in operation, but they were able to view most of the components.

After examining the press, Bill Casey paid Lance Burden—Morris' representative—the $525,000 required before shipping. The press was delivered to Casey on Monday, September 8, 1997, and was examined by Randy Falen, a technician hired by Morris Graphics to install the press. Falen discovered that several parts necessary to make the press operational were missing. Falen ordered the parts from the manufacturer, which billed Casey $2,394.60. …

On Tuesday, September 16, 1997, after installing the parts that he ordered, Falen successfully completed a "dry run" of the press without ink. Falen worked on the press for several more days and left Casey Printing on Friday, September 19, 1997. At the time of Falen's departure, the press was operable; but some minor parts still were missing, and the press was not, yet, functioning in accordance with the required standards.

On Monday, September 22, 1997, Bill Casey sent a fax to Burden informing Burden that the press was not fully operational and listing several items that needed to be fixed or replaced. Casey also informed Burden that Robert Saunders—a Komori mechanic—was scheduled to remove another press from Casey Printing, and he suggested that Morris allow Saunders to complete installation of the L540 press.

Burden agreed but made it clear that he was approving only the work listed on Bill Casey's September 22 fax—except for work on the Lateral Register Control board which Burden stated would be performed by Morris. On September 25, 1997, Saunders began working on the press. He corrected most of the problems referred to in Casey's September 22 fax, but identified additional work necessary to make the press fully operational. Komori charged Casey $10,653.25 for the work performed by Saunders.

On September 30, Bill Casey wrote to Burden requesting that the additional work identified by Saunders be performed. … However, Burden failed to respond to the request for additional work contained in Casey's September 30 letter. Casey hired Tom Sivula, a technician, to fix the cylinders. Sivula's fee was $6,265.19—an amount that Morris concedes should be credited to the balance it claims to be due from Casey. Because the press was important to the conduct of Casey's business, Casey also made arrangements to have the additional work referred to in its September 30 letter done without Morris' authorization.

Most of this additional work consisted of correcting electrical problems, which were alluded to in Casey's September 22 and September 30 letters. Casey hired Rai Gurdev—an electrical technician—who worked on the press from October 1 through October 3, 1997 and again on October 9, 1997. In order to complete his work, Gurdev ordered several parts for which Casey was billed. Gurdev was paid the sum of $3,312 for his labor. Taking into account credits for parts that were returned, the net cost of the parts was $8,246.37.

All of the work performed by Gurdev was necessary to complete the installation of the press in accordance with the terms of the Agreement. The cost of additional work required to correct problems listed in Casey's September 22 and September 30 letters was $9,630.78.

Casey also paid King City Electric to upgrade its electrical service to a level necessary to operate the press. However, even if, as Casey claims, Burden erroneously stated that Casey's service was adequate, Casey is not entitled to recover for the amount paid to King City because, under the Agreement, Casey was responsible for providing the electrical connections required to operate the press.

Until November 28, 1997, the press was not capable of operating in accordance with the standards prescribed in the Agreement. On November 28, 1997, the press was fully operational and performed its first five-color job. The total amount expended by Casey Printing to bring the press into conformity with the requirements specified in the Agreement is $38,107.59.

CONCLUSIONS OF LAW

The agreement between the parties is a contract for the sale of goods, controlled by Article 2 of the Rhode Island Uniform Commercial Code (UCC), R.I.G.L. §§ 6A-2-101, *et. seq*. Under § 2-709(1)(a) of the UCC, a seller is entitled to recover the contract price of accepted goods when the price comes due. Casey's actions constituted acceptance of the press within the meaning of § 2-606.

Under the terms of the agreement, the remainder of the purchase price became due when installation was completed. Installation was completed on November 28, 1997, when the press became fully operational. However, because Morris failed to complete the installation, the press that it delivered did not conform to the requirements of the Agreement.

Under § 2-714 of the UCC, a buyer who has accepted nonconforming goods, and given notification of breach to the seller pursuant to § 2-607(3), may recover damages for the nonconformity determined in any manner which is reasonable. The various telephone calls and faxes from Casey to Burden constituted notice of the breach sufficient to satisfy § 2-607(3). The measure of damages for Morris' breach is the amount reasonably expended by Casey to bring the press into conformity with the requirements of the Agreement, namely, $38,107.59.

Under § 2-717, that amount may be deducted from the $100,000 balance due on the purchase price. Therefore, the net amount owed by Casey Printing to Morris Graphics is $61,892.41. There is no need to consider Casey's claims for breach of warranty because the damages to which Casey would be entitled, if successful, would be the same as the damages recoverable for breach of contract. ...

CONCLUSION

For all of the foregoing reasons, the clerk is directed to enter judgment in favor of Morris Graphics, Inc., in the amount of $61,892.41 plus interest. ...

UNIFORM COMMERCIAL CODE

§ 2-709. ACTION FOR THE PRICE

(1) When the buyer fails to pay the price as it becomes due the seller may recover, together with any incidental damages under the next section, the price

(a) of goods accepted or of conforming goods lost or damaged within a commercially reasonable time after risk of their loss has passed to the buyer; and

(b) of goods identified to the contract if the seller is unable after reasonable effort to resell them at a reasonable price or the circumstances reasonably indicate that such effort will be unavailing.

(2) Where the seller sues for the price he must hold for the buyer any goods which have been identified to the contract and are still in his control except that if resale becomes possible he may resell them at any time prior to the collection of the judgment. The net proceeds of any such resale must be credited to the buyer and payment of the judgment entitles him to any goods not resold.

(3) After the buyer has wrongfully rejected or revoked acceptance of the goods or has failed to make a payment due or has repudiated (Section 2-610), a seller who is held not entitled to the price under this section shall nevertheless be awarded damages for non-acceptance under the preceding section.

§ 2-710. SELLER'S INCIDENTAL DAMAGES

Incidental damages to an aggrieved seller include any commercially reasonable charges, expenses or commissions incurred in stopping delivery, in the transportation, care and custody of goods after the buyer's breach, in connection with return or resale of the goods or otherwise resulting from the breach.

---

2. *Seller Has the Goods and Buyer Breaches the Contract*

Karen v. Cane
578 N.Y.S.2d 85
(N.Y. Civ. Ct. 1991)

ROBERTA L. DUNLOP, JUSTICE. In this action, the plaintiff—Herbert Karen, d/b/a Metro Sales Company—seeks to recover the balance due for goods sold to the defendant (Barbara Cane) pursuant to a sales contract executed by the parties. The court sets forth the following as its findings of facts and conclusions of law.

The credible evidence adduced during this non-jury trial de novo established that the defendant purchased goods from the plaintiff through two shop-at-home sales transactions.

In the first sales transaction, the defendant—after reviewing a sales catalogue—ordered a bedroom set which included a spindle headboard, a queen size mattress with support frame, a triple door dresser and a landscape mirror. The price was $1,675 plus tax. During the same transaction, the defendant ordered carpeting with padding which was subsequently delivered and installed in her master bedroom, den and living room. The price of the carpeting was $1,505 plus sales tax. The defendant had requested a price breakdown for each item ordered, but the plaintiff stated "it's a package deal."

In the second sales transaction, the defendant ordered thirty-four square feet of additional carpeting for the price of $740 plus sales tax. The plaintiff made oral representations that if the defendant was not satisfied he would take the furniture back and replace it. During the trial the parties stipulated that the defendant has paid the plaintiff a total of $2539.45. The amount in dispute is $1,704, which is the difference between the amount of the sales contract and the amount actually paid toward the purchases.

This action arose subsequent to the installation of the carpet ordered pursuant to the first sales transaction. On July 12, 1990, the defendant objected to a partial delivery of the bedroom set and the attempted installation of a black carpet instead of a blush color as ordered in the second sales transaction. The plaintiff only delivered the triple door dresser, the queen size mattress with support frame and the incorrect color carpet. Defendant attempted to have the delivery men return the triple door dresser because it was not solid oak. The delivery men refused to take it back on the truck claiming that they had other furniture which had to be delivered and they told the defendant "you bought it you own it."

After the carpet was installed, the plaintiff saw that it was a black color instead of the blush color which she had ordered. She had the installers remove it immediately. Although they left the padding in place, she claims it also had to be removed due to dry rot and mildew.

After several unsuccessful attempts to reach the plaintiff by telephone, the defendant managed to get a call through to him. He assured her that the remainder of the furniture would be delivered as soon as it arrived from the factory. He blamed his workmen for taking the wrong roll of carpet from the warehouse. He informed her that the carpet she ordered was already cut and he would have it delivered and installed.

At the time of the partial delivery, the defendant turned over a post-dated check—as agreed to—in the amount of $700. After the problems arose regarding the partial delivery and wrong carpet, the defendant stopped payment on the check and refused to make any additional payments to the plaintiff. Within three days she had another carpet delivered and installed by a different merchant. The issue to be resolved in this case is whether the plaintiff has proven his entitlement to damages under the Uniform Commercial Code.

Since this is a transaction for the sale of goods, it is governed by Article 2 of the Uniform Commercial Code (U.C.C.). The plaintiff is seeking $1,704, which is the balance allegedly due on the sales contract with the defendant. Plaintiff is seeking to recover the price of the undelivered goods as well as the price of the triple door dresser. An action for the sale price is essentially one for specific performance of the contract of sale. *Pratt Chuck Co. v. Cresent Insulated Wire & Cable Co.*, 33 F.2d 269 (2d Cir. 1929).

In regard to the undelivered goods, section 2-709(1)(b) of the U.C.C. provides:

> When the buyer fails to pay the price as it becomes due the seller may recover, together with any incidental damages under the next section, the price ... of goods identified to the contract if the seller in unable after reasonable effort to resell them at a reasonable price or the circumstances reasonably indicate that such effort will be unavailing. N.Y. U.C.C. § 2-709(1)(b) (McKinney 1980).

In order for a seller of goods to recover under § 2-709(1)(b), the seller must affirmatively allege and prove—as a condition precedent in an action for the purchase price—that the goods could not readily be resold. The burden of establishing that the goods could not be resold rests with the plaintiff. *Barber-Greene Co. v. M.F. Dollard Jr., Inc.*, 196 N.E. 571 (N.Y. 1935).

In a similar case, a Pennsylvania court rejected a seller's plea for the price on a contract for a dining room suite, a bedroom suite, two sofas, a cocktail table and assorted chairs. While that court acknowledged that it might be difficult to sell the goods due to their unusual colors, the court held that the plaintiff had not proved his inability to sell the goods at "reasonably marked down prices." *Bacon Estate*, 45 Pa. D. & C. 2d 733, 739 (Orphan's Ct. 1968).

In the present case, the plaintiff failed to offer any evidence to prove that he attempted to resell the undelivered goods. The plaintiff stated that the carpet was cut to order and therefore not available for resale. However, the plaintiff did not make any efforts to resell the carpet as a remnant. Thus, the plaintiff has failed to establish that he has attempted to resell the undelivered goods and is therefore not entitled to recovery for them under section 2-709(1)(b) of the U.C.C.

In an action for the price of goods under section 2-709(1)(a) of the U.C.C., "when the buyer fails to pay the price as it becomes due the seller may recover ... the price ... of [the] goods accepted. ..." N.Y. U.C.C. § 2-709(1)(a) (McKinney 1980). The facts indicate that the defendant did not accept the triple door dresser. The defendant rejected this item when it was delivered because it was not made of solid oak, but merely oak veneer. While the sales contract did not specifically state that this item be made of solid oak, there is evidence that the plaintiff made oral representations to the defendant to the effect that if the defendant was dissatisfied he would take the items back. A seller may not recover the purchase price of goods where factual questions have been raised regarding the seller's performance under the contract. *American Elec. Power Co., Inc. v. Westinghouse Elec. Corp.*, 418 F.Supp. 435 (S.D.N.Y. 1976).

The defendant has raised factual issues whether the plaintiff has actually breached the sales contract by his non-compliance with his oral representations. In addition, the defendant offered evidence that the queen size mattress is defective and the carpet installed pursuant to the first sales transaction was incorrectly seamed. Therefore, the plaintiff cannot maintain an action for price of the triple door dresser under § 2-709(1)(a) of the U.C.C.

When a seller is not entitled to maintain an action for the price under § 2-709 of the U.C.C., a seller may nevertheless be awarded damages for a buyer's non-compliance under § 2-708 of the U.C.C., N.Y. U.C.C. § 2-709(3) (McKinney 1980). Section 2-708(1) provides:

> Subject to subsection (2) and to the provisions of this Article with respect to proof of market price (Section 2-723), the measure of damages for non-acceptance or repudiation by the buyer is the difference between the market price at the time and place for tender and the unpaid contract price together with any incidental damages provided in this Article (Section 2-710), but less expenses saved in consequence of the buyer's breach.

In an action to recover damages for the buyer's failure or refusal to accept delivery, the burden of proving market price or the market value of goods refused by the buyer rests on the seller. *Haughey v. Belmont Quadrangle Drilling Corp.*, 29 N.E.2d 649 (N.Y. 1940).

After the plaintiff made a partial delivery of the goods and removed the black carpet, the defendant repudiated the contract. While repudiation of a sales contract would normally result in recovery of damages, the plaintiff failed to establish damages in accordance with § 2-708(1) of the U.C.C., in that, the plaintiff did not offer any evidence establishing the difference between the market price and the unpaid contract price. Subsection (2) of § 2-708 of the U.C.C. provides:

> If the measure of damages provided in subsection (1) is inadequate to put the seller in as good a position as performance would have done, then the measure of damages is the profit—including reasonable overhead—which the seller would have made from full performance by the buyer, together with any incidental damages provided in this Article (Section 2-710), due allowance for costs reasonably incurred and due credit for payments or proceeds of resale.

The plaintiff failed to provide any evidence by which the court could determine his lost profit under § 2-708(2) of the U.C.C. Also, the plaintiff failed to introduce evidence that would entitle him to any incidental damages under § 2-710 of the U.C.C.

Accordingly, judgment is entered in favor of the defendant. The plaintiff may retain the $2539.45 paid by the defendant for goods actually delivered. Since the defendant stated that she wants the triple door dresser removed from her apartment, the defendant is directed to permit the plaintiff access to the defendant's apartment so that the plaintiff may remove the rejected triple door dresser.

UNIFORM COMMERCIAL CODE

§ 2-706. SELLER'S RESALE INCLUDING CONTRACT FOR

> (1) Under the conditions stated in Section 2-703 on seller's remedies, the seller may resell the goods concerned or the undelivered balance thereof. Where the resale is made in good faith and in a commercially reasonable manner the seller may recover the difference between the resale price and the contract price together with any incidental damages allowed under the provisions of this Article (Section 2-710), but less expenses saved in consequence of the buyer's breach.

(2) Except as otherwise provided in subsection (3) or unless otherwise agreed resale may be at public or private sale including sale by way of one or more contracts to sell or of identification to an existing contract of the seller. Sale may be as a unit or in parcels and at any time and place and on any terms but every aspect of the sale including the method, manner, time, place and terms must be commercially reasonable. The resale must be reasonably identified as referring to the broken contract, but it is not necessary that the goods be in existence or that any or all of them have been identified to the contract before the breach.

(3) Where the resale is at private sale the seller must give the buyer reasonable notification of his intention to resell.

(4) Where the resale is at public sale

(a) only identified goods can be sold except where there is a recognized market for a public sale of futures in goods of the kind; and

(b) it must be made at a usual place or market for public sale if one is reasonably available and except in the case of goods which are perishable or threaten to decline in value speedily the seller must give the buyer reasonable notice of the time and place of the resale; and

(c) if the goods are not to be within the view of those attending the sale the notification of sale must state the place where the goods are located and provide for their reasonable inspection by prospective bidders; and

(d) the seller may buy.

(5) A purchaser who buys in good faith at a resale takes the goods free of any rights of the original buyer even though the seller fails to comply with one or more of the requirements of this section.

(6) The seller is not accountable to the buyer for any profit made on any resale. A person in the position of a seller (Section 2-707) or a buyer who has rightfully rejected or justifiably revoked acceptance must account for any excess over the amount of his security interest, as hereinafter defined (subsection (3) of Section 2-711).

§ 2-708. SELLER'S DAMAGES FOR NON-ACCEPTANCE OR REPUDIATION

(1) Subject to subsection (2) and to the provisions of this Article with respect to proof of market price (Section 2-723), the measure of damages for non-acceptance or repudiation

by the buyer is the difference between the market price at the time and place for tender and the unpaid contract price together with any incidental damages provided in this Article (Section 2-710), but less expenses saved in consequence of the buyer's breach.

(2) If the measure of damages provided in subsection (1) is inadequate to put the seller in as good a position as performance would have done then the measure of damages is the profit (including reasonable overhead) which the seller would have made from full performance by the buyer, together with any incidental damages provided in this Article (Section 2-710), due allowance for costs reasonably incurred and due credit for payments or proceeds of resale.

§ 2-719. CONTRACTUAL MODIFICATION OR LIMITATION OF REMEDY

(1) Subject to the provisions of subsections (2) and (3) of this section and of the preceding section on liquidation and limitation of damages,

(a) the agreement may provide for remedies in addition to or in substitution for those provided in this Article and may limit or alter the measure of damages recoverable under this Article, as by limiting the buyer's remedies to return of the goods and repayment of the price or to repair and replacement of non-conforming goods or parts; and

(b) resort to a remedy as provided is optional unless the remedy is expressly agreed to be exclusive, in which case it is the sole remedy.

(2) Where circumstances cause an exclusive or limited remedy to fail of its essential purpose, remedy may be had as provided in this Act.

(3) Consequential damages may be limited or excluded unless the limitation or exclusion is unconscionable. Limitation of consequential damages for injury to the person in the case of consumer goods is prima facie unconscionable but limitation of damages where the loss is commercial is not.

3. Lost-Volume Seller's Damages Awards Under the UCC

Under the lost-volume theory, a seller has an effective response to a breaching buyer's assertion that the seller did not mitigate damages. *See Storage Tech. Corp. v. Trust Co. of N.J.*, 842 F.2d 54, 57 (3d Cir. 1988). Or stated slightly differently, a seller can avoid the consequences of a failure-to-mitigate defense if the seller is a lost-volume seller. A complainant bears the burden of demonstrating that it is a lost-volume seller. In *Ullman-Briggs, Inc. v. Salton*, Inc., 754 F.Supp. 1003, 1008–09 (C.C.S.D.N.Y. 1991), the court outlines the test that tribunals generally apply to determine whether a person qualifies as a lost-volume seller:

> It is well-settled that a plaintiff in a contract action must demonstrate both that his damages were caused by the alleged breach and that the alleged loss is capable of proof with reasonable certainty. Damages in a breach of contract action are intended to put the injured party in the same position they would have been in if the contract had been performed. ... [A] party claiming to be a lost volume seller must establish that it would have had the benefit of both the original contract and the subsequent contracts had there not been a breach. ... This test has both objective and subjective components. First, plaintiff must demonstrate that it had the subjective intent to take on the additional lines—that it acquired—had it retained the [original] account. ... Secondly, as an objective component, [a] plaintiff must also establish that it had the capacity to take on extra lines and adequately service them without additional expenditures for staff and other overhead expenses if the defendant had not breached the original contract.

Put simply, a lost-volume seller has two expectations—the profit from the breached contract and the profit from one or more other contracts that the seller could have performed simultaneously. *See Snyder v. Herbert Greenbaum & Assocs.*, 380 A.2d 618, 624 (Md. Ct. Spec. App. 1977). Or stated another way, "[a] lost volume seller is one who has the capacity to perform the contract that was breached in addition to other potential contracts due to unlimited resources or production capacity." *Precision Pine & Timber, Inc. v. United States*, 72 Fed. Cl. 460, 490 (Fed. Cl. 2006).

In the RESTATEMENT (2D) OF CONTRACTS, §§ 347, 350 (1981), one finds a discussion of lost-volume sellers' rights and burdens. In particular, COMMENT f to section 347 reads in relevant part:

> LOST VOLUME. Whether a subsequent transaction is a substitute for the broken contract sometimes raises difficult questions of fact. If the injured party could and would have entered into the subsequent contract, even if the contract had not been broken, and could have had the benefit of both, he can be said to have "lost volume" and the subsequent transaction is not a substitute for the broken contract. The injured party's damages are then based on the net profit that he has lost as a result of the broken contract.

Furthermore, COMMENT d to section 350 states:

> LOST VOLUME. The mere fact that an injured party can make arrangements for the disposition of the goods or services that he was to supply under the contract does not necessarily mean that by doing so he will avoid loss. If he would have entered into both transactions but for the breach, he has "lost volume" as a result of the breach. *See* Comment f to § 347. In that case the second transaction is not a "substitute" for the first one.

Also, it is important to stress: Under the common law, the lost-volume-seller theory applies to services as well as to sale-of-goods contracts. *See Jetz Service Co. v. Salina Props.*, 865 P.2d 1051, 1055–56 (Kan. Ct. App. 1993) (applying the theory to seller of services), and *Gianetti v. Norwalk Hosp.*, 779 A.2d 847, 853 (Conn. Ct. App. 2001) (applying the theory to provider of medical services). Does the UCC codify the lost-volume-seller doctrine? Or, does the UCC create a "unique" version of the doctrine? Consider the facts, analysis, and conclusion in the next case.

Jewish Federation of Greater Des Moines v.
Cedar Forest Products Company
796 N.W.2d 456
(Iowa App. 2003)

VOGEL, P.J. Cedar Forest Products Company appeals the district court's ruling challenging its finding classifying the company as a lost volume seller but not awarding damages for lost profits. ...

BACKGROUND FACTS

Cedar Forest Products Company (CFP) manufactures pre-cut building packages for shelters, pavilions, gazebos, and other structures typically utilized in park, camp, and recreational facilities. The Jewish Federation of Greater Des Moines (Jewish Federation) contracted with CFP for the manufacture of a 3,500 square foot building with unique and customized schematics. With the signing of the Purchase and Sales Agreement, Jewish Federation sent CFP a deposit of $53,605. Shortly thereafter, it prematurely sent the remaining balance of $160,813 for a total contract price of $214,418.

After a series of redesign discussions and change orders, Jewish Federation informed CFP it was rescinding the contract and requested return of all monies paid. CFP returned $160,530.54, but retained $53,887.46 as lost profits it would have made had Jewish Federation not breached the contract. Jewish Federation filed an action for return of the remaining $53,887.46 claiming there had been no meeting of the minds and the agreement was merely a quote based on preliminary schematic drawings.

CFP counterclaimed alleging breach of contract. Both parties filed motions for summary judgment. At the hearing, the district court found the agreement was a completely integrated contract which Jewish Federation had breached. The only issues at trial were whether CFP was a lost volume seller and what measure of damages, if any, should be awarded due to the breach of Jewish Federation. The district court found that CFP was a lost volume seller but, fashioning an equitable remedy, determined it was only entitled to an award of $13,470.17 for incidental damages. The court further limited CFP's award of attorney fees and costs. CFP appeals.

Discussion

CFP agrees with the district court's finding that it is a lost volume seller but disagrees with the court's subsequent application of the law regarding the damages. CFP argues that because it is a lost volume seller it is entitled to damages for lost profits under 810 Illinois Compiled Statutes 5/2-708(2) (2001). Jewish Federation, while not directly addressing the relevant code sections, contends the incidental damages award is more than adequate under the circumstances.

In anticipation of the building project, CFP purchased cedar paneling, insulation, floor plywood and cedar timber. It had not begun to assemble the building when Jewish Federation breached the contract. After the breach, CFP was able to resell the purchased items to other customers for the same price as called for in the Jewish Federation contract.

While the district court found CFP qualified as a lost volume seller, the court reasoned:

> [I]t would be unjust to allow [CFP] to recoup lost profits in a situation here where it has not even begun to partially assemble component parts into a specialty item. ... [T]his Court does not believe that the lost volume seller theory was intended to apply to sellers who were in the process of preparing to assemble a specialty item.

Accordingly, the district court awarded CFP $13,470.17 in incidental damages rather than allowing lost profits as anticipated under 810 Illinois Compiled Statutes 5/2-708(2).

The primary issue on appeal is the proper measure of damages for a lost volume seller under these particular circumstances. The Illinois Commercial Code—like the Uniform Commercial Code (UCC)—provides for liberal administration such that "the aggrieved party may be put in as good a position as if the other party had fully performed. …" 810 ILL. COMP. STAT. 5/1-106(1). According to the Illinois Code,

> [T]he measure of damages for non-acceptance or repudiation by the buyer is the difference between the market price at the time and place for tender and the unpaid contract price together with any incidental damages provided in this Article (Section 2-710), but less expenses saved in consequence of the buyer's breach. *Id.* 5/2-708(1).

However, if this "amount is inadequate to put the seller in as good a position as performance would have done then the measure of damages is the profit (including reasonable overhead) which the seller would have made from full performance by the buyer, together with any incidental damages provided in this Article (Section 2-710), due allowance for costs reasonably incurred and due credit for payments or proceeds of resale." *Id.* 5/2-708(2).

To resolve this issue, we look to case law construing the Illinois statute or similar statutory law in other jurisdictions. In *R.E. Davis Chem. Corp. v. Diasonics, Inc.*, 826 F.2d 678 (N.D .Ill. 1987), the court used lost profits as the measure of damages pursuant to 810 ILLINOIS COMPILED STATUTES 5/2-708(2) after the buyer repudiated. For the seller to recover lost profits, the court reasoned that the seller must establish that 1) it had the capacity to make the sale to the buyer as well as the sale to the resale buyer and 2) it would have been profitable for it to make both sales. *R.E. Davis Chem. Corp.*, 826 F.2d at 684. Applying this test to the present case, the record reflects CFP was capable of manufacturing the building for Jewish Federation as well as its numerous other customers and it would have been profitable to do so.

Jewish Federation argues that CFP had not begun to assemble the purchased items into the contracted for building at the time of breach, therefore incidental damages were sufficient. However, this position is not supported by case law. Lost profits may be awarded on items yet to be manufactured. *See City of Louisville v. Rockwell Mfg. Co.*, 482 F.2d 159, 165–66 (6th Cir. 1973) (allowing lost profit award on not yet manufactured parking meters); *Anchorage Centennial Dev. Co. v. Van Wormer & Rodrigues, Inc.*, 443 P.2d 596, 599 (Alaska 1968) (holding that lost profit damages extends to items not yet produced); *Kvassay v. Murray*, 808 P.2d 896, 433 (Kan. Ct. App. 1991) (allowing for lost profit damages for items to be manufactured because the goal is to place seller in as good of a position as if the buyer had not breached); *Paramount Lithographic Plate Serv., Inc. v. Hughes Printing Co.*, 22 U.C.C. Rep. Serv. 1129 (Ct. of Common Pleas of Pa. 1977) (applying lost profit damages under UCC § 2-708(2) to a breach of contract for the sale of goods not yet manufactured in light of § 1-106(1) stating that the aggrieved party may be put in as good a position as if the other party had fully performed).

The rationale for these holdings appears to be that a lost volume seller can handle a certain number of sales during the year and when one negotiated sale is lost, the seller simply cannot recoup that anticipated profit. Instead, the seller is one sale short of normal capacity. *See R.E. Davis Chem. Corp.*, 826 F.2d at 683 (defining a lost volume seller as "one that has a predictable and finite number of customers and that has the capacity either to sell to all new buyers or to make the one additional sale represented by the resale after the breach").

So to put the seller in the position he would have been but for the breach, the Illinois statute provides the seller a remedy which includes the anticipated profit as well as incidental expenses and costs incurred. The statutory language in 810 ILLINOIS COMPILED STATUTES 5/2-708(2)—providing for lost profits, "together with ... due credit for payments or proceeds of resale"—does not apply to a lost volume seller. *Teradyne, Inc. v. Teledyne Indus., Inc.*, 676 F.2d 865, 868 (1st Cir. 1982); *Famous Knitwear Corp. v. Drug Fair, Inc.,* 493 F.2d 251, 254 n. 7 (4th Cir. 1974); Snyder v. Herbert Greenbaum & Assoc., Inc., 380 A.2d 618, 625–26 (Md. Ct. Spec. App. 1977).

Therefore, the district court erred in its application of Illinois law. As a lost volume seller, CFP is entitled to its lost profits of $53,887.46 pursuant to 810 ILLINOIS COMPILED STATUTES 5/2-708(2) which includes the incidental damages of $13,470.17 awarded by the district court. *See R.E. Davis Chem. Corp.*, 826 F.2d at 683 (determining that when a "breach effectively cost[s] the seller a 'profit,' ... the seller can only be made whole by awarding it damages in the amount of its 'lost profit' under 2-708(2)"). As such, we reverse the damage portion of the district court ruling by increasing the award to CFP by an additional $40,417.29.

CFP next argues the district court's failure to award lost profits resulted in an improper reduction in the amount of attorney fees and costs awarded. The district court awarded CFP $5,000 in attorney fees and $801.98 in costs, reduced from a requested amount of $38,120.27 in attorney fees and costs. The award of attorney fees and costs is based on the contract language allowing the prevailing party to recoup reasonable attorney fees and costs. As the district court found, CFP was the prevailing party. However, because we reverse the district court by substantially increasing the amount of damages allowed under the statute, we agree with CFP that its award of attorney fees should be substantially increased. We remand for the district court to reconsider the award of reasonable attorney fees in light of the superior prevailing position CFP is in following this decision.

Reversed and remanded with direction.

CHAPTER THIRTEEN

PROOF OF EQUITABLE REMEDIES IN ACTIONS INVOLVING ARTICLE 2 OF THE UNIFORM COMMERCIAL CODE

"Equity will not suffer a wrong to be without a remedy." *Manning v. Potomac Elec. Power Co.*, 187 A.2d 468, 472 (Md. 1963). Consequently, a court of chancery has greater powers to administer "nicer and more perfect justice" than a court of law. *Montana Co. v. St. Louis Mining & Milling Co.*, 152 U.S. 160, 167 (1894). For centuries, English and American courts sitting in equity have exercised those powers and awarded an assortment of equitable remedies. In particular, to reflect contracting parties' intentions, courts of equity have reformed or modified contracts. *See, e.g., Johnson Family Ltd. Partnership v. White Pine Wireless, LLC*, 281 Mich. App. 364, 372 (Mich. Ct. App. 2008). And in instances where contracts were found to be illegal, unconscionable, or fashioned under duress, courts of equity have canceled, disaffirmed, and rescinded those agreements. Furthermore, when disgruntled parties were unable to secure adequate compensatory damages in law, courts of equity used their broad equitable powers to compel offending parties to perform specific promises. *See Crafts v. Pitts*, 162 P.3d 382, 386 (Wash. 2007); and, RESTATEMENT (SECOND) OF CONTRACTS § 360 (1981).

May courts apply equitable principles to achieve "more perfect justice" in lawsuits involving Article 2 of the Uniform Commercial Code? Or stated in a different way, do UCC provisions bar the application of equitable principles to resolve sale-of-goods disputes? Section 1-103—arguably one of the most important provisions in the UCC—provides:

> Unless *displaced* by the particular provisions of this Act, the principles of law and equity, including the law merchant and the law relevant to capacity to contract, principal and agent, estoppel, fraud, misrepresentation, duress, coercion, mistake, bankruptcy, or other validating or invalidating cause shall *supplement* its provisions.

Both "displaced" and "supplement" appear in section 1-103(b) of the UCC. Therefore, which one controls? Does the UCC displace or supplement principles of equity? To understand why this is an important question, consider the commentators' discussion in WHITE & SUMMERS, HANDBOOK OF THE LAW UNDER THE UNIFORM COMMERCIAL CODE. 19–20 (2d ed. 1980).

> Section 1-103 also deals with general equitable principles. It would have been better had the drafters dealt with these in a separate section. The relations between general equitable principles and Code provisions are quite unlike the relations between general legal principles and Code provisions. One primary function of the corpus of Code sections is generally to *displace* prior legal principles. But it is not a primary function of these sections to *displace* prior equitable principles.
>
> To put this another way, Code sections "occupy the legal field" except insofar as they do not "particularly" *displace* pre-existing legal principles. But it is wrong to think of the relation between Code sections and general equitable principles in this way. Code sections do not "occupy the equity field." Rather, general equitable principles remain largely intact, for they are only *rarely "particularly displaced."* In a sense, then, they are the main occupants of the relevant field. This follows from their basic character. Unlike general legal principles, they do not merely *supplement* Code sections; their function is also to carve exceptions from or otherwise modify Code sections, and the courts have recognized as much.
>
> These functions are not peculiar to the bearing of § 1-103 equitable principles on Code rules; they are characteristic of the bearing of equitable principles upon legal rules throughout the law. With § 1-103 and related law on the books, judges can escape the ancient dilemma of either adhering to the legal rule and doing an inequity, or of doing equity but in an unlaw-like fashion. Indeed, § 1-103 imposes a duty on the judge to reach the equitable result *unless* the relevant general equitable principle has been *particularly displaced*. (Emphasis added)

Clearly, White & Summers are emphatic: UCC provisions do not "occupy the equity field." But, COMMENT 2—which accompanies section 1-103(b)—states that the UCC generally preempts the application of "inconsistent" equitable principles to resolve UCC-related disputes. The comment reads:

> [T]he Uniform Commercial Code is the primary source of commercial law rules in areas that it governs, and its rules represent choices made by its drafters and the enacting legislatures about the appropriate policies to be furthered in the transactions it covers. Therefore, while principles of common law and *equity may supplement* provisions of the Uniform Commercial Code, they may not be used to *supplant* its provisions or the purposes and policies those provisions reflect, *unless* a specific provision of the Uniform Commercial Code provides otherwise. In the absence of such a provision, the Uniform Commercial Code *preempts principles of common law and equity* that are inconsistent with either its provisions or its purposes and policies. (Emphasis added)

On the other hand, a consensus has emerged among courts over whether equitable principles preempt, displace, or supplement UCC rules. For example, the New York Court of Appeals declared: The UCC allows courts to consider and apply equitable principles unless a particular UCC provision *displaces* equitable doctrines. *Mouradian v. Astoria Fed. Sav. & Loan*, 689 N.E.2d 1385, 1388 (N.Y. 1997). Similarly, the Minnesota Court of Appeals concluded that the application of equitable principles is unnecessary only if UCC provisions are "determinative." *First Nat. Bank of Blooming Prairie v. Olsen*, 403 N.W.2d 661, 666 (Minn. Ct. App. 1987).

Other federal and state courts have reached fairly similar conclusions as well. *See also*, *S.S. Kresge Co. v. Port of Longview*, 18 Wash. App. 805, 811 (1977) (UCC provisions "do not totally preempt the fields of law"); *Arcon Const. Co., Inc. v. S.D. Cement Plant,* 349 N.W.2d 407, 412 (S.D. 1984) ("[G]eneral principles of law may only supplement the UCC to the extent they are not displaced; they will not be applied where they conflict with particular provisions of the UCC."); and *Morgan Guar. Trust Co. v. American Savs. & Loan Ass'n,* 804 F.2d 1487, 1495 (9th Cir. 1986) (concluding that courts should consider the equities of a case unless an express U.C.C. provision—governing the award of remedies—has displaced equitable principles).

Entrustment, unjust enrichment, specific performance, reformation, reclamation, restitution, rescission, and replevin are some equitable principles that courts have applied to decide disagreements involving construction, services, real estate, employment, and manufacturing contracts. The sections below present cases illustrating how courts have applied some of the same principles to settle sale-of-goods contractual disputes between buyers and sellers under Article 2 of the UCC.

UNIFORM COMMERCIAL CODE

§ 1-103. CONSTRUCTION OF [UNIFORM COMMERCIAL CODE] TO PROMOTE ITS PURPOSES AND POLICIES; APPLICABILITY OF SUPPLEMENTAL PRINCIPLES OF LAW

(a) [The Uniform Commercial Code] must be liberally construed and applied to promote its underlying purposes and policies, which are:

(1) to simplify, clarify, and modernize the law governing commercial transactions;

(2) to permit the continued expansion of commercial practices through custom, usage, and agreement of the parties; and

(3) to make uniform the law among the various jurisdictions.

(b) Unless displaced by the particular provisions of [the Uniform Commercial Code], the principles of law and equity, including the law merchant and the law relative to capacity to contract, principal and agent, estoppel, fraud, misrepresentation, duress, coercion, mistake, bankruptcy, and other validating or invalidating cause supplement its provisions.

SECTION ONE: THE APPLICATION OF THE ENTRUSTMENT DOCTRINE UNDER ARTICLE 2 OF THE UCC

Heinrich v. Titus-Will Sales, Inc.
868 P.2d 169
(Wash. Ct. App. 1994)

SEINFELD, JUDGE. Titus-Will Ford Sales, Inc. appeals a judgment for replevin of a 1990 Ford pickup truck that Titus-Will had previously sold to dealer/broker James Wilson. Upon consideration of the entrustment and voidable title provisions of the Uniform Commercial Code, we agree that Titus-Will must bear the burden of loss of payment for the vehicle. …

In 1989 Michael Heinrich wished to buy a particular model new Ford pickup truck. James Wilson held himself out as a dealer/broker, licensed to buy and sell vehicles. Heinrich retained Wilson to make the purchase, but did not direct Wilson to any particular automobile dealer. Unbeknownst to Heinrich, Wilson had lost his Washington vehicle dealer license the previous year. Wilson negotiated with Titus-Will for the purchase of a Ford pickup truck with Heinrich's desired options. Titus-Will had been involved in hundreds of transactions with Wilson over the years and also was unaware that Wilson was no longer licensed to act as a vehicle dealer.

Heinrich made two initial payments to Wilson: an $1,800 down payment and a $3,000 payment when Titus-Will ordered the truck. Wilson gave Heinrich a receipt using a "Used Car Wholesale Purchase Order" that displayed Wilson's alleged vehicle dealer license number. Wilson then ordered the truck from Titus-Will, using his own check to make a $7,000 down payment. The purchase order indicated the truck was being sold to Wilson. "Dealer" was written in the space on the form for tax. Wilson told the Titus-Will salesman handling the sale that he was ordering the truck for resale.

On October 13, 1989, Wilson told Heinrich the truck was ready for delivery. Heinrich paid Wilson $15,549.55 as final payment, including tax and license fees. Wilson gave Heinrich a copy of the purchase order and of an options checklist with corresponding prices. These documents indicated that Wilson was buying the truck from Titus-Will. The Titus-Will salesman had signed off on the options list; Wilson marked it "paid in full" and signed it after Heinrich paid him. On the same day, at Wilson's behest, Heinrich signed a Washington application for motor vehicle title.

Wilson agreed to deliver the truck to Heinrich at Titus-Will on Saturday, October 21, 1989. He arranged with a Titus-Will salesman to deliver a check on the morning of October 21 to a clerk in the Titus-Will office and, in return, to receive the truck keys and paperwork. The clerk accepted Wilson's check for $11,288.00—post-dated to Monday, October 23, 1989—and delivered to Wilson a packet containing the keys to the truck, the owner's manual, an odometer disclosure statement, and a warranty card. The odometer statement, which Wilson and the Titus-Will salesman signed, showed Wilson as the transferor. Titus-Will did not fill out the warranty card with the name and address of the purchaser because the sale appeared to be dealer to dealer, with the warranty to benefit the ultimate purchaser.

Titus-Will retained the manufacturer's certificate of origin. The certificate of origin is apparently a "pre-title" document used to obtain state title documents when a car is sold to a non-dealer. Titus-Will, believing this to be a dealer to dealer transaction, planned to give the certificate to Wilson when his check cleared. Wilson could then obtain title to the vehicle in the name of his customer. Wilson immediately taped Heinrich's application for title in the rear window of the truck that was parked on the Titus-Will lot. When Heinrich arrived, Wilson gave him the keys and documents and Heinrich drove off in the truck.

Wilson's check did not clear. Titus-Will demanded return of the truck. On November 6, Wilson picked up the truck from Heinrich, telling him he would have Titus-Will make certain repairs under the warranty. Wilson returned the truck to Titus-Will. On November 9, 1989, Wilson admitted to Heinrich that he did not have funds to cover his check to Titus-Will and that Titus-Will would not release the truck without payment. Heinrich then asked Titus-Will for the truck; it refused. By a pretrial arrangement, Heinrich regained possession of, but not clear title to, the truck on April 1, 1990.

Heinrich sued Titus-Will and Wilson, seeking replevin of the truck and damages for his loss of use. Heinrich obtained a default order against Wilson. After a bench trial, the court awarded Heinrich title to the truck and $3,050 in damages for loss of its use. On appeal, Titus-Will argues that the trial court erroneously applied the entrustment doctrine of RCW 62A.2-403; it also argues the law of agency—not the Uniform Commercial Code (UCC)—controls and requires reversal. Heinrich contends that in addition to the entrustment doctrine, the trial court's findings also support application of the voidable title doctrine contained in RCW 62A.2-403. ...

I. The Entrustment Doctrine

RCW 62A.2-403(2) and (3) contain the entrustment provisions of the Uniform Commercial Code (UCC). The statute provides as follows:

> (2) Any entrusting of possession of goods to a merchant who deals in goods of that kind gives him power to transfer all rights of the entruster to a buyer in ordinary course of business.
>
> (3) "Entrusting" includes any delivery and any acquiescence in retention of possession regardless of any condition expressed between the parties to the delivery or acquiescence and regardless of whether the procurement of the entrusting or the possessor's disposition of the goods have been such as to be larcenous under the criminal law.

To prevail under this statute, Heinrich must show 1) Titus-Will "entrusted" the truck to Wilson and, thus, empowered Wilson subsequently to transfer all rights of Titus-Will in the truck to Heinrich; 2) Wilson was a merchant dealing in automobiles; and 3) Heinrich bought the truck from Wilson as a "buyer in ordinary course of business." *See Williams v. Western Sur. Co.*, 6 Wash. App. 300, 302 (1972).

Three general policies support RCW 62A.2-403(2), the UCC provision placing the risk of loss on the entruster. First, it protects the innocent buyer who, based on his observation of goods in the possession of a merchant of those goods, believes that the merchant has legal title to the goods and can, therefore, pass title in the goods to another. *See* OFFICIAL COMMENT 2, RCWA 62A.2.403. The statute carries forward the pre-Uniform Commercial Code law of estoppel under which an owner—who clothes a merchant with apparent ownership of or authority to sell goods—is estopped from denying such authority as against the one's buying the goods from the merchant in good faith. 3 R. ANDERSON, UNIFORM COMMERCIAL CODE § 2-403:29 (3d ed. 1983). *See, e.g., Gramm-Bernstein Motor Truck Co. v. Todd*, 121 Wash. 145, 147–48 (1922).

Secondly, the entrustment clause reflects the idea that the entruster is in a better position than the innocent buyer to protect against the risk that an intermediary merchant will not pay for or not deliver the goods. *Apeco Corp. v. Bishop Mobile Homes, Inc.*, 506 S.W.2d 711, 718–19 (Tex. Civ. App. 1974). Thirdly, the entrustment clause facilitates the flow of commerce by allowing purchasers to rely on a merchant's apparent legal right to sell the goods. *Cugnini v. Reynolds Cattle Co.*, 687 P.2d 962, 967 (Colo. 1984). Without the safeguards of the entrustment provision, a prudent buyer would have to delay the finalization of any sizeable sales transaction for the time necessary to research the merchant's ownership rights to the goods.

A. ENTRUSTING

The UCC definition of "entrusting"—contained in RCW 62A.2-403(3)—is broad. The statute declares that "any delivery and any acquiescence in retention of possession" constitutes entrustment. RCW 62A.2-403(3). A person can entrust goods to a merchant by a variety of methods—such as consigning them, creating a bailment, taking a security interest in inventory, leaving them with the merchant after purchase, and delivering them for purposes of repair. OFFICIAL COMMENT 2, RCWA 62A.2-403. A sale can also constitute an entrustment when some aspect of the transaction remains incomplete.

Titus-Will properly concedes that it entrusted the truck to Wilson. However, it argues Wilson was not a merchant and Heinrich was not a buyer in ordinary course. Further, Titus-Will contends that the timing of the entrusting deprived Wilson of the power to transfer its rights.

B. MERCHANT

Titus-Will argues that Wilson was not a merchant because he had no inventory. However, it is not necessary to possess an inventory to fit within the broad statutory definition of merchant. Article 2 of the UCC defines (in part) "merchant" as "a person who deals in goods of the kind or otherwise by his occupation holds himself out as having knowledge or skill peculiar to the practices or goods involved in the transaction." RCW 62A.2-104(1). Wilson was a merchant who dealt in automobiles; he held himself out as a dealer in automobiles and appeared to be a dealer in automobiles. Both parties treated him as one. Titus-Will processed all the documents as it would for a dealer and understood that Wilson was buying the truck for resale.

Titus-Will also argues that Wilson was not a merchant because he did not have a vehicle dealer license. However, the UCC does not require proper state licensing for merchant status. RCW 62A.2-104(1), 62A.2-403(2). Wilson's apparent violation of state licensing statutes may subject him to penalties, but it does not void an otherwise valid UCC commercial transaction. Indeed, the exclusion of an unlicensed dealer from merchant status under the UCC would be contrary to the statutory purpose of protecting innocent purchasers from the illegal (even larcenous) conduct of the entrustee. *See* RCW 62A.2-403(3); OFFICIAL COMMENT 2, RCWA 62A.2-403.

C. BUYER IN ORDINARY COURSE

There is also substantial evidence that Heinrich was a "buyer in ordinary course of business" although the trial court referred to him as a "good faith purchaser for value." A buyer in ordinary course of business is "a person who in good faith and without knowledge that the sale to him is in violation of the ownership rights or security interest of a third party in the goods buys in ordinary course from a person in the business of selling goods of that kind[.]" RCW 62A.1-201(9). "Buying" includes receiving goods ... under a pre-existing contract for sale". RCW 62A.1-201(9). Good faith is "honesty in fact in the conduct or transaction concerned." RCW 62A.1-201(19).

The amount of the consideration is significant as evidence of good faith. Heinrich gave substantial value for the truck, more than Wilson agreed to pay Titus-Will. Nor did Heinrich know or have a basis to believe that Wilson's sale and delivery of the truck to him violated Titus-Will's ownership or security interest rights. There was no showing that Heinrich acted other than in good faith. As the trial court noted in its memorandum decision, it is not unusual for a buyer to purchase a car that the dealer has acquired from another dealer. Wilson's illegal and fraudulent activity does not taint Heinrich's status as a buyer under RCW 62A.2-403(2). When Heinrich accepted delivery after previously paying Wilson, Heinrich was "buying" as defined by RCW 62A.1-201(9).

D. TIMING OF ENTRUSTMENT

Titus-Will also argues that the UCC entrustment provisions should not apply because it entrusted the truck to Wilson after Heinrich had completely paid Wilson. This is an issue of first impression in this jurisdiction.

Before the completion of the Wilson-Heinrich sales transaction, Titus-Will entrusted Wilson not only with the truck, but also with the signed odometer disclosure statement, the owner's manual, the warranty card, and the keys. By doing so, Titus-Will clothed Wilson with additional indicia of ownership and with the apparent authority to transfer an ownership interest in the truck. It also enabled Wilson to complete the sales transaction. RCW 62A.2-401(2) ("Unless otherwise explicitly agreed title passes to the buyer at the time and place at which the seller completes his performance with reference to the physical delivery of the goods.").

In addition, the entrustment allowed Wilson to continue to deceive Heinrich from October 21, 1989—the date of delivery of possession—to November 9, 1989, when Wilson finally admitted the truth. We believe that under these circumstances, application of the entrustment doctrine, RCW 62A.2-403(2), furthers the policy of protecting the buyer who relies on the merchant's apparent legal ability to sell goods in the merchant's possession.

The second rationale for the entrustment doctrine also supports its application here. Titus-Will, in the business of selling cars, was in a better position than Heinrich to protect itself against another dealer/broker who might fail to pay for the goods. It could have insured against the loss, and it could have adopted preventive procedures. For example, it simply could have advised Wilson to pick up the car Monday after the check had cleared the bank. Although Heinrich might also have taken precautions, as only an occasional purchaser of motor vehicles he was in a less advantageous position to anticipate and protect against Wilson's fraudulent conduct.

The third rationale for the entrustment doctrine focuses on the flow of commerce. Here we consider the potential impact on commercial transactions of requiring purchasers to research their dealer/broker's legal title before accepting possession of the goods. Although the record contains no evidence on this issue, it seems obvious that this requirement would inevitably cause some delay. *Fuqua Homes Inc. v. Evanston Bldg. and Loan Co.*, 370 N.E.2d 780, 784–85 (Ohio App. 1977).

Requiring the entruster to retain the burden of risk, even when the entrustment occurs after a third party purchaser gives value, supports the policies underlying the entrustment doctrine. Thus, we decline to graft a timing requirement onto the statute. Finally, we note a similarity between this case and those cases where entrustment occurs before the purchaser gives value. In either instance, the seller is at risk of loss because of its own conduct in entrusting the goods to another. The trial court did not err in applying the entrustment doctrine and granting replevin.

II. VOIDABLE TITLE DOCTRINE

Notwithstanding our affirmance of the trial court's decision based on the entrustment doctrine, we also consider the voidable title doctrine, also included in RCW 62A.2-403, as an additional basis for recovery. We note that although the voidable title doctrine was argued to the trial court, the trial court did not expressly rely on this theory in its findings of fact and conclusions of law. However, the trial court did make findings and conclusions that address the elements of voidable title. Furthermore, Heinrich, in the respondent's brief, thoroughly argued the elements of the doctrine. Accordingly, we analyze the applicability of the voidable title doctrine to these facts.

Several of the elements of the voidable title doctrine overlap those of the entrustment doctrine. By application of the doctrine, a good faith purchaser for value acquires good title from a seller with "voidable title." The voidable title doctrine, however, does not include a requirement that the buyer purchase from a "merchant" dealing in goods of that kind. Titus-Will contends that the voidable title concept is not applicable here because Wilson did not intend to take title to the truck for himself. It further argues that Heinrich's evidence was insufficient to prove this theory.

RCW 62A.2-403(1) provides that one with "voidable title" can transfer good title to a good faith purchaser for value. Previous Washington statutory law contained an identical principle. The UCC does not define "voidable title." However, statute and case law describe its characteristics, and commentators note that "[t]he title of the seller is voidable whenever by the pre-Code law it would be subject to avoidance as between the original parties."

Voidable title exists only if the title claimant has some legal interest in the property. Thus, a subsequent purchaser acquires no title to stolen goods, despite the consideration paid or good faith of the later transaction. RCW 10.79.050. Voidable title may exist although the claimant acquired an interest in the property through a transaction flawed by a lack of good faith or a technical defect.

Where the original owner parts with the goods voluntarily in circumstances which, while deplorable, do not constitute outright theft, there is always the chance that the transferee will acquire apparent ownership or 'voidable title' and, thanks to this altered state, may be able to pass along better title to a good faith purchaser than he himself may have. *See Linn v. Reid*, 114 Wash. 609, 611–12 (1921). The dictionary defines the term "voidable" as "capable of being voided ... may be set aside usually at the option of one party." WEBSTER'S THIRD INTERNATIONAL DICTIONARY, 2562, (Unabridged ed. 1966).

Wilson's ownership rights to the truck meet the criteria for voidable title. RCW 62A.2-403(1) applies the "voidable title" doctrine to three particular situations. In each of these instances a purchaser who obtains possession of goods through a "transaction of purchase" has the power to convey good title to a good faith purchaser for value. RCW 62A.2-403(1)(b). The portion of the pertinent statute is as follows: "A person with voidable title has power to transfer a good title to a good faith purchaser for value. When goods have been delivered under a transaction of purchase the purchaser has such power even though ... the delivery was in exchange for a check which is later dishonored. ..."

For Heinrich to prevail under this section, he must establish that 1) Titus-Will delivered to Wilson "under a transaction of purchase"; 2) Wilson paid Titus-Will for the truck with a bad check; and 3) Heinrich was a good faith purchaser for value. The trial court found, and Titus-Will does not dispute, that Wilson paid for the truck with a bad check. Titus-Will does contend that the transaction it engaged in with Wilson was not a "purchase" transaction. It further disagrees with the trial court's characterization of Heinrich as a good faith purchaser for value.

A. TRANSACTION OF PURCHASE

Titus-Will argues that it did not deliver the truck to Wilson under a "transaction of purchase." In its brief, Titus-Will refers to Wilson's interest as a "mere possessory interest" rather than a purchaser's interest. It contends that since Wilson was acting as Heinrich's agent, Wilson did not acquire an independent interest in the truck.

The UCC defines "purchase" very broadly as any "voluntary transaction creating an interest in property," including "taking by sale, discount, negotiation, mortgage, pledge, lien, issue or reissue, [or] gift." RCW 62A.1-201(32) Wilson gave Titus-Will two of his own checks in exchange for delivery of the truck. Titus-Will's purchase order was in Wilson's name. Titus-Will's acceptance of Wilson's check coupled with its transfer of possession of the truck satisfied the criteria for a purchase transaction. When a seller delivers goods to a merchant purchaser under a transaction of purchase, but the transaction is in some way incomplete, the seller may have both conveyed voidable title under RCW 62A.2-403(1) and entrusted under RCW 62A.2-403(2), (3). As we discuss below, agency law does not change the outcome here.

B. Good Faith Purchaser for Value

Wilson had power to pass good title to a good faith purchaser for value. Heinrich clearly "purchased" the truck, RCW 62A.1-201(32), and, as we concluded in our discussion of the entrustment doctrine, did so in good faith. He also gave value. Value is defined broadly; among other methods, a person gives value for rights when he acquires them "by accepting delivery pursuant to a pre-existing contract for purchase", "in return for any consideration sufficient to support a simple contract", and even in satisfaction of a preexisting claim. RCW 62A.1-201(44)(b), (c), (d).

Thus, the fact that Wilson paid Titus-Will with a check that the bank later dishonored did not prevent Heinrich from obtaining good title. RCW 62A.2-403(1)(b). Nonetheless, Titus-Will claims that Heinrich cannot be a good faith purchaser because we must impute Wilson's alleged fraudulent conduct to Heinrich. We address and reject that argument below in our discussion of the applicability of agency law. …

III. Agency

Titus-Will emphasizes the trial court's conclusion of law that Wilson was Heinrich's agent "for the purpose of finding from another dealer a specific vehicle." From this conclusion, Titus-Will argues the applicability of two general principles under the law of agency. First, citing *Young v. Globe Indem. Co.*, 156 Wash. 260, 256–66(1930), it contends that Titus-Will, as one who contracted with the agent of an undisclosed principal, believing in good faith that the agent is the real party in interest, may assert any defenses against Heinrich that it could assert against Wilson.

The trial court concluded that a limited agency existed. Heinrich went to Wilson, a vehicle dealer, seeking a particular truck. Wilson became Heinrich's agent for the purpose of finding such a vehicle to purchase so that he could resell it to Heinrich. However, the trial court also found that Wilson represented to Titus-Will that the truck was for "resale" and that "Titus-Will Ford Sales, Inc. [was] aware at that time that the vehicle was intended for use by someone other than Wilson." In other words, Titus-Will did not believe in good faith that Wilson was the real party in interest. Thus, the first proffered agency principle is not applicable here, and the trial court did not err in refusing to allow Titus-Will to assert against Heinrich any defenses it had against Wilson.

Secondly, Titus-Will argues that we must impute the agent Wilson's fraud to Heinrich, Wilson's principal. This would exclude Heinrich from the UCC definition of good faith purchaser or buyer in ordinary course. Heinrich cites the following rule of agency law:

> Generally speaking, a principal is chargeable with notice of facts which are within the knowledge of his agent, acquired within the scope of the agent's authority. A well-recognized exception to this rule is that, where an agent acquires information which it would be to his advantage to conceal from his principal, it is assumed that he did not impart such knowledge to his principal, and accordingly knowledge would not be imputed to the principal. This exception, however, is qualified by the rule that, if the agent is the sole representative of the principal, or the only person or means by which the principal acts, then the knowledge of the agent will be imputed to the principal, and the general rule applies, and not the exception thereto. *Puget Sound Nat'l Bank v. St. Paul Fire & Marine Ins. Co.*, 32 Wash. App. 32, 40 (1982), quoting *Higgins v. Daniel*, 5 Wash.2d 134, 139 (1940).

In its memorandum decision, the trial court explained why it did not apply agency rules in this case, stating: "The Court does not argue with the law of agency as cited by the defendant. It is the Court's conclusion that the agency rules set forth in those cases simply are not applicable to this particular course of commercial dealing."

The applicability of the agency rule cited requires findings and conclusions that the trial court did not make. First, it did not find that Wilson intended to defraud Titus-Will. Rather, the following language of finding of fact 8 suggests that Wilson planned to cover the check but was unable to do so: "Wilson was unable to make good on the check. ..." Further, the applicability of the "sole representative" exception to agency law was not argued to the trial court. Accordingly, the trial court made no conclusions of law as to its applicability. In light of the trial court's reasoning along with its findings and conclusions, we cannot say that it erred in declining to apply agency principles to these facts.

Finally, we note that the mere existence of a limited agency relationship does not provide a rationale for removing the transaction from the purview of § 2-403. *See Couch v. Cockroft*, 490 S.W.2d 713 (Tenn. Ct. App. 1972) (UCC § 2-403 applied where merchant was also the buyer's agent to obtain goods the merchant did not initially possess in inventory). By incorporating the law of principal and agent, as a "supplement [to] its provisions," RCW 62A.1-103, the UCC does not exclude persons with a limited agency relationship from its definitions of good faith purchaser, buyer in ordinary course, and merchant. Heinrich met the definitions of good faith purchaser and buyer in ordinary course, and Wilson met the definition of merchant.

We affirm the trial court's judgment.

UNIFORM COMMERCIAL CODE

§ 2-401. PASSING OF TITLE; RESERVATION FOR SECURITY; LIMITED APPLICATION OF THIS SECTION

Each provision of this Article with regard to the rights, obligations and remedies of the seller, the buyer, purchasers or other third parties applies irrespective of title to the goods except where the provision refers to such title. Insofar as situations are not covered by the other provisions of this Article and matters concerning title become material the following rules apply:

(1) Title to goods cannot pass under a contract for sale prior to their identification to the contract (Section 2-501), and unless otherwise explicitly agreed the buyer acquires by their identification a special property as limited by this Act. Any retention or reservation by the seller of the title (property) in goods shipped or delivered to the buyer is limited in effect to a reservation of a security interest. Subject to these provisions and to the provisions of the Article on Secured Transactions (Article 9), title to goods passes from the seller to the buyer in any manner and on any conditions explicitly agreed on by the parties.

(2) Unless otherwise explicitly agreed title passes to the buyer at the time and place at which the seller completes his performance with reference to the physical delivery of the goods, despite any reservation of a security interest and even though a document of title is to be delivered at a different time or place; and in particular and despite any reservation of a security interest by the bill of lading

(a) if the contract requires or authorizes the seller to send the goods to the buyer but does not require him to deliver them at destination, title passes to the buyer at the time and place of shipment; but

(b) if the contract requires delivery at destination, title passes on tender there.

(3) Unless otherwise explicitly agreed where delivery is to be made without moving the goods,

(a) if the seller is to deliver a tangible document of title, title passes at the time when and the place where he delivers such documents and if the seller is to deliver an electronic document of title, title passes when the seller delivers the document; or

(b) if the goods are at the time of contracting already identified and no documents of title are to be delivered, title passes at the time and place of contracting.

(4) A rejection or other refusal by the buyer to receive or retain the goods, whether or not justified, or a justified revocation of acceptance revests title to the goods in the seller. Such revesting occurs by operation of law and is not a "sale."

§ 2-402. RIGHTS OF SELLER'S CREDITORS AGAINST SOLD GOODS

(1) Except as provided in subsections (2) and (3), rights of unsecured creditors of the seller with respect to goods which have been identified to a contract for sale are subject to the buyer's rights to recover the goods under this Article (Sections 2-502 and 2-716).

(2) A creditor of the seller may treat a sale or an identification of goods to a contract for sale as void if as against him a retention of possession by the seller is fraudulent under any rule of law of the state where the goods are situated, except that retention of possession in good faith and current course of trade by a merchant-seller for a commercially reasonable time after a sale or identification is not fraudulent.

(3) Nothing in this Article shall be deemed to impair the rights of creditors of the seller

(a) under the provisions of the Article on Secured Transactions (Article 9); or

(b) where identification to the contract or delivery is made not in current course of trade but in satisfaction of or as security for a pre-existing claim for money, security or the like and is made under circumstances which under any rule of law of the state where the goods are situated would apart from this Article constitute the transaction a fraudulent transfer or voidable preference.

§ 2-403. POWER TO TRANSFER; GOOD FAITH PURCHASE OF GOODS; "ENTRUSTING"

(1) A purchaser of goods acquires all title which his transferor had or had power to transfer except that a purchaser of a limited interest acquires rights only to the extent of the interest purchased. A person with voidable title has power to transfer a good title to a good faith purchaser for value. When goods have been delivered under a transaction of purchase the purchaser has such power even though

(a) the transferor was deceived as to the identity of the purchaser, or

(b) the delivery was in exchange for a check which is later dishonored, or

(c) it was agreed that the transaction was to be a "cash sale", or

(d) the delivery was procured through fraud punishable as larcenous under the criminal law.

(2) Any entrusting of possession of goods to a merchant who deals in goods of that kind gives him power to transfer all rights of the entruster to a buyer in ordinary course of business.

(3) "Entrusting" includes any delivery and any acquiescence in retention of possession regardless of any condition expressed between the parties to the delivery or acquiescence and regardless of whether the procurement of the entrusting or the possessor's disposition of the goods have been such as to be larcenous under the criminal law.

SECTION TWO: THE APPLICATION OF THE RESCISSION DOCTRINE UNDER ARTICLE 2 OF THE UCC

Prince v. LeVan
486 P.2d 959
(Alaska 1971)

BONEY, CHIEF JUSTICE. The appellants—Earl Prince, Justin V. Fager, and John Steinbeck—were defendants below. They seek reversal of a superior court judgment granting rescission of a sale of a vessel, the CHARBUS, to the appellees who were plaintiffs below. In the interest of clarity, the parties on appeal will be designated in accordance with their respective relationships at trial.

Defendants were joint owners of the CHARBUS, a registered vessel of the United States. Defendants sold the CHARBUS to plaintiffs for $10,000 on May 8, 1968. Defendants executed the bill of sale in exchange for $3,000 cash and a promissory note for $7,000. The promissory note was secured by a marine mortgage, executed by plaintiffs in favor of defendants on May 8, 1968, the date of the sale. Under the terms of the marine mortgage, plaintiffs were required to obtain insurance coverage on the CHARBUS. This insurance inured to the benefit of defendants as security for the marine mortgage held by them.

Prior to the sale, the defendants had carried marine hull insurance with a $500 deductible clause on the CHARBUS. The annual premium was $825.00. This insurance coverage expired on May 6, 1968, two days before the sale. The parties both concede that at the time of the sale they believed adequate insurance coverage could be obtained on the CHARBUS. However, following the sale, the plaintiffs experienced considerable difficulty in obtaining what they considered to be satisfactory insurance, and although they did receive one offer of comparatively less adequate coverage which was subsequently withdrawn, they failed to insure. Defendants, as holders of the marine mortgage, continued to demand that the required coverage be obtained until at least August 28, 1968. Plaintiffs did not assert impossibility as a defense to the demand that they insure. However, in October of 1968, plaintiffs commenced the present action seeking rescission of the sale on two grounds.

As a first ground for relief, plaintiffs claimed that defendants had expressly warranted the condition of the engine of the CHARBUS, and that subsequent difficulties entitled them to rescission. However, the trial court found that plaintiffs had knowledge of the condition of the engine, and that subsequent difficulties did not amount to a breach of warranty. This finding is not contested on appeal.

Plaintiffs' second ground for relief prevailed, and forms the basis for the present appeal. Plaintiffs contended that the sale was conditioned on the CHARBUS being insurable as required by the marine mortgage, that the vessel was not insurable, and that they were entitled to a rescission of the sale. Defendants denied the vessel was not insurable and denied that insurability was a condition of the sale.

The trial court heard the evidence on the question of insurability and concluded that the CHARBUS was not insurable. In addition, the court found that because of the lack of available insurance, the CHARBUS was not usable as a commercial fishing vessel as the parties had intended. However, the court did not find that insurability was a condition of the sale.

Based upon these findings, the trial court decided that there was a mutual mistake of fact as to the insurability of the CHARBUS. In addition, the court concluded that the unavailability of insurance rendered performance of the insurance terms of the marine mortgage impossible, and that the impossibility of performance of the mortgage terms rendered the CHARBUS commercially useless so that the plaintiffs suffered both a frustration of purpose and a failure of consideration. Based upon these findings of fact and conclusions of law, the court determined that the plaintiffs were entitled to rescission of the sale. Judgment was entered accordingly on July 30, 1969. From that judgment, defendants have brought this appeal.

On appeal, defendants make three basic contentions. First, they assert that the trial court erred in findings, as a fact, that insurance coverage was not available on the CHARBUS. Second, they claim that the trial court erred in finding, as a fact, that the lack of available insurance rendered the CHARBUS useless as a commercial vessel. Third, it is contended that even if the CHARBUS was in fact uninsurable, the trial court erred in concluding that rescission was available under the applicable law. ...

In their brief, defendants point out that the trial court decided this case without reference to the Uniform Commercial Code. The trial judge relied instead upon general principles of contract law which defendants assert was improper. The first question confronting us is whether the code is applicable to the sale of a vessel, and if it is, whether reliance upon general contract principles alone, to the exclusion of the code, was improper.

Alaska Statutes, title 45, Trade and Commerce, adopts Article 2 of the Uniform Commercial Code as the applicable law of sales in Alaska. It is this article which concerns us here. AS 45.05.038 provides that the sales article shall "apply to transactions in goods." AS 45.05.044(a) defines goods: "'Goods' means all things (including specially manufactured goods) which are movable at the time of identification to the contract for sale other than the money in which the price is to be paid, investment securities (§§ 612–688) and things in action."

By the plain meaning of the words of the statute, a vessel is covered. Moreover, the official code comment makes it explicit that "[t]he definition of goods is based on the concept of movability," and it is self-evident that a vessel is within that definition and concept. 1 R. Anderson, UNIFORM COMMERCIAL CODE § 2-105:1, at 223 (2d ed. 1970). We conclude that the code was applicable to the sale of the CHARBUS.

We turn now to a consideration of whether the trial court erred in attempting to apply general contract principles to the total exclusion of the code. Defendants contend that the Uniform Commercial Code provided the exclusive basis for a remedy in this case. Plaintiffs respond by asserting that the trial court was authorized to rely upon basic contract principles by AS 45.05.006, which provides:

> Unless displaced by the particular provisions of this chapter, the principles of law and equity, including the law merchant and the law relative to capacity to contract, principal and agent, estoppel, fraud, misrepresentation, duress, coercion, mistake, bankruptcy, or other validating or invalidating cause supplement its provisions. [UCC § 1-103(b)]

Under this provision the principles of equity, including mistake, misrepresentation, and other invalidating grounds "supplement" the code provisions and apply "unless displaced by the particular provision of this chapter." It appears then, that general principles of contract law remain in effect, to some extent, under the code. Nevertheless, even when general principles remain operative, they merely supplement the code; they do not displace it so as to exclude application of its specific provisions where relevant.

Where both the code and general principles are available, the former should always be considered and applied if applicable. By legislative declaration the code is the law, and if general principles appear inconsistent, they must be considered displaced under AS 45.05.006. Moreover, even where inconsistency does not exist, the code must be regarded as supreme; general principles even when consistent with the code are merely supplementary. Specific code provisions were available to deal with the present case; they should have been applied. We proceed to do so.

At the outset, it should be noted that the code does not employ the term "rescission," a word with numerous non-code meanings, in establishing a buyer's remedial courses of action for a seller's default. Other remedies are provided, however, by AS 45.05.214 and AS 45.05.220:

> AS 45.05.214 applies when a buyer rightfully rejects or revokes acceptance of non-conforming goods; under paragraph (a) of this provision "cancellation" of the contract and restitution of "so much of the price as has been paid" is available. [UCC § 2-711(1)].
>
> AS 45.05.162 provides in part: "[U]nless otherwise agreed ... if the goods or the tender of delivery fail in any respect to conform to the contract, the buyer may (1) reject the whole." [UCC § 2-601(a)].
>
> AS 45.05.164(a) provides: "Rejection of goods must be within a reasonable time after their delivery or tender. It is ineffective unless the buyer seasonably notifies the seller." [UCC § 2-602 (1)].
>
> AS 45.05.214(a) provides in part: "If ... the buyer rightfully rejects or justifiably revokes acceptance, then, the respect to goods involved and with respect to the whole if the breach goes to the whole contract (§ 184), the buyer may cancel and, whether or not he has done so, may, in addition to recovering so much of the price as has been paid." [UCC § 2-711(1)].

AS 45.05.176 provides:

> (a) The buyer may revoke his acceptance of a lot or commercial unit whose nonconformity substantially impairs its value to him if he has accepted it

(1) on the reasonable assumption that its nonconformity would be cured and it has not been seasonably cured; or

(2) without discovery of the nonconformity if his acceptance was reasonably induced either by the difficulty of discovery before acceptance or by the seller's assurances.

(b) Revocation of acceptance must occur within a reasonable time after the buyer discovers or should have discovered the ground for it and before a substantial change in condition of the goods which is not caused by their own defects. It is not effective until the buyer notifies the seller of it.

(c) A buyer who so revokes has the same rights and duties with regard to the goods involved as if he had rejected them. [Modified version of UCC § 2A-517].

This remedy is, in effect, one form of rescission; and a notice of rescission may be given effect as a revocation of acceptance and a cancellation—thus giving effect to the intent of the buyer to terminate the contract within the terminology of the code. 2 R. Anderson, UNIFORM COMMERCIAL CODE § 2-711:19 (2d ed. 1970). *See Lanners v. Whitney*, 428 P.2d 398, 403 (Or. 1967).

The remedies available under AS 45.05.220 are to be distinguished from the rescission type remedy provided by AS 45.05.214. The former applies when a buyer neither rejects nor revokes acceptance of non-conforming goods, but seeks instead to accept them and recover damages for the nonconformity. 2 R. Anderson, UNIFORM COMMERCIAL CODE § 2-714:3 (2d ed. 1970). Under this provision, a buyer who has accepted goods under AS 45.05.172(a) has no remedy at all unless he notifies the sellers of breach within a reasonable time as required by AS 45.05.174(c)(1).

AS 45.05.172(a) provides: Acceptance of goods occurs when the buyer

(1) after a reasonable opportunity to inspect the goods, signifies to the seller that the goods are conforming or that he will take or retain them in spite of their nonconformity;

(2) fails to make an effective rejection (§ 164), but this acceptance does not occur until the buyer has had a reasonable opportunity to inspect them; or

(3) does an act inconsistent with the sellers' ownership but if this act is wrongful as against the seller it is an acceptance only if ratified by him.

AS 45.05.174(c)(1) provides: "[T]he buyer must, within a reasonable time after he discovers or should have discovered a breach, notify the seller of the breach or be barred from any remedy. ..." [Therefore,] if proper notification is given following acceptance, damages but not cancellation is the proper remedy.

Returning now to the facts of this case and treating plaintiffs' attempted rescission as an effort to revoke acceptance and cancel the contract, we have concluded that the remedies provided by AS 45.05.214 are not available. Moreover, we have concluded that if plaintiffs are considered to have accepted the CHARBUS, and to be seeking damages, the remedies provided by AS 45.05.220 are not available.

We are compelled to reach this decision because a review of the record convinces us that the CHARBUS may not be viewed as a nonconforming good. AS 45.05.046(b) provides: "Goods ... are 'conforming' or conform to the contract when they are in accordance with the obligations under the contract." In reaching this conclusion, we accept arguendo that the CHARBUS was not insurable. This fact is not, however, dispositive. For the trial court did not find and the record does not reveal any express warranty of insurability by defendants. It then, a warranty of insurability is to be found, it must be implied.

Under the code, two forms of warranty may commonly be implied. The first of these arises under AS 45.05.096, and is known as a warranty of merchantability: it includes a warranty that the goods are fit for ordinary purposes for which such goods are used. However, under AS 45.05.496(a) a warranty of merchantability is implied only "if the seller is a merchant with respect to goods of that kind." AS 45.05.042(a) defines merchant: "'Merchant' means a person who deals in goods of the kind or otherwise by his occupation holds himself our as having knowledge or skill peculiar to the practices or goods involved in the transaction." In the present case we deal with a single isolated transaction. Defendants were not shown to deal in vessels or to possess peculiar knowledge or skill in relation to vessels. Defendants were therefore not merchants and a warranty of merchantability may not be implied.

A second implied warranty may arise under AS 45.05.098. It includes as an element a warranty of fitness for a particular purpose as distinguished from ordinary purposes under the warranty of merchantability. It is not, by its terms, restricted only to merchants. It applies to a seller, whether or not he is a merchant, who "at the time of contracting has reason to know a particular purpose for which the goods are required and that the buyer is relying on the seller's skill or judgment to select or furnish suitable goods."

At trial, the judge found—as a fact—that the CHARBUS was not useful as a commercial fishing vessel because of its uninsurability. If this finding, which is challenged on appeal, is correct, and if it had been shown that defendants knew of plaintiffs' intended use, and that plaintiffs relied upon defendants' skill or knowledge, a warranty might be implied. However, while the record indicates that the defendants knew of plaintiffs' intended commercial use, the record does not reveal that the defendants possessed special knowledge or skill which plaintiffs relied upon. The record reveals quite the opposite; it shows instead that plaintiffs were the ones possessing peculiar skill and knowledge of commercial fishing requirements. It therefore appears that a warranty of fitness for a particular purpose may not be implied. However, the question of whether a warranty of fitness may be implied is not crucial, in this case, for a review of the record convinces us that the CHARBUS was fit for commercial fishing. ...

When one considers the basis on which plaintiffs contend the CHARBUS was commercially useless, the cause of the trial court's error is apparent. That error stems not from a misunderstanding of the facts but from a misunderstanding of the law. There is considerable testimony in the record which seems to indicate that the plaintiffs based their belief that the CHARBUS was not commercially useful on their understanding of the marine mortgage. ...

Viewing the case as a whole, plaintiffs received and accepted the vessel for which they bargained. When plaintiffs discovered and notified defendants of their inability to insure the CHARBUS, impossibility excused further performance. Plaintiffs were free to use the CHARBUS. Defendants, for whose benefit insurance was required under the mortgage, may have been damaged; plaintiffs were not. Any harm suffered by plaintiffs resulted from their own misunderstanding of the law which resulted in their failing to use the CHARBUS when they might have done so. Plaintiffs lack a remedy under AS 45.05.220 for the simple reason that they have failed to prove any damages suffered as a result of the uninsurability of the CHARBUS.

The judgment is reversed, and the case remanded with directions that judgment be entered for the defendants.

UNIFORM COMMERCIAL CODE

§ 2-703. SELLER'S REMEDIES IN GENERAL

Where the buyer wrongfully rejects or revokes acceptance of goods or fails to make a payment due on or before delivery or repudiates with respect to a part or the whole, then with respect to any goods directly affected and, if the breach is of the whole contract (Section 2-612), then also with respect to the whole undelivered balance, the aggrieved seller may

(a) withhold delivery of such goods;

(b) stop delivery by any bailee as hereafter provided (Section 2-705);

(c) proceed under the next section respecting goods still unidentified to the contract;

(d) resell and recover damages as hereafter provided (Section 2-706);

(e) recover damages for non-acceptance (Section 2-708) or in a proper case the price (Section 2-709);

(f) cancel.

§ 2-717. DEDUCTION OF DAMAGES FROM THE PRICE

The buyer on notifying the seller of his intention to do so may deduct all or any part of the damages resulting from any breach of the contract from any part of the price still due under the same contract.

OFFICIAL COMMENT—PURPOSES:

1. This section permits the buyer to deduct from the price damages resulting from any breach by the seller and does not limit the relief to cases of breach of warranty as did the prior uniform statutory provision. To bring this provision into application the breach involved must be of the same contract under which the price in question is claimed to have been earned.

2. The buyer, however, must give notice of his intention to withhold all or part of the price if he wishes to avoid a default within the meaning of the section on insecurity and right to assurances. In conformity with the general policies of this Article, no formality of notice is required and any language which reasonably indicates the buyer's reason for holding up his payment is sufficient.

§ 2-718. LIQUIDATION OR LIMITATION OF DAMAGES; DEPOSITS

(1) Damages for breach by either party may be liquidated in the agreement but only at an amount which is reasonable in the light of the anticipated or actual harm caused by the breach, the difficulties of proof of loss, and the inconvenience or nonfeasibility of otherwise obtaining an adequate remedy. A term fixing unreasonably large liquidated damages is void as a penalty.

(2) Where the seller justifiably withholds delivery of goods because of the buyer's breach, the buyer is entitled to restitution of any amount by which the sum of his payments exceeds

(a) the amount to which the seller is entitled by virtue of terms liquidating the seller's damages in accordance with subsection (1), or

(b) in the absence of such terms, twenty per cent of the value of the total performance for which the buyer is obligated under the contract or $500, whichever is smaller.

(3) The buyer's right to restitution under subsection (2) is subject to offset to the extent that the seller establishes

(a) a right to recover damages under the provisions of this Article other than subsection (1), and

(b) the amount or value of any benefits received by the buyer directly or indirectly by reason of the contract.

(4) Where a seller has received payment in goods their reasonable value or the proceeds of their resale shall be treated as payments for the purposes of subsection (2); but if the seller has notice of the buyer's breach before reselling goods received in part performance, his resale is subject to the conditions laid down in this Article on resale by an aggrieved seller (Section 2-706).

SECTION THREE: SPECIFIC PERFORMANCE UNDER ARTICLE 2 OF THE UCC

Ewanchuk v. Mitchell
154 S.W.3d 476
(Mo. Ct. App. 2005)

JEFFREY W. BATES, CHIEF JUDGE. Sharon Ewanchuk (Ewanchuk) appeals from a judgment denying her claim for specific performance of an oral agreement to buy two rare Boston terrier puppies from Shelley Mitchell (Mitchell). The trial court denied relief because it concluded the oral agreement lacked the necessary definiteness to be enforced, in that there was "no meeting of the minds" between Ewanchuk and Mitchell concerning how the puppies were to be delivered. Ewanchuk claims the trial court should have granted her request for specific performance because all of the required elements of an enforceable contract were present, and Mitchell simply refused to deliver the puppies. ...

FACTS AND PROCEDURAL HISTORY

Ewanchuk and Mitchell are both in the business of breeding and raising registered Boston terriers. Ewanchuk has been licensed in this business for twelve years and resides in Alberta, Canada. Mitchell has been licensed in this business for three years and operates a kennel in Cabool, Missouri. Mitchell sold only puppies, and she mainly marketed her animals to brokers that purchased animals for resale to pet stores.

On January 20, 2003, one of Mitchell's breeding females whelped two male Boston terrier puppies ("the puppies"). Rather than being the black and white color normally found in Boston terriers, the puppies were red and white in color. This made them very unique and desirable animals.

On February 20, 2003, Mitchell offered to sell the puppies by placing an ad on the internet. That same day, Ewanchuk responded to the ad by leaving a message on Mitchell's answering machine. In the message, Ewanchuk expressed her interest in purchasing the puppies. She asked Mitchell to return the call, which Mitchell did. Ewanchuk and Mitchell had several more telephone conversations about the puppies, and Mitchell sent photographs of them to Ewanchuk. During these conversations, Ewanchuk did not commit to purchasing the puppies because they were still too young.

On March 21, 2003, Mitchell called Ewanchuk to inform her that the puppies were eight weeks old and were going to be sold to a broker the following Monday unless Ewanchuk agreed to buy them. The timing of the sale was very important to Mitchell because pet stores would not purchase puppies older than nine weeks of age. So she had to get them to a broker immediately if Ewanchuk did not buy them. Otherwise, the value of the puppies would decline because Mitchell would no longer be able to sell them to a broker or a pet store.

Mitchell initially priced the puppies at $350 each, but she agreed to sell the puppies for a total of $600 because Ewanchuk wanted to buy both of them. Ewanchuk provided Mitchell with a credit card number which was used to charge the $600 payment. Although Ewanchuk and Mitchell were able to agree on the puppies' price, they were unable to agree on when and how the puppies would be delivered to Ewanchuk. Because the puppies were only two months old, Ewanchuk wanted Mitchell to keep the puppies until they were three to four months old and fully vaccinated. Mitchell, however, insisted that Ewanchuk accept delivery by April 15, 2003.

Ewanchuk and Mitchell were unable to reach any agreement concerning the mode of delivery to be used. Ewanchuk initially wanted both puppies shipped to her by air in one container, but Mitchell would not do so. She was concerned that the puppies might fight if they were shipped together. Ewanchuk said that she would try to get her husband or son—who were both truck drivers—to come pick the puppies up from Mitchell. Ewanchuk, however, was unable to make suitable arrangements to get this done. Ewanchuk also proposed that Mitchell bring the puppies to Ewanchuk in Oklahoma while she was on a trip to Texas to pick up some other dogs. Mitchell was willing to do so, but Ewanchuk provided no definite date as to when the trip would occur. Around April 1, 2003, Ewanchuk did travel from Canada to Texas to pick up the other dogs as planned. ... [However,] the planned delivery in Oklahoma did not occur.

After these events took place, Mitchell spoke to Ewanchuk by telephone. During the call, Ewanchuk said she wanted the puppies delivered by air on April 15, 2003. On that date, Ewanchuk telephoned Mitchell to discuss shipping arrangements. In this telephone call, Ewanchuk insisted Mitchell ship the puppies together in one crate. Ewanchuk testified that "I wanted the two puppies shipped together in one kennel, and they [Mitchell and her husband] refused to do that." Mitchell would not ship the three-month-old puppies together because she believed they "would fight and that it was not safe for the puppies to be in the same crate at that age." Mitchell was willing to send one puppy in one crate, but Ewanchuk wanted both delivered together. Ewanchuk testified that Mitchell "repudiated" the contract during that call and said she would refund Ewanchuk's money.

After April 15, 2003, Ewanchuk made no further arrangements to have the puppies delivered to her and had no further direct contact with Mitchell. Ewanchuk later hired an attorney—who filed suit on her behalf on May 16, 2003—seeking specific performance of the oral agreement and injunctive relief to prevent Mitchell from selling the puppies to someone else. After suit was filed but before Mitchell read the petition, she sold both puppies for $350 each to other buyers. After Ewanchuk learned the puppies had been sold, she was granted leave to file an amended petition that added a count seeking actual and punitive damages from Mitchell.

After hearing the foregoing evidence presented at trial on November 26, 2003, the trial court entered judgment for Mitchell and ordered that the $600 she had tendered into court be paid to Ewanchuk. Ewanchuk appealed. The trial court found for Mitchell—in pertinent part—for the following reason:

> [T]here was no meeting of the minds as to one of the essential terms of the contract, namely when the puppies would be shipped to the Plaintiff in Canada, and how the shipment would be arranged. ... Further, a dispute arose as to whether the puppies should be shipped in one crate or two crates. Therefore, the Court finds that all of the essential terms of

the contract were not agreed upon and that the Agreement lacked a definiteness necessary for its enforcement.

III. DISCUSSION AND DECISION

In Ewanchuk's single point on appeal, she claims the trial court should have granted specific performance because: (1) the required elements of an enforceable contract were present; and (2) Mitchell breached the contract by refusing to deliver the puppies. The oral agreement between Ewanchuk and Mitchell was a contract for the sale of goods within the meaning of Missouri's version of the Uniform Commercial Code (UCC). *See* § 400.2-105(1); *Central Production Credit Ass'n v. Hopkins*, 810 S.W.2d 108, 114 (Mo. App. 1991) (oral agreement to purchase 100 cattle was a contract for the sale of goods governed by the UCC). Therefore, this transaction in goods is governed by the law of sales found in Article 2 of the UCC, which is codified in § 400.2-101 through § 400.2-725.

In the first prong of Ewanchuk's bifurcated argument, she contends the trial court misapplied the law by concluding that the parties' failure to agree on the terms of delivery made their agreement too indefinite to be enforceable. We agree. We begin our analysis by noting that under the UCC, "[e]ven though one or more terms are left open a contract for sale does not fail for indefiniteness if the parties have intended to make a contract and there is a reasonably certain basis for giving an appropriate remedy." § 400.2-204(3). *See also Computer Network, Ltd. v. Purcell Tire & Rubber Co.*, 747 S.W.2d 669, 674 (Mo. App. 1988).

Here, it is clear the parties did intend to make a contract because: (1) Mitchell admitted the contract's existence in her answer to the amended petition; and (2) she accepted full payment in advance for the puppies. *See* § 400.2-201(3)(b) and (c); *Cargill Inc., Commodity Marketing Division v. Hale*, 537 S.W.2d 667, 669 (Mo. App. 1976) (defendant's testimony constituted an admission of contract and prohibited defendant from asserting the statute of frauds as a defense). The manner and place of delivery was left unresolved by the parties' negotiation. Because the parties failed to agree upon the terms of delivery, the UCC cured this omission for them by specifying both the time and place of delivery. Section 400.2-309(1) required that the puppies be delivered within a reasonable time. Section 400.2-308(a) required that delivery take place at Mitchell's place of business in Cabool, Missouri.

The trial court misapplied the law by concluding that the parties' agreement "lacked a definiteness necessary for its enforcement." On appeal, however, we are "primarily concerned with the correctness of the trial court's result, not the route taken by the trial court to reach that result." *Business Men's Assur. Co. of America v. Graham*, 984 S.W.2d 501, 506 (Mo. 1999). "[T]he judgment will be affirmed if cognizable under any theory, regardless of whether the reasons advanced by the trial court are wrong or not sufficient." *Id.*

The second prong of Ewanchuk's argument is that Mitchell breached the contract by refusing to deliver the puppies. We reject this aspect of Ewanchuk's argument. The trial court entered judgment for Mitchell after concluding the contract was unenforceable. This conclusion is correct, but for a different reason than the one upon which the trial court relied.

It is well-settled that a party is bound by his own testimony which is not corrected or explained. *Taylor v. Vestal*, 304 S.W.2d 820, 823 (Mo. 1957). At the trial, Ewanchuk testified unequivocally that she had always wanted the puppies shipped to her by air in the same container. She also testified unequivocally that—from the outset of the negotiation—Mitchell absolutely refused to do so because she believed the puppies would fight if they were shipped together. The issue about the mode of shipping came to a head during the telephone call on April 15, 2003. Ewanchuk insisted the puppies be shipped to her in one crate, and Mitchell refused. Mitchell offered to ship one dog in one crate, but Ewanchuk was adamant that she wanted the puppies shipped together. At that point, Mitchell cancelled the contract and said she would refund Ewanchuk's money. Thereafter, Ewanchuk made no further arrangements to have the puppies delivered to her, and she never contacted Mitchell directly again.

As noted above, the parties failed to reach an agreement upon the manner and place of delivery during their negotiation. Therefore, the UCC supplied that term of the agreement by requiring Ewanchuk to pick up the puppies at Mitchell's place of business in Cabool. Ewanchuk did not pick up the puppies by April 15, 2003. Instead, on the date delivery was due to occur, Ewanchuk insisted that Mitchell ship both puppies by air in one crate to Alberta, Canada. It was this demand which caused Mitchell's refusal to deliver the puppies and consequent cancellation of the contract. Absent Mitchell's agreement, the UCC did not give Ewanchuk the right to receive delivery of the puppies in this fashion.

Both by decisional law and statute, Missouri recognizes the doctrine of anticipatory repudiation. *Missouri Public Service Co. v. Peabody Coal Co.*, 583 S.W.2d 721, 724 (Mo. App. 1979); § 400.2-610. A party repudiates a contract by manifesting a positive intention not to perform by words or conduct. *Gateway Aviation, Inc. v. Cessna Aircraft Co.*, 577 S.W.2d 860, 862 (Mo. App. 1978). Section 400.2-610 states in pertinent part that, "[w]hen either party repudiates the contract with respect to a performance not yet due the loss of which will substantially impair the value of the contract to the other, the aggrieved party may ... (b) resort to any remedy for breach (section 400.2-703 or section 400.2-711)."

Upon a buyer's repudiation of the contract, in whole or in part, one of the seller's available remedies is cancellation of the contract. § 400.2-703(f).

Here, Ewanchuk's own testimony demonstrated that she insisted upon a mode of delivery (both puppies in one crate) and a place of delivery—Alberta, Canada, via air transportation—to which Mitchell had not agreed and to which Ewanchuk was not entitled under the UCC. After making this impermissible demand, Ewanchuk also testified that she never contacted Mitchell directly again and made no further arrangements to have the puppies delivered to her.

Thus, Ewanchuk's trial testimony—by which she was bound—proved that she repudiated the contract on April 15, 2003. Since the puppies were then 12 weeks old, Ewanchuk's repudiation impaired the value of the contract to Mitchell because she could no longer sell the puppies to a broker or pet store. Based on this repudiation, Mitchell was authorized to cancel the contract, which she did. *See Scullin Steel Co. v. Paccar, Inc.*, 708 S.W.2d 756, 761 (Mo. App. 1986) (because buyer repudiated contract, the value of the contract to seller was impaired and seller was entitled to resort to statutory remedies for breach found in § 400.2-703).

In conclusion, the trial court properly denied Ewanchuk's request for specific performance and other relief because the contract was unenforceable. The reason the contract was unenforceable, however, was because it had been cancelled by Mitchell after repudiation by Ewanchuk. Although the trial court did not rely on the doctrine of repudiation as the basis for its decision, we may do so to uphold the judgment based on the record before us. *See Fesperman v. Silver Dollar City, Inc.*, 796 S.W.2d 384, 387–88 (Mo. App. 1990). The judgment of the trial court is affirmed.

UNIFORM COMMERCIAL CODE

§ 2-716. BUYER'S RIGHT TO SPECIFIC PERFORMANCE OR REPLEVIN

(1) Specific performance may be decreed where the goods are unique or in other proper circumstances.

(2) The decree for specific performance may include such terms and conditions as to payment of the price, damages, or other relief as the court may deem just.

(3) The buyer has a right of replevin for goods identified to the contract if after reasonable effort he is unable to effect cover for such goods or the circumstances reasonably indicate that such effort will be unavailing or if the goods have been

shipped under reservation and satisfaction of the security interest in them has been made or tendered. In the case of goods bought for personal, family, or household purposes, the buyer's right of replevin vests upon acquisition of a special property, even if the seller had not then repudiated or failed to deliver.

CHAPTER FOURTEEN

AFFIRMATIVE DEFENSES UNDER ARTICLE 2

After plaintiffs commence breach-of-contract or breach-of-warranty actions under the common law, defendants typically file answers—which lists general, global, and/or specific denials as well as affirmative defenses. *See Lasley v. Combined Transport, Inc.* 261 P.3d 1215, 1224–25 (Or. 2011) (stressing that a general denial is required to "fairly meet the substance of the allegations denied" and reiterating that an affirmative defense must be pleaded if a defendant wants to present evidence which does not directly controvert a one of plaintiff's facts or allegations.); and, *Cook Composites, Inc. v. Westlake Styrene Corp.,* 15 S.W.3d 124, 136 (Tex. App.—Houston [14 Dist.] 2000) ("Generally speaking, affirmative defenses are any propositions that a defendant may interpose to defeat the plaintiff's prima facie case. 'They do not rebut any factual propositions asserted in the plaintiff's case, but open the way for the defendant to adduce evidence establishing an independent reason why the plaintiff may not recover.'), citing *W.R. Grace Co. v. Scotch Corp., Inc.*, 753 S.W.2d 743, 746 (Tex. App.—Austin 1988, writ denied).

Defendants also deny various allegations and raise multiple affirmative defenses in UCC Article 2 lawsuits. Many of the defenses mirror those that are advanced in common-law lawsuits. And others are Article 2-specific affirmative defenses. *See, e.g., RM Crowe Prop. Servs. Co. v. Strategic Energy, L.L.C.*, 348 S.W.3d 444, 449 (Tex. App.—Dallas 2011) (raising "contract modification" and "waiver of contractual right"—based on course of dealing and course of performance—as affirmative defenses); *Mobile Hous., Inc. v. Stone*, 490 S.W.2d 611, 615–16 (Tex.Civ. App.—Dallas 1973) (raising "intent to cure" as an affirmative defense); *Freudenberg Spunweb Co. v. Fibervisions L.P.*, 2006 WL 1064173, *20 (Del. Super. 2006) (reporting that the defendant raised multiple affirmative defenses—failure to give timely notice under Delaware Uniform Commercial Code, waiver of breach-of-contract claim, waiver of a breach-of-warranty claim and waiver of a right to reject allegedly non-conforming goods); and *First Hawaiian Bank v. Powers*, 998 P.2d 55, 67 (Hawai'i App. 2000) raising the four-year, statute-of-limitations defense under UCC § 2-725.

This chapter is devoted to discussing some of the affirmative defenses that often appear in UCC Article 2 litigation.

SECTION ONE: STATUTE-OF-FRAUDS DEFENSE UNDER THE UCC

The Parliament of England enacted, "AN ACT FOR PREVENTION OF FRAUDS AND PERJURIES." 29 Car. 2, c. 3 (1677). The statute's stated purpose was to guard against or diminish the likelihood of fraud and perjury when disputes arose over the enforceability of oral contracts. The English Statute of Frauds has been repealed. Yet, the overwhelming majority of legislatures in the United States used the English Statute of Frauds to fashion their unique statutes of frauds. *See Kiely v. St. Germain*, 670 P.2d 764, 768 (Colo. 1983).

Under the English statute, a court would not enforce any agreement unless a plaintiff produced a written and signed contract. The drafters of the Uniform Commercial Code considered the English Statute of Frauds when they crafted U.C.C. § 2-201—the statute of frauds which applies to the sale of goods. To be sure, section 2-201 has generated a considerable amount of controversy. The following case presents an excellent illustration of how courts apply section 2-201 to resolve breach-of-contract disputes under the UCC Article 2.

Robins v. Zwirner
713 F.Supp.2d 367
(C.C.S.D.N.Y. 2010)

WILLIAM H. PAULEY III, DISTRICT JUDGE: Plaintiff Craig Robins (Robins) brings this breach of contract action against Defendants David Zwirner (Zwirner), David Zwirner Gallery, and David Zwirner, Inc. (collectively the Gallery) claiming that Zwirner reneged on a promise to sell certain paintings by the artist Marlene Dumas (Dumas) to Robins. …

BACKGROUND

This lawsuit offers an unflattering portrait of the art world—a realm of self-proclaimed royalty full of "blacklists," "greylists," and astonishing chicanery. Robins is an art patron from Miami Beach, Florida, who has amassed a substantial collection of Dumas' works. Zwirner is an art dealer and the owner of the Gallery bearing his name in the Chelsea section of Manhattan. The Gallery displays and sells works of art and represents contemporary artists. Dumas is a South African artist who Zwirner has represented since April 2008. Before that time, another New York gallerist Jack Tilton (Tilton) represented Dumas for almost two decades and displayed her works at a gallery bearing his name on the Upper East Side of Manhattan.

A. The Confidentiality Agreement

In late 2004, Robins approached Tilton for assistance in selling a Dumas painting titled *Reinhardt's Daughter*. Robins had purchased *Reinhardt's Daughter* in the Secondary Market. Tilton contacted Zwirner—with whom he had done business before—to ascertain whether Zwirner could sell the painting on consignment. Thereafter, Zwirner informed Tilton that he had located a buyer. Tilton told Zwirner repeatedly that Robins wanted the transaction to be kept secret. During a telephone conversation with Tilton, Zwirner agreed to keep the sale confidential (the "Confidentiality Agreement").

According to Robins, the Confidentiality Agreement was intended to prevent Dumas, who opposed Secondary Market sales of her works, from learning of the deal. Dumas did not sell to collectors who "churned" her work in the Secondary Market. Contrary to Robins' and Tilton's statements, Zwirner avers that he "did not enter into any confidentiality agreement, written or oral, with Mr. Robins" and that, although an art sale is usually kept confidential during negotiations, after a piece is sold, "the new ownership of the work is as public or as private as the new owner wishes to make it."

On December 2, 2004, Robins and Zwirner signed a document titled "Robins Exchange No. 1004," which memorialized the sale of *Reinhardt's Daughter* from Robins to Zwirner in a section called "Relinquished Property Contract ('Sales Agreement')." No confidentiality provision was included in the Sales Agreement.

B. The Dumas Blacklist

In early 2005, while Zwirner was collaborating with Dumas on a catalogue, he informed the artist that Robins had sold *Reinhardt's Daughter*. On March 5, 2005, Dumas' studio manager in the Netherlands, Jolie van Leeuwen (van Leeuwen), emailed Tilton inquiring if Robins had sold *Reinhardt's Daughter*. Tilton confirmed that Robins had sold the painting for personal reasons. Tilton testified that when van Leeuwen learned of Robins' sale of *Reinhardt's Daughter*, she was "quite upset" and "hysterical." Upon learning Robins had sold *Reinhardt's Daughter*,

Dumas also "became so incensed that she literally blacklisted [Robins] from purchasing any other work of hers in the Primary Market."

Tilton acknowledged that Dumas "blacklisted" persons suspected of selling her work in the Secondary Market. In early 2005, van Leeuwen circulated to gallerists several lists of collectors forbidden from purchasing Dumas' art (collectively the "Dumas Blacklist"). Names were added to the lists by recipients who contacted Dumas to inform her of sales in the Secondary Market. A March 2005 version of the Dumas Blacklist includes Robins' name under the heading "Grey List." According to Tilton, the Dumas Blacklist was actually two lists—a Blacklist and the Grey List. The two lists were functionally equivalent—persons on either roll were theoretically forbidden by Dumas from purchasing her works.

The March 2005 version of the Dumas Blacklist contains the following passage:

> From all of you [gallerists] I have received names of persons that we consider for a blacklist. Also with the reasons why these people are considered for a black list. We also spoke about the difficulties of making such a list and about personal grieve [sic] about grey lists of names that are not to be called crooks but you will not so quickly sell them another work from Dumas anymore. Most of these grey names are from people that want a new piece or people that sell thru other galleries or sell themselves, but still consider themselves as admirers of DUMAS. But please let [sic] not sell to the grey list persons either, for the time being.

Many of the names on the Dumas Blacklist are accompanied by the informant who disclosed the identity of a seller in the Secondary Market. Robins' name appears on the Grey List, but no informant is listed. Zwirner's name is also on the March 2005 Dumas Blacklist with a notation that Jack Tilton—his competitor—reported him. Tilton admitted he added Zwirner because Zwirner "was actively selling numerous pieces by Marlene, buying and selling in the secondary market." There were only two ways a person could be removed from the Dumas Blacklist. First, Dumas herself could cross someone off the list. Alternatively, if a gallerist was on the list, his name could be removed if he became Dumas' representative and was given "access to her work."

C. The Gallery Agreement

In early 2005, Zwirner told Robins that his name was on the Dumas Blacklist. Robins was "livid" when he learned that Zwirner had revealed his sale of *Reinhardt's Daughter* to Dumas. After telling Tilton that he wished to sue Zwirner, Tilton encouraged Robins to meet with Zwirner to stave off litigation.

In late March 2005, Robins, Zwirner, and Tilton met at the Gallery. According to Robins, as consideration for refraining from legal action, Zwirner agreed to give Robins "first choice, after museums, to purchase one or more" of Dumas' works whenever Dumas had an exhibition at the Gallery and to remove Robins name from the Dumas Blacklist (the "Gallery Agreement"). The Gallery Agreement was oral and concluded with a handshake. Tilton remembers that Robins was given "first choice on something that [Zwirner] would show in his gallery going forward," which could include one or one or more paintings because "sometimes Marlene works in groups."

Not surprisingly, Zwirner recalls the meeting differently. In his version, Tilton was not present and the meeting occurred in May 2005. At that time, Zwirner agreed "in principle" to sell Robins "other unspecified works from upcoming exhibitions of artists that [Zwirner] represented at the time, whose work was in high demand and for whom there were waiting lists." Robins and Zwirner both agree that there is no writing memorializing the meeting or the Gallery Agreement. ... Robins advised Zwirner that he intended to purchase three Exhibition paintings by Dumas: *Figure in a Landscape*, *Under Construction*, and *Wall Weeping* (the "Three Dumas Paintings"). Zwirner refused to sell these paintings to Robins. Instead, he offered Robins a Dumas painting titled *The Grapes of Plenty*, which Robins claims was nothing more than a "glaring sarcastic insult."

On March 29, 2010, Robins commenced this action and sought a temporary restraining order. Robins seeks specific performance of the Gallery Agreement because Dumas' works are "nearly impossible to obtain as Dumas creates a limited amount." Robins also claims the Exhibition is "a unique body of Israeli themed works," and Dumas "may never do similar paintings." Absent an injunction allowing him to purchase the art, Robins claims he "will not have first provenance in any of the subject paintings" which would "materially" impair his collection. In his Amended Complaint, Robins alleges that in, reliance on Zwirner fulfilling the Gallery Agreement, he purchased several Dumas works—a set of seven drawings in June 2005 and a $500,000 oil painting in December 2005. On April 21, 2010, this Court conducted an evidentiary hearing.

DISCUSSION

B. Likelihood of Success on the Merits

Robins' application for injunctive relief rests primarily on Zwirner's alleged breach of the Confidentiality and Gallery Agreements. Defendants contend that the Statute of Frauds bars enforcement of these two oral agreements.

1. Statute of Frauds

Under New York law, "a contract for the sale of goods for the price of $500 or more is not enforceable" without a contemporaneous writing "sufficient to indicate that a contract for sale has been made between the parties and signed by the party against whom enforcement is sought." N.Y. U.C.C. § 2-201(1); *Hoffmann v. Boone*, 708 F.Supp. 78, 80 (S.D.N.Y. 1989) (applying § 2-201 to sale of art). However, where a service component of a contract "predominates" over the incidental sale of personal property, an oral agreement is barred by the Statute of Frauds only if it is incapable of being performed within one year.

Where an "oral agreement between the parties call[s] for performance of an indefinite duration and [can] only be terminated within one year by its breach during that period," it is void under the Statute of Frauds. *D & N Boening, Inc. v. Kirsch Beverages, Inc.*, 483 N.Y.S.2d 164, 472 N.E.2d 992, 995 (1984). New York courts look to "the main objective sought to be accomplished by the contracting parties" to determine whether a contract is for the sale of goods or rendition of services.

a. The Confidentiality Agreement

The Confidentiality Agreement between Tilton—as agent for Robins—and Zwirner was a verbal accord for a service to be performed by Zwirner—non-disclosure of Robins' sale. ... [A]ccording to Tilton, [it] was intended to last for "an unlimited duration." Since the agreement was premised on Dumas never learning that Robins had sold *Reinhardt's Daughter*, the Confidentiality Agreement could not be fully performed within one year. Indeed, the only way the Confidentiality Agreement could terminate within one year was if Zwirner breached the agreement. Enforcement of this contract is barred by the Statute of Frauds. *See Koret, Inc. v. RJR Nabisco, Inc.*, 702 F.Supp. 412, 414–15 (S.D.N.Y. 1988) ("An oral contract that is 'terminable within one year only upon a breach by one of the parties' is not enforceable under New York law").

b. The Gallery Agreement

Under the Gallery Agreement, Robins was to (1) receive first choice, after museums, to purchase one or more Dumas works, (2) be removed from the Dumas Blacklist, and (3) receive access to Dumas' works in the Primary Market. Despite Plaintiff's averments, the primary objective of this agreement was the future sale to Robins of at least one Dumas painting. Plaintiff's assertion that this is a service agreement is undercut by the fact that only Dumas—a non-party to this litigation—can remove Robins from the Blacklist. The only aspect of the Gallery Agreement that Zwirner can control is the sale of the Three Dumas Paintings from the Gallery.

The Gallery Agreement granted Robins a right of first refusal—in essence, an agreement to agree on a future painting. A right of first refusal "requires [an] owner, when and if he decides to sell, to offer the property first to the party holding the preemptive right so that he may meet a third-party offer or buy the property at some other price set by a previously stipulated method." *Metro. Transp. Auth. v. Bruken Realty Corp.*, 501 N.Y.S.2d 306, 492 N.E.2d 379, 382 (1986).

Rights of first refusal and agreements to agree on the sale of a good are both governed by the U.C.C., and it is "well settled that an oral agreement to execute an agreement that is within the [S]tatute of [F]rauds is itself within the statute." *Backus Plywood Corp. v. Commercial Decal, Inc.*, 317 F.2d 339, 343 (2d Cir. 1963) (collecting cases); *Stillman v. Townsend,* 2006 WL 2067035, at *2–3 (S.D.N.Y.) ("[E]ven if the Agreement constitutes an oral 'agreement to agree,' it remains subject to the statute of frauds."). The relevant Statute of Frauds provisions are set forth in U.C.C. sections 2-201—the sale of goods provision—and 1-206, the sale of personal property provision.

Under either § 1-206 or § 2-201, enforcement of the Gallery Agreement is barred by the Statute of Frauds. The Three Dumas Paintings are each priced over $1 million, and Plaintiff has not come forward with any writing signed by Zwirner promising to sell paintings to Robins. Absent a writing signed by Zwirner, enforcement of the oral Gallery Agreement is barred.

2. Promissory Estoppel

As an alternative ground for recovery, Robins submits that Zwirner should be estopped from reneging on his promise to sell the Three Dumas Paintings. To recover under promissory estoppel, a plaintiff must show (1) a clear and unambiguous promise, (2) reasonable and foreseeable reliance by the party to whom the promise was made, and (3) an injury to the party to whom the promise was made by reason of the reliance. *Cyberchron Corp. v. Calldata Sys. Dev., Inc.*, 47 F.3d 39, 44 (2d Cir. 1995). When promissory estoppel is interjected to overcome a valid Statute of Frauds defense, it "has been strictly construed to apply only in those rare cases where 'the circumstances [are] such as to render it unconscionable to deny the oral promise upon which the promisee has relied.'" *Philo Smith & Co. v. USLIFE Corp.,* 554 F.2d 34, 36 (2d Cir. 1977).

Because Robins alleges no injuries sufficiently severe to be "unconscionable," he is unlikely to succeed on estoppel grounds. The Court of Appeals has defined an "unconscionable injury" as "beyond that which flows naturally (expectation damages) from the non-performance of the unenforceable agreement." *Merex A.G. v. Fairchild Weston Sys., Inc.*, 29 F.3d 821, 827 (2d Cir. 1994). Here, any injuries Robins suffers are within the realm one would reasonably expect from the non-performance of a sales contract—Robins does not own the artworks promised to him.

Moreover, when Robins sold *Reinhardt's Daughter*, he was aware Dumas might learn of the transaction and ban him from purchasing in the Primary Market. Indeed, it was for that reason that he sought the Confidentiality Agreement. "To invoke the power that equity possesses to trump the Statute of Frauds," a plaintiff must suffer a greater injury than one that is both predictable and, to a certain degree, the consequences of the Plaintiff's own choices.

The standard of "unconscionability" cannot be judged solely based on Plaintiff's personal tastes. Because Robins has not shown an unexpected and serious injury flowing from the breach of Zwirner's promises, has been able to purchase Dumas art, and has been offered another painting from the Exhibition by Zwirner, he is unlikely to show an unconscionable injury. Accordingly, a preliminary injunction on estoppel grounds is not warranted. ...

CONCLUSION

As the facts of this case make clear, some in the art world desire a market that is neither open nor honest. Thus, collectors in this seemingly refined bazaar should heed the admonition "caveat emptor" and be mindful of the Statute of Frauds.

For the foregoing reasons, Plaintiff Craig Robins' application for a preliminary injunction is denied.

UNIFORM COMMERCIAL CODE

§ 2-201. FORMAL REQUIREMENTS; STATUTE OF FRAUDS

(1) Except as otherwise provided in this section a contract for the sale of goods for the price of $500 or more is not enforceable by way of action or defense unless there is some writing sufficient to indicate that a contract for sale has been made between the parties and signed by the party against whom enforcement is sought or by his authorized agent or broker. A writing is not insufficient because it omits or incorrectly states a term agreed upon but the contract is not enforceable under this paragraph beyond the quantity of goods shown in such writing.

(2) Between merchants if within a reasonable time a writing in confirmation of the contract and sufficient against the sender is received and the party receiving it has reason to

know its contents, it satisfies the requirements of subsection (1) against such party unless written notice of objection to its contents is given within 10 days after it is received.

(3) A contract which does not satisfy the requirements of subsection (1) but which is valid in other respects is enforceable

(a) if the goods are to be specially manufactured for the buyer and are not suitable for sale to others in the ordinary course of the seller's business and the seller, before notice of repudiation is received and under circumstances which reasonably indicate that the goods are for the buyer, has made either a substantial beginning of their manufacture or commitments for their procurement; or

(b) if the party against whom enforcement is sought admits in his pleading, testimony or otherwise in court that a contract for sale was made, but the contract is not enforceable under this provision beyond the quantity of goods admitted; or

(c) with respect to goods for which payment has been made and accepted or which have been received and accepted (Sec. 2-606).

SECTION TWO: THE APPLICATION OF THE PAROL EVIDENCE RULE UNDER THE UCC

An essential principle of contract law is *pacta sunt servanda*. There are various translations of the Latin phrase: (1) "Agreements must be obeyed." *U.S. v. Verdugo-Urquidez,* 939 F.2d 1341, 1362 (9th Cir. 1991); (2) "A deal's a deal." *Industrial Representatives, Inc. v. CP Clare Corp.*, 74 F.3d 128, 132 (7th Cir. 1996); and (3) "Agreements of the parties must be observed." *Laserdynamics Inc. v. Acer Am. Corp.*, 209 F.R.D. 388, 392 (C.C.S.D. Tex. 2002). *See also* JOSEPH M. PERILLO, CALAMARI AND PERILLO ON CONTRACTS § 13.1, at 445 (6th ed. 2009) ("The harsh traditional common law rule was '*pacta sunt servanda*'; promises must be kept though the heavens fall."). Furthermore, this common-law doctrine protects the parties' intentions under both oral and written contracts. *Air Safety, Inc. v. Teachers Realty Corp.*, 706 N.E.2d 882, 884 (Ill. 1999) ("An agreement, when reduced to writing, must be presumed to speak the intention of the parties who signed it. It speaks for itself, and the intention with which it was executed must be determined from the language used. It is not to be changed by extrinsic evidence.").

However, to ensure that a *written* contract is the final expressions of the parties' intent, the parol evidence rule provides even more protection: It precludes the admission of evidence that adds to, modifies, or contradicts a written agreement. Quite simply, the parol evidence rule allows a contracting party "to protect himself against perjury, infirmity of memory, or the death of witnesses." 30 AM. JUR.2D EVIDENCE § 1016 (1967). Or stated slightly differently, the parol evidence rule prevents a court from considering contracting parties' prior or contemporaneous writings or oral statements in a breach-of-contract dispute, if those written or oral statements contradict the parties' final, written contract.

Of course, a few exceptions temper the arguably "harsh effect" of the parol evidence rule. Extrinsic evidence of contracting parties' intentions "may be introduced to prove mutual mistake, conditional delivery, a lack of consideration or fraud." *O'Brien v. Cacciatore*, 591 N.E.2d 1384, 1390 (Ill. App. Ct. 1992). In addition, prior agreements, oral statements, or other forms of extrinsic evidence may be used to explain ambiguities in totally integrated contracts.

Section 2-202 of the UCC is entitled, "Final Written Expression: Parol or Extrinsic Evidence." Does § 2-202 codify all common-law parol-evidence principles? Do common-law parol-evidence exceptions apply to UCC Article 2, sale-of-goods disputes? Consider the analysis and ruling in the following cases.

A. The Parol Evidence Rule and Merger Clauses Under Article 2

L.F. Brands Marketing, Inc. v. Dillard's, Inc.
314 S.W.3d 736
(Ark. Ct. App. 2009)

RITA W. GRUBER, JUDGE. This case involves breach-of-contract claims between appellee Dillard's, Inc., and appellant L.F. Brands Marketing, Inc. (L.F. Brands), one of Dillard's suppliers. A Pulaski County jury awarded Dillard's $1,265,938.98. On appeal, L.F. Brands argues that the written purchase orders between the parties control over prior oral agreements between the parties concerning allowances Dillard's deducted from the account balance between the parties. ...

L.F. Brands sold clothing to Dillard's for many years. Dillard's would submit purchase orders to L.F. Brands, describing the merchandise and price of the goods, among other things. A document—entitled "DILLARD'S, INC. PURCHASE ORDER TERMS, CONDITIONS & INSTRUCTIONS" (purchase order document)—applied to all transactions involving Dillard's purchase orders. Included in that document was the following provision, hereinafter referred to as "Paragraph A2":

> [L.F. Brands] acknowledges by acceptance and shipment against any Dillard Purchase Order that the terms, conditions and instructions stated herein, in the Purchase Order, [and in two other Dillard's documents] (collectively, the Agreement) shall bind [L.F. Brands] and shall constitute the entire agreement between Dillard and [L.F. Brands], which cannot be modified by either party except in a writing executed by both parties, or [another method]; provided, however, that this provision shall not apply to markdown allowance and other credits authorized by [L.F. Brands].

In another provision, Dillard's was allowed to offset all merchandise allowances, chargebacks, and other credits from any invoices or other amounts due L.F. Brands (Paragraph B11). The purchase order document also contained a second merger/integration clause (Paragraph F6), as well as a provision requiring any amendments, modifications, or cancellations to be in writing (Paragraph F7).

L.F. Brands went out of business in December 2003. In February 2004, at the end of its fiscal year, Dillard's deducted markdown allowances and chargebacks from its account balance with L.F. Brands. These allowances and chargebacks are the subject of this appeal. L.F. Brands filed suit for breach of contract on September 15, 2005, alleging that Dillard's owed $2,367,601.19. Dillard's denied the allegations of the complaint and asserted that the amount sought was subject to setoffs for claims, allowances, discounts, and chargebacks in excess of the amount Dillard's owed L.F. Brands. Dillard's also filed a counterclaim seeking to recover the debit balance L.F. Brands owed.

The record before us contains undisputed testimony from several employees of both L.F. Brands and Dillard's that the parties would agree on a gross margin for Dillard's at the beginning of each fashion season. In 2003, the agreement would be that Dillard's would have a 40% margin for L.F. Brands' dresses and a 38% margin for sportswear. The parties would monitor the sales of the clothing throughout the course of the season, and allowances would be processed at various times during the year to make adjustments to the margins. At the end of the year, the parties would determine whether the gross-margin goal had been met. If it had not, the parties would negotiate on further allowances to achieve an acceptable margin less than the goal. In 2002, the parties had agreed on similar margins that were not met. After negotiations between the parties, Dillard's processed allowances that allowed it to achieve margins greater than 30%.

Prior to trial, the circuit court denied motions for summary judgment by both parties, finding that the entirety of the parties' agreement must be determined by looking to both the written documents, as supplemented by their oral agreements. The court further found that there was some ambiguity in Paragraph A2 when read with the rest of the document, particularly Paragraph B11. The court noted that parol evidence could be admitted to explain the ambiguity.

The case was submitted to the jury on instructions that included a definition of "course of dealing" and that course-of-dealing evidence may be used to give particular meaning to and supplement the terms of the agreement. The jury found for Dillard's on L.F. Brands's complaint. The jury also found for Dillard's on its counterclaim and awarded $1,265,938.98. Judgment was entered on the jury's verdict on May 9, 2007. L.F. Brands filed a motion for judgment notwithstanding the verdict, asserting that the merger clause of the purchase order document superceded the prior oral agreements concerning merchandise allowances. The circuit court did not rule upon the motion and it was deemed denied. L.F. Brands timely filed its notice of appeal.

L.F. Brands does not challenge the sufficiency of the evidence. Instead it argues that the merger/integration clause in the purchase order document—as a matter of law—superceded any prior oral agreements between itself and Dillard's. L.F. Brands asserts that the purchase order document was the parties' complete agreement and that—because the document also discussed the merchandise allowances—the circuit court should not have allowed Dillard's to introduce the course-of-dealing and course-of-performance evidence. We disagree.

This argument sweeps too broadly in this case for the sale of goods governed by Article 2 of the Uniform Commercial Code (UCC), which has a specific provision allowing parol evidence to be introduced even in situations involving fully integrated written agreements. Under the UCC's parol evidence rule, a writing intended to be the parties' final expression of their agreement may not be contradicted by evidence of any prior agreement or contemporaneous oral agreement. But it may be explained or supplemented by evidence of the parties' course of dealing or course of performance. ARK. CODE ANN. § 4-2-202(a) (Supp. 2007); *Bank of America v. C.D. Smith Motor Co.*, 106 S.W.3d 425 (Ark. 2003).

ARKANSAS CODE ANNOTATED § 4-1-303 (Supp. 2007), referred to in § 4-2-202(a), provides in relevant part as follows:

> (a) A "course of performance" is a sequence of conduct between the parties to a particular transaction that exists if:
>
> (1) the agreement of the parties with respect to the transaction involves repeated occasions for performance by a party; and
>
> (2) the other party, with knowledge of the nature of the performance and opportunity for objection to it, accepts the performance or acquiesces in it without objection.

> (b) A "course of dealing" is a sequence of conduct concerning previous transactions between the parties to a particular transaction that is fairly to be regarded as establishing a common basis of understanding for interpreting their expressions and other conduct.
>
> ...
>
> (d) A course of performance or course of dealing between the parties ... is relevant in ascertaining the meaning of the parties' agreement, may give particular meaning to specific terms of the agreement, and may supplement or qualify the terms of the agreement.

We need not decide whether the evidence in this case is properly called "course of dealing" evidence or "course of performance" evidence because both terms would apply under the circumstances of this case.

L.F. Brands relies upon the supreme court's decisions in *Farmers Cooperative Association v. Garrison*, 454 S.W.2d 644 (Ark. 1970), and *Ultracuts, Ltd. v. Wal-Mart Stores, Inc.*, 33 S.W.3d 128 (2000), in support of its argument that the purchase order was a complete agreement with a merger/integration clause and, therefore, the parol evidence rule barred introduction of the testimony concerning the merchandise allowances. However, *Farmers Cooperative* and *Ultracuts* were not UCC sales cases and did not involve or discuss parol and course-of-dealing/course-of-performance evidence.

In *Bank of America*, the Arkansas Supreme Court held that the use of course-of-performance and course-of-dealing evidence is allowed even when the written instrument is a final, written expression as to terms and that the writing is a "complete and exclusive statement" because such evidence can be admitted to "explain" the meaning of terms in the writing. 353 Ark. at 244, (quoting 1 White & Summers, UNIFORM COMMERCIAL CODE, § 2-12, at 104 (4th ed. 1995)). In such instances, the evidence of a course of dealing—that explains or supplements a contract—is competent evidence of the parties' intent, and [it] can become a part of a contract. *Precision Steel Warehouse, Inc. v. Anderson-Martin Mach. Co.,* 854 S.W.2d 321 (Ark. 1993).

In the present case, we conclude: The circuit court did not err in finding that the purchase order document and its merger clauses did not preclude course-of-dealing or course-of-performance evidence because that evidence supplemented, not contradicted, the parties' agreement. Although the purchase order document references merchandise allowances, it does not set forth any agreement as to what Dillard's gross margin would be. That was the subject of a separate oral agreement between the parties, negotiated on a yearly basis as to each line of clothing.

The testimony about what Dillard's gross margin would be is consistent with the purchase order document that allows Dillard's to deduct such allowances. Moreover, even if we accept L.F. Brands's argument that the purchase order document was the final and complete integration of the parties' agreement, the course-of-performance/course-of-dealing evidence would still be admissible because merger clauses do not apply to modifications made after the merged agreement is signed. *See In re Estate of Upchurch*, 62 Tenn. App. 634 (1970).

Here, the parties modified the agreements as to Dillard's gross margins at the end of each season. It is also important to note that L.F. Brands failed to object to any of the course-of-dealing and course-of-performance evidence—either at the time Dillard's processed the allowances or at trial. Thus, there was no error. *Lake Village Implement Co. v. Cox*, 478 S.W.2d 36 (Ark. 1972). Finally, according to COMMENT 1 to section 4-2-202, there is no requirement that the writing be declared ambiguous before evidence of the parties' course of dealing and course of performance is admissible.

We cannot say that the circuit court abused its discretion in admitting such course-of-dealing evidence. Accordingly, we affirm the judgment.

B. The Parol Evidence Rule Exceptions Under Article 2

Watkins & Son Pet Supplies v. Iams Co.
254 F.3d 607
(6th Cir. 2001)

ALDRICH, DISTRICT JUDGE. This case arose out of the termination of a longstanding agreement between Watkins, the plaintiff below, and Iams, the defendant, under which Watkins distributed Iams's products in Michigan. In summary, Watkins alleges that Iams made parol representations to Watkins that if it became an exclusive Iams distributor, Iams would make it the exclusive Iams distributor in a territory in Michigan when Iams moved to an exclusive territory distribution system. Watkins alleges that it relied on those representations to its detriment, but that Iams terminated its distributorship agreement and gave an exclusive contract to a competing distributor. ...

FACTS

Iams is in the business of manufacturing and selling pet foods. For many years, Watkins was a non-exclusive distributor of Iams products in Michigan. In 1986 or 1987, Iams began to require Watkins—as well as its other distributors—to sign yearly written distributorship agreements. Until 1987, Watkins was the sole distributor of Iams products in

Michigan, but in 1987, Wolverton, Inc. also began selling Iams products in the state.

In 1989, Iams began offering its distributors a 2% discount on its products in return for a commitment from the distributors to sell Iams products exclusively. The discount was significant, given the low profit margins customary in the business. Watkins alleges that in 1990, Iams promised: If [Watkins] became an exclusive Iams distributor, Iams would grant it an exclusive sales territory in Michigan when Iams changed to a distribution system of exclusive territories. Watkins claims that it became an exclusive distributor in reliance on this promise. It entered into an exclusivity agreement in July 1990 and annually thereafter through 1993. Nevertheless, Iams notified Watkins in September, 1993, that it would not renew its distributorship contract. The contract expired, in accordance with its terms, on January 31, 1994. Iams subsequently entered into an exclusive distribution contract in Michigan with Wolverton.

The contract of January 31, 1993 between Iams and Watkins contains the following provisions:

> Notwithstanding the appointment herein, the Company [Iams] reserves the right for itself to sell Products within the Territory. In addition, the Company may appoint any other distributor to sell Products within the Territory. (§ 2.1).
>
> This Agreement shall be effective on February 1, 1993, and shall automatically expire, without any further action by either party required, on January 31, 1994 unless earlier terminated as set forth in Section 4.2 or 4.3 or otherwise in accordance with the provisions of this Agreement. This Agreement may be renewed thereafter on terms mutually agreeable to the parties only in a writing signed by the parties hereto ... (§ 4.1).
>
> The distributor [Watkins] shall: ... (c) maintain in stock at all times an inventory of products in such quantities as in the Company's opinion, after consultation and review with the Distributor, either directly or through the Company's representative, are needed to meet sales requirements for the Territory. (§ 5.1).
>
> With the exception of Schedule I, which may be unilaterally amended by the Company as provided in this Agreement ... and except as otherwise provided in this Agreement, no change, modification or amendment of any provision of this Agreement will be binding unless made in writing and signed by the parties hereto. (§ 11).

> This Agreement shall be governed by the laws of the State of Ohio (exclusive of its rules on conflict of laws) and the United States of America. (§ 13).
>
> THIS AGREEMENT TOGETHER WITH THE COMPANY'S STANDARD TERMS AND CONDITIONS OF SALE REPRESENT THE ENTIRE AGREEMENT BETWEEN THE PARTIES AND SUPERSEDES ALL PRIOR, EXISTING, AND CONTEMPORANEOUS AGREEMENTS, WHETHER WRITTEN OR ORAL, BETWEEN THE PARTIES HERETO RELATING TO THE DISTRIBUTION OR SALE OF THE COMPANY'S PRODUCTS. ALL SUCH OTHER AGREEMENTS ARE HEREBY TERMINATED, AND EACH PARTY HEREBY RELEASES THE OTHER FROM ANY AND ALL CLAIMS ARISING AS A RESULT OF OR IN ANY WAY RELATING TO THE RELATIONSHIP BETWEEN THE COMPANY AND THE DISTRIBUTOR UNDER SUCH OTHER AGREEMENTS OR AS A RESULT OF SUCH TERMINATION, WITH THE EXCEPTION OF CLAIMS BY THE COMPANY FOR MONEY DUE FOR GOODS AND SERVICES SOLD TO THE DISTRIBUTOR. THE UNDERSIGNED INDIVIDUALS ON BEHALF OF THE COMPANY AND THE DISTRIBUTOR, AS THE CASE MAY BE, HEREBY AFFIRM THAT THEY HAVE CAREFULLY READ THIS AGREEMENT AND FULLY UNDERSTAND THE TERMS CONTAINED IN THE AGREEMENT. (§ 16). ...

DISCUSSION

Applicability of the Uniform Commercial Code

The case appears to have been argued on the assumption that the contract is a contract for the sale of goods within the scope of Article 2 of the Uniform Commercial Code. We agree with the assumption. Whether the contract is a sales contract is of some importance in this case, because (1) the parol evidence rule governing commercial contracts—codified at OHIO REV. CODE § 1302.05—differs from the common-law rule, and (2) the significance of Watkins's allegations that Iams made parol representations after execution of the written contract depends on the application of OHIO REV. CODE § 1302.12(B)—a U.C.C. provision in derogation of the common law that governs oral modification or rescission of written commercial contracts.

[W]e have on occasion discussed the classification of a distributorship agreement as a sales contract when deciding cases [were] not governed by Ohio law. *See, e.g., AB Prods. v. Dampney Co., Inc.*, 1990 U.S. App. LEXIS 12465, *6 (6th Cir.) (holding that under Michigan law, distributorship agreement without a quantity term was not a contract for the sale of goods); *Herman Bros. Sales Corp. v. Hill's Pet Prods.*, 1989 U.S. App. LEXIS 6600, **6–7 (6th Cir.) (holding that under Kansas law, distributorship agreement was not a contract for the sale of goods). [But] we know of no case decided under Ohio law that discusses the question whether a distributorship agreement is a contract for the sale of goods. …

The majority rule is that distributorship contracts are sales contracts. *See Sally Beauty Co., Inc. v. Nexxus Prods. Co., Inc.*, 801 F.2d 1001, 1005–06 (7th Cir. 1986); *Paulson, Inc. v. Bromar, Inc.*, 775 F.Supp. 1329, 1333 (D. Haw. 1991) (both listing jurisdictions in which the majority rule applies). The majority rule should apply in this case, because it is clear from the text of the written agreement between Watkins and Iams that their relationship was primarily about the sale of pet food by Iams to Watkins, and Watkins's resale of the pet food to retail customers. One can imagine a distributorship agreement in which the service component predominates over the goods component, but in the typical case, as here, the service component will not predominate, and the majority rule will apply under Ohio law as under the law of most other jurisdictions.

WATKINS'S CLAIMS OF FRAUD AND PROMISSORY ESTOPPEL

The district court granted Iams's motion for summary judgment on Watkins's claims of fraud and promissory estoppel. We review summary judgments *de novo*. *Peck v. Bridgeport Machs., Inc.*, 237 F.3d 614, 617 (6th Cir. 2001). Summary judgment is proper when there is no genuine issue as to any material fact and the moving party is entitled to judgment as a matter of law. Id.

Reasonable reliance is an element of both promissory estoppel and fraud. *See Nilavar v. Osborn*, 127 Ohio App.3d 1, 16 (1998) (promissory estoppel); *Daup v. Tower Cellular, Inc.,* 136 Ohio App.3d 555, 568 (2000) (fraud). On the facts of this case, we find that Watkins's reliance on Iams's representations was unreasonable as a matter of law. Therefore, we find no error in the district court's decision to grant summary judgment on the two claims.

In this case, the reasonableness of Watkins's reliance depends upon the effect of the integration clause. When a written contract is the final and complete statement of the parties' agreement—when, that is, it is a complete integration—the parol evidence rule prohibits the parties from introducing extrinsic evidence of the terms of their agreement. The rule is not a rule of evidence, but of substantive contract law. In other words, the parol evidence rule does not operate to prohibit proof of terms of the agreement; instead, it provides that parol terms are not terms of the agreement at all. *Galmish v. Cicchini,* 90 Ohio St.3d 22, 27 (2000). If a written contract is completely integrated, it is unreasonable as a matter of law to rely on parol representations or promises within the scope of the contract made prior to its execution. *Bollinger, Inc. v. Mayerson*, 116 Ohio App.3d 702, 712–13 (1996) (fraud); *Harris v. Equilon Enters., L.L.C.*, 107 F.Supp.2d 921, 936 (S. D. Ohio 2000) (promissory estoppel).

We find that the written agreement at issue here was a complete integration. Under Ohio law, the court determines whether a sales contract is completely integrated by considering the "four corners of the document" and evidence extrinsic to the writing. *Carmargo Cadillac Co. v. Garfield Enters., Inc.*, 445 N.E.2d 1141, 1142 (Ohio App. 1982). Here, § 16 of the agreement provides strong evidence that the parties intended their written agreement to be a complete integration. Watkins does not present extrinsic evidence to show otherwise. Instead, it merely argues that the renewal provision in the written agreement does not contain the terms of the proposed renewal, and that therefore the contract is only a partial integration-final, but not complete.

Watkins's argument is without merit. It is clear from the text of the renewal clause that the parties meant to make a final agreement and to leave the terms of a future agreement for later negotiation. This conclusion is made even clearer when one considers the integration clause. As we note in our discussion of Watkins's claim for breach of the duty of good faith clauses such as the renewal clause in this contract may sometimes create a duty to negotiate the renewal in good faith. But a clause leaving open the possibility of a future agreement affects neither the completeness nor the finality of the present agreement.

Since the written agreement between Watkins and Iams is a complete integration, the parol evidence rule applies. There are, however, exceptions to the rule. The exception on which Watkins most heavily relies is the rule that evidence of fraud in the inducement is not barred by the parol evidence rule. *Coal Resources, Inc. v. Gulf & Western Indus., Inc.*, 756 F.2d 443, 447 n. 2 (6th Cir. 1985). But "fraud in the inducement," in the sense intended in *Coal Resources* is a fraudulent misstatement of fact that induces a party to enter a contract, not a fraudulent promise of future performance that is within the scope of the subject matter of the written contract but that was not included in it.

[T]he parol evidence rule does apply to ... promissory fraud if the evidence in question is offered to show a promise which contradicts an integrated written agreement. Unless the false promise is either independent of or consistent with the written instrument, evidence thereof is inadmissible. There is no evidence in the record sufficient to bring this case within the rule of *Williams v. Edwards*, 717 N.E.2d 368, 374 (Ohio App. 1998), which permits claims of fraud despite the parol evidence rule when the promisor had no intention of honoring his promise and thus had actual fraudulent intent.

Watkins's argument that Iams continued to make fraudulent representations after the execution of the agreement avoids the parol evidence rule, which relates only to prior representations. But because the contract is for the sale of goods that provides that modifications must be in writing, Watkins's argument runs up against OHIO REV. CODE § 1302.12(B), which provides: "A signed agreement which excludes modification or rescission except by a signed writing cannot be otherwise modified or rescinded."

Finally, Watkins's argument that Iams's representations are not within the scope of the statutory U.C.C. parol evidence rule is without merit. The statute allows proof of course of dealing, course of performance, or usage of trade to "explain" or "supplement" the written agreement. But Watkins's evidence—evidence of parol promises of an exclusive territory and of renewal—does not explain or supplement the agreement; it contradicts the agreement. As noted above, the written contract explicitly permits Iams to "appoint any other distributor to sell Products within the Territory," and it explicitly provides for expiration of the contract on January 31, 1994, leaving renewal to future agreement of the parties.

For the foregoing reasons, we find that Watkins's reliance on Iams's representations was unreasonable as a matter of law, and therefore, that the district court properly granted summary judgment on Watkins's claims for fraud and promissory estoppel. ...

CONCLUSION

For the foregoing reasons, we affirm the judgment of the district court in all respects.

UNIFORM COMMERCIAL CODE

§ 2-202. FINAL WRITTEN EXPRESSION: PAROL OR EXTRINSIC EVIDENCE

Terms with respect to which the confirmatory memoranda of the parties agree or which are otherwise set forth in a writing intended by the parties as a final expression of their agreement with respect to such terms as are included therein may not be contradicted by evidence of any prior agreement or of a contemporaneous oral agreement but may be explained or supplemented

(a) by course of performance, course of dealing, or usage of trade (Section 1-303); and

(b) by evidence of consistent additional terms unless the court finds the writing to have been intended also as a complete and exclusive statement of the terms of the agreement.

§ 2-316. EXCLUSION OR MODIFICATION OF WARRANTIES

(1) Words or conduct relevant to the creation of an express warranty and words or conduct tending to negate or limit warranty shall be construed wherever reasonable as consistent with each other; but subject to the provisions of this Article on parol or extrinsic evidence (Section 2-202) negation or limitation is inoperative to the extent that such construction is unreasonable.

(2) Subject to subsection (3), to exclude or modify the implied warranty of merchantability or any part of it the language must mention merchantability and in case of a writing must be conspicuous, and to exclude or modify any implied warranty of fitness the exclusion must be by a writing and conspicuous. Language to exclude all implied warranties of fitness is sufficient if it states, for example, that "There are no warranties which extend beyond the description on the face hereof."

(3) Notwithstanding subsection (2)

(a) unless the circumstances indicate otherwise, all implied warranties are excluded by expressions like "as is", "with all faults" or other language which in common understanding calls the buyer's attention to the exclusion of warranties and makes plain that there is no implied warranty; and

(b) when the buyer before entering into the contract has examined the goods or the sample or model as fully as he desired or has refused to examine the goods there is no implied warranty with regard to defects which an examination ought in the circumstances to have revealed to him; and

(c) an implied warranty can also be excluded or modified by course of dealing or course of performance or usage of trade.

(4) Remedies for breach of warranty can be limited in accordance with the provisions of this Article on liquidation or limitation of damages and on contractual modification of remedy (Sections 2-718 and 2-719).

SECTION THREE: THE APPLICATION OF THE UNCONSCIONABILITY DOCTRINE UNDER ARTICLE 2

Once more, section 1-103(b) of the UCC permits courts to apply both legal as well as equitable principles to resolve sale-of-goods disputes. In fact, the UCC codifies many equitable remedies: rescission, restitution, modification, and specific performance. In addition, several equitable defenses also have been codified under the UCC—estoppel, fraud, misrepresentation, duress, coercion, mistake, and double recovery.

Unconscionability is also an equitable doctrine. *See* 1 White & Summers Uniform Commercial Code § 4-2 (3d ed. 1988). Both courts of law and equity apply the doctrine regularly. Like the previously mentioned equitable defenses, the drafters of the Uniform Commercial Code codified the doctrine of unconscionability. It appears in section 2-302. And the doctrine appears in section 2-719(3)—which states that "[c]onsequential damages may be limited or excluded unless the limitation or exclusion is unconscionable." However, as originally fashioned, the doctrine of unconscionability has two prongs—procedural unconscionability and substantive unconscionability. Therefore, one should ask: Do sections 2-302 and 2-719(3) codify both prongs of the doctrine? The next case discusses this issue and provides an answer.

Adams v. American Cyanamid Company
498 N.W.2d 577
(Neb. Ct. App. 1992)

Connolly, Judge.

I. Introduction

This appeal arises from an action based on theories of strict liability and breach of warranty of merchantability under the Uniform Commercial Code. William Timothy "Tim" Adams and Carol Adams brought suit against American Cyanamid Company, and Panhandle Cooperative Association for damages sustained to a crop of edible beans which was lost after a herbicide manufactured by American Cyanamid was applied to the Adamses' fields. The jury awarded a judgment for the Adamses in the amount of $193,500 against American Cyanamid. American Cyanamid appeals. …

II. Factual Background

In 1989, Tim Adams planned to grow beans on 860 acres of center-pivot irrigated fields. He sought the services of Glenn Johnson of Servi-Tech crop consultants to inspect his fields, to make recommendations as to fertilizers, herbicides, and seed, and to observe the crop through the growing season. Johnson recommended a combination of the herbicides Eptam and Prowl. Prowl herbicide is manufactured by the defendant, American Cyanamid. Adams purchased these herbicides from Panhandle Co-op, whose employee applied the herbicides at the application rate specified by Johnson. In early June, the fields were planted with great northern and pinto beans.

At first, the bean crop grew well, but after the first of July, Adams noticed that the plants in field No. 8 began to look weakened, and plants in the other fields followed suit. The beans flourished in a strip of field No. 1 where no herbicide had been applied due to a parked center pivot. The beans also flourished in a 10-acre area of field No. 5 where no herbicide was applied because the sod had recently been brought under cultivation.

Prowl—the trade name for the herbicide used—is a dinitroaniline herbicide. It can destroy plants by causing a swollen hypocotyl—i.e., the plant's main root stem—and a reduction of the secondary root system. Prowl was applied in combination with Eptam, a thiocarbamate herbicide. A thiocarbamate herbicide produces a type of plant injury different from that produced by a dinitroaniline herbicide. A thiocarbamate herbicide causes early leaf effect and lasts in the soil for a few weeks. The Adamses' expert was able to exclude the possibility that Eptam had caused the plant injury.

The jury entered a general verdict for the Adamses for $193,500, the amount of the lost crop. The jury entered special verdicts finding that the defendant was strictly liable in tort and had breached the warranty of merchantability. The defendant moved for judgment notwithstanding the verdict and for a new trial, which motions were overruled. …

IV. ANALYSIS

Breach of Warranty

The defendant also claims that the Adamses presented insufficient evidence to prove there was a breach of the implied warranty of merchantability and that the trial court erred by failing to direct a verdict against the Adamses on this theory of recovery.

NEB. U.C.C. § 2-314 (Reissue 1980) provides:

> (1) Unless excluded or modified (Section 2-316), a warranty that the goods shall be merchantable is implied in a contract for their sale if the seller is a merchant with respect to goods of that kind. …
>
> (2) Goods to be merchantable must be … fit for the ordinary purposes for which such goods are used.

There is no question that American Cyanamid is a merchant, i.e., one that deals in the goods of the kind involved in the transactions under consideration. *See* NEB. U.C.C. § 2-104 (Reissue 1980). After goods are accepted, the buyer has the burden of establishing any breach with respect to those goods. *Laird v. Scribner Coop*, 237 Neb. 532 (1991).

The plaintiffs' *prima facie* case for breach of warranty of merchantability has been described in *Delgado v. Inryco, Inc.*, 230 Neb. 662, 668 (1988):

> "[T]here must be proof that there was a deviation from the standard of merchantability at the time of sale and that such deviation caused the plaintiff's injury both proximately and in fact. Thus, a breach of the warranty has been found to exist where the item sold failed to perform adequately because of a lack of quality inherent within the item itself."

The *Delgado* court also stated, "In proving a deviation from the standard of merchantability, some proof of noncompliance with the warranty must be presented." 230 Neb. at 668. A plaintiff may not rely on the sole fact that an accident occurred.

In the case at bar, the defendant argues that "[t]here was no proof by the plaintiffs that the risk of harm from the Prowl herbicide was any greater than herbicides in its class generally, and there was no evidence as to any breach of a standard of merchantability."

In *Laird v. Scribner Coop, supra*, the Supreme Court held that "reliance on eyewitnesses alone is not fatal when the defect is obvious to a layman, but when standards of performance of the product are not generally known, other evidence, usually expert testimony, is necessary to prove proper or acceptable standards of performance." 237 Neb. at 539. It would seem apparent to a layperson that the standard of merchantability for herbicides is that they should not damage the crops to which they are applied. Therefore, expert testimony was not required to establish a standard of merchantability.

As to the existence of a breach of the standard, the evidence at trial was in conflict. Prof. Eugene Heikes, called by the Adamses, testified that a dinitroaniline herbicide affects plants through their root system, attacking the hypocotyl, or main root, and the secondary roots which branch therefrom. He also testified that the growth of the bean plants he inspected was stunted because of their swollen hypocotyl and the lack of a secondary root system. Dr. Raymond Ward, a soil testing specialist called by the defendant, testified that the injury to the root system was not caused by the herbicide, but by the quality of water from the deep wells used to irrigate the fields. He testified that the irrigation water contained sodium, chlorides, and boron and that dry beans are especially susceptible to injury from the concentration of such salts in the soil.

Whether there was a breach of implied warranty of merchantability is a factual question for jury determination. Professor Heikes testified that injury to the plants was caused by the effects of dinitroaniline substances. It was undisputed that Prowl contained dinitroaniline. Professor Heikes' testimony was sufficient for the jury to have concluded that the herbicide in question was not suitable for its ordinary use in controlling weeds in dry beans.

Therefore, we hold that the Adamses presented sufficient evidence as to a breach of a standard of merchantability. Accordingly, we affirm that portion of the court's judgment overruling the motions for directed verdict and for judgment notwithstanding the verdict to the Adamses' theory of recovery based on implied warranty of merchantability. …

JURY INSTRUCTION ON CONSPICUOUSNESS OF DISCLAIMER

The defendant claims that the court erred by submitting the issue of the conspicuousness of the disclaimer to the jury. In an appeal based on the claim of an erroneous instruction, the appellant has the burden to show that the questioned instruction was prejudicial or otherwise adversely affected a substantial right of the appellant. *Pugh v. Great Plains Ins. Co.*, 239 Neb. 171 (1991).

The "label" in this case was contained in exhibit 166—a 107-page manual on various herbicides. The label applying to Prowl herbicide appears on page 17 of that manual and provides:

> DISCLAIMER
>
> American Cyanamid Company warrants only that the material contained herein conforms to the chemical description on the label and is reasonably fit for the use therein described when used in accordance with the directions for use, subject to the risks referred to above. …
>
> American Cyanamid Company makes no other express or implied warranty, including any other express or implied warranty of FITNESS or MERCHANTABILITY.

At trial, the issue of whether the label was conspicuous was submitted to the jury. Instruction No. 4, given by the trial court, informed the jury that it was required to find whether the disclaimer was conspicuous with respect to the exclusion of the warranty of merchantability, fitness, and consequential damages.

Section 1-201(10) reads: "Whether a term or clause is 'conspicuous' or not is for decision by the court." On the basis of § 1-201(10), we hold that the trial court erred in submitting the issue of the label's conspicuousness to the jury. However, such error would be prejudicial only if it adversely affected the defendant's substantial rights. Since the defendant would have a substantial right affected only if the disclaimer is conspicuous as a matter of law, we first resolve that issue and then return to whether prejudice arose from the jury instruction.

LABEL CONSPICUOUS AS A MATTER OF LAW

The defendant claims that its disclaimer was conspicuous as a matter of law and that the court ought to have directed a verdict against the Adamses on their theory of recovery for breach of warranty. NEB. U.C.C. § 2-316(2) reads:

> Subject to subsection (3), to exclude or modify the implied warranty of merchantability or any part of it the language must mention merchantability and in case of a writing must be conspicuous, and to exclude or modify any implied warranty of fitness the exclusion must be by a writing and conspicuous. ...

The warranty in the instant case mentions merchantability and the heading "DISCLAIMER" is prominently displayed. The disclaimer is sufficiently set off from other material so as to draw attention to itself. Also, the disclaimer is on the third page of the label, although the record establishes that the only label presented to Adams was contained in a manual. Therefore, notwithstanding the fact that the label appears in a manual, we hold that the disclaimer was conspicuous as a matter of law. ...

UNCONSCIONABILITY

In its final assignment of error the defendant claims that the trial court erred (1) by failing to rule on the unconscionability of the limitation of remedy found on its label, pursuant to § 2-302; (2) by failing to find that the Adamses were excluded by the disclaimer from claiming consequential damages; and (3) by failing to instruct the jury that the limitation of remedy clause excluded the Adamses' recovery of consequential damages for breach of warranty.

(a) Consequential Damages Defined

At the outset, we must determine whether this case involves direct or consequential damages. NEB. U.C.C. § 2-719(3) reads: "Consequential damages may be limited or excluded unless the limitation or exclusion is unconscionable. Limitation of consequential damages for injury to the person in the case of consumer goods is *prima facie* unconscionable but limitation of damages where the loss is commercial is not."

American Cyanamid's disclaimer provides, *inter alia*: "Any damages arising from a breach of this warranty shall be limited to direct damages, and shall not include consequential commercial damages such as loss of profits or values or any other special or indirect damages." The Adamses are clearly seeking consequential damages as defined in NEB. U.C.C. § 2-715(2) (Reissue 1980). In *Duyck v. Northwest Chemical Corp.*, 764 P.2d 943, 946 (Or. App. 1988), the Code's definition of consequential damages was explained as follows:

> Consequential damages, as opposed to direct damages, do not arise directly according to the usual course of things from the breach itself; rather, they occur as a consequence of special circumstances known or reasonably supposed to have been contemplated by the parties when the contract was made. In other words, [§ 2-715(2)] includes loss resulting from general or particular requirements which Dupont had reason to know about at the time of the contracting.

In this case, the special circumstances are that Prowl can be injurious to crops when applied to soils with high salinity—according to expert testimony for the defendant. The defendant claimed that damages were a consequence of such special circumstances. The consequences were known or reasonably should have been contemplated by the parties. Therefore, this case is concerned with consequential damages rather than direct damages.

(b) Conspicuousness of Limitation of Remedies

We must also decide as a preliminary to our analysis of the unconscionability issue whether the limitation of consequential damages must also be conspicuous. The issue of the conspicuousness of the limitation of remedy is separate from that of conspicuousness of the disclaimer of warranty. The Code does not require that a limitation of remedy be conspicuous. See 5 RONALD A. ANDERSON, ANDERSON ON THE UNIFORM COMMERCIAL CODE § 2-719:20 (3d ed. 1984). Nevertheless, we believe that the requirement of § 2-316(2) that a disclaimer of warranty of merchantability be conspicuous also applies to limitations of remedies. Section 2-316(2) reads as follows:

> Subject to subsection (3), to exclude or modify the implied warranty of merchantability or any part of it the language must mention merchantability and in case of a writing must be conspicuous, and to exclude or modify any implied warranty of fitness the exclusion must be by a writing and conspicuous. ...

A court will construe statutes relating to the same subject matter together so as to maintain a consistent and sensible scheme. *In re Estate of Morse*, 241 Neb. 40 (1992). We have held above that a disclaimer of warranty must be conspicuous and that the buyer must have an opportunity to see and read it if it is to become part of the bargain of sale. On similar reasoning, in order for a limitation of remedy to be effective, it must also be conspicuous and a buyer must be afforded a reasonable opportunity to read it. Because we have held that the disclaimer of the warranty is conspicuous as a matter of law, we also hold that the limitation of remedies is conspicuous. …

(d) Determination of Unconscionability

The defendant claims that it was error for the trial court not to address the unconscionability of the exclusion. Since the issue is likely to arise again on remand, we provide direction for the lower court by determining in advance whether American Cyanamid's limitation of remedies is unconscionable.

The concept of conscionability is not defined by the Code. The Supreme Court has quoted with approval from the comments to § 2-302: "The basic test is whether in the light of the general commercial background and the commercial needs of the particular trade or case, the clauses involved are so one-sided as to be unconscionable under the circumstances existing at the time of the making of the contract. …" *T.V. Transmission v. City of Lincoln*, 374 N.W.2d 49, 56 (Neb. 1985).

Although the test is stated in *T.V. Transmission*, we have not found a Nebraska case that has applied it. Accordingly, we must determine how the concept of unconscionability is to be applied. The Code's concept of unconscionability [was] developed in the context of consumer transactions. Since our concern here is solely with a commercial contract, we must determine how the concept applies in a commercial setting.

Generally, the issue of unconscionability is divided into substantive unconscionability and procedural unconscionability. "Substantive unconscionability involves those cases where a clause or term in the contract is alleged to be one-sided or overly harsh, while procedural unconscionability relates to impropriety during the process of forming a contract." *Schroeder v. Fageol Motors*, 86 Wash.2d 256, 260 (1975). Generally, a contract is not substantively unconscionable unless the terms are grossly unfair under the circumstances as they existed at the time the contract was formed. *See Guthmann v. La Vida Llena*, 103 N.M. 506 (1985). An often-quoted formulation of substantive unconscionability is the following:

> In determining reasonableness or fairness, the primary concern must be with the terms of the contract considered in light of the circumstances existing when the contract was made. The test is not simple, nor can it be mechanically applied. The terms are to be considered "in the light of the general commercial background and the commercial needs of the particular trade or case." CORBIN suggests the test as being whether the terms are "so extreme as to appear unconscionable according to the mores and business practices

of the time and place." *Williams v. Walker-Thomas Furniture Company*, 350 F.2d 445, 450 (D.C. Cir. 1965).

Accordingly, to determine whether a contract clause is substantively unconscionable, a court asks "whether under the circumstances existing at the time of making of the contract, and in light of the general commercial background and commercial needs of a particular case, clauses are so one-sided as to oppress or unfairly surprise one of the parties." *Barnes v. Helfenbein*, 548 P.2d 1014, 1020 (Okla. 1976).

In the present case, the limitation of consequential damages clause would leave the herbicide user without any substantial recourse for his loss. "One-sided agreements whereby one party is left without a remedy for another party's breach are oppressive and should be declared unconscionable." *Durham v. Ciba-Geigy Corp.*, 315 N.W.2d 696, 700 (S.D. 1982). *See, also, Campbell Soup Co. v. Wentz*, 172 F.2d 80 (3d Cir. 1948). We conclude that the provision excluding consequential damages is substantively unconscionable.

Substantive unconscionability in a commercial setting—standing alone—is insufficient to void a contract or clause. *See, e.g.,* 1 E. ALLAN FARNSWORTH, CONTRACTS § 4.28 (2d ed. 1990). The remaining question, therefore, is whether there is evidence of procedural unconscionability. The factors involved in determination of procedural unconscionability have been formulated in *American Nursery v. Indian Wells,* 115 Wash.2d 217, 797 P.2d 477 (1990). In *American Nursery*, the court stated that a clause excluding damages may be found to be conscionable when "the general commercial setting indicates a prior course of dealing or reasonable usage of trade as to the exclusionary clause." Id. at 223, 797 P.2d at 481.

Otherwise, "[u]nconscionability is determined in light of all the surrounding circumstances, including (1) the manner in which the parties entered into the contract, (2) whether the parties had a reasonable opportunity to understand the terms of the contract, and (3) whether the important terms were hidden in a maze of fine print." Id. at 222, 797 P.2d at 481. None of the factors is conclusive; rather, unconscionability is determined under the totality of the circumstances.

Applying the *American Nursery* analysis, we first look to evidence of a prior course of trade. This inquiry has been explained as follows:

> [A court] must consider whether the plaintiff and [defendant], through prior contracts, had established a consistently adhered to policy of excluding consequential damages, or whether it is a recognized practice within the trade to exclude consequential damages. The presence of either of these elements, unless the trade practice as related to the plaintiff was clearly unreasonable, would support a finding of conscionability in spite of a lack of "negotiations" or the

"inconspicuous" appearance of the clause. *Schroeder v. Fageol Motors*, 86 Wash.2d at 260–61.

Although the evidence supports the conclusion that there is a trade practice among chemical firms related to excluding consequential damages, we find it unreasonable to impose the trade practice on the Adamses. In selecting Prowl herbicide, Adams was merely following the advice of Johnson. He was not independently assessing the risks involved in the use of particular chemicals; and the use of middlemen, as in the case at bar, appears to be a common trade practice in the agricultural industry.

Therefore, we examine the totality of the circumstances. In this case, Adams was in no position to bargain with American Cyanamid. Johnson testified that all herbicide manufacturers place the same disclaimers on their products. Moreover, Adams testified that he did not receive the label containing the exclusion until he had problems with his crops. Even if we disregard the fact that Adams may not have received the contract terms at the time of purchase, the language of the exclusion is not such as to be immediately understandable by a layperson such as Adams. The exclusion specifically excludes "indirect" damages, but allows direct damages without specifying the extent of such damages.

This is a situation where the Adamses had no alternative other than to accept the manufacturer's exclusion. The undisputed evidence is that Adams could not purchase any manufacturer's herbicide without such an exclusion. The Adamses were not in a position to bargain with the defendant for more favorable terms than those set out in the preprinted label. Nor were they in a position to test the effectiveness of the herbicide prior to purchase. As Adams expected, the herbicide he purchased killed the weeds in his crop. However, quite unexpectedly and unfortunately, the herbicide also destroyed his crop.

If the evidence is believed, to permit the defendant to escape all consequential responsibility by inserting a limitation of consequential damage clause, as in this case, would leave a farmer without any substantial recourse for his loss. We conclude that under the circumstances presented here, the exclusion is procedurally unconscionable. Having found the exclusion both substantively and procedurally unconscionable, we decline to enforce it.

V. CONCLUSION

We reverse that portion of the district court's judgment overruling the defendant's motions for directed verdict on the strict liability count. We affirm that portion of the district court's judgment overruling the defendant's motions for directed verdict and for judgment notwithstanding the verdict on the Adamses' theory of recovery based on breach of the implied warranty of merchantability, but we remand because the district court improperly submitted the issue of the disclaimer's conspicuousness to the jury.

Affirmed in part, and in part reversed and remanded for a new trial.

UNIFORM COMMERCIAL CODE

§ 2-302. UNCONSCIONABLE CONTRACT OR CLAUSE

(1) If the court as a matter of law finds the contract or any clause of the contract to have been unconscionable at the time it was made the court may refuse to enforce the contract, or it may enforce the remainder of the contract without the unconscionable clause, or it may so limit the application of any unconscionable clause as to avoid any unconscionable result.

(2) When it is claimed or appears to the court that the contract or any clause thereof may be unconscionable the parties shall be afforded a reasonable opportunity to present evidence as to its commercial setting, purpose and effect to aid the court in making the determination.

§ 2-719. CONTRACTUAL MODIFICATION OR LIMITATION OF REMEDY

(1) Subject to the provisions of subsections (2) and (3) of this section and of the preceding section on liquidation and limitation of damages,

(a) the agreement may provide for remedies in addition to or in substitution for those provided in this Article and may limit or alter the measure of damages recoverable under this Article, as by limiting the buyer's remedies to return of the goods and repayment of the price or to repair and replacement of non-conforming goods or parts; and

(b) resort to a remedy as provided is optional unless the remedy is expressly agreed to be exclusive, in which case it is the sole remedy.

(2) Where circumstances cause an exclusive or limited remedy to fail of its essential purpose, remedy may be had as provided in this Act.

(3) Consequential damages may be limited or excluded unless the limitation or exclusion is unconscionable. Limitation of consequential damages for injury to the person in the case of

consumer goods is prima facie unconscionable but limitation of damages where the loss is commercial is not.

SECTION FOUR: THE APPLICATION OF THE DOCTRINES OF IMPOSSIBILITY AND COMMERCIAL IMPRACTICABILITY UNDER ARTICLE 2

Chapter 6 in Part I of this casebook presents a comprehensive discussion of several interrelated common-law defenses—doctrine of commercial frustration or frustration of venture, the impossibility of performance doctrine, and the defense of impracticability of performance. Briefly, "[t]he doctrine of impossibility operates to excuse performance when the bargained-for performance is no longer in existence or is no longer capable of being performed due to the unforeseen, supervening act of a third party." *Haessly v. Safeco Title Ins. Co. of Idaho*, 825 P.2d 1119, 1121 (Idaho 1992).

On the other hand, "[t]he impracticability doctrine represents an exception to the accepted maxim of *pacta sunt servanda*, in recognition of the fact that certain conditions cannot be met because of unforeseen occurrences. [If a party asserts that a supervening event or contingency excuses a promised performance], the party must demonstrate that: (1) the event made the performance impracticable; (2) the nonoccurrence of the event was a basic assumption on which the contract was made; (3) the impracticability resulted without the fault of the party seeking to be excused; and (4) the party has not assumed a greater obligation than the law imposes." *Dills v. Enfield*, 557 A.2d 517, 523 (Conn. 1989). And, the central principle underlying the doctrine of commercial frustration is this one: A contract may be discharged, if a supervening event or circumstance completely frustrates the purpose of the contract and makes the contract impossible to perform. *Downing v. Stiles,* 635 P.2d 808, 811 (Wyo. 1981).

Article 2 of the UCC has codified the various affirmative defenses or excuses—without embracing the common-law names or labels. The case appearing below illustrates how one court applied the general doctrine of impracticability to decide a buyer and seller's UCC-related sale-of-goods disagreement.

Maple Farms, Inc. v. City School Dist. of City of Elmira
352 N.Y.S.2d 784
(N.Y. Sup. 1974)

CHARLES B. SWARTWOOD, JUSTICE. This is a motion for summary judgment in an action for declaratory judgment whereby the plaintiff seeks, first, a determination that the contract wherein the plaintiff agreed to supply milk to the defendant school district at an agreed price be terminated without further liability on the grounds of legal "impossibility" or "impracticality" because of the occurrence of events not contemplated by the parties which makes performance impracticable and, second, a determination that the defendant school district has authority to unilaterally relieve the plaintiff of its contract without violating Article 8, Section 1 of the New York State Constitution. ...

The background of this dispute is that the price of raw milk at the farm site is and has been controlled for many years in this area by the United States Department of Agriculture through the New York–New Jersey Market Administrator. The president of the plaintiff milk dealer has for at least ten years bid on contracts to supply milk for the defendant school district and is thoroughly conversant with prices and costs. Though the plaintiff avers that the defendant was aware of the prices of raw milk and the profit picture, the fiscal officer of the defendant denies that either the price of raw milk or the profit structure of suppliers was known or of any concern to him or the defendant. The defendant's only concern was the assurance of a steady supply of milk for the school lunch program at an agreed price on which the school's budget had to be based.

The mandated price of raw milk has in the past fluctuated from a cost of $6.73 cwt. in 1969 to a high of $7.58 cwt. in 1972, or 12%—with fluctuation within a calendar year ranging from 1% to 4.5%. The plaintiff agreed to supply milk to the defendant for the school year 1973–1974 by agreement of June 15, 1973 at a price of $.0759 per half pint—at which time the mandated price of raw milk was $8.03 cwt. By November of 1973 the price of raw milk had risen to $9.31 cwt. and by December 1973 to $9.89 cwt.—an increase of 23% over the June 1973 price. However, it should be noted that there was an increase from the low price in 1972 to the June 1973 price—date of the contract—of 9.5%. Because of considerable increase in the price of raw milk, the plaintiff, beginning in October 1973, has requested the defendant to relieve the plaintiff of its contract and to put the contract out for rebidding. The defendant has refused.

The plaintiff spells out in detail its costs based on the June and December prices of raw milk and shows that it will sustain a loss of $7,350.55 if it is required to continue its performance on the same volume with raw milk at the December price. Its contracts with other school districts where it is faced with the same problem will triple its total contemplated loss. The plaintiff further claims that because of the advent of the federally sponsored milk lunch subsidy of $.04 to the defendant, the price per half pint of milk will be dropped to $.05 and the volume of milk sold will increase, thus further increasing the plaintiff's loss. There is no substantiation for this estimated volume increase so that we do not meet that question.

The plaintiff goes to great lengths to spell out the cause of the substantial increase in the price of raw milk, which the plaintiff argues could not have been foreseen by the parties because it came about in large measure from the agreement of the United States to sell huge amounts of grain to Russia and to a lesser extent to unanticipated crop failures.

The legal basis of the plaintiff's request for being relieved of the obligation under the contract award is the doctrine known variously as "impossibility of performance" and "frustration of performance" at common law and as "Excuse by Failure of Presupposed Conditions" under the Uniform Commercial Code, § 2-615. The common law rule is stated in RESTATEMENT (SECOND) OF THE LAW OF CONTRACTS, § 454, as follows:

> Definition of Impossibility—In the Restatement of this Subject impossibility means not only strict impossibility but impracticability because of extreme and unreasonable difficulty, expense, injury or loss involved.

Performance has been excused at common law where performance has become illegal, where disaster wipes out the means of production, and where governmental action prevents performance. In *Mineral Park Land Co. v. Howard*, 172 Cal. 289, 156 P. 458 (1916) the defendants agreed to take all the gravel from the plaintiff's land up to a certain quantity. The defendants took only half the agreed amount because the balance of the gravel was under the water level. The court relieved the defendants from the obligation to pay for the balance under water because it was not within the contemplation of the parties that the gravel under the water level would be taken and secondly because the cost of doing so would be ten to twelve times as expensive. The court stated the common law rule, 172 Cal. 293, 156 P. at page 460:

> A thing is impossible in legal contemplation when it is not practicable; and a thing is impracticable when it can only be done at an excessive and unreasonable cost." (1 BEACH ON CONTRACTS § 216.) We do not mean to intimate that the defendants could excuse themselves by showing the existence of conditions which would make the performance of their obligation more expensive than they had anticipated, or which would entail a loss upon them. But, where the difference in cost is so great as here, and has the effect, as found, of making performance impracticable, the situation is not different from that of a total absence of earth and gravel.

407 E. 61st Garage v. Savoy Corp., 23 N.Y.2d 275, 296 N.Y.S.2d 338 holds that where economic hardship alone is involved, performance will not be excused. This is so even where governmental acts make performance more expensive. *Baker v. Johnson*, 42 N.Y. 126. Existing circumstances and foreseeability also play a part in determining whether a party should be relieved of his contracts. The Uniform Commercial Code § 2-615 states in part:

> Except so far as a seller may have assumed a greater obligation and subject to the preceding section on substituted performance:
>
> (a) Delay in delivery or non-delivery in whole or in part by a seller ... is not a breach of his duty under a contract for sale if performance as agreed has been made impracticable by the occurrence of a contingency the non-occurrence of which was a basic assumption on which the contract was made or by compliance in good faith with any applicable foreign or domestic governmental regulation or order whether or not it later proves to be invalid.

The Official Comment 3 to that section points out that the test of impracticability is to be judged by commercial standards. Official Comment 4 states:

> Increased cost alone does not excuse performance unless the rise in cost is due to some unforeseen contingency which alters the essential nature of the performance. Neither is a rise or a collapse in the market in itself a justification, for that is exactly the type of business risk which business contracts made at fixed prices are intended to cover. But a severe shortage of raw materials or of supplies due to a contingency such as war, embargo, local crop failure, unforeseen shutdown of major sources of supply or the like, which either causes a marked increase in cost or altogether prevents the seller from securing supplies necessary to his performance, is within the contemplation of this section. *See Ford & Sons, Ltd., v. Henry Leetham & Sons, Ltd.*, 21 Com. Cas. 55 (1915, K.B.D.)

Official Comment 10 states in part that "governmental interference cannot excuse unless it truly 'supervenes' in such a manner as to be beyond the seller's assumption of risk." We find little authority dealing with this section based on facts that are similar to those in this case. *See*, however: *Transatlantic Financing Corporation v. United States*, 124 U.S. App. D.C. 183, 363 F.2d 312. The *Transatlantic* case is somewhat analogous to the question raised here. In that case the Suez Canal was closed causing the plaintiff's ship en route to Iran to have to go around Africa to deliver its cargo of wheat. The plaintiff sought to recover the increased expense from the defendant. The court found that shipping dangers in the Suez Canal area could have been anticipated; that the risk should be allocated to the plaintiff and that the increased cost was not of such magnitude to say that it was not within the accepted degree of risk.

The doctrine enunciated by Uniform Commercial Code § 2-615 was explained by the court, 363 F.2d at page 315:

> The doctrine ultimately represents the ever-shifting line, drawn by courts hopefully responsive to commercial practices and mores, at which the community's interest in having contracts enforced according to their terms is outweighed by the commercial senselessness of requiring performance. When the issue is raised, the court is asked to construct a condition of performance based on the changed circumstances, a process which involves at least three reasonably definable steps. First, a contingency—something unexpected—must have occurred. Second, the risk of the unexpected occurrence must not have been allocated either by agreement or by custom. Finally, occurrence of the contingency must have rendered performance commercially impracticable.

Applying these rules to the facts here, we find that the contingency causing the increase of the price of raw milk was not totally unexpected. The price from the low point in the year 1972 to the price on the date of the award of the contract in June 1973 had risen nearly 10%. And any businessman should have been aware of the general inflation in this country during the previous years and of the chance of crop failures.

However, should we grant that the first test had been met and thus the substantial increase in price was due to the sale of wheat to Russia, poor crops and general market conditions which were unexpected contingencies, then the question of allocation of risk must be met. Here, the very purpose of the contract was to guard against fluctuation of price of half pints of milk as a basis for the school budget. Surely had the price of raw milk fallen substantially, the defendant could not be excused from performance. We can reasonably assume that the plaintiff had to be aware of escalating inflation.

It is chargeable with knowledge of the substantial increase of the price of raw milk from the previous year's low. It had knowledge that for many years the Department of Agriculture had established the price of raw milk and that that price varied. It nevertheless entered into this agreement with that knowledge. It did not provide in the contract any exculpatory clause to excuse it from performance in the event of a substantial rise in the price of raw milk. On these facts the risk of a substantial or abnormal increase in the price of raw milk can be allocated to the plaintiff.

As pointed out in the *Transatlantic* case, 363 F.2d at page 319, where the circumstances reveal a willingness on the part of the seller to accept abnormal rises in costs, the question of impracticability of performance should be judged by stricter terms than where the contingency is totally unforeseen. The increase in the price of raw milk from

June to December 1973 was 23%. And the estimated loss to the plaintiff in completing the contract on the same assumed volume and estimated cost of raw milk would be $7,350.55. Based on the plaintiff's December 1973 figures, including increased transportation cost, the cost of a delivered half pint of milk would be 10.4% greater than the bid price. The percentage would be 8.7%—without the increased transportation cost.

There is no precise point—though such could conceivably be reached—at which an increase in price of raw goods above the norm would be so disproportionate to the risk assumed as to amount to "impracticality" in a commercial sense. However, we cannot say on these facts that the increase here has reached the point of "impracticality" in performance of this contract in light of the risks that we find were assumed by the plaintiff.

The plaintiff also seeks a declaratory judgment that the defendant could agree to cancel the contract without violating Article 8, Section 1 of the New York State Constitution. Since the defendant has not indicated any willingness to excuse the plaintiff from performance, there is therefore no issue in that regard before us—since we have held that the plaintiff is not entitled to be excused from performance under the law. We do not pass on any question of the impact of an unexpected increase in volume, if that proves to be true, through the impact of the United States school lunch program.

The plaintiff's motion is denied and the defendant is granted summary judgment dismissing the complaint.

UNIFORM COMMERCIAL CODE

§ 2-613. CASUALTY TO IDENTIFIED GOODS

Where the contract requires for its performance goods identified when the contract is made, and the goods suffer casualty without fault of either party before the risk of loss passes to the buyer, or in a proper case under a "no arrival, no sale" term (Section 2-324) then

(a) if the loss is total the contract is avoided; and

(b) if the loss is partial or the goods have so deteriorated as no longer to conform to the contract the buyer may nevertheless demand inspection and at his option either treat the contract as avoided or accept the goods with due allowance from the contract price for the deterioration or the deficiency in quantity but without further right against the seller.

§ 2-614. SUBSTITUTED PERFORMANCE

(1) Where without fault of either party the agreed berthing, loading, or unloading facilities fail or an agreed type of carrier becomes unavailable or the agreed manner of delivery otherwise becomes commercially impracticable but a commercially reasonable substitute is available, such substitute performance must be tendered and accepted.

(2) If the agreed means or manner of payment fails because of domestic or foreign governmental regulation, the seller may withhold or stop delivery unless the buyer provides a means or manner of payment which is commercially a substantial equivalent. If delivery has already been taken, payment by the means or in the manner provided by the regulation discharges the buyer's obligation unless the regulation is discriminatory, oppressive or predatory.

§ 2-615. EXCUSE BY FAILURE OF PRESUPPOSED CONDITIONS

Except so far as a seller may have assumed a greater obligation and subject to the preceding section on substituted performance:

(a) Delay in delivery or non-delivery in whole or in part by a seller who complies with paragraphs (b) and (c) is not a breach of his duty under a contract for sale if performance as agreed has been made impracticable by the occurrence of a contingency the non-occurrence of which was a basic assumption on which the contract was made or by compliance in good faith with any applicable foreign or domestic governmental regulation or order whether or not it later proves to be invalid.

(b) Where the causes mentioned in paragraph (a) affect only a part of the seller's capacity to perform, he must allocate production and deliveries among his customers but may at his option include regular customers not then under contract as well as his own requirements for further manufacture. He may so allocate in any manner which is fair and reasonable.

(c) The seller must notify the buyer seasonably that there will be delay or non-delivery and, when allocation is required under paragraph (b), of the estimated quota thus made available for the buyer.

INDEX

Uniform Commercial Code

Conventions

A

B

C

D

E

F

G

H

I

L

M

N

O

P

Q

R

CONTRACT LAW

PRACTICE, INTERPRETATION, AND ENFORCEMENT

• • •

Contract Law: Practice, Interpretation, and Enforcement teaches common-law principles regarding the formation, interpretation and enforcement of contracts and stand-alone promises. More specifically, the casebook discusses theories of recovery, and explains the practicable application of those theories in legal complaints and answers. In addition, the casebook covers Article 2 of the Uniform Commercial Code, which governs the formation and enforcement of sale-of-goods contracts.

Most legal casebooks generally focus on the theoretical. *Contract Law*, however, covers legal and statutory theories as well as civil procedures, and the practice of law in everyday life. Therefore, the casebook gives first-year students valuable skills that they can use throughout their legal careers.

Contract Law is literally two textbooks in one and can be used for a full year of instruction. Therefore, it is ideal for law school courses in contracts. And, to re-emphasize, the text teaches students how to construct plaintiffs' complaints, and defendants' answers using common-law and UCC-related theories of recovery and affirmative defenses.

Willy E. Rice earned his Ph.D. at the University of North Carolina at Chapel Hill, completed a postdoctoral fellowship in law, psychiatry and statistics at The Johns Hopkins University, and earned this J.D. at the University of Texas at Austin. Dr. Rice is a professor of law at St. Mary's University School of Law in San Antonio, Texas. He is a past recipient of several Distinguished Faculty Awards for Excellence in Teaching. The author of numerous law publications, Dr. Rice's areas of legal interest include contract law, insurance law, tort law, medical and legal malpractice, and law and econometrics.

cognella academic publishing

www.cognella.com 800-200-3908

ISBN 978-1-62131-241-3

9 781621 312413 90000

www.ingramcontent.com/pod-product-compliance
Lightning Source LLC
LaVergne TN
LVHW080356011026
849161LV00009B/2322